Companion Website Access Instructions

**To access the Companion Website,
follow the instructions below to create an account and log in.**

1   Go to **behavioralneuroscience8e.com**

2   Click "Register Using a Registration Code."

3   Enter the registration code below and follow the on-screen
instructions to create your account.

4   After registering, go to **behavioralneuroscience8e.com** and
log in using your newly-created login information.

Scratch below to reveal your unique registration code:

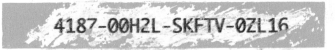

4187-00H2L-SKFTV-0ZL16

This code activates a 180-day subscription.

Important Note: The registration code above is valid for creating one account only. If the code has been
revealed, it may no longer be valid. New codes may be purchased at behavioralneuroscience8e.com.

BioPsychology NewsLink

behavioralneuroscience8e.com/news

This invaluable online resource helps you make connections between the science of behavioral neuroscience and your daily life, and keeps you apprised of the latest developments in
the field. The site is updated 3–4 times per week, so it includes up-to-the-minute information,
and contains thousands of news stories organized both by keyword and by textbook chapter.
Follow news updates on Facebook at Behavioralneuroscience.

Companion Website Resources (behavioralneuroscience8e.com)

The **Behavioral Neuroscience** Companion Website includes the following animations, videos, and activities:

Behavioral Neuroscience
Eighth Edition

I am a brain, Watson.
The rest of me is a mere appendix.

Sherlock Holmes, in *The Adventure of the Mazarin Stone*
(1921) by Sir Arthur Conan Doyle

Behavioral Neuroscience
Eighth Edition

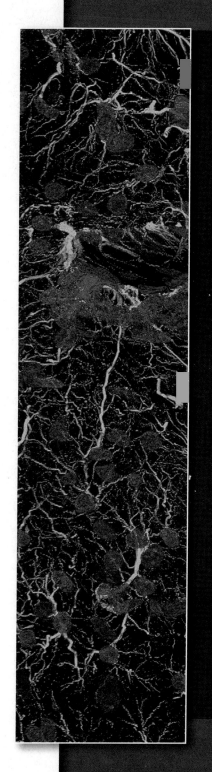

S. MARC BREEDLOVE
Michigan State University

NEIL V. WATSON
Simon Fraser University

Sinauer Associates, Inc. Publishers
Sunderland, Massachusetts

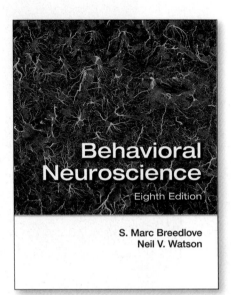

About the Cover:

Confocal digital image of rat cortex. Glial cells have been stained yellow and the nuclei red. © Thomas Deerinck and Mark Ellisman, The National Center for Microscopy and Imaging Research, UCSD.

Behavioral Neuroscience, Eighth Edition

Copyright © 2017 by Sinauer Associates, Inc.
All rights reserved. This book may not be reproduced in whole or in part without permission from the publisher.
For information, address
Sinauer Associates, Inc. P.O. Box 407, Sunderland, MA 01375 U.S.A.
Fax: 413-549-1118
E-mail: publish@sinauer.com
Internet: www.sinauer.com

Library of Congress Catologing-in Publication Data
Names: Breedlove, S. Marc, author. | Watson, Neil V. (Neil Verne), 1962– author.
Title: Behavioral neuroscience / S. Marc Breedlove, Michigan State University, Neil V. Watson, Simon Fraser University.
Other titles: Biological psychology
Description: Eighth edition. | Sunderland, Massachusetts: Sinauer Associates, Inc., Publishers, [2017] | Revision of: Biological psychology. 2013. Seventh edition. | Includes bibliographical references and index.
Identifiers: LCCN 2016033728 | ISBN 9781605354187
Classification: LCC QP360 .B727 2017 | DDC 612.8--dc23
LC record available at https://lccn.loc.gov/2016033728

Printed in U.S.A.
6 5 4 3 2 1

Brief Contents

Contents

PART II
Evolution and Development of the Nervous System 161

6 | Evolution of the Brain and Behavior 163

7 | Life-Span Development of the Brain and Behavior 193

PART III
Perception and Action 227

8 | General Principles of Sensory Processing, Touch, and Pain 229

PART VI
Cognitive Neuroscience 533

17 Learning and Memory 535

18 Attention and Higher Cognition 573

Preface

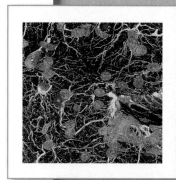

For over 20 years now, we have been striving to make *Biological Psychology* the definitive and comprehensive undergraduate survey of the neuroscience of behavior. Thanks to the explosion of discovery in the neurosciences, each of the past seven editions has included more neural details than the one before. Thus we felt the time had come to revise the title to reflect the evolution of both the book and the field: *Behavioral Neuroscience*. Many courses and degree programs have already made this transition in nomenclature, and for the same reasons. The wealth of data coming from the neurosciences means we spend more time talking, writing, and thinking about neuroscience than any other field of biology while, of course, maintaining our focus on behavior. We're still full-fledged psychologists (between us we have six degrees and all are in psychology), but we're also card-carrying neuroscientists, so the new title seems better suited to our personal outlooks as well as the state of the field. It would have been fine to have a title using both *psychology* and *neuroscience*, but *Neuroscientific Psychology* and *Psychological Neuroscience* both sounded awkward, while the term *neuropsychology* already describes a rather narrow slice of the material we cover. So *Behavioral Neuroscience* it is and will be for the foreseeable future.

As in previous revisions, there have been plenty of new findings to include. In fact, the problem we face is which of the many, many new findings to *leave out*—those that are not quite essential for a survey of the field. We work hard to be judicious in what we add, and still it seems like a waterfall of new information and ideas. Over 600 new papers are cited in this edition. If that sounds like a lot, let us give you a perspective on how many new papers were omitted. On our newsfeed site (behavioralneuroscience8e.com/news or bn8e.com/news) over 1300 new links relevant to behavioral neuroscience were added in 2015 alone. Those are just the findings that were important enough to get the attention of mass media reporters. Over 31,000 new articles indexed under "neuroscience" appeared that year in PubMed, where the pace is set to reach over 44,000 articles in 2016. It would take several textbooks just to list the titles of papers we couldn't include.

Despite being very selective in sampling from this deluge of new information, we have made substantial changes in every chapter. For example, in Chapter 2 we talk about growing concerns that the algorithms guiding fMRI analysis may be faulty, and in Chapter 7 we discuss new brain-scanning methods to visualize Tau as well as amyloid for screening for Alzheimer's. Chapter 13 contains a discussion of new evidence that long-lasting metabolic changes work against permanent weight loss, and in Chapter 17 we outline the growing consensus for a dual-process model of human memory that distinguishes between familiarity and recollection. Several chapters have new Cutting Edge material, like the use of DREADDS in Chapter 5 and the important new insights in pain mechanisms revealed by the study of scorpion venom in Chapter 8. Other additions have been made, not because of new developments but to provide a broader perspective of the field. For example, Chapter 3 now discusses the Nernst and Goldman equations and includes a box on patch clamping, while new figures depict sleep in hunter-gatherer societies (Chapter 14) and the importance of a sense of life purpose for surviving heart disease (Chapter 15). Several chapters include new case studies, like the story of Mary Lou Jepsen, who without endogenous pituitary hormones must titrate her personality as she takes exogenous hormones (Chapter 5); "Bella," who found out the night before starting junior high that she had been born a boy (Chapter 12); and Eleanor, who began hearing voices her first year in college (Chapter 16). As in past revisions, we keep squeezing into the page proofs fascinating tidbits that have just come to light, tempting the patience of the editorial staff. We feel confident in our status as the official "impossible authors" of Sinauer Associates.

We've also retained two very popular changes introduced in the previous edition: **The Cutting Edge** at the end of each chapter, where we explore some of the most exciting examples of recent research, followed by a **Visual Summary**, where students see graphic reminders as they review the principle findings that we just presented. As in the previous edition, we also encourage students to use these Visual Summaries online, where with just a click they can review figures, animations, and quizzes to help them integrate the material. We also continue to open each chapter with a gripping **vignette**, relating someone's real-life experiences that will be better understood as the content of the chapter unfolds, and we continue to replace several of these vignettes as more recent events bring to the surface many of the important issues in behavioral neuroscience. Likewise we've retained the marginal glossary that makes sure students can always find the definitions they need to incorporate the material, as well as two features to guide students when they want to burrow in on a particular subject: the online supplements called **A Step Further** found throughout the text, and the **Recommended Reading** at the close of each chapter.

You might think after 20 years we'd be tired of improving and revising our presentations, but the dynamic and exciting pace of neuroscience research shows no sign of abating soon. As always, we welcome all feedback, praise or criticism, cuts or additions, from our readers. You can email us directly at **bn8e@sinauer.com**.

Acknowledgments

The authors feel privileged to work with the peerless team at Sinauer Associates, whose deep skills and generous guidance transform a collection of Word files and napkin-scribbles into the gorgeous volume you are currently holding. In particular, the book could not exist without the contributions of Editor Syd Carroll, Production Editor Kathaleen Emerson, Production Manager Chris Small, Book Designer Joanne Delphia, and Media and Supplements Editor Jason Dirks and his crew, along with Julie HawkOwl. We'd also like to thank our Copy Editor Lou Doucette, and our longtime art studio, Dragonfly Media.

By now many generous reviewers have provided comments and suggestions that continually improve our efforts, so of course we want to thank them, including: Brian Derrick, Karen De Valois, Russell De Valois, Jack Gallant, Ervin Hafter, Richard Ivry, Lucia Jacobs, Dacher Keltner, Raymond E. Kesner, Joe L. Martinez, Jr., James L. McGaugh, Frederick Seil, Arthur Shimamura, and Irving Zucker for the very first edition. Then, Alfonso Abizaid, Duane Albrecht, Chalon E. Anderson, Michael Antle, Anthony Austin, A. Michael Babcock, Benoit Bacon, John-Paul Baird, Scott Baron, Terence J. Bazzett, Mark S. Blumberg, Charlotte A. Boettiger, Eliot A. Brenowitz, Bruce Bridgeman, Chris Brill, Peter C. Brunjes, Rebecca D. Burwell, Judith Byrnes-Enoch, Kevin A. Corcoran, Joshua D. Cosman, Catherine P. Cramer, Paul J. Currie, Deana Davalos, Heather Dickinson-Anson, Tiffany Donaldson, Kristine Erickson, Marcie Finkelstein, Loretta M. Flanagan-Cato, Robert Flint, Francis W. Flynn, John D. E. Gabrieli, Philip Gasquoine, Matthew Gendle, Kimberley P. Good, Diane C. Gooding, Janet M. Gray, John T. Green, James Gross, Joshua M. Gulley, Derek A. Hamilton, S. E. Hammack, Mary E. Harrington, Michael J. Hawken, Wendy Heller,

Christine Holler-Dinsmore, Mark Hollins, Katherine Hooper, Susan M. Jenks, Janice Juraska, Ilia N. Karatsoreos, Anna Klintsova, Keith R. Kluender, Leah A. Krubitzer, Ryan T. LaLumiere, Joseph E. LeDoux, Michael A. Leon, M. P. Leussis, Simon LeVay, Ming Li, Jeremy L. Loebach, Stephen G. Lomber, Kathleen B. Lustyk, Cyrille Magne, Robert G. Mair, Susan E. Maloney, Donna Maney, Stephen A. Maren, Christopher May, John J. McDonald, Robert J. McDonald, Steven Meier, Robert L. Meisel, Garrett W. Milliken, Ralph Mistlberger, Jeffrey S. Mogil, Andrea M. Morris, Randy J. Nelson, Chris Newland, Miguel Nicolelis, Marilee Ogren, Jaime F. Olavarria, M. Foster Olive, Lee Osterhout, James Pfaus, Kimberley A. Phillips, Helene S. Porte, Joseph H. Porter, Anne E. Powell Anderson, Jason J. Radley, George V. Rebec, Christian G. Reich, Linda Rinaldini Head, Shannon Robertson, Scott R. Robinson, David A. Rosenbaum, Jeanne P. Ryan, Lawrence J. Ryan, Lisa Sanders, Martin F. Sarter, Jeffrey D. Schall, Stan Schein, Erik Schweitzer, Dale R. Sengelaub, Fred Shaffer, Matthew Shapiro, Rae Silver, Cheryl L. Sisk, Laura Smale, David M. Smith, Robert L. Spencer, Steven J. St. John, J. A. Stamp, Steven K. Sutton, Harald K. Taukulis, Jaime L. Tartar, Sheralee Tershner, David G. Thomas, Jeramy Townsley, Franco J. Vaccarino, David R. Vago, Cyma Van Petten, Charles J. Vierck, Charlene Wages, Jonathan D. Wallis, Ryan Wessell, Leonard E. White, Robert Wickesberg, Christoph Wiedenmayer, Walter Wilczynski, S. Mark Williams, Richard D. Wright, and Mark C. Zrull.

In this most recent edition we benefited from the critiques of many colleagues, and we want to express our appreciation to them, too:

Richard Addante, *The University of Texas at Dallas*
Chana Akins, *University of Kentucky*
Daniel J. Brasier, *Carnegie Mellon University*
Melissa Burns Cusato, *Centre College*
Brian Coffman, *University of New Mexico*
Derek Daniels, *The State University of New York at Buffalo*
Darragh P. Devine, *University of Florida*
Marc Dingman, *Pennsylvania State University*
Stan B. Floresco, *University of British Columbia*
Peter J. Gianaros, *University of Pittsburgh*
Ralf R. Greenwald, *Central Washington University*
Matthew Holahan, *Carleton University*
Eric Jackson, *University of New Mexico*
Michael Jarvinen, *Emmanuel College*
Lori Knackstedt, *University of Florida*
Ryan T. LaLumiere, *University of Iowa*
Jennifer Lewis, *University of Oregon*
Scott MacDougall-Shackleton, *University of Western Ontario*
John McDonald, *Simon Fraser University*
Ewan McNay, *University at Albany, State University of New York*
Naomi Nagaya, *Texas A&M University*
Jin Ho Park, *University of Massachusetts, Boston*
Nathan A. Parks, *University of Arkansas*
Linda D. Rice, *Adler University*
Russell D. Romeo, *Barnard College*
Victoria Smith, *University of Calgary*
Sara Taylor, *Hendrix College*
Jan Tornick, *University of New Hampshire*
Donna Toufexis, *University of Vermont*
Lucy J. Troup, *Colorado State University*
Katie Wiens, *Christopher Newport University*
David Yager, *University of Maryland*

As always, we fondly recall our previous coauthors, Mark R. Rosenzweig and Arnold L. Leiman, whose intellectual stamp is still apparent on this, our ever-evolving joint effort. We'd like to think they would be proud of this new edition, too. Finally, our thanks to all those tireless colleagues who keep trying to understand the neural basis of behavior, using techniques that would have seemed like sorcery only a few years ago, and who share their hard-won findings with us all.

S. Marc Breedlove

Neil V. Watson

Media and Supplements

to accompany *Behavioral Neuroscience,* Eighth Edition

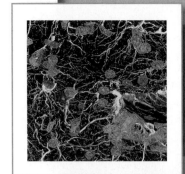

For the Student

Companion Website (behavioralneuroscience8e.com)

The *Behavioral Neuroscience* Companion Website contains a range of study and review resources to help students master the material presented in each chapter of the textbook. Access to the site is included with each new copy of the textbook (see inside front cover). The site includes the following resources:

- Chapter outlines
- Visual summaries
- Study questions
- Animations and videos
- Activities
- "A Step Further" topics
- Online quizzes (multiple-choice and essay questions)
- Flashcards
- Complete glossary

(Note that instructor registration is required in order for students to access the online quizzes.)

BioPsychology NewsLink (behavioralneuroscience8e.com/news)

This invaluable online resource helps students make connections between the science of behavioral neuroscience and their daily lives, and keeps them apprised of the latest developments in the field. The site includes links to thousands of news stories, all organized both by keyword and by textbook chapter. The site is updated 3–4 times per week, so it includes up-to-the-minute information. NewsLink updates are also available on Facebook (facebook.com/behavioralneuroscience).

For the Instructor

Instructor's Resource Library

The *Behavioral Neuroscience* Instructor's Resource Library (available to qualified adopters) includes a variety of resources to aid in course planning, lecture development, and student assessment. The Resource Library includes:

PRESENTATION RESOURCES

- *Figures & Tables*: All of the figures (including photos) and tables from the textbook are provided as both high-resolution and low-resolution JPEGs, all optimized for use in presentations.

- *PowerPoint Presentations*: Two PowerPoint presentations are provided for each chapter of the textbook:
  - Figures: All of the chapter's figures, photos, and tables, with titles and complete captions
  - Lectures: Complete lecture outlines, including selected figures
- *Videos*: New for the Eighth Edition, the instructor video collection has been greatly expanded with a new collection of fascinating segments from BBC programs that illustrate many important concepts from the textbook.
- *Animations*: These detailed animations from the companion website help enliven lectures and illustrate dynamic processes.

INSTRUCTOR'S MANUAL

The Instructor's Manual includes useful resources for planning your course, lectures, and exams. For each chapter of the textbook, the IM includes a chapter overview, a chapter outline, the chapter's key concepts, additional references for course and lecture development, and a list of the chapter's key terms.

TEST BANK

The Test Bank consists of a broad range of questions covering key facts and concepts in each chapter. Multiple choice, fill-in-the-blank, matching, essay, and paragraph development questions are included. The Test Bank also includes the Companion Website online quiz questions. Questions are ranked according to Bloom's Taxonomy and referenced to specific textbook sections.

COMPUTERIZED TEST BANK

The entire Test Bank, including all of the online quiz questions, is provided in Blackboard's Diploma format (software included). Diploma makes it easy to assemble quizzes and exams from any combination of publisher-provided questions and instructor-created questions.

ONLINE QUIZZING

The *Behavioral Neuroscience* Companion Website features pre-built chapter quizzes that report into an online gradebook. Adopting instructors have access to these quizzes and can choose to either assign them or let students use them for review. (Instructors must register in order for their students to be able to take the quizzes.) Instructors also have the ability to add their own questions and create their own quizzes.

COURSE MANAGEMENT SYSTEM SUPPORT

The Test Bank is also provided in Blackboard format, for easy import into campus Blackboard systems. In addition, using the Computerized Test Bank, instructors can create and export quizzes and exams (or the entire test bank) for import into other course management systems, including Moodle, Canvas, and Desire2Learn/Brightspace.

Value Options

eBook

Behavioral Neuroscience, Eighth Edition is available as an eBook, in several different formats, including VitalSource, RedShelf, Yuzu, and BryteWave. The eBook can be purchased as either a 180-day rental or a permanent (non-expiring) subscription. All major mobile devices are supported. For details on the eBook platforms offered, please visit www.sinauer.com/ebooks.

Looseleaf Textbook

(ISBN 978-1-60535-642-6)
Behavioral Neuroscience is also available in a three-hole punched, looseleaf format. Students can take just the sections they need to class and can easily integrate instructor material with the text.

Behavioral Neuroscience
Eighth Edition

Behavioral Neuroscience
Scope and Outlook

1

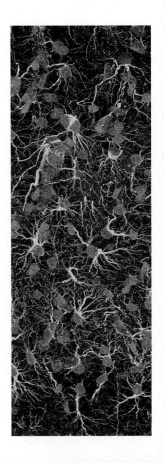

◼ Human or Machine?

In the haunting movie *A.I. Artificial Intelligence*, set late in this century, robots have been developed that imitate humans in a nearly flawless fashion. These humanoid robots, called *Mecha*, fulfill any number of functions, including social interactions where they are programmed to simulate emotional reactions that would be appropriate to the situation. But of course just because Mecha *act* sympathetic, or excited, or happy, displaying the facial and body language of those emotions and saying the words that humans say when they feel them, that doesn't mean that these machines actually *experience* emotions.

A new, advanced model Mecha named David, built to resemble a 10-year-old boy, is programmed to "imprint" upon his adoptive mother, Monica, so that he projects the sort of love and devotion for her that a real boy would display for his mother. Once David has fulfilled his temporary function, his "mother" cannot bring herself to destroy the robot, abandoning him instead. David's subsequent behavior forces the viewer to wonder whether his emotions are simulated or real.

We can't be sure whether David really experiences love or dejection because *A.I.* is, after all, only a movie. But we can reverse the metaphor to ask something else: whether *Monica is actually a machine*. Not a machine made of metal and plastic with a silicon-based computer guiding her behavior, but a machine made of trillions of cells forming flesh and bone, with trillions more cells in her brain that guide her behavior. Those cells in her brain also cause Monica to *experience* love, anguish, and grief as genuinely as any human has ever experienced them. We don't know anything about David or the other Mecha because they don't exist, but modern science has learned a great deal about how Monica's brain—and your brain—works. Our aim in this book is to help you learn what is known so far about how brains work, and how much more we have yet to learn.

In this book we explore the many ways in which the structures and actions of the brain produce mind and behavior. But that is only half of our task. We are also interested in the ways in which behavior and experience in turn modify the structures and actions of the brain. One of the most important lessons we hope to convey is that interactions between brain and behavior are reciprocal. The brain controls behavior and, in turn, behavior and experience alter the brain.

We hope to give an interesting account of the main ideas and research in behavioral neuroscience, which is of great popular as well as scientific interest. Because there are so many strands to tie together, we try to introduce a given piece of information when it makes a difference to the understanding of a subject—especially when it forms part of a story. Most important, we try to communicate our own interest and excitement about the mysteries of mind and body.

Go to **Brain Explorer**
bn8e.com/1.1

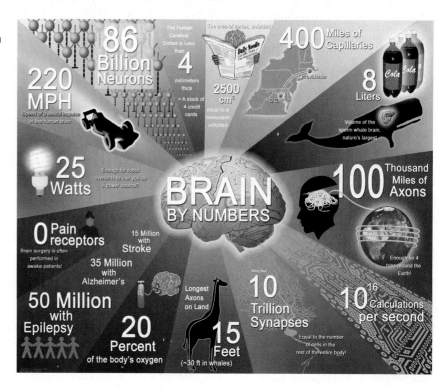

The Brain Is Full of Surprises

I used to think that the brain was the most wonderful organ in my body. Then I realized who was telling me this.

—Emo Philips
(American comedian)

Of course we should always consider the source when evaluating an idea, but even so, the brain seems like a very wonderful organ. For one thing, brains produced the entire extent of human knowledge, everything we understand about the universe, however limited that may be. Brains also produced every written description of that hard-won knowledge (including this book you hold in your hands), as well as every work of visual art, from doodles to sweeping murals on the ceiling of the Sistine Chapel.

Most of us have a hard time grasping the idea of a billion of anything, but your head contains an estimated 86 billion nerve cells, or **neurons** (from the Greek word for "nerve" or "cord") (Herculano-Houzel, 2012). Each neuron contacts many other cells at points called *synapses*, so there are *trillions* of those between your ears. A specialized extension of neurons, called an *axon*, is microscopically slender, yet it may be several feet long. We'll learn that axons produce electrical impulses that travel hundreds of miles per hour. **FIGURE 1.1** offers a list of just a few of the things we will learn about the human brain in the course of this book. All this hardware isn't just for show—it allows you to take in all the information in that figure in less than a minute.

What Is Behavioral Neuroscience?

neuron   Also called *nerve cell*. The basic unit of the nervous system.

neuroscience   The study of the nervous system.

behavioral neuroscience   Also called *biological psychology*. The study of the neural bases of behavior and mental processes.

No treaty or trade union agreement defines the boundaries of behavioral neuroscience. The first people to study the relationships between brain and behavior regarded themselves as philosophers, and their findings contributed to the births of biology and psychology. Those disciplines merged in the twentieth century to form *biological psychology*, the field that relates behavior to bodily processes. With the modern explosion of **neuroscience**, the study of the brain, this research has evolved to the point that **behavioral neuroscience** offers a more accurate description. Whichever name is used, the main goal of this field is to understand the neuroscience underlying behavior and experience.

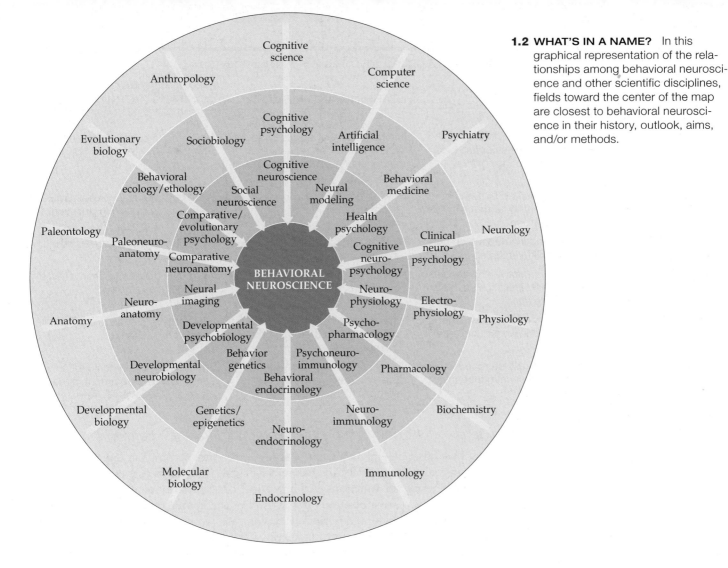

1.2 WHAT'S IN A NAME? In this graphical representation of the relationships among behavioral neuroscience and other scientific disciplines, fields toward the center of the map are closest to behavioral neuroscience in their history, outlook, aims, and/or methods.

Behavioral neuroscience is a field that includes many players who come from quite different backgrounds: psychologists, biologists, physiologists, engineers, neurologists, psychiatrists, and many others. Thus, there are many career opportunities, in both universities and private industry, for people with interests in this field (Hitt, 2007). **FIGURE 1.2** maps the relations of behavioral neuroscience to these many other disciplines. Clearly, the behavioral neuroscience umbrella opens very wide.

Five Viewpoints Explore the Biology of Behavior

In our pursuit to understand the neuroscience bases of behavior, we use several different perspectives. Because each one yields information that complements the others, the combination of perspectives is especially powerful. We will discuss five major perspectives:

1. *Describing* behavior
2. Studying the *evolution* of behavior
3. Observing the *development* of behavior and its biological characteristics over the life span
4. Studying the biological *mechanisms* of behavior
5. Studying *applications* of behavioral neuroscience—for example, its applications to dysfunctions of human behavior

These perspectives are discussed in the sections that follow, and **TABLE 1.1** on the next page illustrates how each perspective can be applied to three kinds of behavior.

TABLE 1.1 Five Research Perspectives Applied to Three Kinds of Behavior

RESEARCH PERSPECTIVE	SEXUAL BEHAVIOR	LEARNING AND MEMORY	LANGUAGE AND COMMUNICATION
DESCRIPTION			
Structural	What are the main patterns of reproductive behavior and sex differences in behavior?	In what main ways does behavior change as a consequence of experience—for example, conditioning?	How are the sounds of speech patterned?
Functional	How do specialized patterns of behavior contribute to mating and to care of young?	How do certain behaviors lead to rewards or avoidance of punishment?	What behavior is involved in making statements or asking questions?
EVOLUTION	How does mating depend on hormones in different species?	How do different species compare in kinds and speed of learning?	How did the human speech apparatus evolve?
DEVELOPMENT	How do reproductive and secondary sex characteristics develop over the life span?	How do learning and memory change as we grow older?	What changes in the brain when a child learns to speak?
MECHANISMS	What neural circuits and hormones are involved in reproductive behavior?	What anatomical and chemical changes in the brain hold memories?	What brain regions are particularly involved in language?
APPLICATIONS	Low doses of testosterone restore libido in some postmenopausal women.	Gene therapy and behavioral therapy improve memory in some senile patients.	Speech therapy, in conjunction with amphetamine treatment, speeds language recovery following stroke.

Behavior can be described according to different criteria

Until we describe what we want to study, we cannot accomplish much. Depending on our goals, we may describe behavior in terms of detailed acts or processes, or in terms of results or functions. An analytical description of arm movements might record the successive positions of the limb or the contraction of different muscles. A functional behavioral description, by contrast, would state whether the limb was being used in walking or running, texting or sexting. To be useful for scientific study, a description must be precise and reveal the essential features of the behavior, using accurately defined terms and units.

We compare species to learn how the brain and behavior have evolved

Charles Darwin's theory of evolution through natural selection is central to all modern biology. From this perspective emerge two rather different emphases: (1) the *continuity* of behavior and biological processes among species because of our common ancestry and (2) the species-specific *differences* in behavior and biology that have evolved as adaptations to different environments.

Nature is conservative. Once particular features of the body or behavior evolve, they may be maintained for millions of years and may be seen in animals that otherwise appear very different. For example, the electrical messages used by nerve cells (see Chapter 3) are essentially the same in a jellyfish, a cockroach, and a human being. Some of the chemical compounds that transmit messages through the bloodstream (hormones) are also the same in diverse animals (see Chapter 5). Species share these **conserved** characteristics because the features first arose in a shared ancestor (**BOX 1.1**). But mere similarity of a feature between species does not guarantee that the feature came from a common ancestral species. Similar solutions to a problem may have evolved independently in different classes of animals.

The body and behavior develop over the life span

Ontogeny is the process by which an individual changes in the course of its lifetime—that is, grows up and grows old. Observing the way in which a particular behavior changes during ontogeny may give us clues to its functions and mechanisms. For example, we know that learning ability in monkeys increases over the first years of life. Therefore, we can speculate that prolonged maturation of brain circuits is re-

conserved In the context of evolution, referring to a trait that is passed on from a common ancestor to two or more descendant species.

ontogeny The process by which an individual changes in the course of its lifetime—that is, grows up and grows old.

We Are All Alike, and We Are All Different

Each person has some characteristics shared by…

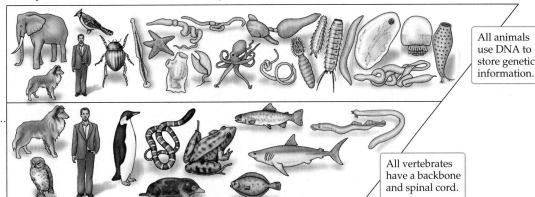

all animals…

All animals use DNA to store genetic information.

all vertebrates…

All vertebrates have a backbone and spinal cord.

all mammals…

All mammals suckle their young.

all primates…

All primates have a hand with an opposable thumb and a relatively large, complex brain.

all humans (people)…

All humans use symbolic language to communicate with each other.

some people…

Some people like to eat beets (no one knows why).

no other person.

No two people, even identical twins, are alike in each and every way, as individual experiences leave their unique stamp on every brain.

How do similarities and differences among people and animals fit into behavioral neuroscience? Each person is in some ways like all other people, in some ways like some other people, and in some ways like no other person. As the figure shows, we can extend this observation to the much broader range of animal life. In some ways each person is like all other animals (e.g., needing to ingest complex organic nutrients), in some ways like all other vertebrates (e.g., having a spinal column), in some ways like all other mammals (e.g., nursing our young), and in some ways like all other primates (e.g., having a hand with an opposable thumb and a relatively large, complex brain).

Whether knowledge gained about a process in another species applies to humans depends on whether we are like that species in regard to that process. The fundamental research on the mechanisms of inheritance in the bacterium *Escherichia coli* proved so widely applicable that some molecular biologists proclaimed, "What is true of *E. coli* is true of the elephant." To a remarkable extent, that statement is true, but there are also some important differences in the genetic mechanisms of *E. coli* and mammals.

With respect to each biological property, researchers must determine how animals are identical and how they are different. When we seek animal models for studying human behavior or biological processes, we must ask the following question: Does the proposed animal model really have some things in common with the process at work in humans (Seok et al., 2013)? We will see many cases in which it does.

Even within the same species, however, individuals differ from one another: cat from cat, blue jay from blue jay, and person from person. Behavioral neuroscience seeks to understand individual differences as well as similarities. Therefore, the way in which each person is able to process information and store the memories of these experiences is another part of our story.

quired for complex learning tasks. In rodents, the ability to form long-term memories lags somewhat behind the maturation of learning ability. So, young rodents learn well but forget more quickly than older ones, suggesting that learning and memory involve different processes. Studying the development of reproductive capacity and of differences in behavior between the sexes, along with changes in body structures and processes, throws light on body mechanisms underlying sexual behaviors.

Biological mechanisms underlie all behavior

To learn about the mechanisms of an individual's behavior, we study how his or her *present* body works. To understand the underlying mechanisms of behavior, we must regard the organism (with all due respect) as a "machine," made up of billions of neurons. We must ask, How is this thing constructed to be able to do all that?

Our major aim in behavioral neuroscience is to examine body mechanisms that make particular behaviors possible. In the case of learning and memory, for example, we would like to know the sequence of electrical and biochemical processes that occur when we learn something and retrieve it from memory. What parts of the nervous system are involved in that process? In the case of reproductive behavior, we also want to understand the neuronal and hormonal processes that underlie mating behaviors.

Research can be applied to human problems

Like other sciences, behavioral neuroscience is also dedicated to improving the human condition. Numerous human diseases involve malfunctioning of the brain. Many of these are already being alleviated as a result of research in the neurosciences, and the prospects for continuing advances are good. Attempts to apply knowledge also benefit basic research. For example, the study of memory disorders in humans has pushed investigators to extend our knowledge of the brain regions involved in different kinds of memory (see Chapter 17).

Three Approaches Relate Brain and Behavior

Behavioral neuroscientists use three approaches to understand the relationship between brain and behavior: somatic intervention, behavioral intervention, and correlation. In the most common approach, **somatic intervention** (**FIGURE 1.3A**), we alter a structure or function of the brain or body to see how this alteration changes behavior. Here, somatic intervention is the **independent variable**, and the behavioral effect is the **dependent variable**; that is, the resulting behavior depends on how the brain has been altered. For example, in response to mild electrical stimulation of one part of her brain, not only did one patient laugh, but she found whatever she happened to be looking at amusing (Fried et al., 1998).

In later chapters we describe many kinds of somatic intervention with both humans and other animals, as in the following examples:

- A hormone is administered to some animals but not to others; various behaviors of the two groups are later compared.
- A part of the brain is stimulated electrically, or by use of lasers to stimulate only a particular class of neurons, and behavioral effects are observed.
- A connection between two parts of the nervous system is cut, and changes in behavior are measured.

The approach opposite to somatic intervention is psychological or **behavioral intervention** (**FIGURE 1.3B**). In this approach, the scientist intervenes in the behavior or experience of an organism and looks for resulting changes in body structure or function. Here, behavior is the independent variable, and change in the body is the dependent variable. Among the examples that we will consider in later chapters are the following:

- Putting two adults of opposite sex together may lead to increased secretion of certain hormones.

somatic intervention An approach to finding relations between body variables and behavioral variables that involves manipulating body structure or function and looking for resultant changes in behavior.

independent variable The factor that is manipulated by an experimenter.

dependent variable The factor that an experimenter measures to monitor a change in response to manipulation of an independent variable.

behavioral intervention An approach to finding relations between body variables and behavioral variables that involves intervening in the behavior of an organism and looking for resultant changes in body structure or function.

(A) Manipulating the body may affect behavior

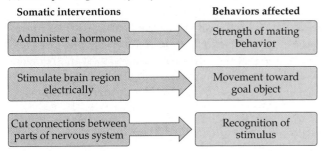

Somatic interventions		Behaviors affected
Administer a hormone	→	Strength of mating behavior
Stimulate brain region electrically	→	Movement toward goal object
Cut connections between parts of nervous system	→	Recognition of stimulus

(B) Experience affects the body (including the brain)

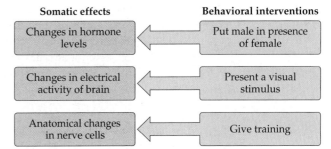

Somatic effects		Behavioral interventions
Changes in hormone levels	←	Put male in presence of female
Changes in electrical activity of brain	←	Present a visual stimulus
Anatomical changes in nerve cells	←	Give training

(C) Body and behavioral measures covary

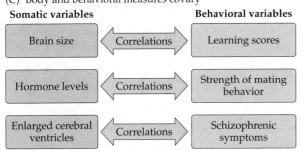

Somatic variables		Behavioral variables
Brain size	Correlations	Learning scores
Hormone levels	Correlations	Strength of mating behavior
Enlarged cerebral ventricles	Correlations	Schizophrenic symptoms

(D) Behavioral neuroscience seeks to understand all these relationships

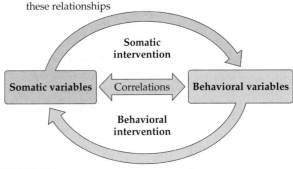

1.3 THREE MAIN APPROACHES TO STUDYING THE NEUROSCIENCE OF BEHAVIOR (A) In *somatic intervention*, investigators change the body structure or chemistry of an animal in some way and observe and measure any resulting behavioral effects. (B) Conversely, in *behavioral intervention*, researchers change an animal's behavior or its environment and try to ascertain whether the change results in physiological or anatomical changes. (C) Measurements of both kinds of variables allow researchers to arrive at *correlations* between somatic changes and behavioral changes. (D) Each approach enriches and informs the others.

- Exposing a person or animal to a visual stimulus provokes changes in electrical activity and blood flow in parts of the brain.

- Training of animals in a maze is accompanied by electrical, biochemical, and anatomical changes in parts of their brains.

The third approach to brain-behavior relations, **correlation** (**FIGURE 1.3C**), consists of finding the extent to which a given body measure varies with a given behavioral measure. Later we will examine the following questions, among others:

- Are people with large brains more intelligent than people with smaller brains (a topic we'll take up later in this chapter)?

- Are individual differences in sexual behavior correlated with levels of certain hormones in the individuals?

- Is the severity of schizophrenia correlated with the magnitude of changes in brain structure?

Such correlations should not be taken as proof of causal relationship. For one thing, even if a causal relation exists, the correlation does not reveal its direction—that is, which variable is independent and which is dependent. For another, two factors might be correlated only because a third, unknown factor affects the two factors measured. If you and your study partner get similar scores on an exam, that's not because your performance *caused* her to get the score she did, or vice versa. What a correlation does suggest is that the two variables are linked in some way—directly or indirectly. Such a correlation often stimulates investigators to formulate hypotheses and to test them by somatic or behavioral intervention. Only by moving on to such

correlation The covariation of two measures.

neuroplasticity Also called *neural plasticity*. The ability of the nervous system to change in response to experience or the environment.

intervention approaches can we establish whether one variable is *causing* changes in the other.

Combining these three approaches yields the circle diagram of **FIGURE 1.3D**, incorporating the basic approaches to studying relationships between bodily processes and behavior. It also emphasizes the theme that the relations between brain and behavior are reciprocal: each affects the other in an ongoing cycle of bodily and behavioral interactions. We will see examples of this reciprocal relationship throughout the book.

Neuroplasticity: Behavior Can Change the Brain

The idea that there is a reciprocal relationship between brain and behavior has embedded within it a concept that is, for most people, startling. When we say that behavior and experience affect the brain, we mean that they, literally, physically alter the brain. The brain of a child growing up in a French-speaking household assembles itself into a configuration different from that of the brain of a child who hears only English. That's why the first child, as an adult, understands French effortlessly while the second does not. In this case we cannot tell you what the structural differences are exactly, but we do know one part of the brain that is being altered by these different experiences (see Chapter 19).

Numerous examples, almost all in animal subjects, show that experience can affect the number or size of neurons, or the number or size of connections between neurons. This ability of the brain, both in development and in adulthood, to be changed by the environment and by experience is called **neuroplasticity** (or *neural plasticity*, or simply *plasticity*).

Today when we hear the word *plastic*, we think of the class of materials found in so many modern products. But originally, *plastic* meant "flexible, malleable" (from the Greek *plassein*, "to mold or form"), and the modern materials were named *plastics* because they can be molded into nearly any shape. In 1890, William James (1842–1910) described plasticity as the possession of a structure weak enough to yield to an influence but strong enough not to yield all at once.

In the ensuing years, research has shown that the brain is even more plastic, more yielding, than James suspected. For example, parts of neurons known as *dendritic spines* (see Chapter 2) appear to be in constant motion, changing shape in the course of seconds (H. Fischer et al., 1998). We will see many examples in which experience alters the structure and/or function of the brain: In Chapter 5, you'll read that hearing a baby cry causes the mother's brain to secrete a hormone. In Chapter 7, we'll see that visual experience in kittens directs the formation of connections in the brain. In Chapter 12, we'll discuss how a mother rat's grooming of her pups affects the survival of spinal cord neurons. And Chapter 17 talks about how a sea slug learning a task changes the connections between two particular neurons.

Behavioral neuroscience and social psychology are related

The plasticity of the human brain has a remarkable consequence: other individuals can affect the physical structure of your brain! Indeed, the whole point of coming to a lecture hall is to have the instructor use words and figures to alter your brain so that you can retrieve that information in the future (in other words, she is teaching you something). Many of these alterations in your brain last only until you take an exam, but every once in a while the instructor may tell you something that you'll remember for the rest of your life. Most aspects of our social behavior are learned—from the language we speak to the clothes we wear and the kinds of food we eat—so the mechanisms of learning and memory (see Chapter 17) are important for understanding social behavior.

For an example from an animal model, consider the fact that rats spend a lot of time investigating the smells around them, including those coming from other rats. Cooke et al. (2000) took young male rats, just weaned from their mother, and raised them in two different ways: either alone in separate cages, or with other males in group cages so they could engage in play (including a lot of sniffing of each other's butts). Examination of these animals as adults found only one brain difference between the groups: a region of the brain known to process odors was smaller in the isolated males than in the males raised with playmates (**FIGURE 1.4**). Was it the lack of play (N. S. Gordon et al., 2003), the lack of odors to investigate, or the stress of isolation that made the region smaller? Whatever the mechanism, social experience affects this brain structure. In Chapter 17 we'll see more examples of social experience altering the brain.

Here's an example of how social influences can affect the human brain. When people were asked to put a hand into moderately hot water (47°C), part of the brain became active, presumably because of the discomfort involved (Rainville et al., 1997). But people who were led to believe the water would be *very* hot had a more activated brain than did those led to believe the discomfort would be minimal (**FIGURE 1.5**), even though the water was the same temperature for everyone. The socially induced psychological expectation affected the magnitude of the brain response, even though the physical stimulus was exactly the same. (By the way, the people with the more activated brains also reported feeling more pain.)

In most cases, biological and social factors continually interact and affect each other in an ongoing series of events as behavior unfolds. For example, the level of the hormone testosterone in a man's circulation affects his dominance behavior and aggression (see Chapter 15). The dominance may be exhibited in a great variety of social settings, ranging from playing chess to physical aggression. In humans and other primates, the level of testosterone correlates positively with the degree of dominance and with the amount of aggression exhibited. Winning a contest, whether a game of chess or a boxing match, raises the level of testosterone; losing a contest lowers the level. Thus, at any moment the level of testosterone is determined, in part, by recent dominant-submissive social experience, and the level of testosterone determines, in part, the degree of dominance and aggression in the future. Of course, social and cultural factors also help determine the frequency of aggression; cross-cultural differences in rates of aggression exist that cannot be correlated with hormone levels, and ways of expressing aggression and dominance are influenced by sociocultural factors.

Perhaps nothing distinguishes behavioral neuroscience from other neurosciences more clearly than this fascination with neuroplasticity and the role of experience. Behavioral neuroscientists have a pervasive interest in how experience physically alters the brain and therefore affects future behavior. We will touch on this theme in every chapter of this book.

> Only in this brain region was growth stunted by the lack of opportunity to play.

1.4 THE ROLE OF PLAY IN BRAIN DEVELOPMENT A brain region involved in processing odors (the posterodorsal portion of the medial amygdala) was smaller in male rats housed individually than in males housed together and allowed to play. Other nearby regions were identical in the two groups. (After Cooke et al., 2000.)

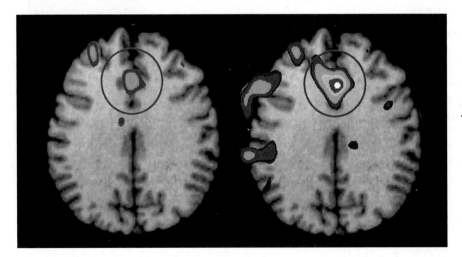

1.5 PICTURES OF PAIN People told to expect only mild discomfort from putting a hand into 47°C water (left) showed less activation in a particular brain region (the anterior cingulate cortex) than did people expecting more discomfort (right) from water of the very same temperature. Areas of high activation are indicated by orange, red, and white. (From Rainville et al., 1997, courtesy of Dr. Pierre Rainville.)

Behavioral Neuroscientists Use Several Levels of Analysis

reductionism The scientific strategy of breaking a system down into increasingly smaller parts in order to understand it.

levels of analysis The scope of experimental approaches. A scientist may try to understand behavior by monitoring molecules, nerve cells, brain regions, or social environments, or some combination of these levels of analysis.

1.6 LEVELS OF ANALYSIS IN BEHAVIORAL NEUROSCIENCE The scope of behavioral neuroscience ranges from the level of the individual interacting with others, to the level of the molecule. Depending on the question at hand, investigators use different techniques to focus on these many levels, but always with an eye toward how their findings apply to behavior.

Scientific explanations usually involve analysis on a simpler or more basic level of organization than that of the structure or function to be explained. This approach is known as **reductionism**. In principle, it is possible to reduce each explanatory series down to the molecular or atomic level, though for practical reasons this extent of reductionism is rare. For example, most chemists deal with large, complex molecules and the laws that govern them; seldom do they seek explanations in terms of subatomic quarks and bosons.

Understanding behavior often requires several levels of biological analysis. The units of each level of analysis are simpler in structure and organization than those of the level above. The **levels of analysis** range from social interactions to the brain, continuing to successively less complex units until we arrive at single nerve cells and their even simpler, molecular constituents.

Naturally, in all fields different problems are carried to different levels of analysis, and fruitful work is often being done simultaneously by different workers at several levels (**FIGURE 1.6**). Thus, in their research on visual perception, cognitive neuroscientists advance analytical descriptions of behavior. They try to determine how the eyes move while looking at a visual pattern, or how the contrast among parts of the pattern determines its visibility. Meanwhile, other behavioral neuroscientists study the differences in visual abilities among species and try to determine the adaptive significance of these differences. For example, how is the presence (or absence) of color vision related to the life of a species? At the same time, other investigators trace out brain structures and networks involved in different kinds of visual discrimination. Still other scientists try to ascertain the electrical and chemical events that occur in the brain during vision.

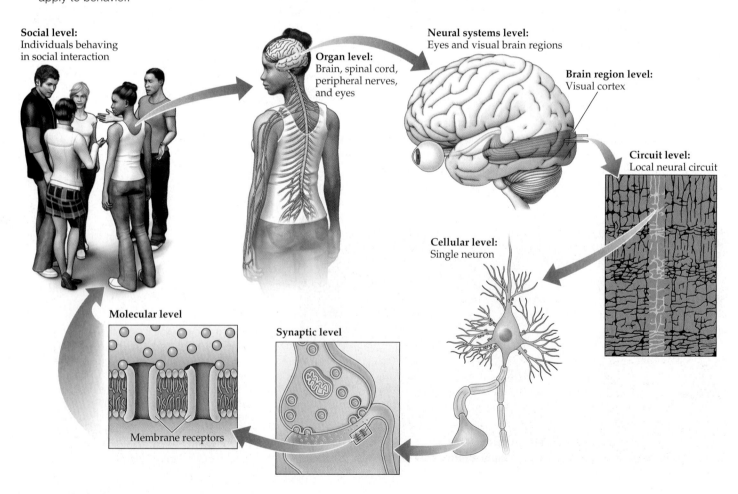

Social level: Individuals behaving in social interaction

Organ level: Brain, spinal cord, peripheral nerves, and eyes

Neural systems level: Eyes and visual brain regions

Brain region level: Visual cortex

Circuit level: Local neural circuit

Cellular level: Single neuron

Molecular level — Membrane receptors

Synaptic level

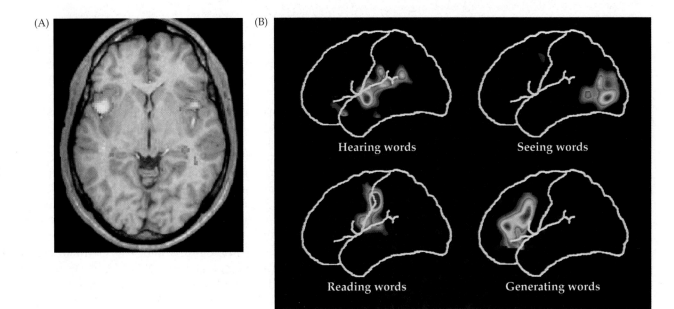

1.7 "TELL ME WHERE IS FANCY BRED, OR IN THE HEART OR IN THE HEAD?" (A) The parts of the brain highlighted here become especially active when a person thinks about his or her romantic partner. (B) Different brain regions are activated when people perform four different language tasks. The techniques used to generate such images are described in Chapter 2. (Part A from A. Bartels and Zeki, 2000; B courtesy of Dr. Marcus Raichle.)

The Brain and Behavior Are Reciprocally Related

Here are some examples of research topics considered in this book:

- How does the brain grow, maintain, and repair itself over the life span (see Chapter 7), and how are these capacities related to the growth and development of the mind and behavior from the womb to the tomb?

- How does the nervous system capture, process, and represent information about the environment? For example, sometimes brain damage causes a person to lose the ability to identify other people's faces (see Chapter 18); what does that tell us about how the brain recognizes faces?

- How does sexual orientation develop? Some brain regions are different in straight versus gay men (see Figure 12.24); what do those differences tell us about the development of human sexual orientation?

- What brain sites and activities underlie feelings and emotional expression? Are particular parts of the brain active in romantic love, for example (**FIGURE 1.7A**)?

- Some people suffer damage to the brain and afterward seem alarmingly unafraid in dangerous situations and unable to judge the fearfulness of other people; what parts of the brain are damaged to cause such changes (see Figure 15.16)?

- How does the brain manage to change during learning (see Chapter 17), and how are memories retrieved?

- Why are different brain regions active during different language tasks (**FIGURE 1.7B**)?

The relationship between the brain and behavior is, on the one hand, very mysterious because it is difficult to understand how a physical device, the brain, could be responsible for our subjective experiences of fear, love, and awe. Yet despite this mystery, we all use our brains every day. Perhaps it is the "everyday miracle" aspect of the topic that has generated so much folk wisdom about the brain. Think of it as "neuromythology."

Sometimes these popular ideas about the brain are in line with our current knowledge, but in many cases we know they are false. For example, the notion that we normally use only 10% of our brain is commonplace—a survey of teachers found that nearly half of them agreed with this notion (Howard-Jones, 2014)—but it is patent nonsense. Brain scans make it clear that the entire brain is activated by even fairly mundane tasks. Indeed, although the areas of activation shown in Figure 1.7 appear rather small and discrete, we will show in Box 2.3 that experimenters must work very hard to create images that separate activation related to a particular task from the background of widespread, ongoing brain activity.

We offer a list of other commonly held beliefs about the brain and behavior on our website in **A Step Further: Neuromythology: Facts or Fables?** Throughout the book we offer such opportunities for you to explore a given topic in more detail on our website, bn8e.com.

Behavioral Neuroscience Contributes to Our Understanding of Human Disorders

One of the great promises of behavioral neuroscience is that it can help us understand brain disorders and devise treatment strategies. Like any other complex mechanism, the brain is subject to a variety of malfunctions and breakdowns. People afflicted by disorders of the brain are not an exotic few—a European survey estimated that at least 38% of the population would suffer from a mental disorder at some point in a typical year (Wittchen et al., 2011). At least one person in five around the world currently suffers from neurological and/or psychiatric disorders that vary in severity from complete disability to significant changes in quality of life. **FIGURE 1.8A** shows the estimated numbers of U.S. residents afflicted by some of the main neurological disorders. **FIGURE 1.8B** gives estimates of the numbers of U.S. adults who suffer from certain major psychiatric disorders. The percentage of U.S. adults suffering from mental illness may be increasing (Twenge, 2015; Twenge et al., 2010).

The toll of these disorders is enormous, in terms of both individual suffering and social costs (Demyttenaere et al., 2004). The National Advisory Mental Health Council has estimated that direct and indirect costs of behavioral and brain disorders amount to $400 billion a year in the United States. For example, the cost for treatment of dementia (severely disordered thinking) exceeds the costs of treating cancer and heart disease combined. The World Health Organization (2004) estimates that over 15% of all disease burden, in terms of lost productivity, is due to mental disorders. The high cost in suffering and expense has compelled researchers to try to understand the mechanisms involved in these disorders and to try to alleviate or even prevent them.

In this quest, the distinction between clinical and laboratory approaches begins to fade away. For example, when clinicians encounter a pair of twins, one of whom has schizophrenia while the other seems healthy, the discovery of structural differences in their brains (**FIGURE 1.9**) immediately raises questions for laboratory scientists: Did the structural differences arise before the symptoms of schizophrenia, or the other way around? Were the brain differences present at birth, or did they arise during puberty? Does medication that reduces symptoms affect brain structure? When genes associated with schizophrenia in people are introduced into mice, will their ventricles

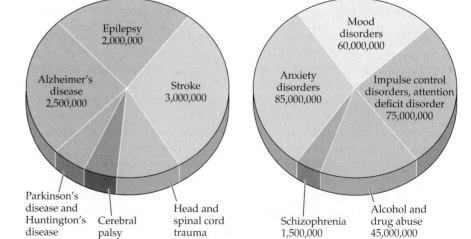

1.8 THE TOLL OF BRAIN DISORDERS Estimated numbers of people in the United States with neurological disorders (A) and psychiatric disorders (B). One in four affected persons in part B appear in more than one of the slices because they will suffer from two or more psychiatric disorders during their lifetimes. (A after Hirtz et al., 2007; B after Kessler et al., 2005.)

(A) Prevalence of neurological disorders

Epilepsy 2,000,000

Alzheimer's disease 2,500,000

Stroke 3,000,000

Parkinson's disease and Huntington's disease 500,000

Cerebral palsy 500,000

Head and spinal cord trauma 1,000,000

(B) Prevalance of psychiatric disorders

Mood disorders 60,000,000

Anxiety disorders 85,000,000

Impulse control disorders, attention deficit disorder 75,000,000

Schizophrenia 1,500,000

Alcohol and drug abuse 45,000,000

grow (see Figure 16.7)? This last question is just one instance of when working with animals is essential, an issue we address next.

Animal Research Makes Vital Contributions

Because we will draw on animal research throughout this book, we should comment on some of the ethical issues of experimentation on animals. Human beings' involvement and concern with other species predates recorded history. Early humans had to study animal behavior and physiology in order to escape some species and hunt others. To study biological bases of behavior inevitably requires research on animals of other species as well as on human beings. Psychology students usually underestimate the contributions of animal research to psychology because the most widely used introductory psychology textbooks often present major findings from animal research as if they were obtained with human participants (Domjan and Purdy, 1995).

Because of the importance of carefully regulated animal research for both human and animal health and well-being, the National Research Council (NRC Committee on Animals as Monitors of Environmental Hazards, 1991) undertook a study on the many uses of animals in research. The study noted that 93% of the mammals used in research are laboratory-reared rodents. It also reported that most Americans believe that animal research should continue. Of course, researchers have an obligation to minimize the discomfort of their animal subjects, and ironically enough, animal research has provided us with the drugs and techniques to make most research painless for the animal subjects (Sunstein and Nussbaum, 2004).

Nevertheless, a very active minority of people believe that research with animals, even if it does lead to lasting benefits, is unethical. For example, in his 1975 book *Animal Liberation*, Peter Singer asserts that research with animals can be justified only if it actually produces benefits. The trick, of course, is how to predict which experiment will lead to a breakthrough. Thus Singer refuses to say that animal experimentation is never justified (Neale, 2006). In the meantime, animal rights groups have vandalized labs, burned down buildings, and exploded bombs in laboratories (Conn and Parker, 2008). In 2008, animal rights extremists set off firebombs at the homes of two scientists in Santa Cruz, California. One scientist's family, including two young children, had to flee their home through a second-story window (**FIGURE 1.10**) (Paddock and

(A) Twin with schizophrenia

(B) Unaffected twin

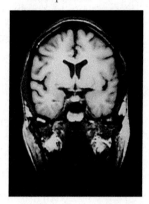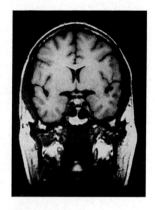

1.9 IDENTICAL TWINS BUT NONIDENTICAL BRAINS AND BEHAVIOR In these images of the brains of identical twins, the fluid-filled cerebral ventricles are prominent as dark "butterfly" shapes. The twin whose brain is imaged in (A) suffers from schizophrenia and has the enlarged cerebral ventricles that some researchers believe are characteristic of this disorder. The other twin does not suffer from schizophrenia; his brain (B) clearly has smaller ventricles. (Courtesy of Dr. E. Fuller Torrey.)

1.10 CAR FIREBOMBED BY ANIMAL RIGHTS ACTIVISTS The extremists targeted the cars and homes of two scientists who work with animals at the University of California in Santa Cruz in 2008. The next year, the car of a researcher at UCLA was torched.

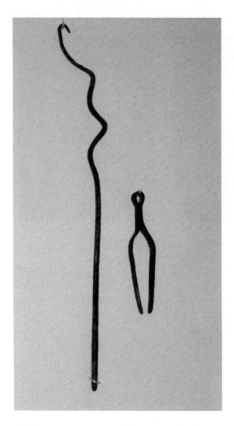

1.11 BRAIN REMOVAL KIT Ancient Egyptians had little regard for the brain. During mummification, they would use tools like these to reach through the nostrils to pick out brain pieces and throw them away. (Photograph by Dr. Neil Watson.)

La Ganga, 2008). These personal attacks on individuals appear to be a new tactic for animal rights activists to intimidate and frighten scientists (Grimm, 2014), which has already hounded at least one researcher out of the field (Nature Neuroscience, 2015).

Perhaps in a future where robots can be made that look and act like humans, methods will be available to clearly see all the processes at work in a living, working human brain. In the meantime, there's no substitute for research with animal subjects. Every chapter in this book is teeming with information that was gathered from humane experiments with animals.

The History of Research on the Brain and Behavior Begins in Antiquity

Only recently have scientists recognized the central role of the brain in controlling behavior. When Egyptian pharaoh Tutankhamen was mummified (about 1300 BCE), five important organs were preserved in his tomb: liver, lungs, stomach, intestines, and heart. All these organs were considered necessary to ensure the pharaoh's continued existence in the afterlife. The brain, however, was picked out through the nostrils (**FIGURE 1.11**) and thrown away. Although the Egyptian version of the afterlife entailed considerable struggle, the brain was not considered an asset.

Neither the Hebrew Bible (written from the twelfth to the second century BCE) nor the New Testament ever mentions the brain. However, the Bible mentions the heart hundreds of times and makes several references each to the liver, the stomach, and the bowels as the seats of passion, courage, and pity, respectively. "Teach us … that we may gain a heart of wisdom" (Psalms 90:12).

The heart is also where Aristotle (about 350 BCE), the most prominent scientist of ancient Greece, located mental capacities. We still reflect this ancient notion when we call people *kindhearted, openhearted, fainthearted, hardhearted,* or *heartless* and when we speak of learning *by heart.* Aristotle considered the brain to be only a cooling unit to lower the temperature of the hot blood from the heart.

Also about 350 BCE, the Greek physician Herophilus (called the "Father of Anatomy") advanced our knowledge of the nervous system by dissecting bodies of both people and animals. He traced nerves from muscles and skin into the spinal cord and noted that each region of the body is connected to separate nerves.

A second-century Greco-Roman physician, Galen (the "Father of Medicine"), treated the injuries of gladiators. His reports of behavioral changes caused by injuries to the heads of gladiators drew attention to the brain as the controller of behavior. Galen advanced the idea that animal spirits—a mysterious fluid—passed along nerves to all regions of the body. But Galen's ideas about the anatomy of the human brain were very inaccurate because he refused to dissect humans.

Renaissance scientists began to understand brain anatomy

The eminent Renaissance painter and scientist Leonardo da Vinci (1452–1519) studied the workings of the human body and laid the foundations of anatomical drawing. He especially pioneered in providing views from different angles and cross-sectional representations. His artistic renditions of the body included portraits of the nerves in the arm and the fluid-filled ventricles of the brain (**FIGURE 1.12**).

Renaissance anatomists emphasized the shape and appearance of the external surfaces of the brain because these were the parts that were easiest to see when the skull was removed. It was immediately apparent to anyone who looked that the brain has an extraordinarily complex shape. To Renaissance artists like Michelangelo (1475–1564), this marvelous structure was God's greatest gift to humankind. So, in Michelangelo's painting on the ceiling of the Sistine Chapel, God seems to ride the form of the human brain when bestowing life to Adam (Meshberger, 1990), while in another scene God's throat resembles the base of the brain (Suk and Tamargo, 2010).

In 1633, René Descartes (1596–1650) wrote an influential book (*De Homine* [*On Man*]) in which he tried to explain how the behavior of animals, and to some extent the behavior of humans, could be like the workings of a machine. In addition to

(A) Early drawing

(B) Later drawing based on observation

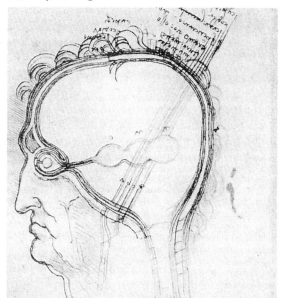
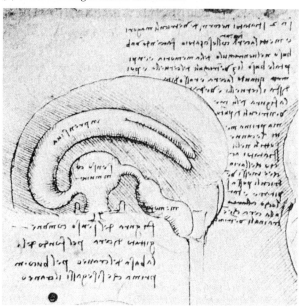

1.12 LEONARDO DA VINCI'S CHANGING VIEW OF THE BRAIN (A) In an early representation, Leonardo simply copied old schematic drawings that represented the fluid-filled cerebral ventricles as a linear series of chambers. (B) Later he made a drawing based on direct observation: after making a cast of the ventricles of an ox brain by pouring melted wax into the brain and letting it set, he cut away the tissue to reveal the true shape of the ventricles.

tackling other topics, Descartes proposed the concept of spinal reflexes and a neural pathway for them (**FIGURE 1.13**). Attempting to relate the mind to the body, Descartes suggested that the two come into contact in the pineal gland, located within the brain. He suggested the pineal gland for this role because (1) whereas most brain structures are double, located symmetrically in the two hemispheres, the pineal gland is single, like consciousness, and (2) he believed, erroneously, that the pineal gland exists only in humans and not in animals.

As Descartes was preparing to publish his book, he learned that the Catholic Church had forced Galileo to renounce his teaching that Earth revolves around the sun, threatening to execute him if he did not recant. Fearful that his own speculations about mind and body could also incur the wrath of the church, Descartes withheld his book from publication. It did not appear in print until 1662, after his death. Descartes believed that if people were nothing more than intricate machines, they could have about as much free will as a pocket watch, and no opportunity to make the moral choices that were so important to the church. He asserted that humans, at least, had a nonmaterial soul as well as a material body. This notion of **dualism** spread widely and left other philosophers with the task of determining how a nonmaterial soul could exert influence over a material body and brain. Mainstream

dualism Here, the notion promoted by René Descartes that the mind is subject only to spiritual interactions while the body is subject only to material interactions.

1.13 AN EARLY ACCOUNT OF REFLEXES In this depiction of an explanation by Descartes, when a person's toe touches fire, the heat causes nervous activity to flow up the nerve to the brain (blue arrows). From there the nervous activity is "reflected" back down to the leg muscles (red arrows), which contract, pulling the foot away from the fire; the idea of activity being reflected back is what gave rise to the word *reflex*. In Descartes's time, the difference between sensory and motor nerves had not yet been discovered, nor was it known that nerve fibers normally conduct in only one direction. Nevertheless, Descartes promoted thinking about bodily processes in scientific terms, and this focus led to steadily more accurate knowledge and concepts.

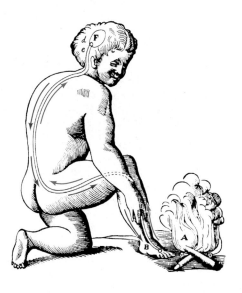

phrenology The outmoded belief that bumps on the skull reflect enlargements of brain regions responsible for certain behavioral faculties.

neuroscientists reject dualism and insist that all the workings of the mind can also, in theory, be understood as purely physical processes in the material world, specifically in the brain.

The concept of localization of function arose in the nineteenth century

By the end of the 1600s, the English physician Thomas Willis (1621–1675), with his detailed descriptions of the structure of the human brain and his systematic study of brain disorders, convinced educated people in the Western world that the brain is the organ that coordinates and controls behavior (Zimmer, 2004). A popular notion of the nineteenth century, called **phrenology**, elaborated on this idea by asserting that the cerebral cortex consisted of separate functional areas and that each area was responsible for a behavioral faculty such as love of family, perception of color, or curiosity. Investigators assigned functions to brain regions anecdotally, by observing the behavior of individuals and noting, from the shape of the skull, which underlying regions of the brain were more or less developed (**FIGURE 1.14A**).

Opponents rejected the entire concept of localization of brain function, insisting that the brain, like the mind, functions as a whole. Today we know that the whole brain is indeed active when we are doing almost any task. When we are performing particular tasks, however (as we saw earlier in this chapter), certain brain regions become even more activated. Different tasks activate different brain regions. Modern brain maps of these places where *peaks* of activation occur (**FIGURE 1.14B**) bear a passing resemblance to their phrenological predecessors, differing only in the specific locations of functions. But unlike the phrenologists, we confirm these modern maps by other methods, such as examining what happens after brain damage.

Even as far back as the 1860s, the French surgeon Paul Broca (1824–1880) argued that language ability was not a property of the entire brain but rather was localized in a re-

(A)

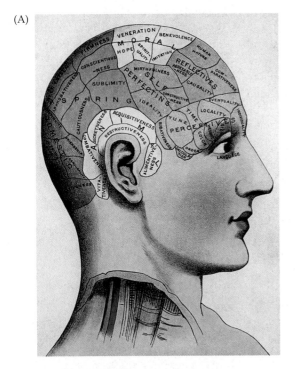

(B)

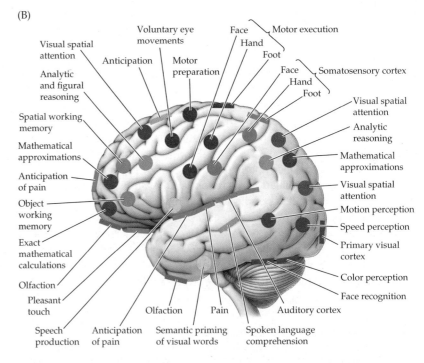

1.14 OLD AND NEW PHRENOLOGY (A) In the early nineteenth century, certain "faculties," such as skill at mathematics or a tendency toward aggression, were believed to be directly associated with particular brain regions. Phrenologists used diagrams like this one to measure bumps on the skull, which they took as an indication of how fully developed each brain region was in an individual, and hence how fully that person should display particular qualities. (B) Today, technology enables us to roughly gauge how active different parts of the brain are when a person is performing various tasks (see Chapter 2). But virtually the entire brain is active during any task, so the localization of function that such studies provide is really a measure of where *peak* activity occurs, rather than a suggestion of a single region involved in a particular task. (B after Nichols and Newsome, 1999.)

stricted brain region. Broca presented a postmortem analysis of a patient who had been unable to talk for several years. The only portion of the patient's brain that appeared damaged was a small region within the frontal portions of the brain on the left side—a region now known as *Broca's area* (labeled "Speech production" in Figure 1.14B). The study of additional patients further convinced Broca that language expression is mediated by this specific brain region rather than reflecting activities of the entire brain.

These nineteenth-century observations form the background for a continuing theme of research in behavioral neuroscience—notably, the search for distinguishing differences among brain regions on the basis of their structure, and the effort to relate different kinds of behavior to different brain regions (M. Kemp, 2001). An additional theme emerging from these studies is the relation of brain size to ability across species (see Figure 6.9), and even across various people (**BOX 1.2**).

In 1890, William James's book *Principles of Psychology* signaled the beginnings of a modern approach to behavioral neuroscience. The strength of the ideas described in this book is evident from the continuing frequent citation of the work, especially by contemporary cognitive neuroscientists. In James's work, psychological ideas such as consciousness and other aspects of human experience came to be seen as properties of the nervous system. A true behavioral neuroscience began to emerge from this approach.

BOX 1.2 — Bigger Better? The Case of the Brain and Intelligence

Does a bigger brain indicate greater intelligence? Brain size does seem to explain many species differences in complex behavior, and the human brain has expanded remarkably over the past few million years (see Chapter 6). But do variations in brain size within our species correlate with intelligence? This question has been the subject of lively controversy for at least two centuries. Sir Francis Galton (1822–1911), who invented the correlation coefficient, stated that the greatest disappointment in his life was his failure to find a significant relationship between head size and intelligence. But Galton had to use head size, when he really wanted to measure brain size. In addition, he had to rely on teachers' estimates of their students' intelligence, and every student knows that teachers can be quite wrong. Other investigators in the nineteenth century measured the volumes of skulls of various groups and estimated intelligence on the basis of people's occupations or other doubtful criteria (S. J. Gould, 1981).

The development and standardization of intelligence quotient (IQ) tests in the twentieth century provided invaluable help for one side of the question, and these scores indeed correlate,

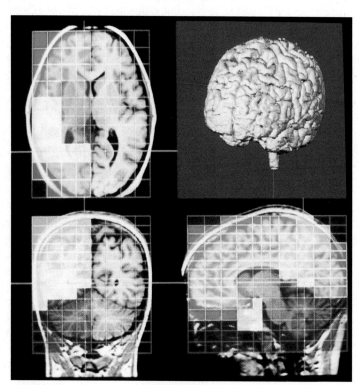

(A) Examples of measuring specific features of brain size from scans.

with ranges from +0.08 to +0.22, with estimates of brain size based on known head size (Van Valen, 1974).

Newer, noninvasive techniques (discussed in detail in Chapter 2) to visualize the brains of healthy people now make it possible to directly measure brain size in living humans. One

study found a significant correlation coefficient of about +0.26 between brain size and IQ (Posthuma et al., 2002). In another study, brain scans were used for measuring the sizes of different brain regions (Figure A).

(continued)

Bigger Better? The Case of the Brain and Intelligence (continued)

BOX 1.2

After correction for body size, the correlation between brain size and IQ scores was +0.38 (Andreasen et al., 1993). IQ seems to correlate better with the volume of the front of the brain than that of the back (Colom et al., 2013). When the brains of children were measured at age 6 and again at 11, those with the highest IQs displayed the greatest thickening of the outer layer of the brain, especially in the front (P. Shaw et al., 2006). Other brain-imaging studies report correlations between IQ scores and the extent of *connectivity* between brain regions of about +0.50 (Figure B) (Haász et al., 2013; Malpas et al., 2016).

Thus, on the basis of modern techniques, the long-standing controversy appears to have been settled in favor of a significant correlation between brain size and intelligence (as shown in Figure B). Note, however, that the modest size of the correla-

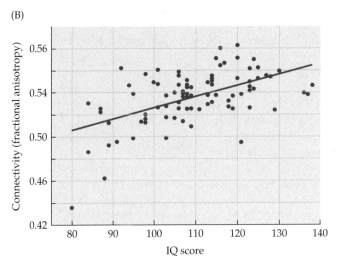

(B) Correlation between IQ and brain connectivity.

tions, while statistically significant, indicates that only about 10–20% of variability in IQ is accounted for by brain size. Thus, there is plenty of room for other factors to contribute to overall IQ. In addition, many people

dispute whether IQ tests really measure a general property of intelligence (Stanovich, 2009). (Figure A courtesy of Nancy Andreasen; B after Malpas et al., 2016.)

Modern behavioral neuroscience arose in the twentieth century

The end of the nineteenth century brought many important developments for behavioral neuroscience. German psychologist Hermann Ebbinghaus showed in 1885 how to measure learning and memory in humans. In 1898, American psychologist Edward L. Thorndike demonstrated how to measure learning and memory in animals. Early in the twentieth century, Russian physiologist Ivan P. Pavlov announced research in his laboratory on conditioning in animals.

American psychologist Shepard I. Franz (1902) sought the site of learning and memory in the brain by removing different brain regions in animal subjects. This work started a search for the traces of experience in the brain—a quest that Karl S. Lashley (1890–1958) referred to as the "search for the engram."

Behavioral neuroscience bears the strong imprint of Canadian psychologist Donald O. Hebb (1904–1985), a student of Lashley (P. M. Milner, 1993). In his book *The Organization of Behavior* (1949), Hebb showed, in principle, how complex cognitive behavior could be accomplished by networks of active neurons. He suggested how brain cell connections that are initially more or less random could become organized by sensory input and stimulation into strongly interconnected groups that he called *cell assemblies*. His hypothesis about how neurons strengthen their connections through use gave rise to the concept of the *Hebbian synapse*, a topic much studied by current neuroscientists (see Chapters 7 and 17).

Consciousness is a thorny problem

Almost anyone using this book has at some time wondered about **consciousness**: the personal, private awareness of our emotions, intentions, thoughts, and movements and of the sensations that impinge upon us. How is it possible that you are aware of the words on this page, the room you are occupying, the goals you have in life?

consciousness The state of awareness of one's own existence and experience.

In his review of theories of consciousness, Adam Zeman (2002) notes that almost all scientists agree on some aspects of consciousness:

- Consciousness matters; it permits us to do certain important things, like planning and mentally "simulating" what might happen in the future.
- Consciousness is bound up somehow with the activity of the brain.
- We are not aware of all of our brain's activities. Some brain activity, and therefore some of our behavior, is unconscious.
- The deepest parts of our brain are important for arousal.
- The topmost parts of the brain are responsible for whatever we experience from moment to moment.

In the chapters to come, we will see many examples of experiments that demonstrate these properties of consciousness. However consciousness is brought about, any satisfying understanding would be able, for example, to explain why a certain pattern of activity in your brain causes you to experience the sensation of blue when looking at the sky (**FIGURE 1.15**), or the smell of cinnamon when entering a bakery. A good theory would let us predict that after messing about with your brain, changing particular connections or activating particular neurons, you would experience yellow when seeing the sky.

Unfortunately, we are nowhere near understanding consciousness this clearly. We describe some intriguing (and disturbing) experiments explicitly directed at human consciousness in Chapter 18. In the rest of the book, we rarely use the words *conscious* or *consciousness*. Normally we cannot say anything about the particulars of what humans or animal subjects are *experiencing*, but only whether their behavior suggests that the brain detected a signal or event. Thus, we are in no position to know whether complicated machines like computers are, or might one day be, conscious.

Both the United States and Europe have begun projects hoping to map an entire human brain, a truly formidable task (Waldrop, 2012), which we discuss in Chapter 2. It will require a computer with vastly more memory and faster processing than any yet devised (**FIGURE 1.16**). Some people even doubt whether our "merely human" brains will ever be able to understand something as complicated as consciousness. Nevertheless, any gains we make in understanding how the brain works, which is the subject of this book, will bring us closer to that goal.

1.15 HOW BLUE IS THE SKY? We would all agree that this sky is the color everyone calls "blue." But in Chapter 18 we will ask whether everyone who sees that sky has the same experience of color.

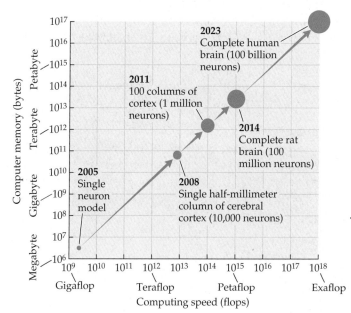

1.16 THE HUMAN BRAIN PROJECT The goal of massive projects in both the United States and Europe is to have a digital re-creation of the neurons and connections found in a human brain. As this projection from the European project (bluebrain. epfl.ch) shows, this would require a computer that is vastly faster than any made to date, as well as a truly staggering amount of computer memory. (After Waldrop, 2012.)

■ The Cutting Edge

Behavioral Neuroscience Is Advancing at a Tremendous Rate

It is difficult to convey the rate at which we are learning new things about the brain. Each year, over 25,000 neuroscientists meet at the annual meeting of the Society for Neuroscience (sfn.org). On our website (bn8e.com), the NewsLink tab directs you to news stories about behavioral neuroscience for a general audience, with more than 20 articles added every week, over a thousand per year. In books, references to *neural*, *neuron*, and *neuroscience* have climbed (**FIGURE 1.17A**). The predominant index for biomedical research, PubMed (pubmed.gov), classified over 31,000 articles under *neuroscience* in 2015 alone (**FIGURE 1.17B**). Somehow, we didn't quite get around to reading them all. This incredible pace of research is driven, in part, by talented young scientists who are more excited by neuroscience than competing fields. Excitement about understanding the brain is also the reason that undergraduate majors in neuroscience are now being offered in dozens of colleges and universities around the United States and the world.

Given this explosion of information in behavioral neuroscience, it is difficult for us to keep this book up to date. We've done our best in every chapter to convey those exciting new concepts that seem to be holding up to the scrutiny of the field, citing over 500 new articles to keep the text current. Each chapter concludes with a special feature: The Cutting Edge. Here we present exciting new findings about the area under discussion. These are the types of findings that have scientists in the field buzzing among themselves. In addition to highlighting new and exciting ideas, we use The Cutting Edge to describe experimental approaches in more detail, to give you a better feel for the process of scientific reasoning and hypothesis testing. We really enjoy writing these breaking news stories about behavioral neuroscience, and we hope that they excite you too.

1.17 NEUROSCIENCE ON THE RISE (A) The term *neuroscience* became increasingly common in books from 1970 to 2008 (the latest year that can be searched with Google Ngram Viewer). (B) In the major index of biomedical journals, PubMed (pubmed.gov), occurrence of the term *neuroscience* has risen sharply in the past 25 years. It seems safe to say that no one has read, or ever will read, the 31,528 such articles published in 2015 alone.

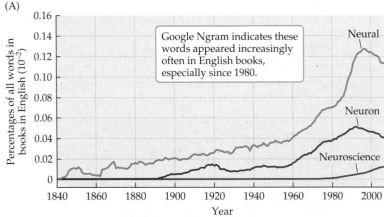

(A) Google Ngram indicates these words appeared increasingly often in English books, especially since 1980.

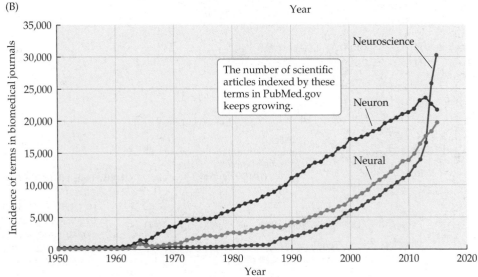

(B) The number of scientific articles indexed by these terms in PubMed.gov keeps growing.

Recommended Reading

Blackmore, S. (2011). *Consciousness: An Introduction* (2nd ed.). New York: Oxford University Press.

Carter, R. (2009). *The Human Brain Book.* London: Dorling Kindersley.

Doidge, N. (2007). *The Brain That Changes Itself.* New York: Penguin.

Finger, S. (1994). *Origins of Neuroscience.* New York: Oxford University Press.

Kaku, M. (2015). *The Future of the Mind: The Scientific Quest to Understand, Enhance, and Empower the Mind.* New York: Random House.

Koch, C. (2012). *Consciousness: Confessions of a Romantic Reductionist.* Cambridge, MA: MIT Press.

Wickens, A. P. (2014). *A History of the Brain: From Stone Age Surgery to Modern Neuroscience.* New York: Psychology Press.

Zimmer, C. (2004). *The Soul Made Flesh: The Discovery of the Brain—and How It Changed the World.* New York: Basic Books.

Go to
bn8e.com
for study questions,
quizzes, activities,
and other resources

1

──── VISUAL SUMMARY ────

You should be able to relate each summary to the adjacent illustration, including structures and processes.
Go to **bn8e.com/vs1** for links to figures, animations, and activities that will help you consolidate the material.

1 **Behavioral neuroscience** is a branch of **neuroscience** that focuses on the biological bases of behavior. It is closely related to many other neuroscience disciplines. Review **Figure 1.2**

2 Behavioral neuroscientists balance three general research perspectives—**correlation**, **somatic intervention**, and **behavioral intervention**—in designing their research. Review **Figure 1.3**

3 Research in behavioral neuroscience is conducted at **levels of analysis** ranging from molecular events to the functioning of the entire brain and complex social situations. Review **Figure 1.6**

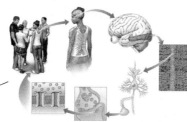

4 The prevalence of neurological and psychiatric disorders exacts a very high emotional and economic toll. Review **Figure 1.8**

5 Although genes can have a major impact on brain function, it is clear that experience physically alters the brain and that genetically identical people will not necessarily suffer from the same brain disorders. Review **Figure 1.9**

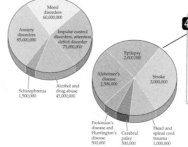

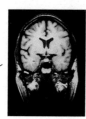

6 Although humans have wondered about the control of behavior for thousands of years, only comparatively recently has a mechanistic view of the brain taken hold. Review **Figure 1.13**

7 The concept of localization of function, which originated in **phrenology**—despite obvious flaws with the phrenologists' methodology—was an important milestone for behavioral neuroscience. Today we know that the part of the brain that shows a peak of activity varies in a predictable way depending on what task we're doing. Review **Figure 1.14**

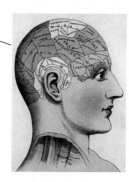

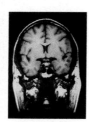

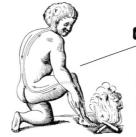

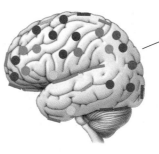

8 Localization of cognitive functions remains a major focus of behavioral neuroscience. With modern imaging technology and a more carefully validated understanding of cognitive abilities, a detailed view of the organization of the brain is emerging. Review **Figure 1.14**

Biological Foundations of Behavior

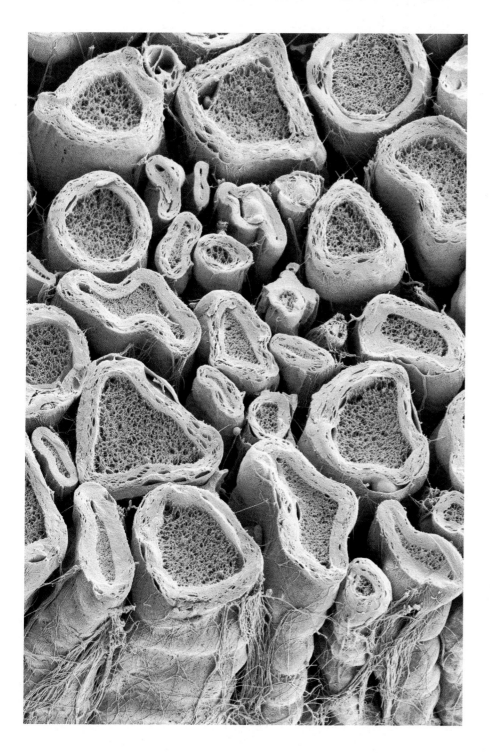

Spinal root nerves Colored scanning electron micrograph (SEM) of a sectioned spinal root nerve bundle, showing individual axons, extensions of nerve cells. Magnification: x1600 when printed at 10cm wide. © Thomas Deerinck and Mark Ellisman, NCMIR, UCSD.

Functional Neuroanatomy

The Nervous System and Behavior

▌ A Stimulating Experience

It was like a scene from a science fiction film. While she remained conscious, comfortable, and aware of her surroundings, Bev's skull was opened and the surface of her brain was exposed. Using a tiny electrode, the surgeon stimulated her brain in precise locations, while sensory experiences and behavioral responses were carefully noted. But this was not make-believe; like thousands of people before her, Bev was undergoing a procedure called *cortical electrical-stimulation mapping*, developed in the mid-twentieth century by neurosurgeon Wilder Penfield (1891–1976). Penfield had learned that mapping the locations of specific functions in someone's brain made it possible to remove diseased brain tissue without harming neighboring regions involved in crucial behaviors like speech or movement. In Bev's case, the target was a patch of diseased tissue that was causing her to experience frequent *seizures*, uncontrollable convulsions of her body.

But beyond its utility as a surgical tool, brain stimulation offered a way to ask more-profound questions about the organization of the human brain. Across many individuals, researchers found that stimulation of some brain regions reliably provoked specific movements; stimulating other regions produced specific sensations, like a tingling hand or flashes of blue light. Elsewhere, stimulations could evoke clear and nuanced vignettes of past experiences, such as the smell of a childhood haunt or a fragment of a favorite song. Furthermore, although some regions are organized much the same from person to person, other regions seem to be organized in ways that are unique to each individual, and at the highest levels the brain's control of complex cognition remains mostly a tantalizing mystery. New brain-imagting technology is improving our ability to map the brain and start answering fundamental questions about brain organization: Does each brain region control a specific behavior, or is the pattern of connections within the brain more important? Do some brain regions act as general-purpose processors? Is everybody's brain organized in the same way?

Thoughts, feelings, behaviors—almost everything that defines you as a person is produced by the three-pound organ inside your head that, despite its unremarkable appearance, is the most complicated object in the known universe. Neuroscientists adopt several different perspectives in describing the physical properties of the brain. Accordingly, in this chapter we look at the structure of the brain from several different perspectives: we open with its cellular composition, go on to its major anatomical divisions, and finally discuss its appearance in computerized brain imaging. In later chapters we'll build on this information as we learn how cells within the brain communicate through electrical (Chapter 3), chemical (Chapter 4), and hormonal (Chapter 5) signals.

Go to Brain Explorer
bn8e.com/2.1

Specialized Cells Make Up the Nervous System

Every organ and muscle in your body is in communication with your nervous system. Like all other living tissue, the nervous system is made up of cells, the most important of which are the **neurons** (or *nerve cells*). Each of the 80–90 billion neurons in the adult human brain (Herculano-Houzel, 2012) is a tiny, discrete information-processing unit, receiving inputs from other cells, integrating those inputs, and then distributing the processed information to other neurons. Arranged in networks that vary enormously in complexity, circuits of neurons define and control all of our abilities and behaviors, from the simplest reflexes to the most complex intellectual processes. An even greater number of **glial cells** (or just *glia*) provide various forms of support and also contribute to information processing. But because neurons produce readily measured electrical signals and do most of the work of the brain, we know much more about them than about glial cells.

The interconnection of nerve cells was a hotly debated question in the early days of modern neuroscience. Rapid advances in microscopy allowed nineteenth-century neuroanatomists to visualize the cells of the brain with high resolution, revealing an astonishing variety of shapes and sizes of neurons. However, the manner in which neurons interacted remained mysterious. Some neuroscientists, like Italian Camillo Golgi (1843–1926), thought that neurons were *continuous* with one another, forming a nearly endless network of connected tubes through which information flowed. But the great Spanish neuroscientist Santiago Ramón y Cajal (1852–1934) developed a convincing alternative. Exploiting Golgi's revolutionary staining techniques (see Box 2.1) to create pen-and-ink studies of neurons so precise that they remain accurate and useful to the present day (**FIGURE 2.1**), Cajal proposed that although neurons come very close to one another (i.e., they are *contiguous*), they are not quite continuous with one another. He argued that at each point of contact between neurons, a tiny gap keeps the cells separate.

From these studies emerged a new perspective—the **neuron doctrine**—which proposed (1) that the cells of the brain are independent from one another structurally, metabolically, and functionally and (2) that information is transmitted from one neuron to the next across tiny gaps. The existence and function of these gaps were later demonstrated by Sir Charles Sherrington (1857–1957), who named them **synapses**.

Although estimates vary somewhat, it is thought that the human brain may have as many as 10^{15} synapses. This number, called a *quadrillion*, is so large that it is hard to comprehend: if you gathered that many grains of sand, each a millimeter in diameter, they would fill a cube with each side longer than an American football field—a million cubic yards (about 750,000 cubic meters)! Such vast networks of connections are responsible for all of humanity's achievements.

The neuron has four structural divisions specialized for information processing

Like any of the other cells of the body, a neuron contains a variety of organelles such as the **mitochondria** (singular *mitochondrion*) that produce energy, the **cell nucleus** that contains genes encoded in DNA, and the **ribosomes** and related machinery that translate genetic instructions from the cell nucleus into proteins (these cellular actions are reviewed in the Appendix). But the neuron also has some unique components that allow it to collect input signals from other sources, process and combine this information, and distribute the result of this processing to other cells by means of its own electrochemical output signals. Therefore, all neurons share some distinctive structures that are directly related to information processing. These structures, illustrated in **FIGURE 2.2**, represent four distinct functional zones that are found in almost all neurons, despite wide variation in shape:

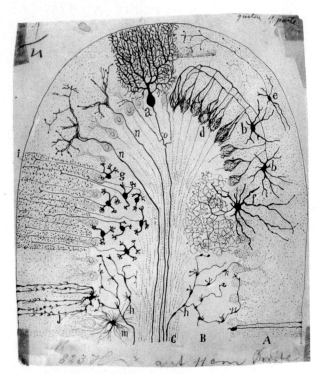

2.1 NINETEENTH-CENTURY DRAWING OF NEURONS The great Spanish neuroanatomist Santiago Ramón y Cajal created detailed renderings of the cells of the nervous system, such as this drawing of mammalian brain neurons.

neuron Also called *nerve cell*. The basic unit of the nervous system, each composed of a cell body, receptive extension(s) (dendrites), and a transmitting extension (axon).

glial cells Also called *glia* or *neuroglia*. Nonneuronal brain cells that provide structural, nutritional, and other types of support to the brain.

neuron doctrine The hypothesis that the brain is composed of separate cells that are distinct structurally, metabolically, and functionally.

synapse The tiny gap between neurons where information is passed from one to the other.

mitochondrion A cellular organelle that provides metabolic energy for the cell's processes.

cell nucleus The spherical central structure of a cell that contains the chromosomes.

ribosomes Structures in the cell body where genetic information is translated to produce proteins.

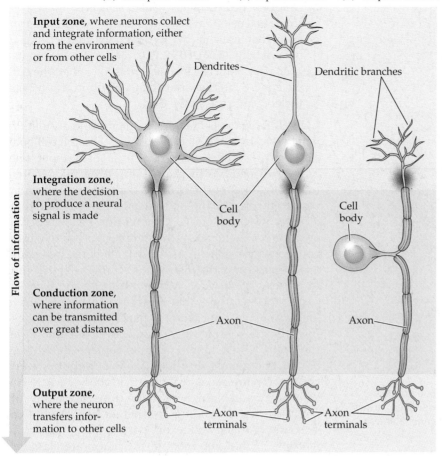

(A) Multipolar neuron (B) Bipolar neuron (C) Unipolar neuron

Input zone, where neurons collect and integrate information, either from the environment or from other cells

Dendrites

Dendritic branches

Integration zone, where the decision to produce a neural signal is made

Cell body

Cell body

Flow of information

Conduction zone, where information can be transmitted over great distances

Axon

Axon

Output zone, where the neuron transfers information to other cells

Axon terminals

Axon terminals

2.2 THE PRINCIPAL COMPONENTS OF NEURONS The dendrites, cell body, axon, and axon terminals are functional zones specialized for the input, integration, conduction, and output of information, respectively. These zones are common to all neurons, despite variation in the forms that neurons take. Three important types of neurons are (A) multipolar neurons with multiple dendrites and a single axon, (B) bipolar neurons with a single dendrite and a single axon, and (C) unipolar neurons with a single process that emerges from the cell body and extends in two directions; in this case the integration zone is not in the cell body but at the base of the dendritic branches.

dendrite   One of the extensions of the cell body that are the receptive surfaces of the neuron.

input zone   The part of a neuron that receives information from other neurons or from specialized sensory structures. Usually corresponds to the cell's dendrites.

cell body   Also called *soma*. The region of a neuron that is defined by the presence of the cell nucleus.

integration zone   The part of the neuron that initiates nerve electrical activity, described in detail in Chapter 3. Usually corresponds to the neuron's axon hillock.

axon   A single extension from the nerve cell that carries action potentials from the cell body to other neurons.

conduction zone   The part of the neuron over which the nerve's electrical signal may be actively propagated. Usually corresponds to the cell's axon.

axon collateral   A branch of an axon from a single neuron.

axon terminal   Also called *synaptic bouton*. The end of an axon or axon collateral, which forms a synapse on a neuron or other target cell.

output zone   The part of a neuron, usually corresponding to the axon terminals, at which the cell sends information to another cell.

multipolar neuron   A nerve cell that has many dendrites and a single axon.

bipolar neuron   A nerve cell that has a single dendrite at one end and a single axon at the other end.

1. Cellular extensions called **dendrites** (from the Greek *dendron*, "tree") serve as an **input zone**, receiving information from other neurons across synapses. Dendrites may be elaborately branched to accommodate synapses from many other neurons.

2. The **cell body** (or *soma*, plural *somata*) contains the cell's nucleus. In addition to receiving additional synaptic inputs, the cell body serves as an **integration zone**, combining (*integrating*) the information that the neuron has received to determine whether or not to send a signal of its own.

3. A single extension, the **axon**, leads away from the cell body and serves as a **conduction zone**, carrying the cell's own electrical signals away from the cell body. Before its end, the axon may split into multiple branches called **axon collaterals**.

4. Specialized swellings at the ends of the axon, called **axon terminals** (or *synaptic boutons*), are a functional **output zone**. They transmit the neuron's activity across synapses to other cells.

Neurons can be classified by shape, size, or function

Neuroscientists use the *shapes* of cell bodies, dendrites, and axons to classify the many varieties of nerve cells into three principal types, each specialized for a particular kind of information processing:

1. **Multipolar neurons** have many dendrites and a single axon, and they are the most common type of neuron (**FIGURE 2.2A**).

2. **Bipolar neurons** have a single dendrite at one end of the cell and a single axon at the other end (**FIGURE 2.2B**). This type of neuron is especially common in sensory systems, such as vision.

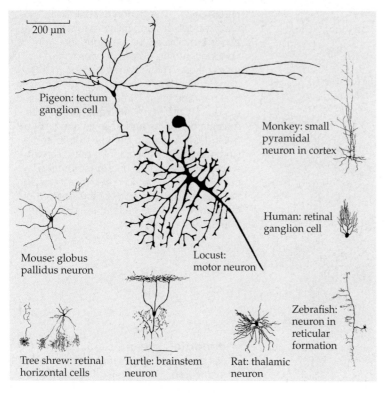

200 μm

Pigeon: tectum
ganglion cell

Monkey: small
pyramidal
neuron in cortex

Mouse: globus
pallidus neuron

Human: retinal
ganglion cell

Locust:
motor neuron

Zebrafish:
neuron in
reticular
formation

Tree shrew: retinal
horizontal cells

Turtle: brainstem
neuron

Rat: thalamic
neuron

2.3 THE GREAT DIVERSITY OF NEURONS Neurons come in a bewildering variety of shapes and sizes. These examples, drawn to scale, are taken from the nervous systems of various species.

unipolar neuron Also called *monopolar neuron*. A nerve cell with a single branch that leaves the cell body and then extends in two directions; one end is the receptive pole, the other end the output zone.

motor neuron Also called *motoneuron*. A nerve cell that transmits motor messages, stimulating a muscle or gland.

sensory neuron A neuron that is directly affected by changes in the environment, such as light, odor, or touch.

interneuron A neuron that is neither a sensory neuron nor a motor neuron; it receives input from and sends output to other neurons.

arborization The elaborate branching of the dendrites of some neurons.

presynaptic Referring to the region of a synapse that releases neurotransmitter.

postsynaptic Referring to the region of a synapse that receives and responds to neurotransmitter.

presynaptic membrane The specialized membrane of the axon terminal of the neuron that transmits information by releasing neurotransmitter.

3. **Unipolar neurons** (also called *monopolar*) have a single extension (or *process*), usually thought of as an axon, that branches in two directions after leaving the cell body (**FIGURE 2.2C**). One end is the input zone with branches like dendrites; the other, the output zone. Such cells transmit touch information from the body into the spinal cord.

In all three types of neurons, the dendrites are in the input zone. In multipolar and bipolar cells, the cell body also receives synapses and so is also part of the input zone.

In many neurons the axon is only a few micrometers (μm) long,* but for the neurons that connect the spinal cord to the rest of the body, axons may be more than a meter in length (in fact, the giraffe has axons that are *several* meters in length). In order for you to wiggle your toes (or for the giraffe to wiggle hers), individual axons must carry the instructions from the spinal cord to muscles of the foot. **Motor neurons** (or *motoneurons*)—the neurons that govern movements—have long axons reaching out to synapse on muscles, causing them to contract in response to commands from the brain. Other motor neurons contact and control organs and glands. The long axons of **sensory neurons** carry messages from the periphery back to the spinal cord and brain. Sensory neurons take many different shapes, depending on whether they detect light or sound or touch and so on. But the great majority of neurons, making up most of the brain, are classified as **interneurons**. These are the neurons that receive information from other neurons, process it, and pass the integrated information to other neurons. Interneurons make up the hugely complex networks and circuits that perform the complex functions of the brain. In contrast with motor neurons and sensory neurons, the axons of interneurons tend to be short. So, neurons are remarkably diverse in shape, their forms reflecting their highly specialized functions. A few of the hundreds of different types of neurons found in the brain are illustrated in **FIGURE 2.3**.

Vertebrate nerve cell bodies range from as small as 10 micrometers (μm) to as large as 100 μm or more in diameter; this variability in neuronal sizes is evident in Figure 2.3. In general, larger neurons tend to have more-complex inputs and outputs, cover greater distances, and/or convey information more rapidly than smaller neurons. The relative sizes of neural structures that we will be discussing throughout the book are illustrated in **FIGURE 2.4**. Some of the wide variety of techniques used to visualize neurons are described in **BOX 2.1**.

Information is received through synapses

The arrangement of a neuron's dendrites—its tree branch–like **arborization**—reflects the complexity of the neuron's information-processing function. Some simple neurons have just a couple of short dendritic branches, while other neurons have huge and complex dendritic trees covered in many thousands of synaptic contacts from other neurons. At each synapse, information is transmitted from the axon terminal of the **presynaptic** neuron to the receptive surface of the **postsynaptic** neuron (**FIGURE 2.5A**). A synapse typically has three principal components (**FIGURE 2.5B AND C**):

*The meter (m), the basic unit of length in the metric system, equals 39.37 inches. A centimeter (cm) is one-hundredth of a meter (10^{-2} m); a millimeter (mm) is one-thousandth of a meter (10^{-3} m); a micrometer, or micron, (μm) is one-millionth of a meter (10^{-6} m); and a nanometer (nm) is one-billionth of a meter (10^{-9} m).

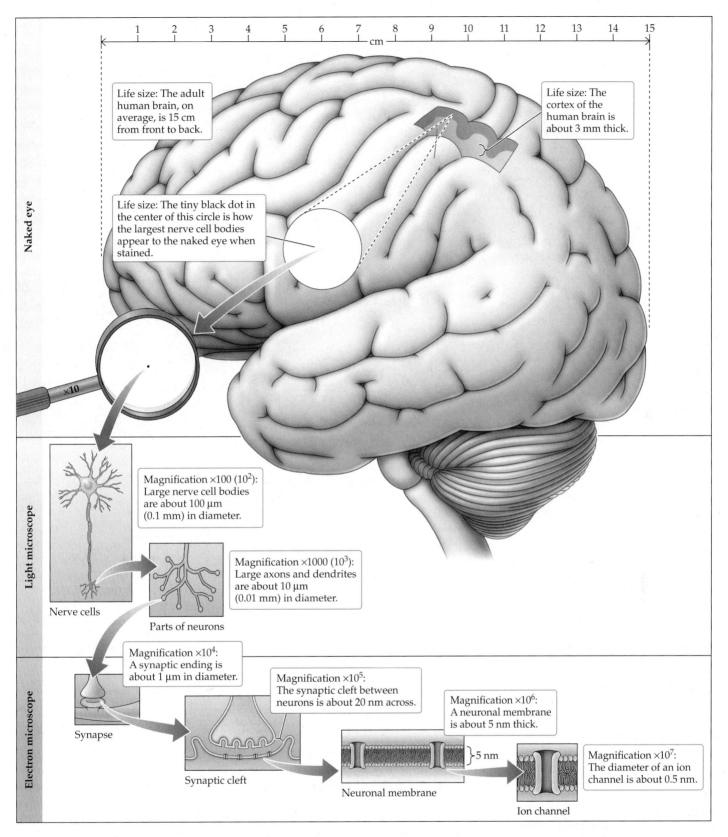

Naked eye

Life size: The adult human brain, on average, is 15 cm from front to back.

Life size: The cortex of the human brain is about 3 mm thick.

Life size: The tiny black dot in the center of this circle is how the largest nerve cell bodies appear to the naked eye when stained.

×10

Light microscope

Magnification ×100 (10^2): Large nerve cell bodies are about 100 μm (0.1 mm) in diameter.

Nerve cells

Magnification ×1000 (10^3): Large axons and dendrites are about 10 μm (0.01 mm) in diameter.

Parts of neurons

Electron microscope

Magnification ×10^4: A synaptic ending is about 1 μm in diameter.

Synapse

Magnification ×10^5: The synaptic cleft between neurons is about 20 nm across.

Magnification ×10^6: A neuronal membrane is about 5 nm thick.

Synaptic cleft

5 nm

Neuronal membrane

Magnification ×10^7: The diameter of an ion channel is about 0.5 nm.

Ion channel

2.4 SIZES OF SOME NEURAL STRUCTURES AND THE UNITS OF MEASURE AND MAGNIFICATION USED IN STUDYING THEM

1. The **presynaptic membrane** of the axon terminal of the presynaptic neuron
2. The **synaptic cleft**, a gap of about 20–40 nanometers (nm) that separates the presynaptic and postsynaptic neurons
3. The specialized **postsynaptic membrane** on the surface of the dendrite or cell body of the postsynaptic neuron

Visualizing the Cells of the Brain

Histology—of the scientific study of the composition of tissue—underwent a revolution beginning in the mid-1800s, when derivatives of fabric dyes were found to vividly stain cells in ways that allowed visualization of previously hidden microscopic structure. In the nervous system, it became possible to selectively stain different parts of neurons and glia, such as cell membranes, the cell body, or the sheaths surrounding axons. Nowadays, scientists use specialized staining procedures to study the numbers, shapes, distribution, and interconnections of neurons within targeted regions of the brain.

(A) Nissl stain

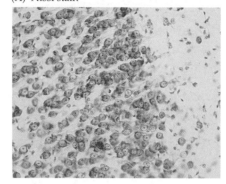

(B) Golgi stain

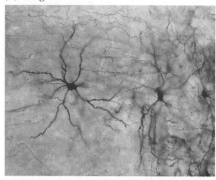

(C) Expression of *c-fos* in activated cells

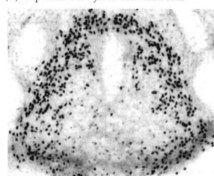

(D) Tract tracing

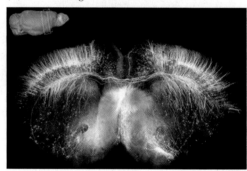

Counting Cells in Brain Regions

Some traditional cell stains, collectively known as **Nissl stains**, outline *all* cell bodies because the dyes are attracted to RNA distributed within the cell. Nissl stains allow us to measure cell body size and the density of cells in particular regions (Figure A). Many types of Nissl stains and other traditional general-purpose cell stains are available.

Examining the Forms of Individual Neurons

Mysteriously, and in contrast to Nissl stains, **Golgi stains** label only a small minority of neurons in a sample,

but the affected cells are stained very deeply and completely, revealing fine details of cell structure such as the branches of dendrites and axons (Figure B). Golgi-stained neurons stand out in sharp contrast to their unstained neighbors, so Golgi staining is useful for quantifying the types and precise shape of neurons in a region. There are a number of variants on

this strategy, such as filling cells with fluorescent molecules.

Mapping the Expression of Cellular Products

Often, neuroscientists would like to know the distribution of neurons that exhibit a specific property, such as sensitivity to a hormone or drug, production of particular proteins, or

---

synaptic cleft The space between the presynaptic and postsynaptic elements.

postsynaptic membrane The specialized membrane on the surface of the cell that receives information by responding to neurotransmitter from a presynaptic neuron.

synaptic vesicle A small, spherical structure that contains molecules of neurotransmitter.

neurotransmitter Also called *synaptic transmitter*, *chemical transmitter*, or simply *transmitter*. The chemical released from the presynaptic axon terminal that serves as the basis of communication between neurons.

Presynaptic axon terminals contain numerous tiny hollow spheres, called **synaptic vesicles**, each 30–140 nm in diameter. Each vesicle contains molecules of a specialized chemical substance, a **neurotransmitter**, which the neuron uses to communicate with postsynaptic neurons. In response to electrical activity in the axon, these vesicles fuse with the presynaptic membrane and rupture, releasing the neurotransmitter molecules into the cleft (see Figure 2.5B). After diffusing across the cleft, the released neurotransmitter interacts with postsynaptic **receptors**: specialized protein molecules that capture and react to molecules of the neurotransmitter. This action results in electrical changes in the postsynaptic cell. If the postsynaptic cell is a neuron (as most are), this electrical event affects the likelihood that the postsynaptic neuron will in turn release its own neurotransmitter. Molecules of neurotransmitter generally do not enter the postsynaptic neuron; they simply bind to the receptors momentarily, and then dissociate. Many different substances are known to act as neurotransmitters; we will discuss them in depth in Chapter 4.

The postsynaptic membrane contains a high density of receptors. And because each synapse occupies a very small patch of the postsynaptic neuron—less than 1

synthesis of the RNA message that indicates that a specific gene has been activated. Numerous clever techniques have been developed to trick neurons into revealing themselves. In **autoradiography**, for example, animals are treated with radioactive versions of experimental drugs, and then thin slices of the brain are placed alongside photographic film. Radioactivity emitted by the labeled compound in the tissue "exposes" the emulsion—as light does striking film—so the brain essentially takes a picture of itself, highlighting the specific brain regions where the drug has become selectively concentrated. An alternative way to visualize cells that have an attribute in common—termed **immunohistochemistry (IHC)**—involves creating antibodies against a protein of interest (we can create antibodies to almost any protein). Equipped with colorful labels, these antibodies can selectively seek out and attach themselves to their target proteins within neurons in a brain slice, selectively revealing the distribution of only those neurons that make the target protein. In the example in Figure C, antibodies have labeled only those cells containing a protein expressed by *c-fos*, which is an immediate early gene (IEG) that is expressed in cells that have been recently active. Localizing IEG proteins allows researchers to identify brain regions that were active during particular behaviors performed by an animal shortly before it was euthanized. A related procedure called **in situ hybridization** goes a step further and, using radioactively labeled lengths of nucleic acid (RNA or DNA, see the Appendix), labels only those neurons in which a gene of interest has been turned on.

Tracing Interconnections between Neurons

Many research questions are more concerned with the pattern of connections between neurons than with their cellular structure (Figure D). But tracing the interconnections between regions is a technical challenge, because axons are profuse and tiny, follow intricate routes, and are difficult to disentangle from one another. To accomplish this goal, scientists have developed many sorts of **tract tracers**, substances that are taken up by neurons and transported over the routes of their axons. In *anterograde labeling* the tract tracer is injected near the dendrites and cell bodies of a region of interest, where it is taken up and transported to the tips of the axons, thus revealing the *targets* of the neurons in the region under study. Conversely, in *retrograde labeling*, when a different kind of tract tracer is injected into a region of interest, it is exclusively taken up by axon terminals and then transported back to their originating cell bodies, thus revealing the *sources* of innervation of the region. A few specialized retrograde tract tracers (such as labeled pseudorabies virus) can even work *trans-synaptically*: they jump backward across synapses and work their way "upstream," back toward higher levels of the nervous system, leaving visible molecules of label all along the way. (Figure B courtesy of Dr. Timothy DeVoogd; C from Sunn et al., 2002; D from Yuan et al., 2015. Courtesy of Dr. Qingming Luo.)

histology   The scientific study of the composition of tissues.

Nissl stain   A cell stain that reveals all cell bodies by staining RNA.

Golgi stain   A cell stain that fills a small proportion of neurons with a dense dark product.

autoradiography   A histological technique that shows the distribution of radioactive chemicals in tissues.

immunohistochemistry (IHC)   A technique in which labeled antibodies are used to visualize the histological distribution of specific proteins.

in situ hybridization   A technique in which labeled complementary nucleic probes are used to identify cells expressing specific messenger RNA transcripts, reflecting the activation of specific genes of interest.

tract tracer   A compound used to identify the routes and interconnections of neuronal projections.

μm²—a large number of synapses can cover the surfaces of the dendrites and cell body. In fact, some neurons receive as many as 100,000 synaptic contacts, although a more common number is about 5,000–10,000. As you might expect, neurons with elaborate dendrites tend to have more synaptic inputs.

The configuration of synapses on a neuron's dendrites and cell body is constantly changing—synapses come and go, and dendrites change their shape—in response to new patterns of synaptic activity and the formation of new neural circuits. We use the general term **neural plasticity** to refer to this continual remodeling of the connections between neurons. Studding the dendrites of many neurons are outgrowths called *dendritic spines* (see Figure 2.5A) that, by effectively increasing the surface area of the dendrites, allow for extra synaptic contacts. Both the number and structure of dendritic spines may be rapidly altered by experience, such as training or exposure to sensory stimuli (see Chapter 17). This plastic property of dendritic spines has made them the focus of intensive research efforts. Some dendritic spines change from minute to minute, while others may be stable for a lifetime (Grutzendler et al., 2002; Trachtenberg et al., 2002).

receptor   Also called *receptor molecule*. A protein that binds and reacts to molecules of a neurotransmitter or hormone.

neural plasticity   Also called *neuroplasticity*. The ability of the nervous system to change in response to experience or the environment.

2.5 SYNAPSES (A) Axon terminals typically form synapses on the cell body or dendrites of a neuron. On dendrites, synapses may form on dendritic spines or on the shaft of a dendrite. (B) Information flows through a synapse from the presynaptic membrane across a gap called the *synaptic cleft* to the postsynaptic membrane. (C) This photomicrograph shows a synapse with some structures color coded.

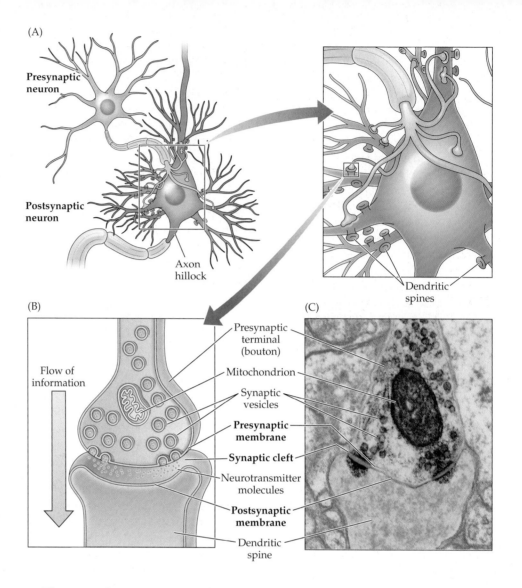

The axon integrates and then transmits information

A typical axon has several distinct regions. The axon arises from the **axon hillock** ("little hill"), a cone-shaped projection of the cell body (see Figure 2.5A). The axon hillock is the neuron's integration zone, gathering and integrating information from all the synapses on the neuron's dendrites and soma, then converting the processed information into a code of electrical impulses that carries the neuron's message down the axon toward its targets (see Chapter 3). The axon beyond the hillock is tubular, with a diameter ranging from 0.2 to 20 μm in mammals, but up to 500 μm or more in the "giant" axons of some invertebrates (Debanne et al., 2011).

With very few exceptions, neurons have only one axon. But as noted earlier, this solitary axon often divides into several axon collaterals, allowing the neuron to influence (or **innervate**) a number of postsynaptic cells. **TABLE 2.1** compares the main structural features of axons and dendrites.

The cell body manufactures various materials, such as enzymes and structural proteins, under the guidance of the DNA (deoxyribonucleic acid) contained in the cell nucleus (see the Appendix). Important substances needed at the axon terminals are loaded into *transport vesicles*—hollow spheres with specialized leglike **motor proteins** on their outer surface (**FIGURE 2.6**). When activated, the motor proteins literally "walk" the vesicles through the inside of the axon, between the cell body and the axon terminals. This movement of material, called **axonal transport**, works in both directions: *anterograde transport* moves material toward the axon terminals, and *retrograde transport* moves used materials back to the cell body for recycling. Furthermore, some materials are transported along axons at a "slow" rate (less than 8 mm

axon hillock A cone-shaped area from which the axon originates out of the cell body. Functionally, the integration zone of the neuron.

innervate To provide neural input.

motor protein A specialized kinetic protein molecule that conveys a load, such as a vesicle, from one location to another within a cell.

axonal transport The transportation of materials from the neuronal cell body to distant regions in the dendrites and axons, and from the axon terminals back to the cell body.

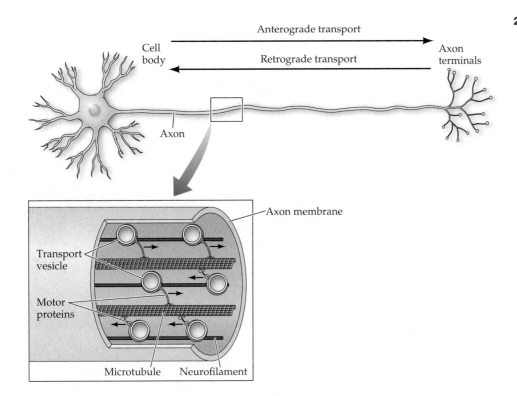

per day); others are transported by a "fast" system (200–400 mm per day). So, the axon has two quite different functions: rapid transmission of electrical signals along the *outside* of the axon, and the much slower transportation of substances *inside* the axon, to and from the axon terminals. You can find links to videos of both types of axonal activity on the website.

Glial cells support and enhance neural activity

Glial cells were originally believed to hold the nervous system together (the Greek *glia* means "glue"). But glial cells can also communicate with each other and with neurons, and they directly affect neuronal functioning by providing neurons with raw materials and chemical signals that alter neuronal structure and excitability (**FIGURE 2.7**). In its exclusion of glial cells, the neuron doctrine was perhaps an oversimplification (Bullock et al., 2005).

There are at least as many glial cells as neurons in the brain—even more than this 1 to 1 ratio in some regions (Azevedo et al., 2009; Herculano-Houzel, 2014)—and yet in contrast to the hundreds of types of neurons, glial cells come in only four basic

TABLE 2.1 Distinctions between Axons and Dendrites

PROPERTY	AXONS	DENDRITES
Number	Usually one per neuron, with many terminal branches	Usually many per neuron
Diameter	Uniform until start of terminal branching	Tapering progressively toward ending
Axon hillock	Present	No hillock-like region
Sheathing	Usually covered with myelin	No myelin sheath
Length	Ranging from practically nonexistent to several meters long	Often much shorter than axons

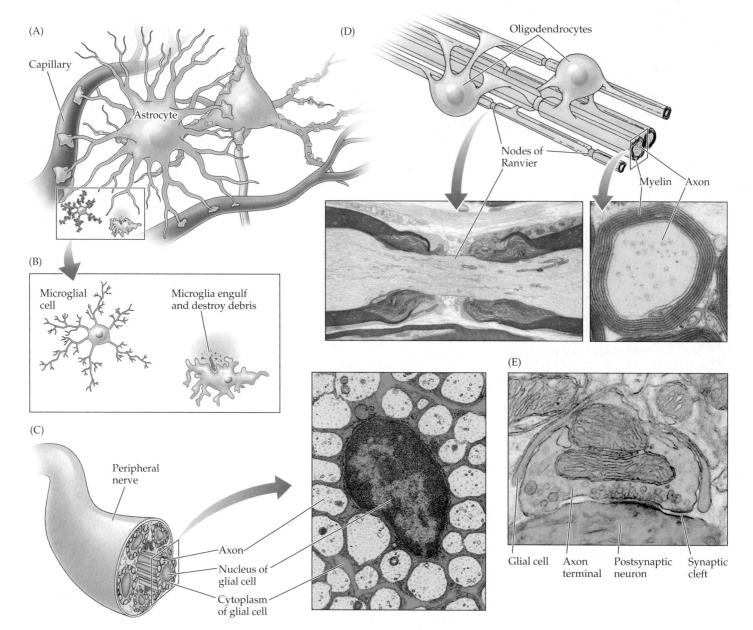

2.7 GLIAL CELLS (A) Star-shaped astrocytes detect neural activity and regulate adjacent capillaries to control blood flow, supplying neurons with more energy when they are active. (B) Tiny microglial cells surround and break down any debris that forms, especially after damage to the brain. (C) Unmyelinated axons are embedded in the troughs of glial cells. The light-colored circular shapes in the photograph are unmyelinated axons surrounded by the cytoplasm (blue) of a glial cell (the large dark area is the glial nucleus). (D) Extensions of oligodendrocytes form myelin wrapping (blue) on axons (yellow). The colorized electron micrograph of a myelinated axon (lower right) shows the many layers of the myelin sheath. The longitudinal micrograph of an axon (lower left) shows a node of Ranvier, the gap between adjacent myelinated segments. (E) Processes from astrocytes (blue) surround and insulate synapses and directly modify synaptic activity. (Micrographs D [left] and E courtesy of Dr. Mark Ellisman and the National Center for Microscopy and Imaging Research; C and D [right] from Peters et al., 1991.)

astrocyte A star-shaped glial cell with numerous processes (extensions) that run in all directions.

forms, three of which are found in the brain. One type, called an **astrocyte** (from the Greek *astron*, "star"), is a star-shaped cell with numerous processes extending in all directions (**FIGURE 2.7A**), weaving among neurons. Some astrocytes form sucker-like end feet on blood vessels, regulating local blood flow to provide more supplies to neurons when they are active (Schummers et al., 2008). Astrocytes receive synapses directly from neurons and surround and monitor the activity of nearby neuronal synapses. There is evidence that cross talk among astrocytes and neighboring neurons constitutes a "tripartite synapse" (*tripartite* means "three-part"), with astrocytes directly participating in the transmission of information between neurons (R. D. Fields and Stevens-Graham, 2002; Perea et al., 2009), although the extent and significance of this sort of "gliotransmission" remains controversial (Agulhon et al., 2010). Astrocytes are also involved in the formation of new synapses, as well as the pruning of surplus synapses that is a normal part of brain development (Chung et al., 2013).

A second type of glial cell is the **microglial cell** (**FIGURE 2.7B**). As the name suggests, microglial cells are very small. They are also remarkably active, continually extending and withdrawing very fine processes that, when they contact a site of damage, form a spherical containment zone around the injury (Davalos et al., 2005). The brain's cleanup crew, microglial cells migrate to sites of injury or disease in the nervous system to remove debris from injured or dead cells. But we are beginning to realize that microglial cells are involved in more than just damage control: for example, microglial cells appear to be a key component of neural pain systems (S. Beggs et al., 2012).

The remaining types of glial cells—**oligodendrocytes** and **Schwann cells**—perform a very different yet vital function called **myelination**. All along the axons of many neurons, these glial cells wrap sections of the axon in multiple layers of **myelin**, a fatty insulating substance, giving the axon the appearance of a string of slender beads (**FIGURE 2.7D**). Between adjacent beads, small uninsulated patches of axonal membrane, called **nodes of Ranvier**, remain exposed.

Within the brain and spinal cord, myelination is provided by the oligodendrocytes, with each cell typically providing myelin beads to several nearby axons (see Figure 2.7D). In the rest of the body, Schwann cells do the ensheathing; a single Schwann cell ensheathes a limited length of a single axon. But whether it is provided by oligodendrocytes or Schwann cells, myelination's result is the same—a large increase in the speed with which electrical signals pass down the axon, jumping from one node to the next (see Chapter 3). Many thin, short axons lack myelin but still are surrounded by oligodendrocytes or Schwann cells, which segregate the unmyelinated axons (**FIGURE 2.7C**). Furthermore, the manner in which glial cells surround some synaptic contacts suggests that one of their roles is to insulate and isolate synapses to prevent one from affecting the other (**FIGURE 2.7E**). Oligodendrocytes also provide chemical signals (*trophic signals*) that enhance the structural integrity of axons (Nave 2010). The process of myelination continues for a long time in humans—in some brain regions for 10–15 years after birth, and possibly throughout life. In fact, more than 75% of the brain's glial cells are oligodendrocytes, reflecting the complexity and importance of myelination. In contrast, about 17% of glia are astrocytes, and microglia make up just 7% of the total (Pelvig et al., 2008).

Glial cells are of clinical interest for a variety of reasons. Unlike neurons, glial cells continue to divide throughout life, and consequently they form many of the types of tumors that may arise in the brain. Some glial cells, especially astrocytes, respond to brain injury by changing in size—that is, by swelling. This **edema** damages neurons and is responsible for many symptoms of brain injuries. Astrocytes also directly influence local brain chemistry, so they have been implicated in diseases that result from changes in neuronal excitability, such as epilepsy (Robel and Sontheimer, 2015). Microglia are also increasingly implicated in disease, especially degenerative processes like Alzheimer's disease. Normally, microglia remove debris and also help maintain synapses, but pathological changes in their microenvironment can cause microglia to show a damaging inflammation response, making them a possible target in the search for Alzheimer's treatments (Graeber, 2010; Perry and Holmes, 2014). Disease processes that interfere with the myelination provided by oligodendrocytes can have a wide variety of effects. For example, in **multiple sclerosis** the loss of the insulating myelin sheath from axons in various regions of the brain can have severe consequences for the individual that vary depending on the region that is affected, just as losing the outer insulation from a computer cable can cause short circuits and the loss of vital information. Changes in all three kinds of glial cells, especially the loss of oligodendrocytes and their associated myelin, are implicated in the onset and symptoms of schizophrenia (Bernstein et al., 2015).

Supported and influenced by glial cells, and sharing information through synapses, neurons form the vast ensembles of circuits that intricately process information, giving the brain its visible form. These major divisions are our next topic.

microglial cells Also called *microglia*. Extremely small glial cells that remove cellular debris from injured or dead cells.

oligodendrocyte A type of glial cell that forms myelin in the central nervous system.

Schwann cell The glial cell that forms myelin in the peripheral nervous system.

myelination The process of myelin formation.

myelin The fatty insulation around an axon, formed by glial cells, that improves the speed of conduction of action potentials.

node of Ranvier A gap between successive segments of the myelin sheath where the axon membrane is exposed.

edema The swelling of tissue, such as in the brain, in response to injury.

multiple sclerosis Literally, "many scars." A disorder characterized by widespread degeneration of myelin.

2.8 THE CENTRAL AND PERIPHERAL NERVOUS SYSTEMS (A) This view of the nervous system is a composite of two drawings. A modern view of the central nervous system (the brain and spinal cord), shown in blue, is superimposed on a rendering of the peripheral nervous system by the great sixteenth-century anatomist Andreas Vesalius (1514–1564). The peripheral nervous system, shown in yellow, courses through the body and connects all body organs and systems to the central nervous system (CNS). (B) The brain and spinal cord together form the CNS. The spinal nerves have been spread out so that they're distinguishable, but they are normally inside the bony spinal column. The solid part of the spinal cord ends in the middle of the lower back. Below this point a spray of fibers called the *cauda equina* (Latin for "horse's tail") continues downward inside the spinal column.

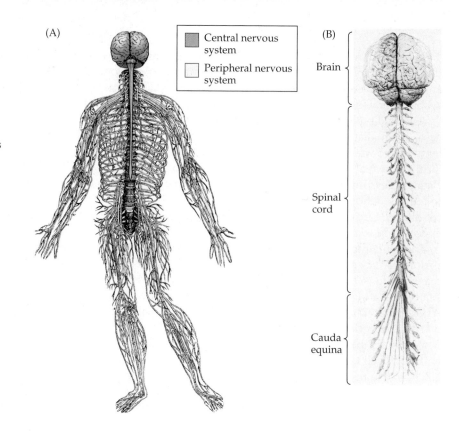

(A)

Central nervous system

Peripheral nervous system

(B)

Brain

Spinal cord

Cauda equina

The Nervous System Consists of Central and Peripheral Divisions

In this section we describe the **gross neuroanatomy** of the nervous system—the components that are visible to the unaided eye. **FIGURE 2.8A** presents a view of the entire human nervous system. This viewpoint reveals a natural subdivision into a **peripheral nervous system** (all nervous system parts that are outside the bony skull and spinal column) and a **central nervous system** (**CNS**), consisting of the brain and spinal cord (**FIGURE 2.8B**).

The peripheral nervous system has two divisions

The peripheral nervous system consists of **nerves**—collections of axons bundled together—that extend throughout the body. Some nerves, called **motor nerves**, transmit information from the spinal cord and brain to the muscles, organs, and glands. Others, called **sensory nerves**, arise from sensory surfaces and convey information from the body to the spinal cord and brain. The various nerves of the body are divided into two distinct systems: (1) the **somatic nervous system**, which consists of nerves that interconnect the brain and the major muscles and sensory systems of the body, and (2) the **autonomic nervous system**, the nerves that primarily control the viscera (internal organs).

THE SOMATIC NERVOUS SYSTEM Taking its name from the Latin word for "body"—*soma*—the somatic nervous system is the main pathway through which the brain controls movement and receives sensory information from the body and from the sensory organs of the head. The nerves that make up the somatic nervous system form two anatomical groups: the **cranial nerves** and the **spinal nerves**.

We each have 12 pairs of cranial nerves—one left-sided and one right-sighted nerve in each pair—that serve the sensory and motor systems of the head and neck (**FIGURE 2.9**). These nerves pass through small openings in the skull, directly entering or leaving the brain without ever joining the spinal cord. Each cranial nerve is known both by name and by Roman numeral.

Three cranial nerves are exclusively sensory pathways to the brain: the olfactory (I) nerve conveys smell, the optic (II) nerve carries visual information, and the vestibulocochlear (VIII) nerve is concerned with hearing and balance. Five pairs of cranial

gross neuroanatomy Anatomical features of the nervous system that are apparent to the naked eye.

peripheral nervous system The portion of the nervous system that includes all the nerves and neurons outside the brain and spinal cord.

central nervous system (CNS) The portion of the nervous system that includes the brain and the spinal cord.

nerve A collection of axons bundled together outside the central nervous system.

motor nerve A nerve that conveys neural activity to muscle tissue and causes it to contract.

sensory nerve A nerve that conveys sensory information from the periphery into the central nervous system.

somatic nervous system The part of the peripheral nervous system that provides neural connections to the skeletal musculature.

autonomic nervous system The part of the peripheral nervous system that supplies neural connections to glands and to smooth muscles of internal organs.

cranial nerve A nerve that is connected directly to the brain.

spinal nerve Also called *somatic nerve*. A nerve that emerges from the spinal cord.

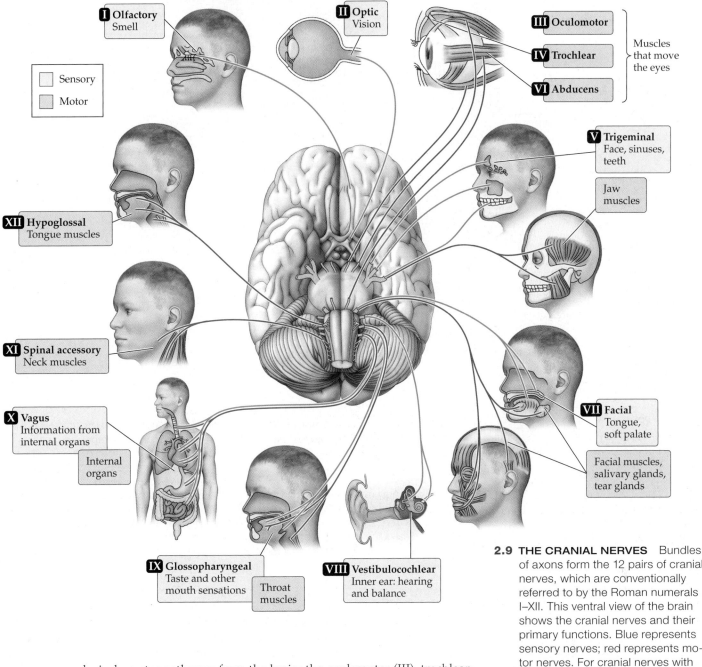

Sensory

Motor

I Olfactory
Smell

II Optic
Vision

III Oculomotor

IV Trochlear

VI Abducens

Muscles that move the eyes

V Trigeminal
Face, sinuses, teeth

Jaw muscles

XII Hypoglossal
Tongue muscles

XI Spinal accessory
Neck muscles

X Vagus
Information from internal organs

Internal organs

VII Facial
Tongue, soft palate

Facial muscles, salivary glands, tear glands

IX Glossopharyngeal
Taste and other mouth sensations

Throat muscles

VIII Vestibulocochlear
Inner ear: hearing and balance

2.9 THE CRANIAL NERVES Bundles of axons form the 12 pairs of cranial nerves, which are conventionally referred to by the Roman numerals I–XII. This ventral view of the brain shows the cranial nerves and their primary functions. Blue represents sensory nerves; red represents motor nerves. For cranial nerves with both types of functions, separate axons within the nerve carry either motor or sensory information.

nerves are exclusively motor pathways from the brain: the oculomotor (III), trochlear (IV), and abducens (VI) nerves innervate muscles to move the eye; the spinal accessory (XI) nerves control neck muscles; and the hypoglossal (XII) nerves control the tongue.

The remaining cranial nerves have both sensory and motor functions. The trigeminal (V), for example, serves facial sensation through some axons, and it controls chewing movements through other axons. The facial (VII) nerves control facial muscles and receive some taste sensation, and the glossopharyngeal (IX) nerves receive additional taste sensations and sensations from the throat, and also control the muscles there. The vagus (X) nerve extends far from the head, running to the heart, liver, and intestines. Its long, convoluted route is the reason for its name, which is Latin for "wandering."

Along the length of the spinal cord, an additional 31 pairs of spinal nerves emerge at regularly spaced intervals through openings in the backbone (**FIGURE 2.10**). As with the cranial nerves, one member of each pair of spinal nerves serves each side of the body. Furthermore, each spinal nerve consists of the fusion of two distinct branches, called *roots*, which are functionally different. The **dorsal** (back) **root** of each spinal nerve consists of sensory projections from the body to the spinal cord. The **ventral** (front) **root** consists of motor projections from the spinal cord to the muscles.

dorsal root The branch of a spinal nerve, entering the dorsal horn of the spinal cord, that carries sensory information from the peripheral nervous system to the spinal cord.

ventral root The branch of a spinal nerve, arising from the ventral horn of the spinal cord, that carries motor messages from the spinal cord to the peripheral nervous system.

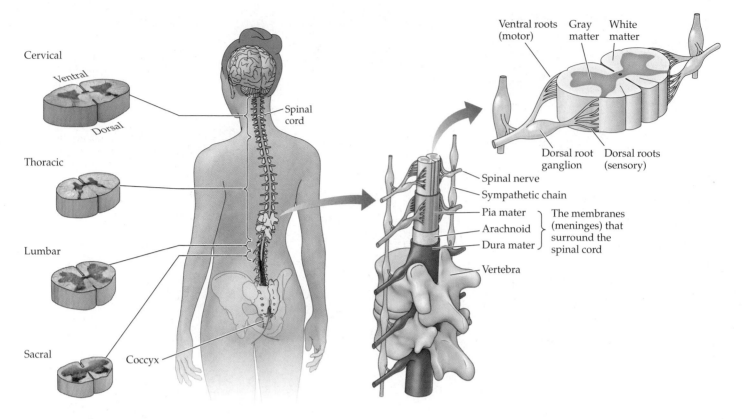

2.10 THE SPINAL CORD AND SPINAL NERVES (Middle) The spinal column runs from the base of the brain to the coccyx (tailbone); a pair of nerves emerges from each level (see Figure 2.8B). (Bottom right) The spinal cord is surrounded by bony vertebrae and is enclosed in three membrane layers (the meninges). Each vertebra has an opening on each side through which the spinal nerves pass. (Top right) The spinal cord gray matter is located in the center of the cord and is surrounded by white matter. In the gray matter are interneurons and the motor neurons that send axons to the muscles. The white matter consists of myelinated axons that run up and down the spinal column. (Left) These stained cross sections show the spinal cord at the cervical, thoracic, lumbar, and sacral levels. (Images from Hanaway et al., 1998.)

cervical   Referring to the topmost eight segments of the spinal cord, in the neck region.

thoracic   Referring to the 12 spinal segments below the cervical (neck) portion of the spinal cord, corresponding to the chest.

lumbar   Referring to the five spinal segments that make up the upper part of the lower back.

sacral   Referring to the five spinal segments that make up the lower part of the lower back.

coccygeal   Referring to the lowest spinal vertebra (also called the *tailbone*).

autonomic ganglia   Collections of nerve cell bodies, belonging to the autonomic division of the peripheral nervous system, that are found in various locations and innervate the major organs.

preganglionic   Literally, "before the ganglion." Referring to neurons in the autonomic nervous system that run from the central nervous system to the autonomic ganglia.

postganglionic   Literally, "after the ganglion." Referring to neurons in the autonomic nervous system that run from the autonomic ganglia to various targets in the body.

sympathetic nervous system   A component of the autonomic nervous system that arises from the thoracic and lumbar spinal cord.

Each spinal nerve is named according to the segment of spinal cord to which it is connected: there are 8 **cervical** (neck), 12 **thoracic** (trunk), 5 **lumbar** (lower back), 5 **sacral** (pelvic), and 1 **coccygeal** (bottom) spinal segments. So, we refer to the spinal nerve that is connected to the twelfth segment of the thoracic portion of the spinal cord as *T12*, the nerve connected to the third segment of the sacral portion as *S3*, and so on. Fibers from different spinal nerves join to form peripheral nerves.

THE AUTONOMIC NERVOUS SYSTEM   Although it is "autonomous" in the sense that we don't have very much conscious, voluntary control over its actions, the autonomic nervous system is the brain's main system for controlling the organs of the body. Supporting these functions are aggregates of neurons called **autonomic ganglia**, found in various locations in the body outside of the CNS. Autonomic neurons within the brain and spinal cord send their axons to innervate neurons in the ganglia, which in turn send their axons to innervate all the major organs. The central neurons that innervate the ganglia are known as **preganglionic** autonomic neurons; the ganglionic neurons that innervate the body are known as **postganglionic** neurons.

The autonomic nervous system has three major divisions: the sympathetic nervous system, the parasympathetic nervous system, and the enteric nervous system. The sympathetic and parasympathetic nervous systems act more or less in opposition (**FIGURE 2.11**). The preganglionic cells of the **sympathetic nervous system** are found in the middle parts of the spinal cord—the thoracic and lumbar regions. They

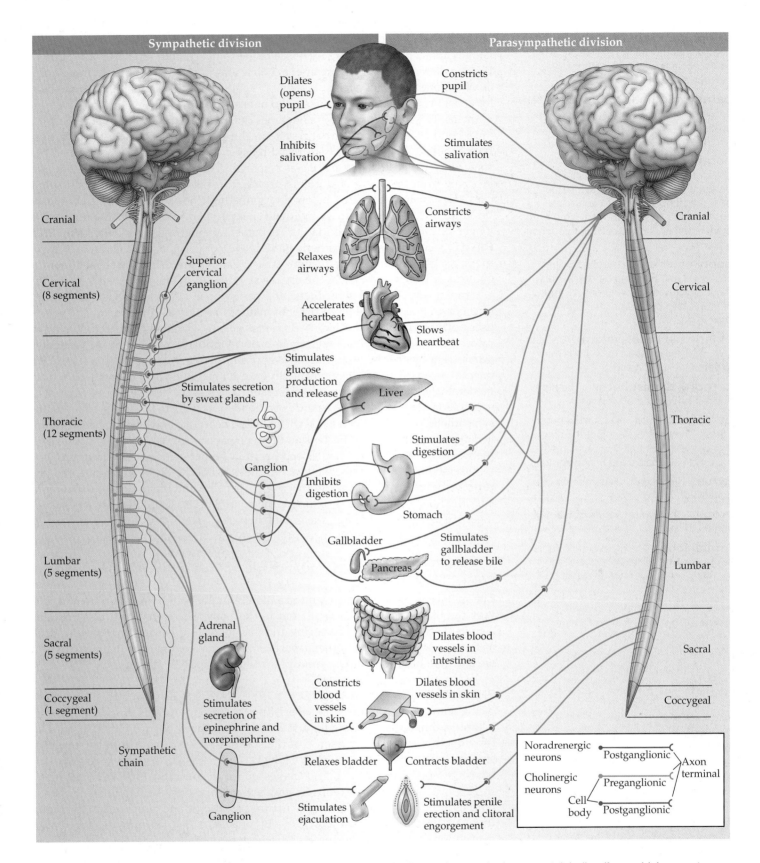

Sympathetic division

Parasympathetic division

Dilates (opens) pupil

Constricts pupil

Inhibits salivation

Stimulates salivation

Cranial

Cervical (8 segments)

Superior cervical ganglion

Constricts airways

Relaxes airways

Accelerates heartbeat

Slows heartbeat

Thoracic (12 segments)

Stimulates glucose production and release

Liver

Stimulates secretion by sweat glands

Ganglion

Stimulates digestion

Inhibits digestion

Stomach

Gallbladder

Stimulates gallbladder to release bile

Pancreas

Lumbar (5 segments)

Sacral (5 segments)

Adrenal gland

Dilates blood vessels in intestines

Coccygeal (1 segment)

Constricts blood vessels in skin

Dilates blood vessels in skin

Stimulates secretion of epinephrine and norepinephrine

Sympathetic chain

Relaxes bladder

Contracts bladder

Ganglion

Stimulates ejaculation

Stimulates penile erection and clitoral engorgement

Cranial

Cervical

Thoracic

Lumbar

Sacral

Coccygeal

Noradrenergic neurons — Postganglionic — Axon terminal

Cholinergic neurons — Preganglionic

Cell body — Postganglionic

2.11 THE AUTONOMIC NERVOUS SYSTEM (Left) The sympathetic division of the autonomic nervous system consists of the sympathetic chains and the nerve fibers that flow from them. (Right) The parasympathetic division arises from both the brain and the sacral parts of the spinal cord. Parasympathetic postganglionic cells and all preganglionic axons, whether sympathetic or parasym- pathetic, produce and release acetylcholine (from which we get the adjective *cholinergic*) as a neurotransmitter. Sympathetic postganglionic cells produce and use norepinephrine (also known as *noradrenaline*; hence the adjective *noradrenergic*) as a neurotransmitter. The different postganglionic transmitters have opposing effects on target organs, allowing precise con- trol. Neurotransmitters are discussed in detail in Chapter 4.

sympathetic chain A chain of ganglia that runs along each side of the spinal column; part of the sympathetic nervous system.

parasympathetic nervous system A component of the autonomic nervous system that arises from both the cranial nerves and the sacral spinal cord.

norepinephrine Also called *noradrenaline*. A neurotransmitter produced and released by sympathetic postganglionic neurons to accelerate organ activity. Also produced in the brainstem and found in projections throughout the brain.

acetylcholine A neurotransmitter produced and released by parasympathetic postganglionic neurons, by motor neurons, and by neurons throughout the brain.

enteric nervous system An extensive mesh-like system of neurons that governs the functioning of the gut.

cerebral hemispheres The right and left halves of the forebrain.

cerebral cortex Also called simply *cortex*. The outer covering of the cerebral hemispheres that consists largely of neuronal cell bodies and their branches.

gyrus A ridged or raised portion of a convoluted brain surface.

sulcus A furrow of a convoluted brain surface.

frontal lobe The most anterior portion of the cerebral cortex.

send their axons only a short distance, innervating the **sympathetic chain** of autonomic ganglia that runs along each side of the spinal column (**FIGURE 2.11, LEFT**). Postganglionic cells of the sympathetic chain course throughout the body, innervating all of the major organ systems. In general, sympathetic activation prepares the body for action: blood pressure increases, the pupils of the eyes dilate, and the heart rate quickens. This set of reactions is sometimes called simply the *fight or flight* response.

In contrast to the sympathetic system, the **parasympathetic nervous system** generally helps the body to relax, recuperate, and prepare for future action, sometimes called the *rest and digest* response. The parasympathetic system gets its name from its anatomical points of origin in the brainstem and sacral spinal cord, thus arising above and below the sympathetic nerves (the Greek *para* means "around"). Compared with sympathetic nerves, parasympathetic axons travel a longer distance before terminating in parasympathetic ganglia (**FIGURE 2.11, RIGHT**), because parasympathetic ganglia are not collected in a chain as sympathetic ganglia are. Instead, parasympathetic ganglia are dispersed throughout the body, usually positioned near the organs affected.

At many organs, the sympathetic and parasympathetic divisions act in opposite directions, because they release different neurotransmitters. The sympathetic system uses **norepinephrine** (also known as *noradrenaline*), which tends to accelerate activity, while the parasympathetic system uses **acetylcholine**, which tends to slow down activity. The balance between these two opposing systems determines the state of the internal organs at any given moment. So, for example, when parasympathetic activity predominates, heart rate slows, blood pressure drops, and digestive processes are activated. As the brain causes the balance of autonomic activity to become predominantly sympathetic, opposite effects are seen: increased heart rate and blood pressure, inhibited digestion, and so on. This tension between parasympathetic and sympathetic activity ensures that the individual is appropriately prepared for current circumstances.

Resembling a mesh embedded within the walls of the digestive organs, the **enteric nervous system** is a local network of sensory and motor neurons that regulates the functioning of the gut, under the control of the CNS. Because it regulates digestive activities of the gut, the enteric nervous system plays a key role in maintaining fluid and nutrient balances in the body (discussed in Chapter 13).

The central nervous system consists of the brain and spinal cord

The spinal cord funnels sensory information from the body up to the brain and conveys the brain's motor commands out to the body. The spinal cord also contains circuits that perform local processing and that control simple units of behavior, such as reflexes. We will discuss other aspects of the spinal cord in later chapters; for now we will limit our focus to the executive portion of the CNS: the brain.

BRAIN FEATURES THAT ARE VISIBLE TO THE NAKED EYE   Given the importance of the adult human brain, it is surprisitng that it only weighs about 1400 grams (about 3 pounds), accounting for just 2% of the average body weight. Put your two fists together and you get a sense of the size of the two **cerebral hemispheres**: smaller than most people expect. However, even casual inspection reveals that what the brain lacks in weight it makes up for in intricacy. **FIGURE 2.12** offers three views of the human brain in standard orientations. Anmatomists use standard terminology to help identify structures, locations, and directions in the brain; these are described in **BOX 2.2**. (It's a bit of a chore, but learning the anatomical conventions now will make our later discussions of brain organization much easier to follow.)

The lumpy convolutions of the paired cerebral hemispheres are the result of elaborate folding together of a thick sheet of brain tissue called the **cerebral cortex** (or sometimes just *cortex*), which is made up mostly of neuronal cell bodies, dendrites, and axons. The resulting ridges of tissue, called **gyri** (singular *gyrus*), are separated from each other by furrows called **sulci** (singular *sulcus*). Folding up the tissue in this

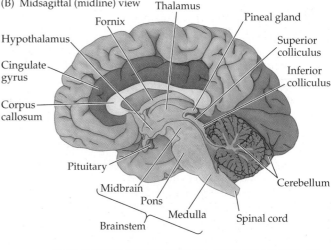

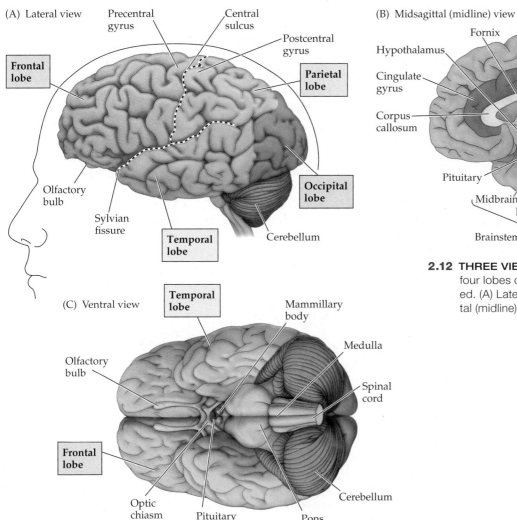

(A) Lateral view

Precentral gyrus — Central sulcus — Postcentral gyrus

Frontal lobe

Parietal lobe

Occipital lobe

Olfactory bulb

Sylvian fissure

Temporal lobe

Cerebellum

(B) Midsagittal (midline) view — Thalamus — Pineal gland

Fornix

Hypothalamus

Cingulate gyrus

Corpus callosum

Superior colliculus

Inferior colliculus

Pituitary

Midbrain

Pons

Medulla

Spinal cord

Cerebellum

Brainstem

2.12 THREE VIEWS OF THE HUMAN BRAIN The four lobes of the cerebral cortex are color coded. (A) Lateral view (from the side). (B) Midsagittal (midline) view. (C) Ventral view (from below).

(C) Ventral view

Temporal lobe

Mammillary body

Medulla

Olfactory bulb

Spinal cord

Frontal lobe

Optic chiasm

Pituitary

Pons

Cerebellum

way greatly increases the amount of cortex that can be jammed into the skull; indeed, about two-thirds of the cerebral surface is hidden in the depths of these folds. The pattern of folding is not random; in fact, it is similar enough between brains that we can name the various gyri and sulci and can group them together into *lobes*.

Neuroscientists rely on a combination of anatomical landmarks and functional differences to distinguish among four major cortical regions called the **frontal**, **parietal**, **temporal**, and **occipital lobes**. These lobes, named after the bones of the skull that overlie them, are distinguished by colors in Figure 2.12. In some cases, the boundaries between adjacent lobes are very clear; for example, the **Sylvian fissure** (a deep sulcus) divides the temporal lobe (just beside your temple) from the other regions of the hemisphere. Likewise, the **central sulcus** provides a distinct landmark dividing the frontal and parietal lobes. The physical boundaries between the occipital lobe and the temporal and parietal lobes are less obvious, but the lobes are quite different with regard to the functions they perform.

The cortex is the seat of complex cognition. Depending on the specific regions affected, cortical damage can cause far-ranging symptoms including impairments of movement or body sensation, speech errors, memory problems, personality changes, or many kinds of visual impairments. Some life-sustaining functions—heart rate and respiration, reflexes, balance, and the like—are governed by lower, subcortical brain regions.

We can identify certain general categories of processing that are particularly associated with specific cortical lobes. For example, the occipital lobes receive and pro-

parietal lobe Large region of cortex lying between the frontal and occipital lobes of each cerebral hemisphere.

temporal lobe Large lateral cortical region of each cerebral hemisphere, continuous with the parietal lobe posteriorly and separated from the frontal lobe by the Sylvian fissure.

occipital lobe Large region of cortex covering much of the posterior part of each cerebral hemisphere.

Sylvian fissure Also called *lateral sulcus*. A deep fissure that demarcates the temporal lobe.

central sulcus A fissure that divides the frontal lobe from the parietal lobe.

Three Customary Orientations for Viewing the Brain and Body

Because the nervous system is a three-dimensional structure, two-dimensional illustrations and diagrams cannot represent it completely. The brain is usually cut in one of three main planes to obtain a two-dimensional section from this three-dimensional object. Although it takes time and practice to master, it is useful to know the terminology that applies to these sections, as shown in the figure.

The plane that bisects the body into right and left halves is called the **sagittal plane** (from the Latin *sagitta*, "arrow"). The plane that divides the body into a front (anterior) and a back (posterior) part is called by several names: **coronal plane** (from the Latin *corona*, "crown"), *frontal plane*, or *transverse plane*. The third main plane, which divides the brain into upper and lower parts, is called the **horizontal plane**.

In addition, several directional terms are used. **Medial** means "toward the middle" and is contrasted with **lateral**, "toward the side." Relative to one location, a second location is **ipsilateral** if it is on the same side of the body, and **contralateral** if on the opposite side of the body. These terms are all relative, as are the terms **superior** (above) and **inferior** (below); for example, the eye is lateral to the nose but medial to the ear, and the mouth is inferior to the nose but superior to the chin.

The head end is referred to as **anterior** or **rostral**, and the tail end is called **posterior** or **caudal** (from the Latin *cauda*, "tail"). **Proximal** means "near the center," and **distal** means "toward the periphery" or "toward the end of a limb." We call an axon, tract, or nerve **afferent** if it carries information into a region that we are interested in, and **efferent** if it car-

ries information away from the region of interest (a handy way to remember this is that **e**fferents **e**xit but **a**fferents **a**rrive, relative to the region of interest).

Dorsal means "toward or at the back," and **ventral** means "toward the belly." In four-legged animals, such as the cat or the rat, *dorsal* refers to both the back of the body and the top of the head and brain. For consistency in comparing brains among species, this term is also used to refer to the top of the brain of a human or of a chimpanzee, even though in such two-legged animals the top of the brain is not at the back of the body. Similarly, *ventral* is understood to designate the bottom of the brain of a two-legged as well as of a four-legged animal. (Photographs courtesy of Drs. S. Mark Williams and Dale Purves, Duke University Medical Center.)

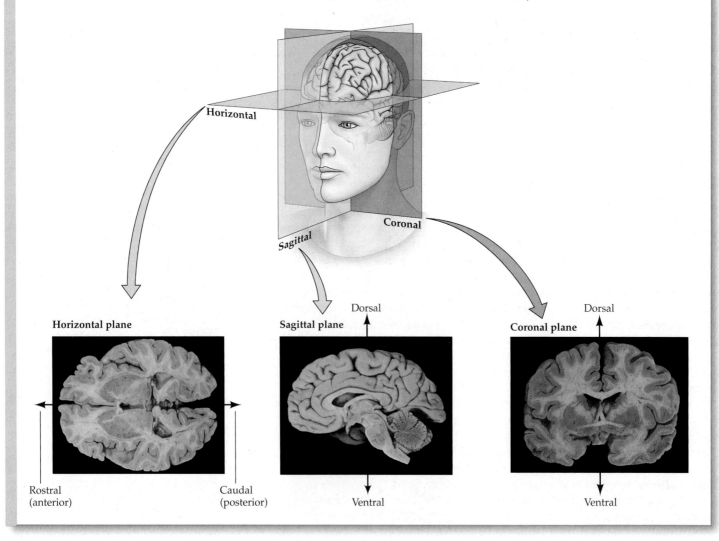

Horizontal plane

Rostral (anterior) — Caudal (posterior)

Sagittal plane

Dorsal — Ventral

Coronal plane

Dorsal — Ventral

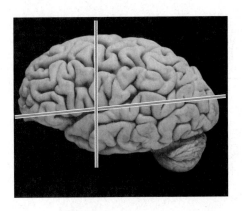

(A) Lateral view showing planes of section

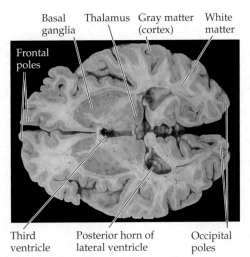

(B) Horizontal section

Basal ganglia   Thalamus   Gray matter (cortex)   White matter

Frontal poles

Third ventricle   Posterior horn of lateral ventricle   Occipital poles

(C) Coronal (transverse) section

Basal ganglia

Corpus callosum   Caudate nucleus   Putamen

Lateral ventricle   Amygdala   Temporal lobe

2.13 INSIDE THE BRAIN (A) The colored lines here indicate the planes of section shown in (B) and (C). The lighter-colored interior is white matter, packed with fatty myelin that surrounds axons sending information in and out of the cortex. Gray matter consists of cell bodies that form the outer layers of the cortex and nuclei within the brain. (Photographs courtesy of Drs. S. Mark Williams and Dale Purves, Duke University Medical Center.)

cess information from the eyes, giving rise to the sense of vision. Auditory information is directed to the nearby temporal lobes, and damage there can impair hearing (the temporal lobes are also particularly associated with the sense of smell and with aspects of learning and memory). The parietal lobes receive sensory information from the body and participate in spatial cognition. The sense of touch is mediated by a strip of parietal cortex that is located just posterior to the central sulcus, and thus cleverly called the **postcentral gyrus**.

In general, the frontal lobes are important for movement and high-level cognition. Immediately anterior to the central sulcus, the **precentral gyrus** of the frontal lobe is crucial for motor control. In fact, Wilder Penfield's experiments with stimulation mapping of the brain, which we discussed at the beginning of the chapter, revealed that the movement-controlling neurons within the precentral gyrus are organized into an orderly map of the muscles of the other side of the body (see Figure 11.13); in general, the left hemisphere controls the right side of the body, and vice versa. Similarly, the postcentral gyrus contains a sensory map of the other side of the body (Penfield and Rasmussen, 1950).

Beyond the generalities presented here, each of the lobes also performs a wide variety of other high-level functions; these will be major topics in later chapters. In people with undamaged brains, the four cortical lobes of each hemisphere are continually communicating among themselves and with their counterparts in the other hemisphere, their collaboration producing the seamless experiences and complex behaviors that distinguish us as individuals. In fact, hundreds of millions of axons cross the midline in a large C-shaped bundle called the **corpus callosum** (see Figure 2.12B), enabling communication between the right and left cerebral hemispheres and allowing the brain to act as a single entity during complex processing.

When you slice into the brain, two distinct shades of color are evident. The darker-colored **gray matter** of the exterior contains a preponderance of neuronal cell bodies and dendrites, which are devoid of myelin (**FIGURE 2.13**). Beneath the outer surface is the lighter-colored **white matter**, which consists mostly of axonal fiber tracts. It gains its appearance from the whitish fatty myelin that ensheathes and insulates the axons of many neurons. A simple view is that gray matter primarily receives and processes information, while white matter mostly transmits information to other locations.

postcentral gyrus The strip of parietal cortex, just behind the central sulcus, that receives somatosensory information from the entire body.

precentral gyrus The strip of frontal cortex, just in front of the central sulcus, that is crucial for motor control.

corpus callosum The main band of axons that connects the two cerebral hemispheres.

gray matter Areas of the brain that are dominated by cell bodies and are devoid of myelin.

white matter A pale-colored layer underneath the cortex that consists largely of axons with white myelin sheaths.

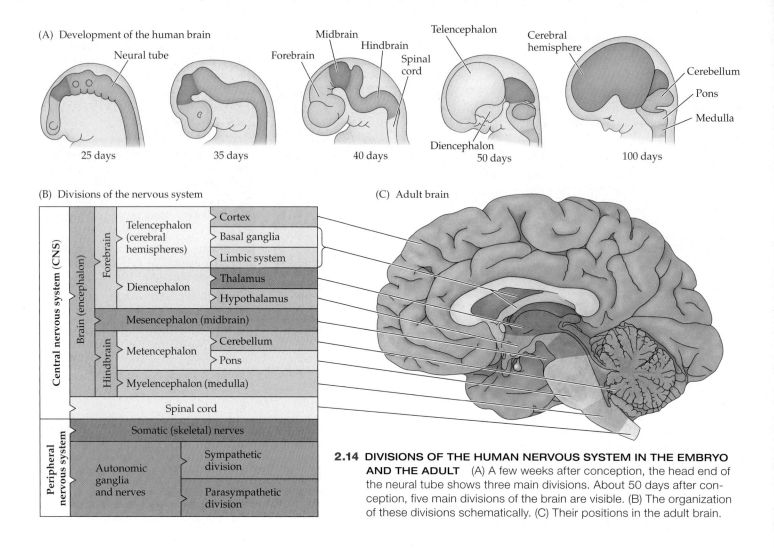

2.14 DIVISIONS OF THE HUMAN NERVOUS SYSTEM IN THE EMBRYO AND THE ADULT (A) A few weeks after conception, the head end of the neural tube shows three main divisions. About 50 days after conception, five main divisions of the brain are visible. (B) The organization of these divisions schematically. (C) Their positions in the adult brain.

neural tube An embryonic structure with subdivisions that correspond to the future forebrain, midbrain, and hindbrain.

forebrain Also called *prosencephalon*. The anterior division of the brain, containing the cerebral hemispheres, the thalamus, and the hypothalamus.

midbrain Also called *mesencephalon*. The middle division of the brain.

hindbrain Also called *rhombencephalon*. The rear division of the brain, which in the mature vertebrate contains the cerebellum, pons, and medulla.

telencephalon The frontal subdivision of the forebrain that includes the cerebral hemispheres when fully developed.

diencephalon The posterior part of the forebrain, including the thalamus and hypothalamus.

metencephalon A subdivision of the hindbrain that includes the cerebellum and the pons.

DEVELOPMENTAL SUBDIVISIONS OF THE BRAIN   It can be difficult to understand some of the anatomical distinctions applied to the adult human brain. For example, the part of the cortex closest to the back of the head is anatomically identified as being part of the *fore*brain. Why? The key to understanding this confusing terminology is to consider how the brain develops early in life.

In a very young embryo of any vertebrate, the CNS looks like a tube. The walls of this **neural tube** are made of cells, and the interior is filled with fluid. A few weeks after conception, the human neural tube begins to show three separate swellings at the head end (**FIGURE 2.14A**): the **forebrain** (or *prosencephalon*), the **midbrain** (or *mesencephalon*), and the **hindbrain** (or *rhombencephalon*). (The term *encephalon*, meaning "brain," comes from the Greek *en*, "in," and *kephale*, "head.")

About 50 days after conception, the forebrain and hindbrain have already developed clear subdivisions. At the very front of the developing brain is the **telencephalon**, which will become the cerebral hemispheres (consisting of cortex plus some deeper structures belonging to two functionally related groups, the basal ganglia and the limbic system). The other part of the forebrain is the **diencephalon** (or "between brain"), which will go on to become the regions called the *thalamus* and the *hypothalamus*. We'll discuss these various forebrain systems later in the chapter.

Behind the midbrain (mesencephalon), the hindbrain further develops into several principle structures: the **metencephalon**, made up of the **cerebellum** ("little brain") and **pons** ("bridge"), and the **medulla**, also called the *myelencephalon*. The term **brainstem** usually refers to the midbrain, pons, and medulla combined (some scientists also include the diencephalon). **FIGURE 2.14C** shows the positions of these structures and their relative sizes in the adult human brain. Even when the brain achieves its adult form, it is still a fluid-filled tube, but a tube of very complicated shape.

Each of the five main sections (telencephalon, diencephalon, mesencephalon, metencephalon, and myelencephalon) can be subdivided in turn. We can work our way from the largest, most general divisions of the nervous system on the left of the schematic in **FIGURE 2.14B** to more-specific ones on the right.

Within and between the major brain regions are aggregations of neurons called **nuclei** (singular *nucleus*) and bundles of axons called **tracts**. (Recall that in the periphery, aggregations of neurons are called *ganglia*, and bundles of axons are called *nerves*.) Unfortunately, the word *nucleus* can mean either "a collection of neurons within the CNS" or "the spherical DNA-containing organelle within a single cell," so you must rely on the context to understand which meaning is intended. Because brain tracts and nuclei are the same from individual to individual, and often from species to species, they have names too.

You are probably more interested in the functions of all these parts of the brain than in their names, but as we noted earlier, each region serves more than one function, and our knowledge of the functional organization of the brain is continually being updated with new research findings. With that caution in mind, we'll briefly survey functions of specific brain structures next, leaving the detailed discussion for later chapters.

cerebellum   A structure located at the back of the brain, dorsal to the pons, that is involved in the central regulation of movement.

pons   A portion of the metencephalon; part of the brainstem connecting midbrain to medulla.

medulla   Also called *myelencephalon*. The posterior part of the hindbrain, continuous with the spinal cord.

brainstem   The region of the brain that consists of the midbrain, the pons, and the medulla.

nucleus   Here, a collection of neurons within the central nervous system (e.g., the caudate nucleus).

tract   A bundle of axons found within the central nervous system.

allocortex   Cortical tissue with three layers or unlayered organization, in contrast with six-layered neocortex.

The Brain Shows Regional Specialization of Functions

Like the rest of our bodies, our brains are *bilaterally symmetrical*—aside from a few midline structures like the corpus callosum, pineal gland, and pituitary (see Figure 2.12B), most structures of the brain are paired, in left- and right-sided mirror-image versions. One important principle of the vertebrate brain is that each side of the brain controls the opposite (or *contralateral*; see Box 2.2) side of the body: as we noted earlier, the right side of the brain controls and receives sensory information from the left side of the body, while the left side of the brain monitors and controls the right side of the body. We'll learn about how the two cerebral hemispheres interact in Chapter 19, but for now let's review the various components of the brain and their functions.

The cerebral cortex performs complex cognitive processing

Neuroscientists agree that understanding human cognition depends on unraveling the structure and fundamental functions of the cerebral cortex. If the cerebral cortex were unfolded, it would occupy an area of about 2000 square centimeters (cm²), or 315 square inches, more than 3 times the area of this book's cover. How are those millions of cells arranged? And how do the arrangements perform particular feats of information processing?

The neurons of the cerebral cortex are arranged in six distinct layers (**FIGURE 2.15A**) (in mammals this tissue is sometimes referred to as *neocortex* or *isocortex*). Each cortical layer has a unique appearance because it consists of either a band of similar neurons or a particular pattern of dendrites or axons. For example, the outermost layer, layer I, is distinct because it has few cell bodies, and layers V and VI stand out because of their many neurons with large cell bodies. While the great majority of the cortex consists of this six-layered tissue, a few

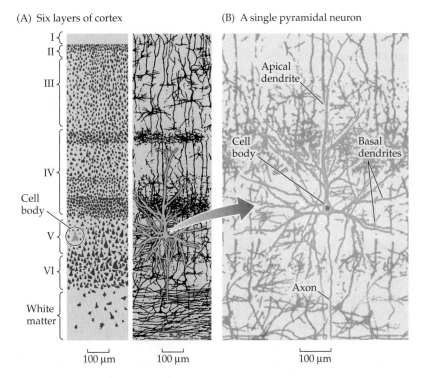

(A) Six layers of cortex

(B) A single pyramidal neuron

Apical dendrite

Cell body

Basal dendrites

Axon

Cell body

White matter

100 µm   100 µm   100 µm

2.15 LAYERS OF THE CEREBRAL CORTEX   (A) The six layers of cortex can be distinguished with stains that reveal all cell bodies (left) or with stains that reveal a few neurons in their entirety (right). (B) This pyramidal cell has been enlarged about 100 times.

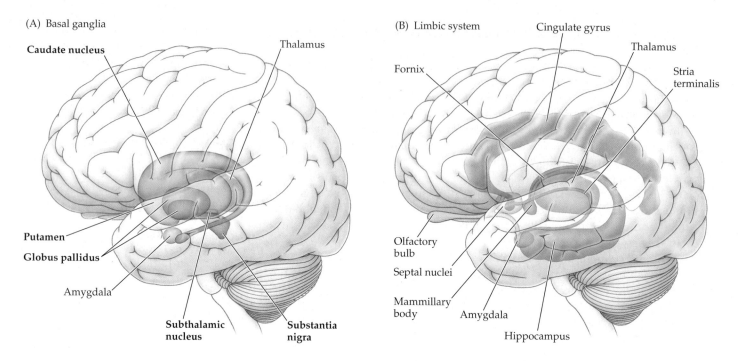

(A) Basal ganglia

Caudate nucleus

Thalamus

Putamen

Globus pallidus

Amygdala

Subthalamic nucleus

Substantia nigra

(B) Limbic system

Cingulate gyrus

Fornix

Thalamus

Stria terminalis

Olfactory bulb

Septal nuclei

Mammillary body

Amygdala

Hippocampus

2.16 TWO IMPORTANT BRAIN SYSTEMS (A) The basal ganglia—caudate nucleus, putamen, globus pallidus, subthalamic nucleus, and substantia nigra—are important in movement. (B) The limbic system—including hippocampus, cingulate gyrus, fornix, septal nuclei, stria terminalis, olfactory bulb, amygdala, and mammillary bodies—is important for emotion, learning, and memory.

pyramidal cell A type of large nerve cell that has a roughly pyramid-shaped cell body; found in the cerebral cortex.

apical dendrite The dendrite that extends from a pyramidal cell to the outermost surface of the cortex.

basal dendrite One of several dendrites on a pyramidal cell that extend horizontally from the cell body.

cortical column One of the vertical columns that constitute the basic organization of the neocortex.

basal ganglia A group of forebrain nuclei, including caudate nucleus, globus pallidus, and putamen, found deep within the cerebral hemispheres.

caudate nucleus One of the basal ganglia; it has a long extension or tail.

putamen One of the basal ganglia.

globus pallidus One of the basal ganglia.

substantia nigra A brainstem structure in humans that innervates the basal ganglia and is named for its dark pigmentation.

limbic system A loosely defined, widespread group of brain nuclei that innervate each other to form a network.

telencephalic structures are instead made up of **allocortex** (from the Greek *allos*, "other"), tissue with three layers or unlayered organization (previously known as *archi*- or *paleocortex*).

The most prominent kind of neuron in the cerebral cortex—the **pyramidal cell** (**FIGURE 2.15B**)—usually has its pyramid-shaped cell body in layer III or V. One dendrite of each pyramidal cell (called the **apical dendrite**) extends from the top of the cell body (its *apex*) to the outermost layer of the cortex. Each pyramidal cell also has several dendrites (called **basal dendrites**) that spread out horizontally from the base of the cell body.

In some regions of the cerebral cortex, neurons are organized into regular columns, perpendicular to the layers, that seem to serve as information-processing units (Horton and Adams, 2005). These **cortical columns** extend through the entire thickness of the cortex, from the white matter to the surface. Within each column, most of the synaptic interconnections of neurons are vertical, although there are some horizontal connections as well (Mountcastle, 1979).

Subcortical structures are involved in movement and the regulation of emotions

Buried within the cerebral hemispheres are several large gray matter structures, richly interconnected with each other and with other brain regions and contributing to a wide variety of behaviors. One prominent cluster—the **basal ganglia**—includes the **caudate nucleus**, the **putamen**, the **globus pallidus** in the telencephalon under the cerebral cortex, and the **substantia nigra** in the midbrain (**FIGURE 2.16A**; see also Figure 2.13B and C). These nuclei (not really ganglia, despite the unfortunate name *basal ganglia*) are reciprocally connected with the cerebral cortex, forming a looping neural system. The basal ganglia are very important in motor control, as we will see in Chapter 11.

Curving through each hemisphere, alongside the basal ganglia, lies a loose network of structures called the **limbic system** (**FIGURE 2.16B**) that is critical for emotion and learning. Limbic components include the **amygdala** (Latin for "almond," because it has that shape), which has several subdivisions with diverse functions such as emotional regulation (Chapter 15) and odor perception (Chapter 9), as well as the **mammillary bodies**, **hippocampus** (from the Greek *hippokampos*, "sea horse," which it resembles), and **fornix**, all of which contribute to learning and memory (Chapter 17). The **septal nuclei** play a role in reward and reinforcement in learning (Chapter 4). Other components of the limbic system include, lying over the corpus callosum in each hemisphere, a strip of cortex called the **cingulate gyrus**, which is implicated in the direction of attention and many other cognitive functions, as well as the **olfactory bulb**, which is involved in the sense of smell. The **stria terminalis** is a fiber pathway that connects the amygdala to limbic structures near the base of the brain, especially the hypothalamus, participating in highly motivated behaviors such as sex and threat responses, as well as the integration of hormonal signals.

The diencephalon directs sensory information and controls basic physiological functions

Toward the medial (middle) and basal (bottom) aspects of the forebrain are found thetow main components of the diencephalon: the **thalamus** and the **hypothalamus** (which simply means "under thalamus"). You can see these structures most clearly in Figures 2.12B, 2.14C, and 2.16B. The thalamus is a complex cluster of nuclei that acts as a switch box, directing almost all incoming sensory information to the appropriate regions of the cortex, to be processed further, and receiving instructions back from the cortex to control which sensory information is transmitted.

The small-but-mighty hypothalamus has a much different role: it is packed with discrete nuclei involved in many vital functions, such as hunger, thirst, temperature regulation, sex, and many more. Furthermore, because the hypothalamus also controls the pituitary gland, it serves as the brain's main interface with the hormonal systems of the body (Chapter 5). We'll encounter the hypothalamus again in several later chapters.

The midbrain has sensory and motor components

In comparison to the forebrain and hindbrain, the midbrain is quite small and contains only a few obvious landmarks. The top part of the midbrain, which is called the **tectum** (from the Latin for "roof," because it's atop the midbrain), features two pairs of bumps—one pair in each hemisphere—with specific roles in sensory processing. The more rostral bumps are called the **superior colliculi** (singular *colliculus*), and they have specific roles in visual processing. The more caudal bumps, called the **inferior colliculi** (see Figure 2.12B), process information about sound.

Two important motor centers are embedded in the midbrain. One, the substantia nigra that we mentioned in discussing the basal ganglia (see Figure 2.16A), contains neurons that release the transmitter dopamine. Loss of this system leads to Parkinson's disease (Chapter 11). The other motor center is the **red nucleus** (named for its reddish tint), which communicates with motor neurons in the spinal cord. Several cranial nerves, including those controlling eye movements, originate in the midbrain.

Also found in the midbrain is a distributed network of neurons collectively referred to as the **reticular formation** (from the Latin *reticulum*, "network"). The reticular formation stretches from the midbrain down to the medulla. The reticular formation is implicated in a variety of behaviors, including sleep and arousal (Chapter 14), temperature regulation (Chapter 13), and motor control.

The cerebellum is attached to the pons and is crucial for motor coordination

The lateral, midsagittal, and ventral views of the brain in Figure 2.12 reveal the cerebellum, the smaller hemispheres tucked up under the posterior cortex and attached

amygdala A group of nuclei in the medial anterior part of the temporal lobe.

mammillary body One of a pair of nuclei at the base of the brain.

hippocampus A medial temporal lobe structure that is important for learning and memory.

fornix A fiber tract that extends from the hippocampus to the mammillary body.

septal nuclei A collection of gray matter structures lying medially below the corpus callosum, implicated in the perception of reward.

cingulate gyrus A cortical portion of the limbic system, found in the frontal and parietal midline.

olfactory bulb An anterior projection of the brain that terminates in the upper nasal passages and, through small openings in the skull, provides receptors for smell.

stria terminalis A limbic pathway connecting the amygdala and hypothalamus.

thalamus The brain regions that surround the third ventricle.

hypothalamus Part of the diencephalon, lying ventral to the thalamus.

tectum The dorsal portion of the midbrain, including the inferior and superior colliculi.

superior colliculi Paired gray matter structures of the dorsal midbrain that receive visual information and are involved in direction of visual gaze and visual attention to intended stimuli.

inferior colliculi Paired gray matter structures of the dorsal midbrain that receive auditory information.

red nucleus A brainstem structure related to motor control.

reticular formation An extensive region of the brainstem (extending from the medulla through the thalamus) that is involved in arousal (waking).

Purkinje cell A type of large nerve cell in the cerebellar cortex.

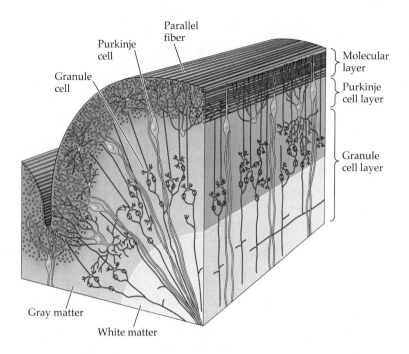

Molecular
layer

Purkinje
cell layer

Granule
cell layer

Parallel
fiber

Purkinje
cell

Granule
cell

Gray matter

White matter

2.17 THE ARRANGEMENT OF CELLS WITHIN THE CEREBELLUM
Large Purkinje cells dominate the cerebellum, dividing it into
three layers. Innervation between the various types of cells in the
cerebellum forms a very consistent pattern. A variety of scattered
cells, depicted here in black, inhibit the activity of other cells.

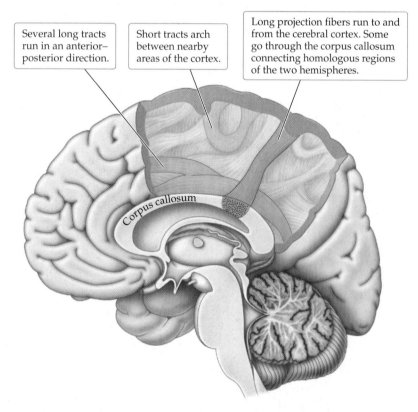

Several long tracts
run in an anterior–
posterior direction.

Short tracts arch
between nearby
areas of the cortex.

Long projection fibers run to and
from the cerebral cortex. Some
go through the corpus callosum
connecting homologous regions
of the two hemispheres.

Corpus callosum

2.18 CORTICAL TRACTS CONNECT CORTICAL REGIONS

to the dorsal brainstem. Like the cortex, the surface of
the cerebellum is elaborately convoluted, giving it more
surface area. The arrangement of cells within this folded sheet is relatively simple, consisting of three layers
(**FIGURE 2.17**). A middle layer is composed of a single
sheet of enormous neurons called **Purkinje cells** after
the anatomist who first described their elaborate, fan-
shaped dendritic patterns. Axons from the small neurons of the **granule cell** layer, lying below the Purkinje
cells, rise to the surface of the cerebellum to form the
parallel fibers of the outermost layer (called the *molecular layer*). The cerebellum has long been known to be
crucial for motor coordination and control, but we now
know it also participates in certain aspects of cognition,
including learning.

Immediately below (ventral to) the cerebellum lies
the pons (see Figure 2.12B and C), a part of the brainstem. Within the pons are important motor control and
sensory nuclei, including several nuclei from which cranial nerves arise. Information from the ear first enters
the brain in the pons, via the nuclei of the vestibulocochlear (VIII) cranial nerves.

The medulla maintains vital basic body functions

The medulla is the most caudal portion of the brainstem,
and it marks the transition from brain to spinal cord (see
Figure 2.12B). Within the medulla are the nuclei of cranial
nerves XI and XII, containing the cell bodies of the neurons that control the neck and tongue muscles, respectively. The reticular formation, which we first saw in the
midbrain, stretches through the pons and ends in the medulla. Because the medulla contains nuclei that regulate
breathing and heart rate, damage there is often fatal. All
axons passing between the brain and spinal cord necessarily course through the medulla, and several medullary
nuclei add their own axons to the descending fiber tracts.

Behaviors and cognitive abilities are determined by functional connections between brain regions

In order to understand the neural origins of our most
complex behaviors and experiences—thought, language,
music—it will be necessary to understand how different brain regions with distinct functions collaborate in
larger-scale networks. This applies to functional units as
small as the individual cortical columns we mentioned
earlier and to much larger assemblages of millions of cells
making up substantial parts of cortical lobes.

Cortical regions communicate with one another via
tracts of axons looping through the underlying white
matter (**FIGURE 2.18**). Some of these connections are
short pathways to nearby cortical regions; others travel longer distances through the cerebral hemispheres.
Some pathways link corresponding areas in the two
hemispheres, traversing the corpus callosum to go from
one hemisphere to the other. Some longer links between cortical regions involve multisynaptic chains of
neurons that loop through subcortical regions such as

the thalamus and the basal ganglia, allowing processing and integration of information at several levels.

Research at the frontier of neuroscience aims to describe the "connectome" of the human brain: the network map that completely describes the functional connections within and between brain regions (Sporns, 2011; Van Essen, 2013). Due to the complexity of the problem, large, international collaborations have been established aimed at (1) developing new technologies for probing brain pathways (such as the BRAIN Initiative, which stands for Brain Research through Advancing Innovative Neurotechnologies; Yuste and Church, 2014) and (2) using available technology to map brain network activity (e.g., the Brain Activity Map [BAM] project), to develop computer simulations of human brain activity (e.g., the Human Brain Project), and to develop other "big science" approaches to the problem (Alivisatos et al., 2013; Huang and Luo, 2015). Dealing with the immense volume of data generated by such approaches, where connections are tracked from the level of individual synapses to large fiber pathways in the brain, is an additional technological challenge for the near future (Lichtman et al., 2014).

Specialized Support Systems Protect and Nourish the Brain

Within the bony skull and vertebrae, the brain and spinal cord are enveloped by three protective membranes called the **meninges** (see Figure 2.10). Between a tough outer sheet called the **dura mater** (in Latin, literally "tough mother") and the delicate **pia mater** ("tender mother") that adheres tightly to the surface of the brain, a webby substance called the **arachnoid** ("spiderweb-like") suspends the brain in a bath of **cerebrospinal fluid (CSF)**. **Meningitis**, an inflammation of the meninges usually caused by viral infection, is a potentially lethal medical emergency characterized in early stages by headache, fever, and stiff neck as the inflamed meninges press on the brain. Sometimes, the meninges can form large tumors called **meningiomas**, which are usually classified as benign in the sense that they are noncancerous, but of course anything that takes up space within the enclosed cranium may cause trouble.

The cerebral ventricles are chambers filled with fluid

Inside the brain is a series of chambers—the **ventricular system**—filled with CSF (**FIGURE 2.19**). The CSF circulating through the ventricular system has at least two main functions. First, it acts mechanically as a shock absorber for the brain: floating in CSF, the brain is protected from sudden movements of the head that would smash

granule cell   A type of small nerve cell.

parallel fiber   One of the axons of the granule cells that form the outermost layer of the cerebellar cortex.

meninges   The three protective sheets of tissue—dura mater, pia mater, and arachnoid—that surround the brain and spinal cord.

dura mater   The outermost of the three meninges that surround the brain and spinal cord.

pia mater   The innermost of the three meninges that surround the brain and spinal cord.

arachnoid   The thin covering (one of the three meninges) of the brain that lies between the dura mater and pia mater.

cerebrospinal fluid (CSF)   The fluid that fills the cerebral ventricles.

meningitis   An acute inflammation of the meninges, usually caused by a viral or bacterial infection.

meningiomas   Several classes of noncancerous tumors arising from the meninges.

ventricular system   A system of fluid-filled cavities inside the brain.

lateral ventricle   A complexly shaped lateral portion of the ventricular system within each hemisphere of the brain.

choroid plexus   A highly vascular portion of the lining of the ventricles that secretes cerebrospinal fluid.

(A) Cerebral ventricles of the brain

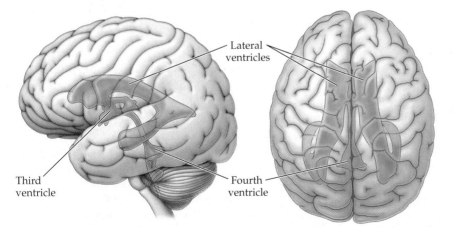

(B) A closer view

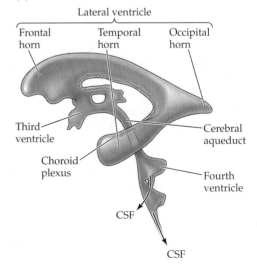

2.19 THE CEREBRAL VENTRICLES   These views of an adult human brain show the position of the cerebral ventricles within it. Cerebrospinal fluid (CSF) is made by the choroid plexus in the lateral ventricles and exits from the fourth ventricle to surround the brain and spinal cord.

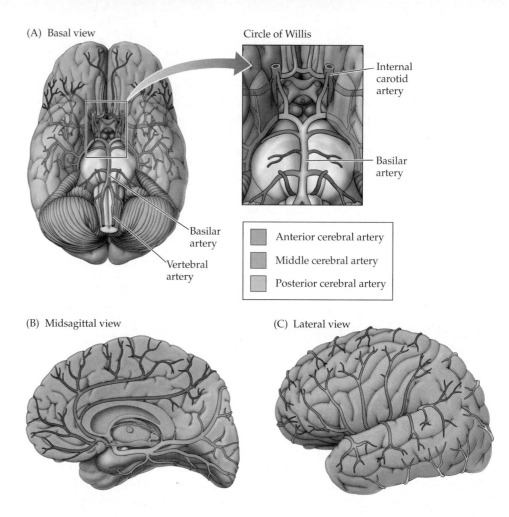

2.20 THE BLOOD SUPPLY OF THE HUMAN BRAIN The anterior, middle, and posterior cerebral arteries—the three principal arteries that provide blood to the cerebral hemispheres—are depicted here in basal (A), midsagittal (B), and lateral (C) views of the brain. The basilar and internal carotid arteries form a circle at the base of the brain known as the *circle of Willis*.

(A) Basal view

Circle of Willis

Internal carotid artery

Basilar artery

Basilar artery

Vertebral artery

Anterior cerebral artery

Middle cerebral artery

Posterior cerebral artery

(B) Midsagittal view

(C) Lateral view

third ventricle The midline ventricle that conducts cerebrospinal fluid from the lateral ventricle to the fourth ventricle.

fourth ventricle The passageway within the pons that receives cerebrospinal fluid from the third ventricle and releases it to surround the brain and spinal cord.

carotid arteries The major arteries that ascend the left and right sides of the neck to the brain, supplying blood to the anterior and middle cerebral arteries.

anterior cerebral arteries Two large arteries, arising from the internal carotid arteries, that provide blood to the anterior poles and medial surfaces of the cerebral hemispheres.

middle cerebral arteries Two large arteries, arising from the internal carotid arteries, that provide blood to most of the lateral surfaces of the cerebral hemispheres.

posterior cerebral arteries Two large arteries, arising from the basilar artery, that provide blood to posterior aspects of the cerebral hemispheres, cerebellum, and brainstem.

it against the inside of the skull. Second, CSF provides a medium for the exchange of materials, including nutrients, between blood vessels and brain tissue.

Each hemisphere of the brain contains a **lateral ventricle**, extending into all four lobes of the hemisphere. The lateral ventricles are lined with a specialized membrane called the **choroid plexus**, which produces CSF by filtering blood. CSF flows from the lateral ventricles into the **third ventricle** (located in the midline) and continues down a narrow passage to the **fourth ventricle**, which lies between the cerebellum and the pons. Just below the cerebellum, three small openings allow CSF to exit the ventricular system and circulate over the outer surface of the brain and spinal cord. CSF is absorbed back into the circulatory system through large veins beneath the top of the skull.

The brain has an elaborate vascular system

Robbed of the oxygen and nutrients that the blood supplies, the brain will swiftly die. That's because the brain is so needy: it accounts for only 2% of the weight of the average human body, but it consumes more than 20% of the body's energy at rest. Supplying these life-giving metabolic fuels to the brain is the job of a complex set of large blood vessels (**FIGURE 2.20**). The **carotid arteries** ascend the left and right sides of the neck and branch into external and internal carotid arteries; these are the major arteries that you can feel pulsing in each side of your neck after exertion. The internal carotid artery enters the skull and branches into **anterior** and **middle cerebral arteries**, which supply blood to about two-thirds of the cerebral hemispheres, indicated in purple and pink in Figure 2.20. The blood supply for the rest of the cortex (indicated in blue in Figure 2.20) is supplied by the **posterior cerebral arteries**. The blood supply for these arteries ascends through the left and right **vertebral arteries**, which course alongside the spinal column into the base of the skull and fuse together to form the **basilar artery**. In addition to feeding the posterior cerebral arteries, the basilar artery has branches supplying blood to the hindbrain.

At the base of the brain, the major cerebral arteries are joined via communicating arteries to form a structure called the **circle of Willis** (see Figure 2.20A). This joining of arterial paths may provide an alternate route for blood flow if any of the main arteries to the brain should be damaged or blocked by disease. The general term **stroke** applies to a situation in which a clot, a narrowing, or a rupture interrupts the supply of blood to a discrete brain region, causing the affected region to stop functioning or die (**FIGURE 2.21**). Although the exact effects of a stroke depend on the region of the brain that is affected, the five most common warning signs are sudden numbness or weakness, altered vision, dizziness, severe headache, and confusion or difficulty speaking. Effective treatments are available to help restore blood flow and minimize the long-term effects of a stroke, but only if the victim is treated immediately.

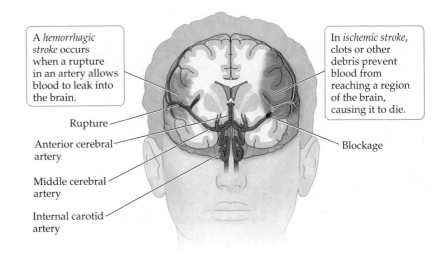

A *hemorrhagic stroke* occurs when a rupture in an artery allows blood to leak into the brain.

In *ischemic stroke*, clots or other debris prevent blood from reaching a region of the brain, causing it to die.

Rupture

Anterior cerebral artery

Middle cerebral artery

Internal carotid artery

Blockage

2.21 STROKE A stroke is the result of any situation that cuts off blood supply to the brain. The exact effects of the stroke depend on the region of the brain that is affected. The impact on the brain can be greatly reduced in some cases if medical attention is obtained promptly.

Fine vessels and capillaries branch off from the main arteries and deliver nutrients and other substances to brain cells and remove waste products. Thanks to regulation by CNS cells that surround the vessels, especially astrocytes and pericytes (small cells that encircle, support, and regulate the brain's capillaries), the endothelial cells that make up the walls of the capillaries in the brain have much tighter junctions than is the case elsewhere in the body (Daneman et al., 2010). As a consequence, brain capillaries are unusually resistant to the passage of large molecules across their walls and into neighboring neurons. This **blood-brain barrier** may have evolved to help protect the brain from infections and blood-borne toxins, but it also makes the delivery of drugs to the brain more difficult. However, the blood-brain barrier is not completely impenetrable. Although scientists believed otherwise for decades, we now know that the brain possesses a lymphatic system just like the rest of the body (Aspelund et al., 2015; Louveau et al., 2015). Because it allows the immune system to access the brain, the brain's lymphatic system may be important in diseases believed to have an immune component, like multiple sclerosis. Researchers also hope to learn how to exploit brain lymphatic mechanisms to deliver drugs to the brain to combat diseases like Alzheimer's disease and cancer.

Brain-Imaging Techniques Reveal the Structure and Function of the Living Human Brain

Researchers have long sought ways to peer into the living human brain to see structures and how they work during different behaviors. X-rays of the head are of limited usefulness because they cannot resolve the brain's small variations in density. Attempts to improve contrast in X-rays through the injection of radiopaque (X-ray-blocking) dye led to a useful technique—**angiography** (from the Greek *angeion*, "blood vessel," and *graphein*, "to write")—that provides detailed views of the cerebral blood vessels and aids in the diagnosis of vascular disease. But more recent technological developments have allowed researchers to study the brains of healthy humans too. These techniques are used in some cases to identify brain structure; other approaches focus more on tracking changes in brain *activity* as behavior occurs. Here we briefly describe the most important brain imaging technologies in use today.

vertebral arteries Arteries that ascend the vertebrae, enter the base of the skull, and join together to form the basilar artery.

basilar artery An artery, formed by the fusion of the vertebral arteries, that supplies blood to the brainstem and to the posterior cerebral arteries.

circle of Willis A vascular structure at the base of the brain that is formed by the joining of the carotid and basilar arteries.

stroke Damage to a region of brain tissue that results from blockage or rupture of vessels that supply blood to that region.

blood-brain barrier The mechanisms that make the movement of substances from blood vessels into brain cells more difficult than exchanges in other body organs, thus affording the brain greater protection from exposure to some substances found in the blood.

angiography A brain-imaging technique in which a specialized X-ray image of the head is taken shortly after the cerebral blood vessels have been filled with a radiopaque dye by means of a catheter.

computerized axial tomography (CAT or CT) A noninvasive technique for examining brain structure in humans through computer analysis of X-ray absorption at several positions around the head.

(A) Computerized tomography (CT)

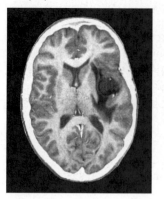

(B) Magnetic resonance imaging (MRI)

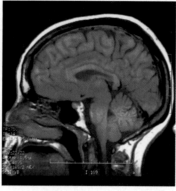

2.22 VISUALIZING THE LIVING HUMAN BRAIN (A) CT scan from a patient with a brain tumor, visible as the dark area in the right hemisphere. (B) Midsagittal MRI image of a healthy brain. (C) An alternative application of MRI called diffusion tensor imaging (DTI) exploits fractional anisotropy—the diffusion of water in axons—to visualize axonal connections between regions. Data from multiple scans can be combined to create 3-dimensional models of the interconnections of brain regions, known as DTI tractography. (D) PET scans from a healthy human brain and the brain of a patient with Alzheimer's, showing levels of metabolic activity. Note the greater level of activity in the normal brain. (E) Functional-MRI images showing changes in regional brain metabolism recorded during the presentation of visual or auditory stimuli (images of a romantic partner; see Figure 1.7). (Images in C from Bernal and Altman, 2010, and Vandermosten et al., 2012; E courtesy of Dr. Semir Zeki, University College London.)

(C) Diffusion tensor imaging (DTI)

Fractional anisotropy

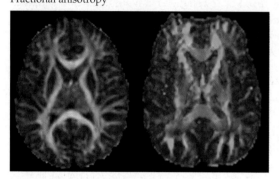

DTI tractography

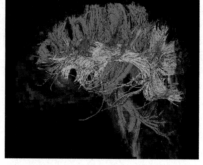

(D) Positron emission tomography (PET)

Normal (horizontal view)   Patient with Alzheimer's disease

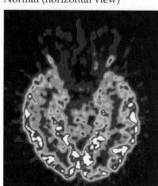
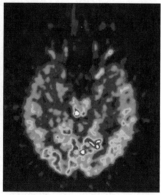

(E) Functional magnetic resonance imaging (fMRI)

Anterior 3-D view   Lateral 3-D view of right hemisphere

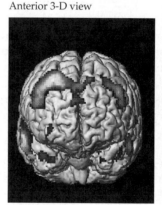
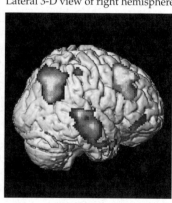

Measurements of density can be used to map the structure of the brain

magnetic resonance imaging (MRI) A noninvasive technique that uses magnetic energy to generate images that reveal some structural details in the living brain.

Go to Animation 2.2
Visualizing the Living Human Brain
bn8e.com/2.2

In **computerized axial tomography (CAT or CT)** (from the Greek *tomos*, "crosscut" or "section"), X-ray energy is used to generate images. In a CT scanner, an X-ray source is moved by steps in an arc around the head. At each point, detectors on the opposite side of the head measure the amount of X-ray radiation that is absorbed; this value is proportional to the density of the tissue through which the X-rays passed. When this process is repeated from many angles and the results are mathematically combined, an anatomical map of the brain based on tissue density can be generated by computer (**FIGURE 2.22A**). CT scans are medium-resolution images, useful for visualizing problems such as strokes, tumors, or cortical atrophy.

Magnetic resonance imaging (MRI) provides higher-resolution images than CT, and because MRI images are derived from radio frequency energy, an additional benefit is that patients are not exposed to potentially damaging X-rays. An MRI scan involves three main steps. First, the patient's head is placed in the center of an extremely powerful circular magnet that causes all the protons in the brain's tissues to line up in parallel, instead of in their usual random orientations. Protons are found in the nuclei of atoms, notably the hydrogen atoms making up water within body tissues. Next, the protons are knocked over by a strong pulse of radio waves. When this pulse is turned off, the protons relax back to their original configuration, emitting radio waves as they go. The emitted radio frequency energy, measured by detectors ringing the head, varies depending on the density of various tissues. Finally, a powerful computer uses this density-based information to generate a detailed cross-sectional map of the brain (**FIGURE 2.22B**) (Elster and Burdette, 2001). With their higher resolution, MRI images can reveal subtle changes in the brain, such as the loss of myelin that is characteristic of multiple sclerosis.

In **diffusion tensor imaging (DTI)**, MRI technology is used in a new way to specifically study white matter tracts—axon bundles—within the living brain. If the water molecules (i.e., their protons) affected by an MRI scanner's magnets are in a relatively unconfined volume, such as a cerebral ventricle, then as they relax, they can diffuse in any direction. This is known as *isotropy*. But water molecules contained within the narrow tubes of axons are constrained, and they diffuse more readily in some directions (lengthwise, for example) than others. This property, known as **fractional anisotropy (FA)** (**FIGURE 2.22C, LEFT**), reflects connections between brain regions and can be mathematically exploited in DTI to produce *structural* images of axonal fiber pathways (**FIGURE 2.22C, RIGHT**), a procedure called **DTI tractography** or *fiber tracking*. Although the technology doesn't have the resolution to portray individual axons, the origin, axon orientation, course, and termination of axonal projections can be effectively visualized using tractographic analysis. DTI has thus become one of the most important tools in efforts to map the human connectome.

Functional-imaging techniques map regional brain activity during behaviors

In **positron emission tomography (PET)** the objective is to obtain images of the brain's *activity* rather than details of its structure, and it has proven to be very valuable for both experimental and medical purposes. Short-lived radioactive chemicals are injected into the bloodstream, and radiation detectors encircling the head map the destination of these chemicals in the brain. A particularly effective strategy is to administer radioactive glucose while a participant is performing a specific cognitive task. Because the radioactive glucose is particularly taken up and used by the brain regions that are most active from moment to moment, a computer-generated, color-coded portrait of brain activity can be created (**FIGURE 2.22D**) (Roland, 1993). Through precise experimental control and the use of special mathematical techniques (described in **BOX 2.3**), we can generate metabolic maps of the brain that identify the regions that contribute to specific functions.

Since its introduction in the 1990s, **functional MRI (fMRI)** has revolutionized cognitive neuroscience research, producing images with reasonable speed (temporal resolution) and excellent sharpness (spatial resolution). Exploiting the same basic technology used in the structural MRI scanning described earlier, fMRI uses high-powered, rapidly oscillating magnetic-field gradients to detect small changes in brain metabolism, particularly the moment-to-moment use of oxygen by the most active regions of the brain. The amount of oxygen available is measured indirectly, on the basis of blood flow or the state of hemoglobin in blood (called the *blood-oxygen-level-dependent*, or *BOLD*, signal). As with PET, scientists can use fMRI data to create computer-generated images that reflect the *activity* of different parts of the brain while people engage in various experimental tasks (see Box 2.3), trading PET's quicker response for the much higher resolution offered by MRI. The detailed activity maps provided by fMRI reveal how networks of brain structures collaborate on complex cognitive processes (**FIGURE 2.22E**). The fMRI image generally reflects synaptic inputs and local processing, rather than the production of neural impulses (Logothetis, 2008) and is altered by aging and disease states (Rypma et al., 2005).

diffusion tensor imaging (DTI) A modified form of MRI in which the diffusion of water in a confined space is exploited to produce images of axonal fiber tracts.

fractional anisotropy (FA) The tendency of water to diffuse more readily along the long axis of an enclosed space, such as an axon. FA is the basis of diffusion tensor imaging.

DTI tractography Also called *fiber tracking*. Visualization of the orientation and terminations of white matter tracts in the living brain via diffusion tensor imaging.

positron emission tomography (PET) A technique for examining brain function by combining tomography with injections of radioactive substances used by the brain.

functional MRI (fMRI) Magnetic resonance imaging that detects changes in blood flow and therefore identifies regions of the brain that are particularly active during a given task.

optical imaging A method for visualizing brain activity in which near-infrared light is passed through the scalp and skull.

Isolating Specific Brain Activity

The advent of modern brain imaging has enabled dramatic images of the brain showing the particular brain regions that are activated during specific cognitive processes; there are many such images in this book. But normally, as you might expect, almost all of the brain is active at any given moment (showing that the old notion that "we use only 10% of our brain" is nonsense). So how do we get these highly specific images of brain activity?

The PET scan shown here beneath the box labeled "Visual stimulus" was made while a person looked at a fixation point surrounded by a flickering checkerboard ring. The scan next to it (beneath the box labeled "Control") was made while a person looked at a fixation point alone. In a comparison of the two, it is hard to see differences, but subtracting the control values from the stimulation values yields an image such as that shown at the upper right ("Difference image"); in this scan it is easy to see that the main difference in activity is in the posterior part of the brain (the visual cortex).

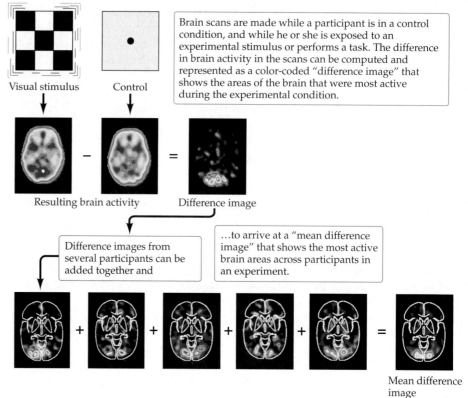

Visual stimulus

Control

Brain scans are made while a participant is in a control condition, and while he or she is exposed to an experimental stimulus or performs a task. The difference in brain activity in the scans can be computed and represented as a color-coded "difference image" that shows the areas of the brain that were most active during the experimental condition.

Resulting brain activity

Difference image

Difference images from several participants can be added together and

...to arrive at a "mean difference image" that shows the most active brain areas across participants in an experiment.

Mean difference image

The PET scans shown in the bottom row are difference images for five individuals who performed the same two stimulation and control tasks. Averaging these five scans yields the mean difference image for all five individuals that is shown at far right.

Averaged images yield more-reliable results than individual images, but they lack some of the specificity of the individual images. (PET scans courtesy of Dr. Marcus Raichle.)

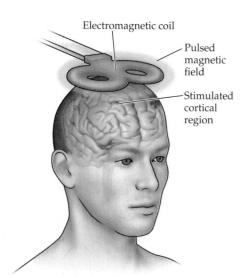

Electromagnetic coil

Pulsed magnetic field

Stimulated cortical region

2.23 TRANSCRANIAL MAGNETIC STIMULATION Magnetic fields induced by electromagnetic coils stimulate neurons of the underlying cortical surface.

Other investigators are using light to make images of brain activity within the head (Gratton and Fabiani, 2001; Villringer and Chance, 1997). In **optical imaging**, researchers capitalize on the observation that near-infrared light (having wavelengths of 700–1000 nm) passes easily through skin, scalp, and skull and penetrates a short distance into the cortex. When such light is transmitted into the brain and detectors pick up the reflections through the scalp, the responses reveal the activity of cortical regions. Some components of the optical responses represent the electrical signals of neurons, and other components represent blood flow. The relatively low expense and small size of the optical imaging apparatus may allow many more laboratories to use brain imaging in their research.

As with light, it is a relatively simple matter to pass magnetic fields into the brain, but it is technically much more challenging to do so in a highly focused and precise manner. In **transcranial magnetic stimulation (TMS)** (**FIGURE 2.23**), strong, focal magnetic currents are used to briefly stimulate the cortex of an alert participant directly, without needing a hole in the scalp or skull. This approach enables experimenters to activate (or interfere with) discrete areas of the cortex through a process of electromagnetic induction. The regions stimulated and the resultant behavioral effects can then be carefully tracked and mapped. In *repetitive TMS* (rTMS), this focal magnetic stimulation of the brain is cycled several times per second, producing transient but measurable changes in behavior that are useful in clinical settings, as well as in research.

2.24 ANIMAL MAGNETISM Using measurements of the minuscule magnetic fields given off by ensembles of cortical cells during specific behavioral functions, magnetoencephalography (MEG) provides a real-time map of brain activity. In these images, MEG data have been superimposed on structural MRIs of a participant's brain, creating maps of brain activity associated with viewing faces (A) versus nonface objects (B). (Images courtesy of Dr. Mario Liotti, Simon Fraser University.)

(A)
Face

(B)
Object

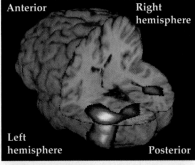
Anterior   Right hemisphere

Left hemisphere   Posterior

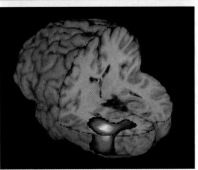

Magnetism and brain function are linked in another way too. Like any electrical system, active circuits of the brain produce their own magnetic fields. Although they are minuscule, the magnetic fields created by activity in local circuits of neurons can be detected by ultrasensitive detectors called *SQUIDs* (superconducting quantum interference devices). In **magnetoencephalography (MEG)**, a large array of SQUIDs is used to create real-time maps of cortical activity during cognitive processing (**FIGURE 2.24**). Because the temporal resolution of MEG is so good—it responds very quickly to moment-by-moment changes in brain activity—it is excellent for studying rapidly shifting patterns of brain activity in cortical circuits, particularly when used in conjunction with MRI (F. H. Lin et al., 2004).

Sophisticated imaging techniques are powerful tools requiring cautious interpretation

In many areas of behavioral neuroscience, technological innovations in brain imaging have provided researchers with exceptional, noninvasive tools that supplement traditional studies of brain **lesions** (regions of damage). They also give us insights into processes that previously were completely hidden. For example, through the use of functional brain imaging, evidence has emerged that someone who appears to be in a coma (or a vegetative state) may be somewhat conscious of her condition and surroundings (**FIGURE 2.25**) (Owen et al., 2006), a topic we return to in Chapter 18. Images made with PET, MEG, fMRI, and DTI are providing us with new appreciation of the organization and dynamics of massive neural circuits involved in all forms of mental life.

It is important to keep in mind that although the colorful images of brain activity that we see everywhere in the popular media seem unambiguous and easy to label, they suffer from a variety of procedural and experimental limitations (Racine et al., 2005).

transcranial magnetic stimulation (TMS) Localized, noninvasive stimulation of cortical neurons through the application of strong magnetic fields.

magnetoencephalography (MEG) A passive and noninvasive functional brain-imaging technique that measures the tiny magnetic fields produced by active neurons, in order to identify regions of the brain that are particularly active during a given task.

lesions Regions of damage within the brain.

(A) Tennis imagery   (B) Spatial navigation imagery

Patient

SMA   PMC

Controls

SMA   PMC

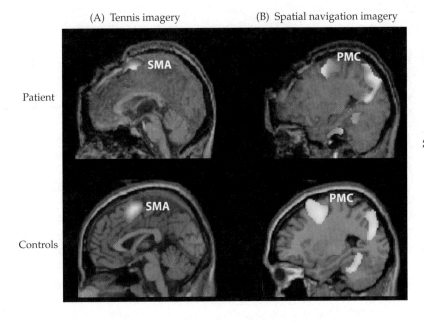

2.25 COMA CONSCIOUSNESS This brain-injured woman was apparently unresponsive and diagnosed as being in a coma, but when researchers asked her to imagine playing tennis (A) or walking through her home (B), fMRI of her brain showed the same patterns of activation as in controls during the same tasks. Note the damage to the patient's skull caused by the accident that caused the coma. SMA, supplementary motor area; PMC, premotor cortex. (Courtesy of Dr. Adrian Owen, Western University.)

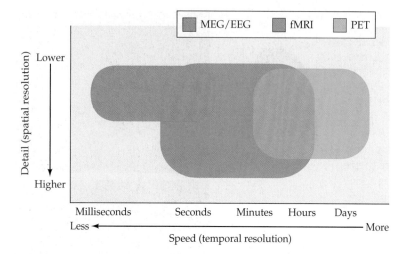

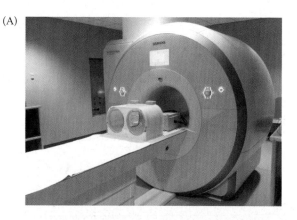

2.26 SPATIAL VERSUS TEMPORAL RESOLUTION IN FUNCTIONAL BRAIN IMAGING No current technique offers both highly detailed imagery and rapid tracking of changes in brain activity. Development of ever-faster and more-accurate technology is a major research focus in neuroscience.

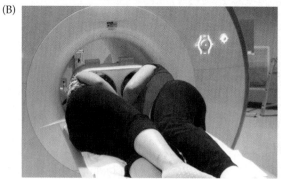

2.27 DYADIC FUNCTIONAL MRI (A) This unique MRI apparatus allows two people to interact while their brains are simultaneously scanned, side by side. (B) Given the narrow confines of the MRI machine, good friendship and a couple of breath mints are probably helpful.

For one thing, technology for functional brain imaging is subject to what the engineers call a "speed-accuracy trade-off": some technologies, like fMRI, provide very fine structural detail (high *spatial resolution*) but are relatively slow to create images and thus are poor at tracking dynamic changes in brain activity (low *temporal resolution*). Electrophysiological measures like MEG and electroencephalography (EEG), conversely, are fast enough to provide excellent temporal resolution but lack the spatial resolution needed to provide highly detailed images. Researchers must weigh these trade-offs carefully in designing experiments (**FIGURE 2.26**).

It is likewise important to realize that these technologies do not produce actual images of the brain, but rather computer-generated composites based on measurements such as density, blood flow, or electromagnetic activity—these measurements are presumed to reflect the structure, metabolism, and electrical activity of the brain. The colors assigned to patterns of activation are arbitrary—obviously, your frontal lobes don't actually glow red hot when you are working on a tricky logic problem—and are based on statistical estimations. The computer algorithms underlying functional brain imaging are the subject of considerable debate and controversy, and there is growing concern that they may have generated false positive results in some studies (Eklund et al., 2016). Further, it is also all too easy to interpret the results of brain imaging as if many behaviors and cognitive processes can be associated with specific locations in the brain; some authors have gone so far as to warn of a modern-day version of phrenology, which we discussed in Chapter 1 (G. A. Miller, 2010). But there is no doubt that modern brain images, interpreted with caution, are helping us to understand the complexities of neural activity. The origins of these neural signals are the topic of Chapter 3.

▌ The Cutting Edge

Two Heads Are Better Than One

Conventional functional-imaging technology does an amazing job of visualizing brain activity during behavior, but the behavior itself is necessarily quite unnatural. For one thing, participants must lie completely motionless in a very narrow, very noisy tunnel. Material for cognitive processing is generally delivered by computer monitor and headphones, and behavioral responses are often limited to button presses. In real life, our behavior is more complex and generally takes place in a social setting, directed toward and shaped by other people.

The burgeoning field of **social neuroscience** aims to understand brain activity as it relates to our interactions with others (McEwen and Akil, 2011). It is relatively easy to study the social interactions of people in the field, where researchers can observe natural behavior at a distance. We can also take measurements of peripheral physiological responses to social interactions, such as salivary measurements of hormonal changes (e.g., van Anders and Watson, 2006). But how can we introduce the social dimension to brain-imaging research?

To approach this question, **dyadic functional MRI (dfMRI)** (R. F. Lee et al., 2012) employs an MRI scanner that is fitted with specially designed dual head coils—a head coil is the part of the apparatus that encircles the head and deals with the radio frequency energy that is used to create brain images. With the use of dfMRI, two people's brains can be scanned while they lie side by side in the machine, interacting through a window linking the two coils (**FIGURE 2.27**). Although previous studies have attempted to simulate social interac-

2.28 DYADIC FUNCTIONAL MRI IMAGES DURING SOCIAL INTERACTION Here, two friends are observing each other's faces while opening and closing their eyes. This is the first time that researchers have imaged the activity of two brains as they are directly interacting. TPJ, temporoparietal junction. (Courtesy of Dr. R. F. Lee, Princeton University.)

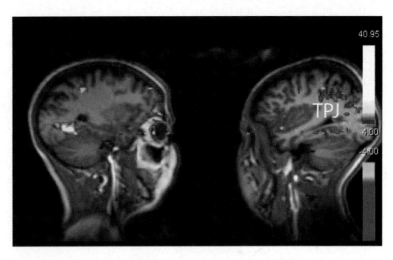

tion using video links between two scanners (Redcay et al., 2010), the dfMRI technique adds an additional level of validity to the interactions—aside from the more intangible aspects of the three-dimensional "realness" of the situation, participants can simultaneously observe small movements, touch each other, and so on.

Initial research with dfMRI has started to reveal some of the subtleties of collaboration between two brains involved in the same behavioral situation. For example, as a pair of friends blinked and gazed at each other's faces, enhanced BOLD signal was observed in the region of the temporoparietal junction (TPJ, a region previously implicated in social cognition), the fusiform face area (see Chapter 19), and in frontal cortex (**FIGURE 2.28**). What is additionally interesting to researchers is how the BOLD responses differ between the participants; as you can see, the left and right individuals in the scans show their own unique patterns of activation, suggesting that individual responses to the social situation may reflect personality and other intrinsic differences and perhaps also differences in the individuals' roles within the pair. Although this approach to social neuroscience is still in its infancy, dfMRI and other emerging technologies hold the promise of unlocking the brain's activity during much richer social behaviors.

social neuroscience The use of neuroscience techniques to understand the neural bases of social processes.

dyadic functional MRI (dfMRI) An fMRI technique in which the brains of two interacting individuals are simultaneously imaged.

Recommended Reading

Allen Brain Atlas, brain-map.org

EU Human Brain Project, humanbrainproject.eu

NIH Brain Research through Advancing Innovative Neurotechnologies (BRAIN) Initiative, braininitiative.nih.gov

Blumenfeld, H. (2010). *Neuroanatomy through Clinical Cases* (2nd ed.). Sunderland, MA: Sinauer.

Cabeza, R., and Kingstone, A. (2006). *Handbook of Functional Neuroimaging of Cognition* (2nd ed.). Cambridge, MA: MIT Press.

Catani, M., and Thiebaut de Schotten, M. (2012). *Atlas of Human Brain Connections*. Oxford, England: Oxford University Press.

Huettel, S. A., Song, A. W., and McCarthy, G. (2014). *Functional Magnetic Resonance Imaging* (3rd ed.). Sunderland, MA: Sinauer.

Mai, J. K., Majtanik, M., and Paxinos, G. (2016). *The Human Brain* (4th ed.). San Diego, CA: Academic Press.

Mendoza, J., and Foundas, A. L. (2010). *Clinical Neuroanatomy: A Neurobehavioral Approach*. Heidelberg, Germany: Springer.

Miller, G. A. (2010). Mistreating psychology in the decades of the brain. *Perspectives on Psychological Science, 5*, 716–743.

Schoonover, C. (2010). *Portraits of the Mind: Visualizing the Brain from Antiquity to the 21st Century*. New York: Abrams.

Vanderah, T. W., and Gould, D. J. (2015). *Nolte's the human brain: An introduction to its functional neuroanatomy* (7th ed.). Philadelphia: Elsevier.

Woolsey, T. A., Hanaway, J., and Gado, M. H. (2007). *The brain atlas: A visual guide to the human central nervous system*. New York: Wiley-Liss.

Go to
bn8e.com
for study questions, quizzes, activities, and other resources

2 — VISUAL SUMMARY

You should be able to relate each summary to the adjacent illustration, including structures and processes.
Go to **bn8e.com/vs2** for links to figures, animations, and activities that will help you consolidate the material.

1 The nervous system is extensive—monitoring, regulating, and modulating the activities of all parts and organs of the body. Review **Figure 2.8**

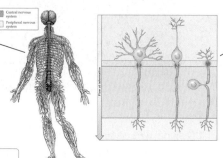

2 At the microscopic level, **neurons** are the basic information-processing units of the nervous system. The typical neuron has four main parts: (1) the **cell body**, which contains the **nucleus**; (2) **dendrites**, which receive information; (3) an **axon**, which conducts information, in the form of electrical potentials, away from the cell body; and (4) **axon terminals**, which transmit the neuron's activity to other cells. Because of the variety of functions they serve, neurons are extremely varied in size, shape, and chemical activity. Review **Figures 2.2 and 2.3**, **Table 2.1**, **Activity 2.1**

3 Neurons make functional contacts with other neurons, or with muscles or glands, at specialized junctions called **synapses**. Synapses may be on dendritic spines, which exhibit **neural plasticity**, changing shape in response to experience. At most synapses a chemical transmitter liberated by the **presynaptic** terminal diffuses across the **synaptic cleft** and binds to special receptor molecules in the **postsynaptic membrane**. Review **Figure 2.5**

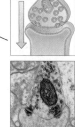

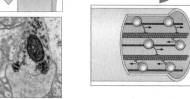

4 The axon is tubular, branching at the end into many collaterals. The primary function of the axon is to conduct action potentials along its membrane. In addition, in the interior of the axon, specialized internal motor proteins "walk" the length of the axon in both directions, carrying vesicles filled with important substances. Review **Figure 2.6**

5 **Glial cells** serve many functions, including the breakdown of transmitters, the production of **myelin** sheaths around axons, the exchange of nutrients and other materials with neurons, the direct regulation of the interconnections and activity of neurons, and the removal of cellular debris. Review **Figure 2.7**

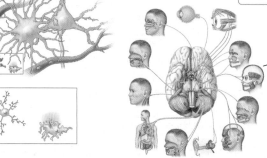

6 At the gross anatomical level (i.e., to the naked eye), the nervous system of vertebrates is divided into **peripheral** and **central nervous systems**. The peripheral nervous system includes the **cranial nerves**, **spinal nerves**, and **autonomic nervous system**. Review **Figures 2.9 and 2.10**, **Activities 2.2 and 2.3**

7 The autonomic nervous system consists of the **sympathetic nervous system**, which tends to ready the body for action; the **parasympathetic nervous system**, which tends to have an effect opposite to that of the sympathetic system; and the **enteric nervous system**, which innervates the gut. Review **Figure 2.11**, **Activity 2.4**

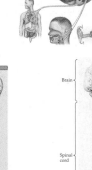

8 The **central nervous system (CNS)** consists of the brain and spinal cord. Review **Figure 2.8**

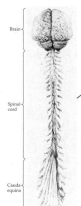

9 The main divisions of the brain are the **forebrain** (**telencephalon** and **diencephalon**), the **midbrain** (mesencephalon), and the hindbrain metencephalon and myelencephalon). Review Figure 2.14, Activity 2.8

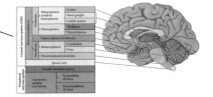

10 The human brain is dominated by the **cerebral hemispheres**, which include the **cerebral cortex**, an extensive sheet of folded tissue. The six-layered cerebral cortex is responsible for higher-order functions such as vision, language, and memory. Other neural systems include the **basal ganglia**, which regulate movement; the **limbic system**, which controls emotional behaviors; and the **cerebellum**, which aids motor control. Review Figures 2.12 and 2.17, Activities 2.5–2.7, 2.9–2.11

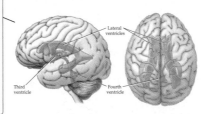

11 The brain and spinal cord, surrounded and protected by the three **meninges**, float in **cerebrospinal fluid (CSF)**, which surrounds and infiltrates the brain (via cerebral ventricles). Review Figure 2.19, Activity 2.12

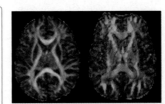

12 The vascular system of the brain is an elaborate array of blood vessels that deliver nutrients and other substances to the brain. The walls of the blood vessels in the brain form the **blood-brain barrier**, restricting the flow of large, potentially harmful molecules into the brain. Disruption of the blood supply to the brain results in a **stroke**. Review Figures 2.20 and 2.21

13 Modern imaging techniques make it possible to visualize the anatomy of the living human brain and regional metabolic differences. These techniques include **computerized axial tomography (CT)**, **positron emission tomography (PET)**, **magnetic resonance imaging (MRI)**, **functional MRI (fMRI)**, **diffusion tensor imaging (DTI)**, near-infrared **optical imaging**, and **magnetoencephalography (MEG)**. Review Figures 2.21 and 2.26, Box 2.3, Animation 2.2

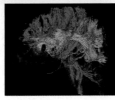

Neurophysiology

The Generation, Transmission, and Integration of Neural Signals

3

The Laughing Brain

Deidre never knew when she might suddenly suffer a seizure, that is, a loss of consciousness accompanied by convulsions, the uncontrollable, rhythmic movements of her whole body. The seizures resulted from electrical malfunctions in her brain and were a symptom of a disorder called *epilepsy*. Medications that usually control epileptic seizures in other people didn't work for Deidre. The seizures weren't just embarrassing—they left her vulnerable to accidents. So Deidre agreed to try something drastic. She let doctors implant tiny wires through her skull to pinpoint exactly where in the brain the electrical problems began. From this information the doctors could decide whether to remove that part of the brain, which should stop the seizures.

When the doctors carefully passed a tiny electrical current through each wire in turn, they found that stimulating the wire to a particular part of the brain elicited a reliable change in Deidre's behavior—she laughed. You might think that Deidre would be puzzled by her own sudden laughter, but she wasn't told when the wires were stimulated and she never seemed to guess they were causing her to laugh. When the doctors asked why she was laughing, Deidre always offered a reason. "You guys standing there, you're so funny!" Stimulating that part of the brain didn't just cause Deidre to laugh, it also affected her mind, causing her to be amused by whatever happened to be going on. If two doctors were standing there in lab coats, she interpreted their behavior as humorous. Presumably this same part of her brain is normally active when Deidre hears a funny joke.

Deidre's behavior demonstrates that even a mental process as elusive as a sense of humor is a product of a machine: give the machine a tiny zap of electricity, and she'll be amused without even hearing a joke. Deidre's epilepsy is also a result of electrical activity—uncontrolled electrical activity—in that marvelously complex machine between her ears. In this chapter we'll find out why electrical activity in the brain affects behavior so profoundly.

In Chapter 2 we learned that the brain consists of billions of neurons that make trillions of elaborate connections with one another. In this chapter we see that each of those neurons is an information-processing device, taking in lots of information, analyzing that information, then passing along the results of that analysis to other cells. To understand how a neuron takes in, analyzes, and transmits information, we delve into **neurophysiology**, the study of electrical and chemical processes in neurons.

We'll learn that information flows *within* a neuron via electrical signals, while information passes *between* neurons through chemical signals. This alternating series of electrical and chemical signaling underlies all neuronal function, including our ability to shoot a basket, or get a joke and laugh. We trace that sequence of electrical and chemical signaling in this chapter. First we explain how neurons produce electrical signals, called *action potentials*, and send them along their axons. Then we describe how such an electrical signal causes axon terminals to release a chemical messenger, called a *neurotransmitter*, into the synapse. Next we discuss how the neurotransmitter affects the electrical state of a neuron on the other side of the synapse. Finally, we talk about how neuronal circuits use these alternating electrical and chemical signals to organize behavior.

Go to Brain Explorer
bn8e.com/3.1

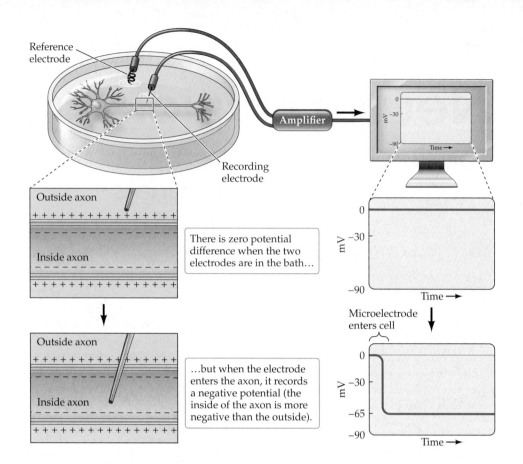

Outside axon

Inside axon

There is zero potential difference when the two electrodes are in the bath…

Outside axon

Inside axon

…but when the electrode enters the axon, it records a negative potential (the inside of the axon is more negative than the outside).

neurophysiology The study of electrical and chemical processes in neurons.

ion An atom or molecule that has acquired an electrical charge by gaining or losing one or more electrons.

anion A negatively charged ion, such as a protein or chloride ion.

cation A positively charged ion, such as a potassium or sodium ion.

intracellular fluid Also called *cytoplasm*. The watery solution found within cells.

extracellular fluid The fluid in the spaces between cells (interstitial fluid) and in the vascular system.

cell membrane The lipid bilayer that ensheathes a cell.

lipid bilayer The structure of the neuronal cell membrane, which consists of two layers of lipid molecules. Various specialized proteins, such as ion channels and receptors, are embedded within the membrane.

microelectrode An especially small electrode used to record electrical potentials from living cells.

resting membrane potential A difference in electrical potential across the membrane of a nerve cell during an inactive period.

Electrical Signals Are the Vocabulary of the Nervous System

All living cells possess an electrical charge—they are more negative on the inside than on the outside—that is a legacy of their evolutionary origins. Early single-celled organisms living in the primordial sea contained many proteins, which are negatively charged. Long ago, neurons began to exploit this electrical property to keep track of information, resulting in a cellular signaling system that is much the same in jellyfish, insects, and human beings. These electrical signals underlie the whole range of thought and action, from composing music to feeling an itch on the skin and swatting a mosquito. To understand this electrical signaling system, we'll first review the physical forces at work and then discuss some details of why neurons are electrically polarized, how neuronal polarity is influenced by other cells, and how a change of polarity in one part of a neuron can spread throughout the cell.

A balance of electrochemical forces produces the resting membrane potential of neurons

Let's start by considering a neuron at rest, neither perturbed by other neurons nor producing its own signals. Of the many **ions** (electrically charged molecules) that a neuron contains, a majority are **anions** (negatively charged ions), especially large protein anions that cannot exit the cell; the rest are **cations** (positively charged ions; to help remember that cations are positive, note the word contains a *t*, which is similar to a plus sign). All of these ions are dissolved in an **intracellular fluid**, which is separated from the **extracellular fluid** by the **cell membrane**, which is made up of a **lipid bilayer**—two layers of linked fatty molecules.

There are more negatively charged ions inside neurons relative to the outside. We can measure that difference in charge across the membrane by inserting a fine **microelectrode** inside a neuron and using a voltmeter to compare the cell's interior with the extracellular fluid surrounding it (as illustrated in **FIGURE 3.1**). Such measures show that a neuron at rest exhibits a characteristic **resting membrane**

(A) Diffusion

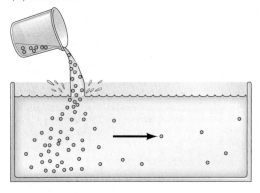

Particles move from areas of high concentration to areas of low concentration. That is, they move down their concentration gradient.

(B) Diffusion through semipermeable membranes

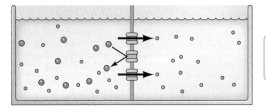

Cell membranes permit some substances to pass through, but not others.

(C) Electrostatic forces

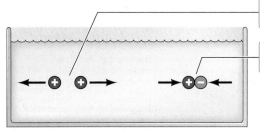

Like charges repel each other.

Opposite charges are attracted to each other.

3.2 FORCES UNDERLYING ELECTRICAL SIGNALING IN NEURONS

potential of about −50 to −80 thousandths of a volt, or **millivolts (mV)** (the negative sign indicates the **negative polarity** of the cell's interior).

To understand why neurons have a resting membrane potential of about −65 mV or so, we need to consider the many sorts of specialized proteins that span the cell membrane. One important type of membrane-spanning protein is the **ion channel**, a tubelike pore that allows ions of a specific type to pass through the membrane. Some ion channels stay open all the time, and the cell membrane of a neuron contains many such channels that selectively allow **potassium ions (K⁺)** to cross the membrane. Because it is studded with these K⁺ channels, we say that the cell membrane of a neuron exhibits **selective permeability** to potassium; that is, K⁺ ions can enter or exit the cell fairly freely, while other ions are impeded by the cell membrane.

The resting potential of the neuron reflects a balancing act between two opposing forces that drive K⁺ ions in and out of the neuron. The first of these is **diffusion** (**FIGURE 3.2A**), which is the force that causes molecules of a substance to diffuse from regions of high concentration to regions of low concentration. For example, if a drop of food coloring is placed in a glass of water, the molecules of dye tend to move from the drop, where they are highly concentrated, into the rest of the glass, where they are less concentrated. In other words, molecules tend to move down their **concentration gradient** until they are evenly distributed. If a selectively permeable membrane divides the fluid, particles that can pass through the membrane, such as K⁺, will diffuse across until they are equally concentrated on both sides (**FIGURE 3.2B**). Other ions, unable to cross the membrane, will remain concentrated on one side (**FIGURE 3.2C**). Now let's consider the situation across a neuron's cell membrane. Neurons use a mechanism, the **sodium-potassium pump**, that pumps three **sodium ions (Na⁺)** out of the cell for every two K⁺ ions pumped in. This action

millivolt (mV) A thousandth of a volt.

negative polarity A negative electrical-potential difference relative to a reference electrode.

ion channel A pore in the cell membrane that permits the passage of certain ions through the membrane when the channel is open.

potassium ion (K⁺) A potassium atom that carries a positive charge because it has lost one electron.

selective permeability The property of a membrane that allows some substances to pass through, but not others.

diffusion The spontaneous spread of molecules of one substance among molecules of another substance until a uniform concentration is achieved.

concentration gradient Variation of the concentration of a substance within a region.

sodium-potassium pump The energetically expensive mechanism that pushes sodium ions out of a cell, and potassium ions in.

3.3 THE IONIC BASIS OF THE RESTING POTENTIAL

Go to Animation 3.2
The Resting Membrane Potential
bn8e.com/3.2

(A) The sodium-potassium pump

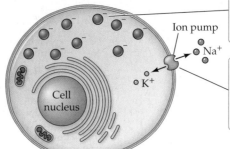

Cells contain many large, negatively charged molecules, such as proteins, that do not cross the membrane.

The sodium-potassium (Na^+-K^+) pump continually pushes Na^+ ions out and pulls K^+ ions in. This ion pump requires considerable energy.

(B) Membrane permeability to ions

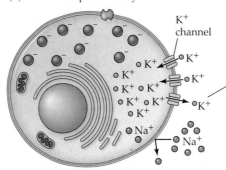

The membrane is permeable to K^+ ions, which pass back out again through channels down their concentration gradient. The departure of K^+ ions leaves the inside of the cell more negative than the outside. Na^+ ions cannot pass back inside.

(C) Equilibrium potential

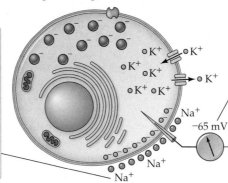

Cations like Na^+ push against the membrane's exterior, attracted to the negative interior. Likewise, anions coat the interior of the cell membrane, attracted to cations on the other side. Most of the cell's potential difference is due to these charges immediately surrounding the membrane.

When enough K^+ ions have departed to bring the membrane potential to −65 mV or so, the electrical attraction pulling K^+ in is exactly balanced by the concentration gradient pushing K^+ out. This is the K^+ equilibrium potential, approximately the cell's resting potential.

sodium ion (Na^+) A sodium atom that carries a positive charge because it has lost one electron.

equilibrium Here, the state in which the number of ions crossing a membrane in one direction is matched by the number crossing in the opposite direction.

electrostatic pressure The propensity of charged molecules or ions to move toward areas with the opposite charge.

Nernst equation An equation predicting the equilibrium potential for a given ion based on the concentrations of the ion on opposite sides of a permeable membrane.

equilibrium potential The voltage across a permeable membrane that exactly counteracts the movement of ions from the side with a high concentration to the side with a low concentration.

consumes energy (**FIGURE 3.3A**). In fact, a large fraction of the energy consumed by the brain is used to maintain these ionic differences across neuronal membranes.

The sodium-potassium pump causes a buildup of K^+ ions inside the cell, but recall that at rest the membrane is much more permeable to K^+ ions than other ions like Na^+. That means K^+ ions will tend to leave the interior, down their concentration gradient, causing a net buildup of negative charges inside the cell (**FIGURE 3.3B**). As negative charge builds up inside the cell, it begins to exert electrostatic pressure to pull positively charged K^+ ions back inside. Eventually these opposing forces—the concentration gradient pushing K^+ ions out and the electrostatic pressure pulling them in—reach **equilibrium**, exactly balancing each other. Any further movement of K^+ ions into the cell (drawn by **electrostatic pressure**) is matched by the flow of K^+ ions out of the cell (moving down the concentration gradient), as **FIGURE 3.3C** depicts. How negative does the neuron's interior need to be to reach this equilibrium?

The **Nernst equation** is a mathematical function predicting the **equilibrium potential**, the voltage difference across a permeable membrane needed to exactly counterbalance the diffusion force pushing an ion from the side of the membrane with a high concentration to the side with a low concentration. The full equation includes several physical constants that can be filled in to simplify the equation at room temperature:

Equilibrium potential for ion X:

$$E_x = \frac{58}{(\text{electrical charge ion } x)} \text{ mV} \times \log \frac{(\text{concentration of } X \text{ outside})}{(\text{concentration of } X \text{ inside})} =$$

$$\frac{58}{(\text{electrical charge ion } x)} \text{ mV} \times \log \frac{[X]_{\text{outside}}}{[X]_{\text{inside}}}$$

Because the K^+ ion has an electrical charge of +1, the Nernst equation for K^+ can be further simplified:

Equilibrium potential for K^+:

$$E_{K^+} = 58\text{mV} \times \log \frac{[K^+]_{\text{outside}}}{[K^+]_{\text{inside}}}$$

The sodium-potassium pump causes the K^+ to be about 24 times more concentrated inside than out, so the equation becomes:

$$E_{K^+} = 58\text{mV} \times \log {}^1\!/_{24} = 58\text{mV} \times -1.38 = -80\text{mV}$$

When the resting membrane potentials of neurons are actually measured, they may sometimes reach this value of −80 mV but are typically closer to −65 mV as indicated in Figures 3.1 and 3.3C. What accounts for this discrepancy? For one thing, the Nernst equation assumes the neuronal membrane is permeable *only* to K^+, but in fact the membrane is *somewhat* permeable to other ions. Another equation, called the **Goldman equation**, takes into account the intracellular and extracellular concentrations of K^+ and Na^+ and several other ions but also accounts for the *degree* of permeability to each. Taking those additional factors into account, the Goldman equation predicts a voltage potential that is quite close to the resting potentials observed in neurons. You can go online to vary the concentration and permeability of various ions across a virtual membrane to see the potentials predicted by the Nernst and Goldman equations: nernstgoldman.physiology.arizona.edu/launch.

The approximate distributions of the most important ions inside and outside neurons are illustrated in **FIGURE 3.4**. Notice the high intracellular concentration of K^+ and the high extracellular concentration of Na^+, which are enforced by the sodium-

Goldman equation An equation predicting the potential difference across a membrane based on the concentrations of ions on opposite sides of the membrane, as well as its relative permeability to each ion.

	Na^+	K^+	Cl^-	Ca^{2+}	Proteins
Concentration outside cell (mM)	145	5	110	1–2	few
Concentration inside cell (mM)	5–15	140	4–30	0.0001	many

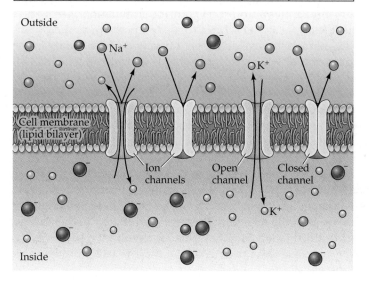

3.4 THE DISTRIBUTION OF IONS INSIDE AND OUTSIDE OF A NEURON Most potassium ions (K^+) are found inside the neuron. Most sodium ions (Na^+), chloride ions (Cl^-), and calcium ions (Ca^{2+}) are in the extracellular fluid. These ions are exchanged through specialized channels in the cell membrane. The large, negatively charged protein molecules stay inside the neuron.

calcium ion (Ca²⁺) A calcium atom that carries a double positive charge because it has lost two electrons.

action potential The propagated electrical message of a neuron that travels along the axon to the presynaptic axon terminals.

hyperpolarization An increase in membrane potential (the interior of the neuron becomes even more negative).

depolarization A reduction in membrane potential (the interior of the neuron becomes less negative).

local potential An electrical potential that is initiated by stimulation at a specific site, which is a graded response that spreads passively across the cell membrane, decreasing in strength with time and distance.

threshold The stimulus intensity that is just adequate to trigger an action potential.

potassium pump. Neurons also keep levels of intracellular **calcium ions (Ca²⁺)** low by using another ion pump to eject Ca^{2+} ions and by using specialized proteins that store Ca^{2+} to use for intracellular signaling, including the synaptic release of neurotransmitter, which we'll take up later in this chapter.

The resting potential of a neuron provides a baseline level of polarization found in all cells. But unlike most other cells, a neuron routinely undergoes a brief but radical *change* in polarization, sending an electrical signal from one end of its axon to the other, as we'll discuss next.

A threshold amount of depolarization triggers an action potential

Action potentials are very brief but large changes in neuronal polarization that arise in the initial segment of the axon and are propagated at high speed along the axon's length. The information that a neuron sends to its postsynaptic targets is encoded in patterns of these action potentials, so we need to understand their properties—where they come from, how they race down the axon, and how they communicate their information across synapses to other cells. Let's turn first to the creation of the action potential.

Two concepts are central to understanding how action potentials are triggered. **Hyperpolarization** is an increasing negativity of the membrane potential (i.e., the neuron becomes even more negative on the inside, relative to the outside). So if the neuron already has a resting membrane potential of, say, −65 mV, hyperpolarization makes it even *farther from zero*, maybe −70 mV. **Depolarization** is the reverse, referring to a decreased polarization of the cell membrane. The depolarization of a neuron from a resting potential of −65 mV to, say, −60 mV makes the inside of the neuron more like the outside. In other words, depolarization of a neuron brings its membrane potential *closer to zero*.

FIGURE 3.5A illustrates an apparatus for experimentally hyperpolarizing and depolarizing a neuron with an electrode. (Later we'll talk about how synapses from other neurons produce similar hyperpolarizations and depolarizations.) Applying a *hyperpolarizing* stimulus to the membrane produces an immediate response that passively follows the stimulus pulse (**FIGURE 3.5B**; the distortions at the beginning and end of the neuron's response are caused by the membrane's ability to store electrical charge, known as *capacitance*). The greater the stimulus, the greater the response, so the neuron's change in potential is called a *graded response*.

If we measured the membrane response at locations successively farther and farther away from the stimulus location, we would see another way in which the membrane response seems passive and graded. Like ripples spreading from a pebble dropped in a pond, the potentials produced by stimulation of the membrane diminish as they spread away from the point of stimulation (see Figure 3.5B, bottom). A simple law of physics describes this phenomenon: as the potential spreads across the membrane, its size decays as a function of the square of the distance. Such **local potentials**, which are graded and diminish over time and distance, also arise at synapses in response to other neurons, as we will see later in this chapter.

Up to a point, the application of *depolarizing* pulses to the membrane follows the same pattern as for hyperpolarizing stimuli, producing local, graded responses. However, the situation changes suddenly if the stimulus depolarizes the cell to −40 mV or so (the exact value varies slightly among neurons). At this point, known as the **threshold**, a sudden and brief (0.5–2.0 millisecond [ms]) response—the action potential—is provoked (**FIGURE 3.5C**). The action potential (sometimes referred to as a *spike* because of its shape) is a rapid reversal of the membrane potential that momentarily makes the inside of the membrane *positive* with respect to the outside. Unlike the passive spread of the graded potentials that we have been discussing, the action potential is actively propagated (or regenerated) down the axon, through ionic mechanisms that we'll discuss shortly.

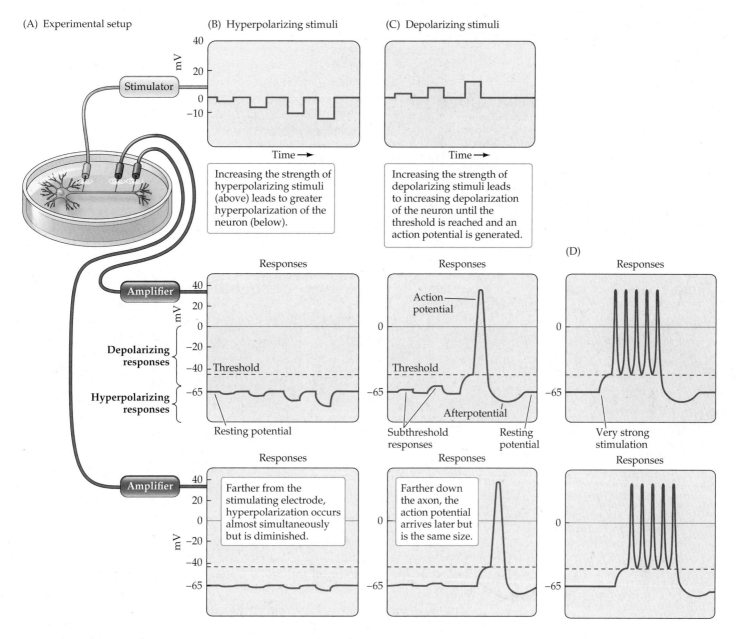

3.5 THE EFFECTS OF HYPERPOLARIZING AND DEPOLARIZING STIMULI ON A NEURON (A) Experimental setup. (B) Effects of hyperpolarizing stimuli at two recording locations. (C) Generation of an action potential with depolarizing stimuli. (D) Note that larger depolarizations trigger more action potentials, not larger action potentials.

Applying strong stimuli to produce depolarizations that far exceed the neuron's threshold reveals another important property of action potentials: larger depolarizations produce *more* action potentials, not larger action potentials (**FIGURE 3.5D**). In other words, the size (or *amplitude*) of the action potential is independent of stimulus magnitude. This characteristic is referred to as the **all-or-none property** of the action potential: either it fires at its full amplitude, or it doesn't fire at all. It turns out that information is encoded by changes in the *frequency* of action potentials rather than in their amplitude.

A closer look at the form of the action potential shows that the return to baseline membrane potential is not simple. Many axons exhibit electrical oscillations immediately following the spike; these changes are called **afterpotentials** (see Figure 3.5C), which are also related to the movement of ions in and out of the cell, as we'll see next.

all-or-none property The fact that the amplitude of the action potential is independent of the magnitude of the stimulus.

afterpotential The positive or negative change in membrane potential that may follow an action potential.

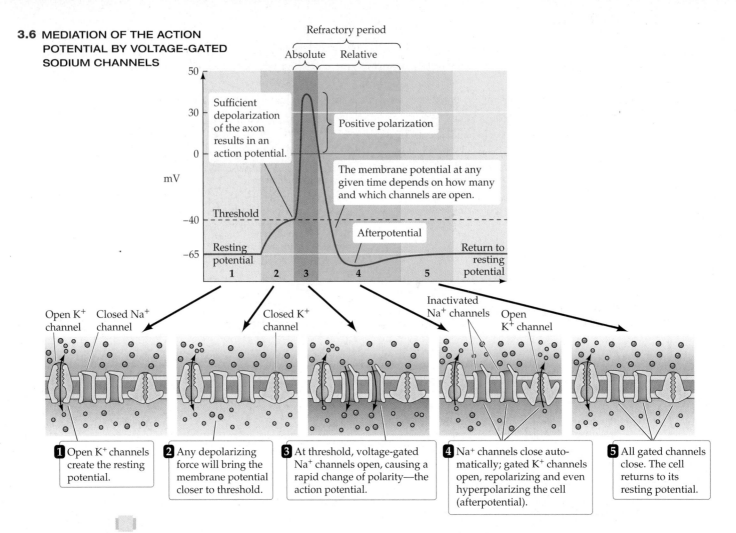

Refractory period

Absolute — Relative

Positive polarization

Sufficient depolarization of the axon results in an action potential.

The membrane potential at any given time depends on how many and which channels are open.

Afterpotential

Threshold

Resting potential

Return to resting potential

mV

50

30

0

−40

−65

1   2   3   4   5

Open K⁺ channel   Closed Na⁺ channel

Closed K⁺ channel

Inactivated Na⁺ channels   Open K⁺ channel

1 Open K⁺ channels create the resting potential.

2 Any depolarizing force will bring the membrane potential closer to threshold.

3 At threshold, voltage-gated Na⁺ channels open, causing a rapid change of polarity—the action potential.

4 Na⁺ channels close automatically; gated K⁺ channels open, repolarizing and even hyperpolarizing the cell (afterpotential).

5 All gated channels close. The cell returns to its resting potential.

Go to Animation 3.3
The Action Potential
bn8e.com/3.3

voltage-gated Na⁺ channel
A Na⁺-selective channel that opens or closes in response to changes in the voltage of the local membrane potential; it mediates the action potential.

Ionic mechanisms underlie the action potential

What events explain the action potential? To answer this question, English neurophysiologists Alan Hodgkin (1914–1998) and Andrew Huxley (1917–2012) took advantage of the giant axon of the squid, from a neuron involved in the animal's emergency escape behavior. More than half a millimeter in diameter, the squid's giant axon is readily apparent to the naked eye and therefore much better suited to experimentation than mammalian axons, which range in size from 0.1 to 20 microns (µm) in diameter (Debanne et al., 2011). Microelectrodes can be inserted into a giant axon without greatly altering the properties of the axon; it is even possible to push the intracellular fluid out of the squid axon and replace it with other fluids to see how that affects the action potential.

Hodgkin and Huxley established that the action potential is created by the movement of sodium ions (Na⁺) into the cell, through channels that open up in the membrane. At its peak, the action potential approaches the equilibrium potential for Na⁺ as predicted by the Nernst and Goldman equations: about +40 mV. At this point, the concentration gradient pushing Na⁺ ions into the cell is exactly balanced by the positive charge pushing them out. The action potential thus involves a rapid shift in membrane properties, switching suddenly from the potassium-dependent resting state to a primarily sodium-dependent active state, and then swiftly returning to the resting state. This shift is accomplished through the actions of a very special ion channel: the voltage-gated Na⁺ channel.

Like other ion channels, the **voltage-gated Na⁺ channel** includes a tubular, membrane-spanning protein, but this Na⁺-selective pore is ordinarily closed. When the cell membrane becomes depolarized to threshold levels, the channel's shape changes, opening the pore to allow Na⁺ ions through. Consider what happens when a patch of axonal membrane depolarizes (**FIGURE 3.6**). As long as the depolarization is below threshold, Na⁺ channels remain closed. But when the depolarization reaches threshold, a few Na$^+$ channels open at first, allowing ions to start entering the neuron, depolarizing the membrane even further and opening still more Na$^+$ channels. Thus, the process accelerates until the barriers are removed and Na$^+$ ions rush in, both because they are attracted to the negatively charged interior of the neuron and because they are flowing down their concentration gradient.

But the voltage-gated Na$^+$ channels stay open for only about a millisecond; then they close again. By this time the membrane potential has approached the Na$^+$ equilibrium potential of about +40 mV. Now, the positive charge inside the nerve cell pushes K$^+$ ions out the channels that are always open, plus voltage-gated K$^+$ channels open as well, making the membrane even more permeable to K$^+$, so the resting potential is quickly restored.

Applying very strong stimuli reveals another important property of axonal membranes. As we bombard the beleaguered axon with ever-stronger stimuli, an upper limit to the frequency of action potentials becomes apparent at about 1200 spikes per second. (Many neurons have even slower maximum rates of response.) Similarly, applying pairs of stimuli that are spaced closer and closer together reveals a related phenomenon: beyond a certain point, only the first stimulus is able to elicit an action potential. The axonal membrane is said to be **refractory** (unresponsive) to the second stimulus.

Refractoriness has two phases: During the **absolute refractory phase**, a brief period immediately following the production of an action potential, no amount of stimulation can induce another action potential, because the voltage-gated Na$^+$ channels are unresponsive (see Figure 3.6, step 3). The absolute phase is followed by a period of reduced sensitivity, the **relative refractory phase**, during which only a very strong stimulation can produce another action potential, because the flow of K$^+$ ions out has temporarily hyperpolarized the neuron, so a stronger stimulus would be needed to reach threshold (see Figure 3.6, step 4).

This tiny protein molecule, the voltage-gated Na$^+$ channel, is really quite a complicated machine. It monitors the axon's polarity, and at threshold it changes its shape to open the channel, shutting down again just a millisecond later. The channel then "remembers" that it was recently open and refuses to open again for a short time. These properties produce and enforce the characteristics of the action potential. As you might expect, anything that alters the functioning of neuronal ion channels will affect action potentials and therefore behavior.

You might wonder if the repeated inrush of Na$^+$ ions would allow them to build up, affecting the cell's resting potential. In fact, relatively few Na$^+$ ions need to enter to change the membrane potential (Alle et al., 2009). Plus, most of the change in ion concentration taking place during an action potential is happening right next to the membrane, leaving the ionic concentrations in the interior of the axon relatively unaffected. In the long run, the sodium-potassium pump enforces the low concentrations of Na$^+$ ions inside the neuron. We've presented the conclusions of Hodgkin and Huxley's research, in which they carefully manipulated the concentration of ions in and out of the axon and also carefully monitored current across the membrane. You can learn about the details of such neurophysiological methods in **BOX 3.1** on the following page.

In general, the transmission of action potentials is limited to axons. Cell bodies and dendrites usually have few voltage-gated Na$^+$ channels, so they do not conduct action potentials. The cell body and dendrites have very different ion channels that are stimulated chemically at synapses, as we'll discuss later in this chapter. Because the axon has many voltage-gated Na$^+$ channels, once an action potential starts just past the **axon hillock** (the slight swelling of the axon where it emerges from the cell body; see Figure 2.6A) it regenerates itself down the length of the axon, as we discuss next.

Action potentials are actively propagated along the axon

Now that we have explored how voltage-gated channels underlie action potentials, we can turn to the question of how action potentials are transmitted down the axon—another function for which voltage-gated channels are crucial. If we use several different

refractory Referring to transiently inactivated or exhausted axonal membrane.

absolute refractory phase A brief period of complete insensitivity to stimuli.

relative refractory phase A period of reduced sensitivity during which only strong stimulation produces an action potential.

axon hillock A cone-shaped area from which the axon originates out of the cell body. Functionally, the integration zone of the neuron.

Go to Animation 3.4
Conduction along Unmyelinated vs. Myelinated Axons
bn8e.com/3.4

BOX 3.1

Voltage Clamping and Patch Clamping

One important tool for Hodgkin and Huxley's study of the action potential in the squid giant axon was the preparation known as **voltage clamping**, in which a stimulator is used to force the axon membrane to remain at a particular potential (voltage) (Figure A). One electrode is placed inside the axon, and another is used as a reference electrode in the bath surrounding the axon. A voltmeter measures the potential difference between the two electrodes and sends that information to a voltage clamp amplifier, which compares the current membrane potential to a command voltage that the experimenter has set. If the membrane potential matches the command potential, the machinery does nothing. But if there's a difference between the two voltages, the clamp amplifier injects electrical current into another electrode inside the axon to force the membrane potential to match the command potential. Importantly, another device measures how much current is being injected into the axon to keep it at the command potential. Initially, injection of a constant amount of current will clamp the axon at the desired voltage. After

that, the machine should not have to change the amount of injected current unless current flows across the axon's membrane, as when another electrode depolarizes the axon to open Na⁺ channels. When that happens, then the apparatus must change the amount of injected current to maintain the voltage clamp. Keeping track of these changes in current from the apparatus tells you how much current passes through the Na⁺ channels.

This tool was originally developed to voltage clamp squid axons, but scientists learned that you can also voltage clamp an entire neuron. By using various tricks to "pop" the tip of a microelectrode into a neuron such that the neuron's membrane forms a seal, you can do whole-cell recording (Figure B, middle). Thus you can either measure various synaptic potentials and action potentials or use the apparatus to voltage clamp the entire neuron and monitor currents across the neuron's membrane.

To get even more detailed information, researchers learned how to pull away a tiny patch of membrane covering the microelectrode tip, a technique called **patch clamping**.

In some cases, you might end up with a single ion channel, such as a voltage-gated Na⁺ channel, on that tiny bit of membrane (see Figure B). Now you voltage clamp this tiny fragment and monitor any current flowing across the channel. When the ion channel opens, you can detect a tiny current passing across the membrane caused by the flow of Na⁺ ions, which stops when the channel closes again (Figure C, top). You can then ask how many channel openings there are during a particular time period, say in one second. Then you can purposely vary the membrane potential by varying the command potential in the voltage clamping apparatus and note how the probability of an opening decreases if the membrane is hyperpolarized, and increases if it is depolarized (see Figure C, bottom).

Several other ingenious variations of patch clamping are possible. Depending on how you manipulate your electrode (and with luck and repeated trials), you can end up with an "inside-out" patch of membrane, where the part of the membrane that had been facing the cytoplasm is now facing the bath (see Figure B, middle). If there is

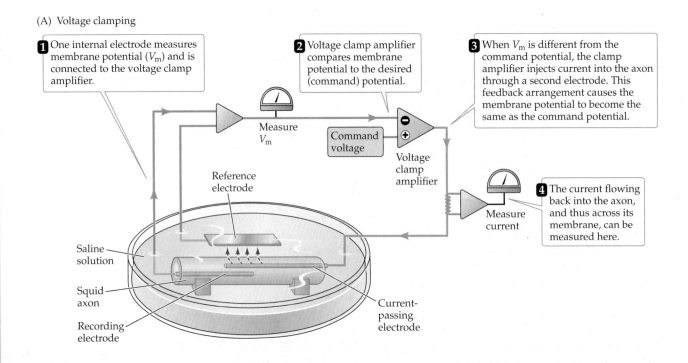

(A) Voltage clamping

1 One internal electrode measures membrane potential (V_m) and is connected to the voltage clamp amplifier.

2 Voltage clamp amplifier compares membrane potential to the desired (command) potential.

3 When V_m is different from the command potential, the clamp amplifier injects current into the axon through a second electrode. This feedback arrangement causes the membrane potential to become the same as the command potential.

Measure V_m

Command voltage

Voltage clamp amplifier

Reference electrode

4 The current flowing back into the axon, and thus across its membrane, can be measured here.

Measure current

Saline solution

Squid axon

Recording electrode

Current-passing electrode

(B) Clamp techniques

Cell-attached recording

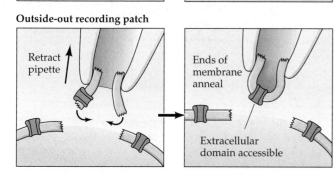

- Recording pipette
- Mild suction
- Tight contact between pipette and membrane

Whole-cell recording

- Strong pulse of suction
- Cytoplasm is continuous with pipette interior

Inside-out recording patch

- Cytoplasmic domain accessible

Outside-out recording patch

- Retract pipette
- Ends of membrane anneal
- Extracellular domain accessible

(C) Studying a single channel

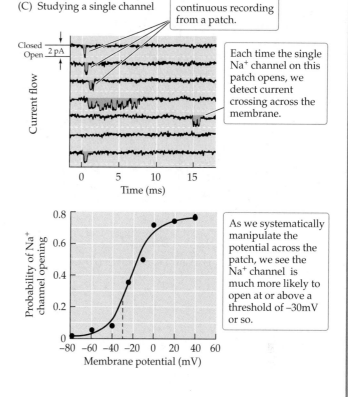

These traces are one continuous recording from a patch.

Each time the single Na⁺ channel on this patch opens, we detect current crossing across the membrane.

Closed / Open — 2 pA

Current flow (vertical axis)

Time (ms) — 0, 5, 10, 15

Probability of Na⁺ channel opening: 0, 0.2, 0.4, 0.6, 0.8

Membrane potential (mV): −80, −60, −40, −20, 0, 20, 40, 60

As we systematically manipulate the potential across the patch, we see the Na⁺ channel is much more likely to open at or above a threshold of −30mV or so.

---

a neurotransmitter receptor on this bit of membrane, you can now expose this cytoplasmic surface to drugs, for example, to see how manipulating second-messenger systems might affect receptor function, again measuring any current that might cross the membrane in response to manipulations. Removing the electrode another way can result in an "outside-out" patch of membrane where the extracellular side is facing the bath (Figure B, bottom). Now you can apply neurotransmitters or drugs to the extracellular portion of the receptor to see how they affect it. Or, you can use this patch of membrane as a "sniffer," moving it around neurons in culture, for example, to see whether any of them are releasing neurotransmitter to that receptor on the tip of your electrode. If so, then bringing the electrode tip nearby should cause current to flow across the membrane as the released transmitter opens up the receptor. (Figure C, top, after Bezanilla and Correa, 1995; bottom, after Correa and Bezanilla, 1994.)

voltage clamping   The use of electrodes to inject current into an axon or neuron to keep the membrane potential at a set value. The apparatus measures how much current must be injected to counteract any ion channel openings.

patch clamp   Use of voltage clamping to monitor current flow across a tiny patch of membrane taken from a neuron.

---

recording electrodes to record an action potential as it races toward the axon terminals, we see that an action potential initiated near the cell body spreads in a sort of chain reaction along the length of the axon, traveling at speeds that range from less than 1 meter per second (m/s) in some axons to more than 100 m/s in others (**FIGURE 3.7**).

How does the action potential travel? It is important to understand that the action potential is *regenerated* along the length of the axon. Remember, the action potential is a spike of depolarizing electrical activity (with a peak of about +40 mV), so it strongly depolarizes the next adjacent axon segment. Because this adjacent segment is similarly covered with voltage-gated Na⁺ channels, the depolarization immediately creates a new action potential, which in turn depolarizes the next patch of membrane, which generates yet another action potential, and so on all down the

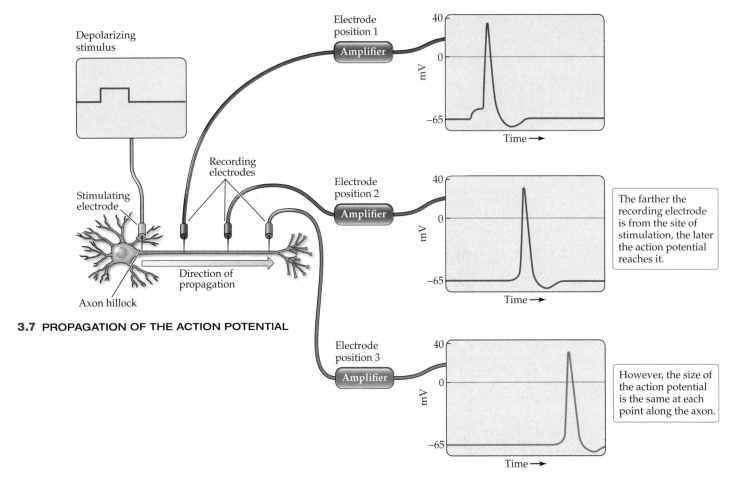

Depolarizing stimulus

Stimulating electrode

Recording electrodes

Axon hillock

Direction of propagation

Electrode position 1

Amplifier

Electrode position 2

Amplifier

The farther the recording electrode is from the site of stimulation, the later the action potential reaches it.

Electrode position 3

Amplifier

However, the size of the action potential is the same at each point along the axon.

3.7 PROPAGATION OF THE ACTION POTENTIAL

length of the axon. An analogy is the spread of fire along a row of closely spaced match heads in a matchbook. When one match is lit, its heat is enough to ignite the next match and so on along the row.

The axon normally conducts action potentials in only one direction—from the axon hillock toward the axon terminals—because as it progresses along the axon, the action potential leaves in its wake a stretch of refractory membrane (**FIGURE 3.8A**). Propagated activity does not spread from the axon hillock back over the cell body and dendrites, because the membranes there have very few voltage-gated Na⁺ channels, so they cannot produce an action potential.

If we record the speed of action potentials along axons that differ in diameter, we see that **conduction velocity** varies with the diameter of the axon. Larger axons allow the depolarization to spread faster through the interior. In mammals, the conduction velocity in large fibers may be as fast as 120 m/s, about one-third the speed of sound in air. We'll discuss axon diameter and conduction velocity again when we describe touch and pain sensation (see Table 8.2).

The highest conduction velocities require more than just large axons. Myelin sheathing also greatly speeds conduction. As we described in Chapter 2, the myelin sheath that encases some axons is interrupted by **nodes of Ranvier**, small gaps spaced about every millimeter along the axon (see Figure 2.7D). Because the myelin insulation offers considerable resistance to the flow of ionic currents across the membrane, the action potential jumps from node to node. This process is called **saltatory conduction** (from the Latin *saltare*, "to leap or jump") (**FIGURE 3.8B**).

The evolution of rapid saltatory conduction in vertebrates gives them a major behavioral advantage over invertebrates, in which axons are unmyelinated and mostly small in diameter and thus slower in conduction. To address this problem, many invertebrates have a few giant axons that mediate essential motor responses, such as escape behavior. The squid's giant axon, which we mentioned earlier, has an unusually high conduction rate for an invertebrate, but that rate is only about 20 m/s, slower than for even small myelinated axons of mammals.

conduction velocity The speed at which an action potential is propagated along the length of an axon (or section of peripheral nerve).

node of Ranvier A gap between successive segments of the myelin sheath where the axon membrane is exposed.

saltatory conduction The form of conduction that is characteristic of myelinated axons, in which the action potential jumps from one node of Ranvier to the next.

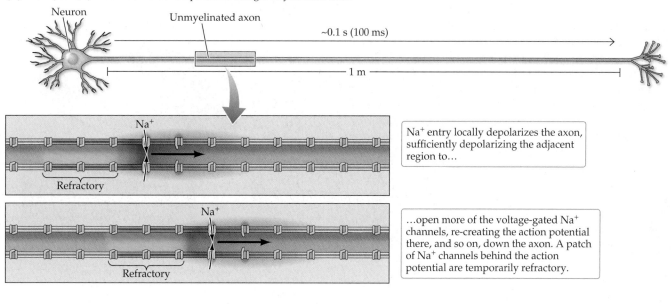

(A) Slow (10 m/s) conduction of action potential along unmyelinated axon

Neuron

Unmyelinated axon

~0.1 s (100 ms)

1 m

Na⁺

Refractory

Na⁺ entry locally depolarizes the axon, sufficiently depolarizing the adjacent region to…

Na⁺

Refractory

…open more of the voltage-gated Na⁺ channels, re-creating the action potential there, and so on, down the axon. A patch of Na⁺ channels behind the action potential are temporarily refractory.

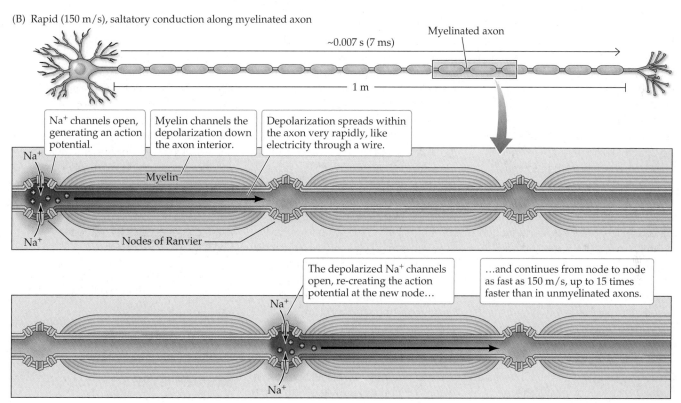

(B) Rapid (150 m/s), saltatory conduction along myelinated axon

~0.007 s (7 ms)

Myelinated axon

1 m

Na⁺ channels open, generating an action potential.

Myelin channels the depolarization down the axon interior.

Depolarization spreads within the axon very rapidly, like electricity through a wire.

Na⁺

Myelin

Na⁺

Nodes of Ranvier

The depolarized Na⁺ channels open, re-creating the action potential at the new node…

…and continues from node to node as fast as 150 m/s, up to 15 times faster than in unmyelinated axons.

Na⁺

Na⁺

3.8 CONDUCTION ALONG UNMYELIN-ATED AXONS AND SALTATORY CONDUCTION ALONG MYELINATED AXONS

To conduct action potentials as swiftly as a myelinated vertebrate axon does, an unmyelinated invertebrate axon would have to be 100 times larger in volume. It has been estimated that at least 10% of the volume of the human brain is occupied by myelinated axons. To maintain the conduction velocity of our cerebral neurons without the help of myelin, our brains would have to be 10 times as large as they are! This fact helps explain why myelination is an important index of maturation of the developing nervous system (see Chapter 7).

There are times when we would rather axons did *not* conduct action potentials, as when a dentist works on an ailing tooth. Then we can turn to drugs that block Na⁺ channels to stop the action potential from propagating pain signals to the brain. Scientists have discovered a host of such drugs and toxins that block specific channels, which have helped us understand neural transmission, as we discuss in **BOX 3.2**.

BOX
3.2

Changing the Channel

The cell membrane is made up of fatty molecules, so it tends to repel water. Because ions in body fluids are usually surrounded by clusters of water molecules, they cannot easily pass directly through neuronal membranes. Instead, they must pass through membrane-spanning ion channels, which are highly selective for particular types of ions. Research has begun to reveal some of the functional details of these channels, such as the K+ channel shown in Figure A (Berneche and Roux, 2001). The inner surfaces of the K+ channel are lined with oxygen atoms that mimic water molecules. With the oxygen atoms substituting for their usual escort of water molecules, K+ ions fit exactly into this *selectivity filter*. Other ions, such as Na+ ions, do not fit as comfortably and thus remain outside, in solution. The end result is a 10,000-fold selectivity for K+ ions!

Given the extreme precision with which these ion channels must operate, it's no surprise that even minor alteration of channel functioning can cause serious health problems (Kass, 2005). **Channelopathies** are medical conditions that arise from abnormalities in the form and function of ion channels, as a result of mutation of the genes that encode those channels. Sodium channelopathy—a problem with sodium channels—is associated with a variety of seizure disorders, as well as heritable muscle diseases and certain types of cardiac ailments (George, 2005; Kass, 2005). Chloride channel disorders can result in deafness, kidney problems, and movement disorders (T. J. Jentsch et al., 2005), as well as seizures. In fact, evidence is mounting that mutations in ion channel genes of all sorts may be a major cause of epilepsy (Ptáček, 2015).

(A) Potassium channel selectivity filter

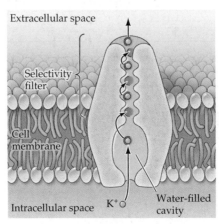

Extracellular space

Selectivity filter

Cell membrane

Intracellular space   K+   Water-filled cavity

(B) Some sources of channel toxins

The critical importance of channels is also exploited by a variety of potent animal toxins (Figure B). For example, **tetrodotoxin** (**TTX**) and **saxitoxin** (**STX**) selectively block voltage-gated sodium channels, thereby preventing the production of action potentials; paralysis and death rapidly follow. Tetrodotoxin is found in the ovaries of the puffer fish, which is esteemed as a delicacy in Japan. If the ovaries of the puffer fish are not removed properly and if the fish is not cleaned with great care, people who eat it may be poisoned by TTX. Saxitoxin is likewise a seafood threat: it derives from "red tide," a bloom of algae that sometimes affects shellfish. The extremely potent neurotoxin **batrachotoxin**, produced by South American poison arrow frogs, has the reverse effect and forces Na+ channels to stay open, with equally lethal results. Scorpions are a rich source of channel-specific toxins; some species produce toxins that specifically block Na+ channels, while others target K+ channels.

Tiny quantities of any of these toxins can dramatically impede the ability of neurons to function. However, the same specificity that makes channel toxins so deadly also makes them use-ful tools in the laboratory. For example, the venom of the tarantula spider contains toxins that very specifically target the voltage sensor of certain voltage-gated ion channels; in the lab, these toxins provided important clues about how those channels work (S.-Y. Lee and MacKinnon, 2004).

Blocking channels isn't always a bad thing. Local anesthetics like lidocaine can be injected into nerves to block voltage-gated sodium channels, stopping action potentials that would otherwise signal pain to the brain. Some visits to the dentist are much more pleasant because of the temporary blockage of *those* channels.

channelopathy   A genetic abnormality of ion channels, causing a variety of symptoms.

tetrodotoxin (TTX)   A toxin from puffer fish ovaries that blocks the voltage-gated sodium channel, preventing action potential conduction.

saxitoxin (STX)   An animal toxin that blocks sodium channels when applied to the outer surface of the cell membrane.

batrachotoxin   A toxin, secreted by poison arrow frogs, that selectively interferes with Na+ channels.

Synapses Cause Graded, Local Changes in the Postsynaptic Membrane Potential

So what is the point of a neuron generating an action potential? The action potential is propagated down the axon, and as the axon splits into many different branches, the action potential is re-created in each axon branch until it reaches the terminal of each branch. The electrical signal of the action potential is converted into a chemical

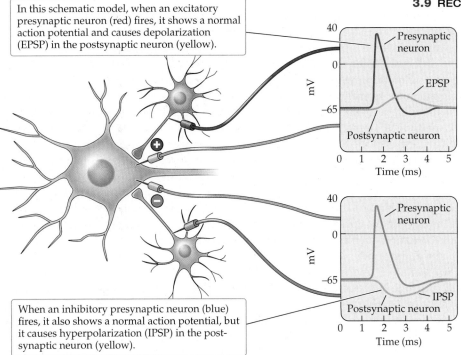

In this schematic model, when an excitatory presynaptic neuron (red) fires, it shows a normal action potential and causes depolarization (EPSP) in the postsynaptic neuron (yellow).

When an inhibitory presynaptic neuron (blue) fires, it also shows a normal action potential, but it causes hyperpolarization (IPSP) in the post-synaptic neuron (yellow).

signal as the axon terminal releases a **neurotransmitter**, a chemical released from a presynaptic terminal that serves to communicate with the postsynaptic cell.

Now we need to understand how neurotransmitters affect the electrical properties of a postsynaptic neuron.

Synapses can be excitatory or inhibitory

Neurotransmitters released into synapses briefly alter the membrane potential of the postsynaptic cell. We call these brief changes **postsynaptic potentials**. A given neuron, receiving synapses from hundreds of other cells, is subject to hundreds or thousands of postsynaptic potentials. When integrated, this massive array of local potentials determines whether the neuron will reach threshold and therefore generate an action potential of its own.

We can study postsynaptic potentials with a setup like that shown in **FIGURE 3.9**. This setup enables us to compare the effects of excitatory versus inhibitory synapses on the local membrane potential of a postsynaptic cell. The responses of the presynaptic and postsynaptic cells are shown on the same graphs in Figure 3.9 for easy comparison of their timing. It is important to remember that excitatory and inhibitory neurons get their names from their actions on *postsynaptic neurons*, not from their effects on behavior.

Stimulation of a presynaptic neuron (red) causes it to produce an all-or-none action potential that spreads to the end of the axon, releasing transmitter. After a brief delay, the postsynaptic cell (yellow) displays a small local depolarization, as Na+ channels open to let the cations in. This local postsynaptic membrane depolarization is known as an **excitatory postsynaptic potential** (**EPSP**) because it pushes the postsynaptic cell a little closer to the threshold for an action potential. Thus the red neuron forms an excitatory synapse upon the yellow target neuron.

Generally, the combined effect of many excitatory synapses is needed to elicit an action potential in a postsynaptic neuron. If EPSPs are elicited by many neurons that converge on the postsynaptic cell, these potentials can produce a depolarization large enough to reach threshold and trigger an action potential. Note that there is a delay: in the fastest cases, the postsynaptic depolarization begins about half a millisecond after the action potential arrives at the presynaptic terminal. This **synaptic delay** reflects the time needed for the neurotransmitter to be released and diffuse across the synapse.

neurotransmitter Also called *synaptic transmitter*, *chemical transmitter*, or simply *transmitter*. The chemical released from the presynaptic axon terminal that serves as the basis of communication between neurons.

postsynaptic potential A local potential that is initiated by stimulation at a synapse, can vary in amplitude, and spreads passively across the cell membrane, decreasing in strength with time and distance.

excitatory postsynaptic potential (EPSP) A depolarizing potential in the postsynaptic neuron that is caused by excitatory connections. EPSPs increase the probability that the postsynaptic neuron will fire an action potential.

synaptic delay The brief delay between the arrival of an action potential at the axon terminal and the creation of a postsynaptic potential.

inhibitory postsynaptic potential (IPSP) A hyperpolarizing potential in the postsynaptic neuron that is caused by inhibitory connections. IPSPs decrease the probability that the postsynaptic neuron will fire an action potential.

chloride ion (Cl⁻) A chlorine atom that carries a negative charge because it has gained one electron.

The action potential of another presynaptic neuron (the blue cell in Figure 3.9) looks exactly like that of the excitatory presynaptic neuron; all neurons use the same kind of propagated signal. But the effect of this neuron on the *post*synaptic cell is quite different. When the blue neuron fires, the postsynaptic effect is an *increase* of the resting membrane potential. This hyperpolarization moves the cell membrane potential away from threshold—*decreasing* the probability that the neuron will fire an action potential—so it is called an **inhibitory postsynaptic potential (IPSP)**.

Usually IPSPs result from the opening of channels that permit **chloride ions (Cl⁻)** to enter the cell. Because Cl⁻ ions are much more concentrated outside the cell than inside (see Figure 3.4), they rush into the cell, making it even more negative. Although in this discussion we have been paying more attention to excitation, inhibition also plays a vital role in the neural processing of information. Just as driving a car requires brakes as well as an accelerator, neural switches must be turned off as well as on. The nervous system treads a narrow path between overexcitation, which leads to seizures such as those that plagued Deidre, and underexcitation, which leads to coma and death.

So, excitatory and inhibitory presynaptic neurons both work in the same way, with only one exception: they have opposite effects on the postsynaptic cell. What determines whether a synapse excites or inhibits the postsynaptic cell? One factor is the particular neurotransmitter released by the presynaptic cell. Some transmitters generate an EPSP in the postsynaptic cells; others generate an IPSP. Plus, as we'll see in Chapter 4, the same neurotransmitter may be excitatory at one synapse and inhibitory at another, depending on the receptors present in the postsynaptic cell.

Whether a neuron fires an action potential at any given moment is decided by the balance between the number of excitatory and the number of inhibitory signals that it is receiving, so let's talk about that next.

Spatial summation and temporal summation integrate synaptic inputs

Complex behavior requires neurons to integrate and transform the messages they receive. In other words, they perform *information processing*: using a sort of neural algebra, each neuron adds and subtracts the myriad inputs it receives from other neurons. These operations are possible because of the characteristics of synaptic inputs, the way in which the neuron integrates the postsynaptic potentials, and the trigger mechanism that determines whether a neuron will fire an action potential.

Postsynaptic potentials are caused by transmitter chemicals that can be either depolarizing (excitatory) or hyperpolarizing (inhibitory). From their points of origin on the dendrites and cell body, these graded EPSPs and IPSPs spread passively over the neuron, decreasing in strength over time and distance. Whether the postsynaptic neuron will fire an action potential is determined by whether a depolarization exceeding threshold reaches the portion of the axon just beyond the hillock, where action potentials begin.

The model in **FIGURE 3.10** illustrates the process of information processing by a neuron. The presynaptic terminals provide excitatory (depolarizing) or inhibitory (hyperpolarizing) stimulation to the postsynaptic cell membrane. An electrode can detect the integrated membrane potential at the axon hillock; if the membrane potential rises (depolarizes) above a threshold level, an action potential is fired.

Suppose two excitatory terminals are activated, as shown in **FIGURE 3.10A**, causing local depolarizations (in red) of the cell body. These depolarizations spread out over the neuron, dissipating as they spread, so only a small proportion of the original depolarization reaches the axon hillock. Taken alone, neither would be sufficient to reach threshold depolarization, but when they both arrive at about the same time, the two depolarizations sum to push the membrane potential of the hillock region to threshold.

FIGURE 3.10B shows what happens when inhibitory synapses also are active, creating postsynaptic hyperpolarizations. These hyperpolarizations also spread passively, dissipating as they travel. Because some potentials excite and others inhibit

(A) Excitatory inputs cause the cell to fire

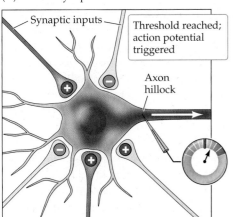

Synaptic inputs

Threshold reached; action potential triggered

Axon hillock

(B) Inhibition also plays a role

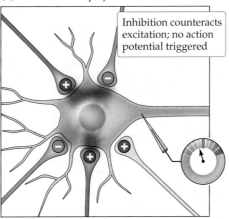

Inhibition counteracts excitation; no action potential triggered

(C) The cell integrates excitation and inhibition

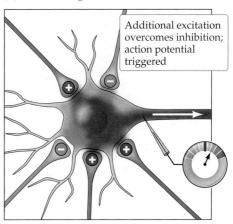

Additional excitation overcomes inhibition; action potential triggered

3.10 INTEGRATION OF EXCITATORY AND INHIBITORY INPUTS

the hillock, these effects partially cancel each other. Thus, the net effect is the difference between the two: the neuron subtracts the IPSPs from the EPSPs and no action potential arises. Simple arithmetic, right?

When summed, EPSPs and IPSPs do tend to cancel each other out. But because postsynaptic potentials spread passively and dissipate as they cross the cell membrane, the resulting sum is also influenced by *distance*. For example, simultaneous EPSPs from two synapses close to the hillock will produce a larger sum there than will two EPSPs from farther away. Only if the overall sum of *all* the potentials—both EPSPs and IPSPs—is sufficient to depolarize the cell to threshold at the axon hillock is an action potential triggered (**FIGURE 3.10C**). Usually the convergence of excitatory messages from many presynaptic neurons is required for a neuron to fire an action potential. This summation of potentials from different physical locations across the cell body is called **spatial summation** (**FIGURE 3.11A**).

Postsynaptic effects that are not absolutely simultaneous can also be summed, because the postsynaptic potentials last a few milliseconds before fading away. The closer they are in time, the greater is the overlap and the more complete is the sum-

spatial summation The summation at the axon hillock of postsynaptic potentials from across the cell body. If this summation reaches threshold, an action potential is triggered.

Go to Animation 3.5
Spatial Summation
bn8e.com/3.5

(A) Spatial summation

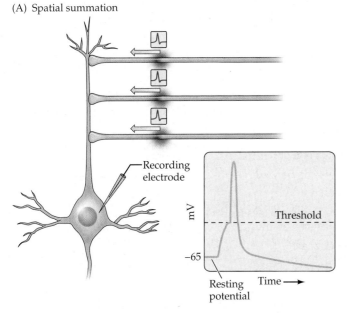

Recording electrode

mV

Threshold

−65

Resting potential

Time →

(B) Temporal summation

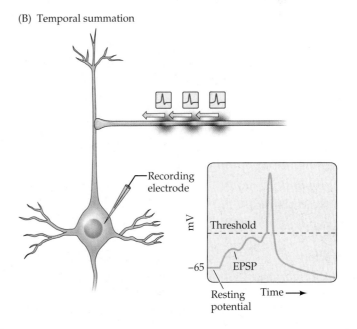

Recording electrode

mV

Threshold

−65 — EPSP

Resting potential

Time →

3.11 SPATIAL VERSUS TEMPORAL SUMMATION

temporal summation The summation of postsynaptic potentials that reach the axon hillock at different times. The closer in time the potentials occur, the more complete the summation.

mation, which in this case is called **temporal summation**. Temporal summation is easily understood if you imagine a neuron with only one input. If EPSPs arrive one right after the other, they sum and the postsynaptic cell eventually reaches threshold and produces an action potential (**FIGURE 3.11B**). If too much time passes between EPSPs, each will fade away before the next occurs, and the neuron will never fire. Likewise, EPSPs from two different synapses may push the target to fire if they arrive at nearly the same time (they sum temporally) but will not if the second arrives after the first EPSP has faded away.

It should now be clear that, although action potentials are all-or-none phenomena, the overall postsynaptic effect is graded in size. The membrane potential at the axon hillock thus reflects the moment-to-moment integration of all the neuron's inputs, which the axon encodes into an ongoing pattern of action potentials.

Dendrites add to the story of neuronal integration. A vast number of synaptic inputs, arrayed across the dendrites and cell body, can induce postsynaptic potentials. Dendrites therefore augment the receptive surface of the neuron and increase the amount of information that the neuron can take in. All other things being equal, the farther out on a dendrite a potential is produced, the less effect the potential should have at the axon hillock, because the potential decreases in amplitude (i.e., strength) as it passively spreads. When the potential arises at a dendritic spine, its effect is further reduced because it has to spread down the shaft of the spine. Thus, information arriving at various parts of the neuron is weighted in terms of the distance and path resistance to the axon hillock.

Interestingly, in some types of neurons, synapses that are distant from the axon hillock compensate by producing larger postsynaptic potentials. These large local potentials boost the effectiveness of the synapse on the integration process occurring at the axon, making distant synapses more comparable to nearer synapses. Furthermore, some neurons have *dendritic* integration zones, featuring voltage-gated ion channels, which sum and amplify local postsynaptic potentials, increasing their eventual impact at the axon hillock (S. R. Williams and Stuart, 2003). And finally, glial cells also play a role in synaptic transmission: they increase the strength of the postsynaptic potential (Pfrieger and Barres, 1997), overlying the presynaptic terminal and thereby preventing neurotransmitter from leaking out of the synaptic cleft.

TABLE 3.1 summarizes the many properties of action potentials, EPSPs, and IPSPs, noting the principal similarities and differences among the three kinds of neural potentials. Now let's look in detail at how the electrical signal arriving at the presynaptic terminal sends a chemical signal to the postsynaptic cell.

TABLE 3.1 Characteristics of Electrical Signals of Nerve Cells

CHARACTERISTIC	ACTION POTENTIAL	TYPE OF SIGNAL	
		EXCITATORY POSTSYNAPTIC POTENTIAL (EPSP)	INHIBITORY POSTSYNAPTIC POTENTIAL (IPSP)
Location	Axon	Dendrites and soma	Dendrites and soma
Signaling role	Conduction along an axon	Transmission between neurons	Transmission between neurons
Typical duration (ms)	1–2	10–100	10–100
Amplitude	Overshooting, 100 mV	Depolarizing, from less than 1 to more than 20 mV	Hyperpolarizing, from less than 1 to about 15 mV
Character	All-or-none, digital	Graded, analog	Graded, analog
Mode of propagation	Actively propagated, regenerative	Local, passive spread	Local, passive spread
Ion channel opening	First Na^+, then K^+, in different channels	Na^+–K^+	Cl^-–K^+
Channel sensitive to:	Voltage (depolarization)	Chemical (neurotransmitter)	Chemical (neurotransmitter)

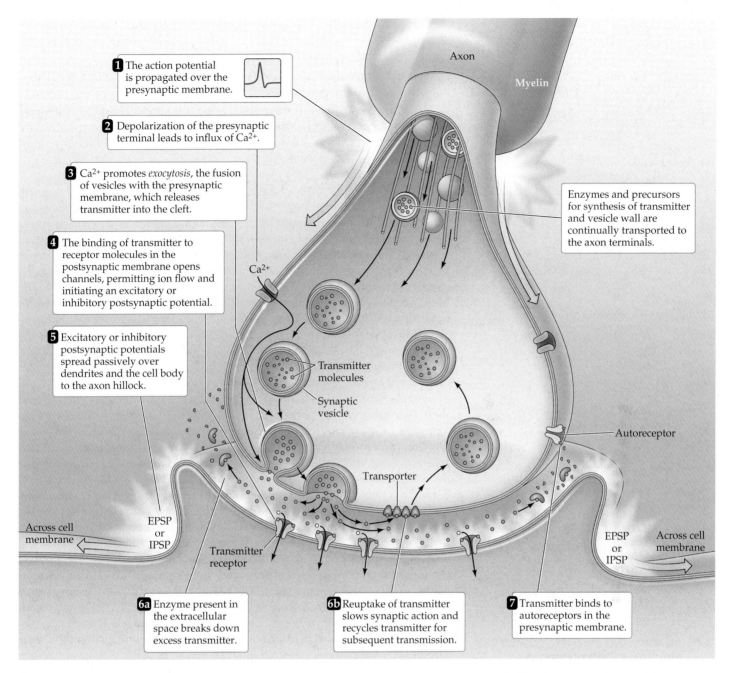

1 The action potential is propagated over the presynaptic membrane.

2 Depolarization of the presynaptic terminal leads to influx of Ca²⁺.

3 Ca²⁺ promotes *exocytosis*, the fusion of vesicles with the presynaptic membrane, which releases transmitter into the cleft.

4 The binding of transmitter to receptor molecules in the postsynaptic membrane opens channels, permitting ion flow and initiating an excitatory or inhibitory postsynaptic potential.

5 Excitatory or inhibitory postsynaptic potentials spread passively over dendrites and the cell body to the axon hillock.

Axon

Myelin

Enzymes and precursors for synthesis of transmitter and vesicle wall are continually transported to the axon terminals.

Ca²⁺

Transmitter molecules

Synaptic vesicle

Autoreceptor

Transporter

Across cell membrane

EPSP or IPSP

Transmitter receptor

EPSP or IPSP

Across cell membrane

6a Enzyme present in the extracellular space breaks down excess transmitter.

6b Reuptake of transmitter slows synaptic action and recycles transmitter for subsequent transmission.

7 Transmitter binds to autoreceptors in the presynaptic membrane.

3.12 STEPS IN TRANSMISSION AT A CHEMICAL SYNAPSE

Synaptic Transmission Requires a Sequence of Events

The transfer of information across a synapse is called *synaptic transmission*. Here's a preview of the steps depicted in **FIGURE 3.12**:

1. The action potential traveling down the axon arrives at the axon terminal.

2. This depolarization opens voltage-gated calcium channels in the membrane of the axon terminal, allowing calcium ions (Ca²⁺) to enter the terminal.

3. The Ca²⁺ causes synaptic vesicles filled with neurotransmitter to fuse with the presynaptic membrane and rupture, releasing the transmitter molecules into the synaptic cleft.

4. Transmitter molecules cross the cleft to bind to special receptor molecules in the postsynaptic membrane, leading to the opening of ion channels in the postsynaptic membrane.

5. This ion flow creates a local EPSP or IPSP in the postsynaptic neuron.

Go to Animation 3.6
Synaptic Transmission
bn8e.com/3.6

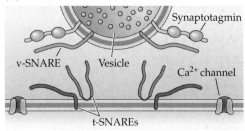

(A) Undocked vesicle

Synaptotagmin

v-SNARE   Vesicle

Ca²⁺ channel

t-SNAREs

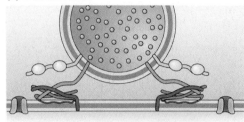

(B) Docked vesicle

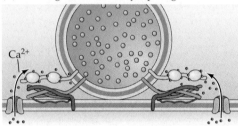

(C) Entering Ca²⁺ binds to synaptotagmin.

Ca²⁺

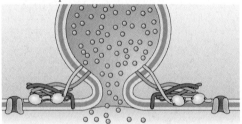

(D) Ca²⁺-bound synaptotagmin catalyzes membrane fusion by binding to SNAREs and the plasma membrane.

3.13 SNARES AND SYNAPTOTAGMIN MEDIATE EXOCYTOSIS

exocytosis The process by which a synaptic vesicle fuses with the presynaptic terminal membrane to release neurotransmitter into the synaptic cleft.

v-SNARE Specialized protein anchored to vesicles to aid their fusing to the presynaptic membrane to release neurotransmitter.

t-SNARE Specialized protein anchored to the presynaptic "target" membrane to bind v-SNAREs to dock vesicles, making them ready for release.

synaptotagmin A specialized protein that responds to calcium ions to trigger vesicular exocytosis.

6. Synaptic transmitter is either (a) inactivated (degraded) by enzymes or (b) removed from the synaptic cleft by *transporters*, so the transmission is brief and accurately reflects the activity of the presynaptic cell.

7. Synaptic transmitter may also activate presynaptic *autoreceptors*, regulating future transmitter release.

The IPSPs and EPSPs in the postsynaptic cell spread throughout its interior. If the integration of all the EPSPs and IPSPs depolarizes the axon hillock enough, the postsynaptic neuron will fire an action potential of its own. Now let's examine these steps in detail.

Action potentials cause the release of transmitter molecules into the synaptic cleft

When an action potential reaches a presynaptic terminal, it opens voltage-gated *calcium* channels that allow an influx of calcium ions (Ca²⁺), rather than K⁺ or Na⁺, into the axon terminal. These Ca²⁺ ions activate enzymes that cause vesicles near the presynaptic membrane to fuse with the membrane and discharge their contents into the synaptic cleft (see Figure 3.12, steps 1–3). The higher the frequency of action potentials arriving at the terminal, the greater the influx of Ca²⁺, and the more vesicles that dump transmitter into the synapse. Most synaptic delay is caused by the time needed for Ca²⁺ to enter the terminal and the vesicles to fuse. Both the diffusion of the transmitter across the cleft and the interaction of transmitter molecules with their receptors also take some time.

Synaptic vesicles, which are about 50 nanometers (nm) in diameter, release their neurotransmitter contents by fusing with the presynaptic membrane, in a process called **exocytosis**. Several specialized proteins mediate exocytosis. One family of proteins, called SNAREs, serve as tethers: those attached to vesicles are called **v-SNAREs**, while those attached to the presynaptic membrane are called **t-SNAREs** (the *t* stands for "target"; **FIGURE 3.13A**). When the v-SNARES on the vesicle attach to the t-SNARES, the vesicle is said to be *docked*, ready to be released (**FIGURE 3.13B**). Another protein attached to the vesicle, called **synaptotagmin**, serves as a Ca²⁺ sensor (Zhou et al., 2015). When the action potential arrives at the axon terminal, the incoming Ca²⁺ ions bind and activate synaptotagmin (**FIGURE 3.13C**), which then triggers the final fusion of the vesicular and presynaptic membranes, allowing the neurotransmitter molecules to enter the synaptic cleft (**FIGURE 3.13D**). **Botulinum toxin** (Botox) and **tetanus toxin** both silence synapses by cutting up SNARE proteins, effectively disabling exocytosis and therefore synaptic transmission.

Because all the synaptic vesicles in an axon terminal contain about the same number of molecules of transmitter, estimated to be tens of thousands, each produces about the same change in postsynaptic potential when it ruptures and releases its contents. Typically, an action potential causes the exocytosis of several hundred vesicles at a time.

The presynaptic terminal normally produces and stores enough transmitter to ensure that it is ready for activity. The rate of production of transmitter is governed by enzymes that are manufactured in the neuronal cell body and transported down the axons to the terminals. Intense activity of the neuron reduces the number of available vesicles, but soon more vesicles are produced to replace those that were discharged. In a variation of regular exocytosis, sometimes a vesicle fuses with the postsynaptic membrane just long enough to spill neurotransmitter into the cleft, then pinches off again to return to the presynaptic terminal, a process termed *kiss and run* (Q. Zhang et al., 2009), and there is increasing evidence for a special, ultrafast process of vesicle formation (Watanabe et al., 2014).

Receptor molecules recognize transmitters

The action of a key in a lock is a good analogy for the action of a transmitter on a receptor protein. Just as a particular key can open a door, a molecule of the correct

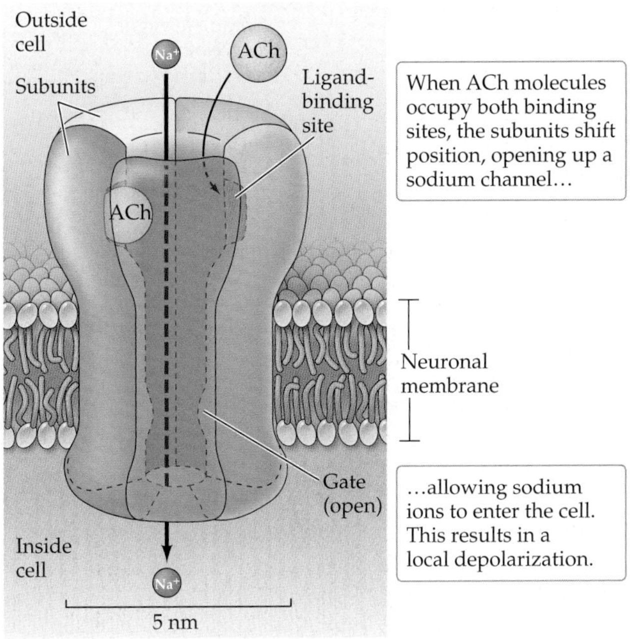

Outside cell

Subunits

Na⁺

ACh

Ligand-binding site

ACh

Inside cell

Na⁺

5 nm

Neuronal membrane

Gate (open)

When ACh molecules occupy both binding sites, the subunits shift position, opening up a sodium channel…

…allowing sodium ions to enter the cell. This results in a local depolarization.

3.14 A NICOTINIC ACETYLCHOLINE (ACH) RECEPTOR Each nicotinic ACh receptor consists of five subunits. The two ligand-binding sites normally bind ACh molecules, but they also bind exogenous ligands like nicotine and other nicotinic drugs. The ACh molecule and Na⁺ ions are enlarged here for diagrammatic purposes.

shape, called a **ligand** (see Chapter 4), can fit into a receptor protein and activate or block it. So, for example, at synapses where **acetylcholine (ACh)** is the transmitter, it fits into *ligand-binding sites* in **receptor molecules** located in the postsynaptic membrane.

The nature of the postsynaptic receptors at a given synapse determines the action of the transmitter (see Chapter 4). For example, ACh can function as either an inhibitory or an excitatory neurotransmitter, at different synapses. At excitatory synapses, binding of ACh opens channels for Na⁺ and K⁺ ions (**FIGURE 3.14**). In this way, ACh released onto muscle fibers excites them to contract. At inhibitory synapses, ACh typically acts on a different type of receptor to open channels that allow chloride ions (Cl⁻) to enter, thereby hyperpolarizing the membrane (i.e., making it more negative and so less likely to create an action potential).

The lock-and-key analogy is strengthened by the observation that various chemicals can fit onto receptor proteins and block the entrance of the key. Neurotransmitters and hormones made inside the body are examples of **endogenous ligands**; drugs and toxins from outside the body are **exogenous ligands**. Some exogenous ligands resemble the ingredients of a witches' brew. As an example, consider a couple of potent poisons that block ACh receptors: curare and bungarotoxin. **Curare** is an arrowhead poison, extracted from a plant, that is used by native South Americans. If the hunter hits any part of the prey, the arrow's poison soon blocks ACh receptors on muscles, paralyzing the animal. **Bungarotoxin**, another blocker of ACh receptors, is found in the venom of the banded krait (*Bungarus multicinctus*), a snake native to Asia. This toxin has proven very useful in research because a radioactive label can be attached to molecules of bungarotoxin without causing any change in their function. The labeled bungarotoxin can then be used to study the number, distribution, and functioning of ACh receptor molecules.

Another poison, muscarine, mimics the action of ACh at some synapses. This poison is extracted from the mushroom *Amanita muscaria*. Molecules such as muscarine and nicotine that act like a transmitter at a receptor are called **agonists** (from the Greek *agon*, "contest" or "struggle") of that transmitter. Conversely, molecules that interfere with or prevent the action of a transmitter—in the manner that curare or bungarotoxin blocks the action of ACh—are called **antagonists**. We'll learn more about agonists and antagonists in Chapter 4.

Just as there are master keys that fit many different locks, there are submaster keys that fit a certain group of locks. Similarly, each chemical transmitter binds to a

botulinum toxin A toxin that cleaves SNAREs, disabling neurotransmitter release.

tetanus toxin A toxin that cleaves SNAREs, disabling neurotransmitter release.

ligand A substance that binds to receptor molecules, such as those at the surface of the cell.

acetylcholine (ACh) A neurotransmitter produced and released by parasympathetic postganglionic neurons, by motor neurons, and by neurons throughout the brain.

receptor molecule Also called *receptor*. A protein that binds and reacts to molecules of a neurotransmitter or hormone.

endogenous ligand Any substance that is produced within the body and selectively binds to the type of receptor that is under study.

exogenous ligand Any substance that originates outside the body and selectively binds to the type of receptor that is under study.

curare An alkaloid neurotoxin that causes paralysis by blocking acetylcholine receptors in muscle.

bungarotoxin A neurotoxin from the venom of the banded krait that selectively blocks acetylcholine receptors.

agonist A molecule, usually a drug, that binds a receptor molecule and initiates a response like that of another molecule, usually a neurotransmitter.

antagonist A molecule, usually a drug, that interferes with or prevents the action of a transmitter.

3.15 LOEWI'S DEMONSTRATION OF A CHEMICAL MESSENGER

Loewi reasoned that some chemical released into the bath by stimulating the nerve to the first heart must have slowed down the second heart. We now know that chemical is the neurotransmitter acetylcholine (ACh) acting on inhibitory muscarinic receptors in heart muscle.

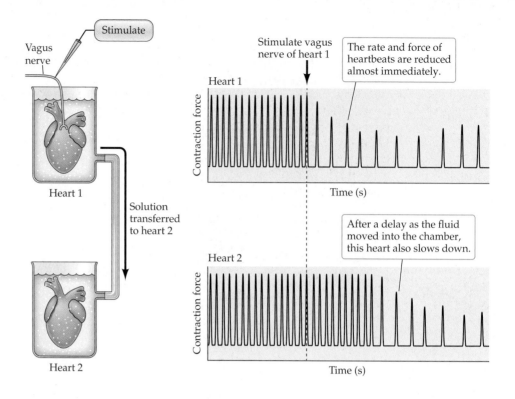

Stimulate

Vagus nerve

Heart 1

Solution transferred to heart 2

Heart 2

Stimulate vagus nerve of heart 1

Heart 1

The rate and force of heartbeats are reduced almost immediately.

Contraction force

Time (s)

After a delay as the fluid moved into the chamber, this heart also slows down.

Heart 2

Contraction force

Time (s)

group of different receptor molecules. ACh acts on at least four kinds of **cholinergic** receptors; nicotinic and muscarinic are the two main kinds.

Most ACh receptors in the brain are muscarinic. Muscarinic cholinergic receptors are also found on organs innervated by the parasympathetic division of the autonomic system (e.g., the intestines, the salivary glands, and heart muscle). These receptors were key to a famous experiment. In the early twentieth century, debate raged over the basic nature of neural communication. The discovery that individual nerve cells contact each other at thousands of points was fresh knowledge. What happened at these synapses to convey information from one cell to the next? How could we find out for sure?

One night in 1921, Otto Loewi (1873–1961) dreamed of a simple experiment that would definitively discriminate between the two candidate modes of transmission—chemical versus electrical. In excitement, Loewi sat up in bed and scribbled a few notes, but in the morning he was disappointed to find the notes indecipherable. When the dream came again the following night, Loewi got up and went straight to the lab, where he performed the experiment while it was still fresh in his mind.

Loewi electrically stimulated the vagus nerve of one frog, which he knew would decrease its heart rate, and collected a sample of the fluid surrounding that frog's heart. Then he bathed a second frog's heart with the fluid sample from the first frog. When the second frog's heart also slowed, Loewi reasoned that the stimulation of the first frog's nerve must have caused the release of a chemical—what Loewi initially called *Vagusstoff* ("substance from the vagus")—into the fluid (**FIGURE 3.15**). Vagusstoff was later found to be ACh. This is how scientists learned that the nervous system, long known to use electrical signals, also uses chemical signals. This breakthrough won Loewi a Nobel Prize in 1936.

Nicotinic cholinergic receptors are found at synapses on muscles and in autonomic ganglia; it is the blockade of these receptors that is responsible for the paralysis caused by curare and bungarotoxin (see Box 3.2). Most nicotinic cholinergic synapses are excitatory, but there are also inhibitory nicotinic synapses (Wersinger and Fuchs, 2011), and there are both excitatory and inhibitory muscarinic synapses, making at least four kinds of acetylcholine receptors. The evolution of many types of receptors for each transmitter enables a given transmitter to have subtly different effects in different parts of the brain.

cholinergic Referring to cells that use acetylcholine as their synaptic transmitter.

The nicotinic ACh receptor resembles a lopsided dumbbell with a tube running down its central axis (see Figure 3.14). The handle of the dumbbell spans the cell membrane (which is about 6 nm thick). The sides of the ion channel that runs through the handle of the receptor consist of five protein subunits arranged like staves in a barrel. Two subunits are alike and, in conjunction with neighboring subunits, provide two recognition sites for ACh (Karlin, 2002); the other three subunits are all different. For the channel to open, both of the ACh-binding sites must be occupied.

After the structure of the nicotinic ACh receptor was determined, similar analyses were carried out for other receptors, including receptors for some other synaptic transmitter molecules such as GABA (gamma-aminobutyric acid), glycine, and glutamate. Several of these receptors resemble each other, suggesting that they all belong to the same family and have a common evolutionary origin.

The coordination of different transmitter systems of the brain is incredibly complex. Each subtype of neurotransmitter receptor has a unique pattern of distribution within the brain. Different receptor systems become active at different times in fetal life. The number of any given type of receptor remains plastic in adulthood: not only are there seasonal variations, but many kinds of receptors show a regular daily variation of 50% or more in number, affecting the sensitivity of cells to the related variety of transmitter. Similarly, the numbers of some receptors have been found to vary with the use of drugs (see Chapter 4). In general, an increase in receptor numbers is referred to as **up-regulation**, and a process that decreases receptor density is called **down-regulation** of that receptor type.

Transmitters bind to receptors, *gating ion channels*

The recognition of transmitter molecules by receptor molecules controls the opening of ion channels in two different ways. **Ionotropic receptors** (**FIGURE 3.16A**) directly control an ion channel. When bound by the transmitter, the ion channel opens and ions flow across the membrane. (Ionotropic receptors are also known as *chemically gated ion channels* or **ligand-gated ion channels**.) **Metabotropic receptors** recognize the synaptic transmitter, but they do not directly control ion channels. Instead, they activate molecules known as **G proteins** (**FIGURE 3.16B**).

up-regulation A compensatory increase in receptor availability at the synapses of a neuron.

down-regulation A compensatory reduction in receptor availability at the synapses of a neuron.

ionotropic receptor A receptor protein that includes an ion channel that is opened when the receptor is bound by an agonist.

ligand-gated ion channel Also called *chemically gated ion channel*. An ion channel that opens or closes in response to the presence of a particular chemical.

metabotropic receptor A receptor protein that does not contain an ion channel but may, when activated, use a G protein system to alter the functioning of the postsynaptic cell.

G proteins A class of proteins that reside next to the intracellular portion of a receptor and that are activated when the receptor binds an appropriate ligand on the extracellular surface.

Go to Animation 3.7
Ionotropic and Metabotropic Receptors
bn8e.com/3.7

(A) Ionotropic receptor (ligand-gated ion channel; fast)

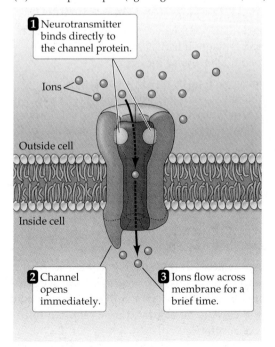

1 Neurotransmitter binds directly to the channel protein.

Ions

Outside cell

Inside cell

2 Channel opens immediately.

3 Ions flow across membrane for a brief time.

(B) Metabotropic receptor (G protein-coupled receptor; slow)

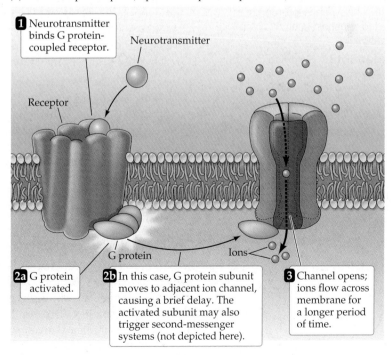

1 Neurotransmitter binds G protein-coupled receptor.

Neurotransmitter

Receptor

G protein

Ions

2a G protein activated.

2b In this case, G protein subunit moves to adjacent ion channel, causing a brief delay. The activated subunit may also trigger second-messenger systems (not depicted here).

3 Channel opens; ions flow across membrane for a longer period of time.

3.16 TWO TYPES OF CHEMICAL SYNAPSES

second messenger A slow-acting substance in the postsynaptic cell that amplifies the effects of synaptic activity and signals synaptic activity within the postsynaptic cell.

degradation The chemical breakdown of a neurotransmitter into inactive metabolites.

reuptake The process by which released synaptic transmitter molecules are taken up and reused by the presynaptic neuron, thus stopping synaptic activity.

transporter Specialized receptor in the presynaptic membrane that recognizes transmitter molecules and returns them to the presynaptic neuron for reuse.

autoreceptor A receptor for a synaptic transmitter that is located in the presynaptic membrane, telling the axon terminal how much transmitter has been released.

axo-dendritic Referring to a synapse in which a presynaptic axon terminal synapses onto a dendrite of the postsynaptic neuron, either via a dendritic spine or directly onto the dendrite itself.

axo-somatic Referring to a synapse in which a presynaptic axon terminal synapses onto the cell body (soma) of the postsynaptic neuron.

axo-axonic Referring to a synapse in which a presynaptic axon terminal synapses onto another axon's terminal.

retrograde synapse A synapse in which a signal (usually a gas neurotransmitter) flows from the postsynaptic neuron to the presynaptic neuron, thus counter to the usual direction of synaptic communication.

dendro-dendritic Referring to a synapse in which a synaptic connection forms between the dendrites of two neurons.

G protein is a convenient designation for proteins that bind the compounds guanosine diphosphate (GDP), guanosine triphosphate (GTP), and other guanine nucleotides. Sometimes the G protein itself acts to open ion channels, as in Figure 3.16B. But in other cases the G protein activates another, internal chemical signal to affect ion channels. If we think of the neurotransmitter as the first, external messenger arriving at the receptor on the cell's surface, then the next chemical signal, activated *inside* the cell, is a **second messenger**. Several different second messengers—such as cyclic adenosine monophosphate (cyclic AMP or cAMP), diacylglycerol, or arachidonic acid—amplify the effect of the first messenger and can initiate processes that lead to changes in electrical potential at the membrane. An important feature of second-messenger systems is their ability to amplify and prolong the synaptic signals that a neuron receives.

About 80% of the known neurotransmitters and hormones activate cellular signal mechanisms through receptors coupled to G proteins, so this coupling device is very important. The G protein is located on the inner side of the neuronal membrane. When a transmitter molecule binds to a receptor that is coupled to a G protein, parts of the G protein complex separate from each other. One part, called the *alpha subunit*, migrates away within the cell and modulates the activity of its target molecules. Depending on the type of cell and receptor, the target may be a second-messenger system, an enzyme that works on an ion channel, or an ion pump. Many combinations of different receptors with different G proteins have already been identified, and more are being discovered at a rapid pace (C. C. Huang and Tesmer, 2011).

The action of synaptic transmitters is stopped rapidly

When a chemical transmitter such as ACh is released into the synaptic cleft, its postsynaptic action is not only prompt but usually very brief as well. This brevity ensures that the message is repeated faithfully. Accurate timing of synaptic transmission is necessary in many neural systems—for example, to drive the rapid cycles of muscle contraction and relaxation essential to many coordinated behaviors.

The prompt cessation of transmitter effects is achieved in one of two ways:

1. *Degradation.* Transmitter can be rapidly broken down and thus inactivated by a special enzyme—a process known as **degradation** (see step 6a in Figure 3.12). For example, the enzyme that inactivates ACh is acetylcholinesterase (AChE). AChE breaks down ACh very rapidly into choline and acetic acid, and these products are recycled (at least in part) to make more ACh in the axon terminal. AChE is found especially at synapses, but also elsewhere in the nervous system. Thus, if any ACh escapes from a synapse where it is released, it is unlikely to reach other synapses intact, where it could start false messages.

2. *Reuptake.* Alternatively, transmitter molecules may be rapidly cleared from the synaptic cleft by being taken up into the presynaptic terminal—a process known as **reuptake** (see step 6b in Figure 3.12). Norepinephrine, dopamine, and serotonin are examples of transmitters whose activity is terminated mainly by reuptake. In these cases, special receptors for the transmitter, called **transporters**, are located on the presynaptic axon terminal and bring the transmitter back inside. Once taken up into the presynaptic terminal, transmitter molecules may be repackaged into newly formed synaptic vesicles. Certain drugs that interfere with reuptake mechanisms are effective in the treatment of depression (see Chapter 16).

Several factors regulate neurotransmitter release

Some neurotransmitter molecules never make it to the postsynaptic membrane. They may bind to receptors on the presynaptic membrane, so-called **autoreceptors** (see Figure 3.12). Through autoreceptors, the presynaptic cell is informed about the net concentration of transmitter in the synaptic cleft and may regulate future neurotransmitter release to adjust that concentration.

For simplicity, we have been focusing on the classic **axo-dendritic** and **axo-somatic** synapses. But many nonclassic forms of chemical synapses exist in the

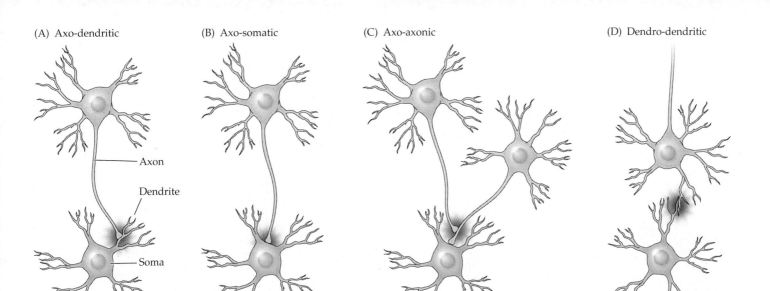

(A) Axo-dendritic (B) Axo-somatic (C) Axo-axonic (D) Dendro-dendritic

Axon

Dendrite

Soma

3.17 DIFFERENT TYPES OF SYNAPTIC CONNECTIONS Most synapses are formed by an axon stimulating a dendrite (A), but axons also sometimes synapse upon cell bodies (B) or even other axons (C). And in some instances, specialized dendrites synapse upon other dendrites (D).

nervous system (**FIGURE 3.17**). As the name implies, **axo-axonic** synapses form on axons, often near the axon terminal, allowing the presynaptic neuron to regulate how much neurotransmitter will be released from the targeted terminal.

At a **retrograde synapse**, transmission starts with classic axo-dendritic synaptic activity, but the postsynaptic cell subsequently releases a gas neurotransmitter, such as carbon monoxide or nitric oxide (see Chapter 4), which signals the presynaptic cell to release more transmitter.

Neurons can also form **dendro-dendritic** contacts, allowing coordination of their activities. Evidence is also mounting that **ectopic transmission** occurs between many neurons; in this mode of transmission, the location of transmitter release and the sites at which the transmitter acts are both well outside the conventional boundaries of nearby synapses (Coggan et al., 2005). And throughout the brain are found axons with regular swellings, called **varicosities**, along their length; like a drip-irrigation system, these **nondirected synapses** steadily release neurotransmitter to broadly affect surrounding areas. Finally, you should know that, in addition to synapses that use chemical neurotransmitters to communicate between cells, there are also electrical synapses between neurons, as we discuss in **BOX 3.3**.

ectopic transmission Cell-cell communication based on release of neurotransmitter in regions outside traditional synapses.

varicosity The axonal swelling from which neurotransmitter diffuses in a nondirected synapse.

nondirected synapse A type of synapse in which the presynaptic and postsynaptic cells are not in close apposition; instead, neurotransmitter is released by axonal varicosities and diffuses away to affect wide regions of tissue.

BOX 3.3

Electrical Synapses Work with No Time Delay

Although we are focusing in this chapter on synapses that require a chemical substance to mediate synaptic transmission, the brain also has widespread *electrical* synapses (Pereda, 2014). At an **electrical synapse** (or *gap junction*) the presynaptic membrane comes even closer to the postsynaptic membrane than it does at a chemical synapse; the gap at an electrical synapse (Figure A) measures only 2–4 nm. In contrast, the synaptic cleft of a chemical synapse is 20–40

nm. At electrical synapses, the facing membranes of the two cells have relatively large channels, called **connexons**, arranged to allow ions to flow from one neuron directly into the other (Figure B). As a consequence, the electrical current that is associated with neural activity in one neuron can flow directly across the gap junction to affect the other neuron.

Transmission at these synapses closely resembles action potential conduction along the axon. Electrical

synapses therefore work with practically no time delay, in contrast to chemical synapses, where the delay is on the order of a millisecond—slow in terms of neurons. Because of the speed of their transmission, electrical synapses are frequently found in neural circuits that mediate escape behaviors in invertebrates. They are also found where many fibers must be activated synchronously, as in the system for moving our eyes.

(continued)

BOX
3.3
Electrical Synapses Work with No Time Delay (continued)

Clinically, it is suspected that electrical synapses contribute to the spread of synchronized seizure discharges in epilepsy (Szente et al., 2002). (Figure A courtesy of Constantino Sotelo.)

electrical synapse Also called *gap junction*. The region between neurons where the membranes are so close that changes in potential can flow from one to the other without being translated into a chemical message.

connexon A protein assembly that provides an open ion channel between two neurons, forming an electrical synapse between them.

(A) Electron micrograph of an electrical synapse

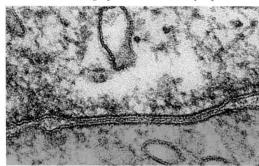

(B) Diagram of an electrical synapse

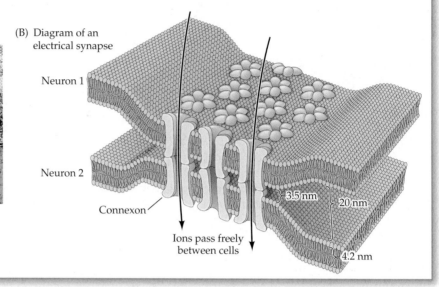

Neuron 1

Neuron 2

Connexon

Ions pass freely between cells

3.5 nm
20 nm
4.2 nm

Neurons and Synapses Combine to Make Circuits

Use of the term *circuit* for a group of neurons and their synaptic interconnections is an analogy to electrical circuits, in which an arrangement of components (e.g., resistors, capacitors, transistors, and their connecting wires) accomplishes a particular function. Electrical circuits can represent signals in either analog or digital ways—that is, in terms of continuously varying values or in terms of integers. Neurons similarly feature two kinds of processes: analog-like signals that vary in strength (such as graded potentials at synapses) and digital-like, all-or-none signals (such as action potentials) that vary in frequency. The nervous system comprises many different types of neural circuits to accomplish basic functions in cognition, emotion, and action—all the categories of behavior and experience.

The simplest neural circuit that is routinely encountered in the nervous system is the **neural chain**, a straightforward linking of a series of neurons. (A look at some other simple neural circuits is presented on the website in A Step Further: Circuits of Neurons Process Information.) From the seventeenth century until well into the twentieth century, most attempts to understand behavior in neural terms were based on chains of neurons, which do indeed account for some behaviors.

For example, the basic circuit for the stretch reflex, such as the **knee-jerk reflex**, consists of a sensory neuron, a motor neuron, and a single synapse where the sensory neuron communicates with the motor neuron. **FIGURE 3.18** details the sequence and timing of events in the knee-jerk reflex. Note that this reflex is extremely rapid: only about 40 ms elapse between the stimulus and the initiation of the response. Three factors account for this rapidity: (1) both the sensory and the motor axons involved are myelinated and of large diameter, so they conduct rapidly; (2) the sensory cells synapse directly on the motor neurons; and (3) both the central synapse and the neuromuscular junction are fast, ionotropic synapses.

For some purposes the afferent (input) parts of the visual system can be represented as a neural chain (**FIGURE 3.19A**) (in reality, however, the retina contains many kinds of neural circuits, which we will discuss in Chapter 10). A more accurate schematic diagram of the visual system (**FIGURE 3.19B**) highlights two other features that are common to many kinds of neural circuits: **convergence** and

neural chain A simple kind of neural circuit in which neurons are attached linearly, end to end.

knee-jerk reflex A variant of the stretch reflex in which stretching of the tendon below the knee leads to an upward kick of the leg.

convergence The phenomenon of neural connections in which many cells send signals to a single cell.

divergence The phenomenon of neural connections in which one cell sends signals to many other cells.

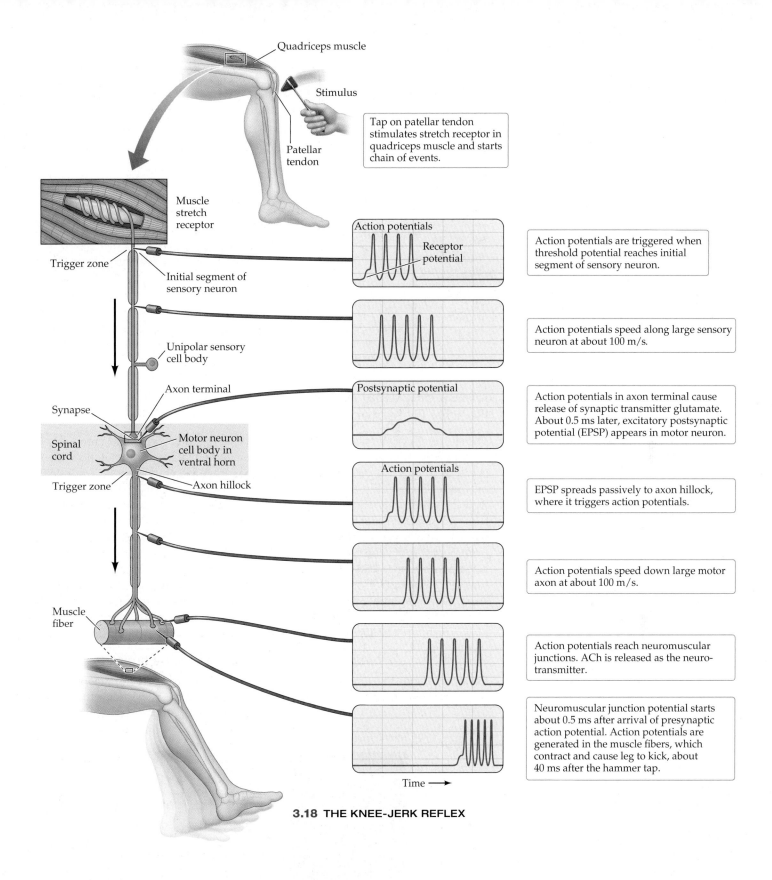

Quadriceps muscle

Stimulus

Patellar tendon

Tap on patellar tendon stimulates stretch receptor in quadriceps muscle and starts chain of events.

Muscle stretch receptor

Trigger zone

Initial segment of sensory neuron

Unipolar sensory cell body

Axon terminal

Synapse

Spinal cord

Motor neuron cell body in ventral horn

Trigger zone

Axon hillock

Muscle fiber

Action potentials

Receptor potential

Postsynaptic potential

Action potentials

Time ⟶

Action potentials are triggered when threshold potential reaches initial segment of sensory neuron.

Action potentials speed along large sensory neuron at about 100 m/s.

Action potentials in axon terminal cause release of synaptic transmitter glutamate. About 0.5 ms later, excitatory postsynaptic potential (EPSP) appears in motor neuron.

EPSP spreads passively to axon hillock, where it triggers action potentials.

Action potentials speed down large motor axon at about 100 m/s.

Action potentials reach neuromuscular junctions. ACh is released as the neurotransmitter.

Neuromuscular junction potential starts about 0.5 ms after arrival of presynaptic action potential. Action potentials are generated in the muscle fibers, which contract and cause leg to kick, about 40 ms after the hammer tap.

3.18 THE KNEE-JERK REFLEX

divergence. In many parts of the nervous system, the axons from large numbers of neurons converge on a small number of cells; in each human eye, about 100 million receptor cells concentrate their information on about 1 million axons that carry the information from the eye to the brain (see Figure 3.19B). Higher in the visual system there is much divergence; the 1 million axons of the optic nerve communicate to billions of neurons in several different specialized regions of the cerebral cortex.

3.19 TWO REPRESENTATIONS OF NEURAL CIRCUITRY (A) This simple representation shows the input part of the visual system. (B) This more realistic representation illustrates convergence and divergence.

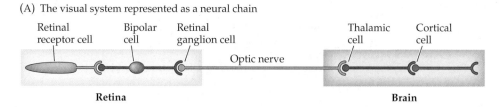

(A) The visual system represented as a neural chain

Retinal receptor cell Bipolar cell Retinal ganglion cell Optic nerve Thalamic cell Cortical cell

Retina Brain

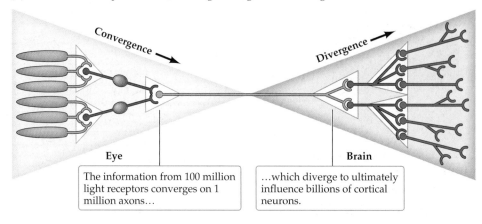

(B) A more realistic representation, showing convergence and divergence

Convergence Divergence

Eye Brain

The information from 100 million light receptors converges on 1 million axons…

…which diverge to ultimately influence billions of cortical neurons.

Gross Electrical Activity of the Brain Is Readily Detected

electroencephalogram (EEG) A recording of gross electrical activity of the brain recorded from electrodes placed on the scalp.

epilepsy A brain disorder marked by major sudden changes in the electrophysiological state of the brain that are referred to as seizures.

The electrical activity of millions of cells working together combines to produce electrical potentials large enough that we can detect them at the surface of the skull. Recordings of electrical activity in the brain that are made with large electrodes either on the scalp or within the brain can provide useful glimpses of the simultaneous workings of large populations of neurons (Buzsáki et al., 2012). Investigators divide these gross brain potentials into two principal classes: those that appear spontaneously without specific stimulation, and those that are evoked by particular stimuli.

A recording of spontaneous brain potentials, or *brain waves*, is called an **electroencephalogram (EEG)** (**FIGURE 3.20**). As we will see in Chapter 14, EEG recordings of a sleeping person allow investigators to detect different kinds and stages of sleep. Brain potentials also provide significant diagnostic data—for example, they may offer predictions about the functional effects of brain injury. EEGs also help distinguish types of seizure disorders, as we discuss next.

Seizure disorders result from electrical storms in the brain

Epilepsy (from the Greek *epilepsia*, a form of the verb meaning "to seize") has provoked wonder and worry since the dawn of civilization. Through the ages the

3.20 GROSS POTENTIALS OF THE HUMAN NERVOUS SYSTEM (Top left) Electrode array for EEG recording. (Bottom left) Each electrode can be assigned a letter on a map of the scalp. (Right) Typical EEG recordings showing potential measured between various points on the scalp.

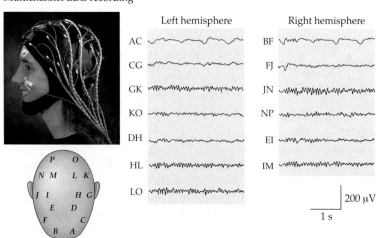

Multichannel EEG recording

Left hemisphere   Right hemisphere

AC   BF
CG   FJ
GK   JN
KO   NP
DH   EI
HL   IM
LO

200 μV
1 s

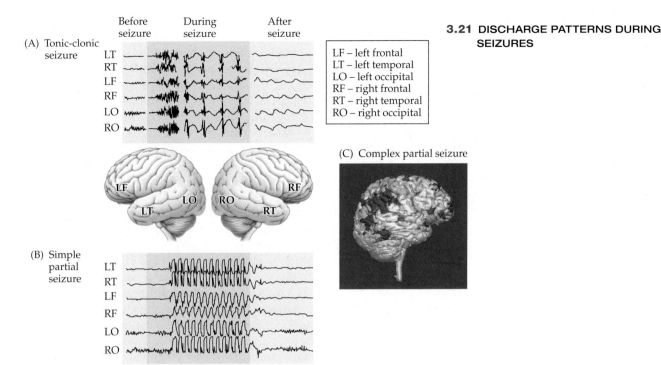

(A) Tonic-clonic seizure

Before seizure
During seizure
After seizure

LT
RT
LF
RF
LO
RO

LF – left frontal
LT – left temporal
LO – left occipital
RF – right frontal
RT – right temporal
RO – right occipital

(C) Complex partial seizure

(B) Simple partial seizure

LT
RT
LF
RF
LO
RO

seizures that accompany this disease have spawned much speculation about the cause—from demons to gods. At least 50 million people, worldwide, suffer from epilepsy (Behr et al., 2016).

Seizures are an unfortunate manifestation of the electrical character of the nervous system. Because of the extensive connections among nerve cells, the brain can generate massive waves of intense nerve cell activity that seem to involve almost the entire brain. In the normal, active brain, electrical activity tends to be desynchronized; that is, different brain regions carry on their functions more or less independently. In contrast, a **seizure** features widespread synchronization of electrical activity: broad swaths of the brain start firing in simultaneous waves of excitation, which are evident in the EEGs as an abnormal "spike-and-wave" pattern of brain activity. Many abnormalities of the brain, such as trauma, injury, or metabolic problems, can predispose brain tissue to produce synchronized epileptiform activity, which can easily spread.

There are several major categories of seizure disorders. Generalized seizures are characterized by loss of consciousness and symmetrical involvement of body musculature. In **tonic-clonic seizures** (previously known as *grand mal seizures*), abnormal EEG activity is evident all over the brain (**FIGURE 3.21A**). The person loses consciousness and makes characteristic movements: an enduring *tonic* contraction of the muscles for 1 or 2 minutes, followed by jerky, rhythmic *clonic* contractions and relaxations. Minutes or hours of confusion and sleep follow the seizure.

Simple partial seizures (also known as *absence attacks*) are a more subtle variant of generalized seizures, in which the characteristic spike-and-wave EEG activity is evident for 5–15 seconds at a time (**FIGURE 3.21B**), sometimes occurring many times per day. The person is unaware of the environment during these periods, and later cannot recall events that occurred during the simple partial episode. Behaviorally, the person does not show unusual muscle activity, except for a cessation of ongoing activity and sustained staring.

Complex partial seizures do not involve the entire brain and thus can produce a wide variety of symptoms, often preceded by an unusual sensation, or **aura**. In one example, a woman felt an unusual sensation in the abdomen, a sense of foreboding, and tingling in both hands before the seizure spread. At the height of it, she was unresponsive and rocked her body back and forth while speaking nonsensically, twisting her left arm, and looking toward the right. **FIGURE 3.21C** is a three-dimensional reconstruction showing where the seizures occurred in her brain. In some individuals, complex partial

seizure An epileptic episode.

tonic-clonic seizure Also called *grand mal seizure*. A type of generalized epileptic seizure in which nerve cells fire in high-frequency bursts.

simple partial seizure Also called *absence attack*. A seizure that is characterized by a spike-and-wave EEG and often involves a loss of awareness and inability to recall events surrounding the seizure.

complex partial seizure In epilepsy, a type of seizure that doesn't involve the entire brain and therefore can cause a wide variety of symptoms.

aura In epilepsy, the unusual sensations or premonition that may precede the beginning of a seizure.

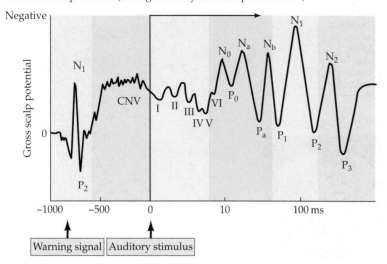

Event-related potentials (average of many stimulus presentations)

Warning signal   Auditory stimulus

3.22 EVENT-RELATED POTENTIALS Following stimulus presentation, a fixed sequence of processing-related potentials is generated. Early components (labeled I–VI) are associated with brainstem activity, followed by large-amplitude negative- and positive-voltage events (labeled N_0–N_2 and P_0–P_3). The later-appearing components are associated with cognitive processing in the cortex.

kindling A method of experimentally inducing an epileptic seizure by repeatedly stimulating a brain region.

event-related potential (ERP) Also called *evoked potential*. Averaged EEG recordings measuring brain responses to repeated presentations of a stimulus.

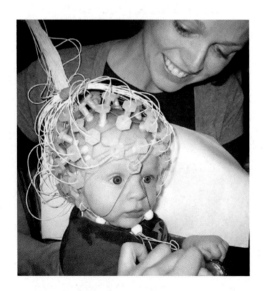

3.23 DID YOU HEAR THAT? If this infant's hearing is normal, presentation of sounds should evoke an ERP from auditory centers in her (his) brain. (Courtesy of Drs. Brett Martin, Jen Gerometta, and Christine Rota-Donahue.)

seizures may be provoked by environmental stimuli and may produce strikingly abnormal behavior.

Seizures affect nonhuman animals too, and such cases are studied as a model of human epilepsy. In **kindling** (McNamara, 1984), animals receive repeated electrical stimulation that is too weak to cause a seizure on its own. Although the individual stimuli are small, eventually their effects accumulate to cause spontaneous seizures. In other words, the kindling stimulations somehow change the tissue and make it more epilepsy-prone. Interestingly, after years of epilepsy some human patients develop multiple foci for the initiation of seizures, perhaps because of a kindling process (Avanzini et al., 2013).

Many seizure disorders can be effectively controlled with the aid of antiepileptic drugs. Although these drugs have a wide variety of different targets, they have in common a tendency to selectively modulate the excitability of neurons, either by counteracting problems with ionic balance (see Box 3.1) or by promoting inhibitory processes (Rogawski and Löscher, 2004). As we learned in Chapter 2, in serious cases of epilepsy that don't respond to medication, the patient may choose to determine the part of the brain where the seizures begin and have it surgically removed. This was the case with Deidre, whom we met at the start of the chapter.

Event-related potentials measure changes resulting from discrete stimuli

Gross potential changes evoked by discrete sensory stimuli, such as light flashes or clicks, are called **event-related potentials** (**ERPs**) (**FIGURE 3.22**). Typically, many ERPs are averaged to obtain a reliable estimate of stimulus-elicited brain activity. Sensory-evoked potentials have very distinctive characteristics of wave shape and latency (time delay) that reflect the type of stimulus, the state of the subject, and the site of recording.

Computer techniques enable researchers to record brain potentials using electrodes that are located far from the sites at which the potentials are generated. For example, *auditory-evoked potentials from the brainstem* (see Figure 3.22) can be recorded through electrodes on the scalp. Decreases in the amplitude of certain waves or increases in their latency have been valuable for the detection of hearing impairments in very young children and noncommunicative persons (**FIGURE 3.23**). Infants with impaired hearing produce reduced auditory ERPs or no ERP at all in response to sounds. ERPs are also used in the assessment of brainstem injury or damage.

The long-latency components of scalp-recorded ERPs reflect the operation of information-processing mechanisms of the brain, such as attention, decision-making, and other complex cognitive processes, as we'll discuss in Chapter 18. In contrast, short-latency responses are determined more by exogenous factors, such as the physical characteristics of the stimulus. For example, dimensions like stimulus intensity have a bigger effect on early components of ERPs than on longer-latency components.

Although it is usually difficult to localize which brain region has produced a given component of the ERP, such changes are detected quickly, within a fraction of a second. In contrast, computer-coordinated imaging of brain activity, such as functional MRI (fMRI) (see Chapter 2), indicates clearly which brain region is active, but because such imaging techniques must average activity over seconds or minutes, they are slower than ERPs. Perhaps the greatest promise for future research is a melding of the two techniques—combining techniques that measure rapid changes in electrical activity, such as ERPs and magnetoencephalography (MEG) (see Chapter 2), with slower but higher-resolution techniques such as fMRI or PET scans to identify probable sites of origin of the evoked activity (Vitali et al., 2015). These techniques have given us a better glimpse of brain functioning than Otto Loewi ever dreamed of.

▌ The Cutting Edge

Optogenetics: Using Light to Probe Brain-Behavior Relationships

At the frontier in neurophysiology is the use of remarkable new tools to precisely stimulate or inhibit electrical activity in the brain. **Optogenetics** uses genetic tools to insert light-sensitive ion channels into neurons so that stimulating the brain with light, delivered by fiber-optic cables, can excite or inhibit those targeted neurons (Tye and Deisseroth, 2012). This breakthrough was made possible by the discovery that various microbial organisms, such as some algae and bacteria, produce light-sensitive proteins called *opsins*, which resemble the mammalian opsins found in light-receptor cells in our eye. Unlike those mammalian opsins underlying vision, which rely on other signaling proteins that we'll describe in Chapter 10, these microbial opsins can themselves open an ion channel in response to light. The first opsin that was studied, **channelrhodopsin**, responds to blue light by allowing Na+ ions to enter the cell, depolarizing it (Kato et al., 2012). Another example is **halorhodopsin**, which when stimulated by yellow light, pumps Cl− ions into the cell, hyperpolarizing it (F. Zhang et al., 2007) (**FIGURE 3.24**).

In the microbes that first made them, these opsins guide light-directed growth. But when neurons are induced to make these opsins, it becomes possible to excite or inhibit the neuron's electrical activity simply by shining a blue or yellow light on the cell, respectively. For example, a scientist might inject into one part of an animal's brain a virus that has been engineered to infect neurons and cause them to make channelrhodopsin. Then a tiny fiber-optic probe can be surgically implanted to provide light stimulation to that same region. When the animal recovers, it can move freely about, and whenever the investigator chooses to direct light to the end of the probe, those neurons will fire (**FIGURE 3.25A**).

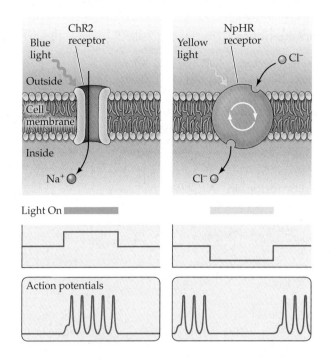

3.24 OPTOGENETIC PROTEINS The protein called *channelrhodopsin* (ChR2), when stimulated by blue light, opens up a channel to let Na+ ions into the neuron, depolarizing it to cause it to fire. In contrast, halorhodopsin (NpHR), in response to yellow light, pumps Cl− ions into the neuron, hyperpolarizing it and preventing it from reaching threshold. (After F. Zhang et al., 2007.)

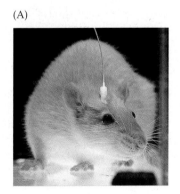

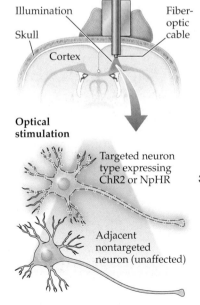

3.25 OPTOGENETIC TOOLS (A) Once the animal recovers from implant surgery, it can move freely about. Then the researcher can stimulate the particular class of cells making the opsin, with either long or short pulses of light, during spontaneous behavior. (B) Using genetic methods, scientists can arrange for only certain types of neurons to make the opsin so that only those cells will respond to the light stimulation. (B after F. Zhang et al., 2007.)

optogenetics The use of genetic tools to induce neurons to become sensitive to light, such that experimenters can excite or inhibit a cell by exposing light.

channelrhodopsin A protein that, in response to light of the proper wavelength, opens a channel to admit sodium ions, which results in excitation of the neuron.

halorhodopsin A protein that, in response to light of the proper wavelength, opens a channel to admit chloride ions, which results in inhibition of neurons.

Go to
bn8e.com
for study questions, quizzes, activities, and other resources

Thus far, optogenetics might seem no different from using electrical wires to stimulate the brain, as with Deidre at the start of the chapter. The difference is that in optogenetic approaches, one can use genetic tricks so that, for example, only neurons that use GABA as a neurotransmitter will make the opsin. Then shining the light will excite only those neurons, not their thousands of neighbors that use other transmitters (**FIGURE 3.25B**). Or the investigator can arrange it so that only those neurons in brain region X that send axons to brain region Y will make the opsin, and therefore only those will respond to the light. One can even use channelrhodopsin and halorhodopsin in the same animal so that sending blue light into the fiber-optic cable into the brain excites the neurons while shining yellow light shuts them down. Or one can have one class of neurons respond to the blue light while another responds to yellow (Deisseroth, 2015). These powerful techniques allow unprecedented control of neural circuits and will, we hope, cast the relationship between brain and behavior in an entirely new light.

Recommended Reading

Hille, B. (2001). *Ion Channels of Excitable Membranes* (3rd ed.). Sunderland, MA: Sinauer.

Kandel, E. R., Schwartz, J. H., Jessell, T. M, Siegelbaum, S.A., et al. (2013). *Principles of Neural Science* (5th ed.). New York: McGraw-Hill.

Nicholls, J. G., Martin, A. R., Fuchs, P. A., Brown, D. A., et al. (2012). *From Neuron to Brain* (5th ed.). Sunderland, MA: Sinauer.

Purves, D., Augustine, G. J., Fitzpatrick, D., LaMantia, A.–S., et al. (2017). *Neuroscience* (6th ed.). Sunderland, MA: Sinauer.

Valenstein, E. S. (2005). *The War of the Soups and the Sparks: The Discovery of Neurotransmitters and the Dispute over How Neurons Communicate.* New York: Columbia University Press.

VISUAL SUMMARY

You should be able to relate each summary to the adjacent illustration, including structures and processes.
Go to bn8e.com/vs3 for links to figures, animations, and activities that will help you consolidate the material.

1 Chemical signals transmit information *between* neurons; electrical signals transmit information *within* a neuron. Neurons exhibit a small **electrical potential** across the cell membrane; neural signals are changes in this **resting potential**. Review **Figure 3.1**

2 Different concentrations of **ions** inside and outside the neuron—especially **potassium ions (K⁺)**, to which the resting membrane is **selectively permeable**—account for the **resting potential**. At the **K⁺ equilibrium potential**, the electrostatic pressure pulling K⁺ ions into the neuron is balanced by the **concentration gradient** pushing them out; at this point, the membrane potential is about –65 mV, the resting potential. Review **Figures 3.2–3.4, Activity 3.1, Animation 3.2**

3 Reducing the resting potential (**depolarization**) of axons until it reaches a **threshold** value opens **voltage-gated sodium (Na⁺) channels**, making the membrane completely permeable to Na⁺. The **sodium ions (Na⁺)** rush in, and the axon becomes briefly more positive inside than outside. This event is called an **action potential**. Review **Figure 3.5, Animation 3.3**

4 Following the action potential, the resting potential is quickly restored by the influx of K⁺ ions. The **sodium-potassium pumps** maintain the resting potential in the long run, counteracting the influx of Na⁺ ions during action potentials. Review **Figure 3.6**

5 The action potential strongly depolarizes the adjacent patch of axonal membrane, causing it to generate its own action potential. In this regenerative manner, the action potential spreads down the axon. **Saltatory conduction** of the action potential along the **nodes of Ranvier** between **myelin** sheaths speeds propagation down the axon. Review **Figure 3.8 and Box 3.2, Animation 3.4**

6 Like all other **local potentials**, **postsynaptic potentials** spread very rapidly but are not regenerated, so they diminish as they spread passively along dendrites and the cell body. **Excitatory postsynaptic potentials (EPSPs)** are **depolarizing** (they decrease the resting potential) and increase the likelihood that the neuron will fire an action potential. **Inhibitory postsynaptic potentials (IPSPs)** are **hyperpolarizing** (they make the cell more polarized), decreasing the likelihood that the neuron will fire. Review **Figure 3.9**

7 Neurons process information by integrating (summing algebraically) the postsynaptic potentials through both **spatial summation** (summing potentials from different locations) and **temporal summation** (summing potentials across time). Review **Figure 3.11, Animation 3.5**

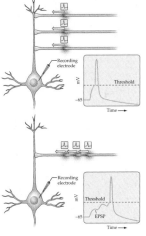

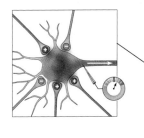

8 Action potentials are initiated just past the **axon hillock** when the excess of EPSPs over IPSPs reaches threshold. During the action potential, the neuron cannot be excited by a second stimulus; it is **absolutely refractory**. For a few milliseconds afterward, the hyperpolarized neuron is **relatively refractory**, requiring a stronger stimulation than usual in order to fire. Review **Figure 3.10**

(continued)

9 Synaptic transmission occurs when a chemical neurotransmitter diffuses across the **synaptic cleft** and binds to **neurotransmitter receptors** in the postsynaptic membrane. **Ionotropic receptors** contain an ion channel; **metabotropic receptors** use **second messengers** to affect the target cell. Review **Figures 3.12 and 3.13, Animations 3.6 and 3.7**

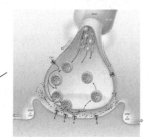

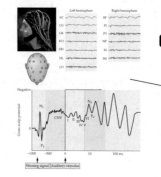

10 Summing electrical activity over millions of nerve cells as detected by electrodes on the scalp, **electroencephalograms** (EEGs) can reveal rapid changes in brain function—for example, in response to a brief, controlled stimulus that evokes an **event-related potential** (ERP). They can also reveal the highly synchronized electrical outbursts of a **seizure** in people with **epilepsy**. Review **Figures 3.20–3.22 and Box 3.3**

The Chemistry of Behavior

Neurotransmitters and Neuropharmacology

4

The Birth of a Pharmaceutical Problem Child

Swiss pharmacologist Albert Hofmann was working for Sandoz Pharmaceuticals and studying compounds derived from ergot, a fungus that grows on grain, in the hope of synthesizing new and useful drugs from it. One day in April of 1943, Dr. Hofmann began to feel unwell at work and, believing he was coming down with a cold, left for home. Soon, however, he began experiencing bizarre visual phenomena: "an uninterrupted stream of fantastic pictures, extraordinary shapes with intense, kaleidoscopic play of colors" (A. Hofmann, 1981). When he closed his eyes, the luridly colored, oddly shifting forms seemed to surge toward him. The state lasted about 2 hours. Suspecting that he had accidentally ingested a small amount of an experimental compound, Hofmann began to research its properties, intentionally taking larger doses and noting the details of its effects.

We can debate the wisdom of testing unknown drugs on yourself, but Hofmann soon realized he had a revolutionary drug on his hands. Even a tiny dose of this stuff caused incapacitating changes in brain function and astonishing, sometimes frightening, visual experiences. In addition to the visual phenomena, he reported sometimes feeling that his sense of self was "loosened." Careful analyses confirmed the new drug to be amazingly potent: a few millionths of a gram was enough to induce substantial effects. What was this substance? How can such a tiny amount of a drug exert so large an effect on the brain?

As far back as we can trace human history, people have experimented with all kinds of **exogenous** substances—animal, vegetable, and mineral compounds from *external* sources—in order to change the functioning of their bodies and brains. From these experiences, people have learned to consume some substances and shun others. Social customs and dietary codes evolved to help people benefit from helpful substances and to protect them from consuming toxins. Our forebears sipped, swallowed, and smoked their way to euphoria, calmness, pain relief, and hallucination. They discovered deadly poisons in frogs, miraculous antibiotics in mold, powerful painkillers in poppies, and all the rest of a vast catalog of helpful and harmful substances.

The brain is an electrochemical system, so it's no surprise that most drugs that affect the nervous system do so by altering brain chemistry and synaptic transmission. We begin our tour of **neurochemistry** and **neuropharmacology** by briefly reviewing the structure and function of the synapse, before delving more deeply into the neurotransmitter mechanisms that we introduced in Chapter 3. Then we discuss many of the major classes of drugs that affect the nervous system and behavior, before we finally turn to mechanisms of drug abuse and dependency.

Go to Brain Explorer
bn8e.com/4.1

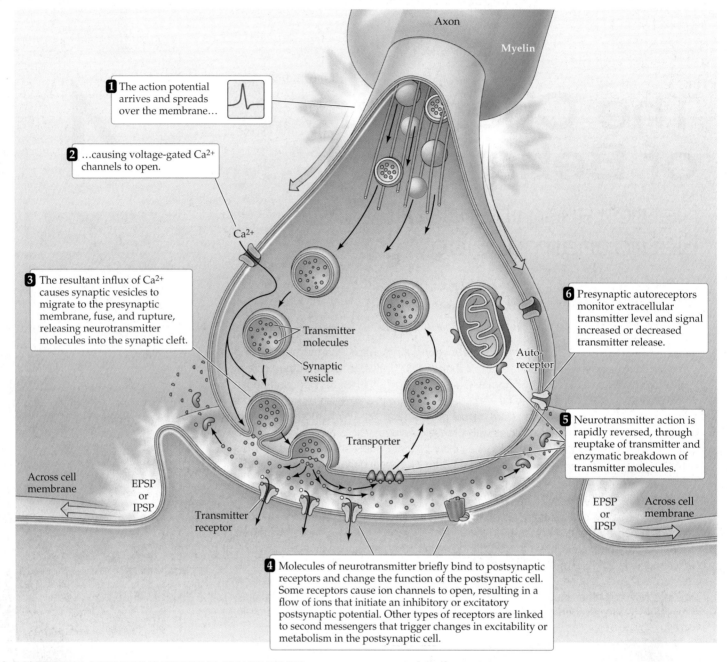

1 The action potential arrives and spreads over the membrane...

2 ...causing voltage-gated Ca^{2+} channels to open.

Axon

Myelin

Ca^{2+}

3 The resultant influx of Ca^{2+} causes synaptic vesicles to migrate to the presynaptic membrane, fuse, and rupture, releasing neurotransmitter molecules into the synaptic cleft.

Transmitter molecules

Synaptic vesicle

Transporter

Auto- receptor

6 Presynaptic autoreceptors monitor extracellular transmitter level and signal increased or decreased transmitter release.

5 Neurotransmitter action is rapidly reversed, through reuptake of transmitter and enzymatic breakdown of transmitter molecules.

Across cell membrane

EPSP or IPSP

Transmitter receptor

EPSP or IPSP

Across cell membrane

4 Molecules of neurotransmitter briefly bind to postsynaptic receptors and change the function of the postsynaptic cell. Some receptors cause ion channels to open, resulting in a flow of ions that initiate an inhibitory or excitatory postsynaptic potential. Other types of receptors are linked to second messengers that trigger changes in excitability or metabolism in the postsynaptic cell.

4.1 SYNAPSES CONVERT ELECTRICAL SIGNALS INTO CHEMICAL SIGNALS

exogenous   Arising from outside the body.

neurochemistry   The branch of neuroscience concerned with the fundamental chemical composition and processes of the nervous system.

neuropharmacology   Also called *psychopharmacology*. The scientific field concerned with the discovery and study of compounds that selectively affect the functioning of the nervous system.

receptor   Also called *receptor molecule*. A protein that binds and reacts to molecules of a neurotransmitter or hormone.

Synaptic Transmission Is a Complex Electrochemical Process

As we learned in Chapter 3, neurons integrate a variety of inputs, and if sufficiently excited (i.e., depolarized), they fire a brief *action potential* that rapidly sweeps down the length of the axon toward the axon terminals. **FIGURE 4.1** recaps the events that follow the arrival of the action potential. Because the action potential strongly depolarizes the axon terminal, voltage-gated calcium (Ca^{2+}) channels in the terminal membrane are induced to open, and the resultant influx of Ca^{2+} ions drives the migration of synaptic vesicles to the presynaptic membrane, where they release their cargo of *neurotransmitter* molecules into the synaptic cleft (a process called *exocytosis*). In Chapter 3 we also saw that following their diffusion across the cleft, neurotransmitter molecules briefly bind to their corresponding **receptors**, which then mediate a response on the postsynaptic side. Receptors are protein molecules embedded in the postsynaptic membrane that recognize a specific transmitter. The transmitter

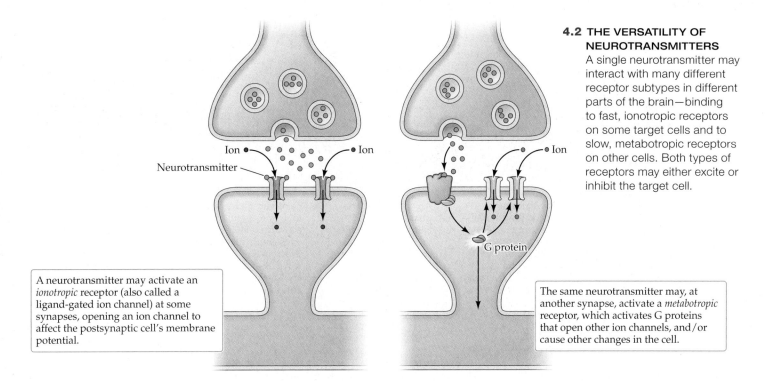

A neurotransmitter may activate an *ionotropic* receptor (also called a ligand-gated ion channel) at some synapses, opening an ion channel to affect the postsynaptic cell's membrane potential.

The same neurotransmitter may, at another synapse, activate a *metabotropic* receptor, which activates G proteins that open other ion channels, and/or cause other changes in the cell.

molecule binds to the receptor, changing its shape to open an ion channel (as with fast, **ionotropic receptors**) or altering chemical reactions within the target cell (as with slow, **metabotropic receptors**) (see Figure 3.15).

Receptors add an important layer of complexity in neural signaling, because any given transmitter may affect various kinds of receptors that differ from one another in structure. This diversity of **receptor subtypes** is true for both metabotropic receptors and ionotropic receptors. In mammals, a gene superfamily encodes hundreds of different **G protein-coupled receptors** (**GPCRs**), many of which are metabotropic neurotransmitter receptors. In the case of ionotropic receptors, families of genes encode a variety of protein subunits that in combination make up the ion channels at the core of the receptors. The characteristics of each subtype of ionotropic receptor, including the specific neurotransmitter it recognizes and the type of ions that it selectively admits, are determined by the unique combination of subunits that make it up. Further, the brain may vary these combinations over time to alter the functioning of synapses—a type of neuroplasticity (Bar-Shira et al., 2015). To get a sense of this complexity, consider that there are at least 14 different subtypes of receptors for the neurotransmitter serotonin, 5 for dopamine, and 5 for norepinephrine.

A neurotransmitter's different receptor subtypes may trigger very different responses in target cells (**FIGURE 4.2**), and in many cases they are also distributed differently within the nervous system. As we will see shortly, drug development capitalizes on the existence of receptor subtypes. Although a given neurotransmitter will interact with *all* the subtypes of its receptors, it is possible to design drugs that selectively affect only one of the subtypes, thereby producing the specific effects associated with that receptor subtype.

Any substance that binds to a receptor is termed a **ligand** and has one of several kinds of effects (**FIGURE 4.3**):

1. A ligand that is classified as an **agonist** initiates the normal effects of the transmitter on that receptor.

2. A receptor **antagonist** is a ligand that binds to a receptor and does not activate it, thereby blocking it from being activated by other ligands (including the native neurotransmitter).

3. An **inverse agonist**—a less common type of ligand—binds to the receptor and initiates an effect that is the *reverse* of the normal function of the receptor.

ionotropic receptor A receptor protein that includes an ion channel that is opened when the receptor is bound by an agonist.

metabotropic receptor A receptor protein that does not contain an ion channel but may, when activated, use a G protein system to alter the functioning of the postsynaptic cell.

receptor subtype Any type of receptor having functional characteristics that distinguish it from other types of receptors for the same neurotransmitter.

G protein-coupled receptor (**GPCR**) A cell surface receptor that, when activated extracellularly, initiates G protein signaling mechanisms inside the cell.

ligand A substance that binds to receptor molecules, such as those at the surface of the cell.

agonist A molecule, usually a drug, that binds a receptor molecule and initiates a response like that of another molecule, usually a neurotransmitter.

antagonist A molecule, usually a drug, that interferes with or prevents the action of a transmitter.

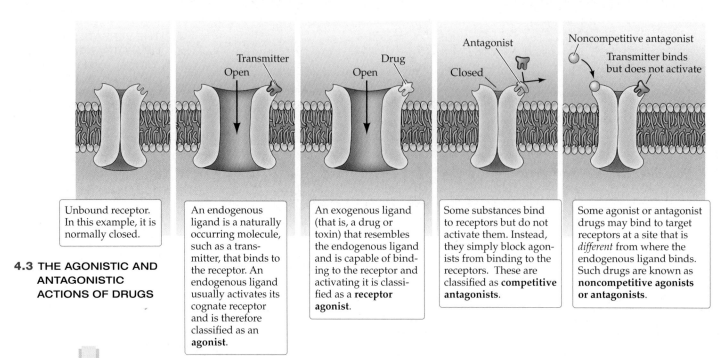

4.3 THE AGONISTIC AND ANTAGONISTIC ACTIONS OF DRUGS

Unbound receptor. In this example, it is normally closed.

An endogenous ligand is a naturally occurring molecule, such as a transmitter, that binds to the receptor. An endogenous ligand usually activates its cognate receptor and is therefore classified as an **agonist**.

An exogenous ligand (that is, a drug or toxin) that resembles the endogenous ligand and is capable of binding to the receptor and activating it is classified as a **receptor agonist**.

Some substances bind to receptors but do not activate them. Instead, they simply block agonists from binding to the receptors. These are classified as **competitive antagonists**.

Some agonist or antagonist drugs may bind to target receptors at a site that is *different* from where the endogenous ligand binds. Such drugs are known as **noncompetitive agonists or antagonists**.

Go to Animation 4.2
Agonists and Antagonists
bn8e.com/4.2

inverse agonist   A substance that binds to a receptor and causes it to do the opposite of what the naturally occurring transmitter does.

competitive ligand   A substance that directly competes with the endogenous ligand for the same binding site on a receptor molecule.

noncompetitive ligand   Also called *neuromodulator*. A substance that alters the response to an endogenous ligand without interacting with the endogenous ligand's recognition site.

modulatory site   A portion of a receptor that, when bound by a compound, alters the receptor's response to its transmitter.

endogenous   Produced inside the body.

But there is one more layer of complexity. Drugs with any of the three actions just described are properly called **competitive ligands** because they compete with the endogenous transmitter for binding to the same part of the receptor complex. But some drugs bind to a part of the receptor complex that does *not* normally bind the transmitter (see Figure 4.3 *far right*). Because this sort of drug does not directly compete with the transmitter for its binding site, we say that the drug is a **noncompetitive ligand** (or *neuromodulator*) binding to a **modulatory site** on the receptor. Noncompetitive ligands may either activate the receptor, thereby acting as noncompetitive agonists, or prevent the receptor from being activated by the transmitter, thus acting as noncompetitive antagonists. We'll see several examples of these actions when we discuss modulatory sites on the GABA$_A$ receptor later in this chapter.

First we will look at some of the substances that the brain itself produces, which we classify as *endogenous ligands*. We will then turn to the major categories of exogenous ligands—drugs—that affect the brain.

Many Chemical Neurotransmitters Have Been Identified

We learned in Chapter 3 that each neuron integrates electrical information from many synapses and may then release a chemical—an **endogenous** substance (a substance from an internal source) called a *neurotransmitter*—that communicates the result of that information processing to the postsynaptic cell. As you might have guessed, most drugs that affect behavior do so by altering this chemical communication process at millions, or even billions, of synapses. Identification of neurotransmitters, their receptors, and the effects of drugs that modify neurotransmission is one of the most active areas of research in all of neuroscience.

To be considered a classic neurotransmitter, a substance should meet the following criteria:

• The substance exists in presynaptic axon terminals.
• The presynaptic cell contains appropriate enzymes for synthesizing the substance.
• The substance is released in significant quantities when action potentials reach the terminals.
• Specific receptors that recognize the released substance exist on the postsynaptic membrane.
• Experimental application of the substance produces changes in postsynaptic cells.
• Blocking release of the substance prevents presynaptic activity from affecting the postsynaptic cell.

TABLE 4.1 Some Synaptic Transmitters and Families of Transmitters

FAMILY AND SUBFAMILY	TRANSMITTER(S)
AMINO ACIDS	Gamma-aminobutyric acid (GABA), glutamate, glycine, histamine
AMINES	
Quaternary amines	Acetylcholine (ACh)
Monoamines	*Catecholamines*: norepinephrine (NE), epinephrine (adrenaline), dopamine (DA)
	Indoleamines: serotonin (5-hydroxytryptamine; 5-HT), melatonin
NEUROPEPTIDES	
Opioid peptides	*Enkephalins*: met-enkephalin, leu-enkephalin
	Endorphins: β-endorphin
	Dynorphins: dynorphin A
Other neuropeptides	Oxytocin, substance P, cholecystokinin (CCK), vasopressin, neuropeptide Y (NPY), hypothalamic releasing hormones
GASES	Nitric oxide, carbon monoxide

TABLE 4.1 summarizes the major categories of some of the many neurotransmitters presently known. Substances that satisfy the criteria for being considered classic transmitters include various **amine neurotransmitters**, such as acetylcholine, dopamine, and serotonin; **amino acid neurotransmitters**, like GABA and glutamate; and a wide variety of **peptide neurotransmitters** (or *neuropeptides*), made up of short chains of amino acids. As the search goes on, the number of probable synaptic transmitters continues to grow, and the effort occasionally yields surprises like the **gas neurotransmitters**: soluble gases that diffuse between neurons to alter ongoing processes.

Even if a substance is known to be a transmitter in one location, proving that it acts as a transmitter at another location may be difficult. For example, acetylcholine was long known to be a transmitting agent in the peripheral nervous system, but it was harder to prove that it serves as a transmitter in the central nervous system as well. Now it is recognized that acetylcholine is widely distributed in the brain, and many scientists study its possible relationship to the cognitive deficits seen in Alzheimer's disease. Considering the rate at which these substances are being discovered and characterized, it would not be surprising if there turned out to be several hundred different neurotransmitters conveying information at synapses in different subsets of neurons.

Neurotransmitter Systems Form a Complex Array in the Brain

Powerful methods for probing the composition of neural tissue (see Box 2.1) reveal that brain activity depends on a remarkably diverse assortment of neurotransmitters, distributed through intricate anatomical networks that overlap and interact in highly complex ways. Although at one time it was thought that each neuron contained only one transmitter, we now know that some neurons contain more than one—a phenomenon known as neurotransmitter **co-localization** or *co-release*. In this section we discuss the distribution of just a few of the major neurotransmitters, and their receptors.

The most abundant excitatory and inhibitory neurotransmitters in the brain are amino acids

The most plentiful excitatory neurotransmitters in the brain are **glutamate** and **aspartate**. **Glutamatergic** transmission employs what are called *AMPA*, *kainate*, and *NMDA* receptors (the names of these receptor subtypes refer to drugs that act as selective agonists), which are ionotropic. Because NMDA-type glutamate receptors are active in a fascinating model of learning and memory, they have been studied

amine neurotransmitter
A neurotransmitter based on modifications of a single amino acid. Examples include acetylcholine, serotonin, and dopamine.

amino acid neurotransmitter
A neurotransmitter that is itself an amino acid. Examples include GABA, glycine, and glutamate.

peptide neurotransmitter Also called *neuropeptide*. A neurotransmitter consisting of a short chain of amino acids. Examples include neuropeptide Y, galanin, and VIP (vasoactive intestinal polypeptide).

gas neurotransmitter A soluble gas, such as nitric oxide or carbon monoxide, that is produced and released by a neuron to alter the functioning of another neuron.

co-localization Also called *co-release*. Here, the appearance of more than one neurotransmitter in a given presynaptic terminal.

glutamate An amino acid transmitter, the most common excitatory transmitter.

aspartate An amino acid transmitter that is excitatory at many synapses.

glutamatergic Referring to cells that use glutamate as their synaptic transmitter.

excitotoxicity The property by which neurons die when overstimulated, as with large amounts of glutamate.

gamma-aminobutyric acid (GABA) A widely distributed amino acid transmitter; the main inhibitory transmitter in the mammalian nervous system.

glycine An amino acid transmitter, often inhibitory.

acetylcholine (ACh) A neurotransmitter produced and released by parasympathetic postganglionic neurons, by motor neurons, and by neurons throughout the brain.

cholinergic Referring to cells that use acetylcholine as their synaptic transmitter.

nicotinic Referring to cholinergic receptors that respond to nicotine as well as to acetylcholine.

muscarinic Referring to cholinergic receptors that respond to the chemical muscarine as well as to acetylcholine.

very closely and will be discussed more fully in Chapter 17. There are also several metabotropic glutamate receptors (mGluR's), which act more slowly because they work through second messengers. Glutamate is also associated with **excitotoxicity**, a phenomenon in which neural injury, such as a stroke or trauma, provokes an excessive release of glutamate that overexcites cells, eventually killing them.

In contrast to glutamate and aspartate, the amino acid transmitters **gamma-aminobutyric acid** (**GABA**) and **glycine** typically have an inhibitory effect. GABA receptors are divided into several large classes: the GABA$_A$, GABA$_B$, and GABA$_C$ receptors. Although they all normally respond to GABA, the subtypes of GABA receptors exhibit quite different properties.

GABA$_A$ receptors are ionotropic (they are ligand-gated chloride channels; see Figure 4.2 *left*), and when activated they produce fast inhibitory postsynaptic potentials. Each GABA$_A$ receptor is made up of five protein subunits surrounding a Cl$^-$ ion channel that can be widened or narrowed depending on the state of the surrounding complex. By mixing and matching of the various protein subunits that make up the GABA$_A$ receptors, the brain may in fact produce dozens of different kinds.

GABA$_B$ receptors are metabotropic receptors, typically producing a slow-occurring inhibitory postsynaptic potential (Tamás et al., 2003). GABA$_C$ receptors are ionotropic with a chloride channel, but they differ from other GABA receptors in certain details of their subunit structure. Given GABA's inhibitory actions, it is not surprising that some GABA agonists are potent tranquilizers (e.g., Valium) and that inverse agonists of GABA receptors can provoke seizures by blocking the important inhibitory influence of GABA. Interestingly, some GABA-ergic neurons appear to co-release the excitatory transmitter glutamate; perhaps these cells continually rebalance their inhibitory versus excitatory influence on postsynaptic targets (El Mestikawy et al., 2011).

Acetylcholine was the first neurotransmitter to be identified

As we saw in Chapter 3, Otto Loewi's dream-inspired experiments of the 1920s famously established that neurons use chemical messages to communicate (see Figure 3.14). The anatomical distribution of **acetylcholine** (**ACh**), the chemical eventually identified as the transmitter at work in Loewi's experiments, was subsequently mapped by staining cells containing the enzymes needed to synthesize ACh. **FIGURE 4.4** shows the distribution of **cholinergic** (ACh-using) neurons and their projections in the brain. Important clusters of cholinergic cells are found in the basal forebrain, including the medial septal nucleus, the nucleus of the diagonal band, and the nucleus basalis. These cholinergic cells project to the hippocampus and amygdala, as well as throughout the cerebral cortex. Widespread loss of cholinergic neurons is evident in Alzheimer's disease, suggesting that cholinergic systems are crucial for learning and memory. Similarly, the cholinergic antagonist scopolamine interferes with learning and memory in experimental settings.

In Chapter 3 we noted that there are two families of ACh receptors in the peripheral and central nervous systems: **nicotinic** (nACh) and **muscarinic** (mACh) receptors. Each family contains subtypes of receptors. Most nicotinic receptors are ionotropic, responding rapidly and usually having an excitatory effect (see Figure 4.2 *left*). Muscles use nACh receptors, so antagonists, such as the drug curare, cause widespread paralysis. The mACh receptors are G protein-coupled (metabotropic) receptors (see Figure 4.2 *right*), so they have slower responses when activated, and they can be either excitatory or inhibitory (see Figure 3.15B). Muscarinic receptors can be blocked by atropine or scopolamine; either drug produces pronounced changes in cognition, including drowsiness, confusion, memory problems, and blurred vision.

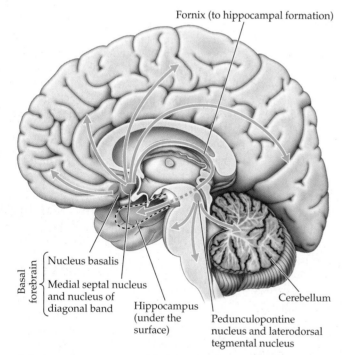

Fornix (to hippocampal formation)

Basal forebrain
Nucleus basalis
Medial septal nucleus and nucleus of diagonal band
Hippocampus (under the surface)
Cerebellum
Pedunculopontine nucleus and laterodorsal tegmental nucleus

4.4 CHOLINERGIC PATHWAYS IN THE BRAIN In this midsagittal view, the brain nuclei containing cell bodies of neurons that release ACh are shown in green; the projections of axons from these neurons are indicated by green arrows. Because they use ACh as a transmitter, these neurons are said to be *cholinergic*.

BOX
4.1

Pathways for Neurotransmitter Synthesis

Here we provide reference information on the chemical pathways by which the classic neurotransmitters are synthesized. By understanding these pathways, researchers can target drug discoveries toward affecting specific transmitter systems. Furthermore, because enzyme action is crucial for transmitter synthesis, neuroanatomists can use the anatomical distribution of these enzymes to determine which transmitters are used by different brain regions. For example, the enzyme **choline acetyltransferase (ChAT)** catalyzes the synthesis of ACh from its precursor, choline:

Acetyl CoA + choline
↓ ChAT
ACh + coenzyme A

The enzyme **acetylcholinesterase (AChE)** breaks down the ACh, leaving choline and acetic acid:

ACh
↓ AChE
Choline + acetic acid

As it turns out, AChE is very widely distributed, but ChAT is found primarily in the nuclei shown in Figure 4.4.

All of the catecholamine transmitters (norepinephrine, epinephrine, and dopamine) are synthesized from the amino acid tyrosine, in a succession of metabolic steps:

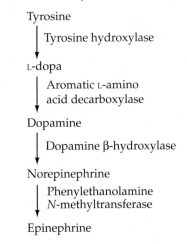

Tyrosine
↓ Tyrosine hydroxylase
L-dopa
↓ Aromatic L-amino acid decarboxylase
Dopamine
↓ Dopamine β-hydroxylase
Norepinephrine
↓ Phenylethanolamine N-methyltransferase
Epinephrine

Note that only neurons that possess the enzyme tyrosine hydroxylase have the capacity to produce any catecholamine transmitter and that L-dopa is a precursor for all three.

The indoleamine serotonin is produced from the amino acid tryptophan in two chemical steps:

Tryptophan
↓ Tryptophan hydroxylase
5-hydroxytryptophan (5-HTP)
↓ Aromatic L-amino acid decarboxylase
5-hydroxytryptamine (5-HT; serotonin)

The monoamines (dopamine, norepinephrine, epinephrine, serotonin, and melatonin) are inactivated through a combination of presynaptic reuptake and enzymatic breakdown. Most of this enzymatic action is performed by a class of enzymes called **monoamine oxidases (MAOs)**.

Neuropeptides are synthesized like any other peptide or protein—through transcription of a gene and translation of messenger RNA (mRNA)—so we can find neurons making those transmitters by looking for the appropriate mRNA transcript (see the Appendix).

choline acetyltransferase (ChAT) An important enzyme involved in the synthesis of the neurotransmitter acetylcholine.

acetylcholinesterase (AChE) An enzyme that inactivates the transmitter acetylcholine both at synaptic sites and elsewhere in the nervous system.

monoamine oxidase (MAO) An enzyme that breaks down and thereby inactivates monoamine transmitters.

Five monoamines act as neurotransmitters

There are two principal classes of neurotransmitters that, because they are modified amino acids, are called *monoamines*: catecholamines and indoleamines. The **catecholamine** neurotransmitters—each derived from the amino acid tyrosine and featuring a six-sided *catechol* ring within its molecular structure—are dopamine, epinephrine, and norepinephrine. The **indoleamine neurotransmitters**—each derived from the amino acid tryptophan, and containing a five-sided *indole* ring— are melatonin and serotonin. Let's take a closer look at three especially important monoamines: dopamine, norepinephrine, and serotonin. (The neuronal synthesis of the monoamines and acetylcholine is summarized in **BOX 4.1**.)

DOPAMINE About a million neurons in the human brain contain **dopamine (DA)**. Several subtypes of DA receptors have been discovered and have been numbered D_1, D_2, D_3, D_4, and D_5, in the order of their discovery. **FIGURE 4.5** shows the locations of dopaminergic neurons and their projections in the brain, focusing on the **mesostriatal pathway** and the **mesolimbocortical pathway**, two of the main groups of these neurons.

catecholamines A class of monoamines that serve as neurotransmitters, including dopamine and norepinephrine.

indoleamine neurotransmitters A class of monoamines, including serotonin and melatonin, that serve as neurotransmitters.

dopamine (DA) A monoamine transmitter found in the midbrain—especially the substantia nigra—and basal forebrain.

mesostriatal pathway A set of dopaminergic axons arising from the midbrain and innervating the basal ganglia, including those from the substantia nigra to the striatum.

mesolimbocortical pathway A set of dopaminergic axons arising in the midbrain and innervating the limbic system and cortex.

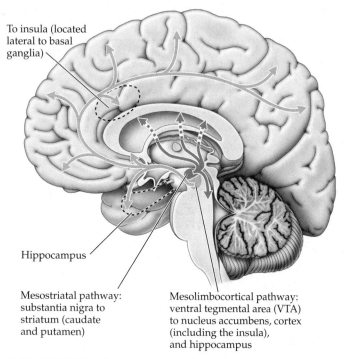

To insula (located lateral to basal ganglia)

Hippocampus

Mesostriatal pathway: substantia nigra to striatum (caudate and putamen)

Mesolimbocortical pathway: ventral tegmental area (VTA) to nucleus accumbens, cortex (including the insula), and hippocampus

4.5 DOPAMINERGIC PATHWAYS IN THE BRAIN Neurons in the pathways represented in this midsagittal view release dopamine and thus are called *dopaminergic*.

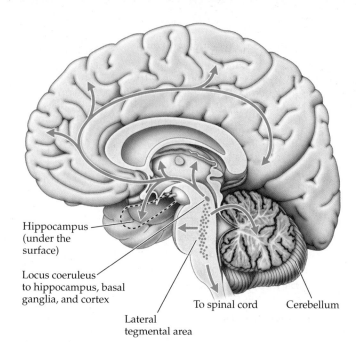

Hippocampus (under the surface)

Locus coeruleus to hippocampus, basal ganglia, and cortex

Lateral tegmental area

To spinal cord

Cerebellum

4.6 NORADRENERGIC PATHWAYS IN THE BRAIN The neurons in the pathways shown in this midsagittal view release norepinephrine (noradrenaline) as a transmitter and thus are said to be *noradrenergic*.

substantia nigra Literally, "black substance." A group of pigmented neurons in the midbrain that provides dopaminergic projections to areas of the forebrain, especially the basal ganglia.

striatum The caudate nucleus and putamen together.

ventral tegmental area (VTA) A portion of the midbrain that projects dopaminergic fibers to the nucleus accumbens.

norepinephrine (NE) Also called *noradrenaline*. A neurotransmitter produced and released by sympathetic postganglionic neurons to accelerate organ activity. Also produced in the brainstem and found in projections throughout the brain.

locus coeruleus Literally, "blue spot." A small nucleus in the brainstem whose neurons produce norepinephrine.

noradrenergic Referring to systems using norepinephrine (noradrenaline) as a transmitter.

serotonin (5-HT) A synaptic transmitter that is produced in the raphe nuclei and is active in structures throughout the cerebral hemispheres.

serotonergic Referring to neurons that use serotonin as their synaptic transmitter.

The mesostriatal pathway, as the name indicates, originates from the mesencephalon (midbrain)—specifically the **substantia nigra** and nearby areas—and ascends as part of the *medial forebrain bundle* to innervate the **striatum**: the caudate nucleus and putamen (see Figure 4.5 *left*). All these structures are part of the *basal ganglia* described in Chapter 2 (see Figure 2.17A). The mesostriatal DA pathway plays a crucial role in motor control, and significant loss of these neurons produces the movement problems of Parkinson's disease (described in Chapter 11).

The mesolimbocortical pathway also originates in the midbrain, in the **ventral tegmental area** (**VTA**) (see Figure 4.5 *right*), and projects to the limbic system (amygdala, nucleus accumbens, hippocampus) and the cortex. This system is important in reward and reinforcement, especially via the dopamine D_2 receptor subtype (Glimcher, 2011); we'll revisit this topic at the end of the chapter. Abnormalities in the mesolimbocortical pathway are associated with some of the symptoms of schizophrenia, as we'll discuss in Chapter 16.

NOREPINEPHRINE The two main clusters of neurons in the brainstem releasing **norepinephrine** (**NE**) are the **locus coeruleus**, in the pons, and the lateral tegmental area of the midbrain (**FIGURE 4.6**). Because norepinephrine is also known as *noradrenaline*, NE-producing cells are said to be **noradrenergic**. Recall from Chapter 2 that sympathetic fibers innervating the body are also noradrenergic (see Figure 2.11).

Fibers from the noradrenergic cells of the locus coeruleus project broadly throughout the cerebrum, including the cerebral cortex, limbic system, and thalamus. The cerebellum and spinal cord also receive noradrenergic innervation. The CNS contains four subtypes of NE receptors—α_1-, α_2-, β_1-, and β_2-adrenoceptors—all of which are metabotropic receptors. Given the brain's wide noradrenergic projections, it's no surprise that there are noradrenergic contributions to diverse behavioral and physiological processes, including mood, overall arousal, and sexual behavior.

SEROTONIN Because its chemical name is *5-hydroxytryptamine*, **serotonin** is abbreviated **5-HT**. Large areas of the brain are innervated by **serotonergic** fibers, although 5-HT cell bodies are relatively few and are concentrated along the midline in the **raphe nuclei** (pronounced "rafay"; Latin for "seam") of the midbrain and brainstem. **FIGURE 4.7** shows the distribution of serotonergic cell bodies and their axonal projections. Only about 200,000 of the 80–90 billion neurons of the human brain are serotonergic, but they exert widespread influence through the rest of the brain.

Serotonin has been implicated in the control of sleep states (see Chapter 14), mood, sexual behavior, anxiety, and many other functions. Several families of drugs that are used as antidepressants share an action on serotonin: they act to increase its synaptic availability. Prozac, for example (see Chapter 16), slows the clearance of serotonin from synapses by inhibiting its reuptake into axon terminals. At least 14 types of 5-HT receptors (5-HT$_1$, 5-HT$_2$, and so on) have been described, and all but one are metabotropic receptors. The effects of serotonergic drugs on behavior depend on which subtypes of 5-HT receptors are affected (Gorzalka et al., 1990; Miczek et al., 2002).

Many peptides function as neurotransmitters

We can't catalog all the peptide neurotransmitters here, but these are some that we'll see again in later chapters:

The **opioid peptides** are a group of endogenous substances with actions that resemble those of opiate drugs like morphine. Some key opioids are met-enkephalin, leu-enkephalin, β-endorphin, and dynorphin (see Chapter 8).

- Another group of peptides that were discovered in the periphery, and especially in the organs of the gut (which explains some of their names), are also made by neurons in the spinal cord or brain where they participate in synaptic transmission. Examples include substance P, cholecystokinin (CCK), vasoactive intestinal polypeptide (VIP), neurotensin, and neuropeptide Y (NPY) (see Chapter 13).

- Pituitary hormones include oxytocin and vasopressin (see Chapters 5 and 12).

Some neurotransmitters are gases

It may surprise you to learn that neurons use certain gas molecules that dissolve in water (and so are called *soluble gases*) to communicate information. The best studied of these is **nitric oxide**, or **NO** (distinct from *nitrous* oxide, or laughing gas, which is N$_2$O).

The actions of NO and other gas neurotransmitters are different from those of the classic transmitters in several important ways. First, nitric oxide is produced in cellular locations other than the axon terminals, especially the dendrites, and molecules of nitric oxide are not held in or released from vesicles; the substance simply diffuses out of the neuron as soon as it is produced. Second, the released NO doesn't interact with membrane-bound receptors on the surface of the target cell, but rather it diffuses into the target cell and stimulates the production of second messengers. And third, NO can serve as a **retrograde transmitter**, diffusing from the postsynaptic neuron back to the presynaptic neuron, where it stimulates changes in synaptic efficacy that may be involved in learning and memory (which will be covered in more detail in Chapter 17). Found widely throughout the body, NO has been implicated in processes as diverse as hair growth and penile erection (Burnett, 2006), in addition to its role in the brain.

The Effects of a Drug Depend on Its Site of Action and Dose

In everyday English, we use the term *drug* in different ways. One common meaning is "a medicine used in the treatment of a disease" (as in *prescription drug* or *over-the-counter drug*). Many *psychoactive drugs*—compounds that alter the function of the brain and thereby affect conscious experiences—fall into this category, and they are useful in psychiatric settings. Other psychoactive drugs are used recreationally with varying

4.7 SEROTONERGIC PATHWAYS IN THE BRAIN The neurons in the nuclei shown in this midsagittal view release serotonin (5-HT) and thus are said to be *serotonergic*.

Go to Animation 4.3
Neurotransmitter Pathways in the Brain
bn8e.com/4.3

raphe nuclei A string of nuclei in the midline of the midbrain and brainstem that contain most of the serotonergic neurons of the brain.

opioid peptide A type of endogenous peptide that mimics the effects of morphine in binding to opioid receptors and producing marked analgesia and reward.

nitric oxide (NO) A soluble gas that serves as a retrograde gas neurotransmitter in the nervous system.

retrograde transmitter A neurotransmitter that diffuses from the postsynaptic neuron back to the presynaptic neuron.

degrees of risk to health; these are *drugs of abuse*. Some drugs affect the brain by altering enzyme action or modifying other internal cellular processes, but as you may have guessed, most drugs of interest to behavioral neuroscience are receptor ligands.

Drugs fit like keys into molecular locks

Because a given neurotransmitter interacts with a variety of different subtypes of receptors—a few are discussed in **TABLE 4.2**—it is possible to develop drugs that primarily interact with just one or a few receptor subtypes. The various subtypes of receptors generally differ in their distribution within the brain, and they also serve very different cellular functions, so selectively activating or blocking specific subtypes of receptors can have widely varying effects. For example, treating someone with serotonin would activate all of her serotonin receptors, regardless of subtype, causing a debilitating constellation of physiological and behavioral changes. But drugs that are selective antagonists of 5-HT$_3$ receptors, showing little activity at other 5-HT receptor subtypes, produce a powerful and specific anti-nausea effect. We have also discussed how a single transmitter, GABA, may have a huge variety of different receptor subtypes, depending on variations in the proteins making up the GABA receptors. Apparently, evolution tinkers with the structure of *receptors* more than with the transmitters themselves.

Drug molecules do not seek out particular receptor molecules; rather, drug molecules spread widely throughout the body, and when they come in contact with a receptor molecule possessing the correct shape, the two molecules bind together briefly and begin a chain of events. The lock-and-key analogy is often used for this

TABLE 4.2   The Bewildering Multiplicity of Transmitter Receptor Subtypes

TRANSMITTER	KNOWN RECEPTOR SUBTYPES	FUNCTION
Glutamate	AMPA, kainate, and NMDA receptors (ionotropic)	Glutamate is the most abundant of all neurotransmitters and the most important excitatory transmitter.
	mGluR's (*m*etabotropic *glu*tamate *r*eceptors)	Glutamate receptors are crucial for excitatory signals, and NMDA receptors are especially implicated in learning and memory.
Gamma-aminobutyric acid (GABA)	GABA$_A$ (ionotropic)	GABA receptors mediate most of the brain's inhibitory activity, balancing the excitatory actions of glutamate. GABA$_A$ receptors are inhibitory in many brain regions, reducing excitability and preventing seizure activity.
	GABA$_B$ (metabotropic)	GABA$_B$ receptors are also inhibitory, by a different mechanism.
Acetylcholine (ACh)	Muscarinic receptors (metabotropic)	Both are involved in cholinergic transmission in the cortex.
	Nicotinic receptors (ionotropic)	Nicotinic receptors are crucial for muscle contraction.
Dopamine (DA)	D$_1$ through D$_5$ receptors (all metabotropic)	Found throughout the forebrain
	D$_6$ and D$_7$ probable	Involved in complex behaviors, including motor function, reward, higher cognition
Norepinephrine (NE)	α_1-, α_2-, β_1-, and β_2-adrenergic receptors (all metabotropic)	NE has multiple effects in visceral organs and is important in sympathetic nervous system and "fight or flight" responses. In the brain, NE transmission provides an alerting and arousing function.
Serotonin	5-HT$_1$ receptor family (5 members)	Different subtypes differ in their distribution in the brain.
	5-HT$_2$ receptor family (3 members)	May be involved in mood, sleep, and higher cognition
	5-HT$_3$ through 5-HT$_7$ receptors	5-HT$_3$ receptors are particularly involved in nausea.
	All but one subtype (5-HT$_3$) are metabotropic.	
Miscellaneous peptides	Many specific receptors for peptides such as opiates (delta, kappa, and mu receptors), cholecystokinin (CCK), neurotensin, neuropeptide Y (NPY), and dozens more (metabotropic)	Peptide transmitters have many different functions, depending on their anatomical localization. Some important examples include the control of feeding, sexual behaviors, and social functions.

binding action, as mentioned in Chapter 3. In the case of receptor-selective drugs, though, we have to think of keys (drug molecules) trying to insert themselves into all the locks (receptor molecules) in the neighborhood; each such key fits into only a particular subset of the locks. Once the drug (the key) binds to the receptor (the lock), it alters the activity of the receptor, activating it or blocking it. But the binding is usually temporary, and when the drug or transmitter breaks away from the receptor, the receptor returns to its unbound shape and functioning.

binding affinity Also called simply *affinity*. The propensity of molecules of a drug (or other ligand) to bind to receptors.

efficacy Also called *intrinsic activity*. The extent to which a drug activates a response when it binds to a receptor.

partial agonist A drug that, when bound to a receptor, has less effect than the endogenous ligand would.

Drug-receptor interactions vary in specificity and activity

The tuning of drug molecules to receptors is not absolutely specific. That is, a particular drug molecule will generally bind strongly to one kind of receptor, more weakly to some other types, and not at all to many others. A drug molecule that has more than one kind of action in the body exhibits this flexibility because it affects more than one kind of receptor molecule. For example, some drugs combat anxiety at low doses without producing sedation (relaxation, drowsiness), but at higher doses they cause sedation, probably because at those doses they activate additional types of receptors.

The degree of chemical attraction between a ligand and a receptor is termed **binding affinity** (or simply *affinity*). A drug with high affinity for a particular type of receptor will selectively bind to that type of receptor even at low doses, and it will stay bound for a relatively long time. The same dose of a lower-affinity drug will bind fewer receptor molecules. **FIGURE 4.8** illustrates how binding affinity is measured. It is interesting to note that the neurotransmitters themselves are low-affinity ligands—their weak binding lets them rapidly dissociate from receptors, allowing the synapse to reset for the next signal's arrival.

After binding, the propensity of a ligand to *activate* the receptor to which it is bound is termed its **efficacy** (or *intrinsic activity*): agonists have high efficacy and antagonists have low efficacy. **Partial agonists** are drugs that produce a middling response. So, it is a combination of affinity and efficacy—where it binds and what it does—that determines the overall action of a drug. To some extent we can compare the effectiveness of different drugs by comparing their affinity for a receptor of interest (see Figure 16.13 for an example).

Dose-response relationships reflect the potency and safety of drugs

As you would probably guess, administering larger doses of a drug increases the proportion of receptors that are bound by the drug. Within certain limits, this increase in receptor binding also increases the response to the drug; in other words, greater doses tend to produce greater effects. When plotted as a graph, the relation-

Receptor   Lower-affinity drug   Higher-affinity drug

  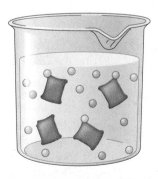

If a particular drug has a low affinity for a receptor, then it will quickly uncouple from the receptor. To bind half the receptors at any given time, a higher concentration of the drug is needed.

If a drug has a high affinity for a receptor, the two will stay together for a longer time, and a lower concentration of drug will be sufficient to bind half the receptors.

If equal concentrations of the two drugs are present, the high-affinity drug will be bound to more receptors at any given time. If the drugs have an equivalent effect on the receptors, then the higher-affinity drug will be more potent.

4.8 USING BINDING AFFINITY TO COMPARE DRUG EFFECTIVENESS

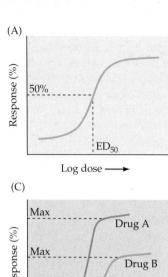

(A) The basic dose-response curve (DRC) plots increasing drug doses (usually on a logarithmic scale) against increasing strength of the response being studied. The dose at which the drug shows half of its maximal effect is termed the effective dose 50% (ED_{50}).

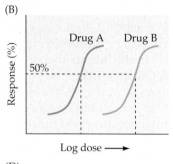

(B) We can assess the relative potencies of two drugs by comparing their ED_{50} values. In this example, both drugs have comparable effects, but drug A (blue) has the effects at lower doses and so is more potent than drug B (yellow).

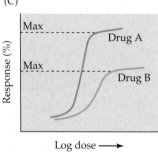

(C) We can compare drug efficacies by evaluating *maximal* responses, rather than doses. Here, drug A (blue) has a much greater maximal effect than drug B, no matter how much of B is given. A drug of only moderate efficacy is termed a *partial agonist* (or, equivalently, a *partial antagonist*).

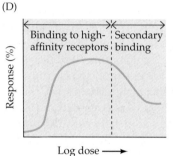

(D) The shape of a *nonmonotonic DRC* is normal up to a point, but then it reverses, and the measured response begins to decrease with larger doses. At that point, the drug is starting to have effects elsewhere than at the drug's highest-affinity receptors.

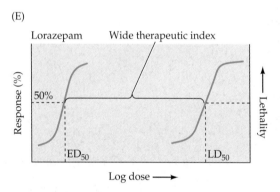

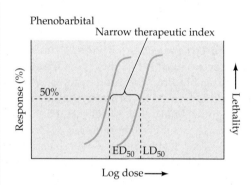

The *therapeutic index* refers to the separation between useful doses of the drug and dangerous doses. This is determined by comparing the ED_{50} dose of the drug with the dose at which 50% of the animals either show symptoms of toxicity (*toxic dose 50%*; TD_{50}) or outright die (*lethal dose 50%*; LD_{50}). In this example, a greater difference between ED_{50} and LD_{50} is observed for the anxiolytic drug lorazepam (Ativan) than for the older anxiolytic phenobarbital, indicating that lorazepam is the safer drug. Many deaths— accidental and not—have resulted from phenobarbital overdose.

4.9 THE DOSE-RESPONSE CURVE (DRC)

dose-response curve (DRC)
A formal plot of a drug's effects (on the *y*-axis) versus the dose given (on the *x*-axis).

pharmacodynamics Collective name for the factors that affect the relationship between a drug and its target receptors, such as affinity and efficacy.

tolerance A condition in which, with repeated exposure to a drug, an individual becomes less responsive to a constant dose.

ship between drug doses and observed effects is called a **dose-response curve (DRC)**. Careful analysis of DRCs reveals many aspects of drug activity and is one of the main tools for understanding **pharmacodynamics** (the functional relationships between drugs and their targets).

FIGURE 4.9 illustrates how DRCs are used to assess many important characteristics of drugs. For example, DRCs reveal the effective dose range of a drug and allow comparison of the potencies and efficacies of different drugs. Sometimes a DRC gives us hints that the drug may be binding more than one type of receptor. By directly comparing the DRCs for two drugs, we can determine which drug would be safer to use.

Repeated treatments may reduce the effectiveness of drugs

Our bodies are impressively adaptable. Many body systems change their functioning in order to accommodate environmental challenges, and in most ways drug treatments can be viewed as changes in the body's chemical environment. This adaptability is evident in the development of drug **tolerance**, where a drug's effectiveness diminishes over repeated treatments. Consequently, successively larger and larger doses of drug are needed to cause the same effect.

Drug tolerance can develop in several different ways. Some drugs provoke **metabolic tolerance**, in which the body's metabolic systems and organs (such as the liver and its specialized enzymes) become increasingly effective at eliminating the drug from the bloodstream before it has a chance to affect the brain or another target. Alternatively, the target tissue itself may show altered sensitivity to the drug, or **functional tolerance**. Although we tend to think of receptors in postsynaptic

(A) Cell's response to agonist

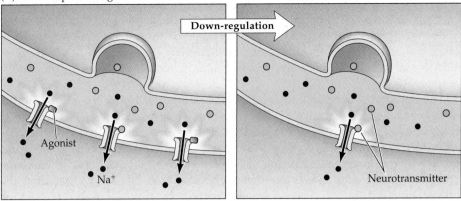

Down-regulation

Agonist

Na⁺

Neurotransmitter

(B) Cell's response to antagonist

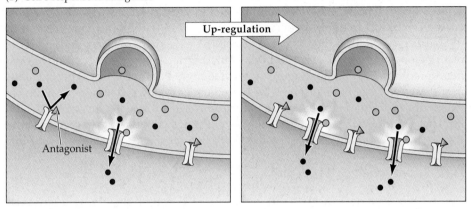

Up-regulation

Antagonist

4.10 RECEPTOR REGULATION Over time, cells respond to the actions of receptor-selective drugs by altering their own sensitivity, through changes in the number of receptors they make available. In (A), the effects of an agonist drug augment the effects of the endogenous ligand, enhancing the effect on the postsynaptic cell. The postsynaptic cell may respond by down-regulating (decreasing) the number of receptors it places into the synapse, in order to become less sensitive and more like the predrug state. In (B), a competitive antagonist instead blocks an endogenous substance from having its usual effect, to which the postsynaptic cell may respond by up-regulating (increasing) the number of its receptors in order to become more sensitive and compensate for the lessened effect of the endogenous ligand.

membranes as being fairly static, in fact the reverse is true—receptor densities are continually waxing and waning as new receptors are inserted into the synapse, or old ones are internalized by the cell for recycling (Anggono and Huganir, 2012; Choquet and Triller, 2013). In neuropharmacology, this dynamic regulation of receptor proteins—changing the number of receptors present in the cell membrane—is an important source of functional tolerance. Receptor regulation tends to alter neuronal sensitivity in the direction opposite to the drug's effect. Thus, over the course of repeated exposures to an *agonist* drug, neurons may **down-regulate** (decrease the number of available receptors to which the drug can bind), thereby becoming less sensitive and countering the drug effect. If the drug is an *antagonist*, target neurons may instead **up-regulate** (increase the number of receptors) and thereby become more sensitive. These actions are illustrated in **FIGURE 4.10**.

Tolerance to a drug often generalizes to other drugs belonging to the same chemical class; this effect is termed **cross-tolerance**. For example, people who have developed tolerance to heroin tend to exhibit a degree of tolerance to all the other drugs in the opiate category, including codeine, morphine, and methadone. For drugs that have multiple effects in the body, tolerance to the various effects may develop at different rates. Once established, drug tolerance is believed to be a major cause of **withdrawal symptoms**, the unpleasant sensations that occur when one stops using a drug. As we will discuss later, one factor that maintains drug addiction is the avoidance of the physical discomfort of withdrawal symptoms.

Furthermore, some drug responses can become *stronger* with repeated treatments, rather than weaker. Termed **sensitization**, this effect is thought to contribute to the drug craving that addicts experience. This heightened sensitivity may last for a prolonged period and is associated with long-term brain changes (Peris et al., 1990), altering the function of the mesolimbocortical DA reward pathway (Vialou et al., 2012).

Drugs are administered and eliminated in many different ways

The amount of drug that reaches the brain and the speed with which it starts acting are determined in part by the drug's route of administration. Some routes, such as

metabolic tolerance The form of drug tolerance that arises when repeated exposure to the drug causes the metabolic machinery of the body to become more efficient at clearing the drug.

functional tolerance Decreased responding to a drug after repeated exposures, generally as a consequence of up- or down-regulation of receptors.

down-regulation A compensatory reduction in receptor availability at the synapses of a neuron.

up-regulation A compensatory increase in receptor availability at the synapses of a neuron.

cross-tolerance A condition in which the development of tolerance for one drug causes an individual to develop tolerance for another drug.

withdrawal symptom An uncomfortable symptom that arises when a person stops taking a drug that he or she has used frequently, especially at high doses.

sensitization A process in which the body shows an enhanced response to a given drug after repeated doses.

bioavailable Referring to a substance, usually a drug, that is present in the body in a form that is able to interact with physiological mechanisms.

biotransformation The process in which enzymes convert a drug into a metabolite that is itself active, possibly in ways that are substantially different from the actions of the original substance.

pharmacokinetics Collective name for all the factors that affect the movement of a drug into, through, and out of the body.

blood-brain barrier The mechanisms that make the movement of substances from blood vessels into brain cells more difficult than exchanges in other body organs, thus affording the brain greater protection from exposure to some substances found in the blood.

smoking or intravenous injection, rapidly increase the concentration of drug in the body that is **bioavailable** (free to act on the target tissue and therefore not bound to other proteins or in the process of being metabolized or excreted). With other routes, such as oral ingestion, drug concentration builds up more slowly over longer periods of time.

The duration of a drug effect is largely determined by the manner in which the drug is metabolized and excreted from the body—via the kidneys, liver, lungs, and other routes. In some cases, the metabolites of drugs are themselves active; this **biotransformation** of drugs can be a source of unwanted side effects. Some drugs may be stored in *depots* (collecting in fat or bone, for example), only to reemerge and have physiological effects after long periods of time. The factors that affect the movement of a drug into, through, and out of the body are collectively referred to as **pharmacokinetics**.

Humans have devised a variety of ingenious techniques for introducing substances into the body; these are summarized in **TABLE 4.3**. In Chapter 2 we discussed the **blood-brain barrier**: the tight junctions between the endothelial cells of blood vessels within the CNS that inhibit the movement of larger molecules out of the bloodstream and into the brain. This barrier poses a major challenge for neuropharmacology because many drugs that might be clinically or experimentally useful are too large to pass the blood-brain barrier to enter the brain. To a limited extent this problem can be circumvented by delivering drugs directly into the brain, but that is a drastic step. Alternatively, some drugs can take advantage of active transport systems that normally move nutrients out of the bloodstream and into the brain.

TABLE 4.3 The Relationship between Routes of Administration and Effects of Drugs

ROUTE OF ADMINISTRATION	EXAMPLES AND MECHANISMS	TYPICAL SPEED OF EFFECTS
INGESTION Tablets and capsules Syrups Infusions and teas Suppositories	Ingestion of many sorts of drugs and remedies depends on absorption by the gut, which is somewhat slower than most other routes, and is affected by digestive processes and the presence of food	Slow to moderate
INHALATION Nasal absorption Inhaled powders and sprays Smoking	Nicotine, cocaine, and organic solvents such as airplane glue and gasoline are inhaled, as are a variety of prescription drugs and hormone treatments. Inhalation methods take advantage of the rich vascularization of the nose and lungs to convey drugs directly into the bloodstream.	Moderate to fast
PERIPHERAL INJECTION Subcutaneous Intramuscular Intraperitoneal (abdominal) Intravenous	Many drugs are injected. Subcutaneous (under the skin) injections tend to have the slowest effects because drugs must diffuse into nearby tissue in order to reach the bloodstream; intravenous injections have very rapid effects because the drugs are placed directly into circulation.	Moderate to fast
CENTRAL INJECTION Intracerebroventricular (into ventricular system) Intrathecal (into spinal CSF) Epidural (under the dura mater) Intracerebral (directly into a brain region)	Central methods involve injection directly into the CNS and are used in order to circumvent the blood-brain barrier, to rule out peripheral effects, or to directly affect a discrete brain location.	Fast to very fast

Drugs Affect Each Stage of Neural Conduction and Synaptic Transmission

Local anesthetics such as procaine (trade name Novocain) block sodium channels and therefore action potentials (see Chapter 3) in pain fibers from, say, that tooth your dentist is working on. But the great majority of drugs that act on the nervous system to produce changes in behavior do so by altering the complex choreography of synaptic transmission.

local anesthetic A drug, such as procaine or lidocaine, that blocks sodium channels to stop neural transmission in pain fibers.

Some drugs alter presynaptic events

One of the ways that a drug may change synaptic transmission is by modifying the behavior of the presynaptic neuron, changing the system that converts an electrical signal (an action potential) into a chemical signal (secretion of neurotransmitter). **FIGURE 4.11** illustrates presynaptic processes that are targeted by CNS drugs, with examples of each kind of drug. The most common presynaptic drug effects can be grouped into three main categories: (1) effects on transmitter production, (2) effects on transmitter release, and (3) effects on transmitter clearance.

TRANSMITTER PRODUCTION In order for the presynaptic neuron to produce neurotransmitter, the axon terminals must receive a steady supply of raw materials and

4.11 DRUG EFFECTS ON PRESYNAPTIC MECHANISMS

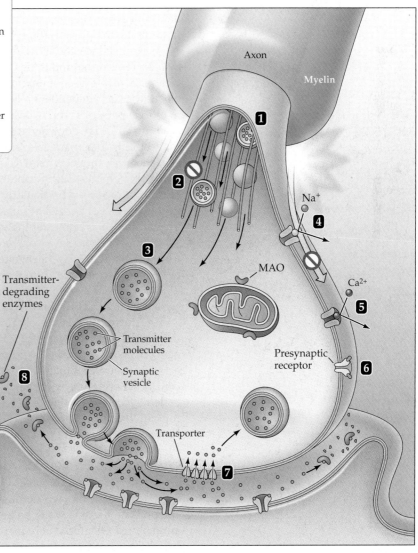

A Effects on Transmitter Production

1 **Inhibition of transmitter synthesis**
Example: *Para*-chlorophenylalanine inhibits tryptophan hydroxylase, preventing synthesis of serotonin from its metabolic precursor.

2 **Blockade of axonal transport**
Example: Colchicine impairs maintenance of microtubules and blocks axonal transport.

3 **Interference with the storage of transmitters**
Example: Reserpine blocks the packaging of transmitter molecules within vesicles, thereby allowing the transmitter to be broken down by enzymes.

B Effects on Transmitter Release

4 **Prevention of synaptic transmission**
Example: Tetrodotoxin, found in puffer fish, blocks voltage-gated Na$^+$ channels and prevents nerve conduction.

5 **Alteration of synaptic transmitter release**
Example: Calcium channel blockers (e.g., verapamil) inhibit release of transmitters. Amphetamine stimulates release of catecholamine transmitters. Black widow causes overrelease, and thus depletion, of ACh.

6 **Alteration of transmitter release through modulation of presynaptic activity**
Example: Caffeine competes with adenosine for presynaptic receptors, thus preventing its inhibitory effects.

C Effects on Transmitter Clearance

7 **Inactivation of transmitter reuptake**
Example: Cocaine and amphetamine inhibit reuptake mechanisms, thus prolonging synaptic activity. Certain antidepressants inhibit serotonin or norepinephrine reuptake.

8 **Blockade of transmitter degradation**
Example: Some drugs (e.g., monoamine oxidase [MAO] inhibitors) inhibit enzymes that normally break down neurotransmitter molecules in the axon terminal or in the synaptic cleft. As a result, transmitter remains active longer and to greater effect.

autoreceptor A receptor for a synaptic transmitter that is located in the presynaptic membrane, telling the axon terminal how much transmitter has been released.

caffeine A stimulant compound found in coffee, cacao, and other plants.

adenosine In the context of neural transmission, a neuromodulator that alters synaptic activity.

the enzymes that use them to synthesize transmitter molecules, vesicles, and other important components.

Some drugs alter this process in various ways (**FIGURE 4.11A**). For example, a drug may inhibit the enzymes that neurons use to synthesize a particular neurotransmitter, resulting in depletion of that transmitter. Alternatively, drugs that block axonal transport prevent materials from reaching the axon terminals in the first place, likewise causing the terminals to run out of neurotransmitter. In both cases, affected presynaptic neurons are prevented from having their usual effects on postsynaptic neurons, with sometimes profound effects on behavior. A third class of drug (e.g., reserpine) doesn't prevent the *production* of transmitter molecules, but instead interferes with the ability of neurons to *store* catecholamine transmitters in synaptic vesicles, for later release. This has the effect of depleting transmitter at catecholaminergic synapses and may have a complicated effect on behavior, depending on whether and how much transmitter reaches the postsynaptic cell.

TRANSMITTER RELEASE Even if a presynaptic terminal has an adequate supply of transmitter stored in vesicles, various agents or conditions can prevent the *release* of transmitter when an action potential reaches the terminal (**FIGURE 4.11B**). For example, compounds that block sodium channels (like the toxin that makes puffer fish a dangerous delicacy, called *tetrodotoxin*) prevent axons from firing action potentials, shutting down synaptic transmission with deadly results. And drugs called *calcium channel blockers* do exactly as their name suggests, blocking the calcium influx that normally drives the release of transmitter into the synapse.

Some toxins prevent the release of *specific* kinds of transmitters (de Paiva et al., 1993). For instance, the active ingredient in Botox—botulinum toxin, which is formed by a bacterium that multiplies in improperly canned food—binds to specialized receptors in nicotinic cholinergic membranes and is transported into the cell, where it blocks the Ca^{2+}-dependent release of acetylcholine (McMahon et al., 1992), resulting in muscle paralysis. The widespread paralysis that occurs after eating contaminated food can be lethal, but when the dilute toxin is selectively injected into facial muscles, the resulting local paralysis reduces wrinkling of the overlying skin. Tetanus (lockjaw) bacteria produce a toxin, called *tetanospasmin*, that interferes with the molecular machinery that causes synaptic vesicles to bind to the presynaptic membrane. By blocking exocytosis, particularly at inhibitory synapses in the CNS, tetanospasmin causes the loss of normal inhibitory influences on motor neurons, resulting in strong involuntary contractions of the muscles.

A different approach involves modifying the systems that the neuron normally uses to monitor and regulate its own transmitter release. For example, presynaptic neurons often use **autoreceptors** to monitor how much transmitter they have released; it's a kind of feedback system. Drugs that alter autoreceptor signals provide a false feedback signal, prompting the presynaptic cell to release more or less transmitter.

The **caffeine** that we obtain from coffee and other beverages (worldwide, we drink more than 2.2 *billion* cups of coffee *every day*) acts by blocking the autoreceptor effect of an endogenous ligand called **adenosine** (Lindskog et al., 2002). Adenosine acts as a neuromodulator: it is normally co-released with primary transmitters to control synaptic activity by inhibiting transmitter release. So, by blocking adenosine, caffeine *increases* catecholamine release, resulting in arousal. Interestingly, consuming caffeine after a period of studying reportedly improves memory consolidation in humans (Borota et al., 2014) and bees (Chittka and Peng, 2013).

TRANSMITTER CLEARANCE Immediately after being released, transmitter is rapidly cleared from the synapse. Obviously, getting rid of the used transmitter is normally an important step because until it is gone, new releases of transmitter from the presynaptic side won't be able to have much extra effect. But under certain circumstances, a significant reduction of synaptic transmitter availability may contribute to disorders such as depression. There are several pharmacological strategies for altering the clearance process. Some drugs interfere with **transmitter reuptake** by blocking the specialized proteins, called **transporters**, that normally remove neurotransmitter from the cleft for reuse (**FIGURE 4.11C**) (see also Chapter 3). For example, we'll see that some very common antidepressants inhibit the reuptake of serotonin, allowing the transmitter to accumulate and have a larger effect on postsynaptic receptors. Such drugs are said to work presynaptically, because the transporters are on the presynaptic terminal.

Other drugs may have a similar effect by inhibiting **degradation**, the chemical process of breaking down neurotransmitter into inactive metabolites, again allowing the transmitter to accumulate and have a greater effect on the postsynaptic cell (see Figure 4.11, step 8). Agents that inhibit the enzyme acetylcholinesterase (AChE), called *acetylcholinesterase inhibitors*, allow ACh to remain active at the synapse and alter the timing of synaptic transmission. They include certain pesticides and chemical weapons, and they produce prolonged contraction of muscles and resultant paralysis, as well as overactivity of the parasympathetic nervous system.

Drugs may act postsynaptically

Another powerful way for drugs to affect synaptic transmission is to modify the activity of the postsynaptic cell. As illustrated in **FIGURE 4.12**, there are two major classes of postsynaptic drug actions: (1) direct effects on transmitter receptors and (2) effects on cellular processes within the postsynaptic cell.

EFFECTS ON TRANSMITTER RECEPTORS   As we discussed earlier in the chapter, receptor antagonists bind directly to postsynaptic receptors and block them from being activated by their neurotransmitters (**FIGURE 4.12A**). This can have immediate and dramatic effects. Curare, for example, blocks the nicotinic ACh receptors found on muscles, resulting in immediate paralysis of all skeletal muscles, including those used for breathing (which is why curare is an effective arrow poison).

transmitter reuptake   The reabsorption of synaptic transmitter by the axon terminal from which it was released.

transporters   Specialized receptors in the presynaptic membrane that recognize neurotransmitter molecules and return to the presynaptic neuron for reuse.

degradation   The chemical breakdown of a neurotransmitter into inactive metabolites.

4.12 DRUG EFFECTS ON POSTSYNAPTIC MECHANISMS

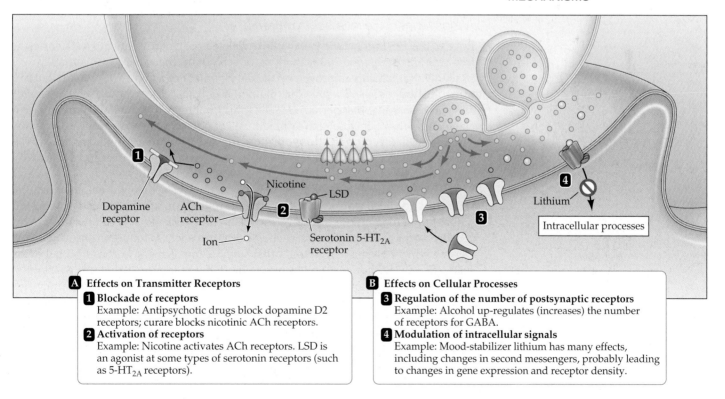

A Effects on Transmitter Receptors
1 Blockade of receptors
Example: Antipsychotic drugs block dopamine D2 receptors; curare blocks nicotinic ACh receptors.
2 Activation of receptors
Example: Nicotine activates ACh receptors. LSD is an agonist at some types of serotonin receptors (such as 5-HT$_{2A}$ receptors).

B Effects on Cellular Processes
3 Regulation of the number of postsynaptic receptors
Example: Alcohol up-regulates (increases) the number of receptors for GABA.
4 Modulation of intracellular signals
Example: Mood-stabilizer lithium has many effects, including changes in second messengers, probably leading to changes in gene expression and receptor density.

antipsychotics A class of drugs that alleviate the symptoms of schizophrenia.

typical antipsychotics A class of antischizophrenic drugs whose principal mode of action is antagonism of dopamine D_2 receptors.

atypical antipsychotics Also called *atypical neuroleptics*. A class of antischizophrenic drugs that have actions other than or in addition to the dopamine D_2 receptor antagonism that characterizes the typical antipsychotics.

antidepressants A class of drugs that relieve the symptoms of depression.

tricyclic antidepressants A class of drugs that act by increasing the synaptic accumulation of serotonin and norepinephrine.

Selective receptor agonists bind to specific receptors and activate them, mimicking the natural neurotransmitter at those receptors. These drugs are often very potent, with effects that vary depending on the particular types of receptors activated. LSD is an example, producing bizarre visual experiences through strong stimulation of a subtype of serotonin receptor (5-HT_{2A} receptors) found in visual cortex.

EFFECTS ON CELLULAR PROCESSES When they bind to their matching receptors on postsynaptic membranes, neurotransmitters can stimulate a variety of changes within the postsynaptic cell, such as activation of second messengers, activation of genes, and the production of various proteins (**FIGURE 4.12B**). For example, as we saw earlier, some drugs induce the postsynaptic cell to up-regulate (increase) its receptors, thus changing the sensitivity of the synapse, while other drugs cause a down-regulation of receptor density. Some drugs directly alter second messenger systems, with widespread effects in the brain; this is one of the ways in which the mood-stabilizing drug lithium chloride is believed to act. Future research will probably focus on drugs to selectively activate, alter, insert, or block targeted genes within the DNA of neurons. These *genomic* effects could produce profound long-term changes in the structure and function of the targeted neurons.

Some Neuroactive Drugs Ease the Symptoms of Injury or Psychiatric Illness

It's hard to believe, but prior to the 1950s about half of all hospital beds in the United States were taken up by psychiatric patients (Menninger, 1948), and there can be little doubt that many historical accounts of sorcery, strange visions, and possession by demons had their foundation in symptoms of severe mental illness, as we discuss in detail in Chapter 16. But where the historical response to psychiatric illness was to lock away the afflicted, neuroscience breakthroughs of the last 70 years have revolutionized psychiatry and liberated millions from the purgatory of institutionalized care. In the sections that follow, we will briefly review some of the major categories of psychoactive drugs, based on how they affect behavior.

Antipsychotics relieve schizophrenia

Prior to the 1950s, a majority of institutionalized psychiatric patients were suffering from the delusions and hallucinations of schizophrenia. This awful situation was suddenly dramatically improved by the development of a family of drugs called **antipsychotics** (or *neuroleptics*). The first of these drugs, chlorpromazine (Thorazine), and successors like haloperidol (Haldol) and loxapine (Loxitane) all share one crucial feature: they act as selective antagonists of dopamine D_2 receptors in the brain. These so-called **typical antipsychotics** are so good at relieving the *positive symptoms* of schizophrenia—emergent abnormalities like hallucinations and delusions—that a dopaminergic model of the disease became dominant.

The 1990s saw the advent of second-generation schizophrenia medications, known as **atypical antipsychotics**, that have both dopaminergic activity and additional, nondopaminergic actions, especially the blockade of certain serotonin receptors. Atypical antipsychotics, such as clozapine, seem to reduce the *negative symptoms* of schizophrenia—symptoms that involve impairment or loss of a behavior, such as social withdrawal and blunted emotional responses—that are resistant to the typical antipsychotics, but this claim has been disputed (Burton, 2006). Emerging evidence that schizophrenia involves additional non-monoaminergic mechanisms has prompted an intense research effort aimed at developing third-generation antipsychotics, with novel targets like glutamatergic synapses, but effective treatments remain elusive (Dunlop and Brandon, 2015). So, although there has been progress in its treatment, schizophrenia remains a difficult, multifaceted disease and a major health problem. We will return to the topic of schizophrenia and its treatment in Chapter 16.

Antidepressants reduce chronic mood problems

Disturbances of mood, or *affective disorders,* are among the most common of all psychiatric complaints (World Health Organization, 2001). The first generation of effective **antidepressant** medications, developed in the 1950s, were the monoamine oxidase (MAO) inhibitors, such as tranylcypromine (Parnate) and isocarboxazid (Marplan). Normally, MAOs break down monoamine neurotransmitters at axon terminals, thereby reducing transmitter activity. By blocking this process, MAO inhibitors allow monoamine neurotransmitters to accumulate at synapses (see Figure 4.11, step 8), with an associated improvement in mood.

Increasing synaptic monoamine availability appears to be a key activity of all antidepressants. The second generation of antidepressants—the **tricyclics**—combat depression by increasing the synaptic content of the monoamines norepinephrine and serotonin. Named for their three-ringed molecular structure, tricyclics such as imipramine (Tofranil) block the reuptake of neurotransmitters into presynaptic axon terminals (see Figure 4.11, step 7), thereby allowing the transmitter to accumulate in the synapse. More recently developed antidepressants, such as fluoxetine (Prozac), sertraline (Zoloft), and citalopram (Celexa), are **selective serotonin reuptake inhibitors** (**SSRIs**) and **serotonin-norepinephrine reuptake inhibitors** (**SNRIs**); as their names indicate, these drugs alleviate depression by selectively allowing serotonin (plus norepinephrine in the case of SNRIs) to accumulate in synapses. These newer antidepressants lack some of the undesirable side effects of older drugs, although they have side effects of their own (such as disturbances of sexual function) and can take as long as 6–8 weeks to have full effect. We will discuss the causes and treatment of affective disorders in more detail in Chapter 16.

Anxiolytics combat anxiety

Most of us occasionally suffer feelings of vague dissatisfaction or apprehension that we call anxiety, but some people are stricken by disabling emotional distress that resembles abject fear and terror. These clinical states of anxiety include panic attacks, phobias (such as the fear of taking an airplane or even of leaving the house), and generalized anxiety (see Chapter 16).

Humans have long sought relief from anxiety through the ingestion of **anxiolytics** (from the word *anxiety* and the Greek *lytikos,* "able to loosen"). Sometimes also called *tranquilizers,* anxiolytics belong to the general category of **depressants**: drugs that depress or reduce nervous system activity. Alcohol and opiates are perhaps the original anxiolytics, but their anxiety-fighting properties come at the cost of intoxication, addiction potential, and neuropsychological impairment with long-term abuse, so they are not suitable for therapeutic use.

Barbiturate drugs ("downers") were originally developed to reduce anxiety, promote sleep, and prevent epileptic seizures. They are still used for those purposes but are also addictive and easily overdosed, often fatally, as illustrated in Figure 4.9E. Since the 1970s the most widely prescribed anxiolytics have been the **benzodiazepine agonists**, which are both more specific and safer than the barbiturates. Members of this class of drug, like diazepam (trade name Valium) and lorazepam (Ativan), bind to specific sites on GABA$_A$ receptors and enhance the activity of GABA (Walters et al., 2000). Because GABA$_A$ receptors are inhibitory, benzodiazepines help GABA to produce larger inhibitory postsynaptic potentials than would be caused by GABA alone. This has the end result of reducing the excitability of neurons.

GABA$_A$ receptors have several different binding sites—some that facilitate and some that inhibit the effect of GABA (**FIGURE 4.13**); therefore, many different drugs can interact with this receptor complex. For example, benzodiazepines bind to a unique modulatory site

selective serotonin reuptake inhibitor (SSRI) A drug that blocks the reuptake of transmitter at serotonergic synapses.

serotonin-norepinephrine reuptake inhibitor (SNRI) A drug that blocks the reuptake of transmitter at both serotonergic and noradrenergic synapses.

anxiolytics A class of substances that are used to combat anxiety.

depressants A class of drugs that act to reduce neural activity.

barbiturate A powerful sedative anxiolytic derived from barbituric acid, with dangerous addiction and overdose potential.

benzodiazepine agonists A class of antianxiety drugs that bind to sites on GABA$_A$ receptors.

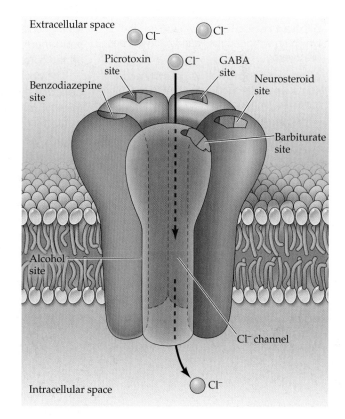

4.13 THE GABA$_A$ RECEPTOR HAS MANY DIFFERENT BINDING SITES The GABA$_A$ complex is made up of five protein subunits that penetrate the cell membrane and surround a Cl$^-$ ion channel at the core. These subunits contain many different recognition and receptor sites; some of the most important ones are labeled here. GABA$_A$ receptors are widespread in the brain and are crucial for normal inhibitory processes. Many depressant drugs work by increasing the responsiveness of GABA$_A$ receptors to GABA.

4.14 THE SOURCE OF OPIUM AND MORPHINE The opium poppy has a distinctive flower and seedpod. The bitter flavor and CNS actions of opium may provide the poppy plant a defense against being eaten.

orphan receptor Any receptor for which no endogenous ligand has yet been discovered.

allopregnanolone A naturally occurring steroid that modulates GABA receptor activity in much the same way that benzodiazepine anxiolytics do.

neurosteroids Steroids produced in the brain.

opium A heterogeneous extract of the seedpod juice of the opium poppy, *Papaver somniferum*.

morphine An opiate compound derived from the poppy flower.

analgesic Referring to painkilling properties.

heroin Diacetylmorphine; an artificially modified, very potent form of morphine.

opioid receptor A receptor that responds to endogenous and/or exogenous opiates.

on the receptor complex that is distant from where GABA itself binds. The benzodiazepine-binding site is thus an **orphan receptor**—a receptor for which an endogenous ligand has not been conclusively identified—and the hunt for its endogenous ligand has been intense. **Allopregnanolone**, a steroid derived from the hormone progesterone, acts on yet another site on the $GABA_A$ receptor. Allopregnanolone is elevated during stress and has a calming effect (Melcangi and Panzica, 2014). Alcohol ingestion also increases brain concentrations of allopregnanolone (VanDoren et al., 2000), so this steroid may mediate some of the calming influence of alcohol. Several other progesterone-like **neurosteroids** (steroids produced in the brain) may act on $GABA_A$ receptors to produce anxiolytic, analgesic, and anticonvulsant effects (Belelli and Lambert, 2005; Gunn et al., 2015).

Other categories of anxiolytics under active investigation affect other transmitter systems, such as serotonergic and neuropeptide mechanisms (Griebel and Holmes, 2013). The serotonergic agonist buspirone (BuSpar) is an effective anxiolytic that lacks the sedative effects of benzodiazepines. Buspirone is a $5\text{-}HT_{1A}$ agonist and a partial agonist of dopamine D_2 receptors, but the exact mechanism of its anxiolytic action remains unknown.

Opiates potently relieve pain

Opium, extracted from poppy flower seedpods (**FIGURE 4.14**), has been used by humans since at least the Stone Age. **Morphine**, the major active substance in opium, is a very effective **analgesic** (painkiller) that has brought relief from severe pain to many millions of people (see Chapter 8). Unfortunately, morphine also has a strong potential for addiction, as does its close relative **heroin** (diacetylmorphine) and powerful opiate painkillers like oxycodone (OxyContin) and fentanyl. Accidental fentanyl overdose is all too common, claiming the life of the musician Prince in 2016.

The opiates morphine, heroin, and codeine bind to specific receptors—**opioid receptors**—that are concentrated in certain regions of the brain. Opioid receptors are found in the limbic and hypothalamic areas of the brain, and they are particularly rich in the locus coeruleus and in the **periaqueductal gray**—the gray matter that surrounds the cerebral aqueduct in the brainstem (**FIGURE 4.15**). Injection of morphine directly into the periaqueductal gray produces strong analgesia, indicating that this is a region where morphine acts to reduce pain perception (see Chapter 8). The discovery of orphan receptors for opiates came as a surprise, and because the presence of these receptors implied that there must be an endogenous ligand produced within the body, it prompted an intense scientific effort to identify **endogenous opioids**.

4.15 THE DISTRIBUTION OF OPIOID RECEPTORS IN THE RAT BRAIN This horizontal section (rostral is at the top) shows opioid receptors widely distributed in the brain (the areas of highest binding are shown in yellow, orange, and red). They are concentrated in the medial thalamus and in some brainstem areas: the periaqueductal gray and the inferior colliculus. (Courtesy of Dr. Miles Herkenham, National Institute of Mental Health.)

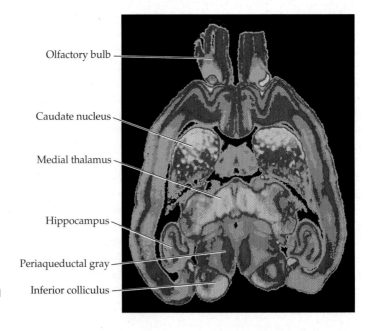

Olfactory bulb

Caudate nucleus

Medial thalamus

Hippocampus

Periaqueductal gray

Inferior colliculus

Researchers have now identified three major families of these potent peptides (see Table 4.1): the **enkephalins** (from the Greek *en*, "in," and *kephale*, "head") (Hughes et al., 1975), the **endorphins** (a contraction of *endogenous morphine*), and the **dynorphins** (short for *dynamic endorphins*, in recognition of their potency and speed of action.) Like morphine, enkephalins relieve pain and are addictive. Only a small part of the enkephalin molecule is the same as the morphine molecule, but this common part is what binds to the opioid receptor.

There are three main kinds of opioid receptors—the delta (δ), kappa (κ), and mu (μ) opioid receptors—all of which are metabotropic receptors. Powerful drugs that block opiate receptors—naloxone and naltrexone are examples—can rapidly reverse the effects of opiates and rescue people from overdose. Opiate antagonists also block the rewarding aspects of drugs like heroin, so they can be helpful for treating addiction, as we'll discuss at the end of this chapter. For some alcoholics, naltrexone treatment blocks the euphoria that normally results from alcohol, suggesting that in these individuals alcohol causes the release of endogenous opioids that brings pleasure. Interestingly, only that minority of alcoholics who carry a gene for a particular variant of the mu opioid receptor benefit from naltrexone treatment (Oroszi et al., 2009).

Some Neuroactive Drugs Are Used to Alter Conscious Experiences

Humans have a long history of tinkering with their conscious experience of the world. Some of the major classes of neuroactive drugs that modify consciousness include cannabinoids, stimulants, alcohol, and hallucinogenic and dissociative drugs.

Cannabinoids have a wide array of effects

Marijuana and related preparations, such as hashish, are derived from the *Cannabis sativa* plant (**FIGURE 4.16**) and have been used in various cultures for thousands of years (E. B. Russo et al., 2008). Typically inhaled via smoking, marijuana contains dozens of active ingredients, chief among which is the compound **Δ9-tetrahydrocannabinol** (**THC**) (Gaoni and Mechoulam, 1964). Marijuana use usually produces pleasant relaxation and mood alteration, although the drug can occasionally cause stimulation and paranoia instead.

Casual use of marijuana seems to be mostly harmless, but as with other substances, heavy use can be harmful. For example, heavy use may be associated with respiratory problems, addiction, psychiatric disorders, and cognitive decline (Maldonado and Rodríguez de Fonseca, 2002; Meier et al., 2012). Adolescents who use marijuana appear to be more likely to develop psychosis in adulthood (Gage et al., 2015; Malone et al., 2010), but it is not clear whether the drug causes psychosis or whether adolescents who are prepsychotic are more likely to turn to marijuana. Several preliminary studies have identified specific gene variants that seem to be associated with greater risk for marijuana-associated psychosis (Caspi et al., 2005; van Winkel et al., 2011); if confirmed, such associations would indicate that a minority of individuals are genetically vulnerable to this severe side effect of marijuana use.

As was the case with opiates and benzodiazepines, researchers found that the brain contains cannabinoid receptors that mediate the effects of compounds like THC. Cannabinoid receptors are concentrated in the substantia nigra, the hippocampus, the cerebellar cortex, and the cerebral cortex (**FIGURE 4.17**) (Devane et al., 1988); other regions, such as the brainstem, show few of these receptors. There are at least two subtypes of cannabinoid receptors—CB_1 and CB_2 (Gerard et al., 1991; Pertwee, 1997)—both of which are G protein-coupled metabotropic receptors. Genetic disruption of CB_1 receptors is sufficient to make mice unresponsive to the rewarding properties of cannabinoid drugs (Ledent et al., 1999). Only the CB_1 receptor is found in the nervous system; CB_2 receptors are especially prominent in the immune system.

The discovery of cannabinoid receptors touched off an intensive search for an endogenous ligand, and several such compounds—termed **endocannabinoids**—were identified. Interestingly, endocannabinoids can function as retrograde messengers, conveying messages from the postsynaptic cell to the presynaptic cell. This

4.16 RELAXATION In many jurisdictions, laws prohibiting the sale and consumption of marijuana are being relaxed. Although legal access to marijuana, via licensed dispensaries like this one, is expected to reduce criminal activity and raise tax revenue, concerns about health risks in adolescents and heavy users remain.

periaqueductal gray The neuronal body–rich region of the midbrain surrounding the cerebral aqueduct that connects the third and fourth ventricles; involved in pain perception.

endogenous opioids A family of peptide transmitters that have been called the body's own narcotics. The three kinds are enkephalins, endorphins, and dynorphins.

enkephalins One of three kinds of endogenous opioids.

endorphins One of three kinds of endogenous opioids.

dynorphins One of three kinds of endogenous opioids.

marijuana A dried preparation of the *Cannabis sativa* plant, typically smoked to obtain THC.

Δ9-tetrahydrocannabinol (THC) The major active ingredient in marijuana.

endocannabinoid An endogenous ligand of cannabinoid receptors; thus, an analog of marijuana that is produced by the brain.

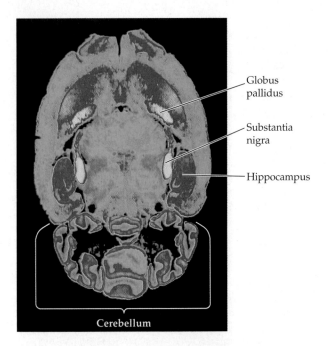

Globus pallidus

Substantia nigra

Hippocampus

Cerebellum

4.17 THE DISTRIBUTION OF CANNABINOID RECEPTORS IN THE RAT BRAIN The areas of highest binding are indicated by yellow, orange, and red in this horizontal section. (Courtesy of Dr. Miles Herkenham, National Institute of Mental Health.)

retrograde signal is thought to modulate the release of neurotransmitter by the presynaptic nerve terminal (Murray et al., 2007). The most studied endocannabinoid is **anandamide** (from the Sanskrit *ananda*, "bliss") (Devane et al., 1992), which has diverse functional effects, including alterations of memory formation, appetite stimulation, reduced sensitivity to pain, and protection from excitotoxic brain damage (Marsicano et al., 2003; P. B. Smith et al., 1994). Other endocannabinoids include 2-arachidonylglycerol (2-AG) (Stella et al., 1997) and oleamide (Leggett et al., 2004). Most CB_1 receptors are found on GABA-ergic axon terminals, and cannabinoids acting on these receptors modulate GABA release. In the case of hippocampal neurons, this action has the result—familiar to chronic marijuana users—of transient amnesia secondary to changes in protein synthesis in the postsynaptic cells (Puighermanal et al., 2012).

Cannabinoids are thus targets of an intense research effort aimed at developing drugs with some of the specific beneficial effects of marijuana: improving mood, relieving pain, lowering blood pressure, combating nausea, lowering eye pressure in glaucoma, and so on. The documented use of cannabis for medicinal purposes spans over 6000 years, but from the early twentieth century until recently, it has remained illegal in most jurisdictions. Several U.S. states have recently legalized the sale and use of marijuana for recreational purposes, and medical marijuana use is now "decriminalized" in many U.S. states, Canada, and other countries. It seems likely that the relaxation of marijuana laws will continue.

Stimulants increase the activity of the nervous system

The degree of activity of the nervous system reflects a balance of excitatory and inhibitory influences. Stimulants are drugs that tip the balance toward the excitatory side; they therefore have an alerting, activating effect. Many naturally occurring and artificial stimulants are widely used, including amphetamine, nicotine, caffeine, and cocaine. Some stimulants act directly by increasing excitatory synaptic potentials. Others act by blocking normal inhibitory processes; we've already seen that caffeine blocks adenosine receptors. Amphetamine-like stimulants called *cathinones* are released when the African shrub **khat** (or *qat*, pronounced "cot") is chewed. Many types of synthetic cathinones—known collectively as "bath salts"—have been developed and marketed (often via the Internet). These new designer drugs have shown rapid growth in popularity as unconventional stimulants; *mephedrone* ("plant food" or "meow-meow"), for example, acts in many ways like amphetamine (J. P. Kelly, 2011; Zawilska, 2014), which we'll discuss shortly. Paradoxically, stimulants such as methylphenidate (Ritalin) have a calming effect in humans with attention deficit hyperactivity disorder (ADHD); this activity may be mediated by changes in serotonergic activity (Gainetdinov et al., 1999).

NICOTINE Tobacco is native to the Americas, where European explorers first encountered smoking; these explorers brought tobacco back to Europe with them. Tobacco use became much more widespread following technological innovations that made it easier to smoke, in the form of cigarettes (W. Bennett, 1983). Exposed to the large surface of the lungs, the **nicotine** from cigarettes enters the blood and brain much more rapidly than does nicotine from other tobacco products. Nicotine increases heart rate, blood pressure, secretion of hydrochloric acid in the stomach, and intestinal activity. In the short run, these effects make tobacco use pleasurable. But these neural effects on body function, quite apart from the effects of tobacco tar on the lungs, make prolonged tobacco use very unhealthful. Smoking and nicotine exposure in adolescence have a lasting impact on attention and cognitive development, likely as a consequence of impairments of glutamatergic synapses in the prefrontal cortex (Counotte et al., 2011).

anandamide An endogenous substance that binds the cannabinoid receptor molecule.

khat Also spelled *qat*. An African shrub that, when chewed, acts as a stimulant.

nicotine A compound found in plants, including tobacco, that acts as an agonist on a large class of cholinergic receptors.

The *nicotinic* ACh receptors didn't get their name by coincidence—it is through these receptors that the nicotine from tobacco exerts its effects in the body. Nicotinic receptors drive the contraction of skeletal muscles and the activation of various visceral organs, but they are also found in high concentrations in the brain, including the cortex. This is one way in which nicotine enhances some aspects of cognitive performance. Astonishingly, the nicotine from one cigarette can occupy 88% of the brain's nicotinic receptors (A. L. Brody et al., 2006). Using a sophisticated genetic model in which certain nicotinic ACh receptors are expressed only in discrete brain regions, researchers found that nicotine acts directly on the ventral tegmental area (see Figure 4.5) to exert its rewarding/addicting effects (Maskos et al., 2005).

COCAINE   For hundreds of years, people in Bolivia, Colombia, and Peru have used the leaves of the coca shrub—either chewed or brewed as a tea—to increase endurance, alleviate hunger, and promote a sense of well-being. This use of coca leaves does not seem to cause problems. The artificially purified coca extract **cocaine**, however, is a powerfully addictive alkaloid stimulant that has harmed millions of lives.

First isolated in 1859, cocaine was added to beverages (such as *Coca*-Cola) and tonics for its stimulant qualities, and subsequently it was used as a local anesthetic (it is in the same chemical family as procaine) and as an antidepressant. But people soon discovered that the rapid hit of cocaine resulting from snorting or smoking (see Table 4.3) has a stimulant effect that is powerful and pleasurable. Unfortunately, it is also very highly addictive. *Crack*, a smokable form of cocaine that appeared in the mid-1980s, enters the blood and the brain more rapidly and thus is even more addictive than cocaine powder. Heavy cocaine use raises the risk of serious side effects such as stroke, psychosis, loss of gray matter, and severe mood disturbances (Franklin et al., 2002). Like other psychostimulants, cocaine acts by blocking monoamine transporters, especially those for dopamine (**FIGURE 4.18**), slowing reuptake of the transmitters and therefore boosting their effects.

As a consequence of sensitization, which we discussed earlier, chronic cocaine use can provoke symptoms similar to psychosis. Cessation of cocaine use often produces very uncomfortable withdrawal symptoms: initial agitation and powerful drug cravings, followed by depression and an inability to enjoy anything else in life. Cerebral glucose metabolism is decreased for months after cocaine use is discontinued and may contribute to that depression. People who use cocaine along with other substances run the added risk of **dual dependence**, in which the interaction of two (or more) drugs produces another addictive state. For example, cocaine metabolized in the presence of ethanol (alcohol) yields an active metabolite called *cocaethylene*, to which the user may develop an additional addiction (D. S. Harris et al., 2003).

AMPHETAMINE   The molecular structure of the synthetic psychostimulant **amphetamine** closely resembles that of the catecholamine transmitters (norepinephrine, epinephrine, and dopamine). Amphetamine and the even more potent methamphetamine ("meth" or "speed") cause the release of these transmitters from presynaptic terminals even in the absence of action potentials, and when action potentials *do* reach the axon terminals, amphetamine also potentiates the subsequent release of transmitter. Once transmitter has been released, amphetamine further enhances activity in two ways: (1) by blocking the reuptake of catecholamines into the presynaptic terminal and (2) by providing an alternative target for the enzyme (monoamine oxidase) that normally inactivates them.

The result of amphetamine's various actions is thus that monoaminergic synapses become unnaturally potent, strongly affecting behavior. Over the short term, amphetamine causes increased vigor and stamina, wakefulness, decreased appetite, and feelings of euphoria. For these reasons amphetamine has historically been used

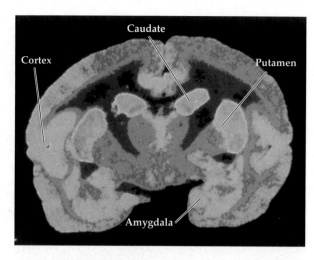

4.18 COCAINE-BINDING SITES IN THE MONKEY BRAIN   This autoradiograph of a coronal section shows the distribution of cocaine-binding sites. The areas of highest binding, shown by orange and yellow, include many regions that receive dopaminergic innervation. (Courtesy of Dr. Bertha K. Madras.)

cocaine   A drug of abuse, derived from the coca plant, that acts by potentiating catecholamine stimulation.

dual dependence   Dependence for emergent drug effects that occur only when two drugs are taken simultaneously.

amphetamine   A molecule that resembles the structure of the catecholamine transmitters and enhances their activity.

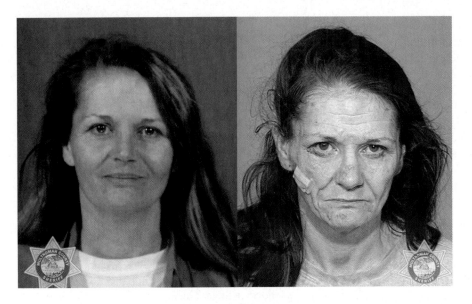

4.19 FACES OF METH These before and after photos, taken just 2½ years apart, are a stark testament to the heavy toll taken by chronic methamphetamine abuse. Meth causes multiple severe problems such as motor disorders, cognitive impairment, psychosis, and rapid changes in appearance due to accelerated tooth decay ("meth mouth"), skin pathology, and excessive weight loss. (Mug shots courtesy of the Multnomah County Sheriff's Office, Oregon.)

in military applications and other settings where intense sustained effort is required. However, the quality of the work being performed may suffer, and the costs of amphetamine use soon outweigh the benefits. Addiction and tolerance to amphetamine and methamphetamine develops rapidly, requiring ever larger doses and leading to sleeplessness, severe weight loss, and general deterioration of mental and physical condition (**FIGURE 4.19**).

Prolonged use of amphetamine may lead to symptoms that closely resemble those of paranoid schizophrenia: compulsive, agitated behavior and irrational suspiciousness. In fact, some amphetamine users have been misdiagnosed as having schizophrenia (see Chapter 16). Amphetamine also acts on the autonomic nervous system to produce high blood pressure, tremor, dizziness, sweating, rapid breathing, and nausea. Worst of all, people who chronically abuse speed display symptoms of brain damage long after they quit using the drug (Ernst et al., 2000).

Alcohol acts as both a stimulant and a depressant

Alcohol has traveled the full route of human history, no doubt because it is so easily produced by the fermentation of fruit or grains and thus is an ingredient of many types of pleasant beverages. Taken in moderation, alcohol is harmless or even beneficial to the health of adults. For example, moderate consumption—one drink per day for women, up to two per day for men—is associated with reduced risk of cardiovascular and Alzheimer's diseases and with improved control of blood sugar levels (Davies et al., 2002; Katsiki et al., 2014; Leroi et al., 2002). *Excessive* alcohol consumption, however, is very damaging and linked to more than 60 disease processes, making it one of the top three risks to health worldwide (the other two being smoking and high blood pressure).

The psychoactive effect of alcohol in the nervous system is biphasic: an initial stimulant phase is followed by a more prolonged depressant phase. In a manner similar to that of the benzodiazepines, but acting via a different recognition site, alcohol activates the $GABA_A$ receptor–coupled chloride channel (see Figure 4.13), thereby increasing postsynaptic inhibition. This action contributes to social disinhibition, as well as the impairment of motor coordination that occurs after a few drinks (Hanchar et al., 2005). Alcohol also affects other transmitters. For example, low doses of alcohol stimulate dopamine pathways, and the resulting increase in dopamine may be related to the slightly euphoric feelings that many people experience when having a drink.

Chronic abuse of alcohol damages neurons. Cells of the superior frontal cortex, Purkinje cells of the cerebellum, and hippocampal pyramidal cells show particularly prominent pathological changes. Some of these degenerative effects of chronic alcohol use may be due to a secondary consequence of alcoholism: poor diet. For example, chronic alcoholism is accompanied by severe thiamine deficiency, which can lead to neural degeneration and Korsakoff's syndrome (see Chapter 17). And alcohol abuse by expectant mothers can cause grievous permanent brain damage to the developing fetus (termed **fetal alcohol syndrome**), a topic to which we will return in Chapter 7 (see Figure 7.17). In fact, it is not clear whether it is safe for pregnant women to consume *any* alcohol, even small quantities; a few studies have suggested subtle changes in the cognitive function of babies exposed to only moderate levels of alcohol in utero (Day et al., 2002; Huizink and Mulder, 2006).

fetal alcohol syndrome A disorder, including intellectual disability and characteristic facial anomalies, that affects children exposed to too much alcohol (through maternal ingestion) during fetal development.

(A) Anterior cortical gray matter

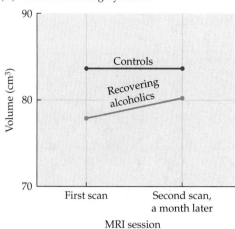

(B) Lateral ventricles

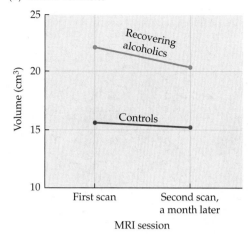

4.20 THE EFFECTS OF ALCOHOL ON THE BRAIN MRI studies of humans with alcoholism show that abstaining from alcohol for 30 days increases the volume of cortical gray matter (A) and decreases the volume of the lateral ventricles (B). (After Pfefferbaum et al., 1995.)

The frontal lobes—especially the superior frontal association cortex—are the brain areas that are most affected by chronic alcohol use (Kril et al., 1997). However, some of the anatomical changes associated with chronic alcoholism may be reversible with abstinence. In rats, chronic exposure to alcohol reduces the number of synapses on neurons in some regions, but this number returns to normal levels after alcohol treatments stop (Dlugos and Pentney, 1997). Similarly, in humans suffering from alcoholism, MRI studies show an increase in the volume of cortical gray matter and an associated reduction in ventricular volume within weeks of giving up alcohol (**FIGURE 4.20**) (Pfefferbaum et al., 1995).

There is a strong hereditary component to alcoholism, as indicated by human studies and selective breeding experiments in rats (Schuckit and Smith, 1997), and a combination of genetic vulnerability and a stressful environment probably explains many cases of alcoholism (McGue, 1999). The transition from intermittent overconsumption to a more stable and treatment-resistant pattern of alcoholism may involve up-regulation of a specific form of NMDA receptor in the nucleus accumbens, part of the brain's reward circuitry (Seif et al., 2013) that we'll discuss shortly.

Even in the absence of clear-cut alcoholism, periodic overconsumption of alcohol—*bingeing* (defined as five or more drinks on a single occasion)—may cause brain damage. After only 4 days of bingeing on alcohol, rats exhibit neural degeneration in several brain regions. Damage is especially evident in the olfactory bulbs and in limbic structures connected with the hippocampus, and it is associated with impairments of cognitive ability (Obernier et al., 2002). Alcohol bingeing also significantly reduces the rate of neurogenesis—the formation of new neurons—in the adult hippocampus (Nixon and Crews, 2002). Alcohol bingeing can depress breathing enough to kill, as happens every year to a few college students. Many additional college students die from alcohol-related accidents (Hingson et al., 2005).

Hallucinogenic and dissociative drugs alter sensory perception

Drugs classified as **hallucinogens** have long been sought out by humans as a way of profoundly altering consciousness. These substances cause bizarre and mysterious sensory phenomena, with the result that users may believe that their experiences have deeper spiritual or psychological meaning. But the term *hallucinogen* is a misnomer because, whereas a hallucination is a novel perception that takes place in the absence of sensory stimulation (hearing voices, or seeing something that isn't there), the drugs in this category tend to alter or distort *existing* perceptions. The effects of lysergic acid diethylamide (**LSD**, or *acid*) and related substances like mescaline (peyote) and psilocybin ("magic mushrooms") are predominantly visual (**FIGURE 4.21**). Users often see fantastic images with intense colors, and they are often aware that these strangely altered perceptions are not real events.

hallucinogens A class of drugs that alter sensory perception and produce peculiar experiences.

LSD Also called *acid*. Lysergic acid diethylamide, a hallucinogenic drug.

These images are portraits produced by a professional artist just after taking LSD (leftmost drawing) and then at three successive time points as the drug took effect. The model for all four drawings is the same man (the researcher, in fact).

20 minutes

Time

3 hours

4.21 PERCEPTUAL ALTERATION WITH LSD These images are portraits produced by a professional artist just after taking LSD (leftmost drawing) and then at three successive time points while the drug was active. The model for all four drawings is the same (the researcher, in fact).

4.22 THE FATHER OF LSD Albert Hofmann discovered LSD in 1943 and devoted the remainder of his career to studying it. A prohibited drug in most jurisdictions, LSD is distributed on colorful blotter paper. This example, picturing Hofmann and the LSD molecule, is made up of 1036 individual doses (or "hits").

Hallucinogenic agents are diverse in their neural actions. For example, the Mexican herb *Salvia divinorum* is unusual among hallucinogens because it acts on the opioid kappa receptor. Other hallucinogens, such as muscarine (another mushroom compound), affect the ACh system. Mescaline, the drug extracted from the peyote plant, affects noradrenergic and serotonergic systems. Many hallucinogens, including LSD, mescaline, and psilocybin, act as serotonin receptor agonists or partial agonists, especially at $5\text{-}HT_{2A}$ receptors. These receptors are found in high concentration in the visual cortex of the brain, which may account for the fantastical images that users experience. People treated with psilocybin also show reduced activity in medial prefrontal cortex and anterior cingulate cortex (Carhart-Harris et al., 2012). These structures inhibit limbic emotion-processing regions, so the drug's emotional, mystical qualities may be the product of an uninhibited limbic system.

You may have guessed that Albert Hofmann (**FIGURE 4.22**), whose story opened this chapter, was the discoverer of LSD. In fact, the study of LSD's activities became the focus of his professional career, summarized in his 1981 book, *LSD: My Problem Child*. Following its discovery, LSD was intensively studied as a possible psychiatric treatment. Starting in the 1950s, research to see if LSD could model psychosis did not bear fruit. But there has been a resurgence of interest in whether hallucinogens may relieve various psychiatric disorders, including depression and obsessive-compulsive disorder (Vollenweider and Kometer, 2010). The neural actions, recreational properties, and possible psychiatric uses of some of the major hallucinogens are summarized in **TABLE 4.4**.

Unlike the hallucinogens we've described so far, **ketamine** (known as *Special K*) is a drug that is already in widespread use in medical settings. Developed in the 1960s as a potent analgesic and anesthetic agent, ketamine is classified as a **dissociative** because at moderate doses it produces feelings of depersonalization and detachment from reality. Ketamine has several actions in the brain, especially blockade of NMDA receptors. PET studies indicate that ketamine increases metabolic activity in the prefrontal cortex (Breier et al., 1997), and while high doses produce transient hallucinogenic effects and occasional psychotic symptoms in volunteers, low doses have a potent antidepressant effect that may help ease symptoms in resistant cases (Williams and Schatzberg, 2016).

Ecstasy is the street name for the hallucinogenic amphetamine derivative **MDMA** (3,4-methylenedioxymethamphetamine). Major actions of MDMA in the brain in-

TABLE 4.4 Possible Clinical Applications for Hallucinogens

DRUG NAME AND DATE OF DISCOVERY	ACTION IN BRAIN	RECREATIONAL USE	POSSIBLE CLINICAL APPLICATION
Psilocybin / Psilocin (*Psilocybe* mushroom) (Archaeological evidence indicates use in prehistory)	Partial agonist of 5-HT receptors, especially 5-HT$_{2A}$ receptors that occur in high density in visual cortex. Modifies activity of frontal and occipital cortex.	Users of "shrooms" often report spiritual experiences and feelings of transcendence, along with intense visual experiences and alterations in the perception of time. The exact effects are strongly influenced by the expectations and surroundings of the user.	Recent studies suggest that psilocybin—administered in controlled settings—can offer substantial and enduring improvements in the symptoms of obsessive-compulsive disorder (OCD), cluster headache (a type of migraine), and debilitating anxiety and anguish (as in a sample of terminal cancer patients) (Grob et al., 2011; E. A. Schindler et al., 2015).
Lysergic acid diethylamide (LSD) (1938)	Activates many subtypes of monoamine receptors, especially DA and 5-HT, resulting in heightened activity in many cortical regions, especially frontal, cingulate, and occipital cortex.	"Acid" produces pronounced perceptual changes that resemble hallucinations. Intense colors in geometric patterns, novel visual objects, and an altered sense of time are common.	LSD may be an effective treatment for alcoholism and other addictions and may also be an effective treatment for some types of debilitating anxiety (Bogenschutz and Johnson, 2016; Gasser et al., 2014).
Ketamine (1962)	Widespread effects in the brain, especially blockade of NMDA receptors, and stimulation of opioid and ACh receptors.	"Special K" creates a detached, trancelike state, in keeping with its routine medical use as an anesthetic. It may also produce hallucinogenic perceptual alterations.	Recent experiments have revealed a potent antidepressant effect of ketamine at lower doses, even in cases that resist other types of treatments (Williams and Schatzberg, 2016).
3,4-Methylenedioxymethamphetamine (MDMA) (1912/1970s)	Stimulates release of monoamine transmitters and the pro-social hormone oxytocin	Users of "Ecstasy" experience intense visual phenomena, empathy, strongly pro-social feelings, and euphoria.	MDMA treatment may effectively reduce symptoms of posttraumatic stress disorder (PTSD), especially in combination with conventional psychotherapy, but concerns remain regarding drug safety (Amoroso, 2015; Parrott, 2014).

clude an increase in the release of serotonin, stimulation of 5-HT$_{2A}$ receptors, and changes in the levels of dopamine and certain peptide hormones, such as oxytocin. Exactly how these activities account for the subjective effects of MDMA—positive emotions, empathy, euphoria, a sense of well-being, and colorful visual phenomena—remains to be established. In lab animals, chronic use of Ecstasy alters the structure and function of serotonergic neurons (T. J. Monks et al., 2004), although it's not clear whether there is lasting damage, at least at the lower doses typically used by humans. Several possible psychiatric and cognitive consequences of chronic MDMA use have been described, including memory disturbances and depression (Parrott, 2013; Sumnall and Cole, 2005). However, shorter-term MDMA treatment is also being studied in clinical settings, as a possible therapy for treatment-resistant posttraumatic stress disorder (Amoroso, 2015; Mithoefer et al., 2013).

ketamine A dissociative anesthetic drug that acts as an NMDA receptor antagonist.

dissociative drug A type of drug that produces a dreamlike state in which consciousness is partly separated from sensory inputs.

MDMA Also called *Ecstasy*. A drug of abuse, 3,4-methylenedioxymethamphetamine.

Drug Abuse and Addiction Are Widespread Problems

Substance abuse and addiction afflict many millions of people and disrupt the lives of their families, friends, and associates. Just one example reveals the extent of the problem: in the United States each year, more men and women die of smoking-related lung cancer than of colon, breast, and prostate cancers *combined*. In addition to the personal impact of so much illness and early death, there are dire social costs: huge expenses for medical and social services, millions of hours lost in the workplace, elevated rates of crime associated with illicit drugs, and scores of children who are damaged by their parents' substance abuse behavior, in the uterine environment as well as in the childhood home.

Researchers have proposed numerous models of substance abuse and addiction that vary in their emphasis on physiological, behavioral, and environmental factors (M. Glantz and Pickens, 1992). Some of these models stem from social forces; others are more deeply rooted in scientific observations and theories. But for any model of drug abuse, the challenge is to come up with a single account that can explain the addicting power of substances as diverse as, for example, cocaine (a stimulant), heroin (an analgesic and euphoriant), and alcohol (largely a sedative).

Addictive substances are no exception to the general rule that any given drug may produce multiple effects, so it is difficult to determine exactly which drug actions are most important in producing dependence. For example, we have already noted that cocaine (1) is a local anesthetic, (2) produces intensely pleasurable feelings, and (3) is a psychomotor stimulant. The opiate drugs, like morphine and heroin, also produce intensely rewarding sensations, but they are depressants, not stimulants. Like cocaine, the opiates produce a strong physical dependence and powerful withdrawal symptoms on cessation of use. But opiates tend to produce only tolerance, whereas at least some of the actions of cocaine induce sensitization. So a comprehensive theory of drug abuse and addiction must be able to account for dependence across this wide and confusing range of addictive compounds and effects.

We will focus primarily on addiction to cocaine, the opiate drugs (such as morphine and heroin), nicotine, and alcohol because these substances have been studied the most thoroughly. According to the 2013 National Survey on Drug Use and Health, some 21.6 million people in the United States alone suffer from substance-related disorders (Substance Abuse and Mental Health Services Administration, 2014). Worldwide, the number is probably in the hundreds of millions. Some terminology specific to substance dependence (addiction) and substance abuse is clarified in **BOX 4.2**.

Several perspectives help us understand drug abuse

Any comprehensive model of drug abuse has to answer several difficult questions: What social and environmental factors in a person's life cause her to start abusing a substance? What factors cause her to continue? What physiological mechanisms make a substance rewarding? What is addiction, physiologically and behaviorally, and why is it so hard to quit?

THE MORAL MODEL   The earliest approach to explaining drug abuse was to simply blame the substance abuser for a failure of moral character or a lack of self-control. Explanations of this sort often have a religious aspect and hold that only divine help will free a person from addiction. Applications based on the moral model can occasionally be effective. For example, the temperance movement in the United States, beginning around the 1830s, is estimated to have cut per capita consumption of alcohol to about one-third its level in the period from 1800 to 1820 (Rorabaugh, 1976). However, despite good intentions, high hopes, and multi-billion dollar budgets, there is little evidence that modern morality-based campaigns—Project D.A.R.E., for example—have any appreciable effect on rates of drug abuse (Vincus et al., 2010; West and O'Neil, 2004).

THE DISEASE MODEL   According to the disease model, the person who abuses drugs requires medical treatment rather than moral exhortation or punishment. This view also justifies spending money to research drug abuse in the same way that money is spent to research other diseases. However, the term *disease* is usually reserved for a state in which we can identify an abnormal physical or biochemical condition that initiates the problem. No abnormal physical or biochemical condition has been found in the case of drug addiction, and the disease model is mute about how

BOX 4.2

Terminology of Substance-Related Disorders

For definitions of mental disorders, psychiatrists, psychologists, and neuroscientists rely on the *Diagnostic and Statistical Manual of Mental Disorders* (5th edition), known as the *DSM-5* (American Psychiatric Association, 2013). The *DSM-5* provides descriptions of a spectrum of substance-related disorders. Within this category, **dependence** (commonly called *addiction*) is a more severe disorder than **substance abuse**. Males are three times more likely than females to be diagnosed, at some point in life, with substance abuse or dependence (see the figure).

The essential feature of dependence on psychoactive substances (e.g., alcohol, tobacco, cocaine, marijuana) is a cluster of cognitive, behavioral, and physiological symptoms indicating that the person continues use of the substance despite significant substance-related problems. To be diagnosed as dependent, a person must meet a certain number of criteria relating to patterns of consumption, craving, expenditure of time and energy in serving the addiction, and impact on the other aspects of the person's life.

When the minimum number of criteria for dependence has not been met but maladaptive patterns of substance use have persisted at least a month or have occurred repeatedly, the diagnosis is substance abuse. The following situations are examples in which a diagnosis of substance abuse is appropriate:

1. A student has substance-related absences, suspensions, or expulsion from school.
2. A person is repeatedly intoxicated with alcohol in situations that are hazardous—for example, when driving a car, operating machinery, or engaging in risky recreational activities such as swimming or rock climbing.
3. A person has recurrent substance-related legal problems—for example, arrests for disorderly conduct, assault and battery, or driving under the influence.

dependence Also called *addiction*. The strong desire to self-administer a drug of abuse.

substance abuse A maladaptive pattern of substance use that has lasted more than a month but does not fully meet the criteria for dependence.

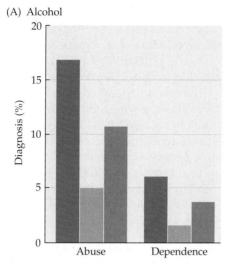
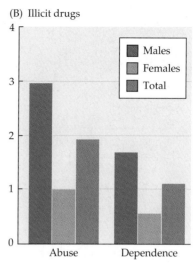

(A) Alcohol

(B) Illicit drugs

Males
Females
Total

PATTERNS OF ABUSE AND DEPENDENCE Proportions of North American men and women diagnosed at some point in their lives with abuse and/or dependence for (A) alcohol and (B) illicit drugs, according to *DSM-5* criteria.

---

addiction arises, although mounting evidence suggests that some people are genetically more susceptible to addiction than others. Nevertheless, this model continues to appeal to many, and an intensive effort is under way to identify the physiological "switch" that establishes addiction after exposure to a drug.

A related formulation of the disease model views drug abuse as a type of self-medication, in which the addict is drawn to specific drugs in an effort to compensate for a deficiency of a corresponding endogenous substance: taking opiates to compensate for a lack of endorphins, for example. The causes of the endogenous shortages are generally unspecified, however.

THE PHYSICAL DEPENDENCE MODEL   The physical dependence model, sometimes called the *withdrawal avoidance model*, argues that people keep taking drugs in order to avoid unpleasant withdrawal symptoms. The specific withdrawal symptoms depend on the drug, but they are often the opposite of the effects produced by the drug itself. For example, withdrawal from morphine causes irritability, a racing

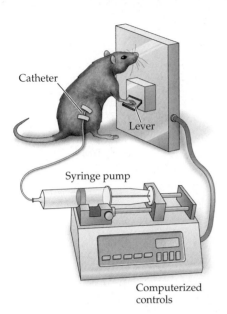

4.23 EXPERIMENTAL SETUP FOR SELF-ADMINISTRATION OF A DRUG BY AN ANIMAL Here a computer is programmed to administer a small dose of an experimental drug after a certain number of lever presses. The number of lever presses that the animal will perform to receive the drug is a measure of its rewarding properties and addictive potential. Lab animals will press the lever many thousands of times to receive a single small dose of a highly addictive compound like cocaine or methamphetamine.

dysphoria Unpleasant feelings; the opposite of euphoria.

nucleus accumbens A region of the forebrain that receives dopaminergic innervation from the ventral tegmental area.

heart, and waves of goose bumps (that's where the term *cold turkey* comes from—the skin looks like the skin of a plucked turkey).

Whereas most drugs of abuse produce pleasurable feelings, withdrawal usually induces the opposite: **dysphoria**. Withdrawal symptoms can develop rapidly; some teenagers can experience withdrawal symptoms within 2 days of starting smoking (DiFranza et al., 2007). And withdrawal symptoms can be suppressed quickly (within a few minutes in the case of morphine) by administration of the withdrawn drug or a chemically similar compound. So the model does a good job of explaining why addicts will go to great lengths to obtain their addicted drug, but it has an important shortcoming: it can't explain how the addiction gets established in the first place. Why do some people, but not all, start to abuse a drug before physical dependence (tolerance) has ever developed? And how is it that some people can become addicted to some drugs even in the absence of clear physical withdrawal symptoms? For example, cocaine withdrawal is not accompanied by the shaking and vomiting seen during heroin withdrawal, yet cocaine seems to be at least as addictive as heroin.

THE POSITIVE REWARD MODEL   The positive reward model of addictive behavior proposes that people get started with drug abuse, and become addicted, because the abused drug provides powerful reinforcement. Using a self-administration apparatus that allows animals to administer drugs to themselves (**FIGURE 4.23**), it is possible to quantify the motivation of animals to consume drugs (McKim, 1991).

Morphine-dependent rats or monkeys quickly learn to repeatedly press a lever in order to receive a small morphine injection (e.g., T. Thompson and Schuster, 1964). The drug infusion therefore acts like any other experimental reward, such as food or water. Furthermore, even animals that are not already morphine-dependent learn to press a lever for morphine, and they will happily self-administer doses of morphine that are so low that no physical dependence ever develops (Schuster, 1970). Animals will also furiously press a lever to self-administer cocaine and other stimulants that do not produce withdrawal symptoms as marked as those that opiates produce (Pickens and Thompson, 1968; Tanda et al., 2000). In fact, cocaine supports some of the highest rates of lever pressing ever recorded.

Experiments using drug self-administration thus suggest that by itself, the physical dependence model is inadequate to explain drug addiction, although physical dependence and tolerance may contribute to drug hunger. The more comprehensive view of drug self-administration interprets it as a behavior controlled by a powerful pattern of positive and negative rewards (a variant of operant conditioning; see Chapter 17), without the need to implicate a disease process.

Many—but not all—addictive drugs cause the release of dopamine in the **nucleus accumbens**, just like more-conventional rewards such as food, sex, or winning money (D'Ardenne et al., 2008; D. J. Nutt et al., 2015); interestingly, dopamine release is also linked to pathological gambling (Dodd et al., 2005; Reuter et al., 2005). As we mentioned previously, dopamine released from axons originating from the VTA, part of the mesolimbocortical dopaminergic pathway illustrated in Figure 4.5, has been widely implicated in the perception of reward (**FIGURE 4.24**). Endocannabinoid actions within the reward circuitry may also contribute to the rewarding aspects of drug use (Parsons and Hurd, 2015).

If the dopaminergic pathway from the VTA to the nucleus accumbens serves as a reward system for a wide variety of experiences, then the addictive power of drugs may come from their artificial stimulation of this pathway. When the drug hijacks this system, providing an unnaturally powerful reward, the user learns to associate the drug-taking behavior with that pleasure and begins seeking out drugs more and more until life's other pleasures fade into the background. These higher-order cognitive aspects of addiction depend on glutamatergic inputs from the prefrontal cortex, integrating aspects of memory, attention, and self-control to regulate the functioning of the dopamine reward system (e.g., R. Z. Goldstein and Volkow, 2011).

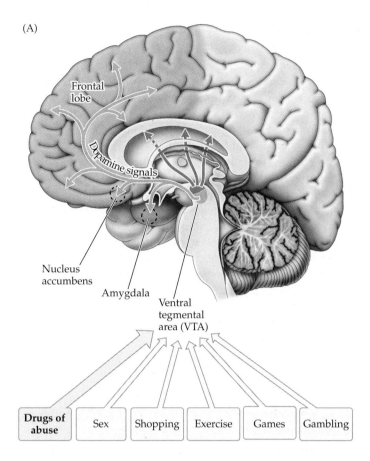

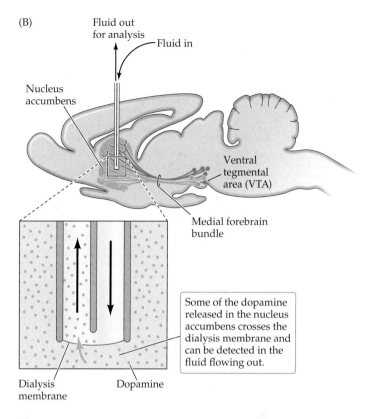

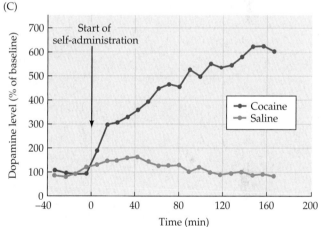

4.24 A NEURAL PATHWAY IMPLICATED IN DRUG ABUSE
(A) A variety of different behaviors, including sexual behavior, gambling, and video game playing, normally activate the dopaminergic pathway that produces the experience of pleasure. Drugs of abuse exert a particularly strong influence on this system and may eclipse other sources of pleasure. (B) The microdialysis technique makes use of a small, permanently implanted probe to monitor neurochemical changes in awake, behaving animals. The microdialysis probe inserted into the nucleus accumbens detects increased dopamine release in response to drug administration. (C) Dopamine levels in the nucleus accumbens rise sharply in rats during self-administration of cocaine (begins at arrow). (Part C after Pettit and Justice, 1991.)

Cocaine produces long-lasting changes in dopaminergic circuitry (Dalley et al., 2007; Volkow et al., 2006), as well as other neurotransmitter systems in the nucleus accumbens (K. L. Conrad et al., 2008; D. L. Graham et al., 2007), which seem to further augment the pleasure associated with drugs while decreasing the pleasure experienced from other behaviors. The drug's "pathological" reinforcement of associated behaviors leads to exclusive, compulsive drug seeking. If natural activities like conversation, eating, and even sex no longer provide appreciable pleasure, addicts may seek drugs as the only source of pleasure available to them.

People suffering damage to a brain region tucked within the frontal cortex called the **insula** (Latin for "island") were able to effortlessly quit smoking (Naqvi et al., 2007), indicating that this brain region is also involved in addiction. The reciprocal connections between the VTA and the insula (Oades and Halliday, 1987) suggest that these two regions normally interact to mediate addiction.

insula A region of cortex lying below the surface, within the lateral sulcus, of the frontal, temporal, and parietal lobes.

cue-induced drug use
An increased likelihood to use a drug (especially an addictive drug) because of the presence of environmental stimuli that were present during previous use of the same drug.

People differ in their vulnerability to drug abuse

Not everyone who uses an addictive drug becomes addicted. For example, very, very few hospitalized patients treated with opiates for pain relief go on to abuse opiates after leaving the hospital (Brownlee and Schrof, 1997). However, prescription pain-killers are highly effective at activating the dopamine reward system, so the use of these drugs outside of medical contexts carries a high risk of addiction. Of Vietnam War veterans who had used heroin overseas, only a minority relapsed to dependence within 3 years after their return (Robins and Slobodyan, 2003). The individual and environmental factors that account for this differential susceptibility are the subject of active investigation and fall into several general categories:

• *Biological factors* Sex is a significant variable; males are more likely to abuse drugs than are females. There is also evidence for genetic predisposition. For example, having a biological parent who suffers from alcoholism makes drug abuse more likely, even for children adopted away soon after birth (Cadoret et al., 1986). A tendency to use opiates and cocaine also appears to be heritable (Kendler et al., 2000), and adolescents carrying a specific version of the gene for a specific serotonin transporter are more likely to abuse drugs (Caspi et al., 2003), although this risk can be mitigated by involved and attentive parenting (G. H. Brody et al., 2009).

• *Family situation* Family breakup, a poor relationship with parents, or the presence of an antisocial sibling are associated with drug abuse.

• *Personal characteristics* Certain traits, such as aggressiveness and poor emotional control, are especially associated with drug abuse. Strong educational goals and maturity are associated with lower likelihood of drug abuse.

• *Environmental factors* A high prevalence of drug use in the community, and especially in the peer group, predisposes an individual toward drug abuse.

It is now clear that environmental stimuli—locations, social settings, sensory stimuli, and so on—can rapidly become strongly associated with the subjective effects of abused substances. These environmental stimuli can then become risk factors for deepening addiction or relapse: simply being in a setting where a person previously used drugs can trigger drug craving in that person (O'Brien et al., 1998). This phenomenon, termed **cue-induced drug use**, is not limited to longer-term users; in rats, exposure to environmental stimuli that were present during their *very first cocaine treatment* effectively and persistently cued drug-seeking behavior later (Ciccocioppo et al., 2004). Emotional aspects of cue-induced drug use may be controlled by the central nucleus of the amygdala (L. Lu et al., 2005, 2006). Neurons that encode learned associations between drugs and drug cues are also found in the nucleus accumbens, a major component of the dopamine reward pathway of the brain. Selectively inactivating these neurons blocks context-cued effects of cocaine in mice (Koya et al., 2009).

Drug abuse and dependence can be prevented or treated in multiple ways

Given the health and social costs of substance abuse, the development of effective treatment programs is a pressing concern. Many of those who become dependent are able to overcome their addiction without outside help: more than 90% of ex-smokers and about half of those who recover from alcoholism appear to have quit on their own (S. Cohen et al., 1989; Institute of Medicine, 1990). Many others gain great benefit from counseling or social interventions such as the 12-step program developed by Alcoholics Anonymous in the 1930s. However, some people are unable to overcome powerful addictions without medical intervention. Medical strategies for treating drug dependence can be grouped into several categories:

• *Lessening the discomfort of withdrawal* Benzodiazepines and drugs that suppress central adrenergic activity (e.g., clonidine) help reduce withdrawal symptoms during the early drug-free period, and anti-nausea medication and sleep aids may also be of benefit. Other medications help reduce uncomfortable cravings for the abused substance; for example, acamprosate (trade name Campral) eases alcohol-associated withdrawal symptoms.

- *Providing alternatives to the addictive drug* Agonist or partial agonist analogs of the addictive drug weakly activate the same mechanisms that the addictive drug activates, allowing the individual to gradually wean off the addictive drug. For example, the opioid receptor agonist methadone reduces heroin appetite and lessens withdrawal symptoms; similarly, nicotine patches provide reduced doses of the addictive compound, without the other harmful components of cigarette smoke. Smoking electronic e-cigarettes (a practice nicknamed "vaping," as the device is actually a vaporizer) provides another way of obtaining nicotine without the many harmful additional ingredients found in tobacco.

- *Directly blocking the actions of the addictive drug* Specific receptor antagonists can prevent an abused drug from interacting with its receptors. For example, the opiate antagonist naloxone (trade name Narcan) blocks heroin's actions, but it also may produce harsh withdrawal symptoms.

- *Altering the metabolism of the abused drug* Changing the breakdown of a drug can change, reduce, or reverse its rewarding properties. Disulfiram (Antabuse) changes alcohol metabolism such that a nausea-inducing metabolite (acetaldehyde) accumulates, counteracting the rewarding aspects of alcohol abuse.

- *Blocking the brain's reward system* Treatment with dopamine receptor blockers reduces the activity of the mesolimbocortical dopamine reward system, causing drugs of abuse to lose much of their pleasurable quality. One problem with this approach is a generalized loss of pleasurable feelings, termed *anhedonia*.

No single approach appears to be uniformly effective, and rates of relapse remain high. Research breakthroughs are therefore badly needed.

◼ The Cutting Edge

The Needle and the Damage Undone

As we've discussed, attempts to develop effective treatments for substance abuse and addiction have focused on a variety of interventions. Some treatments use pharmacological means to block the pleasurable effects of the abused substance, or to ease the discomfort of withdrawal. Behavioral methods often center on educational programs, peer-support systems, and therapy techniques that aim to break the learned associations between drug use, contexts, and reward. But all of these approaches require a significant investment on the part of the substance abuser: he must be motivated, willing to tolerate considerable discomfort, and able to commit the time required to complete the therapy. A rapid, long-lasting, easy-to-administer pharmacological treatment would be more likely to succeed for higher-risk, low-compliance individuals.

What if we could get the user's body to reject the abused substance? Scientists have long had tools for bending the immune system to their will so that it produces highly selective antibodies that seek out and destroy targeted substances—in it's simplest form, that's what we call **vaccination**. Of course, we all know vaccination as a way to combat infectious diseases, but it looks like we can develop effective vaccines against drugs like cocaine, heroin, and nicotine too (Maurer and Bachmann, 2007; Skolnick 2015). Here, the strategy is to prompt the individual's immune system to produce antibodies that remove the targeted drugs from circulation before they ever reach the brain.

The problem is that the immune system evolved to recognize large foreign proteins, not small molecules such as cocaine. So how can you get the immune system to produce antibodies against the drug? The solution is to conjugate (join) molecules of the drug with molecules of a larger carrier protein and get the immune system to react to the new combination. In one such approach, as shown in **FIGURE 4.25A**, cocaine is conjugated with protein from an inactivated virus (this adenovirus provokes a strong immune reaction). The conjugated molecules are then injected and are recognized by blood plasma cells that begin to produce antibodies. Many of these antibodies recognize the part of the conjugate that contained the cocaine molecules, so they become specifically reactive to cocaine. Just as with other forms of vaccination, the immune system has a "memory" for cocaine vaccine and continues to make the anti-cocaine antibodies. Now, when cocaine enters the bloodstream, the antibodies immediately bind to the drug molecules, forming large conglomerates that cannot reach

vaccination Injection of a foreign substance, such as deactivated viruses or conjugated molecules of drugs of abuse like cocaine, in order to provoke the production of antibodies against the foreign substance.

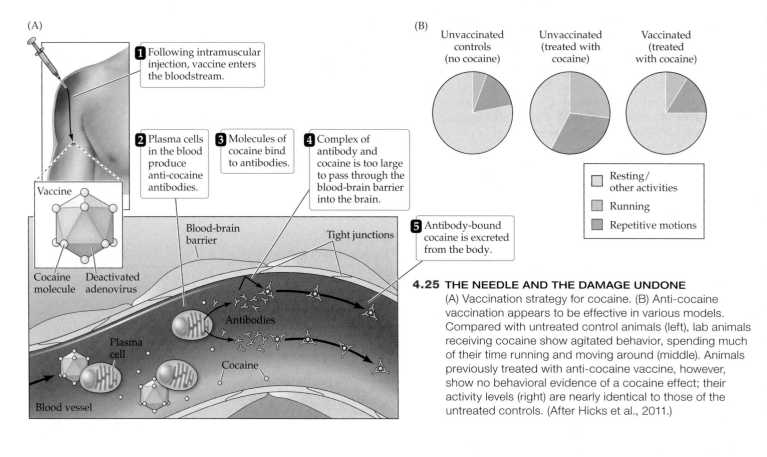

(A)

1. Following intramuscular injection, vaccine enters the bloodstream.

Vaccine

Cocaine molecule   Deactivated adenovirus

2. Plasma cells in the blood produce anti-cocaine antibodies.

3. Molecules of cocaine bind to antibodies.

4. Complex of antibody and cocaine is too large to pass through the blood-brain barrier into the brain.

Blood-brain barrier

Tight junctions

5. Antibody-bound cocaine is excreted from the body.

Antibodies

Plasma cell

Cocaine

Blood vessel

(B)

Unvaccinated controls (no cocaine)

Unvaccinated (treated with cocaine)

Vaccinated (treated with cocaine)

☐ Resting/ other activities
☐ Running
☐ Repetitive motions

4.25 THE NEEDLE AND THE DAMAGE UNDONE
(A) Vaccination strategy for cocaine. (B) Anti-cocaine vaccination appears to be effective in various models. Compared with untreated control animals (left), lab animals receiving cocaine show agitated behavior, spending much of their time running and moving around (middle). Animals previously treated with anti-cocaine vaccine, however, show no behavioral evidence of a cocaine effect; their activity levels (right) are nearly identical to those of the untreated controls. (After Hicks et al., 2011.)

the brain and are subsequently cleared from the body. In mice, the vaccine prevents the hyperactivity normally associated with cocaine exposure (**FIGURE 4.25B**).

Preliminary studies indicate that vaccination is effective for blunting the rewarding properties of cocaine and reducing addiction (Haney et al., 2010; Orson et al., 2014). Other vaccines under study target heroin, nicotine, and methamphetamine, with mixed results to date (Schlosburg et al., 2013; Skolnick, 2015).

Go to
bn8e.com
for study questions, quizzes, activities, and other resources

Recommended Reading

Advokat, C. D., Comaty, J. E., and Julien, R. M. (2014). *Julien's Primer of Drug Action* (13th ed.). New York: Worth.

Erickson, C. K. (2007). *The Science of Addiction: From Neurobiology to Treatment.* New York: Norton.

Grilly, D. M., and Salamone, J. (2011). *Drugs, Brain, and Behavior* (6th ed.). Boston: Allyn & Bacon.

Karch, S. B., and Drummer, O. (2008). *Karch's Pathology of Drug Abuse* (4th ed.). Boca Raton, FL: CRC Press.

Meyer, J. S., and Quenzer, L. F. (2013). *Psychopharmacology: Drugs, the Brain, and Behavior* (2nd ed.). Sunderland, MA: Sinauer.

Nestler, E., Hyman, S., and Malenka, R. (2014). *Molecular Neuropharmacology* (3rd ed.). New York: McGraw-Hill.

Schatzberg, A. F., and Nemeroff, C. B. (Eds.). (2013). *Essentials of Clinical Psychopharmacology.* Arlington, VA: American Psychiatric Publishing.

Thombs, D. L. (2006). *Introduction to Addictive Behaviors* (3rd ed.). New York: Guilford.

You should be able to relate each summary to the adjacent illustration, including structures and processes.
Go to **bn8e.com/vs4** for links to figures, animations, and activities that will help you consolidate the material.

1 The major categories of **neurotransmitters** are **amine**, **amino acid**, **peptide**, and soluble **gas** neurotransmitters. Because many drugs work by acting on **receptor** molecules, investigators search for the receptor molecules and for the **endogenous** substances that work on the receptors. A given neurotransmitter may normally bind several different subtypes of receptors. Review **Figures 4.1 and 4.2**, **Table 4.1**, **Activity 4.1**

2 A **ligand** is any substance that binds to a receptor. **Agonists** activate transmitter pathways, **antagonists** block transmitter pathways, and **inverse agonists** have effects opposite to a transmitter's normal effects. The classic neurotransmitters are found in segregated regions that project widely throughout the brain. Review **Figures 4.3–4.7**, **Animations 4.2 and 4.3**

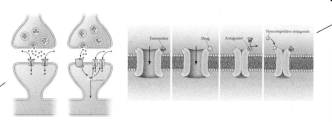

3 Drugs vary in their **binding affinity** for different types of receptors, as well as in **efficacy**—ability to produce effects—once they are bound. The relationship between concentrations of a drug and its physiological effects is studied by use of a **dose-response curve**, which reveals its activity, specificity, potency, and safety. Review **Figures 4.8 and 4.9**

4 Repeated treatments with a drug can produce **tolerance** to its effects, often through the **up-** or **down-regulation** of receptors. Most CNS drugs alter neural transmission. Many drugs selectively affect presynaptic mechanisms, such as by inhibiting axonal transport, affecting **transmitter reuptake**, or acting on presynaptic receptors. Neuromodulators such as **caffeine** may affect the release of the transmitter or the receptor's response to the transmitter. Review **Figures 4.10 and 4.11**

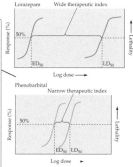

5 Other CNS drugs selectively modify post-synaptic mechanisms, directly blocking or activating receptors, or modifying processes within the postsynaptic cell. **Antipsychotics** (antischizophrenics) generally block D$_2$ receptors; **antidepressants** improve synaptic availability of **serotonin** and **norepinephrine**. Review **Figure 4.12**

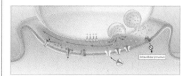

6 The benzodiazepines are potent **anxiolytic** drugs. The benzodiazepines synergize the activity of the inhibitory transmitter **GABA** at some of its receptors. Alcohol acts on GABA receptors to produce some of its effects. Alcohol in moderation has beneficial effects, but in higher doses it is very harmful, damaging neurons in many areas of the brain. Review **Figures 4.13 and 4.20**

7 Opiates are potent painkillers; **endogenous opioids** include the **endorphins**, and **exogenous** opiates include **morphine** and **heroin**. Review **Figures 4.14 and 4.15**

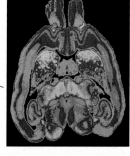

8 The active ingredient in **marijuana**, **THC**, acts on cannabinoid receptors to produce its effects. An endogenous cannabinoid, **anandamide**, serves as a **retrograde transmitter** in some synapses. Review **Figures 4.16 and 4.17**

Cerebellum

9 Some stimulants, such as **nicotine**, imitate an excitatory synaptic transmitter. Others, such as **amphetamine** and **cocaine**, cause the release of excitatory synaptic transmitters and block the reuptake of transmitters. Still others, such as **caffeine**, block the activity of an inhibitory neuromodulator. Review **Figure 4.18**

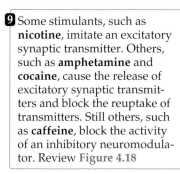

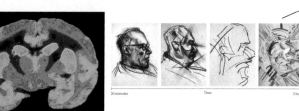

10 Some drugs are called **hallucinogens** because they alter sensory perception and produce peculiar experiences. Different hallucinogens act on different kinds of synaptic receptors, and it is not yet clear what causes the hallucinogenic effects. Review **Figure 4.21 and Table 4.4**

(continued)

11 Substance abuse and addiction are being studied intensively, and several models have been proposed: the moral model, the disease model, the physical dependence model, and the positive reward model. Review Figures 4.23 and 4.24

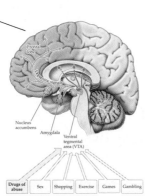

12 People differ in their vulnerability to drug abuse according to several factors: genetic predisposition, personality characteristics, and family and social context. There are several medicinal approaches to treating drug addiction, including antiwithdrawal and anticraving medication and vaccination. Review Figure 4.25

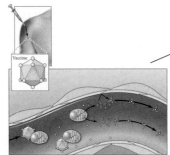

Hormones and the Brain

5

Crafting a Personality Through Hormones

When she was 13, Mary Lou spent a whole summer in the intensive care ward of a hospital with a grave illness that doctors could not diagnose. When she finally got out of the hospital, she assumed that her life would be short, so Mary Lou pursued it with gusto, working as an artist, playing in a band, working on a PhD in electrical engineering at an Ivy League school. But by her early 20s, Mary Lou's medical condition was deteriorating. She was sleeping 20 hours per day, coping with constant headache and repeated vomiting, and periodically wheelchair bound, but the worst part for Mary Lou was that, for the first time in her life, she felt stupid.

Then doctors finally detected a slow-growing brain tumor that had disrupted function of a pea-sized structure called the *pituitary gland*. The tumor was removed, but the pituitary was damaged beyond repair. As we'll learn in this chapter, the lack of a functioning pituitary means Mary Lou fails to make a host of hormones, some of which are crucial for survival. Fortunately, pharmacies can provide many of these missing hormones, so in the 20 years after surgery, a recovered Mary Lou has been able to found several technology start-ups and has headed projects, first for Google then Facebook, where she has led efforts in virtual reality.

Taking hormones saved Mary Lou's life. But in the process of tinkering to get the right doses and combinations of hormones, Mary Lou learned that hormones influence not only her physical health and intelligence, but also her moods and personality. As she says, "It took me years to craft a better 'me' after my personality was essentially killed by the effects of the tumor and surgery" (Jepsen, 2013). What are these hormones that Mary Lou must tinker with, and how can they have such a large effect on her brain and behavior?

The cells in your body use chemicals to communicate, including an extensive array of hormones. Alterations in hormone levels can produce striking changes in brain function. Cognitive abilities, emotions, our appetite for food or drink or sex, our aggressiveness or submissiveness, our care for children—the scope of hormonal influences on behavior is vast. Furthermore, hormones do more than influence adult behavior. Early in life, thyroid and sex hormones regulate brain development. Later in life, the changing outputs of endocrine glands and the body's changing sensitivity to hormones are prominent aspects of adolescence and aging.

In this chapter we consider the major hormones, their anatomical sources, their physiological actions, and their effects on behavior. This discussion sets the stage for topics in later chapters, such as hormonal effects in reproductive behavior (Chapter 12); feeding, drinking, and body maintenance (Chapter 13); and stress and emotion (Chapter 15).

Go to Brain Explorer
bn8e.com/5.1

Hormones Have Many Actions in the Body

hormone A chemical secreted by cells that is conveyed by the bloodstream and regulates target organs or tissues.

endocrine gland A gland that secretes hormones into the bloodstream to act on distant targets.

exocrine gland A gland whose secretions exit the body via ducts.

The ancient Greeks emphasized body *humors*, or fluids, as an explanation of temperament and emotions. It was believed that these fluids—phlegm, blood, black bile, and yellow bile (also known as *choler*)—all interacted to produce health or disease. The notion of body fluids as the basis of human temperament lingers in our language in many now seldom-used terms, such as *phlegmatic* ("sluggish"), *sanguine* ("cheerful"; *sanguis* is Latin for "blood"), *bilious* ("irritable"), and *choleric* ("hot-tempered") to describe personalities.

Today we know there are a lot more than four hormones. Most **hormones** (from the Greek *horman*, "to excite") are chemicals secreted by a group of cells in one part of the body and carried through the bloodstream to other parts of the body, where they act on specific target tissues to produce specific physiological effects. Many hormones are produced by **endocrine glands** (from the Greek *endon*, "within," and *krinein*, "to secrete"), so called because they release their hormones *inside* the body. Endocrine glands are sometimes contrasted with **exocrine glands** (tear glands, salivary glands, sweat glands), which use ducts to secrete fluid outside the body (the Greek *exo* means "out").

Endocrine glands come in a variety of sizes, shapes, and locations in the body (**FIGURE 5.1**). Although the endocrine glands and their hormones are important, the definition of *hormone* is more inclusive than it used to be, recognizing that other tissues, such as the heart and kidneys, secrete hormones too. Even plants, which have no endocrine glands, use chemical signals that are considered to be hormones.

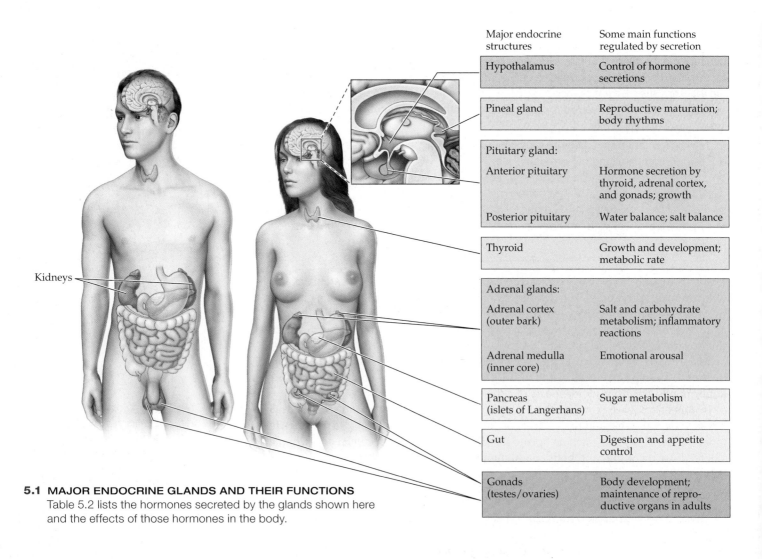

Major endocrine structures	Some main functions regulated by secretion
Hypothalamus	Control of hormone secretions
Pineal gland	Reproductive maturation; body rhythms
Pituitary gland:	
Anterior pituitary	Hormone secretion by thyroid, adrenal cortex, and gonads; growth
Posterior pituitary	Water balance; salt balance
Thyroid	Growth and development; metabolic rate
Adrenal glands:	
Adrenal cortex (outer bark)	Salt and carbohydrate metabolism; inflammatory reactions
Adrenal medulla (inner core)	Emotional arousal
Pancreas (islets of Langerhans)	Sugar metabolism
Gut	Digestion and appetite control
Gonads (testes/ovaries)	Body development; maintenance of reproductive organs in adults

Kidneys

5.1 MAJOR ENDOCRINE GLANDS AND THEIR FUNCTIONS
Table 5.2 lists the hormones secreted by the glands shown here and the effects of those hormones in the body.

The scientific method established the importance of testicular hormones

The importance of hormones was anticipated in ancient civilization. In the fourth century BCE, Aristotle accurately described the effects of **castration** (removal of the testes) in birds, and he compared the behavioral and bodily effects with those seen in *eunuchs* (castrated men). Perhaps this practice built on prehistoric agricultural knowledge of the effects of castration on cattle. Although no one knew what mechanism was involved, clearly the testes were important for the reproductive capacity and sexual characteristics of males.

The first published experiment in behavioral endocrinology showed that the effects of castration were due to a loss of hormones from the testes. In 1849 German physician Arnold Adolph Berthold (1803–1861) tried replicating some studies that were rumored to have been done by English physician John Hunter (Sawin, 1996). When roosters are castrated as juveniles, they fail to develop normal reproductive behavior and secondary sexual characteristics, such as the rooster's comb, in adulthood (**FIGURE 5.2**). Berthold observed, however, that placing one testis (either from the same chick or even from another chick) into the body cavity of a young castrate could preserve normal development of adult anatomy and behavior. Animals so treated began crowing and showed the usual male sexual behaviors. Because the nerve supply to the testis had not been reestablished, Berthold concluded that the testes release a chemical into the blood that affects both male behavior and male body structures. Today we know that the testes make and release the hormone *testosterone*, which exerts these effects.

castration Removal of the gonads, usually the testes.

	Group 1	Group 2	Group 3
	Left undisturbed, young roosters grow up to have large red wattles and combs, to mount and mate with hens readily, and to fight one another and crow loudly.	Animals whose testes were removed during development displayed neither the appearance nor the behavior of normal roosters as adults.	However, if one of the testes was reimplanted into the abdominal cavity immediately after its removal, the rooster developed normal wattles and normal behavior.
Comb and wattles:	Large	Small	Large
Mount hens?	Yes	No	Yes
Aggressive?	Yes	No	Yes
Crowing?	Normal	Weak	Normal

Conclusion
Because the reimplanted testis in group 3 was in an abnormal body site, disconnected from normal innervation, and yet still affected development, Berthold reasoned that the testes release a chemical signal, which we would call a hormone, that has widespread effects.

5.2 THE FIRST EXPERIMENT IN BEHAVIORAL ENDOCRINOLOGY Berthold's nineteenth-century experiment demonstrated the importance of hormones for behavior. The hormone responsible for these changes, testosterone, must be present early in life to have these effects in roosters.

endocrine Referring to glands that release chemicals to the interior of the body. These glands secrete the principal hormones.

neurocrine Referring to secretory functions of neurons, especially pertaining to synapse transmission.

autocrine Referring to a signal that is secreted by a cell into its environment and that feeds back to the same cell.

paracrine Referring to cellular communication in which a chemical signal diffuses to nearby target cells through the extracellular space.

Go to Animation 5.2
Chemical Communication Systems
bn8e.com/5.2

Although Berthold didn't know it, experiments like this also illustrate another distinction in hormonal action. If he had waited until the castrated chicks were adults before transplanting the testes, Berthold would have seen little effect. The testosterone must be present *early* in life to have such dramatic effects on the adult body and behavior. We say that the brain and body are "organized" by exposure to hormones early in life, and sometimes these changes can be dramatic and long lasting. If you wait until adulthood to provide hormones, they still affect the body and behavior, but the changes are less dramatic and tend to be short-lived. In that case, the hormones are said to "activate" behavior. We'll discuss organizational and activational effects of hormones in more detail in Chapter 12.

Organisms use several types of chemical communication

By reviewing the several categories of chemical signals used by the body, we can see how hormonal communication by endocrine glands compares with other methods of communication:

- *Endocrine communication* In **endocrine** communication, our topic for this chapter, the chemical signal is a hormone released into the bloodstream to selectively affect distant target organs (**FIGURE 5.3A**).

- *Synaptic communication* This form of communication was described in Chapters 3 and 4. In synaptic transmission (sometimes called **neurocrine** function), the released chemical signal diffuses across the synaptic cleft and causes a change in the postsynaptic membrane (**FIGURE 5.3B**). Typically, synaptic transmitter function is highly localized.

- *Autocrine communication* In **autocrine** communication, a released chemical acts on the releasing cell itself and thereby affects its own activity (**FIGURE 5.3C**). For example, it is common for a neuron to contain autoreceptors that detect neurotransmitter molecules released by that neuron; the cell can thus monitor its own activity. In this case, the neurotransmitter serves both an autocrine and a synaptic function.

- *Paracrine communication* In **paracrine** communication, the released chemical signal diffuses to nearby target cells (**FIGURE 5.3D**). The strongest impact is on the nearest cells.

5.3 CHEMICAL COMMUNICATION SYSTEMS

(A) Endocrine function

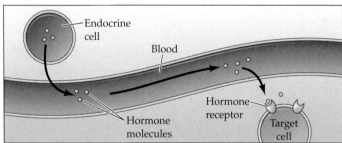

Endocrine cell

Blood

Hormone receptor

Hormone molecules

Target cell

(B) Synaptic transmission (neurocrine function)

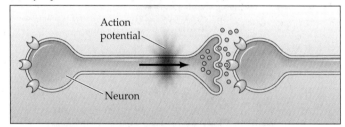

Action potential

Neuron

(C) Autocrine function

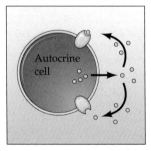

Autocrine cell

(D) Paracrine function

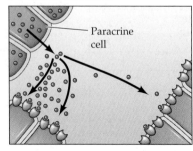

Paracrine cell

(E) Pheromone function

(F) Allomone function

- *Pheromone communication*   Chemicals can be used for communication not only within an individual, but also between individuals. **Pheromones** (from the Greek *pherein*, "to carry") are released into the outside environment to affect other individuals of the same species (**FIGURE 5.3E**). For example, ants produce pheromones that communicate the presence of intruders in the nest or that identify the route to a rich food source (to the annoyance of picnickers). Dogs and wolves urinate on landmarks to designate their territory; other members of the species smell the pheromones in the urine and either respect or challenge the territorial claim. In Chapters 9 and 12 we'll discuss pheromones in more detail.

- *Allomone communication*   Some chemical signals are released by members of one species to affect the behavior of individuals of *another* species. These substances are called **allomones** (from the Greek *allos*, "other") (**FIGURES 5.3F AND 5.4**). Flowers exude scented allomones to attract insects and birds in order to distribute pollen. And the bolas spider—nature's femme fatale—releases a moth sex pheromone to attract male moths to their doom (Eberhard, 1977; Haynes et al., 2002).

5.4 SCENTS AND SENSIBILITY
Skunks produce a very effective allomone.

pheromone   A chemical signal that is released outside the body of an animal and affects other members of the same species.

allomone   A chemical signal that is released outside the body by one species and affects the behavior of other species.

Hormonal actions can be organized according to general principles

Although there are some exceptions, the following rules are general principles of hormonal action:

1. Hormones frequently act in a *gradual* fashion, activating behavioral and physiological responses hours or weeks after entering the bloodstream. The changes may persist for days, weeks, or years after hormone release is over.

2. When hormones alter behavior, they tend to act by changing the *intensity* or *probability* of evoked behaviors, rather than acting as a switch to turn behaviors on or off regardless of context.

3. Both the quantities and the types of hormones released are influenced by environmental factors. Therefore, *the relationship between behavior and hormones is reciprocal*; that is, hormones change behaviors and behaviors change hormone levels. For example, high levels of testosterone are related to aggression, and in some species, males who lose in aggressive encounters show a reduction in testosterone levels, while the winners may show little change in testosterone levels. This example illustrates the reciprocal relation between behavioral and somatic (body) events that we discussed in Chapter 1 (see Figure 1.2).

4. A hormone may have multiple effects on different cells, organs, and behaviors; conversely, a single type of behavior or physiological change can be affected by many different hormones (**FIGURE 5.5**).

5. Hormones are produced in small amounts and often are secreted in bursts. This *pulsatile* secretion pattern is sometimes crucial for the small amount of hormone to be effective.

6. The levels of most hormones vary rhythmically throughout the day, and many hormonal systems are controlled by circadian "clocks" in the brain, as we'll see in Chapter 14. A shortcoming of taking hormones for therapy, as Mary Lou must do, is that we can't really replicate the pulsatile and rhythmic changes in levels seen in naturally released hormones.

7. Hormones interact; the effects of one hormone can be markedly changed by the actions of another hormone.

8. Hormones can affect only those cells that possess corresponding receptor proteins to recognize the hormones and alter cell function.

Neuroendocrine cells blend neuronal and endocrine functions

Synaptic transmission—chemical communication between neurons—and hormonal communication are both secretory events, and they seem similar in several ways. For example, the neuron produces particular transmitter chemicals and releases them, just as an endocrine gland produces and releases hormones. Similarities between

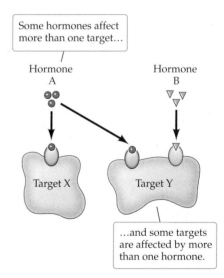

Some hormones affect more than one target…

Hormone A

Hormone B

Target X

Target Y

…and some targets are affected by more than one hormone.

5.5 THE MULTIPLICITY OF HORMONE ACTION   A single hormone (hormone A in this illustration) may affect multiple target tissues in various locations throughout the body. Similarly, a single process or body organ (target Y here) may be sensitive to several hormones.

5.6 NEUROENDOCRINE CELLS BLEND NEU-RONAL AND ENDOCRINE MECHANISMS

(A) Neurons can communicate only with the particular neurons, muscle cells, or glands on which they synapse. The target cell is determined by the synaptic anatomy. (B) Endocrine signals are transmitted through the bloodstream and are recognized by appropriate receptors wherever they occur in the body. (C) Neuroendocrine (neurosecretory) cells are the interface between neurons and endocrine glands. They receive synaptic signals from other neurons, yet they secrete hormones into the bloodstream. In this way electrical signals are converted into hormonal signals.

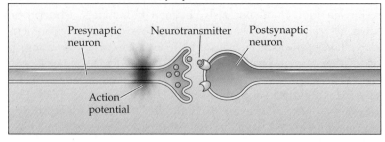

(A) Neurocrine communication (synaptic transmission)

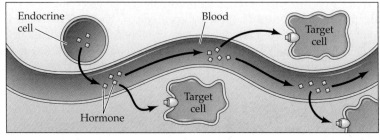

(B) Endocrine communication

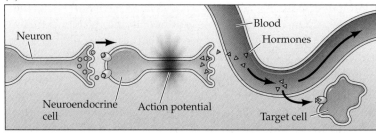

(C) Neuroendocrine communication

neuroendocrine cell   Also called *neurosecretory cell*. A neuron that releases hormones into local or systemic circulation.

neuropeptide   Also called *peptide neurotransmitter*. A peptide that is used by neurons for signaling.

neuromodulator   A substance that influences the activity of synaptic transmitters.

peptide hormones   A class of hormones, molecules of which consist of a string of amino acids. If the string of amino acids is long enough, it may be called a *protein hormone*.

amine hormones   Also called *monoamine hormones*. A class of hormones, each composed of a single amino acid that has been modified into a related molecule, such as melatonin or epinephrine.

steroid hormones   A class of hormones, each of which is composed of four interconnected rings of carbon atoms.

neuronal and hormonal communication are especially exemplified by the **neuroendocrine cells** (or *neurosecretory cells*) of the hypothalamus (**FIGURE 5.6**). These cells are neurons in almost every way—they receive synaptic input, reach threshold, and produce action potentials—except at their axon terminals they release hormone into the bloodstream rather than neurotransmitter into a synapse. Later we'll learn that neuroendocrine cells are crucial for brain control of endocrine glands.

Some peptides are used both as hormones by endocrine glands and as **neuropeptides** (peptides used by neurons) in the brain. Because these same peptides are found in single-celled organisms, the nervous system and the endocrine system may share an evolutionary origin from chemical communication systems in our remote single-celled ancestors (LeRoith et al., 1992).

Whereas neural messages are rapid and are measured in milliseconds, hormonal messages are slower and are measured in seconds and minutes. But this distinction is blurred sometimes: **neuromodulators** alter the reactivity of cells to specific transmitters (see Chapter 4), acting more slowly and having longer-lasting effects than neurotransmitters have. So neuromodulators are something of a blend of neurotransmitter (because they're released into synapses) and hormone (because they act gradually).

Hormones can be classified by chemical structure

Most hormones fall into one of three categories: peptide hormones, amine hormones, or steroid hormones. Like any other protein, a **peptide hormone** is composed of a string of amino acids (**FIGURE 5.7A**). (Recall that a peptide is simply a small protein—a short string of amino acids. Thus these may sometimes be referred to as *protein hormones*.) Different peptide hormones consist of different combinations of amino acids. **Amine hormones** are smaller and simpler, consisting of a modified

(A) Peptide hormone

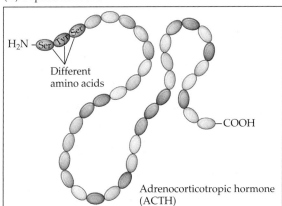

Different amino acids

H_2N —Ser—Tyr—Ser

—COOH

Adrenocorticotropic hormone (ACTH)

(B) Amine hormone

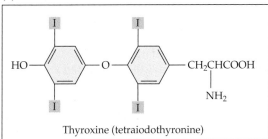

HO— —O— —$CH_2CHCOOH$

NH_2

Thyroxine (tetraiodothyronine)

(C) Steroid hormone

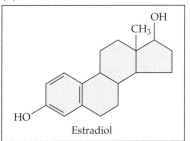

OH
CH_3

HO—

Estradiol

5.7 CHEMICAL STRUCTURES OF THE THREE MAIN HORMONE TYPES (A) Protein hormones consist of strings of amino acids. If the string is short, as it is in adrenocorticotropic hormone (ACTH), it may be referred to as a *peptide hormone*. (B) Amine hormones, such as thyroxine, are modified single amino acids. (C) Steroid hormones, such as estradiol, are derived from cholesterol and consist of four interconnected rings of carbon atoms, to which are attached different numbers and types of atoms.

version of a single amino acid (hence their alias, *monoamine* hormones) (**FIGURE 5.7B**). **Steroid hormones** are derivatives of cholesterol, sharing its structure of four rings of carbon atoms (**FIGURE 5.7C**). Different steroid hormones vary in the number and kinds of atoms attached to the rings. Steroids dissolve readily in lipids, so they easily pass through membranes (recall from Chapter 2 that the cell membrane is a lipid bilayer). **TABLE 5.1** gives examples of each class of hormones.

The different classes of hormones act through very different mechanisms, as we'll see next.

Hormones Have a Variety of Cellular Actions

In later chapters we will be considering the effects of specific hormones on behavior. In preparation for that discussion, let's look briefly at three aspects of hormonal activity: the effects of hormones on cells, the mechanisms by which hormones exercise these effects, and the regulation of hormone secretion.

Hormones affect cells by influencing their growth and activity

By influencing cells in various tissues and organs, hormones affect many everyday behaviors in humans and other animals. Hormones exert these far-reaching effects by (1) promoting the proliferation, growth, and differentiation of cells and (2) modulating cell activity. Hormones

TABLE 5.1 Examples of Major Classes of Hormones

CLASS	HORMONE
Peptide hormones	Adrenocorticotropic hormone (ACTH)
	Follicle-stimulating hormone (FSH)
	Luteinizing hormone (LH)
	Thyroid-stimulating hormone (TSH)
	Growth hormone (GH)
	Prolactin
	Insulin
	Glucagon
	Oxytocin
	Vasopressin (arginine vasopressin, AVP; antidiuretic hormone, ADH)
	Releasing hormones, such as:
	Corticotropin-releasing hormone (CRH)
	Gonadotropin-releasing hormone (GnRH)
Amine hormones	Epinephrine (adrenaline)
	Norepinephrine (NE)
	Thyroid hormones
	Melatonin
Steroid hormones	Estrogens (e.g., estradiol)
	Progestins (e.g., progesterone)
	Androgens (e.g., testosterone, dihydrotestosterone)
	Glucocorticoids (e.g., cortisol)
	Mineralocorticoids (e.g., aldosterone)

second messenger A slow-acting substance in a target cell that amplifies the effects of synaptic or hormonal activity and regulates activity within the target cell.

cyclic adenosine monophosphate (cyclic AMP, or cAMP) A second messenger activated in many target cells in response to synaptic or hormonal stimulation.

shape many processes during development. For example, without thyroid hormones, fewer cells are produced in the developing brain, and mental development is stunted. Later in development, during adolescence, sex hormones cause secondary sexual characteristics to appear: breasts and broadening of the hips in women, facial hair and enlargement of the Adam's apple in men.

In cells that are already differentiated, hormones can modulate the rate of function. Thyroid hormones and insulin, for instance, regulate the metabolic activity of most of the cells in the human body. Other hormones modulate activity in certain types of cells. For example, luteinizing hormone (a hormone from the anterior pituitary gland) promotes the secretion of sex hormones by the testes and ovaries.

Hormones initiate actions by binding to receptor molecules

The three classes of hormones exert their influences on target organs in two different ways. Peptide and amine hormones bind to specific receptors (proteins that recognize only one hormone or class of hormones) that are usually found *on the surface* of target cell membranes. In contrast, steroid hormones easily pass through cell membranes, so they generally bind to specific receptor proteins located *inside* the cell.

Let's look at these two main modes of action in a little more detail and examine the ways in which hormones affect cells.

PEPTIDE AND AMINE HORMONES What determines whether a cell responds to a particular peptide hormone? Only those cells that produce the appropriate receptor proteins for a hormone and insert them into the membrane can respond to that hormone. As we saw with neurotransmitter receptors in Chapters 3 and 4, the receptor protein spans the cellular membrane. When a hormone binds to the extracellular portion of the receptor, the receptor molecule changes its overall shape. The alteration in the intracellular portion of the receptor then changes the internal chemistry of the cell, most often by activating a **second messenger** (**FIGURE 5.8A**). Second-messenger systems within the target cell can bring about changes in metabolism, membrane potentials, and other cellular functions. These same second-messenger systems are activated by metabotropic receptors in neurons, which we learned about in Chapter 4.

One second-messenger compound in particular—**cyclic adenosine monophosphate** (**cyclic AMP or cAMP**)—transmits the messages of many of the peptide and amine hormones. It may seem surprising that the same second messenger can mediate the effects of many different hormones, but a change in cAMP levels

Go to Animation 5.3
Mechanisms of Hormone Action
bn8e.com/5.3

5.8 TWO MAIN MECHANISMS OF HORMONE ACTION (A) Protein hormone receptors are found in the cell membrane. When the hormone binds to the receptor, a second-messenger system is activated, which affects various cellular processes. (B) Steroid hormones diffuse passively into cells. Inside the target cells are large receptor molecules that bind to the steroid hormones. The steroid-receptor complexes then bind to DNA, causing an increase in the production of some gene products and a decrease in the production of others. This is the mechanism by which steroids exert a genomic effect, which is distinct from the nongenomic effects mentioned in the text.

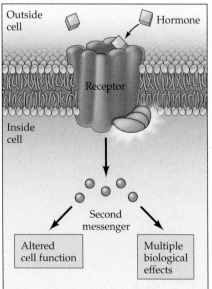

(A) Protein hormone action

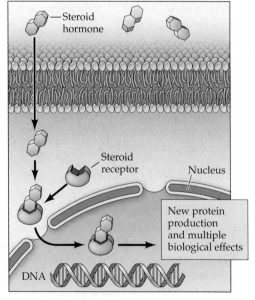

(B) Steroid hormone action

can cause many different outcomes, depending on which cells are affected, on which part of a cell is affected, and on the prior biochemical activity inside the cell. Other widespread second-messenger compounds include **cyclic guanosine monophosphate (cyclic GMP or cGMP)** and **inositol triphosphate (IP₃)**.

The specificity of hormonal effects is determined in large part by the selectivity of receptors. Only a minority of cells produce the receptor that recognizes and reacts to a particular hormone, and thus only those cells can respond to it. For example, adrenocorticotropic hormone (ACTH) interacts with receptors on the membranes of cells in the adrenal gland, and in these cells an increase in cAMP leads to the synthesis and release of other hormones.

Peptide hormones usually act relatively rapidly, within seconds to minutes. (Although rapid for a hormone, this action is much slower than neural activity.) There can also be prolonged effects. For example, ACTH promotes the proliferation and growth of some adrenal cells, thereby increasing their long-term capacity to produce hormones. A cell may increase or decrease the number of hormone receptors it makes, and these changes are sometimes referred to as *up-regulation* and *down-regulation*, respectively.

STEROID HORMONES   Steroid hormones typically act more slowly than protein or amine hormones, usually requiring hours to take effect. The specific actions of steroid hormones are determined by the receptors that reside *inside* target cells. These receptors are truly ancient, in an evolutionary sense, having arisen in primordial invertebrate species a billion years ago (Bridgham et al., 2006).

Steroid hormones pass in and out of many cells in which they have no effect. If appropriate receptor proteins are inside a cell, however, these receptors bind to the hormone (**FIGURE 5.8B**). The resulting steroid-receptor complex then binds to specific regions of the DNA in the nucleus of the cell, where it acts as a **transcription factor**, controlling the expression of specific genes. This action results in an increase or decrease in the production of the protein encoded by the regulated gene (see the Appendix). By regulating gene expression, steroid hormones can affect a vast array of cellular processes.

Simple possession of appropriate steroid receptors is not enough to ensure that a given neuron will respond to the presence of that particular steroid hormone. Cells make a wide variety of **steroid receptor cofactors** that may be required, along with the bound steroid receptors, in order for the cell to respond. Furthermore, the nature of the target cell's response may be determined by the type of cofactor present: two different cells containing the same steroid receptors may respond quite differently to the steroid hormone if they are producing different steroid receptor cofactors (Molenda-Figueira et al., 2006; Tetel, 2000).

By altering protein production, steroids have slow but long-lasting effects on the development or adult function of cells. We will discuss such effects of steroids further in Chapter 12. There is a large "superfamily" of steroid receptor genes (Ribeiro et al., 1995), and some steroids act on more than one receptor. For example, a second estrogen **receptor isoform** (steroid receptor subtype) has been described and named estrogen receptor β (Kuiper et al., 1996) to distinguish it from the previously discovered estrogen receptor α. The brain contains both types of estrogen receptors, and they differ in their anatomical distributions within the brain and in their effects on behavior.

Because steroid-receptor complexes become concentrated in the nuclei of target cells, we can study where a steroid hormone is active by injecting radioactively tagged molecules of the steroid and observing where they accumulate. For example, tagged estrogens accumulate not only in the reproductive tract (as you might expect), but also in the nuclei of some neurons throughout the hypothalamus. Because neurons producing hormone receptors are found in only a limited number of brain regions, we can begin to learn how hormones affect behavior by finding those brain sites and asking what happens when the hormones arrive there. This strategy for learning about hormones and behavior is discussed in **BOX 5.1** on the following page.

cyclic guanosine monophosphate (cyclic GMP, or cGMP)   A second messenger activated in some target cells in response to synaptic or hormonal stimulation.

inositol triphosphate (IP3)   A member of a class of second-messenger compounds (*phosphoinositides*) common in postsynaptic cells.

transcription factor   A substance that binds to recognition sites on DNA and alters the rate of expression of particular genes.

steroid receptor cofactors   Proteins that affect the cell's response when a steroid hormone binds its receptor.

receptor isoform   A version of a receptor protein (here, a hormone receptor) with slight differences in structure that give it different functional properties. Conceptually similar to a receptor subtype.

BOX 5.1

Techniques of Modern Behavioral Endocrinology

To establish that a particular hormone affects behavior, investigators usually begin with the type of experiment that Berthold performed in the nineteenth century: observing the behavior of the intact animal and then removing the endocrine gland and looking for a change in behavior (see Figure 5.2). Berthold was limited to this type of experiment, but modern scientists have many additional options available. Let's imagine that we're investigating a particular effect of hormones on behavior to see how we might proceed.

Which Hormones Affect Which Behaviors?

First we must carefully observe the behavior of several individuals, seeking ways to classify and quantify the different types of behavior and to place them in the context of the behavior of other individuals. For example, most adult male rats will try to mount and copulate with a receptive female placed in their cage. If the testes are removed from a male rat, he will eventually stop copulating with females. We know that one of the hormones produced by the testes is testosterone. Is it the loss of testosterone that causes the loss of male copulatory behavior?

To explore this question, we inject some synthetic testosterone into castrated males and observe whether the copulatory behavior returns. (It does.) Another way to ask whether a steroid hormone is affecting a particular behavior is to examine the behavior of animals that lack the receptors for that steroid. We can delete the gene for a given hormone receptor, making a **knockout organism** (because the gene for the receptor has been "knocked out"), and ask which behaviors are different in the knockouts versus normal animals (see Box 7.3).

Next we might examine individual male rats and ask whether the ones that copulate a lot have more testosterone circulating in their blood than those that copulate only a little. To investigate this question, we measure individual differences in the amount of copulatory behavior, take a sample of blood from each individual, and measure levels of testosterone with **radioimmunoassay** (**RIA**), a technique using an antibody that binds to a particular hormone. By adding many such antibodies to each blood sample and measuring how many of the antibodies find a hormone molecule to bind, we can estimate the total number of molecules of the hormone per unit volume of blood.

It turns out that individual differences in the sexual behavior of normal male rats (and male humans) do *not* correlate with differences in testosterone levels in the blood. In both rats and humans, a drastic loss of testosterone, as occurs after castration, results in a gradual decline in sexual behavior. All healthy males, however, appear to make more than enough testosterone to maintain sexual behavior, so something else must modulate this behavior. In other words, the hormone acts in a permissive manner: it permits the display of the behavior, but something else determines how much of the behavior each individual exhibits.

Where Are the Target Cells?

What does testosterone do to permit sexual behavior? One step toward answering this question is to ask another question: Which parts

1. A rat is injected with molecules of testosterone (an androgen) that have been radioactively labeled.

2. The testosterone molecules enter the bloodstream and accumulate in those cells that have androgen receptors.

3. The brain is removed and frozen to keep the testosterone molecules inside the target cells.

Film

4. The brain is thinly sliced and film is placed on top in the dark. The radioactive molecules release particles that "expose" the film just as light would.

Exposure

5. When the film is developed, small black dots form on the film where the testosterone had accumulated in target cells.

(A) Steps in steroid autoradiography

of the brain are normally affected by this hormone? We have several methods at our disposal for investigating this question.

In one method, we can inject a castrated animal with radioactively labeled testosterone and wait for the hormone to accumulate in the brain regions that have receptors for the hormone (Figure A). Then we can sacrifice the animal, remove the brain, freeze it, cut thin sections from it, and place the thin sections on photographic film. Radioactive emissions from the tissue will expose the film, revealing which brain regions have accumulated the most labeled testosterone. This method is known as **autoradiography** because the tissue "takes its own picture" with radioactivity.

When the labeled hormone is a steroid like testosterone, the radioactivity accumulates in the nuclei of neurons and leaves small black specks on the film (Figure B). When the radiolabeled hormone is a peptide hormone such as oxytocin, the radioactivity accumulates in the membranes of cells and appears in particular layers of the brain. Computers can generate color maps that highlight regions with high densities of receptors (Figure C).

Another method for detecting hormone receptors is **immunocytochemistry (ICC)**. In this method (described in more detail in Box 2.1), we use antibodies that recognize the hormone receptor (Figure D). This method allows us to map the distribution of hormone receptors in the brain. We put the antibodies on slices of brain tissue, wait for them to bind to the receptors, wash off the unbound antibodies, and use chemical methods to visualize the antibodies by creating a tiny dark spot in the nuclei of target brain cells. We can also use **in situ hybridization** (see Box 2.1) to look for the neurons that make the mRNA for the steroid receptor. Because these cells make the transcript for the receptor, they are likely to possess the receptor protein itself.

What Happens at the Target Cells?

Once we have used autoradiography, immunocytochemistry, or in situ hybridization (or, better yet, all three) to identify brain regions that have receptors for the hormone, those regions become candidates for the places at which the hormone works to change behavior. Now we can take castrated

(B) Autoradiogram

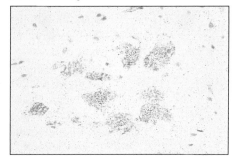

(C) Autoradiogram

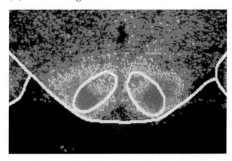

males and implant tiny pellets of testosterone into one of those brain regions. We use RIA to ensure that the pellets are small enough that they have no effect on hormone levels in the blood. Then we ask whether the small implant in that brain region restores the behavior. If not, then in other animals we can implant pellets in a different region or try placing implants in a combination of brain sites.

It turns out that such implants can restore male sexual behavior in rats only if they are placed in the medial preoptic area (mPOA) of the hypothalamus. Thus, we have found so far that testosterone does something to the mPOA to permit individual males to display sexual behavior. Now we can examine the mPOA in detail to learn which changes in the anatomy, physiology, or protein production of this region are caused by testosterone. We have more or less caught up to modern-day scientists who work on this very question. Some of the preliminary answers suggested by their research will be discussed in Chapter 12. (Figure C courtesy of Dr. Bruce McEwen; D courtesy of Dr. Cynthia Jordan.)

(D) Immunocytochemistry

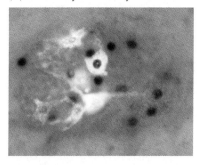

(B) An autoradiogram showing that spinal motor neurons (purple cell profiles) accumulate radioactive testosterone (small dots). (C) An autoradiogram showing the concentration of oxytocin receptors in the ventromedial hypothalamus (oval outlines). (D) Immunocytochemistry revealing cells with nuclei that contain androgen receptors (dark circles), to which testosterone can bind. The somata of these neurons have been labeled with the tracers Fluoro-Gold (white) and Fluoro-Ruby (red).

knockout organism An individual in which a particular gene has been disabled by an experimenter.

radioimmunoassay (RIA) A technique that uses antibodies to measure the concentration of a substance, such as a hormone, in blood.

autoradiography A histological technique that shows the distribution of radioactive chemicals in tissues.

immunocytochemistry (ICC) A method for detecting a particular protein in tissues in which an antibody recognizes and binds to the protein and then chemical methods are used to leave a visible reaction product around each antibody.

in situ hybridization A method for detecting particular RNA transcripts in tissue sections by providing a nucleotide probe that is complementary to, and will therefore hybridize with, the transcript of interest.

OH ... OH (figure top left)

Testosterone → (Aromatase) → Estradiol

Aromatase converts androgens like testosterone into estrogens like estradiol.

5.9 ENZYMATIC CONVERSION OF STEROID HORMONES

nongenomic effect An effect of a steroid hormone that is not mediated by direct changes in gene expression.

neurosteroids Steroid molecules produced within the brain that affect neurons.

aromatase An enzyme that converts some androgens into estrogens.

Steroids can also affect cells through mechanisms other than the classic nuclear steroid receptor. For example, estradiol, in addition to its slow, long-lasting action on gene expression, can have a rapid, brief effect on some neurons without affecting gene expression. This rapid **nongenomic effect** of steroids involves a separate class of receptors in the neuronal *membrane* (Mani et al., 2012), modulating neural excitability. Similarly, testosterone can have effects that are too rapid to involve the transcription of genes and appears instead to involve androgen receptors localized in axons and other sites, distant from the cell nucleus and its DNA (DonCarlos et al., 2006).

Sometimes the brain makes its own steroid hormone. Steroids made in the brain are called **neurosteroids**. We mentioned in Chapter 4 that progesterone-like neurosteroids act as noncompetitive agonists at $GABA_A$ receptors to reduce anxiety (see Figure 4.12). The brain also makes "gonadal" steroids like testosterone and estrogens. Furthermore, the brain may transform one steroid into another. For example, in Chapter 12 we'll see that testosterone released from the testes may, upon entering the brain, be converted into estrogens! An enzyme called **aromatase**, which converts testosterone to estradiol in a single chemical reaction (**FIGURE 5.9**), is abundant in the hypothalamus. In fact, testosterone is the major precursor for making estrogens. The reason ovaries release so much estrogen is because they are loaded with aromatase, rapidly converting most testosterone and other androgens into estrogens. Testes, on

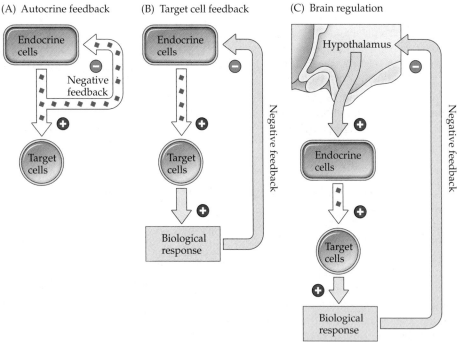

5.10 ENDOCRINE FEEDBACK LOOPS (A) In the simplest type of negative feedback control, an endocrine gland releases a hormone that not only acts on a target, but also feeds back in an autocrine fashion to inhibit further hormone secretion. (B) The hormone from the endocrine gland acts on target cells to produce a specific set of biological effects. The consequences of these effects may be detected by the endocrine gland, inhibiting further hormone release. (C) In many feedback systems the brain becomes involved. The hypothalamic region drives the endocrine gland via either neural or hormonal signals. The target organ signals the brain to inhibit this drive. (D) More complex feedback mechanisms involve the hypothalamus and the anterior pituitary, as well as the endocrine gland. Feedback is regulated by a variety of hormones via multiple routes.

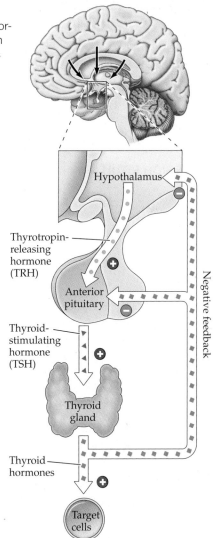

5.11 AN EXAMPLE OF COMPLEX ENDOCRINE REGULATION The brain funnels information to the hypothalamus, which then controls the anterior pituitary, which in turn stimulates the thyroid gland. Note that three hormones and at least four cell groups are interacting in this instance.

the other hand, have far less aromatase on hand and so release smaller amounts of estrogens. That's why there is no steroid hormone found exclusively in one sex.

Feedback control mechanisms regulate the secretion of hormones

One of the major features of almost all hormonal systems is that they don't just manufacture a hormone; they also detect and evaluate the effects of the hormone. Thus, secretion is usually monitored and regulated so that the rate is appropriate to ongoing activities and needs of the body. The basic control used is a **negative feedback** system: output of the hormone *feeds back* to inhibit the drive for more of that same hormone. This negative feedback action of a hormonal system is like that of a thermostat, and just as the thermostat can be set to different temperatures at different times, the set points of a person's endocrine feedback systems can be changed to meet varying circumstances. We'll discuss negative feedback regulation of other processes in Chapter 13 (see Figure 13.1).

In the simplest kind of hormone regulation system, diagrammed in **FIGURE 5.10A**, an endocrine cell releases a hormone that acts on target cells, but the same hormone also feeds back to inhibit the gland that released it. This is an autocrine response.

In other cases, the endocrine cell reacts not to its own hormone, but to the biological response that the hormone elicits from the target cells (**FIGURE 5.10B**). If the initial effect is too small, additional hormone is released; if the effect is sufficient, no further hormone is released. For example, the hormone insulin is released to control the level of glucose circulating in our blood. After a meal, glucose from the food enters the bloodstream, causing insulin to be released from the pancreas. The insulin causes glucose to enter muscle and fat cells. As the level of glucose in the blood falls, the pancreas secretes less insulin, so a balance tends to be maintained (Chapter 13).

A more complex endocrine system includes the brain, usually the hypothalamus, as part of the circuit that controls an endocrine gland (**FIGURE 5.10C**). When we are alarmed, for example, the hypothalamus directs the adrenal medulla to secrete the hormone epinephrine (also called *adrenaline*), which affects many target cells. The brain detects these effects and exerts negative feedback on the hypothalamus to reduce further hormone output.

An even greater degree of complexity is encountered when the anterior pituitary becomes involved (**FIGURE 5.10D**). As we'll see in the next section, several anterior pituitary hormones regulate hormone secretion by other endocrine glands; all of these pituitary hormones are called **tropic hormones**. (*Tropic*, pronounced with a long *o* as in *toe*, means "directed toward." There is nothing "tropical" about tropic hormones.) The hypothalamus uses another set of hormones, called **releasing hormones**, to control the pituitary release of tropic hormones. Thus, the brain's releasing hormones affect the pituitary's tropic hormones, which affect the release of hormones from endocrine glands. Negative feedback in this case goes from the hormone of the endocrine gland to both the hypothalamus and the anterior pituitary (**FIGURE 5.11**).

Each Endocrine Gland Secretes Specific Hormones

We restrict our account in this chapter to some of the main endocrine glands because a thorough treatment would fill an entire book (e.g., Melmed et al., 2016). **TABLE 5.2** gives a fuller but far from complete listing of hormones and their functions. We will discuss hormones from the pancreas and stomach in Chapter 13 when we consider hunger. Keep in mind that most hormones have more functions than are mentioned here.

Go to Animation 5.4
The Hypothalamus and Endocrine Function
bn8e.com/5.4

negative feedback The property by which some of the output of a system feeds back to reduce the effect of input signals.

tropic hormones A class of anterior pituitary hormones that affect the secretion of other endocrine glands.

releasing hormones A class of hormones, produced in the hypothalamus, that traverse the hypothalamic-pituitary portal system to control the pituitary's release of tropic hormones.

TABLE 5.2 Main Endocrine Glands, Their Hormone Products, and Principal Effects of the Hormones

GLAND	HORMONES	PRINCIPAL EFFECTS
POSTERIOR PITUITARY (storage organ for certain hormones produced by hypothalamus)	Oxytocin	Stimulates contraction of uterine muscles; stimulates release of milk by mammary glands
	Vasopressin (AVP), or antidiuretic hormone (ADH)	Stimulates increased water reabsorption by kidneys; stimulates constriction of blood vessels
ANTERIOR PITUITARY	Growth hormone (GH)	Stimulates growth
	Thyroid-stimulating hormone (TSH)	Stimulates the thyroid
	Adrenocorticotropic hormone (ACTH)	Stimulates the adrenal cortex
	Follicle-stimulating hormone (FSH)	Stimulates growth of ovarian follicles and of seminiferous tubules of the testes
	Luteinizing hormone (LH)	Stimulates conversion of follicles into corpora lutea; stimulates secretion of sex hormones by gonads
	Prolactin	Stimulates milk production by mammary glands
HYPOTHALAMUS	Releasing hormones	Regulate hormone secretion by anterior pituitary
	Oxytocin; vasopressin	*See* "Posterior pituitary" above
PINEAL	Melatonin	Regulates seasonal changes; regulates puberty
ADRENAL CORTEX	Glucocorticoids (corticosterone, cortisol, hydrocortisone, etc.)	Inhibit incorporation of amino acids into protein in muscle; stimulate formation and storage of glycogen; help maintain normal blood sugar level
	Mineralocorticoids (aldosterone, deoxycorticosterone, etc.)	Regulate metabolism of sodium and potassium
	Sex hormones (especially androstenedione)	Regulate facial and body hair
ADRENAL MEDULLA	Catecholamines (epinephrine, norepinephrine)	Prepare body for action
GONADS		
Testes	Androgens (testosterone, dihydrotestosterone, etc.)	Stimulate development and maintenance of male primary and secondary sexual characteristics and behavior
Ovaries	Estrogens (estradiol, estrone, etc.)	Stimulate development and maintenance of female secondary sexual characteristics and behavior
	Progestins (progesterone)	Stimulate female secondary sexual characteristics and behavior; maintain pregnancy
THYROID	Thyroxine (tetraiodothyronine); triiodothyronine	Stimulate oxidative metabolism
	Calcitonin	Prevents excessive rise in blood calcium
PANCREAS	Insulin	Stimulates glycogen formation and storage
	Glucagon	Stimulates conversion of glycogen into glucose
STOMACH	Secretin	Stimulates secretion of pancreatic juice
	Cholecystokinin (CCK)	Stimulates release of bile by gallbladder
	Gastrin	Stimulates secretion of gastric juice
	Ghrelin	Provides appetite signal to the hypothalamus
HEART	Atrial natriuretic peptide	Promotes salt loss in urine

pituitary gland Also called *hypophysis*. A small, complex endocrine gland located in a socket at the base of the skull.

anterior pituitary Also called *adenohypophysis*. The front division of the pituitary gland; secretes tropic hormones.

The pituitary gland releases many important hormones

Resting in a socket in the base of the skull is the **pituitary gland** (or *hypophysis*; see Figure 5.1), occupying a volume of about 1 cubic centimeter and weighing about 1 gram. The hypothalamus sits just above it. The term *pituitary* comes from the Latin *pituita*, "mucus," reflecting the erroneous historical belief that waste products dripped down from the brain into the pituitary, which secreted them out through the nose. (The ancients may have thought you could literally sneeze your brains out!) The pituitary used to be referred to as the *master gland* because it controls hormone release from several other endocrine glands. That's why loss of her pituitary left Mary Lou, whom we met at the start of this chapter, with deficits in many hormones. But this gland is itself enslaved by the hypothalamus above it, as we'll see.

The pituitary gland consists of two main parts: the **anterior pituitary** (or *adenohypophysis*) and the **posterior pituitary** (or *neurohypophysis*). The anterior and posterior pituitary develop from different embryonic tissues and are completely separate in function. The pituitary is connected to the hypothalamus by a thin piece of tissue called the **pituitary stalk** (or *infundibulum*). The stalk contains many axons and is richly supplied with blood vessels. The axons extend only to the posterior pituitary, which we will consider next. The blood vessels, as we will see later, carry information exclusively to the anterior pituitary.

THE POSTERIOR PITUITARY   The posterior pituitary gland secretes two principal hormones: **oxytocin** and **arginine vasopressin** (**AVP**), often called just **vasopressin**. Neurons in the **supraoptic nuclei** and the **paraventricular nuclei** of the hypothalamus synthesize these two hormones and transport them along their axons to the axon terminals (**FIGURE 5.12**). Action potentials in these hypothalamic neurosecretory cells travel down the axons in the pituitary stalk and reach the axon terminals in the posterior pituitary, causing release of the hormones from the terminals into the rich vascular bed of the neurohypophysis. The axon terminals abut capillaries (small blood vessels), allowing the hormones to enter circulation immediately.

Some of the signals that activate the nerve cells of the supraoptic and paraventricular nuclei are related to thirst and water regulation, which we will discuss in Chapter 13. Secretion of vasopressin increases blood pressure by causing blood vessels to contract. Vasopressin also inhibits the formation of urine, so it is sometimes called *antidiuretic hormone* (ADH) (a diuretic is a food or drug that promotes urination). This action of vasopressin helps conserve water. In fact, the major physiological role of vasopressin is its potent antidiuretic activity; it exerts this effect with less than one-thousandth of the dose needed to alter blood pressure.

Oxytocin is involved in many aspects of reproductive and parental behavior. One of its functions is to stimulate contractions of the uterus in childbirth (the word *oxytocin* is derived from the Greek *oxys*, "rapid," and *tokos*, "childbirth"). Injections of oxytocin (or the synthetic version, Pitocin) are frequently used in medical settings to induce or accelerate labor and delivery.

Oxytocin also triggers the **milk letdown reflex**, the contraction of mammary gland cells that ejects milk into the breast ducts. This phenomenon exemplifies the reciprocal relationship between behavior and hormone release. When an infant or young animal first begins to suckle, the arrival of milk at the nipple is delayed by 30–60 seconds. This delay is caused by the sequence of steps that precedes letdown. Stimulation of the nipple activates receptors in the skin, which transmit this information through a chain of neurons and synapses to hypothalamic cells that contain oxytocin. Once these cells have been sufficiently stimulated, the oxytocin is released from the posterior pituitary and travels via the bloodstream to the mammary glands, where it produces a contraction of the tissues storing milk, making the milk available at the nipple (**FIGURE 5.13**).

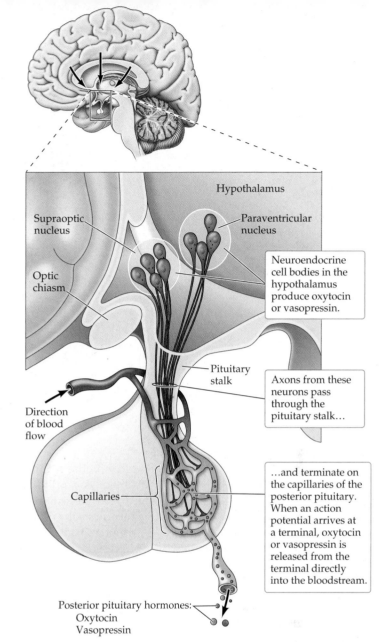

5.12 HORMONE PRODUCTION BY THE POSTERIOR PITUITARY

posterior pituitary   Also called *neurohypophysis*. The rear division of the pituitary gland.

pituitary stalk   Also called *infundibulum*. A thin piece of tissue that connects the pituitary gland to the hypothalamus.

oxytocin   A hormone, released from the posterior pituitary, that triggers milk letdown in the nursing female.

arginine vasopressin (AVP)   Also called *vasopressin* or *antidiuretic hormone* (ADH). A peptide hormone from the posterior pituitary that promotes water conservation.

supraoptic nucleus   A hypothalamic nucleus containing neuroendocrine cells that send axons to the posterior pituitary to release oxytocin or vasopressin.

1 Stimulation of the mother's nipple by the infant's suckling response produces brain activity in the mother.

2 This brain activity stimulates hypothalamic cells to release oxytocin from the posterior pituitary.

Hypothalamus

Nerve impulses to hypothalamus

Oxytocin from pituitary gland

Posterior pituitary

Release of oxytocin

4 The baby, rewarded with milk, continues suckling until sated.

3 The oxytocin causes the cells of the mammary glands to contract, thereby releasing milk.

paraventricular nucleus A nucleus of the hypothalamus implicated in the release of oxytocin and vasopressin and in the control of feeding and other behaviors.

milk letdown reflex The reflexive release of milk in response to suckling or to stimuli associated with suckling.

median eminence Midline feature on the base of the brain marking the point at which the pituitary stalk exits the hypothalamus to connect to the pituitary. Contains elements of the hypophyseal portal system.

hypophyseal portal system A system of capillaries spanning between the neurosecretory cells of the hypothalamus and the secretory tissue of the anterior pituitary.

For mothers, this reflex response to suckling frequently becomes conditioned to baby cries, so milk appears promptly at the start of nursing. Because the mother learns to release oxytocin *before* the suckling begins, sometimes the cries of someone else's baby in public may trigger an inconvenient release of milk. Oxytocin and vasopressin also serve as neurotransmitters from hypothalamic cells (**FIGURE 5.14**), projecting widely through the nervous system. Oxytocin and vasopressin have been implicated in social behaviors, as we'll discuss at the end of this chapter.

THE ANTERIOR PITUITARY   Different cells of the anterior lobe of the pituitary synthesize and release different tropic hormones, which we'll discuss in the next section. Secretion of these tropic hormones, however, is under the control of releasing hormones, as mentioned earlier. Let's discuss how this regulation works.

Hypothalamic releasing hormones govern the anterior pituitary

The neurons that synthesize the different releasing hormones are neuroendocrine cells residing in various regions of the hypothalamus. The axons of these neuroendocrine cells converge on the **median eminence**, just above the pituitary stalk. This region contains an elaborate profusion of blood vessels that form the **hypophyseal portal system** (or *pituitary portal system*). Here, in response to inputs from the rest of the brain, the axon terminals of the hypothalamic neuroendocrine cells secrete their releasing hormones into the local bloodstream (**FIGURE 5.15**).

Blood carries the various releasing hormones only a few millimeters, into the anterior pituitary. The rate at which releasing hormones arrive at their target cells in the anterior pituitary controls the rate at which the anterior pituitary cells, in turn, release their tropic hormones into the general circulation. These tropic hormones then regulate the activity of major endocrine organs throughout the body.

(A) Intact (B) Castrated

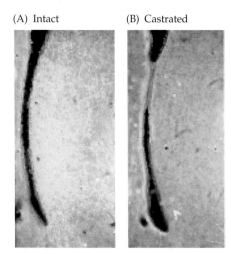

5.14 VASOPRESSIN CAN SERVE AS A NEUROTRANSMITTER   Revealed here by immunocytochemistry are vasopressin-filled axonal fibers (yellow) in the septum of intact (A) and castrated (B) male rats. (Courtesy of Dr. Geert DeVries.)

The hypothalamic neuroendocrine cells that synthesize the releasing hormones are themselves subject to two kinds of influences:

1. They are directly affected by *circulating messages*, such as other hormones (especially hormones that have themselves been secreted in response to tropic hormones), and by blood sugar and products of the immune system. The hypothalamus is not shielded by the blood-brain barrier (see Chapter 2) to the same extent that other brain regions are, which makes it possible for a wide variety of blood-borne material to access the hypothalamic neuroendocrine cells.

2. They receive *synaptic inputs* (either excitatory or inhibitory) from many other brain regions. A wide range of neural signals, reflecting both internal and external events, can thereby influence the endocrine system. As a result, hormonal actions can be coordinated with ongoing events, and conditioning (learning) can alter endocrine status. We saw an example of such influence in our discussion of the milk letdown reflex, and we'll see other examples throughout the book.

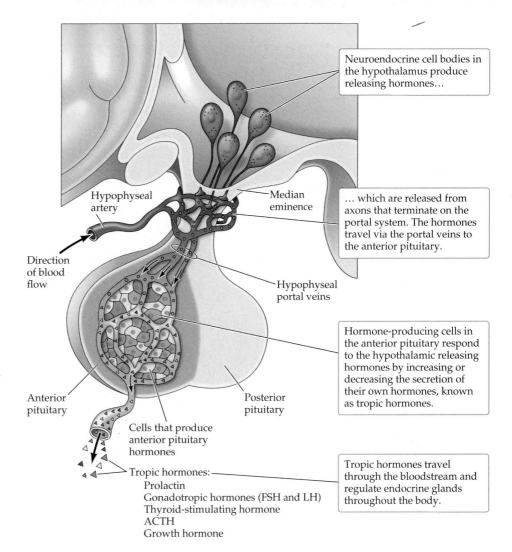

Neuroendocrine cell bodies in the hypothalamus produce releasing hormones...

... which are released from axons that terminate on the portal system. The hormones travel via the portal veins to the anterior pituitary.

Hormone-producing cells in the anterior pituitary respond to the hypothalamic releasing hormones by increasing or decreasing the secretion of their own hormones, known as tropic hormones.

Tropic hormones travel through the bloodstream and regulate endocrine glands throughout the body.

Hypophyseal artery

Direction of blood flow

Median eminence

Hypophyseal portal veins

Anterior pituitary

Posterior pituitary

Cells that produce anterior pituitary hormones

Tropic hormones:
Prolactin
Gonadotropic hormones (FSH and LH)
Thyroid-stimulating hormone
ACTH
Growth hormone

5.15 HORMONE RELEASE BY THE ANTERIOR PITUITARY

The hypothalamic releasing hormone system therefore exerts high-level control over endocrine organs throughout the body and provides a route by which brain activity is translated into hormonal action. Cutting the pituitary stalk interrupts the portal blood vessels and the flow of releasing hormones, leading to profound atrophy of the pituitary and major hormonal disruptions.

TROPIC HORMONES OF THE ANTERIOR PITUITARY   Driven by various releasing hormones from the hypothalamus, the anterior pituitary gland secretes six main tropic hormones (**FIGURE 5.16**; see also Table 5.2). Two of these regulate the function of the adrenal cortex and the thyroid gland:

1. **Adrenocorticotropic hormone** (**ACTH**) controls the production and release of hormones of the adrenal cortex. The adrenal cortex, in turn, releases steroid hormones. The levels of ACTH and adrenal steroids show a marked daily rhythm (see Chapter 14), and respond to stress (see Chapter 15).

2. **Thyroid-stimulating hormone** (**TSH**) increases the release of thyroid hormones from the thyroid gland and markedly affects thyroid gland size.

Two other tropic hormones of the anterior pituitary influence the gonads and consequently are termed **gonadotropins**:

3. **Follicle-stimulating hormone** (**FSH**) gets its name from its actions in the ovary, where it stimulates the growth and maturation of egg-containing **follicles** and the secretion of estrogens from the follicles. In males, FSH governs sperm production.

adrenocorticotropic hormone (ACTH)   A tropic hormone secreted by the anterior pituitary gland that controls the production and release of hormones of the adrenal cortex.

thyroid-stimulating hormone (TSH)   A tropic hormone, released by the anterior pituitary gland, that signals the thyroid gland to secrete its hormones.

gonadotropin   An anterior pituitary hormone that selectively stimulates the cells of the gonads to produce sex steroids and gametes.

follicle-stimulating hormone (FSH)   A gonadotropin, named for its actions on ovarian follicles.

follicles   Ovarian structures containing immature ova.

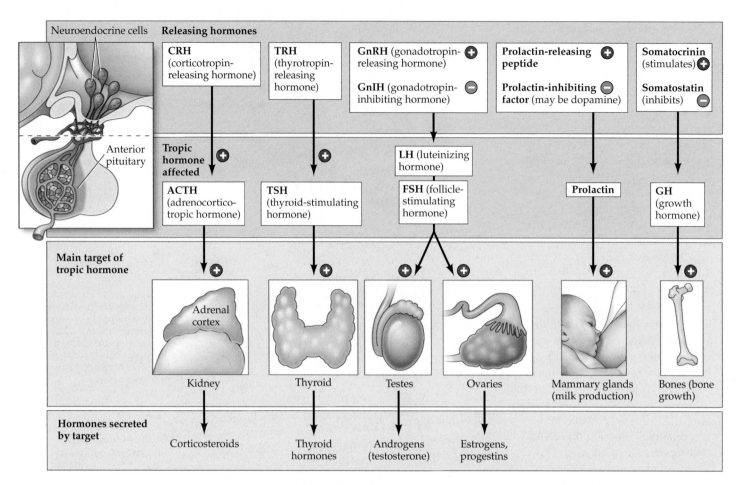

5.16 SECRETIONS OF THE ANTERIOR PITUITARY Hormones produced in the anterior pituitary include tropic hormones, which control endocrine glands and directly affect other structures, such as bones.

luteinizing hormone (LH)
A gonadotropin, named for its stimulatory effects on the ovarian corpora lutea.

corpora lutea The structures formed from collapsed ovarian follicles subsequent to ovulation. The corpora lutea are a major source of progesterone.

prolactin A peptide hormone, produced by the anterior pituitary, that promotes mammary development for lactation in female mammals.

growth hormone (GH) Also called *somatotropin* or *somatotropic hormone*. A tropic hormone, secreted by the anterior pituitary, that influences the growth of cells and tissues.

adrenal gland An endocrine gland atop the kidney.

adrenal cortex The outer rind of the adrenal gland.

4. **Luteinizing hormone (LH)** stimulates the follicles of the ovary to rupture, release their eggs, and form into structures called **corpora lutea** (singular *corpus luteum*) that secrete the sex steroid hormone progesterone. In males, LH stimulates the testes to produce testosterone. We will discuss the gonadal steroid hormones in more detail shortly.

The two remaining tropic hormones control milk production and body growth:

1. **Prolactin** is so named because it promotes lactation in female mammals. But prolactin has a number of roles in addition to its actions on breast tissue. For example, it is closely involved in the parental behavior of a wide variety of vertebrate species.

2. **Growth hormone** (**GH**), also known as *somatotropin* or *somatotropic hormone*, acts throughout the body to influence the growth of cells and tissues by affecting protein metabolism. GH is released almost exclusively during sleep. Other factors also affect GH secretion. The stomach secretes a hormone called *ghrelin* (from the Proto-Indo-European root for "grow"), which evokes GH release from the anterior pituitary (Kojima et al., 1999). Ghrelin is discussed in more detail in Chapter 13. Starvation, vigorous exercise, and intense stress can all profoundly inhibit GH release (**BOX 5.2**).

Now let's consider three of the glands stimulated by tropic hormones of the anterior pituitary: the adrenal gland, the thyroid gland, and the gonads. Each of these glands secretes hormones of its own in response to the pituitary tropic hormones.

BOX 5.2

Stress and Growth: Psychosocial Dwarfism

Genie had a horrifically deprived childhood. For over 10 years, starting from the age of 20 months, she was isolated in a small, closed room, and much of the time she was tied to a potty chair. Her disturbed parents provided food, but nobody held Genie or spoke to her. When she was released from her confinement and observed by researchers at the age of 13, her size made her appear only 6 or 7 years old (Rymer, 1993).

Other less horrendous forms of family deprivation also result in failure of growth. This syndrome is referred to as **psychosocial dwarfism** to emphasize that the growth failure arises from psychological and social factors mediated through the CNS and its control over endocrine functions (W. H. Green et al., 1984). When children suffering from psychosocial dwarfism are removed from stressful circumstances, many begin to grow rapidly. The growth rates of five such children, before and after periods of emotional deprivation, are shown in the figure (an asterisk indicates when each child was removed from the abusive situation). These children seem to have compensated for much of the growth deficit that occurred during prolonged stress periods (Sirotnak et al., 2004).

How do stress and emotional deprivation impair growth? Growth impairments appear to be mediated by changed outputs of several hormones, including cortisol, growth hormone (GH), and other hormones

known as **somatomedins** (normally released by the liver in response to GH).

Some children with psychosocial dwarfism show almost a complete lack of GH release, which may be caused by an absence of the releasing hormone somatocrinin from the hypothalamus (Albanese et al., 1994). Disturbed sleep has also been suggested as a cause of this failure, because GH is typically released during certain stages of sleep and children under stress show disturbed sleep patterns (L. I. Gardner, 1972). Other children who exhibit psychosocial dwarfism show normal levels of GH but low levels of somatomedins, and these hormones, along with GH, appear to be necessary for normal growth. Still other children with this condition show elevated levels of cortisol, probably as a result of stress, that inhibit growth. Some affected children show none of these hormonal disturbances, so there must also be other routes through which emotional experiences affect growth.

Growth is an example of a process that involves many factors—hormonal, metabolic, and dietary—and can

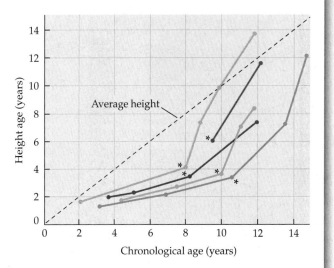

therefore malfunction in a variety of ways. Cases of psychosocial dwarfism are more common than once was thought, and investigators who study this syndrome are calling for further awareness of and attention to it (W. H. Green et al., 1984). For Genie, relief came in time to restore much of her *body* growth, but her mental development remained severely limited; she never learned to say more than a few words and, now in her 50s, she lives in an institution.

psychosocial dwarfism Reduced stature caused by stress early in life that inhibits growth.

somatomedins A group of proteins, released from the liver in response to growth hormone, that aid body growth and maintenance.

Two divisions of the adrenal gland produce hormones

Resting on top of each kidney is an **adrenal gland** (see Figure 5.1), which secretes a large variety of hormones. In mammals, the adrenal structure is divided into two major portions. The outer 80% of the gland, the **adrenal cortex**, is composed of distinct layers of cells, each producing different steroid hormones. The core of the gland is the **adrenal medulla**, which is richly supplied with autonomic nerves.

As part of the "fight or flight" reaction to threat, the adrenal medulla secretes hormones—the catecholamines **epinephrine** (adrenaline) and **norepinephrine** (**NE**) (noradrenaline)—that prepare the body for action, raising heart rate and respiration, among other things. Because emergencies demand quick action, secretion of these hormones is under direct control of the brain, via sympathetic nerve terminals that release acetylcholine in the adrenal medulla. In Chapter 4 we saw that epinephrine and norepinephrine are also synaptic transmitters at certain sites in the nervous system.

adrenal medulla The inner core of the adrenal gland, which secretes epinephrine and norepinephrine.

epinephrine Also called *adrenaline*. A compound that acts both as a hormone (secreted by the adrenal medulla under the control of the sympathetic nervous system) and as a synaptic transmitter.

norepinephrine (**NE**) Also called *noradrenaline*. A neurotransmitter produced and released by sympathetic postganglionic neurons to accelerate organ activity. Also released as a hormone from the adrenal medulla.

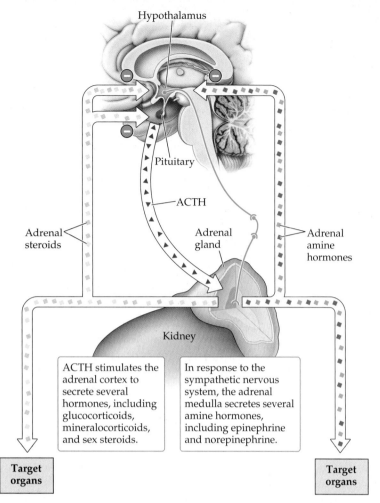

Hypothalamus

Pituitary

ACTH

Adrenal
steroids

Adrenal
gland

Adrenal
amine
hormones

Kidney

ACTH stimulates the adrenal cortex to secrete several hormones, including glucocorticoids, mineralocorticoids, and sex steroids.

In response to the sympathetic nervous system, the adrenal medulla secretes several amine hormones, including epinephrine and norepinephrine.

Target organs

Target organs

5.17 REGULATION OF HORMONES PRODUCED BY THE ADRE-NAL GLANDS Situated above each kidney, each adrenal gland consists of an outer cortex (in yellow) and an inner medulla (blue).

adrenocorticoids Also called *adrenal steroids*. A class of steroid hormones that are secreted by the adrenal cortex.

glucocorticoids A class of steroid hormones, released by the adrenal cortex, that affect carbohydrate metabolism and inflammation.

cortisol A glucocorticoid stress hormone of the adrenal cortex.

mineralocorticoids A class of steroid hormones, released by the adrenal cortex, that affect ion concentrations in body tissues.

aldosterone A mineralocorticoid hormone, secreted by the adrenal cortex, that induces the kidneys to conserve sodium ions.

sex steroids Steroid hormones secreted by the gonads: androgens, estrogens, and progestins.

androstenedione The chief sex hormone secreted by the human adrenal cortex.

The adrenal cortex produces and secretes a variety of steroid hormones, collectively called the **adrenocorticoids** (or *adrenal steroids*). One subgroup consists of the **glucocorticoids**, so named because of their effects on the metabolism of glucose. Hormones of this type, such as **cortisol**, increase the level of blood glucose and accelerate the breakdown of proteins. It was probably the lack of glucocorticoids that caused Mary Lou to feel weak and nauseous from the lack of circulating glucose. She must take glucocorticoids every day to stay healthy.

In high concentrations, glucocorticoids have a marked anti-inflammatory effect; that is, they inhibit the swelling around injuries or infections. This action normally results in the temporary decrease of bodily responses to tissue injury, which is why synthetic glucocorticoids (such as prednisone) are important and useful drugs. However, sustained high levels of circulating glucocorticoids are harmful to the brain (see Chapter 15), so Mary Lou must adjust her dosage to avoid harmful effects of too much hormone.

A second subgroup of adrenal steroids consists of the **mineralocorticoids**, so named because of their effects on minerals such as sodium and potassium. The primary mineralocorticoid hormone is **aldosterone**, which acts on the kidneys to retain sodium and thus reduces the amount of urine produced, conserving water. This action helps maintain a healthful concentration of ions in blood and extracellular fluids (see Chapter 13). The adrenal cortex also produces **sex steroids**, notably **androstenedione**. Androstenedione contributes to the adult pattern of body hair in men and women. In some females the adrenal cortex produces more than the normal amounts of sex hormones, causing a more masculine appearance (see Chapter 12).

Levels of circulating adrenal cortical hormones are regulated in several steps (**FIGURE 5.17**). The pituitary hormone ACTH promotes steroid synthesis in the adrenal gland. Adrenal steroids in turn exert a negative feedback effect on ACTH release. As the level of adrenal cortical hormones increases, the secretion of ACTH is suppressed, so the output of hormones from the adrenal cortex diminishes. When the levels of adrenal steroids fall, the pituitary ACTH-secreting cells are released from suppression, and the concentration of ACTH in the blood rises again.

Thyroid hormones regulate growth and metabolism

Situated in the throat, around the location of the Adam's apple, is the **thyroid gland** (see Figure 5.1). This gland produces and secretes several hormones. Two of these— *thyroxine* (or *tetraiodothyronine*) and *triiodothyronine*—are usually referred to as **thyroid hormones**; a third—*calcitonin*—promotes calcium deposition in bones and will not be discussed further.

The thyroid is unique among endocrine glands because it stores a large amount of hormone—at least a 100-day supply—which it slowly releases. Although thyroid hormones are amines, they behave like steroids. They bind to specialized receptors (part of the steroid receptor superfamily) found inside cells. The thyroid hormone–receptor complex then binds to DNA and regulates gene expression.

Figure 5.11 shows the control network for regulating thyroxine levels in blood. The major control is exerted by thyroid-stimulating hormone (TSH) from the anterior pituitary gland. The secretion of TSH by the pituitary is controlled by the hy-

5.18 ISN'T THAT A STYLISH COLLAR?   Because there is little iodine in the soil in Switzerland, vegetables grown there provide insufficient iodine even for prosperous people like the novelist Jeremias Gotthelf (1797–1854), who suffered from a large goiter that he routinely concealed behind elaborate collars. (Painting by Johann Friedrich Dietler.)

pothalamic release of **thyrotropin-releasing hormone (TRH)**, which stimulates the pituitary to secrete TSH. When the level of circulating thyroid hormone falls, both TRH and TSH are secreted. When TSH reaches the thyroid gland, it stimulates the production and release of thyroid hormones. The thyroid hormones then have a negative feedback effect, inhibiting further TRH and TSH release.

Thyroid hormones are the only substances produced by the body that contain iodine, and their manufacture is critically dependent on the supply of iodine. In parts of the world where foods contain little iodine, many people suffer from hypothyroidism. Driven by higher and higher TSH levels, the thyroid gland swells in its attempt to produce more thyroid hormones, causing a **goiter** to form. Because the soil in Switzerland has little iodine, through the nineteenth century even well-fed citizens there often had goiters (**FIGURE 5.18**). Today the addition of a small amount of iodine to table salt—producing *iodized salt*—ensures that we won't develop goiters even if we get insufficient iodine from our vegetables.

Thyroid hormones have a general effect on the nervous system, maintaining alertness and reflexes. People with hypothyroidism may appear depressed, so the hormonal imbalance is often overlooked in mild cases (C. G. Roberts and Ladenson, 2004). So Mary Lou must also adjust her dosages of thyroid hormones to keep her mind sharp and avoid feeling fatigue.

When thyroid deficiency starts early in life, body growth is stunted and the face malformed. Thyroid deficiency also produces a marked reduction in brain size and in the branching of axons and dendrites. This state, called **cretinism** or *congenital hypothyroidism*, is accompanied by intellectual disability.

The gonads produce steroid hormones, regulating reproduction

Almost all aspects of reproductive behavior, including mating and parenting, depend on hormones. Since Chapter 12 is devoted to reproductive behavior and physiology, at this point we will only briefly note relevant hormones and some pertinent aspects of anatomy and physiology. Female and male **gonads** (ovaries and testes, respectively; see Figure 5.1) contain two different subcompartments—one to produce hormones (the sex steroids we mentioned earlier) and another to produce gametes (eggs or sperm). The gonadal hormones are critical for triggering both reproductive behavior, controlled by the brain, and gamete production.

The hypothalamus controls gonadal hormone production by releasing **gonadotropin-releasing hormone (GnRH)**, which drives the anterior pituitary to release the gonadotropins FSH or LH, which we mentioned earlier. Although named for their effects on ovaries, FSH and LH drive development and steroid production in both testes and ovaries. The GnRH neurons in turn are stimulated by a hypothalamic peptide, **kisspeptin** (Kriegsfeld, 2006; J. T. Smith et al., 2006), which appears to play an important role in governing the onset of puberty (Han et al., 2005).

The hypothalamus uses GnRH to *stimulate* pituitary gonadotropin secretion, but it also uses a hormone to *inhibit* gonadotropin secretion named, sensibly enough, **gonadotropin-inhibiting hormone (GnIH)** (Tsutsui et al., 2006). GnRH and GnIH thus work in opposition, translating inputs from the brain into controls on the pituitary, and therefore the gonads, like an accelerator and a brake, respectively.

THE TESTES   Within the **testes** are Sertoli cells, which produce sperm, and Leydig cells, which produce and secrete the sex steroid **testosterone**. Testosterone and other male hormones are called **androgens** (from the Greek *andro-*, "man," and *gennan*, "to produce").

thyroid gland   An endocrine gland, located in the throat, that regulates cellular metabolism throughout the body.

thyroid hormones   Two hormones, triiodothyronine and thyroxine (also called *tetraiodothyronine*), released from the thyroid gland that have widespread effects, including growth and maintenance of the brain.

thyrotropin-releasing hormone (TRH)   A hypothalamic hormone that regulates the release of thyroid-stimulating hormone from the anterior pituitary.

goiter   A swelling of the thyroid gland resulting from iodine deficiency.

cretinism   Also called *congenital hypothyroidism*. Reduced stature and intellectual disability caused by thyroid deficiency during early development.

gonads   The sexual organs (ovaries in females, testes in males), which produce gametes for reproduction.

gonadotropin-releasing hormone (GnRH)   A hypothalamic hormone that controls the release of luteinizing hormone and follicle-stimulating hormone from the pituitary.

kisspeptin   A hypothalamic peptide hormone that increases gonadotropin secretion by facilitating the release of gonadotropin-releasing hormone.

gonadotropin-inhibiting hormone (GnIH)   A hypothalamic peptide hormone that reduces gonadotropin secretion from the pituitary.

testes   The male gonads, which produce sperm and androgenic steroid hormones.

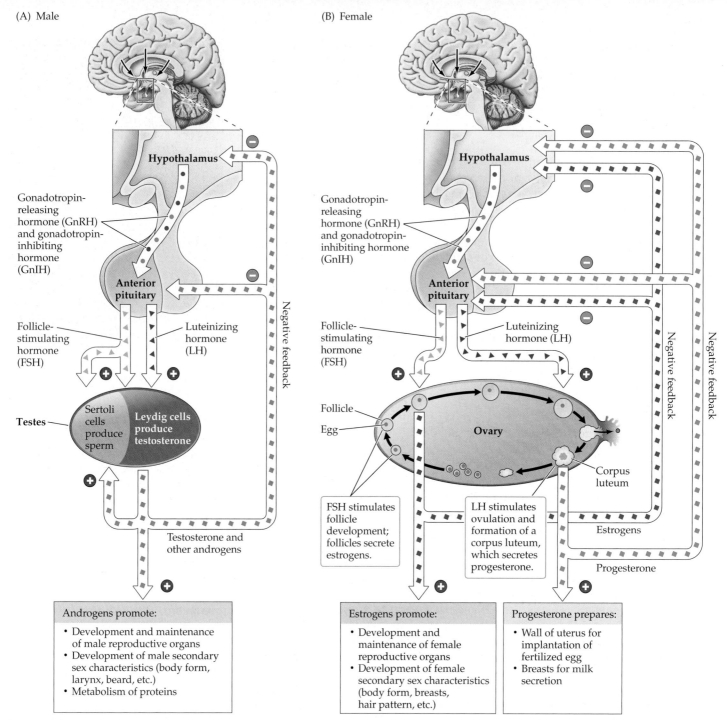

(A) Male

Hypothalamus

Gonadotropin-releasing hormone (GnRH) and gonadotropin-inhibiting hormone (GnIH)

Anterior pituitary

Follicle-stimulating hormone (FSH)

Luteinizing hormone (LH)

Negative feedback

Testes

Sertoli cells produce sperm

Leydig cells produce testosterone

Testosterone and other androgens

Androgens promote:
- Development and maintenance of male reproductive organs
- Development of male secondary sex characteristics (body form, larynx, beard, etc.)
- Metabolism of proteins

(B) Female

Hypothalamus

Gonadotropin-releasing hormone (GnRH) and gonadotropin-inhibiting hormone (GnIH)

Anterior pituitary

Follicle-stimulating hormone (FSH)

Luteinizing hormone (LH)

Negative feedback

Negative feedback

Follicle

Egg

Ovary

Corpus luteum

FSH stimulates follicle development; follicles secrete estrogens.

LH stimulates ovulation and formation of a corpus luteum, which secretes progesterone.

Estrogens

Progesterone

Estrogens promote:
- Development and maintenance of female reproductive organs
- Development of female secondary sex characteristics (body form, breasts, hair pattern, etc.)

Progesterone prepares:
- Wall of uterus for implantation of fertilized egg
- Breasts for milk secretion

5.19 REGULATION OF GONADAL STEROID HORMONES

testosterone A hormone, produced by male gonads, that controls a variety of bodily changes that become visible at puberty.

androgens A class of hormones that includes testosterone and other male hormones.

Testosterone controls a wide range of bodily changes that become visible at puberty, including changes in voice, hair growth, and genital size (**FIGURE 5.19A**). In species that breed only in certain seasons of the year, testosterone has especially marked effects on appearance and behavior—for example, the antlers and fighting between males that are displayed by many species of deer (**FIGURE 5.20**). As men age, testosterone levels tend to decline. Although elderly men who happen to maintain high levels of circulating testosterone perform better on tests of memory and attention than do those with low levels (Yaffe et al., 2002), there have been too few studies to tell whether taking supplemental testosterone actually helps aging men (Harder, 2003; Nair et al., 2006). Furthermore, taking supplemental testosterone can sometimes increase aggressive or manic behaviors (Pope et al., 2000) and may increase prostate cancer risk.

5.20 THE INFLUENCE OF A HORMONE
The antlers and combative behavior of male red deer, a subspecies of the North American elk, are both seasonally affected by testosterone.

THE OVARIES   The paired female gonads, the **ovaries**, also produce both the mature gametes—called *ova* (singular *ovum*) or eggs—and sex steroid hormones. However, hormone secretion is more complicated in ovaries than in testes. Ovarian hormones are produced in cycles, the duration of which varies with the species. Human ovarian cycles last about 4 weeks; rat cycles last only 4 days.

Normally, the ovary produces two major classes of steroid hormones: **progestins** (from the Latin *pro*, "favoring," and *gestare*, "to bear," because these hormones help to maintain pregnancy) and **estrogens** (from the Latin *oestrus*, "gadfly" or "frenzy"—*estrus* is the scientific term for the periodic sexual receptivity of females of many species—and the Greek *gennan*, "to produce"). Estrogens drive the development of female bodily changes at puberty, including the growth of breasts. The most important naturally occurring estrogen is **17β-estradiol** (or just *estradiol*). The primary progestin is **progesterone** (**FIGURE 5.19B**). Interestingly, estrogens make the brain sensitive to progesterone by promoting the production of progestin receptors there.

Oral contraceptives contain small doses of synthetic estrogen and/or progestin, which exert a negative feedback effect on the hypothalamus, inhibiting the release of GnRH. The lack of GnRH prevents the release of FSH and LH from the pituitary, and therefore the ovary fails to release an egg for fertilization.

Estrogens may improve aspects of cognitive functioning (Maki and Resnick, 2000), although this topic is still debated (Dohanich, 2003). Estrogens may also protect the brain from some of the effects of stress and stroke (Suzuki et al., 2009). For these reasons and others, estrogen replacement therapy has been a popular postmenopausal treatment, but evidence that these treatments increase the risk of serious diseases like cancer and heart disease has raised questions about their safety (Hickey et al., 2012; Lisabeth and Bushnell, 2012). Many synthetic estrogens are produced and tested in search of drugs that have only the beneficial effects of the hormone, without its harmful side effects.

RELATIONS AMONG GONADAL HORMONES   As we mentioned earlier, the steroid hormones—androgens, estrogens, progestins, and the adrenal steroids—are all based on the chemical structure of cholesterol, featuring a backbone of four interconnected carbon rings (see Figure 5.7C). Furthermore, progestins can be converted to androgens, and androgens in turn can be converted into estrogens. Each of these conversions is controlled by specific enzymes. The structural similarity among steroids reflects their evolutionary history: as enzymes evolved to modify old steroids, new steroids became available for signaling.

Different organs—and the two sexes—differ in the relative amounts of gonadal hormones that they produce. For example, whereas the testis converts only a rela-

ovaries   The female gonads, which produce eggs for reproduction.

progestins   A major class of steroid hormones that are produced by the ovary, including progesterone.

estrogens   A class of steroid hormones produced by female gonads.

17β-estradiol or estradiol   The primary type of estrogen that is secreted by the ovary.

progesterone   The primary type of progestin secreted by the ovary.

oral contraceptive   A birth control pill, typically consisting of steroid hormones to prevent ovulation.

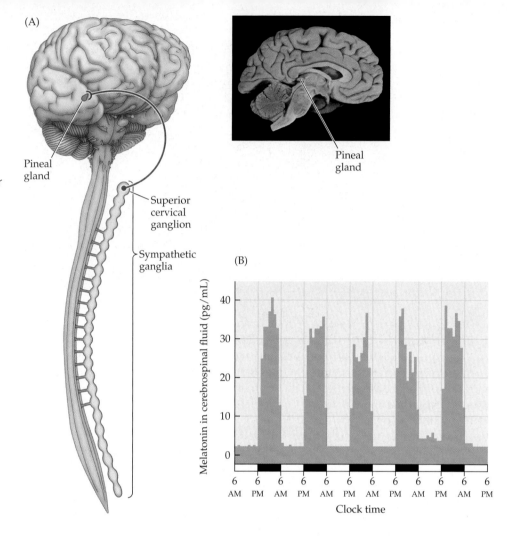

5.21 REGULATION OF THE PINEAL GLAND (A) The pea-shaped pineal gland sits atop the brainstem, tucked under the cerebral hemispheres. Innervated by the sympathetic nervous system, specifically the superior cervical ganglion, the pineal releases melatonin. (B) Melatonin is released almost exclusively during the night in a wide variety of vertebrates, including humans. (After Reppert et al., 1979, photograph courtesy of Drs. S. Mark Williams and Dale Purves, Duke University Medical Center.)

pineal gland   A secretory gland in the brain midline; the source of melatonin release.

melatonin   An amine hormone that is released by the pineal gland.

tively small proportion of testosterone into estradiol, the ovary converts most of the testosterone it makes into estradiol. But it is important to appreciate that *no steroid is found exclusively in either males or females*; rather, the two sexes differ in the proportion of these steroids.

The pineal gland secretes melatonin

The **pineal gland** sits atop the brainstem and in mammals is overlain by the cerebral hemispheres (**FIGURE 5.21A**; see also Figure 5.1). Most brain structures are paired (with symmetrical left and right sides), but the pineal gland is a single structure. It is this unusual aspect of the pineal that led the seventeenth-century philosopher René Descartes to propose it to be "the seat of the soul"; religious dogma of his day held that the soul, like the pineal, is indivisible.

Today we know that the pineal plays a crucial role in biological rhythms. Governed by the superior cervical ganglion—part of the sympathetic nervous system—the pineal releases an amine hormone called **melatonin**. The melatonin receptor is a G protein-coupled receptor residing in cell membranes and is similar to receptors for peptide hormones. Because melatonin is released almost exclusively at night (**FIGURE 5.21B**), it provides a signal that tracks day length and, by extension, the seasons.

Melatonin secretion controls breeding condition in many seasonally breeding mammals. In hamsters, for example, the lengthening of nights in autumn causes the pineal to prolong its nocturnal release of melatonin. The hypothalamus responds to the prolonged exposure to melatonin by releasing less and less GnRH, resulting in atrophy of the gonads (Revel et al., 2009). In the spring, as days lengthen and the breeding season approaches, the process reverses and the animal prepares to breed.

In birds, light from the environment penetrates the thin skull and reaches the pineal gland directly. Photosensitive cells in the bird pineal gland monitor daily light durations (Doyle and Menaker, 2007). In several reptile species the pineal is close to the skull and even has an extension of photoreceptors providing a "third eye" in the back of the head. The pineal photoreceptors do not form images but simply monitor day length to regulate seasonal functions.

Humans are not, strictly speaking, seasonal breeders, but melatonin plays a role in our biological rhythms, especially the timing of sleep onset. Like other vertebrates, we release melatonin at night, and administering exogenous melatonin reportedly induces sleep sooner. This is why melatonin has been used to treat jet lag (Sack et al., 1992). Interestingly, Mary Lou's loss of the pituitary should not affect her pineal function, yet she reports she no longer suffers from jet lag during her frequent international travels (Jepsen, 2013). So perhaps jet lag is caused by shifts in the daily rhythms of hormones other than melatonin (see Chapter 14).

Hormones Affect Behavior in Many Different Ways

In later chapters we will discuss specific examples of the role of hormones in reproductive behavior (Chapter 12), eating and drinking (Chapter 13), biological rhythms (Chapter 14), and stress (Chapter 15). Sometimes hormonal conditions produce symptoms that physicians may mistake for psychiatric disorders, as **A Step Further: Endocrine Pathology Can Produce Extreme Effects on Human Behavior** details on the website. For now, to get an idea of how hormones affect behavior, let's briefly consider the role of hormones in social interaction.

Hormones can affect social behavior

We've already seen the role that the hormone oxytocin plays in the interaction of nursing babies and their mothers (see Figure 5.13). It turns out that this hormone is involved in several other social behaviors too. For one thing, a pulse of oxytocin is released during orgasm in both men and women (Carmichael et al., 1994), adding to the pleasurable feelings accompanying sexual encounters.

In nonhuman animals, oxytocin and vasopressin modulate many social processes (Lim and Young, 2006). Rodents given supplementary doses of oxytocin spend more time in physical contact with each other (Carter, 1992). Male mice with the oxytocin gene knocked out are unable to produce the hormone, and they display social amnesia: they seem unable to recognize the scents of female mice that they have met before (Ferguson et al., 2000). These oxytocin knockout males can be cured of their social amnesia with brain infusions of oxytocin (Winslow and Insel, 2002). In mice, the oxytocin released during delivery appears to protect fetal neurons from injury (Tyzio et al., 2006) and to improve the mother's ability to navigate a maze (Tomizawa et al., 2003).

In another rodent, the prairie vole (*Microtus ochrogaster*), in which couples form stable monogamous pair-bonds, oxytocin infusions in the brains of females help them bond to their mates. In male prairie voles, it is vasopressin rather than oxytocin that facilitates the formation of a preference for a specific female partner. In fact, the distribution of vasopressin receptors in the brains of male prairie voles may be what makes them monogamous.

Supporting this idea is the finding that in the closely related meadow voles (*M. pennsylvanicus*), which do not form pair-bonds and instead have multiple mating partners, the males have far fewer vasopressin receptors in certain brain regions than do prairie voles (**FIGURE 5.22**) (Lim et al., 2004). Furthermore, laboratory mice that have been genetically engineered to produce vasopressin receptors in their brains in the same pattern that is seen in prairie vole males are much more interested in associating with females, almost as if they were trying to form pair-bonds.

Thus, it appears that oxytocin and vasopressin regulate a range of social behaviors and that natural selection sometimes alters the social behaviors of a species through changes in the brain distribution of receptors for these two peptides (Donaldson and Young, 2008).

DIALING UP A PERSONALITY Mary Lou Jepsen has learned to fine-tune her hormone treatments in order to feel like her true self.

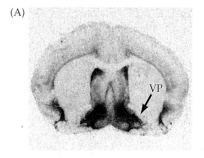

(A)

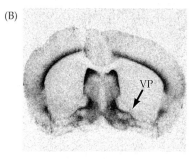

(B)

5.22 VASOPRESSIN AND THE MONOGAMOUS BRAIN (A) Monogamy in male prairie voles seems to be due to the dense concentration of vasopressin receptors in the ventral pallidum (VP). (B) Males of the closely related meadow vole species have fewer vasopressin receptors in the VP (notice lighter area compared to A), which may explain why they are not monogamous. (Photographs courtesy of Drs. Miranda Lim and Larry Young.)

Hormonal and Neural Systems Interact to Produce Integrated Responses

In many ways, the endocrine system and the nervous system can be viewed simply as divisions of a single master control mechanism. The two divisions work together, in an intimate and reciprocal manner, to seamlessly integrate the systems of the body and produce adaptive responses to environmental challenges.

Incoming environmental stimuli elicit activity in sensory pathways that project to a wide variety of brain regions, including the cerebral cortex, cerebellum, and hypothalamus. Our own behavioral responses to environmental circumstances bring further changes in stimulation. For example, if we approach an object or a sound source, we cause the visual image to become larger or the sound to become louder. Meanwhile the endocrine system is tuning our response characteristics to be consistent with the nature of the stimulus. If the stimulus calls for action—that faint buzzing sound turns out to be coming from a nest of angry wasps, for example—energy is mobilized through hormonal routes to prepare for appropriate behaviors (namely, sprinting and swatting and maybe some judicious swearing). The behaviors themselves, of course, are executed under the control of the nervous system. Sensory receptor organs are also subject to continual adjustment, thus modifying further processing of stimuli. Another example of neural and hormonal coordination is the milk letdown reflex (see Figure 5.13).

Four kinds of signals are possible between neurons and endocrine cells: neural-to-neural, neural-to-endocrine, endocrine-to-endocrine, and endocrine-to-neural. All four types are illustrated in the courtship behavior of the ringdove (**FIGURE 5.23**). Experience activates the brain, which alters hormone secretion. The release of one hormone often affects release of other hormones. These hormones in turn can affect brain functioning and therefore future behavior. That behavior will affect the animal's future experience, completing the circle of influences.

5.23 INTERACTIVE SIGNALS BETWEEN THE NERVOUS SYSTEM AND THE ENDOCRINE SYSTEM

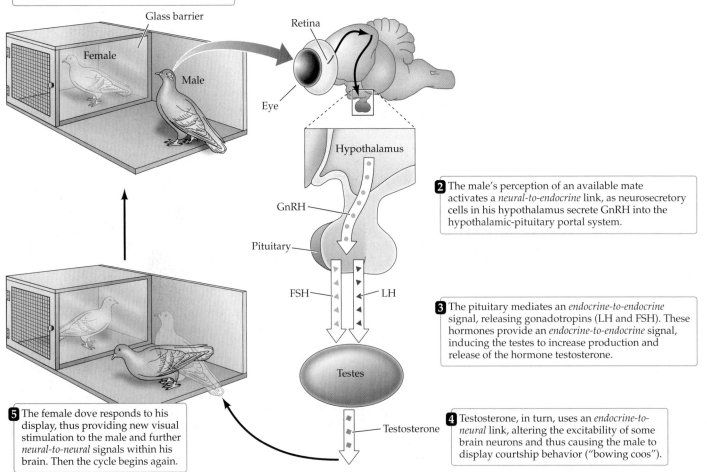

1 The male ringdove sees an attractive female. The stimulation of his retina sets off a chain of *neural-to-neural* transmission of information.

Glass barrier

Female

Male

Retina

Eye

Hypothalamus

GnRH

Pituitary

FSH — LH

Testes

Testosterone

2 The male's perception of an available mate activates a *neural-to-endocrine* link, as neurosecretory cells in his hypothalamus secrete GnRH into the hypothalamic-pituitary portal system.

3 The pituitary mediates an *endocrine-to-endocrine* signal, releasing gonadotropins (LH and FSH). These hormones provide an *endocrine-to-endocrine* signal, inducing the testes to increase production and release of the hormone testosterone.

4 Testosterone, in turn, uses an *endocrine-to-neural* link, altering the excitability of some brain neurons and thus causing the male to display courtship behavior ("bowing coos").

5 The female dove responds to his display, thus providing new visual stimulation to the male and further *neural-to-neural* signals within his brain. Then the cycle begins again.

Thus the interactions between endocrine activity and behavior are cyclical, as depicted by the circle schema in **FIGURE 5.24**. The level of circulating hormones can be altered by experience, which in turn can affect future behavior and future experience. For example, starting to exercise or stepping out in the cold increases the release of thyroid hormones. Men rooting for a sports team will produce more testosterone if their team wins (Bernhardt et al., 1998). Physical stresses, pain, and unpleasant emotional situations decrease thyroid output and trigger the release of adrenal glucocorticoids (see Chapter 15).

Each of these hormonal events will affect the brain, shaping behavior, which will once more affect the person's future hormone production. Any thorough understanding of the relationship between hormones and behavior must include these reciprocal interactions.

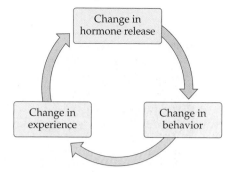

5.24 THE RECIPROCAL RELATIONS BETWEEN HORMONES AND BEHAVIOR

The Cutting Edge

Can Oxytocin Treat Autism?

Autism spectrum disorder (**ASD**) is a developmental disorder characterized by impaired social interactions and language, and a narrow range of interests and activities. As the term *spectrum* indicates, the severity of ASD varies considerably. Severe cases of autism are usually discovered when apparently normal toddlers begin regressing, losing language skills and withdrawing from family interaction. Children with ASD tend to **perseverate** (such as by continually nodding the head or making stereotyped finger movements), actively avoid making eye contact with other people, and have a difficult time judging other people's thoughts or feelings (Senju et al., 2009).

Some children with ASD are helped by highly structured training in language and behavior. The number of children diagnosed with ASD is increasing steadily, and no one knows why. The notion that childhood vaccines may act as a neurotoxin to cause autism has been thoroughly debunked (Aschner and Ceccatelli, 2010), yet celebrities and trial lawyers keep this discredited idea in the public eye.

There is clearly a genetic component to ASD (Weiss et al., 2009), and in a few very rare cases a single gene can cause autism. One such gene is *Cntnap2,* which in mutant forms causes an epilepsy disorder and, about 70% of the time, ASD in humans. Mice with the *Cntnap2* gene knocked out display social deficits reminiscent of ASD (Peñagarikano et al., 2015); they avoid interacting with other mice, for example. Examination of the brains of the *Cntnap2* knockout mice revealed reduced levels of oxytocin, so did the mutation cause social deficits by interfering with oxytocin? Indeed, oxytocin treatment that increased social behavior in other mouse models of ASD also increased social behavior in the *Cntnap2* knockout mice.

To test whether activation of oxytocin neurons in the *Cntnap2* knockout mice can reverse the social deficits, the researchers turned to **designer receptors exclusively activated by designer drugs** (**DREADDs**). This technique requires getting targeted neurons to make a "designer" receptor, a synthetic receptor never found in nature (Urban and Roth, 2015). This receptor is designed to be stimulated only by a synthetic "designer" drug (H. M. Lee et al., 2014). Thus administering the designer drug should only affect neurons expressing the designer receptor (**FIGURE 5.25**). The scientists infused viruses into the hypothalamus to infect cells with a gene for the designer receptor that would be expressed only in neurons that

autism spectrum disorder (ASD)
A disorder, which can run from mild to severe, characterized by deficits in social communication and interaction, accompanied by restricted, repetitive behaviors and interests.

perseverate To continue to show a behavior repeatedly.

designer receptors exclusively activated by designer drugs (DREADDs) An engineered G-protein receptor that responds only to a synthetic ligand, so that scientists can selectively activate neurons made to express the receptor.

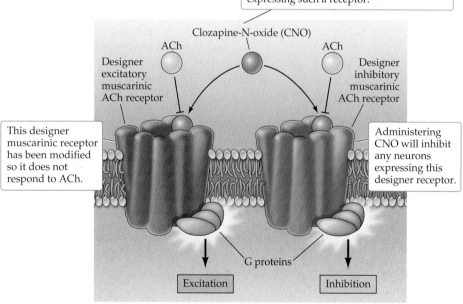

The synthetic compound clozapine-N-oxide (CNO) binds and activates only designer receptors and so would affect only neurons expressing such a receptor.

This designer muscarinic receptor has been modified so it does not respond to ACh.

Administering CNO will inhibit any neurons expressing this designer receptor.

Clozapine-N-oxide (CNO)

ACh — Designer excitatory muscarinic ACh receptor

ACh — Designer inhibitory muscarinic ACh receptor

G proteins

Excitation

Inhibition

5.25 DESIGNER RECEPTORS EXCLUSIVELY ACTIVATED BY DESIGNER DRUGS (DREADDS)

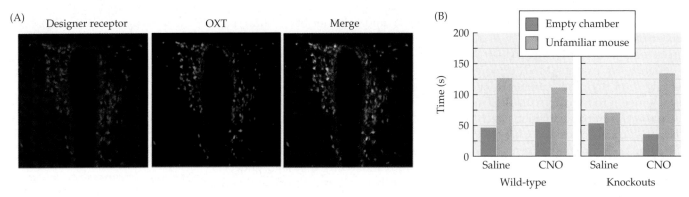

5.26 ACTIVATING OXYTOCINERGIC NEURONS INCREASES SOCIAL BEHAVIOR (From Peñagarikano et al., 2015.)

normally make oxytocin. First they confirmed that only oxytocinergic neurons in the paraventricular nucleus expressed the synthetic receptor (**FIGURE 5.26A**) in both control (wild-type) mice and *Cntnap2* knockouts. As expected, control mice preferred visiting a chamber with another mouse rather than an empty chamber, and they showed this social behavior whether they were given the designer drug (CNO) or saline control. But the *Cntnap2* knockout mice showed a preference for social stimuli *only* when given the designer drug (**FIGURE 5.26B**), showing that direct activation of oxytocinergic neurons, which would cause them to release the hormone, was enough to restore social behavior. Intriguingly, chronic treatment of the knockout mice with oxytocin *early in life* seemed to permanently restore social behavior in adulthood, adding to a growing excitement that prenatal oxytocin treatment of at-risk children might prevent the development of ASD in the first place (Zimmerman and Connors, 2014).

Go to
bn8e.com
for study questions,
quizzes, activities,
and other resources

Recommended Reading

Becker, J. B., Breedlove, S. M., Crews, D., and McCarthy, M. M. (Eds.). (2002). *Behavioral Endocrinology* (2nd ed.). Cambridge, MA: MIT Press.

Fink, G., Pfaff, D. W., and Levine, J. (2011). *Handbook of Neuroendocrinology.* San Diego, CA: Academic Press.

Garcia-Segura, L. M. (2009). *Hormones and Brain Plasticity.* New York: Oxford University Press.

Hadley, M. E., and Levine, J. (2006). *Endocrinology* (6th ed.). Englewood Cliffs, NJ: Prentice Hall.

Melmed, S., Polonsky, K. S., Larsen, P. R., and Kronenberg, H. M. (2016). *Williams Textbook of Endocrinology* (13th ed.). Philadelphia: Elsevier.

Nelson, R. J., and Kriegsfeld, L. J. (2017). *An Introduction to Behavioral Endocrinology* (5th ed.). Sunderland, MA: Sinauer.

VISUAL SUMMARY

You should be able to relate each summary to the adjacent illustration, including structures and processes.
Go to **bn8e.com/vs5** for links to figures, animations, and activities that will help you consolidate the material.

1 **Hormones** are chemicals that are secreted by **endocrine glands** into the bloodstream and are taken up by receptor molecules in target cells. Review **Figures 5.1 and 5.2**

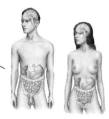

2 Hormones are just one of a variety of modes of chemical communication between cells. Neurotransmitters cross a tiny gap during synaptic transmission. An **autocrine** signal acts upon the cell that released it, while **paracrine** signals act on nearby cells. **Pheromones** are chemical signals to individuals of the same species, while **allomones** communicate with individuals of other species. Review **Figures 5.3 and 5.4, Animation 5.2**

3 Unlike neuronal signaling, hormones spread more slowly and act throughout the body. Some hormones act on **receptors** in a wide variety of cells and can therefore coordinate their influences on the activities of most cells in the body. Other hormones have receptors in only certain special cells or organs. Review **Figures 5.5 and 5.6, Animation 5.3**

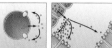

4 **Peptide** and **amine hormones** bind to receptor molecules at the surface of the target cell membrane and activate second-messenger molecules inside the cell. **Steroid hormones** pass through the membrane and bind to receptor molecules inside the cell, ultimately regulating gene expression. Review **Figures 5.7 and 5.8, Animation 5.3**

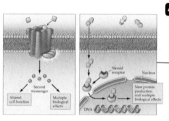

5 A **negative feedback** system monitors and controls the rate of secretion of each hormone. The hormone acts on target cells, leading them to change the amount of a substance they release. In the simplest case the hormone also acts on the endocrine cells, and this regulates further output of the endocrine gland. Review **Figure 5.10, Animation 5.4**

6 Other hormones are controlled by a **releasing hormone** from the **hypothalamus** that regulates the release of an anterior pituitary **tropic hormone**, which in turn controls secretion by an endocrine gland. The endocrine gland hormone then provides negative feedback to the hypothalamus and pituitary. Review **Figures 5.10 and 5.11**

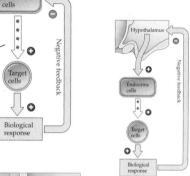

7 **Posterior pituitary** hormones are manufactured by **neuroendocrine** cells in the **supraoptic** and **paraventricular nuclei** of the hypothalamus, which send their axons down the **pituitary stalk** to terminate on capillaries there. When these neuroendocrine cells are stimulated to produce an action potential, they release **oxytocin** or **vasopressin** into circulation. Review **Figures 5.12–5.14**

8 **Anterior pituitary** hormones are controlled by the overlying hypothalamus. Hypothalamic neuroendocrine cells send axons to the **median eminence** to secrete releasing hormones into the **hypophyseal portal system**, which transports the releasing hormones to the pituitary. Different hypothalamic releasing hormones either stimulate or inhibit anterior pituitary cells that secrete tropic hormones. Review **Figures 5.15–5.17**

9 Hypothalamic cells secrete **gonadotropin-releasing hormone (GnRH)** into the hypophyseal portal system to stimulate anterior pituitary cells to release **follicle-stimulating hormone (FSH)** and **luteinizing hormone (LH)**, which stimulate the gonads to release steroid hormones. The principle *gonadal steroids* in males are **androgens** such as **testosterone**, while ovaries release **estrogens** such as **estradiol** and **progestins** such as **progesterone**. Review **Figure 5.19**

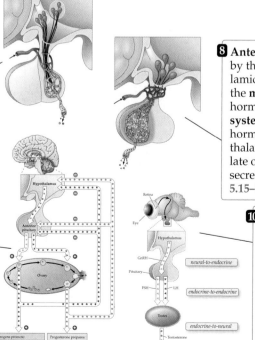

10 Many behaviors require the coordination of neural and hormonal components. Messages may be transmitted in the body via neural-to-neural, neural-to-endocrine, endocrine-to-endocrine, or endocrine-to-neural links. Experience affects hormone secretion, and hormones affect behavior and therefore future experiences. Review **Figures 5.23 and 5.24**

Evolution and Development of the Nervous System

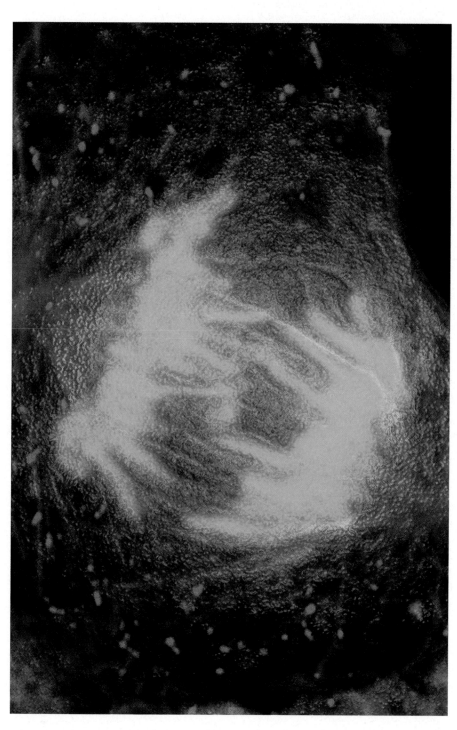

Mitosis Fluorescent light micrograph of a cell during the anaphase stage of mitosis (cell division). Magnification: x800 when printed 10cm wide. © Thomas Deerinck and Mark Ellisman, NCMIR, UCSD.

Evolution of the Brain and Behavior

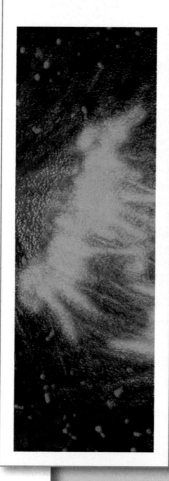

6

We Are Not So Different, Are We?

It probably comes as no surprise that our closest animal relatives are the chimpanzees—so many of their expressions and behaviors seem oddly, well, *human*. But despite the apparent similarities, humans and chimps are also strikingly dissimilar in many fundamental ways. Whereas humans have complex languages, chimps make only a small variety of vocal sounds. And whereas humans walk erect and have long legs, chimps travel mostly on all fours and have relatively long arms. The human brain is about twice the size of the chimp's. Humans have spread wide from their origins in Africa, populating (or overpopulating) the globe, but chimps have remained in Africa, their numbers now dwindling at an alarming rate.

Given the many differences between humans and chimps, it is remarkable that the genetic material of the two species differs by only about 1.2%. One prominent scientist suggested that, since the genes of chimps and humans differ so little, the social context provided during the rearing of human children must be what causes them to come out so different from chimpanzees. If that suggestion strikes you as unlikely, you are probably right. Several people have tried to rear chimpanzees like human children (see Chapter 19), and none of the chimps ever won a spelling bee or got a driver's license (not even a learner's permit).

Of course social rearing is crucial for human development, but it cannot explain the vast differences between chimps and humans. So the problem remains: If human and chimp DNA are nearly 99% identical, how can we explain the striking differences in behavior, anatomy, and neurobiology? In other words, what makes humans human? Progress in neuroscience is suggesting answers to this puzzle, as we will see.

Our major objective in this chapter is to explore the intriguing story of how brains and behavior have evolved. We will see that brain size in primates, especially in humans, increased rapidly in our recent evolution. This enlarged brain doubtless increased our capacity for higher cognitive abilities, yet it is difficult to determine which expanded brain regions brought us which additional abilities. Thus, scientists study the nervous system in a wide variety of animals to understand how the evolution of a particular brain feature affects particular behaviors. Describing the relationships between the nervous system and behavior in even a small fraction of Earth's inhabitants would be an immense (and dull) task unless we had a rationale beyond mere completeness. Choosing the right species to compare, however, reveals principles of nervous system organization.

Go to Brain Explorer
bn8e.com/6.1

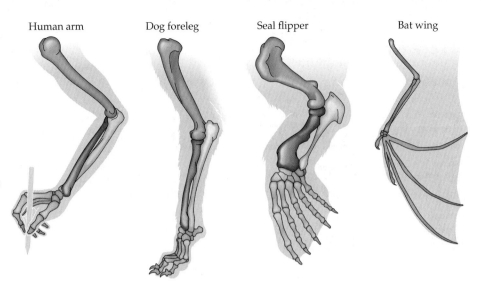

Human arm   Dog foreleg   Seal flipper   Bat wing

6.1 HOMOLOGY OF FORELIMB STRUCTURES Bones of the same sort are shown here in the same color in all species. The sizes and shapes of the bones of the forelimb have evolved so that they are adapted to widely different functions: skilled manipulation in humans, locomotion in dogs, swimming in seals, flying in bats. The similarities among the sets of bones reflect descent from a common ancestor.

naturalist A student of the forms and classification of organisms.

evolution In biology, the process by which a population of interbreeding individuals changes over long periods of time.

evolution by natural selection The Darwinian theory that evolution proceeds by differential success in reproduction.

How Did the Enormous Variety of Species Arise on Earth?

Until about 200 years ago, the dominant view among Western scholars was that each species had been created separately. Then, some **naturalists**—students of the forms and classification of organisms—began to have doubts. For example, researchers observed that the limb bones of all mammals, no matter what the animal's way of life, are remarkably similar in many details (**FIGURE 6.1**). If these species had been specifically created for different ways of locomotion, the naturalists reasoned, they should have been built on different plans rather than all being modifications of the same single plan.

Nineteenth-century geologists showed that Earth has been changing for millions of years, and studies of the fossils of extinct species provided evidence of **evolution**—the process of "descent with modification." It thus became clear that, far from being static categories, animal species are continually changing across the generations, gradually gaining some features and losing others, and sometimes spinning off new species (while others become extinct). But a plausible *mechanism* for evolution was lacking.

Natural selection drives evolution

In 1858, Charles Darwin (1809–1892) and Alfred Russel Wallace (1823–1913) described the process of **evolution by natural selection**. Darwin and Wallace had each hit upon the idea independently. The idea came to Wallace out of the blue, while he was suffering from a fever. In contrast, Darwin had been accumulating and considering evidence for over 20 years, ever since he had voyaged on the HMS *Beagle* to South America and the Galápagos Islands. The governor of the Galápagos had pointed out to Darwin that the giant tortoises differed in their shell patterns from island to island. Later, examining the specimens of finches that he had collected on different Galápagos islands, Darwin observed that the birds also differed from island to island. Although the birds resembled finches on the mainland, those on the Galápagos appeared to represent several different species, suited by their body sizes and beaks to obtaining different kinds of food, such as nuts or seeds or insects. Darwin speculated that the different birds had all descended from a single ancestral species long ago but that, isolated on the various islands, they had gradually diverged from their ancestors and from one another.

In 1859, Darwin published his revolutionary book *On the Origin of Species by Means of Natural Selection*. The hypothesis he stated was based on four main observations and one important inference. The observations were these:

1. Reproduction will tend to increase a population rapidly unless factors limit it.

2. Individuals of a given species are not identical.

3. Some of the variation among individuals is inherited.

4. Not all the offspring of a given generation survive to reproduce.

The inference was that the variations among individuals affect the probability of their surviving long enough to reproduce, thereby passing on their individual characteristics to their offspring. Individuals better suited to the prevailing conditions enjoy more success in reproduction, so their descendants will make up a greater proportion of successive generations. Through this mechanism, new **adaptations**—traits that increase the probability of successful reproduction—will eventually predominate in the population. Over long spans of time and many generations, this process of selection acting at the level of individuals (and their reproductive output) can substantially change a species.

The concept of evolution by natural selection has become the most important organizing principle in the life sciences, directing the study of behavior and its mechanisms, as well as the study of morphology (form and structure). Darwin (1859) felt confident that psychological functions are as much products of evolution as are the organs of the body.

Darwin later proposed an additional mechanism of natural selection: **sexual selection** (1871). This principle holds that members of each sex exert selective pressures on the other in terms of both anatomical and behavioral features that favor reproductive success. For example, choosiness on the part of peahens has led to the ornamental but costly tails of peacocks. We will discuss this principle later in this chapter.

Evolution may converge upon similar solutions

Adaptation to similar ecological features may bring about similarities in behavior or structure among animals that are only distantly related. These similarities are referred to as examples of **convergent evolution**. For example, the body forms of a tuna and a dolphin resemble each other because they each evolved for efficient swimming, even though the tuna is a fish and the dolphin is a mammal descended from terrestrial ancestors. Such a resemblance is an example of **homoplasy**, a resemblance between physical or behavioral characteristics that is due to convergent evolution. By contrast, a **homology** is a resemblance based on common *ancestry*, such as the similarities in forelimb structures of mammals that we described earlier (see Figure 6.1). **Analogy** refers to similar *function*, although the structures may look different (e.g., the hand of a human and the trunk of an elephant are analogous features).

Modern evolutionary theory combines natural selection and genetics

At first, Darwin's theory suffered from uncertainty about two important processes: (1) the mechanism by which an individual inherits its characteristics from its parents, and (2) the source of individual variation upon which natural selection acts. Working with pea plants, an Austrian monk and botanist named Gregor Johann Mendel (1822–1884) provided the needed breakthrough. Mendel's observations on the inheritance of traits across generations resulted in his publication, in 1866, of a set of formal laws of heredity that would eventually form the foundation of the modern science of **genetics**: the study of the mechanisms of inheritance (Mendel, 1967). It wasn't until 1900, however, that Mendel's work was linked to evolution, by the Dutch biologist Hugo de Vries (1848–1935), who was conducting experiments with primroses. De Vries went beyond Mendel in one very important respect. Noting that occasionally a new feature arose spontaneously and was then passed on to successive generations, de Vries reasoned that evolution could proceed by sudden jumps, or **mutations**, as he called these changes (**FIGURE 6.2**).

adaptation Here, a trait that increases the probability that an individual will leave offspring in subsequent generations.

sexual selection A form of evolution through natural selection in which members of one sex favor specific heritable traits in the other sex when choosing a reproductive partner.

convergent evolution The evolutionary process by which responses to similar ecological features bring about similarities in behavior or structure among animals that are only distantly related (i.e., that differ in genetic heritage).

homoplasy A physical resemblance between physical or behavioral characteristics due to convergent evolution, such as the similar body forms of tuna and dolphins.

homology A physical resemblance that is based on common ancestry, such as the similarity in forelimb structures of different mammals.

analogy Similarity of function, although the structures of interest may look different. The human hand and an elephant's trunk are analogous features.

genetics The study of inheritance, including the genes encoded in DNA.

mutation A change in the nucleotide sequence of a gene as a result of unfaithful replication.

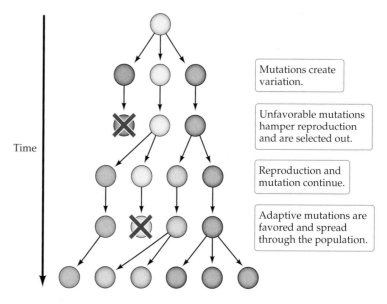

Time

Mutations create variation.

Unfavorable mutations hamper reproduction and are selected out.

Reproduction and mutation continue.

Adaptive mutations are favored and spread through the population.

6.2 NATURAL SELECTION AT THE GENETIC LEVEL A gene mutation that affects behavior may be selected for if the alteration in behavior is adaptive. Thus, not just physical traits, but also behaviors, evolve in a species over time.

chromosome A complex of condensed strands of DNA and associated protein molecules; found in the nucleus of cells.

gene A length of DNA that encodes the information for constructing a particular protein.

epigenetics The study of factors that affect gene expression without making any changes in the nucleotide sequence of the genes themselves.

genus A group of species that resemble each other because of shared inheritance.

species A group of individuals that can readily interbreed to produce fertile offspring.

phylogeny The evolutionary history of a particular group of organisms.

Mutations occur spontaneously and randomly in plants and animals, and because they are the result of changes in the organism's genes, mutations are heritable. (Nowadays, scientists also deliberately induce mutations in plants and animals, as we will discuss in Box 7.3.) Depending on how it modifies the individual, a given mutation may be harmful, neutral, or beneficial. A beneficial mutation will generally give the individual at least a slight reproductive advantage over other individuals of the same species, called *conspecifics*, with the result that the mutation will become more and more widespread as it is passed down through subsequent generations. This gradual, incremental process of selectively transmitting new features and modifications can account for the evolution of even fantastically complex structures, such as eyes or brains—it just takes a lot of generations (and of course the evolutionary timescale runs to millions of generations). It follows from this that evolution has no goal or "endpoint": it is simply a continual remolding of organisms in response to their environments, driven by differential reproductive success.

Progress in genetics research was accelerated by focusing on organisms that reproduce rapidly. An example is the fruit fly *Drosophila melanogaster*, whose generation time is 10 days and whose salivary glands produce giant chromosomes that are visible with a light microscope. **Chromosomes** (from the Greek *chroma*, "color," and *soma*, "body") are the supercoiled lengths of DNA, found within the cell nucleus, that contain the **genes** that encode the tens of thousands of proteins that make up the body (see the Appendix). An additional complexity is the discovery that an individual's experiences and environment can modify the expression of certain genes in a way that can be transmitted to offspring without changing the structure of the affected genes. We'll have more to say about these **epigenetic** modifications in Chapter 7.

Many of the findings about genetic mechanisms based on work with *Drosophila* and even with bacteria hold true for larger organisms, such as humans, that reproduce much more slowly. Gradual changes within a species as well as the formation of new species can now be understood in the light of modern evolutionary theory, which combines Darwin's hypothesis of natural selection with modern genetics and molecular biology.

How closely related are two species?

People have probably always classified the animals around them and realized that some forms resemble each other more closely than others. The Swedish biologist Carolus Linnaeus (1707–1778) proposed the basic classification system that we use today. In Linnaeus's system, each species is assigned two names—the first name identifying the **genus** (plural *genera*), the second name indicating the **species**. Both names are always italicized, and the genus name is capitalized. According to this system, the modern human species is *Homo sapiens*.

The different levels of classification are illustrated and defined in **FIGURE 6.3**. The main trunk of the "tree," the animal kingdom, includes all animal species. As branches divide and subdivide toward the outer reaches of the tree, each successive category includes fewer species, and the species are more closely related. The order of categories, from most broad to most narrow, is this: kingdom, phylum, class, order, family, genus, species. (Here's a handy mnemonic to help you remember them: *k*indly *p*ut *c*lothes *o*n, *f*or *g*oodness' *s*ake.)

Today we understand that the similarities between some species of organisms reflect **phylogeny** (from the Greek *phylon*, "tribe" or "kind," and *genes*, "born"), the evolutionary history of a particular group of organisms. Phylogeny is often represented as a *family tree* that shows which species may have given rise to others. Comparisons among extant animals, coupled with fragmentary but illuminating data from fossils, allow us to hypothesize about the history of the body and brain, and the forces that shaped them through countless generations (Pennisi, 2003). The phylogenetic approach—looking at patterns among related species—also allows scientists to make inferences about the evolution of behaviors (e.g., Delbarco-Trillo et al., 2011).

SPECIES. The basic (most specific) unit of taxonomic classification, consisting of a population or set of populations of closely related and similar organisms capable of interbreeding. The domestic dog is the species *Canis familiaris*. There are about 400 breeds of dogs, all considered to belong to one species.

Canis familiaris. 1 species

Domestic dogs

Dogs

SPECIES
GENUS
FAMILY
ORDER
CLASS
PHYLUM
KINGDOM

All animals alive today shared a common ancestor. Both members of any chosen pair of species have been evolving separately since their last shared ancestor.

GENUS (plural *genera*). The main subdivision of a family; a group of similar, related species. Some genera in the family Canidae are **Canis** (dogs, coyotes, two species of wolves, four species of jackals) and *Vulpes* (ten species of foxes).

Canis. 8 species

Dogs, wolves, coyotes, jackals

FAMILY. The main subdivision of an order; a group of similar, related genera. Some families in the order Carnivora are **Canidae** (dogs, foxes, and related genera) and Felidae (domestic cats, lions, panthers, and related genera). Family names always end in *-idae*.

Canidae. Approximately 35 species

Canids

ORDER. The main subdivision of a class; a group of similar, related families. Some orders of the class Mammalia are **Carnivora** (meat eaters such as dogs, cats, bears, weasels, etc.) and Primates (humans, monkeys, and apes).

Carnivora. Approximately 235 species

Carnivores

CLASS. The main subdivision of a phylum; a group of similar, related orders. Some classes within the phylum Chordata are **Mammalia**, Aves (birds), and Reptilia. Mammals are characterized by production of milk by the female mammary glands and by hair for body covering.

Mammalia. Approximately 4300 species

Mammals

PHYLUM (plural *phyla*). The main—and most inclusive—subdivision of a kingdom; a group of similar, related classes. Some phyla are **Chordata**, Mollusca, and Arthropoda. Chordates differ from members of the other phyla by having an internal skeleton.

Chordata. Approximately 40,000 species

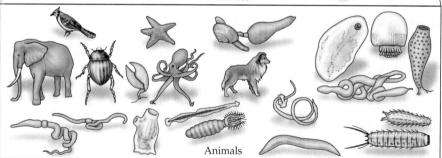

Vertebrates

KINGDOM. All living beings can be divided into five kingdoms: **Animalia**, Plantae, Fungi, Monera (bacteria), and Protista.

Animalia. Approximately 1 million species of animals are known. The total number of existing species has been estimated to be as high as 30 million.

Animals

6.3 LINNAEAN CLASSIFICATION OF THE DOMESTIC DOG

Newer methods aid in classifying animals and inferring evolution

Today the field of **taxonomy** (from the Greek *taxis*, "arrangement," and *nomos*, "law"), or *classification*, makes use of our understanding of genetics to reconstruct phylogeny. DNA appears to change at a relatively steady average rate in all lineages of a given order of animals (Hillis et al., 1996). Thus, the proportion of differences between DNA samples from two species can be used as a "molecular clock" to estimate how long ago they diverged from a common ancestor. For example, **FIGURE 6.4** shows an attempt to reconstruct the family tree of apes and humans according to the genetic similarity of the species (Wildman et al., 2003). The diagram depicts

taxonomy The classification of organisms.

6.4 FAMILY TREE OF APES AND HUMANS This tree was derived from measurements of differences between pairs of species in samples of their genetic material, molecules of deoxyribonucleic acid (DNA). To see how different two species are in their genetic endowments, trace the lines from the two members of a pair to the point that connects them and then match the point with the scale on the left. For example, the line from humans and the line from chimpanzees converge at a point indicating that human DNA differs from chimpanzee DNA by just over 1%. The DNA of humans and of chimpanzees differs from that of gorillas, in turn, by about 2.3%. The scale on the right gives the estimated amount of time, in millions of years, since any pair of species shared a common ancestor. For example, humans and chimpanzees diverged from a common ancestor about 4–6 million years ago. (After Wildman et al., 2003.)

Old World monkeys | Siamang gibbon | Common gibbon | Orangutan | Gorilla | Human | Bonobo | Common chimpanzee

Percentage difference in DNA: 0, 1, 2, 3, 4, 5, 6, 7, 8

4–6
8–10
6–8
12–16
15–20
25–30

Millions of years ago

Common ancestor

ecological niche The unique assortment of environmental opportunities and challenges to which each organism is adapted.

humans and chimpanzees as more closely related to each other than either species is to gorillas. The timelines in Figure 6.4 should be viewed as approximations, however, because scientists are still discussing and testing ideas about calibration of the molecular clocks. For example, some estimates based on mutation rate suggest that humans and chimpanzees may have split from a common ancestor earlier than previously believed, in the range of 7–13 million years ago (Langergraber et al., 2012). If true, the evolutionary tree describing the relatedness of the great apes—including us—will need another revision.

Estimates from fossil and DNA evidence do not always agree completely in dating branches of the evolutionary tree. Fossil dates tend to be too recent, because we can never find the first specimen of a given species. Molecular dates have tended to be too old, because of problems with calibrating rates of change of DNA over time. As technology improves, however, these discrepancies are diminishing (Ho and Duchêne, 2014).

Why Should We Study Other Species?

One old-fashioned reason for comparing species was based on the unfounded assumption that humans were the pinnacle achievement of evolution, as though evolution had an objective (and we were it). This human-centered perspective was properly criticized because it implicitly pictured other animals as incomplete "little humans" or "subhumans" (**FIGURE 6.5**). It also embraced an old notion referred to as *linear descent*: the idea that evolution had proceeded along a single trajectory from simple to complex, culminating in humans. Today, scientists instead understand evolution as a multibranching set of radiations, and we can use comparisons of different species to gather clues about this evolutionary history.

Different kinds of animals have evolved specific behaviors and neural mechanisms that allow them to exploit specific sets of environmental opportunities, or **ecological niches**. The anteater's long face and tongue, for example, allow it to take advantage of the presence of huge ant colonies far more effectively than its precursor species could do. Every species has its own evolutionary history of modification to exploit the ecological niches arising in the local environment. Examples and comparisons of animals in different ecological niches appear in every chapter of this book. Comparing

6.5 WE ARE RELATED, AREN'T WE?

BOX
6.1

Why Should We Study Particular Species?

With all the species that are available, why should we choose certain ones for study? In selecting species for their research, scientists apply several criteria, including the following:

1. *Outstanding features*   Some species are champions at specific behaviors and abilities, such as sensory discrimination (like the incredible auditory localization abilities of the owl) or control of movement (such as the flight behavior of the housefly). These abilities are often linked to highly specialized neuronal structures that incorporate and optimize particular designs that may be less conspicuous in other organisms (Bullock, 1986). Study of such species may yield general principles that apply to other species.

2. *Convenience*   Some species, such as the laboratory rat, are particularly convenient for study because they breed readily, are inexpensive to maintain, are not endangered, have relatively short life spans, and have been studied extensively already, so there is a good base of knowledge about them at the outset. In addition, some (not all) aspects of their brains and behavior are similar enough to other species to allow for generalizations. Some species are convenient for methodological reasons. For example, some mollusks have relatively simple nervous systems that aid in tracing neural circuits, and fruitflies (*Drosophila*) are a classic model species in genetics because they have a simple genome, short generation time, and numerous genes with mammalian homologs (R. Lewis, 1998).

3. *Comparison*   Close relationships between species that behave very differently enable the testing of hypotheses. For example, species of voles that are closely related, and otherwise very similar, show large differences in the size of the hippocampus that appear to reflect differences in the sizes of their home ranges (the hippocampus is implicated in spatial navigation, which is of course more challenging in larger ranges). A similar difference is found in birds, with species that cache food in dispersed spatial locations showing larger hippocampi (see Chapter 17). In New World monkeys, like those in the figure, the structure of the retina differs markedly between species that are active at night and species that are active in daylight (Finlay et al. 2008).

4. *Preservation*   Studies of rare and/or endangered species, conducted in the field or in zoos, can help set priorities and assess options for the conservation of biodiversity (Mace et al., 2003).

5. *Economic importance*   Studying animals that are important for the economy—agricultural animals, food species like fish, predators, and crop-damaging species—can provide information that helps increase production and/or decrease losses.

6. *Treatment of disease*   Some species are subject to the same diseases as other species and therefore are valuable models for investigation. For example, in neuroscience alone there are animal models of Alzheimer's disease, Down syndrome, epilepsy, mood disorders, amyotrophic lateral sclerosis, narcolepsy, stroke, and many other disorders.

Owl monkeys

Howler monkey

The retina of the nocturnal owl monkey features high densities of rod photoceptors for excellent performance in low light. In contrast, the retina of the howler monkey contains a high concentration of cone receptors, giving it excellent acuity and color sensitivity, consistent with its diurnal (daytime) lifestyle.

two or more carefully chosen species leads to a much deeper understanding because the evolutionary framework provides additional explanatory power. Species with varying biological histories show different solutions to the challenges of survival and reproduction. In many cases, these pressures to adapt have led to changes in brain structure. **BOX 6.1** explains some of the factors that scientists consider in choosing particular species to study.

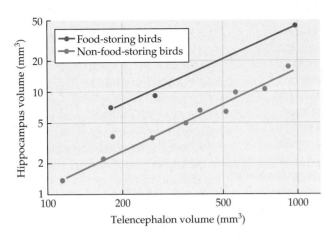

6.6 FOOD STORING IN BIRDS AS RELATED TO HIPPOCAMPAL SIZE Food-storing species of birds have twice as large a hippocampus in relation to their forebrain (telencephalon) as do species that do not store food. Note that both axes on this graph are logarithmic. (After Sherry et al., 1989.)

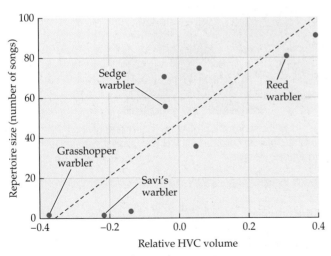

6.7 BRAINY WARBLERS SING MORE SONGS (After Székely et al., 1996.)

One important adaptation is the ability to learn and remember, in order to successfully predict where, when, and how to obtain food and mates and avoid danger. This capability to store information must have arisen early in evolution, because even simple animals show lasting changes in behavior following important experiences. Understanding how simpler animals form and store memories has provided many insights into memory mechanisms in more-complex animals, including human beings, as we will see in Chapter 17. For now, let's look at a few examples of how comparing species can inform us about brain function.

Complicated lives require complicated brains

Most species of animals spend a lot of time and energy in the pursuit of food, often using elaborate strategies. Researchers have found that the strategies that different species use to obtain food are correlated with brain size and structure. For example, mammals that eat food distributed in clusters that are difficult to find (such as ripe fruit) tend to have brains larger than those of related species whose food is more uniformly distributed and thus easy to find (such as grass or leaves). This relationship has been found within families of rodents, insectivores (such as shrews and moles), lagomorphs (such as rabbits and pikas) (Clutton-Brock and Harvey, 1980), and primates (Mace et al., 1981).

Finding novel ways of getting food is related to the size of the forebrain in different orders of birds (Lefebvre et al., 1997). Researchers report a variety of instances where novel food-seeking behavior seems to have emerged in bird species: magpies digging up potatoes, house sparrows searching car radiator grilles for insects, crows dropping palm nuts in the paths of cars that run over and open them, and so on. Data from both North America and the British Isles indicate that the more innovative species have relatively larger forebrains. These results thus suggest that selection pressures favored increased size of the forebrain, allowing these species to cope with environmental challenges and opportunities in new, flexible ways. Later in the chapter we will see an extension of this kind of study to species of primates, showing that increased size of the forebrain seems to be related to innovation and sociality.

Other behavioral adaptations have also been related to differences in relative sizes of certain brain structures. For example, some species of bats find their way and locate prey by hearing; others rely almost entirely on vision. In the midbrain, the auditory center (inferior colliculus) is much larger in bats that depend on hearing; bats that depend on sight have a larger visual center (superior colliculus).

Birds in families that store bits of food for later use (e.g., the acorn woodpecker, Clark's nutcracker, and the black-capped chickadee) have a larger hippocampus relative to the forebrain and to body weight than do birds in families that do not store food (Sherry, 1992). This difference has been found among both North American species (**FIGURE 6.6**) and European species. For more on hippocampal size and memory for food storage, see **A Step Further: Food Storing Depends on Hippocampal Size** on the website.

A different evolutionary pressure affected the brains of songbirds—species in which males sing to attract mates. In some species, each male may sing only a single song, while in other species males have repertoires of ten or more different tunes. The females prefer to mate with males with larger repertoires, so large repertoires are definitely adaptive in those species. Among the closely related species of European warblers, repertoire size correlates with the volume of a brain region known as the *HVC* (**FIGURE 6.7**). This correlation strongly suggests that the HVC is important for song production in birds, an inference that has been confirmed in lab studies (in fact, the HVC is sometimes referred to as the *higher vocal center*). It is

BOX
6.2

To Each Its Own Sensory World

Differences in the lifestyles of various mammals, reflecting the varying ecological niches they occupy, are evident in the organization of the cerebral cortex. The rat (*Rattus norvegicus*) is nocturnal and uses its whiskers to find its way in the dark. About 28% of the cortical representation of the rat's body surface is devoted to the whiskers (vibrissae), compared with only about 9% in the squirrel (*Sciurus carolinensis*) (Figure A) (Huffman et al., 1999). In addition, the nocturnal rat makes little use of vision, and its primary visual cortex (V1) is relatively small compared with that of the squirrel, which is diurnal.

The remarkable platypus (*Ornithorhynchus anatinus*) is an egg-laying mammal that lives in and around streams in eastern Australia and Tasmania. Because of its duck-like bill and webbed feet, some scientists thought it might be a hoax when preserved animals were brought to Europe in the nineteenth century. The platypus is largely nocturnal and dives into murky waters, closing its eyes, ears, and nostrils as it hunts for insects, shrimp, and crayfish. How it senses its prey remained a mystery until the 1980s, when investigators found that the main sensory organ of the platypus is its bill,

which is about 7 centimeters (cm) long in a 160-cm-long adult.

The bill has about 16 longitudinal stripes of receptors: stripes of touch (mechanosensory) receptors alternate with touch-electrical (electrosensory) receptors (Figure B) (Manger et al., 1998). As the platypus moves its bill underwater, it can detect prey by both the mechanical ripples and the changes in electrical fields that they cause. In keeping with the importance of the bill in locating prey, almost all somatosensory cortex (S1 and S2) in the platypus is devoted to the bill (see Figure B), and the primary visual (V1) and auditory (A1) areas are small (Krubitzer et al., 1995).

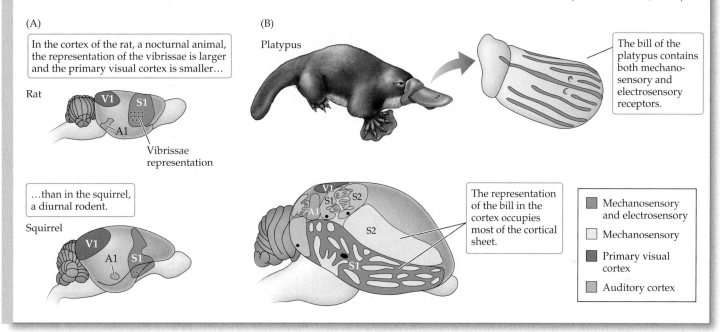

(A) In the cortex of the rat, a nocturnal animal, the representation of the vibrissae is larger and the primary visual cortex is smaller… than in the squirrel, a diurnal rodent.

Rat
V1 · S1 · A1
Vibrissae representation

Squirrel
V1 · A1 · S1

(B) Platypus

The bill of the platypus contains both mechanosensory and electrosensory receptors.

V1 · S1 · S2 · A1 · S2 · S1

The representation of the bill in the cortex occupies most of the cortical sheet.

■ Mechanosensory and electrosensory
□ Mechanosensory
■ Primary visual cortex
■ Auditory cortex

the females that are exerting the evolutionary pressure, by choosing males with large repertoires and thereby also selecting for larger HVCs. This is therefore an example of sexual selection: large song repertoires are adaptive only because the opposite sex prefers them.

BOX 6.2 provides other examples of solutions that different species employ to solve the dilemmas of adaptation. As a general rule, the relative size of a brain region is a rough guide to the importance of the function of that region for the adaptations of the species.

Simpler invertebrate nervous systems provide models of neural function

Most of the animals on Earth are invertebrates—animals without backbones—and they far exceed vertebrates in many ways, including diversity of appearance, variety of habitat, and overall numbers. For each person on Earth, there are at least 1 billion insects, which are just one type of invertebrate!

The gross anatomy of the nervous systems of some representative animals is illustrated in **FIGURE 6.8**. The enormous complexity of the vertebrate brain, with its billions of nerve cells, presents major difficulties for understanding the basic neuronal

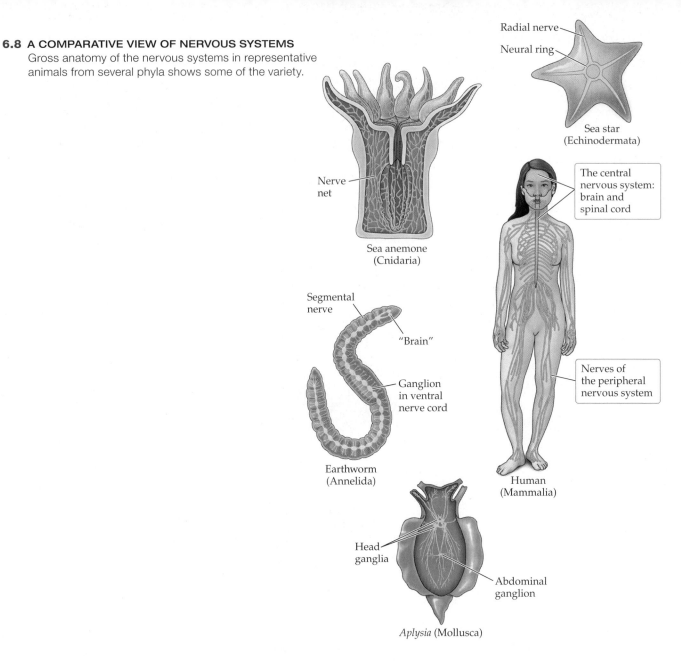

6.8 A COMPARATIVE VIEW OF NERVOUS SYSTEMS Gross anatomy of the nervous systems in representative animals from several phyla shows some of the variety.

Radial nerve

Neural ring

Sea star
(Echinodermata)

Nerve net

Sea anemone
(Cnidaria)

The central nervous system: brain and spinal cord

Nerves of the peripheral nervous system

Segmental nerve

"Brain"

Ganglion in ventral nerve cord

Earthworm
(Annelida)

Human
(Mammalia)

Head ganglia

Abdominal ganglion

Aplysia (Mollusca)

processes underlying simple behaviors. To address this problem, many researchers have turned instead to the much simpler nervous systems of invertebrates that have only hundreds or thousands of neurons. If we can understand how memories are formed in a model system like the worm *Caenorhabditis elegans*, which has only 302 neurons, perhaps we can uncover basic cellular mechanisms of learning and memory that are shared across species (Ardiel and Rankin, 2010). We compare invertebrate and vertebrate nervous systems in **A Step Further: Insect Nervous Systems** on the website. Since we are primarily interested in understanding human behavior, let's focus here on brains more similar to our own.

All Vertebrate Brains Share the Same Basic Structures

Let's look more broadly at the differences and similarities of nervous systems in mammals and other vertebrates.

The main brain structures are the same in all mammals

As you can see in **FIGURE 6.9**, the various orders of mammals all share the same basic set of brain regions devoted to visual, auditory, and somatosensory processing. The regions are also arranged in the same basic pattern. However, the relative

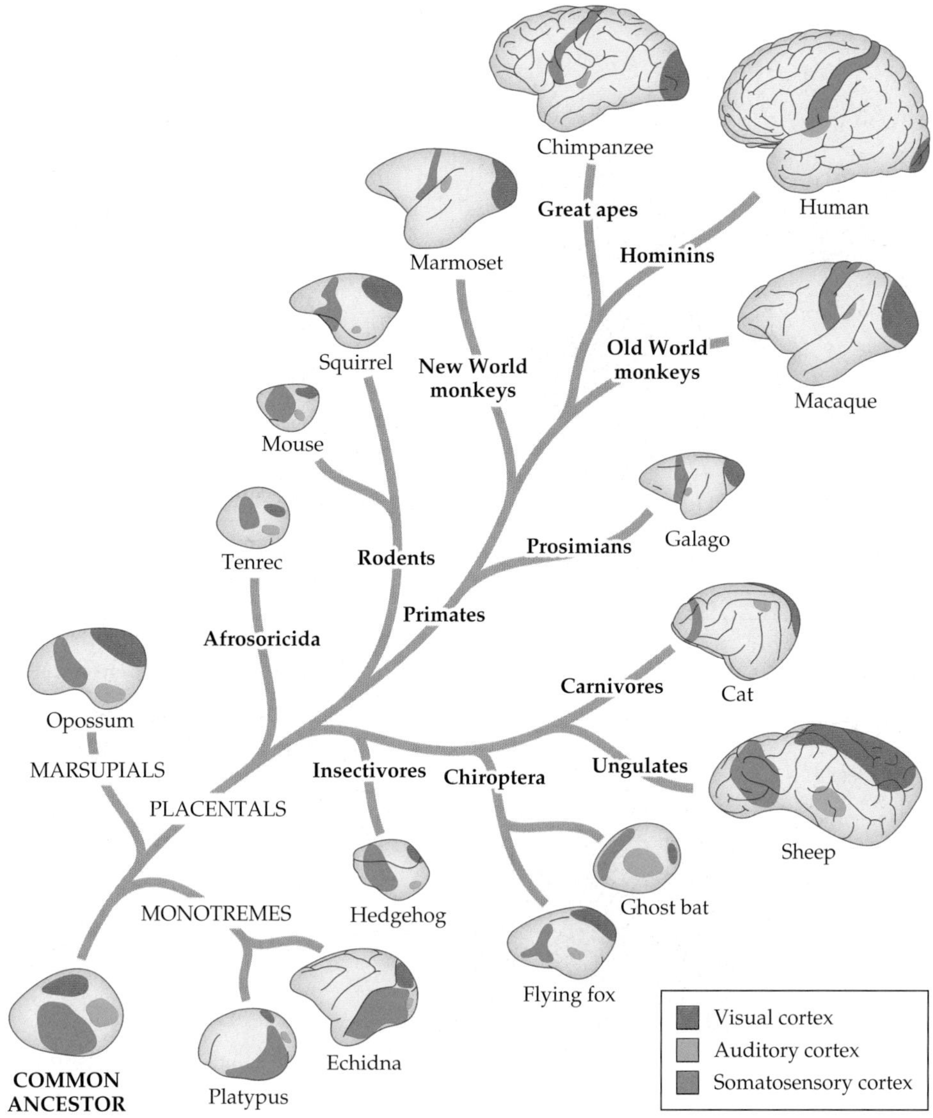

Chimpanzee
Human
Great apes
Marmoset
Hominins
Squirrel
New World monkeys
Old World monkeys
Macaque
Mouse
Galago
Tenrec
Rodents
Prosimians
Primates
Afrosoricida
Opossum
Carnivores
Cat
MARSUPIALS
PLACENTALS
Insectivores
Chiroptera
Ungulates
Sheep
MONOTREMES
Hedgehog
Ghost bat
Flying fox
Echidna
Platypus
COMMON ANCESTOR
Visual cortex
Auditory cortex
Somatosensory cortex

6.9 FUNCTIONS AND RELATIONS This family tree of mammalian brains shows that while we mammals all share the same basic sensory cortical regions, their size and placement are determined by how each species makes its living. Brains are not drawn to scale. (Courtesy of Dr. Leah Krubitzer, UC Davis.)

sizes, proportions, and anatomical locations of these brain regions have been subject to evolutionary modification as the species have adapted to their unique ecological niches (Krubitzer and Seelke, 2012). Our understanding of how these differences in size and structure of the brain promote behavioral specializations should help us to understand neural mechanisms at work in human behavior. For example, the sizes of some regions in the human temporal lobes seem to be related to language function (see Chapter 19). The diversity of mammalian brains can be seen on the Web at brainmuseum.org.

A comparison of the human brain with the brain of the lab rat, perhaps the most completely studied brain, reveals basic similarities and differences (**FIGURE 6.10**). Each of the main structures in the human brain has a counterpart in the rat brain. This comparison can be extended in great detail to include nuclei, fiber tracts, and types of cells and even the many molecules specific to brain function. These similarities in structure and organization of mammalian brains reflect the heritage of our evolution from a common ancestor long ago.

There are differences between the brains of humans and the brains of other mammals, of course, but they are mainly quantitative. Whereas the brain of an adult human being weighs about 1400 grams (g), that of an adult rat weighs a little less than 2 g, but in each case the brain represents about 2% of total body weight. The cerebral hemispheres occupy a much greater proportion of the brain in the human than in the rat, and the human cerebral cortex is highly convoluted (i.e., covered in gyri and sulci) (Chapter 2), whereas the rat cerebral cortex is smooth. The olfactory

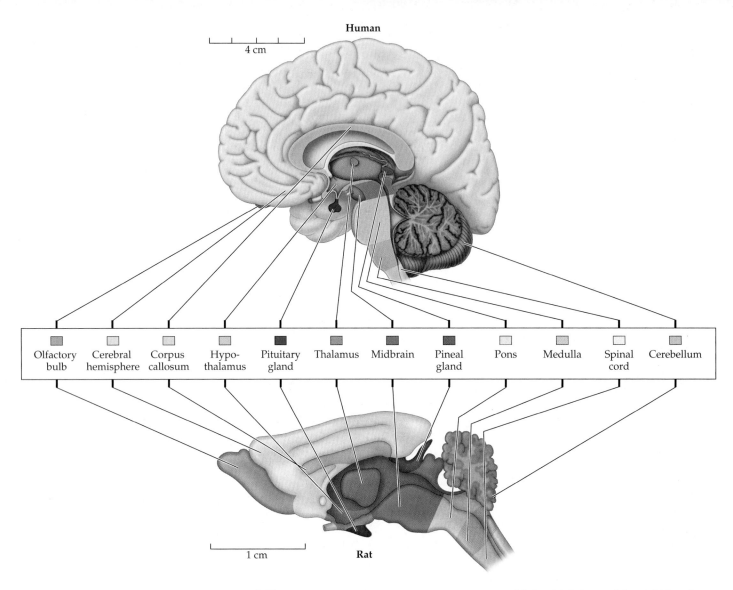

4 cm

| Olfactory bulb | Cerebral hemisphere | Corpus callosum | Hypo-thalamus | Pituitary gland | Thalamus | Midbrain | Pineal gland | Pons | Medulla | Spinal cord | Cerebellum |

1 cm   **Rat**

6.10 HUMAN AND RAT BRAINS COMPARED Midsagittal views of the right hemisphere in human and rat brains show that the main structures are the same in both, and they have the same topological relations to each other. Note, however, that the cerebral hemispheres are relatively much larger in the human brain, whereas the rat has a relatively larger midbrain and olfactory bulb. (The rat brain has been enlarged here about 6 times in linear dimensions relative to the human brain.)

bulb is relatively larger in rats than in humans. This difference is probably related to the rat's much greater use of the sense of smell.

All vertebrate nervous systems share certain main features but differ in others

Let's extend our view to the basic features of the nervous systems of vertebrates more generally, not just mammals. Vertebrate nervous systems share many characteristics:

- *Development from a hollow dorsal neural tube* The head of the embryonic neural tube goes on to form the major subdivisions of the brain, but a fluid series of hollow spaces within the brain—the ventricular system—persists into adulthood (see Chapters 2 and 7).

- *Bilateral symmetry* The cerebral hemispheres are almost mirror images. (We'll see some interesting exceptions in Chapter 19.)

- *Segmentation* Pairs of spinal nerves extend from each level of the spinal cord.

- *Hierarchical control* The cerebral hemispheres control or modulate the activity of the spinal cord.

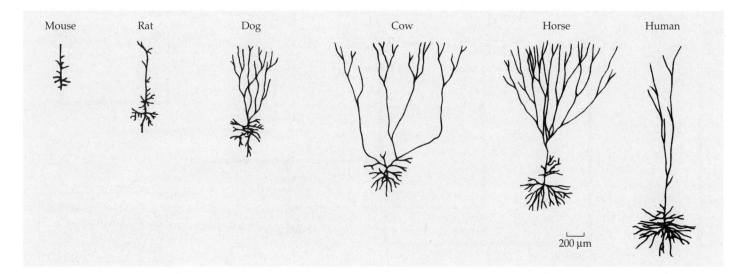

| Mouse | Rat | Dog | Cow | Horse | Human |

200 μm

6.11 THE SAME KIND OF NEURON IN DIFFERENT SPECIES These pyramidal neurons from the motor cortices of different mammals are all drawn to the same scale. (After Barasa, 1960.)

- *Separate systems* The central nervous system (brain and spinal cord) is clearly separate from the peripheral nervous system, as shown for humans in Figure 6.8.
- *Localization of function* Certain functions are controlled by certain locations in the central nervous system.

Vertebrates have all of these features in common because they descended from a common ancestor that possessed them. In general, vertebrate species with larger bodies tend to possess larger brains, with larger neurons and larger dendritic trees, as **FIGURE 6.11** shows for some mammals. However, some classes of vertebrates have proportionately larger brains than others, as we'll see next.

The Evolution of Vertebrate Brains Reflects Changes in Behavior

During the course of evolution, the characteristics of the nervous system changed progressively. One especially prominent change in the last 100 million years has been a general tendency for the brain size of vertebrates to increase, and the brains of our human ancestors have shown a particularly striking increase in size over the last 2 million years. How does evolution of the brain relate to changes in behavior?

Present-day animals and fossils reveal evolution of the brain

Theoretically, we could learn more about the evolution of the brain by studying the brains of fossil animals, but brains themselves do not fossilize—at least, not literally. Two methods of analysis have proven helpful. One is to use the cranial cavity of a fossil skull to make a cast of the brain that once occupied that space. These casts, called **endocasts** (the Greek *endon* means "within"), give a reasonable indication of the size and shape of the brain, but no fine detail.

The other method is to study present-day animals, choosing species that show various degrees of similarity to (or difference from) the ancestral species. Although no modern animal is an ancestor of any other living species—because all species are constantly evolving—some present-day species resemble ancestral forms more closely than others do. For example, present-day salamanders are much more similar to the fossils of vertebrates of 300 million years ago than are any mammals. Among mammals, some species, such as the opossum, resemble fossil mammals of 50 million years ago more than do other species, such as the dog. Thus, a species such as the opossum is said to retain primitive or ancestral states of particular anatomical features. In studying the brains of living species, anatomists can obtain far more detailed information than they get from endocasts, because they can investigate the internal structure of the brain: its nuclei, its fiber tracts, and the circuitry formed by connections of its neurons.

endocast A cast of the cranial cavity of a skull, especially useful for studying fossils of extinct species.

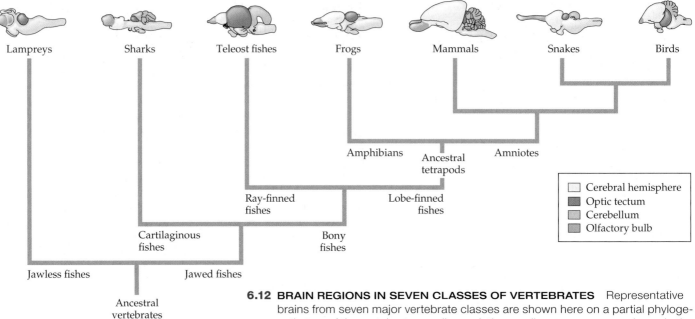

6.12 BRAIN REGIONS IN SEVEN CLASSES OF VERTEBRATES Representative brains from seven major vertebrate classes are shown here on a partial phylogenetic tree of the vertebrates; earlier evolutionary divergences appear lower in the tree. Note the relatively large sizes of the cerebral hemispheres (light blue) and the cerebellum (green) in the bird and mammal brains. (Brains are not drawn to the same scale.)

As we noted earlier, we must be careful not to interpret change over time, including the change in brain size, as if it were a linear evolutionary sequence. The main classes of vertebrates in **FIGURE 6.12** represent different lines or radiations of evolution that have been proceeding separately and simultaneously for at least 200 million years. For example, today's sharks have much larger brains than primitive sharks had, but the evolution of large-brained sharks had nothing to do with the development of large brains in mammals. The line of descent that eventually led to mammals had separated from the shark line long before the large-brained sharks evolved.

Through evolution, vertebrate brains have changed in both size and organization

Let's consider some examples of changes in the size and organization of vertebrate brains. Even the living vertebrate that has the most primitive features—the lamprey (a jawless fish)—has a fairly complex brain. The lamprey has not only the basic neural chassis of spinal cord, hindbrain, and midbrain, but also a diencephalon and a telencephalon. Its telencephalon has cerebral hemispheres and other subdivisions that are also found in the mammalian brain. So all vertebrate brains appear to have these regions.

One difference in basic brain structure between the lamprey and other vertebrates is that the cerebellum in the lamprey is very small (too small to be depicted in Figure 6.12). The evolution of large cerebellar hemispheres in birds and mammals appears to be a case of independent evolution from the small cerebellum in their common reptilian ancestor; the increased size of the cerebellum may be responsible for increased complexity of sensory processing and increased motor agility.

The differences among the brains of vertebrate species, then, lie not in the existence of basic subdivisions, but in their *relative size*. At what stages of vertebrate evolution do various brain regions first become important? Large, paired optic lobes in its midbrain probably represent the lamprey's highest level of visual integration. In bony fishes, amphibians, and reptiles, the relatively large optic tectum in the midbrain (see Figure 6.12) is the main brain center for vision. In birds and mammals, however, complex visual perception requires an enlarged telencephalon.

All mammals have a six-layered **cortex**, sometimes called **neocortex** (from the Greek *neo*, "new," and the Latin *cortex*, "bark of a tree"). In more-recent mammals the cortex accounts for more than half the volume of the brain. In mammals the cortex is mainly responsible for higher-order functions, such as the perception of objects. Regions that were responsible for perceptual functions in animals with less-developed brains—such as the midbrain optic lobes (in the lamprey) or the midbrain optic center (in the frog)—have become visual reflex centers in present-day mammals.

Reptiles were the first vertebrates to exhibit relatively large cerebral hemispheres. Reptiles were also the first vertebrates to have a cerebral cortex, but they have only three cortical layers, unlike the six cortical layers of mammals. (Three-layered cortex is sometimes referred to as *archicortex*, from the Greek *arche*, "ancient.") Part of the cortex in reptiles may be homologous to the three-layered hippocampus in mammals.

Brain size evolved independently in multiple lineages

If we compare animals of similar body size, we see considerable variation in brain size within each line of evolution. For example, within the ancient class of jawless fishes, more-recent members called *hagfishes* have forebrains that are 4 times as large as those of lampreys of comparable body size. Such increases in brain size have been related to behavioral capacity most thoroughly in mammals, as we'll see next.

THE ENCEPHALIZATION FACTOR   The study of brain size across species is complicated by the wide variation in body sizes, raising the question, How are body size and brain size related? A general relationship was found first for present-day species and then applied successfully to fossil species. This function turns out to be useful in understanding relationships between brain and behavior.

We humans long believed our own brains to be the largest, but this belief was upset in the seventeenth century when the elephant brain was found to weigh 3 times as much as our own. Later, whale brains were found to be even larger. Scientists of the day proposed that brain weight should be considered as a fraction of body weight, with the reassuring outcome that humans then outranked elephants, whales, and all other animals of large or moderate body size. But a mouse has about the same ratio of brain weight to body weight as a human, and the tiny shrew outranks a human on this measure. So, from a comparative point of view, what is the general relation between brain size and body size?

When we plot brain weights and body weights for many species of mammals, we see some generalities (**FIGURE 6.13**). There is a distinct overall correlation between body and brain weight across many species, so all of the points on the plot fall within a narrow polygon. Using a statistical procedure called *linear regression*, a "line of best fit" can be created that passes as closely as possible through the collection of points representing mammalian species. This line has a slope of about 0.69 (Harvey and Krebs, 1990), representing the general mathematical relationship between body weight and brain weight across all mammals.

Having created this general model of braininess, relative to body weight, we can then consider how much any individual species deviates from the expectation for mammals as a group. This deviation (known as a *residual* in linear regression procedures) corresponds to the vertical distance for

cortex   The outer covering of the cerebral hemispheres that consists largely of nerve cell bodies and their branches.

neocortex   Cerebral cortex that is made up of six distinct layers.

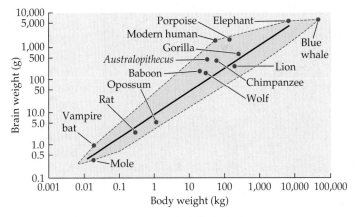

6.13 THE RELATION BETWEEN BRAIN WEIGHT AND BODY WEIGHT   Brain weight is related here to body weight in several mammalian species. Note that both axes are logarithmic, so the graph includes a wide range of brain weights and body weights. A polygon has been drawn to connect the extreme cases and include the whole sample. The black diagonal line is a line of best fit (also known as the *regression line*), indicating a prediction line for brain size among mammals as a group. For each species, the encephalization factor, *k*, corresponds to the distance (the *residual*) between the line and the brain weight value for that species. Although not shown, bird species are about as "brainy" as mammals, but reptile species are substantially less so (Jerison, 1991; H. Stephan et al., 1981).

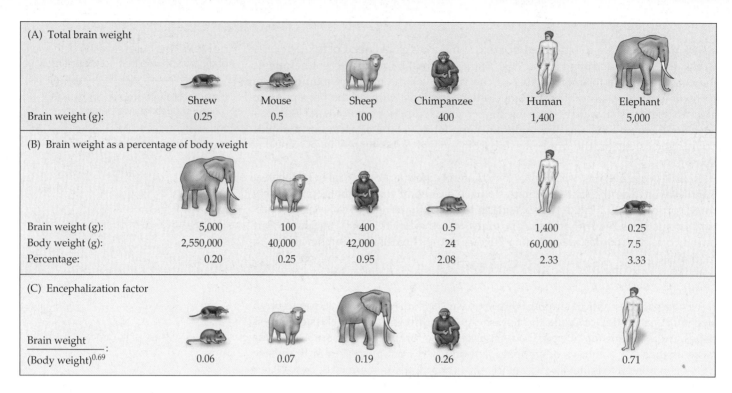

6.14 WHO IS THE BRAINIEST? For this sample of small to large mammals, the answer depends on what measure is used: total brain weight (A), brain weight as a percentage of body weight (B), or the encephalization factor (C). For each measure, the animals are ranked here from lowest value to highest.

THE FAR SIDE By GARY LARSON

"The picture's pretty bleak, gentlemen... The world's climates are changing, the mammals are taking over, and we all have a brain about the size of a walnut."

6.15 WAS THE DINOSAUR BEING TOO MODEST?

that species above or below the diagonal line on the graph. This distance, *k*, is known as the **encephalization factor**. The greater the encephalization factor is for a species—that is, the higher its value is above the diagonal line—the more exaggerated the brain size is for that species relative to the mathematical predication for a mammal of its size. As summarized in **FIGURE 6.14**, among mammals the encephalization factor is greatest for humans and quite a bit less for chimpanzees, despite our evolutionary closeness (see Figure 6.14C). The encephalization factor for opossums indicates that they have *less* brain for their size than would be typical of mammals as a group. Nevertheless, it is important to guard against a tendency to selectively emphasize data that confirm our biased expectation that we are brainier than other species. For example, although our brains are substantially larger than predicted for other animals of the same size, dolphins have comparable proportions, as do some birds; we have also tended to overestimate the number of neurons in the human brain by as much as 15% (Scudellari, 2015). As we'll discuss later, patterns of connectivity and gene expression may be more important for distinguishing the human brain from the brains of related species than are gross anatomical features like size and cell count.

As we've described, brain size can be related to evolutionary adaptive pressures, and you may have heard that dinosaurs became extinct because of their inadequate ("walnut-sized") brains (**FIGURE 6.15**). But is this notion correct? No. The endocasts of dinosaurs indicate that their brain weights are typical of the encephalization of reptiles. The brain of *Tyrannosaurus rex* probably weighed about 700 g: roughly half the size of a human brain, but still a lot larger than a walnut, and appropriate for a reptile of its size (Jerison, 1991). So it seems unlikely that dinosaurs perished due to a lack of brains.

BRAIN SIZE AS ADAPTATION As we saw earlier in the chapter, certain capabilities—navigating by sound, foraging for food, performing a large repertoire of songs—are linked to sizes of particular brain regions. But some capabilities, because they are related to overall cortical volume rather than the volume of any particular region, may have propelled a more general increase in brain size. Most major parts of the brain increase roughly in proportion to total increases in brain size, but even at the gross anatomical level, the rates of increase do show subtle differences (Finlay and Darlington, 1995). For example, the olfactory bulb has a larger relative size in some species, presumably because natural selection pressures have favored a highly developed sense of smell in those species.

As we compare brains across different species of primates, from small to large, it is evident that the medulla becomes *proportionally smaller* relative to brain weight, the cerebellum keeps pace with overall brain weight, and the cortex becomes proportionally larger than any other part (**FIGURE 6.16**). This pattern suggests that the cortex has grown disproportionally over the course of human evolution. It seems that the brain regions that have most expanded over primate evolution are the ones that develop later in life and serve more complex functions (Finlay and Darlington, 1995); for example, the human medulla is fully developed at birth, but the cortex continues adding neurons throughout childhood. This has led theorists to propose that larger brains evolved by prolonging the later stages of development. A mutation that prolonged the last stages of brain development, when neurons are being added almost exclusively in cortex, would result in a larger cortex relative to the rest of the brain. And to the extent that the larger cortex gave individuals advantages over conspecifics, the altered gene that caused it would be favored by natural selection.

Such a "later becomes larger" pattern of evolution may even explain changes in the fine structure of the cortex. During fetal development, the innermost layers of the cortex develop first, and new neurons are added to form each subsequent outer layer. A comparison across mammals suggests that the later-added, outer layers of cortex (e.g., layers I and II) have enlarged more in primates than the innermost layers (**FIGURE 6.17**). Let's consider primate evolution further to see if we can understand what selective pressures favored the expansion of cortex in humans.

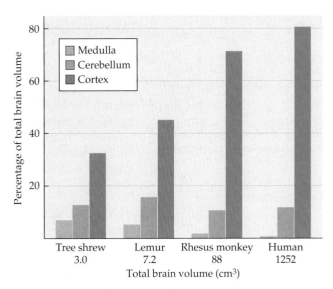

6.16 CHANGES IN THE APPORTIONMENT OF BRAIN REGIONS AMONG PRIMATES This graph shows the percentage of brain volume occupied by three different parts of the brain in four different primates. As the overall size of the brain increases, the sizes of its different parts increase at different rates. The size of the cortex increases steadily as a proportion of total brain size, while that of the cerebellum stays about the same and the relative size of the medulla *decreases*. (Data from H. Stephan et al., 1981.)

encephalization factor A measure of brain size relative to body size.

6.17 EVOLUTION ALLOWS LATER-DEVELOPING BRAIN REGIONS TO GROW LARGER The expansion of cortex that took place in mammals, especially among primates, is due primarily to greater growth of the outermost layers of cortex, which are the last to arise during development. Note that reptiles have three-layered cortex, compared to the basic six-layered cortex in the insectivores and other mammals. (From Hill and Walsh, 2005.)

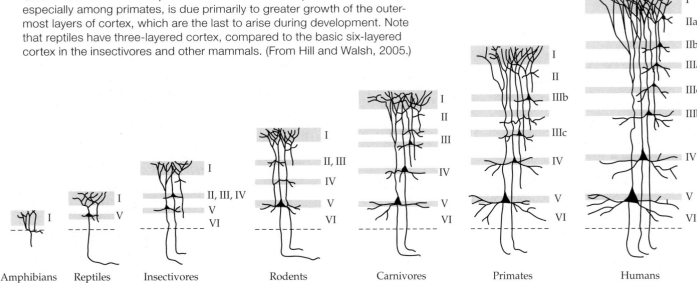

EVOLUTION OF THE BRAIN AND BEHAVIOR **179**

Many Factors Led to the Rapid Evolution of a Large Cortex in Primates

hominin The subgroup of Hominidae that contains modern humans and their ancestral species.

australopithecine Referring to *Australopithecus*, a primate genus, known only from the fossil record, thought to be an ancestor to humans.

We've seen that the comparative approach—studying general principles across different species—reveals that humans are exceptionally brainy for their size, compared with other vertebrates. This additional brain power confers advantages in cognitive abilities, but how did we come to evolve such a large cortex? The study of **hominins** —primates within the family Hominidae (which includes four genera of great apes)— and particularly those hominin species that are ancestral to modern *Homo sapiens*, can help us understand how our body and brain adapted to the vironment through natural selection.

Hominin brains enlarged rapidly in our recent evolution

The structural and behavioral features that we consider characteristic of humans did not develop simultaneously (Falk, 1993). Our large brain is a relatively late development. The trunk and arms of hominins reached their present form about 10 million years ago, and it appears that hominins became bipedal more than 4 million years ago. The fossil record indicates that by at least 2.5 million years ago, hominins were manufacturing and using stone tools in their daily lives (Semaw, 2000).

Yet these early bipedal, tool-making hominins, called **australopithecines**, still had relatively small brains of 350–400 cubic centimeters (cm³), about the size of the modern chimpanzee brain. Wild chimpanzees do not appear to make tools from flaked stone, although they collect stones to use as hammering tools and may inadvertently produce tool-like modifications to stones as they use them to open nuts— perhaps this was a precursor to toolmaking in our own lineage (Bril et al., 2012). But the australopithecines also clearly made and used sharpened stone tools for hunting and butchering animals (Domínguez-Rodrigo et al., 2005). The ability to use tools reduced the selection pressure to maintain large jaws and teeth, and hominin jaws and teeth thus became steadily smaller than those of other apes and more like those of modern human beings. Our australopithecine ancestors were successful, lasting some 2 million years relatively unchanged (**FIGURE 6.18**), living in nomadic social

6.18 HOMININ EVOLUTION The bipedal (two-footed) gait was similar to that of modern humans even in *Australopithecus*, but cerebral volume reached its current size only in *Homo sapiens*. High culture (art, agriculture, cities, writing) emerged only relatively recently and was not associated with any additional change in brain size. (After Tobias, 1980; updated with the assistance of Dr. Tim White.)

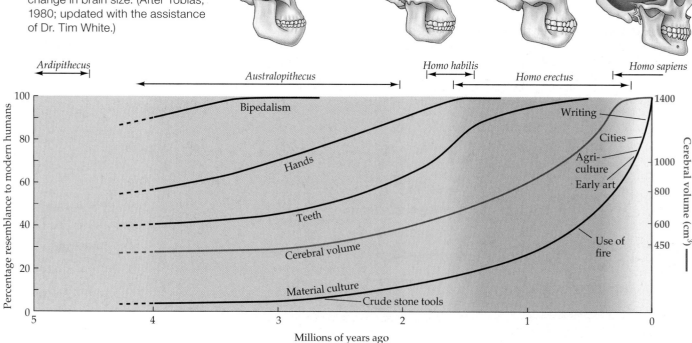

groups of 20–50 individuals, cooperatively hunting and gathering plant foods—a new lifestyle that was continued by later hominins.

By about 2 million years ago, the last of the *Australopithecus* species had developed modern features, such as dexterous hands and smaller teeth, and a trend toward increasing cranial capacity (Berger et al., 2010; Kivell et al., 2011). These features became much more developed as the genus *Homo* appeared (see Figure 6.18). One early representative of the genus, *Homo erectus*, had a cranial capacity of about 700 cm^3 and a smaller face than the australopithecines. As *Homo erectus* evolved, the brain became steadily larger, reaching the present-day volume of about 1400 cm^3, and the face continued to become smaller. *Homo erectus* made elaborate stone tools, used fire, and killed large animals. Fossils and tools of *Homo erectus* are found throughout three continents, whereas australopithecine remains are found only in Africa. *Homo erectus* may have represented a level of capacity and of cultural adaptation that enabled the hominins to expand into new ecological niches and to overcome barriers that kept earlier hominins in a narrower range.

Evolution of the brain and behavior advanced rapidly following the time of *Homo erectus* (see Figure 6.18), through a number of successive *Homo* species. By the time modern *Homo sapiens* appeared, about 150,000 years ago, brain volume had reached the modern level. Thus, after remaining little changed in size during about 2 million years of tool use by the australopithecines, the brain of descendant *Homo* species almost tripled in volume during the next 1.5 million years.

The size of the human brain now appears to be at a plateau. The recent changes in human lifestyle indicated in Figure 6.18—such as the appearance of written language, the introduction of agriculture and animal husbandry (about 10,000 years ago), and urban living (the last few thousand years)—have all been accomplished and assimilated by a brain that does not seem to have altered in size since *Homo sapiens* first appeared. The lack of further increase in brain size may be related to the costs of a large brain, a topic we consider next.

Negative and positive selection pressures affected hominin brain size

Having a large brain entails costs as well as benefits. Growth of a large brain involves a long and burdensome gestation period and difficult birthing. This problem is particularly acute in us bipeds, where the babies of big-brained *Homo* species must pass through the narrow pelvis that our small-brained australopithecine ancestors evolved in order to balance over two feet instead of four. Once that inconvenient baby is born, much of the growth of the brain continues for years after birth, which means prolonged dependence of the infant and prolonged parental care.

Of course, this prolonged dependence reflects the protracted development of humans we mentioned earlier. The extended growth period of humans compared with other primates is obvious in brain weight after birth. While the growth of the chimpanzee brain levels off shortly after birth, the human brain keeps growing after birth, at a rate rivaling that of the fetus (**FIGURE 6.19**). Indeed, the newborn human is, in a sense, continuing fetal development outside the womb. This is also another example of "later becomes larger" that we discussed earlier (see Figure 6.17), as most of the postnatal brain growth is due to expansion of the cortex.

The human brain makes up only about 2% of our total adult body weight, but when we are at rest, it consumes a much bigger proportion of our metabolic budget. Construction and maintenance of the human brain is so complex that more than half of our genes contribute to the task. These complex genetic messages are vulnerable to accidents; mutations of any of them are likely to lead to behavior disorders. Despite all these negative selection pressures, we nonetheless evolved a large brain, so presumably the benefits outweighed the costs.

Any change in an organ during evolution is assumed to confer a fitness advantage, that is, an increased likelihood that the individual will survive and reproduce. A rapid change, as in the increase in size of the hominin brain, implies a strong fitness advantage. One hypothesis is that selection pressure in the social domain may have led to increased brain size. Indeed, across primate species there is a correlation between the average size of a clique (a group of individuals that

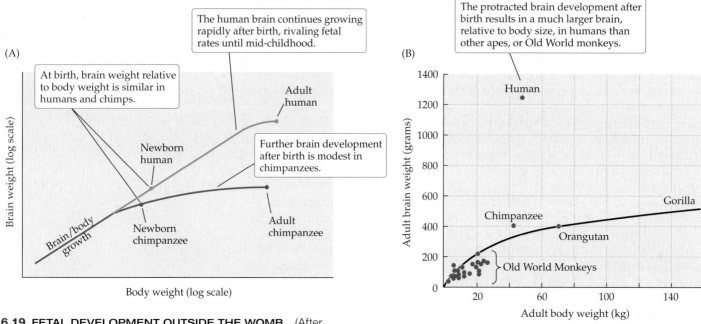

6.19 FETAL DEVELOPMENT OUTSIDE THE WOMB (After Bogin, 1997.)

regularly socialize with one another) and the size of the cortex relative to overall brain size (**FIGURE 6.20**) (Dunbar, 1998). The *social brain hypothesis* suggests that a larger cortex is needed to handle the complex cognitive task of maintaining social relationships with other large-brained individuals (Dunbar, 2009). Based on the correlation between social group size and brain size, it is possible to estimate the maximum size of various species' social groups from the size of the cortex (Dunbar, 2009). For humans, this value is about 150. It's a surprisingly prevalent number in anthropology—for example, the average number of people in many hunter-gatherer societies is about 150, and the same holds true for many functional military units. So the ratio of cortex to brain may indicate the maximum number of individuals with whom we can have a meaningful social relationship. Perhaps our brains are too small to let us really keep tabs on more than about 150 "friends" on Facebook. (If you haven't reached your limit yet, you can "like" us at facebook.com/Behavioralneuroscience, to learn about new developments in behavioral neuroscience.)

An alternative perspective on the positive selection pressures driving expansion of the hominin brain emphasizes skill development. A major study correlated brain size in 116 species of primates with three different factors that have been proposed to account for the enhanced size of primate brains: (1) innovations in behavior, (2) use of tools, and (3) social learning—that is, learning by observing others (Reader and Laland, 2002). Rather than testing animals for these traits or observing them directly, the scholars surveyed about 1000 articles in primate journals and other relevant literature for instances of innovation, tool use, and social learning (**FIGURE 6.21**). In addition to using total brain weights, they used the ratio of what has been called the *executive brain* (the forebrain) to the brainstem.

Both total brain size and relative forebrain size correlated positively with the frequency of each of the three behavioral indices, indicating that each is related to expansion of the primate brain. Thus, the results indicate that these multiple, interrelated sources of selection favored evolution of the large

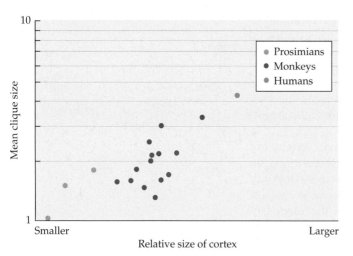

6.20 THE SOCIAL BRAIN HYPOTHESIS In primate species the average size of cliques (groups that individuals regularly associate with) is correlated with the relative size of the cortex. Did sociality drive human brain evolution? (After Dunbar, 1998.)

6.21 TRANSMITTING CULTURE Culture has been observed in nonhuman primates. For example, a population of Japanese macaques developed a set of behaviors that included washing food, playing in water, and eating marine food items, and they transmitted this culture of water-related behaviors from generation to generation.

primate brain. Similar relationships between forebrain size and innovation may apply to birds as well, because members of the crow family have been observed to use tools (Bird and Emery, 2009), and they have relatively larger forebrains than other birds have (Cnotka et al., 2008).

Brain size predicts success in adapting to a novel environment

We have seen that brain size correlates with the complexity of feeding behavior, and with social group size in primates, but is it possible to test the hypothesis that enlarged brains evolved as a more general adaptation to allow us to cope with sudden changes in environmental conditions? One way would be to introduce species with relatively large or small brains into novel environments and see whether they would be able to establish themselves and thrive. However, experimental introductions of species into novel environments would be unethical, because of the unpredictable ecological problems that often occur when nonnative species are released into a new area. An alternative is to study the rich record of past human-mediated introductions. A comprehensive study that used a global database to examine more than 600 examples of introduction involving 195 bird species found that the species with larger brains, relative to body size, tended to be more successful in establishing themselves in novel environments (Sol et al., 2005).

Sexual selection may have contributed to hominin brain expansion

Using a different approach, we can evaluate the rapid expansion of the human brain over the last 1.5 million years in terms of Darwin's second evolutionary principle: sexual selection. Based on a reanalysis of the fossil record, Geoffrey F. Miller (2000) suggested that natural selection to obtain food and shelter is not likely to account completely for the large brain and complex intelligence of *Homo sapiens*. For example, he notes, brain size tripled in our ancestors between 2.5 million years ago and 200,000 years ago, yet during this period our ancestors continued to make the same kind of stone ax (see Figure 6.18). Only well *after* the human brain stopped expanding did technological progress develop, so brain growth did not correlate well with this supposed fitness benefit of enlarged brains.

Rather, Miller proposes, an additional factor accounts for large human brains: in humans, he postulates, much creativity, along with related brain growth, is due to sexual selection for abilities to attract attention, stimulate, and surprise a potential mate. This hypothesis, Miller claims, has the further value of presenting an evolutionary theory for such characteristic human traits as humor, art, music, language, and creativity (**BOX 6.3**).

BOX
6.3

Evolutionary Psychology

Zoologists have long viewed the behavior of animals through an evolutionary prism: just like any other adaptation, the specific behaviors of animals can be seen as a set of adaptations that evolved in response to specific pressures within the species' ecological niche, such as the need to find food, attract mates, and avoid predators. More recently, this perspective has been extended to the study of human behavior, giving rise to a lively and controversial field called **evolutionary psychology** (Buss, 2000; Confer et al., 2010). Applying evolutionary principles to the human mind, researchers in evolutionary psychology view the mind as a large collection of cognitive "modules," each shaped through natural selection to solve a specific adaptive problem that confronted our distant hominin ancestors. But while it's easy to spin plausible tales about how evolution might have shaped our behavior, the challenge for theorists is to come up with ways to test hypotheses that are based on the conditions of the long-gone ancestral

This brightly colored peacock must impress the plain-colored peahen before she will accept his sperm.

environment. Ethical considerations prevent direct experimentation in humans on many of the variables of interest, so studies tend to use indirect surveys and correlational designs (see Chapter 1).

There's no doubt that humans looking for a mate find some traits more attractive than others, and just as

sexual selection pressures have generated sex differences in size and ornamentation in many species (as in the figure), sexual selection has also shaped behaviors such as vocalizations, territoriality, courtship behaviors, and so on. This leads inevitably to questions about the extent to which our own behaviors have been affected

6.22 A BOWERBIRD NEST To attract mates, male bowerbirds build elaborate bowers of twigs, such as this structure, and decorate them with colorful objects. The architectural complexity and ornate decoration of the bowers may be the reason for the relatively large brains of bowerbirds. If a human moves one item while no birds are around, the male bowerbird will promptly put it back in place when he returns.

The hypothesis that sexual selection for artistry and creativity may lead to increased brain size is supported by findings regarding the bowerbird family (Ptilonorhynchidae). To attract and impress females, male bowerbirds construct elaborate structures of twigs, decorated with colorful objects such as shiny beetles, shells, and petals (**FIGURE 6.22**). Bowerbirds have large brains, compared with other birds, and within the bowerbirds, species that build more-elaborate bowers have relatively larger brains (Madden, 2001).

Primate species differ in gene expression

At the start of this chapter, we asked why humans and chimpanzees, which are identical in almost 99% of their genomic DNA sequences, differ in many morphological, behavioral, and cognitive aspects. It is important to understand that humans and their closest relatives can differ on a genetic basis in two principle ways: (1) the DNA *sequences* of specific genes may vary in important ways between the species, and (2) humans and their nonhuman relatives may also differ in how those genes are *expressed* to construct a complex brain.

For example, the gene *ASPM* influences the size of the cerebral cortex. Humans inheriting one version of *ASPM* develop very small brains and are mentally disby the difference between male and female reproductive strategies. For example, *are women inherently more selective than men about choosing mating partners?* Such a difference could be a result of the tremendous investment of time, energy, and resources that a female mammal must make in each offspring. Conversely, men might be more promiscuous than women because of the low cost of producing sperm, zero gestational costs, and potential for a man to expend *no* energy on child rearing. *Is there an "ideal" waist-to-hip ratio that indicates maximal fertility in women?* Correlational studies suggest that a particular ratio is especially attractive to men, across different cultures and historical eras (Singh, 2002). *Are women attracted to power, and men to youth, because natural selection favored these preferences?* Such mate preferences are hypothesized to confer specific advantages for producing numerous strong offspring (youth) or for providing resources and protection to offspring (power).

Geoffrey F. Miller (2000) proposes that sexual selection was crucial for evolution of the human brain. If early hominins had come to favor mates who sang, made jokes, or produced artistic works, such high-order functioning would have evolved rapidly in an "arms race," as the ever more discriminating brains of one sex demanded ever more impressive performances from the brains of the other sex. Did humor, song, and art originate from the drive to be sexually attractive? And does sexual selection account for the large size of the human brain?

Of course, other aspects of natural selection also shape human behavior. For example, the particular forms of learning and memory that we exhibit are presumed to reflect our evolutionary history. Our most striking adaptation is the use of language to communicate concepts between individuals and across generations, so it is perhaps no surprise that one of the greatest feats of human memory is the seemingly effortless learning of language in childhood. Our memory for the symbols and grammar of language is *domain-specific*; that is, we possess evolved mental mechanisms that are specialized for learning to talk, and those mechanisms cannot easily be pressed into the service of behaviors in other domains. Researchers similarly seek adaptation-centered explanations for behaviors as diverse as altruism, religion, sensory perception, emotional expression, innovation, and cultural behaviors (Muthukrishna and Henrich, 2016; Norenzayan et al., 2016). Further, researchers are now rethinking the notion that cognitive modules are *exclusively* highly specialized, and they are broadening the evolutionary view of psychology to include the evolution of at least a few *domain-general* mechanisms, such as memory processes that can function as general-purpose "scratch pads," thus allowing flexible responses to unpredictable circumstances (Heyes, 2012).

evolutionary psychology A field devoted to asking how natural selection has shaped behavior in humans.

---

abled. The protein encoded by *ASPM* differs considerably between humans and chimps, suggesting that the sequence of this gene evolved rapidly in the ancestral line leading to humans (Evans et al., 2004). So, even moderate changes in just a few crucial genes may make a big difference.

In addition to differences in the structure of genes, researchers report that humans differ considerably from other primates in patterns of gene *expression* in the brain (Enard, Khaitovich et al., 2002; Somel et al., 2013). When gene expression in blood cells and liver cells is compared, humans and chimpanzees are more similar to each other than either species is to rhesus monkeys, as **FIGURE 6.23** shows. These relationships probably reflect the well-documented evolutionary relationships among the three species. But when gene expression is studied in the *brain*, we humans are so different from chimpanzees that, mathematically speaking, their expression pattern has more in common with that of the monkeys than with us. These observations suggest that the pattern of gene expression in the brain has changed and accelerated in the human lineage, presumably under selection pressure, since the time we shared a common ancestor with chimpanzees. No such acceleration is evident in the liver or blood.

6.23 GENETIC SIMILARITIES OF PRIMATE SPECIES VARY ACROSS DIFFERENT TISSUES Although the chimpanzee and human genomes are 98.7% identical, the *expression* of these genes differs between species and between organ systems, which may help explain some of the striking differences between the two species. In particular, there has been a 5.5-fold increase in the rate of change in expression levels of genes in the brains of humans, compared with chimpanzees. (After Enard et al., 2002.)

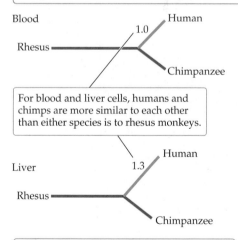

The distance between any two species indicates how different they are in the pattern of gene expression. In each case, the number is the ratio of gene expression changes in humans relative to chimpanzees.

For blood and liver cells, humans and chimps are more similar to each other than either species is to rhesus monkeys.

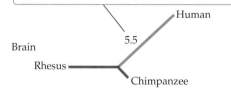

However, for gene expression in the brain, chimps and rhesus monkeys are more similar to each other than either species is to humans.

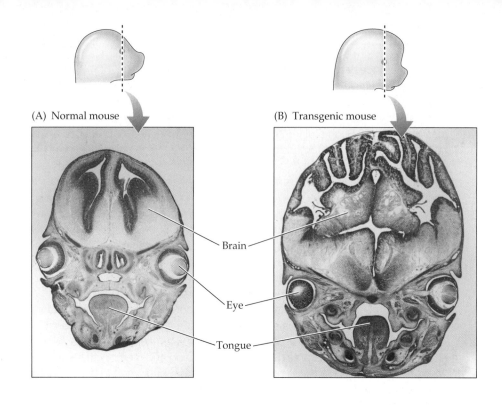

6.24 OVER YOUR HEAD Normally, mice at birth have a fairly simple cortex with no sulci or gyri (A), but increasing the expression of just one gene (that for β-catenin) in transgenic mice results in a monstrously complex, highly folded cortex (B). These animals die shortly after birth. (From Chenn and Walsh, 2002; photographs courtesy of Dr. Anjen Chenn.)

(A) Normal mouse

(B) Transgenic mouse

Brain

Eye

Tongue

Even a small change in gene expression can cause a dramatic difference in brain development (Chenn and Walsh, 2002). For example, overexpression of just one gene in mice causes so much more growth in the cortex that the normally smooth surface develops gyri and sulci (**FIGURE 6.24**). So, to answer the question we raised at the start of this chapter, the *pattern* of gene expression has a tremendous effect on the developing brain and may be what makes humans so different from chimps, despite our nearly 99% identical genomes.

Evolution Continues Today

Although some examples of evolution have occurred slowly—over millions of years, as shown by the aspects of hominin evolution illustrated in Figure 6.18—other examples occur in a matter of years or decades. These rapid instances of evolution would have surprised Darwin, who thought that natural selection required vast periods of time to be effective. In some cases, selection is driven by human behavior; this is sometimes called evolution by *artificial* selection. One obvious example is the selective breeding that farmers have employed for millennia: by deciding which individuals will reproduce, the farmer can encourage specific traits to manifest in the offspring (giving us oranges without seeds, for example, and the small and companionable wolves that we call *dogs*). Humans can also induce evolution accidentally; for example, inappropriate use of antibiotic medicines eliminates all but a very few resistant bacteria, leaving the survivors to reproduce and rapidly spread antibiotic resistance through subsequent generations (B. Holmes, 2005).

Another striking example of human-generated evolution is the case of bighorn rams in the Rocky Mountains of Alberta, Canada. The massive, curling horns of these rams make them a prized hunting trophy (**FIGURE 6.25**). Under strictly enforced laws, only mature rams with horns reaching an almost 360° curl may be hunted. In some areas of Alberta, most rams are shot within a year or two after reaching this status. As a result, selection has worked in favor of rams whose horns never reach trophy status. In fact, the average horn size has dropped by about 25% over the past 30 years (Coltman et al., 2003).

Darwin's finches continue to evolve in the Galápagos Islands. In 1973, the medium ground finch (*Geospiza fortis*) predominated on one small island, eating both large and small seeds. Then, in 1982, a breeding population of the large ground

6.25 BIGGER IS NO LONGER BETTER Because human hunters selectively shoot rams with large horns, the population of bighorn rams has changed. Males these days have smaller horns than males just a few decades ago, providing a clear example of evolution in action.

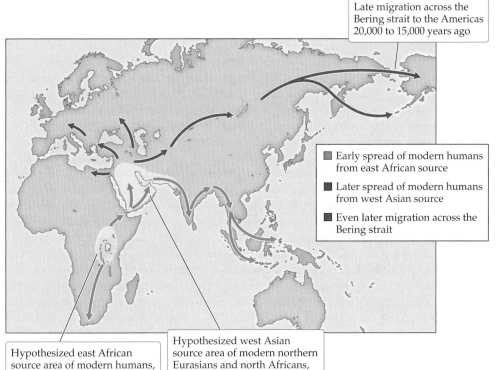

Late migration across the Bering strait to the Americas 20,000 to 15,000 years ago

■ Early spread of modern humans from east African source

■ Later spread of modern humans from west Asian source

■ Even later migration across the Bering strait

Hypothesized east African source area of modern humans, 80,000 to 60,000 years ago

Hypothesized west Asian source area of modern northern Eurasians and north Africans, 50,000 to 45,000 years ago

finch (*G. magnirostris*) became established on that island. These larger birds eat large seeds more easily than the medium ground finches can, even those with relatively large beaks. For two decades there were not enough individuals of the larger species to make much difference. But then in 2004, a drought sharply reduced the food supply. Competition for larger seeds became severe, and many of the medium ground finches with larger beaks died off. The smaller-beaked medium ground finches, however, survived and passed along the small-beaked trait to their offspring (Grant and Grant, 2006).

An economically important case of recent evolution concerns commercial fishing. In many regions, fishermen are allowed to keep only fish that are larger than a particular size. Atlantic cod off the coast of Newfoundland have been maturing at smaller sizes over several decades, probably because the largest fish are the ones being captured (E. M. Olsen et al., 2004). The remaining small fish produce fewer eggs than large fish, and this reduced egg production could help explain the collapse in the cod population.

New developments in radiocarbon dating have shown that the colonization of Europe and Asia by *Homo sapiens* was more rapid than previously believed (Mellars, 2006), occurring less than 50,000 years ago (**FIGURE 6.26**). Thus, the differences in skin color, stature, and facial traits that characterize Asian, African, and European populations evolved in less than 50,000 years in response to different climatic conditions. Human variation, then, is a reminder of both how quickly evolutionary processes can work and how very closely related we all are.

▌ The Cutting Edge

Are Humans Still Evolving?

When we study the evolution of the brain and behavior, we are looking backward through time. The human brain is the product of selection forces encountered over an extended period of time in an ancestral environment thousands of years ago. You can use your brain and muscles to drive a car, but they were optimized by natural selection for life in the African bush. Each of us is doing modern things with an ancient brain, because there hasn't been enough time for evolution to change it very much.

single-nucleotide polymorphisms (SNPs) A minor variation within a gene, or neighboring noncoding DNA, where one nucleotide has been substituted for another.

allele One of two or more different forms of a gene or genetic locus.

So what does the future hold for human evolution? Because big brains have already proven advantageous, science fiction writers sometimes imagine our distant descendants as huge-brained superhumans—but that won't happen as long as the route into the world is through Mother's narrow bipedal pelvis. And anyway, there is a more immediate issue. We are living in a world in which cultural and medical developments have radically altered two main ingredients of evolution: life span and fertility. Historical data suggest a role of natural and sexual selection in our very recent past (Courtiol et al., 2012; Milot et al., 2011), but medical science has now largely replaced natural selection in determining who dies and who gets to reproduce. So if rates of reproduction no longer reflect the genetic fitness of the parents, and all the beneficial mutations they have accumulated, are human beings evolving at all?

Many writers argue that recent changes in human brains and behavior are due to cultural evolution, the ability of humans to pass hard-won knowledge along to the next generation. Are humans also going through genetic changes as a result of recent natural selection? The answer, now that we know how to sequence the genome, appears to be a qualified yes (Sabeti et al., 2006; Stearns et al., 2010).

Recall that a gene is a stretch of DNA, made up of nucleotides, that encodes a particular protein (**FIGURE 6.27**) (also see the Appendix). To determine whether a candidate gene has been under strong natural selection pressure in the recent past, scientists look at the gene bundled together with its neighboring stretches of DNA; collectively, this is known as an individual's *haplotype*. As shown in **FIGURE 6.27A**, minor variations where one nucleotide substitutes for another can occur at certain locations within a gene (or neighboring stretch of DNA); these are called **single-nucleotide polymorphisms** (**SNPs**) (*polymorphism* means "many shapes"). Most SNPs (not all) have just two different versions, or **alleles**. Be-

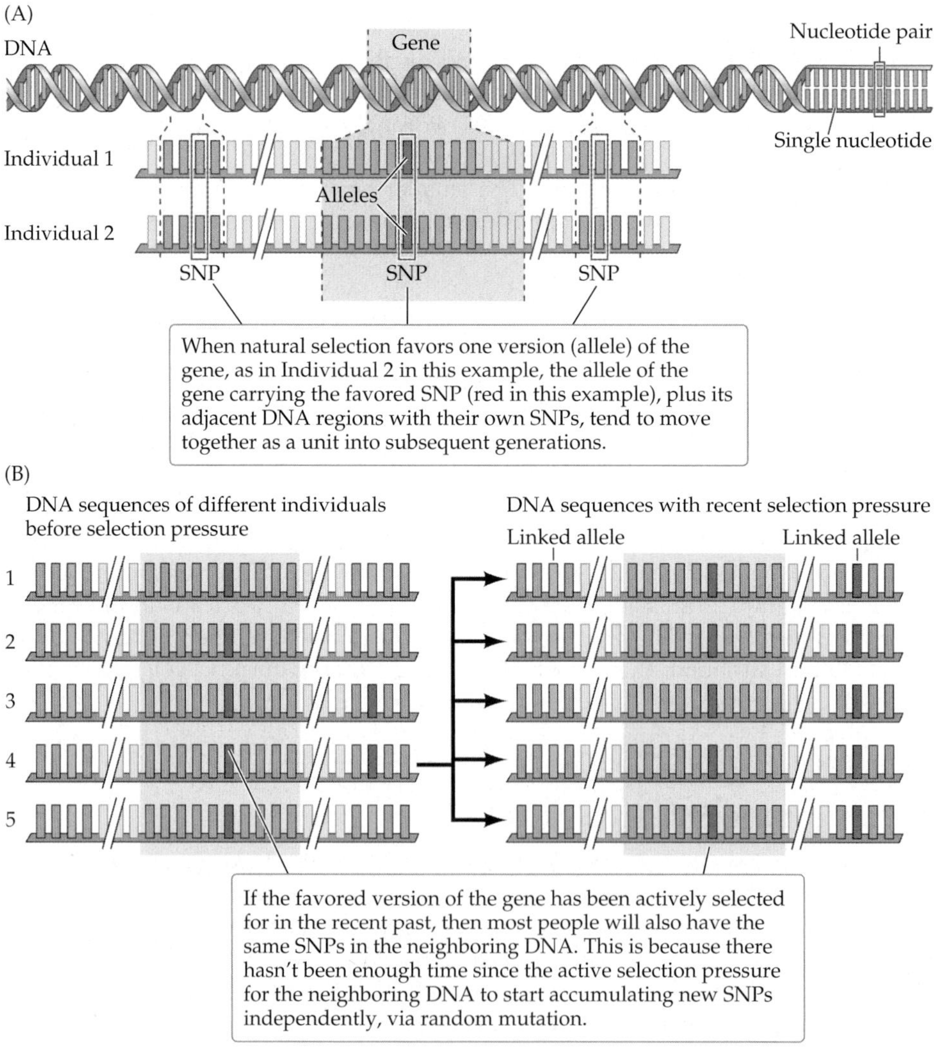

6.27 SNP VARIATION AND NATURAL SELECTION (A) Stretches of DNA that contain genes are bracketed by noncoding regions (lengths of DNA that are not part of a gene) that tend to be passed to offspring along with the gene. If the gene contains an allele that enhances reproductive success (as in Individual 2), that version of the gene (plus the bracketing DNA) will be favored in subsequent generations. (B) In the absence of selection pressure, DNA from different individuals shows a random mix of SNP alleles in the gene and surrounding DNA (left). But recent active selection pressure that favors a specific allele within the gene results in the pattern at right: the SNPs in the gene and its surrounding regions are invariant because they have recently spread from an originating individual (in this case, Individual 2 in part A).

When natural selection favors one version (allele) of the gene, as in Individual 2 in this example, the allele of the gene carrying the favored SNP (red in this example), plus its adjacent DNA regions with their own SNPs, tend to move together as a unit into subsequent generations.

If the favored version of the gene has been actively selected for in the recent past, then most people will also have the same SNPs in the neighboring DNA. This is because there hasn't been enough time since the active selection pressure for the neighboring DNA to start accumulating new SNPs independently, via random mutation.

cause SNPs result in slightly differing versions of genes, they cause variation within traits: eye color variants, susceptibility to disease, levels of enzyme function, and so on.

If one particular allele confers a slight reproductive advantage on those who possess it, it will come under natural selection pressure—it will be "selected for"—as we described earlier in the chapter. Genes thus selected for will gradually spread throughout subsequent generations, until most people possess the same allele. But simply sequencing a gene in a sample of people doesn't reveal whether the gene has been subject to *recent* evolutionary pressure. That additional information comes from looking at SNPs in the DNA that brackets the gene under study. Because these neighboring stretches of DNA tend to "tag along" with genes during the recombination processes of reproduction, geneticists can ask whether the adjacent SNPs show independent variation or whether they appear to be locked to the SNP allele in the gene being studied (**FIGURE 6.27B**). Genes that have been subject to recent natural selection show reduced variation in these adjacent SNPs, as shown in the figure. **TABLE 6.1** provides a sample of genes (and their functions) that show evidence of recent natural selection in humans (Balter, 2005; Kamm et al., 2013).

TABLE 6.1 Examples of Human Genes Subject to Recent Selection Pressure

GENE	BENEFIT OR SELECTION PRESSURE
AGT, CYP3A	Protection against hypertension 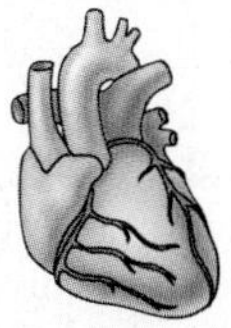
ASPM, NPAS3	Brain development 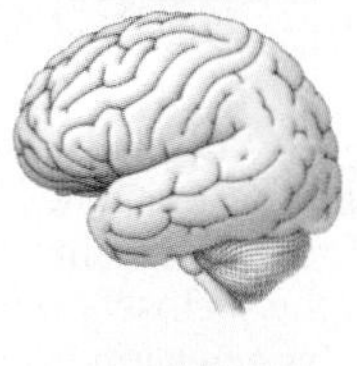
DRD4, MAOA	Cognition and behavior
FOXP2	Language
TAS2R38	Bitter taste perception
CCR5	Protection against smallpox and AIDS 
G6PD, Duffy blood group, HBC (hemoglobin C), TNFSF5	Protection against malaria
Lactase	Improved nutrition from milk 

Of course, not all changes in recent humans are evolutionary, or even genetic. The increased stature of modern humans, for example, has more to do with good nutrition and medical advances than changes in any genes—another form of cultural evolution. And some responses to environmental pressures involve epigenetic modifications of gene expression (see Figure 7.20). For example, early stress produces lasting changes in the expression of genes encoding stress hormone receptors (see Chapter 15). Perhaps the question, Are we still evolving? should be rephrased as, Do we all make equal contributions to the next generations? As long as we don't, and there is a systematic reason, evolution is occurring. Sadly, in the underdeveloped parts of the world, disease and poverty still exert tremendous selection pressure, and new environmental challenges like global warming and infectious diseases like HIV, malaria, and Zika virus may continue to mold our genome.

Recommended Reading

Alcock, J. A. (2013). *Animal Behavior: An Evolutionary Approach* (10th ed.). Sunderland, MA: Sinauer.

Bazzett, T. J. (2008). *An Introduction to Behavior Genetics.* Sunderland, MA: Sinauer.

Darwin, C. R. (1859). *On the Origin of Species by Means of Natural Selection.* London: John Murray. (Note: This classic book, long out of copyright, can be obtained as a free e-book from various Internet sources, including Amazon.com.)

De Waal, F. (2016). *Are We Smart Enough to Know How Smart Animals Are?* New York: Norton.

Futuyma, D. J. (2013). *Evolution* (3rd ed.). Sunderland, MA: Sinauer.

Gray, P. B., and Garcia, J. R. (2013). *Evolution and Human Sexual Behavior.* Cambridge, MA: Harvard University Press.

Shubin, N. (2009). *Your Inner Fish: A Journey into the 3.5-Billion-Year History of the Human Body.* New York: Vintage.

Striedter, G. P. (2005). *Principles of Brain Evolution.* Sunderland, MA: Sinauer.

Understanding Evolution, http://evolution.berkeley.edu.

Go to
bn8e.com
for study questions, quizzes, activities, and other resources

VISUAL SUMMARY

You should be able to relate each summary to the adjacent illustration, including structures and processes.
Go to **bn8e.com/vs6** for links to figures, animations, and activities that will help you consolidate the material.

1 Some species feature similar structures and functions due to shared ancestry; in other cases the similarity is the result of **convergent evolution**. Review **Figure 6.1**

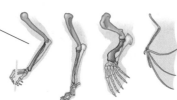

2 Darwin's theory of **evolution by natural selection** posits that individuals with adaptive traits produce more offspring, so species evolve over time. This process of natural selection favors newly arisen **genes** (**mutations**) that confer adaptive traits, including behavioral traits. By these gradual changes, all animal species arose from a common ancestor. Review **Figure 6.2**

3 Studies of the classification of animals help determine how closely related different **species** are. Knowing this relationship, in turn, helps us interpret similarities and differences in the behavior and structure of different species. Review **Figures 6.3 and 6.4**, **Activity 6.1**

4 Comparative studies help us understand the evolution of the nervous system, including the human brain. They also provide a perspective for understanding species-typical behavioral **adaptations**. Review **Box 6.2**

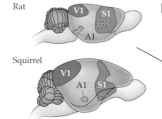

5 The nervous systems of invertebrate animals range in complexity from a simple nerve net to the complex structures of mollusks. The nervous systems of certain invertebrates may provide a simplified model for understanding some aspects of vertebrate nervous systems. Review **Figure 6.8**, **Activity 6.2**

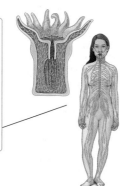

6 Differences in the size and organization of specific brain regions are sometimes related to distinctive forms of behavioral adaptation in different species. Review **Figure 6.9**

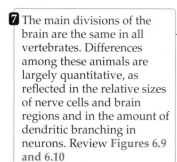

7 The main divisions of the brain are the same in all vertebrates. Differences among these animals are largely quantitative, as reflected in the relative sizes of nerve cells and brain regions and in the amount of dendritic branching in neurons. Review **Figures 6.9 and 6.10**

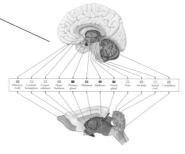

8 Fossil **endocasts** of brains from extinct species indicate that the main result of mammalian evolution has been larger overall brain size. The brain size of a species must be interpreted in terms of body size. As a rough rule of thumb, vertebrate brain weight is proportional to body weight to the 0.69 power. Review **Figure 6.13**

9 Some animals have larger brains and some have smaller brains than the general relation between brain and body weights predicts; that is, they differ in **encephalization factor**. Humans, in particular, have larger brains than their body size would predict. Review **Figure 6.13**

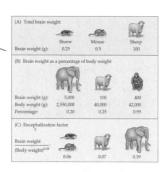

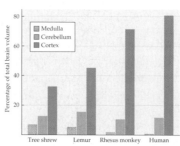

10 Primates have an especially large **cortex** relative to overall brain size. This relative enlargement of the cortex appears to have evolved because the later stages of brain development are prolonged, resulting in a disproportionally large cortex. Review **Figures 6.16 and 6.17**

11 Several factors, including tool use, innovation, and social relationships, are thought to have driven enlargement of the primate cortex. Review **Figures 6.18 and 6.19**

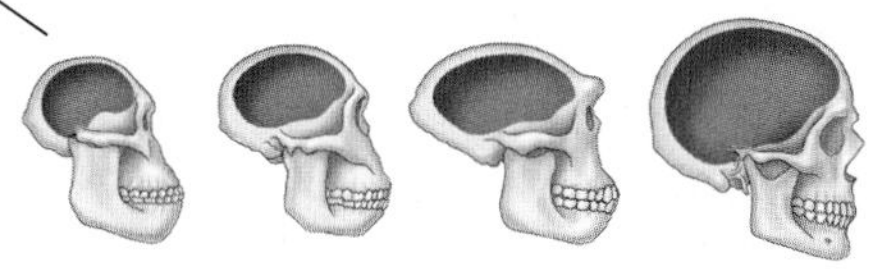

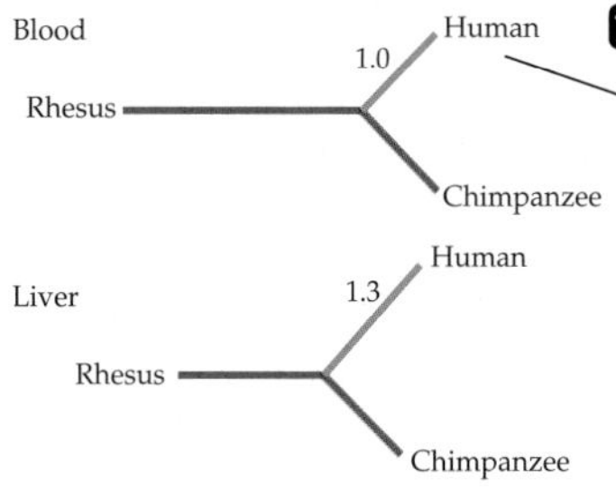

12 Humans more closely resemble their nearest relatives, the chimpanzees, in the blood and liver than in the brain. Review **Figure 6.23**

Blood

Rhesus

Human

1.0

Chimpanzee

Liver

Rhesus

Human

1.3

Chimpanzee

13 Analysis of patterns of reproduction as well as genetic studies of the frequencies of **single-nucleotide polymorphisms** (**SNPs**) in specific chromosomal loci indicate that, while cultural influences have an important impact, evolution through natural selection continues in humans to this day. Review **Figure 6.27 and Table 6.1**

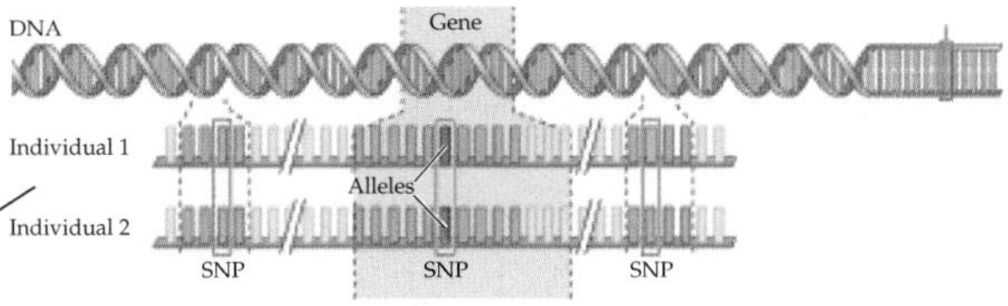

DNA

Gene

Individual 1

Individual 2

Alleles

SNP

SNP

SNP

Life-Span Development of the Brain and Behavior

▌ Overcoming Blindness

As a 3-year-old, Michael May was injured by a chemical explosion that destroyed his left eye and damaged the surface of his right eye so badly that he was blind. He could tell whether it was day or night, but otherwise he couldn't see anything. An early attempt to restore his sight with corneal transplants failed, but Michael seemed undaunted. He learned to play Ping-Pong using his hearing alone (but only on the table at his parents' house, where he learned to interpret the sound cues). Michael also enjoyed riding a bicycle, but his parents made him stop after he crashed his brother's and his sister's bikes.

As an adult, Michael became a champion skier, marrying his instructor and raising two sons. He also started his own company, making equipment to help blind people navigate on their own. Then, when Michael was 46, technical advances made it possible to restore vision in his right eye. As soon as the bandages were removed, he could see his wife's blue eyes and blond hair. But even years later, he could not recognize her face unless she spoke to him, or recognize three-dimensional objects like cubes or spheres unless they were moving. Michael could still ski, but he found that he had to close his eyes to avoid falling over. On the slopes, seeing was more distracting than helpful.

The doctors could tell that images were focusing properly on Michael's retina, so why was his vision so poor?

Age puts its stamp on us all. Although the changes are especially rapid early in life, change is a feature of the entire life span. In this chapter we describe brains in terms of their progress through life from the womb to the tomb. The fertilization of an egg leads to a body with a brain that contains billions of neurons with an incredible number of connections. The pace of this process is extraordinary: during the height of prenatal growth of the human brain, more than 250,000 neurons are added per minute! This chapter describes the emergence of nerve cells, the formation of their connections, and the role of genes in shaping the nervous system. But we show that experience, gained through behavioral interactions with the environment, also sculpts the developing brain.

Picture, if you can, the number of neurons in the mature human brain—over 80 billion (Herculano-Houzel, 2012). There are many types of neurons, and most are connected to many other neurons, forming vast networks. Indeed, there are more than 100 trillion synaptic connections in the brain. Yet each of us began as a single microscopic cell, the fertilized egg. How can one cell divide and grow to form one of the most complicated machines on Earth, perhaps in the universe? Of course, some vital information was packed in the genes of that single cell, but we'll see that the developing nervous system also relies on the environment and experience to guide the construction of this fabulous gadget between our ears.

Go to Brain Explorer
bn8e.com/7.1

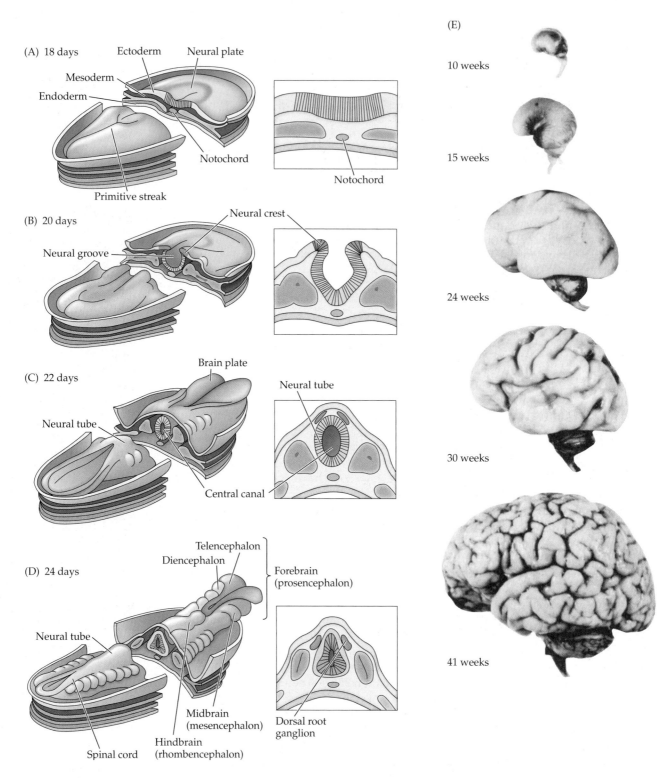

(A) 18 days

Ectoderm · Neural plate · Mesoderm · Endoderm · Notochord · Primitive streak · Notochord

(B) 20 days

Neural crest · Neural groove

(C) 22 days

Brain plate · Neural tube · Neural tube · Central canal

(D) 24 days

Telencephalon · Diencephalon · Forebrain (prosencephalon) · Neural tube · Midbrain (mesencephalon) · Dorsal root ganglion · Hindbrain (rhombencephalon) · Spinal cord

(E)

10 weeks · 15 weeks · 24 weeks · 30 weeks · 41 weeks

Go to Video 7.2
Early Nervous System Development
bn8e.com/7.2

Go to Video 7.3
Brain Development
bn8e.com/7.3

7.1 DEVELOPMENT OF THE NERVOUS SYSTEM IN THE HUMAN EMBRYO AND FETUS (A) At 18 days the embryo has begun to implant in the uterine wall and consists of three layers of cells: endoderm, mesoderm, and ectoderm. A thickening of the ectoderm leads to development of the neural plate (insets). (B) At 20 days the neural groove begins to develop. (C) At 22 days the neural groove has closed to form the neural tube, with the rudimentary beginning of the brain at the anterior end. (D) A few days later, three major divisions of the brain—forebrain (prosencephalon, consisting of the telencephalon and diencephalon), midbrain (mesencephalon), and hindbrain (rhombencephalon)—are discernible. (E) In these lateral views of the human brain (shown at one-third size) at several stages of fetal development, note the gradual emergence of gyri and sulci. (Part E from Larroche, 1977.)

Growth and Development of the Brain Are Orderly Processes

The fertilized egg, or **zygote**, has 46 chromosomes—23 from each parent—which contain genetic recipes for the development of a new individual. (A summary of the life cycle of cells, including a discussion of the basic genetic materials and how they direct cell activities, is provided in the Appendix.) Within 12 hours after fertilization, the single cell begins dividing, so after 3 days it has become a small mass of homogeneous cells, like a cluster of grapes, a mere 200 micrometers (μm) in diameter.

Within a week the emerging embryo shows three distinct cell layers (**FIGURE 7.1A**) that are the beginnings of all tissues. The nervous system develops from the outer layer, called the **ectoderm** (from the Greek *ektos*, "out," and *derma*, "skin"). As the cell layers thicken, they grow into a flat oval plate. Uneven rates of cell division at the head end form the **neural groove**, which will become the midline (**FIGURE 7.1B**).

The pace of events then quickens. The ridges of the groove come together to form the **neural tube** (**FIGURE 7.1C**). At the head end of the neural tube, three subdivisions become apparent. These subdivisions correspond to the future **forebrain** (*prosencephalon*, consisting of the *telencephalon* and *diencephalon*), **midbrain** (*mesencephalon*), and **hindbrain** (*rhombencephalon*, consisting of the *metencephalon* and *myelencephalon*) (**FIGURE 7.1D**), which were discussed in Chapter 2 (see Figure 2.14). The interior of the neural tube becomes the fluid-filled cerebral ventricles of the brain, the central canal of the spinal cord, and the passages that connect them.

By the end of the eighth week, the human embryo shows the rudimentary beginnings of most body organs. The rapid development of the brain is reflected in the fact that by this time the head is half the total size of the embryo. (Note that the developing human is called an **embryo** during the first 10 weeks after fertilization; thereafter it is called a **fetus**.) **FIGURE 7.1E** shows the prenatal development of the human brain from weeks 10–41. Even after this period, there are dramatic local changes as some brain regions mature more than others, well into the teenage years, as we'll see later.

Development of the Nervous System Can Be Divided into Six Distinct Stages

It is useful to consider brain development as a sequence of distinct cellular stages:

1. *Neurogenesis,* the mitotic division of nonneuronal cells to produce neurons
2. *Cell migration,* the movements of cells to establish distinct nerve cell populations (brain nuclei, layers of the cerebral cortex, and so on)
3. *Differentiation,* the transformation of precursor cells into distinctive types of neurons and glial cells
4. *Synaptogenesis,* the establishment of synaptic connections, as axons and dendrites grow
5. *Neuronal cell death,* the selective death of many nerve cells
6. *Synapse rearrangement,* the loss of some synapses and development of others, to refine synaptic connections

The six stages, which we will take up in order, are depicted in **FIGURE 7.2** on the next page.

Cell proliferation produces cells that become neurons or glial cells

The production of nerve cells is called **neurogenesis**. Nerve cells themselves do not divide, but the cells that will give rise to neurons begin as a single layer of cells along the inner surface of the neural tube. These cells divide, in a process called **mitosis**, and gradually form a closely packed layer of cells called the **ventricular zone**. All neurons and glial cells are derived from cells that originate from this ventricular mitosis. Eventually, some cells leave the ventricular zone and begin transforming into either neurons or glial cells.

zygote The fertilized egg.

ectoderm The outer cellular layer of the developing embryo, giving rise to the skin and the nervous system.

neural groove In the developing embryo, the groove between the neural folds.

neural tube An embryonic structure with subdivisions that correspond to the future forebrain, midbrain, and hindbrain.

forebrain Also called *prosencephalon*. The anterior division of the brain, containing the cerebral hemispheres, the thalamus, and the hypothalamus.

midbrain Also called *mesencephalon*. The middle division of the brain.

hindbrain Also called *rhombencephalon*. The rear division of the brain, which, in the mature vertebrate, contains the cerebellum, pons, and medulla.

embryo The earliest stage in a developing animal.

fetus A developing individual after the embryo stage.

neurogenesis The mitotic division of nonneuronal cells to produce neurons.

mitosis The process of division of somatic cells that involves duplication of DNA.

ventricular zone Also called *ependymal layer*. A region lining the cerebral ventricles that displays mitosis, providing neurons early in development and glial cells throughout life.

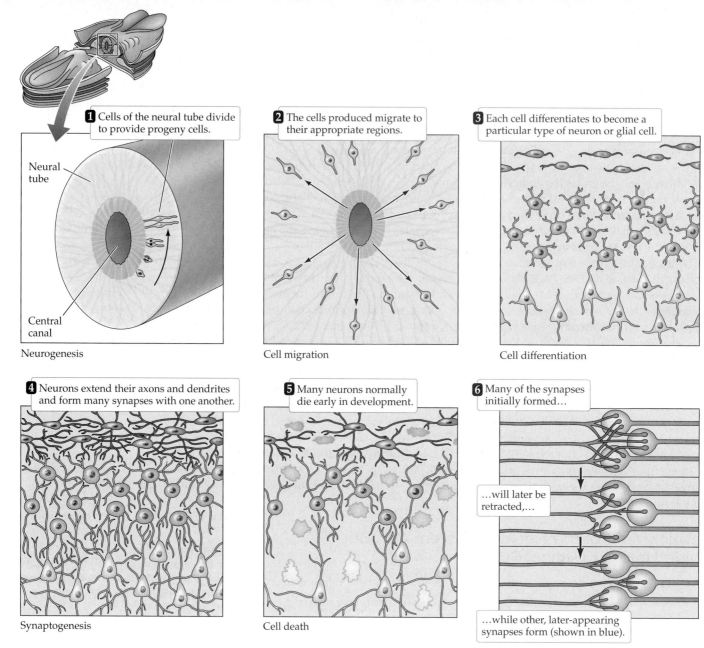

1 Cells of the neural tube divide to provide progeny cells.

Neural tube

Central canal

Neurogenesis

2 The cells produced migrate to their appropriate regions.

Cell migration

3 Each cell differentiates to become a particular type of neuron or glial cell.

Cell differentiation

4 Neurons extend their axons and dendrites and form many synapses with one another.

Synaptogenesis

5 Many neurons normally die early in development.

Cell death

6 Many of the synapses initially formed…

…will later be retracted,…

…while other, later-appearing synapses form (shown in blue).

Synapse rearrangement

7.2 SIX STAGES OF NEURAL DEVELOPMENT

Go to Animation 7.4
Stages of Neuronal Development
bn8e.com/7.4

Each part of an animal's brain has a species-characteristic "birth date." That is, there is an orderly chronological program for brain development, and we know on approximately which days of embryonic development the precursor cells of each group of neurons will stop dividing. Of course, given the complexity of vertebrate brains, it is impossible to trace the development of individual cells from the initial small population of ancestral ventricular cells (**FIGURE 7.3**). Descendants disappear in the crowd. But in some simpler invertebrate nervous systems that have very few neurons, mitotic lineages can be traced more easily and completely.

A favorite animal of researchers who study the lineage of nerve cells is the nematode *Caenorhabditis elegans*, a tiny worm with fewer than 1000 cells, precisely 302 of which are neurons. Because the body of *C. elegans* is almost transparent (**FIGURE 7.4A**), researchers have been able to trace the origin of each neuron (Pines, 1992). By observing successive cell divisions of a *C. elegans* zygote, investigators can exactly predict the fate of each cell in the adult—whether it will be a sensory neuron, muscle cell, skin cell, or other type of cell—on the basis of its mitotic "ancestors" (**FIGURE 7.4B**).

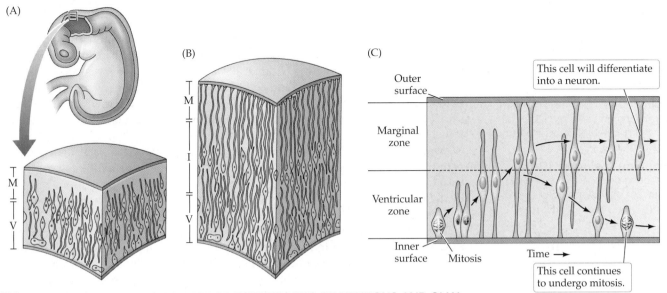

7.3 THE PROLIFERATION OF CELLULAR PRECURSORS OF NEURONS AND GLIAL CELLS (A) In this small section of the wall of the neural tube at an early stage of embryonic development, only ventricular (V) and marginal (M) layers are visible. (B) Later an intermediate (I) layer develops as the wall thickens. (C) Nuclei (within their cells) migrate from the ventricular layer to the outer layers. Some cells then become neurons while others return to the ventricular zone to divide again.

Whereas cell fate in *C. elegans* is a highly predetermined and unvarying result of mitotic lineage, in vertebrates the paths that cells take to form the completed nervous system are more complex. In most other species, and in all vertebrates, the paths of development include more-local regulatory mechanisms. The hallmark of vertebrate development is that cells sort themselves out via **cell-cell interactions**, taking on fates that are appropriate in the context of what neighboring cells are doing. Thus, vertebrate development is less hardwired and more susceptible to being shaped by environmental signals and, as we'll see, experience.

cell-cell interactions The general process during development in which one cell affects the differentiation of other, usually neighboring, cells.

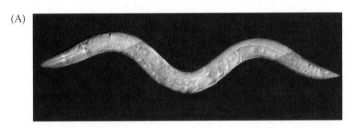

7.4 CELL FATE IN A SIMPLE ORGANISM (A) This photomicrograph shows the transparent body of *Caenorhabditis elegans*. (B) In this mitotic lineage of cells that give rise to the body of the adult *C. elegans*, nervous system cells are highlighted in blue. The structure and function of every cell can be predicted from its mitotic lineage. Such mitotic determination of cell differentiation does not seem important to the development of vertebrates or more complex invertebrates like fruit flies. (Part A courtesy of Drs. Paola Dal Santo and Erik M. Jorgensen; B after Pines, 1992.)

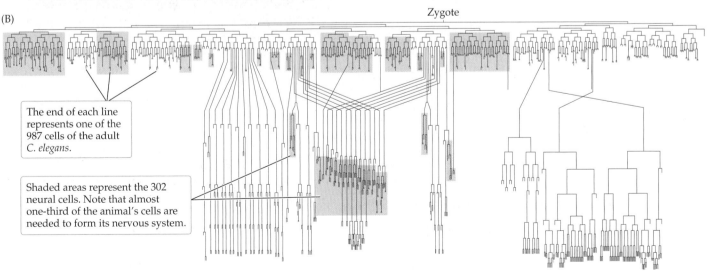

The end of each line represents one of the 987 cells of the adult *C. elegans*.

Shaded areas represent the 302 neural cells. Note that almost one-third of the animal's cells are needed to form its nervous system.

adult neurogenesis The creation of new neurons in the brain of an adult.

cell migration The movement of cells from site of origin to final location.

radial glial cells Glial cells that form early in development, spanning the width of the emerging cerebral hemispheres, and guide migrating neurons.

cell adhesion molecule (CAM) A protein found on the surface of a cell that guides cell migration and/or axonal pathfinding.

Go to Video 7.5
Cell Migration
bn8e.com/7.5

At birth, mammals have already produced most of the neurons they will ever have. The postnatal increase of human brain weight is primarily due to growth in the size of neurons, branching of dendrites, elaboration of synapses (as we'll see in Figure 7.6), increase in myelin, and addition of glial cells. But early reports that new neurons are added just after birth in some brain regions (Altman, 1969) have been supplemented with findings of **adult neurogenesis**, the generation of new neurons in adulthood, in humans (Eriksson et al., 1998) and other animals (E. Gould, Reeves, et al., 1999; Shingo et al., 2003). Adult neurogenesis is particularly prominent in the dentate gyrus of the hippocampal formation, where it's been estimated we add 1400 new neurons per day (Spalding et al., 2013), replacing neurons that have died. Likewise, nerve cells of the olfactory organ (which we use to detect odors) are replaced throughout life (Sawamoto et al., 2006).

While the new neurons acquired in adulthood represent a tiny minority of neurons, there's reason to think they are important. Enriched experience, such as learning, increases the rate of neurogenesis in adult mammals (Opendak and Gould, 2015). So by studying this chapter, you may be giving your brain a few more neurons to use on exam day! Physical exercise also boosts neurogenesis, at least in rats—an effect that can be blocked by stresses such as social isolation (Stranahan et al., 2006)—so invest in exercise and a network of friends too.

New nerve cells migrate

Neurons in the developing nervous system are always on the move. At some stage the cells that form in the ventricular layer through mitotic division move away, in a process known as **cell migration**. In primates, by the time of birth almost all future neurons have completed their migration; but in rats, cells that will become neurons continue to migrate in some regions for several weeks after birth.

Cells do not move in an aimless, haphazard manner. Cells in the developing brain move along the surface of a particular type of glial cell (Rakic, 1985). Like spokes (radii) of a wheel, these **radial glial cells** extend from the inner to the outer surfaces of the emerging nervous system (**FIGURE 7.5**). The radial glial cells act as a series of guides, and the newly formed cells mostly creep along them, as if "riding the glial monorail." Some migrating cells move in a direction perpendicular to the radial glial cells (Parnavelas et al., 2000), like Tarzan swinging from vine to vine; others move in a rostral stream to supply the olfactory bulbs (Eom et al., 2010).

The migration of cells and the outgrowth of nerve cell extensions (dendrites and axons) involve various chemicals that promote the adhesion of developing elements of the nervous system. These **cell adhesion molecules (CAMs)** guide migrating cells and growing axons (McKeown et al., 2013). Genetic abnormalities in CAMs can disrupt cell migration, resulting in either a vastly reduced population of neurons or a disorderly arrangement and, not surprisingly, behavior disorders. CAMs may also guide axons to regenerate when they are cut in adulthood (**BOX 7.1**).

The single-file migration of nerve cell precursors (see Figure 7.5A) is followed by the aggregation of cells into the brain nuclei we discussed in Chapter 2. For example, cells of the cerebral cortex arrive in waves during fetal development, each successive wave forming a new outer layer, until the six layers of the adult cortex are formed, with the latest arrivals on the outside.

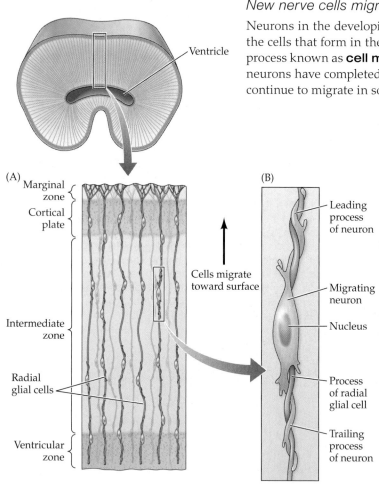

Ventricle

(A) Marginal zone
Cortical plate
Intermediate zone
Radial glial cells
Ventricular zone

Cells migrate toward surface

(B)
Leading process of neuron
Migrating neuron
Nucleus
Process of radial glial cell
Trailing process of neuron

7.5 GLIAL SPOKES GUIDE MIGRATING CELLS Early in development, radial glial cells span the width of the emerging cerebral hemispheres. (A) This enlargement shows how radial glial cells act as guide wires for the migration of neurons. New cells shinny past established neurons to become neurons in successively higher (outer) layers of the cortex. (B) Further enlargement shows a single neuron migrating out along a radial glial fiber. (After Cowan, 1979, based on Rakic, 1971.)

Degeneration and Regeneration of Nervous Tissue

BOX 7.1

When a mature nerve cell is injured, it can regrow in several ways. Complete replacement of injured nerve cells is rare in mammals, but Figures A and B illustrate characteristic forms of degeneration and regeneration in the mammalian peripheral and central nervous systems. Injury close to the cell body of a neuron produces a series of changes resulting in the eventual destruction of the cell; this process is called **retrograde degeneration** (Figure A, 2 and 3). If the injured neuron dies, the target cells formerly innervated by that neuron may show signs of *transneuronal degeneration* (Figure A, 4).

Cutting through the axon also produces loss of the distal part of the axon (the part that is separated from the cell body). This process is called **anterograde degeneration** (Figure B, 2 and 3). The part of the axon that remains connected to the cell body may regrow. Severed axons in the peripheral nervous system regrow readily. Sprouts emerge from the part of the axon that is still connected to the nerve cell body and advance slowly toward the periphery (Figure B, 4). Cell adhesion molecules (CAMs) help guide the regenerating axons. Some fishes and amphibians have an enviable advantage over humans: after an injury to the brain, they can regenerate many of the lost connections. In these cases, CAMs appear to guide the regeneration.

One interesting thing about regeneration of the nervous system is that it involves processes that seem similar to those that take place during an organism's original development. Studying regeneration, then, may increase our understanding of the original processes of growth of the nervous system, and vice versa. From a therapeutic viewpoint, these studies may help scientists learn how to repair and regrow damaged tissue in human brains.

retrograde degeneration
Destruction of the nerve cell body following injury to its axon.

anterograde degeneration   Also called *Wallerian degeneration*. The loss of the distal portion of an axon resulting from injury to the axon.

(A) Retrograde degeneration

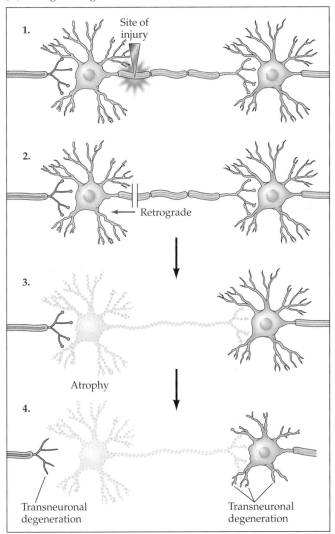

(B) Anterograde degeneration

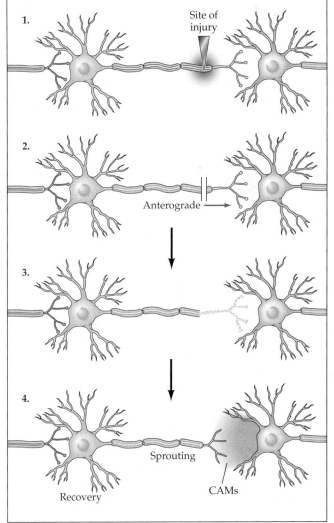

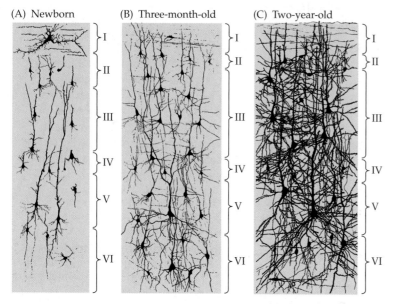

(A) Newborn   (B) Three-month-old   (C) Two-year-old

7.6 CEREBRAL CORTEX TISSUE IN THE EARLY DEVELOPMENT OF HUMANS These representations of cerebral cortex show the extent of neural connections and neuronal differentiation at birth (A), at 3 months of age (B), and at 2 years of age (C). Numerals refer to the six cortical layers. (From Conel, 1939, 1947, 1959.)

Cells in newly formed brain regions differentiate into neurons

Newly arrived cells in the brain bear no more resemblance to mature nerve cells than to the cells of other organs. Once they reach their destinations, however, the cells begin to use, or **express**, particular genes. This means that the cell transcribes a particular subset of genes to make the specific proteins it needs. This process of **cell differentiation** shapes the cell into the distinctive forms and functions of neurons found in that particular region (**FIGURE 7.6**).

What controls differentiation is not completely understood, but two classes of influence are known. First, intrinsic self-organization is an important factor; for example, cerebellar Purkinje cells develop a very specific dendritic tree even **in vitro** (in a glass dish) (Seil et al., 1974). When a cell shows characteristics that are independent of neighboring cells, we say that it is acting in a **cell-autonomous** manner. In cell-autonomous differentiation, presumably only the genes within that cell are directing events.

However, the local environment also greatly influences nerve cell differentiation. In other words, neighboring cells are a second major influence on the differentiation of neurons. In vertebrates (unlike the nematode *C. elegans*), young neural cells seem to have the capacity to become many varieties of neurons, and the particular type of neuron that a cell becomes depends on where it happens to be and what its neighboring cells are. For example, consider spinal motor neurons—cells in the spinal cord that send their axons out to control muscles. Motor neurons are large, multipolar cells found in the left and right sides of the spinal cord in the ventral horn of gray matter. Motor neurons are among the first recognizable neurons in the spinal cord, and they send their axons out early in fetal development. How do these cells "know" they should express motor neuron–specific genes and differentiate into motor neurons?

Examination of the late divisions giving rise to motor neurons makes it clear that the cells are not attending to mitotic lineage (Leber et al., 1990). Instead, some spinal cells are directed to become motor neurons under the influence of other cells lying just ventral to the developing spinal cord—in the **notochord**, a rodlike structure that forms along the midline (see Figure 7.1A) (Miri et al., 2013). The notochord releases a protein (playfully named Sonic hedgehog) that diffuses to the spinal cord and directs some (but not all) cells to become motor neurons (**FIGURE 7.7**).

The influence of one set of cells on the fate of neighboring cells is known as **induction**; the notochord releases a protein that induces some spinal cord cells to differentiate into motor neurons. Induction of this sort has been demonstrated many times in the developing vertebrate body and brain. This is an example of the extensive cell-cell interaction in developing vertebrates, each cell taking cues from its neighbors.

Because each cell influences the differentiation of others, vertebrate neural development is very complex, but also very flexible. For example, cells differentiate into the type of neuron that is appropriate for wherever they happen to be in the brain; thus, cell-cell interaction coordinates development—directing differentiation to provide the right type of neuron for each part of the brain. Another benefit of cell-cell interactions in development is that if a few cells are injured or lost, other cells will "answer the call"—that is, respond to the inducing factors—and fill in for the missing cells.

This phenomenon can be observed in embryos from which some cells have been removed. For example, if cells are removed early enough from a developing limb bud in a chick embryo, other cells pitch in, and by the time the chick hatches, the limb looks nor-

expression The process by which a cell makes an mRNA transcript of a particular gene.

cell differentiation The developmental stage in which cells acquire distinctive characteristics, such as those of neurons, as the result of expressing particular genes.

in vitro Literally "in glass" (in Latin). Outside the body, usually in a laboratory dish.

cell-autonomous Referring to cell processes that are directed by the cell itself rather than being under the influence of other cells.

notochord A midline structure arising early in the embryonic development of vertebrates.

induction The process by which one set of cells influences the fate of neighboring cells, usually by secreting a chemical factor that changes gene expression in the target cells.

regulation An adaptive response to early injury, as when developing individual cells compensate for missing or injured cells.

stem cell A cell that is undifferentiated and therefore can take on the fate of any cell that a donor organism can produce.

7.7 THE INDUCTION OF SPINAL MOTOR NEURONS In this cross section of embryonic chick spinal cord, the notochord (green circle at bottom) lies just beneath the spinal cord and secretes the protein Sonic hedgehog. A moderate concentration of this protein in the ventral spinal cord induces the cells there to develop as motor neurons (gold), forming columns of motor neurons on the left and right sides. Another protein (blue) is expressed only in the dorsal spinal cord. (Courtesy of Dr. Thomas Jessell.)

mal, with no parts missing. Embryologists refer to such adaptive responses to early injury as **regulation** (or *self-regulation*): the developing animal compensates for missing or injured cells. Because cell fate is so tightly coupled with mitotic lineage in *C. elegans*, this organism shows little or no regulation. If a cell in *C. elegans* is killed (with a laser through the microscope), no other cells take its place; the worm must do without that cell.

The more complicated vertebrate system, in which cells take cues from their neighbors to guide their gene expression and functional fate, has another consequence: if cells that have not yet differentiated extensively can be obtained and placed into a particular brain region, they will differentiate in an appropriate way and become properly integrated. Such undifferentiated cells, called **stem cells**, are present throughout embryonic tissues, so they can be gathered from umbilical cord blood, miscarried embryos, or unused embryos produced during in vitro fertilization.

It may be possible to take cells from adult tissue and, by treating them with various factors in a dish, transform them into neurons (Vierbuchen et al., 2010) or into "adult" stem cells (Palmer et al., 2001). Researchers hope that, someday, placing stem cells in areas of brain degeneration—loss of myelination in multiple sclerosis or loss of dopaminergic neurons in Parkinson's disease (see Chapter 11)—might reverse such degeneration as the implanted cells differentiate to fill in for the missing components.

The axons and dendrites of young neurons grow extensively and form synapses

The biggest change in brain cells early in life is the extensive growth of axons and dendrites (termed *process outgrowth*) and the proliferation of synapses, or **synaptogenesis**. At the tips of axons and dendrites alike, specialized swellings called **growth cones** are found. Very fine extensions, called **filopodia** (singular *filopodium*, from the Latin *filum*, "thread," and the Greek *pod*, "foot"), extend from the growth cone (**FIGURE 7.8**). Just as migrating cells are guided by CAMs, the filopodia of growth cones adhere to CAMs in the extracellular environment and then contract to pull the growth cone in a particular direction (the growing axon or dendrite trail-

synaptogenesis The establishment of synaptic connections as axons and dendrites grow.

growth cone The growing tip of an axon or a dendrite.

filopodia Very fine, tubular outgrowths from the growth cone.

(A)

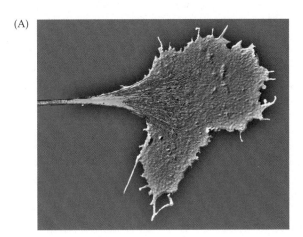

(B)

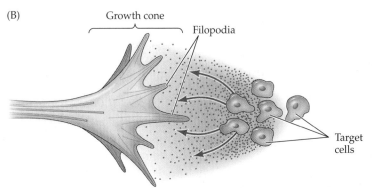

7.8 THE GROWTH CONES OF GROWING AXONS AND DENDRITES (A) The fine, threadlike extensions pictured here are filopodia, which find adhesive surfaces and pull the growth cone, and therefore the growing axon, to the right. (B) Target cells release a chemical that creates a gradient (dots) around them. Growth cones orient to and follow the gradient to the cells. (Part A courtesy of Dr. Paul Bridgman; B after Tessier-Lavigne et al., 1988.)

Go to Video 7.6
Growth Cones
bn8e.com/7.6

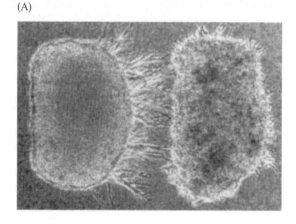

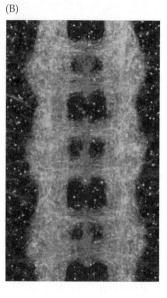

7.9 THE GROWTH CONES OF GROWING AXONS AND DENDRITES (A) The extensions visible here are growing out of a sensory ganglion (left) toward their normal target tissue. (B) The chemorepellent protein Slit (red), shown here in an embryo of the fruit fly *Drosophila*, repels most axons (green), preventing them from crossing the midline. (Part A courtesy of Dr. Marc Tessier-Lavigne; B courtesy of Drs. Julie Simpson and Corey S. Goodman.)

chemoattractants Compounds that attract particular classes of axonal growth cones.

chemorepellents Compounds that repel particular classes of axonal growth cones.

cell death Also called *apoptosis*. The developmental process during which "surplus" cells die.

death gene A gene that is expressed only when a cell becomes committed to natural cell death (apoptosis).

caspases A family of proteins that regulate cell death (apoptosis).

Diablo A protein released by mitochondria, in response to high calcium levels, that activates apoptosis.

inhibitors of apoptosis proteins (IAPs) A family of proteins that inhibit caspases and thereby stave off apoptosis.

ing behind). Dendritic growth cones are found in adults, mediating the continued elongation and change in dendrites that occurs throughout life in response to experience (see Chapter 17).

What guides axons along the paths they take? The CAMs guiding growth cones are released by the target nerve cells or other tissues, such as muscles. The axon growth cone responds to the concentration gradients of these chemicals that provide directional guidance, as illustrated in **FIGURE 7.9**. Chemical signals that attract certain growth cones are called **chemoattractants**; chemicals that repel growth cones are **chemorepellents** (McKeown et al., 2013). For example, because it is important for some axons to remain on one side of the body and for others to cross over, the protein Slit repels some axons to prevent them from crossing the midline (see Figure 7.9B) (Dickson and Gilestro, 2006). The same secreted protein may act as a chemoattractant to some growth cones and a chemorepellent to others (Polleux et al., 2000).

Synapses can form quickly on dendrites and dendritic spines, which proliferate rapidly after birth (see Figure 7.6). These connections can be affected by postnatal experience, as we will see later in this chapter. To support the metabolic needs of the expanded dendritic tree, the nerve cell body grows larger too.

The death of many neurons is a normal part of development

As strange as it may seem, cell death is a crucial phase of brain development, especially during embryonic stages. This developmental stage is not unique to the nervous system. Naturally occurring **cell death**, also called *apoptosis* (from the Greek *apo*, "away from," and *ptosis*, "act of falling"), is a kind of sculpting process in the emergence of other tissues in both animals and plants.

The number of neurons that die during early development is quite large. In some regions of the brain and spinal cord, *most* of the young nerve cells die during prenatal development. In 1958, Viktor Hamburger (1900–2001) first described naturally occurring neuronal cell death in chicks, in which nearly half the originally produced spinal motor neurons die before the chick hatches (**FIGURE 7.10**). Genetically interfering with neural apoptosis in fetal mice causes them to grow brains that are too

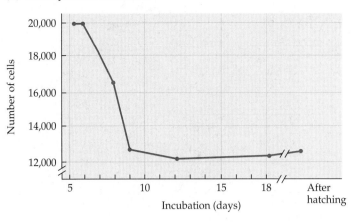

(A) Chick spinal motor neurons

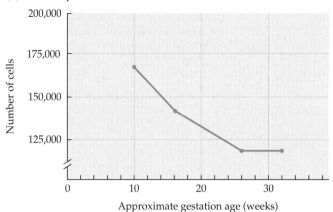

(B) Human spinal motor neurons

7.10 MANY NEURONS DIE DURING NORMAL EARLY DEVELOPMENT The pattern of neuronal cell death in spinal motor neurons of chicks (A) and humans (B). Many neuronal populations show a similar pattern of apoptosis. (Part A from Hamburger, 1975; B from Forger and Breedlove, 1987.)

large to fit in the skull (Depaepe et al., 2005), so we can see how vital it is that some cells die.

These cells are not dying because of a defect. Rather, it appears that these cells have "decided" to die and are actively committing suicide. Your chromosomes carry **death genes**—genes that are expressed only when a cell undergoes apoptosis (Park and Poo, 2013). For example, the **caspases** are a family of proteases (protein-dissolving enzymes) that cut up proteins and nuclear DNA. Apoptosis appears to begin with a sudden influx and release of calcium (Ca2+) ions that cause the mitochondria inside the cell to release a protein called, devilishly enough, **Diablo** (Tait and Green, 2010).

Diablo binds to a family of proteins, the well-named **inhibitors of apoptosis proteins** (**IAPs**) (Earnshaw et al., 1999). The IAPs normally inhibit the caspases, so when Diablo binds the IAPs, the caspases are free to dismantle the cell. **Bcl-2** proteins block apoptosis by preventing Diablo release from the mitochondria. This intricate system of checks and balances, which determines whether a cell gives up the ghost (**FIGURE 7.11**), was established long ago in evolution, because homologs of the genes that produce these proteins function similarly in *C. elegans*. In the worm, mitotic lineage determines which cells are fated to die, but what determines which cells will die in vertebrates?

As you may have guessed, apoptosis in vertebrates is regulated by cell-cell interactions, such as the availability of synaptic targets. Reducing the size of the synaptic target invariably reduces the number of surviving nerve cells. If the leg of a tadpole is removed in development, for instance, many more developing spinal motor neurons die than would die if the leg remained. Conversely, grafting an extra leg onto one side of the body—a technique that is possible with chicken embryos and tadpoles—reduces the usual loss of cells;

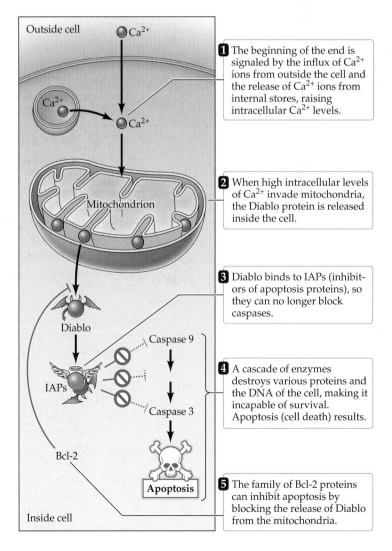

1 The beginning of the end is signaled by the influx of Ca²⁺ ions from outside the cell and the release of Ca²⁺ ions from internal stores, raising intracellular Ca²⁺ levels.

2 When high intracellular levels of Ca²⁺ invade mitochondria, the Diablo protein is released inside the cell.

3 Diablo binds to IAPs (inhibitors of apoptosis proteins), so they can no longer block caspases.

4 A cascade of enzymes destroys various proteins and the DNA of the cell, making it incapable of survival. Apoptosis (cell death) results.

5 The family of Bcl-2 proteins can inhibit apoptosis by blocking the release of Diablo from the mitochondria.

7.11 DEATH GENES REGULATE APOPTOSIS

7.12 THE EFFECTS OF NERVE GROWTH FACTOR If NGF is added to the solution bathing a spinal ganglion grown in vitro, neuronal processes grow outward in an exuberant, radiating fashion. (From Levi-Montalcini, 1963.)

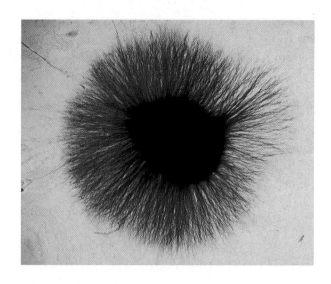

Bcl-2 A family of proteins that regulate apoptosis.

neurotrophic factor Also called *trophic factor*. A target-derived chemical that acts as if it "feeds" certain neurons to help them survive.

nerve growth factor (NGF) A substance that markedly affects the growth of neurons in spinal ganglia and in the ganglia of the sympathetic nervous system.

brain-derived neurotrophic factor (BDNF) A protein purified from the brains of animals that can keep some classes of neurons alive.

neurotrophins A family of proteins, including NGF and BDNF, that prevent different classes of neurons from dying.

in such cases the mature spinal cord has more than the usual number of motor neurons on that side.

Thus neurons compete for connections to target structures (other nerve cells or end organs, such as muscle). Neurons that make adequate synapses survive and grow; those that fail to form synaptic connections die. Apparently the neurons compete not just for synaptic sites, but also for a chemical that the target structure makes and releases. Neurons that receive enough of the chemical survive; those that do not, die. Such target-derived chemicals are called **neurotrophic factors** (or simply *trophic factors*) because they act as if they "feed" the neurons to help them survive (in Greek, *trophe* means "nourishment"). The neurotrophic factor that was the first to be identified prevents the death of developing sympathetic neurons, as we'll discuss next.

Neurotrophic factors allow neurons to survive and grow

In the 1950s, investigators discovered a substance—called **nerve growth factor** (**NGF**)—that markedly affects the growth of neurons in spinal ganglia and in the ganglia of the sympathetic nervous system (Levi-Montalcini, 1982). Administered to a chick embryo, NGF resulted in many more sympathetic neurons than usual. These cells were also larger and had more extensive processes (**FIGURE 7.12**).

Various target organs normally produce NGF during development. It is taken up by the axons of sympathetic neurons that innervate those organs and is transported back to the cell body, where NGF prevents the sympathetic neurons from dying. The amount of NGF produced by targets during development is roughly correlated with the amount of sympathetic innervation that the targets maintain into adulthood. Thus, cell death, controlled by access to NGF, provides each target with an appropriate amount of sympathetic innervation (**FIGURE 7.13**).

There are additional neurotrophic factors, each one affecting the survival of a particular cell type during a specific developmental period. One such factor, named **brain-derived neurotrophic factor** (**BDNF**), is very similar to NGF. Investigators used molecular techniques to search for other NGF-related molecules and found several more. This family of NGF-like molecules—now named the **neurotrophin** family—includes neurotrophin-1 (i.e., NGF), neurotrophin-2 (BDNF), neurotrophin-3, and neurotrophin-4/5 (the fifth neurotrophin discovered turned out to be identical to the fourth—oops). Neurotrophic factors that are unrelated to NGF also have been found, including ciliary neurotrophic factor (named after its ability to keep neurons from ciliary ganglia alive in vitro).

The exact role of these various factors (and other neurotrophic factors yet to be discovered) is under intense scientific scrutiny. One role of neurotrophic factors seems to be guiding the rearrangement of synaptic connections, as we discuss next.

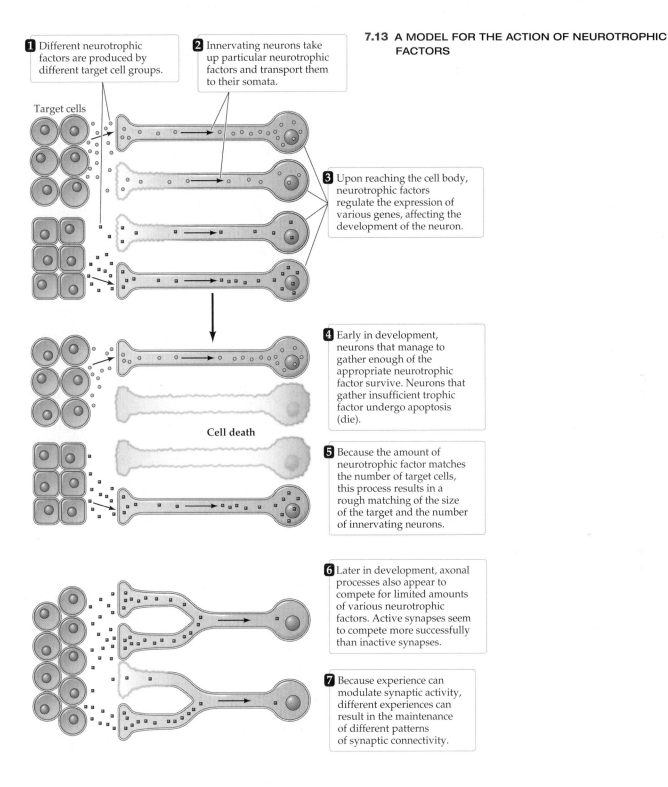

1 Different neurotrophic factors are produced by different target cell groups.

2 Innervating neurons take up particular neurotrophic factors and transport them to their somata.

3 Upon reaching the cell body, neurotrophic factors regulate the expression of various genes, affecting the development of the neuron.

4 Early in development, neurons that manage to gather enough of the appropriate neurotrophic factor survive. Neurons that gather insufficient trophic factor undergo apoptosis (die).

5 Because the amount of neurotrophic factor matches the number of target cells, this process results in a rough matching of the size of the target and the number of innervating neurons.

6 Later in development, axonal processes also appear to compete for limited amounts of various neurotrophic factors. Active synapses seem to compete more successfully than inactive synapses.

7 Because experience can modulate synaptic activity, different experiences can result in the maintenance of different patterns of synaptic connectivity.

Target cells

Cell death

Synaptic connections are refined by synapse rearrangement

Just as not all the neurons produced by a developing individual are kept into adulthood, some of the synapses formed early in development are later retracted. Originally this process was described as synapse elimination, but later studies found that, although some original synapses are indeed lost, many new synapses are also formed as they compete for neurotropic factors (**FIGURE 7.14**). Thus, a more accurate term is **synapse rearrangement**, or *synaptic remodeling*. In most cases, synapse rearrangement takes place after the period of cell death.

synapse rearrangement Also called *synaptic remodeling*. The loss of some synapses and the development of others; a refinement of synaptic connections that is often seen in development.

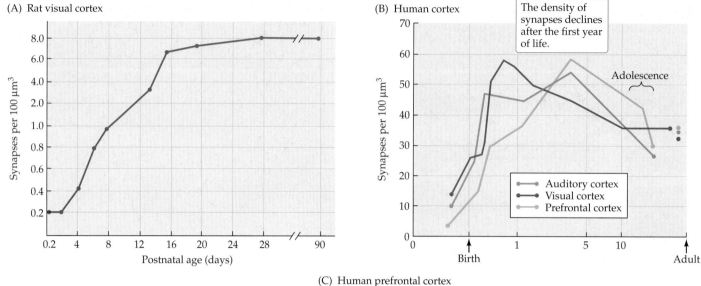

(A) Rat visual cortex

(B) Human cortex

The density of synapses declines after the first year of life.

Adolescence

Auditory cortex
Visual cortex
Prefrontal cortex

Birth

Adult

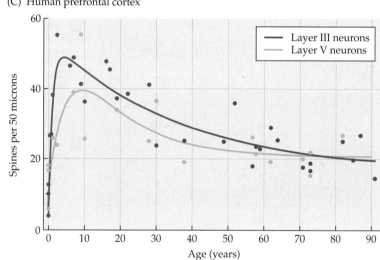

(C) Human prefrontal cortex

Layer III neurons
Layer V neurons

7.14 THE POSTNATAL DEVELOPMENT OF SYNAPSES The rate of synapse development in the visual cortex of rats (A) and humans (B). In humans, note the decline in the density of synapses after the first year of life. (C) For one particular class of synaptic spines on pyramidal neurons in human prefrontal cortex, the elimination of synapses extends even longer, well into adulthood. (Part A after Blue and Parnavelas, 1983; B from Huttenlocher et al., 1982; C after Petanjek et al., 2011.)

For example, as we learned already, about half of the spinal motor neurons that form die later (see Figure 7.10). By the end of the cell death period, each surviving motor neuron innervates many muscle fibers, and every muscle fiber is innervated by several motor neurons. But later the surviving motor neurons retract many of their axon collaterals, until each muscle fiber comes to be innervated by only one motor neuron.

Similar events occur in other neural regions, including the cerebellum (Mariani and Changeaux, 1981), the brainstem (Jackson and Parks, 1982), the visual cortex (Hubel et al., 1977), and the autonomic ganglia (Lichtman and Purves, 1980). In human cerebral cortex there seems to be a net loss of synapses from late childhood through adolescence (see Figure 7.14B and C). This synaptic remodeling is evident in thinning of the gray matter in the cortex as pruning of dendrites and axon terminals progresses. The thinning process continues in a caudal–rostral direction during maturation (**FIGURE 7.15A**), so prefrontal cortex matures last (Gogtay et al., 2004). Indeed, some synapse

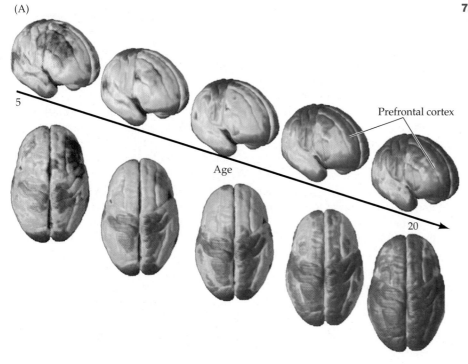

(A)

5

Age

Prefrontal cortex

20

7.15 SYNAPSE REARRANGEMENT IN THE DEVELOPING HUMAN BRAIN (A) Repeated measures from many brains reveal that the layer of gray matter on the exterior of the cortex becomes thinner across development, as synapses are retracted. Purple and blue depict regions with little change in cortical thickness; yellow and red depict areas that are changing rapidly with age. Note that the prefrontal cortex, usually thought to be important in inhibiting behavior, does not finish maturation until late adolescence. (B) A sample from the prefrontal cortex shows how rapidly cortical thickness changes during puberty and well into adulthood. (A from Gogtay et al., 2004, courtesy of Dr. Nitin Gogtay; B from Mills et al., 2014.)

(B)

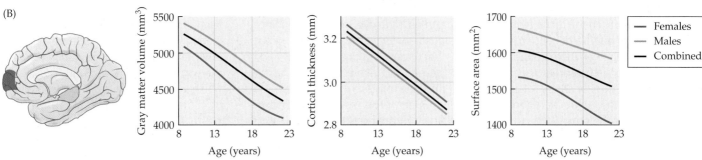

elimination there continues well into adulthood (Mills et al., 2014) (**FIGURE 7.15B**). During this process, connections between prefrontal cortex and some brain regions become more numerous, while others thin out (Dosenbach et al., 2013). Since prefrontal cortex is important for inhibiting behavior (see Chapter 18), this delayed brain maturation may contribute to teenagers' impulsivity and lack of control. Furthermore, because the synaptic pruning going on at this stage is critical for future functioning of the brain, the tendency of psychiatric disorders, such as schizophrenia and mood disorders, to emerge in adolescence reflects the vulnerability of this developmental stage (Paus et al., 2008).

What determines which synapses are kept and which are lost? Although we don't know all the factors, one important influence is neural activity. One theory is that active synapses take up some neurotrophic factor that maintains the synapse, while inactive synapses get too little trophic factor to remain stable (see Figure 7.13 *bottom*). Intellectual stimulation probably contributes, as suggested by the fact that teenagers with the highest IQs show an especially prolonged period of cortical thinning (P. Shaw et al., 2006).

In Chapter 8 we'll review evidence that synapse rearrangement in the cerebral cortex continues throughout life. Later in this chapter we'll see specific examples in which active synapses are maintained and inactive synapses are retracted in the mammalian visual system. Those studies were built on studies of vision in amphibians, as described in **BOX 7.2** on the next page.

BOX 7.2

The Frog Retinotectal System Demonstrates Intrinsic and Extrinsic Factors in Neural Development

In the 1940s Roger Sperry (1913–1994) began a series of experiments that seemed to emphasize the importance of intrinsic factors, such as genes, for determining the pattern of connections in the brain. If the optic nerve that connects an eye to the brain is cut in an adult mammal, the animal is blinded in that eye and never recovers. In fishes and amphibians such as frogs, however, the animal is only temporarily blinded; in a few months the axons from the eye (specifically, from the ganglion cells of the retina) reinnervate the brain (specifically the dorsal portion of the midbrain, called the *tectum*) and the animal recovers its eyesight. When food is presented on the left or right, above or below, the animal flicks its tongue accurately to retrieve it. Thus, either (1) the retina reestablishes the same pattern of connections to the tectum that was there before surgery, and the brain interprets visual information as before, or (2) the retina reinnervates the tectum at random, but the rest of the brain learns to interpret the information presented in this new pattern.

Several lines of evidence established that the first hypothesis is correct. One such piece of evidence is that the first-arriving retinal axons sometimes pass over uninnervated tectum to reach their original targets. In the classic case illustrating this phenomenon, the optic nerve was cut and the eye was rotated 180°; when the animal recovered eyesight, it behaved as if the visual image had been rotated 180°, moving to the left when trying to get food that was presented on the right, and flicking its tongue up when food was presented below. The only explanation for this behavior is that the retinal axons had grown back to their *original* positions on the tectum, ignoring the rotation of the eye. Furthermore, once the original connections had been reestablished, the brain interpreted the information as if the eye were in its original position. Even months later, animals that underwent this treatment had not learned to make sense of information from the rotated eye.

Sperry proposed the **chemoaffinity hypothesis** to explain how retinal axons know which part of the tectum to innervate. Suppose each retinal cell and each tectal cell had a specific chemical identity—an address of sorts. Then each retinal cell would need only to seek out the proper address in the tectum and the entire pattern would be reestablished; many chemical cues (represented by many colors in Figure A, top) or only a few (two colors in Figure A, bottom) may be involved.

After arriving at the roughly appropriate region of tectum, however, retinal connections are fine-tuned by extrinsic factors, specifically by experience. Normally, each retina innervates only the tectum on the opposite side. When implantation of a third eye forces two retinas to innervate a single tectum (Figure B, left), they each do so in the same rough pattern, but they segregate; axons from one retina predominate in one area, and axons from the other retina predominate in neighboring tectum, so there are alternating stripes of innervation from the two eyes (Figure B, right).

This segregation depends on activity (Constantine-Paton et al., 1990). If neural activity in one eye is silenced (by injection of drugs), the eye loses its connections to the tectum and the other eye takes over, innervating the entire tectum. If both eyes are

Glial cells provide myelin, which is vital for brain function

As already noted, glial cells develop from the same populations of immature cells as neurons. Glial cells continue to be added to the nervous system throughout life. (Sometimes, however, the process becomes aberrant, resulting in glial tumors, called *gliomas*, of the brain.) In fact, the most intense phase of glial cell proliferation in many animals occurs *after* birth, when glial cells are added from immature cells located in the ventricular zone.

The development of sheaths around axons—the process of **myelination** (**FIGURE 7.16**)—greatly changes the rate at which axons conduct messages (see Figure 3.8). Myelination has a strong impact on behavior because it allows large networks of cells to communicate rapidly. **Multiple sclerosis** is a disorder in which myelin is destroyed by the person's own immune system in random distinct patches (Lee and Petratos, 2013). The resultant defects in neural communication in these locations can cause devastating disruptions of sensory and motor function.

In humans, the earliest myelination in the peripheral nervous system is evident in cranial and spinal nerves about 24 weeks after conception. But the most *intense* phase of myelination occurs shortly after birth. Furthermore, some investigators believe that myelin can be added to axons throughout life. The first nerve tracts in the

myelination The process of myelin formation.

multiple sclerosis Literally, "many scars"; a disorder characterized by widespread degeneration of myelin.

silenced (by keeping the animal in the dark), neither eye predominates, their axons fail to segregate in the tectum, and the detailed pattern of innervation fails to appear. Presumably the two eyes are competing for limited supplies of neurotrophic factor from the tectum, and active synapses take up more of the factor(s).

Thus, the retinotectal system appears to reestablish the original pattern of innervation in two steps: (1) chemical cues bring retinal axons to the approximately correct region of tectum; and (2) the neural activity of the retinal cells, normally driven by visual experience, directs these axons to innervate or maintain innervation of the precise tectal region. As we'll see later in this chapter, a similar competition goes on in young mammals as information from the two eyes competes to form synapses in visual cortex. (Figure B courtesy of Dr. Martha Constantine-Paton.)

chemoaffinity hypothesis The notion that each cell has a chemical identity that directs it to synapse on the proper target cell during development.

(A) Two possible mechanisms of chemoaffinity

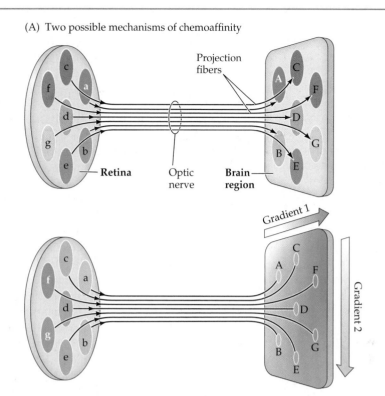

(B) This three-eyed frog has two eyes innervating the left tectum

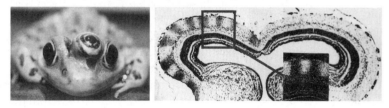

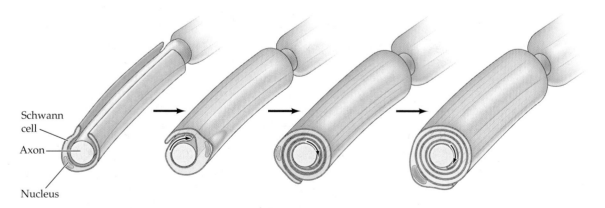

7.16 MYELIN FORMATION The repeated wrapping of the cytoplasm of a Schwann cell around a peripheral axon results in a many-layered sheath that insulates the axon electrically, speeding the conduction of electrical signals along its length.

intellectual disability A disability characterized by significant limitations in intellectual functioning and adaptive behavior.

hypoxia A lack of oxygen.

behavioral teratology The study of impairments in behavior that are produced by embryonic or fetal exposure to toxic substances.

fetal alcohol syndrome (FAS) A disorder, including intellectual disability and characteristic facial anomalies, that affects children exposed to too much alcohol (through maternal ingestion) during fetal development.

human nervous system to become myelinated are in the spinal cord. Myelination then spreads successively into the hindbrain, midbrain, and forebrain. Within the cerebral cortex, sensory zones are myelinated before motor zones; correspondingly, sensory functions mature before motor functions.

Developmental Disorders of the Brain Impair Behavior

Many psychological disorders, like depression and schizophrenia, affect mostly adults. But other disorders are seen primarily in children. **Intellectual disability** refers to a variety of conditions that impede mental growth. Some advocates for the intellectually disabled regard the older term *mental retardation* as demeaning, so it has fallen from use. First we'll consider cases where the disability is known to be caused by environmental factors; then we'll take up cases where genes play a contributing role. That will lead us to a more detailed consideration of how genes can influence brain development.

Environmental factors may limit brain development

Certain basic environmental factors are required for proper brain development. For example, if children experience complicated delivery at birth, when transient **hypoxia** (lack of oxygen) may affect the brain, they are at greater risk for intellectual disability than are children who have a problem-free birth. Similarly, if the mother does not get enough to eat, the fetal brain may have insufficient energy and nutrients to develop properly: Fetuses carried by malnourished Dutch women during the "hunger winter" of 1944 were underweight at birth, as would be expected, and more likely to be intellectually disabled. A similar outcome followed a famine in China (A. S. Brown and Susser, 2008). In Chapter 16 we'll see that these children are also more likely to suffer from schizophrenia in adulthood.

Even when nutrition is not a problem, the embryo and fetus are not immune to outside influence; what is taking place in the mother's body directly affects them. Maternal conditions such as viral infection and exposure to drugs are especially likely to result in developmental disorders in the unborn child. Concern with the maternal environment affecting brain development spawned the field of **behavioral teratology** (*teratology*—from the Greek *teras*, "monster"—is the study of malformations). This field tracks the pathological effects of exposure to environmental contaminants and drugs before birth.

There is a long history of concern about alcohol and pregnancy. About 40% of children born to alcoholic mothers show a distinctive profile of anatomical, physiological, and behavioral impairments known as **fetal alcohol syndrome** (**FAS**) (Abel, 1984). Prominent anatomical effects of fetal exposure to alcohol include distinctive changes in facial features (e.g., a sunken nasal bridge and altered shape of the nose and eyelids) and stunted growth. In severe cases, children with FAS may lack a corpus callosum (**FIGURE 7.17**). Few FAS children catch up in the years following birth. The most common problem associated with FAS is intellectual disability, which varies in severity. No threshold has yet been established for this syndrome, but it can occur with relatively moderate alcohol intake during pregnancy. Even when FAS is not diagnosed, prenatal exposure to alcohol is correlated with impairments in language and fine motor skills (Mattson et al., 1998). Thus there is no level of alcohol use during pregnancy that we can be sure is low enough to be safe for the child.

Genes are important intrinsic factors influencing brain development

Many factors influence the emergence of the form, arrangements, and connections of the developing brain. One influence is that of genes, which direct the production of every protein the cell can make. Genes are also a major influence on the development of the vertebrate brain. An animal that has inherited an altered gene will make an altered protein, which will affect any cell structure that includes that protein. Thus, every neuronal structure, and therefore every behavior, can be altered by changes in the appropriate gene(s). It is useful to think of genes as *intrinsic* factors—

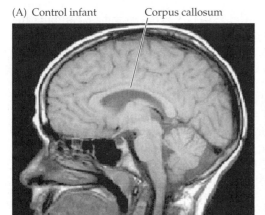

(A) Control infant   Corpus callosum

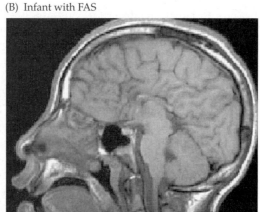

(B) Infant with FAS

7.17 ABNORMAL BRAIN DEVELOPMENT ASSOCIATED WITH FETAL ALCOHOL SYNDROME (A) The brain of a control infant. (B) The brain of an infant of the same age with FAS. This brain shows microcephaly (abnormal smallness), fewer cerebral cortical gyri, and the absence of a corpus callosum connecting the two hemispheres. (Courtesy of Dr. E. Riley.)

that is, factors that originate within the developing cell itself. All other influences can be considered *extrinsic*—originating outside of the developing cell. One extrinsic factor we considered above is exposure to alcohol before birth.

Two terms help illustrate how these intrinsic and extrinsic factors interact. The sum of all the intrinsic, genetic information that an individual has is its **genotype**. The sum of all the physical characteristics that make up an individual is its **phenotype**. Your genotype, some 20,000 genes (Pennisi, 2012), was determined at the moment of fertilization and remains the same throughout your life. But your *phenotype* changes constantly, as you grow up and grow old and even, in a tiny way, as you take each breath. In other words, phenotype is determined by the interaction of genotype and extrinsic factors, including experience. Thus, as we'll see, individuals who have identical genotypes do not have identical phenotypes, because they have not received identical extrinsic influences. And since their nervous system phenotypes are somewhat different, they do not behave exactly the same.

Let's consider some of the best-studied influences of genes on brain development, including one genetic condition that can result in either severe intellectual disability or normal intelligence, depending on extrinsic factors in the diet.

CHROMOSOMAL EFFECTS   A common form of intellectual disability results from a chromosomal abnormality—**Down syndrome (FIGURE 7.18A)**. A person with Down syndrome usually has an extra chromosome 21, for a total of three rather than the typical two copies. This disorder is related to the age of the mother at the time of conception: for women over 45 years old, the chance of having a baby with Down syndrome is nearly one in 40 (Karp, 1976). In most cases an individual who has Down syndrome will have a low IQ, but the rare individual may attain a normal IQ (Karmiloff-Smith et al., 2016). Brain abnormalities in Down syndrome also vary. The cerebral cortex shows abnormal formation of dendritic spines. Mouse models of extra chromosomes result in structural changes that appear analogous

genotype   All the genetic information that one specific individual has inherited.

phenotype   The sum of an individual's physical characteristics at one particular time.

Down syndrome   A syndrome caused by inheriting an extra copy of chromosome 21, usually accompanied by intellectual disability.

(A)

(B)

7.18 ATYPICAL CHROMOSOMES HAVE WIDESPREAD EFFECTS (A) A young woman with Down syndrome. (B) A young man with fragile X syndrome.

fragile X syndrome A condition that is a frequent cause of inherited intellectual disability; produced by a fragile site on the X chromosome that seems prone to breaking because the DNA there is unstable.

trinucleotide repeat Repetition of the same three nucleotides within a gene, which can lead to dysfunction, as in the cases of Huntington's disease and fragile X syndrome.

mutation A change in the nucleotide sequence of a gene as a result of unfaithful replication.

to Down syndrome in humans (Gotti et al., 2011). Chromosome 21 contains the amyloid precursor protein gene (*APP*) that has been implicated in Alzheimer's disease (which we take up at the end of this chapter), so there is speculation that brain abnormalities in Down syndrome may be related to those seen in Alzheimer's (Fonseca et al., 2016; Wiseman et al., 2015).

Probably the most frequent cause of inherited intellectual disability is the condition **fragile X syndrome** (**FIGURE 7.18B**), which is more common in males than in females. At the end of the long arm of the X chromosome is a site that seems fragile—prone to breaking because the DNA there is unstable (Lyons et al. 2015). A person with this condition has a modified facial appearance, including elongation of the face, large prominent ears, and a prominent chin. A wide range of cognitive effects—from mild to severe impairment—are associated with the syndrome. Cortical neurons from the brains of people with fragile X syndrome, as well as mice genetically engineered to have this syndrome, possess an excess of small, immature dendritic spines (Bagni and Greenough, 2005). These findings suggest that the syndrome affects mental development by blocking the normal elimination of synapses after birth (see Figure 7.10).

The molecular basis of fragile X syndrome provided a surprise for geneticists because it demonstrated that we don't always pass on faithful copies of our DNA to our offspring. The fragile site in the DNA consists of three nucleotides (CGG; see the Appendix for a review of nucleotides) repeated over and over. Most people have only 6–50 of these **trinucleotide repeats** at this site. But during the production of sperm or eggs, the number of repeats sometimes changes, so a mother who has only 50 trinucleotide repeats may provide 100 repeats to her son. Any children who receive more than 200 repeats will display fragile X syndrome (Lozano et al., 2014). Trinucleotide repeats in a different gene cause another behavior disorder: Huntington's disease (see Chapter 11).

EFFECTS OF MUTATIONS Sometimes an animal inherits a sudden change in genetic structure, a **mutation**, that results in marked anatomical or physiological change. Researchers can increase the frequency of mutations by exposing animals to radiation or chemicals that produce changes in genes. Animals with mutations are interesting to study because their changed behavioral phenotypes may be quite specific and striking. For example, certain mutants of the fruit fly *Drosophila* seem normal in every way except that they have memory problems. Affectionately labeled *dunce, amnesiac,* and *turnip,* these mutants either fail to learn or can learn but forget rapidly. Biochemical deficits in these mutants (due to mutations that render specific genes, and therefore specific proteins, ineffective) cause the failure of memory (Dudai, 1988).

Many mutations in mice affect the nervous system. One group of mouse mutants includes different single-gene mutations that affect development of the cerebellum (Tissir and Goffinet, 2003). The names of these mutant mice—*reeler, staggerer,* and *weaver*—reflect their locomotor impairment (**FIGURE 7.19**). Today, scientists deliberately delete or introduce a particular gene in mice in order to study the effect of that gene on the nervous system (**BOX 7.3**). At the end of this chapter, we'll consider another gene mutation that results in severe impairment of brain development, in that case by affecting glia.

In humans, many different genes have been identified that can cause intellectual disability (Gilissen et al., 2014). For most of these genes, we know little about how they normally function, but the first gene associated with intellectual disability offers an important lesson on the interaction of intrinsic and extrinsic factors, as we'll see next.

PHENYLKETONURIA Several hundred different genetic disorders affect the metabolism of proteins, carbohydrates, or lipids, having a profound impact on the developing brain (Najmabadi et al., 2011). Characteristically, the genetic defect is the absence of a particular enzyme that controls a critical biochemical step in the synthesis or breakdown of some vital body product.

(A) Normal   (B) *weaver*   (C) *reeler*

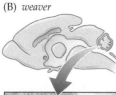
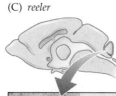

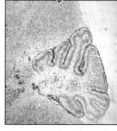

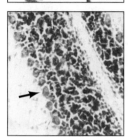
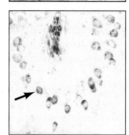
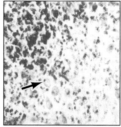

7.19 CEREBELLAR MUTANTS AMONG MICE
The cerebellum in a normal mouse (A) and two mutants (B, C) at two levels of magnification (top: ×25; bottom: ×250). In the mutant *weaver* (B), note the almost complete absence of the tiny granule cells (bottom), while the alignment of the large Purkinje cells (arrow) is normal. The mutant *reeler* (C) shows marked derangement of the customary layering of cells. Both mutants show overall shrinkage of the cerebellum (top). (From Dr. A. L. Leiman, unpublished observations.)

An example is **phenylketonuria (PKU)**, a recessive hereditary disorder of protein metabolism that at one time resulted in many people with intellectual disability. About one out of 100 persons is a carrier; one in 10,000 births produces an affected victim. The basic defect is the absence of an enzyme necessary to metabolize phenylalanine, an amino acid that is present in many foods. As a result, the brain is damaged by an enormous buildup of phenylalanine, which becomes toxic.

The discovery of PKU marked the first time that an inborn error of metabolism was associated with intellectual disability. Screening for PKU looks for excess levels of phenylalanine in children a few days after birth. Early detection is important because brain impairment can be prevented simply by reducing phenylalanine in the diet. Such dietary control of PKU is critical during the early years of life, especially

phenylketonuria (PKU) An inherited disorder of protein metabolism in which the absence of an enzyme leads to a toxic buildup of certain compounds, causing intellectual disability.

Transgenic and Knockout Mice

Animals with mutations in specific genes offer clues about the role of genes in development and brain function. Among the many new tools brought about by the revolution in molecular biology is **site-directed mutagenesis**, the ability to cause a mutation in a particular gene. Researchers using such techniques, including CRISPR, must know the sequence of nucleotides in the gene of interest (see Appendix). Then they can use the tendency of complementary nucleotides to hybridize with that part of the gene to induce changes.

The easiest change to understand is total disruption of the gene, making it nonfunctional. If this is done in embryonic mouse cells, these cells may

form the testes or ovaries of a developing mouse. That mouse can then produce offspring that are missing the gene. We call the resulting animal a **knockout organism** because the gene of interest has been *knocked out*.

By following the development of knockout mice, we can obtain clues about the roles of particular genes in normal animals. For example, the motor neurons of mice whose genes for brain-derived neurotrophic factor (BDNF) have been knocked out survive despite the absence of BDNF (Sendtner et al., 1996), so we know that BDNF is not crucial for motor neuron survival. On the other hand, some parasympathetic ganglia fail to

form in BDNF knockout mice (J. T. Erickson et al., 1996), suggesting that these neurons depend on BDNF for survival. As we'll see in Chapter 17, several genes suspected of playing a role in learning have been knocked out in mice, and the resulting animals indeed show deficits in learning.

There are some problems in interpreting such results, because the missing gene may have contributed only very indirectly to the learning process, or the animal's poor performance may have been due to a distraction caused by the knockout. For that matter, even normal behavior by animals missing the gene does not

(continued)

BOX 7.3 — **Transgenic and Knockout Mice** (continued)

prove that the gene is unimportant for behavior. Perhaps the developing animal, in the absence of that gene, somehow has compensated for the loss and found a new way to solve the problem. This would be another example of the embryonic regulation that is so common in vertebrate development.

In other cases, a functional, manipulated copy of a gene can be introduced into the mouse. This animal is described as **transgenic** because a gene has been *trans*ferred into its genome. Sometimes the introduction of just a single new gene can have a dramatic effect on brain development; for example, compare the brains of newborn mice that are normal with those of transgenic mice carrying a modified gene for β-catenin (see Figure 6.23). Modifying this one gene caused the mouse to make far too

many neurons, so extra gyri and sulci developed (Chenn and Walsh, 2002).

The transgenic approach is often used as a method for improving our understanding of genetic disorders. For example, in Chapter 11 we'll learn that when a gene mutation that causes severe motor impairments in people is transferred into mice, the mice develop symptoms similar to those that appear in humans. It may be possible to study the disease more closely in these mice and test possible therapies.

Knockout and transgenic animals have one limitation: they possess the genetic manipulation from the moment of conception and in every cell in the body. However, molecular neurobiologists have begun knocking out or replacing genes in adult animals—by injecting the animals with a triggering substance such as tetracycline, or

by replacing or knocking out a gene in only one region of the brain. These manipulations allow the animals to develop with a normal genotype, thereby making it easier to interpret the result of the gene manipulation in adulthood. It may even be possible to knock out and then restore a gene in the same individual mouse, tracking its behavior as the gene is lost and regained.

site-directed mutagenesis A technique in molecular biology that changes the sequence of nucleotides in an existing gene.

knockout organism An individual in which a particular gene has been disabled by an experimenter.

transgenic Referring to an animal in which a new or altered gene has been deliberately introduced into the genome.

---

before age 2; after that, diet can be relaxed somewhat. Note this important example of the interaction of genes and the environment in PKU: the dysfunctional gene causes intellectual disability *only* in the presence of phenylalanine. Reducing phenylalanine consumption reduces or prevents this effect of the gene.

Phenylketonuria illustrates one reason why, despite the importance of genes for nervous system development, understanding the genome alone could never enable an understanding of the developing brain. Knowing that a baby is born with PKU doesn't tell you anything about how that child's brain will develop *unless* you also know something about the child's diet. Another reason why genes alone cannot tell the whole story is that experience can affect the activity of genes, as we discuss next.

Genes Interact with Experience to Guide Brain Development

We saw that in the case of PKU, the genotype alone does not determine whether there will be disability. Only if sufficient phenylalanine is in the diet will brain development be impaired. A much more prominent mechanism by which the environment influences gene action concerns gene expression. It turns out that, no matter which version of a gene you inherit, whether and how much that gene will be expressed may depend on experience. In other words, experience can control how genes are used in the developing brain. Thus, every behavior is affected not only by genes, but also by experience.

Experience regulates gene expression in the developing and mature brain

Genetically identical animals, called **clones**, used to be known mainly in science fiction and horror films. But life imitates art. In grasshopper clones, the basic shape of larger cells is similar in all clones, but many neurons show differences in neural

clones Asexually produced organisms that are genetically identical.

epigenetics The study of factors that affect gene expression without making any changes in the nucleotide sequence of the genes themselves.

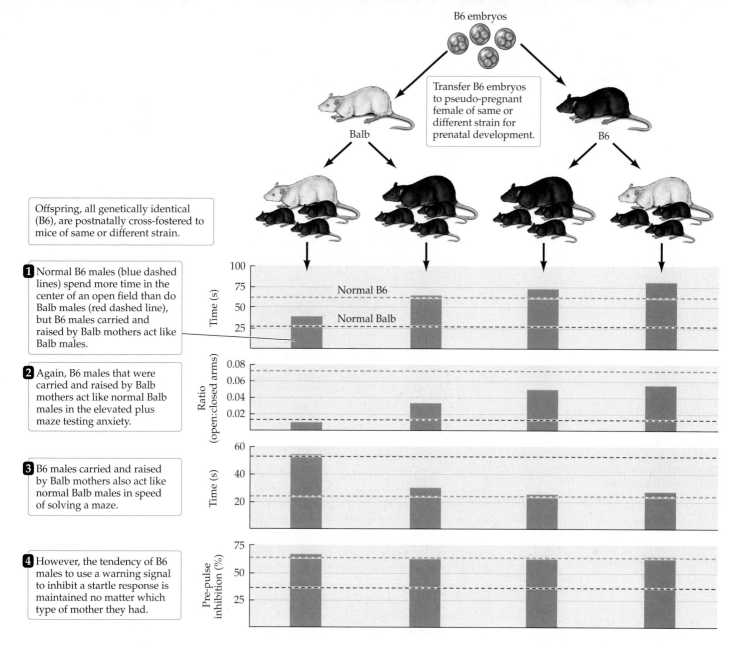

B6 embryos

Transfer B6 embryos to pseudo-pregnant female of same or different strain for prenatal development.

Balb

B6

Offspring, all genetically identical (B6), are postnatally cross-fostered to mice of same or different strain.

1 Normal B6 males (blue dashed lines) spend more time in the center of an open field than do Balb males (red dashed line), but B6 males carried and raised by Balb mothers act like Balb males.

Time (s)

Normal B6

Normal Balb

2 Again, B6 males that were carried and raised by Balb mothers act like normal Balb males in the elevated plus maze testing anxiety.

Ratio (open:closed arms)

3 B6 males carried and raised by Balb mothers also act like normal Balb males in speed of solving a maze.

Time (s)

4 However, the tendency of B6 males to use a warning signal to inhibit a startle response is maintained no matter which type of mother they had.

Pre-pulse inhibition (%)

7.20 EPIGENETIC EFFECTS ON MOUSE BEHAVIOR In this experiment, offspring are weaned at 22 days, and behavioral testing begins at 3 months. All males in the inbred C57Black6 strain (B6) are genetically identical and behave differently than males of the Balb strain. Yet B6 males carried and raised by Balb mothers act like Balb males in some ways. (From Francis et al., 2003.)

connections despite the identical genotypes (Goodman, 1979). Likewise, genetically identical cloned pigs show as much variation in behavior and temperament as do normal siblings (G. S. Archer et al., 2003), and genetically identical mice raised in different laboratories behave very differently on a variety of tests (Finch and Kirkwood, 2000). If genes are so important to the developing nervous system, how can genetically identical individuals differ in their behavior?

EPIGENETICS Recall that although nearly all of the cells in your body have a complete copy of your genome, each cell uses only a small subset of those genes at any one time. We told you earlier that when a cell transcribes a particular gene and makes the encoded protein, we say the cell has *expressed* that gene. **Epigenetics** is the study of factors that affect gene *expression* without making any changes in the nucleotide sequence of the genes themselves. One important epigenetic factor affecting the developing brain in mice is the mothering they receive. If genetically identical embryos of one mouse strain are implanted into the wombs of two foster mothers, of either their own strain or another strain, their behavior is affected (Francis et al., 2003). Strain B6 males carried and raised by mothers from another strain (Balb) show significant differences in several behaviors, including maze running and measures of anxiety (**FIGURE 7.20**). Since the various B6 males are *genetically iden-*

7.21 EARLY EXPERIENCE IMPRINTS GENES TO AFFECT THE STRESS RESPONSE IN ADULTHOOD Attentive mothers prevent methylation of the stress hormone receptor gene in their pups, so their daughters grow up to be attentive mothers themselves. In this way, maternal care can have epigenetic effects that can be transmitted across generations. (After Hackman et al., 2010.)

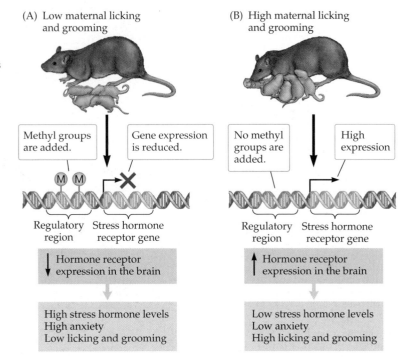

methylation A chemical modification of DNA that does not affect the nucleotide sequence of a gene but makes that gene less likely to be expressed.

tical to one another, their different behaviors must be due to the effect of different prenatal environments and postnatal experiences on how those genes are expressed.

One particular influence of mothering on gene expression has been well documented. **Methylation** is a chemical modification of DNA that does not affect the nucleotide sequence of a gene but makes that gene less likely to be expressed. There are patterns of gene methylation in the developing cortex that are consistent from one individual to another (Lister et al., 2013), indicating that this regulation of gene expression is important for proper development. Neuronal activity can affect the methylation of genes, and therefore the likelihood those genes will be expressed, even in adulthood (Guo et al., 2011). Thus experience at one time in life may affect gene expression later. One well-characterized example is when rodent pups are provided with inattentive mothers, which leads to methylation of the gene for the glucocorticoid receptor (discussed in Chapters 5 and 15) in the pups' brains. This methylation reduces expression of the gene in the pups, so they secrete more glucocorticoids in response to stress (T. Y. Zhang and Meaney, 2010), making them hyperresponsive to stress as adults (**FIGURE 7.21**).

A similar mechanism may apply to humans, because this same gene is also more likely to be methylated in the postmortem brains of suicide victims than of controls, *but only if the victim was subjected to childhood abuse*. Suicide victims who did not suffer childhood abuse were no more likely to have the gene methylated than were others (McGowan et al., 2009). These results suggest that methylation of the gene in abused children may have made them hyperresponsive to stress as adults—a condition that may have led them to take their own lives. This is a powerful demonstration of epigenetic influences on our behavior.

EPIGENETIC REGULATION IN ADULTS Neurons in adults also alter gene expression in response to synaptic stimulation. Some genes, called *immediate early genes*, are briefly expressed by almost any neuron that has been stimulated (see Box 2.1). Neuroscientists exploit this process by exposing an animal to, say, a sound of a particular frequency and then examining the brain to see which neurons altered gene expression in response to different frequencies. Likewise, lights, odors, or touches will all affect neuronal expression of immediate early genes in particular regions of the brain and spinal cord that receive information about those sensations. Experience also affects the expression of many other genes (Mayfield et al., 2002), not just immediate early genes. One reason why genetically identical individuals do not have identical brains or behavior is that they are inevitably exposed to different experiences, so they grow up expressing their identical genes in very nonidentical ways (Ridley, 2003).

Let's explore a system where we can identify the experiences that direct development: the visual system.

Experience Is an Important Influence on Brain Development

The young of many species are born in a very immature anatomical and behavioral state. Varying an individual's experience during early development alters many aspects of behavior, brain anatomy, and brain chemistry in animal models (M. R. Rosenzweig and Bennett, 1977, 1978). Likewise, early-childhood enrichment programs produce long-lasting increases in IQ in humans, especially those from deprived backgrounds (Raine et al., 2002). Work on the developing visual system shows us how experience can guide synaptic connectivity to have such long-lasting effects on behavior.

Visual deprivation can lead to blindness

Some people do not see forms clearly with one of their eyes, even though the eye is intact and a sharp image is focused on the retina. Such impairments of vision are known as **amblyopia** (from the Greek *amblys*, "dull", and *ops*, "eye"). Some people with this disorder have an eye that is turned inward (cross-eyed) or outward. Children born with such a misalignment see a double image rather than a single fused image. By the time an untreated person reaches the age of 7 or 8, pattern vision in the deviated eye is almost completely suppressed. If the eyes are realigned during childhood, the person learns to fuse the two images and has good depth perception. But if realignment is done in adulthood, it's too late to restore acute vision to the turned eye.

Understanding the cause of amblyopia has been greatly advanced by visual-deprivation experiments with animals. Either the eyelids are sutured to prevent any light entry, or frosted contact lenses are implanted to prevent images coming into focus on the retina. These experiments revealed startling changes related to disuse of the visual system in early life. Depriving animals of sight in both eyes (**binocular deprivation**) produces structural changes in visual cortical neurons: a loss of dendritic spines and a reduction in synapses. If such deprivation is maintained for several weeks during development, when the animal's eyes are opened, it will be blind. Although light enters its eyes, and the cells of the eyes send messages to the brain, the brain seems to ignore the messages and the animal is unable to detect visual stimuli. If the deprivation lasts long enough, the animal is *never* able to recover eyesight. Thus, early visual experience is crucial for the proper development of vision, and there is a **sensitive period** during which these manipulations of experience can exert long-lasting effects on the system (**FIGURE 7.22**). These effects are most extensive during the early period of synaptic development in the visual cortex. After the sensitive period, the manipulations have little or no effect.

amblyopia Reduced visual acuity of one eye, that is not caused by optical or retinal impairments.

binocular deprivation Depriving both eyes of form vision, as by sealing the eyelids.

sensitive period The period during development in which an organism can be permanently altered by a particular experience or treatment.

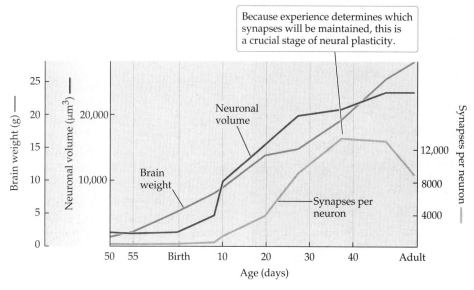

Because experience determines which synapses will be maintained, this is a crucial stage of neural plasticity.

7.22 BRAIN DEVELOPMENT IN THE VISUAL CORTEX OF CATS (After Cragg, 1975.)

monocular deprivation Depriving one eye of light.

ocular dominance histogram A graph that portrays the strength of response of a brain neuron to stimuli presented to either the left eye or the right eye.

Hebbian synapse A synapse that is strengthened when it successfully drives the postsynaptic cell.

Depriving only one eye of light (**monocular deprivation**) produces profound structural and functional changes in the thalamus and visual cortex. Monocular deprivation in an infant cat or monkey causes the deprived eye not to respond when the animal reaches adulthood. The effect of visual deprivation can be illustrated graphically by an **ocular dominance histogram**, which portrays the strength of response of a brain neuron to stimuli presented to either the left or the right eye. Normally, most cortical neurons (except those in layer IV) are excited equally by light presented to either eye (**FIGURE 7.23A**).

Keeping one eye closed or covered in development results in a striking shift from the normal graph; most cortical neurons respond only to input from the nondeprived eye (**FIGURE 7.23B**). In cats the susceptible period for this effect is the first 4 months of life. In rhesus monkeys the sensitive period extends to age 6 months. After these ages, visual deprivation has little effect.

During early development, synapses are rearranged in the visual cortex, and axons representing input from each eye "compete" for synaptic places. Active, effective synapses predominate over inactive synapses. Thus, if one eye is "silenced," synapses carrying information from that eye are retracted while synapses driven by the other eye are maintained. Donald O. Hebb (1949) proposed that effective synapses (those that successfully drive the postsynaptic cell) might grow stronger at the expense of ineffective synapses. Thus, synapses that grow stronger or weaker depending on their effectiveness in driving their target cell are known as **Hebbian synapses** (**FIGURE 7.23D**). In Chapter 17 we will see that the maintenance of active synapses and retraction of inactive synapses may also play a role in learning and memory.

Researchers offer a similar explanation for amblyopia produced by misalignment of the eyes. Hubel and Wiesel (1965) produced an animal replica of this human condition by surgically causing the eyes to diverge in kittens. The ocular dominance histogram of these animals reveals that the normal binocular sensitivity of visual cortical cells is greatly reduced (**FIGURE 7.23C**). A much larger proportion of visual cortical cells is excited by stimulation of either the right or the left eye in these animals than in control animals. The reason for this effect is that, after surgery, visual stimuli falling on the misaligned eyes no longer provide simultaneous, convergent input to the cells of the visual cortex.

Neurotrophic factors may be playing a role in experience-driven synapse rearrangement. For example, if the postsynaptic cells are making a limited supply of a neurotrophic factor, and if active synapses take up more of the factor than inactive synapses do, then perhaps the inactive axons retract for lack of neurotrophic factor. BDNF has been implicated as the neurotrophic factor being competed for in the kitten visual cortex (McAllister et al., 1997) and in the frog retinotectal system (Du and Poo, 2004) (see Box 7.2). So perhaps ineffective synapses wither for lack of neurotrophic support.

Early exposure to visual patterns helps fine-tune connections in the visual system

Human disorders have also proven that early experience is crucial for vision. Babies born with cataracts (cloudy lenses) in industrialized countries usually have them removed a few months after birth and will have good vision. But if such a child grows up with the cataracts in place, removing them in adulthood is much less effective; the adults acquire the use of vision slowly (Ostrovsky et al., 2009) and to only a limited extent (Bower, 2003). Early visual experience is known to be especially crucial for learning to perceive faces, because infants with cataracts that occlude vision for just the first 6 months of life are impaired at recognizing faces even 9 years later (Le Grand et al., 2001). These experience-dependent effects are probably mediated by synapse rearrangement within the visual cortex (Ruthazer et al., 2003) like that seen in kittens.

Why does Michael May, whom we met at the start of the chapter, have such poor vision despite the clear images entering his eye? Had the accident happened to him

LEARNING TO SEE Despite over a decade of vision in one eye, Michael May still has a hard time identifying faces.

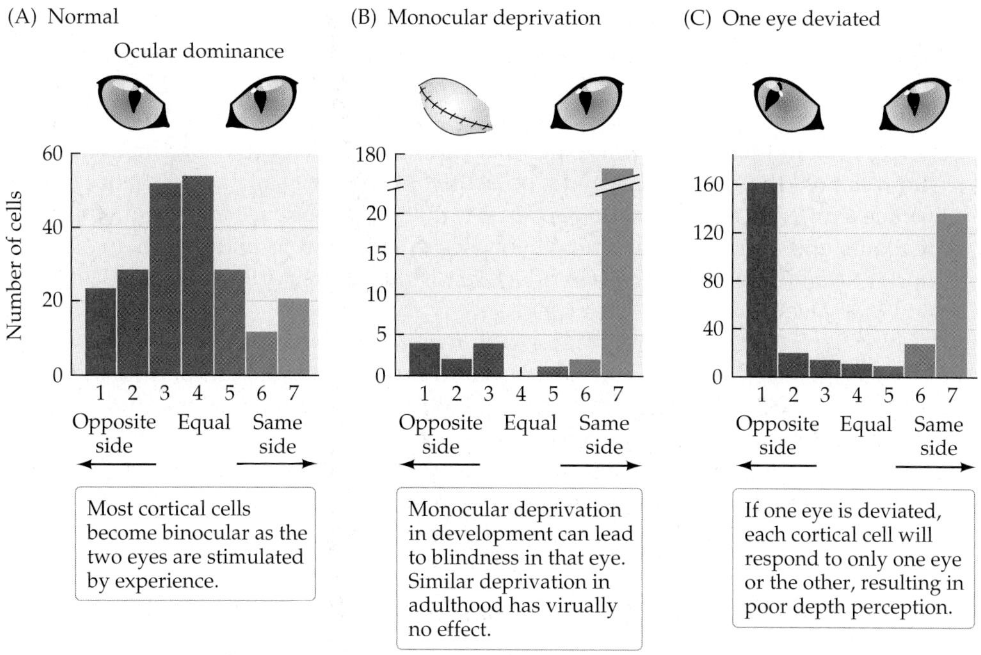

(A) Normal

Ocular dominance

60

40

Number of cells

20

0

1 2 3 4 5 6 7

Opposite Equal Same
side side

Most cortical cells become binocular as the two eyes are stimulated by experience.

(B) Monocular deprivation

180

20

15

10

5

0

1 2 3 4 5 6 7

Opposite Equal Same
side side

Monocular deprivation in development can lead to blindness in that eye. Similar deprivation in adulthood has virually no effect.

(C) One eye deviated

160

120

80

40

0

1 2 3 4 5 6 7

Opposite Equal Same
side side

If one eye is deviated, each cortical cell will respond to only one eye or the other, resulting in poor depth perception.

7.23 OCULAR DOMINANCE HISTO-GRAMS These histograms show responses of cells in the visual cortex of cats: (A) normal adults; (B) after monocular deprivation through the early critical period; (C) after early deviation of one eye (squint). The numbers along the *x*-axis represent a gradation in response: Cells that respond *only* to stimulation of the opposite eye are class 1 cells. Cells that respond *mainly* to stimulation of the opposite eye are class 2. Cells that respond equally to either eye are class 4. Cells that respond only to stimulation of the eye on the same side are class 7, and so on. (D) Hebbian synapses can account for changes after monocular deprivation. (After Hubel and Wiesel, 1965; Wiesel and Hubel, 1965.)

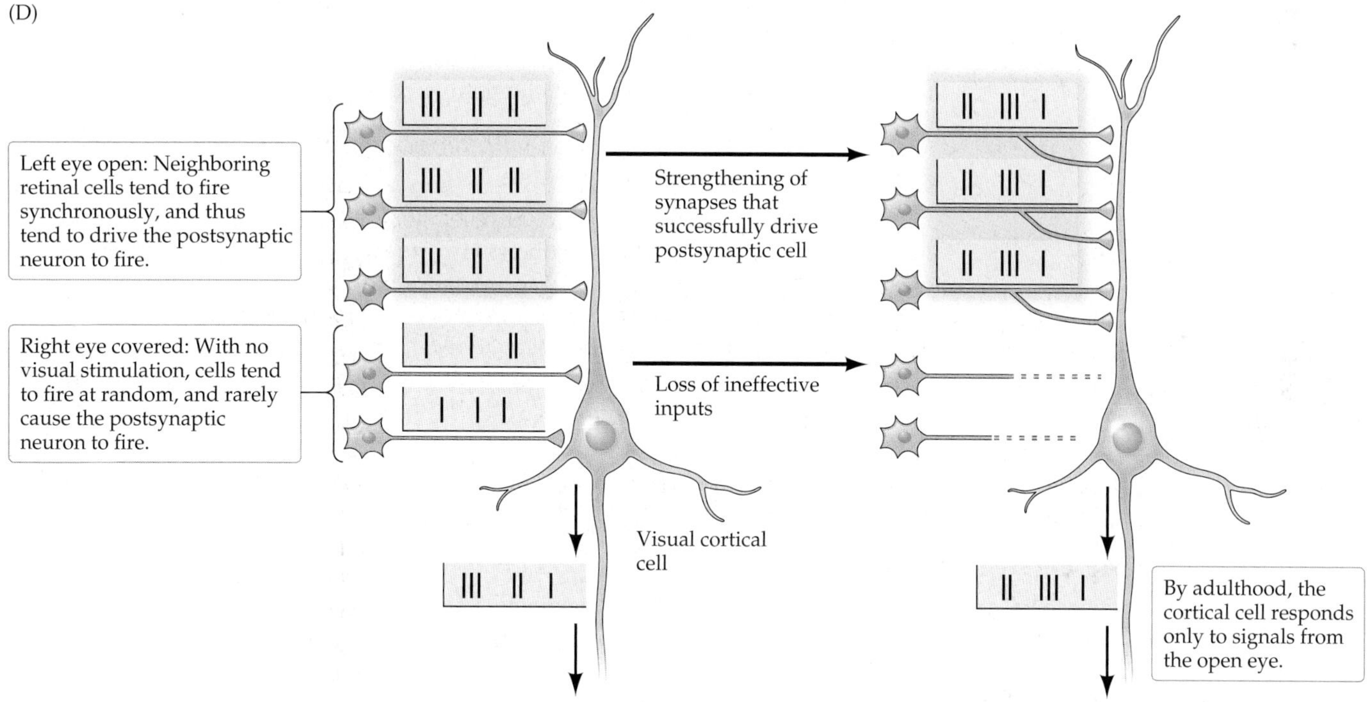

(D)

Left eye open: Neighboring retinal cells tend to fire synchronously, and thus tend to drive the postsynaptic neuron to fire.

Right eye covered: With no visual stimulation, cells tend to fire at random, and rarely cause the postsynaptic neuron to fire.

Strengthening of synapses that successfully drive postsynaptic cell

Loss of ineffective inputs

Visual cortical cell

By adulthood, the cortical cell responds only to signals from the open eye.

as an adult, the surgery to let light back into his eye would have restored normal vision. But, like a kitten fitted with opaque contact lenses, Michael was deprived of form vision—in his case, for over 40 years. Because this deprivation began when he was a child, synaptic connections within his visual cortex were not strengthened by the patterns of light moving across the retina. In the absence of patterned stimulation, synapses between the eye and the brain languished and disappeared.

In one sense, Michael was lucky that his blindness came as late as it did. He had normal form vision for the first 3½ years of his life, and that stimulation may have been sufficient to maintain some synapses that would otherwise have been lost. These residual synapses are probably what allow him to make any sense whatsoever of his vision. Yet, despite more than a decade of visual experience as an adult, Mi-

7.24 WHICH LINE IS MORE SLANTED? The numbers and letters on the lower line look more slanted than those on the upper line, but in fact the characters on the two lines are equally slanted. If you look at them in a mirror, the upper line will look more slanted. Does this optical illusion result from modification of synapses caused by looking at digital clocks and italic font?

chael still has problems distinguishing three-dimensional objects or faces (Huber et al., 2015). Other people who gain vision for the first time as adults have similar difficulties recognizing objects and faces (Gregory and Wallace, 1963; Sikl et al., 2013).

One demonstration shows how visual experience in everyday life may affect our perception. In **FIGURE 7.24**, the numbers and letters along the bottom line appear more slanted than those above, but in fact the slant is the same. One theory of why we see a difference here that doesn't exist is that our experience reading digital clock readouts and italic fonts may tune synapses in the brain to perceive them as more upright than they really are—an effect lost if the figures are backward (Whitaker and McGraw, 2000).

In **A Step Further: Experiences in Nonvisual Senses Also Affect Neural Development** on the website, you can learn how mouse whiskers compete for synapses in the cortex. As you read **TABLE 7.1**, which lists some of the intrinsic and extrinsic factors that we've discussed, consider how all of the extrinsic factors must regulate gene expression in order to have their effects on the developing brain. This review may give you a feel for how genes and environmental influences, including experience, are inextricably joined in their effects on development.

The Brain Continues to Change as We Grow Older

The passage of time brings us an accumulation of joys and sorrows—perhaps riches and fame—and a progressive decline in many of our abilities. Although slower responses seem inevitable with aging, many cognitive abilities show little change during the adult years, until we reach an advanced age. What happens to brain structure from adulthood to the day when we all become a little forgetful and walk more hesitantly?

Memory impairment correlates with hippocampal shrinkage during aging

In a study of healthy people age 55–87, investigators asked whether mild impairment in memory is specifically related to reduction in size of the hippocampal formation (HF) or is better explained by generalized shrinkage of brain tissue. (In Chapter 17 we'll see that the hippocampus is implicated in memory.) Volunteers took a series of memory tests and were scored for both immediate recall and delayed recall. MRI images for each person were measured for three variables (**FIGURE 7.25**): (1) volume of the HF;

TABLE 7.1 Intrinsic and Extrinsic Factors That Affect Neural Development

FACTORS	EXAMPLES OF EFFECTS
INTRINSIC FACTORS (GENES)	
Chromosomal aberrations	Down syndrome, fragile X syndrome
Single-gene effects	Phenylketonuria, *Drosophila* mutations
EXTRINSIC FACTORS	
Basic biological factors	Malnutrition, hypoxia
Drugs, toxins	Fetal alcohol syndrome
Cell-cell interactions	
Induction directs differentiation	Motor neurons induced by notochord
Neurotrophic factors	NGF spares sympathetic neurons
Thyroid hormone	Deficiency causes intellectual disability (see Chapter 5)
Neural activity	
Non-sensory-driven	Eye segregation in layer IV cortex before birth
Sensory-driven (experience)	Ocular dominance outside layer IV after birth, maternal behavior affects gene methylation, increased IQ resulting from childhood enrichment

(2) volume of the supratemporal gyrus, a region that is close to the HF and is known to shrink with age but has not been implicated in memory; and (3) volume of the fluid-filled space between the interior of the skull and the surface of the brain (which yields a measure of overall shrinkage of the brain). Immediate memory showed very little decline with age, but delayed memory did decline. When effects of sex, age, IQ, and overall brain atrophy were eliminated statistically, HF volume was the only brain measure that correlated significantly with the delayed-memory score (Golomb et al., 1994). Later studies confirmed this correlation between volume of the medial temporal lobe, which encases the hippocampus, and memory in the elderly (Bailey et al., 2013).

Two other brain regions show how different the effects of aging can be. In the motor cortex, a type of large neuron—called the *Betz cell*—starts to decline in number by about age 50, and by the time a person reaches age 80, many of these cells have shriveled away (M. E. Scheibel et al., 1977). In contrast, other cells involved in motor circuitry—for example, those in an area of the brainstem called the *inferior olive*— remain about the same in number through at least eight decades of life (Sjöbeck et al., 1999).

PET scans of elderly people add a new perspective to aging-related changes. Studies of healthy people reveal that cerebral metabolism remains almost constant. This stability is in marked contrast to the decline of cerebral metabolism in Alzheimer's disease (see Figure 2.21C), which we will consider next.

Space between brain and skull

Hippocampal formation

Supratemporal gyrus

7.25 HIPPOCAMPAL SHRINKAGE IS CORRELATED WITH AGE-RELATED MEMORY DECLINE MRI images like the one on the right, taken from the sectional plane shown on the left, illustrated that shrinkage of the hippocampal formation was correlated with memory decline in cognitively healthy elderly people. Overall brain shrinkage and shrinkage of the supratemporal gyrus were not. (From Golomb et al., 1994; MRI courtesy of Dr. James Golomb.)

Alzheimer's disease is associated with a decline in cerebral metabolism

The population of elderly people in the United States is increasing dramatically. Most people reaching an advanced age lead happy, productive lives, although at a slower pace than they did in their earlier years. In some elderly people, however, age has brought a particular agony: the disorder called **Alzheimer's disease**, named after Alois Alzheimer (1864–1915), the neurologist who first described a type of **dementia** (drastic failure of cognitive ability, including memory failure and loss of orientation) appearing before the age of 65. Alzheimer's disease is a type of **senile dementia**.

Over 35 million people worldwide suffer from senile dementias (Abbott, 2011), and the progressive aging of our population means that these ranks will continue to swell. The frequency of Alzheimer's increases with aging up to age 85–90 (Rocca et al., 1991), but several people have lived over 110 years without showing signs of mental impairment (Z. Yang et al., 2013). This last finding indicates that Alzheimer's is in fact a disease, and not simply the result of wear and tear in the brain. The fact that remaining physically and mentally active reduces the risk of developing Alzheimer's disease (Smyth et al., 2004) also refutes the notion that brains simply "wear out" with age. Extensive use of the brain makes Alzheimer's *less* likely.

Alzheimer's disease begins as a loss of memory of recent events. Eventually this memory impairment becomes all-encompassing, so extensive that Alzheimer's patients cannot maintain any form of conversation because both the context and prior information are rapidly lost. They cannot answer simple questions such as, What year is it? Who is the president of the United States? or Where are you now? Cognitive decline is progressive and relentless, until the patient needs constant supervision.

The cerebral cortex of a patient with Alzheimer's shows striking atrophy, especially in the frontal, temporal, and parietal areas. PET scans show marked reduction of metabolism in posterior parietal cortex and some portions of the temporal lobe

Alzheimer's disease A form of dementia that may appear in middle age but is more frequent among the aged.

dementia Drastic failure of cognitive ability, including memory failure and loss of orientation.

senile dementia A neurological disorder of the aged that is characterized by progressive behavioral deterioration, including personality change and profound intellectual decline. It includes, but is not limited to, Alzheimer's disease.

7.26 PEOPLE WITH ALZHEIMER'S SHOW STRUCTURAL CHANGES IN THE BRAIN (A) This representation of the brain shows the location of the basal forebrain nuclei and the distribution of their axons, which use acetylcholine as a neurotransmitter. These cells seem to disappear in Alzheimer's patients. (B) Neurofibrillary tangles (the flame-shaped objects) and senile plaques (the darkly stained clusters) are visible in this micrograph of the cerebral cortex of an aged patient with Alzheimer's. (From Roses, 1995; micrograph courtesy of Dr. Gary W. Van Hoesen.)

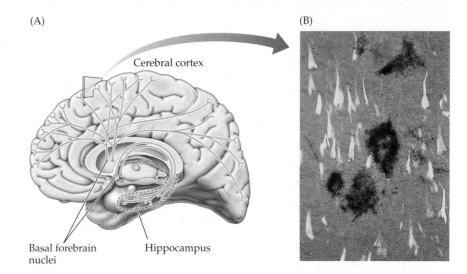

(A)

Cerebral cortex

(B)

Basal forebrain nuclei

Hippocampus

(N. L. Foster et al., 1984) (see Figure 2.22D). The brains of individuals suffering from Alzheimer's also reveal progressive changes at the cellular level (**FIGURE 7.26**):

- Patches termed **senile plaques** appear in the cortex, the hippocampus, and associated limbic system sites. The plaques, formed by the buildup of a substance called β-amyloid, impair synaptic function (Wei et al., 2010).

- Many cells show abnormalities called **neurofibrillary tangles**, which are abnormal whorls of neurofilaments, including a protein called **Tau**, that form a tangled array inside the cell. The number of neurofibrillary tangles is directly related to the magnitude of cognitive impairment (Wang and Mandelkow, 2016), and they may be a secondary response to amyloid plaques.

- These degenerative events cause the cholinergic neurons in the basal forebrain to disappear in Alzheimer's patients, either because the cells die or because they stop producing acetylcholine. The latter possibility is more likely, because providing these neurons with NGF restores their cholinergic characteristics in aged monkeys (D. E. Smith et al., 1999).

The only surefire diagnosis for Alzheimer's at present is postmortem examination of the brain for senile plaques and neurofibrillary tangles. But one innovative approach is to inject a dye, called *Pittsburgh Blue* (PiB), that has an affinity for β-amyloid. Then, a PET scan determines whether the dye has accumulated in the brain (Wolk et al., 2009). The brain of virtually every patient diagnosed with Alzheimer's accumulates the dye, as do the brains of many elderly people showing mild cognitive impairment. Scientists are working on similar scans to monitor Tau tangles, especially in the hippocampus (Maruyama et al., 2013), which might offer even better predictions about the onset of memory problems in people with Alzheimer's (**FIGURE 7.27**).

Amyloid plaques appear to be the primary cause of Alzheimer's disease, but what causes the buildup of β-amyloid? **Amyloid precursor protein** (**APP**) is cleaved by two enzymes—**β-secretase** and **presenilin**—to form extracellular β-amyloid that builds up. Once a buildup of β-amyloid forms, it seems to attract more β-amyloid molecules to join, reminiscent of infectious prion proteins (Jaunmuktane et al., 2015) that we'll discuss in Chapter 11. Perhaps in response to the β-amyloid, some neurons form neurofibrillary tangles of Tau. Another enzyme, **apolipoprotein E** (**ApoE**), works to break down β-amyloid (Bu, 2009). Mutations in each of the genes that produce these proteins can increase the risk of Alzheimer's disease (Bertram and Tanzi, 2008), but most patients have normal copies of the genes (**FIGURE 7.28**). There is growing evidence that β-amyloid normally encases invading microbes (Kumar et al., 2016), so Alzheimer's might be the result of an overly vigorous response to infection.

Several treatment strategies are being explored. For example, injection of antibodies that bind β-amyloid should slow the formation of plaques, but they do not seem to delay symptoms (C. Holmes et al., 2008). Another strategy is to develop drugs that

senile plaques Also called *amyloid plaques*. Senile plaques are small areas of the brain that have abnormal cellular and chemical patterns. Senile plaques correlate with senile dementia.

β-amyloid A protein that accumulates in senile plaques in Alzheimer's disease.

neurofibrillary tangle An abnormal whorl of neurofilaments within nerve cells.

Tau A protein associated with neurofibrillary tangles in Alzheimer's disease.

amyloid precursor protein (APP) A protein that, when cleaved by several enzymes, produces β-amyloid.

β-secretase An enzyme that cleaves amyloid precursor protein, forming β-amyloid, which can lead to Alzheimer's disease.

presenilin An enzyme that cleaves amyloid precursor protein, forming β-amyloid, which can lead to Alzheimer's disease.

apolipoprotein E (ApoE) A protein that may help break down amyloid.

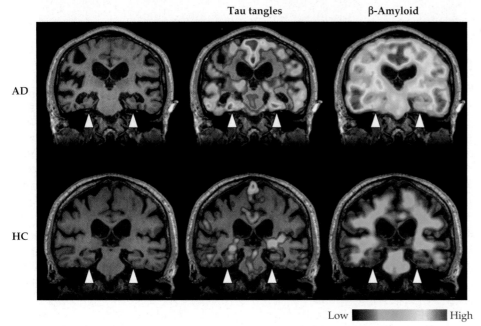

Tau tangles   **β-Amyloid**

AD

HC

Low ▬▬▬ High

7.27 IMAGING TAU TANGLES AND AMYLOID PLAQUES IN THE BRAIN By injecting radiolabeled markers, scientists can image Tau tangles, which are concentrated in the hippocampus (indicated by arrowheads) of an Alzheimer's disease (AD) patient compared to a healthy control (HC). Similarly, Pittsburgh blue can reveal β-amyloid, which is abundant throughout the brain of the AD patient. (From Maruyama et al., 2013.)

interfere with enzymes that produce β-amyloid or that boost enzymes like ApoE that break down the amyloid (Cramer et al., 2012). Unfortunately, all the drug trials to date have been disappointing, which is leading at least some scientists to question the role of amyloid in the disease (Herrup, 2015). In the meantime, and in keeping with the repeated theme of this chapter that genes and experience interact, there is good evidence that physical activity (K. I. Erickson et al., 2011), mental activity (Belleville et al., 2011), and adequate sleep (Ju et al., 2014) can postpone the appearance of Alzheimer's disease.

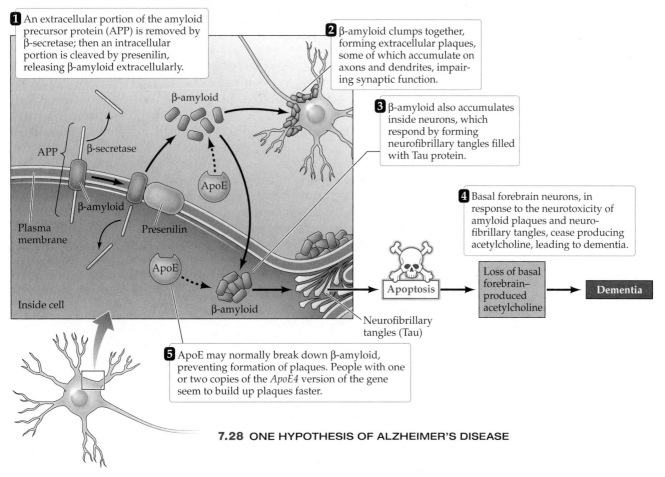

1 An extracellular portion of the amyloid precursor protein (APP) is removed by β-secretase; then an intracellular portion is cleaved by presenilin, releasing β-amyloid extracellularly.

2 β-amyloid clumps together, forming extracellular plaques, some of which accumulate on axons and dendrites, impairing synaptic function.

3 β-amyloid also accumulates inside neurons, which respond by forming neurofibrillary tangles filled with Tau protein.

4 Basal forebrain neurons, in response to the neurotoxicity of amyloid plaques and neurofibrillary tangles, cease producing acetylcholine, leading to dementia.

5 ApoE may normally break down β-amyloid, preventing formation of plaques. People with one or two copies of the *ApoE4* version of the gene seem to build up plaques faster.

β-amyloid

APP

β-secretase

β-amyloid

ApoE

Presenilin

Plasma membrane

ApoE

Inside cell

β-amyloid

Neurofibrillary tangles (Tau)

Apoptosis → Loss of basal forebrain–produced acetylcholine → **Dementia**

7.28 ONE HYPOTHESIS OF ALZHEIMER'S DISEASE

Genetically Reversing an Inherited Brain Disorder

Rett syndrome A rare genetic disorder, occurring almost exclusively in girls, of slowing development resulting in intellectual disability, stereotyped movements, and loss of language.

Rett syndrome is a rare disorder caused by a mutation that disables a gene called *MeCP2* such that it no longer produces a functional protein. Absence of the protein disrupts development in many parts of the body, including the brain. The *MeCP2* gene is on the X chromosome, so males who inherit a dysfunctional copy on their only X cannot make any functional protein and almost always die before birth. Girls inheriting a dysfunctional *MeCP2* on one X chromosome are not as severely affected because they can still make some functioning protein from the gene on their *other* X chromosome. However, their body and brain growth is impaired, and they show severe intellectual disability, typically never learning to speak.

Disrupting the *MeCP2* gene in mice also severely affects body and brain growth, as well as behavior. You might expect that the impaired brain growth would be due to the lack of MeCP2 protein in neurons. However, recent experiments suggest that the problem in brain growth in these knockout mice (see Box 7.3) may be caused by the absence of the protein in *glial cells*. Recall from Chapter 2 that microglia in the brain remain tiny (as their name implies) unless there is damage nearby. In that case, the microglia divide and grow to engulf and clean up any debris.

The strongest evidence that the symptoms of Rett syndrome in these mice are caused by microglia comes from dramatic experiments where animals lacking a functional *MeCP2* gene are rescued by transplants of normal microglia (Derecki et al., 2012). This is possible because microglia are part of the immune system, originating from bone marrow cells that enter the brain, where inducers transform the cells into microglia. The researchers subjected the knockout mice to radiation that is known to destroy the entire immune system, including microglia in the brain. Then they infused the animals with bone marrow cells, which went throughout the body, replacing the entire immune system, including microglia (**FIGURE 7.29A**). When 28-day-old *MeCP2* knockout animals were treated this way and given bone marrow from *normal* mice, their brain and body growth was restored (**FIGURE 7.29B,C**). What's more, the knockout animals given normal microglia also developed more normal behavior (**FIGURE 7.29D**). Notice that when the knockout mice were provided bone marrow from other knockouts, there was no benefit. If researchers waited until the animals were older before replacing the microglia, it was too late. The mice had to get normal microglia in place early in development to be rescued.

This rescue is impressive, but you might wonder whether the benefit really came from replacing microglia. Maybe what helped the knockout mice was replacing the immune system *outside* the brain. But the researchers showed that the benefit came from the brain. When they put a lead shield over the animals' heads during the irradiation, protecting microglia in the brain, then the normal bone marrow cells did not enter the brain (because the abnormal microglia were already there). In that case, infusing normal bone marrow did no good—the animals died young. Only by killing off the microglia lacking the gene, so that invading bone marrow cells would replace them, could they rescue the animals.

These results suggest that the symptoms of Rett syndrome are caused by a failure of microglia to clear away debris in the developing brain. Perhaps the buildup of waste products interferes with synaptic functioning or leads to loss of neurons (Petrelli, Pucci, and Bezzi, 2016). If so, then it might be possible to treat newborns inheriting the mutant gene by harvesting their bone marrow, introducing a functional copy of the *MeCP2* gene into the harvested cells, then implanting them in the brain to provide functional microglia. These results also raise the question of whether other mental disorders might be the result of more subtle dysfunction in microglia. Long ignored by scientists, glia are turning out to be a lot more important to neural development than just as "glue" for neurons.

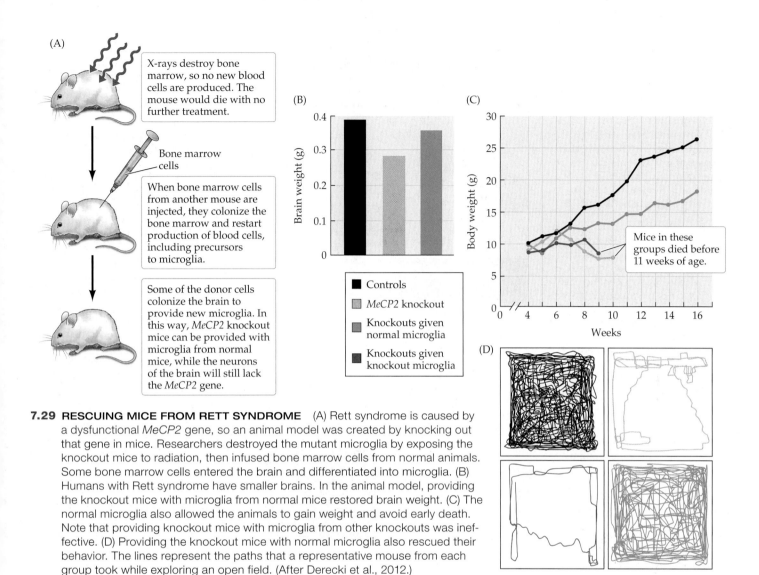

7.29 RESCUING MICE FROM RETT SYNDROME (A) Rett syndrome is caused by a dysfunctional *MeCP2* gene, so an animal model was created by knocking out that gene in mice. Researchers destroyed the mutant microglia by exposing the knockout mice to radiation, then infused bone marrow cells from normal animals. Some bone marrow cells entered the brain and differentiated into microglia. (B) Humans with Rett syndrome have smaller brains. In the animal model, providing the knockout mice with microglia from normal mice restored brain weight. (C) The normal microglia also allowed the animals to gain weight and avoid early death. Note that providing knockout mice with microglia from other knockouts was ineffective. (D) Providing the knockout mice with normal microglia also rescued their behavior. The lines represent the paths that a representative mouse from each group took while exploring an open field. (After Derecki et al., 2012.)

Recommended Reading

Bazzett, T. J. (2008). *An Introduction to Behavior Genetics.* Sunderland, MA: Sinauer.

Breedlove, S. M. *Foundations of Neural Development.* Sunderland, MA: Sinauer. Forthcoming 2017.

Gilbert, S. F., and Barresi, M. J. F. (2016). *Developmental Biology* (11th ed.). Sunderland, MA: Sinauer.

Marcus, G. (2004). *The Birth of the Mind: How a Tiny Number of Genes Creates the Complexities of Human Thought.* New York: Basic Books.

Sanes, D. H., Reh, T. A., and Harris, W. A. (2011). *Development of the Nervous System* (3rd ed.). San Diego, CA: Academic Press.

Steinberg, L. (2014). *Age of Opportunity: Lessons from the New Science of Adolescence.* New York: Houghton Mifflin Harcourt.

Wolfe, M. S. (2016). *Developing Therapeutics for Alzheimer's Disease: Progress and Challenges.* San Diego, CA: Academic Press.

Go to
bn8e.com
for study questions, quizzes, activities, and other resources

VISUAL SUMMARY

You should be able to relate each summary to the adjacent illustration, including structures and processes.
Go to **bn8e.com/vs7** for links to figures, animations, and activities that will help you consolidate the material.

1 The vertebrate brain develops from a **neural tube** with three subdivisions that will become the **forebrain**, **midbrain**, and **hindbrain**. Review **Figure 7.1**, **Activity 7.1**, **Videos 7.2 and 7.3**

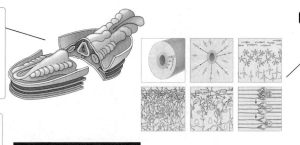

2 Early embryological events in the formation of the nervous system include a sequence of six cellular processes: (1) **neurogenesis**, (2) **cell migration**, (3) **cell differentiation**, (4) **synaptogenesis**, (5) neuronal **cell death**, and (6) **synapse rearrangement**. Review **Figures 7.2 and 7.3**, **Animation 7.4**, **Video 7.5**

3 In simple animals such as the nematode *Caenorhabditis elegans*, neural pathways and synapses form according to a genetic plan that specifies the precise relations between growing axons and particular target cells. In more-complicated animals—including all vertebrates—**cell-cell interactions** determine the fate of individual neurons and glia. Review **Figures 7.4–7.9**, **Table 7.1**, **Video 7.6**

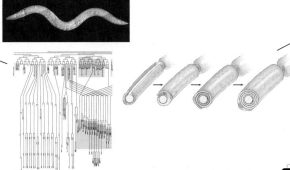

4 Although in humans most neurons are present at birth, most synapses develop *after* birth and continue developing into adulthood. Fetal and postnatal changes in the brain include the **myelination** of axons by glial cells and the development of dendrites and synapses by neurons. Review **Figures 7.10, 7.11, and 7.16**

5 Among the many determinants of brain development are (1) intrinsic genetic information and (2) a multitude of extrinsic factors, such as **neurotrophic factors**, nutrition, and experience. These factors interact extensively because extrinsic factors like experience can affect gene expression. Review **Figures 7.12–7.15, Table 7.1**

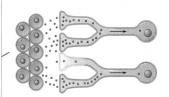

6 Impairments of fetal development that lead to intellectual disability can be caused by the use of drugs such as alcohol during pregnancy. The inheritance of many different genes can lead to **intellectual disability**. Review **Figures 7.17 and 7.18**

7 Maldevelopment of the brain can occur as a result of **mutations** or other genetically controlled disorders. Some, such as **Down syndrome** and **fragile X syndrome**, are related to disorders of chromosomes; others are metabolic disorders, such as **phenylketonuria (PKU)**. Review **Figures 7.18 and 7.19**

8 Gene expression is affected by environmental factors and experience, so **epigenetic** influences can profoundly affect brain development without altering the sequence of nucleotides in any genes. Similarly, genetically identical individuals, either twins or **clones**, do not display identical behaviors. Review **Figures 7.20 and 7.21**

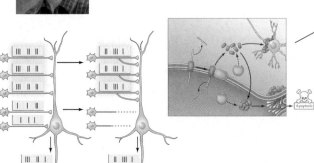

9 Experience affects the growth and development of the brain. Experience can induce and modulate the formation of synapses, maintain synapses that are already formed, or determine which neurons and synapses will survive and which will be eliminated. Review **Figures 7.22–7.24**

10 **Alzheimer's disease** seems to be caused by a buildup of β-**amyloid**, causing degenerative extracellular **senile plaques** and intracellular **neurofibrillary tangles** made up of **Tau**, through much of the cortex. Several genes, including those that encode the enzymes **presenilin** and **apolipoprotein E (ApoE)**, influence the rate of amyloid accumulation and the risk of Alzheimer's. Mental activity, physical activity, and adequate sleep seem to postpone the onset of Alzheimer's. Review **Figures 7.26–7.29**

Perception and Action

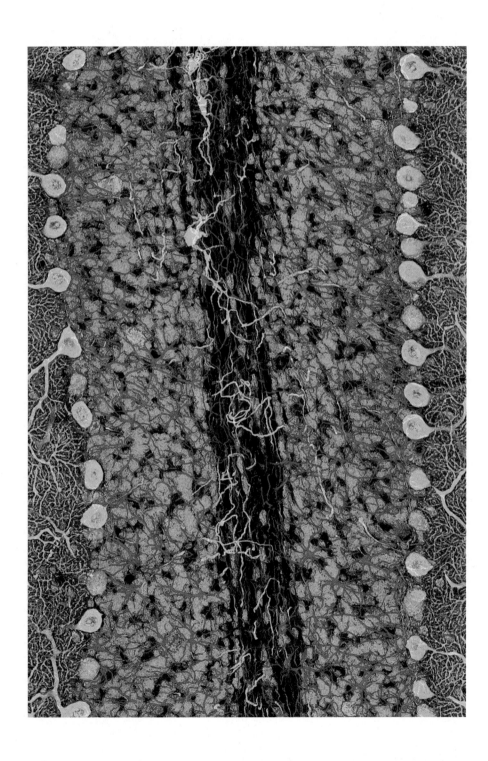

Cerebellar Purkinje cells 2-photon fluorescent micrograph of a section through the cerebellum of the brain. © Thomas Deerinck and Mark Ellisman, NCMIR, UCSD.

General Principles of Sensory Processing, Touch, and Pain

8

What's Hot? What's Not?

What would it be like to never know pain? No one likes pain, so being pain-free might seem like a great blessing—no aches, no throbbing burns, no stings or worse. And would you ever experience fear if you had never felt pain? How would you regard the world around you, including the people in your life, if you'd never experienced hurt from any injury?

Ashlyn Blocker has never felt pain. While most babies cry after the arduous birth process, newborn Ashlyn calmly stared out from her blankets. Later, she developed a terrible diaper rash, and it didn't seem to bother her at all. That seemed strange to her mother, although the doctors dismissed it. But when Ashlyn's teeth came in, she nearly chewed off part of her tongue! When she reached up to her eye and scratched the cornea deeply, that should have been excruciating, but her parents only found out about the injury when the eye swelled and grew bloodshot. Soon her mother had to wrap Ashlyn's hands to keep her from biting them and rubbing her face raw (Heckert, 2012). Despite feeling no pain—in fact *because* she feels no pain—Ashlyn's daily life is full of peril. For instance, as a teenager, she was stirring noodles in boiling water when the spoon slipped in, and Ashlyn reflexively reached in to retrieve it. With wonderful support from her family, Ashlyn has learned to think carefully about what she does to avoid injury because, although she doesn't feel *pain*, she can be *damaged*, just like everyone else, and that could lead to disability or death.

How did Ashlyn come to have this dangerous "gift" of feeling no pain? What's going on inside her so that experiences that would bring us agony cause her no discomfort at all? What can she teach us about the neuroscience of pain, and about the importance of pain for survival?

All around us, many different types of energy affect us in various ways. Some molecules traveling through the air cause us to note particular odors. We detect waves of compressed air molecules as sounds. Our abilities to detect, recognize, and appreciate these varied energies depend on the characteristics of our sensory systems.

For each species, however, certain environmental features have become especially significant for adaptive success. For example, the bat darting through the evening sky is specially equipped to detect ultrasonic cries, which we humans are unable to hear. Some snakes have infrared-sensing organs in their faces that allow them to "see" heat sources, enabling them to locate warm-blooded prey in the dark. How do animals, including humans, detect changes in the world around them?

Go to Brain Explorer
bn8e.com/8.1

8.1 THE VARIETY OF EYES (A) Scanning electron micrograph of blackfly (*Simulium damnosum*) showing the compound eye magnified ×13. (B) The panther chameleon can move its two eyes independently. (C) The eyes of the Philippine tarsier are specialized for nighttime foraging. (D) The vision of the American bald eagle is particularly sharp.

(A)

(B)

(C)

(D)

Sensory Processing

Each species has distinctive windows on the world, based on which energies it detects and how its nervous system processes that information. We open this chapter by considering some of the basic principles of sensory processing. Then we look at how those principles apply first to touch and then to pain.

Sensory Receptor Organs Detect Energy or Substances

All animals have specialized body parts that are particularly sensitive to some forms of energy. These **sensory receptor organs** act as filters of the environment: they detect and respond to some events but not others. We call an event that affects the sensory organ a **stimulus** (plural *stimuli*). Stimuli may be sound waves reaching the ear, light entering the eye, or food touching the tongue. **Receptor cells** within the organs detect particular kinds of stimuli and convert them into the language of the nervous system: electrical signals. Eventually, information from sensory receptor organs enters the brain as a series of action potentials traveling along millions of axons, and our brains must make sense of it all.

Across the animal kingdom, receptor organs offer enormous diversity. For some snakes, detectors of infrared radiation are essential; several species of fishes detect electrical fields; and some animals detect Earth's magnetic field (Czech-Damal et al., 2012; L.-Q. Wu and Dickman, 2012). These specialized sensors evolved to detect signals that are crucial for survival in particular environmental niches. Thus, receptor organs reflect strategies for success in particular worlds.

Even if we consider only a single receptor organ, such as the eye, a wide array of sizes, shapes, and forms reflects the varying survival needs of different animals (**FIGURE 8.1**). Different kinds of energy, such as light and sound, need different

sensory receptor organ An organ (such as the eye or ear) specialized to receive particular stimuli.

stimulus A physical event that triggers a sensory response.

receptor cell A specialized cell that responds to a particular energy or substance in the internal or external environment and converts this energy into a change in the electrical potential across its membrane.

TABLE 8.1 Classification of Sensory Systems

TYPE OF SENSORY SYSTEM	MODALITY	ADEQUATE STIMULI
Mechanical	Touch	Contact with or deformation of body surface
	Pain	Tissue damage
	Hearing	Sound vibrations in air or water
	Vestibular	Head movement and orientation
	Joint	Position and movement
	Muscle	Tension
Visual	Seeing	Visible radiant energy
Thermal	Cold	Decrease in skin temperature
	Warmth	Increase in skin temperature
Chemical	Smell	Odorous substances dissolved in air or water
	Taste	Substances in contact with the tongue or palate
	Common chemical	Changes in CO_2, pH, osmotic pressure
	Vomeronasal	Pheromones in air or water
Electrical	Electroreception	Differences in density of electrical currents

receptor organs to convert them into neural activity, just as taking a photograph requires a camera, not a microphone.

adequate stimulus The type of stimulus for which a given sensory organ is particularly adapted.

TABLE 8.1 classifies sensory systems, identifying the kinds of stimuli detected by sensory receptor organs in each system. An **adequate stimulus** is the type of stimulus for which a given sensory organ is particularly adapted. The adequate stimulus for the eye is photic (light) energy; an electrical shock or pressure on your eye can create an illusory sensation of light (called a *phosphene*), but neither electricity nor mechanical pressure is considered an adequate stimulus for the eye.

Sensory systems of particular animals have restricted ranges of responsiveness

For any single form of physical energy, the sensory systems of a particular animal are quite selective. For example, humans do not hear sounds with frequencies exceeding 20,000 cycles per second (i.e., hertz, or Hz)—a range we call *ultrasonic*. Many bats, however, detect vibrations in air of 50,000 Hz or more. The range of hearing of some larger mammals includes even lower frequencies than humans hear. **FIGURE 8.2** compares the auditory ranges of some animals. In the visual realm, too, some animals can detect stimuli that humans cannot. For example, birds and bees see in the ultraviolet range of light.

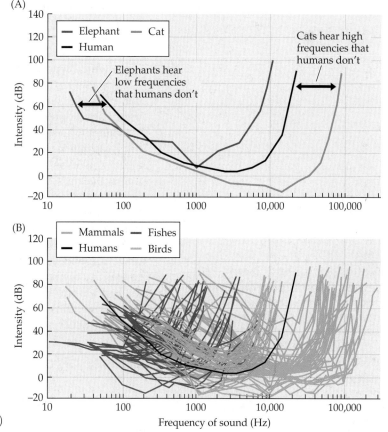

8.2 DO YOU HEAR WHAT I HEAR? For comparison, the auditory sensitivity ranges of three mammals (A) and of many species of fishes, birds, and mammals (B) are plotted here together. Note that the species within a class detect a similar range of frequencies. For a discussion of the measurement of sound, see Box 9.1. (After Fay, 1988.)

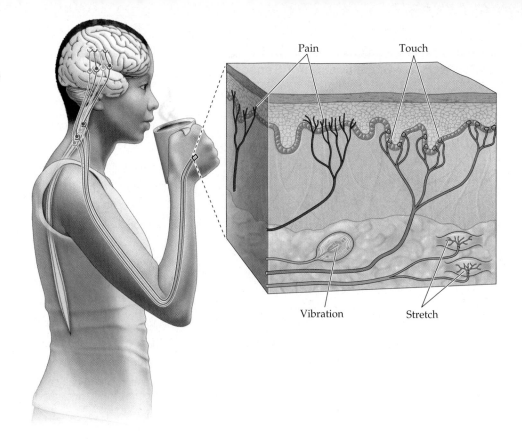

8.3 LABELED LINES Each type of receptor (stretch, vibration, pain, touch) has a distinct pathway to the brain, so different qualities of skin stimulation can be communicated to distinct places in the brain.

Pain Touch Vibration Stretch

What Type of Stimulus Was That?

How do we know whether a sudden event was a noise, a flash, or a slap? The physiologist Johannes Müller (1801–1858) proposed the doctrine of **specific nerve energies**, which states that the receptors and neural channels for the different senses are independent and that each uses a different nerve "energy." For example, no matter how the eye is stimulated—by light or mechanical pressure or electrical shock—the resulting sensation is always visual. Müller formulated his hypothesis before anyone knew about action potentials. He imagined that different receptor organs might each use a different type of energy to communicate with the brain and that the brain knew which type of stimulus had happened by which type of energy was received.

Today we know that the messages for the different senses—such as seeing, hearing, touching, sensing pain, and sensing temperature—all use the same type of "energy": action potentials. But the brain recognizes the different kinds of sensation (modalities) as separate and distinct because *each modality sends its action potentials along separate nerve tracts*. This is the concept of **labeled lines**: particular neurons are, at the outset, labeled for distinctive sensory experiences. Neural activity in one line signals a sound, activity in another line signals a smell, and activity in other lines signals touch. We can even distinguish different types of touch because some lines signal light touch, others signal vibration, and yet other lines signal stretching of the skin (**FIGURE 8.3**).

You can demonstrate this effect right now. If you take your finger and *gently* press on your eyelid, you'll see a dark blob appear on the edge of your field of view (it helps to look at a blank white wall). Of course, your skin also feels the touch of your finger, but why do you *see* a blob with your eye? The energy you applied, pressure, affected action potentials coming from your eye. Because your brain labels that line as always carrying visual information, what you *experienced* was a change in vision.

Sensory Processing Begins in Receptor Cells

Detection of energy starts with receptor cells. A given receptor cell is specialized to detect particular energies or chemicals. Upon exposure to a stimulus, a receptor cell

specific nerve energies The doctrine that the receptors and neural channels for the different senses are independent and operate in their own special ways and can produce only one particular sensation each.

labeled lines The concept that each nerve input to the brain reports only a particular type of information.

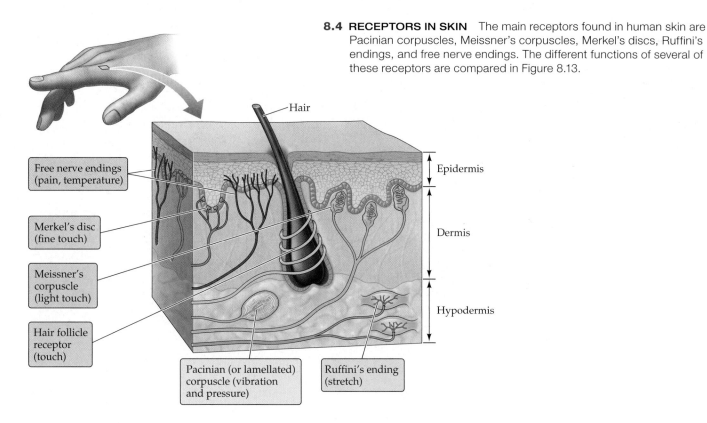

8.4 RECEPTORS IN SKIN The main receptors found in human skin are Pacinian corpuscles, Meissner's corpuscles, Merkel's discs, Ruffini's endings, and free nerve endings. The different functions of several of these receptors are compared in Figure 8.13.

Hair

Free nerve endings (pain, temperature)

Merkel's disc (fine touch)

Meissner's corpuscle (light touch)

Hair follicle receptor (touch)

Pacinian (or lamellated) corpuscle (vibration and pressure)

Ruffini's ending (stretch)

Epidermis

Dermis

Hypodermis

converts that energy or substance into a change in the electrical potential across its membrane. Changing the signal in this way is called **sensory transduction** (devices that convert energy from one form to another are known as *transducers*, and the process is called *transduction*). Receptor cells are transducers that convert energy around us into neural activity that leads to sensory perception. **FIGURE 8.4** shows some different receptor cells in skin. We will look at these types in more detail later in the chapter.

Some receptor cells have axons to transmit information. Other receptor cells have no axons of their own but stimulate associated nerve endings, either mechanically or chemically. For example, various kinds of energy-detecting corpuscles are associated with nerve endings in the skin. The eye has specialized receptor cells that convert light energy into electrical changes that cause neurotransmitter to be released onto nearby neurons. The inner ear has specialized hair cells that transduce mechanical energy into electrical signals that stimulate the fibers of the auditory nerve.

The initial stage of sensory processing is a change in electrical potential in receptor cells

The structure of a receptor determines the forms of energy to which it will respond. The steps between the arrival of energy at a receptor cell and the initiation of action potentials in a nerve fiber involve local changes of membrane potential called **receptor potentials** (or *generator potentials*). In most instances, the receptor potential resembles the excitatory postsynaptic potentials discussed in Chapter 3.

One example of the generator potential can be studied in a receptor called the **Pacinian corpuscle** (or *lamellated corpuscle*) (Loewenstein, 1971). This receptor, which detects vibration, is found throughout the body in skin and muscle. It consists of an axon surrounded by a structure that resembles a tiny onion because it has concentric layers of tissue (**FIGURE 8.5A**).

Mechanical stimuli (in this case vibration) delivered to the corpuscle produce a graded electrical potential with an amplitude that is directly proportional to the strength of the stimulus. When this receptor potential gets big enough, an action

sensory transduction The process in which a receptor cell converts the energy in a stimulus into a change in the electrical potential across its membrane.

receptor potential Also called *generator potential*. A local change in the resting potential of a receptor cell that mediates between the impact of stimuli and the initiation of action potentials.

Pacinian corpuscle Also called *lamellated corpuscle*. A skin receptor cell type that detects vibration.

8.5 THE STRUCTURE AND FUNCTION OF THE PACINIAN CORPUSCLE (A) The Pacinian corpuscle (also called a *lamellated corpuscle*) surrounds an afferent nerve fiber ending. (B) When the nerve membrane is at rest (left), the ion channels are too narrow to admit sodium ions (Na⁺). Vibration applied to the corpuscle (right) stretches part of the neuronal membrane, enlarging the ion channels and permitting the entry of Na⁺, which initiates an action potential (Lumpkin and Caterina, 2007). (C) The neuron shows increasing response to stimuli of increasing intensity until it reaches threshold, triggering an action potential.

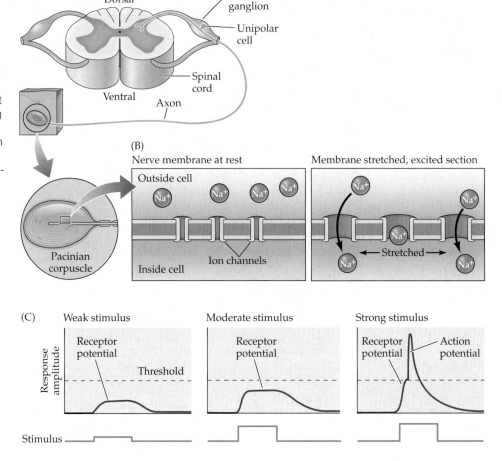

threshold The stimulus intensity that is just adequate to trigger an action potential.

coding The rules by which action potentials in a sensory system reflect a physical stimulus.

range fractionation A hypothesis of stimulus intensity perception stating that a wide range of intensity values can be encoded by a group of cells, each of which is a specialist for a particular range of stimulus intensities.

somatosensory Referring to body sensation, particularly touch and pain sensation.

potential is generated and we say that the receptor has reached **threshold**. The sequence of excitatory events is as follows:

1. Mechanical stimulation deforms the corpuscle.

2. Deformation of the corpuscle stretches the tip of the axon.

3. Stretching the axon opens mechanically gated ion channels in the membrane (Brohawn et al., 2014), allowing positively charged ions to enter (**FIGURE 8.5B**).

4. When the receptor potential reaches threshold amplitude, the axon produces one or more action potentials (**FIGURE 8.5C**).

Sensory Information Processing Is Selective and Analytical

Thinkers in ancient Greece believed that nerves were tubes through which tiny bits of stimulus objects traveled to the brain, to be analyzed and recognized there. (Imagine the nerves in your tongue sending minuscule chunks of garlic to your brain for analysis.) Even after learning about neural conduction in the twentieth century, many investigators thought that the sensory nerves simply transmitted accurate information about stimuli to the brain centers. Now, however, it is clear that the sensory organs and peripheral sensory pathways convey only limited—even *distorted*—information to the brain. A good deal of selection and analysis takes place along sensory pathways. In the discussion that follows, we will examine six aspects of sensory processing: coding, adaptation, suppression, pathways, receptive fields, and attention.

Coding: Sensory events are represented by action potentials

Information about the world is represented in the nervous system by electrical potentials in cells. We have already considered the first steps in this process—the transduction of energy at receptors, the receptor potential, and the creation of action potentials in sensory neurons. But how does this neural activity "stand for" (or represent) the stimuli impinging on the organism? Through some form of **coding**, the pattern of electrical activity in the sensory system must convey information about the original stimulus. Neural codes are limited in that each action potential is always the same size and duration, so sensory information is encoded by other features of neural activity, such as the number and frequency of the action potentials, the rhythm in which clusters of action potentials occur, and so on. Let's examine neural representations of the intensity and location of stimuli.

STIMULUS INTENSITY We respond to sensory stimuli over a wide range of intensities. Furthermore, within this range we can detect small differences of intensity. How are different intensities of a stimulus represented in the nervous system? A single neuron could represent the intensity of the stimulus by changing the frequency of action potentials transmitted, but only up to some limit, which for some neurons may be only up to 150 times per second (**FIGURE 8.6A**). Thus only a limited range of different sensory intensities can be represented in this manner, because neurons can fire only so fast.

As we noted in Chapter 3, the maximal rate of firing for any single neuron is about 1200 action potentials per second, and most sensory fibers do not fire that fast. *Multiple* receptor cells acting in a parallel manner provide a broader range for coding the intensity of a stimulus. As the strength of a stimulus increases, new neurons are "recruited"; thus, intensity can be represented by the number of active cells. **Range fractionation** takes place when different receptor cells are "specialists" in particular segments, or *fractions*, of an intensity scale (**FIGURE 8.6B**). This mode of stimulus coding requires an array of receptors and neurons that differ in threshold to fire. Some sensory neurons have a very low threshold (so they are highly sensitive); others have a much higher threshold (so they are less sensitive). Thus, one clue to the intensity of a stimulus is whether it activates only low-threshold receptors, or both low- and high-threshold receptors.

STIMULUS LOCATION The position of an object or event, either outside or inside the body, is an important piece of information. Did something just poke my foot, or my hand? Some sensory systems reveal this information by the position of excited receptors on the sensory surface. This feature is most evident in the **somatosensory** (body sensation) system. You know that an object is on your back if a receptor in the skin there is stimulated. If a receptor on your palm is stimulated, then the object must be there. Each receptor activates pathways that convey unique positional

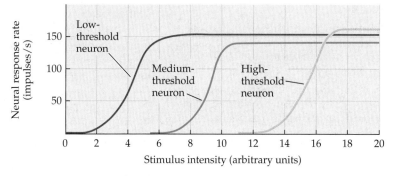

(A) Response rate versus stimulus intensity for three neurons with different thresholds

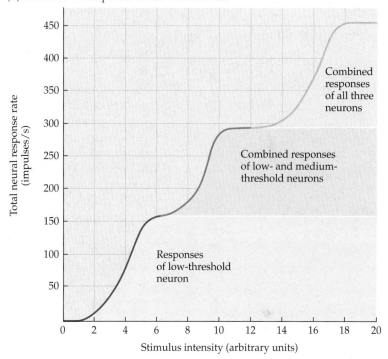

(B) Simulation of responses for the three neurons

8.6 INTENSITY CODING (A) Each of the three nerve cells represented here has a different threshold—low, medium, or high—and thus a different response to stimuli. Each cell varies its response over a *fraction* of the total *range* of stimulus intensities. (B) Although none of these nerve cells can respond faster than 150 times per second, the *sum* of all three can vary in response rate from 0 to 450 action potentials per second, accurately indicating the intensity of the stimulus—an example of range fractionation.

adaptation Here, the progressive loss of receptor sensitivity as stimulation is maintained.

tonic receptor A receptor in which the frequency of action potentials declines slowly or not at all as stimulation is maintained.

phasic receptor A receptor in which the frequency of action potentials drops rapidly as stimulation is maintained.

information. The spatial properties of a stimulus are represented by labeled lines that uniquely convey spatial information. Similarly, in the visual system an object's spatial location determines which receptors in the eye are stimulated.

In both the visual and the touch systems, cells at all levels of the nervous system—from the surface sheet of receptors to the cerebral cortex—are arranged in an orderly, maplike manner. The map at each level is not exact but reflects both position and receptor density. More cells are allocated to the spatial representation of sensitive, densely innervated sites, like the skin of the lips or the center of the eye, than to sites that are less sensitive, such as the skin of the back or the periphery of the eye.

With bilateral receptor systems—the two ears or the two nostrils—the relative time of arrival of the stimulus at the two receptors, or the relative intensity, is directly related to the location of the stimulus. For example, the only time when both ears are excited identically is when the sound source is equidistant from the ears, in the median plane of the head. As the stimulus moves to the left or right, receptors of the left and right sides are excited asymmetrically. The use of inputs from both ears to determine where sounds come from is illustrated in Figure 9.10.

Adaptation: Receptor response can decline even if the stimulus is maintained

Many receptors show progressive loss of response when stimulation is maintained, a process called **adaptation**. We can demonstrate adaptation by recording action potentials in a fiber leading from a sensory receptor that is receiving a constant level of stimulation. The frequency of action potentials progressively declines, even though the stimulus is continued (**FIGURE 8.7**). In terms of adaptation, there are two kinds of receptors: **Tonic receptors** show little or no decrease in the frequency of action potentials as stimulation is maintained; in other words, these receptors show relatively little adaptation. **Phasic receptors** display adaptation, rapidly decreasing the frequency of action potentials when the stimulus is maintained.

Adaptation means that there is a progressive shift in neural activity *away from accurate portrayal* of physical events. Thus, the sensory system may fail to register neural activity even though the stimulus continues. Such a discrepancy is no accident; sensory systems emphasize *change* in stimuli because changes are more likely to be significant for survival. Sensory adaptation prevents the nervous system from becoming overwhelmed by stimuli that offer very little "news" about the world. For example, your pants may press a hair on your leg continually, but you're saved from a constant neural barrage from this stimulus by several mechanisms, including adaptation.

The basis of adaptation includes both neural and nonneural events. For example, in some mechanical receptors, adaptation develops from the elasticity of the receptor cell itself. This situation is especially evident in the Pacinian corpuscle, which detects vibration (see Figure 8.5). Maintained vibration on the receptor results in an initial burst of neural activity and a rapid decrease to almost nothing. But when the corpuscle (which is a separate, accessory cell) is removed, the same constant stimulus applied to the uncovered sensory nerve fiber produces a continuing discharge of action potentials. So for this receptor, at least some adaptation is due to mechanical properties of the nonneural component, the corpuscle rather than the axon.

Suppression: Sometimes we need receptors to be quiet

We have noted that successful survival does not depend on exact reporting of stimuli. Rather, our success as a species demands that our sensory systems accentuate, from among the many things happening about us, the important *changes* of stimuli. We just discussed how sensory receptor adaptation can suppress a constant stimulus, but two other suppression strategies are also available.

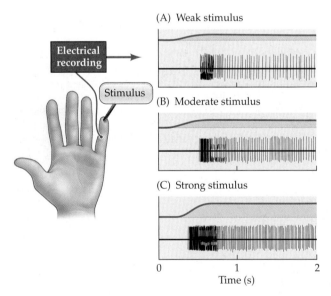

8.7 SENSORY ADAPTATION The neuron represented here responds to a touch on the fifth finger. It fires rapidly when the stimulus—whether weak (A), moderate (B), or strong (C)—is first applied, but then it adapts, slowing to a steady rate. (After Knibestol and Valbo, 1970.)

(A) Weak stimulus

(B) Moderate stimulus

(C) Strong stimulus

In many sensory systems, accessory structures can reduce the level of input in the sensory pathway. For example, closing the eyelids reduces the amount of light that enters the eye. In the auditory system, contraction of the middle-ear muscles reduces the intensity of sounds that reach the inner ear. In this form of sensory control, the relevant mechanisms change the intensity of the stimulus before it reaches the receptors.

In a second form of information control, neural connections descend from the brain to lower stations in the sensory pathway, in some cases as far as the receptor surface. This is sometimes referred to as a **top-down process**—the upper brain regions modulate the activity of lower centers. For example, higher centers in the pain system (discussed later in this chapter) send axons down the spinal cord, where they can inhibit incoming pain signals. Top-down processing is also evident in the auditory system, where cells in the brainstem send axons along the auditory nerve to connect with the base of the receptor cells to dampen their response to certain sounds.

Pathways: Successive levels of the nervous system process sensory information

Sensory information travels from the sensory surface to the highest levels of the brain, and each sensory system has its own distinctive pathway. Pathways from receptors lead into the spinal cord or brainstem, where they connect to distinct clusters of neurons. These cells, in turn, have axons that connect to other groups of neurons. Each sensory modality—such as touch, vision, or hearing—has a distinct hierarchy of tracts and stations in the brain that are collectively known as the **sensory pathway** for that modality.

Each station in the pathway accomplishes a basic aspect of information processing. For example, painful stimulation of the finger leads to reflex withdrawal of the hand, which is mediated by spinal circuits. At the brainstem level, other circuits can turn the head toward the source of pain. Eventually, sensory pathways terminate in the cerebral cortex, where the most complex aspects of sensory processing take place. For most senses, information reaches the **thalamus** before being relayed to the cortex (**FIGURE 8.8**). Information about each sensory modality is sent to a separate division of the thalamus. One way for the brain to suppress particular stimuli is for the cortex to direct the thalamus to emphasize some sensory information and suppress other information (Briggs and Usrey, 2008), another form of top-down processing.

top-down process A process in which higher-order cognitive processes control lower-order systems, often reflecting conscious control.

sensory pathway The chain of neural connections from sensory receptor cells to the cortex.

thalamus The brain regions at the top of the brainstem that trade information with the cortex.

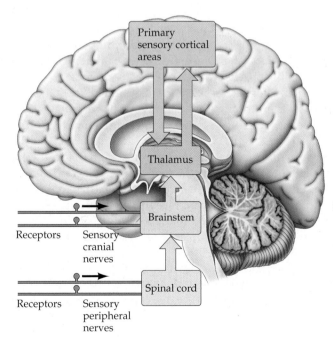

8.8 LEVELS OF SENSORY PROCESSING Sensory information enters the CNS through the brainstem or spinal cord and then reaches the thalamus. The thalamus transmits the information to the cerebral cortex; the cortex directs the thalamus to suppress some sensations. Primary sensory cortex swaps information with nonprimary sensory cortex. This organization is present in all sensory systems except smell, which bypasses the thalamus, going directly to cortex (see Figure 9.26).

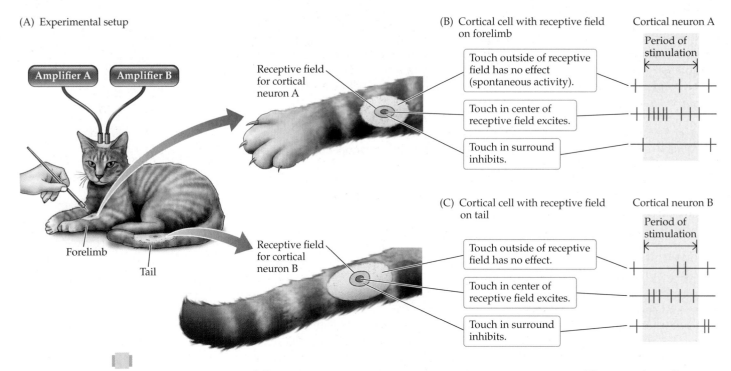

(A) Experimental setup

Amplifier A   Amplifier B

Forelimb

Tail

Go to Animation 8.2
Somatosensory Receptive Fields
bn8e.com/8.2

(B) Cortical cell with receptive field on forelimb

Receptive field for cortical neuron A

Touch outside of receptive field has no effect (spontaneous activity).

Touch in center of receptive field excites.

Touch in surround inhibits.

Cortical neuron A

Period of stimulation

(C) Cortical cell with receptive field on tail

Receptive field for cortical neuron B

Touch outside of receptive field has no effect.

Touch in center of receptive field excites.

Touch in surround inhibits.

Cortical neuron B

Period of stimulation

8.9 IDENTIFYING SOMATOSENSORY RECEPTIVE FIELDS The procedures illustrated here are used to record from somatosensory neurons of the cerebral cortex. Changes in the position of the stimulus affect the rate of action potentials. Neuron A responds to touch on a region of the forepaw; neuron B, only a few centimeters away in the somatosensory cortex, responds to stimulation of the tail. The receptive fields of these neurons include an excitatory center and an inhibitory surround, but other neurons have receptive fields with the reverse organization: inhibitory centers and excitatory surrounds.

Receptive fields: What turns on this particular receptor cell?

receptive field The stimulus region and features that affect the activity of a cell in a sensory system.

The **receptive field** of a sensory neuron consists of a region of space in which a stimulus will alter that neuron's firing rate. To determine this receptive field, investigators record the neuron's electrical responses to a variety of stimuli to see what makes the activity of the cell change from its resting rate. For example, which patch of skin must we vibrate to change the activity of a particular Pacinian corpuscle? Such experiments show that somatosensory receptive fields have either an excitatory center and an inhibitory surround, or an inhibitory center and an excitatory surround (**FIGURE 8.9**). These receptive fields make it easier to detect edges and discontinuities on the objects we feel.

Receptive fields differ also in size and shape and in the quality of stimulation that activates them. For example, some neurons respond preferentially to light touch, while others fire most rapidly in response to painful stimuli, and still others respond to cooling.

Following sensory information from the receptor cell in the periphery into the brain shows that neurons all along the pathway will respond to particular stimuli, so each of these cells has a receptive field too. But as each successive neuron combines information from prior cells in the pathway, the receptive fields change considerably. Receptive fields have been studied for cells at all levels, from the periphery to the brain, and we will see many examples of receptive fields later in this chapter and in Chapters 9 and 10.

RECEPTIVE FIELDS IN THE CEREBRAL CORTEX   For a given sensory modality we can find several different regions (fields) of cortex that receive information about that sense. Each of these cortical regions has a separate map of the same receptive surface, but the different cortical regions process the information differently and make different contributions to perceptual experiences.

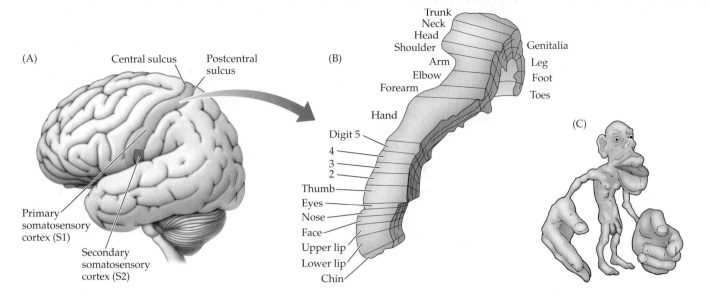

8.10 REPRESENTATION OF THE BODY SURFACE IN SOMATOSENSORY CORTEX (A) The locations of primary (S1) somatosensory cortex on the lateral surface of the parietal cortex. Secondary somatosensory cortex (S2) is much smaller than S1. (B) The order and size of cortical representations of different regions of skin. Note that information from the various parts of the hand and fingers takes up much more room than does information from the shoulder. (C) The *homunculus* (literally, "little man") depicts the body surface with each area drawn in proportion to the size of its representation in the primary somatosensory cortex.

By convention, one of the cortical maps is designated as **primary sensory cortex** for that particular modality. Thus, there is primary somatosensory cortex, primary auditory cortex, and so on. The other cortical maps for a given modality are said to be **secondary sensory cortex**, or *nonprimary sensory cortex* (see Figure 8.8). The primary cortical area is the main source of input to the other fields for the same modality, even though these other fields also have direct thalamic inputs. Information is sent back and forth between the primary and nonprimary sensory cortex through subcortical loops (see Figure 8.8).

Primary somatosensory cortex (*somatosensory 1*, or **S1**) of each hemisphere lies in the postcentral gyrus of the parietal cortex, just behind the central sulcus dividing the parietal lobe from the frontal lobe. Each S1 receives touch information from the opposite side of the body (**FIGURE 8.10**). The cells in S1 are arranged according to the plan of the body surface (Kell et al., 2005). Each region is a map of the body in which the relative areas devoted to body regions reflect the density of body innervation. Thus, parts of the body where we are especially sensitive to touch (like the hand and fingers) send information to a larger area of S1 than do less sensitive body regions (like the shoulder). **Secondary somatosensory cortex** (*somatosensory 2*, or **S2**) maps both sides of the body in registered overlay; that is, the left-arm and right-arm representations occupy the same part of the map, and so forth.

Some mammals have a very different pattern of representation in somatosensory cortex. For example, the nose of the star-nosed mole is a very sensitive organ for touch, and a considerable portion of its somatosensory cortex is devoted to responding to each of the rays of the "star" (**FIGURE 8.11**) (Catania, 2001).

Attention: How do we notice some stimuli but not others?

Attention is the process by which we select or focus on one or more specific stimuli for enhanced processing and analysis. Sometimes attention is a top-down process, when we decide to concentrate our attention on a particular task. In other cases, a sudden loud noise may pull our attention to some dramatic event.

primary sensory cortex For a given sensory modality, the region of cortex that receives most of the information about that modality from the thalamus or, in the case of olfaction, directly from the secondary sensory neurons.

secondary sensory cortex Also called *nonprimary sensory cortex*. For a given sensory modality, the cortical regions receiving direct projections from primary sensory cortex for that modality.

primary somatosensory cortex (S1) Also called *somatosensory 1*. The gyrus just posterior to the central sulcus, in the parietal lobe, where sensory receptors on the body surface are mapped; primary cortex for receiving touch and pain information.

secondary somatosensory cortex (S2) Also called *somatosensory 2*. The region of cortex that receives direct projections from primary somatosensory cortex.

attention A state or condition of selective awareness or perceptual receptivity, by which specific stimuli are selected for enhanced processing.

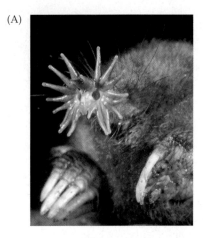

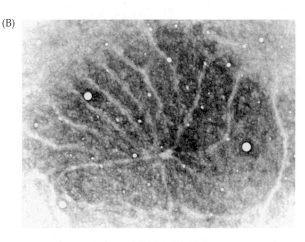

8.11 HEY THERE, YOU WITH THE STAR ON YOUR NOSE (A) The tip of the star-nosed mole's nose is a very delicate organ for touch. (B) In this section from the somatosensory cortex of a star-nosed mole, we can see how each of the 11 rays from one-half of the star-shaped nose projects to its own patch of cortex. The two bottommost rays are the most sensitive; each innervates a larger piece of cortex than do the other rays. (From Catania, 2001, photographs courtesy of Dr. Ken Catania.)

cingulate cortex Also called *cingulum*. A region of medial cerebral cortex that lies dorsal to the corpus callosum.

In sensory processes, a cortical region that plays a special role in attention is the posterior parietal lobe. Many cells here are especially responsive in a trained monkey that is expecting the appearance of a stimulus (Mountcastle et al., 1981), whether auditory or visual. Lesions of this area in monkeys result in inattention, or neglect of stimuli, on the opposite side. (In Chapter 18 we will see that this symptom is especially severe in people with lesions of the right parietal lobe.)

The **cingulate cortex** (the portion of cortex along and just above the corpus callosum; see Figure 2.17) has been implicated in attention. We'll see an example of that later in this chapter when we learn that anterior cingulate cortex seems to mediate the emotional, discomforting aspect of pain. **FIGURE 8.12** shows activation in the cingulate and posterior parietal cortex during a task involving a shift in spatial orientation (Gitelman et al., 1996; Nobre et al., 1997). We'll discuss these and other aspects of attention at some length in Chapter 18.

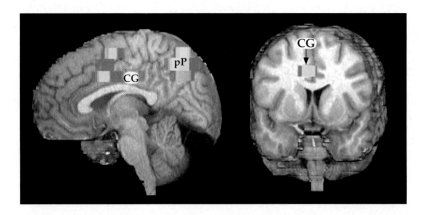

8.12 BRAIN REGIONS ACTIVATED WHEN WE ARE ATTENDING Functional MRI images of a person cued to expect a stimulus in a particular portion of the visual field show right-hemisphere activation in posterior parietal cortex (pP) and cingulate cortex (CG) in midsagittal (left) and frontal (right) views. Areas of highest activation are shown in yellow. (Courtesy of Dr. Darren Gitelman.)

Sensory systems influence one another

Often the use of one sensory system influences perception derived from another sensory system. For example, cats may not respond to birds unless they can both see and hear the birds; neither sense alone may be sufficient to elicit a response (B. Stein and Meredith, 1993). Similarly, humans detect a visual signal more accurately if it is accompanied by a sound from the same part of space (McDonald et al., 2000).

Many sensory areas in the brain—so-called association areas—do not represent exclusively a single modality but show a mixture of inputs from different modalities. Some "visual" cells, for instance, also respond to auditory or touch stimuli. Perhaps loss of input from one modality allows these cells to analyze input from the remaining senses better, as happens, for example, in cases of people who become blind early in life and are better than sighted people at localizing auditory stimuli (Gougoux et al., 2005). The normal stimulus convergence on such **polymodal** cells provides a mechanism for intersensory interactions (B. E. Stein and Stanford, 2008). For a few people, a stimulus in one modality may evoke an additional perception in another modality, as when seeing a letter evokes a color, or hearing different tones evokes different flavors—a situation that is described further in **BOX 8.1**.

polymodal Involving several sensory modalities.

BOX 8.1

Synesthesia

For a few people, stimuli in one modality evoke the involuntary experience of an additional sensation in another modality—a condition known as **synesthesia** (from the Greek *syn*, "union," and *aesthesis*, "sensation"). For example, a person with synesthesia (a "synesthete") may perceive different colors when seeing different letters of the alphabet ("*D* looks green, but *E* is blue") or words for days of the week ("*Tuesday* is a yellow word"). In one documented example, a musician experienced a particular taste whenever she heard a specific musical tone interval (Beeli et al., 2005). Discordant tones evoked unpleasant tastes.

How common synesthesia is depends to some extent on how it's defined, but it is estimated that as much as 2–4% of the population displays some form of synesthesia, and as much as 1% reports experiencing a color along with particular days of the week or numbers (Simner et al. 2006). In a sample of 11 people reporting the common synesthesia of color associated with letters, many associations were identical across the individuals. For example, most reported experiencing red with the letters *A*, *M*, and *S*; yellow with the letters *C*, *O*, and *U*; and green with *D*, *P*, and *V* (Witthoft and Winawer,

(A) Magnetic letter set

2013). The authors noted that these color associations match those in a popular Fisher-Price toy set of magnetic letters (Figure A), which at least some of the synesthetes remembered having as a child. So, did the early exposure to the toy inspire these particular associations of letters with colors? (If you look at Figure A, you'll see the toy letters are colored in the order of the rainbow—red, orange, yellow, green, blue, violet [ROYGBV]—over and over.) Brain imaging shows that such synesthetes have more axonal connections across cortex, especially in the temporal lobe (Rouw and Scholte, 2007), suggesting

that the experience of color is due to extensive connections between brain regions.

Since you probably do not have this experience, you may doubt whether other people really do, if the basis for knowing that they do is self-report alone. For some forms of synesthesia, however, a clever test may confirm whether, for example, "2 is red but 5 is green." Ramachandran and Hubbard (2001) showed a page like that in Figure B to someone who reported having this experience. They asked him to quickly point to all of the

(continued)

BOX 8.1

Synesthesia (continued)

2s. Because the shapes of 2 and 5 are so similar, it takes a certain amount of time for most people (nonsynesthetes) to pick out each 2 among all those 5s. But this person found them much faster than that. For such a synesthete, the numbers look colored, as in Figure C; with the addition of colors, it's certainly much easier to pick out the 2s.

You can test whether *you* have synesthesia online at http://synesthete.org (Eagleman et al., 2007).

synesthesia A condition in which stimuli in one modality evoke the involuntary experience of an additional sensation in another modality.

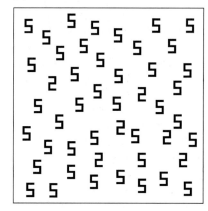

(B) Difficult search

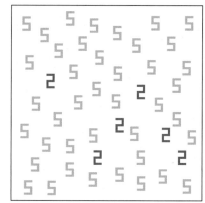

(C) Easy search

Touch: Many Sensations Blended Together

The skin that envelops our bodies is a delicate yet durable boundary that separates us from our surroundings. It also presents to the world a massive array of sensory receptors monitoring many types of stimuli. But touch is not just touch. Careful studies of skin sensations reveal qualitatively different sensory experiences: pressure, vibration, tickle, "pins and needles," and more-complex dimensions, such as smoothness or wetness—all recorded by the receptors in the skin.

Skin Is a Complex Organ That Contains a Variety of Sensory Receptors

epidermis The outermost layer of skin, over the dermis.

dermis The middle layer of skin, between the epidermis and the hypodermis.

hypodermis Also called *subcutaneous tissue*. The innermost layer of skin, under the dermis.

tactile Of or relating to touch.

Meissner's corpuscle A skin receptor cell type that detects light touch.

Merkel's disc A skin receptor cell type that detects fine touch.

Because the average person has about 1–2 square meters (10–20 square feet) of skin, skin is sometimes considered the largest human organ. Skin is made up of three separate layers; the relative thickness of each varies over the body surface. The outermost layer—the **epidermis**—is the thinnest. The middle layer—the **dermis**—contains a rich web of nerve fibers in a network of connective tissue and blood vessels. The innermost layer—the **hypodermis** (or *subcutaneous tissue*)—provides an anchor for muscles, contains Pacinian corpuscles, and helps shape the body (see Figure 8.4).

Pain, heat, and cold at the skin are detected by free nerve endings (see Figure 8.4), which are described later in this chapter. In contrast, light touch is detected by four highly sensitive **tactile** (touch) receptors (**FIGURE 8.13**). We mentioned earlier the Pacinian corpuscles, which are found in the hypodermis. The onion-like outer portion of the corpuscle acts as a filter, shielding the underlying nerve fiber from most stimulation. Only vibrating stimuli of more than 200 Hz will pass through the corpuscle and stretch the nerve fiber to reach threshold. Normally, the skin receives this sort of rapid vibration when it is moving across the *texture* of an object's surface. The ridges provided by fingerprints mechanically filter out vibrations of some frequencies and amplify others, apparently optimizing the stimulation of Pacinian corpuscles (Scheibert et al., 2009). Pacinian corpuscles are fast-responding and fast-adapting receptors (**FIGURE 8.13A**).

Most of our ability to perceive the form of an object we touch comes from the fast-adapting **Meissner's corpuscles** (**FIGURE 8.13B**) and the slow-adapting, oval **Merkel's discs** (**FIGURE 8.13C**). These receptors are densely distributed in skin regions where we can discriminate fine details by touch (fingertips, tongue, and lips).

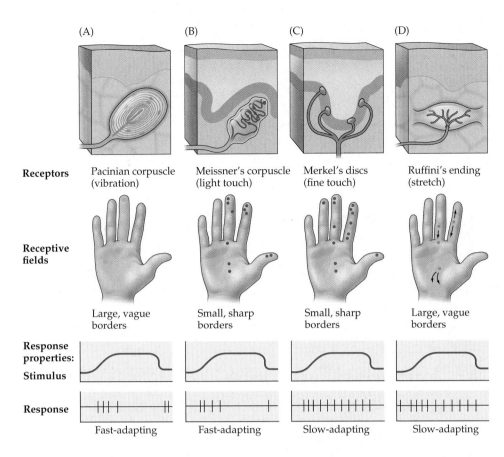

| Receptors | Pacinian corpuscle (vibration) | Meissner's corpuscle (light touch) | Merkel's discs (fine touch) | Ruffini's ending (stretch) |

Receptive fields

| Large, vague borders | Small, sharp borders | Small, sharp borders | Large, vague borders |

Response properties:

Stimulus

Response

| Fast-adapting | Fast-adapting | Slow-adapting | Slow-adapting |

8.13 PROPERTIES OF SKIN RECEPTORS RELATED TO TOUCH Shown here for each skin receptor is the type of receptor (top), the size and type of the receptive field (middle), and the electrophysiological response (bottom). (A) Pacinian corpuscles activate fast-adapting fibers with large receptive fields. (B) Meissner's corpuscles are fast-adapting mechanoreceptors with small receptive fields. (C) Merkel's discs are slow-adapting receptors with small receptive fields. (D) Ruffini's endings are slow-adapting receptors with large receptive fields. The locations of these receptors in the skin are illustrated in Figure 8.4. (After Johansson and Flanagan, 2009.)

The receptive fields of Merkel's discs usually have an inhibitory surround, which increases their spatial resolution. This field also makes them especially responsive to isolated *points* on a surface (such as the dots for Braille characters). Genetically modified mice that lack Merkel's discs no longer respond to light touch (Maricich et al., 2009).

Meissner's corpuscles are more numerous than Merkel's discs but offer less spatial resolution. Meissner's corpuscles seem specialized to respond to *changes* in stimuli (as one would expect from rapidly adapting receptors) to detect localized movement between the skin and a surface (Heidenreich et al., 2012). This sensitivity to change in stimuli provides detailed information about *texture* (K. O. Johnson and Hsiao, 1992).

Both Meissner's corpuscles and Merkel's discs preferentially respond to *edges* on a surface (Pruszynski and Johansson, 2014). These receptors respond to touch because they make a specialized ion channel, called **Piezo2**, which opens when mechanically stretched and so depolarizes the cell. Disabling the *Piezo2* gene in mice severely disrupts their response to light touch, without affecting response to painful stimuli or temperatures (Ranade et al., 2014).

The final touch receptors are the slow-adapting **Ruffini's endings**, which detect *stretching* of the skin when we move fingers or limbs. The very few Ruffini's endings (Pare et al., 2003) have large receptive fields (Johansson and Flanagan, 2009) (**FIGURE 8.13D**).

All four of these light-touch receptors utilize moderately large (so-called Aβ) myelinated fibers (**TABLE 8.2**). Recall from Chapter 3 that large axons conduct action potentials faster than small axons do and that myelination speeds conduction even more. So the light-touch receptors send information very rapidly to the CNS. Later in this chapter we'll learn that some pain fibers are large and conduct rapidly, while others are small and conduct slowly. In Chapter 11 we'll meet a man whose large fibers were destroyed by a virus, so he can no longer feel light touch. He can still feel pain, coolness, and warmth on his skin, however, because those smaller axons were spared. **FIGURE 8.14** compares how the four light-touch receptors respond when a finger is moved across the raised dots of Braille.

Piezo2 A receptor protein in touch receptors that responds to mechanical stretch by opening channels to let cations in to depolarize the cell.

Ruffini's ending A skin receptor cell type that detects stretching of the skin.

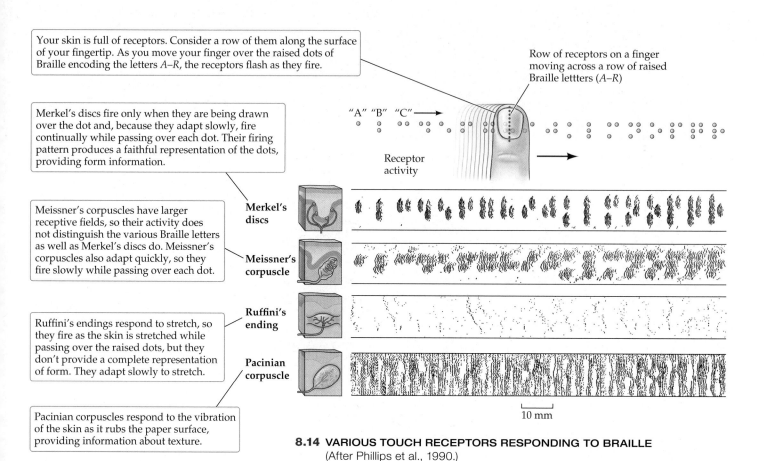

Your skin is full of receptors. Consider a row of them along the surface of your fingertip. As you move your finger over the raised dots of Braille encoding the letters *A–R*, the receptors flash as they fire.

Row of receptors on a finger moving across a row of raised Braille lettters (*A–R*)

"A" "B" "C" →

Merkel's discs fire only when they are being drawn over the dot and, because they adapt slowly, fire continually while passing over each dot. Their firing pattern produces a faithful representation of the dots, providing form information.

Receptor activity

Meissner's corpuscles have larger receptive fields, so their activity does not distinguish the various Braille letters as well as Merkel's discs do. Meissner's corpuscles also adapt quickly, so they fire slowly while passing over each dot.

Merkel's discs

Meissner's corpuscle

Ruffini's endings respond to stretch, so they fire as the skin is stretched while passing over the raised dots, but they don't provide a complete representation of form. They adapt slowly to stretch.

Ruffini's ending

Pacinian corpuscle

Pacinian corpuscles respond to the vibration of the skin as it rubs the paper surface, providing information about texture.

10 mm

8.14 VARIOUS TOUCH RECEPTORS RESPONDING TO BRAILLE
(After Phillips et al., 1990.)

TABLE 8.2 Fibers That Link Receptors to the CNS

SENSORY FUNCTION(S)	RECEPTOR TYPE(S)	AXON TYPE	DIAMETER (µm)	CONDUCTION SPEED (M/S)
Proprioception (body sense)	Muscle spindle (see Chapter 11)	Aα (A alpha)	13–20	80–120
Touch (see Figures 8.13 and 8.14)	Pacinian corpuscles, Ruffini's endings, Merkel's discs, Meissner's corpuscles	Aβ (A beta)	6–12	35–75
Pain, temperature	Free nerve endings	Aδ (A delta)	1–5	5–30
Temperature, pain, itch	Free nerve endings	C	0.2–1.5	< 1

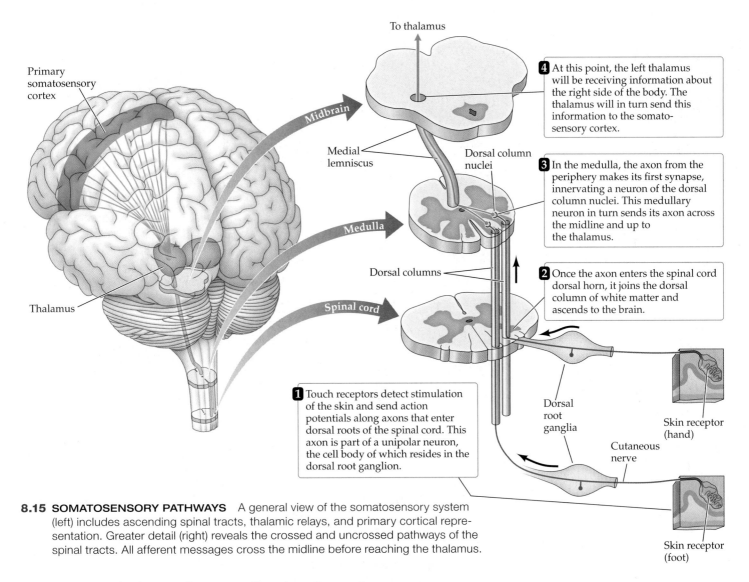

8.15 SOMATOSENSORY PATHWAYS A general view of the somatosensory system (left) includes ascending spinal tracts, thalamic relays, and primary cortical representation. Greater detail (right) reveals the crossed and uncrossed pathways of the spinal tracts. All afferent messages cross the midline before reaching the thalamus.

Labels in figure:

Primary somatosensory cortex

Thalamus

To thalamus

Medial lemniscus

Dorsal column nuclei

Dorsal columns

Dorsal root ganglia

Cutaneous nerve

Skin receptor (hand)

Skin receptor (foot)

Midbrain

Medulla

Spinal cord

4 At this point, the left thalamus will be receiving information about the right side of the body. The thalamus will in turn send this information to the somatosensory cortex.

3 In the medulla, the axon from the periphery makes its first synapse, innervating a neuron of the dorsal column nuclei. This medullary neuron in turn sends its axon across the midline and up to the thalamus.

2 Once the axon enters the spinal cord dorsal horn, it joins the dorsal column of white matter and ascends to the brain.

1 Touch receptors detect stimulation of the skin and send action potentials along axons that enter dorsal roots of the spinal cord. This axon is part of a unipolar neuron, the cell body of which resides in the dorsal root ganglion.

The Dorsal Column System Carries Somatosensory Information from the Skin to the Brain

The touch receptors that we have described (Pacinian corpuscles, Merkel's discs, Meissner's corpuscles, and Ruffini's endings) send their axons to the spinal cord, where they enter the dorsal horn and turn upward, traveling to the brain along the spinal cord's dorsal column of white matter, which is why this is called the **dorsal column system**. These axons go all the way up to the brainstem, where they synapse on neurons of the **dorsal column nuclei** in the medulla (**FIGURE 8.15**). The axons of these medullary neurons then cross the midline to the opposite side and ascend to a group of nuclei of the thalamus. Outputs of the thalamus are directed to primary somatosensory cortex (S1).

The skin surface can be divided into bands corresponding to the spinal nerves that carry the axons from the different regions. A **dermatome** (from the Greek *derma*, "skin," and *tome*, "part" or "segment") is the region of skin innervated by a particular spinal nerve. The pattern of dermatomes is hard to understand in an upright human, but remember that our erect posture is a recent evolutionary development. The mammalian dermatomal pattern evolved among our quadrupedal (four-legged) ancestors. Thus, the dermatomal pattern makes more sense when depicted on a person in a quadrupedal posture. The dermatomes overlap a modest amount (**FIGURE 8.16**).

dorsal column system A somatosensory system that delivers most touch stimuli via the dorsal columns of spinal white matter to the brain.

dorsal column nuclei Collection of neurons in the medulla that receive somatosensory information via the dorsal columns of the spinal cord. These neurons send their axons across the midline and to the thalamus.

dermatome A strip of skin innervated by a particular spinal nerve.

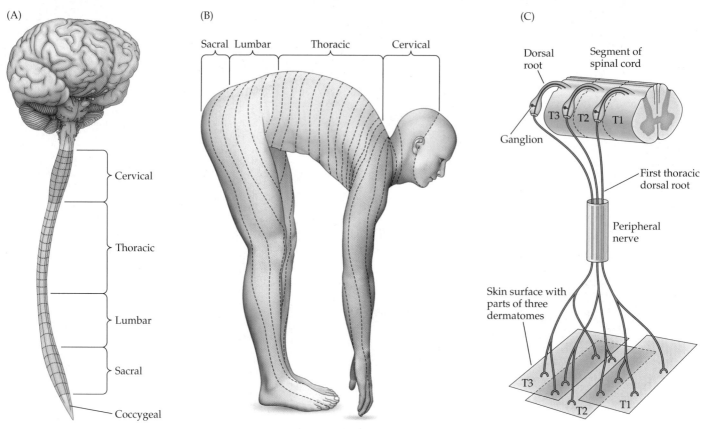

(A)

Cervical

Thoracic

Lumbar

Sacral

Coccygeal

(B)

Sacral Lumbar Thoracic Cervical

(C)

Dorsal root

Segment of spinal cord

T3 T2 T1

Ganglion

First thoracic dorsal root

Peripheral nerve

Skin surface with parts of three dermatomes

T3 T2 T1

8.16 DERMATOMES (A) Bands of skin send their sensory inputs to different dorsal roots of the spinal cord. Each dermatome is the section of skin that is innervated primarily by a given dorsal root. (B) In this side view of the human body in quadrupedal position, the pattern of dermatomes is color-coded to correspond to the spinal regions in A, and it appears more straightforward than it would in the erect posture. (C) Adjacent dorsal roots of the spinal cord collect sensory fibers from overlapping strips of skin, so the boundaries between the dermatomes overlap.

Plasticity in cortical maps: Receptive fields can be changed by experience

At one time, most researchers thought that cortical maps were fixed early in life and were invariant among all members of the same species. Now, however, we know that cortical maps can change with experience (Merzenich and Jenkins, 1993).

In one experiment, the receptive field of a monkey's hand was mapped in detail in the somatosensory cortex (**FIGURE 8.17A**). Then the middle finger was surgically removed. The region of cortex that responded to each remaining, adjacent finger expanded, so the region that had formerly responded to the removed finger now responded to the neighboring fingers (**FIGURE 8.17B**). In another experiment, a monkey was trained to rest two fingers on a rotating disk in order to obtain food rewards. After several weeks of training, the hand area was mapped again, and the stimulated fingers were found to have enlarged representations compared with their previous areas (**FIGURE 8.17C**).

Similar findings were noted in rats exposed to differential tactile experiences (Xerri et al., 1996). Professional musicians who play stringed instruments have expanded cortical representations of their left fingers, presumably because they have been using these fingers to depress the strings for precisely the right note (Elbert et al., 1995; Münte et al., 2002). Brain imaging also reveals cortical reorganization in people who lose a hand in adulthood (**FIGURE 8.18**). One man received a transplanted hand (from an accident victim) 35 years after losing his own. Despite the length of time that had passed, his brain reorganized in just a few months to receive sensation from the new hand in the appropriate part of S1 (S. H. Frey et al., 2008).

Having dealt with the pleasant aspects of touch, we turn now to the mixed blessing of pain.

(A) Representation of the left
    hand in primary somatosensory
    cortex in right hemisphere
    of monkey brain

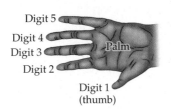

Digit 5
Digit 4
Digit 3
Digit 2

Palm

Digit 1
(thumb)

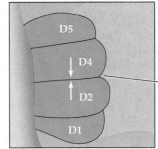

Posterior   Anterior

Body
Face

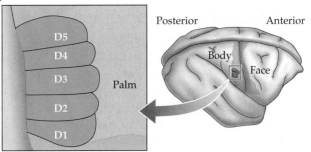

D5
D4
D3
D2
D1

Palm

Details of cortical map
(D5 = digit 5, etc.)

**8.17 THE PLASTICITY OF SOMATOSEN-
SORY REPRESENTATIONS** These
experiments demonstrate that the adult
brains of monkeys can be altered by experience. (After Merzenich and Jenkins,
1993.)

(B) Experiment 1

D3 surgically removed.

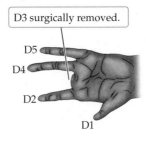

D5
D4
D2

D1

D5
D4
D2
D1

Several weeks later,
areas representing
D2 and D4 have
expanded, replacing
the representation
of D3.

(C) Experiment 2

Monkey trained to keep
two fingers in contact with
rotating stimulus disk.

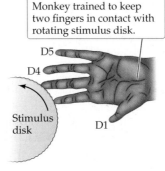

D5
D4

Stimulus
disk

D1

D5
D4
D3
D2
D1

Areas representing
stimulated digits
expand and replace
part of the areas that
formerly represented
adjacent digits.

(A) Typical somatosensory cortex

Hand   Arm

Face

Central
sulcus

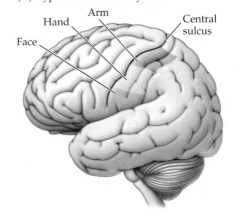

(B) Somatosensory cortex
    reorganized after loss of hand

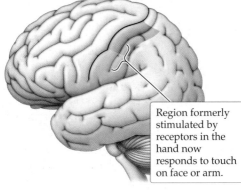

Region formerly
stimulated by
receptors in the
hand now
responds to touch
on face or arm.

**8.18 TYPICAL AND REORGANIZED
SOMATOSENSORY CORTEX** In
humans we can map S1 using functional
brain imaging to determine which parts of
cortex are activated by touch on different
parts of the body. (A) Normally, the region
of S1 receiving information from the hand
is interposed between the regions representing the upper arm and the face. (B)
In a person who, as an adult, loses one
hand, the cortical regions representing the
upper arm and face expand, taking over
the cortical region previously representing
the missing hand. Presumably the loss of
sensory input from the lost hand allows
those cortical neurons to become innervated by neighboring inputs. (Part B after
T. T. Yang et al., 1994.)

Pain: An Unpleasant but Adaptive Experience

The International Association for the Study of Pain defines **pain** as "an unpleasant sensory and emotional experience associated with actual or potential tissue damage, or described in terms of such damage." Because pain is unpleasant and causes great suffering, it may be difficult to imagine a biological role for it. But clues to the adaptive significance of pain can be gleaned from the study of rare individuals with **congenital insensitivity to pain**, who never experience pain (Hirsch et al., 1995), like Ashlyn, whom we met at the start of the chapter.

The first clinically reported person with congenital insensitivity to pain worked on the stage as a "human pincushion" (**FIGURE 8.19**) (Dearborn, 1932). People who display pain insensitivity can discriminate between the touch of the point or head of a pin, but they experience no pain when pricked with the point. Such people show extensive scarring from injuries to fingers, hands, and legs (Manfredi et al., 1981), and they tend to die young of injuries, suggesting that pain guides adaptive behavior by signaling harm to our bodies.

Pain provides us with powerful lessons about how to avoid injury. Dennis and Melzack (1983) list three more ways that pain helps us:

1. Short-lasting pain causes us to withdraw from the source, often reflexively, thus preventing further damage.

2. Long-lasting pain promotes behaviors, such as sleep, inactivity, grooming, feeding, and drinking, that promote recuperation.

3. The expression of pain serves as a social signal to other animals. For example, screeching after a painful stimulus signals the potential harm to genetically related individuals and elicits caregiving behavior from them, such as grooming, defending, and feeding.

Human Pain Can Be Measured

In some parts of the world, people endure, with stoic indifference, rituals (including body mutilation) that would cause most other humans to cry out in pain. Incisions of the face, hands, arms, legs, or chest; walking on hot coals; and other treatments clearly harmful to the body can be part of the ritual. Comparable experiences are also seen in more ordinary circumstances, such as when a highly excited athlete continues to play a game with a broken arm or leg. Learning, experience, emotion, and culture all affect the perception of pain in striking ways.

The mere terms *mild* and *intense* are inadequate to describe the pain that is distinctive to a particular disease or injury. The physician's simple query "Is the pain still there?" has been replaced by a more detailed analysis that provides better clues about how to control pain. For example, the McGill Pain Questionnaire (Melzack, 1984) consists of a list of words arranged into classes that describe three different aspects of pain:

1. The *sensory-discriminative* quality (e.g., throbbing, gnawing, shooting)

2. The *motivational-affective* (emotional) quality (e.g., tiring, sickening, fearful)

3. An overall *cognitive* evaluative quality (e.g., no pain, mild, excruciating)

Patients are asked to select the set of words that best describes their pain. These three components reflect different aspects of pain perception (**FIGURE 8.20**).

One of the interesting aspects of the McGill scale is that it can distinguish among pain syndromes, meaning that patients use a distinctive constellation of words to describe a particular pain ex-

8.19 DOESN'T THAT HURT? The earliest scientific report of a person with congenital insensitivity to pain was of a man working in the theater, like the man shown here, as a "human pincushion." (Photograph by Culver Pictures, Inc.)

THE HUMAN PINCUSHION WHO INCURS CONSTANT RISKS OF BLOOD POISONING.

pain The discomfort normally associated with tissue damage.

congenital insensitivity to pain The condition of being born without the ability to perceive pain.

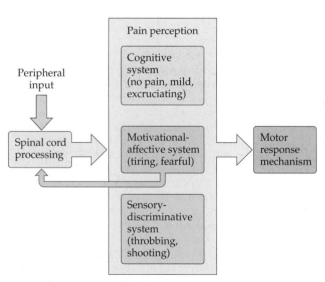

8.20 THE MULTIFACETED CHARACTER OF PAIN

perience. For example, tooth pain is described differently from arthritic pain, which in turn is described differently from menstrual pain.

Contemporary studies of pain mechanisms have revealed receptors in the skin that transmit pain information to the central nervous system. In this section we will discuss some features of peripheral and CNS pathways that mediate pain.

Peripheral receptors get the initial message

In most cases the initial stimulus for pain is the destruction or injury of tissue adjacent to certain nerve fibers. The damaged tissue releases chemicals that activate pain fibers in the skin. Various substances have been suggested as the chemical mediators of pain, including neuropeptides, serotonin, histamine, various proteolytic (protein-metabolizing) enzymes, and prostaglandins (a group of widespread hormones) (**FIGURE 8.21**).

Peripheral receptors and nerve fibers that are specialized to respond to pain are called **nociceptors**. **Free nerve endings** in the dermis display no specialized structures (they look like naked nerve endings), but they have specialized receptor proteins on the cell membrane that respond to various signals. Different free nerve endings produce different receptor proteins, so they report different stimuli, such as pain and/or changes in temperature.

HOT, COLD, OR COOL? The best evidence for specialized pain fibers in the periphery came from studies of **capsaicin**, the chemical that makes chili peppers spicy hot. Investigators isolated a receptor found in some free nerve endings that binds capsaicin, and they found that the receptor also responds to sudden increases in temperature (Caterina et al., 1997). The receptor was cloned and found to be a member of a family of proteins called *transient receptor potential* (TRP) ion channels. They named the capsaicin receptor **transient receptor potential vanilloid type 1 (TRPV1)**, or *vanilloid receptor 1*, because the crucial component of the capsaicin molecule is a chemical known as *vanilloid*. Mice lacking the gene for this receptor still responded to *mechanosensory* pain, but not to mild heat or capsaicin (Caterina et al., 2000). So the reason that chili peppers taste "hot" is that the capsaicin in the peppers activates TRPV1 receptors in the body that normally detect noxious heat.

nociceptor A receptor that responds to stimuli that produce tissue damage or pose the threat of damage.

free nerve ending An axon that terminates in the skin without any specialized cell associated with it and that detects pain and/or changes in temperature.

capsaicin A compound synthesized by various plants to deter predators by mimicking the experience of burning.

transient receptor potential vanilloid type 1 (TRPV1) Also called *vanilloid receptor 1*. A receptor that binds capsaicin to transmit the burning sensation from chili peppers and normally detects sudden increases in temperature.

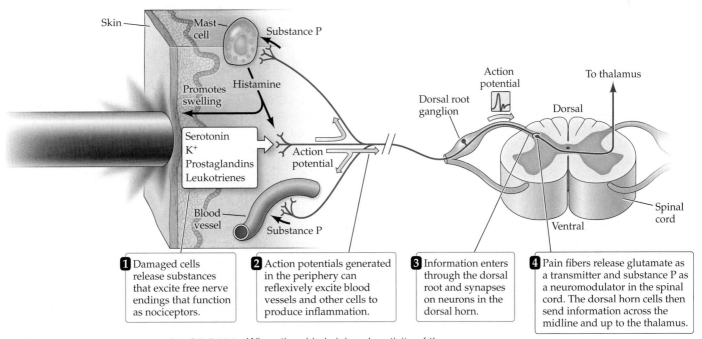

8.21 PERIPHERAL MEDIATION OF PAIN When the skin is injured, activity of the peripheral nervous system causes the local release of various substances.

1. Damaged cells release substances that excite free nerve endings that function as nociceptors.

2. Action potentials generated in the periphery can reflexively excite blood vessels and other cells to produce inflammation.

3. Information enters through the dorsal root and synapses on neurons in the dorsal horn.

4. Pain fibers release glutamate as a transmitter and substance P as a neuromodulator in the spinal cord. The dorsal horn cells then send information across the midline and up to the thalamus.

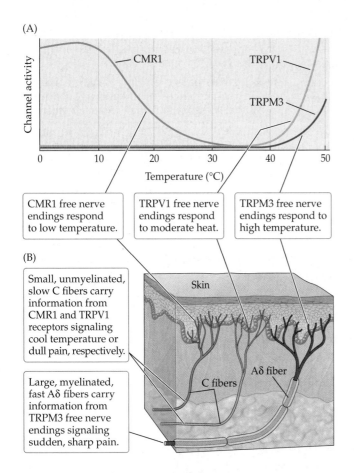

(A)

CMR1 TRPV1

TRPM3

Channel activity

Temperature (°C)
0   10   20   30   40   50

CMR1 free nerve endings respond to low temperature.

TRPV1 free nerve endings respond to moderate heat.

TRPM3 free nerve endings respond to high temperature.

(B)

Small, unmyelinated, slow C fibers carry information from CMR1 and TRPV1 receptors signaling cool temperature or dull pain, respectively.

Large, myelinated, fast Aδ fibers carry information from TRPM3 free nerve endings signaling sudden, sharp pain.

Skin

C fibers

Aδ fiber

8.22 RECEPTORS THAT DETECT PAIN AND TEMPERATURE (A) Free nerve endings with cool-menthol receptor 1 (CMR1) are activated by temperatures below normal body temperature. Free nerve endings with the capsaicin receptor (TRPV1) respond to moderate heat and the capsaicin found in chili peppers. Other free nerve endings, with the related receptor protein TRPM3, detect high temperatures. (B) The TRPM3 free nerve endings transmit a fast action potential along large, myelinated Aδ fibers to the spinal cord. CMR1 and TRPV1 receptors transmit along slower, unmyelinated C fibers. (Part A after Vriens et al., 2014.)

transient receptor potential type M3 (TRPM3) A receptor, found in some free nerve endings, that opens its channel in response to rising temperatures.

Aδ fiber A moderately large, myelinated, and therefore fast-conducting axon, usually transmitting pain information.

C fiber A small, unmyelinated axon that conducts pain information slowly and adapts slowly.

cool-menthol receptor 1 (CMR1) Also called *TRPM8*. A sensory receptor, found in some free nerve endings, that opens an ion channel in response to a mild temperature drop or exposure to menthol.

The venom of a Caribbean tarantula contains peptides that activate this same receptor, causing an intense burning sensation (Siemens et al., 2006).

TRPV1's normal job is to report a drastic rise in temperature to signal burning. Chili peppers evolved the chemical capsaicin to ward off mammalian predators, which is why some people sprinkle chili pepper flakes on their flower bushes to discourage deer from eating them. Capsaicin molecules have the perfect shape to bind to TRPV1 and open its ion channel, which is normally opened by heat. Because the brain interprets action potentials from that nerve as signaling painful heat, we (and the deer) experience painful heat.

Interestingly, the *bird* version of TRPV1 is *not* affected by capsaicin (Tewksbury and Nabhan, 2001). In this case both the animal and the plant benefit from capsaicin: the birds are able to get food from the plants—food that might be gone if mammals were able to eat it—and then fly off to spread the chili seeds far and wide. Clever, clever chili plants.

Why do our lips swell when we have overindulged in capsaicin? As Figure 8.21 illustrates, the action potentials generated by the chemical travel back out other branches of the axon to affect blood vessels and mast cells, triggering the swelling. Paradoxically, rubbing capsaicin into the skin overlying arthritic joints brings some pain relief, perhaps because overactivated pain fibers temporarily run out of transmitter.

A related receptor, **transient receptor potential type M3 (TRPM3)**, detects even higher temperatures than does TRPV1 (Vriens et al., 2014). TRPM3 differs from TRPV1 in two other ways as well: TRPM3 does *not* respond to capsaicin, and TRPM3 receptors are found on nerve fibers larger than those carrying TRPV1. Remember that large axons conduct action potentials more rapidly than do small axons. TRPM3 receptors are found on relatively large axons known as **Aδ** ("A delta") **fibers**: large-diameter, myelinated axons (**FIGURE 8.22**). Because of the relatively large axon diameter and myelination, these fibers report to the spinal cord very quickly. When you burn your finger on a hot skillet, the first, sharp pain you feel is conducted by these fat Aδ fibers that detected the heat with TRPM3 receptors. In contrast, the nerve fibers that possess TRPV1 receptors consist of thin, unmyelinated fibers called **C fibers** (see Figure 8.22B). These C fibers conduct slowly, and TRPV1 adapts slowly, providing the second wave of pain—the dull, lasting ache in that darned finger.

This is the reason for the slight delay between licking the cut surface of a chili pepper and feeling the burn. Only the TRPV1 fibers, with their slowly conducting C fibers, have been activated, not the fast Aδ fibers using TRPM3. Table 8.2 compares these different fibers.

Taking a cue from the success with capsaicin, another group of investigators tried looking for the "coolness" receptor, reasoning that it should respond to the chemical menthol. They found and named **cool-menthol receptor 1 (CMR1)**. CMR1 is also a member of the TRP family (so it is sometimes called *TRPM8*) but responds to *cool* temperatures, and it is found on small C fibers (Bautista et al., 2007), so it transmits information about cool temperatures rather slowly (see Figure 8.22). Another member of the TRP family is expressed by other free nerve endings to make them responsive to the spices oregano, thyme, and clove (H. Xu et al., 2006), while another receptor responds to garlic and onion (Salazar et al., 2008), and yet another receptor from this family responds to the mustard oils that are found in wasabi (Jordt et al.,

2004). Spices add so much to our experience of food because they stimulate these various receptors in our mouth (in addition to the olfactory receptors we'll discuss in Chapter 9).

Yet other free nerve endings provide us with the sensation of itch (gee, thanks!). Some of these fibers respond to histamine that is released from mast cells in the skin (see Figure 8.21). Other causes of itch—like certain medications and plants such as cowhage—do not respond to antihistamines (Gawande, 2008), indicating that a second, histamine-independent mechanism can also provide the sensation of itch (S. R. Wilson et al., 2011). These two itch systems both use the same TRPV1 receptors as heat-detecting neurons and, like those receptors, use slowly conducting C fibers to send action potentials to the spinal cord. But unlike heat sensors, the itch-specific fibers use a particular neurotransmitter, called **natriuretic polypeptide B** (**Nppb**) to stimulate neurons in the dorsal horn (LaMotte et al., 2014). Mice lacking the gene for Nppb fail to show an itch response (Mishra and Hoon, 2013). Scratching the affected area of skin provides temporary relief by silencing those spinal neurons that normally respond to the Nppb fibers and in turn report itch sensation to the brain. This spinal mechanism to suppress response to itch signals uses neuropeptide Y (NPY) (see Chapter 13) for a transmitter (Bourane et al., 2015), so perhaps it will be possible to develop drugs to activate these NPY-sensitive circuits to suppress itch.

THE PAIN RECEPTOR? The search for the protein receptor used by free nerve endings to detect *mechanical* damage was hindered by the fact that so many chemicals are released by damaged tissue. It remains unclear which chemical is crucial for activating nociceptors. However they are initially activated, nociceptors then use a very particular type of voltage-gated sodium channels to produce action potentials to report pain to the brain. We learned this fascinating aspect of nociception from a family in northern Pakistan. A 10-year-old boy there was giving street performances of piercing his arms with knives and walking on hot coals without pain. Before scientists could locate him, he died after jumping off a roof to impress his friends. The boy got up, saying he felt fine, unaware of the internal bleeding that killed him.

This boy's apparent fearlessness, which cost him his life, reminds us that pain, and fear derived from pain, really can be our friend. Six of the boy's relatives also felt no pain. They could detect light touch, coolness, warmth, and other sensations just fine. Scientists isolated the gene, called *SCN9A*, responsible for pain insensitivity in this family and found that it encodes a voltage-gated sodium channel **Na$_v$1.7** that is expressed in many free nerve endings (Cox et al., 2006). For some reason, pain receptors rely primarily on this particular voltage-gated sodium channel to initiate action potentials (Waxman and Zamponi, 2014). A mutation of the *Na$_v$1.7* gene in this family prevents the channel from opening, and so the pain receptors do not produce action potentials. Ashlyn, the teenager we described at the start of the chapter, has a similar mutation in this gene. She can feel light touch, vibrations, coolness, and warmth, but not the high temperatures that cause burns. Axons that would normally signal pain don't produce action potentials to send the message to her brain. Other mutations of the same channel may make it open more readily, causing a life of chronic pain (Catterall and Yu, 2006). Interestingly, this same channel is also used by odor-detecting sensory cells to produce action potentials (J. Weiss et al., 2011), as we'll discuss further in Chapter 9. That is why Ashlyn and others with this mutation cannot detect odors (Heckert, 2012). Why these particular sensory neurons use this particular sodium channel for producing action potentials, while the vast majority of neurons use other sodium channels, remains a mystery. But it's exciting to think that we may be able to synthesize drugs that specifically block that channel, and therefore pain, without silencing the entire brain. At the end of the chapter, we'll learn how natural selection has modified another sodium channel to help grasshopper mice withstand the sting from scorpions.

natriuretic polypeptide B (Nppb) A peptide neurotransmitter used by neurons reporting itch to the spinal cord.

Na$_v$1.7 Also called *SCN9A*. A voltage-gated sodium channel used almost exclusively by nociceptors to initiate action potentials.

A PAINLESS LIFE? Unable to feel pain, Ashlyn must be more vigilant than other teenagers to avoid injury.

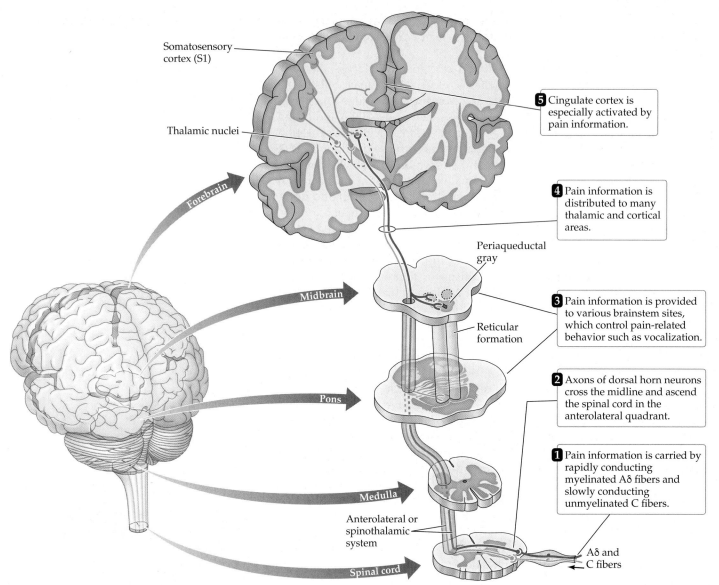

Somatosensory cortex (S1)

Thalamic nuclei

5 Cingulate cortex is especially activated by pain information.

4 Pain information is distributed to many thalamic and cortical areas.

Periaqueductal gray

3 Pain information is provided to various brainstem sites, which control pain-related behavior such as vocalization.

Reticular formation

2 Axons of dorsal horn neurons cross the midline and ascend the spinal cord in the anterolateral quadrant.

1 Pain information is carried by rapidly conducting myelinated Aδ fibers and slowly conducting unmyelinated C fibers.

Forebrain

Midbrain

Pons

Medulla

Anterolateral or spinothalamic system

Spinal cord

Aδ and C fibers

8.23 PAIN ASCENDS THE SPINOTHALAMIC SYSTEM TO REACH THE BRAIN Sensation of pain travels from its origin to the brain via the spinothalamic system, crossing the midline in the spinal cord.

anterolateral system or spinothalamic system A somatosensory system that carries most of the pain and temperature information from the body to the brain.

glutamate An amino acid transmitter, the most common excitatory transmitter.

substance P A peptide transmitter implicated in pain transmission.

Spinal pathways transmit pain information

In the central nervous system, special pathways mediate pain and temperature information. Earlier we discussed the dorsal column system that carries touch information to the brain (see Figure 8.15). The sensations of pain and temperature are transmitted separately by the **anterolateral**, or **spinothalamic**, **system**. Free nerve endings in the skin send their axons to synapse on neurons in the dorsal horn of the spinal cord. These spinal cord neurons send their axons across the midline to the opposite side and up the anterolateral column of the spinal cord to the thalamus (hence the term *spinothalamic*). So, in the spinothalamic system, pain information crosses the midline in the spinal cord before ascending to the brain (**FIGURE 8.23**); recall that touch information, in contrast, first ascends to the brainstem and then crosses the midline (see Figure 8.15). Either way, sensory information from one side of the body ends up in the opposite side of the brain.

The afferent fibers from the periphery that carry nociceptive information probably use **glutamate** as a neurotransmitter to excite spinal cells in the dorsal horn (S. Li and Tator, 2000), but they also release the neuromodulator **substance P**, which is a neuropeptide (the *P* stands for *peptide*). Injection of capsaicin into the skin provides a specific painful stimulus that leads to the release of substance P in the dorsal horn.

There, the postsynaptic neurons take up the substance P and begin remodeling their dendrites; investigators have speculated that this neural plasticity later affects pain perception, as we'll discuss shortly (Mantyh et al., 1997).

Further evidence that substance P plays a role in pain comes from experiments with knockout mice that lack either a gene for substance P (Cao et al., 1998) or the substance P receptor (De Felipe et al., 1998). These mice are unresponsive to certain kinds of intense pain. Interestingly, they still respond to mildly painful stimuli, suggesting that other signals, perhaps the glutamate neurotransmitter, can carry that information.

The reign of pain is mainly in the brain

Sometimes pain persists long after the injury that gave rise to it has healed. The most dramatic example is a person's continued perception of chronic pain coming from a missing limb after loss of an arm or leg. Called *phantom limb pain*, this sensation is an example of **neuropathic pain**, so called because the pain seems to be due to inappropriate signaling of pain by neurons (rather than to tissue damage). The pain experienced may also be called *neuralgia*. Such cases can be seen as a disagreeable example of neural plasticity, because the nervous system seems to have amplified its response to the pain signal (Woolf and Salter, 2000). Some of this amplification is taking place in the cortex (Flor et al., 2006), but changes in the spinal cord also contribute. After peripheral nerve injury (such as a damaged back or lost limb), microglial cells surround the synapses between pain fibers and neurons in the dorsal horn of the spinal cord. These microglial cells release chemicals that make the dorsal horn neurons hyperexcitable (Guan et al., 2016). Nearby astrocytes also boost the effectiveness of the synapses between pain fibers and spinal cells (Gosselin et al., 2010). Thus, the dorsal horn neurons become chronically active, flooding the thalamus with action potentials signaling pain.

Chronic pain can have dramatic effects on the brain. One study found that the gray matter in the dorsolateral prefrontal cortex of people with chronic back pain shrinks faster than in normal aging, averaging 1.3 cubic millimeters more per year of pain (Apkarian et al., 2004). This shrinkage is equivalent to 10–20 years of normal aging.

Cases of phantom limb pain are notoriously difficult to treat. In one type, the patient perceives that a missing limb is twisted and therefore hurts. Vilayanur Ramachandran has pioneered a treatment for this condition: the patient looks at himself in a mirror, positioned in such a way that the reflection of the intact limb seems to have filled in for the missing limb (**FIGURE 8.24**). The patient then repeatedly moves "both limbs" (by moving the remaining one), watching closely the whole while, and sometimes reports that the phantom limb feels as though it has straightened out and no longer hurts (Ramachandran and Rogers-Ramachandran, 2000). This result suggests that the brain interprets the signals coming from the limb stump as painful, but visual stimuli may lead to a reinterpretation.

Pain information is eventually integrated in the cingulate cortex. The cingulate cortex is much more activated by a stimulus if people are led to believe that the stimulus will be painful (see Figure 1.5) (Rainville et al., 1997). The extent of activation in the cingulate (as well as in somatosensory cortex) also correlates with how much discomfort different people report in response to the same mildly painful stimulus (Coghill et al., 2003; Vogt, 2005). In people experiencing pain, both anterior and posterior cingulate were activated; but when they were *empathizing* with a loved one who was experiencing pain, experiencing the *emotional* components of pain, only the *anterior* cingulate was activated (T. Singer et al., 2004).

neuropathic pain Pain caused by damage to peripheral nerves; often difficult to treat.

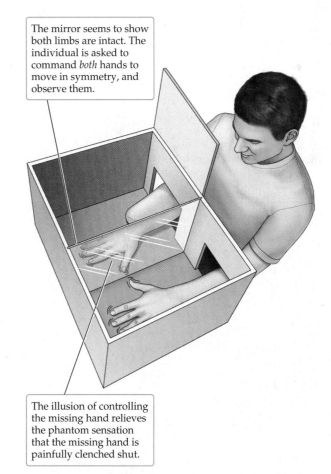

The mirror seems to show both limbs are intact. The individual is asked to command *both* hands to move in symmetry, and observe them.

The illusion of controlling the missing hand relieves the phantom sensation that the missing hand is painfully clenched shut.

8.24 USING A VISUAL ILLUSION TO RELIEVE PHANTOM LIMB PAIN (After Ramachandran and Rogers-Ramachandran, 2000.)

migraines Intense headaches, typically perceived from one half of the head, that recur regularly and can be difficult to treat.

The cingulate cortex is also activated in people experiencing illusory pain (Craig et al., 1996): placing your hand over alternating pipes of cool and warm (not hot) water produces the sensation of pain, as though the pipes were hot. Presumably this illusory pain sensation is produced by the unusual circumstance of neighboring CMR1 and TRPV1 receptors being stimulated at the same time. Since no tissue is actually being damaged, this is a wonderful illustration that "pain is in the brain."

Migraines, intense headaches that typically affect one side of the head and recur at regular intervals, also illustrate the central role of the brain in pain. Some migraines are associated with a wave of neuronal hyperexcitation that spreads across the cortex, leaving in its wake a wave of inhibition or *cortical spreading depression*. The wave of activity stimulates trigeminal nerves that normally signal damage in blood vessels, causing the experience of pain (Pietrobon and Moskowitz, 2014). Another theory is that the trigeminal nerves release a neuropeptide called *CGRP*, which actually causes the pain, so interfering with CGRP might provide relief (Underwood, 2016). Genetic susceptibility to migraine has been traced to genes encoding ion channels and pumps (Chasman et al., 2011) that trigger the hyperexcitation.

Social Rejection Hurts Too

We've noted that while it is very unpleasant, pain is our friend. The neural machinery for pain was favored by natural selection to shape our behavior, causing us to avoid doing things that are bad for us (which might leave us with no descendants). Perhaps natural selection has also exploited that same machinery underlying pain to shape our social behavior (Panksepp, 1998). We are born small and defenseless, utterly dependent on others for protection. In evolutionary times, our dependence on others continued in adulthood—only *groups* of humans could benefit from cooperative hunting and ensure safety from predators whose claws and teeth far outmatch our own. Does being excluded from the group, which could be fatal in those days, activate the emotional component of the pain system (**FIGURE 8.25**)?

Indeed, several findings indicate that social rejection also activates the anterior cingulate cortex and that the extent to which a person is upset by rejection correlates with activation of this region (Eisenberger, 2012). In one study, participants were brought to the lab to play a virtual game of catch with other people through a computer. The other two players were supposed to be on other computers, but in fact the researchers determined whether the participant would get to participate in throwing the ball (social inclusion). For some participants, the other two "players" would toss the ball back and forth exclusively with each other, excluding the participant. This game took place while the participant's head was in an fMRI scanner monitoring brain activity.

As you might expect, being excluded from a virtual ball toss bothered some participants more than others (Eisenberger and Lieberman, 2004). Remarkably, the more distress or feelings of rejection the participant felt, the greater the activity in anterior cingulate cortex (**FIGURE 8.26A**). If in fact social rejection activates the same emotional pain as physical damage, then can the same drugs that relieve the affective discomfort of physical ills also relieve the pain of rejection? Yes. When participants were given either placebos or a painkiller (acetaminophen, often marketed as Tylenol) before playing virtual catch, the ones given placebo reported more hurt feelings from social rejection than those given Tylenol (DeWall et al., 2010). What's more, there was less activation of the anterior cingulate in the participants taking Tylenol before being socially rejected (**FIGURE 8.26B**). Participants taking the painkiller also reported fewer hurt feelings in their everyday lives than those taking placebo.

So, does Ashlyn, the girl who's never felt physical pain, suffer hurt feelings if she is socially rejected? Do the higher brain centers, never receiving signals of physical pain, fail to develop enough for her to have hurt feelings? Ashlyn cried when her dog ran away, so she can feel sad (Heckert, 2012). And surely she can tell if people reject her, but does that hurt?

These findings that social hurt activates the same brain centers as physical pain refute the old saying "sticks and stones may break my bones, but words will never hurt me."

8.25 SOCIAL REJECTION There is evidence that social rejection activates the same emotional brain circuits as physical pain.

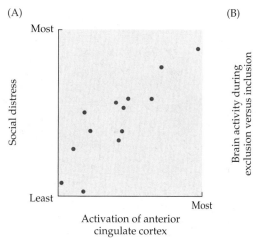

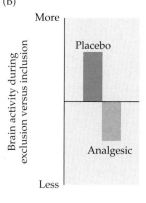

8.26 SOCIAL REJECTION ACTIVATES BRAIN REGIONS FOR AFFECTIVE PAIN (A) Participants' emotional response to social rejection when playing a virtual game of catch correlates with activation in anterior cingulate cortex, the region that mediates the emotional distress of pain from physical damage. (B) People who had been taking Tylenol before experiencing social rejection reported less distress than those taking placebo and also displayed less activation of this brain region. (Part A after Eisenberger and Lieberman, 2004; B after DeWall et al., 2010.)

That outmoded notion may explain why historically our society has been more concerned about physical bullying—pushing, biting, hitting—than verbal bullying such as yelling, name-calling, and social rejection. Playgrounds often display a sex difference in bullying styles. Boys tend to resort to physical bullying, while girls tend to use social rejection to hurt each other (Simmons, 2003). Adults who would quickly intervene if boys were hitting each other might ignore a group of girls rejecting a playmate. But if social rejection activates the same brain regions mediating pain as physical bullying, and if the discomfort experienced is the same, the distinction seems unfounded.

Pain Can Be Difficult to Control

Having learned that there are specific pathways that transmit pain signals to the brain, you might think that simply cutting the axons signaling pain would take care of the problem. But one frustrating, puzzling aspect of neuropathic pain is that cutting the pathway may reduce pain perception only temporarily. After a pathway in the spinal cord is cut, pain is initially diminished, but it returns in a few weeks or months. The usual way that these data are interpreted is that nociceptive input from the remaining intact pathways becomes abnormally effective.

Different strategies can alleviate pain

Here are some of the strategies to control pain, which are prime examples of the interaction between basic research and application.

OPIATE DRUGS Opium has been used for **analgesia** (loss of pain sensation; from the Greek *an-*, "not," and *algesis*, "feeling of pain") for centuries. In attempts to determine how **opiates** (drugs, such as morphine, that are derived from or related to opium) control pain, modern researchers found that the brain contains natural opiate-like substances, or **opioids**. In effect, the brain modulates pain by releasing substances that work the same way as exogenous opioids such as morphine. Three classes of **endogenous opioids—endorphins**, **enkephalins**, and **dynorphins**—have been discovered (see Chapter 4), and several classes of **opioid receptors** have been identified and designated by Greek letters. Of these, the mu (μ) receptor seems to be most affected by morphine. There are interesting individual differences in opioid receptor function. For example, analgesics that act on μ receptors are more effective in men than in women, while drugs that act on the kappa (κ) receptors are more effective in women than in men (Mogil and Chanda, 2005). Furthermore, the κ receptor–specific drugs are especially effective in redheaded women (Mogil et al., 2003).

In an enormously influential paper, Melzack and Wall (1965) suggested that pain is subject to many modulating influences, including some that can close spinal "gates" controlling the flow of pain information from the spinal cord to the brain. Indeed, a brainstem system projects to the spinal cord to close the pain gate. Electri-

analgesia Absence of or reduction in pain.

opiates A class of compounds that exert an effect like that of opium, including reduced pain sensitivity.

opioids A class of peptides produced in various regions of the brain that bind to opioid receptors and act like opiates.

endogenous opioids A family of peptide transmitters that have been called the body's own narcotics. The three kinds are enkephalins, endorphins, and dynorphins.

endorphins One of three kinds of endogenous opioids, substances that reduce pain perception.

enkephalins One of three kinds of endogenous opioids, substances that reduce pain perception.

dynorphins One of three kinds of endogenous opioids, substances that reduce pain perception.

opioid receptor A receptor that responds to endogenous and/or exogenous opioids.

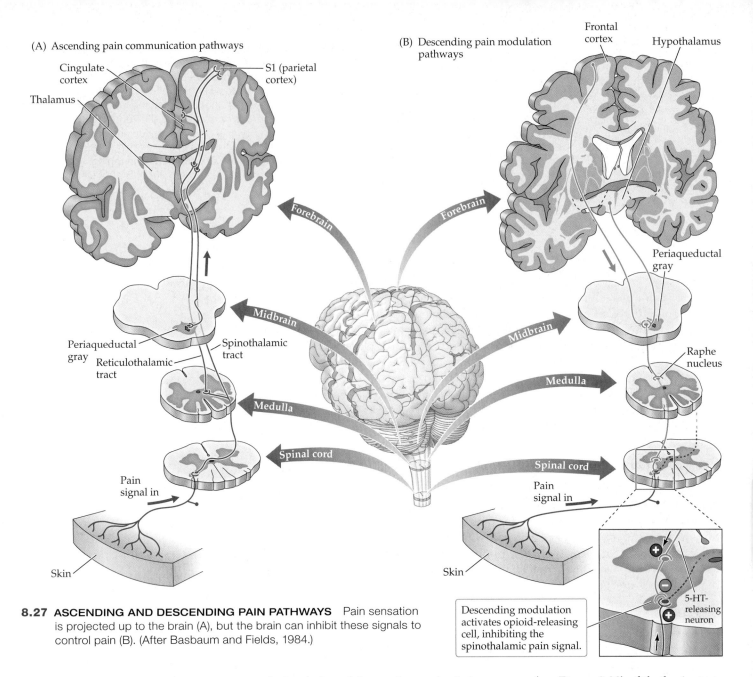

(A) Ascending pain communication pathways

Cingulate cortex

Thalamus

S1 (parietal cortex)

Forebrain

Midbrain

Periaqueductal gray

Reticulothalamic tract

Spinothalamic tract

Medulla

Spinal cord

Pain signal in

Skin

(B) Descending pain modulation pathways

Frontal cortex

Hypothalamus

Forebrain

Periaqueductal gray

Midbrain

Raphe nucleus

Medulla

Spinal cord

Pain signal in

Skin

5-HT-releasing neuron

Descending modulation activates opioid-releasing cell, inhibiting the spinothalamic pain signal.

8.27 ASCENDING AND DESCENDING PAIN PATHWAYS   Pain sensation is projected up to the brain (A), but the brain can inhibit these signals to control pain (B). (After Basbaum and Fields, 1984.)

cal stimulation of the **periaqueductal gray** area (see Figure 8.23) of the brainstem produces potent analgesia. Periaqueductal gray neurons send endorphin-containing axons to stimulate neurons in the medulla. These medullary neurons send axons to the spinal cord, eventually stimulating neurons to release opioids there. In this way, pain information is blocked by a direct gating action in the spinal cord (**FIGURE 8.27**). Electrical stimulation of the descending tract inhibits the response of spinal cord sensory relay cells to noxious stimulation of the skin. Morphine provides analgesia by stimulating the opioid receptors in this descending pain control system, in both the brainstem and the spinal cord.

In addition to their beneficial pain-relieving effects, opiates and other analgesics (painkillers) often produce side effects such as confusion, drowsiness, vomiting, constipation, and depression of the respiratory system. Now that we know the circuitry of the pain relief system, why give large doses of the drug systemically (i.e., throughout the body)? Instead, physicians can administer very small doses of opiates directly to the spinal cord to relieve pain, thus avoiding many of the side effects. The drugs can be administered *epidurally* (just outside the spinal cord's dura mater) or *intrathecally* (between the dura mater and the spinal cord). Both routes are somewhat invasive and therefore are restricted to surgical anesthesia, childbirth, or the management of severe chronic pain (Landau and Levy, 1993).

periaqueductal gray   The neuronal body–rich region of the midbrain surrounding the cerebral aqueduct that connects the third and fourth ventricles; involved in pain perception.

TABLE 8.3 Types of Pain Relief Intervention

MEASURE	MECHANISM	LIMITATIONS/COMMENTS
PSYCHOGENIC		
Placebo	May activate endorphin-mediated pain control system	Ethical concerns of deceiving patient
Hypnosis	Alters brain's perception of pain	Unaffected by opiate antagonists
Stress	Both opioid and non-opioid mechanisms	Clinically impractical and inappropriate
Cognitive (learning, coping strategies)	May activate endorphin-mediated pain control system	Limited usefulness for severe pain
PHARMACOLOGICAL		
Opiates	Bind to opioid receptors in periaqueductal gray and spinal cord	Severe side effects due to binding in other brain regions
Spinal block	Drugs block pain signals in spinal cord	Avoids side effects of systemic administration
Anti-inflammatory drugs	Block prostaglandin and/or leukotriene synthesis at site of injury (see Figure 8.21)	May have side effects
Cannabinoids	Act in spinal cord and on nociceptor endings	Illegal in some regions; smoke damages lungs
STIMULATION		
Acupuncture	Seems similar to placebo	Sometimes affected by opiate antagonists
Central gray	Electrical stimulation activates endorphin-mediated pain control systems, blocking pain signal in spinal cord	Inhibited by opiate antagonists; invasive surgery to implant electrodes
SURGICAL		
Cut peripheral nerve cord	Create physical break in pain pathway	Considerable risk of failure or return of pain
Rhizotomy (cutting dorsal root)	Create physical break in pain pathway	Considerable risk of failure or return of pain
Cord hemisection		
Frontal lobotomy	Disrupts affective response to pain	Irreversible; risky; severe effects on behavior

Because of long-standing concerns about the addictive potential of morphine and other opiates, the traditional standard for using them to relieve pain was to prescribe them only infrequently and in low doses. However, more modern medical standards emphasize swift use of painkillers after surgery. Once chronic pain develops, it is extremely difficult to overcome, so the best approach is to prevent the onset of chronic pain by early, aggressive treatment. The danger of addiction from the use of morphine to relieve surgical pain has been vastly exaggerated; the increase in risk is no more than 0.04% (Brownlee and Schrof, 1997). In the media, people addicted to painkillers are often said to have "gotten hooked" when given a prescription for pain. But further investigations reveal that almost all of these people had been drug abusers *before* they were given a prescription for pain (Szalavitz, 2004). Unfortunately, the myth that opiate treatment leads to addiction results in millions of people being undertreated for pain each year (Quill and Meier, 2006). So we will conclude this chapter by considering alternative means of controlling pain, as summarized in **TABLE 8.3**.

Marijuana's analgesic effect has been known for centuries. Marijuana, the dried leaves and flowers of the plant *Cannabis sativa*, reduces pain by stimulating endogenous cannabinoid receptors (CB_1 receptors), both in the spinal cord (Pernía-Andrade et al., 2009) and, surprisingly, in the free nerve endings of the nociceptors themselves (Clapper et al., 2010). This latter discovery suggests it may be possible to devise topical creams that provide cannabinoid stimulation through the skin to relieve pain. Other non-opioid analgesics may be available soon.

PLACEBOS The search for pain relief has led people to consume many unusual substances; even chemically inert pills alleviate pain in many patients. The term **placebo** (Latin for "I shall please") refers to an inert substance (such as a sugar pill) or other treatment that has no obvious direct physiological effect. In one example,

marijuana Dried leaves and flowers of the plant *Cannabis sativa*, typically smoked to obtain THC for a psychoactive effect.

placebo A substance that is known to be ineffective or inert, but when administered like a drug can sometimes bring relief.

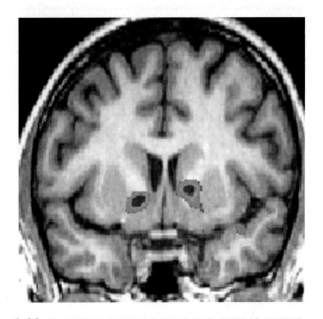

8.28 PLACEBO AFFECTS OPIOID SYSTEMS IN THE BRAIN Volunteers were subjected to a painful procedure and given a placebo for the pain. Some people seemed to respond to the placebo, but others did not. This difference image shows brain regions that were more activated in responders than in nonresponders. These regions are rich in receptors for endogenous opioids (D. J. Scott et al., 2008). (From Wager et al., 2007, courtesy of Dr. Jon-Kar Zubieta.)

naloxone A potent antagonist of opiates that is often administered to people who have taken drug overdoses. It blocks receptors for endogenous opioids.

acupuncture The insertion of needles at designated points on the skin in an attempt to alleviate pain or physiological malfunction, or alter behavior.

volunteers who had just had their wisdom teeth extracted were told that they were being given an analgesic but were not told what kind (J. D. Levine et al., 1978). Some of these patients received morphine-based drugs, and some were given saline solutions—the placebo. One out of three patients given the placebo experienced pain relief. (Morphine produced relief in most, but not all, patients.)

The researchers gave the opioid antagonist **naloxone** to other patients, who were also administered the placebo. Patients given the placebo *and* naloxone did not experience pain relief; this result implies that placebo relieves pain by causing the release of endogenous opioids. Functional brain imaging indicates that opioids and placebos activate the same brain regions (Petrovic et al., 2002) and that both treatments reduce the activity of neural regions responding to pain, including cingulate cortex (Wager et al., 2004) and spinal cord (Eippert et al., 2009). A consistent finding is that some people experience relief from a placebo and others do not. People who respond to placebo show a greater activation of brain regions with opioid receptors than do nonresponders (**FIGURE 8.28**), further implicating endogenous opioids in the placebo effect.

Careful experimentation has revealed many environmental cues that can enhance the placebo effect (Wager and Atlas, 2015) (**TABLE 8.4**). For example, large pills are more effective than small pills, and medicines are more effective if they are thought to be expensive. Having a doctor or nurse in a white coat assert that the treatment will work also boosts the effectiveness of placebos (**FIGURE 8.29A**). In other words, the *expectation* that the treatment will be effective actually contributes to that effectiveness. The expectation of relief may also explain why hypnosis effectively controls pain in many people (Jensen et al., 2014).

ACUPUNCTURE The earliest description of pain relief from **acupuncture** is at least 3000 years old. In some acupuncture procedures, the needles are manipulated once they are in position; in others, electrical or heat stimulation is delivered through the inserted needles. Acupuncture has gained popularity, but only some people achieve continued relief from chronic pain. At least part of the pain-blocking character of acupuncture appears to be mediated by the release of endorphins, because administering opioid antagonists such as naloxone prior to acupuncture blocks or reduces its pain control effects (Z. Q. Zhao, 2008).

Pain relief from acupuncture is also at least partly due to placebo effect. Thousands of years of acupuncture tradition indicate that the points at which needles are

TABLE 8.4 Environmental Cues That Affect the Placebo Effect

TYPE OF CUE	EXAMPLES
EXTERNAL	
Verbal suggestion	"This treatment will make you feel better."
Place	Doctor's office
Social	Body language, eye gaze, voice cues, "White coat"
INTERNAL	
Outcome expectancies	"My pain will go away."
Emotions	Reduced anxiety
Meaning schema	"I am being cared for."
Explicit memories	"This brought relief before."

Source: Wager and Atlas, 2015.

(A)

(B)

8.29 PLACEBOS CAN BE EFFECTIVE (A) Having the doctor express confidence that the treatment will work can boost the placebo effect. (B) In some cases, acupuncture controls pain. Opioid antagonists block this analgesia, indicating that acupuncture, like some placebos, activates endogenous opioids.

inserted must be chosen carefully to match the type of pain and its location on the body (**FIGURE 8.29B**). But one report that acupuncture relieves headaches in many people also found that *where* the needles were inserted *made no difference* (Linde et al., 2009). Again, the expectation that the needles will reduce pain helps bring relief.

STRESS   A deer fleeing an encounter with a mountain lion would do well to ignore any pain from injuries for the moment. Similarly, sometimes people badly hurt in traumatic circumstances report little or no immediate pain (Beecher, 1956). Laboratory studies demonstrate the existence of pain control circuitry, but they don't tell us how the inhibitory systems are normally activated.

To answer this question, researchers have examined pain inhibition that arises in stressful circumstances. It appears that brain systems produce analgesia when pain threatens to overwhelm effective coping strategies. For example, exposing rats to several different kinds of inescapable foot shock induces analgesia (Terman et al., 1984). Stress analgesia may be blocked by the opiate antagonists, depending on the type of stress, indicating that stress activates both an opioid-sensitive analgesic system and a pain control system that does *not* involve opioids but may involve release of endogenous cannabinoids (A. G. Hohmann et al., 2005).

The many types of pain relief strategies, including surgical and pharmacological strategies, psychological treatments, brain and spinal cord stimulation, and sensory stimulation, reflect how powerfully pain affects us. Natural selection can also provide us with new clues about how to control pain, as we'll see next.

■ The Cutting Edge

Evolving an Indifference to Toxins

Because sensory neurons signaling pain use very specific versions of the voltage-gated sodium channel that triggers action potentials, we have the exciting opportunity to produce novel compounds that might reduce pain by interfering with only those sodium channels. But a long-running arms race in the U.S. Southwestern desert between grasshopper mice and the bark scorpions they love to eat beautifully illustrates how natural selection can also produce novel compounds, in this case for *causing* pain. Bark scorpions evolved a toxin that selectively activates that same $Na_v1.7$ that drives pain fibers to fire, so we humans find their sting quite painful (but not fatal for adults). Laboratory mice also seem to find the sting painful—if a tiny bit is injected into a paw, they lick it vigorously. But grasshopper mice that

8.30 AN INDIFFERENCE TO SCORPION TOXIN (After Rowe et al., 2013; photograph courtesy of Drs. Matt and Ashlee Rowe.)

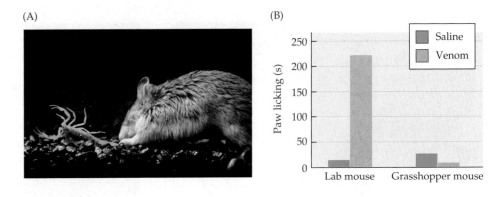

(A)

(B)

normally live in that same desert don't seem to mind the scorpion toxin (**FIGURE 8.30**). When scientists recorded from sensory cells in the two species of mice, they found that the toxin strongly activates sensory cells in lab mice but *inhibits* them in grasshopper mice (Rowe et al., 2013).

Did the grasshopper mice evolve a new $Na_V1.7$ that ignores the toxin? Apparently not, because the current opened by the toxin in grasshopper mice was unaffected by tetrodotoxin (TTX), which blocks the $Na_V1.7$ channel. Instead, the grasshopper mice seem to have evolved a mutation in *another* voltage-gated sodium channel that is found exclusively in pain receptors—$Na_V1.8$. The $Na_V1.7$ channel seems to *initiate* firing of pain sensory neurons, while $Na_V1.8$ mediates the *sustained*, continuous firing of the nociceptive neurons, and the toxin activates both channels in humans. But when the scientists sequenced the $Na_V1.8$ gene from grasshopper mice, they found it differed from that of lab mice in several amino acids. By systematically inducing different mutations in the gene, they identified two amino acid changes that are necessary for the difference in response to scorpion toxin. While the toxin opens the $Na_V1.7$ channel in both species, and also opens the $Na_V1.8$ channel in lab mice, it *blocks* that channel in grasshopper mice. So the grasshopper mice probably feel the first sting of the scorpion toxin, when $Na_V1.7$ responds, but without the sustained firing of nociceptors normally mediated by $Na_V1.8$, they probably never feel the long, slow burn that we feel. Unless the scorpions evolve a new toxin that can activate rather than block the grasshopper mouse $Na_V1.8$ channel, they're going to have to be careful out there. In the meantime, the discovery that $Na_V1.8$ mediates sustained firing of nociceptors offers yet another target for relieving pain if scientists can find a compound that blocks the human version of the channel.

Go to
bn8e.com
for study questions, quizzes, activities, and other resources

Recommended Reading

Ballantyne, J. C., and Fishman, S. M. (Eds.). (2010). *Bonica's Management of Pain* (4th ed.). Philadelphia: Lippincott.

Cytowic, R. E., and Eagleman, D. M. (2009). *Wednesday Is Indigo Blue.* Cambridge, MA: MIT Press.

Delmas, P., Hao, J., and Rodat-Despoix, L. (2011). Molecular mechanisms of mechanotransduction in mammalian sensory neurons. *Nature Reviews Neuroscience, 12*(3),139–153.

McMahon, S., Koltzenburg, M., Tracey, I., and Turk, D. C. (2013). *Wall & Melzack's Textbook of Pain* (6th ed.). Philadelphia: Saunders.

Merskey, H., Loeser, J. D., and Dubner, R. (2005). *The Paths of Pain: 1975–2005.* Seattle, WA: IASP Press.

Wolfe, J. M., Kluender, K. R., Levi, D. M., Bartoshuk, L. M., et al. (2015). *Sensation & Perception* (4th ed.). Sunderland, MA: Sinauer.

VISUAL SUMMARY

You should be able to relate each summary to the adjacent illustration, including structures and processes.
Go to **bn8e.com/vs8** for links to figures, animations, and activities that will help you consolidate the material.

1 A sensory system furnishes selected information to the brain about internal and external events. It captures and processes only information that is significant for the particular organism. Some **stimuli** are detected readily by some species but have no effect on others. Review **Figure 8.2, Table 8.1**

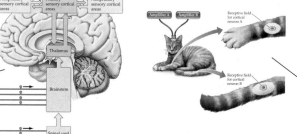

2 **Sensory receptor organs** furnish only selected information to the brain. For example, our skin contains four kinds of touch receptors, each specialized for detecting a specific stimulus. The brain decodes sensory information by using **labeled lines**, nerves that normally transmit only certain types of sensory information. Review **Figures 8.3 and 8.4, Activity 8.1**

3 Energy is transduced at sensory receptors by the production of a **receptor potential** that triggers action potentials. **Coding** translates receptor information into patterns of neural activity. The frequency and pattern of action potentials signal the intensity and type of stimulus encountered. Review **Figures 8.5 and 8.6**

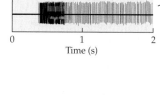

4 In **adaptation**, the rate of action potentials progressively decreases as the same stimulation is maintained. This decline is slow in the case of **tonic receptors** but rapid for **phasic receptors**. Adaptation protects the nervous system from redundant stimulation. Review **Figure 8.7**

5 The succession of levels in a **sensory pathway** allows for increasingly elaborate kinds of processing. Information enters the spinal cord or brain and reaches the **thalamus**, which communicates to the **cortex**. **Attention**, the temporary enhancement of certain sensory messages, is modulated at higher levels of the sensory pathway. Review **Figures 8.8 and 8.12**

6 The **receptive field** of a neuron is the region in space where a stimulus will change the firing of that cell. The receptive fields of neurons may be very different at successive levels of the sensory pathway. Review **Figures 8.9 and 8.13, Animation 8.2**

7 At the level of the cerebral cortex, there are multiple maps of the body surface. **Primary somatosensory cortex**, or **S1**, located in the postcentral gyrus, contains a map of the contralateral body, which overrepresents highly sensitive body regions. Review **Figures 8.10, 8.11, 8.17, and 8.18**

8 Touch information from the body courses through a distinct spinal pathway, the **dorsal column system**. Review **Figures 8.15 and 8.16**

9 Some **sensory receptor cells** are specialized to transduce particular kinds of energy. **Merkel's discs** and **Meissner's corpuscles** detect fine touch, while **Pacinian corpuscles** and **Ruffini's endings** respond to vibration and stretch, providing information about textures. Review **Figures 8.13 and 8.14, Table 8.2, Activity 8.2**

10 **Free nerve endings** act as **nociceptors**, detecting mechanical damage or temperature changes because they have specialized receptor proteins that detect these conditions (such as **transient receptor potential vanilloid 1 [TRPV1]**, which detects heat and is activated by chili peppers), opening up ion channels to trigger action potentials. Review **Figures 8.20–8.22**

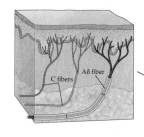

(continued)

11 Some peripheral pain fibers have fairly large, myelinated axons to transmit sharp pain rapidly; others use small, unmyelinated axons to transmit dull, aching pain after injury. Review **Figure 8.21, Table 8.2**

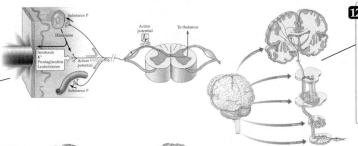

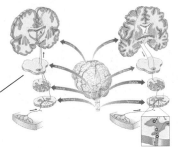

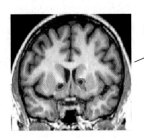

12 Pain, temperature, and itch information enters the spinal cord, crosses the midline, and ascends through the **anterolateral (spinothalamic) system** to the brain. Review **Figure 8.23, Activity 8.3**

13 Pain sensation is subject to many controlling or modulating conditions, including circuitry within the brain and spinal cord that employs **opioid** synapses. One component in the modulation of pain is made up of the descending pathways arising in the brain that inhibit incoming neural activity at synapses within the spinal cord. Review **Figure 8.27, Activity 8.4**

14 Pain control has been achieved by the administration of drugs (including **placebos**), electrical and mechanical stimulation of the skin, **acupuncture**, and surgery, among other methods. Review **Figures 8.24, 8.28, and 8.29, Table 8.3**

Hearing, Vestibular Perception, Taste, and Smell

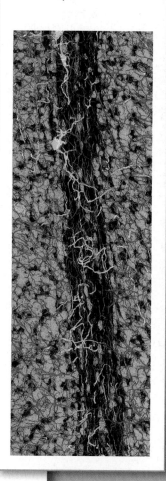

◼ No Ear for Music

Given the category "wedding music," you will probably immediately think of a tune or two that you can hear in your head—perhaps "The Wedding March" or (alas?) "Uptown Funk." The same goes for Beethoven's Symphony No. 5 or the theme from *Star Wars*. These pieces of music, and others like them, are tunes that most people can identify right away, after hearing just a few bars. But Tony is different.

Tony is completely baffled by music. He is much less sensitive than most people to the difference between musical tones. Tony's ability to understand pitch, and the relationships between chords, is nearly at chance level. Although he is happy to try to belt out a song, he is unable to sing in tune and doesn't even recognize that he is singing off-key unless he is told so by a (grimacing) friend. He cannot identify the tune to "Happy Birthday" unless he also hears the lyrics, in which case he can identify it immediately. Yet he has no problem with nonmusical uses of pitch, such as the rising tone at the end of a question.

Tony is a man of better-than-average intelligence, with perfectly normal cognitive functioning, except for his lifelong inability to appreciate music despite years of childhood music lessons. This highly specific difficulty with music is an affliction that Tony shares with many other people; notable examples include Pope Francis, revolutionary Che Guevara, U.S. President Theodore Roosevelt, and Nobel Prize–winning economist Milton Friedman.

What is the nature of this mysterious problem? Is it a kind of hearing problem? A learning disability?

Your existence is a testament to the keen senses of your ancestors—senses that helped them to find food and mates, and to avoid predators and other dangers. In this chapter we consider some of the amazing sensory systems that allow us to monitor important signals from distant sources, especially sounds (audition) and smells (olfaction). We also discuss related systems for detecting position and movement of the body (the vestibular system, related to the auditory system) and tastes of foods (the gustatory or taste sense, which, like olfaction, is a chemical sense). We begin with hearing because audition evolved from special mechanical receptors related to the somatosensory elements that we discussed in Chapter 8.

Go to Brain Explorer
bn8e.com/9.1

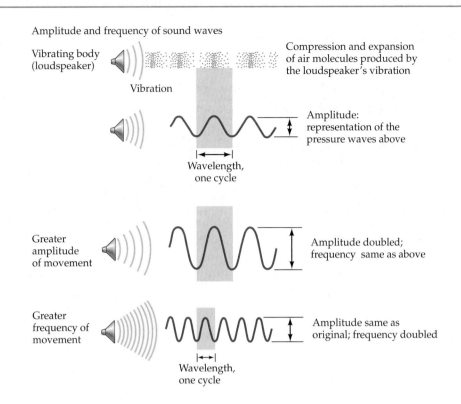

BOX 9.1 · The Basics of Sound

We perceive a repetitive pattern of local increases and decreases in air pressure as sound. Usually this oscillation is caused by a vibrating object, such as a loudspeaker or a person's larynx during speaking. A single alternation of compression and expansion of air is called one *cycle*.

The figure illustrates the fluctuations in pressure produced by loudspeakers, each vibrating at a single frequency. Such sounds, called **pure tones**, are represented by sine waves that plot the oscillation between the compressions (peaks) and expansions (troughs) of air in front of the vibrating cone of the speaker. A pure tone is described physically in terms of two measures:

1. **Amplitude**, or intensity—usually measured as sound pressure, or force per unit area, in dynes per square centimeter (dyn/cm^2). Our perception of amplitude is termed **loudness**.

2. **Frequency**, or the number of cycles per second, measured in hertz (**Hz**). For example, middle A on a piano has a frequency of 440 Hz. Our perception of frequency is termed **pitch**.

Most sounds are more complicated than a pure tone. For example, a sound made by a musical instrument contains a **fundamental** frequency plus one or

Amplitude and frequency of sound waves

Vibrating body (loudspeaker)

Vibration

Compression and expansion of air molecules produced by the loudspeaker's vibration

Amplitude: representation of the pressure waves above

Wavelength, one cycle

Greater amplitude of movement

Amplitude doubled; frequency same as above

Greater frequency of movement

Amplitude same as original; frequency doubled

Wavelength, one cycle

Hearing

Hearing is vital for the survival of many animals. Humans employ an impressive variety of vocalizations—from barely audible murmurs to soaring flights of song—but we especially rely on speech sounds to provide a basis for our social relations and for the transmission of knowledge between individuals. Helen Keller, who was both blind and deaf, said, "Blindness deprives you of contact with things; deafness deprives you of contact with people."

The sounds produced by other animals—from insects to whales—also have a wide range of complexity, in keeping with their adaptive significance. Birds sing and crickets chirp in order to attract mates; monkeys grunt and screech and burble to signal comfort, danger, and pleasure. Elephants employ vocalizations too deep for us to hear, and can recognize individuals by their calls (Herbst et al., 2012; McComb et al., 2000). Owls and bats exploit the directional property of sound to locate prey and avoid obstacles in the dark, and whales employ sounds that can travel hundreds of miles in the ocean. Unlike light, sounds can go around obstacles and can be detected in the darkest night.

Pressure Waves in the Air Are Perceived as Sound

How do small vibrations of air molecules become the speech, music, and other sounds we hear? Your auditory system detects rapid changes in the *intensity* (measured in decibels, dB) and *frequency* (measured in cycles per second, or hertz, Hz) of vibrations in the air. **BOX 9.1** describes basic properties of sound that we will be considering.

more integer multiples of the fundamental, called **harmonics**. So, middle A on the piano has a fundamental frequency of 440 Hz plus some combination of harmonics at 880 Hz, 1320 Hz, 1760 Hz, and so on. When different instruments play the same note, the notes differ in the relative intensities of the various harmonics, and there are subtle qualitative differences between instruments in the way they commence, shape, and sustain the sound; these differences are what gives each instrument its characteristic sound quality, or **timbre**. As a result, most "real-world" sounds have a wave form that is much more complex that the simple sine wave of a pure tone. However, using a mathematical process called **Fourier analysis**, a complex wave form can be decomposed into a sum of simple sine waves. (We will see in Chapter 10 that Fourier analysis can also be applied to visual patterns.)

Because the ear is sensitive to a huge range of sound pressures, sound intensity (a measure of the difference between two pressures) is usually expressed in **decibels (dB)**, on a logarithmic scale. The common reference level for human hearing is 0.0002 dyn/cm², the smallest amplitude at which an average human ear can detect a 1000-Hz tone. A faint whisper is about 10 times as intense, and a jet airliner 500 feet overhead is about a million times as intense. The whisper is about 20 dB above threshold, and the jetliner is about 120 dB above threshold. Normal conversation is about 60 dB above the reference level.

pure tone A tone with a single frequency of vibration.

amplitude The force sound exerts per unit area, usually measured as dynes per square centimeter.

loudness The subjective experience of the pressure level of a sound.

frequency The number of cycles per second in a sound wave; measured in hertz (Hz).

hertz (Hz) Cycles per second, as of an auditory stimulus.

pitch A dimension of auditory experience in which sounds vary from low to high.

fundamental The predominant frequency of an auditory tone or a visual scene.

harmonics Multiples of a particular frequency called the *fundamental*.

timbre The characteristic sound quality of a musical instrument, as determined by the relative intensities of its various harmonics.

Fourier analysis The mathematical decomposition of a complex pattern into a sum of sine waves.

decibel (dB) A measure of sound intensity.

The outer parts of the auditory system have been shaped through evolution to capture biologically important sound vibrations and direct them into the inner parts of the ear, where the mechanical energy of the sound is **transduced** into neural activity: the action potentials that inform the brain. Your ears are incredibly sensitive organs; in fact, one of the main jobs of your powers of attention is to filter out the constant barrage of unimportant little noises that your ears are able to detect (see Chapter 18).

The external ear captures, focuses, and filters sound

The oddly shaped fleshy objects that most people call *ears* are properly known as **pinnae** (singular *pinna*, Latin for "wing"). Aside from their occasional utility as handles and jewelry hangers, the pinnae funnel sound waves into the second part of the **external ear**: the **ear canal**. The pinna is a distinctly mammalian characteristic, and mammals show a wide array of ear shapes and sizes. Furthermore, although humans can move their ears only enough to entertain children, many other mammals deftly shape and swivel their pinnae to help determine the source of a sound (**FIGURE 9.1**). Animals with exceptional auditory localization abilities, such as bats, may have especially mobile ears. In these animals, proprioceptors (position sensors; see Chapter 11) within the pinnae provide information to the auditory system about the positions of the external ears as an aide to localizing sound sources.

The "ridges and valleys" of the pinna modify the character of sound that reaches the middle ear. Some frequencies of sound are enhanced; others are suppressed. For example, the shape of the human ear especially increases the reception of sounds between 2000 and 5000 Hz—a frequency range that is important for speech percep-

transduction The conversion of one form of energy to another.

pinna The external part of the ear.

external ear The part of the ear that we readily see (the pinna) and the canal that leads to the eardrum.

ear canal A tube leading from the pinna to the middle ear.

9.1 THE EARS HAVE IT The external ears, or pinnae, of mammals come in a variety of shapes, each adapted to a particular niche. Many mammals can move their ears to direct them toward a particular sound. In such cases, the brain must account for the position of the ear to judge where a particular sound came from.

middle ear The cavity between the tympanic membrane and the cochlea.

tympanic membrane Also called *eardrum*. The partition between the external ear and the middle ear.

ossicles Three small bones (incus, malleus, and stapes) that transmit sound across the middle ear, from the tympanic membrane to the oval window.

oval window The location on the surface of the cochlea at which vibrations are received from the ossicles.

malleus Latin for "hammer." A middle-ear bone that is connected to the tympanic membrane.

incus Latin for "anvil." A middle-ear bone situated between the malleus and the stapes.

stapes Latin for "stirrup." A middle-ear bone that is connected to the oval window.

tensor tympani The muscle attached to the malleus that modulates mechanical linkage to protect the delicate receptor cells of the inner ear from damaging sounds.

stapedius A middle-ear muscle that is attached to the stapes.

tion. The shape of the external ear is also important in identifying the direction and distance of the source of a sound (discussed later in this chapter).

The middle ear concentrates sound energies

A collection of tiny structures made of membrane, muscle, and bone—essentially a tiny biological microphone—links the auditory canal to the neural receptor cells of the inner ear (**FIGURE 9.2A**). This **middle ear** (**FIGURE 9.2B**) consists of the taut **tympanic membrane** (eardrum), sealing the end of the auditory canal, and a chain of tiny bones, or **ossicles**, that mechanically couple the tympanic membrane to the inner ear at a special location called the **oval window**. These ossicles, the smallest bones in the body, are called the **malleus** (Latin for "hammer"), the **incus** (Latin for "anvil"), and the **stapes** (Latin for "stirrup").

Sound waves in the air strike the tympanic membrane and cause it to vibrate with the same frequency as the sound. The movement of the tympanic membrane moves the chain of ossicles, concentrating the tiny mechanical forces of vibrating air particles, captured from the relatively large tympanic membrane, onto the small oval window. This arrangement vastly amplifies sound pressure so that it can produce movement in the fluid of the inner ear, as we'll see.

Two muscles vary the mechanical linkage between the ossicles to improve auditory perception and protect the delicate inner ear from loud, potentially damaging sounds. One of these muscles, the **tensor tympani** (see Figure 9.2B), is attached to the malleus, which is connected to the tympanic membrane. The other muscle of the middle ear is attached to the stapes and thus is called the **stapedius**. Within 200 milliseconds of the arrival of a loud sound, the brain signals the muscles via a reflex arc in the brainstem, causing the muscles to contract and stiffen the chain of ossicles (Mukerji et al., 2010). Because the stiffened chain of ossicles is less able to transmit energy, the power of the vibrations reaching the inner ear is significantly reduced. The middle-ear muscles also attenuate self-made sounds; without this system, body movement, swallowing, vocalizations, and other internally produced sounds would be painfully loud. Species that produce especially loud calls, such as bats, rely on this system to protect their auditory receptors from physical damage (Avan et al., 1992). Interestingly, the middle-ear muscles activate just *before* we produce self-made sounds like speech or coughing, which is why we don't perceive our own sounds as distractingly loud.

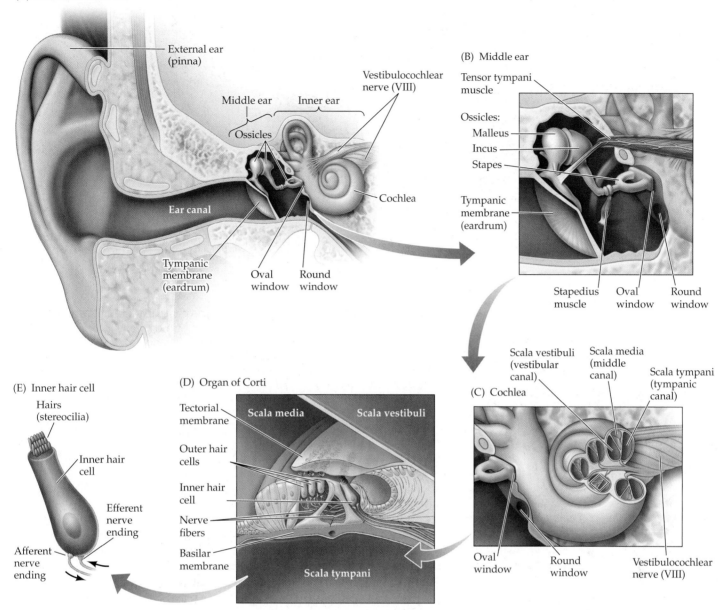

(A) Structures of the ear

External ear (pinna)

Middle ear   Inner ear

Vestibulocochlear nerve (VIII)

Ossicles

Cochlea

Ear canal

Tympanic membrane (eardrum)

Oval window   Round window

(B) Middle ear

Tensor tympani muscle

Ossicles:
Malleus
Incus
Stapes

Tympanic membrane (eardrum)

Stapedius muscle   Oval window   Round window

(C) Cochlea

Scala vestibuli (vestibular canal)   Scala media (middle canal)   Scala tympani (tympanic canal)

Oval window   Round window   Vestibulocochlear nerve (VIII)

(D) Organ of Corti

Tectorial membrane

Scala media   Scala vestibuli

Outer hair cells

Inner hair cell

Nerve fibers

Basilar membrane

Scala tympani

(E) Inner hair cell

Hairs (stereocilia)

Inner hair cell

Efferent nerve ending

Afferent nerve ending

9.2 EXTERNAL AND INTERNAL STRUCTURES OF THE HUMAN EAR

The cochlea converts vibrational energy into waves of fluid

The complex structures of the **inner ear** ultimately convert sound into neural activity. In mammals the auditory portion of the inner ear is a coiled, fluid-filled structure called the **cochlea** (from the Greek *kochlos*, "snail") (**FIGURE 9.2C AND D**). Embedded in the temporal bone of the skull, the human cochlea is a marvel of miniaturization. In an adult, the cochlea measures only about 4 millimeters (mm) in diameter—about the size of a pea. Unrolled, the cochlea would measure about 35–40 mm in length.

The cochlea is a coil of three parallel canals: (1) the **scala vestibuli** (*vestibular canal*), (2) the **scala media** (*middle canal*), and (3) the **scala tympani** (*tympanic canal*). In Figure 9.2C you can see that the width of these canals—and the membranes that divide them—decreases along the length of the spiral. The oval window is adjacent to the *base* of the spiral, where the canals and membranes are narrow; the distant wide end is referred to as the *apex*. Because these canals are filled with noncompressible fluid, movement inside the cochlea in response to a push on the oval window requires a second membrane-covered window that can bulge outward a bit. This membrane is the **round window**, which separates the scala tympani from the middle ear (see Figure 9.2B).

inner ear   The cochlea and vestibular apparatus.

cochlea   A snail-shaped structure in the inner ear that contains the primary receptor cells for hearing.

scala vestibuli   Also called *vestibular canal*. One of the three canals running the length of the cochlea.

scala media   Also called *middle canal*. The central of the three canals running the length of the cochlea, situated between the scala vestibuli and the scala tympani.

scala tympani   Also called *tympanic canal*. One of three canals running the length of the cochlea.

round window   A membrane separating the cochlear duct from the middle-ear cavity.

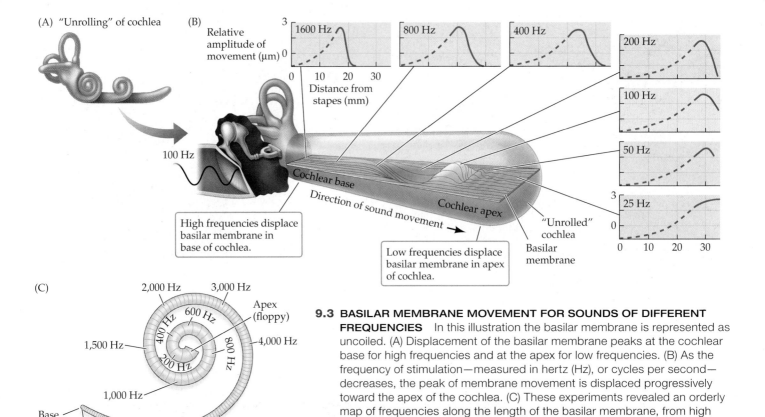

(A) "Unrolling" of cochlea

(B) Relative amplitude of movement (μm)

1600 Hz 800 Hz 400 Hz 200 Hz 100 Hz 50 Hz 25 Hz

Distance from stapes (mm)

Cochlear base

Direction of sound movement

Cochlear apex

High frequencies displace basilar membrane in base of cochlea.

Low frequencies displace basilar membrane in apex of cochlea.

"Unrolled" cochlea

Basilar membrane

(C)

2,000 Hz 3,000 Hz Apex (floppy)

600 Hz 4,000 Hz

400 Hz 800 Hz

1,500 Hz 200 Hz

1,000 Hz

Base (stiff)

20,000 Hz 5,000 Hz

7,000 Hz

9.3 BASILAR MEMBRANE MOVEMENT FOR SOUNDS OF DIFFERENT FREQUENCIES In this illustration the basilar membrane is represented as uncoiled. (A) Displacement of the basilar membrane peaks at the cochlear base for high frequencies and at the apex for low frequencies. (B) As the frequency of stimulation—measured in hertz (Hz), or cycles per second—decreases, the peak of membrane movement is displaced progressively toward the apex of the cochlea. (C) These experiments revealed an orderly map of frequencies along the length of the basilar membrane, from high frequencies at the base (which is narrow and stiff) to low frequencies at the apex (which is broad and floppy).

organ of Corti A structure in the inner ear that lies on the basilar membrane of the cochlea and contains the hair cells and terminations of the auditory nerve.

hair cell A cochlear auditory receptor cell.

basilar membrane A membrane in the cochlea that contains the principal structures involved in auditory transduction.

inner hair cell (IHC) One of the two types of cochlear receptor cells for hearing.

outer hair cell (OHC) One of the two types of cochlear receptor cells for hearing.

stereocilium A relatively stiff hair that protrudes from a hair cell in the auditory or vestibular system.

tectorial membrane A membrane that sits atop the organ of Corti in the cochlear duct.

The principal components that convert sounds into neural activity, collectively known as the **organ of Corti** (see Figure 9.2D), consist of three main structures: (1) the sensory cells (**hair cells**) (**FIGURE 9.2E**), (2) an elaborate framework of supporting cells, and (3) the terminations of the auditory fibers. The base of the organ of Corti is the **basilar membrane**. This flexible membrane separates the scala tympani from the scala media and, most important, vibrates in response to sound. The basilar membrane is about 5 times wider at the apex of the cochlea than at the base, even though the cochlea itself narrows toward its apex.

When the stapes moves in and out as a result of sound waves hitting the eardrum, it sets up waves or ripples in the fluid of the scala vestibuli, which in turn cause the basilar membrane to ripple, like shaking out a rug. Because the basilar membrane is tapered—it's wider at the apex than at the base—different parts of the basilar membrane show their strongest responses to different frequencies of sound (**FIGURE 9.3**). High frequencies have their greatest effect near the base, where the membrane is narrow and relatively stiff, whereas low-frequency sounds produce a larger response near the apex, where the membrane is wider and more flexible (Ashmore, 1994). The hair cells transduce movements of the basilar membrane into electrical signals.

There are two sets of hair cells within the organ of Corti: a single row of about 3500 **inner hair cells** (**IHCs**; called *inner* because they are closer to the central axis of the coiled cochlea) and about 12,000 **outer hair cells** (**OHCs**) in three rows (see Figure 9.2D). From the upper end of each hair cell protrude tiny hairs that range from 2 to 6 micrometers in length (see Figure 9.2E). Each hair cell has 50–200 of these relatively stiff hairs, called **stereocilia** (singular *stereocilium*; from the Greek *stereos*, "solid," and the Latin *cilium*, "eyelid/eyelash") or simply *cilia*. The heights of the stereocilia increase progressively across the hair cell, so the tops form a slope. Atop the organ of Corti is the **tectorial membrane** (see Figure 9.2D). The stereocilia of the OHCs extend into indentations in the bottom of this membrane.

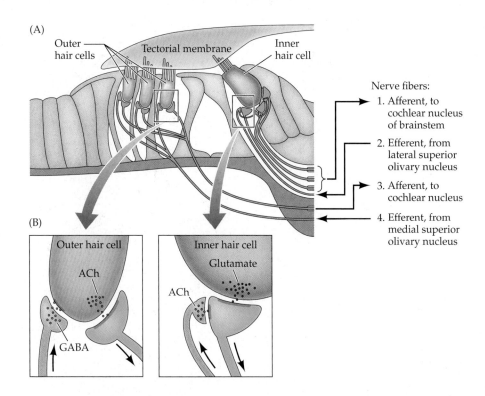

(A)

Outer hair cells

Tectorial membrane

Inner hair cell

Nerve fibers:

1. Afferent, to cochlear nucleus of brainstem

2. Efferent, from lateral superior olivary nucleus

3. Afferent, to cochlear nucleus

4. Efferent, from medial superior olivary nucleus

(B)

Outer hair cell

ACh

GABA

Inner hair cell

Glutamate

ACh

9.4 AUDITORY NERVE FIBERS AND SYNAPSES IN THE ORGAN OF CORTI (A) The inner and outer hair cells form synaptic connections to and from the brain. (B) Different synaptic transmitters are hypothesized to be active at the synapses of inner and outer hair cells in the organ of Corti.

Auditory nerve fibers contact the hair cells at the base (see Figure 9.2E). The organ of Corti has four kinds of synapses and nerve fibers. Two of these (1 and 3 in **FIGURE 9.4A**) are *afferents* that convey messages from the hair cells to the brain; the other two (2 and 4 in Figure 9.4A) are *efferents* that convey messages from the brain to the hair cells. Several different synaptic transmitters—especially glutamate and acetylcholine, but also GABA and dopamine—appear to be involved in activity at the various hair cell synapses (**FIGURE 9.4B**) (Goutman et al., 2015). Each IHC is associated with 16–20 auditory nerve fibers; relatively few nerve fibers contact the many OHCs. In fact, the afferent nerve fibers running from the IHCs account for 90–95% of all afferent auditory fibers and give rise to the perception of sound. Thus, mice with a type of glutamate knockout have nonfunctional IHCs but normal OHCs, and are deaf. Restoration of the knocked out IHC neurotransmission via gene therapy restores their hearing (Akil et al., 2012).

The OHCs don't detect sound; they push on the tectorial membrane in response to commands from the brain via the efferent nerve fibers. The OHCs change their length (Zheng et al., 2000), thereby fine-tuning the organ of Corti, as we'll discuss shortly. The IHCs also receive efferent messages (see Figure 9.4B), probably to inhibit afferent responses to loud sounds.

How do IHCs transduce sound into neural activity? As sounds induce vibrations of the basilar membrane, the vibrations bend the hair cell stereocilia that nestle under the tectorial membrane (see Figure 9.2D). Very small displacements of hair bundles cause rapid changes in ionic channels of the stereocilia. Each hair cell has only about 100 such ion channels, about one or two per stereocilium, located toward the tops of the cilia. Fine, rodlike fibers called **tip links** run along the tips of the stereocilia. These tip links play a key role in the generation of hair cell potentials. Sounds that cause the stereocilia to sway, even only very slightly, increase the tension on the tip links and pop open the ion channels to which they are attached (Hudspeth, 2014) (**FIGURE 9.5**). The channels snap shut again in a fraction of a millisecond as the hair cell sways back. The ion channel of a stereocilium thus resembles a trapdoor or porthole, and it appears that a springlike mechanism in the tip link's anchor in the neighboring stereocilium provides the force to rapidly shut the channel (Powers et al., 2012)—so in a real sense, a stereocilium ion channel is spring-loaded with a hair trigger.

tip link A fine, threadlike fiber that runs along and connects the tips of stereocilia.

Go to Animation 9.2
Sound Transduction
bn8e.com/9.2

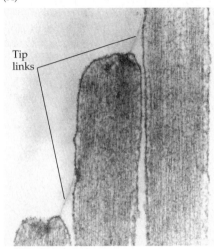

(A)

Tip links

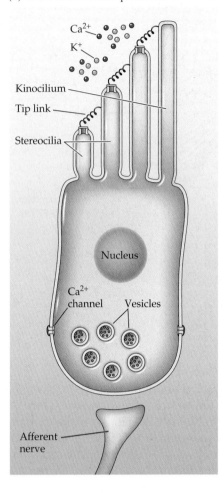

(B) Before stereocilia displacement

Kinocilium

Tip link

Stereocilia

Ca^{2+} channel   Vesicles

Nucleus

Afferent nerve

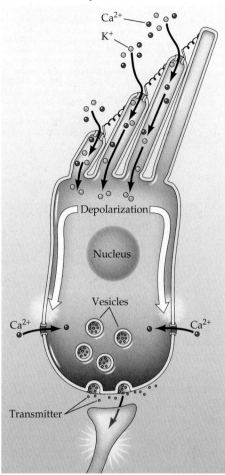

After stereocilia displacement

Ca^{2+}

K^+

Depolarization

Nucleus

Vesicles

Ca^{2+} Ca^{2+}

Transmitter

9.5 HOW STEREOCILIA SENSE AUDITORY STIMULATION   (A) This micrograph of stereocilia shows the threadlike tip links. (B) Bending of the stereocilia (right) opens large, nonselective ion channels, allowing K^+ and Ca^{2+} to enter the stereocilia. The resulting depolarization opens Ca^{2+} channels in the cell's base, causing the release of neurotransmitter to excite afferent nerves (Hudspeth, 1992). Here we depict the channels near the top of each tip link, but they may be near the bottom (Beurg et al., 2009). (Micrograph courtesy of Dr. A. J. Hudspeth.)

Opening of the channels allows an inrush of potassium (K^+) and calcium (Ca^{2+}) ions and rapid depolarization of the entire hair cell. This initial depolarization leads to a rapid influx of Ca^{2+} at the *base* of the IHC, which causes synaptic vesicles there to fuse with the presynaptic membrane and release their transmitter contents—probably glutamate—from the base of the hair cell, stimulating the afferent nerve fiber to trigger action potentials in these afferent axons (see Figure 9.5). The action potentials reach the brain via the vestibulocochlear nerve (cranial nerve VIII), as we'll discuss shortly, but first let's take a closer look at the actions of OHCs.

Active mechanical processes in the cochlea enhance frequency discrimination

Humans can discriminate between sounds that differ in frequency by just 2 Hz. The basic physical characteristics of the basilar membrane cannot account for such sharp discrimination of sounds, so an additional tuning process must be at work. It turns out that the OHCs fine-tune the cochlea to help discriminate frequencies. We mentioned earlier that OHCs show the surprising property of changing length when their membrane potential changes. Hyperpolarization causes the OHCs to lengthen by as much as 5%, using a specialized motor protein called **prestin**; depolarization causes the OHCs to shorten (He et al., 2014; Zheng et al., 2000). Through this electromechanical action, OHCs continually modify the stiffness of regions of the basilar membrane, resulting in both sharpened tuning and pronounced amplification (Hudspeth, 2014). A curious consequence of this mechanical movement of the basilar membrane is that the cochlea itself produces sounds—called **otoacoustic emissions**—by pushing back on the eardrum. (Otoacoustic emissions are discussed in more detail on the website in **A Step Further: The Ears Emit Sounds as Part of the Hearing Process.**)

prestin   A motor protein that allows outer hair cells to change length .

otoacoustic emission   A sound produced by the cochlea itself, either spontaneously or in response to an environmental noise.

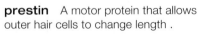

Now that the inner ear has transduced sound waves into trains of action potentials, the auditory signals must leave the cochlea and enter the brain.

Auditory Signals Run from Cochlea to Cortex

On each side of your head, about 30,000–50,000 auditory fibers from the cochlea make up the auditory part of the **vestibulocochlear nerve** (cranial nerve VIII). Recall that most of these afferent fibers are carrying messages from the IHCs, each of which stimulates several nerve fibers. Each auditory neuron responds to a very precise frequency at its threshold, but for more-intense stimuli the neuron responds to a broader range of frequencies. For example, the fiber whose responses are shown in red in **FIGURE 9.6** has its *best frequency* at 1200 Hz; that is, it responds to a very weak tone at 1200 Hz. When sounds are 20 dB louder, however, the fiber responds to any frequency from 500 to 1800 Hz. We call this the **tuning curve** of that cell's response to sounds of various frequencies. Thus, although an auditory nerve fiber transmits exclusively auditory information, it does not respond to just one frequency of stimulation. If the brain received a signal from only one such fiber, it would not be able to tell whether the stimulus was a weak tone of 1200 Hz or a stronger tone of 500 or 1800 Hz, or any frequency in between. Instead, the brain analyzes signals from thousands of such units to calculate the intensity and frequency of each sound.

Input from the auditory nerve is distributed in a complex manner to both sides of the brain, as depicted in **FIGURE 9.7**. Each auditory nerve fiber divides into two main branches as it enters the brainstem. Each branch then goes to one of two groups of neurons, one group in the dorsal **cochlear nucleus** and the other group in the ventral cochlear nucleus. The output of neurons in the cochlear nuclei also travels

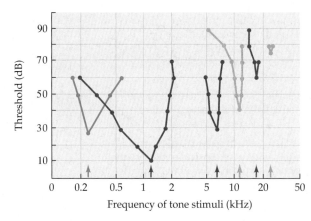

9.6 EXAMPLES OF TUNING CURVES OF AUDITORY NEURONS These curves depict the responses of six different cells of the cat auditory nerve, to sounds of different intensities and frequencies. Because they represent threshold measurements, the *lowest* point on each curve (indicated by arrows on the *x*-axis for six cells) corresponds to that neuron's preferred frequency. (After Kiang, 1965.)

vestibulocochlear nerve   Cranial nerve VIII, which runs from the cochlea to the brainstem auditory nuclei.

tuning curve   A graph of the responses of a single auditory nerve fiber or neuron to sounds that vary in frequency and intensity.

cochlear nuclei   Brainstem nuclei that receive input from auditory hair cells and send output to the superior olivary complex.

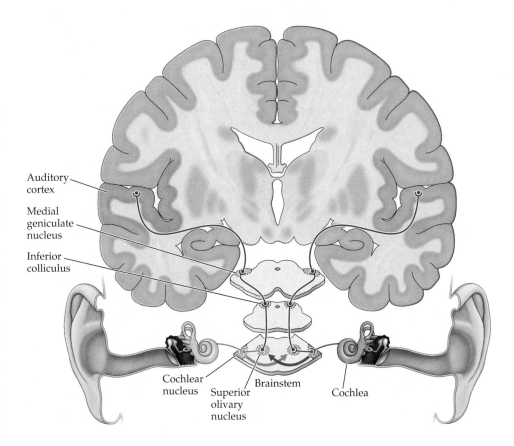

Auditory cortex

Medial geniculate nucleus

Inferior colliculus

Cochlear nucleus

Superior olivary nucleus

Brainstem

Cochlea

9.7 AUDITORY PATHWAYS OF THE HUMAN BRAIN This view from the front of the head shows the first binaural (two-ear) interactions in the brainstem superior olivary nucleus. Most (but not all) of the information from each ear projects to the cortex on the opposite side of the brain, as illustrated here by the colors of the projections to the medial geniculate of the thalamus and then the cortex.

superior olivary nuclei Brainstem nuclei that receive input from both right and left cochlear nuclei and provide the first binaural analysis of auditory information.

inferior colliculi Paired gray matter structures of the dorsal midbrain that receive auditory information.

medial geniculate nuclei Nuclei in the thalamus that receive input from the inferior colliculi and send output to the auditory cortex.

tonotopic organization A major organizational feature in auditory systems in which neurons are arranged as an orderly map of stimulus frequency, with cells responsive to high frequencies located at a distance from those responsive to low frequencies.

primary auditory cortex (A1) The region of superior temporal cortex in which auditory processing occurs.

via multiple paths. One path from each cochlear nucleus goes to both **superior olivary nuclei**, so they both receive inputs from both right and left cochlear nuclei. This bilateral input is the first stage in the CNS at which *binaural* (two-ear) effects are processed; as you might expect, this mechanism plays a key role in localizing sounds by comparing the two ears, as we'll discuss shortly. Several other parallel paths converge on the **inferior colliculi**, which are the primary auditory centers of the midbrain. Outputs of the inferior colliculi go to the **medial geniculate nuclei** of the thalamus. At least two different pathways from the medial geniculate extend to several auditory cortical areas.

Throughout the auditory pathways, neuronal response is frequency-sensitive, as with the vestibulocochlear nerve fibers that we discussed earlier (see Figure 9.6). This ability to discriminate frequencies is even sharper at higher stations of the auditory nervous system. At the medial geniculate nucleus and the auditory cortex, not only are neurons excited by certain frequencies, but they are also *inhibited* by neighboring frequencies. This interplay of excitation and inhibition further sharpens the frequency responses, allowing us to discriminate very small frequency differences.

All levels of the auditory pathway display **tonotopic organization**; that is, they are spatially arranged in an orderly map according to the auditory frequencies to which they respond. This organization begins with the cochlea—remember, frequency is ordered along the length of the basilar membrane (see Figure 9.3), and because the IHC fibers exiting the cochlea are organized according to their points of origin along the basilar membrane, analysis of the auditory projection reveals an orderly map from low to high frequencies. This can be seen when auditory brain regions are mapped using 2-deoxyglucose (2-DG), as shown in **FIGURE 9.8**. Following 2-DG injection, an animal is exposed to a tone of a particular frequency. Because 2-DG is taken up like glucose by neurons, but not metabolized, the most active neurons take up the most 2-DG. Postmortem processing of 2-DG distribution reveals which cells were most active when the stimulus frequency was presented. (The organization of auditory cortical areas in other species is described on the website in **A Step Further: The Auditory Cortical Regions of Many Species Show Tonotopic Organization**.)

Brain-imaging studies in humans have confirmed that many sounds (tones, noises, and so on) result in activation of **primary auditory cortex (A1)**, located on the upper surface of the temporal lobes (**FIGURE 9.9A**). Speech sounds produce similar activation but additionally activate other, more specialized auditory areas (**FIGURE 9.9B**). Interestingly, at least some of these regions are activated when hearing people try to lip-read—that is, to understand someone by watching that person's lips without auditory cues (L. E. Bernstein et al., 2002; Calvert et al., 1997); this result suggests that the auditory cortex integrates other, nonauditory, information with sounds.

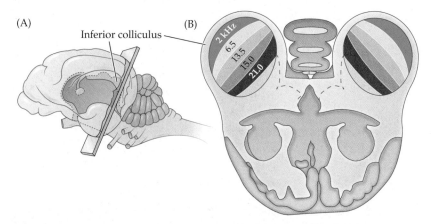

9.8 TONOTOPIC MAPPING IN THE CAT INFERIOR COLLICULUS (A) This lateral view of the cat brain shows the plane of the transverse section through the inferior colliculus shown in part B. (B) Following exposure to tones of different frequencies, 2-DG labeling reveals an orderly tonotopic map within the inferior colliculus (After Serviere et al., 1984.)

Go to Animation 9.3
Mapping Auditory Frequencies
bn8e.com/9.3

(A) Noise

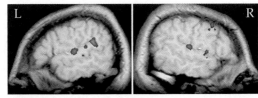

Speech sounds

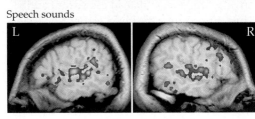

(B) Listening to words

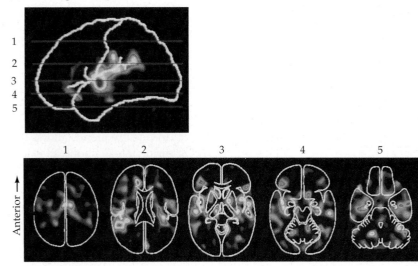

9.9 RESPONSES OF THE HUMAN AUDITORY CORTEX TO RANDOM SOUNDS VERSUS SPEECH (A) Functional MRI scans of the cerebral hemispheres show that pure tones or noise (upper) activate chiefly the primary auditory area on the superior aspect of the temporal lobe, while speech sounds (upper) activate other auditory cortical regions, as well as the primary auditory area. (B) Lateral (upper) and horizontal (lower) PET scans show that listening to words activates not only several regions of the cerebral cortex but also regions of the thalamus and the cerebellum. The numbered horizontal lines in the upper panel correspond to the levels of the horizontal sections in the lower panel. (Part A from Binder et al., 1994, courtesy of Dr. Jeffrey Binder; B from Posner and Raichle, 1994, courtesy of Dr. Marcus Raichle.)

Pitch Information Is Encoded in Two Complementary Ways

Most of us can discriminate very small differences in frequency of sound over the entire audible range—from 20 Hz to 15,000 or even 20,000 Hz. The ability to detect a change in frequency is usually measured as the **minimal discriminable frequency difference** between two tones. The detectable difference is about 2 Hz for sounds up to 2000 Hz; at higher frequencies, larger differences are required.

Note that *frequency* and *pitch* are not synonymous terms. *Frequency* describes a physical property of sounds; *pitch* relates solely to the subjective sensory experience of sounds (see Box 9.1). This is an important distinction because frequency is not the sole determinant of perceived pitch (at some frequencies, higher-intensity sounds may seem higher pitched), and changes in pitch do not precisely parallel changes in frequency.

How do we distinguish pitches? Two signals from the cochlea appear to inform the brain about pitch:

1. In **place coding**, the pitch of a sound is encoded in the physical location of the activated receptors along the length of the basilar membrane: activation of receptors near the base of the cochlea (which is narrow and stiff, and responds to high frequencies) signals **treble**, and activation of receptors nearer the apex (which is wide and floppy, and responds to low frequencies) signals **bass**. For complex sounds with components at several different frequencies, the cochlea maps simultaneous peaks of vibration at different places along the basilar membrane (something like Fourier analysis; see Box 9.1).

2. A complementary process, **temporal coding**, directly encodes the frequency of auditory stimuli in the rate of firing of auditory neurons. So, for example, a 500-Hz sound might cause some neurons to fire 500 action potentials per second. In

minimal discriminable frequency difference The smallest change in frequency that can be detected reliably between two tones.

place coding The encoding of sound frequency as a function of the location on the basilar membrane that is most stimulated by that sound.

treble An aspect of pitch corresponding to the subjective experience of high-frequency sounds (especially musical sounds, such as cymbals).

bass An aspect of pitch corresponding to the subjective experience of low-frequency sounds (especially musical sounds, such as bass guitar).

temporal coding The encoding of sound frequency in terms of the number of action potentials per second produced by an auditory nerve.

infrasound   Very low-frequency sound; in general, below the threshold for human hearing, at about 20 Hz.

ultrasound   High-frequency sound; in general, above the threshold for human hearing, at about 20,000 Hz.

binaural   Referring to two ears.

intensity differences   Perceived differences in loudness between the two ears, which can be used to localize a sound source.

such cases the firing of the action potential is *phase-locked* to the stimulus; that is, it occurs at a particular point in each sound cycle and thus directly reflects the number of cycles per second (i.e., hertz). Because individual cells may miss some cycles, especially as frequencies increase, an accurate phase-locked representation generally requires averaging across several cells rather than a single cell. Recordings from auditory fibers additionally indicate that while lower-frequency sounds are encoded as action potentials on a one-to-one basis, for higher-frequency sounds the frequency of action potentials may instead encode an auditory frequency that is an integer multiple. Encoding a multiple, rather than one-to-one, frequency allows the auditory system to overcome the maximal neuronal firing rate of about 1000 action potentials per second. In general, temporal coding is most evident at the lower end of the hearing range, but it functions up to about 4000 Hz.

Because each mechanism makes up for certain deficiencies in the other, the contemporary view of pitch perception incorporates elements of both models. Thus, the frequency properties of a sound are coded in two ways: (1) according to the distribution of excitation among cells, that is, place coding or tonotopic representation; and (2) according to the temporal pattern of discharge in cells projecting to the auditory cortex.

Mammalian species employ an astonishing range of frequencies in their vocalizations, from less than 10 Hz (called **infrasound**) in some whales to more than 100,000 Hz (**ultrasound**) in some bats. In addition to their importance in social communication, vocalizations are used by many species in other special ways (see Figure 9.1). Bats process the echoes of their loud ultrasonic vocalizations, in order to navigate and hunt in the dark; porpoises likewise employ powerful ultrasonic sonar to scan the ocean around them. Their extraordinary sensitivity and accuracy are conferred by elaborate adaptations of their bodies and brains. At the other end of the spectrum, homing-pigeon races are severely disrupted if the birds encounter the sonic-boom shock wave of a supersonic jet (an infrasound pulse that can travel hundreds of miles), suggesting that the pigeons use infrasound cues to establish a navigational map (Hagstrum, 2000). Elephants' voices include infrasonic components so powerful that they can be detected *seismically* by other elephants (Herbst et al., 2012; O'Connell-Rodwell, 2007), while conveying enough detail to distinguish between human-related threats and bee-related threats (Soltis et al., 2014). Tigers may use infrasound to add impact to their roars (Walsh et al., 2003), and infrasound experimentally inserted into concerts heightens the music's emotional effect on human listeners, but it's not yet known how we detect infrasound.

Brainstem Auditory Systems Are Specialized for Localizing Sounds

Being able to quickly identify where a sound is coming from—be it the crack of a twig under a predator's foot or the alluring murmur of a would-be mate—is a matter of great evolutionary significance. So it's no surprise that we are remarkably good at locating a sound source (our accuracy is within about 1° horizontally around the head, and many animals are even better). The auditory system accomplishes this feat by analyzing two kinds of **binaural** (two-ear) cues that signal the location of a sound source in the horizontal plane (this is called *azimuth*):

1. **Intensity differences** are differences in *loudness* at the two ears. Depending on the species—and the placement and characteristics of their pinnae—intensity differences occur because one ear is pointed more directly toward the sound source or because the head casts what is called a *sound shadow* (**FIGURE 9.10A**), preventing sounds located to one side (called *off-axis sounds*) from reaching both ears with equal loudness. The head shadow effect is most pronounced for higher-frequency sounds. Low-frequency sounds have longer sound waves that reach around the head more effectively, reducing the head shadow (**FIGURE 9.10B**).

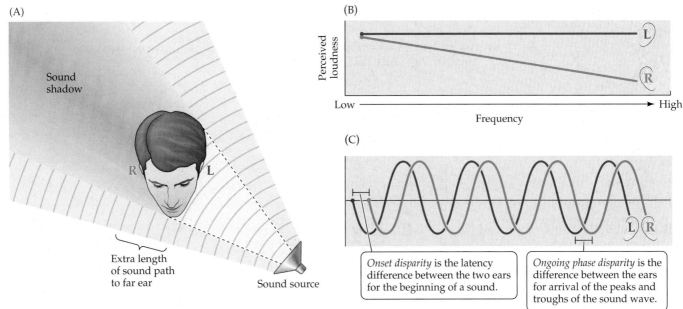

(A)

Sound
shadow

R L

Extra length
of sound path
to far ear

Sound source

(B)

Perceived loudness

Low ——————————————————→ High

Frequency

L

R

(C)

Onset disparity is the latency difference between the two ears for the beginning of a sound.

Ongoing phase disparity is the difference between the ears for arrival of the peaks and troughs of the sound wave.

L R

9.10 CUES FOR BINAURAL HEARING   The two ears receive somewhat different information from sound sources located to one side or the other of the observer's midline. (A) The head casts a sound shadow, producing binaural differences in sound intensity. (B) The resulting differences in perceived intensity are greater at higher frequencies. (C) Sounds also take longer to reach the more distant ear, resulting in binaural differences in time of arrival.

2. **Latency differences** are differences between the two ears in the *time of arrival* of sounds. They arise because one ear is always a little closer to an off-axis sound than is the other ear. Two kinds of latency differences are present in a sound: *onset disparity*, which is the difference between the two ears in hearing the beginning of the sound, and *ongoing phase disparity*, which is the continuous mismatch between the two ears in the arrival of all the peaks and troughs that make up the sound wave (these cues are illustrated in **FIGURE 9.10C**).

Researchers now know that sound localization involves processing of *both* intensity differences and latency differences; this is known as the **duplex theory**. At low frequencies, no matter where sounds are presented horizontally around the head, there are virtually no intensity differences between the ears. For these frequencies, differences in times of arrival are the principal cues for sound localization (and at very low frequencies, neither cue is much help; this is why you can place the subwoofer of an audio system anywhere you want). At higher frequencies, however, the sound shadow cast by the head produces significant binaural intensity differences. Of course, you can't perceive which types of processing you're relying on for any given sound; in general, we are aware of the *results* of neural processing but not the processing itself.

What brain systems analyze binaural cues? Both birds and mammals have highly specialized brainstem mechanisms that receive information from the two ears, and they use arrays of bipolar neurons to derive sound location from the left and right auditory signals. These bipolar neurons are capable of making very precise timing calculations by comparing the inputs to their two dendrites (Agmon-Snir et al., 1998).

In birds, the organization of neurons within the primary sound localization nucleus (called the *nucleus laminaris*) constitutes an auditory map of space. In this model, originally proposed by Lloyd Jeffress (1948), each binaural neuron of the nucleus laminaris functions as a **coincidence detector** and is maximally excited by a particular latency difference between inputs from the two ears, corresponding to a particular place in space (Joris et al., 1998) (**FIGURE 9.11**). This map is further

latency differences   Differences between the two ears in the time of arrival of a sound, which can be employed by the nervous system to localize sound sources.

duplex theory   A theory that we localize sound by combining information about intensity differences and latency differences between the two ears.

coincidence detector   A device that senses the co-occurrence of two events.

9.11 THE CLASSIC (JEFFRESS) MODEL OF SOUND LOCALIZATION IN THE AUDITORY BRAINSTEM OF BIRDS

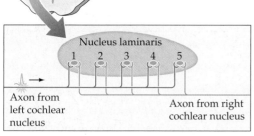

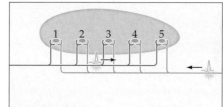

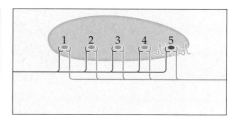

1 A sound occurring to the left of the bird's midline is detected by the left cochlea slightly earlier than the right cochlea.

2 Monaural neurons of the left cochlear nucleus of the brainstem become active, sending action potentials along their axons toward the nucleus laminaris.

3 Slightly later, neurons of the right cochlear nucleus also send action potentials toward the nucleus laminaris…

4 …with the result that the action potential from the left side and the one from the right side arrive simultaneously at neuron 5. Neuron 5 is thus a coincidence detector that signals a particular location to the left of midline. For simplicity, only 5 neurons are shown; in reality, thousands of such neurons make up a detailed map of space.

spectral filtering Alteration of the amplitude of some, but not all, frequencies in a sound.

9.12 ALL EARS As in other mammals, including humans, the ridges and valleys of this bat's outer ear produce precise changes, called *spectral filtering*, in the sounds being funneled into the ear. This process provides additional cues about the location of a sound source. Some moths produce ultrasonic clicks that interfere with these signals (Corcoran et al., 2009), confusing the bat about where to find that tasty moth.

developed at higher levels, especially the *tectum* (equivalent to the mammalian inferior colliculus), which contains a complete map of space.

Mammals apparently do things quite differently (Franken et al., 2015). The superior olivary nucleus is the primary sound localization nucleus in the mammalian brain, and its two main divisions serve different functions. The *lateral superior olive* (LSO) processes intensity differences. The *medial superior olive* (MSO) processes latency differences, but in contrast to the nucleus laminaris in birds, the MSO does not appear to contain a map of auditory space. Instead, sound location is encoded by the relative activity of the *entire* left MSO compared with the *entire* right MSO (Grothe, 2003; McAlpine et al., 2001). So, for example, a sound on the midline would activate the left and right MSOs equally, and the two signals would effectively cancel each other out. But a sound on the right would produce more excitation of the left MSO than the right MSO, and the converse would be true for sounds on the left. The bigger the difference between the left and right MSO is, the farther the sound source is from the midline. This disparity is passed along for further processing at other levels of the auditory system.

The structure of the external ear provides yet another sort of localization cue. As we mentioned earlier, the hills and valleys of the external ear selectively reinforce some frequencies in a complex sound and diminish others (**FIGURE 9.12**). This process is known as **spectral filtering**, and the frequencies that are affected depend on where the sound originates (Kulkarni and Colburn, 1998).

The relationship between spectral cues and location is learned and calibrated during development. Unlike the binaural intensity and latency cues that localize a sound in azimuth (horizontal location), spectral cues provide critical information about *elevation* (vertical location). Researchers can place a speaker directly in the ear canal and, by varying the binaural cues and the spectral filtering of natural sounds, fool a person or animal into believing that the sound came from a particular point in space (L. Xu et al., 1999).

Orchestra conductors are especially good at identifying the spatial location of sound sources (Münte et al., 2001), presumably because of extensive practice ("Ms. Emerson, could you *please* play in tune?"). Single-cell recordings indicate that the multiple binaural and spectral cues involved in sound localization converge in the auditory system at the level of the inferior colliculus (Slee and Young, 2011).

The Auditory Cortex Processes Complex Sounds

The historical view of auditory function was that the various subcortical auditory areas performed only basic processing, serving mostly as stepping-stones in a pathway to the auditory cortex (Masterton, 1993). The cortex, it was believed, was where auditory sensation and discrimination really arose. But behavioral testing suggested otherwise; for example, cats can still discriminate different tones following surgical removal of auditory cortex (M. R. Rosenzweig, 1946). If the auditory cortex is not involved in these basic kinds of auditory discrimination, then what *does* it do?

Early studies relied on simple, but unnatural, pure tones. Most of the sounds in nature, however—such as vocalizations of animals, footsteps, snaps, crackles, and pops—contain many frequencies and change rapidly. The auditory cortex seems to be specialized for the detection of these more complex "biologically relevant" sounds (Theunissen and Elie, 2014). In other words, the auditory cortex evolved to process the sounds of everyday life. Indeed, most cortical auditory neurons habituate rapidly to continuous tones, ceasing to respond after only a few milliseconds; but brief or abruptly changing sounds usually evoke responses from many neurons, from the cochlear nuclei to the auditory cortex. Ablation of the auditory cortex does impair discrimination of temporal *patterns* of sound in cats (Neff and Casseday, 1977) and monkeys (Heffner and Heffner, 1989).

Other cortical regions have rich interconnections with auditory cortex. Two streams of auditory processing are found in the cortex (Kaas and Hackett, 1999): a dorsal stream, involving the parietal lobe, is concerned with spatial *location* of sounds; a ventral stream through the temporal lobe may analyze the various *components* of sounds (Romanski et al., 1999), which in the human left hemisphere might include processing of speech sounds (see Chapter 19). This organization suggests the existence of separate auditory processing streams for *what* versus *where*, neatly paralleling a similar scheme that has been proposed for visual processing (Goodale and Milner, 1992; Recanzone and Cohen, 2010), as we will discuss in Chapter 10. Furthermore, during locomotion the activated motor cortex selectively modifies the responsiveness of auditory cortex, helping it to focus on specific stimuli that are of immediate importance (D. M. Schneider et al., 2014).

Experience affects auditory perception and the auditory pathways

The unique capabilities of the auditory cortex result from hardwired sensitivity that is fine-tuned by experience as we grow (Kandler et al., 2009). Human infants have diverse hearing capabilities at birth, but hearing for complex speech sounds in particular becomes more precise and rapid through exposure to the speech of their family and other people. Similarly, early experience with binaural hearing (via hearing aids), compared with equivalent monaural hearing or no hearing, has a significant effect on the ability of children to localize sound sources later in life (W. D. Beggs and Foreman, 1980). Studies with lab animals confirm that experience with sounds of a particular frequency can cause a rapid retuning of auditory neurons (**FIGURE 9.13**) (Fritz et al., 2003; N. M. Weinberger, 1998). You can also learn about the role of experience in auditory localization by owls on the website in **A Step Further: Auditory Systems Are Calibrated through Polymodal Integration**.

Music is also effective in shaping the responses of auditory cortex. It might not surprise you to learn that

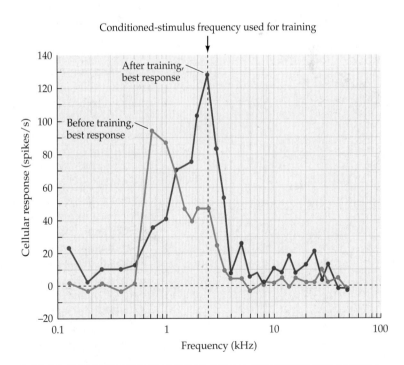

9.13 PLASTICITY IN THE TUNING OF AN AUDITORY RECEPTIVE FIELD This graph plots the response of a single guinea pig auditory cortex neuron to varying frequencies. Before training, the "best" frequency of the cell was about 0.7 kHz (blue line). After training with a 1.1-kHz tone, the best frequency had shifted to 1.1 kHz (red line), and it stayed there for at least 4 weeks. (After N. M. Weinberger, 1998.)

Sound processing   Pattern recognition   Emotional content   Rewarding qualities

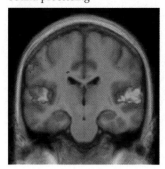 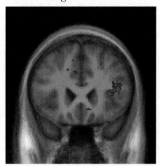 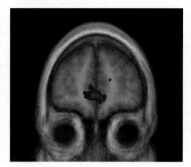 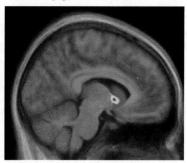

9.14 MAKING SWEET MUSIC These fMRI images show 4 distinct brain mechanisms that are activated when we concentrate on new music. Separable systems analyze complex sounds (green) and process temporal patterns of the music (blue). Frontal cortical regions (red) are associated with processing the emotional content of the music. The overall pleasurableness of a new song is associated with activity in the nucleus accumbens (rainbow), part of the brain's reward system, and the strength of this signal predicts the amount that people will spend in order to buy it. (Courtesy of Dr. V. Salimpoor, McGill University.)

amusia A disorder characterized by the inability to discern tunes accurately.

diffusion tensor imaging (DTI) A modified form of MRI in which the diffusion of water in a confined space is exploited to produce images of axonal fiber tracts.

the auditory cortex of trained musicians shows a bigger response to musical sounds than does the same cortex in nonmusicians. After all, when two people differ in any skill, their brains *must* be different in some way, and maybe people born with brains that are more responsive to complex sounds are also more likely to become musicians. The surprising part is the discovery that the extent to which a musician's brain is extra sensitive to musical notes is correlated with the age at which she began her serious training in music—the earlier the training began, the bigger the difference in auditory cortex in adulthood (Pantev et al., 1998). This finding indicates that intensive musical experience in development potently alters the functioning of auditory cortex later in life.

Certainly there are big differences by adulthood: the portion of primary auditory cortex where music is first processed, called *Heschl's gyrus,* is more than twice as large in professional musicians as in nonmusicians, and more than twice as strongly activated by music (P. Schneider et al., 2002). Debate continues about whether musical ability is a specific and hardwired human trait or just a happy by-product of systems that evolved for other purposes (Balter, 2004), but the existence of disorders in which people cannot accurately discern tunes (called **amusia**, from the Greek *amousia,* "want of harmony") suggests that at least the rudiments of a musical sense are inborn (Münte, 2002). Further, auditory cortex that is involved in perceptual analysis of music interacts directly with the mesolimbic dopamine-based reward circuitry of the brain (see Chapter 4) to attach a reward value to music that is new to us (Salimpoor et al., 2013). The degree of activation of this system predicts an individual's willingness to pay for a music recording (**FIGURE 9.14**).

Tone-deaf Tony, whom we described at the beginning of the chapter, exemplifies the dyslexia-like problem of amusia. Whereas most infants clearly understand the basics of musical relationships almost from birth, people with congenital amusia never develop that ability (Peretz and Hyde, 2003). This seems to be a problem in recognizing pitch, not the timing aspects of music (*rhythm*), since that facet of music sensation may be unaffected in amusia (K. L. Hyde and Peretz, 2004). Brain imaging suggests that the right inferior frontal gyrus, which is normally active in pitch perception, contains less white matter in people with amusia than in people with normal music perception (K. L. Hyde et al., 2006). Images of fiber tracts between brain regions, created using **diffusion tensor imaging (DTI)** (see Chapters 2 and 19), reveal that tone-deaf people have fewer connections between frontal cortex and the temporal auditory cortex (Loui et al., 2009) (**FIGURE 9.15**). The result is an inability to consciously access pitch information, even though cortical pitch processing

(A) Control   (B) Tone-deaf

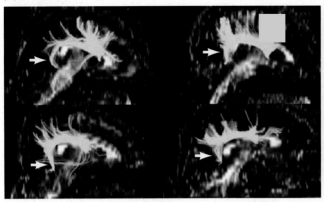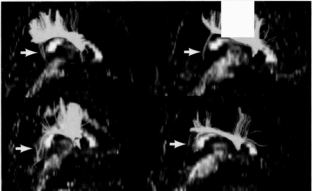

9.15 BRAIN CONNECTIONS IN TONE-DEAF PEOPLE Diffusion tensor imaging (DTI) reveals myelinated tracts in these midsagittal images of people facing to the right. The group of fibers connecting the frontal cortex, which is active during pitch discrimination, to the temporal lobe, where auditory processing begins, is called the *arcuate fasciculus* because it is arc-shaped (arrow). The arcuate fasciculus is much more prominent in four controls (A) than in four people with amusia (B). (From Loui et al., 2009, courtesy of Dr. Psyche Loui.)

systems are intact (Zendel et al., 2015). However, music is a complex stimulus, and many additional regions of the brain are active in people listening to or producing music; dysfunction in some of these other regions may result in other types of musical defects. If you're worried about your own ability to carry a tune, the National Institutes of Health (NIH) provides an online test of pitch perception at nidcd.nih.gov/tunestest/test-your-sense-pitch.

Hearing Loss Is a Major Disorder of the Nervous System

Disorders of hearing include **hearing loss** (defined as decreased sensitivity to sound, ranging from moderate to severe) and **deafness** (a loss of hearing so profound that speech cannot be perceived even with the use of hearing aids). Hearing loss affects as much as 15% of the population—about 37.5 million people in the United States alone (Blackwell et al., 2014)—with more than 3% categorized as experiencing serious hearing loss or deafness. (Mitchell, 2006). The prevalence of hearing loss is probably similar in other developed countries. Auditory problems can come about in several different ways.

There are three main causes of hearing loss and deafness

Many severe hearing impairments arise early in life and impair language acquisition. Others occur later in life as a consequence of environmental factors, such as exposure to loud sounds, infections, or side effects of certain drugs. **FIGURE 9.16** depicts the three categories of problems that lead to hearing loss and deafness: (1) a failure of vibrations to reach the cochlea, (2) problems with the cochlear conversion of sound waves into action potentials, and (3) dysfunction of auditory processing systems in the brain.

Conduction deafness or hearing loss arises when disorders of the outer or middle ear prevent vibrations produced by auditory stimuli from reaching the cochlea (**FIGURE 9.16A**). In one common form of conduction deafness, the ossicles become fused and can no longer transmit sound vibrations effectively. Surgery to free up the ossicles is helpful in some cases. The nervous system is generally not involved in this form of hearing loss.

Sensorineural deafness or hearing loss, a condition in which auditory nerve fibers are unable to become excited in a normal manner, can be caused by noise exposure, metabolic problems, infections, exposure to toxins, trauma, and hundreds of different hereditary disorders (**FIGURE 9.16B**). This type of hearing loss is usu-

hearing loss Decreased sensitivity to sound, in varying degrees.

deafness Hearing loss so profound that speech perception is lost.

conduction deafness A hearing impairment that is associated with pathology of the external-ear or middle-ear cavities.

sensorineural deafness A hearing impairment that originates from cochlear or auditory nerve lesions.

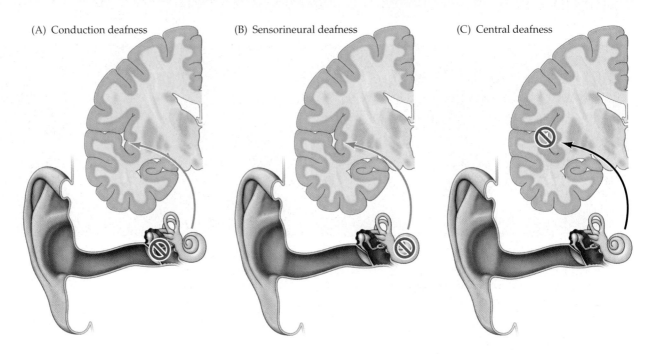

(A) Conduction deafness   (B) Sensorineural deafness   (C) Central deafness

9.16 THREE MAJOR CATEGORIES OF HEARING LOSS AND DEAFNESS Most deafness is the result of either (A) a problem with the outer or middle ear that prevents the transmission of sound energy to the cochlea, called *conduction deafness*, or (B) a problem with the cochlea or its neural projections that interferes with the transduction of mechanical sound energy into action potentials that the brain can understand, termed *sensorineural deafness*. (C) Less commonly, people may also experience hearing difficulties as a result of lesions of auditory areas in the brain.

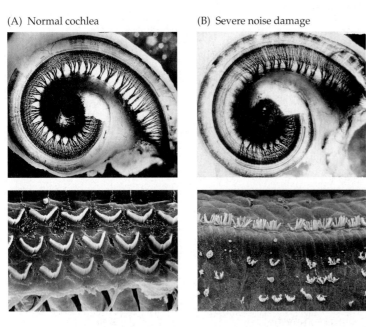

(A) Normal cochlea   (B) Severe noise damage

9.17 COCHLEAR DAMAGE DUE TO LOUD NOISE (A) In a normal cochlea, hair cells line the organ of Corti throughout its length (top). With scanning electron microscopy, the stereocilia are easily visualized as orderly rows of bristles (bottom) protruding into the tectorial membrane. (B) Exposure to excessively loud sounds can have rapid destructive effects in the cochlea. Here, the hair cells are completely missing from a wide extent of the cochlea (top) corresponding to the frequencies of the intense sounds that the person was exposed to. The stereocilia (bottom) have been crushed and flattened by the noise exposure.

ally permanent. Defects in certain genes affecting hair cell structure and function are prominent causes of sensorineural deafness that is present from birth (Petit and Richardson, 2009). For example, mutations in the gene *GJB2* may be responsible for as much as 50% of congenital or early-onset hearing loss (Cryns and Van Camp, 2004); this gene encodes the protein connexin-26, which is involved in the formation of electrical synapses (known as *gap junctions*; see Chapter 3).

Drug-induced hearing loss sometimes results from the toxic properties of the group of antibiotics that includes streptomycin and gentamicin. The **ototoxic** (ear-damaging) properties of streptomycin were discovered when many patients who received it as treatment for tuberculosis subsequently developed cochlear damage. In severe cases the hair cells of the cochlea were completely destroyed, producing total, irreversible loss of hearing.

Noise pollution and loud sounds—industrial noise, loud engines, the firing of guns—can severely damage the cochlea in a short period of time. Once again, the hair cells suffer the brunt of the damage: in the affected part of the cochlea, the stereocilia appear shattered and broken, like a flattened forest (**FIGURE 9.17**). There is growing concern about hearing loss caused by listening to personal music players over headphones, which can produce sounds above 100 dB. Those who listen for more than 5 hours per week at 89 dB or louder are exceeding workplace limits, so they are exposing themselves to levels known to induce permanent hearing loss (SCENIHR, 2008). A comparison of sound sources is depicted in **FIGURE 9.18**; if you are concerned about your own exposure, excellent sound level meter apps for smartphones are available at little or no cost. Loud sounds coupled with the use of some over-the-counter drugs, such as aspirin, can also have profound cumulative effects on hearing (McFadden and Champlin, 1990), reducing sensitivity to certain tones by up to 40 dB and/or leading to the development of **tinnitus**, a sensation of noises or ringing in the ears (Brien, 1993).

Central deafness (hearing loss caused by brain lesions such as stroke) (**FIGURE 9.16C**) is seldom a simple loss of auditory sensitivity. An example illustrating the complexity of changes in auditory perception following cerebral cortical damage is **word deafness**, a disorder in which people show normal speech and hearing for simple sounds but cannot recognize spoken words. Word deafness may be due to an abnormally slow analysis of auditory inputs. Another example of central deafness is **cortical deafness**, in which patients have difficulty recognizing both verbal and nonverbal auditory stimuli. Cortical deafness is a rare syndrome because it requires bilateral damage to the auditory cortex.

Strokes that interrupt all of the projection fibers from the medial geniculate nucleus to the various auditory cortical regions also cause deafness (Y. Tanaka et al., 1991). Patients who suffer from stroke-induced deafness still show various acoustic reflexes mediated by the brainstem—such as a startle response to a sudden, loud noise—although they deny hearing the sounds to which they are reacting. In contrast, patients with bilateral destruction of only the *primary* auditory cortex often have less-severe hearing loss, presumably because other auditory cortical regions contribute to hearing, as discussed earlier. And central hearing impairment doesn't necessarily involve gross tissue damage: for example, long-term exposure to noise that isn't loud enough to hurt the cochlea may degrade hearing by provoking plastic changes in auditory cortex (Gourévitch et al., 2014).

Treatments for deafness focus on replacing missing stimulation

Generations ago, people used ear horns (basically reversed megaphones) to capture sounds and direct them into the ear more loudly than usual; cupping one hand over your ear has a similar but more modest effect. Nowadays, most people are familiar with electronic hearing aids, which are simply miniaturized audio amplifiers—a microphone picks up environmental sounds, amplifies them, and plays the amplified sounds directly into the ear canal. By providing louder than usual sounds, hearing aids effectively overcome the mechanical problems inherent in conduction deafness.

Unfortunately, amplifying sounds can't help as effectively in sensorineural hearing loss, where the hair cells or other neural components of the inner ear are damaged or missing. But while the hair cells may be completely destroyed, the electrical excitability of the auditory nerve often remains unchanged. So one approach for circumventing deafness due to hair cell loss involves directly stimulating the

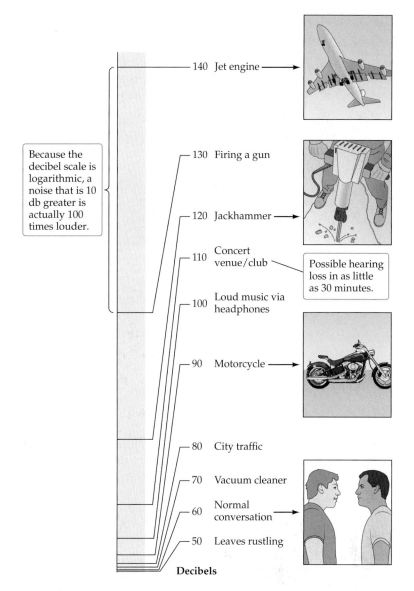

Because the decibel scale is logarithmic, a noise that is 10 db greater is actually 100 times louder.

- 140 Jet engine
- 130 Firing a gun
- 120 Jackhammer
- 110 Concert venue/club
- 100 Loud music via headphones
- 90 Motorcycle
- 80 City traffic
- 70 Vacuum cleaner
- 60 Normal conversation
- 50 Leaves rustling

Decibels

Possible hearing loss in as little as 30 minutes.

9.18 HOW LOUD IS TOO LOUD? Because the decibel scale is logarithmic, each increment of 10 dB represents a 100-fold increase in loudness. Listening to sounds over 85–90 dB for extended periods of time can cause hearing loss, and by 110 dB or so, exposure for as little as 30 minutes can be harmful. Earplugs are available that attenuate all frequencies equally, making concerts a little quieter without muffling the music.

ototoxic Toxic to the ears, especially the middle or inner ear.

tinnitus A sensation of noises or ringing in the ears.

central deafness A hearing impairment that is related to lesions in auditory pathways or centers, including sites in the brainstem, thalamus, or cortex.

word deafness The specific inability to hear words, although other sounds can be detected.

cortical deafness A hearing impairment that is caused by a fault or defect in the cortex.

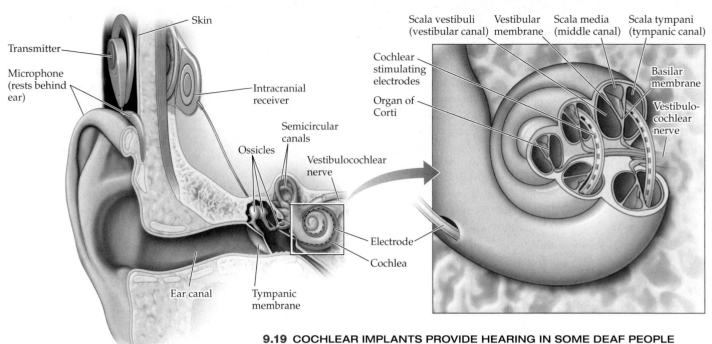

Skin

Transmitter

Microphone
(rests behind
ear)

Intracranial
receiver

Semicircular
canals

Ossicles

Vestibulocochlear
nerve

Ear canal

Tympanic
membrane

Electrode

Cochlea

Scala vestibuli
(vestibular canal)

Vestibular
membrane

Scala media
(middle canal)

Scala tympani
(tympanic canal)

Cochlear
stimulating
electrodes

Organ of
Corti

Basilar
membrane

Vestibulo-
cochlear
nerve

9.19 COCHLEAR IMPLANTS PROVIDE HEARING IN SOME DEAF PEOPLE
A microphone detects sound and directs the cochlear implant circuitry to stimulate
the auditory nerve. Although this apparatus provides only a crude simulation of ordinary auditory nerve activity, the brain can learn to use the information to decipher
speech.

cochlear implant An electromechanical device that detects sounds and
selectively stimulates nerves in different regions of the cochlea via surgically
implanted electrodes.

Go to Video 9.4
**A Baby Hears His
Mother's Voice**
bn8e.com/9.4

auditory nerve with electrical currents. Progress in the development of **cochlear
implants** that deliver such electrical stimulation has been rapid (**FIGURE 9.19**). Cochlear implants provide only a limited range of frequencies and loudness, so they
do not restore normal hearing, but they nonetheless provide stimulation that the
brain can interpret as sound. Functional brain imaging indicates that the stimulation activates auditory cortex in a tonotopic manner, and it appears to be processed
by auditory cortex in similar fashion to "natural" inputs (Lazeyras et al., 2002). For
example, modern cochlear implants provide enough information to allow recipients
to distinguish between voiced and unvoiced speech sounds (e.g., "v" and "f"), which
cannot be distinguished in lip-reading. They likewise allow reasonably good (but
not perfect) perception of tonal aspects of speech, which are especially important
in languages like Mandarin (S. Wang et al., 2013). Although some advocates of deaf
culture oppose the use of such prostheses, studies confirm an increase in speech
perception with continued use of cochlear implants (Skinner et al., 1997), with the
best linguistic outcomes occurring when implants are received early in life (Geers
and Sedey, 2011). The success of these implants seems to be due mainly to the clever-
ness of the brain, not the implant.

Can damaged hair cells be regrown? Although fishes and amphibians produce
new hair cells throughout life, mammals traditionally have been viewed as incapable
of regenerating hair cells. This conclusion may have been too hasty, however (Brigande and Heller, 2009). As in fishes and birds, the supporting cells packed around
the hair cells of the mammalian organ of Corti do remain capable of dividing and
differentiating into hair cells in adulthood (P. M. White et al., 2006). Deletion of the
gene *Rb1* in mice enables hair cells themselves to divide, providing new, functional
hair cells in a deafened cochlea (Sage et al., 2006). Alternatively, a gene therapy that
uses a virus to insert the gene *Atoh1* into the cochlea of deafened mice results in the
growth of new hair cells and significant restoration of hearing within 1–2 months
(Kraft et al., 2013). Human clinical trials of *Atoh1* and other drugs and gene therapies
are currently underway, raising hopes of an effective treatment for sensorineural
hearing loss in the near future.

Now let's consider another sensory system that relies on hair cells, this time to
track the position and motion of the head.

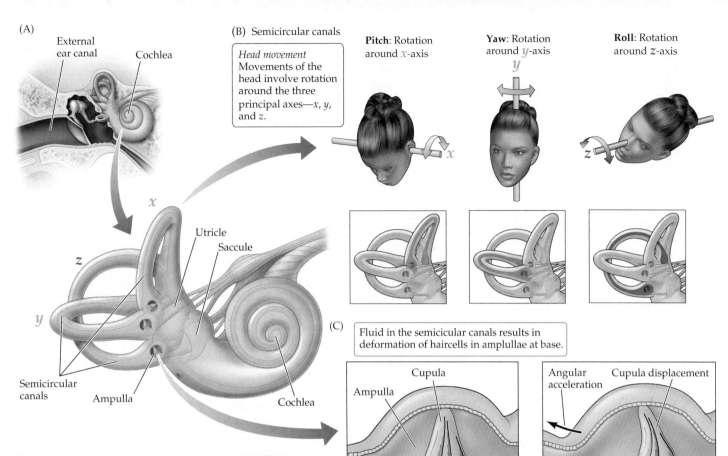

(A) External ear canal · Cochlea

(B) Semicircular canals

Head movement Movements of the head involve rotation around the three principal axes—*x*, *y*, and *z*.

Pitch: Rotation around *x*-axis

Yaw: Rotation around *y*-axis

Roll: Rotation around *z*-axis

Utricle
Saccule

Semicircular canals
Ampulla
Cochlea

(C) Fluid in the semicircular canals results in deformation of haircells in amplullae at base.

Cupula
Ampulla
Semicircular canal
Hair cells

Angular acceleration
Cupula displacement
Endolymph flow

9.20 STRUCTURES OF THE VESTIBULAR SYSTEM
(A) The vestibular apparatus is located in the temporal bone, continuous with the cochlea. The semicircular canals are connected through ampullae to the utricle, which connects to the saccule. (B) The semicircular canals detect rotation in three planes; hair cells in the ampullae detect flow of fluid in the canals when the head is rotated. The utricle and saccule detect linear acceleration and static position, aided by tiny crystals, called *otoliths*, that overlie the hair cells in these structures and maximize the deflection of hair cells in response to movement.

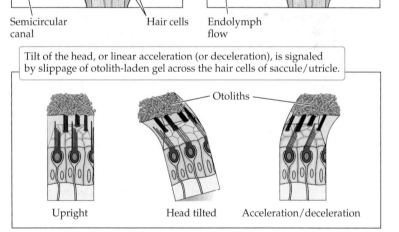

Tilt of the head, or linear acceleration (or deceleration), is signaled by slippage of otolith-laden gel across the hair cells of saccule/utricle.

Otoliths

Upright · Head tilted · Acceleration/deceleration

Vestibular Perception

Without our sense of balance, it would be a challenge to simply stand on two feet. When you use an elevator, you clearly sense that your body is rising or falling, despite the sameness of your surroundings. When you turn your head, take a tight curve in your car, or bounce through the seas in a boat, your continual awareness of motion allows you to plan further movements and anticipate changes in perception due to movement of your head. And of course, too much of this sort of stimulation can make you lose your lunch. It is the vestibular system that informs the brain about gravity, movement, and the position of the body in space.

An Inner Ear System Senses Gravity and Acceleration

The position and movement of the head are detected by the **vestibular system**, which is part of the inner ear, attached to the adjacent cochlea within a hollow in the temporal bone (the Latin term *vestibulum* means "entrance hall"). The most obvious parts of the vestibular system are the three **semicircular canals**, fluid-filled tubes oriented at right angles to each other (**FIGURE 9.20A**). The canals are oriented in the three different planes in which the head can rotate (**FIGURE 9.20B**)—nodding up

vestibular system The inner ear system that encodes the orientation and acceleration of the head in three axes, crucial for the sense of balance.

semicircular canal One of the three fluid-filled tubes in the inner ear that are part of the vestibular system. Each of the tubes, which are at right angles to each other, detects angular acceleration.

utricle A small, fluid-filled sac in the vestibular system above the saccule that responds to static positions of the head.

saccule A small, fluid-filled sac under the utricle in the vestibular system that responds to static positions of the head.

ampulla An enlarged region of each semicircular canal that contains the receptor cells (hair cells) of the vestibular system.

cupula A small gelatinous structure, containing hair cells that detect fluid movement within the semicircular canals of the vestibular system.

otolith A small crystal on the gelatinous membrane in the vestibular system.

lateral-line system A sensory system, found in many kinds of fishes and some amphibians, that informs the animal of water motion in relation to the body surface.

vestibular nuclei Brainstem nuclei that receive information from the vestibular organs through cranial nerve VIII (the vestibulocochlear nerve).

vestibulo-ocular reflex (VOR) The brainstem mechanism that maintains gaze on a visual object despite movements of the head.

Go to Animation 9.5
The Vestibular System
bn8e.com/9.5

and down (technically known as *pitch*), shaking side to side (*yaw*), and tilting left or right (*roll*). The three canals are connected at their ends to a saclike structure called the **utricle** (literally, "little uterus"). Lying below the utricle is another small fluid-filled sac, the **saccule** ("little sac").

Receptors in these structures, just like those of the auditory system, are groups of hair cells, whose stereocilia bend, leading to the excitation of vestibular neurons. Each semicircular canal terminates near the utricle in an enlarged region—the **ampulla** (plural *ampullae*)—that contains the hair cells that signal movement in the corresponding plane (see Figure 9.20B). Here the stereocilia of the hair cells are embedded in a gelatinous structure, the **cupula** (plural *cupulae*). The orientation of the stereocilia is quite precise and determines the direction of mechanical force to which they are especially sensitive. Movement of the head in one axis sets up a relative flow of the fluid in the semicircular canal that lies in the same plane, deflecting the stereocilia in the ampulla and signaling the brain that the head has moved. Working together, the three semicircular canals provide accurate tracking of the rotation of the head. Specialized receptors in the utricle and saccule provide the remaining signal—straight-line acceleration and deceleration—that the brain needs in order to track the precise position and movement of the head in three-dimensional space. On the gelatinous membrane, small crystals called **otoliths** (from the Greek *ot-*, "ear," and *lithos*, "stone") increase the sensitivity of these receptors to movement. At the base of the hair cells are nerve fibers connected much like those that connect auditory hair cells.

It is generally accepted that the auditory organ evolved from the vestibular system, although the ossicles probably evolved from parts of the jaw. Before that, the vestibular system evolved from the **lateral-line system**, a sensory system found in many kinds of fishes and some amphibians. The lateral-line system consists of an array of receptors along the side of the body. Tiny hairs that emerge from sensory cells in the skin are embedded in cupulae, like those in the mammalian ampulla (see Figure 9.20B). Lateral-line systems detect currents of water resulting from movement of the body and from the movements of other animals—maybe prey, maybe predators. It is speculated that the first semicircular canals developed from a stretch of lateral-line canal that migrated inside the body, serving as a sensor for turns to the right or left. The auditory system probably evolved in turn from the early vestibular system.

Nerve Fibers from the Vestibular Portion of the Vestibulocochlear Nerve (VIII) Synapse in the Brainstem

The brain pathways carrying vestibular system information reflect its importance to motor control and posture. Nerve fibers from the vestibular receptors enter lower levels of the brainstem and synapse in the **vestibular nuclei**. Some of the fibers bypass this structure and go directly to the cerebellum, contributing to its motor functions. The outputs of the vestibular nuclei are complex, as is appropriate, considering their influences on the motor system. These outputs go to the motor nuclei of the eye muscles, the thalamus, and the cerebral cortex, among others.

One of the many important functions of the vestibular system is the precise control of eye movements. Try moving your head around while staring at a particular spot on the wall. It seems almost effortless to maintain your gaze on the fixation point, but in reality it is a very complex processing problem; the six muscles that control the movement of each eye must rapidly and precisely counter the movements of the head as they occur. This function is called the **vestibulo-ocular reflex** (VOR), involving a high-speed network within the brainstem that uses vestibular information about head rotations to move the eyes in compensation (**FIGURE 9.21**). The VOR functions accurately even when the eyes are closed, showing that vestibular inputs—rather than visual ones—control the accuracy of gaze as we move through the world.

Some Forms of Vestibular Excitation Produce Motion Sickness

There is one aspect of vestibular activation that many of us would gladly do without. Too much strong vestibular stimulation—as when riding in a boat, car, plane, or roller coaster—can produce the misery of **motion sickness**. Motion sickness is caused especially by movements of the body that we cannot control. For example, passengers in a car are more likely to suffer from motion sickness than is the driver.

Why do we experience motion sickness? The **sensory conflict theory** argues that we feel bad when we receive contradictory sensory messages, especially a discrepancy between vestibular and visual information. When an airplane bounces around in turbulence, for instance, the vestibular system signals that various changes in direction and accelerations are occurring, but as far as the visual system is concerned, nothing is happening; the plane's interior is a constant. One hypothesis is that the stimulation is activating a system that originally evolved to rid the body of swallowed poison (M. Treisman, 1977). According to this hypothesis, discrepancies in sensory information might normally signal a dangerous neurological impairment, triggering dizziness and vomiting to get rid of potentially toxic food. However, data to support the "poison hypothesis" are scanty at best, and overall the evolutionary origins of motion sickness remain a mystery (Oman, 2012).

A different type of vestibular disorientation can strike airplane pilots. Note from Figure 9.20B that linear acceleration and an upward head tilt produce the same stimulation of the otolith organs (the saccule and utricle). So in conditions of very low visibility, an acceleration of the plane may be misinterpreted as a climb (an upward tilt of the plane) (P. R. MacNeilage et al., 2007). This *false-climb illusion* can be very compelling, leading pilots to force their planes into a dive because they mistakenly believe they are climbing. Because the dive itself produces further acceleration, heightening the illusion of climbing, an even steeper dive may be adopted, with tragic consequences. Fortunately, pilots of modern aircraft making landings in low-visibility conditions learn to rely on a variety of instruments rather than on their vestibular systems.

The Chemical Senses: Taste and Smell

Detecting chemicals in the environment is vital for the survival of organisms throughout the animal kingdom. The sense of taste provides an immediate assessment of foods (Lindemann, 1995): sweet indicates high-calorie foods; savory tastes signal a protein source; salty and sour relate to important aspects of homeostasis;

motion sickness The experience of nausea brought on by unnatural passive movement, as in a car or boat.

sensory conflict theory A theory of motion sickness suggesting that discrepancies between vestibular information and visual information simulate food poisoning and therefore trigger nausea.

bitter warns of toxic constituents. The sense of smell is critical for appreciating the rich and complex flavors of individual foods but has additional important functions as well, such as signaling the presence of prey, predators, or potential mates. This section will explore the many roles of the chemical senses—taste and smell—in guiding behavior.

Chemicals in Foods Are Perceived as Five Basic Tastes

Most people derive great pleasure from eating delicious food, and because we recognize many substances by their distinct flavors, we tend to think that we can discriminate many tastes. In reality, though, humans detect only five basic tastes: salty, sour, sweet, bitter, and umami. (*Umami*, Japanese for "delicious taste," is the term for the savory, meaty taste that is characteristic of gravy or soy sauce.) These tastes are determined genetically, as we will see shortly, but there is considerable genetic variation across the globe in both the strength and pleasurable qualities of the basic tastes (Pirastu et al., 2016; Robino et al., 2014). Further, the hunt continues for additional basic tastes: one such candidate, called *kokumi*, is described as the full-bodied, thick, mouth-filling quality of foods, and reportedly the product of newly discovered calcium-sensing receptors on the tongue (Brennan et al., 2014).

The sensations uniquely aroused by an apple, a steak, or an olive are *flavors* rather than simple tastes; they involve smell as well as taste. Block your nose, and a raw potato tastes the same as an apple. Our ability to respond to many odors—incredibly, it is estimated that humans can distinguish more than 1 trillion different odors (Bushdid et al., 2014)—is what produces the complex array of flavors that we normally think of as tastes.

Tastes excite specialized receptor cells on the tongue

It is a common misconception that the myriad little bumps on the tongue are taste buds, but they aren't. They are actually **papillae** (singular *papilla*, Latin for "nipple") (**FIGURE 9.22**), tiny lumps of tissue that serve to increase the surface area of the tongue. There are three kinds of papillae, distributed on the tongue as shown in **FIGURE 9.23**. Each of the relatively few **circumvallate papillae** and **foliate papillae** contains many taste buds in its sides. **Fungiform papillae**, which contain only about six taste buds each, resemble button mushrooms in shape (*fungus* is Latin for "mushroom"). The tongue contains hundreds of fungiform papillae, but we'll see that the numbers vary greatly among individuals.

Each papilla holds one or more **taste buds**, and each taste bud consists of a cluster of 50–150 taste receptor cells (**FIGURE 9.23A**). At the surface end of the taste bud

papilla A small bump that projects from the surface of the tongue. Papillae contain most of the taste receptor cells.

circumvallate papillae One of three types of small structures on the tongue, located in the back, that contain taste receptors.

foliate papillae One of three types of small structures on the tongue that contain taste receptors, located along the sides of the tongue.

fungiform papillae One of three types of small structures on the tongue that contain taste receptors, located in the front of the tongue.

taste bud A cluster of 50–150 cells that detects tastes. Taste buds are found in papillae.

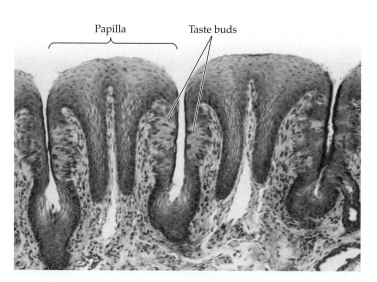

9.22 A CROSS SECTION OF THE TONGUE

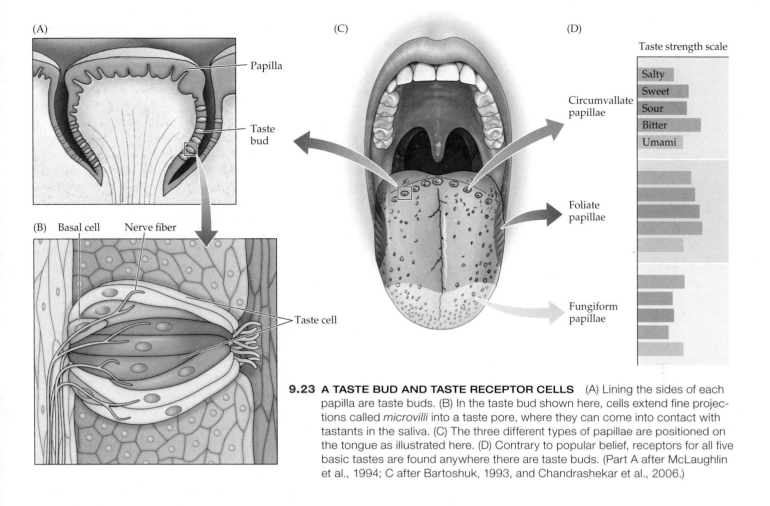

(A) Papilla

Taste bud

(B) Basal cell   Nerve fiber

Taste cell

(C) Circumvallate papillae

Foliate papillae

Fungiform papillae

(D) Taste strength scale

Salty
Sweet
Sour
Bitter
Umami

9.23 A TASTE BUD AND TASTE RECEPTOR CELLS (A) Lining the sides of each papilla are taste buds. (B) In the taste bud shown here, cells extend fine projections called *microvilli* into a taste pore, where they can come into contact with tastants in the saliva. (C) The three different types of papillae are positioned on the tongue as illustrated here. (D) Contrary to popular belief, receptors for all five basic tastes are found anywhere there are taste buds. (Part A after McLaughlin et al., 1994; C after Bartoshuk, 1993, and Chandrashekar et al., 2006.)

is an opening called the **taste pore**. The taste cells extend fine cilia into the taste pore, and these come into contact with **tastants** (substances that can be tasted). Each taste cell is sensitive to just one of the five basic tastes, and with a life span of only 10–14 days, taste cells are constantly being replaced. Each taste bud contains immature taste cells that eventually become new taste cells (**FIGURE 9.23B**); it's not clear whether this turnover is a normal process or the result of damage from daily use. As our varied experience with hot drinks, frozen flagpoles, or spicy foods informs us, taste is not the only sensory capability of the tongue. Some of the sensory cells within taste buds signal heat, pain, and touch.

Many books show a map of the tongue indicating that each taste is perceived mainly in one region (sweet at the tip of the tongue, bitter at the back, and so on), but this map is erroneous. All five basic tastes can be perceived *anywhere* on the tongue where there are taste receptors (Collings, 1974; Yanagisawa et al., 1992). The areas do not differ greatly in the strength of taste sensations that they mediate (**FIGURE 9.23D**).

The ability to taste many substances is already well developed in humans at birth. Even premature infants seem to show a clear preference for sweet substances, and aversion to bitter substances (Steiner, 1974). Newborns seem to be relatively insensitive to salty tastes, but a preference for mildly salty substances develops in the first few months. This preference does not seem to be related to experience with salty tastes; rather it probably indicates maturation of the mechanisms of salt perception (Beauchamp et al., 1994).

Different cellular processes transduce the basic tastes

The tastes salty and sour are evoked when taste cells are stimulated by simple ions acting on ion channels in the membranes of the taste cells. Sweet and bitter tastes

taste pore The small aperture through which tastant molecules are able to access the sensory receptors of the taste bud.

tastant A substance that can be tasted.

are perceived by specialized receptor molecules and communicated by second messengers. At least two types of receptor proteins may be involved in the perception of umami.

SALTY   The transduction of the taste of salt (NaCl) is perhaps the easiest to understand, because it mostly relies on ion channels of the sort we have seen in previous chapters. Sodium ions (Na^+) from salty food enter taste cells via sodium channels in the cell membrane, causing a depolarization of the taste cell and release of neurotransmitter that stimulates the afferent neurons that relay the information to the brain. We know that this is a crucial mechanism for perceiving saltiness, because blocking the sodium channels with a drug greatly reduces our ability to taste salt (Schiffman et al., 1986). Blockade of sodium channels does not completely eradicate salt taste, however. A second salt receptor, a variant of the receptor TRPV1 (transient receptor potential vanilloid type 1), may provide this additional sensitivity to Na^+, along with sensitivity to cations from other salts in foods, such as potassium (K^+) and calcium (Ca^{2+}) (Lyall et al., 2004). Transient receptor potential (TRP) proteins form a large family of receptors that are sensitive to external stimuli of many kinds, including temperature detectors in skin, as we discussed in Chapter 8. Mice in which TRPV1 has been genetically knocked out show little change in salt sensitivity, however (Treesukosol et al., 2007), so the search for additional, possibly redundant salt receptors continues. One strong candidate for this role is TMC-1, an ionotropic sodium receptor that acts as a salt sensor in invertebrates and is also found in mammals, including humans (Chatzigeorgiou et al., 2013). Interestingly, while the other tastes are generally *either* appetizing (sweet and umami) *or* unpalatable (sour and bitter), salt is *both*: it is appetizing at lower concentrations but powerfully aversive at high concentrations. It turns out that the aversive quality of strong salt taste is accomplished by temporarily recruiting the aversive taste pathways through activation of sour- and bitter-sensing cells (Oka et al., 2013).

SOUR   Acids in food taste sour—the more acidic the food, the sourer it tastes—but no one knows exactly how sour tastants are detected. The property that all acids share is that they release protons (H^+; also called *hydrogen ions*). A number of mechanisms have been proposed for sour detection, especially acid-sensing ion channels (thus resembling the ionotropic receptors described in Chapters 3 and 4). For example, one type of potassium channel is blocked by H^+, preventing the release of K^+ ions from taste cells and causing depolarization and neurotransmitter release. Although the exact mechanisms of sour detection are not completely understood, it seems that all sour-sensitive taste cells contain a particular type of ion channel protein (called PKD2L1) and share an inward flow of protons that depolarizes the cell (Bushman et al., 2015; A. L. Huang et al., 2006). Interestingly, this same receptor detects the taste of carbonation in drinks (Chandrashekar et al., 2009).

SWEET   The molecular mechanisms in the transduction of sweet, bitter, and umami tastes are more complex than those responsible for salty and sour tastes. Sweet, bitter, and umami tastants appear to stimulate specialized G protein-coupled receptor molecules on membranes of the taste cells, resulting in intracellular activation of second messengers. These receptors are made up of simpler protein subunits belonging to two families—designated **T1R** and **T2R**—that are combined in various ways, as we'll see shortly. The receptors function much like the slow metabotropic receptors that we considered in Chapter 3, although they may employ a different G protein alpha subunit, called *gustducin* (McLaughlin et al., 1994).

When two members of the T1R family—T1R2 and T1R3—combine (heterodimerize), they make a receptor that selectively detects sweet tastants (G. Nelson et al., 2001). Mice lacking T1R2 or T1R3—and particularly knockout mice that lack both components—are insensitive to sweet tastes (G. Q. Zhao et al., 2003). Dozens of substances taste sweet, so how can a single receptor be sensitive to sweet molecules that are as different as, for example, sugar, aspartame, and saccharin? Different sweet

T1R   A family of taste receptor proteins that, when particular members heterodimerize, form taste receptors for sweet flavors and umami flavors.

T2R   A family of bitter taste receptors.

tastants appear to interact with different recognition sites within the T1R2+T1R3 receptor complex (Cui et al., 2006). Furthermore, certain sweet tastes may be sensed independently of the T1R2+T1R3 system, via a different receptor that has yet to be characterized (Treesukosol and Spector, 2012).

If you've spent any time around cats, you may be aware that most of them seem to be indifferent to sweets. It turns out that all cats, from tabbies to tigers, share a mutation in the gene that encodes T1R2; their sweet receptors don't work (X. Li et al., 2009). Your cat may like ice cream, but that's more likely because of the fat in it than the sugar.

BITTER   Bitter sensations are evoked by many different tastants. The association of bitter tastes with many toxic substances—such as nicotine, caffeine, strychnine, and morphine—provided strong evolutionary pressure to develop a high sensitivity to bitterness. The fact that different bitter substances can be discriminated—as shown by psychophysical work with human tasters (McBurney et al., 1972) and with animal subjects (Lush, 1989)—suggested that there is more than one receptor protein for bitterness.

Members of the T2R family of G protein-coupled receptors appear to be bitter receptors (Chandrashekar et al., 2000; Matsunami et al., 2000). The T2R family has about 30 members, and this large number may reflect the wide variety of bitter substances encountered in the environment, as well as the adaptive importance of being able to detect and avoid them. Interestingly, each bitter-sensing taste cell produces most or all of the different types of T2R bitter receptors (E. Adler et al., 2000). This means that these taste cells serve as broadly tuned bitter sensors: they are maximally sensitive to any of a wide variety of bitter substances but not very good at encoding qualitative distinctions *between* them. Nonetheless, behavioral and electrophysiological data indicate that at least certain broad classes of subjectively bitter substances *are* discriminable (St. John and Spector, 1998; Travers and Geran, 2009). The full details of bitter sensitivity remain to be established.

About 25% of people in the United States cannot taste the chemical phenylthiocarbamide (PTC) and the related compound 6-*n*-propylthiouracil (PROP), even though they can taste other bitter substances. Family studies indicate that tasters and nontasters are genetically different. Furthermore, some people, referred to as *supertasters*, exhibit heightened sensitivity to some bitter tastes, suggesting that they are genetically different as well (Bartoshuk and Beauchamp, 1994). In fact, supertasters also enjoy stronger sweet sensations from some substances. Nontasters of PROP have the fewest fungiform papillae, averaging 96 per square centimeter (cm²) on the tongue tip, medium tasters have an intermediate number (184), and supertasters have the most (425) (**FIGURE 9.24**).

UMAMI   The fifth basic taste, **umami**, is described as a meaty, savory flavor. For most of the twentieth century, researchers argued about whether a distinct umami taste existed, but at least two types of receptors appear to be specialized to respond to exactly this sort of tastant. One of these, a variant of the metabotropic glutamate receptor, is expressed in certain taste buds (Chaudhari et al., 2000; Maruyama et al., 2006) and most likely responds to the amino acid glutamate, which is found in high concentrations in meats, cheeses, kombu, and other savory foodstuffs (that's why MSG—monosodium glutamate—is used as a "flavor enhancer").

A second probable umami receptor is a heterodimer of T1R1 and T1R3 receptors. Despite the similarity to the T1R2+T1R3 sweet receptor described already, the T1R1+T1R3 receptor selectively responds to most of the 20 standard amino acids that might be encountered in the diet (G. Nelson et al., 2002).

In mice lacking the gene that encodes the T1R3 receptor, sensitivity to sweet and umami tastants is greatly reduced but not abolished (Damak et al., 2003), implying that there must be additional receptor systems for these tastes that are T1R3-independent. It also suggests that the receptors for things that taste especially good—sweet and umami—may have shared evolutionary origins. In giant pandas, the

umami   One of the five basic tastes (along with salty, sour, sweet, and bitter), probably mediated by amino acids in foods.

(A) Nontaster

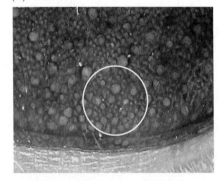

(B) Supertaster

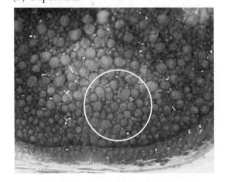

9.24 IT'S ALL A MATTER OF TASTE BUDS   We can count the number of fungiform papillae (larger blue-green circles) in a unit area (the white circle is about the size of a hole made by a paper punch). (A) The tongue of this person has only about 22 fungiform papillae in the defined area. (B) This supertaster's tongue has about twice as many. Some individuals have as few as 5 fungiform papillae in this space, while others pack in as many as 60. (Courtesy of Dr. Linda Bartoshuk and the Bartoshuk Lab.)

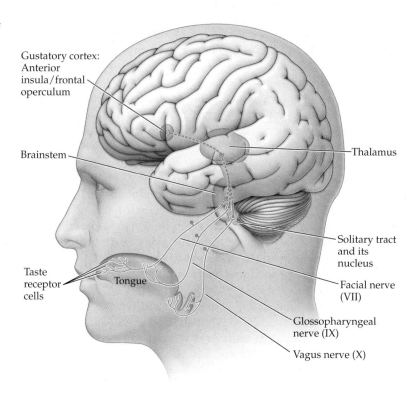

Gustatory cortex:
Anterior
insula/frontal
operculum

Brainstem

Thalamus

Solitary tract
and its
nucleus

Facial nerve
(VII)

Glossopharyngeal
nerve (IX)

Vagus nerve (X)

Taste
receptor
cells

Tongue

T1R1 gene became a nonfunctional "pseudogene" around the time in the animals'
evolutionary history when they switched from a carnivorous diet to an exclusive diet
of bamboo (H. Zhao et al., 2010). This is another illustration of the ecological mold-
ing of the senses. Similarly, birds (like their housecat enemies) lack the *T1R2* gene
and thus ordinarily can't taste sweet, so evolution repurposed the hummingbirds'
T1R1+T1R3 umami receptor into a new class of sweet receptor (Baldwin et al., 2014),
allowing them to sense the nectar they need for survival.

Taste information is transmitted to several parts of the brain

The **gustatory system** (from the Latin *gustare*, "to taste") extends from the taste
receptor cells through brainstem nuclei and the thalamus to the cerebral cortex
(**FIGURE 9.25**). Each taste cell transmits information to several afferent fibers, and
each afferent fiber receives information from several taste cells. The afferent fibers
run along three different cranial nerves—the facial (VII), glossopharyngeal (IX), and
vagus (X) nerves (see Figure 2.9). The gustatory fibers in each of these nerves run to
the brainstem. Here they synapse with second-order gustatory neurons that project
to the ventral posterior medial nucleus of the thalamus. Those thalamic neurons extend their third-order gustatory fibers to the cortical taste area located in the insula,
just anterior to the central sulcus. Even within the cortical taste area, a "gustatopic"
map is preserved—the different tastes are represented in distinct areas within gustatory cortex (X. Chen et al., 2011). Researchers have used optogenetic techniques
(see Chapter 3) to control the behavior of mice by selectively stimulating different
cortical taste representations: activation of neurons in the sweet area elicits behavioral signs of attraction, whereas activation of neurons in the bitter area provokes
strong behavioral avoidance (Peng et al., 2015).

A longstanding debate among sensory neuroscientists concerns the encoding of
incoming information in the nerves leading to the brain. Some gustation researchers
argue that the brain extrapolates taste information from **pattern coding**, the relative activity across ensembles of axons from different taste receptor cells. This type
of encoding provides great capacity for distinguishing subtle differences between
stimuli, and it provides a rich, parallel set of inputs upon which the brain can act to
tune the stimulation it receives (as we will see again in describing color perception in

gustatory system The taste system.

pattern coding Coding of information
in sensory systems based on the temporal
pattern of action potentials.

Chapter 10). Other researchers believe that taste sensation involves a simple system of **labeled lines** (which we touched on in Chapter 8), in which there are five distinct types of axon "lines" corresponding to five classes of taste receptor cells—one line for each taste (plus the sensors for heat, pain, and so on that we discussed earlier). Imagine five separate telephone lines, one for each taste. In this case, taste perception is believed to be determined simply by which line is active, rather than by the pattern of activity across groups of axons (Chandrashekar et al., 2006).

It has been reported that selectively inactivating taste cells that express receptors for just one of the five tastes tends to eradicate sensitivity to that one taste while leaving the other four tastes unaffected (A. L. Huang et al., 2006). This result would seem to support the position that taste is a labeled-line system, where the line for the knocked-out taste has been lost. However, the results are not inconsistent with the pattern-coding account, either, because when one of the five taste categories is knocked out, *patterns* of activity must also be affected. In other words, how could pattern coding work properly if one-fifth of the pattern had been inactivated? Furthermore, it remains to be established how a purely labeled-line system could account for the ability to discriminate different forms of salty, or different forms of sweet. In fact, it is difficult to imagine an experiment that would allow us to unambiguously establish whether labeled lines or pattern coding accounts for taste perception. The resolution of the debate, if there is to be one, will require new technical developments in sensory neuroscience.

Chemicals in the Air Elicit Odor Sensations

Many aspects of an animal's world are determined by chemicals carried in the air. Olfactory sensitivity varies widely across species of mammals: cats and mice, dogs and rabbits—all have a sharper sense of smell than humans. In the 1980s, a large survey of olfaction revealed widespread partial **anosmia** (odor blindness) among humans, with men exhibiting slightly worse olfaction than women (Gilbert and Wysocki, 1987). Most birds have only basic olfactory abilities, and dolphins don't have olfactory receptors at all (Freitag et al., 1998). These differences evolved because of differences between species in the importance of smell for survival and reproduction. Nevertheless, different species of mammals, including humans, accomplish olfaction in much the same way, as we will describe next.

The sense of smell starts with receptor neurons in the nose

In humans, a sheet of cells called the **olfactory epithelium** (**FIGURE 9.26**) lines the dorsal portion of the nasal cavities and adjacent regions, including the septum that separates the left and right nasal cavities. Within the 5–10 cm^2 of olfactory epithelium that we possess, three types of cells are found: supporting cells, basal cells, and about 6 million **olfactory receptor neurons**. In many other mammals this number is an order of magnitude greater; for example, popular dog breeds generally have about 100–200 million receptor neurons in the olfactory epithelium, and in bloodhounds the number is closer to 300 million. This is one reason why they can follow an odor trail so much better than we can, although, interestingly, people can learn to do this pretty well too (J. Porter et al., 2007). In fact, dogs possess a sense of smell that is so sensitive that they can detect the banana-like scent of *n*-amyl acetate at less than 2 parts per *trillion*—like tasting a small pinch of sugar dissolved in a billion cups of tea (King, 2013).

Each olfactory receptor cell has a long, slender apical dendrite that extends to the outermost layer of the epithelium, the mucosal surface. There, numerous **cilia** (singular *cilium*) emerge from the **dendritic knob** and extend along the mucosal surface. At the opposite end of each bipolar olfactory receptor cell, a fine, unmyelinated axon, which is among the smallest-diameter axons in the nervous system, runs to the olfactory bulb (to be discussed shortly).

In contrast with many other receptor neurons in the body, olfactory receptor neurons can be replaced in adulthood (Costanzo, 1991). One theory is that these receptor

labeled lines The concept that each nerve input to the brain reports only a particular type of information.

anosmia The inability to smell.

olfactory epithelium A sheet of cells, including olfactory receptors, that lines the dorsal portion of the nasal cavities and adjacent regions, including the septum that separates the left and right nasal cavities.

olfactory receptor neuron A type of neuron, found in the olfactory epithelium, that senses airborne odorants via specialized receptor proteins.

cilium A hairlike cellular extension.

dendritic knob A portion of an olfactory receptor cell present in the olfactory epithelium.

9.26 ANATOMY AND MAIN PATHWAYS OF THE HUMAN OLFACTORY SYSTEM The schematic at lower right indicates the main olfactory pathways in the brain.

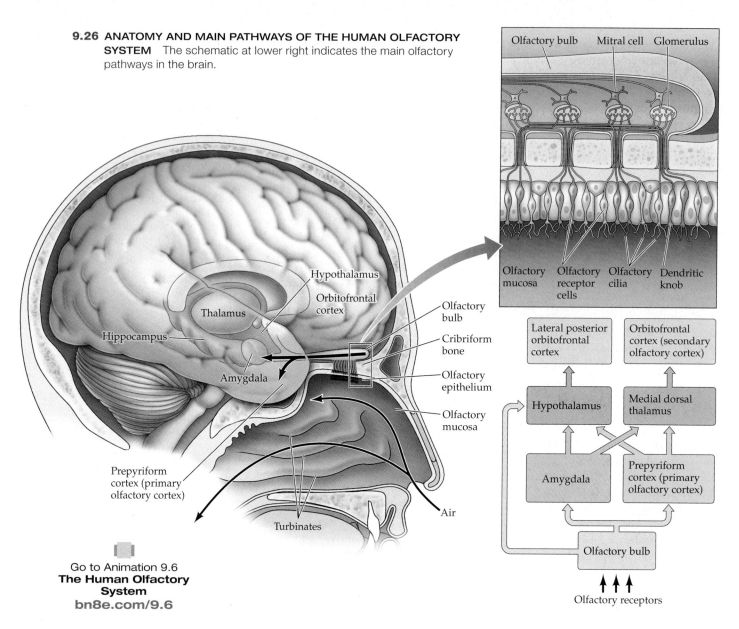

Go to Animation 9.6
The Human Olfactory System
bn8e.com/9.6

neurons normally degenerate after a few weeks because they are in direct contact with external irritants, such as chemicals and viruses, so they must constantly be replaced. It's clear that, if destroyed, an olfactory receptor cell will be replaced as an adjacent basal cell differentiates into a neuron and extends dendrites to the mucosal surface and an axon into the brain that ultimately forms new synapses in the correct portion of the olfactory bulb (C. T. Leung et al., 2007). What's not clear is whether receptor cells are *normally* "disposable," subject to constant turnover even in the absence of a particular trauma.

If the olfactory epithelium is damaged, it can be regenerated and will properly reconnect to the olfactory bulb. The functional capability of these new connections has been clearly demonstrated in both behavioral and electrophysiological studies of animals with completely regenerated olfactory epithelium. Investigators are trying to determine how these neurons can regenerate while those in most other parts of the nervous system cannot.

Odorants excite specialized receptor molecules on olfactory receptor neurons

Odorants enter the nasal cavity during inhalation and especially during periods of sniffing; they also rise to the nasal cavity from the mouth when we chew food. The direction of airflow in the nose is determined by complex curved surfaces called *turbinates* that form the nasal cavity (see Figure 9.26). Airborne molecules initially

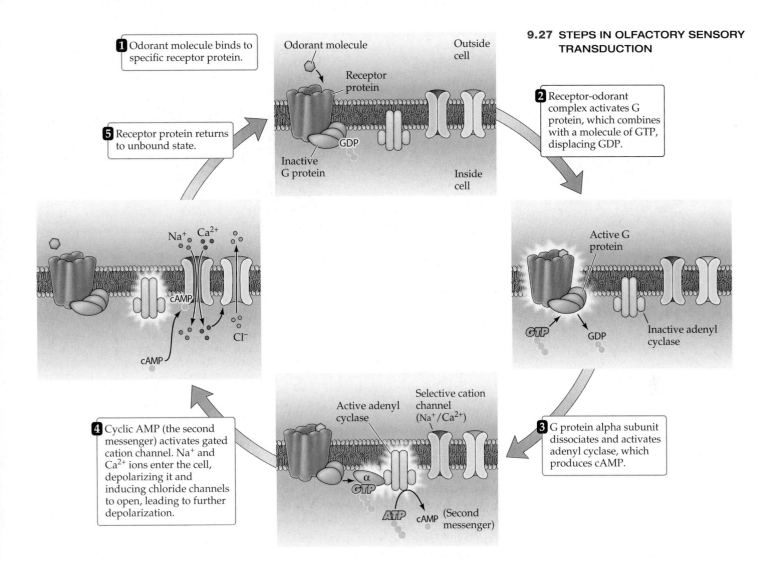

1 Odorant molecule binds to specific receptor protein.

5 Receptor protein returns to unbound state.

2 Receptor-odorant complex activates G protein, which combines with a molecule of GTP, displacing GDP.

3 G protein alpha subunit dissociates and activates adenyl cyclase, which produces cAMP.

4 Cyclic AMP (the second messenger) activates gated cation channel. Na$^+$ and Ca^{2+} ions enter the cell, depolarizing it and inducing chloride channels to open, leading to further depolarization.

encounter the fluids of the mucosal layer, which contain binding proteins that transport odorants to receptor surfaces (Farbman, 1994).

Once at a receptor cell, the odorant stimulus interacts with receptor proteins located on the surface of the olfactory cilia and the dendritic knob. These receptor proteins are members of a superfamily of G protein-linked receptors (Buck and Axel, 1991). Interactions of odorants with their receptors trigger the synthesis of second messengers, such as cyclic AMP (cAMP). Cyclic AMP opens cation channels (L. J. Brunet et al., 1996), resulting in depolarization of the olfactory receptor neuron, which in turn leads to the generation of action potentials.

This sensory transduction process, portrayed in **FIGURE 9.27**, is similar to the activation of other sensory systems, such as those for sweet and bitter tastes and those in the eye (see Chapter 10). A specific G protein, named G$_{olf}$ in recognition of its importance in olfaction, must be used by all the olfactory receptors, because mice in which the gene that encodes G$_{olf}$ is knocked out are generally anosmic (Belluscio et al., 1998).

Mice have about 2 million olfactory receptor cells, each of which expresses only one of about 1000 different receptor proteins. These receptor proteins can be divided into four different subfamilies of about 250 receptors each (Mori et al., 1999). Within each subfamily, members have a very similar structure and presumably recognize similar odorants. In rodents, each subfamily of receptors is synthesized in a separate band of the epithelium, as shown in **FIGURE 9.28** (Vassar et al., 1993).

Now that it has been fully mapped, we know that the human genome also contains about 1000 apparent olfactory receptor genes, but only a subset appear to be fully functional, perhaps as few as 400 (Gilad et al., 2003). The rest have apparently

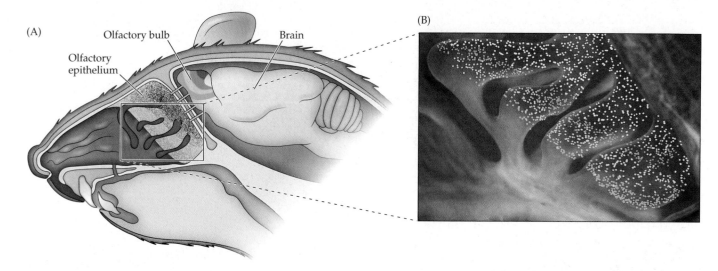

(A)

Olfactory bulb

Brain

Olfactory epithelium

(B)

9.28 DIFFERENT KINDS OF OLFACTORY RECEPTOR MOLECULES ON THE OLFACTORY EPITHELIUM (A) In this diagram showing the anatomy of the rat olfactory organ, color swathes correspond to the distribution of four receptor subfamilies. (B) The different colors in this photograph of rat olfactory epithelium show receptor locations for the four receptor subfamilies and also correspond to the topographic representation in the olfactory bulb. The different receptor types have distinct but overlapping spatial distributions. (After Vassar et al., 1993; B courtesy of Dr. Robert Vassar.)

accumulated mutations and become nonfunctional during the course of evolution, implying that whatever they detected ceased to be important to our ancestors' survival and reproduction.

For a long time the orthodox view was that humans could distinguish between, at most, 5,000–10,000 different odors. However, psychophysical experiments using multiple combinations of odorants in varying concentrations indicate that, in fact, we can discriminate more than 1 trillion olfactory stimuli! To accomplish this feat, each type of functional odorant receptor must interact with a significant number of different odorants in order to make up the many distinct patterns that encode this vast spectrum of scents (Bushdid et al., 2014; Duchamp-Viret et al., 1999). Furthermore, any two people differ by about 30% in the makeup of their olfactory receptors (Frumin et al., 2014), suggesting that to some extent we each inhabit a personalized olfactory environment.

Olfactory axons connect with the olfactory bulb, which sends its output to several brain regions

The numerous axons of the olfactory nerve terminate in a complex structure at the anterior end of the brain called the **olfactory bulb**. The olfactory bulb, in relation to the rest of the brain, is much smaller in humans than in animals, such as rats, that depend extensively on olfaction (compare Figures 9.26 and 9.28). The olfactory bulb is organized into many roughly spherical neural circuits called **glomeruli** (singular *glomerulus*, from the Latin *glomus*, "ball"), within which the axon terminals of olfactory receptor neurons synapse on the dendrites of the specialized **mitral cells** of the olfactory bulb (see Figure 9.26). The intrinsic circuitry within and between these glomeruli contributes to an elaborate system for modulating, tuning, and sharpening olfactory bulb activity (Aungst et al., 2003).

Mice have about 1800 glomeruli. Each one receives inputs exclusively from olfactory neurons that are expressing the same type of olfactory receptor, and the glomeruli are organized in functional zones according to the four receptor protein subfamilies described in the previous section (Mori et al., 1999). So there appears to be a topographic distribution of smells in the bulb, and within each functional zone neighboring glomeruli tend to receive inputs from receptors that are closely related.

olfactory bulb An anterior projection of the brain that terminates in the upper nasal passages and, through small openings in the skull, receives axons from olfactory receptor neurons.

glomerulus A complex arbor of dendrites from a group of olfactory cells.

mitral cell A type of cell in the olfactory bulb that conducts smell information from the glomeruli to the rest of the brain.

This glomerular map of the olfactory bulb is established during an early developmental critical period, becoming essentially immutable in early postnatal life (Ma et al., 2014; Tsai and Barnea, 2014).

Perhaps surprisingly, olfactory receptors are found in the axon terminals of olfactory neurons, as well as in their dendrites (Barnea et al., 2004). Experiments with knockout mice (see Box 7.3) suggest that the olfactory receptor proteins help guide the innervating axons to their corresponding glomeruli (Imai et al., 2009). Disruptions of the receptor protein prevent newly generated olfactory receptor axons from reaching their normal targets (F. Wang et al., 1998).

Output from the olfactory bulb consists of the axons from mitral cells, which extend to a variety of brain regions. These include the prepyriform and entorhinal cortex (note that smell is the only sensory modality that can synapse directly in the cortex rather than having to pass through the thalamus), the amygdala, and the hypothalamus. This close relation between olfactory inputs and limbic system structures involved in memory and emotion may help explain the potent ability of odors to evoke strong nostalgic memories of childhood (M. Larsson and Willander, 2009).

Functional MRI studies suggest that the human prepyriform cortex is activated during sniffing, whether or not an odor is present, because the airflow induced by sniffing provides somatosensory stimulation. When an odor is present during a sniff, primary olfactory cortex (prepyriform cortex) and secondary olfactory cortex (orbitofrontal cortex) are both activated (Sobel et al., 2000). Furthermore, the same chemical mix may produce a different odor perception, depending on how fast the air enters during a sniff (Sobel et al., 1999). So the brain gauges the airflow rate during a sniff in order to interpret olfactory information properly. In addition, the size of the sniff appears to reflect attentional processes: larger sniffs occur during sampling of *pleasant* odors even when they are only imagined, that is, when no odor is present (Bensafi et al., 2003).

pheromone A chemical signal that is released outside the body of an animal and affects other members of the same species.

vomeronasal system A specialized chemical detection system that detects pheromones and transmits information to the brain.

vomeronasal organ (VNO) A collection of specialized receptor cells, near to but separate from the olfactory epithelium, that detect pheromones and send electrical signals to the accessory olfactory bulb in the brain.

Many vertebrates possess a vomeronasal system

Many vertebrates have a second chemical detection system that appears to specialize in detecting **pheromones**, the odor signals or trails that many animals secrete (see Chapter 5). This **vomeronasal system** (**FIGURE 9.29**), as it is called, is present in most terrestrial mammals, amphibians, and reptiles. The receptors for the system are found in a **vomeronasal organ** (**VNO**) of epithelial cells near the olfactory epithelium.

Rodents express two major families of vomeronasal receptors—V1R and V2R—that encode hundreds of different types of receptors (Dulac and Torello, 2003). Although both are families of G protein-coupled receptors, they are quite different from each other; in fact, the V1Rs are more similar to the T2R bitter taste receptors (discussed earlier) than they are to the receptors of the main olfactory system. Interestingly, the distribution of certain V2Rs differs between male and female rats, in keeping with the critical role of pheromones in organizing rodent reproductive behavior (Herrada and Dulac, 1997). V2Rs are also sensitive to certain major histocompatibility complex (MHC) molecules (Loconto et al., 2003); detection of MHCs is thought to be one of the main ways in which animals can assess their degree of relatedness to other animals, which has implications for mating

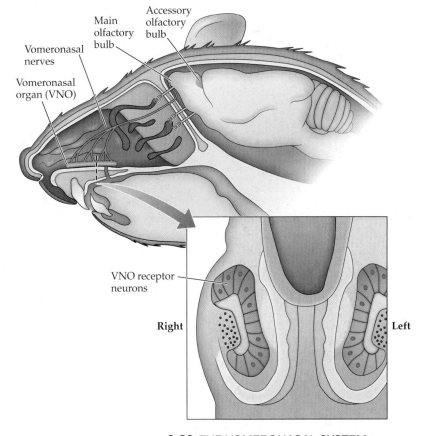

9.29 THE VOMERONASAL SYSTEM

A family of probable pheromone receptors produced by neurons in the main olfactory epithelium.

strategies (see Chapter 6). The VNO-specific ion channel TRPC2 (transient receptor potential, subfamily C, 2)—a member of the TRP family of sensory receptors that we mentioned earlier—is also essential for VNO function (Stowers et al., 2002).

VNO receptors are remarkably sensitive, detecting extremely low concentrations of pheromone molecules (Leinders-Zufall et al., 2000). The receptors send their information to the accessory olfactory bulb (adjacent to the main olfactory bulb), which projects to the medial amygdala, which in turn projects to the hypothalamus. Relying in part on MHCs, hamsters (Mateo and Johnston, 2000) and mice (Isles et al., 2001) can distinguish relatives from nonrelatives just by smell, even if they were raised by foster parents. Presumably these animals compare whether other animals smell like themselves, perhaps to avoid mating with kin.

In humans, molecular and anatomical evidence for a functional VNO is scanty at best. Humans have a structure that resembles a VNO and show behavioral evidence of some pheromone-like capabilities: for example, early work found that simple exposure to bodily odors of other women can cause the women's menstrual cycles to synchronize (Stern and McClintock, 1998), and exposure to female tears reportedly can cause reductions in testosterone and sexual arousal in men (Gelstein et al., 2011). However, analysis of the genome indicates that almost all of the human variants of the genes that encode the V1R and V2R vomeronasal receptors, and the TRPC2 channel, have become nonfunctional pseudogenes over evolutionary time, and the question of whether humans and other mammals really employ pheromonal cues that significantly affect behavior remains controversial (Doty, 2010; Lübke and Pause, 2015).

The discovery of a new class of olfactory receptors within the main olfactory epithelium (Liberles and Buck, 2006) adds a new dimension to the question of pheromone sensitivity. Called **TAARs**, for **trace amine–associated receptors**, these receptors are expressed in specific olfactory neurons within the main olfactory epithelium, just like the regular olfactory receptors, but at least in mice they seem to respond to volatile sex-specific urinary compounds that may be pheromones. Mice in which the TAAR genes have been knocked out lose their normal aversion to certain urinary volatiles, even including the urine of predators (Dewan et al., 2013). Thus it seems that the old dichotomy that the olfactory epithelium detects odors while the VNO detects pheromones is an oversimplification, and the prior evidence suggesting that humans respond to pheromones, despite a vestigial or nonfunctional VNO, isn't necessarily paradoxical. If rodents can detect pheromones through the main olfactory epithelium, perhaps we can too.

■ The Cutting Edge

More Than a Matter of Taste

For most people, the concept of "taste" doesn't extend beyond the tongue; after all, our conscious experience of the gustatory sense is limited to the things we have in our mouth. Scientists have historically shared this bias until fairly recently, perhaps limiting the extent of taste research. But now that we know how to search for some of the molecular components of taste-sensing cells, such as the taste-associated G protein gustducin and the T1R- and T2R-based taste receptors, objective analyses are revealing that taste-like chemosensation is astonishingly widespread within the body. Within the oral cavity, taste receptors are found outside the tongue, such as in the soft palate (the posterior roof of the mouth) (Tomonari et al., 2012). Perhaps that's not too surprising, considering that food contacts all parts of the mouth. But how about taste cells in the stomach? In the colon? In the lungs, brain, and gonads? Although they don't give rise to conscious sensations of taste, "taste" cells have now been found in all of those locations and more (**FIGURE 9.30**). If flies can taste the surfaces they land on, do we mammals have similar subconscious capabilities?

The initial discovery of cells in the stomach and intestine that express gustducin and T1R3 sweet receptors (S. V. Wu et al., 2002) suggested that the gut actively samples the composition of food. These cells help organize appropriate digestive responses, such as the mobilization of insulin from the pancreas in response to sweet substances (Jang et al., 2007; Kokrashvili et al., 2009). Other cells in the stomach and colon express T2R bitter receptors that may alter the transit time of foods or cause diarrhea, possibly in response to the presence of bitter toxins (Glendinning et al., 2008; Kaji et al., 2009). Further, by altering the release of the appetite-related hormone ghrelin (see Chapter 13) and inhibiting stomach activity (Janssen et al., 2011), bitter taste cells of the gut may protectively adjust appetite and slow the absorption of ingested material.

Taste-transducing cells are also found in components of the airways, such as the nasal cavity and the bronchioles, and in the cilia that line the airways. These taste-sensitive cells, which primarily express T2R bitter receptors, appear to regulate protective reflexes like sneezing and coughing, probably to protect from noxious substances and infectious agents (Tizzano and Finger, 2013). Bitter and sweet receptors throughout the upper respiratory tract help to activate and direct innate immune responses against microbial infections (Lee and Cohen, 2015). Because the taste-transducing cells of the lungs likewise mediate bronchial inflammation (Deshpande et al., 2010), drugs that interact with these receptors may provide a new generation of asthma drugs.

The role of bitter taste receptors in the testes remains somewhat mysterious, but as elsewhere, they may serve to sense toxins (J. Xu et al., 2013). In any case, these taste receptors appear to play a crucial role—genetic knockout of testis bitter receptors in mice results in small testes and a great reduction in spermatogenesis (Li and Zhou, 2012). Likewise, the recent discovery of bitter taste transduction cells in the mammalian brain (Dehkordi et al., 2012) raises more questions than it answers, especially because the brain is more insulated from environmental substances than any other organ in the body (see Chapter 2). Perhaps we will eventually find that the gustatory sensing and transduction molecules play a more fundamental role in cellular signaling apart from gustation—and we can begin accounting for taste.

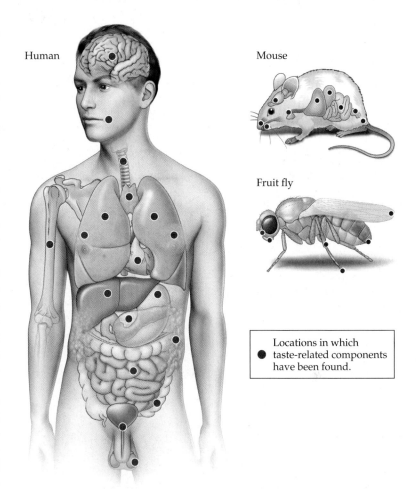

9.30 LOCATIONS EXPRESSING TASTE RECEPTORS The search for molecular components of taste-transducing cells has revealed taste-like sensors in a surprising variety of tissues. (After Ehrenberg, 2010.)

Locations in which taste-related components have been found.

Recommended Reading

Bartoshuk, L. M., and Beauchamp, G. K. (2005). *Tasting and Smelling* (2nd ed.). New York: Academic Press.

Doty, R. L. (2015). *Handbook of Olfaction and Gustation* (3rd ed.). New York: Wiley-Blackwell.

Finger, T. E., Silver, W. L., and Restrepo, D. (Eds.). (2000). *The Neurobiology of Taste and Smell* (2nd ed.). New York: Wiley-Liss.

Horowitz, S. S. (2012). *The Universal Sense: How Hearing Shapes the Mind*. London: Bloomsbury.

Menini, A. (2009). *The Neurobiology of Olfaction*. Boca Raton, FL: CRC Press.

Musiek, F. E., and Baran, J. A. (2007). *The Auditory System: Anatomy, Physiology, and Clinical Correlates*. Boston: Pearson.

Palmer, A., and Rees, A. (2010). *Oxford Handbook of Auditory Science*. Oxford, England: Oxford University Press.

Wolfe, J. M., Kluender, K. R., Levi, D. M., Bartoshuck, L. M., et al. (2015). *Sensation & Perception* (4th ed.). Sunderland, MA: Sinauer.

Wyatt, T. D. (2014). *Pheromones and Animal Behavior: Chemical Signals and Signatures* (2nd ed.). Cambridge, England: Cambridge University Press.

Yost, W. A. (2006). *Fundamentals of Hearing* (5th ed.). San Diego, CA: Academic Press.

Go to
bn8e.com
for study questions, quizzes, activities, and other resources

VISUAL SUMMARY

You should be able to relate each summary to the adjacent illustration, including structures and processes.
Go to **bn8e.com/vs9** for links to figures, animations, and activities that will help you consolidate the material.

1 The **external ear** captures, focuses, and filters sound. Vibrations of the **tympanic membrane** (eardrum) are focused by the three **ossicles** of the **middle ear** onto the **oval window** to stimulate the **cochlea**. Review **Figure 9.2, Animation 9.2**

2 Sound arriving at the oval window causes ripples on the **basilar membrane** of the cochlea. High-frequency sounds affect the basilar membrane near the base of the cochlea; low-frequency sounds affect the apex. Review **Figure 9.3**

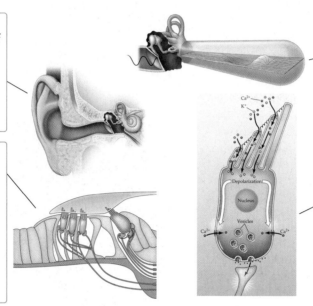

3 The **organ of Corti** has both **inner hair cells** and **outer hair cells**. The inner hair cells convey most of the information about sounds. The outer hair cells change their length with the help of a specialized motor protein called **prestin**, under the control of the brain, tuning the basilar membrane. Review **Figure 9.4, Activity 9.1**

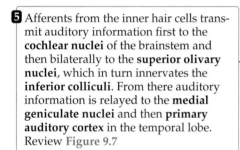

4 Movement of the **stereocilia** of the hair cells causes the opening and closing of ion channels, thereby **transducing** mechanical movement into changes in electrical potential. These changes in potential stimulate the nerve cell endings that contact the hair cells. Review **Figure 9.5**

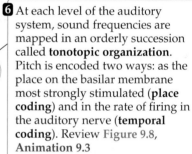

5 Afferents from the inner hair cells transmit auditory information first to the **cochlear nuclei** of the brainstem and then bilaterally to the **superior olivary nuclei**, which in turn innervates the **inferior colliculi**. From there auditory information is relayed to the **medial geniculate nuclei** and then **primary auditory cortex** in the temporal lobe. Review **Figure 9.7**

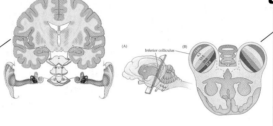

6 At each level of the auditory system, sound frequencies are mapped in an orderly succession called **tonotopic organization**. Pitch is encoded two ways: as the place on the basilar membrane most strongly stimulated (**place coding**) and in the rate of firing in the auditory nerve (**temporal coding**). Review **Figure 9.8, Animation 9.3**

7 Auditory localization depends on differences in the sounds arriving at the two ears. For low-frequency sounds, differences in time of arrival at the two ears (**latency differences**) are especially important. For high-frequency sounds, **intensity differences** are especially important. Review **Figure 9.10**

8 Birds and mammals evolved different neural mechanisms for localizing sounds; in mammals the lateral superior olivary nucleus of the brainstem processes differences in intensity, and the medial superior olivary nucleus processes differences in time of arrival. Review **Figure 9.11**

9 Deafness can be caused by changes at any level of the auditory system. **Conduction deafness** consists of impairments in the transmission of sound through the external or middle ear to the cochlea. **Sensorineural deafness** arises in the cochlea, often because of the destruction of hair cells, or in the auditory nerve. **Central deafness** stems from brain damage. Some forms of deafness may be alleviated by direct electrical stimulation of the auditory nerve (by a **cochlear implant**). Review **Figures 9.16–9.19, Video 9.4**

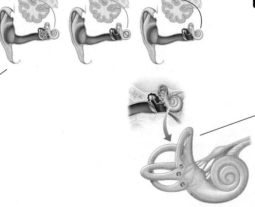

10 The receptors of the vestibular system lie within the inner ear next to the cochlea. In mammals the vestibular system consists of three **semicircular canals**, plus the **utricle** and the **saccule**. Within these structures hair cells detect rotation of the body in three planes, and the utricle and saccule sense static positions and linear accelerations. Review **Figure 9.20, Animation 9.5**

11 Nerve fibers from the vestibular receptors enter the brainstem and synapse in the **vestibular nuclei**, which send their outputs to the motor nuclei of numerous structures. One important function of the vestibular system is the **vestibulo-ocular reflex** (**VOR**), which uses vestibular information about head rotations to precisely move the eyes to keep our gaze fixed. Review **Figure 9.21**

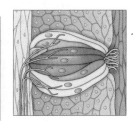

12 Humans detect only five main tastes: salty, sour, sweet, bitter, and **umami**. In mammals, most taste receptor cells are located in clusters of cells called **taste buds**, situated within small projections from the surface of the tongue called **papillae**. Review **Figures 9.22 and 9.23**, **Activity 9.2**

13 The tastes of salty and sour are evoked primarily by the action of simple ions on ion channels in the membranes of taste cells. Sweet and bitter tastes are perceived by specialized receptor molecules belonging to the **T1R** and **T2R** families, which are coupled to G proteins. Heterodimers of T1R proteins function as sweet and umami receptors. The **gustatory system** extends from the taste receptor cells through brainstem nuclei to the thalamus and then to the cerebral cortex. Review **Figure 9.25**

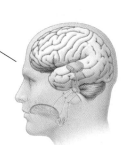

14 Humans can detect thousands of different odors, but some other species have more **olfactory receptor neurons** and larger **olfactory bulbs**. Each olfactory receptor neuron has dendrites in the **olfactory epithelium** in the nose and a fine, unmyelinated axon that runs to a **glomerulus** within an olfactory bulb. If an olfactory receptor cell dies, an adjacent cell will replace it. Review **Figure 9.26**, **Animation 9.6**

15 All olfactory neurons expressing a particular receptor synapse in the same glomerulus in the olfactory bulb. The projection from the epithelium to the bulb and then to the brain maintains a zonal distribution for different kinds of receptor molecules. Review **Figure 9.28**

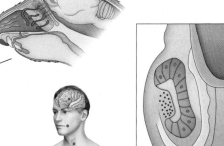

16 The **vomeronasal organ** contains receptors to detect **pheromones** released from other individuals of the species. These receptors transmit signals to the accessory olfactory bulb, which in turn communicates with the amygdala. Pheromones can also be detected by specialized receptors in the main olfactory epithelium. Review **Figure 9.29**

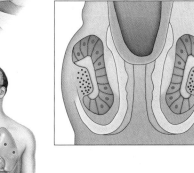

17 Taste-transducing cells have been located throughout the body. These cells may serve a variety of chemosensory and other functions. Review **Figure 9.30**

Vision

From Eye to Brain

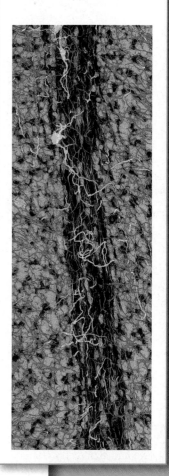

▮ When Seeing Isn't Seeing

It was cold in the bathroom, so the young woman turned on a small heater before she got in the shower. She didn't know that the heater was malfunctioning, filling the room with deadly, odorless carbon monoxide gas. Her husband found her unconscious on the floor and called for an ambulance to rush her to the emergency room. When she regained consciousness, "D.F." seemed to have gotten off lightly, avoiding what could have been a fatal accident. She could understand the doctors' questions and reply sensibly, move all her limbs, and perceive touch on her skin. But something was wrong with her sight.

D.F. couldn't recognize faces, even her husband's, nor could she name any objects presented to her view. D.F. still cannot recognize objects today, decades after her accident. Yet she is not entirely blind. Show her a flashlight and she can tell you that it's made of shiny aluminum with some red plastic, but she doesn't recognize it ("Is it a kitchen utensil?"). Without telling her what it is, if you ask her to pick it up, D.F.'s hand goes directly to the flashlight and holds it exactly as one normally holds a flashlight. Show D.F. a slot in a piece of plastic and she cannot tell you whether the slot is oriented vertically, horizontally, or diagonally; but if you hand her a disk and ask her to put it through the hole, D.F. invariably turns the disk so that it goes smoothly through the slot (Goodale et al., 1991).

Can D.F. see or not?

Vision offers tremendous benefits for vital behaviors such as finding food, avoiding predators, finding a mate, and locating shelter, so a variety of visual systems have evolved. Beyond serving basic needs, vision affords most of us the pleasures of nature and art, reading and writing, and watching videos. Because vision is so important, a lot of effort is exerted to prevent its deterioration, and even to restore vision to the blind.

However, the sheer volume of visual information poses a serious problem. Seeing the surrounding world has been compared to drinking from a waterfall. How does the visual system avoid being overwhelmed by the flood of information entering the eyes? The answer seems to be that the visual perceptions of each species depend on how their eyes and brains evolved to process information about light and attend to the aspects likely to be important for survival in that particular species.

Research on vision is one of the most active fields of neuroscience, as it should be, since about one-third of the human cerebral cortex is devoted to visual analysis and perception.

The Visual System Extends from the Eye to the Brain

To understand how the visual system constructs our vision, let's follow the path of information triggered by light, starting with the optical properties of the eye. Next, we'll look at the cells and processes intrinsic to the back of the eye that encode light

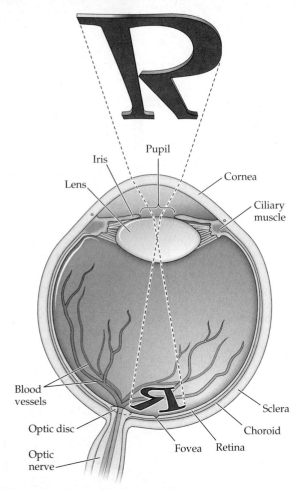

10.1 STRUCTURES OF THE HUMAN EYE Here the right eye is viewed in cross section from above. The visual image focused on the retina is inverted top to bottom and reversed right to left. The gap in the retina where the optic nerve leaves the eyeball is called the *optic disc*. The optic disc is also shown in Figure 10.5A.

cornea The transparent outer layer of the eye, whose curvature is fixed. It bends light rays and is primarily responsible for forming the image on the retina.

lens A structure in the eye that helps focus an image on the retina.

refraction The bending of light rays by a change in the density of a medium, such as the cornea and the lens of the eye.

ciliary muscle One of the muscles that controls the shape of the lens inside the eye, focusing an image on the retina.

accommodation The process of focusing by the ciliary muscles and the lens to form a sharp image on the retina.

pupil The aperture, formed by the iris, that allows light to enter the eye.

iris The circular structure of the eye that provides an opening to form the pupil.

extraocular muscle One of the muscles attached to the eyeball that controls its position and movements.

as neural activity, allowing vision across an astonishingly wide range of light intensities. Then we'll trace the information flowing from the eye to cortex.

The vertebrate eye acts in some ways like a camera

The eye is an elaborate structure with optical functions (capturing light and forming detailed spatial images) and neural functions (transducing light into neural signals and processing those signals). Accurate optical images are crucial for discerning the shapes of objects; that is, light from a point on a target object must end up as a point—rather than a blur—in the retinal image. Without optical images, light-sensitive cells would be able to detect only the presence or absence of light and would not be able to see forms.

To produce optical images, the eye has many of the features of a camera, starting with the **cornea** and **lens** to focus light (**FIGURE 10.1**). Light travels in a straight line until it encounters a change in the density of the medium, which causes light rays to bend. This bending of light rays, called **refraction**, is the basis of such instruments as eyeglasses, telescopes, and microscopes. The cornea of the eye—the curvature of which is fixed—bends light rays and is primarily responsible for forming the image on the retina.

In a camera, the lens moves in or out to adjust focus, and the same system is used in the eyes of fishes, amphibians, and reptiles. In mammals and birds, however, focus is adjusted by changes in the *shape* of the lens, which is controlled by the **ciliary muscles** inside the eye. As the degree of contraction of the ciliary muscles varies, the lens focuses images of nearer or farther objects so that they form sharp images on the retina; this process of focusing is called **accommodation**. As mammals age, their lenses become less elastic and therefore less able to change curvature to bring nearby objects into focus. Aging humans correct this problem by wearing reading glasses (or holding the menu farther away).

The amount of light that enters the eye is controlled by the size of the **pupil**, which is an opening in the colorful disc called the **iris** (see Figure 10.1). In Chapter 2 we mentioned that dilation of the pupils is controlled by the sympathetic division of the autonomic nervous system, and constriction is controlled by the parasympathetic division. Because usually both divisions are active, pupil size reflects a balance of influences.

During an eye examination, the doctor may use a drug to block acetylcholine transmission in the parasympathetic synapses of your iris; this drug relaxes the sphincter muscle fibers and permits the pupil to open widely. One drug that has this effect got its name—*belladonna* (Italian for "beautiful lady")—because it was thought to make a woman more beautiful by giving her the wide-open pupils of an attentive person. Other drugs, such as morphine, constrict the pupils.

The movement of the eyes is controlled by the **extraocular muscles**, three pairs of muscles that extend from the outside of the eyeball to the bony socket of the eye, known as the *orbit*.

Visual processing begins in the retina

The first stages of visual-information processing occur in the **retina**, the receptive surface inside the back of the eye (**FIGURE 10.2A**). The retina is only 200–300 micrometers (μm) thick—not much thicker than the edge of a razor blade—but it contains several types of cells in distinct layers (**FIGURE 10.2B**). The receptor cells that detect light are called **photoreceptors**. There are two kinds of photoreceptors: some are called **rods** because of their relatively long, narrow form; others are called **cones** (**FIGURE 10.2C**). There are several different types of cones, which respond differently to light of varying wavelengths, providing us with color vision, as described later in the chapter. Both rod and cone photoreceptors release neurotrans-

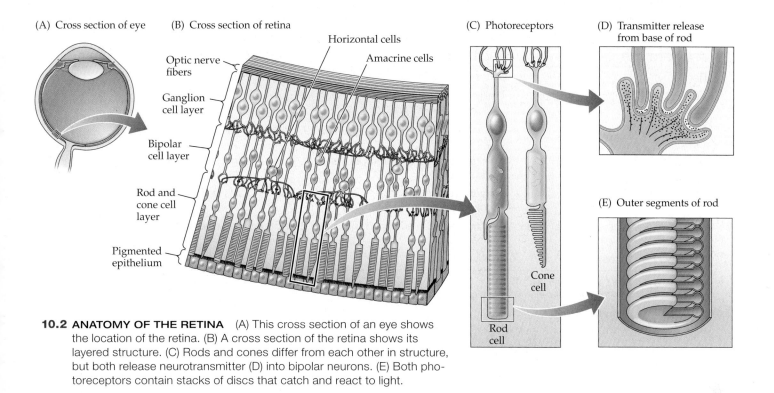

10.2 ANATOMY OF THE RETINA (A) This cross section of an eye shows the location of the retina. (B) A cross section of the retina shows its layered structure. (C) Rods and cones differ from each other in structure, but both release neurotransmitter (D) into bipolar neurons. (E) Both photoreceptors contain stacks of discs that catch and react to light.

Labels in figure:
(A) Cross section of eye
(B) Cross section of retina
Horizontal cells
Amacrine cells
Optic nerve fibers
Ganglion cell layer
Bipolar cell layer
Rod and cone cell layer
Pigmented epithelium
(C) Photoreceptors
(D) Transmitter release from base of rod
(E) Outer segments of rod
Cone cell
Rod cell

mitter molecules (**FIGURE 10.2D**) that control the activity of the **bipolar cells** that synapse with them (see Figure 10.2B). The bipolar cells, in turn, connect with **ganglion cells**. The axons of the ganglion cells form the **optic nerve**, which carries information from the eyes to the brain.

Horizontal cells and **amacrine cells** are especially significant in lateral interactions within the retina, which we'll discuss later. The horizontal cells make contacts among the receptor cells and bipolar cells; the amacrine cells contact both the bipolar and the ganglion cells.

Interestingly, the rods, cones, bipolar cells, and horizontal cells generate only graded local potentials; they do not produce action potentials. These neurons affect each other through the graded release of neurotransmitters in response to graded changes in electrical potentials. The ganglion cells, on the other hand, do conduct action potentials. Because the ganglion cells have action potentials and are relatively large, they were the first retinal neurons to have their electrical activity recorded. From the receptor cells to the ganglion cells, enormous amounts of data converge and are compressed; the human eye contains about 100 million rods and 4 million cones, but there are only 1 million ganglion cells to transmit that information to the brain. Thus, a great deal of information processing is done in the eye.

Two different functional systems arise from the two different populations of receptors (rods and cones) in the retina. One system uses the rods and works in dim light, so it is called the **scotopic system** (from the Greek *skotos*, "darkness," and *ops*, "eye"). The scotopic system has only one receptor type (rods) and therefore does not respond differentially to different colors, which is the basis for the saying "at night, all cats are gray." There is a lot of convergence in the scotopic system, as many rods provide information to each ganglion cell.

The other system requires more light and, in some species, shows differential sensitivity to wavelengths, enabling color vision. This system uses the cones and is called the **photopic system** (from the Greek *phos*, "light"). Compared with the scotopic system, the photopic system has less convergence, as some ganglion cells report information from only a single cone.

At moderate levels of illumination, both rods and cones function, providing us the benefit of both the scotopic and photopic systems, which are compared in **TABLE 10.1** on the following page.

retina The receptive surface inside the eye that contains photoreceptors and other neurons.

photoreceptors Neural cells in the retina that respond to light.

rods A class of light-sensitive receptor cells (photoreceptors) in the retina that are most active at low levels of light.

cones A class of photoreceptor cells in the retina that are responsible for color vision.

bipolar cells A class of interneurons of the retina that receive information from rods and cones and pass the information to retinal ganglion cells.

ganglion cells A class of cells in the retina whose axons form the optic nerve.

optic nerve Cranial nerve II; the collection of ganglion cell axons that extend from the retina to the optic chiasm.

horizontal cells Specialized retinal neurons that contact both the receptor cells and the bipolar cells.

amacrine cells Specialized retinal neurons that contact both the bipolar cells and the ganglion cells and are especially significant in inhibitory interactions within the retina.

scotopic system A system in the retina that operates at low levels of light and involves the rods.

photopic system A system in the retina that operates at high levels of light, shows sensitivity to color, and involves the cones.

TABLE 10.1 Properties of the Human Photopic and Scotopic Visual Systems

PROPERTY	PHOTOPIC SYSTEM	SCOTOPIC SYSTEM
Receptors[a]	Cones	Rods
Approximate number of receptors per eye	4 million	100 million
Photopigments[b]	Three classes of cone opsins; the basis of color vision	Rhodopsin
Sensitivity	Low; needs relatively strong stimulation; used for day vision	High; can be stimulated by weak light intensity; used for night vision
Location in retina[c]	Concentrated in and near fovea; present less densely throughout retina	Outside fovea
Receptive field size and visual acuity	Small in fovea, so acuity is high; larger outside fovea	Larger, so acuity is lower
Temporal responses	Relatively rapid	Slow

[a]Cones and rods are illustrated in Figure 10.2.
[b]Figure 10.24 shows the spectral sensitivities of the photopigments.
[c]See Figure 10.5.

Photoreceptors transduce light into chemical reactions

The extraordinary sensitivity of rods and cones is the result of their unusual structure and biochemistry. A portion of these cells, when magnified, looks like a large stack of pancakes (**FIGURE 10.2E**) and is where light particles are detected. Because light is reflected in many directions by the lens and the fluid inside the eye, only a fraction of the light that passes through the cornea actually reaches the retina. The stacking of discs increases the likelihood that one will capture those light particles, called *photons* (**BOX 10.1**), that reach the retina.

BOX 10.1 The Basics of Light

The physical energy to which our visual system responds is a band of electromagnetic radiation. This radiation comes in very small packets of energy called **quanta** (singular *quantum*). Each quantum can be described by a single number, representing its **wavelength** (the distance between two adjacent crests of vibratory activity).

The human visual system responds only to quanta whose wavelengths lie within a very narrow section of the total electromagnetic range, from about 400 to 700 nm, as the figure shows. Quanta in this range are called **photons** (from the Greek *phos*, "light"). This band of radiant energy visible to animals may be narrow, but it provides for accurate reflection from the surface of objects in the size range that matters for survival. Among the other wavelengths of electromagnetic radiation, radio waves are good for imaging objects of astronomical size, and X-rays penetrate below the surfaces of objects. Each photon has a tiny

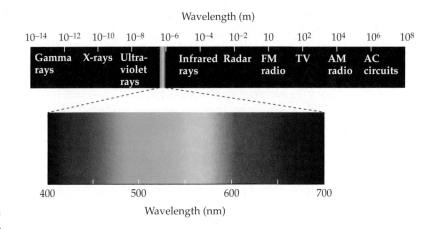

amount of energy; the exact amount depends on the wavelength. A 100-watt (W) incandescent lightbulb gives off only about 3 W of visible light; the rest is heat. But even the 3 W of light amounts to 8 quintillion (8×10^{18}) photons per second.

When quanta within the visible spectrum enter the eye, they can evoke visual sensations. The exact nature of such sensations depends both on the wavelengths of the pho-

tons and on the number of photons per second.

quantum (pl. quanta) A discrete unit of electromagnetic energy.

wavelength The length between two peaks in a repeated stimulus such as a wave, light, or sound.

photon A quantum of electromagnetic energy in the range of wavelengths we call light.

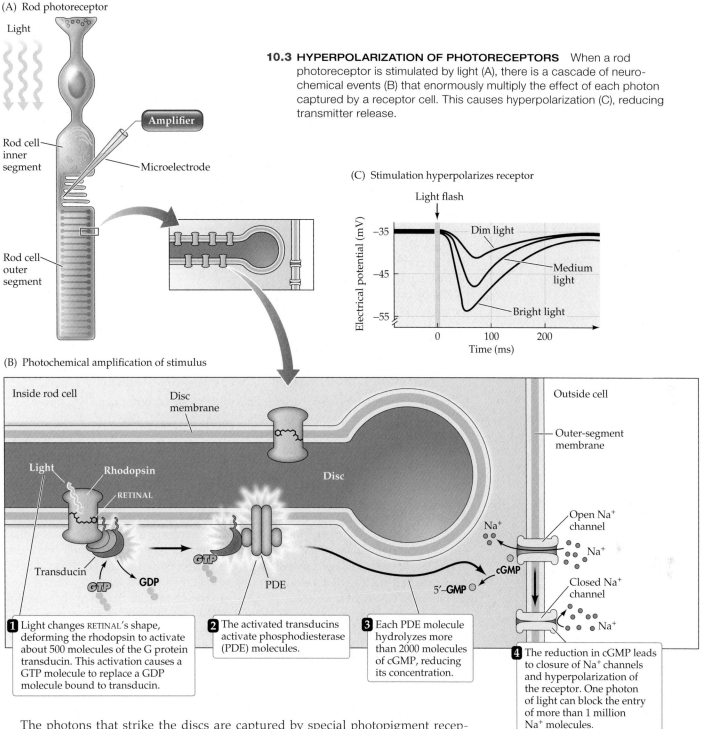

(A) Rod photoreceptor

Light

Rod cell inner segment

Amplifier

Microelectrode

Rod cell outer segment

10.3 HYPERPOLARIZATION OF PHOTORECEPTORS When a rod photoreceptor is stimulated by light (A), there is a cascade of neuro-chemical events (B) that enormously multiply the effect of each photon captured by a receptor cell. This causes hyperpolarization (C), reducing transmitter release.

(C) Stimulation hyperpolarizes receptor

Light flash

Dim light

Medium light

Bright light

Electrical potential (mV)

−35

−45

−55

0   100   200

Time (ms)

(B) Photochemical amplification of stimulus

Inside rod cell

Disc membrane

Disc

Outside cell

Outer-segment membrane

Light   Rhodopsin

RETINAL

Transducin

GTP   GDP

GTP

PDE

cGMP

5′-GMP

Na⁺

Open Na⁺ channel

Na⁺

Closed Na⁺ channel

Na⁺

1 Light changes RETINAL's shape, deforming the rhodopsin to activate about 500 molecules of the G protein transducin. This activation causes a GTP molecule to replace a GDP molecule bound to transducin.

2 The activated transducins activate phosphodiesterase (PDE) molecules.

3 Each PDE molecule hydrolyzes more than 2000 molecules of cGMP, reducing its concentration.

4 The reduction in cGMP leads to closure of Na⁺ channels and hyperpolarization of the receptor. One photon of light can block the entry of more than 1 million Na⁺ molecules.

The photons that strike the discs are captured by special photopigment receptor molecules. In the rods this photopigment is **rhodopsin** (from the Greek *rhodon*, "rose," and *opsis*, "vision"). Cones use similar photopigments, as we will see later. The rod and cone photopigments in the eye consist of two parts: RETINAL (an abbreviated name for *retinaldehyde*) and **opsin**. (In this book the noun RETINAL, standing for the molecule, is printed in small capital letters to distinguish it from the adjective *retinal*, meaning "pertaining to the retina.") The visual receptor molecules span the membranes of receptor discs and have structures that are similar to those of the G protein-coupled neurotransmitter receptors that we discussed in Chapter 3.

When rhodopsin is hit by light (**FIGURE 10.3A**), RETINAL dissociates rapidly from the opsin molecule to reveal an enzymatic site. This altered opsin molecule rapidly activates many molecules of the G protein transducin (**FIGURE 10.3B**). Transducin, in turn, acts through an enzyme, phosphodiesterase (PDE), to break apart cyclic GMP (cyclic guanosine monophosphate, or cGMP) to 5′-GMP. Cyclic GMP

rhodopsin The photopigment in rods that responds to light.

RETINAL Abbreviation for *retinaldehyde*, one of the two components of photopigments in the retina. Also called *vitamin A aldehyde*.

opsin One of the two components of photopigments in the retina.

holds channels for sodium ions (Na^+) open; stimulation by light initiates a cascade of events that *closes* these channels. Capture of a single quantum of light can lead to the closing of hundreds of Na^+ channels in the photoreceptor membrane, thereby blocking the entry of more than a million Na^+ ions (Schnapf and Baylor, 1987). Closing the Na^+ channels creates a hyperpolarizing potential (**FIGURE 10.3C**).

This change of potential is the first electrical signal activating the visual pathway: light hitting rhodopsin hyperpolarizes the rods. In the same way, stimulation of the cone pigments by light hyperpolarizes the cones. For both rods and cones, the size of the hyperpolarizing photoreceptor potential determines how much *less* synaptic transmitter will be released (see Figure 10.3C).

It may seem puzzling at first that stimulation by light *hyper*polarizes vertebrate retinal photoreceptors and causes them to release *less* neurotransmitter, since sensory stimulation depolarizes most other receptor cells. But remember that the visual system responds to *changes* in light. Either an increase or a decrease in the intensity of light can stimulate the visual system, and hyperpolarization is just as much a neural signal as depolarization.

The cascade of processes required to stimulate the visual receptors helps account for three characteristics of the visual system:

1. Its *sensitivity*, because weak stimuli are amplified to produce physiological effects (one photon blocks *millions* of Na^+ ions)

2. The *integration* of the stimulus over time, which makes vision relatively slow (compared, for example, to audition) but increases its sensitivity

3. The *adaptation* of the visual system to a wide range of light intensities, as we will discuss next

Different mechanisms enable the eyes to work over a wide range of light intensities

Many sensory systems have to work over wide ranges of stimulus intensity, as we learned in Chapter 8. This is certainly true of the visual system: a very bright light is about 10 billion times as intense as the weakest lights we can see. How do we do it?

One way the visual system deals with a large range of intensities is by adjusting the size of the pupil. In bright light the pupil constricts quickly to admit less light. Interestingly, the pupillary response to light is controlled not by rods or cones, but by specialized retinal ganglion cells that possess their own photopigment, which makes them sensitive to light (Xue et al., 2011). These ganglion cells project to the superior colliculus to control pupil diameter, matching the level of ambient light (Lucas et al., 2003). We'll see in Chapter 14 that these same ganglion cells also help control daily cycles of behavior called *circadian rhythms*. Although rapid, this pupillary response reduces light only about 16-fold, so it cannot account for the billionfold range of visual sensitivity (**FIGURE 10.4**).

Another mechanism for dealing with different light intensities is **range fractionation**, the handling of different intensities by different receptors—some with low thresholds (rods) and others with high thresholds (cones) (see Table 10.1). Figure 8.6 illustrated range fractionation for the somatosensory system. Additional range fractionation would carry an unacceptable cost: If, at a particular light level, several sets of receptors were not responding, sharpness of vision would be impaired. If only a fraction of the receptors responded to the small changes in the intensity of light around a given level, the active receptors would be spaced apart from each other in the retina, and the image would be "grainy" or "pixelated."

Natural selection solved this problem by giving every photoreceptor an enormous range of **adaptation**; that is, each photoreceptor adjusts its sensitivity to match the ambient illumination. At any given time, a photoreceptor operates over a range of intensities of about a hundredfold; that is, it is completely depolarized by a stimulus about one-tenth the ambient level of illumination, and a light 10 times brighter than the ambient level will completely hyper-

range fractionation A hypothesis of stimulus intensity perception stating that a wide range of intensity values can be encoded by a group of cells, each of which is a specialist for a particular range of stimulus intensities.

adaptation Here, the progressive loss of receptor sensitivity as stimulation is maintained.

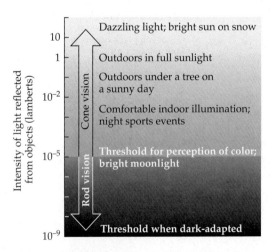

10.4 THE WIDE RANGE OF SENSITIVITY TO LIGHT INTENSITY

(A) Distributions of rods and cones across the retina

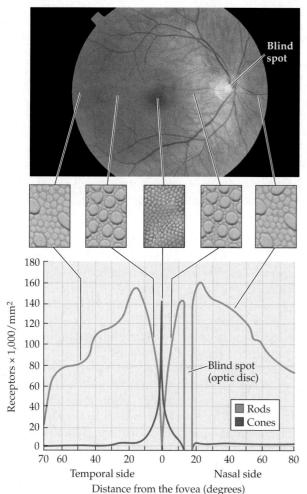

(B) Variation of visual acuity across the retina

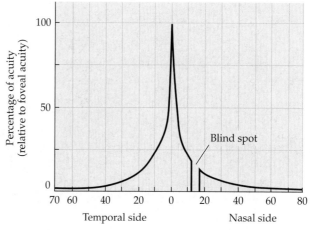

10.5 DENSITIES OF RETINAL RECEPTORS AND VISUAL ACUITY
(A) The photograph of the retina was taken through the pupil. The yellow circle is the optic disc, the point where ganglion cell axons exit the eye. The absence of photoreceptors there is responsible for the blind spot in our vision. The rods and cones vary in size (middle panel) and density (bottom graph) across the retina. (B) The variation of visual acuity across the retina reflects the distribution of cones.

polarize it. But the receptors constantly shift their whole range of response, to work around the prevailing level of illumination. This tremendous range of **photoreceptor adaptation** is the main reason we can see over such wide ranges of light. Thus, the visual system is concerned with *differences*, or changes, in brightness—not with the absolute level of illumination.

Two main factors account for most of the adaptation of photoreceptors. Probably the most important factor is one shared by other sensory modalities: varying the concentration of calcium (Ca^{2+}) ions (E. N. Pugh and Lamb, 1990). The photoreceptors regulate the release and storage of intracellular Ca^{2+} ions to control their sensitivity to light. Also, when the photoreceptor pigment is split apart by light, its two components—RETINAL and opsin—recombine slowly. This recombination takes time, affecting how much photopigment is available to respond to light. If you go from bright daylight into a dark theater, it takes several minutes until enough rhodopsin recombines to restore your dark vision (E. N. Pugh and Lamb, 1993). Further adaptation occurs in the ganglion cells and the thalamus and probably at higher levels too.

Acuity is best in foveal vision

The **visual field** is the whole area you can see without moving your head or eyes. You may think that your vision is equally good across the visual field, but this is an illusion. **Visual acuity**, the sharpness of vision, is especially fine in the center of the visual field and falls off rapidly toward the periphery. We can understand this difference in visual acuity by learning more about the retina and successive levels of the visual system.

FIGURE 10.5A shows a photograph of the back of the eye seen through the pupil. The central region, called the **fovea** (Latin for "pit"), has a dense concentration

photoreceptor adaptation The tendency of rods and cones to adjust their light sensitivity to match ambient levels of illumination.

visual field The whole area that you can see without moving your head or eyes.

visual acuity Sharpness of vision.

fovea The central portion of the retina, packed with the most photoreceptors and therefore the center of our gaze.

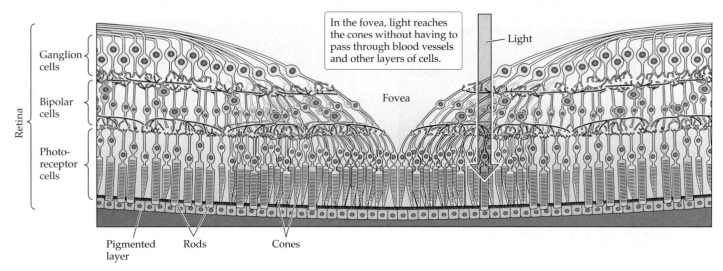

In the fovea, light reaches the cones without having to pass through blood vessels and other layers of cells.

Light

Fovea

Ganglion cells

Bipolar cells

Retina

Photo-receptor cells

Pigmented layer   Rods   Cones

10.6 AN UNOBSTRUCTED VIEW

optic disc   The region of the retina devoid of receptor cells because ganglion cell axons and blood vessels exit the eyeball there.

blind spot   The portion of the visual field from which light falls on the optic disc. Because there are no receptors in this region, light striking it cannot be seen.

saccades   Fast movements of the eyes that present various parts of the visual scene to the fovea. When we fix our gaze, small saccades that we are unaware of avert photoreceptor adaptation.

lateral inhibition   The phenomenon by which interconnected neurons inhibit their neighbors, producing contrast at the edges of regions.

of cones. The **optic disc**, to the nasal side of the fovea, is where blood vessels and ganglion cell axons leave the eye. There are no photoreceptors at the optic disc, so there is a **blind spot** here that we normally do not notice. To locate your blind spot and experience firsthand some of its interesting features, see **A Step Further: The Blind Spot** on the website.

The high concentration of cones in the fovea provides high visual acuity in this region (**FIGURE 10.5B**). People differ in their concentrations of cones (Curcio et al., 1987), and this variation may be related to individual differences in visual acuity. Species differences in visual acuity also reflect the density of cones in the fovea. For example, hawks, whose acuity is much greater than that of humans, have much narrower and more densely packed cones in the fovea than we do. In the human retina, both cones and rods are larger toward the periphery. Therefore, our acuity falls off about as rapidly in the horizontal direction as in the vertical direction. But species that live in open, flat environments (such as the cheetah and the rabbit) have fields of acute vision that extend farther horizontally than vertically. In all vertebrates, there are fewer blood vessels overlying the foveal region of the retina (**FIGURE 10.6**), so more light reaches the photoreceptors there.

Quick movements of the eyes, called **saccades**, bring various parts of the visual scene to the fovea to take advantage of the sharp visual acuity there. Even when we think we are holding our eyes still to fixate on a scene, they are in fact making tiny saccades (Martinez-Conde et al., 2013), constantly shifting the scene to different parts of the retina to be detected by fresh photoreceptors. Otherwise, the photoreceptors would adapt and stop responding to the light, causing the scene to disappear.

Rods are distributed differently than cones: rods are absent in the fovea but more numerous than cones in the periphery of the retina (see Figure 10.5A). They are the most concentrated in a ring about 20° away from the center of the retina. This is why if you want to see a dim star, you do best to search for it a little off to the side of your center of gaze. This directs the dim light to the periphery of your visual field, onto rods driving the scotopic system. Not only are the rods more sensitive to dim light than the cones, but as we mentioned earlier, input from many rods converges on ganglion cells in the scotopic system, further increasing the system's sensitivity to weak stimuli. On the other hand, that greater convergence of information from photoreceptors to ganglion cells in rods than in cones is another reason why acuity is greater in the cone-rich fovea. A cone here is more likely to have exclusive control over a single ganglion cell. Rods provide high sensitivity with limited acuity; cones provide high acuity with limited sensitivity.

Brightness is created by the visual system

The brightness dimension of visual perception is created in part by the visual system, not simply by the amount of light reflected. **FIGURE 10.7** presents two examples. The enhancement of the boundaries of the bars in **FIGURE 10.7A**, each of which is uniformly gray but looks as though it varies in brightness, is based on a neural process called **lateral inhibition**.

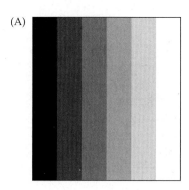
(A)

(B)

10.7 THE EFFECT OF CONTEXT ON THE PERCEPTION OF BRIGHTNESS (A) Each bar shown here is uniform in color, but each of the gray bars appears lighter on its left edge and darker on its right. (B) Shading around a patch of light affects the perception of brightness. For example, even though the two tiles in the middle are the same shade of gray, one appears darker than the other. If you don't believe this, place your pinky finger over the place where the two tiles meet. See? (Part B from Purves and Lotto, 2010.)

Lateral inhibition occurs where the neurons in a region—in this case, retinal cells—are interconnected, either through their own axons or by means of interneurons, and each neuron tends to inhibit its neighbors (**FIGURE 10.8**). The photoreceptors stimulated by the right edge of each gray bar in Figure 10.7A are inhibited by the neighboring photoreceptors stimulated by the lighter bar next door. Thus, photoreceptors on the right edge report receiving less light than they actually do (i.e., that edge looks darker to us).

In **FIGURE 10.7B**, two tiles that clearly differ in brightness *reflect the same amount of light*. If you use your pinkie to cover the boundary between the upper and lower tiles, they appear equally dark. How are such puzzling effects produced? Although the contrast effect in Figure 10.7A is determined, at least in part, by lateral inhibition among adjacent retinal cells, the two indicated patches of the tiles in Figure 10.7B are not immediately adjacent (they are separated by shading), so the effect must be produced higher in the visual system (Purves and Lotto, 2010). The important point is that our visual experience is not a simple reporting of the physical properties of light. Rather, our experience of light versus dark is created by the brain in response to many factors, including surrounding stimuli. Later in the chapter we'll find that our experience of color is also created by the visual system, and not a simple reporting of the wavelengths of light.

Neural Signals Travel from the Retina to Several Brain Regions

The ganglion cells in each eye produce action potentials that are conducted along their axons to send visual information to the brain. These axons make up the optic nerve (also known as *cranial nerve II*) that brings visual information into the brain on each side, eventually reaching visual cortex in the occipital lobe at the back of the brain. Primary visual cortex passes along the information to other visual cortical regions, as we discuss shortly.

In all vertebrates, some or all of the axons of each optic nerve cross to the opposite cerebral hemisphere. The optic nerves cross the midline at the **optic chiasm** (named for the Greek letter χ [chi] because of its crossover shape). In humans, axons from the half of the retina toward the nose (called the *nasal hemiretina*) cross over to the opposite side of the brain (**FIGURE 10.9A**). The half of the retina toward the side of the head (the *temporal hemiretina*) projects its axons to its own side of the head. This distribution of retinal fibers means the right side of the brain receives input from the left half of the visual field, while the left side of the brain receives input from the right half of the visual field.

optic chiasm The point at which the two optic nerves meet.

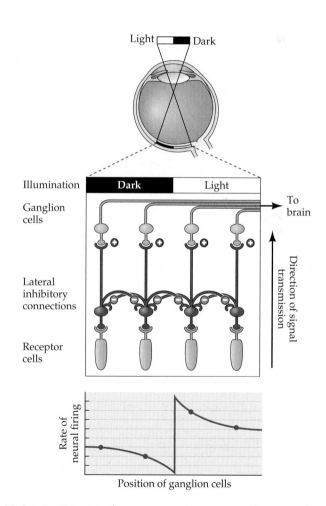

10.8 LATERAL INHIBITION IN THE RETINA Because of lateral inhibitory connections, the two central receptor cells differ more in their rates of firing than do either the two left-hand cells or the two right-hand cells, as the graph shows. This is a simplified view; in fact, each purple cell inhibits many of its neighbors and not just those directly adjacent.

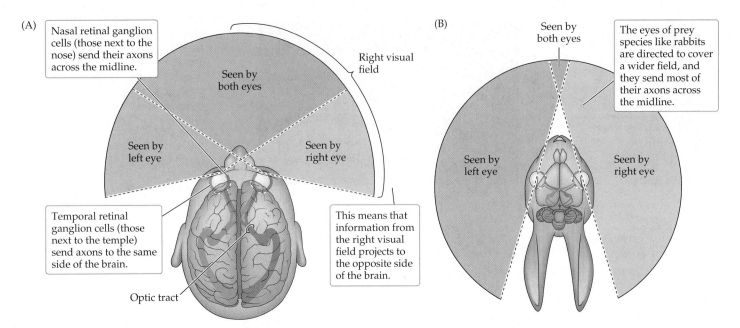

(A) Nasal retinal ganglion cells (those next to the nose) send their axons across the midline.

Right visual field

Seen by both eyes

Seen by left eye

Seen by right eye

Temporal retinal ganglion cells (those next to the temple) send axons to the same side of the brain.

This means that information from the right visual field projects to the opposite side of the brain.

Optic tract

(B) Seen by both eyes

The eyes of prey species like rabbits are directed to cover a wider field, and they send most of their axons across the midline.

Seen by left eye

Seen by right eye

10.9 THE VISUAL FIELDS OF THE TWO EYES OVERLAP TO SOME EXTENT (A) In humans, both eyes receive information from both the left and right visual field. This means that the central portion of the visual field projects to both eyes. However, since axons from the portion of the retina next to the nose (nasal retina) cross the midline on the way to the brain while the portion of the retina next to the temple (temporal retina) projects to the same side of the brain, informa- tion from the left visual field reaches the right side of the brain, and information from the right visual field reaches the left side. (B) In prey species that need to be on the lookout for predators, the eyes may be farther apart so they can scan more of the space around them, and consequently almost all retinal ganglion cells send their axons across the midline.

optic tract The axons of retinal ganglion cells after they have passed the optic chiasm; most terminate in the lateral geniculate nucleus.

lateral geniculate nucleus (LGN) The part of the thalamus that receives information from the optic tract and sends it to visual areas in the occipital cortex.

optic radiation Axons from the lateral geniculate nucleus that terminate in the primary visual areas of the occipital cortex.

primary visual cortex (V1) Also called *striate cortex* or *area 17*. The region of the occipital lobe where most visual information first arrives in the cortex.

occipital lobe Large region of cortex covering much of the posterior part of each cerebral hemisphere, specialized for visual processing.

extrastriate cortex Visual cortex outside of the primary visual (striate) cortex.

Having our eyes cover overlapping sections of the visual field helps us judge the distance of objects, by (unconsciously) comparing the inputs from the two eyes. In prey species such as rabbits, natural selection has sacrificed some of this binocular depth perception, favoring instead the broader visual field that results from having the eyes positioned farther apart (**FIGURE 10.9B**); this broader visual field helps the rabbit detect approaching predators. In such species, most of the optic nerve fibers cross the midline.

After they pass the optic chiasm, the axons of the retinal ganglion cells are known collectively as the **optic tract**. As **FIGURE 10.10** shows, most axons of the optic tract in mammals terminate on cells in the **lateral geniculate nucleus** (**LGN**), which is the visual part of the thalamus (step 4a in Figure 10.10). The axons of neurons in the LGN form the **optic radiations** (step 5), which terminate in **primary visual cortex** (**V1**) of the **occipital lobe** at the back of the brain (step 6). The primary visual cortex is often called *striate cortex* because a broad stripe, or *striation*, is visible in anatomical sections through this region; the stripe represents layer IV of the cortex, where the optic-radiation fibers arrive. Information from the two eyes converges on cells beyond layer IV of the primary visual cortex, making binocular, three-dimensional vision possible, as we discussed in Chapter 7.

Some retinal ganglion cells send their optic-tract axons to the superior colliculus in the midbrain (see Figure 10.10, step 4b), to help coordinate rapid movements of the eyes toward a target and to control the size of the pupil, as we mentioned earlier.

In addition to V1 shown in Figure 10.10, numerous surrounding regions of the cortex are also largely visual in function. These visual cortical areas outside the striate cortex are sometimes called **extrastriate cortex**. These different cortical regions work in parallel to process different aspects of visual perception, such as form, color, location, and movement, as we will discuss later in this chapter. In striate cortex, as well as most extrastriate regions, there is a topographic projection of the retina, which means there's a topographic projection of the visual field, discussed next.

Don't understand.

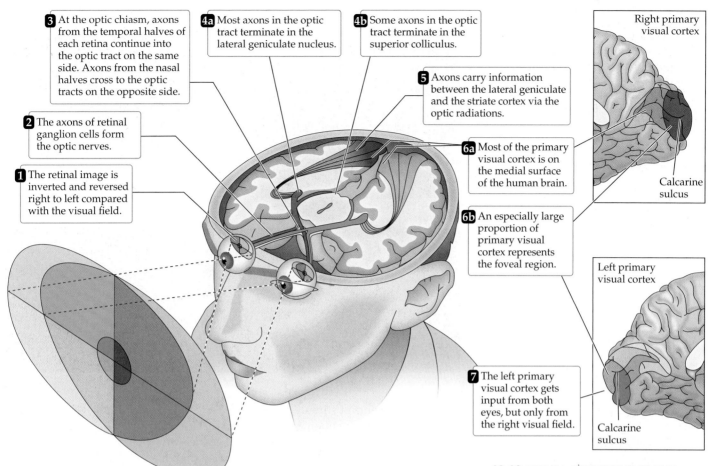

3 At the optic chiasm, axons from the temporal halves of each retina continue into the optic tract on the same side. Axons from the nasal halves cross to the optic tracts on the opposite side.

2 The axons of retinal ganglion cells form the optic nerves.

1 The retinal image is inverted and reversed right to left compared with the visual field.

4a Most axons in the optic tract terminate in the lateral geniculate nucleus.

4b Some axons in the optic tract terminate in the superior colliculus.

5 Axons carry information between the lateral geniculate and the striate cortex via the optic radiations.

6a Most of the primary visual cortex is on the medial surface of the human brain.

6b An especially large proportion of primary visual cortex represents the foveal region.

7 The left primary visual cortex gets input from both eyes, but only from the right visual field.

Right primary visual cortex

Calcarine sulcus

Left primary visual cortex

Calcarine sulcus

10.10 VISUAL PATHWAYS IN THE HUMAN BRAIN Visual fields are represented on the retinas and project to the cerebral hemispheres. The right visual field, which falls on parts of both retinas, projects to the left cerebral hemisphere. Similarly, the left visual field projects to both eyes and then to the right cerebral hemisphere.

Go to Animation 10.2
Visual Pathways in the Human Brain
bn8e.com/10.2

The retina projects to the brain in a topographic fashion

The retina represents a two-dimensional map of visual space. As this information courses through the brain, the point-to-point correspondence between neighboring parts of visual space is maintained, forming a maplike projection (see Figure 10.10). Much of this topographic projection of visual space is devoted to the foveal region (**FIGURE 10.11A**) (Tootell et al., 1982). Although the monkey V1 is located on the lateral surface of the occipital area, human V1 is located mainly on the medial surface of the cortex (**FIGURE 10.11B**; see also Figure 10.19D). The fact that about half of the human V1 is devoted to the fovea and the retinal region just around the fovea does not mean that our spatial perception is distorted. Rather, this representation makes possible the great acuity of spatial discrimination in the central part of the visual field. One reason we see better in this region of visual space is because we devote more brain circuits to analyzing it. Apparently those brain circuits are somewhat plastic, benefiting from practice, because people who intensively play "point and shoot" video action games display improved visual acuity (R. Li et al., 2009).

Because of the orderly mapping of the visual field (known as *retinotopic mapping*) at the various levels of the visual system, damage to parts of the visual system can be diagnosed from defects in perception of the visual field. If we know the site of injury in the visual pathway, we can predict the location of such a perceptual gap, or **scotoma** (plural *scotomas* or *scotomata*), in the visual field. Although the word *scotoma* comes from the Greek *skotos*, meaning "darkness," a scotoma is not perceived as a dark patch in the visual field; rather, it is a spot where nothing can be perceived, and usually rigorous testing is required to demonstrate its existence.

Within a scotoma, a person cannot consciously perceive visual cues, but some visual discrimination in this region may still be possible; this paradoxical phenomenon has been called *blindsight*. In other cases, stimuli that cannot be seen within a scoto-

scotoma A region of blindness caused by injury to the visual pathway or brain.

10.11 LOCATION OF THE PRIMARY VISUAL CORTEX   (A) A pattern of flickering lights (left) was shown in a monkey's visual field, and a map of the visual field (right) was revealed by autoradiography in a flattened portion of the primary visual cortex. (B) Maps of human visual cortex derived from fMRI measurements show primary visual cortex as the innermost yellow region on each of these medial views. (Part A from Tootell et al., 1988; B from Tootell et al., 1998; both courtesy of Dr. Roger Tootell.)

(A) Monkey

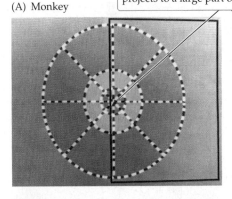

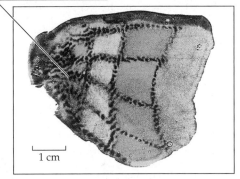

The small central region of the visual field projects to a large part of primary visual cortex.

1 cm

(B) Human

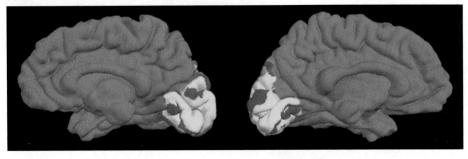

receptive field   The stimulus region and features that affect the activity of a cell in a sensory system.

on-center bipolar cell   A retinal bipolar cell that is excited by light in the center of its receptive field.

off-center bipolar cell   A retinal bipolar cell that is inhibited by light in the center of its receptive field.

ma affect judgments of stimuli outside it (Stoerig and Cowey, 1997). Blindsight may also be related to the phenomenon known as *hemispatial neglect*—neglect of the side opposite to an injured cerebral hemisphere—which we will discuss in Chapter 18.

When we look at a complex organ like the eye of a mammal, an octopus, or a fly, it is hard at first to understand how it could have evolved. But inspection of different living species reveals a gradation from very simple light-sensitive cells to increasingly complex organs with focusing devices (**BOX 10.2**), and each gradation of a visual system helps the animal survive.

BOX 10.2

Eyes with Lenses Have Evolved in Several Phyla

Phylogenetic studies indicate that the evolution of eyes with lenses, like those of a mammal or an octopus, included the following steps (Fernald, 2000), as illustrated in the figure:

1. *Concentrating light-sensitive cells* into localized groups that serve as photoreceptor organs. Animals with such photoreceptor organs have better chances of surviving and reproducing, because photoreceptor organs make it easier to respond differently to stimuli that strike different parts of the body surface.

2. *Clustering light receptors* at the bottom of pitlike or cuplike depressions in the skin. Animals with this adaptation can discriminate better among stimuli that come from different directions.

3. *Narrowing the top of the cup* into a small aperture so that, like a pinhole camera, the eye can focus well.

4. *Closing the opening with transparent skin or filling the cup with a transparent substance.* This covering protects the eye against the entry of foreign substances that might injure the receptor cells or block vision.

5. *Forming a lens* either by thickening the transparent skin or by modifying other tissue in the eye. This adaptation improves the focusing of the eye while allowing the aperture to be relatively large to let in more light.

The only requirement for the evolution of eyes to begin appears to be the existence of light-sensitive cells. Natural selection then favors the de-

velopment of auxiliary mechanisms to improve vision.

Eyes evolved independently in many different phyla (Salvini-Plawen and Mayr, 1977)—an example of convergent evolution. The fact that the cephalopods (such as squid and octopuses) evolved a visual system that in many ways resembles that of vertebrates (from fishes to humans) suggests that major constraints limit the development of a visual system for a large, rapidly moving animal. In both cephalopods and vertebrates, the eyes are relatively large, allowing for many receptors and the ability to gather large amounts of light. The incoming light is regulated by a pupil and focused by a lens. In both cephalopods and vertebrates, three

Neurons at Different Levels of the Visual System Have Very Different Receptive Fields

As we noted in Chapter 8, the **receptive field** of a sensory cell consists of the stimulus region and the features that excite or inhibit the cell. The nature of the receptive field of a cell gives us good clues about its function(s) in perception. In the next sections we will see that neurons at lower levels in the visual system seem to account for some perceptual phenomena while neurons at higher levels account for others.

Photoreceptors excite some retinal neurons and inhibit others

At their resting potentials, both rod and cone photoreceptors steadily release the synaptic neurotransmitter glutamate. Light always hyperpolarizes the photoreceptors, causing them to release *less* glutamate. But the response of the bipolar cells that receive this glutamate differs, depending on what type of glutamate receptor they possess. Glutamate depolarizes one group of bipolar cells but hyperpolarizes another group. These groups differ in their receptive fields.

One group of bipolar cells contains **on-center bipolar cells**: turning *on* a light in the center of an on-center bipolar cell's receptive field excites the cell because it receives *less* glutamate, which otherwise inhibits on-center bipolar cells (**FIGURE 10.12** *left*). The second group contains **off-center bipolar cells**: turning *off* light in the center of an off-center bipolar cell's receptive field excites the cell because it receives *more* glutamate, which depolarizes off-center bipolar cells (**FIGURE 10.12** *right*).

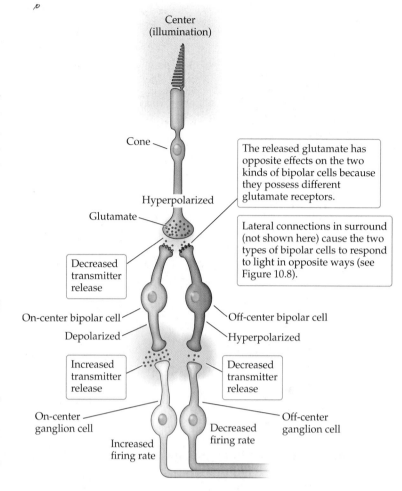

The released glutamate has opposite effects on the two kinds of bipolar cells because they possess different glutamate receptors.

Lateral connections in surround (not shown here) cause the two types of bipolar cells to respond to light in opposite ways (see Figure 10.8).

10.12 CONNECTIONS OF CONES TO BIPOLAR CELLS Light falling on a given photoreceptor may increase the firing of one ganglion cell and reduce the firing of another.

sets of extraocular muscles move the eyeballs.

However, it is still uncertain whether eyes of all species have evolved from a single progenitor or have arisen more than once during evolution (Fernald, 2000). The eyes of all seeing animals share at least two important genetic features: First, they all use opsin pigments. Second, from the compound eye of the fruit fly *Drosophila*, to the vertebrate eye, to the cephalopod eye, they all develop through genes of the *Pax* family. The finding that homologous molecules are key regulators of eye development in different phyla suggests that eyes in all phyla share a common origin.

1 Cluster of light-sensitive cells

2 Light-sensitive cells clustered in a pitlike depression in the skin

3 Pinhole eye

4 Opening closed with transparent skin

5 Cornea / Lens / Eye with cornea and lens

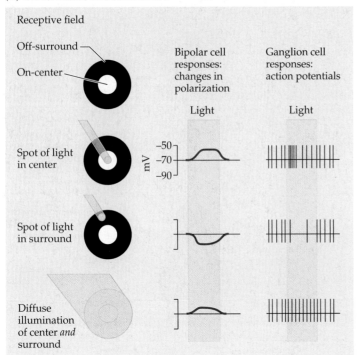

(A) An on-center/off-surround cell

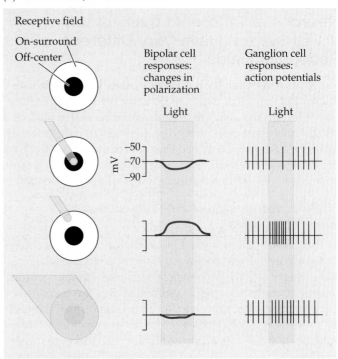

(B) An off-center/on-surround cell

10.13 RECEPTIVE FIELDS OF RETINAL CELLS In primates, each retinal bipolar cell, as well as each retinal ganglion cell, has a concentric receptive field, with antagonistic center and surround. Bipolar cells respond by changes in local membrane potentials; ganglion cells respond with action potentials. (A) An on-center/off-surround cell is excited by an increase of illumination in the center of its receptive field and inhibited by illumination in the surround. (B) Changes in illumination have the opposite effects on an off-center/on-surround cell. Note that uniform light across the entire receptive field (bottom) has little effect on the firing of either type of ganglion cell.

Go to Animation 10.3
Receptive Fields in the Retina
bn8e.com/10.3

on-center ganglion cell A retinal ganglion cell that is activated when light is presented to the center, rather than the periphery, of the cell's receptive field.

off-center ganglion cell A retinal ganglion cell that is activated when light is presented to the periphery, rather than the center, of the cell's receptive field.

on-center/off-surround Referring to a concentric receptive field in which the center excites the cell of interest while the surround inhibits it.

off-center/on-surround Referring to a concentric receptive field in which the center inhibits the cell of interest while the surround excites it.

Bipolar cells also *release* glutamate, and glutamate always depolarizes the ganglion cells. Therefore, when light is turned on, on-center bipolar cells depolarize (excite) **on-center ganglion cells**; and when light is turned off, off-center bipolar cells depolarize (excite) **off-center ganglion cells** (see Figure 10.12). The stimulated on-center and off-center ganglion cells then fire nerve impulses and report "light" or "dark" to higher visual centers.

Neurons in the retina and the LGN have concentric receptive fields

The pattern of connections of photoreceptors to bipolar cells shapes the receptive fields of the ganglion cells. Scientists can record from single ganglion cells while moving a small spot of light across the visual field, keeping the animal's eye still. These studies show that the receptive fields of retinal ganglion cells are concentric, consisting of a roughly circular central area and a ring around it. Through various retinal connections, including the lateral inhibition we discussed earlier (see Figure 10.8), the photoreceptors in the central area and those in the ring around it tend to have the opposite effects on the next cells in the circuit. Thus, both bipolar cells and ganglion cells have two basic types of retinal receptive fields: **on-center/off-surround** (**FIGURE 10.13A**) and **off-center/on-surround** (**FIGURE 10.13B**). These antagonistic effects of the center and its surround explain why uniform illumination of the visual field is less effective in activating a ganglion cell than is a well-placed small spot or a line or edge passing through the center of the cell's receptive field.

We told you earlier that most ganglion cell axons synapse in the LGN of the thalamus in mammals. The primate LGN has six main layers and some smaller layers in between (**FIGURE 10.14**). The structure is called *geniculate* because the layers are bent like a knee, which in Latin is *genu*. The four dorsal, or outer, layers of the primate

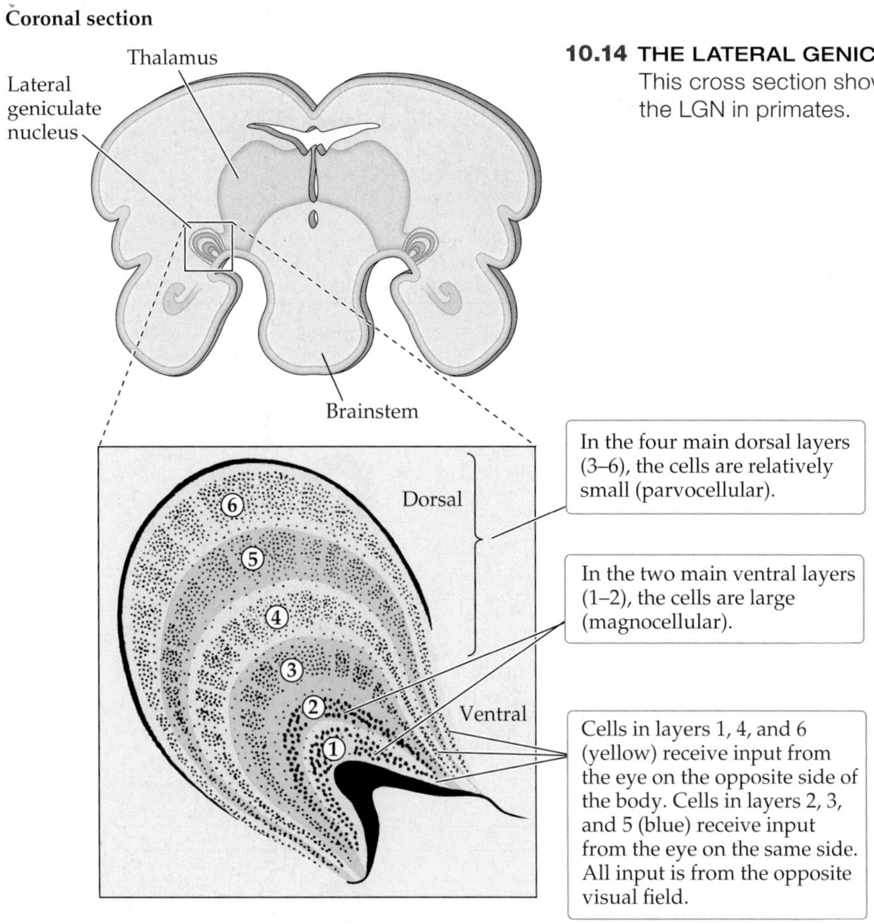

Thalamus

Lateral
geniculate
nucleus

Brainstem

10.14 THE LATERAL GENICULATE NUCLEUS
This cross section shows the layered structure of
the LGN in primates.

Dorsal

Ventral

In the four main dorsal layers
(3–6), the cells are relatively
small (parvocellular).

In the two main ventral layers
(1–2), the cells are large
(magnocellular).

Cells in layers 1, 4, and 6
(yellow) receive input from
the eye on the opposite side of
the body. Cells in layers 2, 3,
and 5 (blue) receive input
from the eye on the same side.
All input is from the opposite
visual field.

LGN are called **parvocellular** (from the Latin *parvus*, "small") because their cells are relatively small. The two ventral, or inner, layers are called **magnocellular** (from the Latin *magnus*, "large") because their cells are large. LGN neurons of all six layers have concentric receptive fields. For most neurons in the magnocellular layers, these concentric receptive fields are relatively large, receiving input from large ganglion cells, which receive their input from bipolar cells contacting many neighboring photoreceptors. Most magnocellular LGN neurons do not show differential wavelength responses; that is, they cannot be involved in color discrimination. In contrast, the neurons of the parvocellular layers have relatively small receptive fields, whose input can be traced back to cones. These LGN neurons discriminate wavelengths.

Neurons in the visual cortex have varied and complicated receptive fields

The next level of the visual system, the primary visual cortex, provided a puzzle to vision researchers. Neurons from the LGN send their axons to cells in V1, but the spots of light that are effective stimuli for ganglion cells and LGN cells are not very effective for cortical cells. In 1959, David Hubel and Torsten Wiesel reported that visual cortical cells require more-specific stimuli that are more elongated than those that activate LGN cells. Most cells in area V1 respond best to lines or bars in a particular position and at a particular orientation in the visual field. Some cortical cells also require movement of the stimulus to make them respond actively. For some of these cells, any movement in their field is sufficient; others are more demanding, requiring motion in a specific direction (**FIGURE 10.15**).

Cortical cells can be categorized according to which of these types of stimuli produce maximum responses. So-called **simple cortical cells** respond best to an edge or a bar that has a particular width and a particular orientation and location in the visual field. Therefore these cells were sometimes called *bar detectors* or *edge detectors*. Like the simple cells, **complex cortical cells** have elongated receptive fields,

parvocellular   Referring to relatively small cells.

magnocellular   Referring to relatively large cells.

simple cortical cell   Also called *bar detector* or *edge detector*. A cell in the visual cortex that responds best to an edge or a bar that has a particular width, as well as a particular orientation and location in the visual field.

complex cortical cell   A cell in the visual cortex that responds best to a bar of a particular size and orientation anywhere within a particular area of the visual field.

10.15 RECEPTIVE FIELDS OF CELLS AT VARIOUS LEVELS IN THE CAT VISUAL SYSTEM
Microelectrode recordings reveal that cells differ greatly in their receptive fields. (A) Visual cells in the lateral geniculate nucleus (LGN) have concentric receptive fields, like those of retinal bipolar cells and ganglion cells (see Figure 10.13). (B) Visual cells in the cerebral cortex are more responsive to bars of light and may show orientation specificity or respond only to motion, or (C) they may respond only to motion in a particular direction.

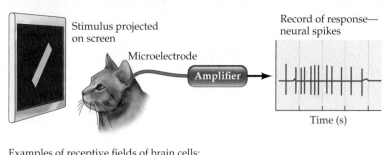

Stimulus projected on screen

Record of response—neural spikes

Microelectrode

Amplifier

Time (s)

Examples of receptive fields of brain cells:

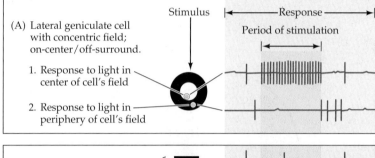

Stimulus

Response

Period of stimulation

(A) Lateral geniculate cell with concentric field; on-center/off-surround.

1. Response to light in center of cell's field

2. Response to light in periphery of cell's field

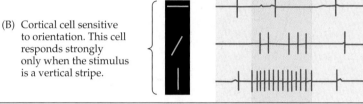

(B) Cortical cell sensitive to orientation. This cell responds strongly only when the stimulus is a vertical stripe.

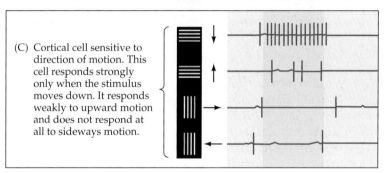

(C) Cortical cell sensitive to direction of motion. This cell responds strongly only when the stimulus moves down. It responds weakly to upward motion and does not respond at all to sideways motion.

but in addition they show some latitude for location; that is, they respond to a bar of a particular size and orientation anywhere within a larger area of the visual field.

This categorization of receptive fields can be described as hierarchical; that is, more-complex events are built up from inputs of simpler ones. For example, a simple cortical cell can be thought of as receiving input from a row of LGN cells, and a complex cortical cell can be thought of as receiving input from a row of simple cortical cells (**FIGURE 10.16**). Other theorists extrapolated from this model, suggesting that higher-order circuits of cells could detect any possible form. Thus it was suggested that, by integration of enough successive levels of analysis, a neuron could be constructed that would enable a person to recognize his or her grandmother, and such hypothetical "grandmother cells" were frequently mentioned in the literature. According to this view, whenever such a cell was excited, up would pop a mental picture of one's grandmother. This hypothesis was given as a possible explanation for facial recognition.

Critics soon pointed out both theoretical and empirical problems with this hierarchical model of vision. For one thing, a hierarchical system like this would require a vast number of cells—perhaps more neurons than the cortex possesses—in order to account for all the visual objects that we may encounter. Although some neurons are activated by the sight of very specific faces (e.g., "Halle Berry neurons" are some neurons that were activated by photos of that actress) in both humans (Pedreira et

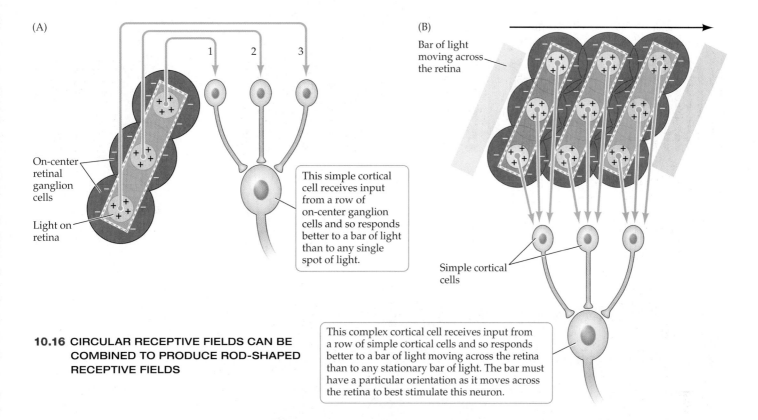

(A)

On-center retinal ganglion cells

Light on retina

This simple cortical cell receives input from a row of on-center ganglion cells and so responds better to a bar of light than to any single spot of light.

10.16 CIRCULAR RECEPTIVE FIELDS CAN BE COMBINED TO PRODUCE ROD-SHAPED RECEPTIVE FIELDS

(B)

Bar of light moving across the retina

Simple cortical cells

This complex cortical cell receives input from a row of simple cortical cells and so responds better to a bar of light moving across the retina than to any stationary bar of light. The bar must have a particular orientation as it moves across the retina to best stimulate this neuron.

al., 2010) and monkeys (Freiwald et al., 2009), these neurons do not respond to specific features of the face, as you would expect if they were feature detectors. Rather, they respond only when the whole face or most of the face is presented (Freiwald et al., 2009). Thus, we need an alternative model of vision, which we describe next.

spatial-frequency filter model
A model of pattern analysis that emphasizes Fourier analysis of visual stimuli.

Most cells in the primary visual cortex are tuned to particular spatial frequencies

Concepts of pattern analysis in terms of lines and edges have largely given way to what is known as the **spatial-frequency filter model**, which is more powerful but less intuitive than the hierarchical model it replaces (R. L. De Valois and De Valois, 1988). By *spatial frequency of a visual stimulus* we mean the number of light-dark (or color) cycles that the stimulus shows per degree of visual space. For example, **FIGURE 10.17A AND B** differ in the spacing of the bars: Figure 10.17A has twice as many bars in the same horizontal space and is therefore said to have double the spatial frequency of Figure 10.17B. The spatial-frequency technique applies Fourier analysis (see Box 9.1) or linear systems theory, rather than analyzing visual patterns into bars and angles.

In Box 9.1 we saw that we can produce any complex, repeating auditory stimulus by adding together simple sine waves. Conversely, using Fourier analysis, we can determine which combination of sine waves would be needed to make any particular complex waveform. The same principle of Fourier analysis can be applied to visual patterns. If the dimension from dark to light varies according to a sine wave function, visual patterns like the ones in **FIGURE 10.17C AND D** result. Any series of dark and light stripes, like those in Figure 10.17A and B, can be analyzed into the sum of a visual sine wave and its odd harmonics (multiples of the basic frequency).

A complex visual pattern or scene can also be analyzed by the Fourier technique; in this case, frequency components at different angles of orientation are also used. A given spatial frequency can exist at any level of contrast; Figure 10.17C and D show examples of high and low contrast, respectively. To reproduce or perceive a complex pattern or scene accurately, the system has to handle all the spatial frequencies present. If the high frequencies are filtered out, the small details and sharp contrasts are lost; if the low frequencies are filtered out, the large uniform areas and gradual

(A) High-frequency square wave

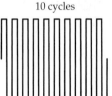

10 cycles

(B) Low-frequency square wave

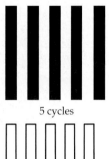

5 cycles

(C) High-contrast sinusoidal spatial grid

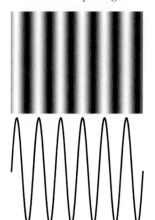

(D) Low-contrast sinusoidal spatial grid

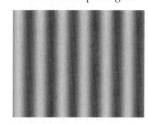

(E) Normal

(F) High frequencies filtered out

(G) Low frequencies filtered out

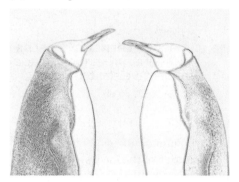

10.17 SPATIAL FREQUENCIES (A, B) The spacing between dark and light stripes shows that the grating in part A has double the spatial frequency of the grating in part B. (C, D) These visual grids show sinusoidal modulation of intensity: (C) high contrast; (D) low contrast. (E) A photograph of two penguins. (F) Filtering out high spatial frequencies fuzzes out edges. (G) Conversely, when low spatial frequencies are filtered out, contrasting edges are emphasized.

Go to Animation 10.4
Spatial Frequencies
bn8e.com/10.4

transitions are lost. **FIGURE 10.17E–G** shows how the filtering of spatial frequencies affects a photograph. The photograph is still recognizable after either the high visual frequencies (Figure 10.17F) or low frequencies (Figure 10.17G) are filtered out.

The suggestion that the nervous system detects different spatial frequencies (F. W. Campbell and Robson, 1968) was soon supported by experiments on selective adaptation to spatial patterns. In these experiments a person spent a minute or more inspecting a visual grating with a given spacing (spatial frequency), such as those in Figure 10.17A and B. Looking at the grating made the cells that are tuned to that frequency adapt (become less sensitive). Then the person's sensitivity to gratings of different spacings was determined.

The results showed that sensitivity to the subsequent gratings was reduced briefly at the particular frequency to which the person had adapted. The suggestion of multiple spatial-frequency channels had revolutionary impact because it led to entirely different conceptions of how the visual system might go about dealing with spatial stimuli. The idea suggests that, rather than specifically detecting such seminatural-istic features as bars and edges, the system is breaking down complex stimuli into their individual spatial-frequency components in a kind of crude Fourier analysis (R. L. De Valois and De Valois, 1988, p. 320). In such a system, we might require a view of the whole face, which includes the low-frequency components, for recognition. This could explain why "Halle Berry neurons" do not respond to small portions of a face, because those have only high-frequency components.

Similarly, Leonardo da Vinci's *Mona Lisa* is famous because sometimes the model seems to be smiling but other times she doesn't (**FIGURE 10.18**). That ambiguity may be due to differences in spatial frequency (Livingstone, 2000). The low-spatial-frequency components of the picture (left two panels in the figure) make it look as if she is smiling, but the high-spatial-frequency components (right) give her a rueful, almost sad expression. As we run our eyes over the original, views from the fovea re-

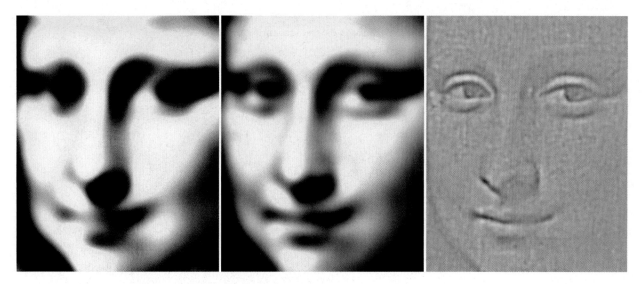

10.18 MONA LISA'S AMBIGUOUS SMILE Leonardo da Vinci's *Mona Lisa* sometimes seems to be smiling, but other times she doesn't. Filtering that reveals very low spatial frequencies (left panel) or moderately low spatial frequencies (middle) makes it look as if she is smiling, but the high-spatial-frequency components (right) make her look almost sad. Is this why when we see her from the corner of our eye, she seems to be smiling, but when we look directly at her mouth, it conveys sadness? (Courtesy of Dr. Margaret Livingstone, Harvard University.)

port the sad, high-frequency components; but views from the peripheral vision, with large receptor fields that can detect only low-frequency components, emphasize the smile (Bohrn et al., 2010). The spatial-frequency approach has proven useful in the analysis of many aspects of human pattern vision, and it provides the basis of high-definition television (HDTV).

Area V1 is involved in the formation of mental images

Neurons of V1 appear to be involved not only in perceiving objects and events, but also in forming mental images. For example, imagined objects activate regions that correspond to the retinotopic mapping of V1; when people imagined small letters, PET recording showed activation of the foveal representation; when they imagined large letters, the parafoveal representation was also activated (Kosslyn et al., 1993).

Impairing the function of V1 through repetitive transcranial magnetic stimulation (rTMS) also affected mental imagery. Before each set of trials in which participants formed and inspected mental images, rTMS was administered for 10 minutes. This stimulation did not prevent the formation of images, but it significantly impaired the process (Kosslyn et al., 1999), thus adding further evidence of the necessity of V1 for the formation of images.

Neurons in the visual cortex beyond area V1 have complex receptive fields and contribute to the identification of forms

Area V1 is only a small part of the portion of cortex that is devoted to vision. Area V1 sends axons to other visual cortical areas, including areas that appear to be involved in the perception of form: V2, V4, and the inferior temporal area (see Figure 10.19C). Some of these extrastriate areas also receive direct input from the LGN. The receptive fields of the cells in many of these extrastriate visual areas are even more complex than those of cells in area V1. Anatomical, physiological, and behavioral investigations with macaque monkeys reveal at least 32 distinct cortical areas that are directly involved in visual function (Van Essen and Drury, 1997) (**FIGURE 10.19A–C**).

The visual areas of the human brain (**FIGURE 10.19D**) have been less thoroughly mapped than those of the monkey brain, and mainly by neuroimaging (the spatial resolution of which is not as fine as that of the electrophysiological recording used in

(A) Macaque brain, lateral view

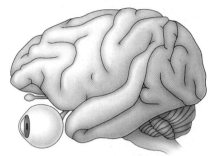

(B) Macaque brain, medial view

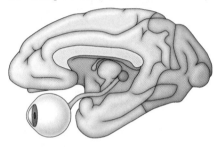

(C) Visual areas in the macaque cortex, unfolded view

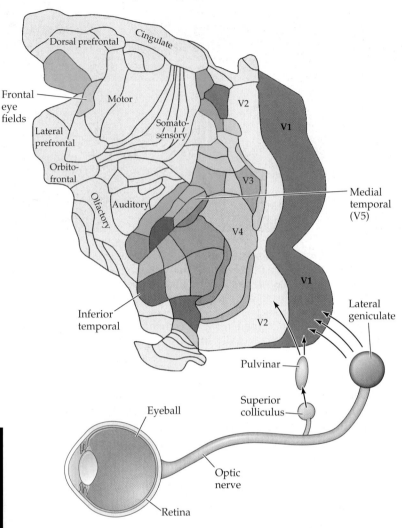

(D) Visual areas in the human occipital cortex, "flattened" by computational techniques

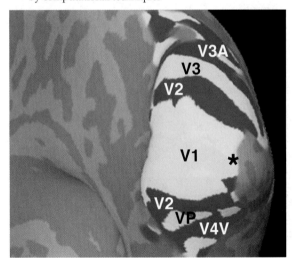

10.19 MAIN VISUAL AREAS IN MONKEY AND HUMAN BRAINS (A, B) Macaque visual areas in occipital and temporal cortex are shown in purple. (C) All the known visual areas of the macaque on a flattened cortex in color. (D) Through computational techniques, the occipital regions of human brain shown in Figure 10.11B were "inflated," flattening the brain and bringing sulci in the cortex to the surface, thus revealing the relative size and extent of various cortical visual areas. The asterisk identifies the representation of the center of the fovea. (Parts A–C after Van Essen and Drury, 1997; D from Tootell et al., 1998, courtesy of Dr. Roger Tootell.)

the monkey brain), but the general layout appears to be similar in the two species, especially for V1 (Tootell et al., 2003).

An astonishing proportion of primate cortex analyzes visual information. The areas that are largely or entirely visual in function occupy about 55% of the surface of the macaque cortex, and about 30% of human cortex (Tootell et al., 2003). We will discuss only a few of the main visual cortical areas and their functions.

Area V2 is adjacent to V1, and many of its cells respond to *textures* in naturalistic scenes (Freeman et al., 2013). Many V2 cells can respond to illusory contours, which may help explain how we perceive contours such as the boundaries of the upright triangle in **FIGURE 10.20** (Peterhans and von der Heydt, 1989). Clearly, such cells respond to complex relations among the parts of their receptive fields.

Area V4 receives axons from V2 and has cells that give their strongest responses to the sinusoidal frequency gratings that we discussed earlier (see Figure 10.17C and D). However, many V4 cells give even stronger responses to concentric and radial stimuli, such as those in **FIGURE 10.21A** (Gallant et al., 1993). Area V4 also has many cells that respond most strongly to wavelength differences, as we will see later when we discuss color vision. Area V5, also called the *medial temporal area*, appears to be specialized for the perception of motion, as we will also discuss later in the chapter.

Most cells in inferior temporal visual cortex do not require a natural object such as a face to activate them; instead, they require moderately complex shapes, sometimes combined with color or texture, such as those in **FIGURE 10.21B**.

Area V1 Is Organized in Columns

The primary visual cortex has separate representations for at least four dimensions of the visual stimulus: (1) location in the visual field, with larger, finer mapping of the central region of the visual field than of the periphery; (2) ocular dominance; (3) orientation; and (4) color.

Ocular dominance columns were first discovered by electrophysiological recording. Although the receptive field of an individual V1 neuron is the same for vision through either eye, some cells are equally activated by the two eyes while other cells respond preferentially (i.e., more strongly) to stimulation of one eye. However, all the cells in a vertical column of cells have the same ocular dominance. The vertical columns are arranged into **ocular dominance slabs** about 0.5 millimeters wide, all cells of which respond preferentially to stimulation of one eye. A given point in the visual field elicits responses in cells in adjacent left-eye-preferring and right-eye-preferring ocular dominance slabs. Ocular dominance is especially clear in layer IV, where each cell is monocular, responding to only one eye. Above and below the (monocular) ocular dominance stripes in layer IV, most of the cells respond to stimulation of both eyes but still prefer one eye over the other.

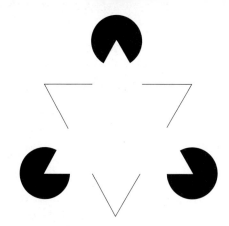

10.20 A GEOMETRIC FIGURE WITH "ILLUSORY" OR "SUBJECTIVE" CONTOURS Cells have been found in visual cortical areas that respond to illusory contours such as those of the upright triangle shown here. These contours thus have neurophysiological meaning.

ocular dominance column A region of cortex in which one eye or the other provides a greater degree of synaptic input.

ocular dominance slab A slab of visual cortex, about 0.5 mm wide, in which the neurons of all layers respond preferentially to stimulation of one eye.

10.21 COMPLEX STIMULI EVOKE STRONG RESPONSES IN VISUAL CORTEX
(A) These concentric and radial stimuli evoke maximal responses from some cells in visual cortical area V4. The stimuli that evoked the highest response rates are shown in red and orange. (B) These 12 examples illustrate the critical features of stimuli that evoke maximal responses from cells in the anterior inferior temporal area. (Part A from Gallant et al., 1993, courtesy of Jack Gallant; B from K. Tanaka, 1993, courtesy of Keiji Tanaka.)

10.22 VISUALIZATION OF OCULAR DOMINANCE COLUMNS AND ORIENTATION COLUMNS BY OPTICAL IMAGING (A) In this method for visualization of ocular dominance, a camera records changes in light reflected from the cortex when the monkey views a twinkling checkerboard with one eye. Small differences in reflected light are amplified, and intensity is coded by color (red for strong intensity, blue for weak). (B) After the recording is processed, regions activated by the active eye are seen as red stripes. (C) In this method for visualization of orientation preference, stimuli at different orientations (vertical, horizontal, diagonal) are presented to reveal groups of neurons that respond most strongly to a particular orientation. The stimuli are usually black or white, but here they are color coded to correspond to color-coded responses to four different orientations combined into a single pattern. (D) Although the pattern at first seems disorderly, closer inspection reveals several regions where four orientations converge in a pinwheel pattern (inset). The foci of pinwheels occur at regular intervals, each orientation is represented only once within a pinwheel, and the sequence of orientations is consistent across pinwheels. (After T. Bonhoeffer and Grinvald, 1991; B and D courtesy of Dr. A. Grinvald.)

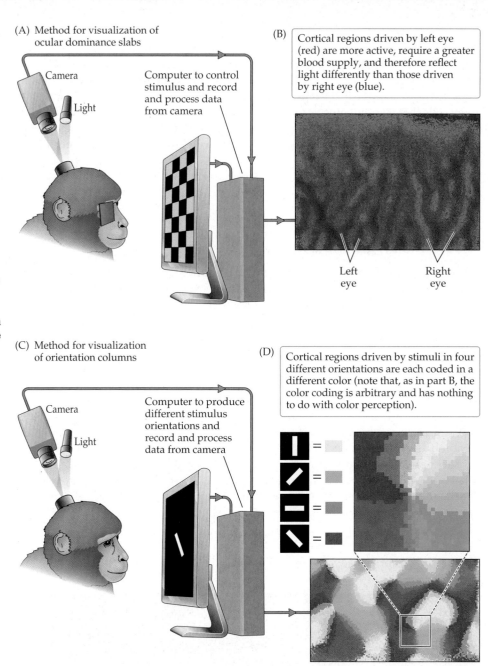

(A) Method for visualization of ocular dominance slabs

Camera
Light
Computer to control stimulus and record and process data from camera

(B) Cortical regions driven by left eye (red) are more active, require a greater blood supply, and therefore reflect light differently than those driven by right eye (blue).

Left eye   Right eye

(C) Method for visualization of orientation columns

Camera
Light
Computer to produce different stimulus orientations and record and process data from camera

(D) Cortical regions driven by stimuli in four different orientations are each coded in a different color (note that, as in part B, the color coding is arbitrary and has nothing to do with color perception).

orientation column A column of visual cortex that responds to rod-shaped stimuli of a particular orientation.

Optical imaging of cortical activity (T. Bonhoeffer and Grinvald, 1991; Ts'o et al., 1990) allows us to see the ocular dominance stripes in the primary visual cortex of an awake monkey (**FIGURE 10.22A AND B**). Ocular dominance columns develop during the first months of life in cats and monkeys. As we saw in Chapter 7, both eyes must be exposed to the visual environment if each eye is to obtain its own cortical representation (see Figure 7.23). Up to the age of 3 or 4 months, human infants are unimpressed by stereograms (pairs of pictures showing somewhat different left-eye and right-eye views that most adult observers perceive as a three-dimensional view). Beginning at the age of 3 or 4 months, however, most infants are captivated by stereograms (Held, 1993). Presumably, before that age the cortex is unable to separate the information from the two eyes because the information reaches the same cortical neurons.

Primary visual cortex has a columnar organization for stimulus orientation as well (**FIGURE 10.22C AND D**). That is, in one **orientation column** all the cells may be "tuned" to upright stimuli (at an orientation of 0°); in an adjacent column, all cells may respond best to another orientation, perhaps at 10° from the vertical; in the next column, perhaps at 25°; and so forth. There are also columns of cells in V1 that respond to particular spatial frequencies (Nauhaus et al., 2012), which we discussed earlier.

These columns are organized parallel to the surface of the cortex. In Figure 10.22D, optical recordings of the surface show the regions of primary visual cortex that respond best to stimuli of four different orientations. Adjacent orientation columns shift by 90°, creating regularly spaced "pinwheels" in which responses to the different stimulus orientations pivot around a center (Paik and Ringach, 2011).

Color Vision Depends on Special Channels from the Retinal Cones through Cortical Area V4

For most people, color is a fundamental aspect of vision. Here we discuss four stages of color perception. In the first stage, the cones—the retinal receptor cells that are specialized to respond to certain wavelengths of light—receive visual information. In the second stage, this information is processed by neurons in the local circuits of the retina, leading to retinal ganglion cells that are excited by light of some wavelengths and inhibited by light of other wavelengths. The ganglion cells send the wavelength information via their axons to the LGN, mainly in the parvocellular layers. From there this information goes to area V1, from which it is relayed to other visual cortical areas, where additional stages of color perception take place.

Color is created by the visual system

What most people mean when they use the term *color* is **hue**, which varies continuously from blue to green, yellow, and red and their intermediates. These hues appear different because the reflected light that reaches our eyes can vary in wavelength (see Box 10.1), and we can detect some of these differences. For about 8% of human males and about 0.5% of human females, however, some of these color distinctions are either absent or at least less striking. Even though the term *color blindness* is commonly used, most people with impaired color vision are able to distinguish some hues. Complete color blindness can be caused by brain lesions or by the congenital absence of specialized receptors, but in humans it is extremely rare.

Animals exhibit different degrees of color vision. Many species of birds, fishes, and insects have excellent color vision. Humans and Old World monkeys also have an excellent ability to discriminate wavelengths, but many other mammals (e.g., cats) cannot discriminate wavelengths very well. We'll see more about the distribution of color vision among mammals later in this chapter.

Perception of hue does not simply depend upon a particular stimulus (a wavelength of light), because we perceive a patch illuminated by a particular wavelength as various different hues, depending on factors such as the intensity of illumination, the surrounding field, and prior exposure to a different stimulus. As illumination fades, the blues in a painting or a rug appear more prominent and the reds appear duller, even though the wavelength distribution in the light has not changed. In addition, the hue perceived at a particular point is strongly affected by the pattern of wavelengths and intensities in other parts of the visual field. For example, our interpretation of a particular hue depends on what we perceive about the light illuminating the scene (**FIGURE 10.23A–C**). To understand how the visual system creates our experience of color, we must understand how cone photoreceptors work.

Color perception requires receptor cells that differ in their sensitivities to different wavelengths

Artists have long known that all the hues can be obtained from a small number of primary colors. On the basis of observations of mixing pigments and lights, scientists at the start of the nineteenth century hypothesized that three separate kinds of receptors in the retina provide the basis for color vision. Endorsed in 1852 by the great physiologist-physicist-psychologist Hermann von Helmholtz, this **trichromatic hypothesis** (from the Greek *tri-*, "three," and *chroma*, "color") became the dominant position.

hue A dimension of light perception, varying around the color circle through blue, green, yellow, orange, and red.

trichromatic hypothesis A hypothesis of color perception stating that there are three different types of cones, each excited by a different region of the spectrum and each having a separate pathway to the brain.

(A)

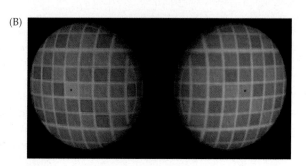
(B)

(C)

10.23 COLOR PERCEPTION

Our perception of color is *not* a simple reflection of the wavelength of light reaching the retina, as the following illusions show. (A) The young woman's two eyes are the same shade of gray in both pictures. But when a red screen is placed over one eye, we perceive the gray eye as blue, while superimposing a blue screen causes us to perceive the gray eye as red. (B) Here the dotted squares in the figures reflect the exact same wavelength of light, but most of us perceive one as green and the other as yellow. (C) The dress that broke the internet. People perceive this dress as either white and gold or as blue and black, depending on how they interpret the lighting of the scene. If you cut a rectangle 2 cm × 1 cm out of a sheet of paper and place the opening over the dress, you'll see it's the same color in the two panels. (Part A courtesy of Dr. Akiyoshi Kitaoka; B courtesy of Drs. Dale Purves and Beau Lotto. C from Lafer-Sousa et al., 2015, courtesy of Dr. Rosa Lafer-Sousa.)

opponent-process hypothesis
The theory that color vision depends on systems that produce opposite responses to light of different wavelengths.

Helmholtz predicted that blue-sensitive, green-sensitive, and red-sensitive receptors would be found; that each would be sharply tuned to its part of the spectrum; and that each type would have a separate path to the brain. The color of an object would be recognized, then, on the basis of which color receptors were activated. This system would be like the mechanisms for discriminating touch and temperature on the basis of which skin receptors and labeled neural lines are activated (see Chapter 8).

Later in the nineteenth century, physiologist Ewald Hering proposed a different explanation. He argued, on the basis of visual experience, that there are four unique hues and three opposed pairs of colors—blue versus yellow, green versus red, and black versus white—and that three physiological processes with opposed positive and negative values must therefore be the basis of color vision. As we will see, both this **opponent-process hypothesis** and the trichromatic hypothesis are encompassed in current color vision theory, but neither of the old hypotheses is sufficient by itself.

Measurements of photopigments in cones have borne out the trichromatic hypothesis, in part. Each cone of the human retina has one of three types of pigments. These pigments do not, however, have the narrow spectral distributions that Helmholtz predicted. The color system that Helmholtz postulated would have given rather poor color vision and poor visual acuity. Color vision would be poor because only a few different hues would be discriminable; within the long-wavelength region of the spectrum, there would be only red, not the whole range of hues that we see. Acuity would be poor because the grain of the retinal mosaic would be coarse; a red stimulus would be able to affect only one-third of the receptors. (In reality, though, acuity is as good in red light as it is in white light.)

The human visual system does not have receptors that are sensitive to only a narrow part of the visible spectrum. Two of the three retinal cone pigments show some response to light of almost *any* wavelength. The pigments have different *peaks* of sensitivity, but even the peaks are not as far apart as Helmholtz predicted. As **FIGURE 10.24** shows, the cone pigment peaks occur at about 420 nanometers (nm) (in the part of the spectrum where we usually see violet under photopic conditions), about 530 nm (where most of us see green), and about 560 nm (where most of us see yellow-green). Despite Helmholtz's prediction, none of the curves peak in the

long-wavelength part of the spectrum, where most of us see red (about 630 nm).

Under ordinary conditions, almost any visual object stimulates at least two kinds of cones, thus ensuring high visual acuity and good perception of form. The spectral sensitivities of the three cone types differ from each other, and the nervous system detects and processes these *differences between cones* to extract the color information. Thus, certain ganglion cells and certain cells at higher stations in the visual system are color-specific, even though the receptor cells are not. Similarly, photoreceptors are not form-specific (they respond to single points of light), but form is detected later in the system by comparison of the outputs of different receptors.

Because the cones are not color detectors, the most appropriate brief names for them can be taken from their peak areas of wavelength sensitivity: *short* (S) for the receptor with peak sensitivity at about 420 nm, *medium* (M) for peak sensitivity at about 530 nm, and *long* (L) for 560 nm (see Figure 10.24). There are typically twice as many L as M receptors, but far fewer S receptors (Brainard et al., 2000; Carroll et al., 2000); this difference explains why acuity is much lower with short-wavelength illumination (blue light) than in the other parts of the visible spectrum. Inheriting genes that cannot produce functional opsins (sometimes called *photopigments*) can affect color discrimination, as **BOX 10.3** explains.

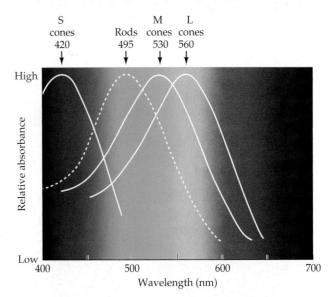

10.24 SPECTRAL SENSITIVITIES OF HUMAN PHOTO-PIGMENTS Each pigment has a different *peak* sensitivity (S, short-wavelength; M, medium-wavelength; L, long-wavelength) but responds to a wide range of wavelengths. Knowing only that an M cone is active, you cannot tell whether it was stimulated by weak light at 530 nm ("green") or by strong light anywhere from 450 nm ("blue") to 620 nm ("red"). Only by *comparing* responses of *different* cones can the brain extract color information.

BOX 10.3 Most Mammalian Species Have Some Color Vision

Animals exhibit different degrees of color vision. Many species of birds, fishes, and insects have excellent color vision. Humans and Old World monkeys also have an excellent ability to discriminate wavelengths, but many other mammals (e.g., cats) cannot discriminate wavelengths very well. Still, most mammals have at least some degree of color vision (G. H. Jacobs, 1993). Although only certain primates have good *trichromatic* color vision based on *three* classes of cone photopigments (each of which is an opsin), most mammalian species have at least *dichromatic* color vision (based on *two* classes of cone pigments). Most so-called color-blind humans (actually color-*deficient* humans) have dichromatic vision and can distinguish short-wavelength stimuli (blue) from long-wavelength stimuli (not blue). When a gene encoding a third photopigment was introduced into photoreceptors of adult male squirrel monkeys with such dichromatic vision, they soon displayed excellent trichromatic vision (Mancuso et al., 2009). Likewise,

introducing photopigment genes in adult mice (G. H. Jacobs et al., 2007) enabled them to discriminate colors they normally could not see, so it may be possible to correct dichromatic vision in people one day (Neitz and Neitz, 2014).

There is a continuum of color vision capabilities, including at least four categories among mammalian species:

1. *Excellent trichromatic color vision* is found in diurnal primates such as humans and the rhesus monkey.

2. *Robust dichromatic color vision* is found in species that have two kinds of cone photopigments and a reasonably large population of cones. Examples of such species include the dog, the pig, and males of the South American squirrel monkey.

3. *Feeble dichromatic color vision* occurs in species that have two kinds of cone pigments but very few cones. An example is the domestic cat.

4. *Minimal color vision* is possessed by species that have only a single kind of cone pigment and that must rely on interactions between rods and

cones to discriminate wavelength. Examples include the owl monkey and the raccoon.

Among those species of South American monkeys that are generally dichromats, some females are actually trichromatic. Why? Because the gene encoding one photopigment is on the X chromosome. Since females have two X chromosomes, if the two chromosomes carry *different* genes for the photopigment, the female will possess a total of three different kinds of cones and will therefore have trichromatic vision.

Unlike South American monkeys that carry a single gene on the X chromosome for photopigment, many other primates, like humans, have *two different* photopigment genes on the X chromosome: one for medium- and one for long-wavelength cones. The short-wavelength photopigment gene is on an autosome rather than on the X. Women are less likely than men to have color deficiency, because if one of their X chromosomes has a defective gene for a photopigment, the copy on the other X is likely to be fine.

(continued)

BOX 10.3

Most Mammalian Species Have Some Color Vision (continued)

(A)

(B)

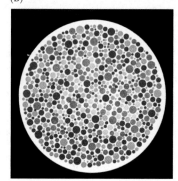

SIMULATING COLOR BLINDNESS   The photograph on the right has been adjusted to simulate the experience of the most common form of color blindness in humans, which is the absence of cones sensitive to medium-wavelength light (M cones). For such individuals, the world's colors consist of blue (detected by short-wavelength photopigment encoded on chromosome 7) and *not* blue (detected by the long-wavelength photopigment encoded on the X chromosome). (B) In a typical test for color vision, dichromats may have a difficult time detecting the numerals displayed in a figure like this. (A [right] was produced by software available from Vischeck [vischeck.com]).

Because men have only one X, if they have a defective copy of the gene for the medium- or long-wavelength pigment, there's no backup copy to compensate. They will see blue (light stimulating the short-wavelength cones) and not blue (light stimulating the other functioning cones), as the figure illustrates. A company selling special glasses that correct this type of color deficiency explains the technology on their website (EnChroma.com/technology).

Interestingly, a woman may carry slightly different genes for the long-wavelength photopigment on her two X chromosomes (Neitz et al., 1998) and therefore have *four* different kinds of cones. Such so-called *tetra*chromats tend to be very good at discriminating colors and very sensitive to clashing colors (G. Jordan et al., 2010). It's interesting to speculate whether such women have a different experience of, for example, green than those of us who are trichromats and dichromats. We will take up the question of our subjective experience of color again in Chapter 18. For a real mind-bender, consider what color perception might be like for mantis shrimp, which have 12 different photoreceptors, each responding to a different range of wavelengths (Thoen et al., 2014)!

Some retinal ganglion cells and parvocellular LGN cells show spectral opponency

Recordings made from retinal ganglion cells in Old World monkeys reveal the second stage of processing of color vision. Most ganglion cells and cells in the parvocellular layers of the LGN fire in response to some wavelengths and are inhibited by other wavelengths. In other words, they show the sort of opponent process that Hering predicted.

FIGURE 10.25A shows the response of an LGN cell as a large spot of light centered on its receptive field changes from one wavelength to another. The neuron responds to wavelengths above 600 nm, where the L cones are most sensitive, and is inhibited at shorter wavelengths, where the L cones are less sensitive than the M cones. A cell exhibiting this response pattern is therefore called a *plus L/minus M*

10.25 RESPONSES OF THE FOUR MAIN TYPES OF SPECTRALLY OPPONENT CELLS IN MONKEY LGN

The four main types of spectrally opponent cells are (A) +L/−M, (B) +M/−L, (C) +(L+M)/−S, and (D) +S/−(L+M). Each type is excited by one band of wavelengths and inhibited by another.

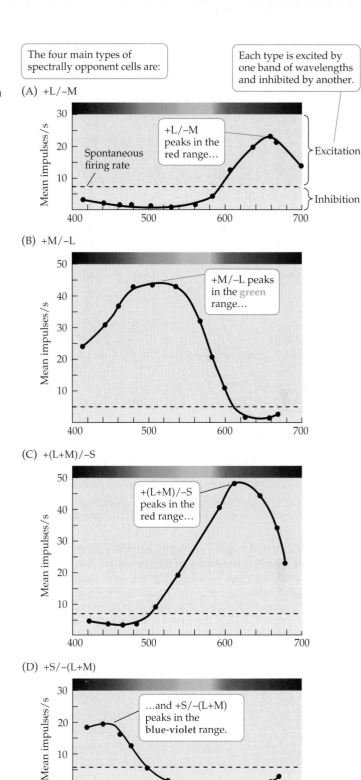

The four main types of spectrally opponent cells are:

Each type is excited by one band of wavelengths and inhibited by another.

(A) +L/−M

Spontaneous firing rate

+L/−M peaks in the red range...

Excitation

Inhibition

(B) +M/−L

+M/−L peaks in the green range...

(C) +(L+M)/−S

+(L+M)/−S peaks in the red range...

(D) +S/−(L+M)

...and +S/−(L+M) peaks in the blue-violet range.

Wavelength (nm)

cell (+L/−M). This is an example of a **spectrally opponent cell** because two regions of the spectrum have opposite effects on the rate at which the neuron fires action potentials.

Each spectrally opponent ganglion cell receives input from two or three different kinds of cones through bipolar cells. The connections from at least one type of cone are excitatory, and those from at least one other type are inhibitory. The spectrally opponent ganglion cells thus record the *difference* in stimulation of different populations of cones. For example, a plus M/minus L (+M/−L) cell responds to the difference in the excitation of M and L cones.

The peaks of the sensitivity curves of the M and L cones are not very different (see Figure 10.24). However, whereas the M-minus-L difference curve (**FIGURE 10.25B**) shows a clear peak at about 500 nm (in the green part of the spectrum), the L-minus-M difference function (see Figure 10.25A) shows a peak at about 650 nm (in the red part of the spectrum). Thus, +M/−L and +L/−M cells yield distinctly different neural response curves. LGN cells excited by the L and M cells but inhibited by S cells—that is, +(L+M)/−S cells—peak in the red range (**FIGURE 10.25C**); while cells excited by S but inhibited by L and M—that is, +S/−(L+M) cells—peak in the blue-violet range (**FIGURE 10.25D**). These spectrally opponent neurons are the second stage in the system for color perception, but they still cannot be called *color cells*, because their peak wavelength sensitivities do not correspond precisely to the wavelengths that we see as the principal hues.

FIGURE 10.26 diagrams the presumed inputs to not only the four kinds of spectrally opponent ganglion cells, but also the ganglion cells that detect brightness and darkness. The brightness detectors receive stimulation from both M and L cones (+M/+L); the darkness detectors are inhibited by both M and L cones (−M/−L).

In the monkey LGN, 70–80% of the cells are spectrally opponent; in the cat, very few spectrally opponent cells are found—only about 1%. This difference explains why it is easy to train monkeys to discriminate wavelengths, and why it is so hard to train cats to notice even large differences in wavelength.

Some visual cortical cells and regions appear to be specialized for color perception

In the cortex, spectral information appears to be used for various kinds of information processing. Forms are segregated from their background by differences in color or intensity (or both). The most important role that color plays in our perception is to denote which parts of a complex image belong to one object and which belong to another. Some animals use displays of brightly colored body parts to call attention to themselves, but color can also be used as camouflage.

spectrally opponent cell A visual receptor cell that has opposite firing responses to different regions of the spectrum.

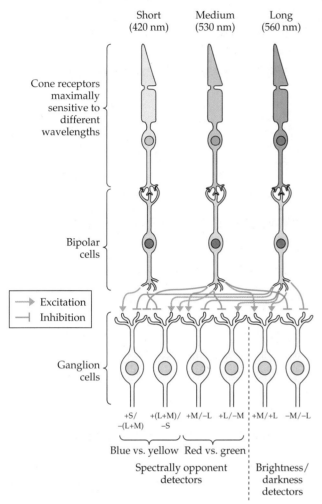

Short
(420 nm)

Medium
(530 nm)

Long
(560 nm)

Cone receptors
maximally
sensitive to
different
wavelengths

Bipolar
cells

→ Excitation
⊣ Inhibition

Ganglion
cells

+S/
−(L+M)

+(L+M)/
−S

+M/−L

+L/−M

+M/+L

−M/−L

Blue vs. yellow   Red vs. green

Spectrally opponent
detectors

Brightness/
darkness
detectors

10.26 A MODEL OF THE CONNECTIONS OF WAVE-LENGTH DISCRIMINATION SYSTEMS IN THE PRIMATE RETINA The connections from the cones yield four kinds of spectrally opponent ganglion cells, as well as ganglion cells that detect brightness or darkness. (After R. L. De Valois and De Valois, 1980.)

Some *spectrally opponent cortical cells* contribute to the perception of color, providing the third stage of the color vision system. Adding and subtracting the outputs of spectrally opponent ganglion cells can yield cortical cells that are perceptually opponent: red versus green, blue versus yellow, and black versus white (R. L. De Valois and De Valois, 1993). The spectral responses of these cells correspond to the wavelengths of the principal hues specified by human observers. Visual cortical region V4 is particularly rich in color-sensitive cells (Schein and Desimone, 1990). These cells provide a fourth stage of color perception that may be important for color constancy and for discrimination between a figure and background (Zeki et al., 1991), but cells in V4 are also tuned in the spatial domain, for orientation and for spatial frequency (Tanigawa et al., 2010).

Perception of Visual Motion Is Analyzed by a Special System That Includes Cortical Area V5

Some retinal ganglion cells respond preferentially to a certain direction of motion of objects; for example, they may respond to stimuli that move to the left but not to stimuli that move to the right (Barlow and Levick, 1965). Motion is analyzed by the cortex, partly in regions close to those that control eye movements. In monkeys, all of the neurons in area V5 (also called the *medial temporal area* or *MT*; see Figure 10.19C) respond to moving visual stimuli, indicating that they are specialized for the perception of motion and its direction. PET studies show that moving stimuli also evoke responses in human area V5.

Experimental lesions of area V5 in monkeys trained to report the direction of perceived motion impaired their performance, at least temporarily (Newsome et al., 1985). Altering the activity of V5 neurons can affect a monkey's perception of movement. Electrically stimulating an area of V5 that normally responds to stimuli moving upward caused the monkeys to report that dots on the screen were moving upward even when they were actually moving in another direction.

One striking case study described a woman who had lost the ability to perceive motion after a stroke damaged her area V5 (Zihl et al., 1983). The woman was unable to perceive continuous motion and saw only separate, successive still images. This impairment led to many problems in her daily life. She had difficulty crossing streets, because she could not follow the positions of automobiles in motion: "When I'm looking at the car at first, it seems far away. But then when I want to cross the road, suddenly the car is very near." She also complained of difficulties in following conversations because she could not see the movements of speakers' lips.

The Many Cortical Visual Areas Are Organized into Two Major Streams

Many investigators have wondered why primate visual systems contain so many distinct regions. Certain regions specialize in processing different attributes of visual experience (such as shape, location, color, motion, and orientation). But the number of visual fields—over 30—is larger than the number of basic attributes. Perhaps the reason that so many separate visual regions have been found is simply that investigators, being visually oriented primates themselves, have lavished special attention on the visual system.

Earlier work with hamsters led to the hypothesis that there are two visual systems: one, for *identification* of objects, involves especially the visual cortex; the other, for *location* of objects, involves especially the superior colliculus (Kravitz et al., 2011). Mortimer Mishkin and Leslie Ungerleider (1982) proposed that primates also have two main cortical processing streams, both originating in primary visual cortex: a ventral processing stream responsible for visually identifying objects, and a dorsal stream responsible for perceiving the location of objects and for guiding movement toward them (**FIGURE 10.27**). These processing streams were called, respectively, the *what* and *where* streams (Ungerleider et al., 1998). The two streams are not completely separate, because there are normally many cross-connections between them. In the ventral stream, including regions of the occipitotemporal, and inferior temporal areas, information about faces is analyzed (Courtney et al., 1996), as we'll discuss in further detail in Chapter 18.

These separate visual cortical streams help us understand the case of patient D.F., described at the start of this chapter. Recall that after carbon monoxide poisoning, she lost the ability to perceive faces and objects while retaining the ability to reach and grasp under visual control. The investigators who studied her (A. D. Milner et al., 1991) hypothesized that D.F.'s ventral visual stream had been devastated but that her dorsal stream was unimpaired. An opposite kind of dissociation had already been reported: damage to the posterior parietal cortex often results in **optic ataxia** in which patients have difficulty using vision to reach for and grasp objects, yet these patients may retain the ability to correctly identify objects (Perenin and Vighetto, 1988).

Investigation with MRI supports the idea that D.F.'s ventral stream was damaged while her dorsal stream was relatively unaffected (T. W. James et al., 2003). High-resolution MRI of D.F.'s brain (**FIGURE 10.28A**) reveals damage concentrating in the ventrolateral occipital cortex. Throughout her brain, there is evidence of atrophy, indi-

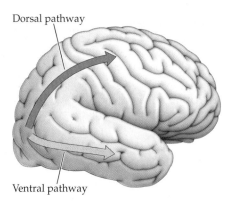

10.27 PARALLEL PROCESSING PATHWAYS IN THE VISUAL SYSTEM The dorsal *where* pathway (shown in blue) and the ventral *what* pathway (shown in yellow) serve different functions.

optic ataxia Difficulty using vision to reach and manipulate objects.

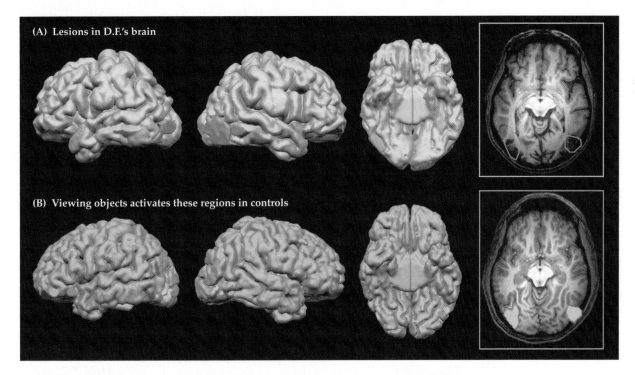

10.28 OBJECT RECOGNITION CENTERS IN THE BRAIN (A) In this reconstruction from MRI images, the brain region that was damaged in patient D.F. (blue) is seen from lateral views and from below (outlined in orange on the right). (B) In neurologically intact people, this same brain region is activated (yellow) when they are looking at recognizably intact pictures of various objects rather than scrambled pictures. D.F.'s inability to recognize the objects she sees appears to be due to the damage to this region on the border of the occipital and temporal cortices. (From T. W. James et al., 2003, courtesy of Dr. Thomas James.)

mirror neuron A neuron that is active both when an individual makes a particular movement and when that individual sees another individual make that same movement.

myopia Nearsightedness; the inability to focus the retinal image of objects that are far away.

cated by shrunken gyri and enlarged sulci. **FIGURE 10.28B** shows the area activated in fMRI recordings when controls viewed pictures of objects; it corresponds to D.F.'s lateral occipital lesion. When D.F. reached for and grasped objects, her fMRI activation in the parietal lobe was similar to that of controls, indicating that her dorsal stream is largely intact. D.F.'s intact dorsal pathway not only tells her where objects are but also guides her movements to use these objects properly.

It is still puzzling that one part of D.F. knows exactly how to grasp a pencil put before her, while another part of her—the part that talks to you—has no idea whether it's a pencil, a ruler, or a bouquet of flowers. Imagining what this disjointed visual experience must be like for D.F. allows us to appreciate how effortlessly our brains usually bind together information to give us the marvelous sense of sight.

The anterior part of the dorsal stream includes mirror neurons

The anterior part of the dorsal visual stream merges with the motor cortex and includes neurons that have both visual and motor functions. These neurons were discovered by investigators who were recording the activity of neurons in the motor cortex of monkeys. To their surprise, the investigators found cells that fired not only when the monkey grasped and moved an object but also when the monkey observed *another monkey*, or even a person, grasping and moving an object.

It took the investigators several years to believe and publish their finding (Di Pelligrino et al., 1992). They proposed that these **mirror neurons** mediate the understanding of actions performed by others: when an individual sees an action performed by another, neurons that represent that action are activated in the observer's premotor cortex (see Figure 11.18) (Rizzolatti and Craighero, 2004).

Several studies provide data for the existence of a mirror neuron system in humans (e.g., Buccino et al., 2004). The discovery of mirror neurons has stimulated much research and speculation, so you are likely to see more about them in the future. The mirror neuron system has been related to topics as varied as empathy, learning by imitation, and the evolution of language; damage to the mirror neuron system has been proposed as a cause of autism, which is characterized by impairments in understanding other people's behavior. We will consider additional aspects of mirror neurons in Chapter 11 in the context of the motor system.

Visual Neuroscience Can Be Applied to Alleviate Some Visual Deficiencies

We humans are a very vision-oriented species, so it's no surprise that a great deal of research effort goes into finding ways to prevent impairment, to improve inadequate vision, and to restore sight to the blind. In the United States, half a million people are blind. Recent medical advances have reduced some causes of blindness but have increased blindness from other causes. For example, medical advances permit people with diabetes to live longer, but because we don't know how to prevent blindness associated with diabetes, there are more people alive today with diabetes-induced blindness. We'll first consider ways of avoiding impairment of vision. Then we'll take up ways of training that are designed to improve an impaired visual system.

Impairment of vision often can be prevented or reduced

Studies of the development of vision in children and nonhuman animals show that the incidence of **myopia** (nearsightedness, from the Greek *myein*, "to be closed," and *ops*, "eye") can be reduced. Myopia develops if the eyeball is too long, causing the eye to focus objects in front of the retina rather than on the retina (**FIGURE 10.29**). As a result, distant objects appear blurred. Considerable evidence suggests that the reason some children develop myopia is that certain environmental factors cause the eyeball to grow excessively. Previously it was thought that the modern habit of looking closely at nearby objects (books, computer screens, and so on) might be responsible for myopia (Marzani and Wallman, 1997), but mounting evidence suggests that indoor lighting may be to blame.

(A) Normal vision   (B) Myopia   (C) Myopia with correction

Glasses or contacts correct focus to restore a sharp image on the retina.

In myopia, the eyeball is too long, so the image reaching the retina is blurred.

10.29 FOCUSING IMAGES ON THE RETINA (A) Normally, the cornea and lens refract light to focus a sharp image of the outside world on the retina. (B) In myopia, the eyeball is too long, so the image is in focus in front of the retina. In this case, the image that actually reaches the retina is blurred. (C) Eyeglasses refract the light before it reaches the cornea, to bring the image into sharp focus on the retina.

Before civilization, most people spent the bulk of their time outdoors, looking at objects illuminated by sunlight. But with the advent of indoor lighting, we've come to spend a lot of time looking at things with light that, while containing many wavelengths, does not exactly match the composition of sunlight and is much less bright than outdoor light. Several studies found that children with myopia spend less time outdoors than do other children, but that correlation could be caused by genes that favor both myopia and indoor activities, like reading. Indeed, the advent of public schools in various nations is accompanied by increased rates of myopia. However, one of these studies focused on people of Chinese origin who lived in either Singapore, where crowded conditions mean that people spend little time outdoors, or Sydney, Australia. Even though these populations should be genetically very similar, 30% of the Chinese children living in Singapore, who average only 30 minutes a day outdoors, were myopic, versus only 3% of those living in Sydney, who average 2 hours a day outdoors (Rose et al., 2008). What's more, in these populations myopia correlates much more strongly with time spent indoors than with time spent reading. In another study, requiring Taiwanese children to spend their entire 80 minutes of recess outdoors significantly reduced the incidence of myopia compared with a nearby control school (Wu et al., 2013).

Of course, too much sunlight can be a bad thing, especially for our skin. But researchers note that almost all children in Australia wear hats to shield their faces when outdoors, yet they still benefit from being outdoors in terms of avoiding myopia. Likewise, there's no evidence that wearing glasses blocks the benefit of light from the sun. The next challenge will be determining what it is about indoor lighting, as opposed to sunlight, that encourages the eyeball in children to grow excessively, leading to myopia. One possibility is simply the higher illumination levels encountered outdoors, since greater light exposure can slow experimentally induced myopia in animals (Norton and Siegwart, 2013).

Increased exercise can restore function to a previously deprived or neglected eye

In Chapter 7 we considered the misalignment of the two eyes (*lazy eye*), which can lead to the condition called **amblyopia** (from the Greek *amblys*, "dull" or "blunt," and *ops*, "eye"), in which acuity is poor in one eye even though the eye and retina are normal. If the two eyes are not aligned properly during the first few years of life, the primary visual cortex of the child tends to suppress the information that arrives in the cortex from one eye, and that eye becomes functionally blind. Studies of the development of vision in children and other animals also show that most cases of amblyopia are avoidable.

amblyopia Reduced visual acuity of one eye, that is not caused by optical or retinal impairments.

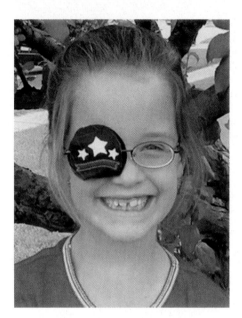

10.30 HEY THERE, YOU WITH THE STARS IN YOUR EYE As a treatment for amblyopia, this girl is wearing a patch over her "good" eye—the one she has been relying on while ignoring information from her other, "weak" eye. Visual experience through the weak eye will strengthen its influence on the cortex.

The balance of the eye muscles can be surgically adjusted to bring the two eyes into better alignment. Alternatively, if the weak eye is given regular practice, with the good eye covered, then vision can be preserved in both eyes. Attempts to alleviate amblyopia by training, however, have produced mixed results and a great deal of controversy. In a study sponsored by the American Academy of Ophthalmology, 507 patients, age 7–17, were separated at random into two groups. The participants in one group were given eyeglasses. Those in the other group were given not only eyeglasses but also a patch covering the good eye (**FIGURE 10.30**), and they participated in visual exercises for 26 weeks. One-fourth of those who received only eyeglasses showed improvement, but among those who also had eye patches and engaged in visual exercises, half improved (Pediatric Eye Disease Investigator Group, 2005).

Other studies have reported considerable improvement, even with adults, if the eye is exercised sufficiently and if the amblyopia is not too severe. In Chapter 7 we saw that Michael May, who was blind from the age of 3 to 46, regained some aspects of vision quickly following surgery to let light back into one of his eyes. Other aspects, such as depth perception and the perception of faces, remain severely impaired.

Frequent causes of visual impairment, especially with age, include diseases that damage the rods and cones. A variety of strategies are being followed to reverse these disorders, representing a cutting edge of visual science, as we'll discuss next.

◼ The Cutting Edge

Seeing the Light

Macular degeneration is a visual impairment caused by damage to the retina, specifically the photoreceptors. The most common type, "dry" macular degeneration, is caused by atrophy of the retinal pigmented epithelium (see Figure 10.2B), resulting in death of the overlying photoreceptors. In the more severe, "wet" macular degeneration, abnormal growth of retinal capillaries leads to detachment of the retina and/or death of photoreceptors.

It might be possible to restore vision in these cases by transplanting new photoreceptors to replace those that have been lost. In one dramatic "proof of principle," scientists were able to provide vision to mice with a mutation that had disabled their rod photoreceptors (R. A. Pearson et al., 2012). The scientists gathered retinas from normal mice that were 3 days old, then injected the young rod cells into the retinas of the mutant adults. Some of the transplanted rod cells integrated into the retinal circuitry (**FIGURE 10.31A**). To test whether the transplanted rods actually allowed the mice to see, each animal was surrounded by computer monitors showing black vertical bars moving either clockwise or counterclockwise, to determine whether the mouse would move its head to follow the bars (**FIGURE 10.31B**). The researchers could vary the contrast of the bars to ask how much contrast was needed before the mouse could see them. They could also vary the width of the bars to measure the animal's visual acuity—how wide the bars must be for the mouse to see them (**FIGURE 10.31C**). These measures of each individual mouse's contrast sensitivity and acuity correlated with how many rods had integrated into its retinas (**FIGURE 10.31D**). Because the extent of vision following the procedure actually reflects the transplanted rods, the current challenge is how to maximize the number of rods that get incorporated into the retina.

Thus it may be possible someday to restore vision in people who have lost their photoreceptors to macular degeneration, but the big problem is where to get young human photoreceptors (Schwartz et al., 2012). It might be possible to culture cells from a blind person needing a transplant and get the cells to differentiate into photoreceptors. Then these transformed photoreceptors could be injected back into the blind person's eyes.

An alternative method for restoring vision does not require introducing more cells at all. One study used viruses to induce retinal bipolar cells to express a light-sensitive ion channel (channelrhodopsin, which we discussed in The Cutting Edge of Chapter 3). Then the bipolar cells themselves fired in response to light, without need of photoreceptor cells to stimulate them. This procedure restored vision in several mouse models of blindness, including mice that had no photoreceptor cells (Doroudchi et al., 2011).

macular degeneration A progressive loss of central vision due to death or obstruction of photoreceptors in the retina.

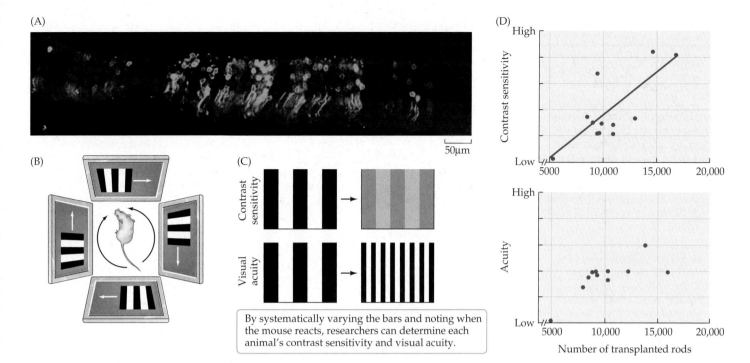

10.31 TRANSPLANTED PHOTORECEPTORS ALLOW BLIND MICE TO SEE (A) Pearson et al. (2012) harvested photoreceptors from 3-day-old mice and transplanted them into adult mice with a mutation that eliminates photoreceptors. After a few weeks, the transplanted rods (green cells) were integrated into the retina, making synaptic contact with bipolar cells and horizontal cells. (B) To see if the transplanted photoreceptors provided the blind mice with vision, the animals were placed in a chamber surrounded by computer monitors that displayed bars moving around the mouse, either clockwise or counterclockwise. If the mouse moved its head to follow the bars, that demonstrated that it could see them. (C) The bars could be systematically altered to vary either contrast (top) or spatial frequency (bottom) to measure each animal's contrast sensitivity and acuity. (D) There was a correlation between the number of integrated rod cells found in an individual mouse's retina and the animal's contrast sensitivity and acuity. Efforts are under way to optimize the procedures to provide as many rods as possible. (After Pearson et al., 2012.)

Recommended Reading

De Valois, R. L., and De Valois, K. K. (1988). *Spatial Vision.* New York: Oxford University Press.

Dowling, J. E., and Dowling, J. L. (2016). *Vision: How It Works and What Can Go Wrong.* Cambridge, MA: MIT Press.

Ings, S. (2008). *A Natural History of Seeing: The Art and Science of Vision.* New York: Norton.

Purves, D., and Lotto, R. B. (2011). *Why We See What We Do Redux: A Wholly Empirical Theory of Vision.* Sunderland, MA: Sinauer.

Sacks, O. (2010). *The Mind's Eye.* New York: Knopf.

Schiller, P. H., and Tehovnik, E. J. (2015). *Vision and the Visual System.* New York: Oxford University Press.

Wolfe, J. M., Kluender, K. R., Levi, D. M., Bartoshuk, L. M., et al. (2015). *Sensation & Perception* (4th ed.). Sunderland, MA: Sinauer.

Go to
bn8e.com
for study questions,
quizzes, activities,
and other resources

VISUAL SUMMARY

You should be able to relate each summary to the adjacent illustration, including structures and processes.
Go to **bn8e.com/vs10** for links to figures, animations, and activities that will help you consolidate the material.

1 Light is bent, or **refracted**, by the transparent outer layer of the eye, the **cornea**, focusing an image on the **retina** in the back of the eye. We vary the thickness of the **lens** to fine-tune that refraction, sharpening the focus of the image. The image on the retina is upside down and reversed. Review **Figure 10.1**, **Activity 10.1**

2 The retina contains two different types of **photoreceptors** to detect light forming the focused image. **Rods** are very sensitive, working even in very low light, and respond to light of any wavelength. They drive the **scotopic** system, which can work in dim light. Each of the three different types of **cones** responds better to some wavelengths of light than others, allowing us to detect colors. The cones provide information for the **photopic system**, which needs more light to function. Photoreceptors **adapt** to function across a wide range of light intensities. Review **Figures 10.2–10.6**, **Table 10.1**

3 The retina consists of layers of neurons, with the photoreceptors in the very back stimulating **bipolar cells**, which stimulate **ganglion cells**. The ganglion cells of the retina project their axons to the brain via the **optic nerve**. **Amacrine cells** and **horizontal cells** communicate across the retina, using processes such as **lateral inhibition** to analyze brightness. Review **Figures 10.2, 10.6–10.8**

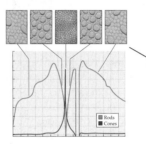

4 The center of our **visual field** lands on the **fovea**, the portion of the retina with the greatest density of photoreceptors, an absence of overlying cell layers, and more direct synaptic connections to ganglion cells, providing us with our greatest **visual acuity** (sharpness of vision). Cones are concentrated in the fovea, and rods in the peripheral retina, so our peripheral vision is best for seeing dim objects but provides no color information. Review **Figures 10.5, 10.9–10.11**, **Animation 10.2**

5 The left visual field falls upon the nasal retina of the left eye and the temporal retina of the right eye. Only nasal retinal ganglion cells of each eye send their axons across the midline, forming the **optic chiasm**, so the left visual field projects to the right hemisphere and the right visual field projects to the left hemisphere. Review **Figures 10.9 and 10.10**

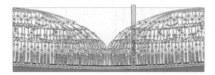

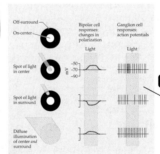

6 The **receptive fields** of bipolar cells and ganglion cells consist of a circular center and a surround that have opposing effects: either **on-center/off surround** or **off-center/on-surround**. Review **Figures 10.12 and 10.13**, **Animation 10.3**

7 Ganglion cells of the retina synapse upon neurons in the **lateral geniculate nucleus (LGN)** of the thalamus. The LGN neurons send axons to synapse on neurons in layer IV of the **primary visual cortex** (also called **V1** or **striate cortex**) in the **occipital lobe**. V1 sends information to many different cortical areas, called **extrastriate cortex** (nearly one-third of the human cortex), to further analyze visual information. Review **Figures 10.14 and 10.19**

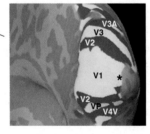

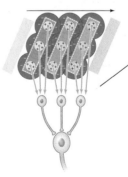

8 Receptive fields of cells at successively higher levels in the visual system change in two main ways: (1) they become larger (occupy larger parts of the visual field), and (2) they require increasingly specific stimuli to evoke responses. For example, they best respond to a bar of light at a particular angle, or bars that move in a particular direction. Review **Figures 10.15–10.22**, **Animation 10.4**

9 Our detection of **hue** (color) depends on the three different cone **opsins**, or photopigments. Each cone responds to a wide range of wavelengths, not just a single color. Our perception of hue results from the relative activity of each type of cone. One way of assessing this *relative activity* is by retinal connections that yield **spectrally opponent** retinal ganglion cells. Review **Figures 10.23–10.26**

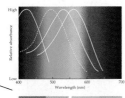

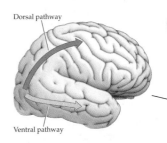

10 Visual cortical areas are organized into two main streams: a dorsal *where* stream that serves in location and visuomotor skills, and a ventral *what* stream that serves in the recognition of faces and objects. Review **Figures 10.27 and 10.28**

11 Myopia (near-sightedness) results when the eyeball is too long to focus the visual image onto the retina properly. Prolonged exposure to indoor lighting during childhood may favor such growth. Review **Figure 10.29.**

12 Treating **amblyopia** works best when the retraining starts early in life, but the visual nervous system retains some plasticity even in adults. Review **Figures 10.30–10.31**

Motor Control and Plasticity

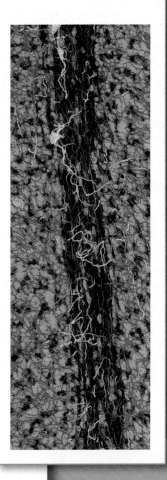

11

■ What You See Is What You Get ───────────

Ian Waterman had a perfectly ordinary life until he caught a viral infection at age 19. For reasons that no one understands, the infection targeted a very specific set of nerves sending information from his body to his brain. Ian can still feel pain or deep pressure, as well as warm and cool surfaces on his skin, but he has no sensation of light touch below his neck. What's more, although Ian can still move all of his muscles, he receives no information about muscle activity or body position (Cole, 1995). You might think this deficiency wouldn't cause any problem, because you've probably never thought much about your "body sense"; it's not even one of the five senses that people talk about, is it?

In fact, however, the loss of this information was devastating. Ian couldn't walk across a room without falling down, and he couldn't walk up or down stairs. The few other people suffering a loss like this spent the rest of their lives in wheelchairs. But Ian was young and determined, so he started teaching himself how to walk using another source of feedback about his body: his vision. Now, as long as the lights are on, Ian can carefully watch his moving body and gauge what motor commands to send out to keep walking. If the lights go out, however, he collapses; and he has learned that he just has to lie where he is until the lights come on again. He has so finely honed this ability to guide movements with vision that if asked to point repeatedly to the same location in the air, he does so more accurately than other people do. Still, it's a mental drain to have to watch and attend constantly to his body just to do everyday tasks.

Ian has a good job and an active, independent life, but he is always vigilant. Lying in bed, he has to be very careful to remain calm, tethering his limbs with the covers to prevent them from flailing about.

And the lights are always on at Ian's house.

Our emphasis in this chapter shifts to the motor system as we complete the circuit from sensory input to behavior. It is important to consider sensory and motor functions together. Just as we saw in Chapters 8–10 that motor activities are important for sensory and perceptual functions—movements of the fingers in active touch perception, sniffing in smell, and movements of the eyes and head in vision—so we will see in this chapter that sensory and perceptual processes guide and correct our actions.

In addition, just as our apparently effortless perception turns out to depend on intricate sensory mechanisms and perceptual processes, so, too, our apparently effortless adult motor abilities—such as reaching out and picking up an object, walking across the room, sipping a cup of coffee—require complex muscular systems with constant feedback from the body, as Ian's case shows. After examining movements and their coordination from the behavioral view and the control systems view, we'll integrate these into the neuroscience view.

The Behavioral View Considers Reflexes versus Plans

By the early nineteenth century, scientists knew that the dorsal roots of the spinal cord transmit sensory information and that the ventral roots contain motor fibers;

Go to Brain Explorer
bn8e.com/11.1

spinal animal   An animal whose spinal cord has been surgically disconnected from the brain to enable the study of behaviors that do not require brain control.

reflex   A simple, highly stereotyped, and unlearned response to a particular stimulus (e.g., an eye blink in response to a puff of air).

motor plan   Also called *motor program*. A plan for action in the nervous system.

electromyography (EMG)   The electrical recording of muscle activity.

closed-loop control mechanism   A control mechanism that provides a flow of information from whatever is being controlled to the device that controls it.

open-loop control mechanism   A control mechanism in which feedback from the output of the system is not provided to the input control.

ballistic movement   A rapid muscular movement that is generally preprogrammed.

connections between the two seemed to provide the basis for simple movements. Research with **spinal animals** (animals in which the spinal cord has been disconnected from the brain) led British physiologist Sir Charles Sherrington (1857–1952) to argue that the basic units of behavior are **reflexes**: simple, unvarying, and unlearned responses to sensory stimuli such as touch, pressure, and pain. We analyzed the famous knee jerk reflex in Figure 3.17.

Sherrington's work inspired a rush to catalog the various reflexes and their neural circuitry, particularly in the spinal cord. These studies showed that some reflexes involve only short pathways in the spinal cord, directly linking dorsal and ventral roots; others involve longer loops, connecting spinal cord segments to each other or to brain regions.

Is normal behavior simply the connecting together of different reflexes, the sensation from one reflex triggering the next? No. The limitations of this perspective are apparent when we think about complex sequences of behavior, such as speech. A speaker has a *plan* in which several units (speech sounds and words) are placed in a larger pattern (the intended complete statement). Sometimes the units are misplaced, although the pattern is preserved: "Our queer old dean," said history professor William Spooner when he meant "Our dear old queen." Or, "You hissed all my mystery lectures." (Spooner was so prone to mixing up the order of sounds in his sentences that this type of error is called a *spoonerism*.) Such mistakes reveal the overall plan: the speaker is *anticipating* a later sound and executing it too soon. A chain of reflexes, each one triggering the next, could not generate such an error.

The **motor plan**, also called the *motor program,* is a complex set of commands to muscles that is established *before* the behavior starts. Feedback from movements informs and fine-tunes the motor program as it unfolds, but the basic sequence of movements is planned. Examples of behaviors that exhibit this kind of internal plan range from highly skilled acts, such as piano playing, to the simple escape behaviors of animals such as crayfish.

Motor behavior can be analyzed and measured in a variety of ways

We can readily analyze movements using high-speed video, which provides an intimate frame-by-frame portrait of even the most rapid events. To deal with the large amounts of data produced, methods of simplification or numerical analysis have been devised. For example, sports trainers use detailed analyses of athletic acts based on time-lapse photographs or information derived from sensors attached at joints. Computer programs process images to help quantify performance, enabling detailed measurement of the positions of different body parts in successive instants. Other devices record the direction, strength, and speed of motions. **FIGURE 11.1** illustrates the paths of normal and impaired reaching movements, which we will consider at several points in this chapter.

Another approach to the fine-grained analysis of movements is to record the electrical activity of muscles—a procedure called **electromyography** (**EMG**). Like neurons, muscles produce action potentials when they contract, as we'll see later in this chapter. Therefore, fine needle electrodes placed in a muscle, or electrodes placed on the skin over a muscle, can detect electrical indications of muscle activity. If electrodes are placed over several different muscles, we get a record of the timing and strength of contraction of the muscles involved in a movement (Hanakawa et al., 2003). The EMGs in **FIGURE 11.2** show that a person pulling a knob will adjust his legs just before moving his arm—another example of motor planning.

The Control Systems View Considers Accuracy versus Speed

One way to look at the mechanisms that regulate and control our movements employs the language of engineering. In designing machines, engineers commonly have two goals: (1) accuracy, to prevent or minimize error, and (2) speed, to complete a task quickly and efficiently. It is difficult to accomplish both these goals at once; usually there is a trade-off between the two. Two forms of control mechanisms—closed-loop and open-loop—are used to optimize one at the expense of the other.

(A) Visually guided reaching task

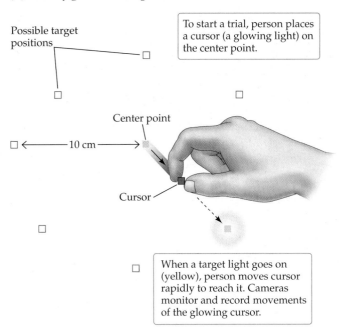

Possible target positions

To start a trial, person places a cursor (a glowing light) on the center point.

Center point

← 10 cm →

Cursor

When a target light goes on (yellow), person moves cursor rapidly to reach it. Cameras monitor and record movements of the glowing cursor.

(B) Examples of cursor movements after 200 practice trials

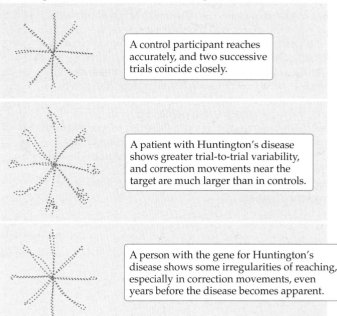

A control participant reaches accurately, and two successive trials coincide closely.

A patient with Huntington's disease shows greater trial-to-trial variability, and correction movements near the target are much larger than in controls.

A person with the gene for Huntington's disease shows some irregularities of reaching, especially in correction movements, even years before the disease becomes apparent.

11.1 MEASUREMENT OF REACHING MOVEMENTS (A) An experimental setup to study reaching movements. (B) Recorded movement trajectories of a control (top), a patient with Huntington's disease (middle), and a carrier of the gene for Huntington's disease (bottom). We'll discuss this disorder in detail later in this chapter. (Part B courtesy of Dr. Maurice R. Smith.)

Closed-loop control mechanisms maximize *accuracy*: information from whatever is being controlled flows back to the device that controls it. Driving a car is an example of a closed-loop motor system; in this case the variable being controlled is the position of the car on the road (**FIGURE 11.3**). Continual information is provided by the driver's visual system, which guides corrections.

Open-loop control mechanisms maximize *speed*; there are no external forms of feedback, and the activity is preprogrammed. Open-loop controls are needed in systems that must respond so rapidly that there is no time to wait for a feedback signal. For example, once a baseball pitcher begins throwing a fastball, the pitch will be completed as programmed no matter what sensory feedback is received. Such open-loop movements are called **ballistic movements**. Because there is no feedback, open-loop systems need other ways to reduce error and variability. They must anticipate potential error. As living systems, we learn to anticipate and avoid error, so (for example) we can learn to rapidly type our names with our eyes shut. That's fast, but it's no way to drive a car.

11.2 ELECTROMYOGRAPHY For these recordings made from biceps and gastrocnemius (calf) muscles, the study participant was instructed to pull the handle as soon as a tone sounded. He sets his legs before pulling the knob, evidence of a motor plan.

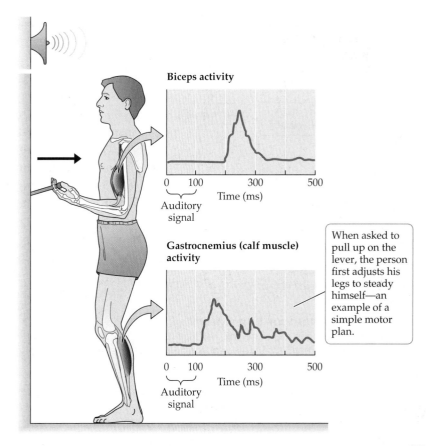

Biceps activity

0   100   300   500
Time (ms)

Auditory signal

Gastrocnemius (calf muscle) activity

0   100   300   500
Time (ms)

Auditory signal

When asked to pull up on the lever, the person first adjusts his legs to steady himself—an example of a simple motor plan.

11.3 A CLOSED-LOOP SYSTEM (A) Automobile driving provides an example of feedback control. (B) In the example in part A, the *controlled system* is the automobile. The *control signal* (i.e., the input) to the controlled system is the position of the steering wheel; the *output* is the position of the car on the road. In any closed-loop system, the transducer is an element that measures output, and the error detector measures differences between actual output and desired output (the control signal). In this example the *transducer* (the visual system), the *error detector* (the perceptual system), and the *controller* (the muscles) are all properties of the person driving the car. The driver compares the actual position of the car on the road with the desired position and makes corrections to minimize the discrepancy. Closed-loop systems emphasize accuracy and flexibility at the expense of speed.

(A) Feedback control during driving

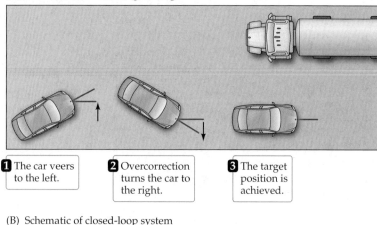

1 The car veers to the left.   **2** Overcorrection turns the car to the right.   **3** The target position is achieved.

(B) Schematic of closed-loop system

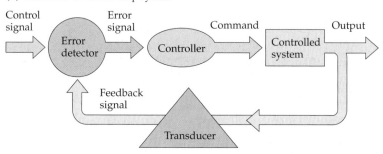

Most of our movements blend these two types of systems: preprogrammed sequences of movements (open-loop) are fine-tuned by sensory feedback (closed-loop).

The Neuroscience View Reveals Hierarchical Systems

We can distinguish several different levels of hierarchically organized motor control systems:

- The *skeletal system* and the muscles attached to it determine which movements are possible.
- The *spinal cord* controls skeletal muscles in response to sensory information. In the simplest case, the response may be a reflex. The spinal cord also implements motor commands from the brain.
- The *brainstem* integrates motor commands from higher levels of the brain and transmits them to the spinal cord. It also relays sensory information about the body from the spinal cord to the forebrain.
- Some of the main commands for action are initiated in the *primary motor cortex*.
- Areas adjacent to the primary motor cortex, *nonprimary motor cortices*, provide an additional source of motor commands, acting indirectly via primary motor cortex and through direct connections to lower levels of the motor hierarchy.
- Other brain regions—the *cerebellum* and *basal ganglia*—modulate the activities of these hierarchically organized control systems. Some of their contributions are routed via the *thalamus* in a loop back to the cortex.

We will examine each of these levels of control, outlined in **FIGURE 11.4**, in the following discussions, beginning with the skeletal system.

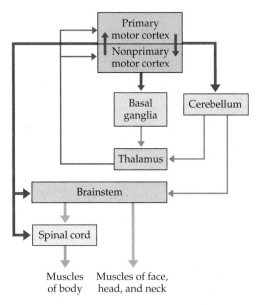

11.4 THE HIERARCHY OF MOVEMENT CONTROL The motor cortex receives information from other cortical areas and sends commands to the thalamus and brainstem, which pass commands to the spinal cord. Both the cerebellum and the basal ganglia adjust these commands.

The skeletal system enables particular movements and precludes others

Some properties of behavior arise from physical characteristics of the skeleton. For example, the length, form, and weight of the limbs shape an animal's stride. The primary sites for bending are the joints, where bones meet. Some joints, such as the hip, are almost "universal" joints, permitting movement in many planes. Others, like the elbow or knee, are more limited and swing mostly in one direction. **FIGURE 11.5** illustrates the human skeleton and shows examples of joints and their possible movements. Interestingly, the octopus has no bones or joints, yet when it grabs food with a tentacle, the octopus will place "bends" in the tentacle, as if it had an elbow and wrist, to bring the food to its mouth (Sumbre et al., 2005), suggesting that joints may be the optimal solution for precise movements.

Muscles control the actions of the skeletal system

Our bare skeleton must now be clothed with muscles. Muscles work solely through contraction (shortening), so the skeletal connections of a muscle give us clues about the particular movements it causes. Muscles have springlike properties that influence the timing of behavior and the forces that can be generated; the rate and force of muscular contractions limit some responses. A variety of visceral organs and blood vessels also employ a type of muscle, called **smooth muscle** (because of its appearance), but since its functions and control are very different from those of the skeletal muscles and since smooth muscle is not generally involved in voluntary behavior, we will not concern ourselves with smooth muscle in this chapter.

Muscles are connected to bone by **tendons**. Around a joint, different muscles are arranged in a reciprocal fashion: when one muscle group contracts, it stretches the other group; that is, the muscles are **antagonists**. Muscles that act together are called **synergists**. For example, several synergistic muscles act together to extend the arm at the elbow. Another set of muscles that flex the arm are antagonists to those that extend it. Movement around a joint requires one set of **motor neurons** (the neurons that send axons to activate muscle contraction) to be excited while the antagonistic set of motor neurons is inhibited (**FIGURE 11.6**). We can lock a limb in position by contracting antagonistic muscles simultaneously.

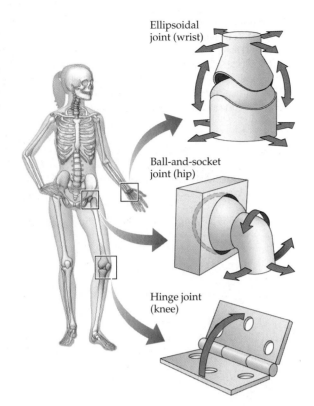

11.5 JOINTS AND MOVEMENTS Enlarged mechanical models indicate the kinds of movements that each type of joint can perform. The wrist joint moves in two principal planes: lateral and vertical. The hip joint is a "universal" joint, moving in all three planes. The knee joint has a single plane of motion.

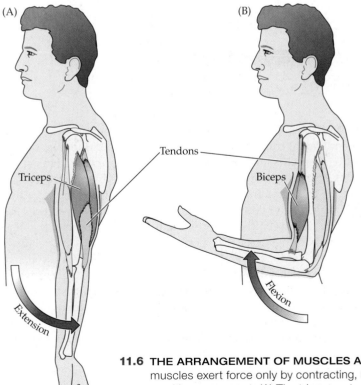

11.6 THE ARRANGEMENT OF MUSCLES AROUND THE ELBOW Because muscles exert force only by contracting, muscle attachments determine the resulting movement. (A) The triceps extends the arm. (B) When the biceps contracts, it flexes the arm. Because these two muscles mediate opposite movements, they are known as *antagonists*.

smooth muscle A type of muscle fiber, as in the heart, that is controlled by the autonomic nervous system rather than by voluntary control.

tendon Strong tissue that connects muscle to bone.

antagonist A muscle that counteracts the effect of another muscle.

synergist A muscle that acts together with another muscle.

motor neuron Also called *motoneuron*. A neuron in the brain or spinal cord that transmits motor messages to a muscle.

11.7 THE COMPOSITION OF MUSCLES AND THE MECHANISM OF MUSCLE CONTRACTION Muscle fibers are shown here at progressively greater magnifications, with the bottom image 2 million times life size. The actions of myosin and actin cause muscle contraction.

Go to Animation 11.2
Muscle Contraction
bn8e.com/11.2

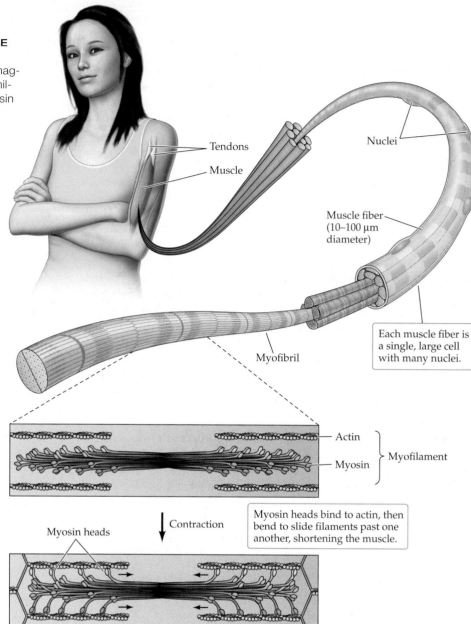

Tendons

Muscle

Nuclei

Muscle fiber
(10–100 µm
diameter)

Each muscle fiber is a single, large cell with many nuclei.

Myofibril

Actin

Myosin

Myofilament

Myosin heads

Contraction

Myosin heads bind to actin, then bend to slide filaments past one another, shortening the muscle.

muscle fiber A collection of large cylindrical cells, making up most of a muscle, that can contract in response to neurotransmitter released from a motor neuron.

striated muscle A type of muscle with a striped appearance, generally under voluntary control.

myosin A protein that, along with actin, mediates the contraction of muscle fibers.

actin A protein that, along with myosin, mediates the contraction of muscle fibers.

fast-twitch muscle fiber A type of striated muscle that contracts rapidly but fatigues readily.

slow-twitch muscle fiber A type of striated muscle fiber that contracts slowly but does not fatigue readily.

THE MOLECULAR MACHINERY OF MUSCLES   A skeletal muscle is composed of thousands of individual **muscle fibers** working together under voluntary control. Each muscle fiber contains many filaments of two kinds arranged in a regular manner (**FIGURE 11.7**), giving the fibers a striped, or "striated," appearance. In this **striated muscle** the thick and thin filaments (made up of the complex proteins **myosin** and **actin**, respectively) overlap. Contraction of the muscle increases the overlap: the filaments slide past each other, shortening the overall length of the muscle fiber.

Because of the varying tasks they perform, different muscles require different speeds, precision, strength, and endurance. So there are two main types of striated muscle fibers: fast-twitch and slow-twitch. Eye movements, for example, must be quick and accurate so that we can follow moving objects and shift our gaze from one target to another. But fibers in the extraocular muscles, which control eye movements, do not have to maintain tension for long periods of time; accordingly, they are mostly **fast-twitch muscle fibers**. In leg muscles, fast-twitch fibers react promptly and strongly but tire rapidly; they are used mainly for activities in which muscle tension changes frequently, as in walking or running. Mixed in with the fast-twitch muscle fibers are **slow-twitch muscle fibers**, which are not as fast but have greater resistance to fatigue; they are used chiefly to maintain posture. These properties of muscle fibers are determined, in part, by use. Athletes who train for endurance boost the proportion of their muscle fibers that display slow-twitch properties (Putman et al., 2004).

If you eat chicken or turkey, you've already contrasted fast-twitch and slow-twitch muscles. The "white meat" of the breast is fast-twitch muscle for the rapid wing beats needed for flight. These birds fly for only short periods, so there's no need for these muscles to resist fatigue. In contrast, the "dark meat" of the leg is slow-twitch muscle, which continually supports the animals as they walk about. These muscles contract slowly but have lots of endurance. Most muscles consist of a mixture of slow-twitch and fast-twitch muscle fibers.

MUSCULAR DYSTROPHY   Numerous muscle diseases are characterized by biochemical abnormalities that lead to structural changes in muscle; collectively, these disorders are referred to as **muscular dystrophy** (MD) (from the Greek *dys*, "bad," and *trophe*, "nourishment"). As the name implies, in various muscular dystrophies the muscles waste away (Blake et al., 2002).

Duchenne muscular dystrophy, the most prevalent form of MD, strikes almost exclusively boys, beginning at the age of about 4 to 6 years and usually leading to death in early adulthood. Studies of family pedigrees show that the disorder is a simple Mendelian trait—caused by a single gene—carried on the X chromosome. When the gene was identified, it was named *dystrophin*. In some ways the name is unfortunate because the dystrophin protein, when normal, does *not* lead to dystrophy. **Dystrophin** is normally produced in muscle cells and is part of a vital structural component of muscle fibers. Because women have two X chromosomes, even if one carries the defective copy of the *dystrophin* gene, the other X chromosome can still direct production of sufficient normal dystrophin. But about 50% of the sons of such women will receive the defective gene and, because they have only the one X chromosome, will be afflicted with the disease. In the hope of halting the loss of muscle fibers in Duchenne, scientists are trying to use gene therapy to induce the muscles of boys with this disease to produce normal dystrophin. One approach, using viruses to infect muscles with the *dystrophin* gene, worked in a dog model of Duchenne muscular dystrophy (Yue et al., 2015), so human clinical trials are being planned.

Neural messages reach muscle fibers at the neuromuscular junction

As each motor neuron integrates the information bombarding it through hundreds or thousands of synapses, it may produce an action potential. The action potential travels down the axon, which splits into many branches near the target muscle (**FIGURE 11.8A AND B**). Each axonal branch carries an action potential to its axon terminal, which then (in vertebrates) releases the neurotransmitter **acetylcholine (ACh)**. Muscle fibers respond to the ACh by producing action potentials of their own. The action potentials travel along the muscle fibers, permitting sodium (Na^+) and calcium (Ca^{2+}) ions to enter and then trigger the molecular changes in actin and myosin that produce contraction.

The region where a motor neuron terminal and adjoining muscle fiber meet is called the **neuromuscular junction (NMJ)** (**FIGURE 11.8C–E**). The NMJ is large and very effective: normally every action potential that reaches an axon terminal releases enough ACh to trigger an action potential and contraction in the innervated muscle fiber.

The **motor unit** consists of a single motor neuron and all the muscle fibers innervated by its various axonal branches (see Figure 11.8C). When the motor neuron fires, each of the muscle fibers that it innervates is stimulated. The **innervation ratio** is the number of muscle fibers innervated by one motor neuron. Low innervation ratios characterize delicate muscles involved in fine movements, like those that move the eye—which have one motor neuron for every three fibers (a 1:3 ratio). Motor units of massive muscles such as those of the leg have high innervation ratios, with each motor neuron innervating hundreds of muscle fibers, so a single motor neuron contracts many muscle fibers at once and produces a lot of force.

muscular dystrophy (MD)   A disease that leads to degeneration of and functional changes in muscles.

dystrophin   A protein that is needed for normal muscle function.

acetylcholine (ACh)   A neurotransmitter produced and released by parasympathetic postganglionic neurons, by motor neurons, and by neurons throughout the brain.

neuromuscular junction (NMJ)   The region where the motor neuron terminal and the adjoining muscle fiber meet; the point where the nerve transmits its message to the muscle fiber.

motor unit   A single motor axon and all the muscle fibers that it innervates.

innervation ratio   The ratio expressing the number of muscle fibers innervated by a single motor axon.

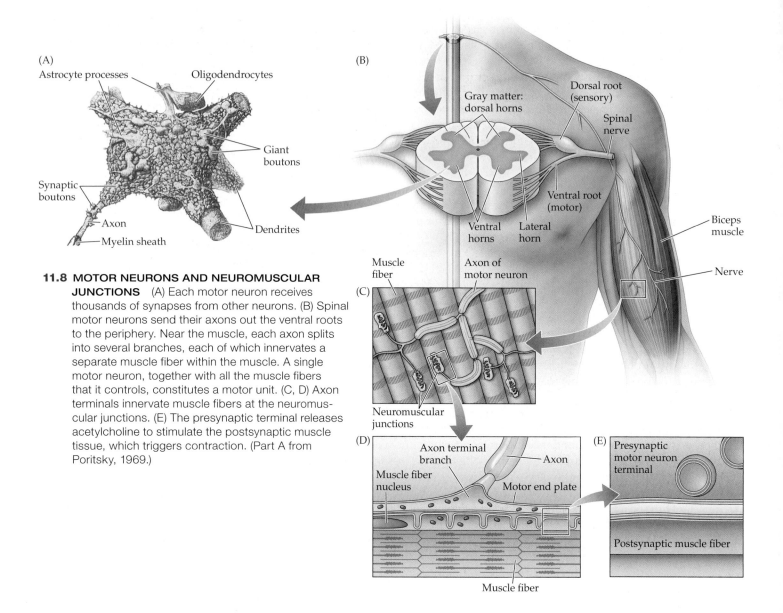

(A)
Astrocyte processes
Oligodendrocytes
Giant boutons
Synaptic boutons
Axon
Myelin sheath
Dendrites

(B)
Gray matter: dorsal horns
Dorsal root (sensory)
Spinal nerve
Ventral root (motor)
Ventral horns
Lateral horn
Biceps muscle
Nerve

(C)
Muscle fiber
Axon of motor neuron
Neuromuscular junctions

(D)
Axon terminal branch
Axon
Muscle fiber nucleus
Motor end plate
Muscle fiber

(E)
Presynaptic motor neuron terminal
Postsynaptic muscle fiber

11.8 MOTOR NEURONS AND NEUROMUSCULAR JUNCTIONS (A) Each motor neuron receives thousands of synapses from other neurons. (B) Spinal motor neurons send their axons out the ventral roots to the periphery. Near the muscle, each axon splits into several branches, each of which innervates a separate muscle fiber within the muscle. A single motor neuron, together with all the muscle fibers that it controls, constitutes a motor unit. (C, D) Axon terminals innervate muscle fibers at the neuromuscular junctions. (E) The presynaptic terminal releases acetylcholine to stimulate the postsynaptic muscle tissue, which triggers contraction. (Part A from Poritsky, 1969.)

Thus, motor neurons are the **final common pathway**: the sole route through which the spinal cord and brain can control our many muscles. Because they respond to inputs from so many sources, motor neurons often have very widespread dendritic fields, and they are the largest cells in the spinal cord. Furthermore, while motor neurons *release* only ACh, they respond to a tremendous variety of synaptic transmitters, both excitatory and inhibitory, released by the diverse inputs that each motor neuron receives. Virtually all motor neuron axons are myelinated (Kaar and Fraher, 1985), so their action potentials are conducted quickly.

ATTACKS ON THE NEUROMUSCULAR JUNCTION Several poisons affect neuromuscular junctions. For example, snake bites can cause neuromuscular blocks because the venom of some highly poisonous snakes contains substances (such as bungarotoxin) that block postsynaptic ACh receptors. If the neuromuscular junctions of the muscles for breathing are blocked, the victim suffocates.

Studies of bungarotoxin led to an understanding of a debilitating neuromuscular disorder, **myasthenia gravis** (from the Greek *mys*, "muscle," and *asthenes*, "weak," and the Latin *gravis*, "grave" or "serious"). This disorder is characterized by a profound weakness of skeletal muscles. The disease often first affects the muscles of the head, producing symptoms such as drooping of the eyelids, double vision, and slowing of

final common pathway The information-processing pathway consisting of all the motor neurons in the body. Motor neurons are known by this collective term because they receive and integrate all motor signals from the brain and then direct movement accordingly.

myasthenia gravis A disorder characterized by a profound weakness of skeletal muscles; caused by a loss of acetylcholine receptors.

speech. In later stages, paralysis of the muscles that control swallowing and respiration becomes life-threatening. The weakness happens because the neuromuscular junctions are not working—the muscles aren't getting the message to contract.

Myasthenia gravis is an **autoimmune disorder**: most cases result when antibodies develop and attack a patient's own ACh receptors, disrupting neuromuscular junctions. In other cases, the antibodies are directed toward other proteins that are associated with the ACh receptor. Treatment often consists of prescribing drugs to suppress the immune system (Richman and Agius, 2003).

Sensory feedback from muscles, tendons, and joints monitors movements

To produce rapid coordinated movements of the body, the brain and spinal cord must continually monitor the state of the muscles and the positions of the limbs. This perception of body movements and positions is called **proprioception** (from the Latin *proprius*, "own," and *recipere*, "to receive"). Because it is crucial for coordinating movement, this information is transmitted to the brain by large, myelinated axons, which conduct action potentials swiftly (see Chapter 3). For some reason, the virus that attacked Ian, whom we met at the start of this chapter, killed only these large axons, leaving him without proprioception below the neck. His predicament illustrates how important this "sixth sense" is for movement.

Two major kinds of proprioceptive receptors that report the state of muscles and joints to the brain are (1) muscle spindles, which monitor muscle *length*, and (2) Golgi tendon organs, which monitor muscle *tension*. We'll discuss each in turn.

THE MUSCLE SPINDLE   The **muscle spindle** is a complicated structure consisting of both afferent and efferent elements. Each spindle (a tapered cylinder) contains small muscle fibers called **intrafusal fibers** (from the Latin *intra*, "within," and *fusus*, "spindle"); the ordinary muscle fibers that lie outside the spindles are called **extrafusal fibers** (**FIGURE 11.9**).

The muscle spindle contains two kinds of receptor endings: **primary sensory endings** (also called *annulospiral endings*) and **secondary sensory endings** (also called *flower spray endings*). These endings are related to different parts of the spindle (see Figure 11.9C). The primary ending wraps in a spiral fashion around the central region of the intrafusal fiber. The secondary endings terminate toward the thin

autoimmune disorder   A disorder caused when the immune system mistakenly attacks a person's own body, thereby interfering with normal functioning.

proprioception   Body sense; information about the position and movement of the body that is sent to the brain.

muscle spindle   A muscle receptor that lies parallel to a muscle and sends action potentials to the central nervous system when the muscle is stretched.

intrafusal fiber   One of the small muscle fibers that lie within each muscle spindle.

extrafusal fiber   One of the ordinary muscle fibers that lie outside the spindles and provide most of the force for muscle contraction.

primary sensory ending   Also called *annulospiral ending*. The axon that transmits information from the central portion of a muscle spindle.

secondary sensory ending   Also called *flower spray ending*. The axon that transmits information from the ends of a muscle spindle.

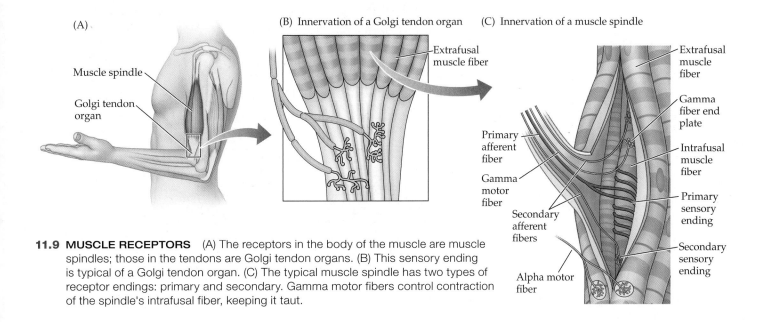

11.9 MUSCLE RECEPTORS   (A) The receptors in the body of the muscle are muscle spindles; those in the tendons are Golgi tendon organs. (B) This sensory ending is typical of a Golgi tendon organ. (C) The typical muscle spindle has two types of receptor endings: primary and secondary. Gamma motor fibers control contraction of the spindle's intrafusal fiber, keeping it taut.

gamma motor neuron   Also called *gamma efferent*. A motor neuron that innervates the contractile tissue (the intrafusal fiber) in a muscle spindle.

alpha motor neuron   A motor neuron that controls the main contractile fibers (extrafusal fibers) of a muscle.

Golgi tendon organ   One of the receptors located in tendons that send action potentials to the central nervous system reporting muscle tension.

ends of the spindle. These different receptor elements of the muscle spindle respond to two different aspects of changes in muscle length. The primary (annulospiral) endings show a maximum discharge early in stretch and then adapt and show a lower discharge rate. They therefore communicate *velocity of muscle stretch* to the nervous system. In contrast, the secondary (flower spray) endings are slow to change their rate during the early phase of stretch and are maximally sensitive to maintained, or *static*, muscle length. In this way, they communicate *muscle length* to the nervous system. The nervous system thus has information about the length and movement of every muscle.

For these receptors to work properly, the overall muscle spindle needs to be about the same length as the muscle. But muscles change their length as they contract or relax. To keep the muscle spindle about the same length as the muscle, a special motor neuron stimulates the intrafusal fiber portion of the spindle, altering the tension, thus controlling the sensitivity of its receptors. These motor neurons are called **gamma motor neurons**, or *gamma efferents*, to distinguish them from the larger **alpha motor neurons**, which go to the extrafusal muscle fibers that do all the work (see Figure 11.9C).

How do the muscle spindle afferents become excited? Suppose a muscle is stretched, as when a load is placed on it. For example, imagine that you hold out your hand and someone hands you a heavy book. The additional load would move your arm downward, stretching the biceps muscle and the spindles it contains. The resulting deformation of the endings on the spindle would trigger action potentials in the afferent fibers. These afferents would inform the spinal cord, and the spinal cord would tell the brain about the muscle stretch and therefore the load imposed. The afferents will also trigger changes in the motor neurons, as part of the stretch reflex we'll discuss shortly.

THE GOLGI TENDON ORGAN   While muscle spindles respond primarily to stretch, the other proprioceptive receptors in muscle—Golgi tendon organs—are especially sensitive to muscle *tension* (**FIGURE 11.10**). Structurally, Golgi tendon organs consist of sensory nerve endings interwoven through the tough proteins that give tendons their strength and elasticity. Because they are part of a robust structure, **Golgi tendon organs** are relatively insensitive to passive muscle lengthening (see Figures 11.9 and 11.10), such as simply extending an arm. But large loads (requiring strong contractions) will stretch the tendon organ and stimulate the nerve endings to fire.

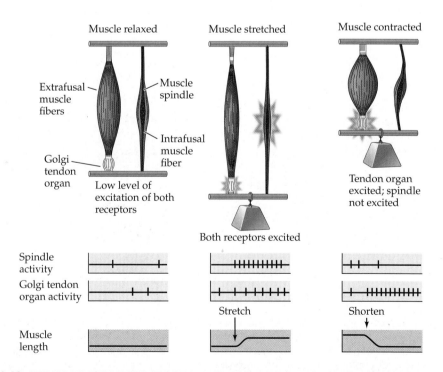

11.10 SPINDLES MEASURE STRETCH, TENDON ORGANS MEASURE TENSION

Thus, the Golgi tendon organs monitor the force of muscle contractions, providing a second source of sensory information about the muscles that aids in precisely controlling movement. This arrangement makes the tendon organs useful in another important way: they detect overloads that threaten to tear muscles and tendons. Strong stimulation of the Golgi tendon organs inhibits the motor neurons supplying the muscles that pull on the tendon and thus, by relaxing the tension, prevents mechanical damage. The afferent neurons in both muscle spindles and Golgi tendon organs use the same stretch-sensitive ion channel protein (Piezo2) as the touch receptor (see Chapter 8) to trigger action potentials (Woo et al., 2015).

Classic studies in physiology emphasized the importance of information from muscle spindles and Golgi tendon organs for controlling movement. Cutting the afferent fibers from muscles in monkeys caused them to stop using the deafferented limb, even if the efferent connections from motor neurons to muscles were preserved (Mott, 1895; Sherrington, 1898). The deafferented limb was not paralyzed, since it could be activated (the motor neurons still innervated the muscles), but lack of information from the muscle led to relative disuse. The arm dangled, apparently useless. However, if the good arm was restrained (by a ball placed around the hand), the animal soon learned to use the deafferented arm and could become quite dexterous (Taub, 1976). Monkeys managed to do this the way Ian does, guiding movements by using vision for feedback about their arm movements.

Probably all of us use visual information to guide the motor system without being aware that we're doing so. Remember the young woman D.F. from Chapter 10? She could not report whether a slot was vertical or horizontal; yet when she was asked to insert a disk in the slot, she consistently rotated her hand to put it in smoothly. This finding suggests that even neurologically intact people unknowingly use visual cues to guide their movements (Goodale and Haffenden, 1998). These are the only cues available for Ian.

The Spinal Cord Is a Crucial Link in Controlling Body Movement

Motor neurons are the final common pathway for behavior, because all action depends on activating these cells to determine the onset, coordination, and termination of muscle activity. But to really understand the physiology of movement, we need to know the source of the inputs to motor neurons. First we'll consider the organization of the spinal cord, and the disorders that disrupt that organization, before considering the descending brain pathways that activate this final common pathway.

Spinal reflexes mediate "automatic" responses

A good example of automatic control at the spinal level is the **stretch reflex**—the contraction that results when a muscle stretches. One version of the stretch reflex is the knee-jerk reflex we discussed in Chapter 3 (see Figure 3.17). This reflex isn't just present to give doctors (or comedians) something to do—it evolved to help us with load control. That might be more obvious if we consider the stretch reflex in an arm rather than a leg. Adding a weight to the hand in **FIGURE 11.11** imposes a sudden stretch on muscle A (M_A). The circuit that keeps us from dropping the load is one that links muscle spindles and the relevant muscles:

1. Weight is added, pulling the hand down.

2. The muscle is stretched.

3. Afferents from the muscle spindle are excited (SN_A in Figure 11.11).

4. The spindle afferents connect directly—that is, monosynaptically—to the motor neurons that control the stretched muscle, exciting them.

5. The motor neurons stimulate the muscle to oppose muscle stretch, keeping the hand from dropping farther.

stretch reflex The contraction of a muscle in response to stretch of that muscle.

11.11 THE STRETCH REFLEX CIRCUIT

MN_A is the motor nerve to muscle A (M_A); MN_B is the motor nerve to muscle B (M_B), an antagonist to M_A. SN_A is the sensory nerve from the muscle spindle of M_A. Characteristic responses at different stages in the circuit are shown at right.

■ Go to Animation 11.3
The Stretch Reflex Circuit
bn8e.com/11.3

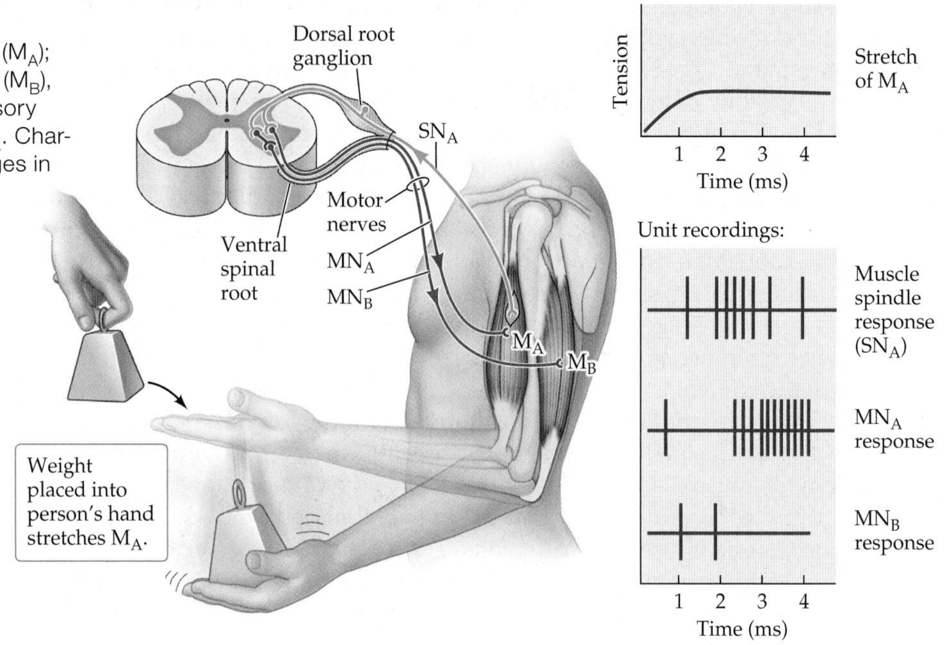

This sequence describes a simple negative feedback system that tends to restore the limb to its "desired" position. Muscle spindle afferents also inhibit the motor neurons that supply the antagonistic muscle (M_B in Figure 11.11). Two synapses are required for this inhibition of the antagonistic motor neuron. Spindle information terminates on an interneuron, which inhibits the motor neuron that supplies M_B. The relaxation of antagonistic muscles prevents them from being injured by the sudden movement. In these and other movements, spinal circuits modulate the inputs from muscle spindles to produce smooth movements (Fink et al., 2014).

Other spinal circuits can generate more-complex movements. Most locomotion is rhythmic, consisting of repetitive cycles of the same movement, whether it be the beating of wings or the swinging of legs. Many such rhythmic movements are generated by mechanisms within the spinal cord (Kiehn, 2016). These endogenous rhythms are normally modulated by sensory feedback, but they can function independently of brain influences or afferents. The term **central pattern generator** refers to the neural circuitry responsible for generating rhythmic patterns of behavior, as seen in walking. The central pattern generators for walking seem much the same in cats, birds, and humans (Dominici et al., 2011). This essential rhythm of walking generated by spinal cord mechanisms is activated and modulated by the brain.

Spinal cord injuries cause severe motor impairments

Vehicular accidents, falls, violence, and sports injuries cause many human spinal injuries that result in motor impairment. Injuries to the human spinal cord commonly develop from force to the neck or back, breaking a bone that then compresses the spinal cord. If the spinal cord is severed completely, immediate paralysis results, and reflexes below the level of injury may be lost—a condition known as **flaccid paralysis**. Flaccid paralysis generally results only when a considerable length of the spinal cord has been destroyed. When the injury severs the spinal cord without causing extensive destruction of spinal cord tissue, reflexes below the level of injury may become abnormally strong because the intact tissue has been disconnected from descending inhibitory projections from the brain.

Over 250,000 individuals in the United States have spinal cord injuries, and about 10,000–12,000 new traumatic spinal injuries occur each year. Tragically, most traumatic spinal injuries occur in young people, with automobile accidents and falls accounting for the majority of cases. Although much remains to be discovered, the

central pattern generator Neural circuitry that is responsible for generating the rhythmic pattern of a behavior such as walking.

flaccid paralysis A loss of reflexes below the level of transection of the spinal cord.

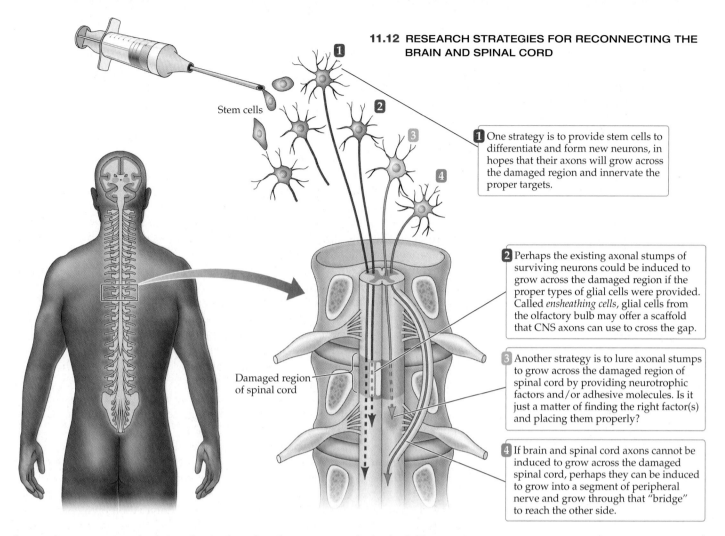

Stem cells

1 One strategy is to provide stem cells to differentiate and form new neurons, in hopes that their axons will grow across the damaged region and innervate the proper targets.

2 Perhaps the existing axonal stumps of surviving neurons could be induced to grow across the damaged region if the proper types of glial cells were provided. Called *ensheathing cells*, glial cells from the olfactory bulb may offer a scaffold that CNS axons can use to cross the gap.

3 Another strategy is to lure axonal stumps to grow across the damaged region of spinal cord by providing neurotrophic factors and/or adhesive molecules. Is it just a matter of finding the right factor(s) and placing them properly?

Damaged region of spinal cord

4 If brain and spinal cord axons cannot be induced to grow across the damaged spinal cord, perhaps they can be induced to grow into a segment of peripheral nerve and grow through that "bridge" to reach the other side.

hope of reconnecting the injured spinal cord no longer seems farfetched. Four main strategies for reconnecting the brain and spinal cord in humans are being investigated (**FIGURE 11.12**):

1. Inserted stem cells might differentiate into new neurons to send new axons across the break (Okano et al., 2003).

2. Transplanted glial cells can promote regeneration in the CNS. Recall from Chapter 9 that olfactory receptor neurons are continually produced, and somehow the axons of the new neurons find the way to their proper targets. Specialized glial cells called olfactory *ensheathing cells* appear to play a central role in guiding this axon growth, so researchers have tried transplanting ensheathing cells from the olfactory bulbs into spinal cord cuts in rats. In most cases, and for various forms of spinal cord damage, at least some function is restored (Raisman and Li, 2007; Khankan et al., 2016).

3. Neurotrophic factors and/or cell adhesion molecules (see Chapter 7) can be used to entice the axons of surviving neurons to grow across the damaged region of spinal cord (Anderson et al., 2015) and reconnect to their targets (Lang et al., 2015; Ruschel et al., 2015). In dogs, a nonspecific polymer, polyethylene glycol, seems to repair broken membranes when injected into spinal cord within a few days of injury. Dogs given this treatment were more than twice as likely to walk again (Laverty et al., 2004).

4. Implanting special "regeneration-friendly" materials at the injury site may allow nerves to regenerate past the break (Orive et al., 2009). A variant of this is to transplant peripheral nerves to connect the brain and lower spinal cord by forming a "bridge" around the injured spinal cord (Bernstein-Goral and Bregman, 1993). This approach centers on the observation that axons in peripheral nerves,

polioviruses A class of viruses that destroy motor neurons of the spinal cord and brainstem.

amyotrophic lateral sclerosis (ALS) Also called *Lou Gehrig's disease*. A disease in which motor neurons and their target muscles waste away.

pyramidal system Also called *corticospinal system*. The motor system that includes neurons within the cerebral cortex that send axons to form the pyramidal tract.

when cut by injury, will regrow and reconnect to their targets; yet cut axons in the CNS almost never accomplish this feat. No one really knows why peripheral and central axons differ in this regard, but it might be possible to exploit regeneration-friendly peripheral nerves to reconnect the spinal cord.

While spinal injuries severely impair movement, another movement disorder amounts to a death sentence, as we'll see next.

Motor neuron pathology leads to motor impairments and death

Virus-induced destruction of motor neurons—for example, by the disease known as *polio*—was once a frightening prospect around the world. **Polioviruses** destroy motor neurons of the spinal cord and, in more severe types of the disease, cranial motor neurons of the brainstem. Because the muscles are no longer called on to contract, they atrophy. If the muscles controlling breathing deteriorate sufficiently, the person must rely on a ventilator to stay alive.

Sometimes, for reasons that remain elusive, the motor neurons of the brainstem and spinal cord spontaneously start to die and their target muscles waste away. In this disease, called **amyotrophic lateral sclerosis** (**ALS**; sometimes called *Lou Gehrig's disease* after the 1930s baseball player who lost his life to the disorder), the afflicted person experiences gradually worsening paralysis until most skeletal muscle ceases to function. There is currently no treatment for ALS (Perrin, 2014), so premature death is the usual outcome, although a few people with ALS can survive for long periods; celebrated British physicist Stephen Hawking, who was diagnosed with ALS in the early 1960s, is an example. A wide range of possible causal factors are under investigation, including premature aging, neurotoxins, viruses, immune responses, and endocrine dysfunction (Al-Chalabi and Hardiman, 2013).

About 10% of ALS cases are hereditary (Cirulli et al., 2015). The pedigrees of several afflicted families indicate that mutation in a single gene, called *SOD1*, account for about 20% of the heritable cases of ALS. This gene was isolated (P. M. Andersen et al., 1995) and found to encode an enzyme: copper/zinc superoxide dismutase. When scientists produced transgenic mice that, in addition to their own normal copies of the enzyme, carried a copy of the defective human *SOD1* gene, these animals displayed an ALS-like syndrome (Gurney et al., 1994). Their muscles wasted away and their motor neurons died, leading to an early death. Because the mice still had their own *SOD1* genes to produce the normal enzyme, these findings suggest that the familial ALS resulted not from the loss of enzyme action but rather from what is called a *toxic gain of function*—a harmful new action of the mutant protein. The abnormal SOD1 protein does not act within the motor neurons themselves (Philips and Rothstein, 2015), but rather acts through nearby astrocytes (Nagai et al., 2007) or through the muscle targets (Wong and Martin, 2010) to kill the motor neurons.

Another protein that has been implicated in ALS is TDP43, and again the mutant protein seems to have a toxic gain of function when expressed in mice (E. B. Lee et al., 2012). Understanding how the mutant TDP43 and SOD1 proteins cause ALS in that minority of cases that are inherited may shed light on what goes wrong in the more common, uninherited forms of ALS.

The brain sends its commands to the spinal cord through two major pathways: the pyramidal system and the extrapyramidal motor system, which we'll discuss in turn.

Pathways from the Brain Control Different Aspects of Movements

Some muscles are controlled directly by the brain. The cranial motor nuclei of the brainstem send their axons to innervate muscles of the head and neck (**FIGURE 11.13**; see also Figure 2.9). But for all the other muscles, the brain has to send commands to the spinal cord, and then the spinal cord controls the muscles.

The **pyramidal system** (or *corticospinal system*) consists of neuronal cell bodies within the cerebral cortex and their axons, which pass through the brainstem, form-

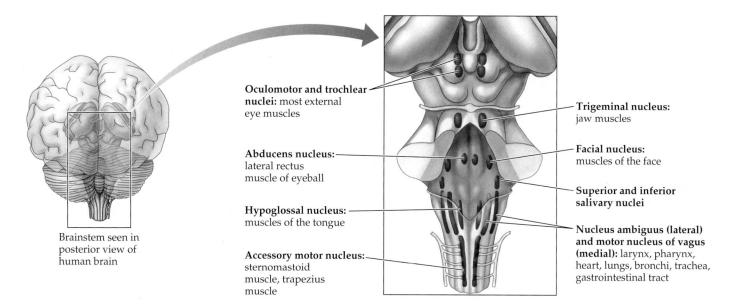

Oculomotor and trochlear nuclei: most external eye muscles

Abducens nucleus: lateral rectus muscle of eyeball

Hypoglossal nucleus: muscles of the tongue

Accessory motor nucleus: sternomastoid muscle, trapezius muscle

Brainstem seen in posterior view of human brain

Trigeminal nucleus: jaw muscles

Facial nucleus: muscles of the face

Superior and inferior salivary nuclei

Nucleus ambiguus (lateral) and motor nucleus of vagus (medial): larynx, pharynx, heart, lungs, bronchi, trachea, gastrointestinal tract

11.13 MOTOR NUCLEI IN THE BRAINSTEM Shown here from the rear, motor nuclei in the brainstem control muscles of the head and neck. The cranial nerves corresponding to these muscles are shown in Figure 2.9.

ing the pyramidal tract to the spinal cord (**FIGURE 11.14A**). The pyramidal tract is seen most clearly where it passes through the floor of the medulla. In a cross section of the medulla, the tract is a wedge-shaped ventral protuberance (pyramid) on each side of the midline. In the medulla the pyramidal tract from the right hemisphere crosses the midline to innervate the left spinal cord, and vice versa. Because the pyramidal tract crosses the midline (technically known as a *decussation*) in the medulla, the right cortex controls the left side of the body while the left cortex controls the right.

Many of the axons of the pyramidal tract originate from neurons in the **primary motor cortex (M1)**, which consists mainly of the precentral gyrus, just anterior to the central sulcus (**FIGURE 11.14B**; see also Figure 2.12B). The cell bodies of many of these large neurons are found in layer V of the primary motor cortex.

Primary motor cortex is an executive motor control mechanism—and more

In humans, brain damage to M1 produces partial paralysis on the side of the body opposite the brain lesion (i.e., the contralateral side of the body). The disturbance is greatest in distal muscles, such as those of the hand. Humans with these lesions are generally disinclined to use the affected limb.

Early-twentieth-century researchers like Wilder Penfield, whom we discussed in Chapter 2, used electrical stimulation to develop functional maps of human primary motor cortex. Disproportionately large regions in the maps of M1 are devoted to the body parts involved in the most elaborate and complex movements. For example, humans and other primates have extremely large cortical fields concerned with hand movements (**FIGURE 11.14C**).

Using nonhuman primates, it is possible to trace motor pathways in a retrograde manner from specific muscles back to corresponding regions of motor cortex, using a type of virus that can jump backward across synapses. This research shows that the organization of M1 is far less discrete than was originally thought; for example, the cortical neurons controlling the individual fingers are extensively intermingled and arise from a variety of locations (Rathelot and Strick, 2006). This arrangement likely aids the coordination of movements that involve multiple muscles. In primates the pyramidal tract has some monosynaptic connections with spinal motor neurons

primary motor cortex (M1) The apparent executive region for the initiation of movement; primarily the precentral gyrus.

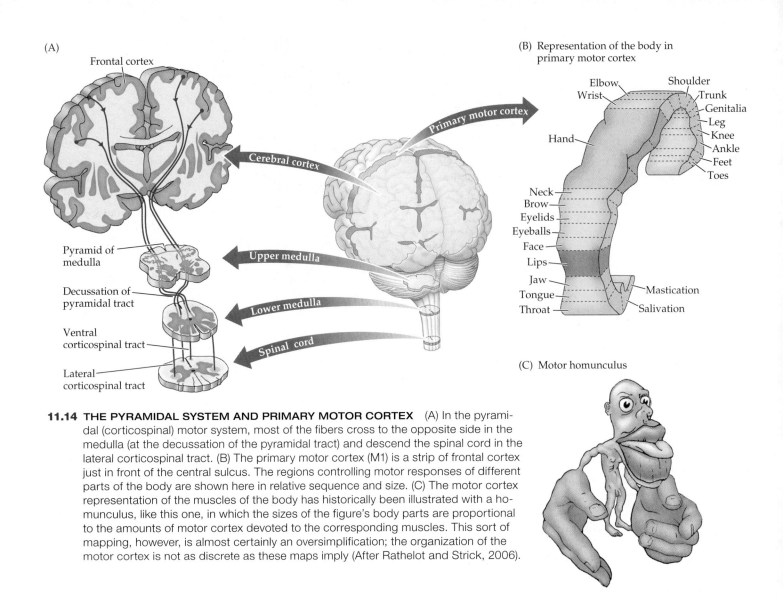

(A)

Frontal cortex

Pyramid of medulla

Decussation of pyramidal tract

Ventral corticospinal tract

Lateral corticospinal tract

Cerebral cortex

Upper medulla

Lower medulla

Spinal cord

Primary motor cortex

(B) Representation of the body in primary motor cortex

Elbow
Wrist
Shoulder
Trunk
Genitalia
Leg
Knee
Ankle
Feet
Toes
Hand

Neck
Brow
Eyelids
Eyeballs
Face
Lips
Jaw
Tongue
Throat

Mastication
Salivation

(C) Motor homunculus

11.14 THE PYRAMIDAL SYSTEM AND PRIMARY MOTOR CORTEX (A) In the pyramidal (corticospinal) motor system, most of the fibers cross to the opposite side in the medulla (at the decussation of the pyramidal tract) and descend the spinal cord in the lateral corticospinal tract. (B) The primary motor cortex (M1) is a strip of frontal cortex just in front of the central sulcus. The regions controlling motor responses of different parts of the body are shown here in relative sequence and size. (C) The motor cortex representation of the muscles of the body has historically been illustrated with a homunculus, like this one, in which the sizes of the figure's body parts are proportional to the amounts of motor cortex devoted to the corresponding muscles. This sort of mapping, however, is almost certainly an oversimplification; the organization of the motor cortex is not as discrete as these maps imply (After Rathelot and Strick, 2006).

(Griffin et al., 2015), but most pyramidal-tract neurons influence spinal motor neurons through polysynaptic routes and share control with other descending influences.

By recording from M1 neurons of monkeys that were trained to make free arm movements in eight possible target directions (Georgopoulos et al., 1993), we have been able to eavesdrop on the commands originating there. Many M1 cells change their firing rates according to the direction of the movement, but for any one cell, discharge rates are highest in one particular direction. **FIGURE 11.15** shows a cell with a preference for leftward movement, but other cells may have a preference for upward, downward, rightward, or diagonal movement or any angle in between. Therefore, each cell carries only partial information about the direction of reaching, but collectively they represent any direction of reaching. When we average the activity of several hundred M1 neurons at once, we can predict fairly well the direction toward which the animal will reach with its arm. Given the millions of neurons in this region, a larger sampling would presumably provide an even more accurate prediction.

A long-standing controversy raged over whether *muscles* or *movements* are represented in M1 (Shenoy et al., 2013). That is, does activity of a cortical motor neuron encode a relatively simple parameter, such as contraction of a particular muscle, or does it encode a more abstract parameter, such as a particular movement of the hand through space? To address this controversy, experimenters trained a monkey to perform rapid tracking movements using the hand and wrist (Kakei et al., 1999). As **FIGURE 11.16** shows, the animal grasped a handle that could be rotated along the two axes of wrist

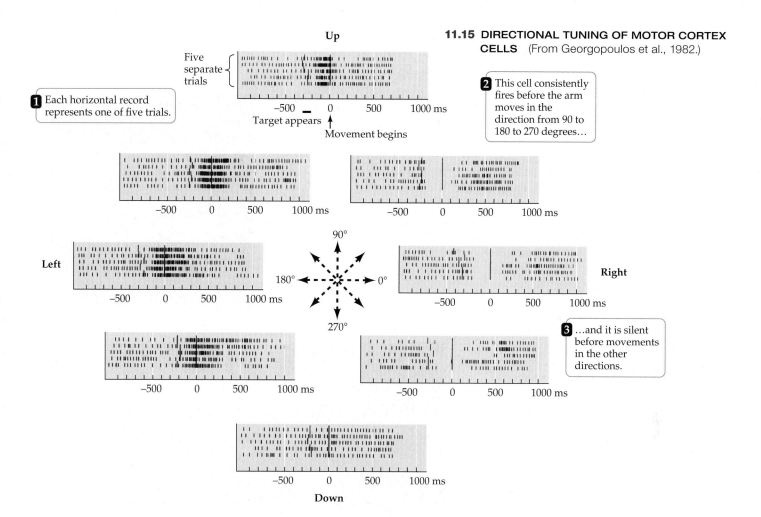

11.15 DIRECTIONAL TUNING OF MOTOR CORTEX CELLS (From Georgopoulos et al., 1982.)

Up

Five separate trials

1 Each horizontal record represents one of five trials.

−500   0   500   1000 ms

Target appears ↑ Movement begins

2 This cell consistently fires before the arm moves in the direction from 90 to 180 to 270 degrees...

Left

90°

180° ◄─────► 0°

270°

Right

3 ...and it is silent before movements in the other directions.

Down

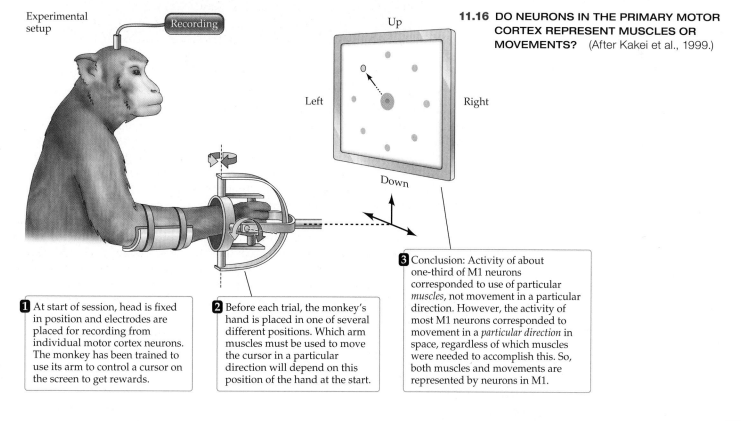

Experimental setup

Recording

11.16 DO NEURONS IN THE PRIMARY MOTOR CORTEX REPRESENT MUSCLES OR MOVEMENTS? (After Kakei et al., 1999.)

Up

Left   Right

Down

1 At start of session, head is fixed in position and electrodes are placed for recording from individual motor cortex neurons. The monkey has been trained to use its arm to control a cursor on the screen to get rewards.

2 Before each trial, the monkey's hand is placed in one of several different positions. Which arm muscles must be used to move the cursor in a particular direction will depend on this position of the hand at the start.

3 Conclusion: Activity of about one-third of M1 neurons corresponded to use of particular *muscles*, not movement in a particular direction. However, the activity of most M1 neurons corresponded to movement in a *particular direction* in space, regardless of which muscles were needed to accomplish this. So, both muscles and movements are represented by neurons in M1.

Cortical Neurons Can Guide a Robotic Arm

With the help of recordings such as those in Figure 11.15, signals from neurons in the motor cortex of an owl monkey (Figure A) can be used to control a robotic arm in three dimensions, reproducing movements to reach for pieces of food placed in different positions, pick them up, carry them to the mouth, and return to the start position (Wessberg et al., 2000). The results of such studies suggested that paralyzed patients might learn to operate a robotic arm by cortical activity, even though they couldn't move their own limbs.

One system, BrainGate, uses many microwires to record the activity of neurons in M1. Two people who had lost control of all four limbs volunteered to have the wires implanted into their brains. They then underwent training where they would watch a robot arm make regular, repetitive movements and *imagine* that the arm was *their* arm and that they were commanding the movements. The researchers carefully monitored the activity of the many M1 neurons during this phase, to "decode" the pattern of activity that signaled when the person was sending commands for movements up or down, left or right, and so on. The next phase of training was to monitor the person's

M1 activity and decode those virtual commands to actually move the robot arm. Watching the arm as it moved, the volunteers could then learn to fine-tune their mental commands to move the robot arm the way they wanted. One person was able to use this system for relatively fine movements, using the robot arm to drink coffee from a bottle (Figure B).

Animal work indicates that recording more neurons should give an even better idea of the intended direction of movement, as well as

(A) Owl monkey perched atop a robotic arm

(B)

motion. Movement of the handle controlled the position of a cursor on a computer screen. After much training (over 8 years!), the monkey performed well.

The experimenters then recorded the activity of single cells in M1 as the monkey performed from different starting positions. A substantial group of M1 neurons displayed changes in activity that corresponded to *muscle contractions*, but an even larger group of neurons showed activity that corresponded to *particular movements*, regardless of which muscles had to be used to accomplish those movements (which could vary depending on the position of the hand at the start). In other words, these cells were active whenever the monkey moved its hand in a particular direction, no matter which muscles were needed to accomplish that movement. Thus, *both* movements (Kaufman et al., 2014) and, to a lesser extent, muscles (Griffin et al., 2015) are represented in M1. Recordings of the activity of motor cortex, to predict what movement the person is calling for, can guide a robotic arm—the subject of **BOX 11.1**.

PRIMARY MOTOR CORTEX AND LEARNING   Several studies with both experimental animals and humans demonstrated that motor representations in M1 change as a result of training. Maps prepared from electrical stimulation in M1 show changes as an animal learns new skills—for example, a visually guided tracking movement with the

(C)

providing the data needed to control grip strength and other more subtle aspects of reaching and grasping (Velliste et al., 2008). Another possibility is to implant the electrodes in premotor cortex, with the idea that these are the neurons that call on primary motor cortex, so the neuronal signals for the intent to move the arm may be detected sooner. Perhaps recording from neurons in even more posterior parietal cortex will reveal even more high-level motor plan-

ning—the person's intent (Aflalo et al., 2015). Again, the neuronal activity would be detected by a computer and used to move the computer cursor or a robotic limb. Monkeys given such an implant became very proficient at moving a cursor on a computer screen (Santhanam et al., 2006). A more difficult approach, still in the early stages, is to use the cortical activity to control electrical stimulation of muscles in the paralyzed arm itself (Bouton et al., 2016), rather than in a robot arm.

Plasticity in motor cortices is gaining new appreciation in the field of neural prosthetics. It takes months for a human to learn to move a robotic arm (Hochberg et al., 2012). During this training, it is vital that the person be able to see how the robotic device is moving, so motor cortex can reorganize to work with the device (Koyama et al., 2010). Monkey research on brain-computer interfaces has shown a remapping of the direction preferences of cortical neurons to work with specific computational decoders; in other words, closed-loop control (seeing the arm move) is vital for motor plasticity to allow individuals to operate an artificial limb. Optimized computational solutions can improve performance, but equal or

better performance can be reached with simple algorithms if the individuals have visual feedback (i.e., they are in a closed-loop control situation). The next challenge is to provide closed-loop control by providing the client with robotically generated sensory feedback from the artificial limb (Bensmaia and Miller, 2014). Otherwise, people using the robotic arms or legs will be like Ian, whom we met at the start of the chapter, dependent on vision to regulate movement.

Given these successes, it is conceivable that people may learn to use devices such as these to control a prosthetic "exoskeleton" (Figure C). No longer an idea limited to science fiction, it is now possible that one day people who have lost the ability to command their own bodies to move may be able to move robotic bodies so they can take care of themselves. (Figure A courtesy of Dr. Miguel Nicolelis; B from Hochberg et al., 2012, courtesy of braingate2.org.)

arm (J. N. Sanes and Donoghue, 2000) or a precision grasping task (Nudo et al., 1996). As monkeys learn a particular skill, the total metabolic activity in M1 declines (Picard et al., 2013), as if it has become more efficient at producing the required movements.

In humans, the width of the precentral gyrus as seen with MRI offers an estimate of the size of M1. The gyrus is significantly wider in piano players, especially in the hand representation area (see Figure 11.14B and C), than in nonmusicians. The younger the musician was at the start of musical training, the larger the gyrus is in adulthood (Amunts et al., 1997), so this expansion of M1 seems to be in response to the experience of musical training.

Transcranial magnetic stimulation (TMS) uses a brief magnetic field to stimulate cortical neurons beneath the skin and skull (see Chapter 2). In one study (Classen et al., 1998), focal TMS was used in human volunteers to evoke isolated thumb movements in a particular direction. Then the people practiced moving the thumb in a different direction for 15–30 minutes. The same TMS was then found to evoke thumb movement in the *new* direction for several minutes before the response reverted to the original direction. (This rapid change seems similar to the retuning of auditory cortical receptors during stimulation at another frequency, as noted in Chapter 9.) It seems likely that the change in response to TMS reflected at least the beginning of

11.17 MOTOR LEARNING CAUSES REMAPPING OF MOTOR CORTEX (A) A map of forelimb control in rat motor cortex, prior to training (green areas control digits and wrist; blue areas, shoulder and elbow). (B) The same rat's motor cortex, following 10 days of training on a task requiring precise reaching and grasping with the forepaw. The representation of the digits and wrist (green) has expanded into areas previously associated with the shoulder and elbow. (Courtesy of Dr. J. Kleim.)

(A) Before training

(B) After training

Digits and wrist
Shoulder and elbow

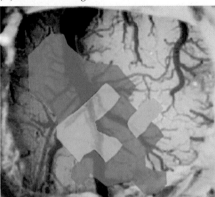

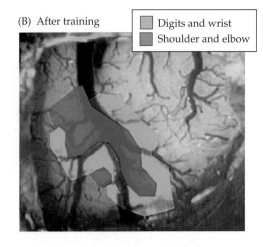

plastic changes in motor cortex in response to practice. In rats, cortical remodeling due to motor learning has been directly observed by means of sophisticated mapping of the motor cortex before and after training of a new skill (Monfils et al., 2005) (**FIGURE 11.17**).

Nonprimary motor cortex aids complex behaviors

Just anterior to M1 are cortical regions that are also important for motor control. Because they are not primary motor cortex, they are called **nonprimary motor cortex**. Despite the name, nonprimary motor systems can contribute to behavior directly, through communication with lower levels of the motor hierarchy in the brainstem and spinal cord systems, as well as indirectly through M1. The traditional account of nonprimary motor cortex emphasizes two main regions: the **supplementary motor area** (**SMA**), which lies mainly on the medial aspect of the hemisphere, and the **premotor cortex**, which is anterior to the primary motor cortex (**FIGURE 11.18**). A rough idea of the different functions of these two nonprimary motor regions is that the SMA is important for planning movements that are internally generated, while the premotor cortex directs movement in response to external cues.

Patients with bilateral damage to the SMA are unable to move voluntarily (only some automatic and reflex movements remain), suggesting that this region is important for planning movement sequences (Tanji, 2001). In one example, cerebral blood flow was measured during simple tasks, such as keeping a spring compressed between two fingers of one hand (P. E. Roland, 1984). As you might expect, this task produced a marked increase in blood flow to the contralateral M1, but increasing the complexity of the tasks to form a sequence of behaviors extended the area of

nonprimary motor cortex Frontal lobe regions adjacent to the primary motor cortex that contribute to motor control and modulate the activity of the primary motor cortex.

supplementary motor area (SMA) A region of nonprimary motor cortex that receives input from the basal ganglia and modulates the activity of the primary motor cortex.

premotor cortex A region of nonprimary motor cortex just anterior to the primary motor cortex.

11.18 HUMAN MOTOR CORTICAL AREAS (A) The primary motor cortex (M1) lies just anterior to the central sulcus. Anterior to the primary motor cortex are the premotor cortex and the supplementary motor area (SMA), which together make up the nonprimary motor cortex. Although we show the premotor cortex here as a unitary structure for the sake of clarity, recent evidence from non-human primates indicates that it is a mosaic of subareas with distinct properties. (B) The SMA lies mainly on the medial surface of the cerebral hemispheres.

(A) Lateral view

Premotor cortex

Supplementary motor area

Primary motor cortex

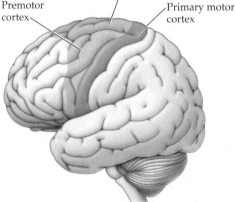

(B) Medial view

Supplementary motor area

Primary motor cortex

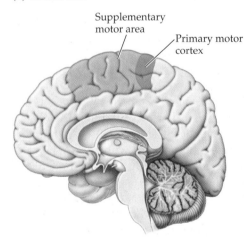

increased blood flow to include the SMA. When people simply mentally *rehearse* the complex movement sequence without actually doing it, the enhanced blood flow is seen only in the SMA, not in M1.

In contrast to the observations from the SMA, the premotor cortex is activated when motor sequences are guided externally by stimuli (Halsband et al., 1994; J. Larsson et al., 1996) rather than generated internally. The premotor cortex is not a single system, but really a mosaic of different units serving separate but overlapping functions in organizing complex motor behavior (Graziano, 2006; Graziano and Aflalo, 2007). These behaviors cluster together in major categories: defensive movements, feeding behavior, and so on. For example, a subset of premotor neurons is activated when objects are brought close to a monkey's face or hand. If the lights are then turned off, some of these neurons continue to fire even if the object is silently moved away, suggesting that the cells are coding for where the monkey *thinks* the object is (Graziano et al., 1997). When the lights are turned back on and the monkey sees that the object is gone, the neurons cease firing. Such neurons may help us reach out for objects that are no longer visible.

In general, evidence is mounting that we should think of the organization of motor and premotor areas in terms of the mapping of behaviors, rather than the mapping of specific movements (Graziano and Aflalo, 2007). It's an idea that is nicely illustrated by recent discoveries about a unique population of premotor neurons, called *mirror neurons*, which we'll discuss next.

Mirror neurons in premotor cortex track movements in others

One of the subregions making up the mosaic of premotor cortex, an area known as *F5*, contains a population of remarkable neurons that seem to fulfill two functions. These neurons fire shortly before a monkey makes a very particular movement of the hand and arm to reach for an object; different neurons fire during different reaching movements. These results suggest that these neurons trigger specific movements. But these neurons also fire whenever the monkey sees *another* monkey (or a human) make that same movement. These cells are called **mirror neurons** because they fire as though the monkey were imitating the movements of the other individual (**FIGURE 11.19**). They are matching the observed behavior with an internal motor representation of that behavior, as if the monkey were imagining doing the same thing as the individual it is watching.

MRI and EEG studies indicate that mirror neurons are also found in adult humans (Buccino et al., 2004) and children (J. F. Lepage and Theoret, 2006). In the classic "mirror game," in which one person moves slowly and the other tries to imitate the first person as closely as possible, these neurons are probably at work. They have also been seen in other areas of frontal cortex (Nelissen et al., 2005) and parietal cortex (Fogassi et al., 2005). The activity of these neurons suggests that they are important in the understanding of other individuals' actions and in attempts to imitate those actions (Rizzolatti and Craighero, 2004). Indeed, using TMS to disrupt premotor cortex made it more difficult for participants to guess what sort of actions other people were miming (Michael et. al., 2014). It's possible that this function of mirror neurons is the basis for acting jointly with others to accomplish a cooperative task.

mirror neuron A neuron that is active both when an individual makes a particular movement and when that individual sees another individual make that same movement.

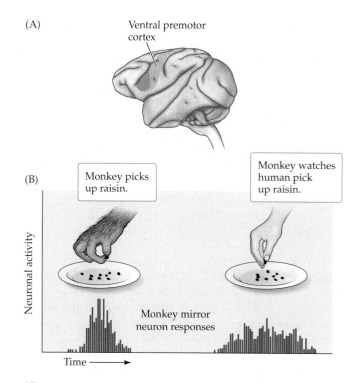

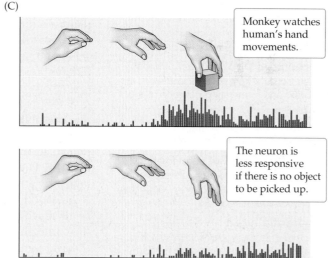

11.19 MIRROR NEURONS (A) In the ventral portion of premotor cortex known as *area F5*, many mirror neurons are found. (B) This neuron fires just before a monkey reaches for an object, such as a raisin (left), or when the monkey sees a human experimenter reach for that object in the same manner (right). (C) This mirror neuron fires when the monkey reaches for a box or, as here, it observes a human reaching for a box (top). The mirror neuron also fires, but much less vigorously, if there is no box for the human to grasp (bottom) (Umilta et al., 2001). (After Rizzolatti et al., 2006.)

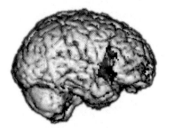 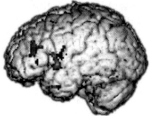

Right hemisphere   Left hemisphere

11.20 UNDERACTIVATION OF MIRROR CELLS IN AUTISM When control children and children with autism are asked to imitate the emotional facial expressions displayed in photographs of other people, many brain regions show activation in both groups. But the indicated region, the pars opercularis region, is less activated in children with autism than in controls. This is the region that contains "mirror neurons." Perhaps deficits in activating brain regions underlying imitation and empathy contribute to the social impairments of autism. (After Dapretto et al., 2006, courtesy of Dr. Mirella Dapretto.)

extrapyramidal system A motor system that includes the basal ganglia and some closely related brainstem structures.

reticulospinal tract A tract of axons arising from the brainstem reticular formation and descending to the spinal cord to modulate movement.

reticular formation An extensive region of the brainstem (extending from the medulla through the thalamus) that is involved in arousal and motor control.

rubrospinal tract A tract of axons arising from the red nucleus in the midbrain and innervating neurons of the spinal cord.

red nucleus A brainstem structure related to motor control.

basal ganglia A group of forebrain nuclei, including caudate nucleus, globus pallidus, and putamen, found deep within the cerebral hemispheres.

substantia nigra A brainstem structure in humans that innervates the basal ganglia and is named for its dark pigmentation.

subthalamic nucleus A nucleus just ventral to the thalamus that interacts with the basal ganglia; a favored site for deep brain stimulation to treat Parkinson's disease.

striatum The caudate nucleus and putamen together.

It is intriguing to think that mirror neurons may help us understand what other people are doing, because the idea suggests a neural basis for empathy. Thus, there has been a great deal of speculation about the function of mirror neurons in the imitating behavior of human infants, the evolution of language, and other behavior (Caramazza et al., 2014). Some have speculated that people with autism, which is characterized by a failure to anticipate other people's thinking and actions, may have a deficit in mirror neuron activity (J. H. Williams et al., 2006). When people with autism make "copycat" movements of the fingers or body, which they find difficult, a brain region that contains mirror neurons (the inferior frontal cortex) is less activated than in people without autism (Villalobos et al., 2005). The same region is also underactivated when people with autism try to mimic emotional facial expressions of others (**FIGURE 11.20**) (Dapretto et al., 2006). Perhaps a deficit in mirror neurons in such a brain region renders other people's behaviors so bewildering that the child withdraws from social relations and language.

Extrapyramidal Systems Also Modulate Motor Commands

In addition to the corticospinal outflow from primary and nonprimary motor cortices through the pyramidal tract, many other motor tracts run from the forebrain to the brainstem and spinal cord. Because these tracts are outside the pyramids of the medulla, they and their connections are called the **extrapyramidal system**. The two most important components of the extrapyramidal system are the basal ganglia and the cerebellum.

How do these components of the extrapyramidal system communicate with the spinal cord? Their messages are transmitted via two brainstem pathways: the **reticulospinal tract**, which originates in the **reticular formation** of the brainstem, and the **rubrospinal tract**, which originates from the midbrain's **red nucleus** (the Latin *ruber* means "red"). Both tracts send axons down the spinal cord to synapse on spinal interneurons.

Using these brainstem pathways, the basal ganglia and cerebellum play slightly different roles in controlling motor output, as we'll see next.

The basal ganglia modulate movements

The **basal ganglia** include a group of interconnected forebrain nuclei: the caudate nucleus, putamen, and globus pallidus. Closely associated with these structures are two nuclei in the midbrain: the **substantia nigra** and the **subthalamic nucleus**. **FIGURE 11.21** shows the locations of these structures. The caudate nucleus and putamen together are referred to as the **striatum**.

Each of these structures receives input from wide areas of the cerebral cortex and sends much of its output back to the cortex via the thalamus, forming a loop from the cortex through the basal ganglia and thalamus and back to the cortex. Lesions of basal ganglia in humans produce movement impairments that seem quite different from those that follow interruption of the pyramidal system. Two disorders described later in the chapter—Parkinson's disease and Huntington's disease—are caused by degeneration of the basal ganglia.

Lesions and recordings of single neurons during motor responses indicate that each structure of the basal ganglia contains a topographic representation of body musculature (DeLong et al., 1984). The basal ganglia play a role in determining the amplitude and direction of movement and the initiation of movement (Yttri and Dudman, 2016). Much of the motor function of the basal ganglia appears to be accomplished by modulating other brain circuits, such as the motor pathways of the cortex (see Figure 11.4). The basal ganglia are especially important in the performance of movements influenced by memories, in contrast to those guided by sensory control

(Graybiel et al., 1994). The basal ganglia are also important in skill learning (Rueda-Orozco and Robbe, 2015), as we'll discuss in Chapter 17 (see Figure 17.17).

The cerebellum affects programs, coordination, and learning of acts

Across vertebrate groups, the size of the cerebellum varies according to the range and complexity of movements. For example, the cerebellum is much larger in fishes with extensive locomotor behavior than it is in less active fishes; it is also larger in flying birds than in bird species that do not fly.

The outer layers of the cerebellum are called the *cerebellar cortex* and are dominated by a sheet of large multipolar cells called *Purkinje cells* (see Figure 2.18). All output of the cerebellar cortex travels via the axons of Purkinje cells, all of which synapse with the deep cerebellar nuclei. At these synapses, Purkinje cells produce only inhibitory postsynaptic potentials. Hence, all the circuitry of the extensive cortical portion of the cerebellum, which also includes 10–20 billion granule cells in humans, guides movement by *inhibiting* neurons.

Inputs to the cerebellar cortex come both from sensory sources and from other brain motor systems. Sensory inputs include the muscle and joint receptors and the vestibular, somatosensory, visual, and auditory systems. Both pyramidal and nonpyramidal pathways contribute inputs to the cerebellum and in turn receive outputs from the deep nuclei of the cerebellum. It has been suggested that the cerebellum elaborates neural "programs" for the control of skilled movements, particularly rapid, repeated movements that become automatic. In fact, we now know that the cerebellum is crucial for a wide variety of motor (Brooks et al., 2015) and nonmotor learning (Katz and Steinmetz, 2002), as discussed in more detail in Chapter 17 (see Figure 17.17).

Despite the importance of the cerebellum in movement and learning, sometimes people are born without a cerebellum and the plasticity of the developing brain compensates so well that the missing structure may be discovered only by accident, as at routine autopsy (Boyd, 2010) or from a brain scan (F. Yu et al., 2015) (**FIGURE 11.22**).

The cerebellum and the basal ganglia contribute differently to the modulation of motor functions

The foregoing discussion and Figure 11.4 indicate that the cerebellum and the basal ganglia occupy rather similar positions in modulating motor functions. However, Yijun Liu et al. (1999) found differences in the activity of these brain regions when they examined fMRI responses of people performing a tactile discrimination task. The people were given two similarly shaped objects—one in each hand—and they had to decide by active touching whether the objects were the same or different.

Changing patterns of activity during this task were found in M1, the SMA, the cerebellum, and the basal ganglia. Cerebellar activity correlated significantly with activity of the SMA but not with activity of M1, whereas basal ganglia activity correlated more strongly with activity of M1 than of the SMA. The difference in times of activation of the two regions reinforces the notion that cerebellum and basal ganglia play different roles in behavior. The basal ganglia work with motor cortex to initiate and terminate movements (Cui et al., 2013), while the cerebellum and SMA (Bonini et al., 2014) monitor ongoing activity to produce smooth movements (**FIGURE 11.23**).

We'll see these different contributions of the cerebellum and basal ganglia in the task of reaching, when we consider brain disorders of move-

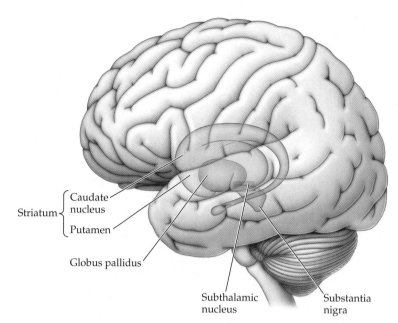

11.21 BASAL GANGLIA INVOLVED IN MOVEMENT Several structures within the basal ganglia are involved in modulating and tuning the movements programmed by other systems.

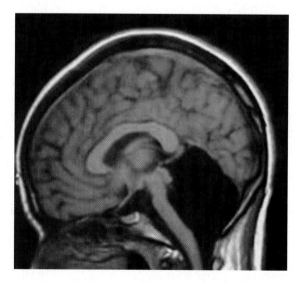

11.22 A WOMAN WITHOUT A CEREBELLUM (From F. Yu et al., 2015.)

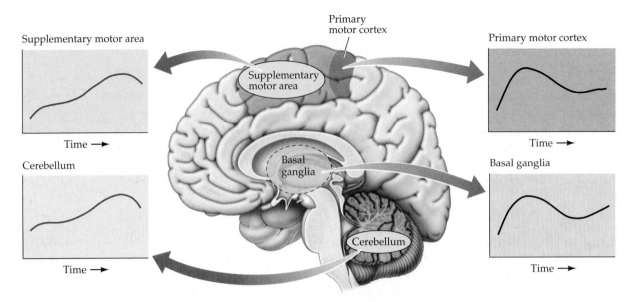

11.23 CONTRIBUTIONS OF THE CEREBELLUM AND BASAL GANGLIA TO THE MODULATION OF MOVEMENTS Cerebellar activity correlates with that of the supplementary motor area; basal ganglia activity correlates with that of primary motor cortex. (After Y. Liu et al., 1999.)

ment, next. As we saw in Figure 11.1B, patients with Huntington's disease, who suffer from damage to the basal ganglia, show impairment especially *terminating* a reach, because their movements become ballistic and sensorimotor feedback is delayed. Parkinson's disease, which damages the basal ganglia in a different way, is characterized by difficulty *initiating* a reach but smooth movement once the reach has been started (because, once the movement begins, the intact cerebellum takes over ongoing coordination). In contrast, people with cerebellar damage are able to initiate movements without difficulty and typically stop at the final target, but they take serpentine paths to the target, suggesting difficulty in *ongoing* motor control.

Brain Disorders Can Disrupt Movement

We've already described movement impairment caused by disorders of muscle, motor neuron, and neuromuscular junctions, as well as spinal cord injury. Other movement disorders are caused by disorders of the brain, including the cortex, basal ganglia, and cerebellum, which we'll discuss in order.

Cerebral cortex pathology causes some motor impairments

The most common motor impairments that follow strokes or injury to the human cerebral cortex are paralysis (**plegia**) or weakness (**paresis**) of voluntary movements, usually on one side of the body (known as *hemiplegia* and *hemiparesis*). Generally the paralysis appears on the side of the body opposite the injured hemisphere. In addition, affected patients show some **spasticity**: increased rigidity in response to forced movement of the limbs. This rigid spasticity after cortical damage contrasts with the flaccid paralysis seen when the spinal cord is damaged.

Spasticity reflects the exaggeration of stretch reflexes that have been released from the inhibition they usually receive from the cortex. Abnormal reflexes occur, such as the flaring and extension of the toes elicited by stroking the sole of the foot (the Babinski reflex). In the months following cerebral cortical injury, the clinical picture changes. The initial paralysis slowly diminishes, and some voluntary movements of the limbs return, although fine motor control of fingers is seldom regained. In humans the symptoms are more severe than in many other mammals.

Damage to nonmotor zones of the cerebral cortex, such as some regions of parietal or frontal association cortex, produces more-complicated changes in motor control.

plegia Paralysis, the loss of the ability to move.

paresis Partial paralysis.

spasticity Markedly increased rigidity in response to forced movement of the limbs.

One condition characterized by such damage is **apraxia** (from the Greek *a-*, "not," and *praxis*, "action"), the inability to carry out complex movements even though paralysis or weakness is not evident and language comprehension and motivation are intact. Apraxia is illustrated in the following example: When asked to smile, a patient is unable to do so, although he certainly attempts to. If asked to use a comb placed in front of him, he seems unable to figure out what to do. But things aren't as simple as they might appear. At one point in the discussion, the patient spontaneously smiles, and at another point he retrieves a comb from his pocket and combs his hair with ease and accuracy. Apraxia is a symptom of a variety of disorders, including stroke, Alzheimer's disease, and developmental disorders of children.

Neurologists studying patients who have suffered strokes have discovered several different types of apraxia. **Ideomotor apraxia** is characterized by the inability to carry out a *simple* motor activity, either in response to a verbal command ("Smile" or "Use this comb") or by copying someone else's gesture, even though this same activity is readily performed spontaneously. **Ideational apraxia** is an impairment in carrying out a *sequence* of actions, although each step can be done correctly (Zadikoff and Lang, 2005). Patients with ideational apraxia have difficulty carrying out instructions for a sequence of acts—"Push the button, then pull the handle, then depress the switch"—but they can do each of these tasks in isolation. Apraxia may be somewhat independent of language deficits; the patients may be perfectly good at naming objects (Rosci et al., 2003) yet unable to perform the requested sequence of actions with those objects.

In Parkinson's disease the death of dopaminergic neurons alters activity of the basal ganglia

About 200 years ago, physician James Parkinson noted people in London who moved quite slowly, showed regular tremors of the hands and face while at rest, and walked with a rigid bearing. Another feature of what is now known as **Parkinson's disease** is a loss of facial muscle tone, which gives the face a masklike appearance. Patients who suffer from Parkinson's also show few spontaneous actions and have great difficulty in all motor efforts, no matter how routine. The hands may display tremors while at rest but move smoothly while performing a task. Parkinson's disease afflicts almost 1% of the U.S. population age 65 and older, but it sometimes unaccountably occurs in younger people, such as actor Michael J. Fox (**FIGURE 11.24**).

Patients with Parkinson's show progressive degeneration of dopamine-containing cells in the substantia nigra that project to the basal ganglia, particularly the caudate nucleus and putamen. The loss of cells in this area is continual, but symptoms begin

apraxia An impairment in the ability to begin and execute skilled voluntary movements, even though there is no muscle paralysis.

ideomotor apraxia The inability to carry out a simple motor activity in response to a verbal command, even though this same activity is readily performed spontaneously.

ideational apraxia An impairment in the ability to carry out a sequence of actions, even though each element or step can be done correctly.

Parkinson's disease A degenerative neurological disorder, characterized by tremors at rest, muscular rigidity, and reduction in voluntary movement, that involves dopaminergic neurons of the substantia nigra.

11.24 LEADERS IN THE CAMPAIGN AGAINST PARKINSON'S DISEASE Parkinson's disease can strike at any point in adulthood. Actor Michael J. Fox was just 30 years old when he was diagnosed with Parkinson's, in 1991. Shown here testifying before a U.S. Senate health committee with fellow Parkinson's sufferer Muhammad Ali (1942–2016), Fox heads a research foundation (michaeljfox.org) that provides funding and advocacy for Parkinson's disease research.

BOX 11.2

Prion-Like Neurodegeneration May Be at Work in Parkinson's

Over two centuries ago, shepherds in Europe recognized a fatal disease in sheep that was called *scrapie* because the animals "scraped" their skin, presumably in an attempt to relieve itching. The shepherds learned that the only way they could stop an outbreak was to kill all the sheep, burn the carcasses and the fields they had used, and keep new sheep away from those fields for years. They didn't know it, but these drastic measures were needed because the disease is not transmitted by a virus or bacterium, which would rely on relatively fragile DNA or RNA for reproduction. Rather, scrapie arises when a particular endogenous protein that normally takes one shape takes on a new, abnormal shape. Once one protein molecule is misfolded, it induces the other molecules of that protein to fold abnormally around it. The accumulation of abnormally folded proteins forms toxic clumps that lead to brain degeneration. These infectious protein particles were named **prions** (pronounced "PREE-ons").

At some point, feed that contained protein derived from sheep with scrapie was fed to some cows in England and caused the cow version of the prion protein to fold abnormally. The result was a bovine version of scrapie called **bovine spongiform encephalopathy** (BSE, or *mad*

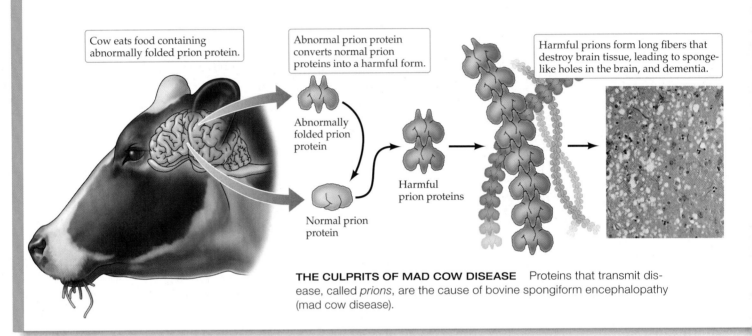

Cow eats food containing abnormally folded prion protein.

Abnormal prion protein converts normal prion proteins into a harmful form.

Abnormally folded prion protein

Normal prion protein

Harmful prion proteins

Harmful prions form long fibers that destroy brain tissue, leading to sponge-like holes in the brain, and dementia.

THE CULPRITS OF MAD COW DISEASE Proteins that transmit disease, called *prions*, are the cause of bovine spongiform encephalopathy (mad cow disease).

---

to appear only after extensive cell death (Coelho and Ferreira, 2012). The discovery of a form of the disorder induced by illicit drugs (Kopin and Markey, 1988) suggests that exposure to toxins over a prolonged period underlies the development of the disorder.

Most cases of Parkinson's disease are not inherited (Trinh and Farrer, 2013), but in one large Italian family, Parkinson's disease develops in members who inherit a defective copy of the gene that encodes **α-synuclein** (Polymeropoulos et al., 1997), a protein normally expressed in the basal ganglia. Another family with inherited Parkinson's disease turned out to have a defective copy of another gene, named *parkin*, which encodes the protein **parkin** (Lucking et al., 2000; Shimura et al., 2001).

Mutation of the α-synuclein gene, or having an overabundance of the protein due to a duplication of the normal gene (Kim et al., 2012; Soldner et al., 2016), leads to abnormal accumulation of α-synuclein into clumps called *Lewy bodies* in the dopaminergic cells. The misfolding of α-synuclein to form these clumps is reminiscent of prion diseases, where misfolded proteins can transmit disease from one individual to another (**BOX 11.2**).

In the noninherited cases of Parkinson's, other factors, such as toxins or brain injury, may accelerate the formation of Lewy bodies that are associated with the death of the dopaminergic cells. Thus, it might be possible someday to prevent Parkinson's by developing drugs to stop or reverse the accumulation of α-synuclein (Hebron et al., 2015; Menzies et al., 2015).

There was no treatment for Parkinson's disease until the late 1960s, when administration of a precursor to dopamine was found to enhance the dopamine levels of

α-synuclein A protein that has been implicated in Parkinson's disease.

parkin A protein that has been implicated in Parkinson's disease.

L-dopa The immediate precursor of the transmitter dopamine.

deep brain stimulation (DBS) Mild electrical stimulation through an electrode that is surgically implanted deep in the brain.

cow disease) because the massive brain degeneration leaves the brain "spongy" (figure). Unfortunately, before BSE was detected, infected cows provided beef for Britons and caused a similar disorder called **Creutzfeldt-Jakob disease (CJD)**, infecting over 100,000 people in the United Kingdom. CJD is fatal, causing widespread brain degeneration and therefore dementia, sleep disorders (see Chapter 14), schizophrenia-like symptoms, and death. Although a few cases of BSE have now been detected in North American cattle, currently they are believed to pose little risk to human health, thanks to changes in screening and feed production procedures.

There is increasing speculation that similar misfolding of other proteins, leading to clumping and toxicity, might underlie other neurodegenerative diseases, including Alzheimer's disease (Walsh and Selkoe, 2016), which we discussed in Chapter 7, and Parkinson's (Theillet et al., 2016). As we noted in the main text, mutations in α-synuclein can cause Parkinson's disease, and these mutations make the protein more likely to misfold and form toxic fibrils that clump to form Lewy bodies. Infusing misfolded α-synuclein fibrils into the brain of healthy mice or rats recapitulates the Lewy bodies and motor defects seen in mutant mice (Luna and Luk 2015). Thus progressive misfolding of more and more α-synuclein molecules may spread degeneration, in which case therapies to prevent or reverse misfolding may one day halt or reverse Parkinson's.

prion   A protein that can become improperly folded and thereby can induce other proteins to follow suit, leading to long protein chains that impair neural function.

bovine spongiform encephalopathy (BSE)   Also called *mad cow disease*. A disorder caused by improperly formed prion proteins, leading to dementia and death.

Creutzfeldt-Jakob disease (CJD)   A brain disorder in humans, leading to dementia and death, that is caused by improperly folded prion proteins; the human equivalent of mad cow disease.

surviving cells. The precursor, called **L-dopa**, markedly reduces symptoms in patients with Parkinson's; notably, it decreases tremors and increases the speed of movements. Although L-dopa can reverse some symptoms of Parkinson's disease, neuron loss in the substantia nigra is relentless. Because the cell bodies in the brainstem degenerate, dopamine-containing terminals in the caudate nucleus and putamen also disappear. Eventually, too few dopamine-containing neurons remain in the substantia nigra, and L-dopa stops being effective.

Electrical stimulation of sites within the basal ganglia, often the subthalamic nucleus, can reduce the symptoms of Parkinson's disease (de Hemptinne et al., 2015). This **deep brain stimulation (DBS)** requires the surgical implantation of electrodes into the brain (**FIGURE 11.25**),

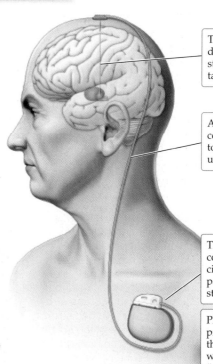

Thin wire electrodes deliver mild electrical stimulation to the target region.

An insulated wire connects the electrode to the stimulation unit.

The stimulation unit contains a battery and circuitry to act like a pacemaker to stimulate the brain.

Physicians can program and adjust the stimulator settings with a handheld "remote control."

11.25 DEEP BRAIN STIMULATION TO TREAT PARKINSON'S DISEASE   For many patients, mild electrical stimulation of the brain brings relief of symptoms such as tremors and slow movement. The most common brain targets are the globus pallidus and the subthalamic nucleus (see Figure 11.21).

and it carries the risk of cognitive side effects such as impulsivity and difficulty making decisions (M. J. Frank et al., 2007).

Another way to compensate for the loss of dopaminergic neurons might be to replace them with new ones. In several experimental treatments, fetal neurons or stem cells have been transplanted into the brains of people with severe Parkinson's in the hope that enough of the cells would establish dopaminergic synaptic connections in the basal ganglia to alleviate the symptoms of the disease. Although significant symptom relief has been reported in some people with Parkinson's (Barker et al., 2015), it's not clear whether these transplants will become a viable treatment option. For one thing, evidence suggests that the transplanted cells may somehow go on to develop Parkinson's disease themselves (Kordower et al., 2008). And although the graft of fetal cells clearly improves the condition of some patients, other patients with grafts become afflicted with severe involuntary movements (Olanow et al., 2003). Debate about this procedure will continue for the foreseeable future.

Another aspect of Parkinson's disease is that some patients show marked cognitive decline during the course of their illness (J. L. Cummings, 1995). Depression in patients with Parkinson's is also common; some researchers have attributed such depression to the consequences of reduced mobility and the general stress of such incapacity. However, L-dopa treatment for Parkinson's disease sometimes produces impulsive behaviors such as gambling (Szarfman et al., 2006), probably by enhancing dopamine signaling in the pathway from the ventral tegmental area (VTA) to the nucleus accumbens that we discussed in Chapter 4 (see Figure 4.22). So depression in Parkinson's may be a direct effect of depleted dopamine in that pathway.

Huntington's disease is characterized by excessive movement caused by deterioration of the basal ganglia

Whereas damage to the basal ganglia in Parkinson's disease *slows* movement, other kinds of basal ganglia disorders cause *excessive* movement. An example of the latter type was reported by George Huntington, a physician whose publication (1872) described a strange motor affliction. The first symptoms of **Huntington's disease** are subtle behavior changes: clumsiness, and twitches in the fingers and face. Subtlety is rapidly lost as the illness progresses; a continuing stream of involuntary jerks engulfs the entire body. Aimless movements of the eyes, jerky leg movements, and writhing of the body turn the routine activities of the day into insurmountable obstacles. Worse yet, as the disease progresses, marked behavior changes include intellectual deterioration, depression, and, in a minority of patients, a psychotic state that resembles schizophrenia. In some patients, cognitive and emotional changes may appear many years before obvious motor impairments do (Wexler et al., 1991). Huntington's disease usually develops over a period of 15–20 years. The neuroanatomical basis of this disorder is the profound, progressive destruction of the basal ganglia, especially the caudate nucleus and the putamen (**FIGURE 11.26**).

George Huntington correctly deduced that the disorder is inherited, passed from generation to generation. Careful analysis of family pedigrees eventually revealed

Huntington's disease Also called *Huntington's chorea*. A progressive genetic disorder characterized by abrupt, involuntary movements and profound changes in mental functioning.

huntingtin A protein produced by a gene (called *HTT*) that, when containing too many trinucleotide repeats, results in Huntington's disease in a carrier.

trinucleotide repeat Repetition of the same three nucleotides within a gene, which can lead to dysfunction, as in the cases of Huntington's disease and fragile X syndrome (see Chapter 7).

11.26 NEUROPATHOLOGY IN HUNTINGTON'S DISEASE Compared with the control (A), a coronal MRI section through the brain of a patient suffering from Huntington's disease (B) shows marked enlargement of the lateral ventricles, caused by atrophy of the neighboring caudate nucleus and putamen. Note also the shrunken cortical gyri and enlarged sulci of the patient compared with those of the brain of a healthy person. (MRI images courtesy of Drs. Terry L. Jernigan and C. Fennema Notestine.)

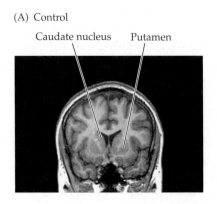

(A) Control

Caudate nucleus   Putamen

(B) Patient with Huntington's disease

Lateral ventricles

that Huntington's disease is transmitted by a single dominant gene on chromosome 4 (Gusella and MacDonald, 1993). Because we have two copies of every gene but pass only one of them on to any one child, each child of a person with Huntington's has a 50% chance of inheriting the bad gene and eventually developing the disease. The affected gene, *HTT*, normally encodes a protein called **huntingtin**. In Huntington's disease, the huntingtin protein that is produced is abnormally lengthened because of a series of three nucleotides (CAG; see the Appendix) that is repeated over and over in the *HTT* gene. If the gene contains fewer than 30 of these **trinucleotide repeats**, no symptoms appear, but if there are 35 or more CAG trinucleotide repeats in the *HTT* gene, the person will develop Huntington's disease (Squitieri, 2013).

We don't yet know what the function of the normal huntingtin protein is, or how the abnormal version of the protein causes the symptoms of Huntington's disease (Bates et al., 2015). It's possible that the elongated protein binds inappropriately to other molecules, somehow gumming up important cellular processes (Martinez-Vicente, 2010). Another mystery concerns the tissue specificity of Huntington's disease: why does the mutant huntingtin protein selectively damage the basal ganglia, when it is also being expressed in neurons and glial cells throughout the brain as well as in cells in muscle, liver, and testes? There's evidence that the abnormal protein, after killing one neuron, spreads to neurons that had innervated the dying cell (Pecho-Vrieseling et al., 2014), spreading the damage within the basal ganglia.

The example of Huntington's disease, with its increased movements, demonstrates the major role that inhibition plays in normal motor control. Without adequate inhibition, a person is compelled to perform a variety of unwanted movements. We saw in Figure 11.1B that patients with Huntington's disease are less accurate in reaching for a target. People whose genetic tests reveal that they will develop Huntington's disease show some impairment in accuracy of reaching several years before apparent onset of the disease (M. A. Smith et al., 2000).

Cerebellar damage causes many types of impairment

Because the cerebellum modulates many aspects of motor performance, it is not surprising that its impairment leads to many abnormalities of behavior. These symptoms permit an examiner to identify with considerable accuracy which part of the cerebellum is damaged (Dichgans, 1984).

The cerebellum has three major functional divisions (**FIGURE 11.27**), and a unique pattern of impairment results from damage to each. The uppermost part of the cerebellum, or **spinocerebellum** (consisting mostly of structures called the *vermis* and *anterior lobe*), receives sensory information about the current spatial locations of the parts of the body and anticipates subsequent movement. The spinocerebellum has rich connections with descending motor pathways, which it modulates. Damage here produces characteristic abnormalities of gait and posture, especially **ataxia** (loss of coordination) of the legs. Long-term alcoholism can cause degeneration of the anterior lobe of the cerebellum, resulting in characteristic weaving and erratic gait.

The lowermost part of the cerebellum (consisting especially of the lateral part of each cerebellar hemisphere) is called the **cerebrocerebellum** in recognition of its close relationship with the cerebral cortex. The cerebrocerebellum is implicated in planning complex movements, so damage here can cause diverse motor problems, such as **decomposition of movement**, in which gestures are broken up into individual segments instead of being executed smoothly. Because the cerebrocerebellum also functions in higher-level cognition, such as motor learning, damage here can also cause cognitive deficits.

spinocerebellum The uppermost part of the cerebellum, consisting mostly of the vermis and anterior lobe.

ataxia An impairment in the direction, extent, and rate of muscular movement; often caused by cerebellar pathology.

cerebrocerebellum The lowermost part of the cerebellum, consisting especially of the lateral part of each cerebellar hemisphere.

decomposition of movement Difficulty of movement in which gestures are broken up into individual segments instead of being executed smoothly; a symptom of cerebellar lesions.

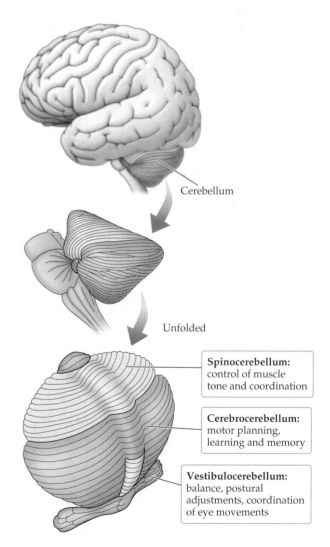

Cerebellum

Unfolded

Spinocerebellum: control of muscle tone and coordination

Cerebrocerebellum: motor planning, learning and memory

Vestibulocerebellum: balance, postural adjustments, coordination of eye movements

11.27 FUNCTIONAL ORGANIZATION OF THE CEREBELLUM

vestibulocerebellum The middle portion of the cerebellum, sandwiched between the spinocerebellum and the cerebrocerebellum and consisting of the nodule and the flocculus.

Cre-recombinase An enzyme normally made by bacteria that removes a segment of DNA flanked by two lox sites.

loxP A specific sequence of nucleotides recognized by the enzyme Cre-recombinase. If the enzyme encounters a pair of loxP sites in a gene, it will remove the DNA between the two sites and recombine the gene, usually rendering the gene product dysfunctional.

Sandwiched between the two major divisions of the cerebellum is the **vestibulocerebellum**, made up of small and somewhat primitive structures called the *nodule* and *flocculus*. As its name suggests, the vestibulocerebellum has close connections with the vestibular nuclei of the brainstem, through which it receives information about body orientation. Its outputs help the motor systems to maintain posture and guide eye movements (Herzfeld et al., 2015); for example, damage to this system produces errors in gaze and difficulty with tracking visual objects as the head moves.

With more research, we are coming to realize that the cerebellum plays a crucial role in an astonishingly wide variety of behaviors. So maybe we shouldn't be too surprised by the report that this compact structure contains more than half of all the neurons in the human nervous system (B. B. Andersen et al., 1992).

▊ The Cutting Edge

Cerebellar Glia Play a Role in Fine Motor Coordination

As we noted above, damage to the cerebellum often results in disruption of locomotion—the person may have difficulty walking, or navigating stairs. Historically, neuroscientists focused their attention on the activity of neurons to understand such behaviors. However, recent years have brought a greater appreciation for the importance of glial cells in neural function, including those in the cerebellum. For example, we now know that many glial cells possess receptors that respond to neurotransmitter released from nearby synapses. Neuroscientists are eager to understand what, if any, contribution these glial cells make to synaptic signaling and behavior.

In the cerebellum, special astrocytes called *Bergmann glia* send processes along Purkinje cell dendrites, surrounding synapses between parallel fibers from granule cells and the Purkinje cell dendrites (**FIGURE 11.28A**). These Bergmann glia possess AMPA-type receptors that normally recognize the neurotransmitter glutamate (see Chapter 4). Do those AMPA receptors on the glia have any effect on cerebellar function? To address this issue, Saab et al., (2012) produced mice in which they could disable genes for the AMPA receptor in Bergmann glia but leave AMPA receptors functioning normally in other cells, including the two neurons making the synapse.

To accomplish this neat trick, the researchers exploited an enzyme, normally found only in bacteria, called **Cre-recombinase**. This enzyme recognizes certain very specific sequences of nucleotides in DNA called **loxP**. When the enzyme encounters a pair of lox sites in DNA, it snips the DNA at those points, throws out the intervening bit of DNA, then joins the cut ends of DNA back together (see Appendix). If the lox sites are placed properly, the recombined gene will be disabled, unable to make a functional protein. This Cre-lox system can be used to "knock out" particular genes in some cells while leaving the gene alone in other cells in the same mouse.

In this case, the researchers first made mice that express the bacterial recombinase gene, called *Cre*, only in glial cells. Then they bred these mice with mice in which lox sites had been inserted into the genes for AMPA receptors. In offspring that received all these genes, *Cre* was expressed only in glia, which meant that AMPA receptors were knocked out of Bergmann glia but were undisturbed in cerebellar neurons (**FIGURE 11.28B**).

Did the absence of AMPA receptors in the Bergmann glia make any difference to cerebellar function? Yes. First, the researchers found that synapses between parallel fibers and Purkinje cells were weaker in animals without AMPA receptors on Bergmann glia. And while the genetically manipulated animals' behavior was relatively normal, when they were given a challenging locomotor task (walking along a special ladder), they made more mistakes than control mice (**FIGURE 11.28C**). Thus the AMPA receptors in Bergmann glia somehow strengthen synaptic connections between parallel fibers and Purkinje cells, and this appears to be important for fine motor coordination. Now researchers are eager to find out how AMPA receptors in Bergmann glia accomplish all this. As usual with cutting-edge science, answering one question brings up many more.

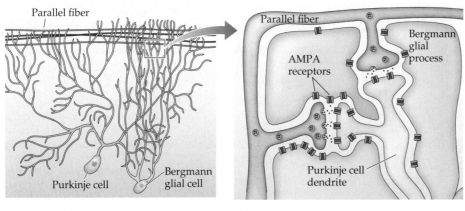

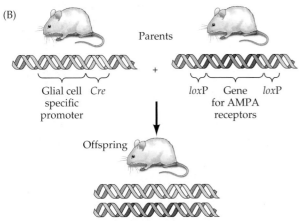

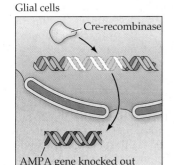

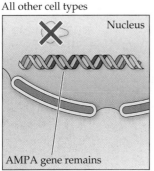

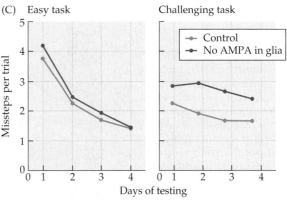

11.28 GLIAL CELLS CONTRIBUTE TO CEREBELLAR FUNCTION
(A) Bergmann glia send processes toward the cerebellar surface to "cap" over synapses from parallel fibers onto the Purkinje cell dendrites. These glia possess AMPA-type receptors that normally respond to the transmitter glutamate. (B) Researchers created mice that would produce a recombinase enzyme, Cre, only in glial cells when injected with a drug. The genes for AMPA receptor subunits in these mice had been altered so that Cre would knock out those genes. The mice were injected with the triggering drug at 2 weeks of age, which produced Cre only in glia, thereby knocking out AMPA receptor genes in Bergmann glia, but not in neurons. (C) Given an easy locomotor task (left), mice missing AMPA receptors in their Bergmann glia learned it as well as control mice. But when the loco-motor task was made more challenging (right), mice without AMPA receptors in their Bergmann glia made more mistakes than controls. (After Saab et al., 2012.)

Recommended Reading

Bates, G., Tabrizi, S., and Jones, L. (2014). *Huntington's Disease* (4th ed.). Oxford, England: Oxford University Press.

Graziano, M. (2006). The organization of behavioral repertoire in motor cortex. *Annual Review of Neuroscience, 29,* 105–134.

Merchant, H., and Georgopoulos, A. P. (2006). Neurophysiology of perceptual and motor aspects of interception. *Journal of Neurophysiology, 95,* 1–13.

Palfreman, J. (2015). *Brain Storms: The Race to Unlock the Mysteries of Parkinson's Disease.* New York: Farrar, Straus and Giroux.

Purves, D., Augustine, G. J., Fitzpatrick, D., Hall, W., et al. (Eds.). (2017). *Neuroscience* (6th ed.). Sunderland, MA: Sinauer. (See Unit III: Movement and Its Central Control, Chapters 16–21.)

Shenoy, K. V., Sahani, M., and Churchland, M. M. (2013). Cortical control of arm movements: A dynamical systems perspective. *Annual Review of Neuroscience, 36,* 337–359.

Vogel, S. (2002). *Prime Mover: A Natural History of Muscle.* New York: Norton.

Go to
bn8e.com
for study questions, quizzes, activities, and other resources

VISUAL SUMMARY

You should be able to relate each summary to the adjacent illustration, including structures and processes.
Go to **bn8e.com/vs11** for links to figures, animations, and activities that will help you consolidate the material.

1 **Reflexes** are patterns of relatively simple and stereotyped movements elicited by the stimulation of sensory receptors. More-complex motor behaviors indicate the existence of a motor plan. Review **Figures 11.1 and 11.2**

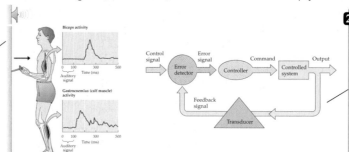

2 In **closed-loop control**, movements may be corrected while they are being produced on the basis of feedback from sensory systems. Some behaviors are so rapid, however, that they are controlled by **open-loop** systems; that is, the pattern is preset and not modified by feedback once it has started. Review **Figure 11.3**

3 Muscles around a joint work in pairs. **Antagonists** work in opposition; **synergists** work together. **Smooth muscles**, such as those in the intestines, are under involuntary control; **striated muscles** are under voluntary control. Action potentials travel over motor nerve fibers (axons from motor neurons) and reach **muscle fibers** at the **neuromuscular junction**, releasing **acetylcholine** to trigger muscle contraction. Review **Figures 11.5–11.7**, **Animation 11.2**

4 The final common pathway for action potentials to skeletal muscles consists of **motor neurons** whose cell bodies in vertebrates are located in the ventral horn of the spinal cord and within the brainstem. The motor neurons receive information from a variety of sources, including sensory input from the dorsal spinal roots, other spinal cord neurons, and descending fibers from the brain. Review **Figures 11.8 and 11.13**

5 **Muscle spindles** and **Golgi tendon organs** transmit crucial information about muscle activities to the CNS. The sensitivity of the muscle spindle can be adjusted by efferent impulses that control the length of the spindle. When a muscle is stretched, a reflex circuit triggers contraction, which works to restore the muscle to its original length; this response is called the **stretch reflex**. Review **Figures 11.9–11.11**, **Animation 11.3**

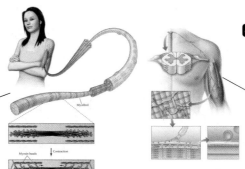

6 Motor control systems are organized into a hierarchy that includes primary and nonprimary motor cortex, the cerebellum, and the basal ganglia. The fibers of the **pyramidal** (corticospinal) **system** originate mainly in the **primary motor cortex** (**M1**) and run directly to spinal motor neurons or to interneurons in the spinal cord. Review **Figures 11.4 and 11.14–11.16**

7 **Nonprimary motor cortex** includes the **supplementary motor area** (**SMA**), which helps control the sequence of internally generated movements, and the **premotor cortex**, which guides movement in response to external cues. Premotor cortex and other frontal lobe regions contain **mirror neurons**, which are active when an individual is moving an object in a particular fashion or when the individual sees someone else moving an object in that manner. Review **Figures 11.18–11.20**

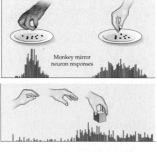

8 **Extrapyramidal** brain regions that modulate movement include the **basal ganglia** (caudate nucleus, putamen, and globus pallidus, **substantia nigra**, and **subthalamic nucleus**), some major brainstem nuclei (thalamic nuclei, **reticular formation**, and **red nucleus**), and the cerebellum. Review **Figures 11.21–11.23**, **Activity 11.1**

9 Movement disorders, such as **muscular dystrophy**, **amyotrophic lateral sclerosis** (**ALS**), and **Parkinson's** and **Huntington's diseases**, can result from impairment at any of several levels of the motor system: muscles, neuromuscular junctions, motor neurons, spinal cord, brainstem, cerebral cortex, basal ganglia, or cerebellum. Review **Figures 11.12 and 11.24–11.26**

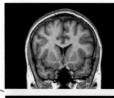
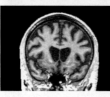
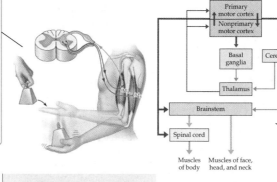
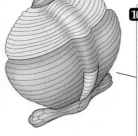

10 The cerebellum is made up of three major functional divisions: **spinocerebellum**, **cerebrocerebellum**, and **vestibulocerebellum**. Damage in each division is associated with specific motor impairments. Cerebellar glia also contribute to fine motor coordination. Review **Figure 11.27 and 11.28**

Regulation and Behavior

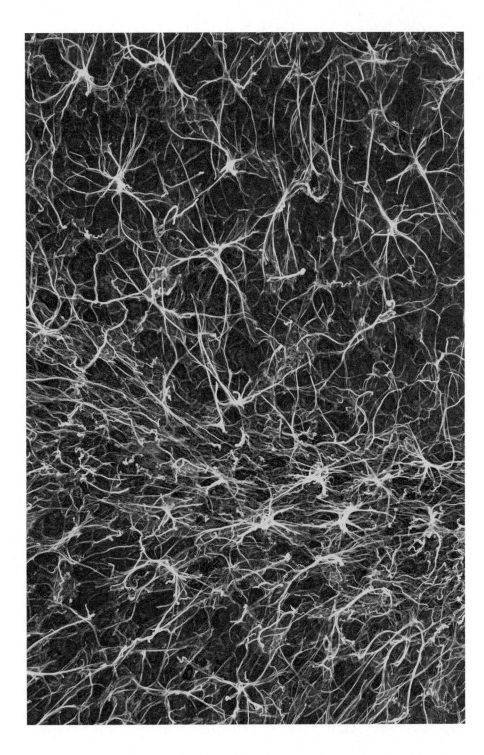

Cerebellar glia Confocal light micrograph of glial cells from the cerebellum of the brain. © Thomas Deerinck and Mark Ellisman, NC-MIR, UCSD.

Sex

Evolutionary, Hormonal, and Neural Bases

12

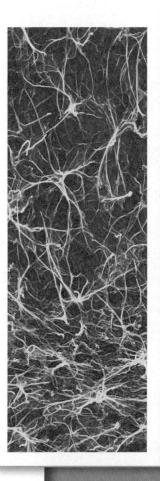

Genitals and Gender: What Makes Us Male and Female?

The night before "Bella" was to start 6th grade, her parents finally told her a secret. She had been born a boy with testes, but with a life-threatening condition called *cloacal exstrophy*, a developmental defect that affects about one in 400,000 live births. Basically, the skin covering the lower abdomen and forming the genitalia was missing. Surgery was needed immediately to cover the exposed intestines to avoid injury and infection, but like other genetic males born with this condition, Bella had been born without a penis. The parents had faced a terrible dilemma: Would it be better to raise the child as a boy without a penis, despite the emotional costs of the deformity? Or would it be better for the child to be unambiguously assigned to the female gender, to have early surgery to remove the testes and fashion female-looking genitals, and then to be raised as a girl? In the end, Bella's parents had decided on the surgery to remove the testes and make her genitalia appear like that of a girl, and to raise her as their daughter.

You might think Bella would have found this story hard to believe. But in fact, she believed them immediately. "I knew that it was true. Even if it had been another person that had told me I would have believed them because it made sense to me" (Reiner and Gearhart, 2004). Too confused to start school the next morning, "Benjamin" began school a week later as a boy. How did Benjamin make the transition from girl to boy? "Cut my hair. That's all I did."

Sexual behaviors are almost as diverse as the species that employ them, and they are the products of millions of years of evolution that has favored continual mixing of genes in an attempt to outrun parasites and other threats (Morran et al., 2011). But in every case, males and females must produce a specific set of behaviors, in a precise and intricately coordinated sequence, in order to reproduce successfully. In this chapter we review sexual behaviors, which include the sex act itself—copulation—as well as the parental behaviors required for the newborns of many species, including our own, to survive. Then we consider sexual differentiation, the process by which an individual's body and brain develop in a male or female fashion. For humans, an important aspect of sexual differentiation is the emergence of sexual orientation. Do we *decide* to be attracted to men or to women, are we *taught* whom we should find attractive, or do prenatal events have an influence?

Go to Brain Explorer
bn8e.com/12.1

Sexual Behavior

We wish we could explain exactly why and how humans and other animals engage in the three Cs—courting, copulating, and cohabiting—but relatively little practical knowledge of such matters exists. Two barriers have limited our understanding of sexual behavior: (1) cultural barriers to the dissemination of knowledge about sexual behavior and (2) the remarkable variety of sexual behaviors in which various species engage.

Reproductive Behavior Can Be Divided into Four Stages

There are four major stages of reproductive behavior: (1) sexual attraction, (2) appetitive behavior, (3) copulation, and (4) postcopulatory behavior.

Sexual attraction is the first stage in bringing males and females together. In many species, females are attracted to males that display the best assortment of species-typical ornaments or traits, such as the feathers of the peacock in **FIGURE 12.1**. Such traits are the products of sexual selection pressures exerted by the opposite sex across many generations (see Chapter 6). Sexually selected traits may signal superior genetic fitness or other characteristics that make the individual desirable as a mate, and thus attractive. The process of attraction and mate selection can have high stakes: for example, in some species (such as voles) mated males and females will form lasting **pair bonds**, living together before and long after copulation (see Chapter 5). Interestingly, there is a distinction between social pair bonds and sexual (or genetic) pair bonds. In the case of voles, the formation of exclusive social pair bonds leads to the greatest reproductive success, even though the partners may occasionally engage in extrapair copulation (Ophir et al., 2008). They are *socially* monogamous (having one partner) but not quite *sexually* monogamous.

In many species, sexual attraction is closely synchronized with physiological readiness and appetite for sex. That's not to say that we are perfectly accurate in gauging sexual interest—in fact, it seems that men overestimate women's interest, and women underestimate men's interest (Perilloux et al., 2012). Attraction and sexual response are also strongly shaped by learned associations, varying from one individual to the next on the basis of life experience (Pfaus et al., 2001). This process, by which a previously neutral item becomes sexually attractive, is the foundation of the fashion industry.

In experiments we gauge an individual's attractiveness by observing the responses of potential mates: how rapidly they approach, how hard they work to gain access, and so on. By manipulating the appearance of individuals, we can deduce which special features are most attractive. For example, males of many primate species are strongly attracted to the "sex skin" that swells on a female's rump when her ovaries are secreting estrogens. Most male mammals are attracted by particular female odors, which also tend to reflect estrogen levels. Because estrogen secretion is associated with the release of eggs, these mechanisms tend to synchronize female sexual attractiveness with peak

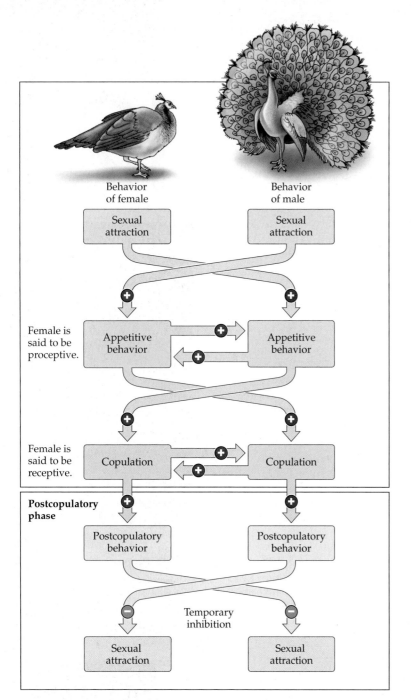

12.1 STAGES OF REPRODUCTIVE BEHAVIOR Interaction between male and female partners in sexual reproduction is extensive, progressing in four stages: sexual attraction, appetitive behavior, copulation, and postcopulatory behavior. The postcopulatory phase includes a temporary decrease in the sexual attractiveness of the partner. (After Beach, 1977.)

sexual attraction The first step in the mating behavior of many animals, in which animals emit stimuli that attract members of the opposite sex.

pair bond A durable and exclusive relationship between a male and a female.

Guinea pig Don Juan sires 43 offspring in 2 nights

PONTYPRIDD, WALES, 1 DECEMBER 2000

HAVING ESCAPED from captivity at Little Friend's Farm earlier this year, a male guinea pig named Sooty chose to re-enter captivity immediately—in the nearby cage housing 24 females. Two months later he is now the father of 43 offspring.

According to his owner, Carol Feehan, Sooty was missing for two whole days before the staff checked the females' pen. "We did a head count and found 25 guinea pigs," she told the press. "Sooty was fast asleep in the corner.

"He was absolutely shattered. We put him back in his cage and he slept for two days."

Sooty enjoyed two nights of passion among 24 females.

12.2 THE COOLIDGE EFFECT By reducing the refractory period when a sexually exhausted male encounters an unfamiliar female, the Coolidge effect permits him to take advantage of a new reproductive opportunity and sire more offspring. (Of course, encountering 24 lovelorn females at once is a situation few males—guinea pig or otherwise—could even dream of.)

fertility. Of course, the female may find a particular male to be unattractive—perhaps his feathers are underwhelming—and refuse to mate with him. Although apparent rape has been described in some nonhuman species, including such close relatives of ours as orangutans (Maggioncalda and Sapolsky, 2002), for most species copulation is controlled by the female and requires her active cooperation.

If the animals are mutually attracted, they may progress to the next stage: **appetitive behaviors**—species-specific behaviors that establish, maintain, or promote sexual interaction (see Figure 12.1). A female displaying these behaviors is said to be **proceptive**: she may approach males, remain close to them, or show alternating approach and retreat behavior. Proceptive female rats typically exhibit "ear wiggling" and a hopping and darting gait that induce a male to mount. Male appetitive behaviors usually consist of staying near the female. In many mammals the male may sniff around the female's face and vagina. Male birds may engage in elaborate songs or nest-building behaviors.

If both animals display appetitive behaviors, they may progress to the third stage of reproduction: **copulation**, also known as *coitus*. In many vertebrates, including all mammals, copulation involves one or more **intromissions**, in which the male inserts his penis into the female's vagina, followed by a variable amount of genital stimulation, usually through pelvic thrusting. When stimulation reaches a threshold level, the male **ejaculates** sperm-bearing **semen** into the female; the length of time and quantity of stimulation that are required vary greatly between species and between individuals.

After one bout of copulation, the animals will not mate again until a **refractory period** has elapsed. The refractory period varies from minutes to months, depending on the species and circumstances. Many animals will resume mating sooner if they are provided with a new partner—a phenomenon known as the **Coolidge effect** (**FIGURE 12.2**).

The female often appears to be the one to choose whether copulation will take place; when she is willing to copulate, she is said to be **sexually receptive**, in heat, or in **estrus**. In some species the female may show proceptive behaviors days before she will participate in copulation itself. In most (but not all) species, females are receptive only when mating is likely to produce offspring. Most species are seasonal breeders, with females that are receptive only during the breeding season, and some—such as salmon, octopuses, and cicadas—reproduce only once, at the end of life.

Finally, the fourth stage of reproductive behavior consists of **postcopulatory behaviors**. These behaviors are especially varied across species. In some mam-

appetitive behavior The second stage of mating behavior; helps establish or maintain sexual interaction.

proceptive Referring to a state in which an animal advertises its readiness to mate through species-typical behaviors, such as ear wiggling in the female rat.

copulation Also called *coitus*. The sexual act.

intromission Insertion of the erect penis into the vagina during copulation.

ejaculation The forceful expulsion of semen from the penis.

semen A mixture of fluids and sperm that is released during ejaculation.

refractory period A period following copulation during which an individual cannot recommence copulation.

Coolidge effect The propensity of an animal that has appeared sexually satiated with a present partner to resume sexual activity when provided with a novel partner.

sexually receptive Referring to the state in which an individual (in mammals, typically the female) is willing to copulate.

estrus The period during which female animals are sexually receptive.

postcopulatory behavior The final stage in mating behavior. Species-specific postcopulatory behaviors include rolling (in the cat) and grooming (in the rat).

copulatory lock Reproductive behavior in which the male's penis swells after ejaculation so that the male and female are forced to remain joined for 5–15 minutes; occurs in dogs and some rodents, but not in humans.

internal fertilization The process by which sperm fertilize eggs inside the female's body, as in all mammals, birds, and reptiles.

gamete A sex cell (sperm or ovum) that contains only unpaired chromosomes and therefore has only half the usual number of chromosomes in other cells.

sperm The gamete produced by males for fertilization of eggs (ova).

ovum An egg, the female gamete.

zygote The fertilized egg.

external fertilization The process by which eggs are fertilized outside of the female's body, as in many fishes and amphibians.

parthenogenesis "Virgin birth," a process of reproduction by which a female produces live offspring without need of a male.

ovulation The production and release of an egg (ovum).

mals—dogs and southern grasshopper mice, for example—the male's penis swells so much after ejaculation that he can't remove it from the female for a while (10–15 minutes in dogs), and the animals are said to be in a **copulatory lock** (Dewsbury, 1972)—just one of the many strategies employed by males of different species to try and ensure their paternity. (Despite wild stories you may have heard or read, humans never experience copulatory lock; that urban myth started in 1884 when a physician submitted a fake report as a practical joke on a journal editor [Nation, 1973].) For mammals and birds, postcopulatory behaviors include extensive parental behaviors to nurture the offspring, which we'll discuss later in this chapter.

Copulation brings gametes together

All mammals, birds, and reptiles employ **internal fertilization**: the fusion of their **gametes**—**sperm** and **ovum** (plural *ova*)—within the female's body to form a **zygote**. Although there is room for only one or a few zygotes to grow, the safe and stable internal environment maximizes the probability that each of these balls of cells will eventually develop into a new individual. Other vertebrates—aquatic species including most fishes and amphibians—employ **external fertilization**, releasing their gametes into the outside world in a reproductive gamble that pits sheer numbers against a high rate of loss. Of course, the reproductive behavior of each species is shaped by its particular ecological niche, accounting for the impressive diversity that we observe in the sex lives of different species. **TABLE 12.1** summarizes the different types of sexual reproduction in animals.

You may be surprised to learn that a few vertebrate species, including turkeys, Komodo dragons, and pit vipers (Booth et al., 2012), can reproduce without sex—the female lays an unfertilized egg that hatches a clone of herself. This asexual mode of reproduction is **parthenogenesis** ("virgin birth"). Even more surprising, there are about 90 vertebrate species, including fish called Amazon mollies as well as some species of whiptail lizards and mole salamanders (Lampert and Schartl, 2010), that rely *exclusively* on parthenogenesis, so there are no males of these species. Interestingly, no such "unisexual" species of birds or mammals have been found.

Most of what we know about the copulatory behavior of mammals derives from studies of lab animals, especially rats. Like most other rodents, rats do not engage in lengthy courtship, nor do the partners tend to remain together after copulation. Rats are attracted to each other largely through odors. Females are spontaneous ovulators; that is, even when left alone, they **ovulate** (release eggs from the ovary) every 4–5 days. For those few hours around the time of ovulation, the female seeks out a male and displays proceptive behaviors, and both animals produce *ultrasonic vocalizations*: sounds in the range of 22–50 kilohertz that are too high-pitched for humans to detect but audible to each other (Holy and Guo, 2005; N. R. White et al., 1993).

These behaviors prompt the male to mount the female from the rear, grasp her flanks with his forelegs, and rhythmically thrust his hips against her rump. If she

TABLE 12.1 Types of Sexual Reproduction in Animals

TYPE	STRATEGY	EXAMPLES
EXTERNAL FERTILIZATION		
Aquatic species	Many gametes are released into the environment	Many invertebrates, fishes, amphibians
INTERNAL FERTILIZATION		
Oviparous species	Female lays a few eggs	Insects, all birds, many reptiles
Viviparous species	Female nourishes embryos in her body, giving birth to a few, relatively mature young	Some fishes, some reptiles, all mammals except monotremes (echidna and platypus)
Ovoviviparous species	Female gives birth to live young that developed from eggs carried internally	Some fishes, some reptiles

is receptive, the female adopts a stereotyped posture called **lordosis** (**FIGURE 12.3**), elevating her rump and moving her tail to one side, allowing intromission. Once intromission has been achieved, the male rat makes a single deep thrust and then springs back off the female. During the next 6–7 minutes the male and female orchestrate seven to nine such intromissions; then, instead of springing away, the male raises the front half of his body up for a second or two while he ejaculates. Finally, he falls backward off the female.

After copulation, the male and female separately engage in grooming their genitalia, and the male pays little attention to the female for the next 5 minutes or so, until, often in response to the female's proceptive behaviors, the two engage in another bout of intromissions and ejaculation. This pattern of multiple intromissions before ejaculation is an obligatory part of rat fertility: only after repeated intromissions will the female's brain cause the release of hormones to support pregnancy. In this instance, then, the behavior of the male rat directly affects the hormonal secretions of his mate.

12.3 COPULATION IN RATS The raised rump and deflected tail of the female (the lordosis posture) make intromission possible in rats.

Gonadal steroids activate sexual behavior

Hormones play an important role in almost all aspects of rat mating behaviors. Testosterone mediates the male's interest in copulation: if he is **castrated** (his testes removed), he will eventually stop mounting receptive females. Although testosterone disappears from the bloodstream within a few hours after castration, the hormone's effects on the nervous system take days or weeks to dissipate. Treating a castrated male with testosterone eventually restores mating behavior; if testosterone treatment is stopped, the mating behavior fades away again. This is an example of a hormone exerting an **activational effect**: the hormone transiently promotes certain behaviors. In normal development, the rise of androgen secretion at puberty activates masculine behavior in males.

Although individual male rats and guinea pigs differ considerably in how eagerly they will mate, blood levels of testosterone clearly are *not* responsible for these differences. For one thing, animals displaying different levels of sexual vigor do not show reliable differences in blood levels of testosterone. Furthermore, when these males are castrated and subsequently all treated with exactly the same doses of testosterone, their precastration differences in sexual activity persist (**FIGURE 12.4**). Not only that, it also turns out that a very small amount of testosterone—one-tenth the amount normally produced by the animals—is enough to fully maintain the mating behavior of male rats. Thus, since all male rats make more testosterone than is re-

lordosis A female receptive posture in quadrupeds in which the hindquarters are raised and the tail is turned to one side, facilitating intromission by the male.

castration Removal of the gonads, usually the testes.

activational effect A temporary change in behavior resulting from the administration of a hormone to an adult animal.

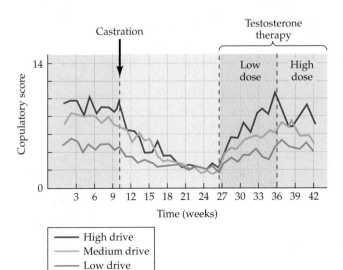

12.4 ANDROGENS PERMIT MALE COPULATORY BEHAVIOR Although androgens—especially testosterone—are important for normal male sexual function, individual differences in sexual activity are *not* determined by differences in androgen levels. Even after testosterone levels were made uniform in all the male guinea pigs in a study group, they returned to the individual levels of sexual activity that they had exhibited prior to castration. Even doubling the amount of hormone at week 36 did not increase the mating activity of any group. Presumably Sooty from Figure 12.2 would have fallen into the "high drive" group. (After Grunt and Young, 1953.)

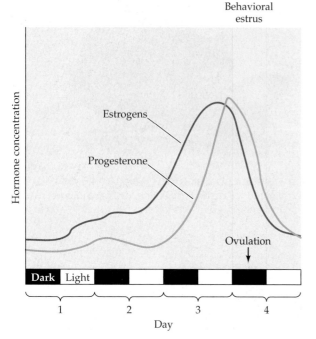

12.5 THE OVULATORY CYCLE OF RATS

quired to maintain their copulatory behavior, some other factor, which we can call *drive*, must differ across individual males.

Estrogens secreted at the beginning of the 4- to 5-day **ovulatory cycle** facilitate the proceptive behavior of the female rat, and the subsequent production of progesterone increases proceptive behavior and activates receptivity (**FIGURE 12.5**). An adult female whose ovaries have been removed will show neither proceptive nor receptive behaviors. However, 2 days of estrogen treatment followed by a single injection of progesterone will, about 6 hours later, make the female rat proceptive and receptive for a few hours. Only the correct combination of estrogens and progesterone will fully activate copulatory behaviors in female rats—another example of activational effects of gonadal steroids.

The Neural Circuitry of the Brain Regulates Reproductive Behavior

Although most of what we know about the neural circuitry of sexual behavior comes from studies of rats, steroid receptors are found in the same specific brain regions across a wide variety of vertebrate species. Steroid-sensitive regions include the cortex, brainstem nuclei, medial amygdala, hippocampus, and many others. And as we'll see, the hypothalamus plays a particularly important role in regulating copulatory behavior.

Estrogens and progesterone regulate a lordosis circuit that spans from brain to muscle

ovulatory cycle The periodic occurrence of ovulation.

ventromedial hypothalamus (VMH) A hypothalamic region involved in eating and sexual behaviors.

periaqueductal gray The neuronal body–rich region of the midbrain surrounding the cerebral aqueduct that connects the third and fourth ventricles.

medullary reticular formation The hindmost portion of the brainstem reticular formation, implicated in motor control and copulatory behavior.

reticulospinal tract A tract of axons arising from the brainstem reticular formation and descending to the spinal cord to modulate movement.

medial preoptic area (mPOA) A region of the anterior hypothalamus implicated in the control of many behaviors, including thermoregulation, sexual behavior, and gonadotropin secretion.

Scientists have exploited the steroid sensitivity of the rat lordosis response to develop a map of the neural circuitry that controls this behavior (**FIGURE 12.6B**). In particular, the **ventromedial hypothalamus** (**VMH**) is crucial for lordosis, because lesions there abolish the response. Furthermore, tiny quantities of estradiol implanted directly into the brain can induce receptivity in females, but only when placed in the VMH (Lisk, 1962; Pleim and Barfield, 1988).

Estrogens potently affect neurons of the VMH, causing elaboration of some parts of their dendritic trees (Meisel and Luttrell, 1990) and the production of progesterone receptors. However, estrogens also act to *retract* the long primary dendrite of each VMH neuron, and they reorganize the oxytocin input received by this dendrite from neighboring lateral regions (G. D. Griffin and Flanagan-Cato, 2011). Later, when both estrogens and progesterone are present in the VMH, the effect of estrogens on the length and connectivity of the dendrite is reversed.

The VMH sends axons to the **periaqueductal gray** region of the midbrain, where again, lesions greatly diminish lordosis. The periaqueductal gray neurons project to the **medullary reticular formation**, which in turn projects to the spinal cord via the **reticulospinal tract**. In the spinal cord, this descending signal from the brain is integrated with sensory inputs from the flanks and rump, which are stimulated by the grasping and mounting behavior of the male. The result of this processing is a pattern of motor activity that produces lordosis. So the role of the VMH is to monitor steroid hormone concentrations and, at the right time in the ovulatory cycle, activate a multisynaptic pathway that induces spinal motor neurons to contract back muscles, producing lordosis in response to male mounting (Pfaff, 1997). Figure 12.6B schematically represents this neural pathway and its steroid-responsive components.

Androgens act on a neural system for male reproductive behavior

As with the lordosis circuit, mapping the sites of steroid action has provided important clues about the neural circuitry controlling male copulatory behavior in rodents (**FIGURE 12.6A**). The hypothalamic **medial preoptic area (mPOA)** is chock-full of steroid-sensitive neurons, and lesions of the mPOA abolish male copulatory behavior

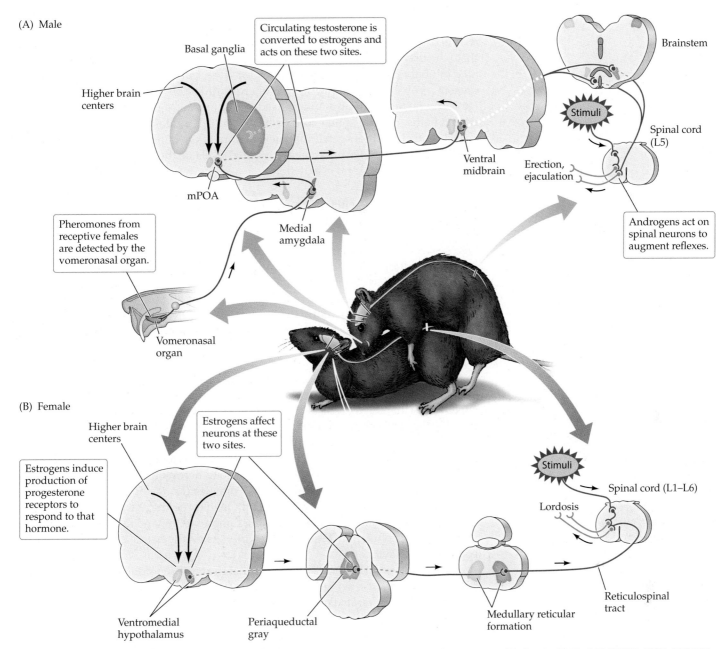

(A) Male

Basal ganglia

Higher brain centers

Circulating testosterone is converted to estrogens and acts on these two sites.

Brainstem

mPOA

Ventral midbrain

Stimuli

Spinal cord (L5)

Erection, ejaculation

Pheromones from receptive females are detected by the vomeronasal organ.

Medial amygdala

Androgens act on spinal neurons to augment reflexes.

Vomeronasal organ

(B) Female

Higher brain centers

Estrogens affect neurons at these two sites.

Estrogens induce production of progesterone receptors to respond to that hormone.

Stimuli

Spinal cord (L1–L6)

Lordosis

Ventromedial hypothalamus

Periaqueductal gray

Medullary reticular formation

Reticulospinal tract

12.6 NEURAL CIRCUITS FOR REPRODUCTION IN RODENTS (Part B after Pfaff, 1980.)

in a wide variety of vertebrate species (Meisel and Sachs, 1994). Furthermore, mating can be reinstated in castrated males by small implants of testosterone placed directly in the mPOA, but not in other brain regions. Note that lesions of the mPOA do not interfere with males' *motivation* for copulating with females; they will still press a bar to gain access to a receptive female (Everitt and Stacey, 1987), but they seem unable to commence mounting. Thus, the mPOA seems to be a final common pathway for the production of male copulatory behaviors; motivation relies on other systems, notably the dopamine reward pathway (see Figure 4.22) that appears to mediate the pleasurable aspects of various behaviors and drugs (Everitt, 1990; Pfaus et al., 1990).

The mPOA coordinates copulatory behavior by sending axons to the ventral midbrain, which in turn projects (1) to the basal ganglia to coordinate mounting behaviors (recall that the basal ganglia are key regulators of motor behavior) and (2) to the spinal cord, via several brainstem nuclei (Hamson and Watson, 2004) that regulate various reflexes of copulation. One of these brainstem nuclei, the **paragigantocellular nucleus (PGN)** in the pons, sends serotonergic fibers down into the spinal cord, where they inhibit a circuit responsible for penile erection (McKenna, 1999).

paragigantocellular nucleus (PGN) A region of the brainstem reticular formation implicated in sleep and modulation of spinal reflexes.

So, in order for erections to occur, the mPOA must inhibit the inhibitory PGN projection, thereby releasing the spinal circuit to permit erection. Antidepressant drugs that boost serotonergic activity in the brain—for example, selective serotonin reuptake inhibitors like Prozac (see Chapter 16)—can cause problems with erection and orgasm, probably by enhancing serotonergic inhibition of the spinal cord circuitry. (In case you're wondering, Viagra [sildenafil] promotes erection by acting directly on the penis, not the spinal cord or brain [Boolell et al., 1996].) Because the reflex circuits and ejaculation-generating neurons are in the lumbar spinal cord (Truitt and Coolen, 2002), men with damage at higher levels of the spinal cord often remain capable of copulation and ejaculation.

Pheromones Guide Reproductive Behavior in Many Species

When steroid hormones from the gonads affect the brain to activate mating behavior, the activation is not absolute; individuals are simply *more likely* to engage in mating behaviors when steroid levels are adequate. This activation can be thought of as communication between the gonads and the brain: by producing steroids to make gametes, the gonads also inform the brain that the body is ready to mate. This signaling takes place inside the individual, while **pheromones** (see Chapters 5 and 9) are chemical signals that communicate information *between* animals to help coordinate their reproductive activities.

An additional branch of male copulatory circuitry in rodents involves the sensory system detecting pheromones to activate male arousal. The **vomeronasal organ (VNO)** (see Chapter 9) consists of specialized receptor cells near to but separate from the olfactory epithelium. These sensory cells send axons to the accessory olfactory bulb in the brain. Neurons in the accessory olfactory bulb project to the **medial amygdala**, which depends on circulating sex steroids to maintain a masculine form and function (Cooke et al., 1999, 2003). Lesions here will abolish the penile erections that normally occur around receptive females (Kondo et al., 1997). The medial amygdala, in turn, sends axons to the mPOA. So the mPOA appears to integrate hormonal and sensory information, such as pheromones, and to coordinate the motor patterns of copulation. Figure 12.6A summarizes the neural circuitry for male rat copulatory behavior.

In many species, chemicals that are part of the basic reproductive physiology have been co-opted to also serve as pheromones. In female goldfish, for example, a hormone called *F prostaglandin* that is required for normal ovulation also escapes the female's body and passes into her watery surroundings, where it acts as a pheromone to stimulate mating behaviors in male goldfish (Sorensen and Goetz, 1993). The most likely scenario for the evolution of this relationship is that long ago, females released F prostaglandin only as a by-product of ovulation, but because the presence of the hormone conveyed important information about the female's reproductive status, natural selection favored males that detected the hormone and began courting in response to the signal. Even very simple unicellular organisms, such as yeasts, prepare each other for mating by releasing and detecting pheromones (S. Fields, 1990).

There are multiple examples of probable sex pheromones in rodents. Pheromones in the urine of male mice can accelerate puberty in young females (Drickamer, 1992; M. A. Price and Vandenbergh, 1992), and females have a specific type of vomeronasal receptor protein that detects a lordosis-inducing pheromone in the tears of male mice (Haga et al., 2010). Female mice can also uniquely identify an individual male by the particular mix of pheromones in his urine, and if the pheromones come from a dominant male—but not a subordinate male—they can induce the birth of new neurons in the olfactory bulbs and hippocampus of the female mouse (Mak et al., 2007). When prairie voles mate, the female is exposed to pheromones from her mate's mouth and urine. If she is then isolated and has urine from that male or any other male applied to her snout, pregnancy will be blocked; the fetuses will be resorbed by the female, and she will soon be ready to mate again. So when the female remains with her original

pheromone A chemical signal that is released outside the body of an animal and affects other members of the same species.

vomeronasal organ (VNO) A collection of specialized receptor cells, near to but separate from the olfactory epithelium, that detect pheromones and send electrical signals to the accessory olfactory bulb in the brain.

medial amygdala A portion of the amygdala that receives olfactory and pheromonal information.

mate, she is careful not to let her mate's urine touch her vomeronasal organ; otherwise she will lose their offspring (Smale, 1988). Terminating pregnancy and absorbing the fetuses in the presence of a new male, a phenomenon known as the *Bruce effect*, may be an attempt to make the best of a bad situation: if her original mate is gone, a female may be better off beginning a new litter with a different male. The Bruce effect has even been observed in primates, specifically the gelada, an African monkey (E. K. Roberts et al., 2012).

Pheromones can also convey important information between individuals of the same sex. During **musth**, the mating season of elephants, males secrete a pheromone-laden liquid from glands on their temples, just behind their eyes (**FIGURE 12.7**). In pubescent males, this substance has a distinctive honey-like odor that may attract bees and birds, but mature bulls signal their rank and attract females with a stronger-smelling secretion that contains a pheromone called *frontalin* (curiously, frontalin is also an important pheromone in insects). By broadcasting their low rank and avoiding mature-smelling males, the honey-scented juveniles thus avoid aggressive encounters (Rasmussen and Greenwood, 2003; Rasmussen et al., 2002).

The Hallmark of Human Sexual Behavior Is Diversity

How much of what we've described so far about sexual behavior in animals is relevant to human sexuality? Until the 1940s, when biology professor Alfred Kinsey began to ask friends and colleagues about their sexual histories, there was virtually no scientific study of human sexual behavior. Kinsey constructed a standardized set of questions and procedures to obtain information for samples of the U.S. population categorized by sex, age, religion, and education. Eventually he and his collaborators published extensive surveys (based on thousands of respondents) of the sexual behavior of American males (Kinsey et al., 1948) and females (Kinsey et al., 1953).

Controversial in their time, these eye-opening surveys indicated that nearly all men masturbated, that college-educated people were more likely to engage in oral sex than were non-college-educated people, that many people had at one time or another engaged in sex with people of the same sex, and that a stable proportion of the population preferred such sex over heterosexual sex.

Another way to investigate human sexual behavior is to make behavioral and physiological observations of people engaged in sexual intercourse or masturbation, but the squeamishness of the general public impeded such research for many years. Finally, after Kinsey's surveys were published, physician William Masters and psychologist Virginia Johnson began a large, famous project of this kind (Masters and Johnson 1966, 1970; Masters et al., 1994), documenting the impressively diverse sexuality of humans.

Among most mammalian species, including most nonhuman primates, the male mounts the female from the rear; but among humans, face-to-face postures are most common. A great variety of coital positions have been described, and many couples vary their positions from session to session or even within a session. It is this variety in reproductive behaviors, rather than differences in reproductive anatomy (**FIGURE 12.8**), that distinguishes human sexuality from that of most other species.

Another difference between species is that, unlike other animals, humans can report their subjective experiences of sexual behavior—specifically **orgasm**, the brief, extremely pleasurable sensations experienced by most men during ejaculation and by most women during copulation. In the original conceptual model of human sexuality, Masters and Johnson (1966) summarized the typical response patterns of both men and women as consisting of four phases: increasing excitement, plateau, or-

12.7 MUSTH During the reproductive season, bull elephants secrete a pheromone-laden fluid from glands behind the eyes. You can see the darkened skin where the fluid is trickling down.

musth An annual period of heightened aggressiveness and sexual activity in male elephants.

orgasm The climax of sexual experience, marked by extremely pleasurable sensations.

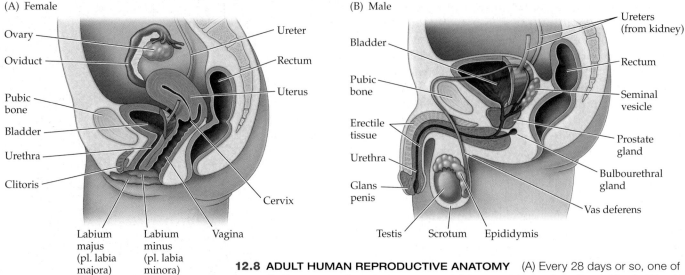

(A) Female

Ovary
Oviduct
Pubic bone
Bladder
Urethra
Clitoris

Ureter
Rectum
Uterus
Cervix

Labium majus (pl. labia majora)
Labium minus (pl. labia minora)
Vagina

(B) Male

Bladder
Pubic bone
Erectile tissue
Urethra
Glans penis

Ureters (from kidney)
Rectum
Seminal vesicle
Prostate gland
Bulbourethral gland
Vas deferens

Testis Scrotum Epididymis

12.8 ADULT HUMAN REPRODUCTIVE ANATOMY (A) Every 28 days or so, one of the human ovaries releases an ovum into an oviduct, where it must be fertilized if pregnancy is to occur. The fertilized zygote implants in the wall of the uterus, and a placenta develops. If no pregnancy occurs, the uterine wall (endometrium) sloughs off during menstruation. Most mammalian species lose less endometrial tissue than humans do and thus do not menstruate. (B) In males, sperm originate in the testes, mature in the adjacent epididymis, and are expelled during ejaculation via the muscular vas deferens. Along the way, structures such as the seminal vesicles and prostate gland add their secretions, forming semen.

phallus The clitoris or penis.

gasm, and resolution (**FIGURE 12.9**). During the excitement phase, the **phallus** (the penis in men, the clitoris in women) becomes engorged with blood, making it erect. In women, parasympathetic activity during the excitement phase causes changes in vaginal blood vessels, resulting in the production of lubricating fluids that facilitate intromission. Stimulation of the penis, clitoris, and vagina during rhythmic thrusting accompanying intromission may lead to orgasm. In both men and women, orgasm is accompanied by waves of contractions of genital muscles (mediating ejaculation in men and contractions of the uterus and vagina in women).

In spite of some basic similarities, the sexual responses of men and women differ in important ways. For one thing, women show a much greater variety of commonly observed copulatory sequences. Whereas men have only one basic pattern, captured by the linear model of Masters and Johnson (**FIGURE 12.9A**), women have at least three typical patterns (**FIGURE 12.9B**). Another important aspect of human sexuality is that most men, but not most women, have an absolute refractory period following orgasm (see Figure 12.9A). That is, most men can-

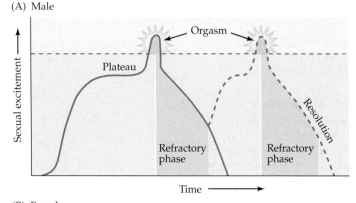

(A) Male

Sexual excitement

Orgasm

Plateau

Refractory phase

Refractory phase

Resolution

Time

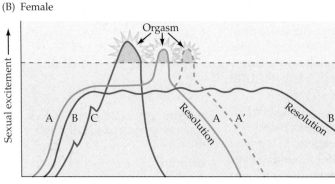

(B) Female

Sexual excitement

Orgasm

A B C

Resolution

A A'

Resolution B

Time

12.9 HUMAN SEXUAL RESPONSE PATTERNS (A) The typical male pattern includes an absolute refractory period after orgasm, which may be followed by renewed arousal (dotted line). (B) These three patterns (A, B, C) are often observed in women. These diagrams are schematic and do not represent a particular physiological measure, although heart rate varies in roughly this manner. The patterns vary considerably from one individual to another. (After Masters and Johnson, 1966.)

not achieve full erection and another orgasm until some time has elapsed—the length of time varying from minutes to hours, depending on individual differences and other factors. Many women, on the other hand, can have multiple orgasms in rapid succession. Functional imaging of the brains of men and women during sexual activity suggests that, although the brain circuitry associated with orgasm itself is quite similar between the sexes (a topic we return to at the end of this chapter), substantially different networks are active in men's and women's brains during sexual activity *prior* to orgasm (Georgiadis et al., 2009).

Taking a broader perspective on sexuality reveals additional distinctions between men and women (Peplau, 2003). Research has generally found that basic sex drive is greater in men, reflected in more frequent masturbation, sexual fantasies, and pursuit of sexual contacts. There are closer links between sexuality and aggression in men than in women, ranging from differences in sexual assertiveness to the most extreme manifestation: rape.

Emotional components and cognitive factors play a stronger role in the sex lives of women than of men. In addition to a somewhat flexible sexuality that adapts to new experiences and situations over time, most women place more emphasis on sexual intimacy within the context of committed relationships. These observations and others have led sex researchers to adopt a more nuanced view of female sexuality. While Masters and Johnson simply adapted the linear model of male sexuality to women, the more modern perspective views women's sexuality as a cycle, governed in large measure by emotional factors (Basson, 2001, 2008). According to this model, emotional intimacy and desire (more than physiological arousal) are crucial in the initiation of sexual responses, and following a sexual encounter, a combination of both emotional and physical satisfaction affects the likelihood of further sexual activity (**FIGURE 12.10**).

Although male and female sexuality may bear the imprint of our evolutionary history, on an individual basis it is also shaped by sociocultural pressures and experience. Sexual therapy, for example, usually consists of helping the person to relax, to recognize the sensations associated with coitus, and to learn the behaviors that produce the desired effects in both partners. Masturbation during adolescence, rather than being harmful as suggested in previous times, may help prevent sexual problems in adulthood. As with other behaviors, practice, practice, practice helps.

Sexual behavior may also aid overall health; epidemiological studies indicate that men who have frequent sex tend to live longer than men who do not (Davey-Smith et al., 1997), and sexual experiences effectively induce adult neurogenesis in the hippocampus in lab animals, suggesting that sexual behaviors may be directly beneficial to the brain (Leuner et al., 2010). Of course, it is also important to one's health to take precautions (such as using condoms) to avoid contracting sexually transmitted infections.

Hormones play only a permissive role in human sexual behavior

We saw that a little bit of testosterone must be in circulation to activate male-typical mating behavior in rodents. The same relation seems to hold for human males. For example, boys who fail to produce testosterone at puberty show little interest in sex unless they receive androgen supplements. These males, as well as men who have lost their testes as a result of cancer or accident, have made it possible to conduct experiments showing that testosterone indeed stimulates sexual interest and activity, as well as a sense of heightened energy, in men (J. M. Davidson et al., 1979).

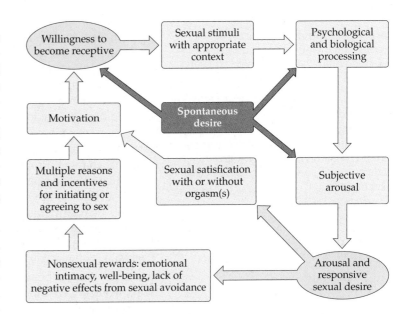

12.10 WOMEN'S SEXUAL/EMOTIONAL RESPONSE According to one model of female sexual responses (Basson, 2008), a willingness to become receptive (top left) interacts with sexual drive (red arrows). A combination of sexual stimuli (top) and biological factors result in feelings of arousal and desire (bottom right). A variety of factors, including rewarding nonsexual intimacy and/or sexual gratification from this encounter, provide feedback that affects levels of motivation (left) for subsequent sexual behavior.

parental behavior   Behavior of adult animals with the goal of enhancing the well-being of their own offspring, often at some cost to the parents.

altricial   Referring to animals that are born in an undeveloped state and depend on maternal care, as human infants do.

precocial   Referring to animals that are born in a relatively developed state and that are able to survive with relatively little maternal care.

parabiotic   Referring to a surgical preparation that joins two animals to share a single blood supply.

Recall that, in rats, additional testosterone has no effect on the vigor of mating. Consequently, there is no correlation between the amount of androgens produced by an individual male rat and his tendency to copulate. In humans, too, just a little testosterone is sufficient to restore behavior, and despite popular misconceptions, there is no correlation between systemic androgen levels and sexual activity among men, provided they have at least *some* androgen. Some women experience sexual dysfunction after menopause, reporting decreased sexual desire and difficulty achieving comfortable coitus. There are many possible reasons for such a change, including several hormonal changes. Providing postmenopausal women with low doses of both estrogens and androgens can have beneficial effects on the genital experience of sex and a modest increase in women's sexual interest (Basson, 2008; Sherwin, 1998, 2002). Attempts by pharmaceutical companies to find a "female Viagra," a drug that would more effectively boost sexual desire in women, have failed so far (Jaspers et al., 2016; Tavernise, 2016).

There have been several attempts to determine whether women's interest or participation in sexual behavior varies with the menstrual cycle. For example, one study found women were more likely to wear red when at the peak of their fertility (Beall and Tracy, 2013). But in general, such effects are small, and several studies have failed to see any significant change in interest in sex across the menstrual cycle.

For Many Vertebrates, Parental Care Determines Offspring Survival

In many vertebrate species, copulation is not enough to ensure reproduction. Extensive **parental behavior** is necessary for the survival of many young vertebrates, and all newborn mammals. This is especially true of species with **altricial** young, which start life with poorly developed motor or sensory systems (e.g., songbirds, humans) and are so generally helpless that a very substantial parental investment, perhaps by both parents, is required just for them to survive. Although **precocial** young (e.g., ducks, horses) likewise require parental investments in the form of food and protection, at least they can move around, see, and keep themselves warm. In these species the female alone may care for the offspring.

In Chapter 5 we discussed the milk letdown reflex, when the infant's suckling on the nipple triggers the secretion of oxytocin to promote the release of milk (see Figure 5.12). In rats, the pregnant female prepares for her pups by licking all of her nipples. Doing so probably helps clean the nipples before the pups arrive, but it also makes them more sensitive to touch. This self-grooming actually expands the amount of sensory cortex that responds to skin surrounding the nipples (Xerri et al., 1994), which probably sets the stage for the letdown reflex. This is a wonderful example of an animal's behavior altering its own brain and therefore changing its future behavior.

Rat mothers (called *dams*) show four easily measured maternal behaviors: nest building, crouching over pups, retrieving pups, and nursing (**FIGURE 12.11**). A virgin female or male rat won't normally show these behaviors toward rat pups. In fact, a virgin female finds the smell of newborn pups aversive. Information about the odor from pups projects via the olfactory bulb to the medial amygdala and on to the VMH. Lesions anywhere along that path will cause a virgin rat to show maternal behavior right away (Numan and Numan, 1991), because she no longer detects the smell.

However, if a virgin female is exposed to newborn pups a few hours a day for several days in a row, she (or almost any adult rat, male or female) will start building a nest, crouching over pups, and retrieving them. As the rat gradually habituates to the smell of the pups, it starts taking care of them. But the rat dam that gives birth to her first litter will instantly show these behaviors. It turns out that the rather complicated pattern of hormones during pregnancy shapes her brain to display maternal behaviors before she is exposed to the pups.

The effect of hormones on a rat's maternal behaviors is demonstrated by a **parabiotic** preparation in which two female rats are surgically joined, sharing a single blood supply, such that each is exposed to any hormones secreted by the other (**FIGURE 12.12**). If one of those females is pregnant, then at the end of her pregnancy, the oth-

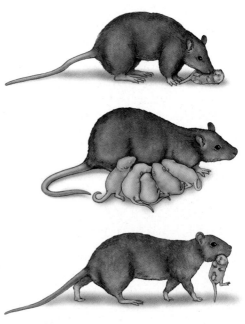

12.11 PARENTAL BEHAVIOR IN RATS

er female, who was never pregnant but was exposed to the pregnant rat's hormones, will also immediately show maternal behavior (Terkel and Rosenblatt, 1972). Which hormone is responsible for promoting maternal behavior? No single hormone alone can do it; the combination of several hormones, including estrogens, progesterone, and prolactin, is required. There is ample evidence that the hormones of pregnancy also prepare human mothers to nurture their newborns (A. S. Fleming et al., 2002).

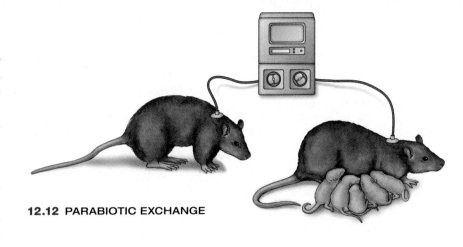

12.12 PARABIOTIC EXCHANGE

The network of brain regions that controls maternal behavior shows considerable overlap with the circuitry for sexual behavior. It's not too surprising that the same brain regions are involved in mating and maternal behavior, when you consider that these behaviors are simply successive stages in the overall process of reproduction. One brain region that regulates maternal behavior is the anteroventral periventricular nucleus (AVPV), which is larger in females than males and which grows even larger after pregnancy (Scott et al., 2015). As we noted earlier, the mPOA is sensitive to many steroid hormones, and lesions there severely reduce or eliminate oral maternal behaviors such as licking and pup retrieval, but they have relatively little effect on crouching or nursing. Lesioning the periaqueductal gray, conversely, has no effect on the oral maternal behaviors, but it virtually eliminates the crouching position for nursing pups (Lonstein and Stern, 1997). Some of the mPOA neurons that play a role in regulating pup care, in both mother and father mice, express the neuropeptide galanin (Dulac et al., 2014). Interestingly, men who are interested in babies show less of a spike in testosterone secretion in response to erotic videos (Zilioli et al., 2015).

Now that we've described the hormonal and neural interactions that influence male and female reproductive behaviors, let's discuss how males and females come to be different in the first place.

Sexual Differentiation

Sexual differentiation is the process by which individuals develop either male or female bodies and behaviors. In mammals this process begins before birth and continues into adulthood. As we'll see, some people may be very male-like (masculine) in some parts of the body and very female-like (feminine) in others, so sometimes a person is neither male nor female but may be a blend of the two sexes.

Sex Determination and Sexual Differentiation Occur Early in Development

In mammals, every egg carries an X chromosome from the mother; fusion with an X- or Y-bearing sperm is the key event in **sex determination**, the developmentally early event that establishes the course of subsequent sexual differentiation of the body. With only occasional exceptions, mammals that receive an X chromosome from the father will become females with XX sex chromosomes; those that receive the father's Y chromosome will become XY males.

In vertebrates the first major consequence of sex determination is in the gonads. Very early in development each individual has a pair of **indifferent gonads**, glands that vaguely resemble both testes and ovaries. During the first month of gestation in humans, differential genetic instructions determine whether the indifferent gonads begin changing into ovaries or testes. In mammals with a Y chromosome, a gene called **SRY** (for *s*ex-determining *r*egion on the *Y* chromosome) is responsible for the development of testes. The Sry protein causes the cells in the core of the indifferent gonad to proliferate at the expense of the outer layers, and the indifferent gonad develops into a testis.

sexual differentiation The process by which individuals develop either male-like or female-like bodies and behavior.

sex determination The process by which the initial decision is made for a fetus to develop as a male or a female.

indifferent gonads The undifferentiated gonads of the early vertebrate fetus, which will eventually develop into either testes or ovaries.

SRY gene A gene on the Y chromosome that directs the developing gonads to become testes. The name SRY stands for *s*ex-determining *r*egion on the *Y* chromosome.

wolffian ducts A duct system in the embryo that will develop into male structures (the epididymis, vas deferens, and seminal vesicles) if testes are present.

müllerian ducts A duct system in the embryo that will develop into female reproductive structures (oviduct, uterus, and inner vagina) if testes are not present.

In XX individuals (or if the *SRY* gene is defective) no Sry protein is produced, and the indifferent gonad takes a different course: cells of the outer layers of the gonad proliferate more than those of the inner core, and an ovary forms. This early decision of whether to form testes or ovaries has a domino effect, setting off a chain of events that usually results in either a male or a female.

Gonadal hormones direct sexual differentiation of the body

For all mammals, including humans, the sexual differentiation of the bodies of males and females is the product of differential hormone secretion. Whereas developing testes produce several hormones, fetal ovaries produce very little hormone. When exposed to testicular hormones, many tissues of the body begin developing masculine characters; if the cells are not exposed to testicular hormones, they develop feminine characters. As a result of their differential exposure to steroid hormones, thousands of genes in tissues throughout the body are expressed differently in males and females (van Nas et al., 2009).

We can chart masculine or feminine development by examining the structures that connect the gonads to the outside of the body. The internal reproductive tracts are quite different in adult males and females (see Figure 12.8), but at the embryonic stage all individuals have the precursor tissues of both systems. The early fetus has a genital tubercle that can form either a clitoris or a penis, as well as two sets of ducts—the **wolffian ducts** and the **müllerian ducts** (**FIGURE 12.13A**)—that connect the indifferent gonads to the outer body wall. In females, the müllerian

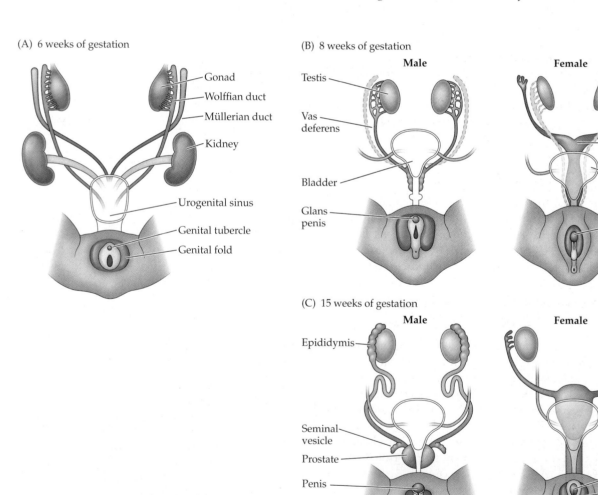

12.13 SEXUAL DIFFERENTIATION IN HUMANS
(A) Undifferentiated fetus. (B, C) Male (left) and female (right) fetuses at 8 weeks (B) and 15 weeks (C) of gestation.

ducts develop into the oviducts (also called *fallopian tubes*), uterus, and inner vagina (**FIGURE 12.13B AND C**, right), and most of the wolffian system degenerates. In males, hormones secreted by the testes orchestrate the converse outcome: the wolffian ducts develop into epididymis, vas deferens, and seminal vesicles (**FIGURE 12.13B AND C**, left), while the müllerian ducts shrink to mere remnants.

Two testicular secretions drive masculinization: testosterone, which promotes the development of the wolffian system, and **anti-müllerian hormone** (**AMH**), which causes regression of the müllerian system. In the absence of testes and their secretions, the genital tract develops in a feminine pattern, as the wolffian ducts regress and the müllerian ducts develop into components of the female internal reproductive tract.

Testosterone also masculinizes other, non-wolffian-derived structures such as the fetal genitalia. Local conversion of testosterone into a more potent androgen, **dihydrotestosterone** (**DHT**), accomplished by the enzyme **5α-reductase** in the genital skin, induces the bipotential genitals to form a scrotum and penis (see Figure 12.13). We'll see later that without local conversion into DHT, testosterone is able to masculinize the genitalia only partially. If androgens are absent altogether, the genital tissues grow into the female labia and clitoris.

In general, unless the indifferent gonad becomes a testis and begins secreting hormones, an immature mammal develops as a female in most respects. As noted earlier, immature ovaries produce few hormones. So the sex chromosomes determine the sex of the gonad, and differential exposure to gonadal hormones controls subsequent sexual differentiation of the rest of the body (**FIGURE 12.14A**). Later in life, hormones and experience act in concert to guide further sexual differentiation and the development of gender identity (**FIGURE 12.14B**).

anti-müllerian hormone (AMH)
A protein hormone secreted by the fetal testis that inhibits müllerian duct development.

dihydrotestosterone (DHT) The 5α-reduced metabolite of testosterone; a potent androgen that is principally responsible for the masculinization of the external genitalia in mammalian sexual differentiation.

5α-reductase An enzyme that converts testosterone into dihydrotestosterone (DHT).

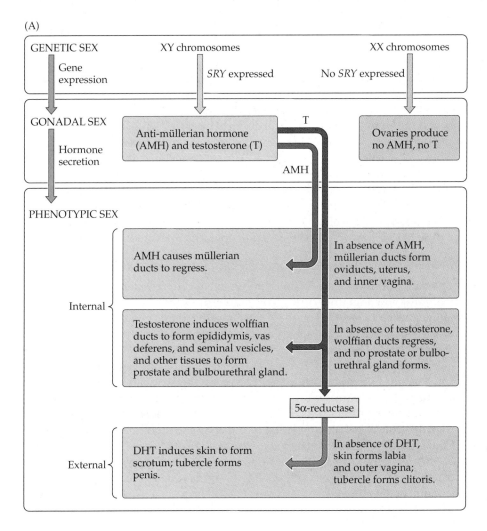

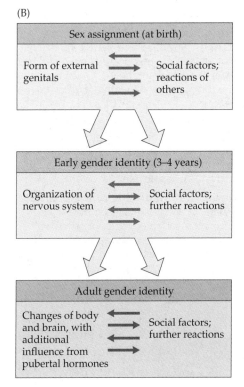

12.14 SEXUAL DIFFERENTIATION AND GENDER IDENTITY (A) Genetic and hormonal mechanisms of embryonic sexual differentiation. (B) Steps toward adult gender identity in humans.

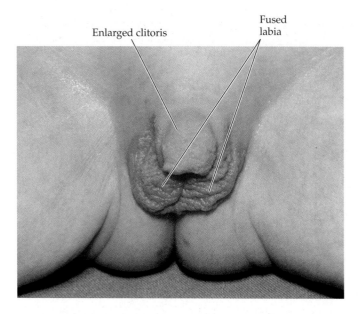

Enlarged clitoris   Fused labia

12.15 AN INTERSEX PHENOTYPE The partially masculinized genitalia of this girl with CAH are the result of excessive androgen production by the adrenals.

Turner's syndrome A condition seen in individuals carrying a single X chromosome but no other sex chromosome.

congenital adrenal hyperplasia (CAH) Any of several genetic mutations that can result in exposure of a female fetus to adrenal androgens, which results in a clitoris that is larger than typical at birth.

intersex Referring to an individual with atypical genital development and sexual differentiation that generally resembles a form intermediate between typical male and typical female genitals.

androgen insensitivity syndrome (AIS) A syndrome caused by a mutation of the androgen receptor gene that renders tissues insensitive to androgenic hormones like testosterone. Affected XY individuals are phenotypic females, but they have internal testes and regressed internal genital structures.

Changes in the sequence of sexual differentiation result in predictable changes in development

Some people have only one sex chromosome: a single X (embryos containing only single Y chromosomes do not survive). This genetic makeup results in **Turner's syndrome**, in which an apparent female has underdeveloped but recognizable ovaries, as you might expect because no *SRY* gene is present.

Sometimes XX individuals with well-formed ovaries are exposed to androgens in utero and, depending on the degree of exposure, they may be masculinized. For example, most fetal rats develop in the uterus sandwiched between two siblings. If a female is bracketed by brothers, some of the androgen from the siblings must reach the female, because although her gross appearance will be feminine at birth, her anogenital distance (the distance from the tip of the clitoris [or penis in a male] to the anus) will be slightly greater (i.e., more male-like) than that of a female developing between two sisters (Clemens et al., 1978).

In humans, **congenital adrenal hyperplasia (CAH)** can cause a developing female to be exposed to excess androgens before birth. In CAH, the adrenal glands fail to produce sufficient corticosteroids, producing instead considerable amounts of androgens. In XX individuals with this condition, the androgen levels produced are usually intermediate between those of typical females and males, and the newborn often has an **intersex** appearance: a phallus that is intermediate in size between a typical clitoris and a typical penis, and skin folds that resemble both labia and scrotum (**FIGURE 12.15**). In severe cases the individual may appear to have well-formed penis and scrotum, but no testes are present in the "scrotum"; instead, these individuals have abdominal ovaries. Once children with CAH are born, the excess adrenal androgen production can be corrected, but by then substantial sexual differentiation has already occurred.

The result is a vigorous controversy over the best course of action for the parents of girls with CAH: to opt for immediate surgical modification of the genitalia, or to wait until adulthood, when the CAH-affected individuals can decide for themselves whether to have surgery, which is, after all, purely cosmetic. Females with CAH are much more likely to be described by their parents (and themselves) as tomboys than are other girls, and they exhibit enhanced spatial abilities on cognitive tests that usually favor males (Berenbaum, 2001). In adulthood, although a majority of females with CAH describe themselves as heterosexual, a much higher proportion report a lesbian orientation than among the general population of women.

Dysfunctional androgen receptors can block male masculinization

The importance of androgens for masculine sexual differentiation is illustrated by the condition known as **androgen insensitivity syndrome (AIS)**. The gene for the androgen receptor is found on the X chromosome. If this gene is dysfunctional in XY individuals, they will be incapable of producing normal androgen receptors, and their tissues will fail to respond to androgens. Because they have normal *SRY* function, such people develop normal testes that secrete AMH and testosterone.

In the absence of working androgen receptors, the wolffian ducts fail to sense testosterone and thus regress; the external genital tissue forms labia and a clitoris. At puberty women with AIS develop breasts; breast development depends on the ratio of estrogenic to androgenic stimulation at puberty, and since androgen-insensitive individuals receive little androgenic *stimulation*, the functional estrogen-to-androgen ratio is high. However, lacking ovaries or uterus, women with AIS do not start menstruating and are infertile with a shallow vagina (due to the missing müllerian contribution). But in almost all other respects, women with AIS look like other women (**FIGURE 12.16**) and, as we'll see shortly, behave like other women.

Some people seem to change sex at puberty

Babies are occasionally born with a rare genetic mutation that disables the enzyme (5α-reductase) that converts testosterone to DHT. An XY individual with this condition will develop testes and normal male internal reproductive structures (because testosterone and AMH function normally), but the external genitalia will not masculinize fully (**FIGURE 12.17**). The reason for this is that the genital epithelium, which normally possesses 5α-reductase, is unable to amplify the androgenic signal by converting the testosterone to the more active DHT. Consequently, the phallus is only slightly masculinized and resembles a large clitoris, and the genital folds resemble labia, although they contain the testes. Usually there is no vaginal opening. The prostate and seminal vesicles are also affected, resulting in abnormalities of semen production, but paternity can be achieved with medical assistance (H. J. Kang et al., 2011).

A particular village in the Dominican Republic is home to several families that carry the mutation causing 5α-reductase deficiency. Children born with this appearance seem to be regarded as girls in the way they are dressed and raised (Imperato-McGinley et al., 1974). At puberty, however, the testes increase androgen production, and the external genitalia become more fully masculinized. The phallus grows into a small but recognizable penis; the body develops narrow hips and a muscular build, without breasts; and the individuals begin acting like young men. The villagers have nicknamed such individuals **guevedoces**, meaning "eggs (testes) at 12 (years)."

guevedoces Literally, "eggs at 12" (in Spanish). A nickname for individuals who are raised as girls but at puberty change appearance and begin behaving as boys do.

(A) Newborn

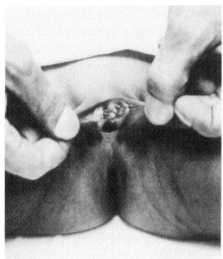

(B) Adolescent

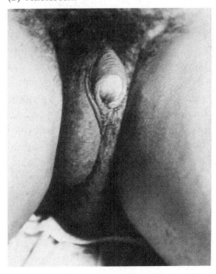

12.17 GUEVEDOCES In the Dominican Republic, some individuals, called *guevedoces*, are born with ambiguous genitalia (A) and are raised as girls. At puberty, however, the phallus grows into a recognizable penis (B), and the individuals begin acting like young men. (Courtesy of Dr. Julianne Imperato-McGinley.)

These men never develop facial beards, but they usually have girlfriends, indicating that they are sexually interested in women. We will discuss the sexual identities of *guevedoces,* as well as women with CAH or AIS, a little later.

How Should We Define Gender— by Genes, Gonads, Genitals, or the Brain?

Most people are either male or female, and whether we examine their chromosomes, gonads, external genitalia, or internal structures, we see a consistent pattern: all are either feminine or masculine in character. Compared with physical features, behavior is much more difficult to define as feminine or masculine. The only behavior displayed *exclusively* by one sex is childbirth. Even behaviors that are very rarely displayed by members of one sex or the other (e.g., sexual assault by women or breast-feeding by men) occur sometimes in the unexpected sex. For behaviors that can be measured and studied experimentally in humans or other animals, we have to resort to group means and statistical tests to see the differences. Almost all individuals display some behaviors that are more common in the opposite sex.

The various syndromes that we have been discussing show us that even physical features can be confusing criteria by which to judge sex (see Figure 12.16), and they indicate that sex, gender, and sexual orientation are distinct and independent from one another. Androgen-insensitive humans have male XY sex chromosomes and internal testes, and like most males they do not have oviducts or a uterus. But they do have a vagina and breasts, and in most respects their behavior is typical of females: they dress like females, they are attracted to and marry males, and perhaps most important, even after they learn the details of their condition, they strongly identify themselves as women (Money and Ehrhardt, 1972).

As we will see next, there is evidence that the same hormones that masculinize the genitalia of male animals in utero also masculinize the brain to affect later behavior. We'll also see that there are structural sex differences in the brains of humans and other animals. In androgen-insensitive rats, some brain regions are masculine and others are feminine. Thus, from a scientific standpoint we cannot regard an animal, especially a human, as simply masculine or feminine. Rather we must specify which structure or behavior we are talking about when we say it is typical of females or of males. As we turn our attention to the effects of hormones on the brain, it is especially important to maintain the perspective that individuals may be relatively masculine in some traits and more feminine in others.

Gonadal Hormones Direct Sexual Differentiation of the Brain and Behavior

As scientists began discovering that testicular hormones direct masculine development of the body, behavioral researchers found evidence for a similar influence on the brain. A female guinea pig, like most other rodents, normally displays the lordosis posture in response to male mounting for only a short period around the time of ovulation, when her fertility is highest. If a male mounts her at other times, she does not show lordosis. Experimenters can induce female rodents to display lordosis by injecting ovarian steroids in the sequence that normally occurs during ovulation— giving her estrogens for a few days and then progesterone. A few hours after the progesterone injection, the female will display lordosis in response to male mounting.

Phoenix et al. (1959) exposed female guinea pigs to testosterone in utero. As adults, these females did *not* show lordosis. Even if their ovaries were removed and they were given the steroidal regimen that reliably activated lordosis in female guinea pigs, these fetally androgenized females did not show lordosis. On the basis of these data, the researchers inferred that the same testicular steroids that masculinize the genitalia during early development also masculinize the developing brain. In other words, they proposed that the brain was just one more target tissue that is masculinized by androgens acting early in life (**FIGURE 12.18**). This type of lasting change due to steroid exposure is known as an **organizational effect**.

organizational effect A permanent alteration of the nervous system, and thus permanent change in behavior, resulting from the action of a steroid hormone on an animal early in its development.

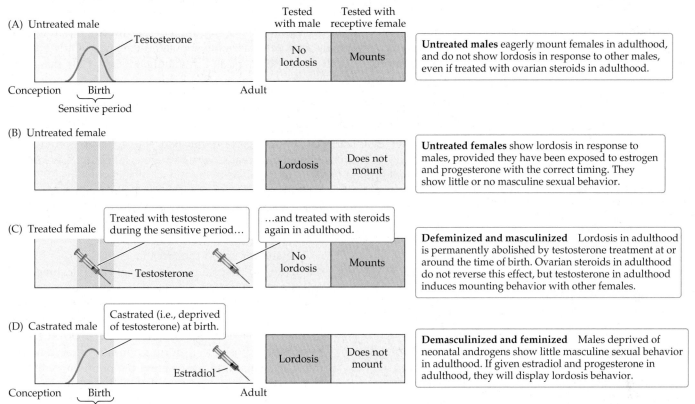

(A) Untreated male

Testosterone

Conception | Birth | Adult

Sensitive period

	Tested with male	Tested with receptive female
	No lordosis	Mounts

Untreated males eagerly mount females in adulthood, and do not show lordosis in response to other males, even if treated with ovarian steroids in adulthood.

(B) Untreated female

Lordosis	Does not mount

Untreated females show lordosis in response to males, provided they have been exposed to estrogen and progesterone with the correct timing. They show little or no masculine sexual behavior.

(C) Treated female

Treated with testosterone during the sensitive period...

...and treated with steroids again in adulthood.

Testosterone

No lordosis	Mounts

Defeminized and masculinized Lordosis in adulthood is permanently abolished by testosterone treatment at or around the time of birth. Ovarian steroids in adulthood do not reverse this effect, but testosterone in adulthood induces mounting behavior with other females.

(D) Castrated male

Castrated (i.e., deprived of testosterone) at birth.

Estradiol

Lordosis	Does not mount

Demasculinized and feminized Males deprived of neonatal androgens show little masculine sexual behavior in adulthood. If given estradiol and progesterone in adulthood, they will display lordosis behavior.

Conception | Birth | Adult

Sensitive period

12.18 ORGANIZATIONAL EFFECTS OF SEX HORMONES ON RODENT BEHAVIOR Untreated males (A) produce a testosterone surge around birth and go on to develop normal adult sexual behavior. Untreated females (B) that are not exposed to gonadal hormones during the perinatal sensitive period develop normal adult female sexual behavior. However, (C) providing steroids to females during the sensitive period or (D) preventing neonatal steroid exposure in males can cause abnormal organization of sexual control mechanisms and the expression of cross-sex sexual behavior in adulthood.

A steroid has an organizational effect only when present during a specific **sensitive period**, generally in early development. Unlike the transient nature of activational effects of hormones, which we discussed earlier, the organizational effects of hormones tend to be permanent. The exact boundaries of the sensitive period of development depend on which behavior and which species are being studied. For rats, androgens given just after birth (the **neonatal** period) can affect later behavior. Guinea pigs, however, must be exposed to androgens *before* birth for adult lordosis behavior to be affected. In mammals, puberty can be viewed as a second sensitive period; for example, steroid exposure during puberty causes the addition of new cells (an organizational effect) to sex-related brain regions of rats (Ahmed et al., 2008).

Early testicular secretions result in masculine behavior in adulthood

The *organizational hypothesis* provides a unitary explanation for sexual differentiation: that a single steroid signal (androgen) diffuses through all tissues, masculinizing the body, the brain, and behavior. From this point of view the nervous system is simply another type of tissue listening for the androgenic signal that will instruct it to organize itself in a masculine fashion. If the nervous system does not detect androgens, it will organize itself in a mostly feminine fashion.

What was demonstrated originally for the lordosis behavior of guinea pigs has been observed in a variety of vertebrate species and for many behaviors. Exposing female rat pups to testosterone either just before birth or during the first 10 days after birth greatly reduces their lordosis responsiveness as adults. This explains the observation that adult male rats show very little lordosis even when given estrogens and progesterone. However, male rats that are castrated on the day of birth display excellent lordosis responses in adulthood if injected with estrogens and progesterone.

In most cases, full masculine behavior requires androgens both in development (to organize the nervous system to enable the later behavior) and in adulthood (to activate that behavior). For example, the copulatory behavior of male rats can be quantified in terms of how often they mount a receptive female and how often such mounting results in intromission. Androgens must be present in adulthood to activate this behav-

sensitive period The period during development in which an organism can be permanently altered by a particular experience or treatment.

neonatal Referring to newborns.

aromatization The chemical reaction that converts testosterone to estradiol, and other androgens to other estrogens.

aromatase An enzyme that converts some androgens into estrogens.

aromatization hypothesis The hypothesis that testicular androgens enter the brain and are converted there into estrogens to masculinize the developing nervous system in some rodents.

α-fetoprotein A protein found in the plasma of fetuses. In rodents, α-fetoprotein binds estrogens and prevents them from entering the brain.

ior: adult males that have been castrated stop mounting in a few weeks; injecting them with testosterone eventually restores masculine copulatory behavior. Only animals exposed to androgen both in development and in adulthood show fully masculine behavior (see Figure 12.4).

The estrogenic metabolites of testosterone masculinize the nervous system and behavior of rodents

Soon after the organizational hypothesis was published, researchers reported a paradoxical finding: newborn female rats treated with estrogens failed to show lordosis behavior in adulthood (Feder and Whalen, 1965). In fact, if such females were also treated with testosterone in adulthood, they would show *mounting* behavior, indicating that the early estrogens had masculinized their brains. Why would estradiol, regarded (incorrectly) as a *female* hormone, cause a *masculinization* of the brain's sexual circuitry in females?

The answer lies in the fact that estradiol is a principle metabolite of testosterone. In a single chemical reaction, called **aromatization**, the enzyme **aromatase** converts testosterone to estradiol (and other androgens to other estrogens). The ovaries normally contain a great deal of aromatase, but so does the brain. The **aromatization hypothesis** posits that during normal rodent development, testicular androgens enter the brain and are there converted into estrogens, and that these estrogens are what act on neurons to *masculinize* the developing rodent nervous system.

All rat fetuses are exposed to high levels of estrogens that originate in the mother and cross the placenta, so why aren't the brains of females masculinized by the maternal estrogens? A blood protein called **α-fetoprotein** binds estrogens and prevents them from entering the brain (Bakker et al., 2006), but it does not bind testosterone. So the male rat's brain is masculinized when testosterone from his testes bypasses the α-fetoprotein and enters his brain, where it is aromatized to estradiol within individual neurons. This newly synthesized estrogen binds to local estrogen receptors, and the steroid-receptor complex regulates gene expression to cause the brain to develop in a masculine fashion (**FIGURE 12.19**). If no androgens are present, there can be no estrogenic action in the brain (because α-fetoprotein has blocked estrogens of peripheral origin), so the fetus develops in a feminine fashion. The reason that the injections of estrogens in rat pups affected lordosis in the original research was that the injection flooded the bloodstream with estradiol molecules and overwhelmed the circulating α-fetoprotein, allowing many estrogen molecules to enter the brain. A lack of aromatase seems to play a role in the unusual sexual differentiation of the spotted hyena (**BOX 12.1**).

The aromatization hypothesis is fully applicable to masculine copulatory behavior in rats. If a male rat is castrated at birth, it grows up to have a small penis and show few intromissions, even when given replacement testosterone in adulthood. Castration plus the androgen DHT, which cannot be aromatized into an estrogen, results in a male with normal genitalia but little or no masculine sexual behavior, because of the lack of organizational estrogenic stimula-

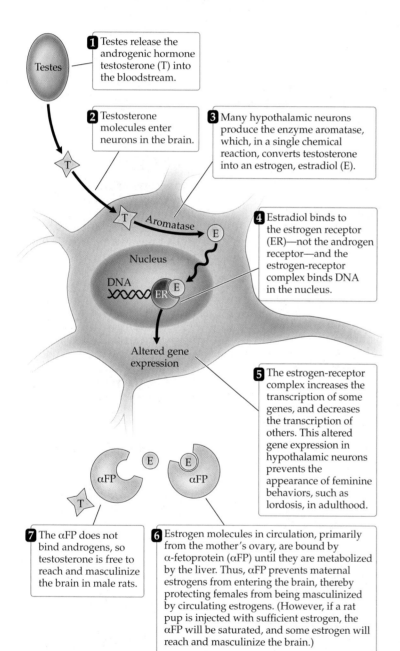

1 Testes release the androgenic hormone testosterone (T) into the bloodstream.

2 Testosterone molecules enter neurons in the brain.

3 Many hypothalamic neurons produce the enzyme aromatase, which, in a single chemical reaction, converts testosterone into an estrogen, estradiol (E).

4 Estradiol binds to the estrogen receptor (ER)—not the androgen receptor—and the estrogen-receptor complex binds DNA in the nucleus.

5 The estrogen-receptor complex increases the transcription of some genes, and decreases the transcription of others. This altered gene expression in hypothalamic neurons prevents the appearance of feminine behaviors, such as lordosis, in adulthood.

6 Estrogen molecules in circulation, primarily from the mother's ovary, are bound by α-fetoprotein (αFP) until they are metabolized by the liver. Thus, αFP prevents maternal estrogens from entering the brain, thereby protecting females from being masculinized by circulating estrogens. (However, if a rat pup is injected with sufficient estrogen, the αFP will be saturated, and some estrogen will reach and masculinize the brain.)

7 The αFP does not bind androgens, so testosterone is free to reach and masculinize the brain in male rats.

12.19 THE AROMATIZATION HYPOTHESIS

BOX
12.1

The Paradoxical Sexual Differentiation of the Spotted Hyena

Scholars of antiquity believed that spotted hyenas were **hermaphrodites** (both male and female). The mistake is understandable because from birth the female hyena has a clitoris that is as large as the penis of the male (as the photograph shows), through which she urinates, receives semen, and gives birth. Female hyenas are also larger than, more aggressive than, and socially dominant over males.

What difference in the hyena's prenatal development causes females to develop a "penis"? In other mammals the placenta rapidly aromatizes androgens into estrogens; this conversion may be a way to protect the mother and fetal females from androgens produced by fetal males. But the placenta of the spotted hyena is remarkably deficient in the aromatase enzyme (Licht et al., 1992).

Because the hyena mother produces large amounts of the androgen androstenedione (Glickman et al., 1987) and the placenta fails to convert the androstenedione to estrogens, all the fetuses are exposed to high concentrations of androgens, which may help account for their masculine appearance. (However, female hyenas treated prenatally with androgen-blocking drugs still develop masculinized exteriors [Drea et al., 1998], suggesting that an additional mechanism must be involved.) One

remarkable observation is that female pups, which are born with teeth, fight viciously with siblings immediately from birth. Sisters fight particularly violently, and in wild populations it is common for one pup to kill its sibling (L. G. Frank et al., 1991), at least when food is scarce (Smale et al., 1999). It remains to be established whether this extreme aggression is due to prenatal stimulation of the brain with androgens.

Even if the extreme aggressiveness of the female hyena is due to fetal androgens, females do mate with males, so their brains have not been made permanently unreceptive (as would happen in prenatally androgen-

ized rats). Indeed, female hyenas seem to have a typically feminine SDN-POA (Fenstemaker et al., 1999) and SNB (Forger et al., 1996). Just the same, mating in the spotted hyena is a tense affair: the female seems to just barely tolerate the male's proximity, and the male alternates between approaching and retreating from his alluring but dangerous mate. (Photograph courtesy of Stephen Glickman.)

hermaphrodite   An individual possessing the reproductive organs of both sexes, either simultaneously or at different points in time.

---

tion of the brain. Conversely, males castrated and treated with estrogens as newborns mount and show intromission behavior when treated with testosterone in adulthood, despite having very small penises (due to the lack of early DHT). The important point in all this is that it is hormonal masculinization of the *brain*, not the genitalia, that organizes male rat copulatory behavior.

In primates, including humans, aromatization cannot play an important role in masculinization of the nervous system. The human brain produces significant quantities of aromatase, but men who have mutations in the aromatase gene—and are thus unable to produce aromatase and therefore estrogens—nonetheless have masculine gender identities and sexual development (Grumbach and Auchus, 1999). Men with defective estrogen receptors nevertheless develop masculine gender attributes; likewise people with AIS display feminine behavior and gender identity, even though they produce lots of testosterone and have functional estrogen receptors. The details of the masculinization of the primate nervous system remain to be worked out, but hormonal masculinization must be accomplished through androgen receptors rather than estrogen receptors. And whichever specific steroid receptor is involved, many vertebrate species display distinct sex differences in the brain, as we'll see next.

Go to Animation 12.2
**The Aromatization
Hypothesis**
bn8e.com/12.2

Several regions of the nervous system differ between males and females

sexual dimorphism The condition in which males and females show pronounced sex differences in appearance.

syrinx The vocal organ in birds.

sexually dimorphic nucleus of the preoptic area (SDN-POA) A region of the preoptic area that is 5 to 6 times larger in volume in male rats than in females.

The fact that male and female animals behave differently means that their brains must be different in some way, and according to the organizational hypothesis, this difference results primarily from androgenic masculinization of the developing brain. The exact form of these neural sex differences can be very subtle; the same basic circuit of neurons will produce very different behavior if the pattern of synapses varies. Sex differences in the number of synapses were identified in the preoptic area (POA) of the hypothalamus as early as 1971 (Raisman and Field, 1971). But scientists soon found that there are much more obvious sex differences in the brain, including differences in neuronal numbers, sizes, and shapes. Darwin coined a term, **sexual dimorphism**, to describe the condition in which males and females show pronounced sex differences in appearance. Let's discuss a few well-known models of sexual dimorphism in the brain.

SONG CONTROL REGIONS IN MALE SONGBIRDS   Male canaries and zebra finches produce elaborate songs to attract mates, but females do not, and the brain nuclei controlling song are 5 to 6 times larger in males than in females (Nottebohm and Arnold, 1976). One of these nuclei, called the *robustus archistriatum* (RA), controls motor neurons innervating the muscular singing organ, called the **syrinx**. The RA is controlled, in turn, by the *high vocal center* (HVC), so named because it exerts top-level control over the song production hierarchy. As we would expect, lesions of RA or HVC disrupt singing, and electrical stimulation can elicit song snippets. (Details of the song system can be seen in Figure 19.3.)

Exposing a hatchling female zebra finch to either testosterone or estradiol causes the development of a larger, male-like HVC and RA, in keeping with the organizational hypothesis, and if she receives additional testosterone in adulthood, she will sing like a male (Gurney and Konishi, 1979). Female zebra finches treated with androgens *only* in adulthood do not sing, so we know that early hormone organizes a masculine song system and adult hormone activates it. Singing in canaries, in contrast, requires only *adult* androgen treatment; previously untreated female canaries start singing after a few weeks of androgen treatment in adulthood. The androgens cause both HVC and RA to become larger, and their neurons grow and form new synaptic connections.

The difference in the hormonal controls of song in zebra finches and canaries may be related to the ecological niche occupied by each. Zebra finches are ready to breed at any time of the year, but canaries are seasonal breeders whose reproductive tracts shut down in the fall. The male canary song system tracks this ebb and flow: HVC and RA grow large in the spring, when the males are singing and their testosterone levels are high, and shrink again in the fall, as testosterone levels and singing decline.

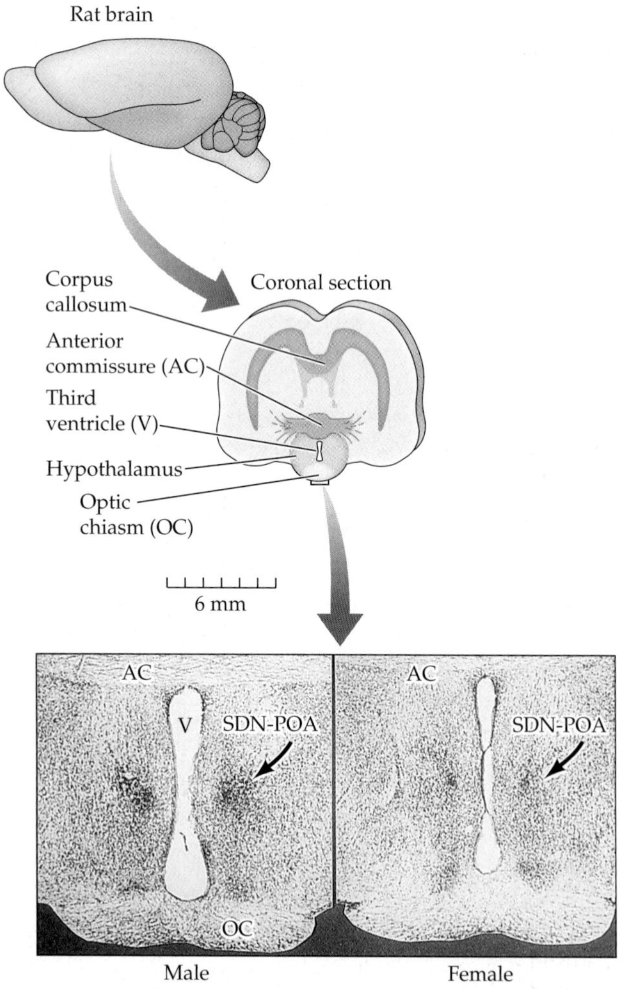

THE PREOPTIC AREA OF RATS   Where else might there be neural sex differences? Roger Gorski et al. (1978) examined the POA of the hypothalamus in rats because of the earlier reports that the numbers of synapses in this region were different in males and females, and because lesions of the POA disrupt ovulatory cycles in female rats and reduce copulatory behavior in males. Sure enough, the investigators found a nucleus within the POA that has a much larger volume in males than in females.

This nucleus, dubbed the **sexually dimorphic nucleus of the POA (SDN-POA)**, is much more evident in male rats than in females (**FIGURE 12.20**). Like the song control nuclei in zebra finches, the SDN-POA conformed beautifully to the organizational hypothesis: males castrated at birth had much smaller SDN-POAs in adulthood, while females androgenized at birth had large, male-like SDN-POAs

Rat brain

Corpus callosum

Coronal section

Anterior commissure (AC)

Third ventricle (V)

Hypothalamus

Optic chiasm (OC)

6 mm

AC — V — SDN-POA — OC — Male

AC — SDN-POA — Female

12.20 A SEX DIFFERENCE IN THE HYPOTHALAMUS
The sexually dimorphic nucleus of the preoptic area (SDN-POA) is much larger in male rats than in females. (Courtesy of Dr. Roger Gorski.)

as adults. Castrating male rats in adulthood, however, did not alter the size of the SDN-POA. Thus, testicular androgens somehow alter the development of the SDN-POA, resulting in a nucleus permanently larger in males than in females (**FIGURE 12.21**). There is growing evidence that androgens exert epigenetic effects of the sort described in Chapter 7, controlling the methylation of genes during development, and thus affecting their expression in adulthood (McCarthy and Nugent, 2015).

The rat SDN-POA system also conforms to the aromatization hypothesis: testosterone is converted to an estrogen in the brain and binds estrogen receptors to masculinize the nucleus. For example, XY rats that are androgen-insensitive (like the people with AIS discussed earlier) have testes but a feminine exterior. These rats have a masculine SDN-POA because their estrogen receptors are normal. Androgen-insensitive rats also do not display lordosis in response to estrogens and progesterone, because the testosterone that they secreted early in life was converted to an *estrogen* in the brain and masculinized their behavior (K. L. Olsen, 1979). Instead, the androgen-insensitive rats show normal male attraction to receptive females, with whom they may attempt to mate despite the lack of a penis (Hamson et al., 2009).

THE SPINAL CORD IN MAMMALS In rats, the bulbocavernosus (BC) muscles that surround the base of the penis are innervated by motor neurons in the **spinal nucleus of the bulbocavernosus (SNB)**. Male rats have about 200 SNB cells, but females have far fewer motor neurons in this region of the spinal cord.

On the day before birth, female rats have BC muscles attached to the base of the clitoris that are nearly as large as those of males and that are innervated by motor neurons in the SNB region (Rand and Breedlove, 1987). In the days just before and after birth, however, many SNB cells die, especially in females (Nordeen et al., 1985), and the BC muscles of females die.

A single injection of androgens given to a newborn female rat permanently spares some SNB motor neurons and their muscles: a powerful organizational effect. Castration of newborn males, accompanied by prenatal blockade of androgen receptors, causes the BC muscles and SNB motor neurons to die as in females. The system also dies in newborn androgen-insensitive rats, so aromatization seems to be unimportant for masculine development of the SNB.

Androgens act on the BC muscles to prevent their demise, and this sparing of the muscles likewise causes the innervating SNB motor neurons to survive (Fishman et al., 1990; C. L. Jordan et al., 1991). The exact site within the BC muscle where androgen has its effects is still unknown (Niel et al., 2009). But whatever the site of action is, the likely result is that the muscles are induced by androgen to provide a signal, such as a neurotrophic factor, that prevents SNB motor neurons from dying (**FIGURE 12.22**) (Forger et al., 1997).

The developmental rescue of SNB motor neurons is accomplished indirectly as a consequence of actions on muscle, but androgens can also directly affect the neurons themselves. SNB neurons contain androgen receptors and retain androgen sensitivity throughout life. In adulthood, androgen acts directly on the neurons to cause them to grow (Watson et al., 2001) and start producing substances to aid in the formation of

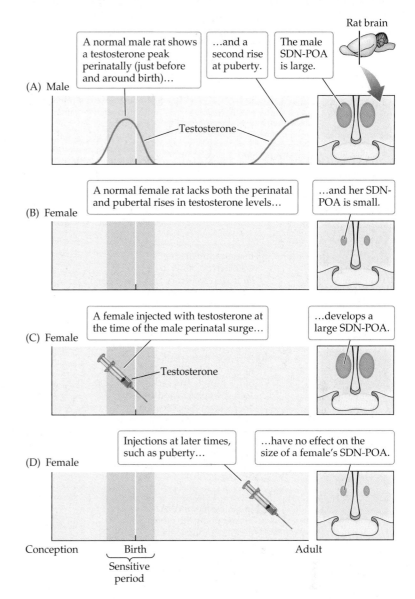

12.21 SEXUALLY DIMORPHIC NUCLEUS OF THE PREOPTIC AREA (SDN-POA) Testosterone can permanently enlarge the SDN-POA in rats, but only if given during a "sensitive period" early in life.

spinal nucleus of the bulbocavernosus (SNB) A group of motor neurons in the spinal cord of rats that innervate striated muscles controlling the penis.

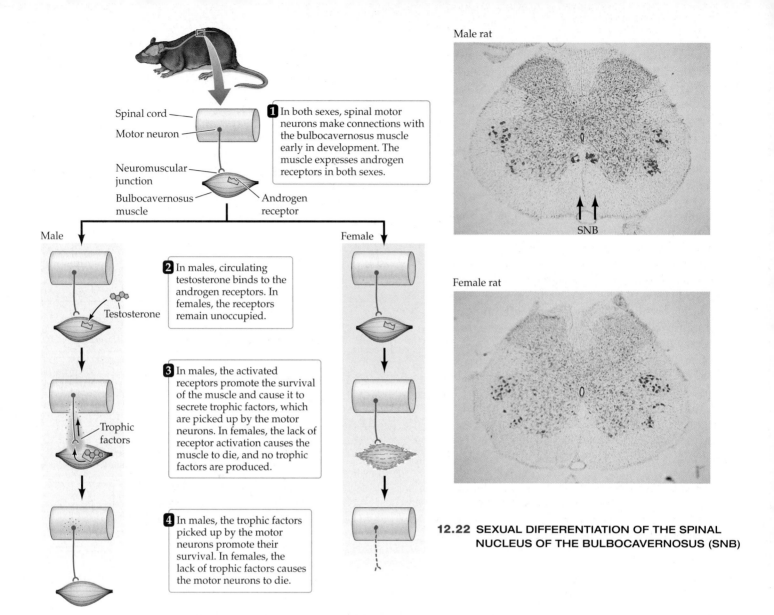

1 In both sexes, spinal motor neurons make connections with the bulbocavernosus muscle early in development. The muscle expresses androgen receptors in both sexes.

Spinal cord
Motor neuron
Neuromuscular junction
Bulbocavernosus muscle
Androgen receptor

Male

Female

2 In males, circulating testosterone binds to the androgen receptors. In females, the receptors remain unoccupied.

Testosterone

3 In males, the activated receptors promote the survival of the muscle and cause it to secrete trophic factors, which are picked up by the motor neurons. In females, the lack of receptor activation causes the muscle to die, and no trophic factors are produced.

Trophic factors

4 In males, the trophic factors picked up by the motor neurons promote their survival. In females, the lack of trophic factors causes the motor neurons to die.

Male rat

Female rat

SNB

12.22 SEXUAL DIFFERENTIATION OF THE SPINAL NUCLEUS OF THE BULBOCAVERNOSUS (SNB)

new connections. For example, androgens directly stimulate SNB neurons to produce N-cadherin, a cell adhesion molecule that mediates the formation of new contacts between cells (D. A. Monks and Watson, 2001). These are examples of activational effects of androgens.

All male mammals have BC muscles, but in nonrodents the BC motor neurons are found in a slightly different spinal location and are known as **Onuf's nucleus**. Surprisingly, most female mammals retain a BC muscle into adulthood; in women, for example, the BC (also known as *constrictor vestibule*) helps constrict the vaginal opening. But, as in rodents, the system is profoundly sexually dimorphic. Men have larger BC muscles and more numerous Onuf's motor neurons, most likely determined by androgen exposure during fetal development (Forger and Breedlove, 1986, 1987).

These model systems, and others like them, demonstrate the power of androgens to mold the brain in sex-typical ways. By controlling the amount and timing of testosterone exposure, researchers can make the various brain structures as masculine or feminine as they like. However, despite the crucial role of androgens in masculinizing sexually dimorphic nuclei in the nervous system, there's evidence that experience affects these systems too.

Environmental influences also affect sexual differentiation of the nervous system

Environmental factors of many sorts, ranging from the chemical composition of the environment to the behaviors of other individuals, can potently modulate the

Onuf's nucleus The human homolog of the spinal nucleus of the bulbocavernosus (SNB) in rats.

development of sexual dimorphism. Neonatal exposure to the ubiquitous plastics component bisphenol A (BPA), for example, interferes with the development of adult sexual behaviors and demasculinizes male rats in tests of emotional behavior (B. A. Jones and Watson, 2012; B. A. Jones et al., 2011). BPA, which acts as a steroid mimic, is found in manufactured products ranging from drinking bottles and baby toys to food can liners.

Purely social inputs can likewise alter the sexual differentiation of the nervous system. The development of the SNB system offers a clear example: newborn rat pups can neither urinate nor defecate on their own; the mother (dam) must lick the anogenital region of each pup to elicit a spinal reflex to empty the bladder and colon. (Incidentally, the dam ingests at least some of the wastes to monitor pheromones from the pups, adjusting the composition of her milk as the pups mature. Another reason not to be a rat!)

Celia Moore et al. (1992) noticed that dams spend more time licking the anogenital regions of male pups than of females. If the dam is anosmic (unable to smell), she licks all the pups less and does not distinguish between males and females. Males raised by anosmic mothers thus receive less anogenital licking, and remarkably, fewer of their SNB cells survive the period around birth. The dam's stimulation of a male's anogenital region helps to masculinize his spinal cord.

On the one hand, this masculinization is still an effect of androgens because the dam identifies male pups by detecting androgen metabolites in their urine. On the other hand, this effect is clearly the result of a social influence: the dam treats a pup differently because he's a male, and thereby she masculinizes his developing nervous system. This example illustrates the futility of trying to distinguish "biological" from "social" influences. Any social influence that alters the individual's future behavior *must* have exerted a physical effect on the brain.

Attention from the dam has a different organizing effect on female rat pups. In adulthood, females who were licked frequently as pups show enhanced estrogen and oxytocin sensitivity in brain regions associated with maternal behavior, and they tend to be attentive mothers themselves. Females who are licked less as pups are less attentive mothers later (Champagne et al., 2001).

What about humans? (No, no, not the licking part, the social influence part.) Humans are at least as sensitive to social influences as rats are. In every culture, most people treat boys and girls differently, even when they are infants. Such differential treatment undoubtedly has some effect on the developing human brain and contributes to later sex differences in behavior. Of course, this is a social influence, but testosterone instigated the influence when it induced the formation of a penis.

If prenatal androgens have even a very subtle effect on the fetal brain, then older humans interacting with a baby might detect such differences and treat the baby differently. Thus, originally subtle sex differences might be magnified by social experience, especially early in life. Such interactions of steroidal and social influences are probably the norm in the sexual differentiation of human behavior. Whether hormones or social influences determine human sexual orientation is our final topic.

Do Fetal Hormones Masculinize Human Behaviors in Adulthood?

Overall, men and women are more similar than different on most psychological parameters (J. S. Hyde, 2005; Petersen and Hyde, 2011). Nevertheless, a variety of behavioral differences between men and women have been documented, as shown in **TABLE 12.2**. Some of these sex differences, especially those pertaining to sexual development, are quite substantial. Others, such as sex differences in cognition, tend to be smaller, but still reliable. Yet others, such as the sex difference in math abilities, seem to have disappeared over the past 30 years. And as with rats and other animals, the fact that men and women behave differently implies that something about them, probably something about their brains, must also be different. Indeed, many parts of the brain are different between men and women. But are these sexual dimorphisms in the human brain caused by prenatal hormone exposure, as in other animals, or

TABLE 12.2 Sex Differences in Human Cognition

BEHAVIORAL CHARACTERISTIC	DIRECTION	MAGNITUDE (IN STANDARD DEVIATIONS)
COGNITIVE AND MOTOR ABILITIES		
Targeting	M > F	1.1–2.0
Fine motor skill	F > M	0.5–0.6
Mental rotations	M > F	0.3–0.9
Spatial perception	M > F	0.3–0.6
Spatial visualization	M > F	0.0–0.6
Verbal fluency	F > M	0.5
Perceptual speed	F > M	0.3–0.7
Computational skill	F = M	0
Math concepts	F = M	0
Vocabulary	F = M	0
PERSONALITY ATTRIBUTES		
Tendencies to physical aggression	M > F	0.4–1.3
Empathy	F > M	0.3–1.3
Dominance/assertiveness	M > F	0.2–0.8
OTHER TRAITS		
Core gender identity	Not applicable	11.0–13.2
Sexual orientation	Not applicable	6.0–7.0
Adult height	M > F	2.0

Source: Hines, 2010.

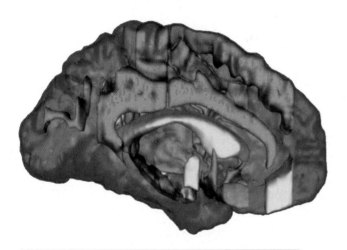

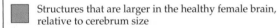

Structures that are larger in the healthy female brain, relative to cerebrum size

Structures that are larger in the healthy male brain, relative to cerebrum size

12.23 VIEW OF SEXUAL DIMORPHISM IN THE HUMAN BRAIN This composite image is based on data obtained from MRI scans of numerous male and female volunteers. Overall, sex differences tend to be evident in regions that are known to possess receptors for sex steroids. (Courtesy of Dr. Jill Goldstein, based on data from J. M. Goldstein et al., 2001).

by social influences? In other words, does prenatal steroid exposure affect the adult behavior of humans (**FIGURE 12.23**)? This is a tricky problem because although prenatal androgens may or may not act on the human brain, they certainly act on the periphery.

For example, recall that people with AIS are usually raised as girls, with their XY genotype and infertility typically discovered at puberty. We said earlier that individuals with AIS tend to have feminine gender identity, which includes being sexually attracted to men and often seeking a family through adoption. Are they feminine because they received the social tutoring to be females, or because their brains, without androgen receptors, could not respond to testosterone? Their behavior is consistent with either hypothesis.

But what about females with CAH, who are exposed to androgens before birth? We saw earlier that CAH females play more like boys than other females do and are more likely than other females to be lesbians in adulthood. Do women with CAH exhibit those behaviors because early androgens partially masculinized their brains? Or did their ambiguous genitalia cause parents and others to treat them differently from infancy?

We've also seen that the *guevedoces* of the Dominican Republic, who are raised as girls but grow a penis at puberty, behave like males as adults, dressing as men and seeking girlfriends. There are two competing explanations for why these people raised as girls later behave as men. First, prenatal testosterone may masculinize their brains; thus, despite being raised as girls, when they reach puberty, their brains lead them to seek out females for mates. This explanation suggests that the social influences of growing up—

assigning oneself to a gender and mimicking role models of that gender, as well as gender-specific playing and dressing—are unimportant for later behavior and sexual orientation. An alternative explanation is that early hormones have no effect—that this culture simply recognizes and teaches children that some people can start out as girls and change to boys later. If so, then the social influences on gender role development might be completely different in this society from those in ours. Of course, a third option is that both mechanisms contribute to the final outcome; for example, early androgens may affect the brain to masculinize the child's behavior and predispose later sexual orientation toward females, and these masculine qualities of the child could alter the behavior of parents and others in ways that promote the emergence of male gender identity as the child develops.

At the opening of the chapter, we discussed the dilemma of **cloacal exstrophy**, in which genetic boys are born with functional testes but without penises. Historically in these cases, neonatal sex reassignment has been recommended on the assumption that unambiguously raising these children as girls, and surgically providing them with the appropriate external genitalia, could produce a more satisfactory psychosexual outcome. In a long-term follow-up of 14 such cases, however, Reiner and Gearhart (2004) found that 8 of these "girls" eventually declared themselves to be boys, even though several were unaware that they had ever been operated on. Although this finding indicates that prenatal exposure to androgens strongly predisposes to subsequent male gender identity, 5 of the 14 individuals were apparently content with their female identities, suggesting that socialization can also play a strong role. On the other hand, at least some of those 5 girls were romantically attracted to other girls. In fact, one of the reasons "Bella," whom we met at the beginning of this chapter, was unsurprised to learn she'd been born a boy was that she was sexually attracted to girls. As he said after becoming "Benjamin," "I was not sad about me being a boy, it was just telling my friends that got me down." So the prenatal androgen may have predisposed all of these individuals to be sexually attracted to females.

Seen alone, the studies of people with these various conditions might leave room for doubt about whether prenatal hormones influence sexual orientation in humans. But these are just part of a growing body of evidence that prenatal testosterone does in fact influence sexual orientation in humans, as we'll see next.

What determines a person's sexual orientation?

There are two classes of possible influence on human sexual orientation. One class encompasses the sociocultural influences that may instruct developing children about how they should behave when they grow up (think of all those charming princes wooing princesses in Disney movies). The other class of influences includes the endogenous factors—especially differences in fetal exposure to testosterone—that could organize developing brains to be attracted to females or males in adulthood. For that great majority of people who are heterosexual, there's no way to distinguish between these two influences, because they both favor the same outcome. Gay men and lesbians provide a test, because same-sex attractions (and other sexual minorities) remain stigmatized by various social groups and cultural institutions (Herek and McLemore, 2013). Is there evidence that early hormones are responsible for causing some people to ignore society's proscription and become gay? If so, then maybe hormones play a role in heterosexual development too.

Certainly, homosexual behavior is seen in other species—mountain sheep, swans, gulls, and dolphins, to name a few (Bagemihl, 1999). Interestingly, homosexual behavior is more common among anthropoid primates—apes and monkeys—than in prosimian primates like lemurs and lorises (Vasey, 1995), so greater complexity of the brain may make homosexual behavior more likely. In the most studied animal model—sheep—some rams consistently refuse to mount females but prefer to mount other rams. There is growing evidence of differences in the POA of "gay" versus "straight" rams (Roselli et al., 2004), apparently organized by testosterone

cloacal exstrophy A rare medical condition in which XY individuals are born completely lacking a penis.

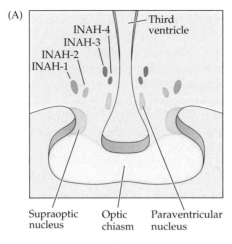

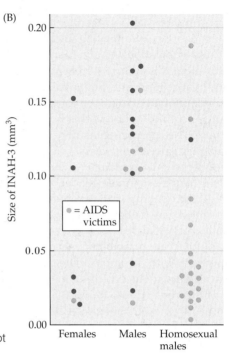

(A)

Third ventricle

INAH-4
INAH-3
INAH-2
INAH-1

Supraoptic nucleus

Optic chiasm

Paraventricular nucleus

(B)

Size of INAH-3 (mm³)

● = AIDS victims

Females   Males   Homosexual males

12.24 INTERSTITIAL NUCLEI OF THE ANTERIOR HYPOTHALAMUS (A) These nuclei in humans are seen in the same part of the hypothalamus where the SDN-POA is found in rats. (B) INAH-3 is larger in men than in women, and larger in straight men than in gay men. Although most of the gay men in this study had died of AIDS, note that heterosexual men who died of AIDS still had a larger INAH-3, indicating that the differences between straight and gay men are not due to AIDS.

acting on the brain via neuronal steroid receptors during fetal development (Roselli and Stormshak, 2009).

Simon LeVay (1991) performed postmortem examinations of the POA in humans and found a nucleus (the third interstitial nucleus of the anterior hypothalamus, or INAH-3) (**FIGURE 12.24A**) that is larger in men than in women, and larger in heterosexual men than in gay men (**FIGURE 12.24B**). All but one of the gay men in the study had died of AIDS, but the brain differences could not be due to AIDS pathology, because the straight men with AIDS still had a significantly larger INAH-3 than did the gay men. To the press and the public, this finding sounded like strong evidence that sexual orientation is "built in." It's still possible, however, that early social experience affects the development of INAH-3 to determine later sexual orientation. Furthermore, sexual experiences as an adult could affect INAH-3 structure, so the smaller nucleus in some gay men may be the *result* of their becoming gay, rather than the *cause*, as LeVay himself was careful to point out.

In women, apparent markers of fetal androgen exposure—otoacoustic emissions from the ears (McFadden and Pasanen, 1998) (see Chapter 9), patterns of eye blinks (Rahman, 2005), and skeletal features (J. T. Martin and Nguyen, 2004)—all indicate that lesbians, as a group, were exposed to slightly more fetal androgen than were heterosexual women. Another adult marker of prenatal androgen, the ratio of the length of the second digit (2D) to the length of the fourth digit (4D) (Breedlove, 2010), also indicates lesbians were exposed to greater prenatal androgen than straight women (**FIGURE 12.25**) (T. J. Williams et al., 2000) and has been replicated many times (Grimbos et al., 2010). These findings indicate that fetal exposure to androgen increases the likelihood that a girl will grow up to be gay. There is always considerable overlap between the two groups, so you cannot use these features to predict whether a *particular* woman will be gay, and clearly fetal androgens cannot account for all lesbians.

Those same markers of fetal androgen do not indicate any difference between gay versus straight men (Grimbos et

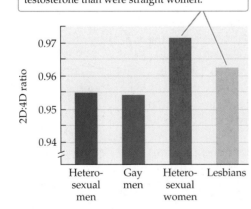

2D
4D

The ratio of the length of the index finger divided by the ring finger (2D:4D) is affected by prenatal androgen, and indicates that lesbians, on average, were exposed to more prenatal testosterone than were straight women.

2D:4D ratio

0.97
0.96
0.95
0.94

Hetero-sexual men   Gay men   Hetero-sexual women   Lesbians

12.25 BODILY INDICATORS OF PRENATAL ANDROGEN Note that these are group differences seen in averages; you cannot reliably determine an *individual's* orientation by examining digit ratios. (After T. J. Williams et al., 2000.)

al., 2010). Thus any difference between gay and straight men would be in their *response* to prenatal androgen rather than *amount* of prenatal androgen. However, another nonsocial factor influences the probability of men being gay: the more older brothers a boy has, the more likely he is to grow up to be gay (Blanchard et al., 2006). Your first guess might be that this is a social influence of older brothers, but it turns out that older stepbrothers who are raised with the boy have no effect, while biological brothers (sharing the same mother) increase the probability of the boy's being gay *even if they are raised apart* (Bogaert, 2006). Furthermore, this "fraternal birth order effect" is seen in boys who are right-handed, but not in boys who are non-right-handed (Blanchard et al., 2006; Bogaert, 2007), providing another indication of differences in early development between the two sexual orientation groups (**FIGURE 12.26**). Statistically, the birth order effect is strong enough to estimate that about one in every seven gay men in North America—about a million people—are gay because their mothers had sons before them (Cantor et al., 2002).

Genetic studies in fruit flies (*Drosophila melanogaster*) have identified genes that control whether courtship behaviors are directed toward same- or opposite-sex individuals (Grosjean et al., 2008), although no one knows the extent to which similar mechanisms are operational in mammals, including humans. Still, there is good evidence that human sexual orientation is at least partly heritable, reinforcing the notion that both biological and social factors have a say. About 50% of variability in human sexual orientation is accounted for by genetic factors, leaving ample room for early social influences. Monozygotic twins, who have exactly the same genes, do not always have the same sexual orientation (J. M. Bailey et al., 1993). In the unusual case of two nontwin brothers who are both gay, they are much more likely than chance would dictate to have both inherited the same X chromosome region (Xq28) from their mother (Hamer et al., 1993; Sanders et al., 2015); but again the genetic explanation accounts for only some, not all, of the cases. It seems clear that there are several different pathways to homosexuality.

From a political viewpoint, the scientific controversy—whether sexual orientation is determined before birth or determined by early social influences—is irrelevant. Laws and prejudices against homosexuality are based primarily on religious views that homosexuality is a sin that some people "choose." But almost all gay and straight men report that, from the beginning, their interests and romantic attachments matched their adult orientation. So any social influence would have to be acting very early in life and without any conscious awareness (do you remember "choosing" whom to find attractive?). Furthermore, despite extensive efforts, no one has come up with a reliable way to change sexual orientation (LeVay, 1996). These findings, added to evidence that older brothers and prenatal androgens affect the probability of being gay, have convinced most scientists that we do not choose our sexual orientation.

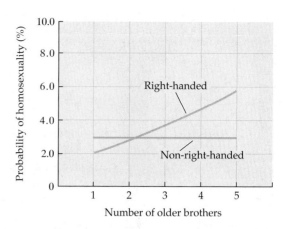

12.26 FRATERNAL BIRTH ORDER AND ORIENTATION Having older biological brothers (but not sisters or foster brothers) increases the likelihood of same-sex orientation in right-handed males. (After Blanchard et al., 2006.)

◼ The Cutting Edge

Sex on the Brain

Although a century of experimentation has provided researchers with a good understanding of the neural bases of sexual behavior in lab animals, the same cannot be said for the sexual circuitry in humans. It was not until the latter part of the twentieth century that curiosity overcame public squeamishness about the topic of human sexuality. Now, however, technological advances in noninvasive imaging are pulling back the curtain on this very private topic. Through careful planning (and a measure of contortion) it is possible to fit a copulating couple into an MRI machine and make detailed cross-sectional images, gaining insights about the genital anatomy of copulation and orgasm that Masters and Johnson could only have dreamed of (Faix et al., 2001; Schultz et al., 1999). Of course, the bigger story in most respects is what's going on in the head. Perhaps the most striking observation so far is how widespread the changes in brain activation are. In men and women, dozens of brain sites are

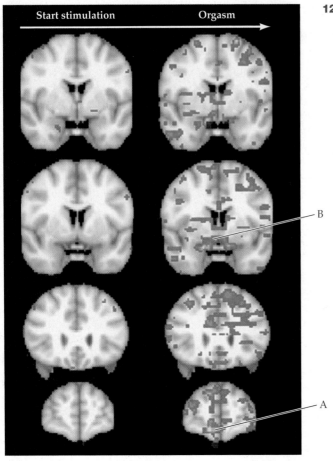

Start stimulation → Orgasm

12.27 SEXY PICTURES These coronal images of a woman's brain reveal widespread activation during orgasm. Notice, in particular, activation of prefrontal cortex (A), associated with conscious, self-aware aspects of sexual experiences, and of the basal forebrain (B), associated with pleasure and reward. (Courtesy of Dr. Barry Komisaruk, Rutgers University.)

active during sex; nonetheless, the findings map onto some of what we know about sexual circuitry in lab rats.

In men, sexual arousal, and especially ejaculation, activates subcortical sites that include the ventral tegmental area and right basal forebrain (Georgiadis et al., 2010; Holstege et al., 2003). These structures are part of the dopamine-based reward system discussed in this chapter in the context of sexual reward and in Chapter 4, where we talked about the role of this reward system in drug abuse (see Figure 4.24). Penile stimulation activates the right insula and secondary somatosensory cortex (Georgiadis and Holstege, 2005). Subcortically, penile stimulation first activates a part of the basal ganglia, followed by activation in the lateral hypothalamus and anterior middle cingulate cortex. Loss of erection following ejaculation is associated with increased activity in the ventral hypothalamus and the anterior cingulate, suggesting that penile erection and stimulation may involve a balance between the two systems (Georgiadis et al., 2010).

In women, orgasms change activity in a variety of brain regions, as shown in **FIGURE 12.27**. Subcortically, clitoral stimulation and orgasm are associated with alterations in activity in the hypothalamus, amygdala, cerebellum, cingulate, and brainstem. Notably, in parallel with men, several sites in the basal forebrain are active during female orgasm, including the nucleus accumbens, likewise implicating the brain's reward system in sexual responses (Komisaruk and Whipple, 2005). Activation is also seen in somatosensory cortex and particularly in the insula, where the degree of change may be associated with orgasm intensity (Ortigue et al., 2007). Interestingly, sexual activity also results in pronounced increases in activity of orbitofrontal cortex and the anterior cingulate, suggesting alteration of consciousness during sex.

Although research into human sexual circuitry is in its infancy, it promises to reveal new insights into consciousness and the perception of pleasure. Functional imaging studies like these reinforce the old adage that "the most important sex organ is between your ears."

Go to
bn8e.com
for study questions, quizzes, activities, and other resources

Recommended Reading

Balthazart, J. (2011). *The Biology of Homosexuality*. Oxford, England: Oxford University Press.

Becker, J. B., Berkeley, K. J., Geary, N., Hampson, E., et al. (2007). *Sex Differences in the Brain: From Genes to Behavior*. Oxford, England: Oxford University Press.

Buss, D. M., and Meston, C. M. (2009). *Why Women Have Sex: Understanding Sexual Motivation—from Adventure to Revenge*. New York: Henry Holt and Company.

Kronenberg, H. M., Melmed, S., Polonsky, K. S., and Larsen, P. R. (2007). *Williams Textbook of Endocrinology* (11th ed.). Philadelphia: Saunders.

LeVay, S. (2016). *Gay, Straight and the Reason Why: The Science of Sexual Orientation* (2nd ed.). Oxford, England: Oxford University Press.

LeVay, S., and Baldwin, J. (2011). *Human Sexuality* (4th ed.). Sunderland, MA: Sinauer.

Nelson, R. J., and Kriegsfeld, L. J. (2017). *An Introduction to Behavioral Endocrinology* (5th ed.). Sunderland, MA: Sinauer.

VISUAL SUMMARY

You should be able to relate each summary to the adjacent illustration, including structures and processes.
Go to **bn8e.com/vs12** for links to figures, animations, and activities that will help you consolidate the material.

1 Reproductive behaviors are divided into four stages: **sexual attraction**, **appetitive behavior**, **copulation**, and **postcopulatory behavior**, including parental behaviors in some species. Review **Figure 12.1**

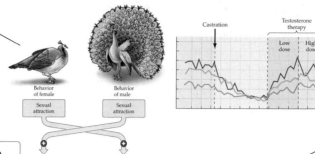

2 Alterations in circulating gonadal steroids alter sexual behavior in male and female mammals. Review **Figures 12.4 and 12.5**

3 In the female rat, a steroid-sensitive **lordosis** circuit extends from the **ventromedial hypothalamus (VMH)** to the spinal cord, via the **periaqueductal gray** and **medullary reticular formation**. In the male rat, neurons of the **medial preoptic area (mPOA)** exert descending control of sexual behavior, integrating inputs from the **medial amygdala** and **vomeronasal organ (VNO)**. These projections, via ventral midbrain and brainstem nuclei, terminate on motor neurons involved in **copulation**. Review **Figure 12.6**

4 Human copulatory behavior is remarkably varied. Most men show a single copulatory pattern; women show much more varied sexual responses. The classic model of sexuality emphasizes four stages: (1) increasing excitement, (2) plateau, (3) **orgasm**, and (4) resolution. Review **Figure 12.9**, **Activities 12.1 and 12.2**

6 **Parental behavior** is a crucial aspect of reproduction and is significantly influenced by hormones. Brain mechanisms for parental behavior show considerable overlap with mechanisms implicated in sexual behavior. Review **Figures 12.11 and 12.12**

5 Modern models identify emotional factors and desire as crucial aspects of female sexuality, whereas male sexuality may involve feelings of power. However, male and female sexuality overlap, and both are heavily influenced by sociocultural factors. Review **Figure 12.10**

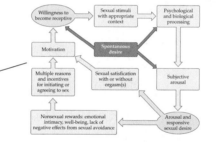

8 People can be classified on the basis of their sex chromosomes, their genitalia, or the gender they identify with. The options within each of these categories are complex and sometimes overlap, so attempts to classify all individuals into just two gender groups oversimplify the real situation. Review **Figures 12.15 and 12.16**

7 In birds and mammals, genetic sex determines whether testes or ovaries develop, and hormonal secretions from the gonads determine whether the rest of the body, including the brain, develops in a feminine or masculine fashion. In the presence of testicular secretions, a male develops; in the absence of testicular secretions, a female develops. Review **Figures 12.13 and 12.14**

10 Among the prominent examples of **sexual dimorphism** in the nervous system, gonadal steroids have been shown to alter characteristics such as neuronal survival, structure, and synaptic connections. Review **Figures 12.20–12.22**

9 The brains of vertebrates are masculinized by the presence of testicular steroids during early development. Such **organizational effects** of steroids permanently alter the structure and function of the brain and therefore permanently alter the behavior of the individual. Review **Figure 12.18, Animation 12.2**

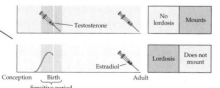

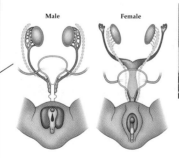

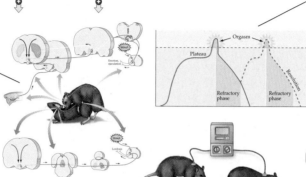

(continued)

11 Several regions of the human brain are sexually dimorphic. However, we do not know whether these dimorphisms are generated by fetal steroid levels or by sex differences in the early social environment. Review **Figure 12.23, Table 12.2**

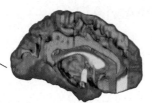

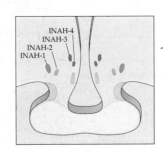

INAH-4
INAH-3
INAH-2
INAH-1

12 Although no perfect animal model of sexual orientation has been developed, all research indicates that sexual orientation is determined early in life and, especially in men, is not a matter of individual choice. Review **Figure 12.24**

Homeostasis

Active Regulation of the Internal Environment

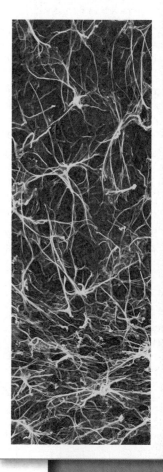

13

▋ Harsh Reality

In 2004, NBC's reality television show *The Biggest Loser* became a prime-time staple. The premise of the show is simple enough—the contestant who loses the most weight during the season wins—but the effort required from the contestants is immense. The biggest loser of them all in season 8 (2009) was Danny C. Through a punishing combination of near-starvation dieting and all-day exercise, Danny shed an incredible 239 pounds, dropping from 430 pounds to a svelte 191 pounds in just 7 months. Other initially obese contestants similarly accomplished exceptional weight loss, clearly delighting in revealing their new and slimmer silhouettes to their friends, families, and viewers.

Recognizing an unusual opportunity, a group of scientists followed Danny and other *Biggest Loser* contestants for 6 years following their weight loss: the longest-term study of its kind ever conducted (Fothergill et al., 2016; Kolata, 2016). The results are discouraging. In the years after his appearance on the show, and despite exceptional ongoing efforts, Danny regained more than 100 pounds of the weight he had lost. In fact, all but one of the 14 contestants in the study regained significant weight; some were even heavier after than they were before the show. The pattern of results confirms the common observation that it is hard to keep the weight off after dieting, but what could explain the additional discovery that even after 6 years of hard work, the bodies of these contestants continued to strive to return to their original obese state?

Millions of years of evolution have endowed our bodies with complex physiological mechanisms, under the control of the brain, that regulate the conditions required for optimal cellular functioning. But in the context of modern society, some of these ancient systems are making trouble for us; obesity, for example, is reaching epidemic proportions and placing a severe burden on health care resources. The physiological and behavioral processes governing the physiological state of the body, and their role when things go wrong, are our topic in this chapter.

Homeostasis Maintains a Consistent Internal Environment: The Example of Thermoregulation

Building on discoveries about cellular physiology, scientists in the nineteenth century realized that the body can be viewed as a self-contained environment, carefully regulated so as to provide optimal conditions for cells to live and grow. Variables such as acidity, saltiness, water level, oxygenation, temperature, and energy availability, among others, are closely monitored and maintained by an elaborate system of behavioral and physiological mechanisms. Collectively these processes are responsible for **homeostasis**, the active regulation of the monitored physical attributes at appropriate levels, resulting in a relatively stable, balanced internal envi-

▋
Go to Brain Explorer
bn8e.com/13.1

homeostatic Referring to the active process of maintaining a particular physiological parameter relatively constant.

motivation Here, a drive state that prompts homeostatic behaviors.

obligatory losses Unavoidable loss of regulated variables, such as energy, water, or temperature, as a consequence of life processes.

thermoregulation The active process of closely regulating body temperature around a set value.

endotherm An animal whose body temperature is regulated chiefly by internal metabolic processes. Examples include mammals and birds.

ectotherm An animal whose body temperature is regulated by, and whose heat comes mainly from, the environment. Examples include snakes and bees.

negative feedback The property by which some of the output of a system feeds back to reduce the effect of input signals.

set point The point of reference in a feedback system. An example is the setting of a thermostat.

set zone The range of a variable that a feedback system tries to maintain.

Go to Animation 13.2
Negative Feedback
bn8e.com/13.2

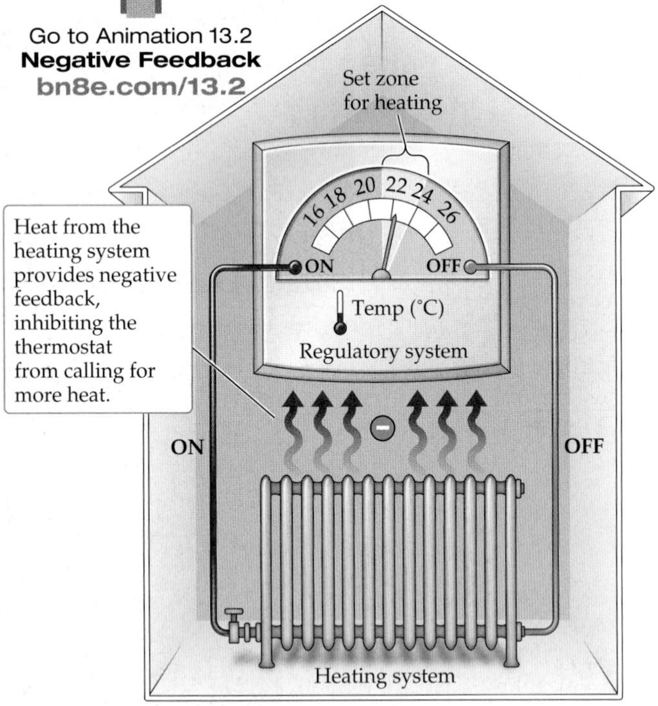

Set zone for heating

16 18 20 22 24 26

ON   OFF

Temp (°C)
Regulatory system

Heat from the heating system provides negative feedback, inhibiting the thermostat from calling for more heat.

ON   OFF

Heating system

13.1 NEGATIVE FEEDBACK The thermostat controlling a home heating system employs negative feedback. All such systems have a sensor (in this example, a thermometer) to monitor the variable (temperature) and a device (the heating system) to change the variable (e.g., by heating the room). The changed variable (heat) provides a negative feedback signal to the sensor, turning the system off.

ronment. Alterations in the internal environment can have an effect on **motivation**, the psychological process that induces or sustains a particular behavior. According to this view, the mismatch between the actual internal state and the regulated, intended state (e.g., becoming dehydrated) produces a *drive* to restore balance (by having a drink of water). And as we all know, drive can rapidly escalate as the mismatch worsens, from a minor distraction (like having a couple of sips if a glass of water happens to be present) to an overwhelming, all-consuming desire (like the raging thirst of someone lost in the desert). And the regulation of our internal resources is complicated by the fact that staying alive requires us to use up some of them. Our homeostatic mechanisms are continually challenged by these **obligatory losses**, which require us to gain and conserve heat, water, and food constantly.

Because it is a relatively simple system, let's start by using **thermoregulation**, the regulation of body temperature, to look at some important general concepts in homeostasis: negative feedback, redundancy, behavioral homeostasis, and the concept of allostatic load. These concepts will arise again when we talk about fluid regulation, appetite, and body weight regulation, later in the chapter.

Homeostatic systems share several key features

We mammals are **endotherms**, species that make our own heat from *inside* our bodies, using metabolism and muscular activity (and if our muscles aren't making enough heat, they shiver to make more). Endothermy gives us clear advantages over the **ectotherms**: animals that get their heat mostly from the environment. For one thing, endotherms can range more widely than ectotherms, such as lizards and snakes, that need to stay nearer sources of warmth. Furthermore, because endotherms have evolved a greater capacity for oxygen utilization (in order to generate heat through metabolism), we mammals can sustain high levels of muscular activity for much longer periods of time: endothermic hares will always outrun ectothermic tortoises. (For more on the pros and cons of endothermy and ectothermy, see **A Step Further: Some Animals Generate Heat but Others Must Obtain Heat from the Environment** on the website.)

So it's no surprise that our body temperature is carefully regulated. The systems that govern body temperature operate according to several general principles common to almost all homeostatic systems.

NEGATIVE FEEDBACK The homeostatic mechanisms that regulate temperature, body fluids, and metabolism are primarily **negative feedback** systems, where deviation from a desired value, called the **set point**, triggers a compensatory action of the system. Restoring the desired value turns off the response (this is why it is called *negative* feedback). A simple analogy for this mechanism is a household thermostat (**FIGURE 13.1**): a temperature drop below the set point activates the thermostat, which turns on the heating system. The heat that is produced has a negative feedback effect on the thermostat, so it stops calling for heat. Most systems have at least a little bit of tolerance built in—otherwise the system would be going on and off too frequently—so there is generally a **set zone** rather than a rigid set *point*.

The setting of the thermostat in your home can be changed; for example, it can be turned down at night to save energy. Similarly, although the body temperature for most mammals is usually held within a narrow range—about 36–38°C (97–100°F)—most mammals reduce their temperature during sleep. Sometimes, your set zone may be temporarily elevated, producing a fever to help your body fight off an infection. But there remain narrow limits. Too hot, and proteins begin to lose their correct shape, link together, and malfunction or die (this is called *denaturing* or, if it is really hot, *cooking*). Too cool, and chemical reactions of the body occur too slowly; at very low body temperatures, ice crystals may disrupt cellular membranes, killing the cells. Some animals that cannot avoid subfreezing temperatures—for example, some species of fishes and beetles (**FIGURE 13.2**)—produce "antifreeze" consisting of special protein molecules that suppress the formation of ice crystals and prevent damage to membranes (Duman, 2015; C. B. Marshall et al., 2004).

REDUNDANCY Just as human engineers equip critical equipment with several backup systems, our bodies tend to have multiple mechanisms for monitoring our stores, conserving remaining supplies, obtaining new resources, and shedding excesses. Loss of function in one part of the system usually can be compensated for by the remaining parts. This redundancy attests to the importance of maintaining a stable inner environment, but it also complicates the lives of scientists who are trying to figure out exactly how the body normally regulates temperature, water balance, and food intake.

The body has multiple systems for the generation of heat, as well as multiple systems for cooling if it gets overheated (**FIGURE 13.3**). There is also substantial redundancy in thermoregulatory control systems in the nervous system. It has long been

(A)

(B)

(C)

13.2 BRAVING THE COLD Mealworm beetles (A) and winter flounder (B) are two species that sometimes have body temperatures below 0°C. These animals produce an "antifreeze" protein in body fluids to prevent ice crystals from forming in their cell membranes. Through mechanisms not yet understood, the arctic ground squirrel (C) is also able to withstand subzero temperatures during hibernation.

Go to Animation 13.3
Thermoregulation in Humans
bn8e.com/13.3

13.3 THERMOREGULATION IN HUMANS Some of the primary ways that our bodies gain (left), conserve, and lose (right) heat, and their neural controls.

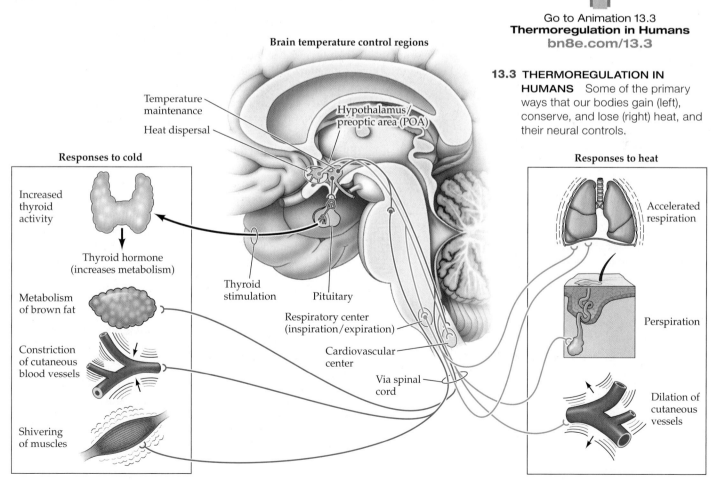

Brain temperature control regions

Temperature maintenance

Heat dispersal

Hypothalamus/ preoptic area (POA)

Responses to cold

Increased thyroid activity

Thyroid hormone (increases metabolism)

Metabolism of brown fat

Constriction of cutaneous blood vessels

Shivering of muscles

Thyroid stimulation

Pituitary

Respiratory center (inspiration/expiration)

Cardiovascular center

Via spinal cord

Responses to heat

Accelerated respiration

Perspiration

Dilation of cutaneous vessels

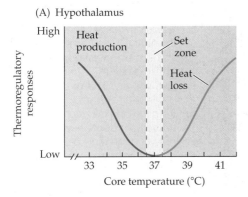

(A) Hypothalamus

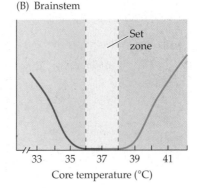

(B) Brainstem

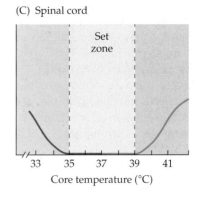

(C) Spinal cord

13.4 MULTIPLE THERMOSTATS IN THE NERVOUS SYSTEM The set zones of thermoregulatory systems are narrower at higher levels of the nervous system than at lower levels. (After Satinoff, 1978.)

known that the hypothalamus senses and controls body temperature, but lesion experiments eventually showed that different hypothalamic sites controlled two separate thermoregulatory systems. Lesions in the preoptic area (POA) impaired the physiological responses to cold, such as shivering and constriction, but did not interfere with such behaviors as pressing levers to control heating lamps or cooling fans (Satinoff and Rutstein, 1970; Van Zoeren and Stricker, 1977). Lesions in the lateral hypothalamus of rats abolished behavioral regulation of temperature but did not affect the physiological responses (Satinoff and Shan, 1971; Van Zoeren and Stricker, 1977). This is a clear example of homeostatic redundancy: two different systems for regulating the same variable. Furthermore, there seems to be a hierarchy of thermoregulatory circuits, some located at the spinal level, some centered in the brainstem, and others in the hypothalamus (**FIGURE 13.4**).

BEHAVIORAL HOMEOSTASIS Organisms also use behavioral measures to help them regulate and acquire more heat, water, or food. In general, ectotherms and endotherms can employ three kinds of behaviors to regulate temperature. They can (1) *change exposure of the body surface*, for example by huddling or extending limbs; (2) *change external insulation*, such as by using clothing or nests; and (3) *change surroundings*, moving into the sun, into the shade, or into a burrow.

Because ectotherms generate little heat through metabolism, behavioral methods of thermoregulation are especially important for them. In the laboratory, iguanas carefully regulate their temperature by moving toward or away from a heat lamp, and when infected by bacteria, they even produce a fever through such behavioral means (**FIGURE 13.5**), which helps their immune system fight off the infection. Endotherms use internal processes to generate a fever; it's a harmful quirk of human nature that we try so hard to suppress fevers, when they may very well improve outcomes when battling infectious diseases like pneumonia (Schulman et al., 2005).

Many ectotherms regulate body temperature using specialized behaviors. Some snakes, for example, adjust their coils to expose

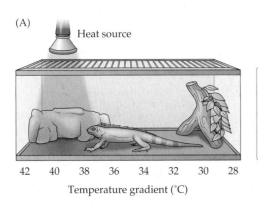

(A) Heat source

The lizard controls its body temperature by moving around the cage.

Temperature gradient (°C)

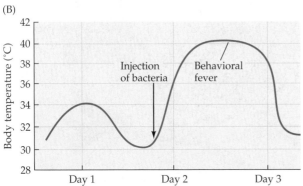

(B)

13.5 BEHAVIORAL THERMOREGULATION IN BACTERIA-CHALLENGED LIZARDS (A) By positioning themselves along the temperature gradient between the cool and warm ends of a terrarium, iguanas exert precise behavioral control over their body temperature. (B) Body temperature recorded from iguanas over the course of 3 days is plotted here. Day 1 shows the normal daily cycle of body temperature, averaging 34°C during the day and slightly cooler at night (similar to the daily temperature cycle of endotherms). Early on day 2, the iguanas were injected with bacteria, to which they reacted by moving closer to the heat source and allowing their body temperature to rise to more than 40°C for about 16 hours. This "behavioral fever" closely resembles the fever that endotherms like humans experience during infection, and it similarly helps fight off infection. (After Kluger, 1978.)

more or less surface to the sun and thus keep their internal temperature relatively constant during the day. On cold days, bees crowd into the hive and shiver, thus generating heat; on hot days, the bees fan the hive with their wings instead, thereby keeping it cool. As a result of these behavioral measures, hive temperature is regulated at about 35°C.

Endotherms such as mammals and birds likewise control their exposure to the sun and to hot or cold surfaces to avoid overtaxing their internal regulatory mechanisms. Throughout history, humans have busily devised adaptations to hot and cold, ranging from the use of fans and swimming pools to the creation of heating systems and highly insulating clothing.

FIGURE 13.6 summarizes the basic mammalian thermoregulatory system: receptors in the skin, body core, and hypothalamus detect temperature and transmit that information to three neural regions (spinal cord, brainstem, and hypothalamus). If the body temperature moves outside the set zone, each of these neural regions can initiate physiological and behavioral responses to return it to the set zone. **BOX 13.1** gives an example of the close integration of physiological and behavioral homeostatic mechanisms.

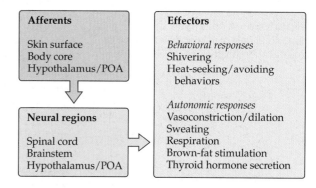

13.6 BASIC ELEMENTS OF MAMMALIAN THERMO-REGULATORY SYSTEMS

Physiological and Behavioral Thermoregulation Are Integrated

Ectothermic animals produce some heat through physiological processes, but not enough to overcome losses to the environment. Instead, like the marine iguana (Figure A), they rely principally on behavioral solutions, either seeking out sources of warmth or, if too warm, shielding themselves from heat. The young of many endothermic species likewise lack the ability to create heat or physiologically regulate their temperature, often because they are small and lose heat rapidly, so they rely on their mothers to gestate, cuddle, and/or incubate them and keep them warm.

Like other mammals, including infant and adult humans (Cypess et al., 2009), newborn rat pups are able to generate heat via thermogenic brown-fat deposits like the one between the shoulder blades, shown in Figure B (Blumberg et al., 1997). Nonetheless, one problem for newborn rats is insulating their hairless bodies to conserve the heat they generate. To tackle this problem, they huddle together. The effectiveness of this behavioral strategy is easily demonstrated: placed in a room-temperature environment, an isolated 5-day-old pup will soon cool to less than 30°C, but as part of a group of four, the same pup can maintain a temperature above 30°C

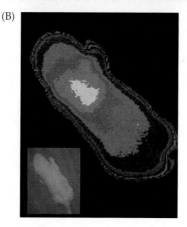

for 4 hours or more (Alberts, 1978). Pups frequently change their positions in the huddle, regulating their temperature by moving to the inside or the outside of the clump, such that all of the animals benefit: an example of cooperative homeostasis.

BEHAVIORAL AND PHYSIOLOGICAL THERMOREGULATION (A) Having been cooled by the sea, the Galápagos marine iguana raises its body temperature by hugging a warm rock and lying broadside to the sun (left). Once its temperature is sufficiently high, the iguana reduces its surface contact with the rock and faces the sun to minimize its exposure (right). (B) This infrared thermograph shows the dorsal surface of a 1-week-old rat pup oriented as shown in the inset. Areas of highest heat production are coded in orange and yellow, and the prominent yellow "hot spot" between the shoulder blades overlies a deposit of brown fat, a thermogenic (i.e., heat-producing) organ. When rat pups are placed in a cold environment, they begin producing heat by using brown fat. (Photographs in A by Dr. Mark R. Rosenzweig; B courtesy of Dr. Mark S. Blumberg.)

allostasis A coordinated set of behavioral and physiological changes to maintain homeostasis.

A wide array of sensors continuously monitor the many internal and external threats to our physiological stability. At any given moment, depending on what's happening in the environment, simultaneous perturbations in multiple regulated systems cause a degree of physiological stress that ranges from mild and healthy to severe and overwhelming. Prior experience with challenges allows us to make predictions and activate a coordinated set of behavioral and physiological changes in order to ward off serious homeostatic deviations: this dynamic process is termed **allostasis** (McEwen, 2012; McEwen and Wingfield, 2010). The associated cost of these responses—the wear and tear of daily life—is called *allostatic load*. Further, homeostatic regulation pervades many physiological and behavioral processes beyond the ones described in this chapter. For example, homeostatic adjustments affect drug actions by changing neuronal sensitivity (Chapter 4), regulate sleep onset and character (Chapter 14), modify hormones and sexual motivation (Chapter 12), and so on. Allostatic adjustments are a normal part of life, but the heavy allostatic load of chronically stressed individuals puts them at risk of pathology, a topic we turn to in Chapter 15.

Fluid Regulation

The water that you drink on a hot day is carefully measured and partitioned by the brain. A precise balance of fluids and dissolved salts bathes the cells of the body and enables them to function.

The composition of body fluids reflects the evolutionary origins of life on Earth. The first living organisms were the unicellular inhabitants of the ancient oceans, so fundamental cellular processes like metabolism and gene expression were optimized, via evolution by natural selection, for operation in the oceanic environment. By the time more-complex multicellular species arose and began to exploit opportunities on land, their only choice was to bring along the watery environment needed by their cells. For this reason, most organisms have evolved homeostatic mechanisms that ensure that the composition of body fluids closely resembles diluted seawater (**FIGURE 13.7**) (Bourque, 2008). Even relatively minor deviation from this optimal concentration of salt in water is generally lethal, with only rare exceptions; the salmon, for example, has unique adaptations that allow it to live in freshwater at hatching, to grow up in salt water, and to return again to freshwater to spawn.

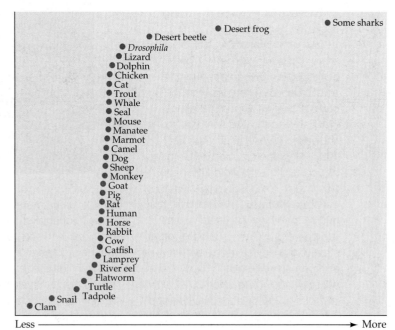

13.7 SEA INSIDE Despite many millions of years of evolution, the concentration of extracellular fluid has remained remarkably constant among different species of animals, with only a few exceptions. (After Bourque, 2008.)

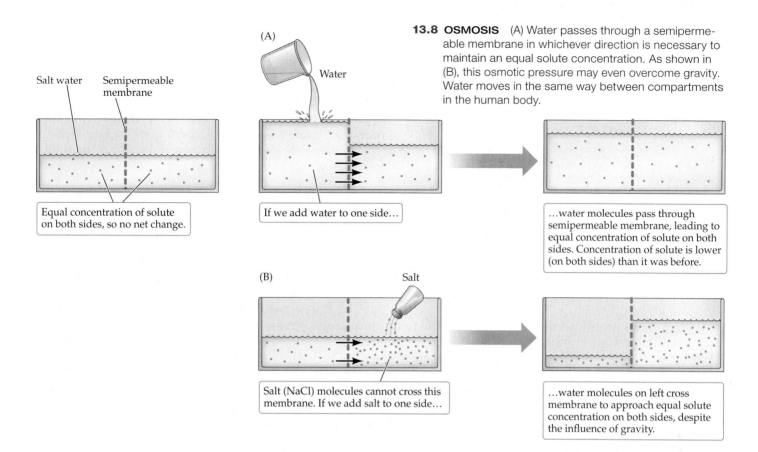

(A)

Salt water   Semipermeable
              membrane

Equal concentration of solute
on both sides, so no net change.

Water

If we add water to one side...

...water molecules pass through
semipermeable membrane, leading to
equal concentration of solute on both
sides. Concentration of solute is lower
(on both sides) than it was before.

13.8 OSMOSIS (A) Water passes through a semipermeable membrane in whichever direction is necessary to
maintain an equal solute concentration. As shown in
(B), this osmotic pressure may even overcome gravity.
Water moves in the same way between compartments
in the human body.

(B)

Salt

Salt (NaCl) molecules cannot cross this
membrane. If we add salt to one side...

...water molecules on left cross
membrane to approach equal solute
concentration on both sides, despite
the influence of gravity.

Because we consist of trillions of cells living in a salty seawater-like bath, scientists typically describe water balance by contrasting the inside versus the outside of our cells. Most of our water is contained within our cells; this combined region is termed the **intracellular compartment**. The fluid outside of our cells, collectively referred to as the **extracellular compartment**, is divided between the *interstitial fluid* (the fluid between cells) and *blood plasma* (the protein-rich fluid that carries red and white blood cells). Water is continually moving back and forth between these compartments, in and out of cells, via specialized protein channels called **aquaporins** that stud the cell membrane (Agre et al., 2002; Knepper et al., 2015). A single aquaporin channel can selectively conduct about 3 *billion* molecules of water per second!

To understand the forces driving the movement of water, we must understand diffusion and osmosis. In **diffusion**, molecules of a substance like salt (a *solute*) dissolved in a quantity of another substance, such as a glass of water (a *solvent*), will passively spread through the water because of the random jiggling and movement of the molecules until they are more or less uniformly distributed throughout the glass (**FIGURE 13.8A**). If we divide a container of water with a membrane that is impermeable to water and salt, and we put the salt in the water on one side, the molecules will diffuse only within that half. If instead the membrane impedes salt molecules only a little, then the salt will distribute itself evenly within the initial half but will also—more slowly—invade and distribute itself across the other half.

A membrane that is permeable to some molecules but not others is referred to as *selectively permeable* or *semipermeable*. As we saw in Chapter 3, cell membranes are very selective in their permeability: for example, neurons normally allow very few sodium ions (Na^+) to pass through their membrane unless the voltage-gated Na^+ channels are opened during the action potential.

Osmosis is the movement of water molecules that occurs when a semipermeable membrane separates solutions containing different concentrations of solute and the solute cannot spread itself evenly across both sides. This is the case we examine in **FIGURE 13.8B**, in which the semipermeable membrane blocks the passage of salt molecules. Here, the water molecules are moving into the compartment where they

intracellular compartment The fluid space of the body that is contained within cells.

extracellular compartment The fluid space of the body that exists outside the cells.

aquaporins Channels spanning the cell membrane that are specialized for conducting water molecules into or out of the cell.

diffusion The spontaneous spread of molecules of one substance among molecules of another substance until a uniform concentration is achieved.

osmosis The passive movement of water molecules from one place to another until a uniform concentration is achieved.

TABLE 13.1 Average Daily Water Balance

SOURCE	QUANTITY (LITERS)
APPROXIMATE INTAKE	
Fluid water	1.2
Water from food	1.3
TOTAL	**2.5**
APPROXIMATE OUTPUT	
Urine	1.4
Evaporative loss	0.9
Feces	0.2
TOTAL	**2.5**

osmotic pressure   The tendency of a solvent to move through a membrane in order to equalize the concentration of solute.

osmolality   The number of solute particles per unit volume of solvent.

isotonic   Referring to a solution with a concentration of salt that is the same as that found in interstitial fluid and blood plasma (about 0.9% salt).

hypertonic   Referring to a solution with a higher concentration of salt than that found in interstitial fluid and blood plasma (more than about 0.9% salt).

hypotonic   Referring to a solution with a lower concentration of salt than that found in interstitial fluid and blood plasma (less than about 0.9% salt).

osmotic thirst   A desire to ingest fluids that is stimulated by a high concentration of solute (like salt) in the extracellular compartment, reducing intracellular fluid.

hypovolemic thirst   A desire to ingest fluids that is stimulated by a reduced volume of extracellular fluid.

osmosensory neuron   A specialized neuron that measures the movement of water into and out of cells.

are less concentrated (because the salt molecules are there), eventually resulting in equal concentrations of solution on both sides of the membrane. The physical force that pushes or pulls water across the membrane is called **osmotic pressure**.

We refer to the concentration of solute in a solution as **osmolality**. Normally, the concentration of salt (NaCl) in the extracellular fluid of mammals is about 0.9% (weight to volume, which means there's about 0.9 grams [g] of NaCl for every 100 milliliters of water). A solution with this concentration of salt is called *physiological saline* and is described as **isotonic**, having the same concentration of salt that mammalian fluids have. A solution with more salt is **hypertonic**; a solution lower in salt is **hypotonic**.

Because water moves so as to produce uniform saltiness (see Figure 13.8B), cells will lose water if placed in a saltier solution, and they will gain water in a less salty solution. If excessive, this movement of water will damage or kill the cell. To prevent such damage, the extracellular fluid serves as a *buffer*, a reservoir of isotonic fluid that provides and accepts water molecules so that cells can maintain proper internal conditions.

We cannot fully seal our bodies from the outside world, so we experience constant obligatory losses of water and salts. Many body functions require that we use up some water (and some salt molecules), as, for example, when we produce urine to rid ourselves of waste molecules. These losses require us to actively replenish the body's water and salts (**TABLE 13.1**). The nervous system uses two cues to ensure that the extracellular compartment has about the right amount of water and solute to allow cells to absorb or shed water molecules readily, as we'll see next.

Two Internal Cues Trigger Thirst

In addition to acting as a buffer, the extracellular fluid is an indicator of conditions in the intracellular compartment. In fact, the nervous system carefully monitors the extracellular compartment to determine whether we should seek water. Two different states can signal that more water is needed: (1) a high extracellular concentration of solute (resulting in **osmotic thirst**) or (2) a low extracellular volume due to the loss of body fluids (triggering **hypovolemic thirst**). We'll consider each in turn.

Osmotic thirst is triggered by increased saltiness of the extracellular fluid

Most of the time, we experience thirst as a result of the obligatory water losses we mentioned earlier: normal physiological processes through which we lose more water than salt, such as in respiration, perspiration, and urination. In this case, not only is the *volume* of the extracellular fluid decreased, but also the solute *concentration* of the extracellular fluid increases. As a result of this increased extracellular saltiness, water is pulled out of cells through osmosis.

Another way that the extracellular fluid can become more concentrated is by ingestion of a lot of salty food. Once again, water will be drawn out of cells through osmosis. In general, an increase in solute concentration of the extracellular fluid triggers a thirst that is independent of extracellular volume: *osmotic thirst* (**FIGURE 13.9A**). Osmotic thirst causes us to seek water to return the extracellular fluid to an isotonic state and protect the intracellular compartment from becoming dangerously depleted of water.

Injecting a small amount of hypertonic (extra-salty) solution into the hypothalamus causes animals to start drinking, suggesting that some hypothalamic cells might be specialized to respond to changes in osmotic pressure. Single-cell recordings confirm that there are **osmosensory neurons** in several regions of the

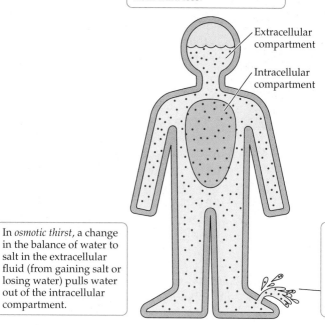

(A) Osmotic thirst

Osmosensory neurons in the brain detect the increased saltiness of the extracellular fluid.

In *osmotic thirst*, a change in the balance of water to salt in the extracellular fluid (from gaining salt or losing water) pulls water out of the intracellular compartment.

(B) Hypovolemic thirst

Baroreceptors in major blood vessels detect any pressure drop from fluid loss.

Extracellular compartment

Intracellular compartment

Hypovolemic thirst results from loss of fluids containing both water and solutes, such as through hemorrhage, intense sweating, or diarrhea.

13.9 TWO KINDS OF THIRST (A) Osmotic thirst is triggered when the total volume of water is constant but an increase in solute concentration in the extracellular compartment (as after a very salty meal) exerts osmotic pressure that pulls water out of the intracellular compartment. (B) Hypovolemic thirst is triggered by the loss of a significant volume of blood or other body fluids (such as through diarrhea or vomiting) that contain both solutes and water. As there is no change in solute concentration in either the intracellular or the extracellular compartment, there is no osmotic pressure to push water from one compartment to the other.

hypothalamus, including the preoptic area, the anterior hypothalamus, the supraoptic nucleus, and the organum vasculosum of the lamina terminalis, one of the circumventricular organs that we will discuss shortly.

Osmosensory neurons have some unusual features that help them detect the concentration of extracellular fluid (Z. Zhang and Bourque, 2003). For one thing, they are stretchy. Most cells in the body and brain actively maintain a constant size in the face of osmotic challenges, but osmosensory neurons don't do this: instead, they balloon or shrink as the concentration of the extracellular fluid changes. The stretching and shrinking of the cell membrane physically opens and closes special mechanically gated ion channels that stud the membrane, causing changes in cell membrane potentials that track the changes in extracellular concentration. This information is then relayed to other parts of the brain, resulting in thirst and homeostatic responses to conserve water, such as through hormone release.

Homeostatic regulation of salt is required for effective regulation of water

Salt (NaCl) is crucial for fluid balance. We cannot maintain water in the extracellular compartment without solutes. If the extracellular compartment contained pure water, osmotic pressure would drive it into the cells, causing them to rupture; consequently, if the extracellular fluid lacks salt, we shed water (through urination) until it returns to isotonic concentration. So, the amount of water that we can retain is determined primarily by the amount of salt contained in the extracellular fluid. That's why thirst is quenched more effectively by very slightly salty drinks (as long as they are still hypotonic, like sports drinks) than by pure water.

Saltier water, such as seawater, has the reverse effect. Seawater is *hyper*tonic, so just as eating salty food makes us thirsty, drinking seawater causes ever-worsening osmotic thirst. We simply can't get rid of the excess salt fast enough, unlike species that have evolved adaptations to dump excess sodium. Some seabirds, for example, have specialized salt glands near the nostrils that can excrete highly con-

13.10 EXCRETION OF EXCESS SALT Marine birds, such as this giant petrel, have only seawater to drink for long periods of time. To compensate, they have salt glands that pull excess salt out of plasma and release it out the nostrils.

aldosterone An adrenal steroid that promotes conservation of sodium by the kidneys.

baroreceptor A pressure receptor in the heart or a major artery that detects a fall in blood pressure.

atrial natriuretic peptide (ANP) A hormone, secreted by the heart, that normally reduces blood pressure, inhibits drinking, and promotes the excretion of water and salt at the kidneys.

vasopressin Also called *antidiuretic hormone* (ADH). A peptide hormone from the posterior pituitary that promotes water conservation.

angiotensin II A substance that is produced in the blood by the action of renin and that may play a role in the control of thirst.

centrated salt solutions (**FIGURE 13.10**) (Schmidt-Nielsen, 1960), so they can drink seawater.

Some Na⁺ loss is inevitable, as during urination or sweating. But when water is at a premium, the body tries to conserve Na⁺ in order to also retain water. Released from the adrenals in response to thirst signals, the steroid hormone **aldosterone** directly stimulates the kidneys to conserve Na⁺ rather than dumping it into the urine. Nonetheless, animals must find additional salt in their environments in order to retain sufficient water to survive.

Hypovolemic thirst is triggered by a loss of water volume

The second signal that triggers thirst doesn't involve salt balance or osmosis, but rather a decrease in the overall volume of the extracellular fluid, called *hypovolemia* (literally "low volume"). Normal everyday obligatory losses cause moderate decreases in extracellular fluid volume (in addition to increased saltiness), but more sudden and dramatic losses of fluid from the body—due to hemorrhage, vomiting, sustained diarrhea—may trigger thirst that is *primarily* hypovolemic in nature (**FIGURE 13.9B**). In this condition, blood vessels that would normally be full and slightly stretched no longer contain their full capacity. Blood pressure drops, and the individual becomes thirsty—powerfully so, if the hemorrhage or other volume loss is severe enough.

Note that suddenly losing fluids from blood loss (or from diarrhea or vomiting) does not change the *concentration* of the extracellular fluid, at least at first, because salts and other solutes are lost along with the water. Rather, only the *volume* of the extracellular fluid is affected in these instances. This tells us that changes in volume alone are sufficient to induce drinking behavior, providing another example of redundancy in a homeostatic system. The initial drop in extracellular volume is detected by pressure receptors, called **baroreceptors**, which are located in major blood vessels and in the heart. In response to the signal from the baroreceptors, the brain activates a variety of responses, such as thirst (to replace the lost water) and salt hunger (to replace the solutes that have been lost along with the water). Replacing the water without also replacing the salts would result in hypotonic extracellular fluid. The sympathetic nervous system also stimulates muscles in artery walls to constrict, reducing the size of the vessels to increase blood pressure and partly compensate for the reduced volume. In addition, several hormonal systems are activated, as we will see next.

HORMONAL RESPONSES TO DEHYDRATION Physiological responses to hypovolemia are coordinated by a set of peptide hormones originating in several different organs. Immediately after the baroreceptors detect a drop in blood pressure, the heart decreases its secretion of **atrial natriuretic peptide** (**ANP**), which normally reduces blood pressure, inhibits drinking, and promotes the excretion of water and salt at the kidneys. At the same time, the brain steps up its release of the peptide hormone **vasopressin** from the posterior pituitary gland. Vasopressin induces additional constriction of blood vessels. Furthermore, vasopressin instructs the kidneys to reduce the flow of water to the bladder. At night, inputs from the circadian clock system of the suprachiasmatic nucleus (see Chapter 14) promote vasopressin release, slowing urine production and preventing dehydration during sleeping (Colwell, 2010). Because of its role in reducing urine production, vasopressin has also been called *antidiuretic hormone* (ADH; *diuresis* is the production of urine), but in light of new knowledge of this hormone's role in love and relationships, perhaps that name is too mundane (L. J. Young, 2009) (see Chapter 5).

A third hormonal response to conserve water comes from the kidneys, which release an enzyme called *renin* into the circulation, triggering a hormonal cascade that culminates in the circulation of a hormone called **angiotensin II** (from the Greek *angeion*, "blood vessel," and the Latin *tensio*, "tension or pressure") (**FIGURE 13.11**). Angiotensin II has several water-conserving actions. In addition to constricting blood vessels and increasing blood pressure, angiotensin II triggers the release of two additional hormones that affect fluid balance: vasopressin and aldosterone (both discussed earlier). Furthermore, circulating angiotensin II directly regulates behavior through actions at neural sites located in the forebrain (Daniels and Marshall, 2012), especially the **circumventricular organs**. As their name suggests, these structures lie in the walls of the cerebral ventricles (**FIGURE 13.12**) and feature *fenestrated capillaries*—blood vessels that lack the usual blood-brain barrier (see Chapter 3)—allowing neurons in these regions to monitor hormones in the bloodstream (Miyata, 2015). Neurons of the circumventricular organs possess specific angiotensin receptors and send signals to other neural regions when angiotensin II is detected. The **organum vasculosum of the lamina terminalis** (**OVLT**) and **subfornical organ** (**SFO**) are circumventricular organs that prompt a particularly large drinking response to the presence of angiotensin II (Lebrun et al., 1995). Further, using optogenetic activation of neurons (see Chapter 3), researchers have identified a population of cells within the SFO that strongly elicits drinking, and a second, genetically separable population of neurons that strongly *suppresses* drinking behavior—indicating that the SFO contains an on/off switch for drinking (Oka et al., 2015). Angiotensin II may also act directly on regions of the hypothalamus, such as the POA, to elicit drinking (Fitzsimmons, 1998). Note that angiotensin II is just one of several redundant systems for provoking thirst and is not active under all conditions (McKinley and Johnson, 2004).

13.11 THE ANGIOTENSIN CASCADE   Renin, released by the kidneys, catalyzes the conversion of angiotensinogen (already present in blood) to angiotensin I. Angiotensin I is converted to angiotensin II (the most biologically active of the angiotensins).

We don't stop drinking just because the throat and mouth are wet

Although plausible, the most obvious explanation of why we stop drinking—that we have dampened our previously dry throat and mouth—is all wet (sorry). Classic research showed that thirsty animals allowed to drink water but not consume water—because the water is diverted out of the esophagus—remain thirsty and continue drinking. However, it was also found that a drink of water is more thirst quenching if taken by mouth than if infused directly into the stomach (Miller et al., 1957). So, provided that water actually reaches the stomach, oral sensations must play *some* role in satiety (*satiety* is the feeling that a hunger has been satisfied). Further, we stop drinking before water has left the gastrointestinal tract and entered the extracellular compartment. Taken together, the research suggests that we use a combination of signals to monitor how much water we have ingested and stop in *anticipation* of correcting the extracellular volume and/or osmolality. Experience may teach us and other animals how to gauge accurately whether we've ingested enough to counteract our thirst (hypovolemic or osmotic). Normally, all the signals—blood volume, osmolality, moisture in the mouth, estimates of the amount of water we have ingested that's "on the way"—agree, but the cessation of one signal alone will not stop thirst; in this way, animals ensure against dehydration.

circumventricular organ   An organ that lies in the wall of a cerebral ventricle and monitors the composition of body fluids.

organum vasculosum of the lamina terminalis (OVLT)   One of the circumventricular organs.

subfornical organ (SFO)   One of the circumventricular organs.

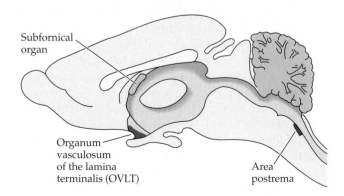

13.12 CIRCUMVENTRICULAR ORGANS   In keeping with their name, the circumventricular organs, seen here in a midsagittal view of the rat brain, lie in the walls of the ventricular system (blue). The blood-brain barrier is greatly reduced in the subfornical organ and the OVLT, so neurons there can monitor the concentration and composition of body fluids.

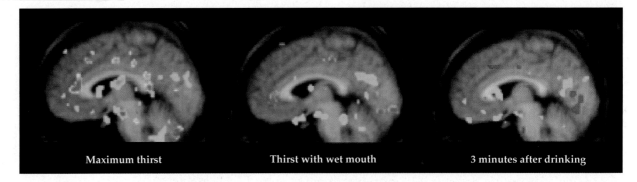

13.13 AHHHHHHH! The experience of strong thirst, induced by injection of hypertonic saline, is associated with activity in several brain regions, especially the cingulate cortex and cerebellum (left). Wetting the mouth reduces this activation only slightly (middle), but drinking a glass of water (right) reduces activation in these brain regions dramatically. (From Denton et al., 1999.)

Thirst is a homeostatic signal that intrudes forcefully into consciousness, with associated strong activation of certain brain regions, particularly in the limbic system (**FIGURE 13.13**) (Denton et al., 1999). The two types of thirst (hypovolemic and osmotic), the two fluid compartments (extracellular and intracellular), and the multiple redundant methods to conserve water make for a fairly complicated system that is not yet fully understood. The current conceptualization of this system is depicted in **FIGURE 13.14**. Our need to compensate for obligatory losses is also crucial to understanding energy regulation, our next topic.

Food and Energy Regulation

Feast or famine—these are poles of human experience. Hunger for the food that we need to build, maintain, and fuel our bodies is a compelling drive, and flavors are powerful reinforcers. The behaviors involved in obtaining and consuming food shape our daily schedules, and our mass media feed us a steady diet of information about food: crop reports, stories about famines and droughts, cooking shows, and restaurant ads.

Our reliance on food for energy and nutrition is shared with all other animals. In the remainder of this chapter, we will look at the regulation of feeding and energy expenditure, as well as some species-specific aspects of food-related behavior.

Nutrient Regulation Helps Prepare for Future Needs

The regulation of eating and of body energy involves numerous redundant mechanisms and complex homeostatic controls. Overall, the system for controlling food intake and energy balance is significantly more complex than those controlling thermoregulation and fluid balance. One important reason for this greater complexity is that we need food to supply not only energy, but also crucial **nutrients** (chemicals required for the effective functioning, growth, and maintenance of the body). We do not know all the nutritional requirements of the body—even for humans. Of the 20 amino acids found in our bodies, 9 are difficult or impossible for us to manufacture, so we must find these *essential amino acids* in our diet. From food we must also obtain a few fatty acids, as well as about 15 vitamins and a variety of minerals.

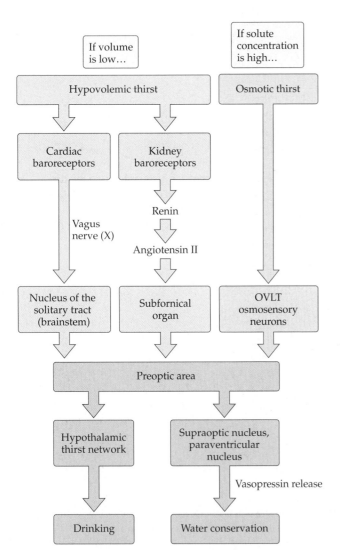

13.14 AN OVERVIEW OF FLUID REGULATION
A hierarchical system of central and peripheral mechanisms prompts behavioral and physiological measures to maintain optimal hydration.

No animal can afford to run out of energy or nutrients; there must be a reserve on hand at all times. If the reserves are too large, however, mobility (for avoiding predators or securing prey) will be compromised. For this reason, the nervous system not only monitors nutrient and energy levels and controls **digestion** (the process of breaking down ingested food), but also has complex mechanisms for *anticipating* future requirements.

Most of our food is used to provide us with energy

All the energy that we need to move, think, breathe, and maintain body temperature is derived in the same way: it is released when the chemical bonds of complex molecules are broken and smaller, simpler compounds form as a result. In a sense we "burn" food for energy just as a car burns gasoline. To raise body temperature, we release chemical-bond energy as heat. For other bodily processes, such as those in the brain, the energy is utilized by more-sophisticated biochemical processes.

Metabolic studies indicate that lab animals lose about 33% of the energy in food during digestion (through excretion of indigestible material or the digestive process itself). Another 55% of food energy in a meal is consumed by **basal metabolism**—processes such as heat production, maintenance of membrane potentials, and all the other basic life-sustaining functions of the body. The remainder, only about 12% of the total, is utilized for active behavioral processes, although this proportion is increased in more-complex environments or during intense activity.

In general, the rate of basal metabolism follows a rule, devised by Max Kleiber (1947), that relates energy expenditure to body weight:

$$\text{kilocalories/day} = 70 \times \text{weight}^{0.75}$$

where weight is expressed in kilograms. This relationship applies across a vast range of body sizes (**FIGURE 13.15**). However, although Kleiber's equation fits nicely at the population level, it is not very accurate for *individuals* within a species, because body weight is only one factor affecting metabolic rate. For example, food-deprived people experience a significant decrease in basal metabolism. In fact, severe food restriction affects metabolic rate much more than it affects body weight, presumably reflecting the operation of an evolved homeostatic mechanism for conserving energy when food is scarce.

nutrient A chemical that is needed for growth, maintenance, and repair of the body but is not used as a source of energy.

digestion The process by which food is broken down to provide energy and nutrients.

basal metabolism The consumption of energy by the basic life-sustaining functions of the body.

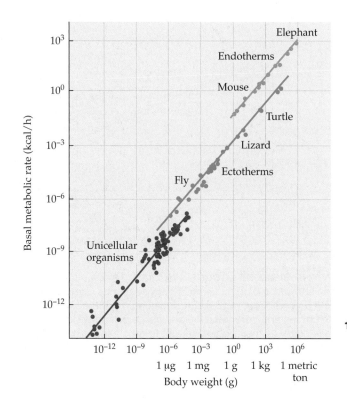

13.15 THE RELATION BETWEEN BODY SIZE AND METABOLISM Basal metabolic rate increases in a very regular, predictable fashion over a wide range of body weights. However, endotherms have a higher metabolic rate than ectotherms of a similar body weight. (After Hemmingsen, 1960.)

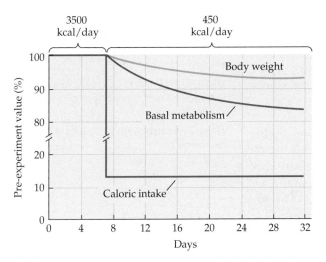

13.16 WHY LOSING WEIGHT IS SO DIFFICULT After 7 days on a diet of 3500 kilocalories (kcal) per day, the intake of six obese participants was restricted to a measly 450 kcal/day—a drop of 87%. However, basal metabolism also declined by 15%, so after 3 weeks, body weight had declined by only 6%. (After Bray, 1969.)

trophic factor A substance that promotes cell growth and survival.

glucose A sugar molecule used by the body and brain for energy.

Because people and animals adjust their metabolism in response to under- or overnutrition, they tend to resist either losing or gaining weight (**FIGURE 13.16**). To the frustration of dieters everywhere, many studies show that a calorie-reduced diet prompts a reduction in basal metabolic rate that *prevents* weight loss (Bray, 1969; C. K. Martin et al., 2007). Along with the other *Biggest Loser* contestants, Danny C., whom we met at the outset of the chapter, has learned the hard way that our brains and bodies vigorously defend our body weight, even if we are obese. Due to a dramatic decrease in his basal metabolism following weight loss—a process called *metabolic adaptation*—Danny now needs to consume 800 *fewer* calories per day than the typical man, just to maintain his current 295-pound body weight. And to make matters worse, this metabolic adaptation is annoyingly persistent; even after 6 long years, the metabolisms of the contestants remained very low (**FIGURE 13.17**), as their brains continued to try to regain the lost weight (Fothergill et al., 2016). A major concern for researchers is thus to discover a way to reset the body weight set point (or set zone) to avoid triggering the brain's body weight defense mechanisms. Mice whose basal metabolic rate has been increased (by a transgenic increase in the energy used by mitochondria) eat more and weigh less than normal mice, without increased locomotor activity (Clapham et al., 2000). Perhaps someday a drug will be developed to exert this effect on human mitochondria and produce such wonderful results in humans as well.

However difficult dieting might be, the only proven way to extend the average life expectancy of lab animals is to reduce their caloric intake to levels that are about 50–75% of what they would eat if food were always available (Weindruch and Walford, 1988). This benefit from reducing calorie intake may be related to the decrease in basal metabolism that is induced by food restriction. Both the body and the brain

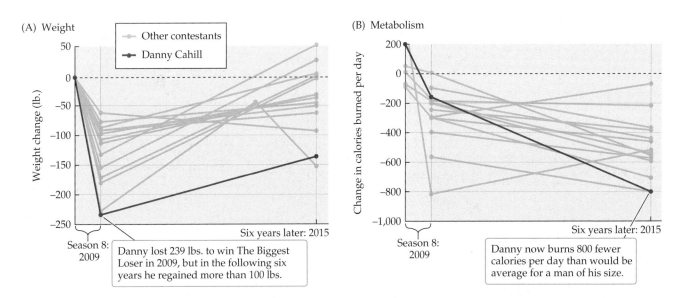

13.17 METABOLIC ADAPTATION IN THE BIGGEST LOSERS (A) Of the 14 contestants from season 8 of the reality television show *The Biggest Loser*, 13 subsequently regained significant weight over the following 6 years. Four contestants weighed more than they had before the competition. (B) The contestants' dramatic weight losses prompted large compensatory decreases in metabolic rate, as their bodies sought to regain the lost weight. Alarmingly, this strong metabolic suppression still persisted 6 years after their weight losses; in fact, it even increased over time. (After Fothergill et al., 2016.)

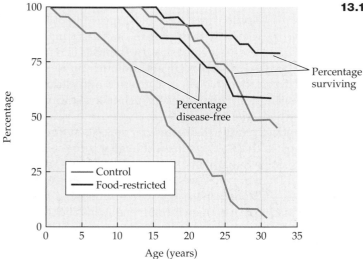

13.18 THE BENEFITS OF CALORIC RESTRICTION IN MONKEYS Twenty years of moderate caloric restriction in rhesus monkeys resulted in significant reductions in age-related diseases and associated mortality. (After Colman et al., 2009.)

give evidence of slower aging under such circumstances (C.-K. Lee et al., 2000). No one knows exactly how food deprivation enhances longevity, but research in invertebrates has identified a pair of genes for transcription factors (substances that control other genes) that are involved (Bishop and Guarente, 2007; Panowski et al., 2007). These genes, which are conserved across many species of animals, may in turn control production of hormones and **trophic factors** (substances that promote cell growth and survival) important for longevity.

During caloric restriction, production of the protein SIRT1, a marker for increased longevity in various vertebrates and invertebrates, is increased (Anson et al., 2003; Holzenberger et al., 2003). Although no one is likely to do full studies on human longevity (because they would take a century or so to complete), evidence that caloric restriction also increases SIRT1 production in humans raises the possibility that restricting intake—while maintaining healthy nutrition—could have the same life-span benefits in humans as it has in lab animals (Allard et al., 2008). Long-term caloric restriction has been found to slow aging and prevent disease and early death in rhesus monkeys (**FIGURE 13.18**) (Colman et al., 2014).

We can store energy for future needs

The most immediate source of energy for the body is the complex carbohydrates in our diet that are rapidly broken down into the simple sugars that cells can use. **Glucose** is the principal sugar used by the body for energy, and it is especially important for fueling the brain. Because we need a steady supply of glucose between meals and may also experience elevated demand for fuel at other times—for example, during intense physical activity—several mechanisms have evolved to store excess fuel for later use.

For short-term storage, glucose can be converted into a more complicated molecule called **glycogen** and stored as reserve fuel in several locations, most notably the liver and skeletal muscles. This process, called **glycogenesis**, is promoted by the pancreatic hormone **insulin** (see Chapter 5). A second pancreatic hormone, **glucagon**, mediates the conversion of glycogen back into glucose, a process known as **glycogenolysis** (**FIGURE 13.19**), which is triggered when blood concentrations of glucose drop too low.

glycogen A complex carbohydrate derived from glucose.

glycogenesis The physiological process by which glycogen is produced.

insulin A hormone, released by beta cells in the islets of Langerhans, that lowers blood glucose.

glucagon A hormone, released by alpha cells in the islets of Langerhans, that increases blood glucose.

glycogenolysis The conversion of glycogen back into glucose, triggered when blood concentrations of glucose drop too low.

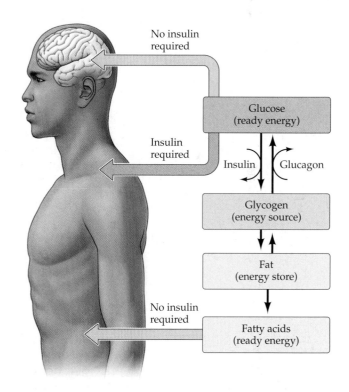

13.19 THE ROLE OF INSULIN IN ENERGY UTILIZATION The body can make use of either fatty acids or glucose for energy. The brain, however, can use only glucose; the brain therefore requires a constant supply of glucose, which it can use without the aid of insulin. On the other hand, the body needs insulin to use glucose, so in the absence of insulin, the body must use fatty acids for energy.

lipids Large molecules (commonly called *fats*) consisting of fatty acids and glycerol that are insoluble in water.

adipose tissue Tissue made up of fat cells.

gluconeogenesis The metabolism of body fats and proteins to create glucose.

ketones A metabolic fuel source liberated by the breakdown of body fats and proteins.

glucose transporter A molecule that conducts glucose molecules through the external membrane of a cell for use inside.

glucodetector A cell that detects and informs the nervous system about levels of circulating glucose.

vagus nerve Cranial nerve X, which regulates the viscera (organs) and transmits signals from the viscera to the brain.

nucleus of the solitary tract (NST) A brainstem nucleus that receives visceral and taste information via several cranial nerves.

diabetes mellitus Excessive glucose in the urine, caused by the failure of insulin to induce glucose absorption by the body.

For longer-term storage, fats (or **lipids**, large molecules consisting of fatty acids and glycerol that are insoluble in water) are deposited in the fat-storing cells that form **adipose tissue**. Some stored fats are created directly from fats in our food, but others are synthesized in the body from surplus sugars and other nutrients. Under conditions of prolonged food deprivation, fat can be converted into glucose (a process called **gluconeogenesis**) and a secondary form of fuel, called **ketones**, which can similarly be utilized by the body and brain.

The debate about the most effective ways to decrease fat deposition through dieting is an endlessly popular topic in the mass media. Although it is counterintuitive, evidence has accumulated to suggest that diets low in carbohydrates, and correspondingly high in proteins and fats, are effective in helping people lose weight and also may increase serum levels of "good" cholesterol while decreasing fats (G. D. Foster et al., 2003; Samaha et al., 2003). Although recommendations about fat intake are evolving, it's worth noting that the only *certain* way to lose weight is to decrease the number of calories eaten and/or increase the calories spent in physical activity. For the weight loss to be permanent, these changes in diet and activity must be permanent too, and as we are seeing in this chapter, our metabolism sometimes works against us in this regard.

Insulin Is Crucial for the Regulation of Body Metabolism

We have already mentioned the importance of insulin for converting glucose into glycogen. Another important role of insulin is enabling the body to use glucose. Most cells regulate the import of glucose molecules via **glucose transporters**: specialized proteins that span the cell membrane and bring glucose molecules from outside the cell into the cell for use. The glucose transporters must interact with insulin in order to function. (Brain cells are an important exception; they can use glucose without the aid of insulin.)

Each time you eat a meal, the foods are broken down and glucose is released into the bloodstream. Most of your body requires insulin to make use of that glucose, so three different, sequential mechanisms stimulate insulin release:

1. The sensory stimuli from food (sight, smell, and taste) evoke a conditioned release of insulin in anticipation of glucose arrival in the blood. This release, because it is mediated by the brain, is called the *cephalic phase* of insulin release (recall that *cephalon* means "head").

2. During the *digestive phase*, food entering the stomach and intestines causes them to release gut hormones, some of which stimulate the pancreas to release insulin. The digestive tract contains taste receptors like those found on the tongue; these provide further regulation of insulin release (Kokrashvili et al., 2009).

3. During the *absorptive phase*, special cells in the liver, called **glucodetectors**, detect the glucose entering the bloodstream and signal the pancreas to release insulin.

The newly released insulin enables the body to make use of some of the glucose immediately and prompts the conversion of extra glucose into glycogen, which is then stored in the liver and muscles. The liver communicates with the pancreas via the nervous system. Information from glucodetectors in the liver travels via the **vagus nerve** to the **nucleus of the solitary tract** (**NST**) in the brainstem and is relayed to the hypothalamus (Powley, 2000). This system informs the brain of circulating glucose levels and contributes to hunger, as we'll discuss shortly. Efferent fibers carry signals from the brainstem back out the vagus nerve to the pancreas. These efferent fibers modulate insulin release from the pancreas.

Lack of insulin causes the disease **diabetes mellitus**. In *type I* (or *juvenile-onset*) *diabetes*, the pancreas stops producing insulin. Although the brain can still make use of glucose from the diet, the rest of the body cannot and is forced to use energy from fatty acids, with the result that lots of glucose is left in the bloodstream. Some of the excess glucose is secreted into the urine, making it sweet, which is how we get the name *diabetes mellitus* (literally "passing honey").

An untreated person with diabetes eats a great deal and yet loses weight because the body cannot make efficient use of the ingested food, and the reliance on fatty acids for energy causes damage to some tissues. People suffering from diabetes also drink and urinate copiously in an attempt to rid the body of the excess circulating glucose. Replacement of the missing insulin (via injection) allows the glucose to be utilized. Another, more common type of diabetes mellitus, called *type II* (or *adult-onset*) *diabetes*, is primarily a consequence of reduced *sensitivity* to insulin. Particularly associated with obesity, type II diabetes often leads to further health problems.

Despite their importance, neither insulin nor glucose is the sole signal for hunger or satiety

Given the crucial role of insulin in mobilizing and distributing food energy, you might think that the brain monitors circulating insulin levels to decide when it's time to eat and when it's time to stop eating. For example, high levels of insulin, secreted because there is food in the pipeline, might signal the brain to produce the sensation of satiety. Conversely, low levels of insulin between meals could signal the brain to make us feel **hunger**, impelling us to find food and eat. Indeed, lowering an animal's blood insulin levels causes it to become hungry and eat a large meal. If moderate levels of insulin are injected, the animal eats much less. These results suggest that insulin can provide a satiety signal to the brain.

Investigators tested this simple hypothesis by injecting a large amount of insulin into animals. But rather than appearing satiated, the animals responded by eating a large meal! That's because high insulin levels direct much of the glucose out of circulation and into storage, resulting in *hypoglycemia*, which the brain detects. So is it the change in circulating glucose that signals satiety and hunger to the brain? Glucose levels are certainly an additional appetite signal, but circulating glucose can't be the only source of information, because people with untreated diabetes have very high levels of circulating glucose, yet they are constantly hungry. Somehow the brain integrates insulin and glucose levels with other sources of information to decide whether to initiate eating. This has become a central theme in research on appetite control—that the brain integrates many different signals rather than relying exclusively on any single signal to trigger hunger.

The Hypothalamus Coordinates Multiple Systems That Control Hunger

Although no single brain region has exclusive control of appetite, decades of research has confirmed that the hypothalamus is critically important to the regulation of metabolic rate, food intake, and body weight. In this classic research, scientists found that lesions in the hypothalamus of rats could induce either chronic hunger and massive weight gain, or chronic satiety and severe weight loss, depending on the location of the lesion. Bilateral lesions of the **ventromedial hypothalamus (VMH)** (**FIGURE 13.20A**) resulted in animals that ate to excess, a behavior called **hyperphagia**, and became obese (Hetherington and Ranson, 1940), leading researchers to suggest that the VMH is a "satiety center" in the brain (because the rats ceased to experience satiety once the VMH was gone). Conversely, rats with lesions of the **lateral hypothalamus (LH)** (**FIGURE 13.20B**) exhibited **aphagia**—a cessation of eating—and rapidly lost weight. This suggested that the LH acts as a hunger center (Anand and Brobeck, 1951). Thus, an early model of appetite control featured the VMH and LH acting in opposition to govern feeding.

Subsequent research soon showed that appetite control is more complicated than can be accounted for by the simple dual-center hypothesis. For one thing, VMH-

hunger The internal state of an animal seeking food.

ventromedial hypothalamus (VMH) A hypothalamic region involved in eating and sexual behaviors.

hyperphagia Excessive eating.

lateral hypothalamus (LH) A hypothalamic region involved in the control of appetite and other functions.

aphagia Refusal to eat.

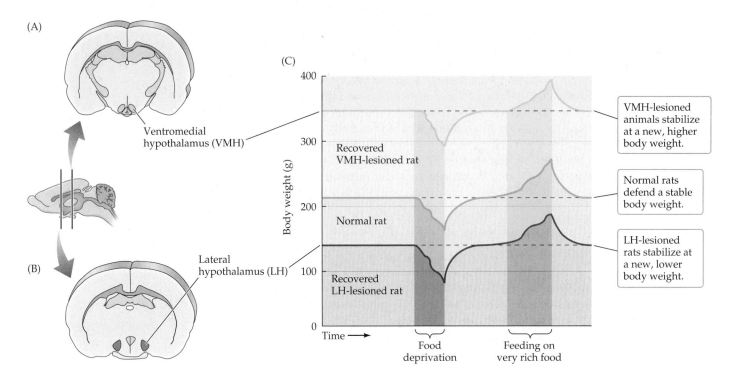

(A)

Ventromedial
hypothalamus (VMH)

(B)

Lateral
hypothalamus (LH)

(C)

Body weight (g)

400

300

200

100

0

Recovered
VMH-lesioned rat

Normal rat

Recovered
LH-lesioned rat

Time →

Food
deprivation

Feeding on
very rich food

VMH-lesioned
animals stabilize
at a new, higher
body weight.

Normal rats
defend a stable
body weight.

LH-lesioned
rats stabilize at
a new, lower
body weight.

13.20 CHANGES IN BODY WEIGHT AFTER HYPOTHALAMIC LESIONS (A) Rats in which the ventromedial hypothalamus (VMH) has been lesioned overeat and gain weight; (B) rats with lesions in the lateral hypothalamus (LH) stop eating and lose weight. (C) Both VMH- and LH-lesioned rats eventually stabilize at a new body weight, which they defend in the face of either forced feeding or food deprivation. (After Keesey and Boyle, 1973; Sclafani et al., 1976.)

arcuate nucleus An arc-shaped hypothalamic nucleus implicated in appetite control.

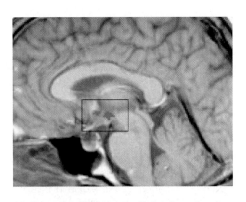

13.21 SWEET SPOT Following glucose ingestion, changes in activity in the hypothalamus (inside the black rectangle) are evident in this midsagittal fMRI image. Blue indicates a significant decrease in activity; yellow indicates a significant increase. (From Y. Liu et al., 2000.)

lesioned animals exhibited a period of rapid weight gain but then stabilized at a new, higher body weight and would eat only to the extent needed to defend the new weight. This indicated that the VMH-lesioned rats experienced satiety (**FIGURE 13.20C**), so the VMH cannot be the sole satiety controller. Likewise, the LH can't be the sole hunger center, because LH-lesioned rats kept alive at first with a feeding tube soon resumed spontaneous eating sufficient to maintain their new, lower body weight (Keesey, 1980). As with the VMH-lesioned animals, LH-lesioned animals that were forced to gain or lose weight would swiftly return to their new set point for body weight once they were allowed to eat at will.

The early research thus demonstrated that the hypothalamus contains distinct components of an appetite control network and provided a framework for subsequent studies. For example, fMRI studies show that increasing circulating glucose after a period of fasting produces large changes in the activity of the human hypothalamus (**FIGURE 13.21**) (Y. Liu et al., 2000), probably acting via hypothalamic glucodetector neurons that directly monitor blood levels of glucose (Parton et al., 2007).

Today it is clear that the hypothalamic control of feeding is quite complicated and, like other homeostatic systems, exhibits redundancy as a safety measure. However, as we'll see next, researchers have uncovered many of the details of the hypothalamic appetite control network and its integration of multiple signals from sites throughout the body.

Multiple peripheral signals are integrated by a hypothalamic appetite network

A spate of discoveries indicates that the **arcuate nucleus** of the hypothalamus contains a highly specialized appetite controller that is governed by circulating levels of a variety of hormones (**TABLE 13.2**). We have already discussed how the pancreatic hormone insulin signals the state of glucose circulating in the blood. Other

TABLE 13.2   Peripheral Hormone Signals for Body Weight Regulation

HORMONE	PRIMARY SOURCE	SIGNAL
Insulin	Beta islet cells of the pancreas	Provides the arcuate appetite controller with information about blood glucose level
Leptin	Fat cells	Signals current long-term energy stores (in fat)
$PYY_{3\text{-}36}$	Cells of the ileum (small intestine) and colon	Provides a rapid signal that food has been consumed, prompting the arcuate system to suppress appetite
Ghrelin	Cells of the stomach and duodenum	Provides a "fasting" signal, indicating to the arcuate system that the digestive system is empty, prompting the arcuate system to increase appetite
CCK	Cells of the duodenum	Suppresses appetite via direct action on the vagus nerve (cranial nerve X)

information about energy balance—especially short-term and long-term reserves—comes in the form of hormonal secretions from elsewhere in the body, including the peptides leptin, ghrelin, and a hormone with a cumbersome name, peptide $YY_{3\text{-}36}$ ($PYY_{3\text{-}36}$). We will discuss each in turn and then look at the possible organization of the hypothalamic appetite controller.

LEPTIN   Mice that receive two copies of the gene called *obese* (abbreviated *ob*) regulate their body weight at a high level (**FIGURE 13.22**), as you might have guessed from the gene's name. These mice have larger and more numerous fat cells than their heterozygous littermates (*ob/+*; the plus sign indicates the wild-type, normal allele). The fat mice (*ob/ob*) maintain their obesity even when given an unpalatable diet or when required to work hard to obtain food (Cruce et al., 1974).

The *ob/ob* mice have defective genes for the peptide **leptin** (from the Greek *leptos*, "thin"). Fat cells produce leptin and then secrete the protein into the bloodstream (Y. Zhang et al., 1994). Leptin receptors (ObR; *r*eceptors to the *obese* gene product, leptin) have been identified in the choroid plexus, the cortex, and several hypothalamic nuclei (Hâkansson et al., 1998), to be discussed shortly. Animals with defects in the gene that encodes ObR likewise become obese (al-Barazanji et al., 1997).

Thus, the brain seems to monitor circulating leptin levels to measure and regulate the body's energy reserves in the form of fat. Defects in leptin production or leptin sensitivity cause a false underreporting of body fat and lead to overeating, especially high-fat or sugary foods.

leptin   A peptide hormone released by fat cells.

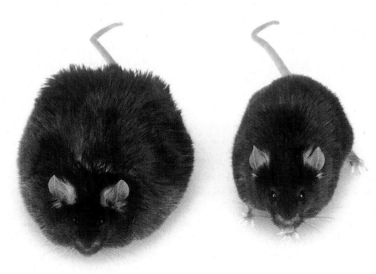

13.22 INHERITED OBESITY   Both of these mice have two copies of the *obese* gene, which impairs the production of leptin by fat cells. The mouse on the left weighs about 67 g; a normal (wild-type) mouse at this age weighs about 25 g. The mouse on the right has been treated with leptin and weighs about 35 g.

ghrelin A peptide hormone emanating from the gut.

PYY$_{3-36}$ A peptide hormone, secreted by the intestines, that probably acts on hypothalamic appetite control mechanisms to suppress appetite.

pro-opiomelanocortin (POMC) A pro-hormone that can be cleaved to produce the melanocortins, which also participate in feeding control.

POMC neurons Neurons involved in the hypothalamic appetite control system, so named because they produce pro-opiomelanocortin (POMC) along with cocaine- and amphetamine-related transcript (CART).

NPY neurons Neurons involved in the hypothalamic appetite control system, so named because they produce neuropeptide Y (NPY) along with agouti-related peptide (AgRP).

neuropeptide Y (NPY) A peptide neurotransmitter that may carry some of the signals for feeding.

GHRELIN **Ghrelin**, released into the bloodstream by endocrine cells of the stomach (Kojima et al., 1999), was named in recognition of its effects on growth hormone secretion (***GH rel****easing*). But we now know that ghrelin is a powerful appetite *stimulant* (Nakazato et al., 2001). Circulating levels of ghrelin rise during fasting and immediately drop after a meal is eaten. Treating either rats or humans with exogenous ghrelin produces a rapid and large increase in appetite (Wren et al., 2000, 2001).

Curiously, obese participants reportedly have lower baseline levels of ghrelin than do lean participants prior to eating, but following a meal their circulating levels of ghrelin do not drop (their leptin levels remain high too). So one mechanism of obesity may involve a ghrelin system that is unresponsive to feeding and thus always slightly elevated, prompting continual hunger (English et al., 2002).

PYY$_{3-36}$ Secreted into the circulation by cells of the small and large intestines, the small peptide **PYY$_{3-36}$** is at a low level in the blood prior to eating, but that level rises rapidly on ingestion of a meal. Systemic injections of PYY$_{3-36}$ curb appetite in both rats and humans, as do injections directly into the arcuate nucleus of the hypothalamus of rats (Batterham and Bloom, 2003; Baynes et al., 2006; Chelikani et al., 2005). Interestingly, lower-than-average levels of circulating PYY$_{3-36}$ are associated with a tendency toward obesity in mice and humans, and postmeal increases in this peptide have been closely linked to feelings of satiety in normal-weight people (see Karra et al., 2009, for a review). It therefore appears that PYY$_{3-36}$ may act in opposition to ghrelin, providing a potent appetite-*suppressing* stimulus to the hypothalamus. The discoveries of PYY$_{3-36}$ and ghrelin have provided important clues about the appetite control mystery, and these hormones converge on the arcuate nucleus of the hypothalamus, which we describe next.

THE ARCUATE APPETITE SYSTEM A streamlined view of the organization of appetite control neurons in the arcuate nucleus is sketched in **FIGURE 13.23**. The appetite system relies on two sets of arcuate neurons with opposing effects, which are named according to the types of neurotransmitters they produce. When activated, arcuate neurons that produce the peptides **pro-opiomelanocortin (POMC)** and cocaine- and amphetamine-regulated transcript (CART)—called **POMC neurons** for short—act as satiety neurons, inhibiting appetite and increasing metabolism. In contrast, the other set of neurons—called **NPY neurons** because they produce **neuropeptide Y (NPY)** along with agouti-related peptide (AgRP)—act as hunger neurons when activated, stimulating appetite directly, inhibiting POMC neurons (thereby blocking satiety signals), and reducing metabolism, a set of actions that promotes eating and weight gain. Projections from the POMC neurons and NPY neurons also leave the arcuate and make contact with neurons in other hypothalamic sites (see Figure 13.23B). It is through these projections that the arcuate system ultimately modulates food intake. But before we turn to those mechanisms, let's first consider how the peripheral hormones interact with the appetite controller in the arcuate.

Because it is made by fat cells, leptin (and to a lesser extent, insulin) conveys information about the body's energy reserves. Both types of appetite neurons in the arcuate system have leptin receptors, but leptin affects them in opposite ways. High circulating levels of leptin *activate* the appetite-suppressing POMC neurons but *inhibit* the appetite-increasing NPY neurons, so in both systems leptin is working to suppress hunger. In keeping with its role as an indicator of the body's current composition, leptin seems to mostly affect the appetite system over the longer term, perhaps by promoting the remodeling of neurons in the arcuate nucleus (Bouret et al., 2004). To add to the difficulties of the *Biggest Loser* contestants, long-term studies have found that their drastically lowered metabolic rates are accompanied by equally striking decreases in circulating leptin levels (Knuth et al., 2014). So their bodies keep telling the arcuate that fat reserves are low, even when they've regained a lot of weight. For reasons that remain a mystery, leptin levels are not similarly suppressed when the weight is shed because of gastric bypass surgery (a topic we explore toward the end of the chapter).

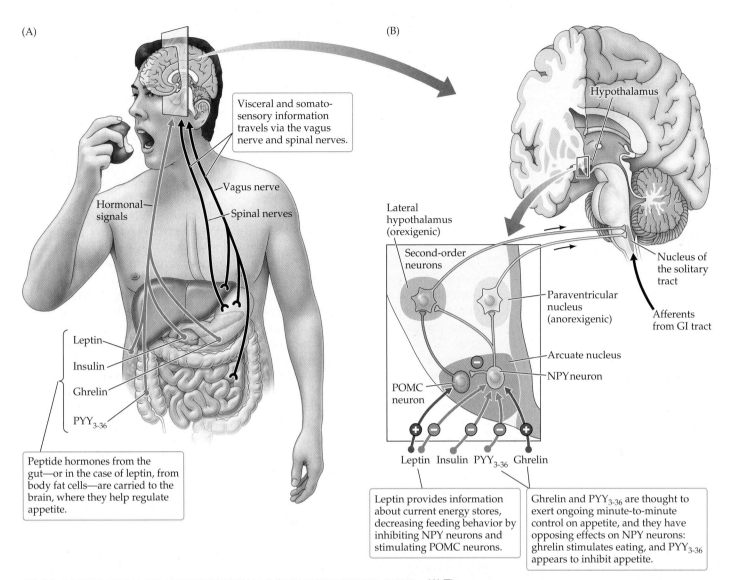

(A)

Visceral and somato-sensory information travels via the vagus nerve and spinal nerves.

Vagus nerve

Hormonal signals

Spinal nerves

Leptin

Insulin

Ghrelin

PYY$_{3-36}$

Peptide hormones from the gut—or in the case of leptin, from body fat cells—are carried to the brain, where they help regulate appetite.

(B)

Hypothalamus

Lateral hypothalamus (orexigenic)

Second-order neurons

Paraventricular nucleus (anorexigenic)

Arcuate nucleus

POMC neuron

NPY neuron

Nucleus of the solitary tract

Afferents from GI tract

Leptin   Insulin   PYY$_{3-36}$ Ghrelin

Leptin provides information about current energy stores, decreasing feeding behavior by inhibiting NPY neurons and stimulating POMC neurons.

Ghrelin and PYY$_{3-36}$ are thought to exert ongoing minute-to-minute control on appetite, and they have opposing effects on NPY neurons: ghrelin stimulates eating, and PYY$_{3-36}$ appears to inhibit appetite.

13.23 INTEGRATION OF APPETITE SIGNALS IN THE HYPOTHALAMUS   (A) The brain integrates a number of peripheral signals to determine appetite. Among these are numerous gut peptides secreted into the bloodstream, especially (1) leptin, secreted by fat cells; (2) insulin, secreted by the pancreas; (3) ghrelin, secreted by the stomach; and (4) PYY$_{3-36}$, secreted by the intestines. In addition, visceral and somatosensory information is transmitted via spinal nerves and the vagus nerve. (B) Two types of neurons in the arcuate nucleus are sensitive to pep-tides from the periphery: POMC neurons signal a decrease in food intake; NPY neurons promote increased feeding. Both types of arcuate neurons exert their effects via second-order neurons in the paraventricular nucleus and lateral hypo-thalamus. POMC neurons signal satiety by releasing α-melanocyte-stimulating hormone (α-MSH). NPY neurons stimulate appetite through the release of NPY but also by releasing AgRP, which directly competes for the melanocortin recep-tors, reducing the effectiveness of α-MSH in suppressing appetite.

In contrast to leptin, ghrelin and PYY$_{3-36}$ provide more-rapid, hour-to-hour hun-ger signals from the stomach and gut. Both peptides act primarily on the appetite-stimulating NPY neurons of the arcuate. Ghrelin stimulates these cells, leading to a corresponding increase in appetite. PYY$_{3-36}$ works in opposition, inhibiting the same NPY cells to *reduce* appetite. Short-term control of appetite thus reflects a balance between ghrelin and PYY$_{3-36}$ concentrations in circulation.

Although much progress has been made in understanding the control of appetite, the story is not yet complete. Further research will clarify the role of additional newly

orexigenic neurons Neurons of the hypothalamic appetite system that promote feeding behavior.

anorexigenic neurons Neurons of the hypothalamic appetite system that inhibit feeding behavior.

paraventricular nucleus (PVN) A nucleus of the hypothalamus implicated in the release of oxytocin and vasopressin, and in the control of feeding and other behaviors.

α-melanocyte-stimulating hormone (α-MSH) A peptide that binds the melanocortin receptor.

melanocortins One category of endogenous opioid peptides.

melanocortin type-4 receptors (MC4Rs) A specific subtype of melanocortin receptor.

orexins Also called *hypocretins*. Neuropeptides produced in the hypothalamus that are involved in switching between sleep states, in narcolepsy, and in the control of appetite.

cholecystokinin (CCK) A peptide hormone, released by the gut after ingestion of food high in protein and/or fat, that also serves as a signaling molecule in the brain.

discovered satiety signals from the gut (Neary and Batterham, 2009), along with new discoveries about the hypothalamic appetite controller. Ultimately, the arcuate appetite controller exerts its effects on feeding behavior via other brain sites, which we discuss next.

Second-order hypothalamic neurons integrate appetite signals

Having identified the main components of the arcuate appetite controller, we can turn to the functional connections of these cells to "downstream" sites involved in feeding. Two hypothalamic sites appear to be primary targets of projections from the arcuate. **Orexigenic neurons** (from the Greek *orexis*, "appetite," and *genein*, "to produce"), located in the lateral hypothalamus, act to increase appetite and food intake. In contrast, **anorexigenic neurons** of the **paraventricular nucleus** (**PVN**) act to decrease appetite and feeding (refer to Figure 13.23B for help in understanding this circuit).

One set of projections from the appetite-suppressing POMC neurons of the arcuate terminates in the PVN. Here they release **α-melanocyte-stimulating hormone** (**α-MSH**), a peptide hormone belonging to a small family of substances, called **melanocortins**, that are derived from POMC. Acting via specific **melanocortin type-4 receptors** (**MC4Rs**) located on the PVN neurons, α-MSH activates the PVN's appetite-suppressant activity, resulting in a net decrease in feeding (Garfield et al., 2015; Krashes et al., 2016). Other POMC projections inhibit the orexigenic neurons of the LH.

The NPY neurons that are essential for increases in feeding (Gropp et al., 2005) likewise exert their effects through the PVN and the LH (see Figure 13.23B) in a complex manner. By inhibiting anorexigenic PVN neurons, the NPY-releasing neurons promote increased appetite. Furthermore, AgRP released by these neurons into the LH competes with α-MSH (from POMC neurons) for receptors. By blocking the α-MSH signal, AgRP thus counters the appetite-suppressing influence from the POMC neurons that we just described, and thus again acts to *increase* feeding behavior, via the LH.

The net result of all this is a constant balancing act between the appetite-stimulating effects of the NPY neurons and the appetite-suppressing effects of the POMC neurons, spread across both the PVN and the LH. It seems that multiple parallel signaling systems influence this balance: for example, increased serotonergic activity within the PVN reverses the hunger-stimulating effects of ghrelin (Currie et al., 2010). The peptide **orexin** (from the Greek *oregein*, "to desire") (**FIGURE 13.24**), which is produced by neurons in the lateral hypothalamus, appears to participate in the subsequent control of feeding. Direct injection of orexin into the hypothalamus of rats causes up to a sixfold increase in feeding (Sakurai et al., 1998), and evidence is emerging that hypothalamic orexin is regulated to some extent by circulating leptin (Ohno and Sakurai, 2008). Orexins (which are also known as *hypocretins*) are also involved in the sleep disorder narcolepsy (see Chapter 14), but whether that function relates to hunger is unknown.

Other systems also play a role in hunger and satiety

Appetite signals from the hypothalamus converge on the nucleus of the solitary tract (NST) in the brainstem (see Figure 13.23B). The NST can be viewed as part of a common pathway for feeding behavior, and it receives and integrates appetite signals from a variety of sources in addition to the hypothalamus. For example, the sensation of hunger is affected by a wide variety of peripheral sensory inputs, such as oral stimulation and the feeling of stomach distension, transmitted via spinal and cranial nerves. Information about nutrient levels is conveyed directly from the body to the NST via the vagus nerve (Tordoff et al., 1991). For example, the peptide **cholecystokinin** (**CCK**),

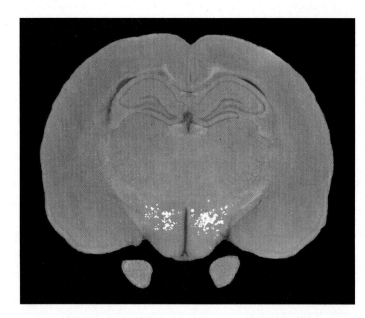

13.24 NEUROPEPTIDES THAT INDUCE HUNGER? In situ hybridization indicates that orexin mRNA (white spots) is made only in the lateral hypothalamus. Infusion of orexin (also known as *hypocretin*) into this region causes rats to eat more food. (Courtesy of Dr. Masashi Yanagisawa.)

released by the gut after feeding, acts directly on receptors of the vagus nerve to inhibit appetite (H. Fink et al., 1998).

In keeping with one of the central themes of this chapter—the concept of multiple redundancy in key systems—it will come as no surprise to you that a variety of other brain locations also participate in controlling feeding behavior, either directly or through indirect effects on related processes. For example, as you might expect, the brain's reward system appears to be intimately involved with food intake. Activity of a circuit including the amygdala and the mesolimbic dopamine-mediated reward system (see Chapter 4) is intimately coordinated with the activity of the lateral hypothalamus, and it is hypothesized to mediate pleasurable aspects of feeding (Stuber and Wise, 2016).

The **endocannabinoid** system likewise has a potent influence on appetite and feeding. Endocannabinoids, such as anandamide, are endogenous substances that act much like the active ingredient in marijuana (*Cannabis sativa*) and, like marijuana, can potently stimulate hunger. Acting both in the brain and in the periphery, endocannabinoids may stimulate feeding by affecting the mesolimbic dopamine reward system. However, injection of anandamide directly into the PVN stimulates eating (C. D. Chapman et al., 2012), confirming that endocannabinoids act directly on hypothalamic appetite mechanisms, while also inhibiting satiety signals from the gut (Di Marzo and Matias, 2005). Paradoxically, one of the actions of cannabinoids in the hypothalamus is a *stimulation* of POMC neurons, despite the fact that POMC neurons normally promote satiety. It appears that in this case, activation of cannabinoid receptors on POMC neurons selectively increases the release of β-endorphin from these neurons, which affects brain reward mechanisms, rather than the release of the α-MSH that would otherwise signal satiety in the hypothalamic circuit (Koch et al., 2015).

Hypothalamic feeding control must be strongly influenced by inputs from higher brain centers, but little is known about these mechanisms. During development, for example, our feeding patterns are increasingly influenced by social factors such as parental and peer group pressures (Birch et al., 2003). Understanding the nature of cortical influences on feeding mechanisms is a major challenge for the future. The list of participants in appetite regulation is long and growing longer each day (**TABLE 13.3**), revealing overlapping and complex controls with a high degree of redundancy, as befits a behavioral function of such critical importance to health and survival. With each new discovery, we draw nearer to finally developing safe and effective treatments for eating disorders, as we discuss next.

endocannabinoid An endogenous ligand of cannabinoid receptors; thus, an analog of marijuana that is produced by the brain.

TABLE 13.3 Hormones and Neurotransmitters Involved in Regulating Feeding and Body Weight

INCREASED FEEDING AND WEIGHT GAIN	DECREASED FEEDING AND WEIGHT LOSS
Agouti-related peptide (AgRP)	α-Melanocyte-stimulating hormone (α-MSH)
β-Endorphin	Brain-derived neurotrophic factor (BDNF)
Corticosterone/cortisol	Cholecystokinin (CCK)
Dopamine	Cocaine- and amphetamine-regulated transcript (CART)
Dynorphin	Corticotropin-releasing hormone (CRH)
Endocannabinoids	Estrogens
Ghrelin	Glucagon-like peptide-1 (GLP-1)
Melanin-concentrating hormone	Histamine
Neuropeptide Y	Insulin
Norepinephrine	Leptin
Orexin/hypocretin	Nesfatin-1
Testosterone	Oxyntomodulin
	PYY_{3-36}
	Serotonin

Note: Many of the members of this partial list are targets for anti-obesity drug development.

BOX 13.2 Body Fat Stores Are Tightly Regulated, Even after Surgical Removal of Fat

As any dieter will attest, the body seems to know how much it wants to weigh, and it defies our efforts to change that value. As in other mammals, our homeostatic mechanisms defend a set value for weight. Perhaps the most striking demonstration of this phenomenon is exhibited by golden-mantled ground squirrels, which show an extreme seasonal variation in body weight, greatly fattening up in the spring.

When these squirrels are brought into the laboratory, they continue to show an annual rhythm in body weight, even when food is always available (Figure A) (I. Zucker, 1988). Force-feeding the squirrels or depriving them of food will cause a temporary increase or decrease in body weight, but as soon as food access returns to normal, body weight returns to the value that is normal for the season.

Even more impressive is the fact that, if body fat is surgically removed, the animals will eat until they regain—with remarkable precision—the amount of fat that would be normal for that point in the season (Figure B) (Dark et al., 1984). Needless to say, these results are not encouraging to humans considering liposuction. Usually the fat simply returns a few months after the procedure (Seretis et al., 2015).

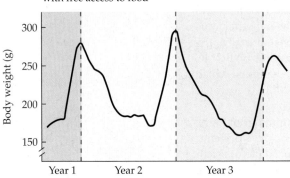

(A) Annual body weight cycles of three ground squirrels with free access to food

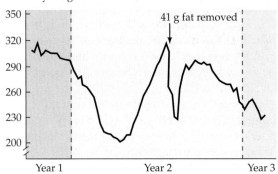

(B) Surgical fat removal has only a transient effect on body weight

41 g fat removed

Obesity Is Difficult to Treat

epigenetic transmission
The passage of epigenetic modifications of a gene from one generation to another.

Unfortunately, effective interventions for combating obesity have been elusive. Our multiple redundant systems for appetite and energy management work all too well in fighting against weight loss (**BOX 13.2**). Like it or not, our evolutionary history has optimized our bodies for obtaining and storing energy, and protecting against accumulating *too much* energy was not much of a concern for our distant ancestors.

The tendency to accumulate excess energy is exacerbated by our ever more sedentary lifestyles. Obesity is certainly a major health problem: almost 65% of the adults in the United States are overweight, and one in three qualify as obese. These categories are based on body mass index (BMI), which is defined in **TABLE 13.4**. The higher incidence of cardiovascular disease, diabetes, and other disorders that accompany obesity will be an increasingly heavy burden on health care services in the future. Parental obesity may program metabolic disadvantages in offspring via **epigenetic transmission** (Ng et al., 2010), so the problem may worsen in future generations.

In Lewis Carroll's *Alice's Adventures in Wonderland*, Alice quaffs the contents of a small bottle in order to shrink. The quest for a real-life shrinking potion—but one that makes you thin rather than short—is the subject of intense scientific activity, and several major strategies or targets are emerging.

TABLE 13.4 Body Mass Index (BMI)

BMI VALUE	BODY WEIGHT CATEGORY
<15	Starvation
15–18.5	Underweight
18.5–25	Ideal weight
25–30	Overweight
30–40	Obese
>40	Morbidly obese

Note:

$$BMI = \frac{weight\ (kg)}{height \times height\ (m \times m)}\ or$$

$$BMI = 703\frac{weight\ (lb)}{height \times height\ (in. \times in.)}$$

APPETITE CONTROL   Hopes are high that drugs designed to modify the functioning of the hypothalamic appetite system will be safe and potent obesity treatments. Unfortunately, alteration of leptin signals has not proven to be an effective strategy; only a tiny minority of obese people have abnormal leptin levels, and most have *higher* levels of circulating leptin than do thin people (Montague et al., 1997).

Interestingly, leptin appears to regulate endogenous cannabinoid levels in the hypothalamus (Di Marzo and Matias, 2005; Di Marzo et al., 2001). Therefore, drugs that are cannabinoid antagonists might effectively suppress appetite by causing "anti-munchies"—the reverse of the hunger experienced by marijuana users. As predicted, a drug that interferes with signaling via CB_1 cannabinoid receptors, rimonabant (classified as an *inverse agonist*; see Chapter 4), effectively reduces appetite and feeding behavior, leading to weight loss (Thornton-Jones et al., 2006; Van Gaal et al., 2005). Unfortunately, rimonabant also has a depressant effect (an "anti-high"?), so was removed from the market in Europe.

Drugs also can be designed to target some of the signaling systems integral to the arcuate appetite controller. For example, we saw earlier that α-MSH activity effectively reduces hunger, so drugs that activate the MC4R melanocortin receptor may be effective appetite suppressants. One such drug, lorcarserin, activates the serotonin 5-HT2C receptors found on many POMC neurons in the hypothalamic appetite controller; lorcarserin produces modest but significant weight loss and has been approved for use in humans since 2012 (Burke and Heisler, 2015). Similarly, treatment with PYY_{3-36} (via nasal spray), or a drug that mimics its actions, may act directly on arcuate neurons to reduce appetite (see Figure 13.23) (Batterham et al., 2003; Sileno et al., 2006). Simply spraying a PYY_{3-36} solution into the mouths of lab mice is apparently not aversive yet powerfully suppresses their appetite (Hurtado et al., 2013). Other newly discovered satiety signals, such as nesfatin-1, oxyntomodulin, and glucagon-like peptide-1, similarly provide excellent targets for drug development; numerous compounds targeting these systems are in clinical trials (Neary and Batterham, 2009).

INCREASED METABOLISM   An alternative approach to treating obesity is to raise the body's metabolic rate and thus expend extra calories in the form of heat. For example, the thyroid hormone thyroxine increases metabolic rate, so scientists are trying to devise drugs that mimic thyroxine's metabolic actions while avoiding its undesirable cardiovascular side effects (Grover et al., 2003). Another approach may be to increase the activity of brown fat, which is rich in special mitochondria containing a protein, called **thermogenin** (or *UCP1*), that allows mitochondria to turn energy directly into heat. Several signaling pathways can activate brown fat, suggesting new targets for drug development (Boström et al., 2012; Symonds et al., 2015). Furthermore, hormone or drug treatments, or even environmental manipulations such as cold exposure, may induce the formation of "beige" fat: fat cells that resemble (or even originate as) white fat but which express larger numbers of thermogenin-containing mitochondria (Berglund et al., 2014; Gnad et al., 2014). Because beige fat is found throughout the body, like white fat, it has the potential to burn excess stored energy at a high rate.

INHIBITION OF FAT TISSUE   A third approach to treating obesity involves interfering with the formation of new white fat tissue. For example, in order for fat tissue to grow, it needs to add new blood vessels—a process called *angiogenesis*—so blocking this process may inhibit fat formation (Rupnick et al., 2002). Blockade of one type of receptor for vascular endothelial growth factor (VEGF)—a signaling protein that normally stimulates angiogenesis—effectively inhibits the growth of fat tissue in mice (Tam et al., 2009). Other modifications of the vasculature in fat tissue, in concert with the delivery of brown fat tissue markers, provide an additional way to induce white fat cells to transform into beige or brown fat (Xue et al., 2016).

REDUCED ABSORPTION   One of only a few currently approved obesity medications, orlistat (Xenical) works by interfering with the digestion of fat. However, this approach has generally produced only modest weight loss, and it often causes intestinal discomfort.

REDUCED REWARD   A different perspective on treating obesity focuses on the rewarding properties of food. Not only is food delicious, but "comfort foods" also directly reduce circulating stress hormones, thereby providing another reward. Chronic food restriction makes rewarding brain stimulations even more rewarding than usual, and this effect is reversed by treatment with leptin (Fulton et al., 2000). Drugs that affect the brain's reward circuitry (see Chapter 4), reducing the rewarding properties of food, may prove beneficial for weight loss (Volkow and Wise, 2005). However, although obesity

thermogenin   Also called *UCP1*. A specialized protein that allows mitochondria to turn energy directly into heat.

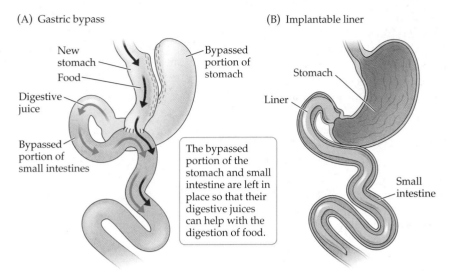

(A) Gastric bypass

New stomach
Food
Digestive juice
Bypassed portion of small intestines

Bypassed portion of stomach

The bypassed portion of the stomach and small intestine are left in place so that their digestive juices can help with the digestion of food.

(B) Implantable liner

Stomach
Liner
Small intestine

13.25 SURGICAL OPTIONS FOR OBESITY (A) In gastric bypass (also called *Roux-en-Y bypass*), the stomach is surgically reduced to a small pouch and connected to the small intestine at some distance, thereby bypassing the initial stretch of small intestine. This reduces the ability of the digestive system to absorb nutrients from food. (B) A less invasive option is the implantation of a plastic liner into the small intestine. It acts as a barrier to prevent the absorption of food, so fewer calories are absorbed from the diet. Both bypass and implantation result in weight loss and improvements in secondary problems like diabetes.

resembles drug addiction in certain ways, it also differs enough that the food addiction model has been called into question (Ziauddeen et al., 2012).

ANTI-OBESITY SURGERY The surgical removal of fat tissue, particularly through liposuction, is a popular approach to controlling weight, but it is generally only moderately successful and temporary (see Box 13.2). Because of the propensity of fat tissue to regrow after excision, people increasingly are turning to **bariatric** procedures that reduce the volume and absorptive capacity of the digestive system (**FIGURE 13.25**). Although gastric bypass surgery doesn't directly target appetite control mechanisms, alterations in appetite hormones such as ghrelin reportedly accompany the surgery (Baynes et al., 2006; D. E. Cummings, 2006). As the only current intervention that produces significant and lasting weight loss, gastric bypass surgery can offer hope of substantial weight loss and reversal of comorbid conditions like type II diabetes and hypertension, but it is accompanied by significant complications and risks.

Less-invasive surgical procedures are under study, such as the use of gastric stimulators that activate the gut's satiety signals to reduce appetite (Miras et al., 2015). Curiously, simply implanting inert weights into the abdominal cavities of mice causes them to lose a proportionate amount of weight, apparently by fooling the body into thinking it is heavier than it actually is (Adams et al., 2003). Perhaps some of us, someday, will be able to lose weight simply by taking on extra ballast!

Eating Disorders Are Life-Threatening

Sometimes people shun food, despite having no apparent aversion to it. These people are usually young, become obsessed with their body weight, and become extremely thin—generally by eating very little and sometimes also by vomiting, taking laxatives, overexercising, or drinking large amounts of water to suppress appetite. This condition, which is more common in adolescent girls and women than in males, is called **anorexia nervosa**. The name of the disorder indicates (1) that the patients have no appetite (*anorexia*) and (2) that the disorder originates in the nervous system (*nervosa*).

People who suffer from anorexia nervosa tend to think about food a good deal, and physiological evidence suggests that they respond even *more* than healthy people to the presentation of food (Broberg and Bernstein, 1989); for example, food stimuli provoke a large release of insulin, despite cognitive denial of any feelings of hunger. So, in a physiological sense their hunger may be normal or even exaggerated, but this hunger is somehow absent from the conscious perceptions of these individuals and they refuse to eat. The idea that anorexia nervosa is primarily a nervous system disorder stems from this mismatch between physiology and cognition and from the distorted body image of the patients (they may consider themselves fat when others see them as emaciated). The observation that agouti-related peptide (AgRP) levels are abnormal in women with anorexia nervosa (Moriya et al., 2006) suggests that the hypothalamic appetite system described earlier may be abnormal in this condition. Studies of the incidence of eating disorders in twins indicate that a predisposition toward anorexia is heritable (Klump et al., 2001), and leading candidates for underlying physiological causes include abnormalities in serotonergic neurotransmission and alterations in the functioning of the dopamine-based reward system (see Chapter 4) that persist even after recovery (Kaye et al., 2009).

bariatric Having to do with treatment of obesity.

anorexia nervosa A syndrome in which individuals severely deprive themselves of food.

Anorexia nervosa is notoriously difficult to treat, because it appears to involve an unfortunate combination of genetic, endocrine, personality, cognitive, and environmental variables. One approach that is successful in some cases is a family-based treatment (sometimes termed *Maudsley therapy* after the hospital where it was introduced) that de-emphasizes the identification of causal factors and instead focuses on intensive, parent-led "refeeding" of the anorexic person (Le Grange, 2005).

Bulimia (or *bulimia nervosa*, from the Greek *boulimia*, "great hunger") is a related disorder. Like those who suffer from anorexia nervosa, people with bulimia may believe themselves fatter than they are, but they periodically gorge themselves, usually with "junk food," and then either vomit the food or take laxatives to avoid weight gain. Also like sufferers of anorexia nervosa, people with bulimia may be obsessed with food and body weight, but not all of them become emaciated. Both anorexia nervosa and bulimia can be fatal because the patient's lack of nutrient reserves damages various organ systems and/or leaves the body unable to battle otherwise mild diseases.

In **binge eating**, people spontaneously gorge themselves with far more food than is required to satisfy hunger, often to the point of illness. Such people are often obese, and the causes of the bingeing are not fully understood. In susceptible people, the strong pleasure associated with food activates opiate and dopaminergic reward mechanisms to such an extent that bingeing resembles drug addiction. Indeed, "binge eating disorder" is now recognized as a psychiatric diagnosis in the *Diagnostic and Statistical Manual of Mental Disorders*, 5th edition, or *DSM-5* (American Psychiatric Association, 2013). Mutation of the gene encoding the MC4R receptor is also associated with binge eating (Branson et al., 2003). Recall that α-MSH acts on MC4R to signal satiety, so people with the mutation may be failing to receive the signal to stop eating.

Despite the epidemic of obesity in our society, or perhaps because of it, our present culture emphasizes that women, especially young women, must be thin to be attractive (**FIGURE 13.26A**). This cultural pressure is widely perceived as one of the causes of eating disorders. In earlier times, however, when plump women were considered the most beautiful (witness Renaissance paintings, such as the one shown in **FIGURE 13.26B**), some women still fasted severely and may have suffered from anorexia nervosa. The origins of these disorders remain elusive, and to date, the available therapies help only a minority of patients.

13.26 CHANGING IDEALS OF FEMALE BEAUTY (A) Actress Angelina Jolie exemplifies modern society's emphasis on thinness as an aspect of beauty. (B) In contrast, Flemish painter Peter Paul Rubens's painting of his wife in *Helena Fourment as Aphrodite* (circa 1630) illustrates the very different ideal for the feminine form during her era. Could pressures around modern weight-conscious notions of female beauty be responsible for some cases of anorexia nervosa and bulimia?

▌ The Cutting Edge

Friends with Benefits

The last decade has seen rapid progress in understanding how various signals from the gut are integrated in the hypothalamus to control appetite and energy balance, as we have explored in this chapter. But recent research is finding that the contents of the gut may play a role as well.

Most people know that the gut is normally inhabited by helpful bacteria, but the extent of that occupation may surprise you. You probably contain in the range of 2.5–5 *pounds* of gut microbes: *trillions* of individual bacteria belonging to dozens (perhaps hundreds) of different species, making up more than half the contents of your large intestine (Guarner and Malagelada, 2003). Put another way, you have more gut microbes than body cells, and they weigh more than your brain. This huge population, known as the **gut microbiota** or, collectively, as the **microbiome**, normally provides a variety of beneficial actions in return for their comfortable lodgings (the gut microbiota are sometimes referred to as *normal flora* in medicine, but this is a misnomer because *flora* refers to plants). Considering new discoveries about the metabolic and signaling activity of the microbiome, some researchers feel that we should start treating it as a "virtual organ"—participating in bidirectional signaling with the brain (Grenham et al., 2011).

bulimia Also called *bulimia nervosa*. A syndrome in which individuals periodically gorge themselves, usually with "junk food," and then either vomit or take laxatives to avoid weight gain.

binge eating The paroxysmal intake of large quantities of food, often of poor nutritional value and high in calories.

gut microbiota Also called *normal flora*. The microorganisms that normally inhabit the digestive tract.

microbiome The collective term for the population of microbes found in the gut.

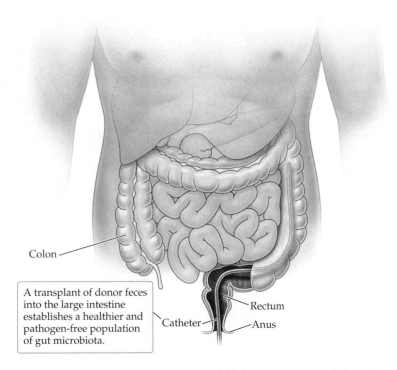

Colon

A transplant of donor feces into the large intestine establishes a healthier and pathogen-free population of gut microbiota.

Rectum

Catheter

Anus

13.27 FECAL TRANSPLANTATION Initial results suggest that replacing abnormal gut microbiota with a sample from a healthy donor may aid in diverse problems, including severe infection, Parkinson's disease, and obesity.

enterotype Each individual's personal composition of gut microbiota.

fecal transplantation A medical procedure in which gut microbiota, via fecal matter, are transferred from a donor to a host.

Each of us possesses a distinct microbial **enterotype**—a personal combination of different species of microbiota. Your enterotype reflects your dietary history: changes in your diet—changing the balance of plant and animal sources, for example, or of fiber, fat, and carbohydrates—potently alter the composition of the enterotype (David et al., 2014; G. D. Wu et al., 2011), with uncertain long-term consequences. Preliminary evidence has linked the microbiome enterotype to such diverse functions as mood, anxiety, cognitive functions, and various disease processes (Cryan and Dinan, 2012; Kelly et al., 2016). Infections in the gut may drastically affect the balance of microbiota, but antibiotic treatments can be harmful too. Changes in the gut microbiota due to antibiotic treatments (such as for *Helicobacter pylori*, a gut bacterium that causes ulcers if too abundant) may be associated with Parkinson's disease (Nielsen et al., 2012), for example. But one of the areas where an effect of changes in the gut microbiota is most evident is obesity.

Feeding antibiotics to young mice, even at relatively low doses, changes gut microbiota and circulating hormones, leading to weight gain (I. Cho et al., 2012). Similarly, two studies looking at almost 40,000 babies have found that human infants given antibiotics in their first 6 months were statistically more likely to be overweight at age 7 (Ajslev et al., 2011; Trasande et al, 2013). It remains to be seen how much adult obesity is accounted for by long-lasting changes to our enterotypes, but it is at least possible that early exposure to antibiotics, and even chlorinated drinking water (after all, chlorine is added to swimming pools to kill bacteria), is making some of us fat. What can we do about it?

One promising avenue for rebalancing the gut microbiota involves a gross-sounding procedure: **fecal transplantation**. Yes, it is just what it sounds like: feces are collected from carefully screened, uh, "donors," processed to create a liquid suspension, and then passed through a catheter into the colon of the recipient (**FIGURE 13.27**), where the donor's healthy enterotype establishes itself. Just one transplant can cure dangerous intestinal infections with bacteria such as *Clostridium difficile*, but intriguingly, fecal transplantation also effectively reversed insulin insensitivity (the hallmark of type II diabetes) in an initial study of obese men (Vrieze et al., 2012). Although research on the topic is just beginning, perhaps manipulation of the gut microbiota will present a treatment for weight loss in humans, as has been seen in mice. The procedure is promising enough that some enterprising scientists have created optimized (and perhaps less nasty) synthetic feces for transplantation (Petrof et al., 2013), showing that in this field, some researchers just make crap up.

Go to
bn8e.com
for study questions, quizzes, activities, and other resources

Recommended Reading

DeSalle, R., and Perkins, S. L. (2015). *Welcome to the Microbiome: Getting to Know the Trillions of Bacteria and Other Microbes In, On, and Around You.* New Haven, CT: Yale University Press.

Flouris, A. (2009). *On the Functional Architecture of the Human Thermoregulatory System: A Guide to the Biological Principles and Mechanisms of Human Thermoregulation.* Berlin: VDM.

Jessen, C. (2001). *Temperature Regulation in Humans and Other Mammals.* Berlin: Telos.

Kirkham, T., and Cooper, S. J. (Eds.). (2006). *Appetite and Body Weight: Integrative Systems and the Development of Anti-Obesity Drugs.* Burlington, MA: Academic Press.

Logue, A. W. (2014). *The Psychology of Eating and Drinking* (4th ed.). New York: Routledge.

McNab, B. K. (2012). *Extreme Measures: The Ecological Energetics of Birds and Mammals.* Chicago: University of Chicago Press.

Schulkin, J. (Ed.). (2012). *Allostasis, Homeostasis, and the Costs of Physiological Adaptation.* Cambridge, England: Cambridge University Press.

Thompson, J. K. (2003). *Handbook of Eating Disorders and Obesity.* New York: Wiley.

VISUAL SUMMARY

You should be able to relate each summary to the adjacent illustration, including structures and processes.
Go to **bn8e.com/vs13** for links to figures, animations, and activities that will help you consolidate the material.

1 The nervous system plays a crucial role in maintaining the **homeostasis** that the body requires for proper functioning. Temperature, fluid concentration, chemical energy, and nutrients must all be maintained within a critical range. These systems often feature **negative feedback** control and redundancy. Review **Figure 13.1**, **Animation 13.2**

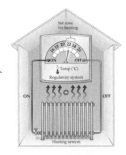

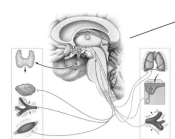

2 Both **endotherms** and **ectotherms** regulate body temperature, but ectotherms depend more on behaviors to capture heat from the environment, while endotherms generate most of their body heat through the metabolism of food. Review **Figure 13.3**, **Animation 13.3**

3 The preoptic area of the hypothalamus, the brainstem, and the spinal cord monitor and help regulate body temperature. Review **Figure 13.4**

4 Both endotherms and ectotherms use behavioral methods to help regulate body temperature at optimal levels. Young animals particularly depend on this form of **thermoregulation**. Review **Figure 13.5, Box 13.1**

5 Our cells function properly only when the concentration of salts and other solutes (the **osmolality**) of the **intracellular compartment** of the body is within a critical range. The **extracellular compartment** is a source of replacement water and a buffer between the intracellular compartment and the outside world. Review **Figure 13.8**

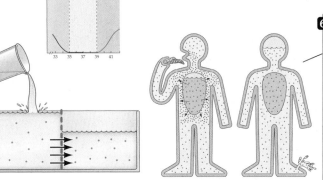

6 Thirst can be triggered either by an increase in the osmolality of the extracellular compartment (**osmotic thirst**) or by a drop in the volume of the extracellular compartment (**hypovolemic thirst**). Because of the importance of osmolality, we must regulate salt intake in order to regulate water balance effectively. Review **Figure 13.9**

7 A drop in blood volume triggers at least three responses: (1) **Baroreceptors** in the major blood vessels signal the brain via the autonomic nervous system. (2) **Vasopressin** from the posterior pituitary reduces blood vessel volume and urination. (3) The kidneys release renin, providing circulating **angiotensin II**, which narrows blood vessels to maintain blood pressure and provides a thirst signal to the brain. Review **Figures 13.11 and 13.12**

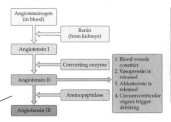

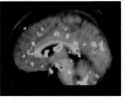

8 The hypothalamus contains **osmosensory neurons** that detect the concentration of extracellular fluid. Increased solute concentration of the extracellular fluid triggers an intake of water. The conscious perception of thirst involves activation of a network of limbic system sites and is a powerful motivator. Review **Figures 13.13 and 13.14**

9 Body weight is actively regulated by multiple redundant systems, making it hard to lose weight by dieting. Review **Figures 13.16 and 13.17**

10 Although brain cells can use **glucose** directly, body cells can import glucose only with the assistance of **insulin** secreted by the pancreas. Insulin also promotes the storage of glucose as **glycogen** and provides a signal to the brain regarding current glucose levels. Another pancreatic hormone, **glucagon**, helps convert glycogen back into glucose. Review **Figure 13.19**

(continued)

11 Lesion studies showed that the hypothalamus plays a special role in appetite regulation. Damage to the **ventromedial hypothalamus** caused animals to become obese, while lesions aimed at the **lateral hypothalamus** caused animals to stop eating and lose weight. Review **Figure 13.20**

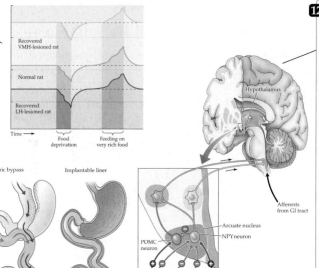

13 Obesity is a pervasive problem that is difficult to treat through diet, drugs, or surgery. The most effective long-lasting medical intervention for obesity is **bariatric** surgery, but several drug strategies based on a new understanding of appetite control offer promise. Review **Figure 13.25**

12 An appetite controller located in the **arcuate nucleus** of the hypothalamus responds to levels of several peptide gut hormones. **Leptin**, providing a chronic signal about fat levels, stimulates arcuate **POMC neurons** to release α-MSH in the **paraventricular nucleus** to activate **MC4Rs** to decrease appetite. Leptin inhibits arcuate **NPY neurons**, decreasing their release of **NPY** and AgRP to suppress appetite further. **Ghrelin** and **PYY**$_{3-36}$ provide more-acute signals from the gut. Ghrelin stimulates and PYY$_{3-36}$ inhibits the arcuate appetite control system. Review **Figure 13.23**

Biological Rhythms, Sleep, and Dreaming

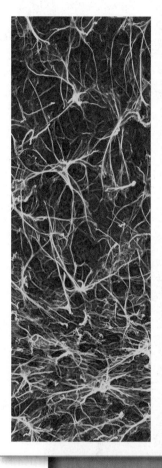

14

■ When Sleep Gets Out of Control

Starting college always brings its share of new experiences and adjustments, but "Barry" knew something was wrong freshman year when he seemed to be sleepy all the time (S. Smith, 1997). Barry napped so often that his friends called him the hibernating bear. Of course, college can be exhausting, and many students seek refuge in long snooze sessions. But one day while Barry was camping with his pals, an even odder thing happened: "I laughed really hard, and I kind of fell on my knees.... After that, about every week I'd have two or three episodes where if I'd laugh… my arm would fall down or my muscles in my face would get weak. Or if I was running around playing catch and someone said something, I would get weak in the knees. And there was a time there that my friends kinda used it as a joke. If they're going to throw me the ball and they didn't want me to catch it, they'd tell me a joke and I'd fall down and miss it."

It was as if any big surge in emotion in Barry might trigger a sudden paralysis lasting anywhere from a few seconds to a few minutes, affecting either a body part or his whole body. Sex became something of a challenge because sometimes during foreplay, Barry's body would just collapse. "Luckily, you're probably laying down, so it's not that big a deal. But it just puts a damper on the whole thing."

What was happening to Barry?

All living systems show repeating, predictable changes over time. These rhythms vary from rapid (e.g., brain potentials) to slow (e.g., annual changes like hibernation). Daily rhythms, the first topic of this chapter, have an intriguing clocklike regularity. The second topic of the chapter is that familiar daily rhythm known as the sleep-waking cycle. By age 60, most humans have spent 20 years asleep (some, alas, on one side or the other of the classroom podium). We'll find that sleep is not a passive state of "nonwaking," but rather the interlocking of several different states orchestrated by the activity of many brain regions.

Biological Rhythms

Biological rhythms range in length from minutes to seconds, and some extend from months to years. We discuss daily rhythms first because they have been studied the most.

Many Animals Show Daily Rhythms in Activity

Most functions of any living system display a rhythm of approximately 24 hours. Because these rhythms last about a day, they are called **circadian rhythms** (from the Latin *circa*, "about," and *dies*, "day"). Circadian rhythms have been studied in a host of creatures at behavioral, physiological, and biochemical levels.

Go to Brain Explorer
bn8e.com/14.1

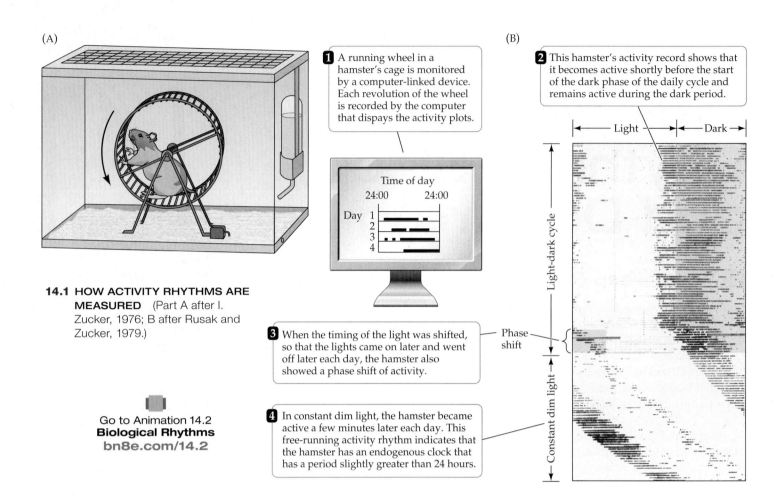

(A)

1 A running wheel in a hamster's cage is monitored by a computer-linked device. Each revolution of the wheel is recorded by the computer that dispays the activity plots.

Time of day

24:00   24:00

Day 1
2
3
4

14.1 HOW ACTIVITY RHYTHMS ARE MEASURED (Part A after I. Zucker, 1976; B after Rusak and Zucker, 1979.)

Go to Animation 14.2
Biological Rhythms
bn8e.com/14.2

3 When the timing of the light was shifted, so that the lights came on later and went off later each day, the hamster also showed a phase shift of activity.

4 In constant dim light, the hamster became active a few minutes later each day. This free-running activity rhythm indicates that the hamster has an endogenous clock that has a period slightly greater than 24 hours.

(B)

2 This hamster's activity record shows that it becomes active shortly before the start of the dark phase of the daily cycle and remains active during the dark period.

← Light → ← Dark →

Light-dark cycle

Phase shift

Constant dim light

Humans and most other primates are **diurnal**—active during the day. Most rodents, including hamsters, are **nocturnal**—active during dark periods. In either case, almost all physiological measures—hormone levels, body temperature, drug sensitivity—change in a regular repeating fashion over the course of the day. A convenient way to study circadian rhythms exploits rodents' love of running wheels. A switch attached to the wheel registers each revolution, revealing an activity rhythm, as in **FIGURE 14.1A**.

These circadian activities show extraordinary precision: the beginning of activity may vary only a few minutes from one day to another. For humans using watches and clocks, this regularity may seem uninteresting, but other animals display such regularity by attending to a *biological clock*.

Circadian rhythms are generated by an endogenous clock

A hamster placed in a dimly lit room continues to show a daily rhythm in wheel running despite the absence of day versus night, suggesting that the animal has an internal clock. But even if the light is always dim, the animal may detect other external cues (e.g., outside noises, temperature, barometric pressure) that signal the time of day. Arguing for an internal clock, however, is the fact that in constant light or dark the circadian cycle is not *exactly* 24 hours: activity starts a few minutes later each day, so eventually the hamster is active while it is daytime outside (**FIGURE 14.1B**, bottom). The animal is said to be **free-running**, maintaining its own cycle, which, in the absence of external cues, is not exactly 24 hours long.

The free-running period is the animal's natural rhythm. A **period** is the time between two similar points of successive cycles, such as sunset to sunset. Because the free-running period does not *quite* match the period of Earth's rotation, and because it differs slightly among individual hamsters in the same room, the free-running

circadian rhythm A pattern of behavioral, biochemical, or physiological fluctuation that has a 24-hour period.

diurnal Active during the light periods of the daily cycle.

nocturnal Active during the dark periods of the daily cycle.

free-running Referring to a rhythm of behavior shown by an animal deprived of external cues about time of day.

period The interval of time between two similar points of successive cycles, such as sunset to sunset.

period cannot simply be reflecting an external cue. So the animal has some sort of endogenous clock, and this clock runs a bit slow in hamsters (and in humans, but not all species).

Normally the internal clock is set by light. If we expose a free-running hamster to periods of light and dark, it soon does most of its wheel running in the dark period. The shift of activity produced by a synchronizing stimulus is referred to as a **phase shift** (see Figure 14.1B, middle), and the process of shifting the rhythm is called **entrainment**. Any cue that an animal uses to synchronize its activity with the environment is called a **zeitgeber** (German for "time giver"). Light acts as a powerful zeitgeber, and we can easily manipulate it in the laboratory. Because light stimuli can entrain circadian rhythms, the endogenous clock must have inputs from the visual system, as we'll confirm shortly. We humans experience phase shifts when we fly from one time zone to another. Flying three time zones east (say, from California to New York) means that sunlight awakens us 3 hours sooner than the brain expects. In addition to light, the availability of food can serve as a cue to entrain the circadian clock (Fuller et al., 2008; Mistlberger and Skene, 2004).

Circadian rhythms allow animals to anticipate changes in the environment

The major value of circadian rhythms is that they synchronize behavior and body states to changes in the environment. Day and night have great significance for survival. The endogenous clock enables animals to *anticipate* an event, such as darkness, and to begin physiological and behavioral preparations before that event (in this case, *before* it gets dark—see Figure 14.1B). A snack in the den at the end of the day may prepare the animal for a long night of foraging. In other words, circadian rhythms provide the temporal organization of an animal's behavior.

The Hypothalamus Houses a Circadian Clock

Where is the endogenous clock that drives circadian rhythms, and how does it work? Early work showed that while removing various endocrine glands has little effect on the free-running rhythm of rats, experimental lesions of the hypothalamus interfere with circadian rhythms (Richter, 1967). It was subsequently discovered that a tiny subregion of the hypothalamus—the **suprachiasmatic nucleus (SCN)**, named for its location above the optic chiasm—serves as the biological clock. Lesions confined to the SCN portion of the hypothalamus interfere with circadian rhythms of drinking and locomotor behavior (**FIGURE 14.2**) (F. K. Stephan and Zucker, 1972) and hormone secretion (R. Y. Moore and Eichler, 1972). So, is the SCN just one part of some neural system that generates a circadian rhythm, or is the rhythm generated within the SCN itself?

Transplants prove that the SCN produces a circadian rhythm

Ralph and Menaker (1988) found a male hamster that exhibited an unusually short free-running activity rhythm in constant conditions. Normally, hamsters free-run at a period slightly longer than 24 hours, but this male showed a period of 22 hours. Half of the offspring of this male also had a shorter circadian rhythm, so the researchers concluded that he had a genetic mutation

phase shift A shift in the activity of a biological rhythm, typically provided by a synchronizing environmental stimulus.

entrainment The process of synchronizing a biological rhythm to an environmental stimulus.

zeitgeber Literally "time giver" (in German). The stimulus (usually the light-dark cycle) that entrains circadian rhythms.

suprachiasmatic nucleus (SCN) A small region of the hypothalamus above the optic chiasm that is the location of a circadian oscillator.

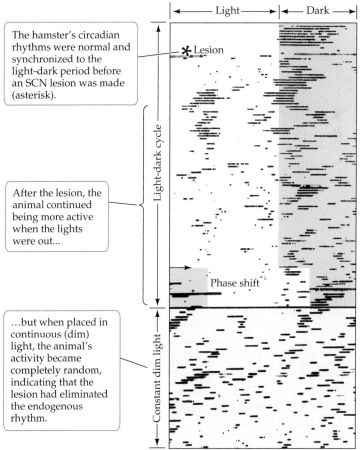

The hamster's circadian rhythms were normal and synchronized to the light-dark period before an SCN lesion was made (asterisk).

After the lesion, the animal continued being more active when the lights were out...

...but when placed in continuous (dim) light, the animal's activity became completely random, indicating that the lesion had eliminated the endogenous rhythm.

14.2 THE EFFECTS OF LESIONS IN THE SCN (From I. Zucker, 1976; based on Rusak and Zucker, 1979.)

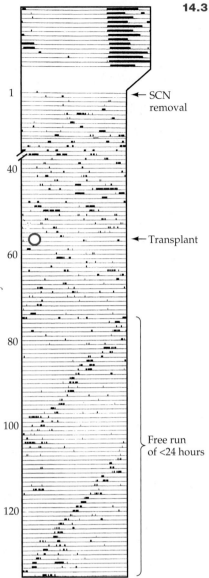

14.3 BRAIN TRANSPLANTS PROVE THAT THE SCN CONTAINS A CLOCK
A wild-type hamster, when kept in constant dim light, displayed an endogenous circadian rhythm 24.05 hours in duration (top). After the SCN was lesioned, the animal became arrhythmic. Later, an SCN from a fetal hamster with two copies of the *tau* mutation was transplanted into the lesioned adult hamster (circle). Soon thereafter, the adult hamster began showing a free-running activity rhythm of 19.5 hours, matching the SCN of the donor animal. This response to the transplant showed that the period of the clock is determined within the SCN. (From Ralph et al., 1990.)

affecting the endogenous clock. Animals with two copies of this mutation had an even shorter period: 20 hours. The mutation was named *tau*, after the Greek symbol used by scientists to represent the period of a rhythm. These animals entrained to a normal 24-hour light-dark period just fine; their abnormal endogenous circadian rhythm was revealed only in constant conditions.

Dramatic evidence that this endogenous period is produced within the SCN was provided by transplant experiments. Nonmutant hamsters with lesions of the SCN were placed in constant conditions, and as expected, their circadian activity rhythms were abolished (**FIGURE 14.3**) (Ralph et al., 1990). The hamsters then received transplants of SCN taken from fetal hamsters with two copies of the mutant *tau* gene. About a week later the hamsters that had received the transplants began showing a free-running activity rhythm again, but the new rhythm matched that of the *donor* SCN: it was about 20 hours rather than the original 24.05.

Reciprocal transplants gave comparable results: the endogenous rhythm following the transplant was always that of the *donor* SCN, not the recipient, so the SCN must be the source of an endogenous circadian rhythm. This is the only known type of transplant of brain tissue from one individual to another in which the recipient displays the donor's behavior!

Intriguingly, transplants of fetal SCNs can drive circadian rhythms in SCN-lesioned hamsters even if the donor cells are encapsulated in polymer (Silver et al., 1996). In such a capsule, the donor SCN is unable to make any synaptic connections with the surrounding hypothalamus, so its only means of communicating is by releasing chemical signals. These signals must act rather locally, because the capsule only works if placed near the normal site of the SCN. Despite the relatively small size of the SCN, it contains several anatomically distinct subregions that make different contributions to the circadian system (Antle and Silver, 2005). Now let's take up the question of how the SCN is informed about day and night.

In mammals, light information from the eyes reaches the SCN directly

The pathway that entrains circadian rhythms to light-dark cycles varies depending on the species (Rusak and Zucker, 1979). Many vertebrates have photoreceptors outside the eye that are part of the mechanism of light entrainment. For example, the **pineal gland** of some amphibians is itself sensitive to light (Jamieson and Roberts, 2000) and helps entrain circadian rhythms to light. Because the skull over the pineal is especially thin in some amphibian species, we can think of them as having a primitive "third eye" in the back of the head (some elementary school teachers also seem to have an eye in the back of the head, but this has not been proven to be the pineal gland). In birds, too, the pineal possesses photoreceptors that can detect daylight through the skull. In mammals, however, cells in the *eye* tell the SCN when it is light out.

Certain retinal ganglion cells send their axons along the **retinohypothalamic pathway**, splitting off at the optic chiasm to synapse directly within the SCN (**FIGURE 14.4**). This tiny pathway carries information about light to the hypothalamus to entrain behavior (R. Y. Moore, 1983). Most of the retinal ganglion cells that extend their axons to the SCN do not rely on the traditional photoreceptors—rods and cones—to learn about light. Rather, these retinal ganglion cells themselves contain a special photopigment, called **melanopsin**, that makes them sensitive to light (Do et al., 2009). Even transgenic mice that lack rods and cones, and thus are blind

pineal gland A secretory gland in the brain midline; the source of melatonin release.

retinohypothalamic pathway The projection of retinal ganglion cells to the suprachiasmatic nuclei.

melanopsin A photopigment found within particular retinal ganglion cells that project to the suprachiasmatic nucleus.

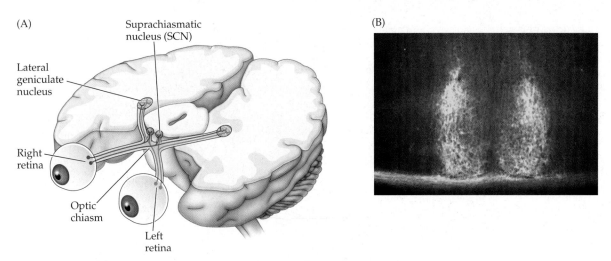

(A) Suprachiasmatic nucleus (SCN)

Lateral geniculate nucleus

Right retina

Optic chiasm

Left retina

(B)

14.4 THE RETINOHYPOTHALAMIC PATHWAY IN MAMMALS (A) This pathway carries information about the light-dark cycle in the environment to the SCN. For clarity of synaptic connections, the SCNs are shown proportionally larger than other features. (B) In this image, axons are shown at the bottom. Those from the left eye are shown in green, and those from the right in red. Both eyes project so diffusely to the two overlying SCNs that they appear to be outlined in yellow. (Photograph courtesy of Dr. Andrew D. Huberman.)

in almost every respect, still entrain their behavior to light (Freedman et al., 1999) because their intrinsically photosensitive retinal ganglion cells still function. These ganglion cells send their axons to the SCN, but other melanopsin-containing retinal ganglion cells project to the brainstem, informing the brain about light to control pupil diameter (S. K. Chen et al., 2011). Melanopsin is most sensitive to light frequencies in the blue range, which explains why blue light has the largest effect on human circadian systems (Gooley et al., 2010).

FIGURE 14.5 provides a schematic outline of the mammalian circadian system, including entrainment by light.

Circadian rhythms have been genetically dissected in flies and mice

The fruit fly *Drosophila melanogaster* displays diurnal circadian rhythms in activity. Flies with a mutation that disabled the gene called *period* (*per*) were arrhythmic when transferred to constant dim light, indicating that their internal clocks weren't running. Subtle mutations of *per* could, depending on the exact change in the gene, cause the animals to have a free-running period that was longer or shorter than

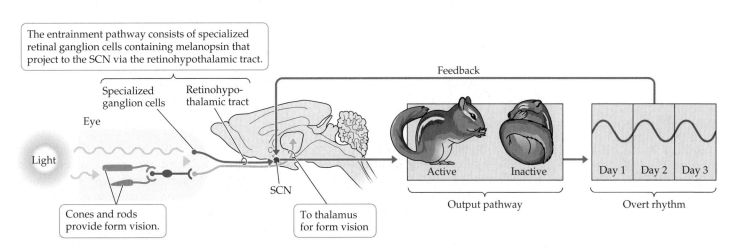

The entrainment pathway consists of specialized retinal ganglion cells containing melanopsin that project to the SCN via the retinohypothalamic tract.

Feedback

Specialized ganglion cells

Retinohypothalamic tract

Eye

Light

Cones and rods provide form vision.

SCN

To thalamus for form vision

Active Inactive

Output pathway

Day 1 Day 2 Day 3

Overt rhythm

14.5 COMPONENTS OF A CIRCADIAN SYSTEM

14.6 A MOLECULAR CLOCK IN FLIES AND MICE In flies, light passing through the head degrades Cry protein to help entrain the animal to the day. In mammals, information about light reaches the SCN via the eyes. This is a simplified view of the clock in mammals, which have several *per* and *cry* genes. The mammalian version of Cycle is called Bmal1.

Go to Animation 14.3
A Molecular Clock
bn8e.com/14.3

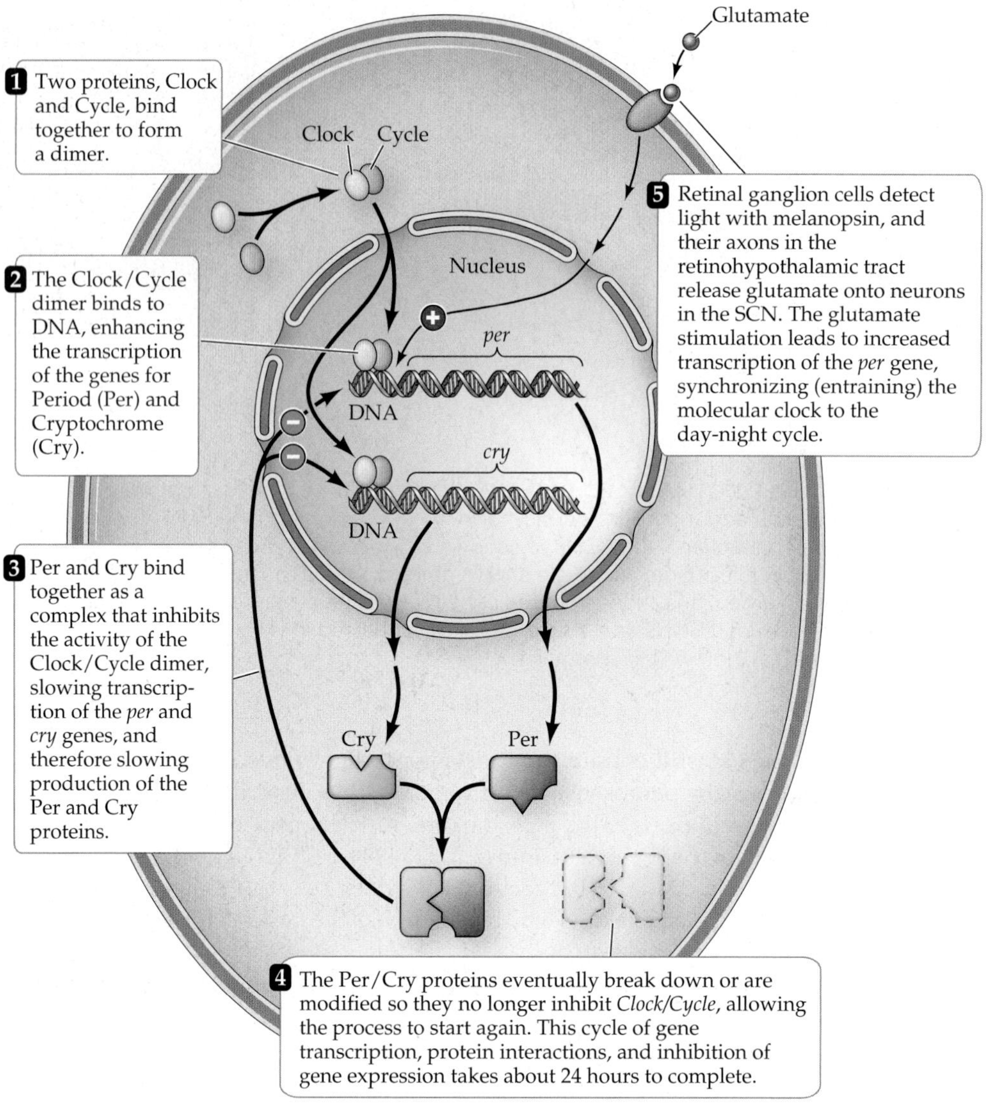

1 Two proteins, Clock and Cycle, bind together to form a dimer.

2 The Clock/Cycle dimer binds to DNA, enhancing the transcription of the genes for Period (Per) and Cryptochrome (Cry).

3 Per and Cry bind together as a complex that inhibits the activity of the Clock/Cycle dimer, slowing transcription of the *per* and *cry* genes, and therefore slowing production of the Per and Cry proteins.

5 Retinal ganglion cells detect light with melanopsin, and their axons in the retinohypothalamic tract release glutamate onto neurons in the SCN. The glutamate stimulation leads to increased transcription of the *per* gene, synchronizing (entraining) the molecular clock to the day-night cycle.

4 The Per/Cry proteins eventually break down or are modified so they no longer inhibit *Clock/Cycle*, allowing the process to start again. This cycle of gene transcription, protein interactions, and inhibition of gene expression takes about 24 hours to complete.

normal (R. J. Konopka and Benzer, 1971). Eventually, more genes were discovered that affect the circadian cycle in *Drosophila*, and mammals were found to have one or more versions of each of them.

These genes provide a *molecular clock*, regulating each other's expression such that their protein products wax and wane in a cycle that takes about 24 hours. Cells in the SCN make the two proteins Clock and Cycle (actually, it is called Cycle in *Drosophila* and Bmal1 in mammals). These two proteins bind together to form a **dimer** (a pair of molecules joined together). This dimer binds to the cell's DNA to promote the transcription of two other genes (*per* and *cryptochrome* [*cry*]). The resulting Per and Cry proteins then dimerize, and now they inhibit expression of the *Clock/Cycle* genes that began the whole process.

Because the Per/Cry proteins either degrade or become chemically modified (Larrondo et al., 2015) with time, eventually the inhibition is lifted, starting the whole cycle over again (**FIGURE 14.6**). The entire cycle takes about 24 hours to complete, and it is this 24-hour molecular cycle that drives the 24-hour activity cycle of SCN cells. Each SCN neuron uses this mechanism to keep time approximately, and then all the neurons communicate with each other through electrical synapses (see Chapter 3). They synchronize their activity to produce a very consistent period of about 24 hours (M. A. Long et al., 2005), which then drives circadian processes throughout the body (Jones et al., 2015). Interestingly, the same molecular clock operates in almost ev-

dimer A complex of two proteins that have bound together.

ery cell in the body, and they are all in sync as long as the SCN is intact. One possibility is that the circadian rhythm in body temperature, driven by pacemakers in the SCN, could serve as a body-wide cue to entrain the molecular clock in all the other cells (Buhr et al., 2010).

How does light entrain the molecular clock to the light-dark cycle? In fruit flies, light passes through the fly's body into brain cells to degrade the Cry protein and synchronize the molecular clock. But things are different in thick-headed mammals like us. We use the retinohypothalamic tract to get light information to the SCN. The retinal ganglion cells containing melanopsin detect light and release the neurotransmitter glutamate in the SCN. Glutamate triggers a chain of events in SCN cells that promotes the production of Per protein. When the animal's photoperiod is shifted, this light-mediated boosting of Per production shifts the phase of the molecular clock and therefore the animal's behavior.

Mutations in the genes involved in the molecular clock affect circadian behavior. We've already seen that hamsters with a *tau* mutation have a shorter free-running rhythm than normal hamsters have. Mice in which both copies of the *Clock* gene are disrupted show severe arrhythmicity in constant conditions (**FIGURE 14.7**). People who feel energetic in the morning ("larks") are likely to carry a different version of the *Clock* gene than "night owls" have (Katzenberg et al., 1998). Different alleles of the *per* gene are also associated with being a lark versus a night owl (Carpen et al., 2005).

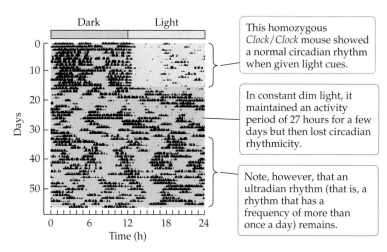

This homozygous *Clock/Clock* mouse showed a normal circadian rhythm when given light cues.

In constant dim light, it maintained an activity period of 27 hours for a few days but then lost circadian rhythmicity.

Note, however, that an ultradian rhythm (that is, a rhythm that has a frequency of more than once a day) remains.

14.7 WHEN THE ENDOGENOUS CLOCK GOES KAPUT (From J. S. Takahashi, 1995.)

infradian   Referring to a rhythmic biological event whose period is longer than that of a circadian rhythm—that is, longer than a day.

circannual   Occurring on a roughly annual basis.

Some Biological Rhythms Are Longer or Shorter than a Day

Some biological rhythms have periods longer than a day. Such rhythms are called **infradian** because their frequency is less than once per day (the Latin *infra* means "below"). A familiar infradian rhythm is the 28-day human menstrual cycle. Recall that many animals display a seasonal cycle in body weight (see Box 13.2). The importance of annual rhythms for humans is evident in the prevalence of seasonal disorders of behavior (see Chapter 16).

Many other animal behaviors are also characterized by annual rhythms; for example, most animals breed only during a particular season. Some of these rhythms are driven by exogenous factors, such as food availability and temperature. But in the laboratory, seasonal animals exposed to short days and long nights (mimicking winter) will often change to the nonbreeding condition (**FIGURE 14.8**). Furthermore, many annual rhythms, including body weight, persist under constant conditions in the lab. As with circadian rhythms in constant light, seasonal animals in isolation show free-running annual rhythms of a period not quite equal to 365 days. Thus, there also seems to be an endogenous **circannual** clock.

How does an animal know that a year has passed? Does it simply count the days being measured by the SCN until 365 have gone by? No. Irving Zucker et al. (1983) measured activity rhythms, reproductive cycles, and body weight cycles of animals that were free-running in both their circadian and their circannual rhythms. SCN lesions clearly disrupted circadian activity cycles, but in at least some animals these lesions did *not* affect circannual changes in body weight and reproductive

14.8 WINTER IS COMING   Siberian hamsters in the wild suppress their reproductive systems and develop a silvery fur coat (left) for camouflage in the snow each fall. In the laboratory, they will undergo identical changes, despite warm temperatures and abundant food, if the lights are on only 10 hours per day. They seem to interpret these short days as an indication that winter is coming. (Photograph courtesy of Dr. Carol D. Hegstrom.)

ultradian Referring to a rhythmic biological event whose period is shorter than that of a circadian rhythm, usually from several minutes to several hours long.

electroencephalography (EEG) The recording and study of gross electrical activity of the brain recorded from large electrodes placed on the scalp.

electro-oculography (EOG) The electrical recording of eye movements.

electromyography (EMG) The electrical recording of muscle activity.

rapid-eye-movement (REM) sleep Also called *paradoxical sleep*. A stage of sleep characterized by small-amplitude, fast-EEG waves, no postural tension, and rapid eye movements. *REM* rhymes with "gem."

status. Circannual cycles, then, do not arise from the circadian clock, and they seem to involve a mechanism that is separate from the SCN (Sáenz de Miera et al., 2014). Light cycles (which of course are a measure of day length) can entrain this circannual rhythm by affecting how long the nightly bout of melatonin secretion lasts (see Figure 5.20).

Some biological rhythms have periods *shorter* than a day. Such rhythms are referred to as **ultradian** (designating a frequency greater than once per day; the Latin *ultra* means "beyond"), and their periods are usually from several minutes to hours. Ultradian rhythms are seen in such behaviors as bouts of activity, feeding, and hormone release. These ultradian rhythms may be superimposed on a circadian rhythm. For example, humans show a 90-minute cycle of daydreaming that is characterized by vivid sensory imagery (P. Lavie and Kripke, 1981). Ultradian rhythms in performance on various boring tasks reflect fluctuations in alertness (Broughton, 1985). We'll also see this same ultradian rhythm of about 90 minutes imposed on the circadian sleep-wake cycle, which we consider next.

Sleeping and Waking

The most obvious circadian rhythm in human behavior is the bout of sleep that starts late in the evening and lasts until morning. The beginning and end of sleep are synchronized to many external events, including light and dark. What happens when all the customary synchronizing or entraining stimuli are removed? To investigate this question, volunteers spent weeks in a dark cave with all cues to external time removed (Wever, 1979). They displayed a circadian rhythm of the sleep-waking cycle, but the rhythm slowly shifted from 24 to 25 hours. In other words, people in constant conditions free-run just as a hamster does (**FIGURE 14.9**), indicating that we too have an endogenous circadian clock (Czeisler et al., 1999). External cues (lights, meals, jobs, alarm clocks) entrain our clock to a 24-hour period, and this circadian clock encourages the brain to sleep at some times of the day and to remain awake at others (Mistlberger, 2005). Because the free-running period is greater than 24 hours, some people in these studies have been surprised when told that the experiment has ended. They may have experienced only 19 sleep-waking cycles during a 21-day study.

Human Sleep Exhibits Different Stages

In the 1930s, experimenters found that brain potentials recorded from electrodes on the scalp by **electroencephalography (EEG)** (see Figure 3.19) provided a way to define, describe, and classify levels of arousal and states of sleep. This measure of brain activity is usually supplemented with recordings of eye movements by **electro-oculography (EOG)** and of muscle tension by **electromyography (EMG)**. Electrophysiological measurement led to the groundbreaking discovery that there are two distinct classes of sleep: **rapid-eye-movement sleep**, or **REM sleep**, and **non-REM (NREM) sleep** (Aserinsky and Kleitman, 1953). In humans, NREM sleep can be divided further into distinct stages, which we'll discuss next.

What are the electrophysiological distinctions that define different stages of NREM? To begin, the pattern of electrical activity in a fully awake, vigilant person is a mixture of many frequencies dominated by waves of relatively fast frequencies (greater than 15–20 cycles per second, or hertz [Hz]) and low amplitude; this type of wave activity is sometimes referred to as **beta activity** or **desynchronized EEG** (**FIGURE 14.10A**).

14.9 HUMANS FREE-RUN TOO These sleep-waking patterns were recorded in a participant who, after 5 days, was isolated from cues about the time of day. During this period the person displayed a free-running rhythm that was a bit longer than 24 hours, getting the equivalent of 74 "nights" of sleep over the 77 days. (From Weitzman et al., 1981.)

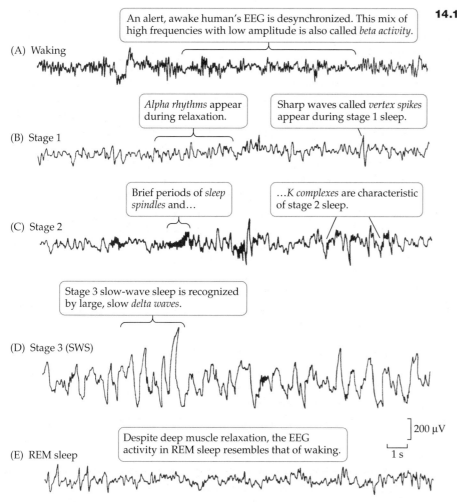

(A) Waking

An alert, awake human's EEG is desynchronized. This mix of high frequencies with low amplitude is also called *beta activity*.

(B) Stage 1

Alpha rhythms appear during relaxation.

Sharp waves called *vertex spikes* appear during stage 1 sleep.

(C) Stage 2

Brief periods of *sleep spindles* and...

...*K complexes* are characteristic of stage 2 sleep.

(D) Stage 3 (SWS)

Stage 3 slow-wave sleep is recognized by large, slow *delta waves*.

(E) REM sleep

Despite deep muscle relaxation, the EEG activity in REM sleep resembles that of waking.

200 μV
1 s

14.10 ELECTROPHYSIOLOGICAL CORRELATES OF SLEEP AND WAKING These are the characteristic EEG patterns seen during waking (A) and different stages of sleep in humans. Note the similarity of EEG activity during waking, stage 1 sleep, and REM sleep (F). (After Rechtschaffen and Kales, 1968.)

non-REM (NREM) sleep Stage of sleep without rapid eye movements. In humans this is divided into stages 1, 2, and 3 sleep.

beta activity EEG activity seen in wakefulness, comprising a mix of many different high frequencies with low amplitude.

desynchronized EEG Also called *beta activity*. A pattern of EEG activity comprising a mix of many different high frequencies with low amplitude.

alpha rhythm A brain potential of 8–12 Hz that occurs during relaxed wakefulness.

vertex spike A sharp-wave EEG pattern that is seen during stage 1 slow-wave sleep.

stage 1 sleep Also called *NREM 1*. The initial stage of NREM sleep, which is characterized by small-amplitude EEG waves of irregular frequency, slow heart rate, and reduced muscle tension.

stage 2 sleep Also called *NREM 2*. A stage of NREM sleep that is defined by bursts of regular 14- to 18-Hz EEG waves called *sleep spindles*.

sleep spindle A characteristic 14- to 18-Hz wave in the EEG of a person in stage 2 sleep.

K complex A sharp negative EEG potential that is seen in stage 2 sleep.

stage 3 sleep Also called *NREM 3*. A stage of NREM sleep that is defined by the presence of large amplitude, very slow waves (delta waves).

delta wave The slowest type of EEG wave, about 1 Hz, characteristic of stage 3 sleep.

slow-wave sleep (SWS) Also called *NREM 3*. A stage of NREM sleep characterized by large amplitude delta waves (in humans, this also called stage 3 sleep).

When you relax and close your eyes, a distinctive EEG rhythm appears, consisting of a regular oscillation at a frequency of 8–12 Hz, known as the **alpha rhythm**. As drowsiness sets in, the time spent in the alpha rhythm decreases, and the EEG shows events of much smaller amplitude and irregular frequency, as well as sharp waves called **vertex spikes**. This is the beginning of NREM, called **stage 1 sleep** (or *NREM 1*) (**FIGURE 14.10B**), which is accompanied by a slowing of heart rate and a reduction of muscle tension; in addition, under the closed eyelids the eyes may roll about slowly. Stage 1 sleep usually lasts several minutes and gives way to **stage 2 sleep** (or *NREM 2*) (**FIGURE 14.10C**), defined by waves of 12–14 Hz called **sleep spindles**, which occur in periodic bursts, and **K complexes**. If awakened during these first two stages of sleep, many participants deny that they were asleep, even though they failed to respond to signals while in those stages.

Stage 2 sleep leads to (can you guess?) **stage 3 sleep** (or *NREM 3*) (**FIGURE 14.10D**), which is defined by the appearance of large-amplitude, *very* slow waves (so-called **delta waves**, about one per second). In the past, researchers defined a stage 4 of sleep, when delta waves were present more than half the time. But because stages 3 and 4 are so similar, researchers today lump them together simply as stage 3 or **slow-wave sleep** (**SWS**). The slow waves of electrical potential that give SWS its name represent a widespread synchronization of cortical activity that has been likened to a room of people who are all chanting the same phrase over and over. From a distance you would be able to hear the rise and fall of the cadence of speech in a slow rhythm. But if each person were saying something different, you would hear only a buzz—the rapid frequencies of many desynchronized voices, which is like the desynchronized EEG, the beta activity of wakefulness when many parts of the cortex are saying different things to different target brain regions. During SWS, neighbor-

(A)

(B)

14.11 SLEEP STAGE POSTURES The kitten in (A) is enjoying slow-wave sleep, with enough muscle tone to maintain a sphinxlike posture. The kitten in (B), with profoundly relaxed muscle tone, may be in REM sleep.

ing cortical neurons tend to have synchronized activity (Poulet and Petersen, 2008), as if they were all "chanting" together rather than fulfilling different functions as they do in waking.

After about 90 minutes—the time usually required for progression through these stages, with a brief return to stage 2—something totally different occurs. Quite abruptly, scalp recordings display a pattern of small-amplitude, high-frequency activity similar in many ways to the pattern of an awake individual (**FIGURE 14.10E**), but the skeletal muscles are completely relaxed and limp. The active-looking EEG coupled with deeply relaxed muscles is typical of REM sleep. If you see a cat sleeping in the sitting, sphinx position, it cannot be in REM sleep; in REM, it will be sprawled limply on the floor (**FIGURE 14.11**).

As we'll see later, this flaccid muscle state appears despite intense brain activity, because during this stage of sleep, brainstem regions are profoundly inhibiting motor neurons. Because of this seeming contradiction—the brain waves look awake, but the musculature is flaccid and unresponsive—another name for this state is *paradoxical sleep*. In addition to the rapid eye movements under closed lids that give REM sleep its name, breathing and pulse rates become irregular. It is also during REM sleep that we experience vivid dreams. EEG activity shows that sleep consists of a complex series of brain states, not just an "inactive" period. **TABLE 14.1** compares the properties of NREM and REM sleep.

How much do we sleep, and when?

The total sleep time of young adults usually ranges from 7 to 8 hours, about half in stage 2 sleep. REM sleep accounts for about 20% of total sleep. The typical night of adult human sleep shows repeating cycles about 90–110 minutes long, recurring four or five times in a night. These cycles change in a subtle but regular manner through

TABLE 14.1 Properties of NREM and REM Sleep

PROPERTY	NREM SLEEP	REM SLEEP
AUTONOMIC ACTIVITIES		
Heart rate	Slow decline	Variable with high bursts
Respiration	Slow decline	Variable with high bursts
Thermoregulation	Maintained	Impaired
Brain temperature	Decreased	Increased
Cerebral blood flow	Reduced	High
SKELETAL MUSCULAR SYSTEM		
Postural tension	Progressively reduced	Eliminated
Knee jerk reflex	Normal	Suppressed
Phasic twitches	Reduced	Increased
Eye movements	Infrequent, slow, uncoordinated	Rapid, coordinated
COGNITIVE STATE	Vague thoughts	Vivid dreams, well organized
HORMONE SECRETION		
Growth hormone secretion	High	Low
NEURAL FIRING RATES		
Cerebral cortex activity	Many cells reduced and more phasic	Increased firing rates; tonic (sustained)
EVENT-RELATED POTENTIALS		
Sensory-evoked	Large	Reduced

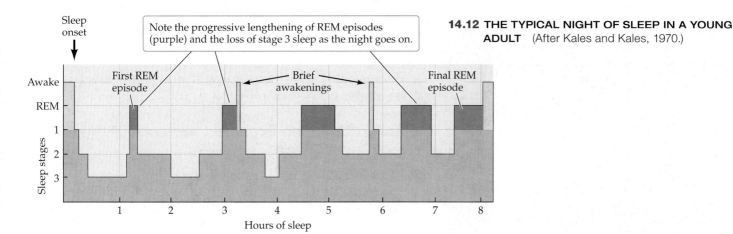

14.12 THE TYPICAL NIGHT OF SLEEP IN A YOUNG ADULT (After Kales and Kales, 1970.)

Note the progressive lengthening of REM episodes (purple) and the loss of stage 3 sleep as the night goes on.

First REM episode

Brief awakenings

Final REM episode

the night. Cycles early in the night are characterized by greater amounts of stage 3 SWS (**FIGURE 14.12**). The latter half of the night has less stage 3 sleep. In contrast, REM sleep is typically more prominent in the later cycles of sleep. The first REM period is the shortest, while the last REM period, just before waking, may last up to 40 minutes.

A brief arousal (yellow in Figure 14.12) occasionally occurs immediately after a REM period, and the sleeper may shift posture at this time (Aaronson et al., 1982). The sleep cycle of 90–110 minutes has been viewed as reflecting a basic ultradian rest-activity cycle (Kleitman, 1969); cycles of similar duration occur during waking periods, such as the cycles of daydreaming we mentioned earlier.

At puberty, the circadian rhythm of sleep shifts in most people, so they get up later in the day (**FIGURE 14.13**), but many school systems require students to come to school *earlier* in the day when they hit adolescence. One group of high schools shifted their start from 7:15 to 8:40 and noted improved student attendance and enrollment, with reduced depression and sleeping in class (Wahlstrom, 2002). You may think of sleep as a simple event in your life, but for neuroscientists sleep is a remarkably complex, multifaceted set of behaviors. As one example, let's consider a fascinating aspect of REM sleep: dreaming.

We do our most vivid dreaming during REM sleep

We can record the EEGs of participants, awaken them at a particular stage (1, 2, 3, or REM), and question them about thoughts or perceptions immediately prior to awakening. Early studies of this sort suggested that dreams happen only during REM sleep, but we now know that dreams also occur in other sleep stages. What is distinctive about the dreams during REM sleep is that they are characterized by visual imagery, whereas dreams during NREM sleep are of a more "thinking" type. REM dreams are apt to include a story that involves odd perceptions and the sense that the dreamer "is there" experiencing sights, sounds, smells, and acts. Participants awakened from NREM sleep report thinking about problems rather than seeing themselves in a stage presentation (Cartwright, 1979).

Almost everyone has terrifying dreams on occasion (Hartmann, 1984). **Nightmares** are defined as long, frightening dreams that awaken the sleeper from REM sleep. Many medications make nightmares more frequent (Pagel and Helfter, 2003), but they are quite prevalent even without such influences. At least 25% of college students report having one or more nightmares per month. Have you had the common one, which Sigmund Freud had, of suddenly remembering that you must take a final exam that is already in progress?

Nightmares are occasionally confused with **night terror**, in which a sudden arousal from NREM sleep is marked by intense fear and

nightmare A long, frightening dream that awakens the sleeper from REM sleep.

night terror A sudden arousal from stage 3 slow-wave sleep that is marked by intense fear and autonomic activation.

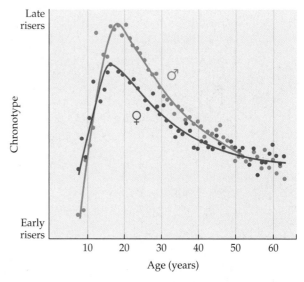

14.13 OH, HOW I HATE TO GET UP IN THE MORNING By comparing the time of day that people of differing ages wake up each day, Roenneberg et al. (2004) confirmed the tendency for humans to become late risers at puberty.

14.14 NIGHT TERROR This 1781 painting by Henry Fuseli is called *The Nightmare*. It also aptly illustrates night terrors, or even sleep paralysis, discussed later in the chapter, as the demon crushes the breath from his victim.

autonomic activation. After a night terror the sleeper does not recall a vivid dream but may remember a sense of a crushing feeling on the chest, as though being suffocated (**FIGURE 14.14**). Night terrors, common in children during the early part of an evening's sleep, seem to have a genetic component (D. Petit et al., 2015).

Different Species Provide Clues about the Evolution of Sleep

Sleep has been studied in a wide assortment of mammals and, to a lesser extent, in reptiles, birds, and amphibians (S. S. Campbell and Tobler, 1984). Many invertebrates also have clear periods of behavioral quiescence that include heightened arousal thresholds and distinctive postures (Koh et al., 2008; Thimgan et al., 2015), and there's growing acceptance that this is indeed sleep (Donelson and Sanyal, 2015; Trojanowski and Raizen, 2016). It's even possible to record slow waves from the nervous systems of crayfish (Ramon et al., 2004) and fruit flies (Nitz et al., 2002) during their periods of inactivity. Sleep is an ancient adaptation.

REM sleep evolved in some vertebrates

REM sleep does not seem quite as ancient as NREM. Nearly all mammalian species that have been investigated thus far, including the platypus (J. M. Siegel, Manger et al., 1999), the mammal most phylogenetically distant from us, display both REM sleep and NREM (**FIGURE 14.15**). Among the other vertebrates, only birds display clear signs of both SWS and REM sleep. These comparisons suggest that either REM sleep was present in an ancestor common to birds and mammals or that REM evolved independently in mammals and birds.

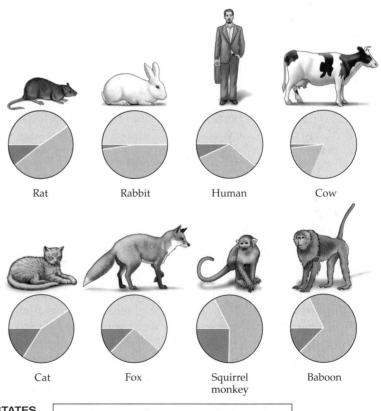

14.15 AMOUNTS OF DIFFERENT SLEEP STATES IN VARIOUS MAMMALS

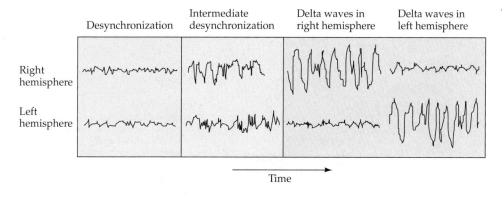

Desynchronization | Intermediate desynchronization | Delta waves in right hemisphere | Delta waves in left hemisphere

Right hemisphere

Left hemisphere

Time

14.16 SLEEP IN MARINE MAMMALS EEG patterns in right and left brain hemispheres in a dolphin (*Tursiops truncatus*) from recordings of the parietal cortex suggest that the two cerebral hemispheres take turns sleeping. (From Mukhametov, 1984.)

Dolphins don't display REM sleep, but their lack of REM sleep is probably a later adaptation that evolved when their land-dwelling ancestors took to the water, because they must come to the surface of the water to breathe. That requirement may be incompatible with the deep relaxation of muscles during REM sleep. Another dolphin adaptation to living in water is that only one side of the dolphin brain engages in SWS at a time (Mukhametov, 1984). It's as if one whole hemisphere is asleep while the other is awake (**FIGURE 14.16**). During these periods of "unilateral sleep," the animals continue to come up to the surface occasionally to breathe. Birds can also display unilateral sleep—one hemisphere sleeping while the other hemisphere watches for predators (Rattenborg, 2006). Unilateral sleep while gliding may also enable birds to fly long distances (e.g., 10,000 miles!) without stopping (Gill et al., 2009). In humans, the left hemisphere displays less slow-wave activity than the right during the first night in a sleep lab, suggesting that side of the brain remains more vigilant in this unfamiliar locale. The second night in the lab, when people usually sleep better (Agnew et al., 1966), sleep depth is again equivalent between the hemispheres (Tamaki et al., 2016).

Species differ in their patterns and types of sleep

A **sleep cycle** is a period of NREM sleep followed by an episode of REM sleep. For laboratory rats, one sleep cycle lasts an average of 10–11 minutes; for humans, one cycle lasts 90–110 minutes, as we said earlier. Across species, cycle duration is inversely related to metabolic rate; that is, small animals, which tend to have high metabolic rates (see Chapter 13), have short sleep cycles, and large species have long sleep cycles. Although almost everybody sleeps, the quantity and quality of sleep are not the same throughout life, as we'll see in the next section.

Our Sleep Patterns Change across the Life Span

How much sleep and what kind of sleep we get change across our lifetime. These changes are most evident during early development.

Mammals sleep more during infancy than in adulthood

A clear cycle of sleeping and waking takes several weeks to become established in human infants (**FIGURE 14.17**). A 24-hour rhythm is generally evident by 16 weeks of age. Infant sleep is characterized by shorter sleep cycles than those of adults. This probably reflects the relative immaturity of the brain; sleep cycles in premature infants are even shorter than in full-term babies.

sleep cycle A period of slow-wave sleep followed by a period of REM sleep. In humans, a sleep cycle lasts 90–110 minutes.

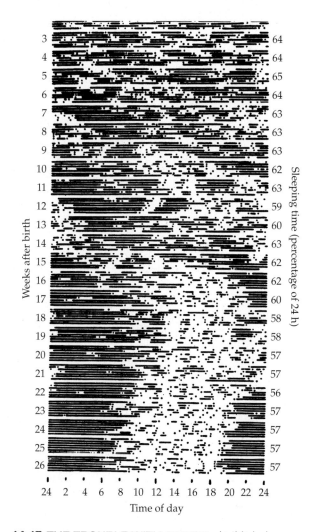

14.17 THE TROUBLE WITH BABIES In this baby, a stable pattern of sleep at night does not appear to be consolidated until about 16 weeks of age. The dark portions here indicate time asleep; the blank portions, time awake. (From Kleitman and Engelmann, 1953.)

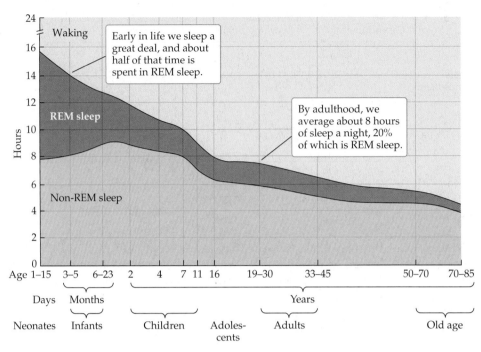

14.18 HUMAN SLEEP PATTERNS CHANGE WITH AGE (After Roffwarg et al., 1966.)

Early in life we sleep a great deal, and about half of that time is spent in REM sleep.

By adulthood, we average about 8 hours of sleep a night, 20% of which is REM sleep.

Infant mammals show a large percentage of REM sleep. In humans, for example, 50% of sleep in the first 2 weeks of life is REM sleep. REM sleep is even more prominent in premature infants, accounting for up to 80% of total sleep. Unlike healthy adults, human infants can move directly from an awake state to REM sleep for the first few months of life. The REM sleep of infants is quite active, accompanied by muscle twitching, smiles, grimaces, and vocalizations. The preponderance of REM sleep early in life (**FIGURE 14.18**) suggests that this state provides stimulation that is essential to maturation of the nervous system. For example, maybe sensory feedback from those twitches guides synaptic development in the brain (Blumberg, 2015). On the other hand, killer whales and bottlenose dolphins appear to spend little or no time sleeping for the first month of life (Lyamin et al., 2005), presumably because they have to surface often to breathe. So either REM sleep does not fill a crucial need in mammalian infants, or dolphin and whale infants have found a different way to fill that need.

Most people sleep appreciably less as they age

The parameters of sleep change more slowly in old age than in early development. **FIGURE 14.19** shows the pattern of the typical night of sleep in an elderly person. The total amount of sleep declines, while the number of awakenings increases (compare with Figure 14.12). Lack of sleep, or insomnia (which we will discuss at the end of this

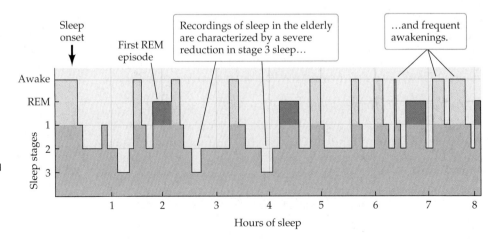

14.19 THE TYPICAL PATTERN OF SLEEP IN AN ELDERLY PERSON Compare this recording with the young-adult sleep pattern shown in Figure 14.12. (After Kales and Kales, 1974.)

Recordings of sleep in the elderly are characterized by a severe reduction in stage 3 sleep…

…and frequent awakenings.

chapter), is a common complaint of the elderly, and a substantial literature suggests fragmented sleep leads to deficits in cognitive function (Scullin and Bliwise, 2015).

In humans and other mammals, the most dramatic progressive decline is in stage 3 sleep; people at age 60 spend only about half as much time in stage 3 as they did at age 20 (Bliwise, 1989). By age 90, stage 3 sleep has disappeared. This decline in stage 3 sleep with age may be related to diminished cognitive capabilities, since an especially marked reduction of stage 3 characterizes the sleep of people who suffer from senile dementia (Kondratova and Kondratova, 2012). Growth hormone is secreted primarily during stage 3, so perhaps the loss of growth hormone from disrupted sleep in the elderly leads to the cognitive deficits.

Most elderly people fall asleep easily enough, but then they may have a hard time staying asleep, causing sleep "dissatisfaction." As in so many things, attitude may be important for the experience of sleep loss in the elderly. Objective measures of sleep suggest that elderly people who complain of poor sleep may actually sleep more than those who are satisfied with their sleep (McCrae et al., 2005). Perhaps, as you grow older, if you can regard waking up at 3:00 AM as a "bonus" (a little more time awake before you die), you will be more satisfied with the sleep you get.

Manipulating Sleep Reveals an Underlying Structure

Sleep is affected by many environmental, social, and biological influences. From one viewpoint, though, sleep is an amazingly stable state: major changes in our waking behavior have only a minor impact on subsequent sleep. The effects of sleep deprivation are especially interesting because they give insight into the underlying mechanisms of sleep.

Sleep deprivation predictably alters sleep patterns

Most of us at one time or another have been willing or not-so-willing participants in informal **sleep deprivation** experiments. Thus, most of us are aware of the effect of partial or total sleep deprivation: it makes us sleepy (**FIGURE 14.20**). The study of sleep deprivation is also a way to explore the regulatory mechanisms of sleeping and waking. Studies of **sleep recovery** ask questions such as, does a sleep-deprived organism somehow keep track of the amounts and types of lost sleep? When the organism is given the opportunity to compensate, is recovery partial or complete? Can you pay off sleep debts?

sleep deprivation The partial or total prevention of sleep.

sleep recovery The process of sleeping more than is normal, after a period of sleep deprivation, as though in compensation.

THE EFFECTS OF SLEEP DEPRIVATION   Early reports from sleep deprivation studies suggested a similarity between "bizarre" behavior provoked by sleep deprivation and schizophrenia. A frequent theme in this work was the functional role of dreams as a "guardian of sanity." But examination of patients suffering from schizophrenia does not confirm this view. For example, these patients can show sleep-waking cycles similar to those of healthy adults, and sleep deprivation does not exacerbate their symptoms.

The behavioral effects of prolonged, total sleep deprivation vary appreciably and may depend on some general personality factors and on age. In several studies employing prolonged total deprivation—205 hours (8.5 days)—a few participants showed occasional episodes of hallucinations. But the most common behavior changes noted in these experiments were increases in irritability, difficulty in concentrating, and episodes of disorientation. The participant's ability to perform tasks was summarized by L. C. Johnson (1969): "His performance is like a motor that after much use misfires, runs normally for a while, then falters again" (p. 216).

You don't need to resort to total sleep deprivation to see effects. Moderate sleep debt can accumulate with successive nights of little sleep. Volunteers who got 6 or 4 hours of sleep per night for 2 weeks showed ever-mounting deficits in attention tasks and in speed of re-

14.20 I NEED SLEEP! Doing without sleep has one clear effect: you feel sleepy.

Sleep Deprivation Can Be Fatal

Sleep that knits up the ravell'd sleave of care.

—William Shakespeare, *Macbeth*, Act II, Scene 2

Although some people seem to need very little sleep, most of us feel the need to sleep 7–8 hours a night. In fact, sustained sleep deprivation in rats causes them to increase their metabolic rate, lose weight, and, within an average of 19 days, die (Everson et al., 1989). Allowing them to sleep prevents their death.

After the fatal effect of sleep deprivation had been shown, researchers undertook studies in which they terminated the sleep deprivation before the fatal endpoint and looked for pathological changes in different organ systems (Rechtschaffen and Bergmann, 1995). No single organ system seems affected in chronically sleep-deprived animals, but early in the deprivation they develop sores on their bodies. These sores mark the

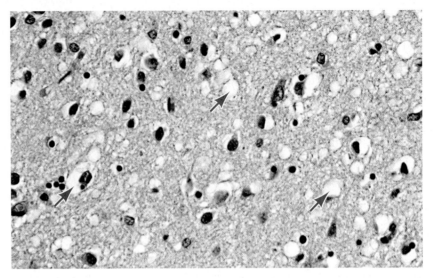

Note the large holes (arrows) that have developed in this section of frontal cortex from a victim of fatal familial insomnia. (Micrograph courtesy of H. Budka.)

beginning of the end; shortly thereafter, blood tests reveal infections from a host of bacteria, which probably enter through the sores (Everson, 1993).

These bacteria are not normally fatal, because the rat's immune system and body defenses keep them in check; but severely sleep-deprived rats fail to develop a fever in response to these infections. (Fever helps the body fight infection.) In fact, the sleep-deprived animals show a *drop*

---

action compared with those sleeping 8 hours per night (Van Dongen et al., 2003). Interestingly, the sleep-deprived participants often reported not feeling sleepy, yet their performance was still impaired. By the end of the study, the people getting less than 8 hours of sleep per night had cognitive deficits equivalent to people who had been totally sleep-deprived for 3 days!

Airline employees who work on schedules that give them little time to adapt to new time zones show deficits in cognitive tasks (Caldwell, 2012) and reduced volume of the brain's temporal lobe compared with employees on a schedule that permits more time to recover from jet lag (K. Cho, 2001). Is it the disruption of circadian rhythms or accumulated sleep debt that caused the difference? We don't know.

Finally, it is clear that prolonged, total sleep deprivation in mammals compromises the immune system and leads to death (**BOX 14.1**). Even fruit flies need sleep, as evidenced by the fact that a particular mutation of the *Cycle* gene (which is part of the circadian molecular clock; see Figure 14.6) causes the flies to die after only 10 hours of sleep deprivation (P. J. Shaw et al., 2002).

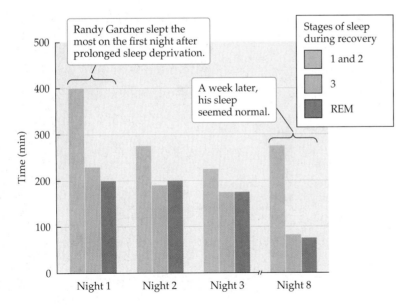

14.21 SLEEP RECOVERY AFTER 11 DAYS AWAKE (After Gulevich et al., 1966.)

SLEEP RECOVERY **FIGURE 14.21** provides data on sleep recovery in a young man named Randy

in body temperature, which probably speeds bacterial infections, which in turn leads to diffuse organ damage. The decline of these severely sleep-deprived rats is complicated, but it seems clear that getting sleep improves immune system function (Everson et al., 2008). So perhaps Shakespeare's folk theory of the function of sleep, quoted above, isn't so far from the truth.

What about the rare humans who sleep only 1 or 2 hours a night? Why aren't their immune systems and inflammatory responses compromised? We don't know, but since the distinguishing trait of these people is that they don't need much sleep, perhaps their immune systems and inflammatory responses don't need much sleep either. Or perhaps the small amount of sleep they have almost every night is more efficient at doing whatever sleep does.

Some unfortunate humans inherit a defect in the gene for the prion protein (which can transmit mad cow disease, discussed in Chapter 11), and although they sleep normally at the beginning of life, in midlife they simply stop sleeping—with fatal effect. People with this disease, called **fatal familial insomnia**, die 7–24 months after the insomnia begins (Mastrianni et al., 1999; Medori et al., 1992). Autopsy reveals degeneration of the cortex (shown in the figure) and thalamus, which may cause the insomnia (Manetto et al., 1992). Like sleep-deprived rats, sleep-deprived humans with this disorder don't have obvious damage to any single organ system but suffer from diffuse bacterial infections. Apparently these patients die because they are chronically sleep-deprived, and these results, combined with research on rats, certainly support the idea that prolonged insomnia is fatal.

fatal familial insomnia   An inherited disorder in which humans sleep normally at the beginning of their life but stop sleeping in midlife and die 7–24 months later.

Gardner following 11 days of sleep deprivation. No evidence of a psychotic state was noted, and the incentive for this unusually long act of not sleeping was simply his own curiosity. Researchers became involved only after he had started his deprivation schedule, which is the reason for the absence of predeprivation sleep data.

In the first night of sleep recovery, stage 3 sleep shows the greatest relative difference from normal. This increase in stage 3 sleep is usually at the expense of stage 2 sleep. However, the rise in stage 3 sleep during recovery never completely makes up for the deficit accumulated over the deprivation period. In fact, the amount is no greater than for deprivation periods of 11 days than for 5 days. REM sleep after prolonged sleep deprivation shows its greatest recovery during the *second* postdeprivation night. REM recovery may also involve another form of compensation—greater intensity: REM sleep in recovery nights is more "intense" than normal, with a greater number of rapid eye movements per period of time. So you never recover all lost sleep time, but you may make up for the loss by having more intense sleep for a while. The sooner you get to sleep, the sooner you recover.

What Are the Biological Functions of Sleep?

Why do most of us spend one-third of our lifetime asleep? The functions of sleep are a subject of great debate. Keep in mind that the proposed functions, or biological roles, of sleep are not mutually exclusive; sleep may have acquired more than one function during evolution. The four functions most often ascribed to sleep are energy conservation, niche adaptation, body restoration, and memory consolidation; we will consider each in turn.

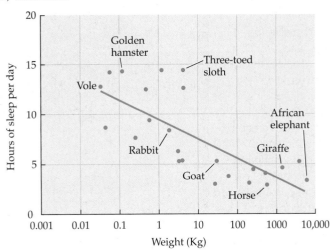

(A) Plant eaters

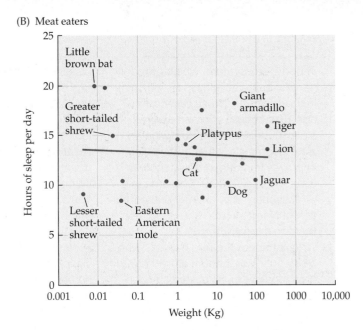

(B) Meat eaters

14.22 RELATIONSHIP BETWEEN BODY SIZE AND SLEEP TIME (A) Among plant eaters, the larger the body is, the less time is spent asleep. (B) Meat eaters sleep a lot, no matter what their body size—presumably because they are more secure when asleep than plant eaters. (From J. M. Siegel, 2005.)

Sleep conserves energy

We use up less energy when we sleep than when we're awake. For example, stage 3 sleep is marked by reduced muscular tension, lowered heart rate, reduced blood pressure, reduced body temperature, and slower respiration. This diminished metabolic activity during sleep suggests that one role of sleep is to conserve energy.

We can see the importance of this function by looking at the world from the perspective of small animals. Small mammals have very high metabolic rates (see Chapter 13), and demand for energy can easily outstrip supply. Reduced activity can be especially valuable if food is scarce. There is also a high correlation between total amount of sleep per day and waking metabolic rate: small animals sleep more than large species, at least among plant-eating species (**FIGURE 14.22A**). Since smaller mammals lose heat faster (see Chapter 13), they burn more energy per gram of body weight just to maintain body temperature, and so perhaps they sleep more to conserve more energy. Interestingly, predatory species show no such correlation, perhaps because meat eaters tend to get more sleep than prey species do (**FIGURE 14.22B**). In zoos and labs, where animals don't have to spend time looking for food, the herbivores, eating low-calorie food, have to spend more time actually eating their food than do the omnivores, which in turn need more time to eat than the carnivores that exclusively eat high-calorie meat (namely, herbivores and omnivores!). Consequently, carnivores sleep more than omnivores, which sleep more than herbivores in these settings (Siegel, 2012).

Sleep enforces niche adaptation

Almost all animals are either nocturnal or diurnal. This specialization for either nighttime or daytime activity is part of each species' **ecological niche**, that unique assortment of environmental opportunities and challenges to which each organism is adapted. Thanks to these adaptations, each species is better at gathering food either at night or in the daytime, and each species is also better at avoiding predators either during the day or at night (**FIGURE 14.23**). If you're a nocturnal mammal, like a mouse, you are adept at sneaking around in the dark, using acute hearing and smell to navigate and find food. The rest of the time, during daylight, you should spend holed up somewhere safe to stay away from diurnal predators. So, one important function of sleep is to force the individual to conform to a particular ecological niche for which it is well adapted (Meddis, 1975). If it is adaptive to forego sleep, as it is during the 3

ecological niche The unique assortment of environmental opportunities and challenges to which each organism is adapted.

weeks of the year when male pectoral sandpipers compete intensively for mates in the round-the-clock daylight of an Arctic summer, then animals can do without sleep. Those males that sleep the least sire the most offspring (Lesku et al., 2012). But as the breeding season ends and periods of dark return, they might as well sleep at night. From this perspective, sleep debt and the unpleasant feelings of sleepiness are simply tools that evolved to enforce inactivity (J. M. Siegel, 2009). This certainly is a function of sleep, and it must have played an important role in the evolution of sleep.

Sleep restores the body and brain

If someone asked you why you sleep, chances are you would answer that you sleep because you're tired. Indeed, one of the proposed functions of sleep is simply the rebuilding or restoration of materials used during waking, such as proteins (Moruzzi, 1972). Maybe this is why most growth hormone release happens during SWS.

If simple wear and tear from activity triggered the need for sleep, then you'd expect exercise to result in more sleep. But while exercise during the day may cause people to fall asleep more quickly, it generally does *not* help them sleep longer. We've seen that prolonged and total sleep deprivation—either forced on rats or as a result of inherited pathology in humans—interferes with the immune system and leads to death (see Box 14.1). Even relatively mild deprivation, having sleep shortened or disrupted (e.g., by a nurse taking vital signs every hour), makes people more sensitive to pain the following day (R. R. Edwards et al., 2009). A study of over a million Americans found that those sleeping less than 6 hours per night were more likely to die in the next year, although, interestingly, people who slept *more than 8* hours per night were also at greater risk (Kripke et al., 2002). People who sleep less than 5 hours per night are more likely to develop diabetes (Gangwisch et al., 2007). Perhaps the most impressive link between sleep and health is the finding that people who work at night and sleep in the daytime are more likely to develop cancer (Erren et al., 2009). So the widespread belief that sleep helps us ward off illness is well supported by research (S. Cohen et al., 2009; Imeri and Opp, 2009).

Sleep also restores the brain by allowing it to get rid of waste products. Glia control the flow of cerebrospinal fluid through a microscopic network of channels throughout the brain, collecting and disposing of toxins that build up. This flow is much faster during sleep than wakefulness (Xie et al., 2013), flushing out brain waste products as we snooze. One of the waste products that is cleared much faster during sleep is β-amyloid. Because the buildup of β-amyloid is a suspected cause of Alzheimer's disease (see Figure 7.28), adequate sleep may postpone the disorder. Or perhaps the brain's clearance system slows down in both wakefulness and sleep in some people, allowing the buildup of β-amyloid and Alzheimer's.

Sleep aids memory consolidation

A peculiar property of dreams is that, unless we tell them to someone or write them down soon after waking, we tend to forget them (Dement, 1974), as though the brain refuses to consolidate information presented during REM sleep. It is probably beneficial that most dreams are not stored in long-term memory, because it would be counterproductive to squander permanent memory storage space on events that never happened.

How about learning during sleep? Despite ads you might read in the backs of magazines, you cannot learn new material while you're sleeping (Druckman and Bjork, 1994). Putting a speaker under your pillow to recite material for a final exam will not work unless you stay awake to listen (J. M. Wood et al., 1992).

In 1924, however, Jenkins and Dallenbach reported an experiment suggesting that sleep helps you learn or remember material or events experienced *before* you go to bed. They trained some participants in a verbal learning task at bedtime and tested them 8 hours later on arising from sleep; other participants they trained early in the day and tested 8 hours later (with no intervening sleep). Participants displayed better retention when a period of sleep intervened between the learning period and the test, suggesting that sleep aids the *consolidation* of memory. More-modern research confirms that sleep helps consolidate memories in a wide variety of tasks, not just verbal memory tasks (Diekelmann and Born, 2010). Performance on nonverbal tasks, such as the in-

14.23 SLEEP HELPS ANIMALS TO ADAPT TO AN ECOLOGICAL NICHE Many diurnal primates sleep in trees to avoid predators at night.

(A) Initial odor exposure

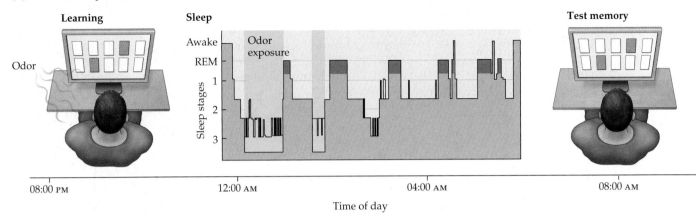

(B) Odor re-exposure

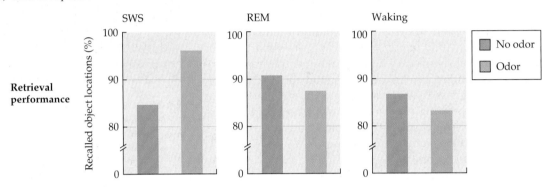

14.24 MEMORY CONSOLIDATION IN SLOW-WAVE SLEEP (A) Participants learned the location of various objects in a concentration game on a computer screen while exposed to an odor. That night they were exposed to the same odor while asleep, during either SWS, as shown here, or REM sleep, then tested upon awakening. (B) Participants exposed to the odor during SWS showed improved memory for the task, while those exposed to the odor during REM sleep or while awake showed no benefit. (After Diekelmann and Born, 2010).

sight that there is a "hidden rule" in a sequence of seemingly random digits, is better if participants sleep between the first and second set of trials (Ellenbogen et al., 2007; U. Wagner et al., 2004). Conversely, sleep deprivation makes people more susceptible to forming false memories (see Chapter 17) (Frenda et al., 2014), which may explain why sleep-deprived suspects sometimes confess to crimes they have not committed.

NREM aids consolidation of memory (Nishida and Walker, 2007), specifically declarative memory (i.e., memory that can be stated or described, as was tested in the verbal learning task experiment by Jenkins and Dallenbach). In fact, boosting cortical slow-voltage oscillations during NREM, using stimulating electrodes over the skull, enhances consolidation of declarative memories (L. Marshall et al., 2006). In contrast, REM sleep may help consolidation of nondeclarative memory (see Chapter 17). For example, humans learning to discriminate different visual textures show little improvement in a single training session but show considerable improvement 8–10 hours after the session. If deprived of REM sleep after training, however, people fail to show the later improvement (C. Smith, 1995).

Patterns of neuronal activity seen while a task is being learned during wakefulness are re-created during subsequent NREM sleep, as if the brain were "rehearsing" the material (Euston et al., 2007; Horikawa et al., 2013; Ji and Wilson, 2007). Similarly, the patterned activity of neurons observed in birdsong nuclei while male zebra finches are learning to sing appears to be repeated during subsequent bouts of sleep (Shank and Margoliash, 2009). Further supporting the idea that declarative memory is consolidated during NREM are studies using a cue to "reactivate" learning during sleep. Participants learned the placement of objects on a computer screen while being exposed to an odor, say of roses. Participants who were later reexposed to that same odor while in NREM showed improved consolidation of memory upon awakening (Diekelmann and Born, 2010). Exposure to the odor in REM sleep, or while awake, had no effect (**FIGURE 14.24**). In another study, exposure to the odor while awake actually impaired performance (Diekelmann et al., 2011).

The memory consolidation function of sleep may involve determining which synapses are gained or lost. In one study, neurons in motor cortex that were activated when mice were learning to run on a rotating rod formed new dendritic spines. Sleep deprivation after a training session reduced the number of new spines formed and impaired learning. In contrast, allowing the mice to sleep after a learning session increased the number of spines formed and made the spines more likely to persist a day later (G. Yang et al., 2014). Thus there's something about sleep that helps the brain form and retain synapses, aiding memory.

Some humans sleep remarkably little, yet function normally

One challenge to all the theories about the function of sleep is the existence of a few people who seem perfectly healthy, yet sleep hardly at all. These cases are more than just folktales. William Dement (1974) described a Stanford University professor who slept only 3–4 hours a night for more than 50 years and died at age 80. Sleep researcher Ray Meddis (1977) found a cheerful 70-year-old retired nurse who said she had slept little since childhood. She was a busy person who easily filled up her 23 hours of daily wakefulness. During the night, she sat in bed reading or writing, and at about 2:00 AM she fell asleep for an hour or so, after which she readily awakened.

For her first 2 days in Meddis's laboratory, she did not sleep at all, because it was all so interesting to her. On the third night she slept a total of 99 minutes, and her sleep contained both SWS and REM sleep periods. Later her sleep was recorded for 5 days, when she slept an average of 67 minutes a day. She never complained about not sleeping more, and she did not feel drowsy during either the day or the night (**FIGURE 14.25**). Meddis described several other people who slept only an hour or two per night. Some of these people reported having parents who slept little. Whatever the function of sleep is, these people possessed some way of fulfilling it with a brief nap. They showed less of stages 1 and 2 sleep, so perhaps they were more efficient sleepers. Most important, though, is that no healthy person has ever been found who does not sleep at all.

14.25 A NONSLEEPER When Ray Meddis brought this 70-year-old nurse into the lab for sleep recording, he confirmed that she slept only about an hour per night. Yet she was a healthy and energetic person. Upon death in her mid-70s, she had been awake for a total of 20 years longer than someone who had slept 8 hours a night. Here she is strolling in the garden with Meddis's son.

At Least Four Interacting Neural Systems Underlie Sleep

At one time sleep was regarded as a passive state, as though most of the brain simply stopped working while we slept, leaving us unaware of events around us. We now know that sleep is an active state mediated by at least four interacting neural systems:

1. A *forebrain* system that by itself can display SWS
2. A *brainstem* system that activates the forebrain into wakefulness
3. A *pontine* system that triggers REM sleep
4. A *hypothalamic* system that affects the other three brain regions to determine whether the brain will be awake or asleep

The forebrain generates slow-wave sleep

General anesthetics—drugs such as barbiturates and anesthetic gases that render people unconscious during surgery—produce slow waves in the EEG that resemble those seen in SWS (Franks, 2008). This finding suggests that general anesthetics tap into existing brain networks promoting sleep. While some general anesthetics are glutamate antagonists and therefore block neuronal excitation throughout the brain, virtually *all* general anesthetics are noncompetitive agonists at $GABA_A$ receptors (**FIGURE 14.26**). Because they boost $GABA_A$ receptors' inhibitory effect on neurons, the action of these anesthetics suggests that some brain system normally uses GABA to inhibit neuronal activity and promote SWS. But where is that system?

Some of the earliest studies of sleep indicated that the system promoting SWS is in the forebrain. These were experiments in which the brain was transected—literally cut into two parts: an upper part and a lower part. The entire brain can be isolated from the body by an incision between the medulla and the spinal cord. This prepara-

general anesthetic A drug that renders an individual unconscious.

14.26 NEUROTRANSMITTER SYSTEMS AFFECTED BY GENERAL ANESTHETICS Note that all general anesthetics increase GABA$_A$ receptor signaling—a clue that these receptors, which tend to inhibit neuronal activity, may play a role in sleep. Some anesthetics also inhibit glutamate receptors, which usually excite neurons, while they stimulate glycine receptors, which usually inhibit neurons. Singer Michael Jackson died of an overdose of propofol that was given to him to induce sleep, but the drug does not provide the normal stages of sleep. (After Alkire et al., 2008.)

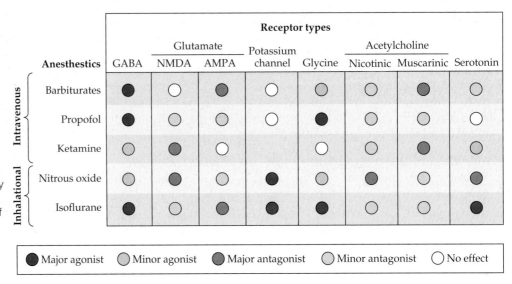

tion was first studied by the Belgian physiologist Frédéric Bremer (1892–1982), who called it the **isolated brain** (Bremer, 1938).

The EEGs of animals with such transections show signs of waking alternating with sleep (**FIGURE 14.27A**). During EEG-defined wakeful periods, the pupils are dilated and the eyes follow moving objects. During EEG-defined sleep, the pupils are small, as in normal sleep. REM sleep can also be detected in the isolated brain by measuring other local electrical signals. These results demonstrate that wakefulness, SWS, and REM sleep are all mediated by *networks within the brain*.

If the transection is made higher along the brainstem—in the midbrain—a very different result is achieved. Bremer referred to such a preparation as an **isolated forebrain**, and he found that the EEG from the brain in front of the cut displayed constant SWS (**FIGURE 14.27B**). The isolated forebrain does not show REM sleep, so it appears that the forebrain alone can generate SWS, with no contributions from the lower brain regions.

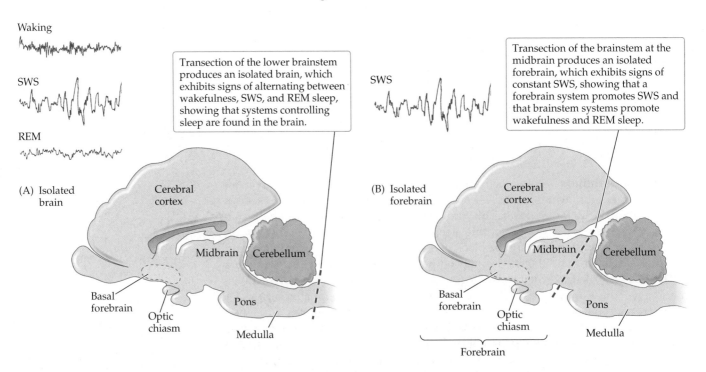

14.27 TRANSECTING THE BRAIN AT DIFFERENT LEVELS

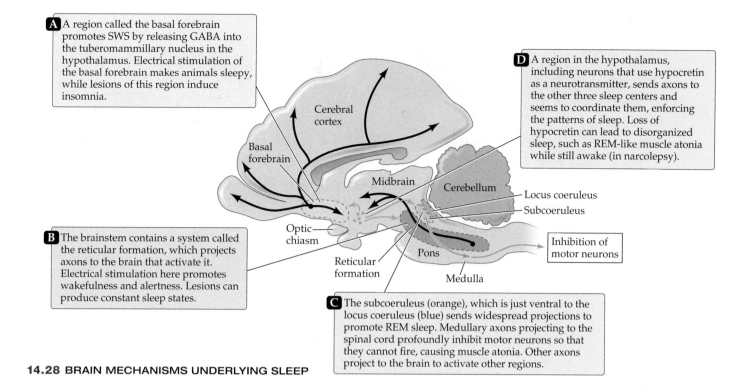

A A region called the basal forebrain promotes SWS by releasing GABA into the tuberomammillary nucleus in the hypothalamus. Electrical stimulation of the basal forebrain makes animals sleepy, while lesions of this region induce insomnia.

D A region in the hypothalamus, including neurons that use hypocretin as a neurotransmitter, sends axons to the other three sleep centers and seems to coordinate them, enforcing the patterns of sleep. Loss of hypocretin can lead to disorganized sleep, such as REM-like muscle atonia while still awake (in narcolepsy).

B The brainstem contains a system called the reticular formation, which projects axons to the brain that activate it. Electrical stimulation here promotes wakefulness and alertness. Lesions can produce constant sleep states.

C The subcoeruleus (orange), which is just ventral to the locus coeruleus (blue) sends widespread projections to promote REM sleep. Medullary axons projecting to the spinal cord profoundly inhibit motor neurons so that they cannot fire, causing muscle atonia. Other axons project to the brain to activate other regions.

Cerebral cortex

Basal forebrain

Midbrain

Cerebellum

Locus coeruleus

Subcoeruleus

Inhibition of motor neurons

Optic chiasm

Reticular formation

Pons

Medulla

14.28 BRAIN MECHANISMS UNDERLYING SLEEP

The constant SWS seen in the cortex of the isolated forebrain appears to be generated by the **basal forebrain** in the ventral frontal lobe and anterior hypothalamus, including the ventrolateral preoptic area (**FIGURE 14.28A**). Electrical stimulation of the basal forebrain can induce SWS activity (Clemente and Sterman, 1967), while lesions there suppress sleep (McGinty and Sterman, 1968). Within the basal forebrain, neural circuits regulate activity of GABA-ergic neurons (M. Xu et al., 2015) that send their axons to two important targets. One target is the nearby **tuberomammillary nucleus** in the posterior hypothalamus where stimulation of $GABA_A$ receptors promotes sleep. These seem to be the $GABA_A$ receptors that general anesthetics act on to make us unconscious and induce slow waves in the EEG (see Figure 14.26). The other target of basal forebrain GABA-ergic inhibition is an ascending arousal system in the brainstem that we consider next.

The reticular formation wakes up the forebrain

In the late 1940s, electrical stimulation of an extensive region of the brainstem known as the **reticular formation** was shown to activate the cortex (**FIGURE 14.28B**). The reticular formation consists of a diffuse group of cells whose axons and dendrites course in many directions, extending from the medulla through the thalamus. Electrically stimulating the reticular formation awakens animals rapidly (Moruzzi and Magoun, 1949). Lesions of these regions produced persistent sleep in the animals. The basal forebrain region actively imposes sleep on the brain in part by inhibiting the reticular formation. Between them, the basal forebrain and the brainstem reticular formation push the brain back and forth from NREM to wakefulness. Now let's consider the systems triggering REM.

The pons triggers REM sleep

Several methods pinpointed the region of the pons that is important for REM sleep. Large lesions of the pons abolish REM sleep (**FIGURE 14.28C**) (L. Friedman and Jones, 1984). Electrical stimulation of the same region, or pharmacological stimulation of this region with cholinergic agonists, can induce or prolong REM sleep. Eventually research pinpointed a specific region of the pons, just ventral to the locus coeruleus, which is therefore called the **subcoeruleus**, where some neurons are active only during REM sleep (J. M. Siegel, 1994).

isolated brain Sometimes referred to by the French term *encéphale isolé*. An experimental preparation in which an animal's brainstem has been separated from the spinal cord by a cut below the medulla.

isolated forebrain Sometimes referred to by the French term *cerveau isolé*. An experimental preparation in which an animal's nervous system has been cut in the upper midbrain, dividing the forebrain from the brainstem.

basal forebrain A ventral region in the forebrain that has been implicated in consciousness and sleep.

tuberomammillary nucleus A region of the basal hypothalamus, near the pituitary stalk, that plays a role in generating SWS.

reticular formation An extensive region of the brainstem (extending from the medulla through the thalamus) that is involved in arousal (waking).

subcoeruleus A brain region just ventral to the locus coeruleus, associated with REM sleep.

Go to Video 14.4
**Cat, Dog, and Human
Sleep Activity**
bn8e.com/14.4

Go to Video 14.5
Rat Sleep Activity
bn8e.com/14.5

(A)

(B)

14.29 ACTING OUT A DREAM (A) This cat received a lesion near the locus coeruleus that blocked the complete paralysis (atonia) that normally accompanies REM sleep. Following a bout of SWS, the cat in REM rises up as though about to pounce, but its eyes are closed and nothing is there. (B) The standing cat is wobbly, "looking" at something we cannot see. These behaviors indicate the cat is dreaming—seeing and interacting with objects that aren't really there. (From A. R. Morrison et al., 1995, photographs courtesy of Dr. Adrian Morrison.)

One job of the subcoeruleus is to profoundly inhibit motor neurons to keep them from firing. Glutamatergic neurons in the subcoeruleus excite neurons in the medulla, which in turn project axons down the spinal cord to release the inhibitory transmitters GABA and glycine to deeply inhibit spinal motor neurons (Hayashi et al., 2015; Weber et al., 2015). This descending inhibition prevents motor neurons from reaching threshold and producing an action potential (Kodama et al., 2003). Thus, the dreamer's muscles are not just relaxed, but flaccid.

This loss of muscle tone during REM sleep is sometimes abolished by small lesions in the subcoeruleus (A. R. Morrison, 1983). Cats with such lesions seem to act out their dreams. They enter NREM sleep like a normal cat, but as they begin to display the desynchronized EEG of REM sleep, instead of becoming completely limp as a normal cat does, these cats stagger to their feet (**FIGURE 14.29**). Are they awake or in REM sleep? They move their heads as though visually tracking moving objects (that aren't there), bat with their forepaws at nothing, and ignore objects that are present. In addition, the cat's inner eyelids, the translucent nictitating membranes, partially cover the eyes. Thus, the cat appears to be in REM sleep, but motor activity is not being inhibited by the brain. You can watch one of these cats acting out its dream on the website for this book.

So far we've described three interacting brain systems controlling sleep: an NREM-promoting region in the forebrain, an arousing reticular formation in the brainstem, and subcoeruleus in the pons to trigger paralysis of the body during REM. There is a fourth important system, which seems to act as a "switch" among these three centers, in the hypothalamus. To understand how we learned about this fourth system, you need to consider the rare but fascinating condition called *narcolepsy*.

A hypothalamic sleep center was revealed by the study of narcolepsy

You might not consider getting lots of sleep an affliction, but many people are either drowsy all the time or suffer sudden attacks of sleep. At the extreme of such tendencies is **narcolepsy**, an unusual disorder in which the patient is afflicted by frequent, intense attacks of sleep that last 5–30 minutes and can occur at any time during usual waking hours. These sleep attacks occur several times a day—usually about every 90 minutes (Dantz et al., 1994).

Most people display NREM for an hour or more before entering REM; individuals who suffer from narcolepsy, however, tend to enter REM in the first few minutes of sleep. People with this disorder exhibit a disrupted pattern of sleep at night, and they suffer abrupt, overwhelming sleepiness during the day. Many people with narcolepsy also show **cataplexy**, a sudden loss of muscle tone, leading to collapse of the body without loss of consciousness. Cataplexy can be triggered by sudden, intense emotional stimuli, including both laughter and anger. Narcolepsy usually manifests itself between the ages of 15 and 25 years and continues throughout life. Remember

narcolepsy A disorder that involves frequent, intense episodes of sleep, which last from 5 to 30 minutes and can occur anytime during the usual waking hours.

cataplexy Sudden loss of muscle tone, leading to collapse of the body without loss of consciousness.

hypocretins Also called *orexins*. Neuropeptides produced in the hypothalamus that are involved in switching between sleep states, in narcolepsy, and in the control of appetite.

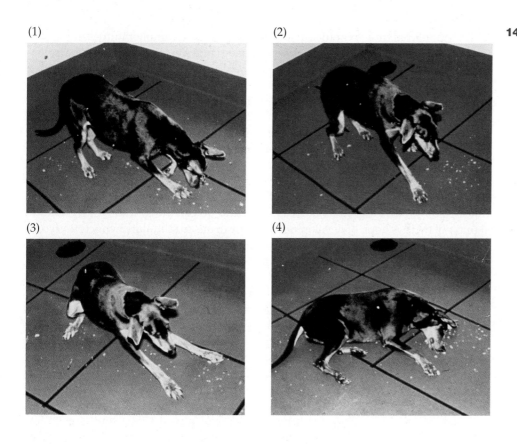

Go to Video 14.6
Narcolepsy
bn8e.com/14.6

14.30 NARCOLEPSY IN DOGS A narcoleptic dog that suffers cataplexy when excited is offered a food treat (1), becomes wobbly (2), lies down (3), and finally falls limply to the floor (4). (Courtesy of Dr. Seiji Nishino.)

Barry from the start of this chapter? His narcolepsy symptoms began in his freshman year of college, when he started showing the classic signs of excessive daytime sleepiness and cataplexy.

Several strains of dogs exhibit narcolepsy (Aldrich, 1993), complete with sudden collapse and very short latencies to sleep onset (**FIGURE 14.30**). (You can watch these dogs displaying cataplexy on our website.) Just like humans who suffer from narcolepsy, the dogs often show REM immediately upon falling asleep. Abrupt collapsing in these dogs is suppressed by the same drugs (discussed shortly) that are used to treat human cataplexy.

The mutation responsible for narcolepsy in one of these strains of dogs was found to be in a gene that encodes receptors for the neuropeptide **hypocretin** (also called *orexin*) (L. Lin et al., 1999). Mice with the *hypocretin* gene knocked out also display narcolepsy (Chemelli et al., 1999). Genetically normal rats can be made narcoleptic if injected with a toxin that destroys neurons that possess hypocretin receptors (Gerashchenko et al., 2001). No one knows why interfering with hypocretin signaling leads to narcolepsy, but the narcoleptic dogs show signs of neural degeneration in the amygdala and nearby forebrain structures (J. M. Siegel, Nienhuis, et al., 1999).

Similarly, humans with narcolepsy have lost about 90% of their hypocretin neurons (**FIGURE 14.31**) (Scammell, 2015; Thannickal et al., 2000). This degeneration of hypocretin neurons seems to cause inappropriate activation of the cataplexy pathway that is normally restricted to REM sleep. So hypocretin normally keeps sleep at bay and prevents the transition from wakefulness directly into REM sleep.

The neurons that normally produce hypocretin are found almost exclusively in the hypothalamus. Where do these neurons send their axons to release the hypocretin? Not so coincidentally, they send their axons to each of the three brain centers that we mentioned before: basal forebrain, reticular formation, and subcoeruleus (Sutcliffe and de Lecea, 2002). The hypocretin neurons also project axons to the hypothalamic tuberomammillary nucleus that is inhibited by the basal forebrain to induce NREM. So, the hypothalamic hypocretin neurons normally control our switching between wakefulness, NREM, and REM (see Figure 14.28D). Loss of these neurons in narcolepsy results in abrupt transitions, rather than orderly progression, through various sleep states.

(A) Normal

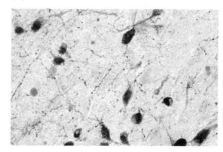

(B) Narcoleptic

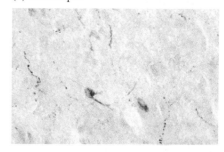

14.31 NEURAL DEGENERATION IN HUMANS WITH NARCOLEPSY (A) Immunocytochemistry reveals hypocretin-containing neurons in the lateral hypothalamus of a person who did not have narcolepsy. (B) This same region of the brain from someone who suffered from narcolepsy has far fewer hypocretin neurons. (Courtesy of Dr. Jerome Siegel.)

sleep paralysis A state during the transition to or from sleep, in which the ability to move or talk is temporarily lost.

sleep enuresis Bed-wetting.

somnambulism Sleepwalking.

The traditional treatment for narcolepsy was the use of amphetamines in the daytime. The drug GHB (γ-hydroxybutyrate, trade name Xyrem) helps some narcoleptics (although there are concerns about potential abuse of this drug [Tuller, 2002]). A newer drug, modafinil (Provigil), is sometimes effective for preventing narcoleptic attacks. There is a debate about whether modafinil should be available to anyone who feels sleepy or needs to stay awake (Pack, 2003), but at least one study found the drug no more effective than caffeine in this regard (Wesensten et al., 2002). Our friend Barry, from the beginning of the chapter, eventually found a combination of mild stimulants that worked for him, and he later earned his MD degree. Antidepressants (see Table 16.3) are often prescribed to suppress episodes of cataplexy (Dauvilliers et al., 2014), although it is not clear they are more effective than placebo (Swick, 2015). Now that narcolepsy is known to be caused by a loss of hypocretin signaling, there is hope of developing synthetic drugs to stimulate hypocretin receptors, both for the relief of symptoms in narcolepsy and to combat sleepiness in people without narcolepsy.

One common symptom of narcolepsy is experienced by many people (whether or not they suffer from narcolepsy) on occasion (Fukuda et al., 1998). **Sleep paralysis** is the (temporary) inability to move or talk either just before dropping off to sleep or, more often, just after waking. In this state people may experience sudden sensory hallucinations (Cheyne, 2002). Sleep paralysis never lasts more than a few minutes, so it's best to relax and avoid panic. One hypothesis is that sleep paralysis results when the pontine center (see Figure 14.28C) continues to impose paralysis for a short while after the person awakens from a REM episode.

Sleep Disorders Can Be Serious, Even Life-Threatening

Narcolepsy is just one of several sleep disorders (**TABLE 14.2**) that have made sleep disorder clinics common in major medical centers. For some people, the peace and comfort of regular, uninterrupted sleep is routinely disturbed by the inability to fall asleep, by prolonged sleep, or by unusual awakenings.

Some minor dysfunctions are associated with sleep

Some dysfunctions associated with sleep are much more common in children than in adults. Two sleep disorders in children—night terrors (described earlier) and **sleep enuresis** (bed-wetting)—are associated with SWS. Most people grow out of these conditions without intervention, but pharmacological approaches can be used to reduce the amount of stage 3 sleep (as well as REM time) while increasing stage 2 sleep. For sleep enuresis, some doctors prescribe a nasal spray of the hormone vasopressin (antidiuretic hormone) before bedtime, which decreases urine production.

Somnambulism (sleepwalking) consists of getting out of bed, walking around, and appearing awake. Although more common in childhood, it sometimes persists into adulthood. These episodes last a few seconds to minutes, and the person usually does not remember the experience. Because such episodes occur during

---

TABLE 14.2 Classification of Sleep Disorders

DISORDERS OF INITIATING AND MAINTAINING SLEEP (INSOMNIA)

Ordinary, uncomplicated insomnia

  Transient

  Persistent

Drug-related insomnia caused by

  Use of stimulants

  Withdrawal of depressants

  Chronic alcoholism

Insomnia associated with psychiatric disorders

Insomnia associated with sleep-induced respiratory impairment (sleep apnea)

DISORDERS OF EXCESSIVE DROWSINESS

Narcolepsy

Drowsiness associated with psychiatric problems

Drug-related drowsiness

Drowsiness associated with sleep-induced respiratory impairment (sleep apnea)

DISORDERS OF SLEEP-WAKING SCHEDULE

Transient disruption caused by

  Time zone change by airplane flight (jet lag)

  Shift work, especially night work

Persistent disruption (irregular rhythm)

DYSFUNCTIONS ASSOCIATED WITH SLEEP, SLEEP STAGES, OR PARTIAL AROUSALS

Sleepwalking (somnambulism)

Sleep enuresis (bed-wetting)

Night terrors

Nightmares

Sleep-related seizures

Teeth grinding

REM behavior disorder (RBD)

Source: After Weitzman, 1981.

stage 3 SWS, they are more common in the first half of the night (when those stages predominate).

Most sleepwalkers are not acting out a dream (Parkes, 1985). The main problem is the inability of sleepwalkers to wake into full contact with their surroundings. At least one person was acquitted of murder after suggesting that he had suffered from "homicidal somnambulism," but such claims are difficult to evaluate (Broughton et al., 1994). Some people, however, do seem to be acting out their dreams during REM sleep. **REM behavior disorder** (**RBD**) is characterized by organized behavior—such as fighting an imaginary foe, eating a meal, acting like a wild animal—in a person who appears to be asleep (Schenck and Mahowald, 2002). Sometimes the person remembers a dream that fits well with this outward behavior (C. Brown, 2003). This disorder usually begins after the age of 50 and is more common in men than in women. Individuals with RBD are reminiscent of the cats with a lesion in the subcoeruleus (see Figure 14.29) that were no longer paralyzed during REM and so acted out their dreams. The onset of RBD is often followed by the early symptoms of Parkinson's disease and dementia (Postuma et al., 2009), suggesting that the disorder is the beginning of a widespread neurodegeneration. RBD is usually controlled by antianxiety drugs (benzodiazepines) at bedtime.

Insomniacs have trouble falling asleep or staying asleep

Almost all of us experience an occasional inability to fall asleep, and a very few individuals die apparently because they stop sleeping altogether (see Box 14.1). But many people persistently find it difficult to fall asleep and/or stay asleep as long as they would like. Estimates of the prevalence of insomnia range from 15% to 30% of the adult population (Parkes, 1985). Insomnia is more commonly reported by people who are older, female, or users of drugs like tobacco, caffeine, and alcohol. Insomnia seems to be the final common outcome for various situational and medical conditions. It is not a trivial disorder; recall that adults who regularly sleep for short periods show a higher mortality rate than those who regularly sleep 7–8 hours each night (Kripke et al., 2002). People with **sleep state misperception** (McCall and Edinger, 1992) report that they didn't sleep even when an EEG showed signs of sleep and they failed to respond to stimuli. On the other hand, EEG readings of people who claim they are not sleeping show fewer slow waves, and more of the alpha and beta activity typical of wakefulness, than other sleepers (Edinger and Krystal, 2003), so perhaps they really are more conscious than other sleepers during NREM.

Situational factors that contribute to insomnia include shift work, time zone changes, and environmental conditions such as novelty (that hard motel bed). Usually these conditions produce transient **sleep-onset insomnia**, a difficulty in falling asleep. Drugs, as well as neurological and psychiatric factors, seem to cause **sleep-maintenance insomnia**, a difficulty in remaining asleep. In this type of insomnia, sleep is punctuated by frequent nighttime arousals. This form of insomnia is especially evident in disorders of the respiratory system.

In some people, respiration becomes unreliable during sleep. Breathing may cease for a minute or so, or it may slow alarmingly; blood levels of oxygen drop markedly. This syndrome, called **sleep apnea**, arises either from the progressive relaxation of muscles of the chest, diaphragm, and throat cavity (*obstructive* apnea) or from changes in the pacemaker respiratory neurons of the brainstem (*central* apnea). In the former instance, relaxation of the throat obstructs the airway—a kind of self-choking. For some people, breathing through a special machine (called a *continuous positive airway pressure*, or *CPAP, machine*) maintains air pressure in their airways and prevents the collapse of those airways (**FIGURE 14.32**). Central apnea is common in very obese people, but it also occurs, often undiagnosed, in nonobese people. Sleep

REM behavior disorder (RBD)
A sleep disorder in which a person physically acts out a dream.

sleep state misperception
Commonly, a person's perception that he has not been asleep when in fact he has. Typically occurs at the start of a sleep episode.

sleep-onset insomnia Difficulty in falling asleep.

sleep-maintenance insomnia
Difficulty in staying asleep.

sleep apnea A sleep disorder in which respiration slows or stops periodically, waking the person. Excessive daytime sleepiness results from the frequent nocturnal awakening.

14.32 A MACHINE THAT PREVENTS SLEEP APNEA By supplying continuous positive airway pressure (CPAP), this machine prevents the collapse of the airway that otherwise causes this man to stop breathing for a while several times each night. It also stops his snoring. (Photograph by Christopher Breedlove.)

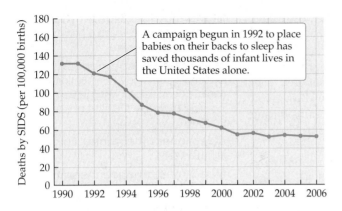

14.33 BACK TO SLEEP (Task Force on Sudden Infant Death and Moon, 2011.)

A campaign begun in 1992 to place babies on their backs to sleep has saved thousands of infant lives in the United States alone.

sudden infant death syndrome (SIDS) Also called *crib death*. The sudden, unexpected death of an apparently healthy human infant who simply stops breathing, usually during sleep.

apnea is frequently accompanied by loud, interrupted snoring, so loud snorers should consult a physician about the possibility that they suffer from sleep apnea.

Each episode of apnea arouses the person enough to restore breathing, but in rats such interruptions in oxygen kill neurons in the hippocampus and impair learning ability (Row et al., 2007), so apnea may lead to brain damage. What's more, the frequent nighttime arousals make such people sleepy in the daytime. Untreated sleep apnea may lead to any of several cardiovascular disorders, including hypertension and diabetes (Rakel, 2009).

Investigators have speculated that **sudden infant death syndrome** (**SIDS**, or *crib death*) arises from sleep apnea as a result of immaturity of systems that normally pace respiration. Autopsies of SIDS victims reveal abnormalities in brainstem serotonin systems (Kinney, 2009), and interfering with this system in young mice renders them unable to regulate respiration effectively. What's more, some of these mice spontaneously stopped breathing and died (Audero et al., 2008). The incidence of SIDS has been cut almost in half by the Back to Sleep campaign, which urges parents to place infants on their backs to sleep rather than on their stomachs (**FIGURE 14.33**). Placing the baby facedown may lead to suffocation if the baby cannot regulate breathing or arouse properly.

Although many drugs affect sleep, there is no perfect sleeping pill

Throughout recorded history, humans have reached for substances to enhance the prospects of sleep. Ancient Greeks used the juice of the poppy to obtain opium and used products of the mandrake plant that we recognize today as the anticholinergic drugs scopolamine and atropine (Hartmann, 1978). The preparation of barbituric acid in the mid-nineteenth century by the discoverer of aspirin, Adolph von Bayer, started the development of many drugs—*barbiturates*—that were once used to help people get to sleep. Unfortunately, none of these substances can provide a completely normal night of sleep in terms of time spent in various sleep states, such as REM sleep, and none of them remain effective when used repeatedly.

Most modern sleeping pills—including the benzodiazepine triazolam (Halcion) and newer drugs like Ambien, Sonata, and Lunesta—bind to various sites on GABA$_A$ receptors (see Figure 4.13), making them more responsive to the neurotransmitter and thus inhibiting broad regions of the brain. But reliance on sleeping pills poses many problems (Mignot, 2013). There is hope that drugs that block both of two known hypocretin receptors may offer another route to sleepiness (Tannenbaum et al., 2016). But viewed solely as a way to deal with sleep problems, drugs fall far short of being a suitable remedy, for several reasons.

First, continued use of sleeping pills causes them to lose effectiveness, and this declining ability to induce sleep often leads to self-prescribed increased dosages that can be dangerous. A second major drawback is that sleeping pills produce marked changes in the pattern of sleep, both while the drug is being used and for days afterward.

Use of sleeping pills may lead to a persistent "sleep drunkenness," coupled with drowsiness, that impairs waking activity or may lead to memory gaps about daily activity. Police report cases of "the Ambien driver," a person who takes a sleeping pill and then gets up a few hours later to go for a spin, with sometimes disastrous results, while apparently asleep (Saul, 2006). In other cases, people taking such medicines eat snacks, shop over the Internet, or even have sex, with no memory of these events the next day (Dolder and Nelson, 2008).

Because the hormone melatonin is normally released from the pineal gland at night (see Figure 5.20), the administration of exogenous melatonin has been suggested to aid the onset of sleep. In fact, melatonin does have a weak hypnotic effect soon after administration (Chase and Gidal, 1997), perhaps because it lowers body temperature, reducing arousal and causing drowsiness (Dawson and Encel, 1993). In contrast, caffeine is an

TABLE 14.3 Some Simple Tips to Promote Sleep Hygiene

RECOMMENDATIONS

Keep your internal clock set with a consistent sleep schedule (get up at the same time each day).

Seek sunlight in the daytime, avoid lights at night.

Turn your bedroom into a sleep-inducing environment.

Avoid caffeine, alcohol, and nicotine before bedtime.

Establish a soothing presleep routine.

Only go to sleep when you're truly tired.

If you're going to nap, do it early in the day.

Lighten up on evening meals.

Balance fluid intake to avoid night trips to the bathroom.

Avoid using computer screens before bedtime.

Don't exercise late in the day.

Source: Healthy Sleep, http://healthysleep.med.harvard.edu/healthy/getting/overcoming/tips

antagonist for the neuromodulator **adenosine**, which generally reduces neural activity (Bjorness and Greene, 2009). Thus caffeine boosts brain activity and, taken at night, delays the circadian clock (Burke et al., 2015).

Certainly, the treatment for insomnia that has the fewest side effects, and that is very effective for many people, is not to use any drug but to practice **sleep hygiene**, habits that promote healthy sleep (Irish et al., 2015). The best advice for insomniacs is to use an alarm clock to wake up faithfully at the same time each day (weekends included!) and then simply go to bed once they feel sleepy. Other sleep hygiene habits include establishing a bedtime routine in a quiet, dark environment, to condition sleep onset, and avoiding daytime naps, caffeine at night, and looking at computer screens (whose bluish light stimulates melanopsin in retinal ganglion neurons; Gooley et al., 2010) before bedtime (**TABLE 14.3**). An important adjunct to this strategy is to ignore preconceived notions about how much sleep you "need." If you get out of bed every day at 6:00 AM and don't feel sleepy until midnight, then your body is telling you that you need only 6 hours of sleep, no matter what millions of dollars in annual pharmaceutical advertising might say. A study of three hunter-gatherer societies found that people in those groups tend to wake just before sunrise, rarely take naps, and go to sleep about 3 hours after sunset. Subtracting awakenings at night, these people sleep an average of 6.4 hours per night (Yetish et al., 2015). Is this the "natural" sleep pattern of our species?

In contrast, in our society, most people sleep longer on weekends, presumably because they are sleep-deprived during the work week (**FIGURE 14.34**). This irregular cycle in sleep patterns has been likened to "social jet lag" (Roenneberg, 2013), which is not conducive to good sleep hygiene.

The Cutting Edge

Can Individual Neurons Be "Sleepy"?

We are used to thinking of sleep as a global state of the brain—either the whole brain is asleep or it's not. But some recent findings are suggesting not only that the two hemispheres can be in different sleep states, but also that one part of cortex may be partially asleep while the patch of cortex next to it is still awake. In fact, some are suggesting that individual cortical neurons may be "awake" or "asleep" and that the ability of a cortical region to perform its function may depend on the proportion of neurons that are awake.

Vyazovskiy et al. (2011) implanted lots of tiny wires into both the frontal and the parietal lobes in rats, which were free to move around, and recorded firing of many neurons in each site for 2–3 weeks. When the animals were awake, most neurons were actively firing. But some neurons would occasionally stop firing for a while, as if the cell had gone "off-line" for a bit

adenosine An endogenous neuro-modulator that generally reduces neural activity; caffeine interferes with adenosine binding.

sleep hygiene Habits, such as avoiding caffeine shortly before bedtime, that promote healthy sleep.

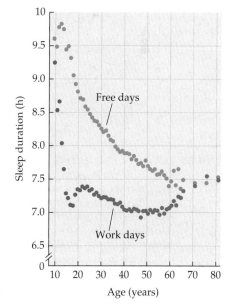

14.34 SLEEPING IN ON THE WEEKEND Such patterns represent poor sleep hygiene, because sleeping late on weekend mornings may make it difficult to fall asleep early enough the night before a work day. (After Roenneberg, 2013.)

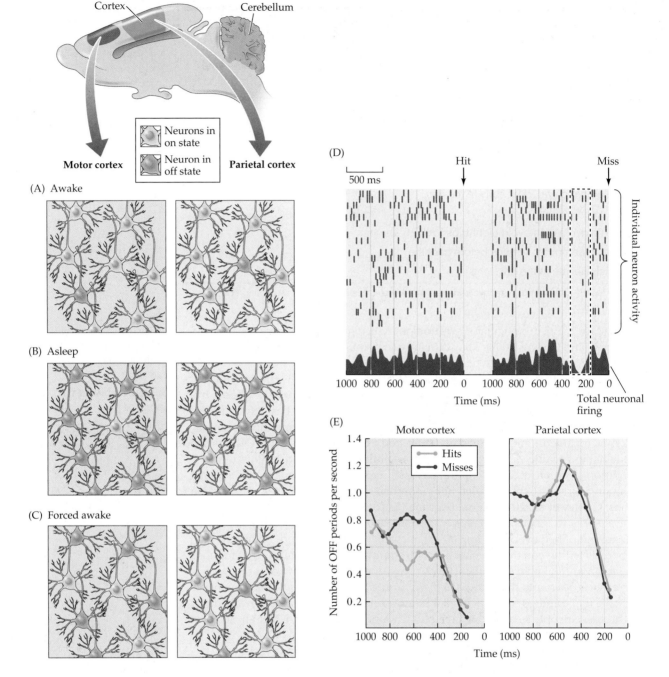

14.35 LOCAL SLEEP IN THE BRAIN (A) By recording both local EEG activity and the firing of individual neurons in two different areas of rat cortex, researchers learned that neurons alternate between being in an "on" state (yellow), when they are firing often, and being in an "off" state (blue), when they fire very rarely, when the animals are awake. (B) During SWS, most neurons are in an off state but switch from off to on and back again in synchrony, which probably generates the slow waves in EEG that give SWS its name. (C) As animals are kept awake, build-ing up pressure to sleep, the proportion of neurons in the off state increases continually. Interestingly, the proportion of off neurons may differ from one cortical region to another. (D) Neu-ron firing is active in motor cortex before a successful reach (a hit) in rats taught to reach for a sugar pellet, but in the time just before a miss (dashed box), many neurons are silent, indicating they are off-line. (E) The proportion of neurons in the off state in motor cortex is greater just before a miss than a hit. In nearby parietal cortex of the same animals, the proportion of neurons in the off state is the same before a miss as before a hit.

(**FIGURE 14.35A**). The researchers suggest this brief period of quiet may be caused by fa-tigue, as if each neuron needs to rest a bit before resuming activity. The picture that emerges is that each neuron alternates between being in an active, "on," state and an inactive, "off," state.

As you might expect, neurons spend more time in the on state when the animal is awake than when it is in SWS (**FIGURE 14.35B**). In fact, during SWS cortical neurons become syn-chronized in this switching from on to off, which seems to be the source of the slow waves that give SWS its name. Even while the animals are awake, a group of neurons in one cortical region may go off-line at the same time, and when they do, a slow wave can be detected with local EEG electrodes. What's fascinating is that depriving the rats of sleep (by giving them new toys to play with) results in more neurons in the off state (**FIGURE 14.35C**). The more pressure there is to sleep (i.e., the longer the animals have been awake), the more neurons go off-line.

So can one group of cortical neurons be asleep while neighboring neurons are still awake? Maybe, because when the researchers had the rats learn to reach for a sugar pellet, they noticed a very interesting phenomenon. There was a different pattern of neuronal activity in motor cortex (in the frontal lobe) just before a reach when the animal successfully got the pellet (a "hit") than when it didn't (a "miss") (**FIGURE 14.35D**). When the animals missed, there was more likely to be a high proportion of neurons off-line in the contralateral motor cortex (i.e., the part of the cortex directing that paw) (**FIGURE 14.35E**, left). Strengthening the idea that having off-line neurons in motor cortex might have caused the miss, there was no relationship between misses and the proportion of neurons off-line in parietal cortex (see Figure 14.35E, right).

The idea that various regions of cortex may be asleep while neighboring regions are awake and functional is controversial and takes some getting used to (Vyazovskiy and Harris, 2013). But it could explain how dolphins and birds can have one cortical hemisphere asleep while the other is awake (see Figure 14.16). Also, it could explain why a sleep-deprived person is impaired in some cognitive tasks, if progressively more neurons have gone off-line in whichever particular cortical region underlies that behavior. It also helps us understand various dissociations in sleep, such as sleepwalking (motor cortex must be working, but the person is not fully conscious). Likewise, sleep talking, RBD, and sleep state misperception can all be understood if parts of the cortex are functioning while others are sleeping.

Recommended Reading

Dunlap, J. C., Loros, J. J., and DeCoursey, P. J. (2003). *Chronobiology: Biological Timekeeping.* Sunderland, MA: Sinauer.

Kryger, M. K., Roth, T., and Dement, W. C. (Eds.). (2016). *Principles and Practice of Sleep Medicine* (6th ed.). Philadelphia: Elsevier.

Lavie, P. (2003). *Restless Nights: Understanding Snoring and Sleep Apnea.* New Haven, CT: Yale University Press.

Max, D. T. (2007). *The Family That Couldn't Sleep: A Medical Mystery.* New York: Random House.

Schenk, C. H. (2008). *Sleep: A Groundbreaking Guide to the Mysteries, the Problems and the Solutions.* New York: Avery.

Stickgold, R., and Walker, M. P. (Eds.). (2009). *The Neuroscience of Sleep.* San Diego, CA: Academic Press.

Go to
bn8e.com
for study questions,
quizzes, activities,
and other resources

VISUAL SUMMARY

You should be able to relate each summary to the adjacent illustration, including structures and processes.
Go to **bn8e.com/vs14** for links to figures, animations, and activities that will help you consolidate the material.

1 Animals show **circadian rhythms** of activity that can be **entrained** by light. These rhythms synchronize behavior to changes in the environment. In constant dim light, animals **free-run**, displaying a **period** of about 24 hours. Review **Figures 14.1 and 14.9, Animation 14.2**

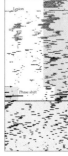
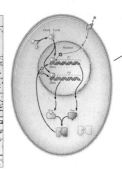

2 Lesions of the **suprachiasmatic nucleus (SCN)** abolish activity rhythms in constant conditions. Transplanting the SCN from one animal into another results in a free-running rhythm of the donor, demonstrating that the SCN contains a clock that can drive circadian activity. Several proteins (Clock, Cycle, Period) interact, increasing and decreasing in a cycle that takes about 24 hours. This molecular clock, pooled from many SCN neurons, drives circadian rhythms. Review **Figures 14.2–14.7, Animation 14.3**

3 Almost all mammals show two sleep states: **rapid-eye-movement (REM) sleep** and **non-REM sleep (NREM)**. Human NREM has three distinct stages (**stages 1, 2, 3**) defined by **electroencephalography (EEG)** criteria, including **sleep spindles** and in stage 3 large, slow **delta waves** during **slow-wave sleep (SWS)**. Muscle tension, heart rate, respiratory rate, and temperature all decline during NREM. Review **Figure 14.10, Table 14.1, Activity 14.1**

4 REM sleep is characterized by rapid, low-amplitude EEG (almost like an EEG while awake) but also by profound muscle relaxation because motor neurons are inhibited. People awakened from REM frequently report vivid dreams, while people awakened from NREM report ideas or thinking. Review **Figure 14.11, Table 14.1**

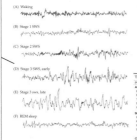

TABLE 14.1 Properties of NREM and REM Sleep

5 Sleep stages cycle through the night, with stage 3 SWS prominent early and REM predominant later. Infants sleep a lot, with lots of REM, but as we grow up we sleep less, with less REM. Elderly people sleep even less, and stage 3 sleep (SWS) eventually disappears. Review **Figures 14.12–14.18**

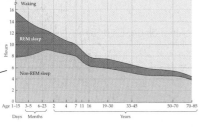

6 Four proposed functions of sleep are energy conservation, **ecological niche** adaptation, body restoration, and memory consolidation. A few people sleep only an hour per night, suggesting that they accomplish the function(s) of sleep very efficiently, but all healthy people sleep. Review **Figures 14.20–14.24**

7 **Sleep deprivation** leads to impairments in vigilance and reaction times. It also incurs sleep debt, although the lost NREM and REM may be partially restored in subsequent nights. Prolonged sleep deprivation compromises the immune system and leads to death. Review **Box 14.1**

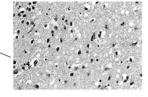

8 Four brain systems control sleep and waking. The **basal forebrain** promotes SWS, the brainstem **reticular formation** promotes arousal, the **subcoeruleus** of the pons triggers REM sleep, and hypothalamic neurons releasing **hypocretin** regulate these three centers. Review **Figures 14.26–14.28, Activity 14.2, Videos 14.4 and 14.5**

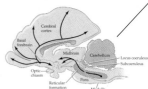

9 **Narcolepsy** is the disorder that involves sudden, uncontrollable periods of sleep, which may be accompanied by **cataplexy**, paralysis while remaining conscious. Disruption of hypocretin signaling causes narcolepsy. Review **Figures 14.29–14.31, Video 14.6**

10 Sleep disorders fall into four categories: trouble falling or staying asleep (**insomnia**); excessive drowsiness (e.g., narcolepsy); disruption of the sleep-waking schedule; and dysfunctions associated with sleep, sleep stages, or partial arousals (e.g., **somnambulism**). No pill guarantees a normal night's sleep. Review **Figures 14.32–14.34, Tables 14.2–14.3**

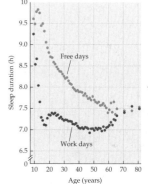

Emotions and Mental Disorders

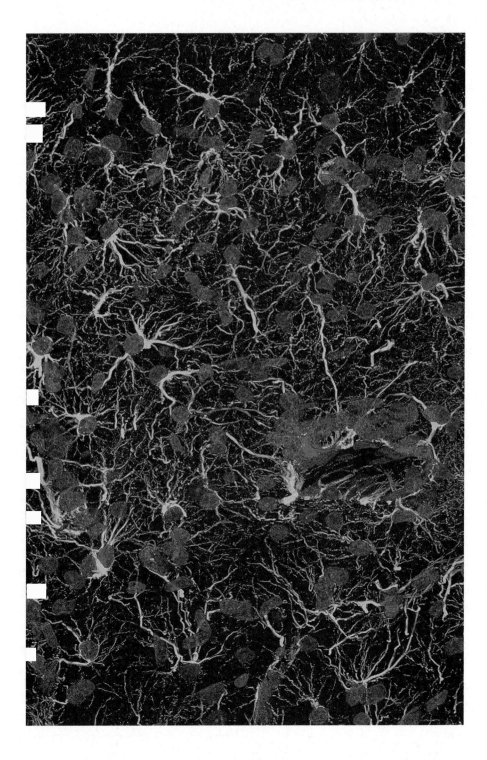

Emotions, Aggression, and Stress

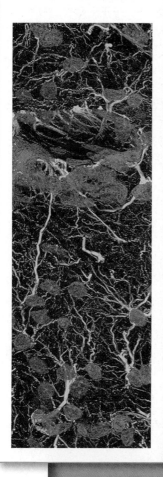

15

▌ The Hazards of Fearlessness

No one enjoys being afraid, so you might think it would be great to never know fear. But recall from Chapter 8 that absence of another unpleasant experience, pain, can be hazardous to your health. When we say that heroes are "fearless," what we really mean is that they manage to function effectively *despite* the fear they experience, not that they never feel afraid. However, there really are people who *literally* do not experience fear. One such woman, a patient known as S.M., lost her fear in late childhood because of a genetic disorder so rare, fewer than 300 cases have been reported (Feinstein et al., 2011). S.M. shows us the value of being afraid. Not only is she unafraid of snakes or spiders, but she once walked right up to a knife-wielding drug addict who was trying to rob her and basically dared him to stab her. He was so disquieted by her strange response that *he* ran away. Another time she was nearly killed in an act of domestic violence. While her behavioral responses and self-report appear typical for other emotions, S.M. shows very little sympathetic response to fearful stimuli and produces almost no startle response to a sudden, loud noise (Aschwanden, 2013).

S.M. is not deliberately reckless; she has learned to follow simple safety rules like looking both ways before crossing the street. But there are other consequences of S.M.'s fearlessness that you might not predict. When talking to someone, she tends to get much closer than other people do, sometimes just a foot away (Kennedy et al., 2009), suggesting she has a distorted sense of personal space. When strangers talk to her in public, like the mugger she encountered, she tends to stroll right up to them. S.M. also fails to perceive risk in more mundane social situations, so she's an easy target for Internet scams. Although she's very outgoing, and might fondly address a waiter she'd only met once before, she has few long-term friendships, perhaps because she speaks without fear. Maybe being fearless isn't all it's cracked up to be.

What happened to S.M. to make her this way, and is there really nothing she is afraid of?

The sound of unexpected footsteps in the eerie quiet of the night brings fear to many of us. But the sound of music we enjoy and the voice of someone we love summons feelings of warmth. For some of us, feelings and emotions can become vastly exaggerated; fears, for example, can become paralyzing attacks of anxiety and panic. No story about our behavior is complete without considering the everyday events that involve feelings.

Our chapter begins with emotions, the bodily responses and brain mechanisms underlying happiness and joy, fear and loathing. We'll discuss both the development of emotions in individuals and the evolution of emotions. The first section's examination of brain mechanisms related to emotional states emphasizes fear and aggression because both are important for survival and they are readily studied in

▌
Go to Brain Explorer
bn8e.com/15.1

emotion A subjective mental state that is usually accompanied by distinctive behaviors, feelings, and involuntary physiological changes.

sympathetic nervous system A component of the autonomic nervous system that arises from the thoracic and lumbar spinal cord.

parasympathetic nervous system A component of the autonomic nervous system that arises from both the cranial nerves and the sacral spinal cord.

James-Lange theory The theory that our experience of emotion is a response to the physiological changes that accompany it.

animals. That discussion leads us to the second section, where we consider stress. Stress is associated with a variety of health problems because it involves not only the nervous and endocrine systems but also the immune system. We find that the nervous, endocrine, and immune systems interact extensively.

What Are Emotions?

The topic of emotions is complicated by the fact that we apply the word *emotion* to several different things. Emotion is a private, subjective feeling that we may have without anyone else being aware of it. But the word *emotional* is also used to describe many behaviors that people show, such as fearful facial expressions, frantic arm movements, or angry shouting. Furthermore, during strong emotion we often experience physiological changes, such as a rapidly beating heart, shortness of breath, or excessive sweating. To encompass all three of these aspects, we will define **emotion** as a subjective mental state that is usually accompanied by distinctive behaviors as well as involuntary physiological changes. Typically, we experience an emotion for only a brief time, but we'll see later in the chapter that prolonged experience of negative emotions, which is the hallmark of stress, can be very bad for our health.

We begin this section by discussing the major theories of how we experience emotions, including efforts to figure out whether emotional experience causes the physiological arousal or vice versa. Then we discuss the different types of emotions and how they relate to one another. Normally we display a very distinctive facial expression for each of the different emotions, and we'll see that people from very different cultures recognize these expressions. This near-universal recognition of emotional faces suggests that emotions are evolved characteristics and that facial displays of emotional experience may help us get along with others. We conclude this section by considering brain circuits for emotion, including a rather specialized brain circuit for fear, before talking about aggression.

Broad Theories of Emotion Emphasize Bodily Responses

In many emotional states the heart races, the hands and face become warm, the palms sweat, and the stomach feels queasy. Common expressions capture this emotional-physical association: "my hair stood on end" or "a sinking feeling in my stomach." These sensations are the result of activation of the autonomic nervous system—either the **sympathetic nervous system** (the "fight or flight" system that generally activates the body for action) or the **parasympathetic nervous system** (which generally prepares the body to relax and recuperate) (see Figure 2.11).

Several theories have tried to explain the close ties between the subjective feelings of emotions and the autonomic activity. Folk wisdom suggests that the autonomic reactions are caused by the emotion—"I was so angry, my stomach was churning," as though the anger produces the churning sensation (**FIGURE 15.1A**). Yet research indicates that the relationship between emotion and physiological arousal is more subtle.

Do emotions cause bodily changes, or vice versa?

William James (1842–1910) and Carl G. Lange (1834–1900) turned the folk notion on its head, suggesting that the emotions we experience are *caused by* the bodily changes. From this perspective, we experience fear because we perceive the activity that dangerous conditions trigger in our body (**FIGURE 15.1B**). Different emotions thus feel different because they are generated by different constellations of physiological responses.

The **James-Lange theory** inspired many attempts to link specific emotions to specific bodily responses. These attempts mostly failed because it turns out that there is no distinctive autonomic pattern for each emotion. Fear, surprise, and anger, for example, all tend to be accompanied by sympathetic activation, while parasympathetic activation tends to accompany both joy and sadness.

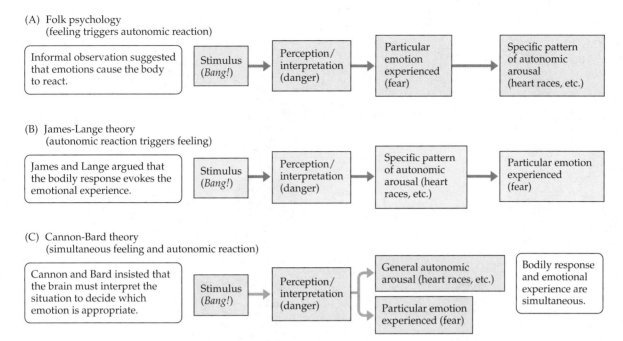

(A) Folk psychology
(feeling triggers autonomic reaction)

| Informal observation suggested that emotions cause the body to react. | → | Stimulus (*Bang!*) | → | Perception/ interpretation (danger) | → | Particular emotion experienced (fear) | → | Specific pattern of autonomic arousal (heart races, etc.) |

(B) James-Lange theory
(autonomic reaction triggers feeling)

| James and Lange argued that the bodily response evokes the emotional experience. | → | Stimulus (*Bang!*) | → | Perception/ interpretation (danger) | → | Specific pattern of autonomic arousal (heart races, etc.) | → | Particular emotion experienced (fear) |

(C) Cannon-Bard theory
(simultaneous feeling and autonomic reaction)

| Cannon and Bard insisted that the brain must interpret the situation to decide which emotion is appropriate. | → | Stimulus (*Bang!*) | → | Perception/ interpretation (danger) | → | General autonomic arousal (heart races, etc.) / Particular emotion experienced (fear) | | Bodily response and emotional experience are simultaneous. |

15.1 DIFFERENT VIEWS OF THE CHAIN OF EVENTS IN EMOTIONAL RESPONSES

In addition, the physiological reactions are rather slow, as physiologists Walter B. Cannon (1871–1945) and Philip Bard (1898–1977) pointed out (W. B. Cannon, 1929). In the **Cannon-Bard theory**, the brain decides which particular emotion is an appropriate response to the stimuli. According to this model, the cerebral cortex *simultaneously* decides on the appropriate emotional experience (fear, surprise, joy) and activates the autonomic nervous system to prepare the body, using either the sympathetic system, to ready the body for action, or the parasympathetic system to help the body rest (**FIGURE 15.1C**).

Stanley Schachter proposed a cognitive interpretation of stimuli and visceral states

Like Cannon and Bard, Stanley Schachter (1975) emphasized cognitive mechanisms in emotion. Under Schachter's **cognitive attribution model**, however, emotional labels (e.g., *anger, fear, joy*) are attributed to relatively nonspecific feelings of physiological arousal. *Which* emotion we experience depends on *cognitive* systems that assess the context—our current social, physical, and psychological situation.

In a famous test of this idea, people were injected with epinephrine (adrenaline) and told either that there would be no effect or that their hearts would race (Schachter and Singer, 1962). Participants who were warned of the reaction reported no emotional experience, but some participants who were not forewarned experienced emotions when their bodies responded to the drug.

However, *which* emotion was experienced could be affected by whether a confederate in the room acted angry or happy. The unsuspecting people injected with epinephrine were much more likely to report feeling angry when in the presence of an "angry" confederate, and more likely to report feeling elated when with a "happy" confederate (**FIGURE 15.2A**). These findings contradict the James-Lange prediction that feelings of anger or happiness should each be associated with a unique profile of autonomic reactions. Schachter and Singer concluded that the misinformed participants experienced their physiological arousal as whichever emotion seemed appropriate based on their cognitive assessment of the situation—"My heart's really pounding; I'm so angry!" or "My heart's really pounding; I'm so elated!" depended on the environment. Thus, Schachter and Singer saw emotional state as the result of an interaction between physiological arousal and cognitive interpretation of that

Cannon-Bard theory The theory that our experience of emotion is independent of the simultaneous physiological changes that accompany it.

cognitive attribution model The theory that our emotional experience results from cognitive analysis of the context around us, such that physiological changes may accentuate emotions but not specify which emotion we experience.

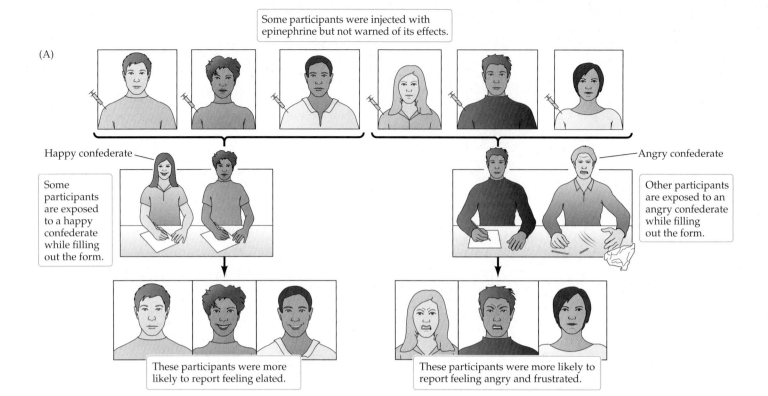

Some participants were injected with epinephrine but not warned of its effects.

(A)

Happy confederate

Some participants are exposed to a happy confederate while filling out the form.

Angry confederate

Other participants are exposed to an angry confederate while filling out the form.

These participants were more likely to report feeling elated.

These participants were more likely to report feeling angry and frustrated.

(B) Schachter's cognitive attribution model

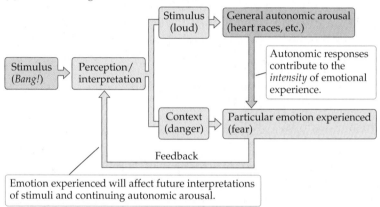

Stimulus (loud) → General autonomic arousal (heart races, etc.)

Autonomic responses contribute to the *intensity* of emotional experience.

Stimulus (*Bang!*) → Perception/ interpretation

Context (danger) → Particular emotion experienced (fear)

Feedback

Emotion experienced will affect future interpretations of stimuli and continuing autonomic arousal.

15.2 COGNITION PLAYS A ROLE IN THE EXPERIENCE OF EMOTION
(A) Schachter and Singer found that participants' emotional experiences after having been (unknowingly) injected with epinephrine could vary depending on how people around them were acting. (B) These results suggest that cognitive analysis of the situation affects what emotion we experience. Thus, sympathetic activation may increase the *intensity* of emotion we experience, but it does not completely determine *which* emotion we experience.

arousal. This cognitive theory of emotions proposes that our interpretation of the context, including social factors such as other people's emotions, determines which emotion we'll experience. Thus being in a theater full of laughing people may help us find the movie funny. The cognitive theory also suggests that our emotional experience at one time may affect how we interpret later events (**FIGURE 15.2B**).

Another interesting outcome of the experiment is that the people receiving epinephrine reported experiencing *more intense* emotions than other participants who were given saline, as would be predicted by the James-Lange theory that bodily reactions are experienced as emotion. The autonomic responses did not specify *which* emotion was being experienced, but awareness of the body's autonomic responses intensified that experience (G. W. Hohmann, 1966).

Schachter's theory has its critics. For example, the theory asserts that physiological arousal is nonspecific, affecting only the intensity of a perceived emotion but not its quality. Yet when people were asked to adopt facial expressions distinctive for particular emotions, autonomic patterns of the participants were different for several emotions, such as fear versus sadness (Levenson et al., 1990). Indeed, positive emotions elicit a different array of autonomic responses than do negative emotions (Cacioppo et al., 2000), although, within those categories, different emotions elicit approximately the same autonomic profile. The fact that all negative emotions involve the same physiological responses is one reason why the **polygraph**—which measures various aspects of autonomic arousal, such as heart rate, blood pressure, sweating, and so on—is so poor at distinguishing liars from, say, anxious innocents (**BOX 15.1**).

polygraph Also called a *lie detector*. A device that measures several bodily responses, such as heart rate and blood pressure.

BOX 15.1 · Lie Detector?

One of the most controversial attempts to apply biomedical science is the so-called lie detector test. In this procedure, properly called a *polygraph* test (from the Greek *polys*, "many," and *graphein*, "to write"), multiple physiological measures are recorded in an attempt to detect lying during a carefully structured interview. The test is based on the assumption that people have emotional responses when lying because they fear detection and/or feel guilty about lying. Emotions are usually accompanied by bodily responses that are difficult to control, such as changes in respiratory rate, heart rate, blood pressure, and skin conductance (a measure of sweating). In polygraph recordings like the one in Figure A, each wiggly line, called a *trace*, provides a measurement of one of these physiological variables,

and taken together, the measures are assumed to track the participant's physiological arousal over time. When participants lie in response to direct questions (arrows), momentary changes in several of the measured variables may occur.

People who administer polygraph examinations for a living claim that polygraphs are accurate in 95% of tests, but the estimate from impartial research is an overall accuracy of about 65% (A. Eriksson and Lacerda, 2007; Nietzel, 2000). Even if the higher figure were correct, the fact that these tests are widely used would mean that thousands of truthful people could be branded as liars and fired, disciplined, or not hired. On the other hand, many criminals and spies have been able to pass the tests without detection. For example,

longtime CIA agent Aldrich Ames, who was sentenced in 1995 to life in prison for espionage, successfully passed polygraph tests after becoming a spy. (His Russian spymaster's advice for passing? Make small talk with the person conducting the test.) In the wake of the terrorist attacks of 2001, a federally appointed panel of scientists noted that even if polygraphs were correct 80% of the time (which is much higher than impartial research suggests), then giving the test to 10,000 people that included 10 spies would condemn 1,600 innocent people, and let 2 spies go free (National Academy of Sciences, 2003)!

Some scientists believe that modern neuroscience may provide new methods of lie detection someday.

(continued)

(A) The polygraph measures signs of arousal. (B) PET images reveal selective activation of prefrontal cortex in a participant engaged in lying (relative to a control scan). (Figure B from Abe et al., 2007, courtesy of Dr. Nobuhito Abe.)

(A)

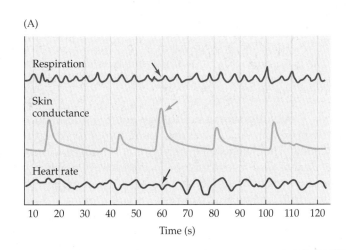

(B)

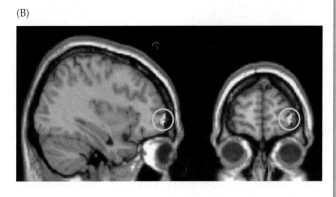

BOX
15.1

Lie Detector? (continued)

Conscious lying may trigger unusual activation of executive control mechanisms of the prefrontal cortex (Figure B) (Abe et al., 2007). Fear results in activation of the amygdala (as we'll discuss later in this chapter) that, in the case of deception, also might be visible with fMRI (see Chapter 2). Functional MRI shows that the anterior cingulate cortex (another region asso-ciated with executive control) becomes more active when participants are lying (Langleben et al., 2002). Although such initial results from brain-imaging studies of deception are intriguing, much more work will be required to establish that brain imaging can detect lies with enough reliability to be useful in making important decisions about individual people. In a major court case, the judge emphasized that there are "no known error rates for fMRI-based lie detection… in the real world" (G. Miller, 2010). Even if such lie detectors are someday validated, they will be more costly and less widely available than polygraphs.

evolutionary psychology A field devoted to asking how natural selection has shaped behavior in humans and other animals.

Emotions from the Evolutionary Viewpoint

In his book *The Expression of the Emotions in Man and Animals* (1872), Charles Darwin presented evidence that certain expressions of emotions are universal among people of all regions of the world. Furthermore, Darwin asked whether nonhuman animals show comparable expressions of some emotions and argued that aspects of emotional expression may have originated in a common ancestor.

Darwin's perspective encompassed behavioral phenomena—the apparent emotional expressions of various mammals (**FIGURE 15.3**)—as well as the physiological mechanisms of emotional display, such as facial muscles and their innervation. Earlier scholars had believed the facial muscles were given uniquely to humans so that they could express their feelings, but Darwin emphasized that nonhuman primates have the same facial muscles that humans have. A century later, Redican (1982) noted distinct facial expressions in nonhuman primates: (1) *grimace*, perhaps analogous to human expressions of fear or surprise; (2) *tense mouth*, akin to human expressions of anger; and (3) *play face*, homologous to the human laugh. Particular facial expressions may represent similar emotions across primate species (**FIGURE 15.4**). This connection may even extend beyond primates: for example, tickling and playing with rats can elicit ultrasonic vocalizations that resemble laughter in some ways, and that may facilitate social contact and learning (Burgdorf et al., 2008; Panksepp, 2007).

How may emotion and emotional displays have evolved?

How do emotions and their expression help individuals survive and reproduce? Darwin offered several suggestions:

> The movements of expression in the face and body… are… of much importance for our welfare. They serve as the first means of communication between the mother and her infant; she smiles approval, and thus encourages her child on the right path, or frowns disapproval. We readily perceive sympathy in others by their expression; our sufferings are thus mitigated and our pleasure increased; and mutual good feeling is thus strengthened. The movements of expression give vividness and energy to our spoken words. They reveal the thoughts and intentions of others more truly than do words, which may be falsified. (Darwin, 1872, p. 365)

Current proponents of **evolutionary psychology** point to additional ways in which emotions are adaptive and could have developed through natural selection (Cosmides and Tooby, 2000). They suggest that emotions are broad motivational programs that coordinate various responses to solve specific adaptive problems, including maintaining cooperative relations with other members of your group, choosing a mate, avoiding predators, and finding food sources.

For example, most of us have experienced the frightening nighttime perception of being stalked by a predator, real or imagined, human or nonhuman. The intensity of the experience may be a legacy of the ancestral environment in which our

(A)

(B)

15.3 EMOTIONAL EXPRESSION IN ANIMALS (A) Crested black macaque monkey "in a placid condition." (B) "The same when pleased by being caressed." (From Darwin, 1872, p. 136.)

15.4 FACIAL EXPRESSION OF EMOTIONS IN NONHUMAN PRIMATES (A) A juvenile bonobo (pygmy chimpanzee) shows a play face while being tickled. According to Frans de Waal (2003), bonobo laughter reveals both upper and lower teeth, making it closer in appearance to human laughter than that of chimpanzes, who tend to reveal only the lower teeth while laughing. (B) The female chacma baboon on the left bares her teeth, grinning to signal submission to a dominant male. In some primates, including humans, teeth baring has gained a different, friendlier meaning.

behavioral systems evolved, where the presence of an unseen predator would be a situation of utmost urgency. Individuals would have differed in their responses to this life-threatening situation. Some individuals' poor choices would have resulted in reduced reproductive success. Other individuals would have made more-effective choices, and to the extent that this behavior was heritable, their descendants would also be more likely to survive in similar situations. Thus, through natural selection, an effective program for dealing with danger could have evolved: fear. The emotion of fear calls forth shifts in perception, attention, cognition, and action that focus on avoiding danger and seeking safety, as well as physiologically preparing for fighting or flight, while other activities, such as seeking food, sleep, or mates, are suppressed. From an evolutionary perspective, in the face of an imminent threat to life, it is better to be afraid, calling on this recipe for action, developed and tested over the ages, than to ad-lib something.

Viewed in this way, emotions can be seen as evolved preprogramming that helps us deal quickly and effectively with a wide variety of situations. To give you another example, feelings of disgust for body fluids may help us avoid exposure to germs (Curtis et al., 2004), so it would be adaptive to recognize disgust in others. Our human tendency to make snap judgments about other people, based on their appearance and facial expressions, may be an overgeneralization of mechanisms that evolved to help us recognize signs of threat or danger in others (Todorov et al., 2008).

Individuals differ in their emotional responsiveness

Even as newborns, people differ in their emotional reactivity and physiological responses to emotional situations—a characteristic known as **individual response stereotypy** (Lacey and Lacey, 1970). In longitudinal studies (extending over many years), researchers tracked the emotional reactivity of people from early childhood through adulthood, using stimuli that provoke autonomic responses, such as immersion of the hand in ice-cold water, performance of rapidly paced arithmetic calculations, and intense stimulation of the skin. Across these conditions, investigators have observed individual profiles of response that are evident even in newborns. For example, some newborns respond vigorously with heart rate changes, others with gastric contractions, and still others with blood pressure responses.

individual response stereotypy
The tendency of individuals to show the same response pattern to particular situations throughout their life span.

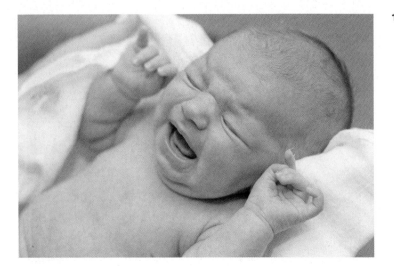

Some infants, when swabbed with rubbing alcohol, react more strongly than others to the unpleasant cold sensation. As adults, these people are more likely to be shy and have phobias. They also show greater activation of the amygdala in response to photographs of strangers.

The response patterns remain remarkably consistent throughout life. When newborns were classified on the basis of their behavioral responses to being swabbed with rubbing alcohol (the sudden cold sensation surprises and sometimes upsets babies), about 20% of the infants were classified as "high reactives" because they gave especially strong reactions to the stimuli (**FIGURE 15.5**) (Kagan, 1997). Many of these high reactives went on to develop anxiety disorders, such as social anxiety (severe shyness), and to become extremely shy children, so by the time they were old enough for school, about a third of them displayed diagnosable extreme phobias (compared with fewer than 10% of the other children). In adulthood, high reactives show an exaggerated activation of the amygdala in response to photographs of strangers' faces (C. E. Schwartz et al., 2003). Because the amygdala has been implicated in fear (as we'll see later in this chapter), high reactives may have a lifelong aversion to new acquaintances, which would certainly affect many aspects of life. These infants may have inherited greater vigilance for danger, which might have been more adaptive in the past than it is today. We've been emphasizing negative emotions, but how many emotions are there, exactly?

How Many Emotions Do We Experience?

There may be a basic core set of emotions underlying the more varied and delicate nuances of our world of feelings. One formulation (Plutchik, 1994) suggests there are eight basic emotions, grouped in four pairs of opposites—joy/sadness, affection/disgust, anger/fear, and expectation/surprise—with all other emotions arising from combinations of this basic array (**FIGURE 15.6**). But investigators do not yet agree about the number of basic emotions (six, seven, eight?). Although there is no way to determine once and for all the number of basic emotions, one clue comes from examining the number of different kinds of facial expressions that we produce and can recognize in others.

Facial expressions have complex functions in communication

How many different emotions can be detected in facial expressions? According to Paul Ekman and collaborators, there are distinctive expressions for anger, sadness, happiness, fear, disgust, surprise, contempt, and embarrassment (**FIGURE 15.7**) (Keltner and Ekman, 2000). Facial expressions of these emotions are interpreted similarly across many cultures without explicit training. (In case you're keeping track, whereas Plutchik included affection and expectation in his eight basic emotions, Keltner and Ekman include, instead, facial expressions of contempt and embarrassment. The other six emotions—anger, sadness, happiness, fear, disgust, and surprise—are recognized in both schemes.)

Cross-cultural similarity is also noted in the *production* of expressions specific to particular emotions. For example, people in a preliterate New Guinea society show emotional facial expressions like those of people in industrialized societies. However, facial expressions apparently are not unfailingly universal. For example, although there was significant agreement across cultures in the recognition of most emotional states from facial expressions, isolated nonliterate groups did not agree with Westerners about recognizing expressions of surprise and disgust (**FIGURE**

Levels of intensity

High

Ecstasy
Vigilance
Adoration
Rage
Terror
Loathing
Amazement
Grief

Medium

Joy
Expectation
Affection
Anger
Fear
Disgust
Surprise
Sadness

Low

Happiness
Alertness
Regard
Annoyance
Apprehension
Boredom
Distraction
Pensiveness

15.6 BASIC EMOTIONS According to one popular scheme, the eight basic emotions are arrayed as four pairs of opposite emotions. Lower- and higher-intensity forms of each basic emotion appear at the bottom and top levels, respectively. (After Plutchik, 1994.)

Anger   Sadness   Happiness   Fear

Disgust   Surprise   Contempt   Embarrassment

15.7 UNIVERSAL FACIAL EXPRESSIONS OF EMOTION   According to Paul Ekman and colleagues, the eight basic emotional facial expressions shown here are displayed in all cultures.

15.8). These subtle cultural differences suggest that cultures prescribe rules for facial expression and that they control and enforce those rules by cultural conditioning (**FIGURE 15.9**). Everyone agrees that cultures affect the facial display of emotion; the remaining controversy is over the extent of the cultural influence. In everyday life we do not see emotional faces in isolation, so context normally colors our judgment about what emotion a person is experiencing (Barrett et al., 2011).

According to Fridlund (1994), a major role of facial expression is paralinguistic; that is, the face is accessory to verbal communication, providing emphasis and direction in conversation. For example, people display few facial responses to odor when smelling alone but significantly more in a social setting (Gilbert et al., 1986).

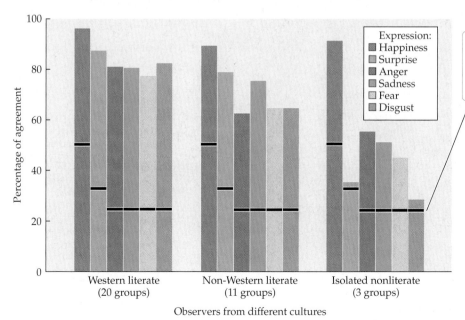

Expression:
- Happiness
- Surprise
- Anger
- Sadness
- Fear
- Disgust

Observers from different cultures

The black bar is the level of agreement expected if the participants were simply guessing which emotion is portrayed.

15.8 CULTURAL DIFFERENCES IN RECOGNIZING FACIAL EXPRESSIONS OF EMOTION   Within Western and non-Western literate groups (left and middle), there is widespread agreement about the emotions represented by photographs of basic facial expressions. But people from isolated nonliterate groups (right) are much less likely to agree with literate people's judgments of some facial expressions, especially those of surprise and disgust. The black horizontal bars indicate the percentage of agreement that would be expected by chance alone. (After Russell, 1994.)

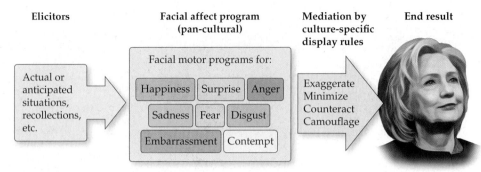

Elicitors

Actual or anticipated situations, recollections, etc.

Facial affect program (pan-cultural)

Facial motor programs for:

Happiness	Surprise	Anger
Sadness	Fear	Disgust
Embarrassment	Contempt

Mediation by culture-specific display rules

Exaggerate
Minimize
Counteract
Camouflage

End result

Similarly, bowlers tend to smile after making a strike only after they turn around to meet the faces of onlookers (Kraut and Johnston, 1979). In simulations, participants take a threat more seriously if it is accompanied by an angry face (Reed et al., 2014). Another important cue about a person's emotional state is their "body language," which is especially effective at conveying whether someone is having negative or positive emotions (Aviezer et al., 2012).

Facial expressions are mediated by muscles, cranial nerves, and CNS pathways

How are facial expressions produced? Within the human face is an elaborate network of finely innervated muscles whose functional roles, in addition to facial expression, include speech production, eating, and respiration, among others. Facial muscles can be divided into two categories:

1. *Superficial facial muscles* attach to facial skin (**FIGURE 15.10**). On contraction they change the shape of the mouth, eyes, or nose, for example; or they pull on their attachment to the skin. One such muscle, the frontalis, wrinkles the forehead and raises the eyebrow.

2. *Deep facial muscles* attach to bone. These muscles enable movements such as chewing and large movements of the face. An example of a deep muscle is the temporalis, a powerful jaw muscle.

facial nerve Cranial nerve VII, which receives information from the face and controls the superficial muscles there.

Human facial muscles are innervated by two cranial nerves: (1) the **facial nerve** (VII), which innervates the superficial muscles of facial expression (see Figure 2.9);

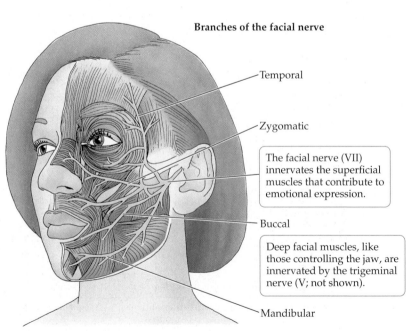

Branches of the facial nerve

Temporal

Zygomatic

The facial nerve (VII) innervates the superficial muscles that contribute to emotional expression.

Buccal

Deep facial muscles, like those controlling the jaw, are innervated by the trigeminal nerve (V; not shown).

Mandibular

15.10 FACIAL MUSCLES AND THEIR NEURAL CONTROL

Several studies indicate that when people are manipulated into mimicking facial expressions of sadness...

...or happiness, their emotional mood is actually affected.

So putting on a happy, cheerful expression may actually help you to feel better.

and (2) the motor branch of the **trigeminal nerve** (V), which innervates muscles that move the jaw (e.g., the temporalis). As Figure 15.10 shows, the main trunk of the facial nerve (yellow) divides into upper and lower divisions shortly after entering the face. These nerve fibers originate in the brainstem in the nucleus of the facial nerve.

Lending support to the James-Lange notion that sensations from our body inform us about our emotions, the **facial feedback hypothesis** suggests that sensory feedback from our facial expressions can affect our mood. In some tests of this idea, a person is given a task such as holding a pencil under her nose or between her teeth (**FIGURE 15.11**), which effectively has her take on a sad or happy face, respectively. The participant is then asked how happy or sad she feels, or how funny she finds a cartoon. Typically, people who have been simulating smiles report more positive feelings than the folks who have been simulating frowns (Davis et al., 2009). So it is possible that forcing yourself to take on a cheerful expression may actually help you feel happier, and the old song that advises "just put on a happy face" may have its basis in fact. Conversely, people who receive Botox injections, paralyzing facial muscles to relieve wrinkles and look younger, experience emotions less intensely after the treatment than before (Davis et al., 2010).

Impaired facial expression may affect social interactions. Chronic selective inhibition of the facial musculature is one symptom of Parkinson's disease (which is discussed in Chapter 11) and of schizophrenia (Kring, 1999). Sometimes viruses infect the facial nerve and damage it enough to cause paralysis of facial muscles. This condition, known as **Bell's palsy**, usually affects just one side, resulting in a variety of symptoms, including drooping eyelid and mouth (**FIGURE 15.12**). There is no standard treatment, but happily most people recover on their own within a few weeks, and almost everyone recovers within 6 months.

Do Distinct Brain Circuits Mediate Different Emotions?

This question has been explored in studies involving either localized brain lesions or electrical stimulation. Taken together, these studies make it clear that particular brain regions are involved in emotions, but often the same regions seem to be involved in many different emotions.

trigeminal nerve Cranial nerve V, which receives information from the face and controls jaw musculature.

facial feedback hypothesis The hypothesis that our emotional experience is affected by the sensory feedback we receive during particular facial expressions, such as smiling.

Bell's palsy A disorder, usually caused by viral infection, in which the facial nerve on one side stops conducting action potentials, resulting in paralysis on one side of the face.

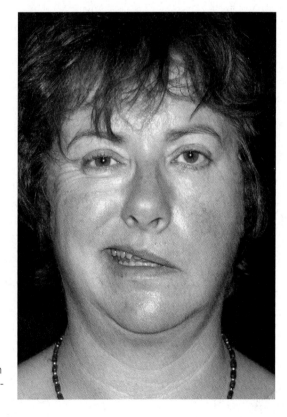

15.12 BELL'S PALSY LEAVES HALF OF THE FACE PARALYZED This woman is smiling, but only the muscles on the right side of her face (left half of photograph) respond to her commands.

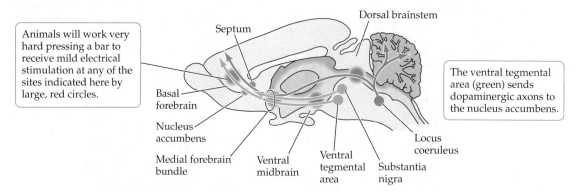

Animals will work very hard pressing a bar to receive mild electrical stimulation at any of the sites indicated here by large, red circles.

The ventral tegmental area (green) sends dopaminergic axons to the nucleus accumbens.

Septum

Dorsal brainstem

Basal forebrain

Nucleus accumbens

Medial forebrain bundle

Ventral midbrain

Ventral tegmental area

Substantia nigra

Locus coeruleus

15.13 BRAIN SELF-STIMULATION SITES IN RODENTS

Electrical stimulation of the brain can produce emotional effects

One way to study the neuroanatomy of emotion is to electrically stimulate sites in the brains of awake, freely moving animals and then observe the effects on behavior. Such stimulation can have either rewarding or aversive effects, or it may elicit sequences of emotional behavior. Such experiments in the 1950s produced an intriguing finding: rats will readily press a lever in order to receive a brief burst of electrical stimulation in a brain region called the *septum* (Olds and Milner, 1954) (**FIGURE 15.13**). This phenomenon, called **brain self-stimulation**, can also happen in humans. Patients receiving electrical stimulation in this region feel a sense of pleasure or warmth, and in some instances stimulation in this region provokes sexual excitation (Heath, 1972).

The discovery of brain self-stimulation was one of those rare scientific moments that launch a new field; many investigators have since employed similar stimulation techniques, mapping the distribution of brain sites that yield self-stimulation responses. Animals will work to receive electrical stimulation of many different subcortical sites, but stimulation of the cortex does not seem to have such rewarding effects. Effective stimulation sites for self-stimulation are concentrated in a large tract that ascends from the midbrain through the hypothalamus—the **medial forebrain bundle**. This bundle of axons is characterized by widespread origins and innervates an extensive set of forebrain regions. One important target for the axons is the nucleus accumbens, which we discussed in Chapter 4. Dopaminergic stimulation of this site appears to be very pleasurable.

One theory is that electrical stimulation taps into the circuits mediating more-customary rewards, such as the arrival of food to a hungry animal or water to a thirsty animal (N. M. White and Milner, 1992). As we discussed in Chapter 4, there is a growing belief that drugs of abuse are addictive because they activate these same neural circuits (Ranaldi and Beninger, 1994; Wise et al., 1992).

Brain lesions affect emotions

Early in the twentieth century, decorticate dogs (dogs from which the cortex had been removed) were found to respond to routine handling with sudden intense **decorticate rage**—snarling, biting, and so on—sometimes referred to as *sham rage* because it seemed undirected. Clearly, then, emotional behaviors of this type must be organized at a subcortical level, with the cerebral cortex normally providing *inhibition* of emotional responsiveness. On the basis of studies of the spread of rabies virus in the brains of cats, combined with observations from brain autopsies of humans with emotional disorders, James W. Papez (1937) proposed a subcortical circuit of emotion. Papez (which rhymes with "capes") noted associations between emotional changes and specific sites of brain damage. These interconnected regions, known as the *Papez circuit*, include the mammillary bodies of the hypothalamus, the anterior thalamus, the cingulate cortex, the hippocampus, and the fornix. The arrows in **FIGURE 15.14** schematically depict this circuit. Later, Paul MacLean (1949)

brain self-stimulation The process in which animals will work to provide electrical stimulation to particular brain sites, presumably because the experience is very rewarding.

medial forebrain bundle A collection of axons traveling in the midline region of the forebrain.

decorticate rage Also called *sham rage*. Sudden intense rage characterized by actions (such as snarling and biting in dogs) that lack clear direction.

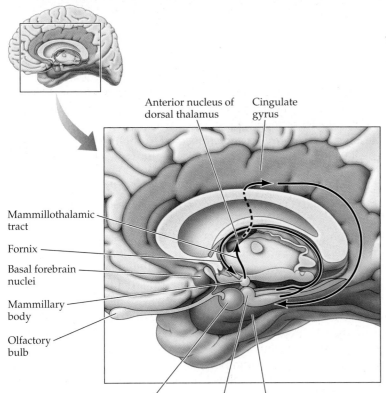

Anterior nucleus of dorsal thalamus

Cingulate gyrus

Mammillothalamic tract

Fornix

Basal forebrain nuclei

Mammillary body

Olfactory bulb

Amygdala   Hippocampus   Parahippocampal gyrus

suggested that the amygdala and several other regions also interacted with the components of this circuit, and he proposed that the entire system be called the **limbic system**.

Reports of an unusual emotional syndrome in primates with temporal lobe lesions provided early support for the limbic model of emotion (Klüver and Bucy, 1938). While studying cortical mechanisms of perception, the researchers removed large portions of the temporal lobes of monkeys. They were surprised to see that the animals' behavior changed dramatically after surgery; the highlight of what is now known as the **Klüver-Bucy syndrome** was an extraordinary taming effect. Animals that had been wild and fearful of humans prior to surgery became tame and showed neither fear nor aggression afterward. They also showed strong oral tendencies, eating a variety of objects, including rocks! Frequent mounting behavior was observed and was described as *hypersexuality*.

Because lesions restricted to the cerebral cortex did not produce these results, deeper regions of the temporal lobe, including sites within the limbic system (see Figure 15.14), were implicated, and more-detailed investigation focused on the amygdala. When the amygdala was destroyed bilaterally in monkeys (Emery et al., 2001), the animals demonstrated increased social affiliation, decreased anxiety, and increased confidence, compared with control animals. In other words, the animals with amygdala lesions appeared to be much less fearful than control monkeys. These reports led to study of the amygdala in rats, which confirmed the importance of this region for fear, as we'll see next.

Fear is mediated by circuitry that includes the amygdala

There is nothing subtle about fear. Many animals display similar behavior under conditions that provoke fear, such as danger posed by a predator. This lack of subtlety and the similarity of fear-related behavior across species may explain why we know much more about the neural circuitry of fear than of any other emotion (LeDoux, 1995). For example, it is very easy to reliably elicit fear by using a type of classical conditioning called **fear conditioning** (see Chapter 17), in which the person or animal is presented with a stimulus such as light or sound that is paired with a brief aversive stimulus such as mild electrical shock. After several such pairings, the

limbic system A loosely defined, widespread group of brain nuclei that innervate each other to form a network. These nuclei are implicated in emotions.

Klüver-Bucy syndrome A condition, brought about by bilateral amygdala damage, that is characterized by dramatic emotional changes including reduction in fear and anxiety.

fear conditioning A type of classical conditioning where a previously neutral stimulus is repeatedly paired with shock or some other unpleasant experience, causing the individual to act fearful in response to the stimulus.

amygdala A group of nuclei in the medial anterior part of the temporal lobe.

response to the sound or light itself is the typical fear portrait, including freezing and autonomic signs such as cardiac and respiratory changes (**FIGURE 15.15A**).

Studies of such fear conditioning have provided a map of the neural circuitry that implicates the **amygdala** as a key structure in the mediation of fear (**FIGURE 15.15B**). Located at the anterior medial portion of the temporal lobe, the amygdala is composed of about a dozen different nuclei, each with a distinct set of connections. Recall that lesions of the entire amygdala seemed to abolish fear in monkeys. Lesioning just the central nucleus of the amygdala has the same effect, preventing blood pressure increases and freezing behavior in response to a conditioned fear stimulus.

On its way to the amygdala, via various sensory channels, information about fear-provoking stimuli reaches a fork in the road at the level of the thalamus (recall from Chapter 2 that the thalamus acts like a switchboard, directing sensory information to specific brain regions). A direct projection from the thalamus to the amygdala, nicknamed the "low road" for fear responses (LeDoux, 1996), bypasses conscious processing and allows for immediate reactions to fearful stimuli (de Gelder et al., 2012) (**FIGURE 15.15C**). An alternate "high road" pathway routes the incoming information through sensory cortex, allowing for processing that, while slower, is conscious, fine-grained, and integrated with higher-level cognitive processes, such as memory (see Figure 15.15B). Contributions from prefrontal cortex and anterior cingulate offer an additional level of fear conditioning called *observational fear learning*, in which fear of potentially harmful stimuli is learned through social transmission (Olsson and Phelps, 2007). So, to extend our example, an individual can learn to fear scorpions by observing signs of fear and pain in others, without personally experiencing a scorpion attack. Given the considerable adaptive benefits that it confers, it's not surprising that observational fear learning is seen in species as diverse as mice, cats, cows, and primates, including humans.

Interconnections within the amygdala also form an important part of the story. Information about the stimulus (the sound in Figure 15.15A) from several brain regions, including sensory cortex, reaches the lateral portion of the amygdala first, and evidence suggests that neurons here encode the *association* between specific stimuli and aversive events like electrical shock (Maren and Quirk, 2004). The lateral amygdala triggers a network within the amygdala, ultimately activating the central nucleus (Namburi et al., 2015). The central nucleus then transmits information to various brainstem centers to evoke three different aspects of emotional responses (see Figure 15.15C): pathways through the central gray (or periaqueductal gray) evoke emotional behaviors, those through the lateral hypothalamus evoke autonomic responses, and those through the bed nucleus of the stria terminalis evoke hormonal responses. Different types of fearful stimuli, such as odors from an aggressive male versus odors from a predator, may activate slightly different pathways to and from the amygdala (C. T. Gross and Canteras, 2012).

Learned fears are notoriously slow to extinguish; in our example (see Figure 15.15A), once the shock and the sound have been paired, the auditory tone must be presented without shock many times before animals stop freezing in response. During such extinction training, activity in the prefrontal cortex, which projects to the amygdala, is necessary for the animal to benefit (Adhikari et al., 2015). If the prefrontal cortex is silenced during extinction training, the next day the animal responds to the sound as if no extinction trials took place (Do-Monte et al., 2015). Mice missing one of the two types of cannabinoid receptors (see Chapter 4) also have a harder time unlearning their fearful reaction to a tone (Marsicano et al., 2002), suggesting that stimulation of these receptors normally extinguishes learned fears. If so, then it may be possible to develop cannabinoid drugs to treat phobias in humans.

The data highlighting the importance of the amygdala for fear in rats and mice fit well with observations in humans. When humans are shown visual stimuli associated with pain or fear, blood flow to the amygdala increases (LaBar et al., 1998), even in the absence of conscious perception of the stimuli (Pegna et al., 2005). People who suffer from temporal lobe seizures that include the amygdala commonly report that

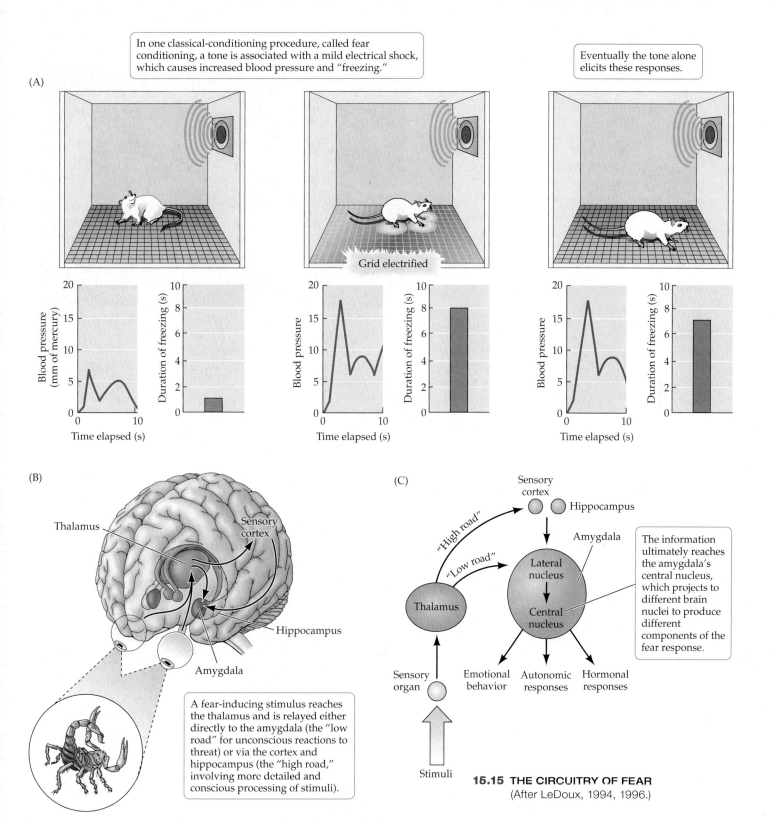

In one classical-conditioning procedure, called fear conditioning, a tone is associated with a mild electrical shock, which causes increased blood pressure and "freezing."

Eventually the tone alone elicits these responses.

(A)

Grid electrified

(B)

Thalamus

Sensory cortex

Hippocampus

Amygdala

A fear-inducing stimulus reaches the thalamus and is relayed either directly to the amygdala (the "low road" for unconscious reactions to threat) or via the cortex and hippocampus (the "high road," involving more detailed and conscious processing of stimuli).

(C)

Sensory cortex

Hippocampus

Amygdala

"High road"

"Low road"

Lateral nucleus

Thalamus

Central nucleus

The information ultimately reaches the amygdala's central nucleus, which projects to different brain nuclei to produce different components of the fear response.

Sensory organ

Emotional behavior

Autonomic responses

Hormonal responses

Stimuli

15.15 THE CIRCUITRY OF FEAR
(After LeDoux, 1994, 1996.)

intense fear heralds the start of a seizure (Engel, 1992). Likewise, electrical stimulation of temporal lobe sites may elicit feelings of fear in patients (Bancaud et al., 1994).

But perhaps the most compelling evidence that the amygdala is important for fear in our species comes from people like patient S.M., the woman we met at the start of the chapter, who is literally fearless. The fearlessness that she and other people suffering from the disorder display seems almost certainly due to the loss of the amygdala. Her very rare genetic disorder causes the accumulation of calcium deposits in the amygdala, starting in late childhood, which eventually destroys the nuclei

15.16 THE LOCUS OF FEAR Unlike a control participant (left), patient S.M. (right) displays dark deposits of calcium in the amygdala of both hemispheres. This remarkably specific lesion seems to have made her fearless without affecting other behaviors. (Courtesy of Dr. J. Feinstein.)

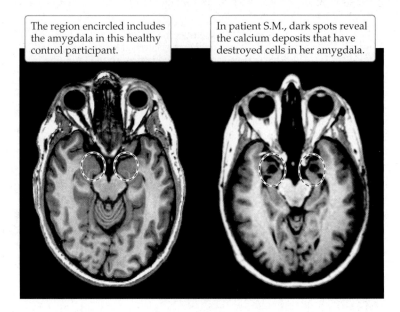

The region encircled includes the amygdala in this healthy control participant.

In patient S.M., dark spots reveal the calcium deposits that have destroyed cells in her amygdala.

in both cerebral hemispheres (**FIGURE 15.16**). When S.M. is shown movie clips that other people find frightening, she reports being unmoved (**FIGURE 15.17**). S.M. is also very poor at recognizing the facial expressions of fear in other people, but she recognizes other emotional expressions—a pattern seen in other people with damaged amygdalas (Adolphs et al., 2005). Her inability to recognize fear may be caused by her tendency not to look at people's eyes (Kennedy and Adolphs, 2011), so she doesn't see fear cues like wide eyes.

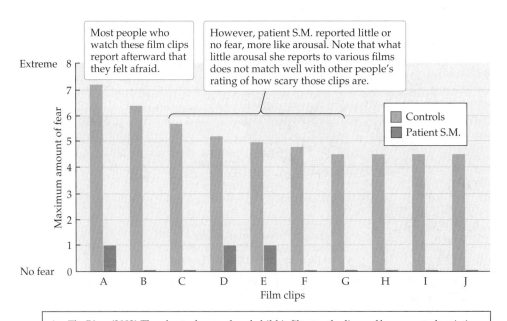

Most people who watch these film clips report afterward that they felt afraid.

However, patient S.M. reported little or no fear, more like arousal. Note that what little arousal she reports to various films does not match well with other people's rating of how scary those clips are.

A – *The Ring* (2002) The ghost of a murdered child infiltrates the lives of her soon-to-be victims.
B – *Blair Witch Project* (1999) Campers are attacked by an unknown apparition during the middle of the night.
C – *CSI* (2009) A man struggles to survive after being buried alive.
D – *The English Patient* (1996) A man is tortured during World War II.
E – *Se7en* (1995) A mutilated man awakes from the dead.
F – *Cry Freedom* (1987) Armed trespassers attack a woman who is home alone during the night.
G – *Arachnophobia* (1990) A large poisonous spider attacks a girl in the shower.
H – *Halloween* (1978) A woman is being chased by a murderer.
I – *The Shining* (1980) A young boy hears voices in the hallway of a haunted hotel.
J – *The Silence of the Lambs* (1991) A female FBI agent tries to capture a twisted serial killer who is hiding in a dark basement.

15.17 WHAT SCARY MOVIE? (After Feinstein et al., 2011.)

What's fascinating about patients like S.M. is that they have never known fear since the disease destroyed their amygdalas in late childhood. But they *can* be made afraid—by being given only air with a high concentration of carbon dioxide. Within 10 seconds, S.M. was flailing her hands and feeling a strong, panicky fear (Feinstein et al., 2013), crying out, "Help me" (Aschwanden, 2013). Similarly, a pair of monozygotic twins with the same genetic disorder and fearless behavior as S.M. both showed evidence of panic, including a full-blown panic attack in one twin, when injected with an epinephrine-like drug (Khalsa et al., 2016). So despite the central role of the amygdala in most fear, the brain has an alternative way of making us very afraid and inducing panic. One possibility is that the amygdala is important for recognizing and responding to *external* threats, but the brain relies on other systems, perhaps in the brainstem, to detect and respond to signs of *internal* threats, like inadequate oxygen.

Different emotions activate different regions of the human brain

Several forebrain areas are consistently implicated in varying emotions (**FIGURE 15.18**) (for research examples, see Canli et al., 2001; A. R. Damasio et al., 2000; H. Takahashi et al., 2009). Andreas Bartels and Semir Zeki (2000) recruited volunteers who professed to be "truly, deeply, and madly in love." Each participant furnished four color photographs: one of his or her boy- or girlfriend, and three of friends who were the same sex as the loved partner and were similar in age and length of friendship. Functional MRI brain scans were taken while each participant was shown counterbalanced sequences of the four photographs. Brain activity elicited by viewing the loved person was compared with that elicited by viewing friends.

Love, compared with friendship, involved increased activity in the insula and anterior cingulate cortex (see Figure 15.18A and C) and, subcortically, in the caudate and putamen—all bilaterally. It also led to *reduced* activity in the posterior cingulate and amygdala, and in the right prefrontal cortex. This combination of sites differs from those found in other emotional states, suggesting that a unique network of brain areas is responsible for the emotion of love. In contrast, feelings of envy reportedly involve increased activity of anterior cingulate cortex activity; and the feeling of schadenfreude (literally "dark joy" in German), experienced when an envied rival falls from grace, is associated with activation of reward-related regions of the ventral forebrain, including the nucleus accumbens (H. Takahashi et al., 2009).

Antonio Damasio et al. (2000) compared brain activation during four different kinds of emotion, and again, the insula, cingulate cortex, and prefrontal cortex (see Figure

15.18 THE EMOTIONAL BRAIN Brain regions implicated in emotions are depicted here in midsagittal (A), anterior coronal (B), and posterior coronal (C) sections. (From Dolan, 2002.)

(A) Orbitofrontal region of prefrontal cortex   Anterior cingulate cortex   Posterior cingulate cortex

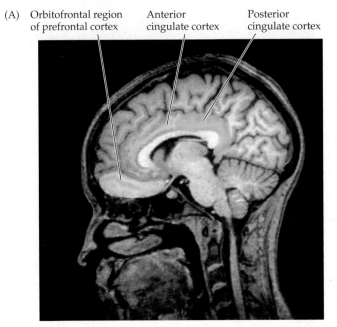

(B) Orbitofrontal region of prefrontal cortex

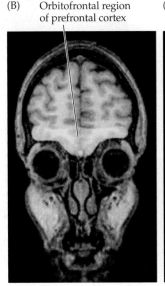

(C) Anterior cingulate cortex   Amygdala

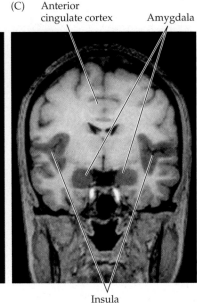

Insula

15.19 BRAIN REGIONS ACTIVE IN FOUR EMOTIONS Red and yellow indicate areas of increased activity; purple indicates areas of decreased activity. For the identified sites, an upward arrow indicates increased activity; a downward arrow, decreased activity. (Courtesy of Dr. Antonio Damasio.)

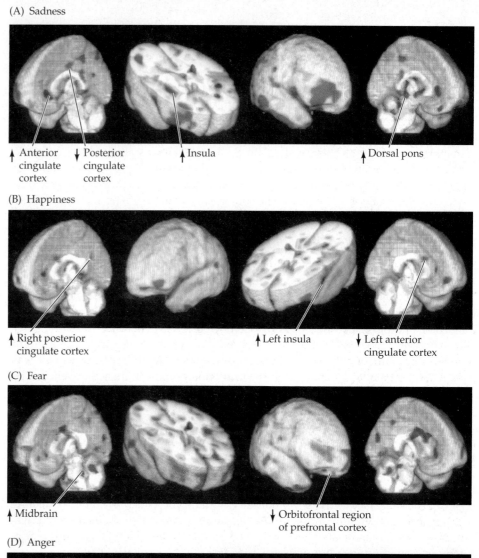

(A) Sadness

↑ Anterior cingulate cortex ↓ Posterior cingulate cortex ↑ Insula ↑ Dorsal pons

(B) Happiness

↑ Right posterior cingulate cortex ↑ Left insula ↓ Left anterior cingulate cortex

(C) Fear

↑ Midbrain ↓ Orbitofrontal region of prefrontal cortex

(D) Anger

↑ Pons ↑ Left anterior cingulate cortex

15.18) were among the regions implicated. In a screening session, adults were asked to recall and attempt to reexperience episodes involving sadness, happiness, fear, or anger, as well as an equally specific but emotionally neutral episode. During the experimental session, the participant was asked to signal as soon as the desired emotion was experienced, and PET images of brain activity were made. Interestingly, physiological responses (skin conductance response and change in heart rate) *preceded* the signal, supporting the idea that at least some physiological responses precede the feeling of emotion (as the James-Lange theory would predict). The PET images were averaged for all participants experiencing a given emotion, and activity during the neutral state was subtracted from activity during the emotion (see Box 2.3). Results showed that activity was altered in many brain regions during emotional experience, and even though we don't understand what role each region plays, it does appear that the four emotions were accompanied by significantly different patterns of brain activity (**FIGURE 15.19**).

These studies confirm that there is no simple, one-to-one relation between a specific emotion and changed activity of a brain region. There is no "happy center" or "sad center." Instead, each emotion involves differential patterns of activation across a network of brain regions associated with emotion. For example, activity of the cingulate cortex is altered in sadness, happiness, and anger; the left somatosensory cortex is deactivated in both anger and fear. Feelings of regret over costly decisions (a topic we'll return to in Chapter 18) apparently involve activation of the amygdala and orbitofrontal cortex (see Figure 18.27). Although different emotions are associated with different patterns of activation, there is a lot of overlap among patterns for different emotions.

Neural Circuitry, Hormones, and Synaptic Transmitters Mediate Violence and Aggression

Violence, assaults, and homicide exact a high toll in many human societies; for example, homicide is a prominent cause of death among young adults in the United States. Many different approaches have been used to investigate the psychological, anthropological, and biological dimensions of aggression.

What is aggression?

The all-too-familiar term *aggression* has many different meanings. We commonly use it in a general sense to refer to strong inner feelings, often involving hate or a desire to inflict harm on others. But when we limit our view of aggression to overt, objectively observable forms of aggressive behavior, we see several different categories, ranging from physical attack, to verbal jousting, to the behavior of corporations and armed forces. We will focus primarily on physical aggression and violence between individuals, excluding the aggression of predators toward their prey, which is perhaps better viewed as feeding behavior (Glickman, 1977).

Intermale aggression (aggression between males of the same species) is observed in most vertebrates, and in many species, males must fight one another to gain access to mates. In the wild, groups of male chimpanzees sometimes band together to kill a rival male (Wilson et al., 2014), increasing the attackers' chances of mating in the future. Men don't generally have to fight (at least physically) to get mates, but they are more physically aggressive than women. Males are 5 times as likely as females to be arrested on charges of murder in the United States. Further, aggressive behavior between boys, in contrast to that between girls, is evident early, in the form of vigorous and destructive play behavior. These large sex differences in aggression indicate that sex hormones play a role (J. Archer, 2006; R. J. Nelson, 2006).

Androgens seem to increase aggression

Because aggressive behavior in males is adaptive for gaining access to food and mates in many species, it makes sense that the same testosterone that prepares males for reproduction would also make them more aggressive. For example, at sexual maturity, when levels of circulating androgens such as testosterone rise, intermale aggression markedly increases in many species (McKinney and Desjardins, 1973). In seasonally breeding species as diverse as birds and primates, male aggression waxes and wanes in concert with changes in testosterone across the seasons (Wingfield et al., 1987). In spotted hyenas, the females are more aggressive than the males (see Box 12.1), and the more androgen a female is exposed to before birth, the more aggressive she will be growing up (Dloniak et al., 2006). In more-typical mammals, such as mice or rats, decreasing circulating androgens by castration usually reduces intermale aggressive behavior profoundly (**FIGURE 15.20**). Treating castrated males with testosterone restores fighting behavior. Fruit flies don't make testosterone, but the same genes that trigger male courtship and copulatory behavior also promote intermale aggression (Vrontou et al., 2006), so the link between reproduction and intermale aggression seems to extend throughout the animal kingdom.

The relationship between testosterone and aggression in humans is less clear-cut (J. Archer, 2006). Treating adult volunteers with extra testosterone does not increase their aggression (O'Connor et al., 2004). Similarly, young men going through puber-

intermale aggression Aggression between males of the same species.

15.20 THE EFFECTS OF ANDRO-GENS ON THE AGGRESSIVE BEHAVIOR OF MICE Counts of the number of biting attacks initiated by males before and after castration (A) and by females before and after removal of the ovaries (B) reveal significantly higher aggression in males before castration. When castrated males are treated with testosterone (C), aggressive behavior is reinstated. (After G. C. Wagner et al., 1980.)

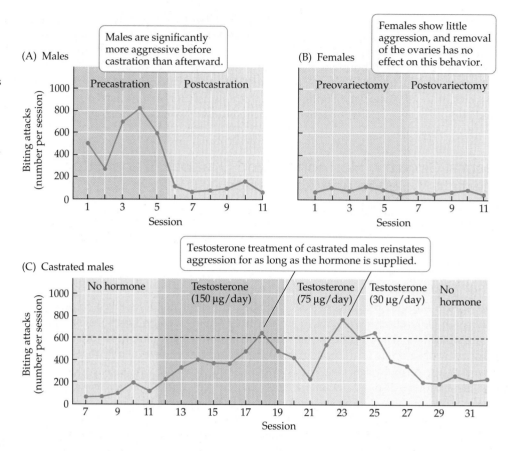

ty experience a sudden large increase in circulating testosterone and yet do not show a correlated increase in aggressive behavior (J. Archer, 2006). Nevertheless, some human studies have shown a positive correlation between testosterone levels and the magnitude of hostility, as measured by behavior rating scales. Comprehensive studies of military veterans suggest that testosterone *is* related to antisocial behavior (Dabbs and Morris, 1990). Nonaggressive tendencies in males are associated with satisfaction in family functioning and with lower levels of serum testosterone (Julian and McKenry, 1979). Among female convicts, testosterone concentrations are highest in women convicted of unprovoked violence and lowest among women convicted of defensive violent crimes (Dabbs et al., 1988).

At least two variables complicate the correlations between testosterone and aggression. First is the observation that experience can affect testosterone levels. In mice and monkeys, the loser in aggressive encounters shows reduced androgen levels (I. S. Bernstein and Gordon, 1974; Lloyd, 1971), so measured levels of testosterone sometimes may be a *result*, rather than a *cause*, of behavior. In men, testosterone levels rise in the winners and fall in the losers after competitions ranging from wrestling to chess. Male sports fans even show a vicarious competition effect in response to simply watching "their" team win or lose a sporting event (Bernhardt, 1997), and as poll results rolled in during the 2008 U.S. presidential election, male McCain voters experienced a sharp drop in circulating testosterone, compared with backers of Obama, who won (Stanton et al., 2009).

These observations suggest that a second confounding variable between testosterone and aggression is *dominance* (Mazur and Booth, 1998), since most chess players could hardly be said to be physically aggressive. For example, women treated with testosterone reportedly spend more time staring into the eyes of threatening faces (Terburg et al., 2012), which is a socially dominant behavior. According to this model, testosterone levels should be associated with behaviors that confer or protect the individual's social status (and thus reproductive fitness). These behaviors may *sometimes*, but not always, involve overt aggression. While surgical or "chemical" castration may reduce violence in some sex offenders (Brain, 1994), the main effect is a reduction in sexual motivation more than a direct effect on aggression. Many ethical issues raised by this approach to the rehabilitation of sex offenders and the intricacies of such intervention have yet to be worked out.

Aggression has several neurochemical correlates

Aggressive behavior in various animals, including humans, is modulated by activity in several neurotransmitter systems. In particular, studies show a negative correlation between brain serotonin activity and aggression. For example, Higley et al. (1992) observed aggressive behavior and fight injuries in monkeys from a large, free-ranging colony, to rank the animals from least to most aggressive. The researchers then gauged serotonin activity by measuring a serotonin metabolite, 5-HIAA (5-hydroxyindoleacetic acid), in cerebrospinal fluid. The most aggressive monkeys had the lowest levels of serotonin metabolites, suggesting that they had the least serotonin being released at synapses in the brain. In agreement with this finding, mice with one of the serotonin receptor genes knocked out are hyper-aggressive (Bouwknecht et al., 2001), as one would expect if serotonin normally inhibits aggression (Siever, 2008). This inhibitory role of serotonin in aggression is probably evolutionarily ancient, as it is evident even in invertebrates: for example, enhanced serotonergic activity prompts solitary locusts to overcome their usual aversion to one another and form the huge swarms that decimate broad swaths of cropland (Anstey et al., 2009).

Serotonin is not the only neurotransmitter involved in aggression. Other substances have been implicated in various forms of aggression in both humans and other animals. For example, the balance between the inhibitory neurotransmitter GABA and the excitatory neurotransmitter glutamate appears to be important in aggressive responses to stimuli. A drug that enhances GABA transmission significantly reduced aggressive behavior in humans (Lieving et al., 2008). Likewise, a variety of peptide hormones, including vasopressin, oxytocin, and the endogenous opioids, have all been implicated in the control of aggression (Siever, 2008). Increased aggression is often seen in knockout mice (see Box 7.3), no matter which of several genes is deleted (R. J. Nelson et al., 1995). So it's clear that aggression is regulated by many systems. Development of antiaggression treatments based on these mechanisms is an active area of research.

There is also growing evidence that in mice a particular brain region, the ventro-lateral portion of the **ventromedial hypothalamus** (**VMH**), serves as a switch to trigger aggression. When experimenters optogenetically stimulated neurons in the VMH in male mice, the animals would stop mounting a receptive female and begin attacking her. Conversely, optogenetically inhibiting VMH activity reduced the likelihood that the subject would attack a male (Falkner et al., 2016; Lee et al., 2014).

The biopsychology of human violence is a topic of controversy

Some forms of human violence are characterized by sudden, intense physical assaults. A long-standing controversy surrounds the idea that some forms of intense human violence are derived from temporal lobe disorders (Mark and Ervin, 1970). Aggression is sometimes a prominent symptom in patients with temporal lobe seizures, and a significant percentage of people arrested for violent crimes have abnormal EEGs or other forms of neuropathology, often associated with temporal lobe function (D. O. Lewis, 1990).

These abnormalities may contribute to a behavior disorder sometimes labeled **emotional dyscontrol syndrome**. Devinsky and Bear (1984) examined a group of patients with seizures involving the limbic system, especially the temporal lobes. These patients showed aggressive behavior that occurred after limbic seizures developed. In another case, a babysitter's violent murder of a child supposedly happened during a temporal lobe seizure provoked by the child's laughter, which was a specific seizure-eliciting stimulus for this person (Engel, 1992).

Psychopaths are intelligent people with superficial charm who have poor self-control, a grandiose sense of self-worth, and little or no feeling of remorse (Hare et al., 1990) and who sometimes commit very violent acts (**FIGURE 15.21**). Compared

ventromedial hypothalamus (VMH) A hypothalamic region involved in eating, sexual, and aggressive behaviors.

emotional dyscontrol syndrome A condition consisting of temporal lobe disorders that may underlie some forms of human violence.

psychopath An individual incapable of experiencing remorse.

15.21 PSYCHOPATHIC IMPULSIVITY Serial killer Theodore Bundy displayed many characteristics of a psychopath. He was superficially charming and, as shown here acting out in the courtroom when the judge was away, impulsive in nature. This scene also hints that, like other psychopaths, Bundy felt little or no remorse for his actions.

stress Any circumstance that upsets homeostatic balance.

alarm reaction The initial response to stress.

adrenal medulla The inner core of the adrenal gland, which secretes epinephrine and norepinephrine.

epinephrine Also called *adrenaline*. Here, a hormone secreted by the adrenal medulla under the control of the sympathetic nervous system, which prepares the body for action.

norepinephrine Also called *noradrenaline*. Here, a hormone secreted by the adrenal medulla under the control of the sympathetic nervous system, which prepares the body for action.

adrenal cortex The outer rind of the adrenal gland, which secretes steroid hormones, including cortisol.

adrenal steroids Steroid hormones secreted by the adrenal cortex, including glucocorticoids such as cortisol and mineralocorticoids such as aldosterone.

cortisol A glucocorticoid stress hormone of the adrenal cortex.

with controls, psychopaths do not react as negatively to words about violence (Gray et al., 2003), and they show little autonomic response to cues that have been associated with aversive stimuli during fear conditioning (Glenn and Raine, 2014). Imaging studies suggest that psychopaths have reduced activity in the prefrontal cortex and a smaller prefrontal cortex than controls (Yang and Raine, 2009), which may impair their ability to control impulsive behavior.

Undoubtedly, human violence and aggression stem from many sources. Biological studies of aggression have been vigorously criticized by both politicians and social scientists. These critics argue that, as a result of emphasizing biological factors such as genetics or brain mechanisms, the most evident origins of human violence and aggression (poverty and lack of education) might be overlooked, and odious forms of biological controls of social dysfunction might be instituted. However, the quality of life of some violent persons might be significantly improved if biological factors could be identified and addressed. For example, treatments that enhance serotonin activity in the brain might be an important addition to a social-environmental or psychotherapeutic intervention (E. Hollander, 1999).

Stress Activates Many Bodily Responses

We all experience stress, but what is it? Attempts to define *stress* have not overcome a certain vagueness implicit in this term. Hans Selye (1907–1982), whose work launched the modern field of stress research, broadly defined stress as "the rate of all the wear and tear caused by life" (Selye, 1956). Nowadays, researchers try to sharpen their focus by treating **stress** as a multidimensional concept that encompasses stressful stimuli, the stress-processing system (including cognitive assessment of the stimuli), and the responses to stress. While many different parts of the body respond to stress, it's clear that the brain carefully monitors and controls those responses (McEwen et al., 2015).

The stress response has multiple stages

Selye emphasized a close connection between stress and disease that he termed "general adaptation syndrome." He called the initial response to stress the **alarm reaction**. As one part of the alarm reaction, the hypothalamus activates the sympathetic nervous system to ready the body for action; this is the "fight or flight" system we mentioned at the start of the chapter. The fight or flight response includes sympathetic stimulation of the core of the adrenal gland, which is called the **adrenal medulla**, to release the hormones **epinephrine** (also known as *adrenaline*) and **norepinephrine** (*noradrenaline*). These hormones act on many parts of the body to boost heart rate, breathing, and other physiological processes that prepare the body for action. As another part of the alarm reaction, the hypothalamus stimulates the anterior pituitary to release a hormone that drives the outer layer of the adrenal gland, the **adrenal cortex**, to release **adrenal steroids** such as **cortisol** (**FIGURE 15.22**). These hormones act more slowly than epinephrine, but they also ready the body for action, including releasing body stores of energy.

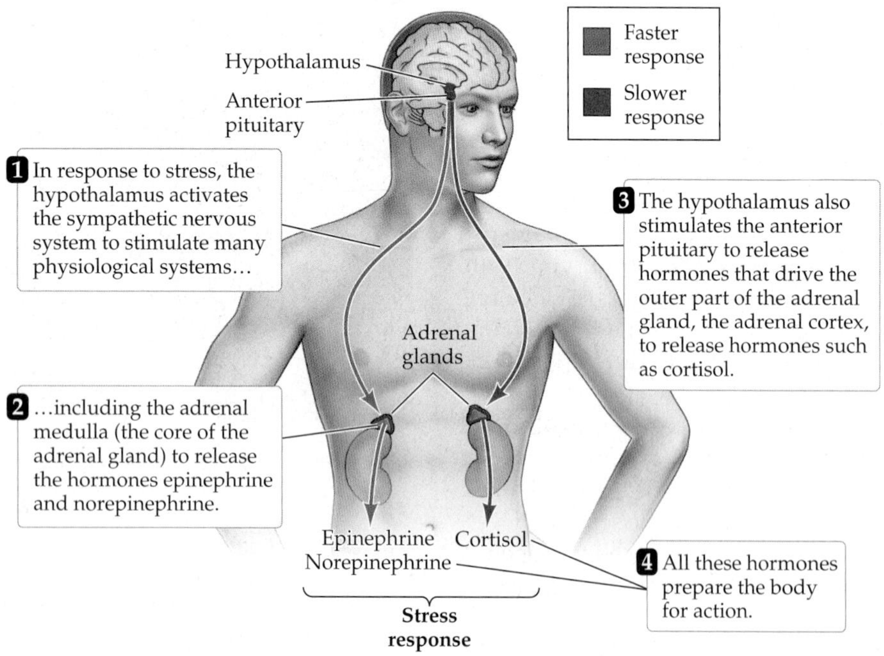

These hormonal responses to stress were studied in a group of young recruits in the Norwegian military both before

Faster response

Slower response

Hypothalamus
Anterior pituitary

1 In response to stress, the hypothalamus activates the sympathetic nervous system to stimulate many physiological systems…

Adrenal glands

3 The hypothalamus also stimulates the anterior pituitary to release hormones that drive the outer part of the adrenal gland, the adrenal cortex, to release hormones such as cortisol.

2 …including the adrenal medulla (the core of the adrenal gland) to release the hormones epinephrine and norepinephrine.

Epinephrine Norepinephrine Cortisol

4 All these hormones prepare the body for action.

Stress response

15.22 STRESS ACTIVATES TWO HORMONAL SYSTEMS

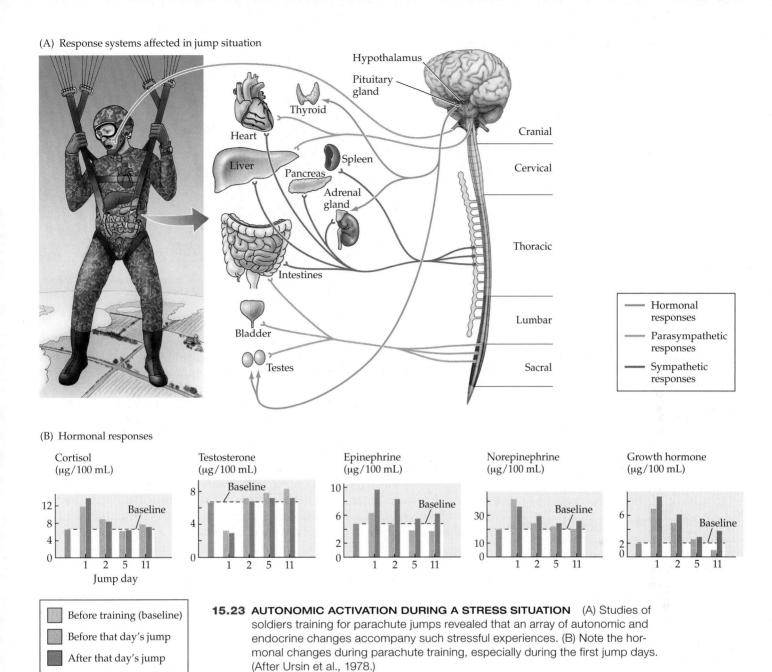

(A) Response systems affected in jump situation

Hypothalamus
Pituitary gland
Thyroid
Heart
Liver
Spleen
Pancreas
Adrenal gland
Intestines
Bladder
Testes

Cranial
Cervical
Thoracic
Lumbar
Sacral

— Hormonal responses
— Parasympathetic responses
— Sympathetic responses

(B) Hormonal responses

Cortisol (μg/100 mL)
Baseline
12
8
0
1 2 5 11
Jump day

Testosterone (μg/100 mL)
Baseline
8
4
0
1 2 5 11

Epinephrine (μg/100 mL)
10
Baseline
6
2
0
1 2 5 11

Norepinephrine (μg/100 mL)
Baseline
30
10
0
1 2 5 11

Growth hormone (μg/100 mL)
6
Baseline
2
0
1 2 5 11

Before training (baseline)
Before that day's jump
After that day's jump

15.23 AUTONOMIC ACTIVATION DURING A STRESS SITUATION (A) Studies of soldiers training for parachute jumps revealed that an array of autonomic and endocrine changes accompany such stressful experiences. (B) Note the hormonal changes during parachute training, especially during the first jump days. (After Ursin et al., 1978.)

and during scary parachute training (Ursin et al., 1978). On each jump day, the anterior pituitary released enhanced levels of hormones, and both the sympathetic and parasympathetic systems were activated (**FIGURE 15.23A**). Initially, cortisol levels were elevated in the blood before each jump, but with more and more successful jumps over successive days, the pituitary-adrenal response soon declined. Epinephrine and norepinephrine were also elevated before the first jumps, but eventually they returned to normal before jumps. Testosterone showed the reverse pattern, falling far below control levels on the first day of training but returning to normal with subsequent jumps (**FIGURE 15.23B**). Once the soldiers mastered the jumps, they no longer showed hormonal responses, having reached the adaptation stage that Selye had described.

Less-dramatic real-life situations also evoke clear endocrine responses (Frankenhaeuser, 1978). Factory work leads to the release of epinephrine; the shorter the work cycle—that is, the more frequently the person has to repeat the same operations—the higher the levels of epinephrine. Riding in a commuter train provokes the release

15.24 HORMONAL CHANGES IN HUMANS IN RESPONSE TO SOCIAL STRESSES (A) Small changes in crowding on a morning commuter train ride affect hormone levels in humans. A 10% increase in the number of passengers during a period of gasoline rationing (right) resulted in a much higher level of epinephrine secretion. (B) Levels of epinephrine and norepinephrine in a graduate student in the weeks before, during, and after a thesis exam reflect levels of stress. (After Frankenhaeuser, 1978.)

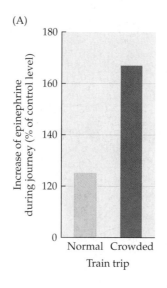

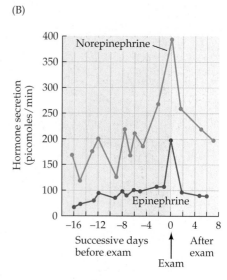

stress immunization The concept that mild stress early in life makes an individual better able to handle stress later in life.

epigenetic regulation Process affecting the expression of a particular gene or genes without affecting the sequence of nucleotides making up the gene itself.

psychosomatic medicine A field of study that emphasizes the role of psychological factors in disease.

health psychology Also called *behavioral medicine*. A field that studies psychological influences on health-related processes, such as why people become ill or how they remain healthy.

hostility Here, the angry, antagonistic personality characteristic associated with a greater risk for heart disease.

psychoneuroimmunology The study of the immune system and its interaction with the nervous system and behavior.

of epinephrine; the longer the ride and the more crowded the train, the greater the hormonal response (**FIGURE 15.24A**). Young people with asthma who are subjected to rejection by their peers have more responsive adrenal systems and more severe symptoms (Murphy et al., 2015). The stress of a PhD oral exam leads to a dramatic increase in both epinephrine and norepinephrine (**FIGURE 15.24B**).

Individual differences in the stress response

Why do individuals differ in their responses to stress (Infurna and Luthar, 2016)? One hypothesis focuses on early experience. Rat pups clearly find it stressful to have a human pick them up and handle them. Yet several studies found that rats that had been briefly handled as pups were *less* susceptible to adult stress than were rats that had been left alone as pups (S. Levine et al., 1967). For example, the previously handled rats secreted lower adrenal steroid amounts in response to a wide variety of adult stressors. This effect was termed **stress immunization** because a little stress early in life seemed to make the animals more resilient to later stress.

Follow-up research showed there was more to the story. The pups did not benefit because they were stressed; they benefited because their mothers *comforted* them *after* the stress. When pups are returned to their mother after a separation, she spends considerable time licking and grooming them. And she will lick the pups much longer if they were handled by humans during the separation. Michael Meaney and colleagues suggest that this gentle tactile stimulation from Mom is crucial for the stress immunization effect. They found that, even among undisturbed litters, the offspring of mother rats that exhibited more licking and grooming behavior were more resilient in their responses to adult stress than other rats were (D. Liu et al., 1997). So the "immunizing" benefit of early stressful experience happens only if the pups are promptly comforted after each stressful event.

If the pups are deprived of their mother for long periods, receiving very little of her attention, then as adults they exhibit a greater stress response, have difficulty learning mazes, and show reduced neurogenesis in the hippocampus (Mirescu et al., 2004). Maternal deprivation exerts this negative effect on adult stress responses by causing long-lasting changes in the expression of adrenal steroid receptors in the brain. This change is termed **epigenetic regulation** because it represents a change in the *expression* of the gene, rather than a change in the encoding region of the gene (see Figure 7.21).

Dramatic evidence for the same phenomenon has been seen in humans. Examination of the brains of suicide victims has revealed the same epigenetic change in expression of the adrenal steroid receptor, but only in those victims who had a history of being abused or neglected as children (McGowan et al., 2009). The implication is that the early abuse epigenetically modified expression of the gene, making the person less able to handle stress and thus more likely to become depressed and commit suicide. Suicide victims who had no history of early neglect did not show the epigenetic change, so their depression may have been a response to other influences.

Stress and Emotions Affect the Immune System

During the past 50 years, researchers and clinicians have begun to understand some of the ways in which psychological, behavioral, and social factors play a role in health and disease, forming a field known as **psychosomatic medicine**. The related field called **health psychology** (or *behavioral medicine*) emphasizes the role of psychological factors in the cause, progression, and consequences of health and illness (Ogden, 2012). **FIGURE 15.25** shows how several factors interact to affect human health and disease.

Some consistent correlations between stressful events and illness have been found (N. Adler and Matthews, 1994). For example, men who reported frequent and severe stress during a period of 1–5 years prior to interviews were more likely to experience heart disease during the next 12 years than were those who reported little stress (Rosengren et al., 1991). Health psychology studies have inspired researchers to try to understand why individuals differ in their resilience in the face of stress (S. J. Russo et al., 2012).

Emotions and stress influence cardiac function

"Calm down before you blow a fuse!" People have long understood that there's a link between strong emotions and heart attacks. An important development in understanding this relationship was the identification of two general behavior patterns and their correlation to the development and maintenance of heart disease (M. Friedman and Rosenman, 1974). *Type A* behavior is characterized by excessive competitive drive, impatience, hostility, and accelerated speech and movements, while *type B* behavior patterns are more relaxed. Initial work indicated that type A people were more likely to develop heart disease than type B individuals. Most of these associations between type A/B personalities were later accounted for by a single factor, **hostility**: angry, mistrustful, antagonistic behavior. So studies asking why people who display hostility are more likely to suffer heart disease (Almada et al., 1991) have largely replaced investigations of the type A/B concept (Matthews, 2005). Other risk factors for dying of heart disease include poor sleep, depression, stressful jobs and/or primary relationships (Rozanski, 2014), and social isolation (Holt-Lunstad et al., 2010). Another psychological factor that appears to affect heart disease is a *sense of life purpose* (Sone et al., 2008). Among people diagnosed with heart disease, those who had a low sense of purpose in life were more likely to die within a few years than people with a strong sense of purpose (**FIGURE 15.26**).

Emotions and stress influence the immune system

Researchers once viewed the immune system as an automatic mechanism: a pathogen, such as a virus, arrived on the scene, and soon the defense mechanisms of the immune system went to work, usually prevailing with their armory of immunological devices. Few investigators thought of the nervous system as involved in the process.

In the 1980s there appeared a new field, **psychoneuroimmunology**, emphasizing that the immune system—with its collection of cells that recognize and attack intruders—interacts with other systems, especially hormone systems and the nervous system (Ader, 2001). Studies of both human and nonhu-

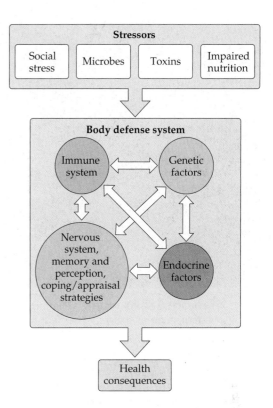

15.25 FACTORS THAT INTERACT DURING THE DEVELOPMENT AND PROGRESSION OF DISEASE

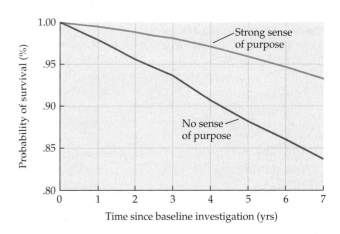

15.26 A SENSE OF PURPOSE People who felt they had little or no sense of purpose in their lives were more likely to die within a few years after diagnosis of heart disease than people with a strong sense of life purpose. (From Sone et al., 2008.)

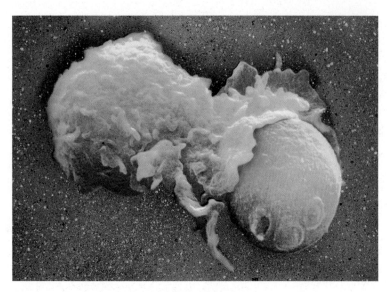

15.27 A PHAGOCYTE AT WORK Phagocytes engulf and consume invaders, such as this yeast cell (right).

phagocyte An immune system cell that engulfs invading molecules or microbes.

B lymphocyte Also called *B cell*. An immune system cell, formed in the bone marrow (hence the *B*), that mediates humoral immunity.

antibody Also called *immunoglobulin*. A large protein that recognizes and permanently binds to particular shapes, normally as part of the immune system attack on foreign particles.

T lymphocyte Also called *T cell*. An immune system cell, formed in the thymus (hence the *T*), which includes killer T cells that attack foreign microbes, and helper T cells that secrete cytokines.

cytokine A protein that induces the proliferation of other cells, as in the immune system.

man subjects now clearly show psychological and neurological influences on the immune system. For example, people with happy social lives are less likely to develop a cold when exposed to the virus (S. Cohen et al., 2006). In fact, social support seems to buffer against social stress. People exposed to a cold virus have more severe symptoms if they are experiencing conflict with others. But individuals who feel they have more social support, and who *receive more hugs from others*, are protected from that effect of conflict (S. Cohen et al., 2015). Likewise, people who tend to feel positive emotions will also produce more antibodies in response to a flu vaccination (Rosenkranz et al., 2003), which should help them fight off sickness. These interactions go in both directions: the brain influences responses of the immune system, and immune cells and their products affect brain activities.

THE IMMUNE SYSTEM   To understand this intriguing story, we need to consider some of the main features of the immune system. In your blood are different classes of white blood cells (leukocytes). The **phagocytes** ("eating" cells) are specialized to engulf and destroy invading germs (**FIGURE 15.27**). But phagocytes rely on other white blood cells (the lymphocytes) to tell them what to attack. **B lymphocytes** (or *B cells*, because they form in the *b*one marrow), produce proteins called **antibodies** (or *immunoglobulins*). Antibodies latch onto foreign molecules such as viruses or bacteria and summon phagocytes and circulating proteins to destroy the invaders. **T lymphocytes** (*T cells*), so called because they form in the *t*hymus gland, include some that act as *killer T cells*, forming a strong part of the body's attack against foreign substances. Other T lymphocytes called *helper T cells* secrete **cytokines**, cell-signaling proteins that regulate the activity of B lymphocytes and phagocytes. These immune system cells form in the thymus gland, bone marrow, spleen, and lymph nodes (**FIGURE 15.28**), which release the cells into the bloodstream.

COMMUNICATION AMONG THE NERVOUS, IMMUNE, AND ENDOCRINE SYSTEMS The brain can affect the immune system through autonomic nerve fibers that innervate immune system organs such as the spleen and thymus gland. These fibers are usually noradrenergic, sympathetic postganglionic axons that affect antibody production and immune cell proliferation (Bellinger et al., 1992). This system may explain why simply seeing photographs of people displaying infectious disease symptoms, such as a runny nose and cough, can quickly trigger an increased release of cytokines (Schaller et al., 2010). Likewise, people who are lonely show an exaggerated release of cytokines in response to stress (Jaremka et al., 2013).

The brain also carefully monitors immune reactions to make sure they are not too extreme and ultimately harmful to the body. For example, peripheral axons of the vagus nerve have receptors to detect high levels of cytokines and relay the information to the brain. Then, brainstem neurons with axons that lead back out the vagus nerve release acetylcholine, which inhibits cytokine release from immune cells (H. Wang et al., 2003). Hypothalamic neurons and neurons located in the walls of cerebral ventricles also monitor cytokines in circulation (Dantzer et al., 2008; Samad et al., 2001). Thus, the brain is directly informed about the actions of the immune system, which serves as an early warning system to alert the brain when microbes invade the body.

There is an interesting theory about why our brains monitor the immune system so closely. Although that achy, lethargic feeling that we have with the flu is unpleasant, it is also adaptive because it forces us to rest and keep out of trouble until we recover (Hart, 1988). Perhaps high levels of cytokines are what cause the brain to enforce that sick feeling. This suggestion has given rise to the idea that some people's

(A) Immune system

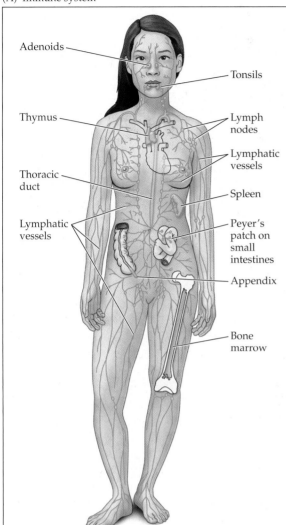

Adenoids

Tonsils

Thymus

Lymph nodes

Thoracic duct

Lymphatic vessels

Spleen

Peyer's patch on small intestines

Appendix

Bone marrow

(B) Humoral immune response system

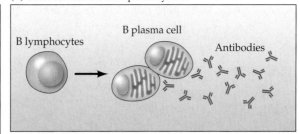

B lymphocytes

B plasma cell

Antibodies

(C) Cell-mediated immune response system

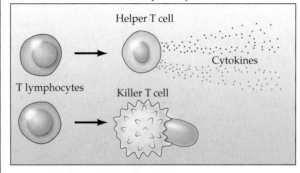

Helper T cell

Cytokines

T lymphocytes

Killer T cell

(D) Phagocytes engulf invading germs and foreign substances

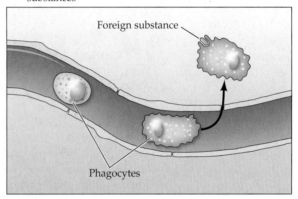

Foreign substance

Phagocytes

15.28 MAIN COMPONENTS OF THE HUMAN IMMUNE SYSTEM (A) The various components of the immune system protect us by means of three classes of white blood cells: B lymphocytes (B) produce antibodies to attack invading microbes. T lymphocytes (C) form helper cells that release cytokines to regulate B cells to divide or die. T cells also form killer cells that, together with phagocytes ("eating" cells) (D), directly attack foreign tissues or microbes.

depression may be due to a broad set of physiological changes in the brain, including large alterations in availability of several neurotransmitters, that are brought about by excessive quantities of cytokines in circulation and penetrating the brain (Hodes et al., 2015). Indeed, one action of antidepressant drugs is to reduce cytokine production (Dantzer et al., 2008).

The immune system and nervous system also interact extensively with the endocrine system (**FIGURE 15.29**). All three systems interact reciprocally, so there is a constant state of flux, carefully tuning the immune system so that it vigorously attacks foreign cells but leaves the body's own cells alone.

PSYCHOLOGICAL STRESS AND IMMUNITY The anatomical and physiological systems described in the previous sections give us some hints about ways in which psychological factors can alter immune system responses. For example, several lines of evidence indicate that the immune system is compromised during depression

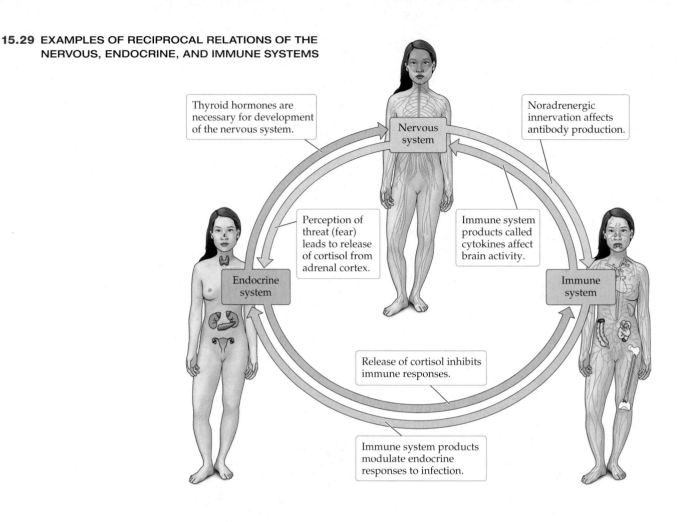

Thyroid hormones are necessary for development of the nervous system.

Noradrenergic innervation affects antibody production.

Nervous system

Perception of threat (fear) leads to release of cortisol from adrenal cortex.

Immune system products called cytokines affect brain activity.

Endocrine system

Immune system

Release of cortisol inhibits immune responses.

Immune system products modulate endocrine responses to infection.

(M. Stein et al., 1991)—a situation that, if sustained, could increase susceptibility to infectious diseases, cancer, and autoimmune disorders. Altered immune function is also observed in people who are grieving the death of a relative, especially a spouse (M. Stein and Miller, 1993).

Stressful exam periods usually produce a decline in the number of immune cells and in levels of cytokines (Glaser et al., 1986). Most important, some studies have noted that the student's *perception* of the stress of the academic program is a predictor of the level of circulating antibody: those who perceive the program as stressful show the lowest levels. One experiment considered the effects of university examinations on wound healing in dental students (Marucha et al., 1998). Two small wounds were placed on the roof of the mouth of 11 dental students (sounds like revenge, doesn't it?). The first wound was timed during summer vacation; the second was inflicted 3 days before the first major examination of the term. Two independent daily measures showed that no student healed as rapidly during the exam period, when healing took 40% longer. A measure of immunological response declined 68% during the exam period. The experimenters concluded that even something as transient, predictable, and relatively benign (do students agree with this description?) as examination stress can have significant consequences for wound healing.

Another connection between the nervous and immune systems was described in Chapter 14, where we learned that sleep deprivation impairs the responsiveness of the immune system (see Box 14.1).

Why does stress suppress the immune system?

Under stressful conditions, as noted earlier, the brain causes adrenal steroid hormones such as cortisol to be released from the adrenal cortex. These adrenal steroids directly suppress the immune system. But doesn't it seem like a bad idea to suppress immunity just when you are more likely to sustain an injury, and maybe an infection? Modern evolutionary theory offers some possible explanations for this seemingly maladaptive situation (for a very readable account, see Sapolsky, 2004).

To the extent that stress might be a sudden emergency, the *temporary* suppression of immune responses makes some sense because the stress response demands a rapid mobilization of energy. Slow and long-lasting immune responses consume energy that otherwise could be used for dealing with the emergency at hand. A zebra wounded by a lion must first escape and hide, and only then does infection of the wound pose a threat. So the stress of the encounter first suppresses the immune system, conserving resources until a safe haven is found. Later the animal can afford to mobilize the immune system to heal the wound. The adrenal steroids also suppress the swelling (inflammation) of injuries, especially of joints, to help the animal remain mobile long enough to find refuge. It is precisely this action that makes adrenal steroids like prednisone such useful medicines.

In the wild, animals are under stress for only a short while; any animal stressed for a *prolonged* period dies. So natural selection favored stress reactions as a drastic effort to deal with a short-term problem. What makes humans "special" is that, with our highly social lives and keen analytical minds, we are capable of experiencing stress for prolonged periods—months or even years. The bodily reactions to stress, which evolved to deal with short-term problems, become a handicap when extended too long (Sapolsky, 2004). Chronic stress leads to degeneration in the hippocampus (Egeland et al., 2015) and prefrontal cortex, while the amygdala may expand (Radley and Sawchenko, 2011). **TABLE 15.1** lists a variety of stress responses that are beneficial in the short term but detrimental in the long term.

What we have described so far is a really depressing picture. If you are stressed for long periods of time, your health suffers, which brings another source of stress to your life. But don't give up hope. Even if there are some sources of stress you cannot avoid altogether, there are things you can do to reduce the impact of stress. *Relaxation training* involves focusing your attention on something calming while becoming more aware of your body, trying to relax muscles as much as you can (McGuigan and Lehrer, 2007). A program of therapy to deal with stress, partially inspired by various practices of meditation, is **mindfulness-based stress reduction (MBSR)**. MBSR pairs relaxation with efforts to focus attention on the present moment, including current sensations, thoughts, and bodily states, in an open, nonjudgmental way. MBSR is focused on results and does not require practitioners to adopt any particular religious or spiritual views. It has been shown to reduce activity in the amygdala (Goldin and Gross, 2010) and prevent relapses of anxiety disorders or depression (Hofmann et al., 2010). You can learn more about MBSR at umassmed.edu/cfm.

mindfulness-based stress reduction (MBSR) A therapy to reduce stress that pairs relaxation with efforts to focus attention on the present moment, rather than past or future problems.

TABLE 15.1 The Stress Response and Consequences of Prolonged Stress

PRINCIPAL COMPONENTS OF THE STRESS RESPONSE	COMMON PATHOLOGICAL CONSEQUENCES OF PROLONGED STRESS
Mobilization of energy at the cost of energy storage	Fatigue, muscle wasting, steroid diabetes
Increased cardiovascular and cardiopulmonary tone	Hypertension (high blood pressure)
Suppression of digestion	Ulcers
Suppression of growth	Psychogenic dwarfism, bone decalcification
Suppression of reproduction	Suppression of ovulation, impotence, loss of libido
Suppression of immunity and of inflammatory response	Impaired disease resistance
Analgesia	Apathy
Neural responses, including altered cognition and sensory thresholds	Neural degeneration in hippocampus and prefrontal cortex

Source: Sapolsky, 1992.

The Cutting Edge

Synaptic Changes during Fear Conditioning

two-photon excitation microscopy Method of providing many low-energy photons that can penetrate deep into tissues, such that the simultaneous arrival of two photons at a fluorescent molecule is sufficient to elicit a visible photon in response.

When microscopes use infrared light, it penetrates deep into tissue, and when the light is finally absorbed, it is unlikely to do any damage. Normally such light is also too weak to bounce back to our eye to let us see anything. If a fluorescent molecule is in the tissue, an infrared photon is also too weak to stimulate it to fluorescence so we can see it. To get around this problem, **two-photon excitation microscopy** uses lasers to shine a *lot* of infrared light onto tissue so that when two infrared photons hit a fluorescent molecule at the same time, they excite it enough to cause it to emit a higher-powered photon that we can see (**FIGURE 15.30A**). If such a microscope is centered over the cortex of a living mouse (**FIGURE 15.30B**), fluorescent molecules (either fluorescent proteins, produced by a

(A)

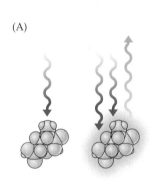

A single photon of low-energy, infrared light striking a fluorescent molecule does not have enough energy to make anything happen. But when two infrared photons arrive at the same time, their combined energy excites the fluorescent molecule enough to make it release a high-energy photon that we can see.

(B)

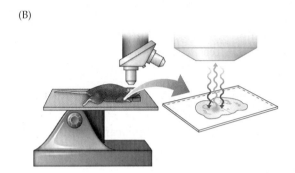

The surgically exposed frontal cortex of an anesthetized mouse can be examined with such a scope to reveal fluorescently labeled neurons beneath the surface. After imaging, the mouse wakes up, is subjected to fear conditioning, and is returned to its cage. A few days later, scientists can examine the same cortical neurons again.

(C)

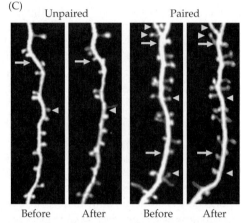

Normally, dendritic spines on these cortical neurons arise and disappear in the course of days. In animals that are exposed to the auditory tone and footshock in an unpaired fashion, the number of new spines that are formed (arrows) 2 days later is about the same as the number of old spines that are eliminated (arrowheads). However, in mice repeatedly exposed to the pairing of tone followed by footshock, many more spines are eliminated than usual.

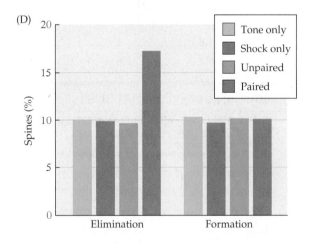

(D)

Only the pairing of tone followed by footshock increases spine elimination. The percentage of new spines that arise is unaffected.

(E)

Across individual mice, those that freeze more often in response to the tone also tend to have more dendritic spine elimination, suggesting that the elimination of these spines and their synapses underlies the fear response.

15.30 CHANGES IN DENDRITIC SPINES DURING FEAR CONDITIONING (Part C from Lai et al., 2012.)

transgenic mouse, or fluorescent neuroanatomical tracers implanted by the scientist) can be excited and seen deep under the cortical surface (Helmchen and Denk, 2005).

Using this method, scientists visualized changes in the brain that may underlie fear conditioning. They directed their two-photon microscope on the dendritic spines of neurons in the frontal cortex of mice (C. S. W. Lai et al., 2012). Repeated observations revealed that dendritic spines on frontal cortex neurons normally wax and wane over time. After recording images of these dendritic spines in many mice, the researchers looked for changes in mice that were subjected to fear conditioning, when an auditory tone was repeatedly followed by footshock (see Figure 15.15). Examining the dendritic spines of the cortical neurons in these mice 2 days later revealed that more spines than normal had been eliminated (**FIGURE 15.30C**). Most important, this increased elimination of dendritic spines was not seen in mice exposed to the tone alone, or to footshock alone, or to both the tone and footshock presented in an unpaired fashion. Only the *pairing* of the tone followed by footshock resulted in more spines being eliminated (**FIGURE 15.30D**). Of course, these were also the only mice that became afraid of the tone, as indicated by their freezing in place when it occurred. In fact, among the mice that were subjected to fear conditioning, those that showed the greatest fear response to the tone (freezing) also showed the most dendritic spine elimination (**FIGURE 15.30E**).

Thus the elimination of these dendritic spines, along with the loss of synaptic input on the spines, may play a role in learning to freeze in response to the fearful signal. Later studies found that if the fear-conditioned animals were repeatedly exposed to the tone *without* shock, as they learned to stop freezing in response to the sound, more dendritic spines were formed on these cortical neurons, which confirms the studies we discussed earlier that the prefrontal cortex is required for extinguishing fear. With powerful techniques like these, scientists may someday uncover the entire circuit underlying fear.

Recommended Reading

Davidson, R. J., and Begley, S. (2012). *The Emotional Life of Your Brain.* New York: Hudson Street Press.

Ekman, P. (2007). *Emotions Revealed: Recognizing Faces and Feelings to Improve Communication and Emotional Life.* New York: Owl Books.

Gilbert, D. (2007). *Stumbling on Happiness.* New York: Vintage.

Hodgins, S., Viding, E., and Plodowski, A. (2009). *The Neurobiological Basis of Violence: Science and Rehabilitation.* New York: Oxford University Press.

LeDoux, J. (2015). *Anxious: Using the Brain to Understand and Treat Fear and Anxiety.* New York: Viking.

Nelson, R. J. (2006). *The Biology of Aggression.* New York: Oxford University Press.

Oatley, K., Keltner, D., and Jenkins, J. M. (2013). *Understanding Emotions* (2nd ed.). New York: Wiley.

Sapolsky, R. (2004). *Why Zebras Don't Get Ulcers* (3rd ed.). New York: Holt.

Go to
bn8e.com
for study questions, quizzes, activities, and other resources

15
—VISUAL SUMMARY—

You should be able to relate each summary to the adjacent illustration, including structures and processes.
Go to **bn8e.com/vs15** for links to figures, animations, and activities that will help you consolidate the material.

1 **Emotions** are feelings, actions, physiological arousal, and motivational programs. The **James-Lange theory** considered emotions to be the perceptions of stimulus-induced autonomic activity, while the **Cannon-Bard theory** emphasized *simultaneous* emotional experience and bodily response. Review **Figure 15.1**

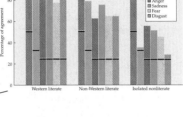

2 According to Schachter's **cognitive attribution model**, autonomic activity may intensify the emotion we feel, but not *which* emotion we experience. We attribute sympathetic arousal to specific emotions by analyzing the physical and social context, including the emotions of those around us. Emotions evolved as adaptations to help in our social relations. Individuals differ, even as babies, in how much they react to unpleasant stimuli. Review **Figures 15.2 and 15.5**

3 Distinctive facial expressions represent anger, sadness, happiness, fear, disgust, surprise, contempt, and embarrassment, which are interpreted similarly across many cultures. **Polygraphs** actually measure activation of the sympathetic nervous system and therefore reflect stress, not lying. Review **Figures 15.6–15.9, Box 15.1**

4 Facial expressions are controlled by distinct sets of facial muscles controlled by the **facial** and **trigeminal nerves**. The **facial feedback hypothesis** suggests our emotions are colored by the facial expressions we display. Review **Figures 15.10–15.12**

5 Lesions revealed an interconnected brain circuit, the **limbic system** (which includes the amygdala) that mediates and controls emotions. Electrical **self-stimulation** of some brain regions is rewarding. Review **Figures 15.13 and 15.14**

6 Fear is mediated by circuitry involving the **amygdala**, which receives information both through a rapid direct route and via cortical sensory regions, allowing for both immediate responses and cognitive processing. The prefrontal cortex is important for the extinction of fear responses to a stimulus. Review **Figures 15.15–15.19, Table 15.1, Activity 15.1**

7 **Intermale aggression** is increased by androgens such as testosterone. Stimulation of some limbic system regions elicits a species-typical pattern of aggression. Serotonin levels are negatively correlated with aggression. Review **Figures 15.20 and 15.21**

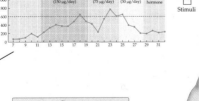

8 **Stress** elevates levels of hormones from the **adrenal cortex** (**cortisol**) and the **adrenal medulla** (**epinephrine** and **norepinephrine**), while suppressing other hormones (testosterone). Review **Figures 15.22–15.24**

9 Physiological responses to stress are adaptive in the short run. However, in socially complex species that can experience stress for long periods, including humans, these hormonal responses decrease immune system competence, damaging our health. Review **Figure 15.25**

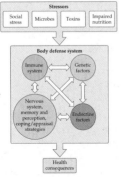

10 The nervous, endocrine, and immune systems interact reciprocally to monitor and maintain health. Emotional traits such as **hostility** and depression can damage our health by, for example, increasing the risk of heart attack. Review **Figures 15.26 –15.29, Activity 15.2**

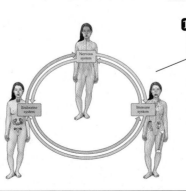

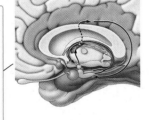

Psychopathology
Biological Basis of Behavioral Disorders

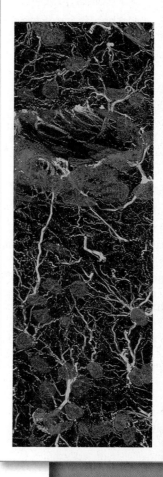

 "The Voice"

Eleanor was off to a great start in college, eager to partake of a life of lectures and parties. The first crack in her optimism came when she was packing up to leave a classroom and heard a voice calmly say, "She is leaving the building." No one was in the room with her, yet the voice was so distinct. Spooked, Eleanor hurried home only to hear, as she arrived, the same voice say, "She is opening the door." For weeks, this disembodied voice dispassionately narrated everything Eleanor did, in the third person. When she finally told a friend about the "Voice," Eleanor was met with suspicion and fear. She went to a physician, getting his full attention when she started talking about the Voice. Thus began Eleanor's struggle with *schizophrenia*, a disorder that afflicts about 1% of individuals in every human society.

Eleanor came to hate the Voice that brought her so much attention and suspicion. It seemed as if her hostility to the Voice was soon reciprocated. She began hearing not just one, but several voices, and they become progressively more menacing and demanding. They began goading Eleanor to injure herself, so her parents started hiding the cutlery. When a voice told Eleanor to pick up the glass of water on her instructor's desk and throw it in his face, he was not amused. Eleanor became a target, someone marked as different and disturbed, suffering ostracism and verbal taunts from her peers. The life she had hoped for seemed lost forever. One psychiatrist said, "Eleanor, you'd be better off with cancer because cancer is easier to cure than schizophrenia" (Longden, 2013, p. 37).

Was Eleanor's life really over?

Debilitating mental afflictions have plagued humankind throughout history, plunging their victims into an abyss of disordered thought and emotional chaos. Psychopathology affects hundreds of millions of people worldwide, not just an exotic few.

The seeds for a biological perspective in psychiatry were sown at the start of the twentieth century, when thousands of patients in mental hospitals suffered from a disorder called *paralytic dementia*. It was characterized by the sudden onset of **delusions** (false beliefs strongly held in spite of contrary evidence), grandiosity (boastful self-importance), euphoria, poor judgment, and impulsive and capricious behavior. One sign of the disease was the "Argyll-Robertson pupil": the pupil in the eye did not constrict in response to light (as pupils normally do) but could still constrict when the patient tried to look at something close up (Argyll-Robertson, 1869).

Recognized for centuries, this disorder was often attributed to "weak character." In 1911, however, microbiologist Hideyo Noguchi (1876–1928) discovered that the brains of people suffering from this disorder had been extensively damaged by syphilis, a sexually transmitted bacterial disease. The mental disorder got a new name, *syphilitic psychosis*, and the subsequent discovery of antibiotic drugs soon made syphilitic psychosis (and the Argyll-Robertson pupil) a rarity. This success

Go to Brain Explorer
bn8e.com/16.1

TABLE 16.1 Standardized 12-Month and Lifetime Prevalence of Disorders in the United States

| | RATE (%) | |
DISORDERS	PREVIOUS 12 MONTHS	LIFETIME
ANY PSYCHIATRIC DISORDER	26.2	46.4
ANY SUBSTANCE USE DISORDER	3.8	14.6
Alcohol abuse	3.1	13.2
Drug abuse	1.4	7.9
ANY MOOD DISORDER	9.5	20.8
Major depressive episode	6.7	16.6
Minor depression (dysthymia)	1.5	2.5
Manic episode	2.6	3.9
ANY ANXIETY DISORDER	18.1	28.8
Phobia	15.5	24.6
Panic	2.7	4.7
OBSESSIVE-COMPULSIVE DISORDER (OCD)	1.0	1.6

Note: The rates are from surveys of the noninstitutionalized adult population of the United States.
(Data from Kessler, Berglund, et al., 2005 and Kessler, Chiu, et al., 2005.)

delusion A false belief strongly held in spite of contrary evidence.

epidemiology The statistical study of patterns of disease in a population.

dissociative thinking A condition, seen in schizophrenia, that is characterized by disturbances of thought and difficulty relating events properly.

schizophrenia A severe psychopathology characterized by negative symptoms such as emotional withdrawal and impoverished thought, and by positive symptoms such as hallucinations and delusions.

positive symptom In psychiatry, a behavior that is gained in a disorder. Examples include hallucinations, delusions, and excited motor behavior in schizophrenia.

negative symptom In psychiatry, a symptom that reflects insufficient functioning. Examples include emotional and social withdrawal, blunted affect, and slowness and impoverishment of thought and speech.

encouraged researchers to consider whether other psychiatric disorders result from biological processes.

In this chapter we explore the biological underpinnings of the most prevalent psychiatric disorders: schizophrenia, depression, and the anxiety disorders. Several other disorders are discussed in other chapters, such as autism (Chapter 5), attention deficit hyperactivity disorder (Chapter 18), and Alzheimer's disease (Chapter 7). Although the biological perspective has not (yet) led to the prevention of any of these disorders, as happened with syphilitic psychosis, modern discoveries have restored millions of people to normal life.

The Toll of Psychiatric Disorders Is Huge

Because they are mostly diagnosed on the basis of behavioral symptoms rather than physical laboratory tests, the precise classification of psychiatric disorders is subject to periodic revision, but we know from **epidemiology** (the scientific study of disease incidence) that psychiatric disorders are startlingly prevalent in modern society. More than one-third of the U.S. population *at some point in life* reports symptoms that match the defining features of a major psychiatric disorder (**TABLE 16.1**). At any one time, men and women show comparable prevalence of mental disorders, although depression is somewhat more prevalent in females, and drug dependency and alcoholism are more prevalent in males. Certain psychiatric disorders—for example, schizophrenia—tend to appear in adolescence and young adulthood. Peaks for depression and antisocial personality appear in 25- to 44-year-olds (**FIGURE 16.1**), whereas cognitive impairment occurs especially in people older than 65. Clearly, mental disorders exact an enormous toll on us throughout our lives.

Schizophrenia Is the Major Neurobiological Challenge in Psychiatry

Medical records tell us that around the world and across the centuries, certain people's lives have been shattered by bizarre and debilitating symptoms—hearing voices that aren't there, feeling intense fear, paranoia, and acting strangely (Heinrichs, 2003). For some people with schizophrenia, this state lasts a lifetime, but some 30–40% will recover (Harrow et al., 2012). Schizophrenia is also a "public" disorder

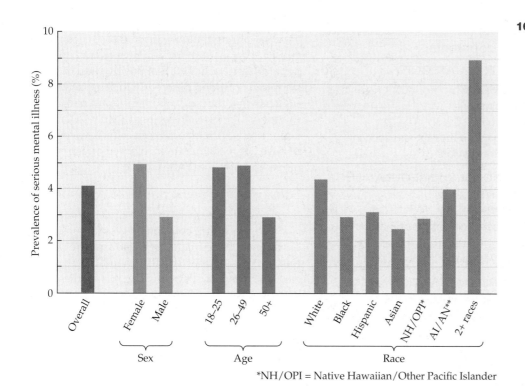

16.1 PREVALENCE OF SERIOUS MENTAL ILLNESS AMONG U.S. ADULTS Prevalence is the percentage of people suffering from a disorder at any one point in time. The greater prevalence of mental illness in females is mostly due to their greater susceptibility to depression. (Males, on the other hand, are more susceptible to drug addiction.) Episodes of schizophrenia are most common in young adults. Note that mental illness occurs in every racial group. (From the National Institute of Mental Health, nimh.nih.gov/health/statistics/prevalence/serious-mental-illness-smi-among-us-adults.shtml.)

*NH/OPI = Native Hawaiian/Other Pacific Islander

because many people who suffer from it become homeless on our streets. Epidemiological surveys of schizophrenia reveal a prevalence of about 1% of the population—about 3 million people in the United States alone. This disorder consumes a disproportionate share of community health resources because of its chronic and overwhelming character.

Schizophrenia is characterized by an unusual array of symptoms

Eugen Bleuler (1857–1939) introduced the term *schizophrenia* (from the Greek *schizein*, "to split," and *phren*, "mind") in 1911 (Bleuler, 1950 translation). Despite the name he chose, Bleuler was not thinking of a "split personality." Rather, he identified the key symptom as **dissociative thinking**, a major impairment in the logical structure of thought, as well as emotional disturbance, delusions, and hallucinations. German psychiatrist Emil Kraepelin (1856–1926) described numerous clinical features common to the varied forms of schizophrenia: paranoia, grandiose delusions, abnormal emotional regulation, bizarre disturbances of thought, and auditory hallucinations (Kraepelin, 1919). Although movies often portray people with schizophrenia experiencing elaborate visual hallucinations (**FIGURE 16.2**), in fact the hallucinations are almost always purely auditory (Javitt and Sweet, 2015), like the Voice heard by Eleanor, whom we met at the start of the chapter.

Today, the major symptom categories associated with **schizophrenia** include (1) auditory hallucinations, (2) highly personalized delusions (false beliefs), (3) changes in affect (emotion), and (4) cognitive changes. An additional major division of schizophrenic symptoms distinguishes positive and negative symptoms (Andreasen, 1991). The term **positive symptoms** refers to behavioral states that have been *gained*; examples include hallucinations, delusions, and excited motor behavior. The term **negative symptoms** refers to behavioral functions that have been *lost*—for example, slow and impoverished thought and speech, emotional and social withdrawal (Green et al., 2015). Since people who suffer from schizophrenia report experiencing very strong emotions, the blunted emotions

16.2 NOT SO BEAUTIFUL VOICES Mathematician John Nash's struggle with schizophrenia is depicted in the Academy Award–winning movie *A Beautiful Mind*. The movie portrays him as having elaborate visual hallucinations, but in fact his hallucinations were exclusively auditory, and he suffered from delusions that fueled his paranoid thinking. Auditory hallucinations are common in schizophrenia; visual hallucinations are quite rare.

TABLE 16.2 Symptoms of Schizophrenia

SYMPTOM DIMENSION	SYMPTOM CATEGORY
POSITIVE SYMPTOMS Refers to symptoms that are present but should not be	**PSYCHOSIS** Hallucinations Delusions Disorganized thought and speech Bizarre behaviors
NEGATIVE SYMPTOMS Refers to characteristics of the individual that are absent but should be present	**EMOTIONAL DYSREGULATION** Lack of emotional expression Reduced facial expression (flat affect) Inability to experience pleasure in everyday activities (anhedonia)
	IMPAIRED MOTIVATION Reduced conversation (alogia) Diminished ability to begin or sustain activities Social withdrawal
COGNITIVE SYMPTOMS Refers to problems with processing and acting on external information	**NEUROCOGNITIVE IMPAIRMENT** Memory problems Poor attention span Difficulty making plans Reduced decision-making capacity Poor social cognition Abnormal movement patterns

in schizophrenia may be limited to emotional *expression*—facial and body signals (Kring and Caponigro, 2010). The fact that positive and negative symptoms respond differently to drug treatments suggests that they arise from different neural disruptions. Likewise, there are probably several different kinds of schizophrenia, which vary in the relative degree of paranoia, blunted affect, or cognitive impairment (**TABLE 16.2**).

Schizophrenia has a heritable component

A variety of approaches make it clear that there is a strong genetic component to schizophrenia, but later we'll see that there's also strong evidence that stress increases the likelihood of the disorder. Thus you should consider the studies we'll take up next as evidence of a genetic *susceptibility* to stress that can lead to schizophrenia.

FAMILY STUDIES   If schizophrenia is inherited, relatives of people with schizophrenia should show a higher incidence of the disorder than is found in the general population. In addition, the risk of schizophrenia among relatives should increase with the closeness of the relationship, because closer relatives share a greater number of genes. Indeed, parents and siblings of people with schizophrenia have a higher risk of developing schizophrenia than do individuals in the general population (**FIGURE 16.3**) (Gottesman, 1991). However, the mode of inheritance of schizophrenia is not simple; that is, it does not involve a single recessive or dominant gene (Tamminga and Schulz, 1991). Rather, many genes play a role in the emergence of schizophrenia.

ADOPTION STUDIES   It is easy to find fault with family studies. They confuse hereditary and environmental factors because members of a family share both. But what about children who are not raised with their biological parents? In fact, studies of adopted persons confirm the significance of genetic factors in schizophrenia. The biological parents of adoptees who suffer from schizophrenia are far more likely than the adopting parents to have suffered from this disorder (Kety et al., 1994).

TWIN STUDIES   In twins, nature provides researchers with what seem to be the perfect conditions for a genetic experiment. Human twins from the same fertilized egg—called **monozygotic** (*identical*) twins—share an identical set of genes. Twins from two different eggs—**dizygotic** (*fraternal*) twins—have only half of their genes in common, like other full siblings. When both individuals of a twin pair suffer from schizophrenia, they are described as being **concordant** for this trait. If only one member of the pair ex-

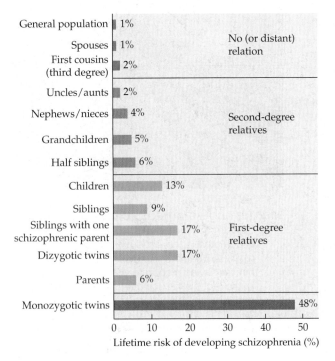

16.3 THE HERITABILITY OF SCHIZOPHRENIA   The more closely related a person is to a patient with schizophrenia, the greater are that person's chances of also developing schizophrenia. (After Gottesman, 1991.)

hibits the disorder, the pair is described as **discordant**. Whereas about half of the monozygotic twins of people with schizophrenia are concordant for the disorder, the rate of concordance for dizygotic twins is only about 17% (see Figure 16.3) (Cardno and Gottesman, 2000; Gottesman, 1991). The significantly higher concordance rate among monozygotic twins (who are twice as closely related genetically as dizygotic twins are) is strong evidence of a genetic factor. After all, environmental variables like family structure and socioeconomic stress would presumably be comparable for the two kinds of twins.

Even with identical twins, however, the concordance rate for schizophrenia is only about 50% (see Figure 16.3), so genes alone cannot fully explain whether a person will develop schizophrenia. What accounts for the discordance of the other 50% of monozygotic twins? In studying discordant cases, E. Fuller Torrey noted that the twin who went on to develop schizophrenia tended to be the one who was more abnormal throughout life. The symptomatic twin frequently weighed less at birth and had an early developmental history that included more instances of physiological distress (Torrey et al., 1994). During development, this twin was more submissive, tearful, and sensitive than the identical sibling and often was viewed by the twins' parents as being more vulnerable.

The childhood difficulties of twins who later suffer from schizophrenia are reflected in behavioral, cognitive, and other neurological signs, such as impairments in motor coordination (Torrey et al., 1994). Elaine Walker (1991) found that these early signs are sufficiently evident that observers watching home videos of children can, with uncanny accuracy, pick out the child who went on to suffer from schizophrenia in adulthood.

These sorts of behavioral distinctions can be objectively measured by various neuropsychological tests. For example, eye-tracking measurements, recording eye movements while the person's gaze follows a moving target on a computer screen, are abnormal in patients with schizophrenia (Stuve et al., 1997). These patients tend to be unable to use smooth movements of the eyes to follow the moving target and instead show an intrusion of rapid, jerky eye movements (**FIGURE 16.4**). These findings suggest that schizophrenia may have an associated **endophenotype**: a group of behavioral or physical characteristics that accompany an inherited susceptibility to a particular disorder. We'll revisit the concept of endophenotypes at the end of the

monozygotic Referring to twins derived from a single fertilized egg (*identical* twins). Such individuals have the same genotype.

dizygotic Referring to twins derived from separate eggs (*fraternal* twins). Such twins are no more closely related genetically than are other full siblings.

concordant Referring to any trait that is seen in both individuals of a pair of twins.

discordant Referring to any trait that is seen in only one individual of a pair of twins.

endophenotype Behavioral or physical characteristics accompanying susceptibility to a particular disorder, which may be used to identify those at risk.

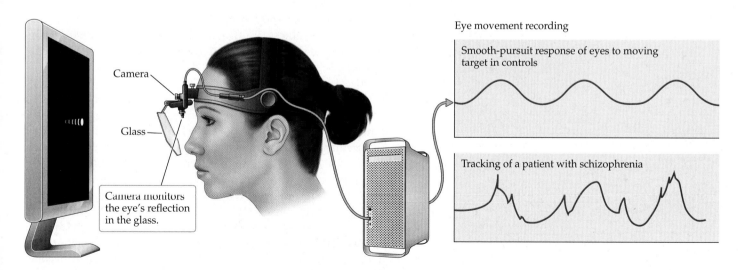

16.4 EYE TRACKING IN PATIENTS WITH SCHIZOPHRENIA VERSUS CONTROLS
People with schizophrenia have greater difficulty making smooth-pursuit movements with their eyes than do controls. Eye movement recordings indicate that the eyes of people who suffer from schizophrenia move in jerks and fits rather than smoothly tracking the moving object as most people's eyes do.

chapter when we describe cutting-edge efforts to find a way to identify people at risk for schizophrenia in hopes of averting it.

INDIVIDUAL GENES   It has proven difficult to identify any single gene that causes schizophrenia to develop or increases susceptibility (Mowry et al., 2004). In fact, genetic analyses suggest that over 100 genes influence the development of schizophrenia (Schizophrenia Working Group of the Psychiatric Genomics Consortium, 2014; Stefansson et al., 2009). Nonetheless, a few genes have been identified that appear to be abnormal in some cases of schizophrenia. These include the genes encoding neuregulin 1, which participates in NMDA (*N*-methyl-D-aspartate), GABA (gamma-aminobutyric acid), and ACh (acetylcholine) receptor regulation (Mei and Xiong, 2008); dysbindin, which is implicated in synaptic plasticity; and catechol-O-methyltransferase (COMT), which is involved in metabolizing dopamine. In one large Scottish family, the several members who had schizophrenia shared a mutant, disabled version of a gene now known as *disrupted in schizophrenia 1* (*DISC1*). The DISC1 protein normally interacts with many other proteins during brain development (Brandon and Sawa, 2011), including some known to be important for synaptic plasticity (Tsuboi et al., 2015). In fact, several genes that seem to increase the risk of schizophrenia are known to be involved in synapse rearrangement (see Figure 7.2) (Sekar et al., 2016).

An interesting *epigenetic* factor (see Chapter 7) in schizophrenia is paternal age: older fathers are more likely than younger men to have children with schizophrenia (Rosenfield et al., 2010). The sperm of older men, which are the product of more cell divisions than the sperm of younger men, have accumulated more mutations caused by errors in copying the chromosomes (Kong et al., 2012); these de novo mutations may increase the likelihood of schizophrenia (Fromer et al., 2014). Another epigenetic difference between people with schizophrenia and controls is the likelihood that certain genes will be methylated (Jaffe et al., 2016), which would make them less likely to be expressed.

The brains of some patients with schizophrenia show structural and functional changes

Because the symptoms of schizophrenia can be so marked and persistent, investigators hypothesized early in the twentieth century that people with this illness would show distinctive and measurable structural anomalies in the brain (Trimble, 1991). Only with the advent of CT and MRI scans, however, has it become possible to study brain anatomy in living patients at all stages of their illness (T. M. Hyde and Weinberger, 1990). Such studies reveal the presence of significant, consistent anatomical differences in the brains of many patients with schizophrenia.

VENTRICULAR ABNORMALITIES   Many patients with schizophrenia have enlarged cerebral ventricles, especially the lateral ventricles (**FIGURE 16.5**) (T. M. Hyde and Weinberger, 1990). Ventricular enlargement is not related to length of illness or to duration of hospitalization. In patients with ventricular enlargement, the extent of enlargement predicts responsiveness to antipsychotic drugs: patients with more-enlarged ventricles tend to show poorer response to these drugs (Garver et al., 2000).

Enlargement of the ventricles appears to be a stable trait in patients, remaining for many years after the initial onset of the disease (Andreasen, 1994). Studies of identical twins discordant for schizophrenia have yielded startlingly clear results: twins with schizophrenia have decidedly enlarged lateral ventricles compared with their well counterparts, whose ventricles are of normal size (**FIGURE 16.6**; also see Figure 1.9) (Torrey et al., 1994).

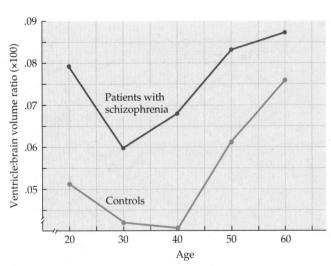

16.5 VENTRICULAR ENLARGEMENT IN SCHIZOPHRENIA The volume of the cerebral ventricles, relative to overall brain volume, is greater in male patients with schizophrenia than in control males. (After T. M. Hyde and Weinberger, 1990.)

MRI brain images of twins discordant for schizophrenia

35-year-old female identical twins

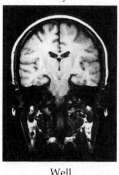 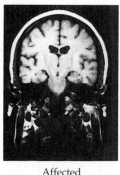

Well   Affected

28-year-old male identical twins

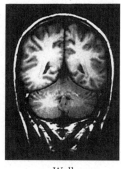 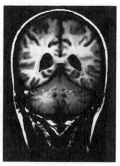

Well   Affected

16.6 IDENTICAL GENES, DIFFERENT FATES   Although the two members of each set of monozygotic twins shown here have the same genes, only one of the twins (the one with larger ventricles) developed schizophrenia. (After Torrey et al., 1994; MRIs courtesy of Dr. E. Fuller Torrey.)

Recall that a disabled version of the gene *DISC1* is associated with schizophrenia in one large family. Producing transgenic mice that express the mutant version of *DISC1* that is associated with schizophrenia in humans has a dramatic effect: the mice develop enlarged lateral ventricles (**FIGURE 16.7**) (Pletnikov et al., 2008) that are very reminiscent of the enlarged ventricles in people with schizophrenia.

What is the significance of enlarged ventricles? Because overall brain size does not seem to be affected in people with schizophrenia or mice expressing mutant *DISC1*, the enlarged ventricles must come at the expense of brain tissue. Therefore, interest has centered on brain structures that run alongside the lateral ventricles, as we discuss next.

LIMBIC SYSTEM ABNORMALITIES   Because the hippocampus and amygdala help form some of the walls of the lateral ventricles, atrophy in these regions could cause the ventricular enlargement in patients with schizophrenia. Indeed, among twins who are discordant for schizophrenia, the hippocampus and the amygdala are smaller in the twin who is ill.

Postmortem studies of patients with schizophrenia reveal abnormalities in several parts of the limbic system, including the hippocampus, amygdala, and parahip-

Control

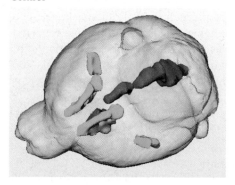

Mutant

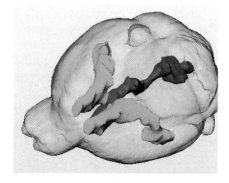

16.7 ENLARGED VENTRICLES IN A MOUSE MODEL   Transgenic mice that express the mutant version of *DISC1*, the gene associated with schizophrenia in humans, develop enlarged lateral ventricles (green region in these reconstructions) reminiscent of enlarged lateral ventricles in people with schizophrenia. (From Pletnikov et al., 2008.)

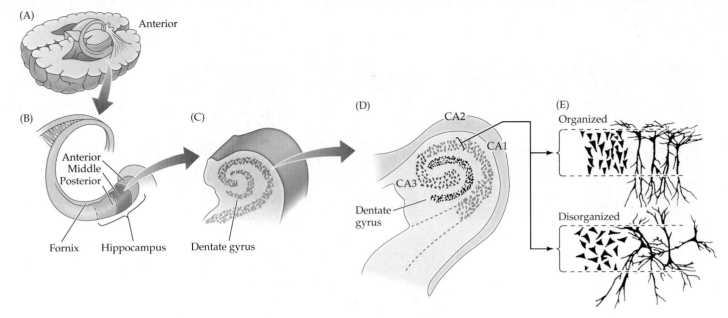

16.8 CELLULAR DISARRAY OF THE HIPPOCAMPUS IN CHRONIC SCHIZOPHRENIA
(A) This horizontal section of the cerebral hemispheres shows the location of the hippocampus (green). (B) Enlargements of the hippocampus and fornix show the location of anterior, middle, and posterior hippocampal segments. (C) The hippocampus and dentate gyrus are enlarged in this cross section. (D) The hippocampus is subdivided into three regions: CA1, CA2, and CA3 ("CA" stands for *cornu ammonis*, or "Ammon's horn," another name for the hippocampus). (E) Orientations of the pyramidal cells of a control (top) and a patient with schizophrenia (bottom) are compared in these hippocampal cross sections. (After Kovelman and Scheibel, 1984.)

pocampal regions. The hippocampal pyramidal cells of people with schizophrenia appear disorganized (**FIGURE 16.8**), possibly resulting from abnormal synaptic arrangements of both the inputs and outputs of these cells (A. J. Conrad et al., 1991; Kovelman and Scheibel, 1984). Abnormalities are also evident in other limbic system structures, including the entorhinal cortex, parahippocampal cortex, and cingulate cortex (R. M. Shapiro, 1993).

The cellular disorganization of schizophrenia probably arises during early cell development (Mednick et al., 1994). But because we now know that humans make new neurons throughout life, especially in the hippocampus (see Chapter 7), abnormal neurogenesis or disordered integration of newly born cells could contribute to the development of schizophrenia.

CORTICAL ABNORMALITIES   People with schizophrenia differ from controls in the structure and functional activity of the corpus callosum (Rotarska-Jagiela et al., 2008) that connects the two cortical hemispheres. Several studies have reported a more accelerated loss of gray matter at adolescence in schizophrenia patients than in controls (Chung et al., 2015; Karlsgodt et al., 2010; P. M. Thompson et al., 2001) (**FIGURE 16.9**). This thinning of gray matter is thought to reflect the net loss of synapses during development (see Figures 7.14 and 7.15), which is intriguing when you recall that several genes associated with schizophrenia are known to be involved in synapse rearrangement. In addition to structural changes in the cortex, what about the *activity* of cortex in schizophrenia?

DIFFERENCES IN BRAIN ACTIVATION   People with schizophrenia tend to be impaired on neuropsychological tests that are sensitive to frontal cortical lesions. These findings raised the possibility that frontal cortex was impaired in schizophrenia. Early observations using PET indicated that patients with schizophrenia show relatively less metabolic activity in the frontal lobes (compared with their posterior lobes), while controls have more-equal activation of frontal and posterior cortex (M. S. Buchsbaum

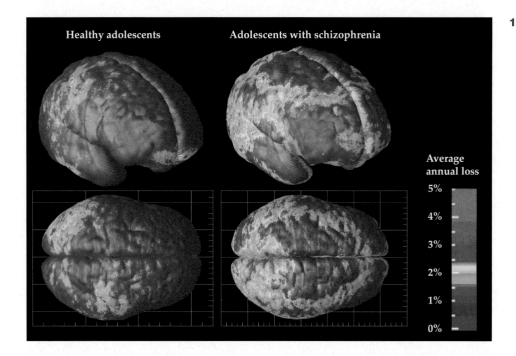

16.9 ACCELERATED LOSS OF GRAY MATTER IN ADOLESCENTS WITH SCHIZOPHRENIA Although neuron loss is a normal part of development, adolescents with schizophrenia (right) lose gray matter over wide regions at a faster rate than do unaffected adolescents (left). (From P. M. Thompson et al., 2001, courtesy of Dr. Paul Thompson.)

et al., 1984). This observation, referred to as the **hypofrontality hypothesis**, fueled interest in the role of the frontal lobes in schizophrenia (Minzenberg et al., 2009; D. R. Weinberger et al., 1994). In discordant identical twins, frontal blood flow is reduced only in the twin who suffers from schizophrenia (Andreasen et al., 1986; Morihisa and McAnulty, 1985).

Some experiments show the hypofrontality effect only during difficult cognitive tasks that particularly depend on the frontal lobes for accurate performance, such as the Wisconsin Card Sorting Task (**FIGURE 16.10**). Unlike controls, people with schizophrenia show no increase in their prefrontal activation above resting levels during the task (D. R. Weinberger et al., 1994). Treatment with drugs that alleviate symptoms of schizophrenia, discussed in the next section, is associated with increased activation of frontal cortex (Honey et al., 1999). Neurons in the frontal cortex of patients with schizophrenia have dendrites with a reduced density of synaptic

hypofrontality hypothesis
The hypothesis that schizophrenia may result from underactivation of the frontal lobes.

(A) At rest

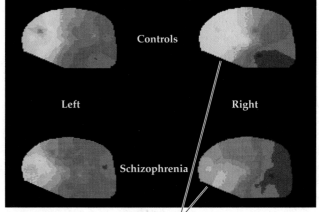

In these PET scans, cooler (blue-green) colors reflect less activation. In the twins with schizophrenia, the frontal cortex (left side of each brain profile) is less activated than in their unafffected twins, both at rest…

(B) During card-sorting task

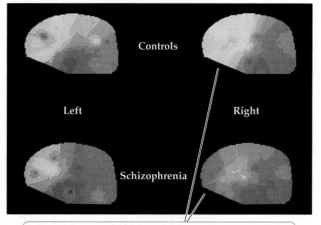

…and during the Wisconsin Card Sorting Task, which is very difficult for people with damage to the frontal lobes.

16.10 HYPOFRONTALITY IN SCHIZOPHRENIA (Courtesy of Dr. Karen Berman.)

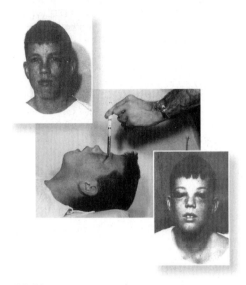

16.11 THE TEENAGED HOWARD DULLY BEFORE, DURING, AND AFTER HIS LOBOTOMY These photographs appear in Mr. Dully's memoir, *My Lobotomy*.

lobotomy The surgical detachment of a portion of the frontal lobe from the rest of the brain, once used as a treatment for schizophrenia and many other ailments.

psychosurgery Surgery in which brain lesions are produced to alleviate severe psychiatric disorders.

chlorpromazine An antipsychotic drug, one of the class of phenothiazines.

antipsychotics Also called *neuroleptics*. A class of drugs that alleviate symptoms of schizophrenia, typically by blocking dopamine receptors.

dopamine hypothesis The hypothesis that schizophrenia results from either excessive levels of synaptic dopamine or excessive postsynaptic sensitivity to dopamine.

spines compared with controls (L. A. Glantz and Lewis, 2000), which may contribute to a less active frontal cortex.

Perhaps the most revolutionary insights into schizophrenia came not from studies of structural or functional differences, but from the discovery of antipsychotic drugs, as we discuss next.

Antipsychotic medications revolutionized the treatment of schizophrenia

In the 1930s, there were no effective treatments for schizophrenia. Because patients were often unable to take care of themselves, they were placed in caregiving institutions. In many cases, the health and welfare of patients in these (poorly funded) institutions were badly neglected, leading to recurrent scandals. So perhaps it was in desperation that psychiatrists turned to **lobotomy**, the surgical separation of a portion of the frontal lobes from the rest of the brain, as a treatment for schizophrenia. Certainly there was little scientific evidence to think the surgery would be effective. But early practitioners reported nearly miraculous recoveries that, in retrospect, must be regarded as wishful thinking on the part of the physicians. The surgery may well have made the patients easier to handle, but they were rarely able to leave the mental institution. Used for almost any mental disorder, not just schizophrenia, lobotomies were performed on some 40,000 people in the United States alone (Kopell et al., 2005). One of the last people to be given a lobotomy was Howard Dully, whose stepmother took the rebellious 12-year-old boy to several psychiatrists until finding one who was willing to say he had schizophrenia. That was used to justify giving the boy a lobotomy in 1960 (**FIGURE 16.11**). Not until he was 50 was Howard able to find out what had happened to him as a child, a journey he recounts movingly in his memoir, *My Lobotomy* (Dully and Fleming, 2007).

Today **psychosurgery**, surgical modification of the brain to treat psychiatric disorders, involves much smaller lesions and is rarely performed, and then only as a last resort. For example, for some people with severe epilepsy, surgical removal of the damaged brain tissue can help, as we discussed in Chapter 3. Psychosurgery is also being explored for other disorders, as we'll note later in this chapter.

By the 1950s, more and more physicians were skeptical that lobotomy was effective for any disorder, and a drug discovered in 1954—**chlorpromazine** (trade name Thorazine)—quickly replaced lobotomy as a treatment for schizophrenia. Although chlorpromazine was originally developed as an anesthetic, a lucky observation revealed that it could powerfully reduce the "positive" symptoms of schizophrenia, including auditory hallucinations, delusions, and disordered thinking. Ironically, the drug was first promoted as "a lobotomy in a bottle" because at the time, that was viewed as a good thing! But chlorpromazine was much better than a lobotomy, not only because drug treatment is reversible while lobotomy is not, but because the drug actually worked. In fact, the symptoms of schizophrenia that responded to chlorpromazine were exactly those that kept people in mental institutions. The introduction of chlorpromazine truly revolutionized psychiatry, relieving symptoms for millions of sufferers and freeing them from a lifetime in psychiatric hospitals.

THE DOPAMINE HYPOTHESIS Chlorpromazine and other antipsychotic drugs, known as **antipsychotics**, that came along a little later were eventually found to share a specific action: they block postsynaptic dopamine receptors, particularly dopamine D_2 receptors. Because all of the earliest antipsychotic drugs blocked dopamine D_2 receptors, researchers proposed the **dopamine hypothesis**: that people with schizophrenia suffer from an excess of either dopamine release or dopamine receptors.

At about the same time, support for the dopamine hypothesis came from another source: people who were abusing drugs. As a consequence of drug tolerance (see Chapter 4), some daily users of amphetamine reach the point of taking astonishingly high doses—as much as 3000 milligrams (mg) per day—in order to experience the drug's "high." (Compare this with the normal 5-mg dose used to combat sleepiness.) Many individuals taking these large doses of amphetamine develop symptoms of paranoia, often involving delusions of persecution with auditory hallucinations, and

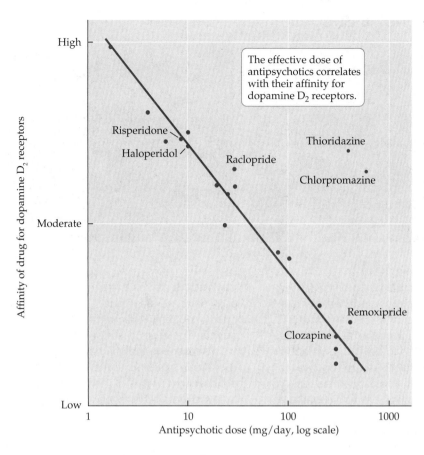

The effective dose of antipsychotics correlates with their affinity for dopamine D$_2$ receptors.

(Graph, vertical axis: Affinity of drug for dopamine D$_2$ receptors; labels High, Moderate, Low. Horizontal axis: Antipsychotic dose (mg/day, log scale); values 1, 10, 100, 1000. Data points labeled: Risperidone, Haloperidol, Raclopride, Thioridazine, Chlorpromazine, Remoxipride, Clozapine.)

they exhibit suspiciousness and bizarre motor behavior. These symptoms strikingly resemble those of schizophrenia and are referred to as **amphetamine psychosis**. What's more, amphetamine exacerbates the symptoms of schizophrenia. It turns out that amphetamine promotes the release of dopamine and prolongs the action of the released transmitter by blocking reuptake (see Chapter 4). Chlorpromazine treatment rapidly reverses amphetamine psychosis.

In contrast, while drugs such as LSD and mescaline produce some perceptual, cognitive, and emotional changes that resemble psychosis in some ways, the resemblance is superficial at best. For instance, the hallucinations produced by these drugs are usually visual, in contrast to the predominantly auditory hallucinations of schizophrenia. Patients with schizophrenia who are given LSD report that the experience produced by the drug is very different from their experiences of the disorder.

All of the various antipsychotic drugs that are now classified as **typical antipsychotics** are D$_2$ receptor antagonists. In fact, the clinically effective dose of the typical neuroleptic can be predicted from its affinity for D$_2$ receptors (**FIGURE 16.12**), as the dopamine hypothesis would predict. For example, haloperidol, discovered a few years after chlorpromazine, has a greater affinity for D$_2$ receptors and quickly became the more widely used drug. Other clinical findings bolster the dopamine hypothesis; for example, treating patients who suffer from Parkinson's disease with L-dopa (the metabolic precursor of dopamine) may induce schizophrenia-like symptoms, presumably by boosting the synaptic availability of dopamine.

Although some evidence supports the dopamine hypothesis of schizophrenia, there are also several problems with the hypothesis. For example, there is no correspondence between the speed with which drugs block dopamine receptors (quite rapidly—within hours) and how long it takes for the symptoms to diminish (usually on the order of weeks). Thus, the relation of dopamine to schizophrenia is more complex than just hyperactive dopamine synapses. Another weakness of the dopamine model of schizophrenia is that some people with schizophrenia don't respond to dopamine antagonists at all (Alpert and Friedhoff, 1980).

amphetamine psychosis
A delusional and psychotic state, closely resembling acute schizophrenia, that is brought on by repeated use of high doses of amphetamine.

typical antipsychotics   A major class of antischizophrenic drugs that share an antagonist activity at dopamine D$_2$ receptors.

BOX
16.1

Long-Term Effects of Antipsychotic Drugs

Clearly, antipsychotic drugs have revolutionized the treatment of schizophrenia. With these drugs, many people who might otherwise have been in mental hospitals their whole lives can take care of themselves in nonhospital settings. The drugs can justly be regarded as "miracle drugs."

Unfortunately, traditional antipsychotic drugs can have other, undesirable effects. Soon after beginning to take these drugs, some people develop maladaptive motor symptoms (**dyskinesia**, from the Greek *dys*, "bad," and *kinesis*, "motion"). Although many of these symptoms are transient and disappear when the dosage of drug is reduced, some drug-induced motor changes emerge only after prolonged drug treatment—after months, sometimes years—and are effectively permanent. The condition, called **tardive dyskinesia** (the Latin *tardus* means "slow"), is characterized by repetitive, involuntary movements, especially involving the face, mouth, lips, and tongue. Elaborate, uncontrollable movements of the tongue are particularly prominent (see figure), including incessant rolling movements and sucking or smacking of the lips. Some patients show twisting and sudden jerking movements of the arms or legs.

The underlying mechanism for tardive dyskinesia continues to be a puzzle. Some researchers claim that

it arises from the chronic blocking of dopamine receptors, which results in receptor site supersensitivity. But tardive dyskinesia frequently takes a long time to develop and tends to be irreversible—a time course that is different from dopamine receptor supersensitivity. In addition, there is no difference in D_1 or D_2 receptor binding between patients with tardive dyskinesia and those without these symptoms.

Long-term treatment with traditional antipsychotic drugs has another unusual effect: Prolonged blockage of dopamine receptors seems to increase the number of dopamine receptors and lead to receptor supersensitivity. In some patients, discontinuation of the drugs or a lowering of dosage results in a sudden, marked increase in positive symptoms of schizophrenia, such as delusions or hallucinations. This **supersensitivity**

psychosis can often be reversed by administration of increased dosages of dopamine receptor–blocking agents. The atypical antipsychotics discussed in the text have fewer dyskinesia side effects than traditional antipsychotics have, but unfortunately they are more likely to lead to weight gain. (Photographs courtesy of Steven J. Frucht.)

dyskinesia   Difficulty or distortion in voluntary movement.

tardive dyskinesia   A disorder characterized by involuntary movements, especially involving the face, mouth, lips, and tongue. It can be caused by prolonged use of antipsychotic drugs, such as chlorpromazine.

supersensitivity psychosis   An exaggerated psychosis that may emerge when doses of antipsychotic medication are reduced, probably as a consequence of the up-regulation of receptors that occurred during drug treatment.

---

atypical antipsychotics   A class of antischizophrenic drugs that have actions other than the dopamine D_2 receptor antagonism that characterizes the typical antipsychotics.

clozapine   An atypical antipsychotic.

The search for new antipsychotics to avoid motor side effects, which are debilitating in some patients (**BOX 16.1**), led to the development of drugs called **atypical antipsychotics**. These drugs generally don't have the selective high affinity for dopamine receptors that is the hallmark of the typical antipsychotics, and they feature high affinity for other types of receptors. For example, the atypical antipsychotic **clozapine** selectively blocks serotonin receptors (especially 5-HT_{2A} receptors), as well as other receptor types (**FIGURE 16.13**).

Atypical antipsychotics are just as effective as the older generation of drugs for relieving the symptoms of schizophrenia. So, if the problem is as simple as an overstimulation of dopamine receptors, why are the atypical antipsychotics effective? For example, clozapine can *increase* dopamine release in frontal cortex (Hertel et al., 1999)—hardly what we would expect if excess dopaminergic activity lies at the root of schizophrenia. In fact, it seems that supplementing antipsychotic treatments with L-dopa (thereby increasing dopaminergic activity) actually helps reduce symptoms of schizophrenia (Jaskiw and Popli, 2004).

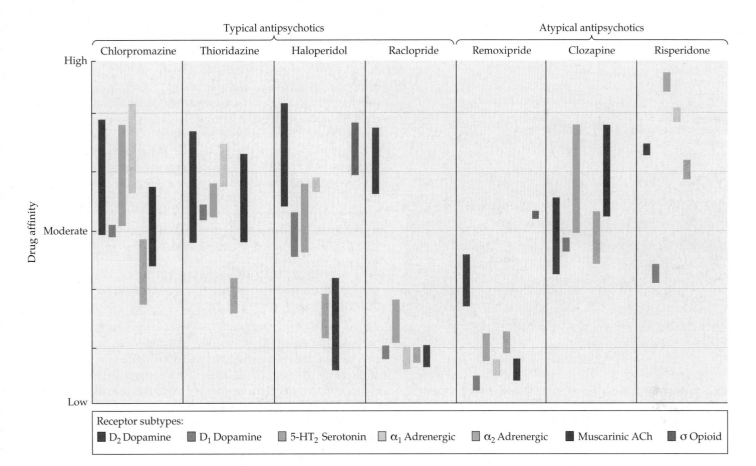

Typical antipsychotics   Atypical antipsychotics

16.13 ANTIPSYCHOTIC DRUGS THAT AFFECT DOPAMINE RECEPTORS Drugs vary widely in the affinity with which they bind to various neurotransmitter receptors. Drugs that block dopamine receptors, specifically the D_2 variety (purple), are more effective at combating symptoms of schizophrenia. Atypical antipsychotics such as clozapine tend to block $5\text{-}HT_2$ receptors (green) more effectively than they block D_2 receptors. (After Seeman, 1990.)

Until recently, almost all clinicians believed that atypical antipsychotics were more effective than typical antipsychotics for treating schizophrenia, especially for relieving negative symptoms. But a large British study comparing the outcome for patients who had been given the two types of drugs found no difference (P. B. Jones et al., 2006). Although the atypical antipsychotics are less likely than typical antipsychotics to cause side effects in motor function (see Box 16.1), they are more likely to cause weight gain (Sikich et al., 2008), which causes other health problems.

THE GLUTAMATE HYPOTHESIS Another drug that, like chlorpromazine, was initially developed as an anesthetic has a much different relationship to schizophrenia. **Phencyclidine (PCP)** was soon found to be a potent **psychotomimetic**; that is, PCP produces phenomena strongly resembling both the positive and negative symptoms of schizophrenia. Users of PCP ("angel dust") often experience auditory hallucinations, strange depersonalization, and disorientation; and they may become violent as a consequence of their drug-induced delusions. Prolonged psychotic states can develop with chronic use of PCP.

PCP acts as an NMDA receptor antagonist, blocking the NMDA receptor's central calcium channel, thereby preventing the endogenous ligand—glutamate—from having its usual effects (**FIGURE 16.14**). Treating monkeys with PCP for 2 weeks produces a schizophrenia-like syndrome, including poor performance on a test that is sensitive to prefrontal damage (J. D. Jentsch et al., 1997). Other antagonists of NMDA receptors, such as **ketamine**, have similar effects. These and other observations prompted researchers to propose a **glutamate hypothesis** of schizophrenia

phencyclidine (PCP) Also called *angel dust*. An anesthetic agent that is also a psychedelic drug. PCP makes many people feel dissociated from themselves and their environment.

psychotomimetic A drug that induces a state resembling schizophrenia.

ketamine A dissociative anesthetic drug, similar to PCP, that acts as an NMDA receptor antagonist.

glutamate hypothesis The hypothesis that schizophrenia may be caused, in part, by understimulation of glutamate receptors.

A model of PCP action on the NMDA receptor

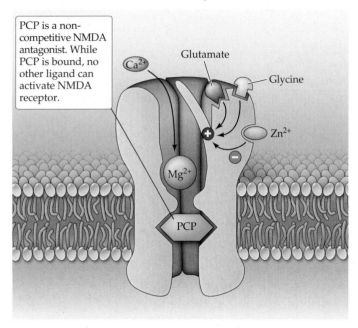

PCP is a non-competitive NMDA antagonist. While PCP is bound, no other ligand can activate NMDA receptor.

16.14 THE EFFECTS OF PCP ON THE NMDA RECEPTOR The resemblance of PCP-induced psychosis to schizophrenia prompted the development of a glutamate hypothesis of schizophrenia.

(Moghaddam and Adams, 1998), that schizophrenia results from an underactivation of glutamate receptors (Hardingham and Do, 2016). If this hypothesis is true, you might ask whether compounds that increase glutamatergic activity would be effective antischizophrenic drugs. Unfortunately, selective NMDA receptor agonists tend to produce seizures, so glutamatergic-boosting compounds are not an option.

The glutamate hypothesis has been expanded to suggest that underactivation of *all* glutamate receptors, not just the NMDA subtype, contributes to schizophrenia (González-Maeso et al., 2008). There are at least eight different subtypes of metabotropic glutamate receptors (mGluR's) (see Chapter 4), so direct stimulation of the proper class of mGluR's might someday provide a third generation of antipsychotics.

An integrative psychobiological model of schizophrenia emphasizes the interaction of multiple factors

We've established that there is genetic influence on schizophrenia, but also that genes alone cannot account for the disorder. What environmental factors contribute to the probability of developing schizophrenia? Research suggests that a variety of stressful events significantly increase the risk. For example, schizophrenia usually appears during a time in life that many people find stressful—the transition from childhood to adulthood, when people deal with physical, emotional, and lifestyle changes (e.g., going away to college).

Prenatal stress—for example, if the mother has an infection while carrying the child—is also a risk factor. The baby of a pregnant woman who contracts influenza in the first trimester of pregnancy is 7 times more likely to develop schizophrenia (P. H. Patterson, 2007). Several other maternal infections also increase chances that the fetus will develop schizophrenia one day (A. S. Brown, 2011). This correlation may be why people born in late winter and early spring are more likely to develop schizophrenia (Messias et al., 2004) (**FIGURE 16.15**): their mothers may be more likely to have gotten sick during the winter before, perhaps at some fetal stage that is particularly vulnerable. Likewise, if the mother and baby have incompatible blood types, or if the mother develops diabetes during pregnancy, or if for some other reason there is a low birth weight, the baby is more likely to develop schizophrenia (King et al.,

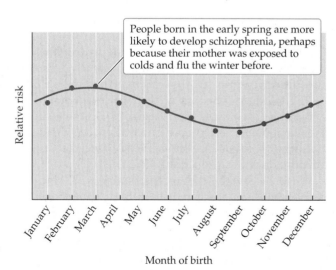

People born in the early spring are more likely to develop schizophrenia, perhaps because their mother was exposed to colds and flu the winter before.

16.15 SEASONAL BIRTH EFFECT ON SCHIZOPHRENIA (After Mortensen et al., 1999.)

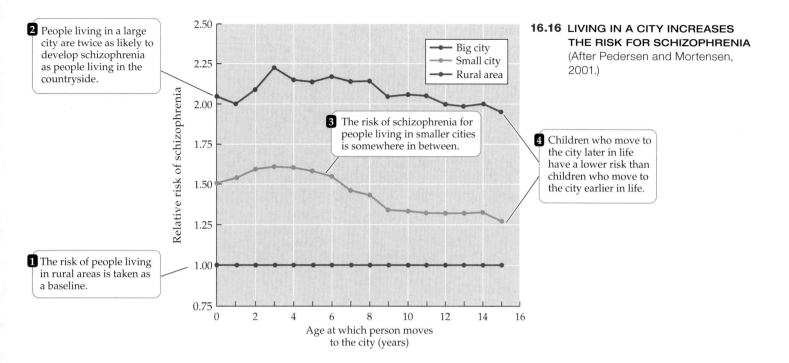

16.16 LIVING IN A CITY INCREASES THE RISK FOR SCHIZOPHRENIA (After Pedersen and Mortensen, 2001.)

2 People living in a large city are twice as likely to develop schizophrenia as people living in the countryside.

3 The risk of schizophrenia for people living in smaller cities is somewhere in between.

4 Children who move to the city later in life have a lower risk than children who move to the city earlier in life.

1 The risk of people living in rural areas is taken as a baseline.

2010). Birth complications that deprive the baby of oxygen also increase the probability of schizophrenia (Clarke et al., 2011).

Because we know that some people are genetically more susceptible to schizophrenia than others, these findings suggest that relatively minor stress during development can make the difference in whether schizophrenia emerges. It is fascinating, and frightening, to think that events in the womb can affect the outcome 16 or 20 years later, when the schizophrenia appears.

Another risk factor seen in multiple studies is the stress of city living. As **FIGURE 16.16** shows, people born and raised in a medium-size city are about 1½ times more likely to develop schizophrenia than people living in the country. What's more, the earlier in life a person begins living in the city, the greater the risk. People moving into a big city are even more likely to develop the disorder (Pedersen and Mortensen, 2001). Conversely, children who move from the city to the country have a *reduced* risk of developing schizophrenia (van Os et al., 2010). We don't know what it is about living in a city that makes schizophrenia more likely. Pollutants, greater exposure to minor diseases, crowded conditions, tense social interactions—all of these could be considered stressful. That may be why people who live in cities show increased activity of the amygdala compared with people living in rural areas, and why adults who grew up in cities show greater activity in the anterior cingulate (Lederbogen et al., 2011), which communicates extensively with the amygdala.

Thus, the modern view is that schizophrenia is caused by the interaction of genetic factors and stress. Each life stage has its own specific features that increase vulnerability to schizophrenia: infections before birth, complications at delivery, urban living in childhood, social stress in adolescence and adulthood (Powell, 2010). From this perspective, the emergence of schizophrenia and related disorders depends on whether a person who is genetically susceptible to schizophrenia is subjected to environmental stressors (**FIGURE 16.17**). The models of genes interacting with environmental stressors also suggest that we may someday be able to reduce the likelihood that a child at risk will develop schizophre-

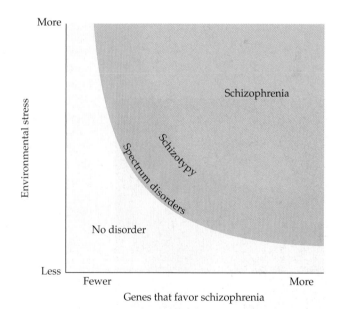

16.17 A MODEL OF THE INTERACTION BETWEEN STRESS AND GENETIC INFLUENCES IN SCHIZOPHRENIA Environmental stress and genetic susceptibility may combine to produce a schizophrenic disorder. Disorders ranging from more mild to more severe are called, respectively, *spectrum disorders*, *schizotypy*, and *schizophrenia*. (After Mirsky and Duncan, 1986.)

16.18 LONG-TERM RELAPSE RATES WITH AND WITHOUT ANTIPSYCHOTICS (After Wunderink et al., 2013.)

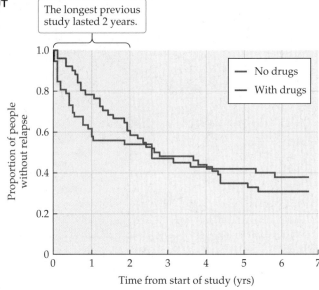

The longest previous study lasted 2 years.

nia. New biological aids, such as functional brain imaging and genetic tools, might help us identify and understand the at-risk child early in life, when interventions to reduce stress might prevent schizophrenia later in life.

There is a controversial question of whether continued use of antipsychotics is the best pathway to recover from schizophrenia. For one thing, people who develop schizophrenia in developing countries are twice as likely to recover as people in industrialized nations like the United States (Hopper and Wanderling, 2000; Jablensky et al., 1992; Myers, 2010; Sartorius et al., 1972), even though the latter are more likely to receive medication. Plus programs that only provide medication are less successful than those that wean people with schizophrenia from medication and help them become reintegrated in society (DeSisto et al., 1995). Long-term studies indicate that, no matter how useful antipsychotics are for controlling symptoms at the onset of schizophrenia, relapses are less common in people who have weaned themselves from the drugs (Wunderink et al., 2013 (**FIGURE 16.18**). There is also growing support for cognitive behavioral therapy to help people with schizophrenia reduce stress (and therefore reduce outbreaks of symptoms), and to help them feel less disturbed by the voices they hear (Morrison et al., 2014). This allows them to disengage from the voices and realize the voices have no power over them.

That was the approach that worked for Eleanor, whom we met at the start of the chapter. She eventually decided that the voices were a result of childhood traumas she had experienced. She began to regard the voices as ways to understand what had happened and how she could cope with the consequences. Eleanor weaned herself from medication and returned to school, finishing her bachelor's degree. As she began regarding the voices more positively, they became less hostile, even helpful (Longden, 2013). During one of her exams, a voice dictated the answers to Eleanor, prompting her to wonder if that was cheating! She went on to earn a master's degree and doctorate in psychology and has published a dozen scientific articles already in her young career. As you may have guessed, the main topic of Eleanor's research is the role of early life adversity in schizophrenia (Longden and Read, 2016a) and the incidence of adverse reactions to antipsychotics (Longden and Read, 2016b). She also serves on the board of the international Hearing Voices Movement (intervoiceonline. org), working to generate acceptance and understanding of people like herself, who hear voices.

bipolar disorder Formerly called *manic-depressive illness*. A psychiatric disorder characterized by periods of depression that alternate with excessive, expansive moods.

HEARING VOICES? Once Eleanor learned the voices she heard had no control over her life, she no longer feared them.

Bipolar disorder has a lot in common with schizophrenia

Bipolar disorder is characterized by periods of depression alternating with periods of excessively expansive mood (or *mania*) that includes sustained overactivity, talkativeness, strange grandiosity, and increased energy. Imaging confirms that the brain is more active during these bouts, too (**FIGURE 16.19**). The rate at which the alternation occurs varies between individuals: Some patients exhibit *rapid-cycling* bipolar disorder, defined as consisting of four or more distinct cycles in one year (and some individuals have many more cycles than that; some may even show several cycles per *day*). Other people experience a milder, subclinical, related state called *cyclothymia*, in which the patient experiences less-extreme moods, cycling between *dysthymia* (poor mood or mild depression) and *hypomania* (a state of increased energy and positive mood that lacks some of the bizarre aspects of frank mania).

Many researchers believe that bipolar disorder has more in common with schizophrenia than with "ordinary" depression (which we'll take up shortly). This is one reason why old terms for bipolar disorder—*bipolar depression* and *manic depression*—have fallen out of favor. For example, the self-aggrandizing ideas and extreme talkativeness of people in the manic phase of bipolar disorder (e.g., "The president called me this morning to thank me for my efforts") resemble the delusions of those in schizophrenia. In addition, families in which some individuals have been diagnosed with bipolar disorder are more likely than other families to have individuals with a diagnosis of schizophrenia (Lichtenstein et al., 2009; van Os and Kapur, 2009).

The neural basis of bipolar disorder is not fully understood, but patients with bipolar disorder exhibit enlarged ventricles (Arnone et al., 2009), which is also reminiscent of changes seen in schizophrenia (see Figures 16.5 and 16.6). The more manic episodes the person has experienced, the greater the ventricular enlargement, suggesting a worsening of brain loss over time. The changes probably include subcortical limbic structures, such as the amygdala (DelBello et al., 2004) and hippocampus (Moorhead et al., 2007). Although typical antipsychotics do not seem to help people with bipolar disorder, the newer, atypical antipsychotics may dampen the manic phase.

However, most people suffering from bipolar disorder benefit from treatment with the element **lithium** (Kingsbury and Garver, 1998). The benefits of lithium for bipolar disorder were discovered by accident when it was intended as an inert control for another drug, and the mechanism of action remains mysterious. Lithium has wide-ranging effects on the brain, including interacting with a protein that is part of the circadian molecular clock (L. Yin et al., 2006) (see Chapter 14), boosting activity of BDNF (brain-derived neurotrophic factor) (Rowe and Chuang, 2004), and reducing neuronal activity (Mertens et al., 2015). Lithium occurs naturally in low levels in drinking water, and there's evidence that communities with more lithium in their water have a lower incidence of depression and suicide (Sugawara et al., 2013; Vita et al., 2015). For people taking lithium medications, care must be taken to avoid overdose, because it has a narrow therapeutic index (the range of safe doses; see Figure 4.9E). Nevertheless, well-managed lithium treatment produces marked relief for many patients and even has been reported to increase the volume of gray matter in the brain (G. J. Moore et al., 2000).

Perhaps the fact that the manic phases blocked by lithium are so exhilarating is the reason that some bipolar clients stop taking the medication. Unfortunately, doing so means that the depressive episodes return as well. But other drug treatments are available, and transcranial magnetic stimulation may provide a nonpharmacological treatment alternative in difficult cases of bipolar disorder (Michael and Erfurth, 2004). Furthermore, evidence suggests that cognitive behavioral therapy can be as effective as drug treatments (Hollon et al., 2002) and perhaps can be beneficially combined with other forms of treatment.

Men and women are equally affected by bipolar disorder, and the age of onset is usually much earlier than that of unipolar depression. Bipolar disorder has a complex heritability: many different genes affect the probability of the disorder (Faraone et al., 2004; Smoller and Finn, 2003). One specific gene implicated in bipolar disorder is the gene that encodes BDNF (E. Green and Craddock, 2003; Neves-Pereira et al., 2002), which we discussed in Chapter 7. Many of the genes that increase the risk of bipolar disorder also increase the risk of schizophrenia, another indication that the

(A) Manic

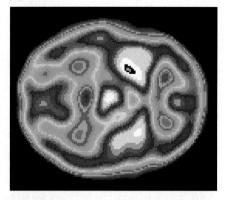

(B) Depressive

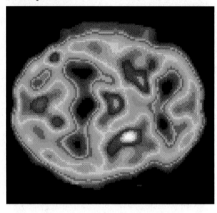

16.19 FUNCTIONAL IMAGES OF BIPOLAR DISORDER Dramatic differences in brain activity are evident between the manic (A) and depressive (B) phases of this patient's bipolar illness. (Courtesy of Dr. Robert G. Kohn, Brain SPECT.)

lithium An element that, when administered as a drug, often relieves the symptoms of bipolar disorder.

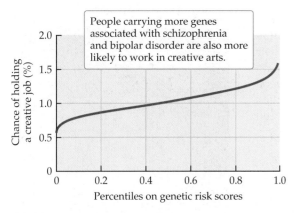

16.20 A CONNECTION BETWEEN SCHIZO-PHRENIA/BIPOLAR DISORDER AND CREATIVITY? (After Keller and Visscher, 2015.)

depression A psychiatric condition characterized by such symptoms as an unhappy mood; loss of interests, energy, and appetite; and difficulty concentrating.

disorders may be related. Finally, it seems that people who are susceptible to schizophrenia and bipolar disorder are more likely to be creative, artistic types. Based on two mega-analyses of genes associated with increased risk for schizophrenia and bipolar disorder, researchers assigned risk scores to 100,000 people in Iceland and Sweden (who were not part of the previous analyses). Then they ascertained which of those people held creative positions, based on whether they were members of societies of actors, dancers, musicians, writers, or visual artists. In this population, the more genes associated with schizophrenia or bipolar disorder people carried, the more likely they were to be associated with one of those creative enterprises (**FIGURE 16.20**). There was no such relationship to creative occupations when the population was ranked for genetic risk for 20 other (nonpsychiatric) disorders (Power et al., 2015).

Mood Disorders Are a Major Psychiatric Category

Disturbances of mood are a fact of life for humans; most of us experience periods of unhappiness that we commonly describe as depression. But for some people, an unhappy mood state is more than a passing malaise. This condition is most common in people over 40 years of age, especially women, but it can affect people of any age, race, or ethnicity (CDC, 2010).

Depression is the most prevalent mood disorder

Clinically, **depression** is characterized by an unhappy mood; loss of interests, energy, and appetite; difficulty in concentration; and restless agitation. Pessimism seems to seep into every act (Solomon, 2001). Periods of such *unipolar depression* (i.e., depression that alternates with normal emotional states) can occur with no readily apparent stress. Without treatment, the depression often lasts several months. Depressive illnesses of this sort are estimated to afflict 13–20% of the population at any one time (Cassens et al., 1990).

Depression can be lethal, as it may lead to suicide. About 80% of all suicide victims are profoundly depressed. Whether or not the person is depressed, many suicides appear to be impulsive acts. For example, one classic study found that of the more than 500 people who were prevented from jumping off the Golden Gate Bridge in San Francisco, only 6% later went on to commit suicide (Seiden, 1978). Similarly, suicide rates went down by a third in Britain when the switch was made in the 1960s and 70s from coal gas, which contains lots of deadly carbon monoxide, to natural gas for heating and cooking. The suicide rate has remained at that reduced level since. Apparently those thousands of Britons who would have found it easy to follow a suicidal impulse by turning on the kitchen oven did not kill themselves when more planning was required. Thus, it is important for society to erect barriers, either literally (e.g., on bridges) or metaphorically, to make it difficult for people suffering from depression to kill themselves. If suicide is averted the first time it is seriously attempted, the person is very unlikely to ever try it again.

Inheritance is an important determinant of depression

Genetic studies of depressive disorders reveal strong hereditary contributions. The concordance rate for monozygotic twins (about 60%) is substantially higher than the concordance rate for dizygotic twins (about 20%) (Kendler et al., 1999). The concordance rates for monozygotic twins are similar whether the twins are reared apart or together. Adoption studies show higher rates of depression in the *biological* parents of a depressed patient than in the foster parents. Although several early studies implicated specific chromosomes, subsequent linkage studies have failed to identify any particular gene (Risch et al., 2009). As is the case for schizophrenia, there probably is no single gene for depression. Rather, *many* genes contribute to making a person more or less susceptible, and environmental factors determine whether depression results (Gotlib et al., 2014).

The brain changes with depression

Most reports of differences in the brains of depressed people focus on functional changes. PET scans of depressed patients show increases in blood flow, suggesting greater activity, in the prefrontal cortex and the amygdala compared with controls (**FIGURE 16.21**) (Drevets, 1998). In addition to increasing in the prefrontal cortex, blood flow decreases in the parietal and posterior temporal cortex and in the anterior cingulate, systems that have been implicated in attention (see Chapter 18). The increase in blood flow in the amygdala—a structure involved in mediating fear (see Chapter 15)—persists even after the alleviation of depression over time.

Descendants of people with severe depression also have a thinner cortex across large swaths of the right hemisphere than do controls (B. S. Peterson et al., 2009), which might make them vulnerable to depression. Many studies report hippocampal volume is reduced in people with depression (Sexton et al., 2013), and there is reduced activation of the hippocampal region in depressed people during memory tasks (K. D. Young et al., 2011). But whether these changes in the hippocampus are present before the depression, and therefore may be a contributing cause of the disorder, or are a result of the depression remains unknown. In any case, there are effective treatments for depression, as we discuss next.

A wide variety of treatments are available for depression

Electroconvulsive therapy (**ECT**)—the intentional induction of a large-scale seizure (Weiner, 1994)—was originally deployed during the 1930s in a desperate and unsuccessful attempt to relieve the symptoms of schizophrenia. Despite ECT's failure at helping sufferers of schizophrenia, however, clinical observations soon revealed that it *could* rapidly reverse severe depression. Demonizing portrayals of ECT in popular entertainment, and the advent of antidepressant drugs, have made ECT less common, but it remains an important tool for treating severe, drug-resistant depression (M. Fink and Taylor, 2007). ECT may work by reducing functional connectivity between prefrontal cortex and other cortical regions (Perrin et al., 2012). A more modern technique for altering cortical electrical activity, *transcranial magnetic stimulation* (TMS; see Chapter 2), is also being explored as a treatment for depression (D. R. Kim et al., 2009), but it appears to be less effective than ECT (Health Quality Ontario, 2016). The milder treatment of direct current stimulation through the skull appears to be effective for relieving depression in some studies (Brunoni et al., 2016), but not in others (Murphy et al., 2009).

Today, the most common treatment for depression is the use of drugs that affect monoamine transmitters. The **monoamine hypothesis** (Schildkraut and Kety, 1967) was suggested by the first antidepressants, which were inhibitors of **monoamine oxidase** (**MAO**), the enzyme that normally inactivates the monoamines: norepinephrine, dopamine, and serotonin. The fact that MAO inhibitors raise the level of monoamines present in synapses suggests that depressed people do not get enough stimulation at those synapses. This would also explain why the drug **reserpine**, which reduces norepinephrine and serotonin release in the brain, can cause profound depression. Inducing the release of monoamines may be the way ECT helps depression. Second-generation antidepressants called **tricyclics** conform to the monoamine hypothesis because they inhibit the reuptake of monoamines, boosting their synaptic activity.

Among the monoamines, serotonin may play the most important role in depression. A major class of modern antidepressants is the **selective serotonin reuptake inhibitors** (**SSRIs**), such as Prozac (**TABLE 16.3**) (see Chapter 4). These drugs are more effective than MAO inhibitors and tricyclics and have fewer side effects. In rats and mice, SSRIs increase neurogenesis in the hippocampus (Sahay and Hen, 2007; Samuels et al., 2015), which may mediate some of the mood effects of the drugs. SSRI treatment also increases the production of brain steroids (L. D. Griffin and Mellon, 1999), such as allopregnanolone, which may contribute to the effectiveness of SSRIs by stimulating GABA receptors and reducing anxiety.

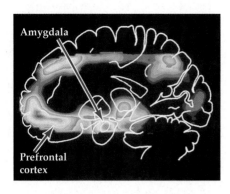

16.21 BRAIN ACTIVITY PATTERNS IN DEPRESSION This PET scan reveals increased activity in the prefrontal cortex and the amygdala of depressed patients. This combined image is the result of the subtraction of brain scans of controls from those of depressed individuals. Areas of highest activation are shown in red and orange. (Courtesy of Dr. Wayne C. Drevets.)

electroconvulsive therapy (ECT) Also called *shock therapy*. A last-resort treatment for intractable depression, in which a strong electrical current is passed through the brain, causing a seizure.

monoamine hypothesis The hypothesis that depression is caused by reduced activity of one or more monoamine transmitters, such as serotonin.

monoamine oxidase (MAO) An enzyme that breaks down and thereby inactivates monoamine transmitters.

reserpine A drug that causes the depletion of monoamines and can lead to depression.

tricyclics A class of drugs that act by increasing the synaptic accumulation of serotonin and norepinephrine.

selective serotonin reuptake inhibitors (SSRIs) A class of drugs that block the reuptake of transmitter at serotonergic synapses; commonly used to treat depression.

TABLE 16.3 Drugs Used to Treat Depression

DRUG CLASS	MECHANISM OF ACTION	EXAMPLES[a]
Monoamine oxidase (MAO) inhibitors	Inhibit the enzyme mono-amine oxidase, which breaks down serotonin, norepinephrine, and dopamine	Marplan, Nardil, Parnate
Tricyclics and heterocyclics	Inhibit the reuptake of norepinephrine, serotonin, and/or dopamine	Elavil, Wellbutrin, Aventyl, Ludiomil, Norpramin
Selective serotonin reup-take inhibitors (SSRIs)	Block the reuptake of serotonin, having little ef-fect on norepinephrine or dopamine synapses	Prozac, Paxil, Zoloft

[a]The more commonly used trade names rather than chemical names are used.

However, there are problems with the theory that reduced serotonin stimulation causes depression. We know that SSRI drugs increase synaptic serotonin within hours of administration. Yet it typically takes several weeks of SSRI treatment before people feel better. This paradox suggests that it is the brain's *response* to increased synaptic serotonin that relieves the symptoms, and that this response takes time. One suggestion is that SSRIs may immediately improve a person's emotional outlook (Capitão et al., 2015) but that several weeks of experiencing this rosier outlook may be required to overturn the depression. Thus, even though boosting serotonin helps some people, their depression may originally have been caused by other factors in the brain.

While SSRIs help many people who are depressed, they do not help everyone. In placebo-controlled trials, although a slightly higher proportion of people taking the drug report relief than do not (Turner et al., 2008), about a third of the people taking the *placebo* also feel better. This result suggests that some people helped by SSRI treatment are actually benefiting from a placebo effect (Berton and Nestler, 2006). One review concluded that only a minority of depressed patients, the 13% constituting the most severe cases, responded significantly better to SSRIs than to placebos (Fournier et al., 2010) (**FIGURE 16.22**). Furthermore, only about half of the people getting the drug are completely "cured," and about 20% show no improvement at all. Finally, there is no evidence that SSRIs or any other antidepressant drugs do better than placebos

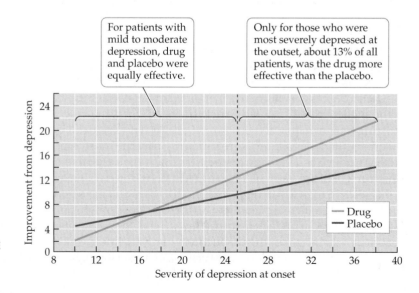

16.22 WHEN ARE ANTIDEPRESSANTS MORE EFFECTIVE THAN PLACEBO? (After Fournier et al., 2010.)

when given to children or teenagers (Bower, 2006), yet millions of American children have been given prescriptions for SSRIs. This is unfortunate, because SSRIs increase the risk of suicide in children and adolescents (Olfson et al., 2006), a finding that the drug companies tried to hide (Ramchandani, 2004). Another risk of SSRIs, for patients of all ages, is that a variety of over-the-counter drugs may synergize with the drugs to push synaptic serotonin levels too high, triggering **serotonin syndrome**, which includes confusion, muscle spasms, and fever. Thousands of cases are reported each year, causing over 100 deaths (Dvir and Smallwood, 2008).

Other drugs being studied as potential antidepressants are the glutamate receptor antagonist ketamine, which acts much like PCP (see Figure 16.14) and relieves depression almost instantly (N. Li et al., 2010; Shah et al., 2014). There are also reports that hallucinogens like psilocybin can rapidly relieve depression (Baumeister et al., 2014; Carhart-Harris et al., 2012).

An unusual treatment for depression is vagal nerve stimulation. In this treatment, electrodes are surgically wrapped around the vagus nerve (see Chapter 2) in the neck, and a pacemaker provides mild electrical stimulation at intervals. The treatment is offered for people who have not experienced relief from drugs or ECT, but it is an expensive procedure and there is little evidence that it actually works (Grimm and Bajbouj, 2010; Vonck et al., 2014). The effectiveness of vagal nerve stimulation for depression is difficult to evaluate because trials have few participants and most have no placebo control (R. Robinson, 2009). The lack of such controls is unfortunate because we know depression is very susceptible to placebo effects (see Figure 16.22).

Deep brain stimulation (**DBS**), mild electrical stimulation of brain sites through a surgically implanted electrode, directed at several different brain target regions (Crowell et al., 2014), is also being tried to treat depression that resists other treatments (Kringelbach et al., 2007). Despite over 10 years of reports using DBS for depression (Mayberg et al., 2005), double-blind controlled studies are only recently being published, and they call into question whether it is more effective than placebo at reducing depression (Bergfeld et al., 2016; Dougherty et al., 2015).

Despite the overwhelming popularity of SSRIs for treating depression, a course of 20 or so sessions of **cognitive behavioral therapy** (**CBT**)—psychotherapy aimed at correcting negative thinking, reducing stress, and improving interpersonal relationships—is about as effective as SSRI treatment (Butler et al., 2006). Furthermore, the rate of relapse is lower for CBT than for SSRI treatment (DeRubeis et al., 2008; Kuyken et al., 2016). Interestingly, CBT and SSRI treatment together are more effective in combating depression than either one is alone (March et al., 2004). Typically, CBT helps the client to recognize self-defeating modes of thinking and encourages breaking out of a cycle of self-fulfilling depression (**FIGURE 16.23**).

The hypothalamic-pituitary-adrenal axis is involved in depression

People who have very high levels of circulating glucocorticoids such as cortisol are prone to depression. This condition, called **Cushing's syndrome**, may have several different causes, including hormone-secreting tumors or therapeutic treatments with synthetic glucocorticoids. In more than 85% of patients with Cushing's syndrome, depression appears quite early, even before other typical signs, such as obesity or unusual growth and distribution of body hair (Krystal et al., 1990). These observations suggest that dysfunction of the hypothalamic-pituitary-adrenal axis (**FIGURE 16.24A**) may be involved in depression, perhaps as part of a depression-inducing stress reaction (Herbert, 2013).

Suicide victims show very high levels of circulating cortisol (Pompili et al., 2010), and hospitalized patients with depression show elevated cortisol levels (**FIGURE 16.24B**).

serotonin syndrome Syndrome of confusion, muscle spasms, and fever that may occur when brain levels of serotonin are too high; a risk of taking SSRIs.

deep brain stimulation (DBS) Mild electrical stimulation through an electrode that is surgically implanted deep in the brain.

cognitive behavioral therapy (CBT) Psychotherapy aimed at correcting negative thinking and improving interpersonal relationships.

Cushing's syndrome A condition in which levels of adrenal glucocorticoids are abnormally high.

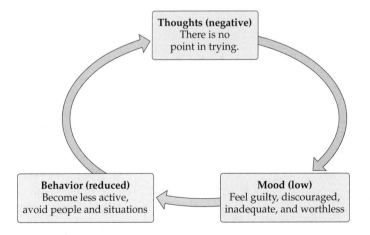

16.23 THE TREADMILL OF DEPRESSION Cognitive behavioral therapy (CBT) aims to break the cycle at one or more points. Thus even a modest program of physical exercise may help because it interrupts the "actions" or "behavior" part of the cycle.

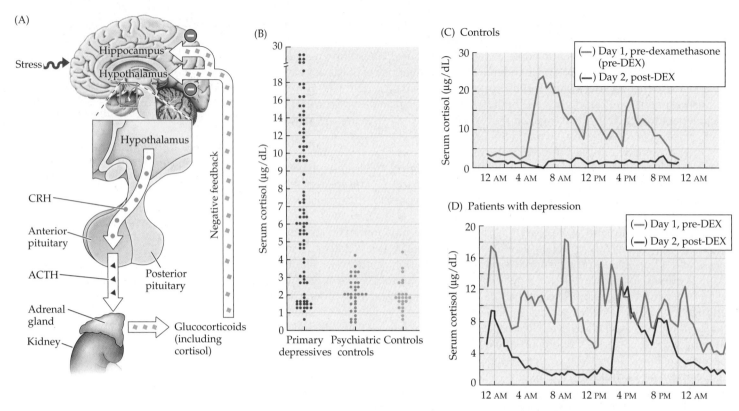

16.24 THE HYPOTHALAMIC-PITUITARY-ADRENAL AXIS IN DEPRESSION (A) Evidence shows that the hypothalamic-pituitary-adrenal system is involved in depression. ACTH, adrenocorticotropic hormone; CRH, corticotropin-releasing hormone. (B) Circulating cortisol levels are usually higher in depressed people than in psychiatric or healthy controls. In this plot, each dot represents an individual case. (C) The normal circadian rhythm in the secretion of cortisol (day 1) is abolished by treatment with the synthetic glucocorticoid dexamethasone (day 2). (D) The same dose of dexamethasone is far less effective in patients with depression. (After Schatzberg et al., 1983.)

dexamethasone suppression test
A test of pituitary-adrenal function in which the participant is given dexamethasone, a synthetic glucocorticoid hormone, which should cause a decline in the production of adrenal corticosteroids.

These findings suggest that adrenocorticotropic hormone (ACTH) is released in excessive amounts by the anterior pituitary. A standard method for assessing hypothalamic-pituitary-adrenal function—the **dexamethasone suppression test**—can reveal a tendency to release excess cortisol.

Dexamethasone is a potent synthetic glucocorticoid that ordinarily suppresses the early-morning rise in ACTH that is typical in most people. When given late at night, dexamethasone seems to "fool" the hypothalamus into believing that there is a high level of circulating cortisol. In healthy individuals, the dexamethasone suppresses cortisol release the next day (**FIGURE 16.24C**), but in many individuals suffering from depression it fails to have this effect (**FIGURE 16.24D**)(Belvederi et al., 2014). As depression is relieved, dexamethasone again suppresses cortisol normally, no matter what caused the relief—passage of time, psychotherapy, pharmacotherapy, or electroconvulsive shock therapy.

Why do more females than males suffer from depression?

Studies all over the world show that more women than men suffer from major depression. In the United States, women are twice as likely as men to suffer major depression (CDC, 2010). Some researchers suggest that the apparent sex difference reflects patterns of help-seeking by males and females—notably, that women use health facilities more than men do. But sex differences in the incidence of depression also are evident in door-to-door surveys (Robins and Regier, 1991), which would appear to rule out the simple explanation that women seek treatment more often than men do.

Some researchers have emphasized gender differences in endocrine physiology. The occurrence of clinical depression often is related to events in the female repro-

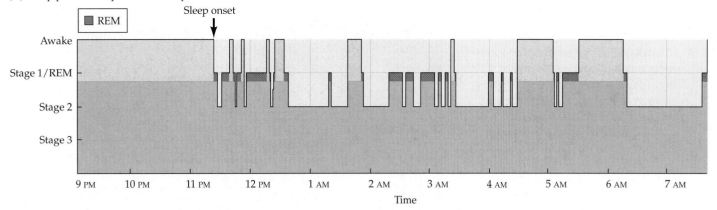

(A) Sleep pattern of a patient with depression

REM

Sleep onset

Awake

Stage 1/REM

Stage 2

Stage 3

9 PM 10 PM 11 PM 12 PM 1 AM 2 AM 3 AM 4 AM 5 AM 6 AM 7 AM

Time

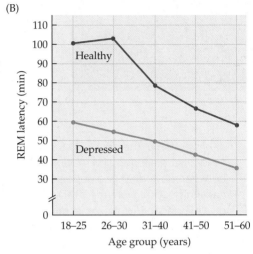

(B)

REM latency (min)

Healthy

Depressed

18–25 26–30 31–40 41–50 51–60

Age group (years)

16.25 SLEEP AND DEPRESSION (A) Depressed people spend little or no time in stage 3 sleep. (Compare with Figure 14.12.) (B) Patients suffering from depression also enter their first REM period earlier in the night. Thus, REM sleep seems to be distributed differently in people with depression.

ductive cycle—for example, before menstruation, during use of contraceptive pills, following childbirth, and during menopause. Although there is little relation between circulating levels of individual hormones and measures of depression, the phenomenon of **postpartum depression**, a bout of depression either immediately preceding or following childbirth, suggests that some combination of hormones can precipitate depression. About one out of every seven pregnant women will show symptoms of depression (Dietz et al., 2007).

Because postpartum depression may affect the mother's relationship with her child, causing long-lasting deleterious effects on the child's behavior (Tronick and Reck, 2009), there is growing alarm about this problem. Unfortunately, there is evidence that prenatal exposure to SSRIs may affect the child's later behavior (Oberlander et al., 2010), and no one knows whether SSRIs in breast milk affect the child. Thus CBT offers the safest treatment for postpartum depression, and it is difficult to weigh the costs and benefits of supplementing that therapy with SSRIs. One intriguing notion is that postpartum depression is a disorder of modern civilization, like obesity and diabetes, caused by modern practices of early weaning, low levels of physical activity and exposure to the sun, and isolation from kin support networks (Hahn-Holbrook and Haselton, 2014).

postpartum depression A bout of depression that afflicts a woman around the time she gives birth.

Sleep characteristics change in affective disorders

Difficulty falling asleep and inability to maintain sleep are common in depression. In addition, EEG sleep studies of depressed patients show certain abnormalities that go beyond difficulty falling asleep. The sleep of patients with major depressive disorders is marked by a striking reduction in stage 3 of slow-wave sleep (SWS) and a corresponding increase in stages 1 and 2 (**FIGURE 16.25A**). Alterations of REM sleep patterns seem to have a special relationship with depression. Depressed patients en-

The Season to Be Depressed?

Seasonal rhythms characterize the behavior and physiology of many animals, including humans. For some unfortunate people, winter seems to bring a low period that may become a profound depression. Sometimes the winter depression alternates with summertime mania (Blehar and Rosenthal, 1989). In wintertime, affected people feel depressed, slow down, generally sleep a lot, and overeat. Come summer, they are elated, energetic, and active, and they become thinner. This syndrome—called **seasonal affective disorder** (**SAD**)—appears predominantly in women and generally starts in early adulthood.

Seasonal rhythms in animals are controlled by the length of the day, so researchers asked whether seasonal changes in exposure to sunlight might cause SAD. Some SAD sufferers were treated with doses of bright light, to see whether it acts as an antidepressant. The efficacy of light therapy, also called *phototherapy*, in SAD is fairly well established (Golden et al., 2005), and in many ways light therapy resembles treatment with traditional antidepressant drugs (A. Moscovitch et al., 2004). Light therapy may be most effective when administered immediately upon awakening in the morning (Lewy et al., 1998). A person receiving phototherapy is shown in the figure.

Light therapy for SAD

However, given the known susceptibility of depression to placebo effects (see Figure 16.22), it is possible that light is only effective because people diagnosed with SAD expect it to be. In fact, we have known for over a century that the seasonal peak in suicide is not in winter (and certainly not around the December holidays, as a persistent myth indicates), but in the spring (Durkheim, 1897), when days are getting *longer*. That well-replicated finding seems difficult to reconcile with the idea that short days can cause depression in any signifi-

cant fraction of the population. In fact, several studies found no relationship between daylength and depression, casting doubt on whether SAD is a valid concept (Brancaleoni et al., 2009; Mersch et al., 1999; Traffanstedt et al., 2016). (Photo courtesy of Uplift Technologies.)

seasonal affective disorder (SAD)   A depression putatively brought about by the short days of winter.

---

ter REM sleep much sooner after sleep onset (**FIGURE 16.25B**)—the latency to REM sleep correlates with the severity of depression—and their REM sleep is unusually vigorous. Furthermore, the temporal distribution of REM sleep is altered, with an increased amount of REM sleep occurring during the first half of sleep, as though REM sleep were displaced toward an earlier period in the night (Wehr et al., 1985). In addition to these links between the daily rhythm of sleep and depression, seasonal rhythms have been implicated in a particular depressive condition known as *seasonal affective disorder* (SAD), which is described in **BOX 16.2**.

Scientists are still searching for animal models of depression

Because a monkey or a cat or a rat can't tell us if it has delusions of persecution or if it hears voices telling it what to do, animal models of schizophrenia are limited. But many of the signs of depression—such as decreased social contact, problems with eating, and changes in activity—are behaviorally overt (Nestler and Hyman, 2010).

In one type of stress model—**learned helplessness**—an animal is exposed to a repetitive stressful stimulus, such as an electrical shock, that it cannot escape (Seligman and Beagley, 1975). Like depression, learned helplessness has been linked to

learned helplessness   A learning paradigm in which individuals are subjected to inescapable, unpleasant conditions.

a decrease in serotonin function (Petty et al., 1994) and also dopamine (B. Li et al., 2011). Removing the olfactory bulb from rodents also creates a model of depression: the animals display irritability, preferences for alcohol, and elevated levels of corticosteroids—all of which are reversed by many antidepressants. A strain of rats created through selective breeding—the Flinders-sensitive line—has been proposed as a model of depression because these animals show reduced locomotor activity, reduced body weight, increased REM sleep, learning difficulties, and exaggerated immobility in response to chronic stress (Overstreet, 1993). These varied animal models may be useful in finding the essential mechanisms that cause and maintain depression in humans.

There Are Several Types of Anxiety Disorders

All of us have at times felt apprehensive and fearful. Some people experience this state with an intensity that is overwhelming and includes irrational fears, a sense of terror, unusual body sensations such as dizziness, difficulty breathing, trembling, shaking, and a feeling of loss of control. Anxiety can be lethal: a follow-up of patients with panic disorder revealed an increased mortality in men with this disorder, resulting from cardiovascular disease and suicide (Coryell et al., 1986).

The American Psychiatric Association distinguishes several major types of **anxiety disorders**. **Phobic disorders** are intense, irrational fears that become centered on a specific object, activity, or situation that the person feels compelled to avoid. Anxiety disorders also include *generalized anxiety disorder*, in which persistent and excessive anxiety and worry are experienced for months, and *panic disorder*, characterized by recurrent transient attacks of intense fearfulness. Some patients who suffer from recurrent panic attacks have temporal lobe abnormalities, and overall temporal lobe volumes tend to be lower in patients with panic disorder (van Tol et al., 2010), while hippocampal volumes are normal. Given the special role of the amygdala in mediating fear (see Chapter 15), changes in the amygdala and associated circuitry may underlie the symptoms (Rauch et al., 2003).

Other anxiety-related disorders that we'll consider shortly are posttraumatic stress disorder and obsessive-compulsive disorder. There is a strong genetic contribution to each of these disorders (Oler et al., 2010; Shih et al., 2004).

Drug treatment of anxiety provides clues to the mechanisms of this disorder

Throughout history, people have consumed all sorts of substances in the hopes of controlling anxiety. The list includes alcohol, bromides, scopolamine, opiates, and barbiturates. In the 1960s the tranquilizing agent meprobamate (Miltown) was introduced and became an instant best seller, ushering in the modern age of anxiety pharmacotherapy. Soon researchers discovered a new class of drugs called **benzodiazepines**, which quickly became the favored drugs for treating anxiety. One type of benzodiazepine—*diazepam* (Valium)—is one of the most prescribed drugs in history. Other commonly prescribed benzodiazepines include Xanax, Halcion, and Ativan. These drugs are so widely used that they can be detected in lakes and streams at concentrations that have been demonstrated to inhibit social behaviors in fish (Brodin et al., 2013). Such drugs that combat anxiety are termed **anxiolytics** ("anxiety dissolving"), although at high doses they also have anticonvulsant and sleep-inducing properties. The anxiolytic drugs are also discussed in Chapter 4.

Anxiolytic benzodiazepines bind to GABA receptors, where they act as noncompetitive agonists (recall from Chapter 4 that GABA is the most common inhibitory transmitter in the brain). This interaction with GABA receptors results in the enhancement of GABA's action at inhibitory synapses in the brain. In other words, GABA-mediated postsynaptic inhibition is facilitated by benzodiazepines. Benzodiazepines preferentially bind to the many $GABA_A$ receptors that are widely distributed throughout the brain, especially in the cerebral cortex and some subcortical areas, such as the hippocampus and the amygdala (**FIGURE 16.26**).

anxiety disorder Any of a class of psychological disorders that include recurrent panic states and generalized anxiety disorders.

phobic disorder An intense, irrational fear that becomes centered on a specific object, activity, or situation that a person feels compelled to avoid.

benzodiazepines A class of anti-anxiety drugs that bind with high affinity to receptor molecules in the central nervous system. One example is diazepam (Valium).

anxiolytics A class of substances that are used to combat anxiety. Examples include alcohol, opiates, barbiturates, and the benzodiazepines.

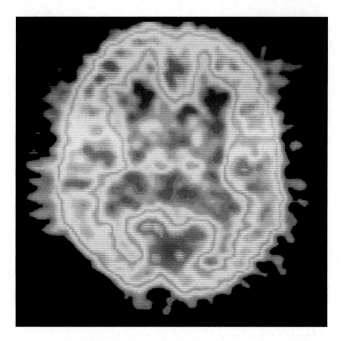

16.26 THE DISTRIBUTION OF BENZODIAZEPINE RECEPTORS IN THE HUMAN BRAIN This PET scan of benzodiazepine receptors shows their wide distribution in the brain, especially the cortex. Highest concentrations are in orange and red. (Courtesy of Dr. Goran Sedvall.)

The ultimate function of the benzodiazepine–GABA$_A$ receptor complex is to regulate the permeability of neuronal membranes to chloride ions (Cl$^-$). When GABA is released from a presynaptic terminal and activates postsynaptic receptors, chloride ions are allowed to move from the outside to the inside of the nerve cell, creating a local hyperpolarization (an inhibitory postsynaptic potential, or IPSP) and therefore inhibiting the neuron from firing. Benzodiazepines alone do little to change chloride conductance, but in the presence of GABA, they markedly enhance GABA-provoked increases in chloride permeability and thus potentiate the inhibitory effect of GABA. Interestingly, the brain probably makes its own anxiety-relieving substances that interact with the benzodiazepine-binding site; the neurosteroid allopregnanolone is a prime candidate for this function (see Chapter 4). Drugs developed to act at this site are effective anxiolytics in both rats and humans (Rupprecht et al., 2009).

Although the benzodiazepines remain an important category of anxiolytics, other types of anxiety-relieving drugs have been developed. A notable example is the drug buspirone (Buspar), an agonist at serotonin 5-HT$_{1A}$ receptors that has been shown to provide relief from anxiety. This observation is consistent with findings from functional-imaging research confirming that 5-HT$_{1A}$ receptor density is abnormal in anxiety disorders (Neumeister et al., 2004). SSRI antidepressants, such as paroxetine (Paxil) and fluoxetine (Prozac), which increase stimulation of serotonin receptors, are also sometimes effective treatments for anxiety disorders.

In posttraumatic stress disorder, horrible memories won't go away

Some people experience especially awful moments in life that seem indelible, resulting in vivid impressions that persist the rest of their lives. The kind of event that seems particularly likely to produce subsequent stress disorders is one that is intense and usually associated with witnessing abusive violence and/or death. Examples include the sudden loss of a close friend, rape, torture, kidnapping, or profound social dislocation, such as in forced migration. In these cases, memories of horrible events intrude into consciousness and produce the same intense visceral arousal—the fear and trembling and general autonomic activation—that the original event caused. These traumatic memories are easily reawakened by stressful circumstances and even by seemingly benign stimuli that somehow prompt recollection of the original event. An ever-watchful and fearful stance becomes the portrait of individuals afflicted with what is called **posttraumatic stress disorder** (**PTSD**, formerly called *combat fatigue, war neurosis,* or *shell shock*).

Analysis of a random sample of Vietnam War veterans indicates that 19% had PTSD at some point after service. This was the rate for all Vietnam veterans; of those exposed to high levels of war zone stressors, more than 35% developed PTSD at some point, and most of them were still suffering from the disorder decades later (Dohrenwend et al., 2006). Familial factors affect vulnerability, as shown in twin studies of Vietnam veterans who had seen combat. Monozygotic twins were more similar than dizygotic twins, and the specific contribution of inheritance to PTSD may account for one-third of the variance. People who display combat-related PTSD show (1) memory changes such as amnesia for some war experiences, (2) flashbacks, and (3) deficits in short-term memory (Bremner et al., 1993). These memory disturbances suggest involvement of the hippocampus, and indeed the volume of the right hippocampus is smaller in combat veterans with PTSD than in controls, with no differences in other brain regions (Bremner et al., 1995). It was once widely assumed that the stressful episode(s) caused the hippocampus to shrink, but some veterans suffering PTSD left a monozygotic twin at home, and it turned out that the nonstressed twin without PTSD also tended to have a smaller hippocampus (Gilbertson

posttraumatic stress disorder (PTSD) Formerly called *combat fatigue, war neurosis,* or *shell shock.* A disorder in which memories of an unpleasant episode repeatedly plague the victim.

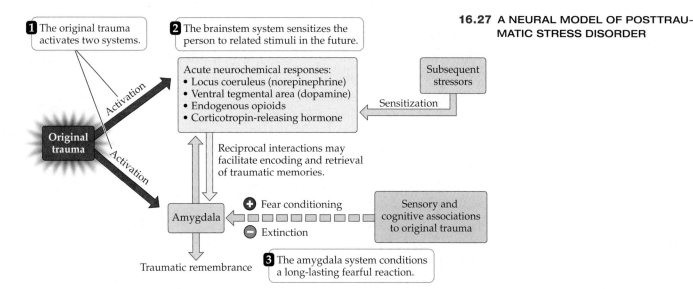

1 The original trauma activates two systems.

2 The brainstem system sensitizes the person to related stimuli in the future.

Original trauma

Activation

Activation

Acute neurochemical responses:
• Locus coeruleus (norepinephrine)
• Ventral tegmental area (dopamine)
• Endogenous opioids
• Corticotropin-releasing hormone

Subsequent stressors

Sensitization

Reciprocal interactions may facilitate encoding and retrieval of traumatic memories.

Amygdala

+ Fear conditioning

− Extinction

Sensory and cognitive associations to original trauma

Traumatic remembrance

3 The amygdala system conditions a long-lasting fearful reaction.

et al., 2002). So an inherited tendency to have a small hippocampus, and perhaps lower rates of adult neurogenesis (J. S. Snyder et al., 2011), may be what makes a person more susceptible to PTSD if exposed to stress.

A comprehensive psychobiological model of the development of PTSD draws connections among the symptoms and the neural mechanisms of fear conditioning, behavioral sensitization, and extinction (Charney et al., 1993). Perhaps patients learn to avoid a large range of stimuli associated with the original trauma. Work in animals has revealed that this type of memory—**fear conditioning**—is very persistent and involves the amygdala (see Chapter 15).

Finally, the persistence of memory and fear in PTSD may depend on the failure to *forget*. In experimental animals, NMDA antagonists delivered to the amygdala prevent the extinction of fear-mediated startle. Sites projecting to the amygdala, such as the hippocampus and prefrontal cortex, may also lose their effectiveness in suppressing learned fear responses (**FIGURE 16.27**). There is also a hormonal link, because PTSD sufferers exhibit a paradoxical long-term *reduction* in cortisol levels (Yehuda, 2002). One possibility is that patients with PTSD have persistent increases in *sensitivity* to cortisol. If, as a result, they feel the effect of stress hormones more strongly than other people do, it might be harder for them to forget stressful events. In Chapter 17 we will discuss research-based methods that have been proposed to help people forget traumatic life events. For now, the most effective treatment for PTSD is cognitive behavioral therapy involving prolonged exposure, gradually increasing the client's (imagined or real) exposure to those stimuli and conditions that trigger flashbacks, until they no longer trigger responses (Foa et al., 2013).

In obsessive-compulsive disorder, thoughts and acts keep repeating

Neatness, orderliness, and similar traits are attributes we tend to admire, especially during those chaotic moments when we realize we have created another tottering pile of papers, bills, or the like. But when does orderliness and routine cross the line into pathology? People with **obsessive-compulsive disorder** (**OCD**) lead lives riddled with repetitive rituals and persistent thoughts that they are powerless to control or stop, despite recognizing that the behaviors are abnormal. In OCD patients, routine acts that we all engage in, such as checking whether the door is locked when we leave our home, become *compulsions*, acts that are repeated over and over. Recurrent thoughts, or *obsessions*, such as fears of germs or other potential harms in the world, invade the consciousness. These symptoms progressively isolate a person from ordinary social engagement with the world. For many patients, hours of each day are consumed by compulsive acts such as repetitive handwashing. The symptoms of OCD are summarized in **TABLE 16.4** on the following page.

fear conditioning A form of learning in which fear comes to be associated with a previously neutral stimulus.

obsessive-compulsive disorder (OCD) A syndrome in which the affected individual engages in recurring, repetitive acts that are carried out without rhyme, reason, or the ability to stop.

TABLE 16.4 Symptoms of Obsessive-Compulsive Disorders

SYMPTOMS	PERCENTAGE OF PATIENTS
OBSESSIONS (THOUGHTS)	
Dirt, germs, or environmental toxins	40
Something terrible happening (fire, death, or illness of self or loved one)	24
Symmetry, order, or exactness	17
Religious obsessions	13
Body wastes or secretions (urine, stool, saliva)	8
Lucky or unlucky numbers	8
Forbidden, aggressive, or perverse sexual thoughts, images, or impulses	4
Fear of harming self or others	4
Household items	3
Intrusive nonsense sounds, words, or music	1
COMPULSIONS (ACTS)	
Performing excessive or ritualized handwashing, showering, bathing, teeth brushing, or grooming	85
Repeating rituals (going in or out of a door, getting up from or sitting down on a chair)	51
Checking (doors, locks, stove, appliances, emergency brake on car, paper route, homework)	46
Engaging in miscellaneous rituals (writing, moving, speaking)	26
Removing contaminants from contacts	23
Touching	20
Counting	18
Ordering or arranging	17
Preventing harm to self or others	16
Cleaning household or inanimate objects	6

Source: Swedo et al., 1989.

Determining the number of persons afflicted with OCD is difficult, especially because many people with this disorder tend to hide their symptoms. It is estimated that nearly 1% of adults will suffer from "severe" OCD in the United States in any given year (Kessler, Chiu et al., 2005). In many cases, the initial symptoms of this disorder appear in childhood; the peak age group for onset of OCD, however, is 25–44 years. Patients with OCD display increased metabolic rates in the orbitofrontal cortex, cingulate cortex, and caudate nuclei (Chamberlain et al., 2008).

Happily, OCD responds to treatment in most cases. It responds well to CBT (Olatunji et al., 2013) and also to several drugs. What do effective OCD drugs—like fluoxetine (Prozac), fluvoxamine (Luvox), and clomipramine (Anafranil)—tend to have in common? They share the ability to inhibit the reuptake of serotonin at serotonergic synapses, thereby increasing the synaptic availability of serotonin. This observation suggests that dysfunction of serotonergic neurotransmission plays a central role in OCD. Recall that we already discussed SSRIs like Prozac that inhibit the reuptake of serotonin when we discussed treatments for depression. How can the same drug help two disorders that seem so different? For one thing, depression often accompanies OCD, so the two disorders may be related. Furthermore,

(A) Horizontal view

(B) Sagittal view

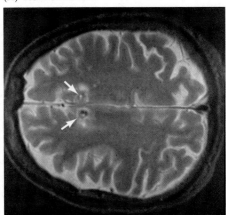 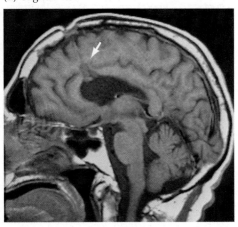

16.28 NEUROSURGERY TO TREAT OBSESSIVE-COMPULSIVE DISORDER These horizontal (A) and sagittal (B) MRIs show the brain of a patient who underwent a cingulotomy—the disruption of cingulate cortex connections (arrows)—in an attempt to treat OCD. (From Martuza et al., 1990, courtesy of Dr. Robert L. Martuza.)

functional brain imaging suggests that the same SSRI drugs alter the activity of the orbitofrontal prefrontal cortex in people with OCD (Saxena et al., 2001) and also affect primarily ventrolateral prefrontal cortex in people with depression (see Figure 16.21).

About one-third of severely disabled OCD patients who underwent *cingulotomy*, surgical disruption of circuits in the cingulate cortex (**FIGURE 16.28**), appeared to benefit from this intervention (Jenike et al., 1991; Martuza et al., 1990). A similar surgery, making small, discrete lesions in the anterior part of the internal capsule (the white matter projections underlying the cortex), may be beneficial in some cases of severe anxiety disorders, but the patients were also more likely to suffer from apathy, a common symptom of lobotomy (Rück et al., 2008). There is growing evidence that overactivity of a circuit from prefrontal cortex to striatum to thalamus and back to cortex may underlie OCD. Induced overactivity of this circuit in mice resulted in prolonged stereotyped grooming behavior that was relieved by SSRI treatment (Ahmari et al., 2013; Burguière et al., 2013). Deep brain stimulation of the nucleus accumbens in people suffering from OCD disrupted this same circuit and relieved symptoms (Figee et al., 2013; van Westen et al., 2015).

Many researchers also believe that OCD and another disease involving repetitive behaviors, known as *Tourette's syndrome*, are part of a spectrum of related disorders (Olson, 2004). Tourette's and OCD are often **comorbid** (occurring together), and both disorders involve abnormalities of the basal ganglia. However, drug therapy in Tourette's syndrome has typically focused on modifying the actions of dopamine rather than of serotonin (**BOX 16.3**).

There is a heritable genetic component to OCD; again, several genes may contribute to susceptibility to this disorder (Grados et al., 2003). For example, genes affecting serotonergic, dopaminergic, and glutamatergic systems have been implicated (Pauls et al., 2014). There is also evidence that perinatal events and infections can trigger OCD. Upon observing that numerous children exhibiting OCD symptoms had recently been treated for strep throat, R. C. Dale et al. (2005) found that many children with OCD were producing antibodies to brain proteins. They theorized that, in mounting an immune response to the streptococcal bacteria, these children also made antibodies that attacked their own brains. The genetic link may be that some people are more likely than others to produce antibodies to the brain proteins.

comorbid Referring to the tendency of certain diseases or disorders to occur together in individuals.

BOX 16.3 Tics, Twitches, and Snorts: The Unusual Character of Tourette's Syndrome

Their faces twitch in an insistent way, and every now and then, out of nowhere, they blurt out odd sounds. At times they fling their arms, kick their legs, or make violent shoulder movements. Sufferers of **Tourette's syndrome** are also supersensitive to tactile, auditory, and visual stimuli (A.

J. Cohen and Leckman, 1992). Many patients report that an urge to emit verbal or phonic tics builds up and that giving in to the urge brings relief. Although popular media often portray people with Tourette's as shouting out insults and curse words (coprolalia), verbal tics of that sort are rare.

Tourette's syndrome begins early in life; the mean age of diagnosis is 6–7 years (de Groot et al., 1995), and the syndrome is 3 to 4 times more common in males than in females. Figure A draws a portrait of the chronology of symptoms. Often people with Tourette's also exhibit attention

(A) The chronology of Tourette's symptoms

Motor tics
- Eyes, face, head
- Shoulder, neck
- Arms, hands
- Trunk
- Legs

Vocal tics
- Low noises
- Loud noises
- Stuttering
- Repetition
- Obscenities
- Syllables
- Blocking
- Words out of context
- Repeating others

Compulsive actions
- Head banging
- Kissing
- Touching objects
- Kicking
- Tapping
- Touching self or others
- Biting self
- Touching sexual organs
- Mimicking others

Mean age at onset (years)

(B) D$_2$ receptor binding in Tourette's syndrome. (Left) PET scan of D$_2$ binding. (Right) MRI scan illustrating the location of the caudate nuclei.

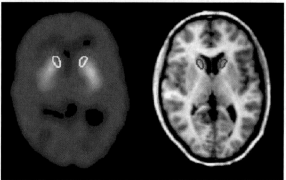

The Cutting Edge

Are Abnormal Eye Movements an Endophenotype for People at Risk for Schizophrenia?

The modern view of schizophrenia is that no inherited gene inevitably leads to the condition. Rather, some people inherit a susceptibility to schizophrenia that may be triggered by stress, especially in the transition from adolescence to adulthood. Thus there is a lot of interest in finding an endophenotype, a normally hidden characteristic that can objectively identify people at risk for schizophrenia, in order to intervene and, perhaps, avoid schizophrenia.

We noted earlier that people with schizophrenia have difficulty with smooth-pursuit eye movements. One group devised a series of eye-tracking tasks. The participants' eye movements were monitored while they performed three tasks: (1) watching a cursor on a computer screen travel a complex weaving pathway (smooth pursuit), (2) freely viewing a series of photographs, and (3) trying to fix their gaze on one point while distracting stimuli appeared deficit hyperactivity disorder (ADHD) or OCD (S. Park et al., 1993). Children with Tourette's display a thinning of primary somatosensory and motor cortex representing facial, oral, and laryngeal structures (Sowell et al., 2008), suggesting that the tics mediated by these regions may be under-inhibited by cortex.

Family studies indicate that genetics plays an important role in this disorder. Twin studies of the disorder reveal a concordance rate among monozygotic twins of 53–77%, contrasted with a concordance rate among dizygotic twins of 8–23% (T. M. Hyde et al., 1992). Among discordant monozygotic twin pairs, the twin with Tourette's has a greater density of dopamine D_2 receptors in the caudate nucleus of the basal ganglia than the unaffected twin has (Wolf et al., 1996). This observation suggests that differences in the dopaminergic system, especially in the basal ganglia, may be important (D_2 receptor binding in an affected twin is illustrated in Figure B). The contemporary view is that Tourette's syndrome is mediated in a complex manner by more than one gene, but the precise genes that are involved remain unidentified (Abelson et al., 2005; Pauls, 2003).

Treatment with haloperidol, a dopamine D_2 receptor antagonist that is an effective antischizophrenic drug, significantly reduces tic frequency and is a primary treatment for Tourette's syndrome. Unfortunately, this treatment has the side effects we mentioned when discussing schizophrenia, and as with people who suffer from schizophrenia, some people with Tourette's respond well to the atypical antipsychotics, which bring fewer side effects. Behavior modification techniques that aim at reducing the frequency of some symptoms, especially tics, help some patients learn to substitute more subtle or more socially acceptable behaviors in place of the more obvious tics (Himle et al., 2006). Some people with Tourette's that has not responded to medication have gained relief from deep brain stimulation (DBS) (Baldermann et al., 2016; Porta et al., 2009), but there has yet to be a consensus on which brain targets are most effective for combating symptoms (Fraint and Pal, 2015). (Figure B courtesy of Dr. Steven Wolf.)

Tourette's syndrome A heightened sensitivity to tactile, auditory, and visual stimuli that may be accompanied by the buildup of an urge to emit verbal or phonic tics.

elsewhere on the screen. A training set of 88 people with schizophrenia and 88 controls performed the tasks, and as in previous studies, people with schizophrenia had a hard time controlling eye movements, as we saw in Figure 16.4.

But then the researchers used mathematical models based on the performance of the participants to see whether some combination of parameters would discriminate between those who did and those who did not have schizophrenia. They found one model that would indeed correctly classify every participant. But of course this might be a trivial matter of picking up on the particular patterns of those participants. Perhaps some mathematical model could correctly discriminate between people randomly assigned to two groups. The big question was whether the model based on the training set could correctly discriminate between people with and people without schizophrenia in *another* set of participants. In fact, the model identified those who had received a diagnosis of schizophrenia with 88% accuracy (P. J. Benson et al., 2012). When the researchers fine-tuned their mathematical model further, it discriminated the 298 total cases with 98% accuracy! No people with schizophrenia were misclassified by the model. Five controls showed abnormalities, but you have to wonder

Smooth pursuit of moving cursor	Free viewing of a photograph	Fixing gaze on a single point

People diagnosed as having schizophrenia

Controls

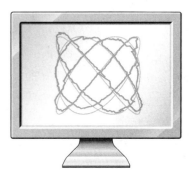 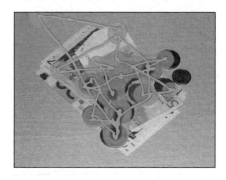 

16.29 A SIMPLE SCAN FOR SCHIZOPHRENIA? People who have been diagnosed with schizophrenia have a more difficult time visually tracking moving objects than controls do. Can this characteristic be used to identify people at risk of developing schizophrenia? (After P. J. Benson et al., 2012, courtesy of Dr. Philip Benson.)

whether they were, in fact, at risk for schizophrenia. Mathematical analysis showed that the differences in eye movement (**FIGURE 16.29**) were seen in both sexes and were not due to differences in whether the patients were in remission, or whether they were receiving antipsychotics, or any other factor examined.

If confirmed, this test could have a big impact on the diagnosis of schizophrenia, as the test itself takes only a few minutes, can be analyzed in real time, and could be administered by a person with only a few hours of training. Thus it may one day be possible to quickly screen lots of people and see whether the test accurately predicts who will develop schizophrenia, and then to test interventions to avert the condition. We already know a key component of any intervention—try to buffer the child from physiological or psychological stress.

Go to
bn8e.com
for study questions,
quizzes, activities,
and other resources

Recommended Reading

Charney, D., and Nestler, E. J. (Eds.). (2014). *Neurobiology of Mental Illness* (4th ed.). New York: Oxford University Press.

Hersen, M., and Beidel, D. C. (2014). *Adult Psychopathology and Diagnosis* (7th ed.). New York: Wiley.

Huettel, S. A., Song, A. W., and McCarthy, G. (2014). *Functional Magnetic Resonance Imaging* (3rd ed.). Sunderland, MA: Sinauer.

Kessler, D. A. (2016). *Capture: Unraveling the Mystery of Mental Suffering.* New York: HarperCollins.

Meyer, J. S., and Quenzer, L. F. (2013). *Psychopharmacology: Drugs, the Brain, and Behavior* (2nd ed.). Sunderland, MA: Sinauer.

Solomon, A. (2001). *The Noonday Demon: An Atlas of Depression.* New York: Scribner.

16

VISUAL SUMMARY

You should be able to relate each summary to the adjacent illustration, including structures and processes.
Go to **bn8e.com/vs16** for links to figures, animations, and activities that will help you consolidate the material.

1 Psychiatric disorders are prevalent in modern society. Studies of families, twins, and adoptees demonstrate a strong role of genetic factors in schizophrenia. Rather than a single gene determining whether a person will develop **schizophrenia**, many genes contribute to the risk. Review **Figures 16.1–16.3, Tables 16.1 and 16.2**

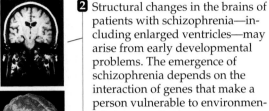

2 Structural changes in the brains of patients with schizophrenia—including enlarged ventricles—may arise from early developmental problems. The emergence of schizophrenia depends on the interaction of genes that make a person vulnerable to environmental stressors. Review **Figures 16.4–16.9, 16.15–16.17**

3 The frontal lobes are less active in people with schizophrenia than in controls. Biochemical theories of schizophrenia emphasize the importance of the dopamine, glutamate, and serotonin receptors. **Typical antipsychotics** block dopamine D_2 receptors, while **atypical antipsychotics** block $5HT_{2A}$ receptors. Review **Figures 16.10–16.14, 16.18, Box 16.1**

4 **Bipolar disorder** is characterized by extreme mood swings and subtle changes in the brain and is commonly treated with **lithium**. As in schizophrenia, many genes contribute to the risk of bipolar disorder, and genetic risk for both disorders seems to be associated with creativity. Review **Figures 16.19 and 16.20**

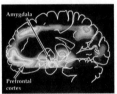

5 **Depression** also has a strong genetic factor. In general, females are more likely than males to suffer from depression. People suffering from depression show increased activity in the frontal cortex and the amygdala, as well as disruption of sleep patterns and adrenal hormone regulation. Review **Figures 16.21, 16.24, 16.25, Box 16.2**

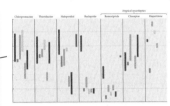

6 The most effective treatment for most cases of depression is a combination of **cognitive behavioral therapy** (CBT) and a **selective serotonin reuptake inhibitor** (SSRI). Review **Figures 16.22 and 16.23, Table 16.3**

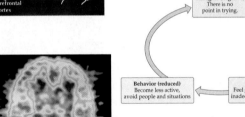

7 Anxiety states are characterized by functional changes in the temporal lobes, particularly the amygdala. **Benzodiazepine** antianxiety drugs (**anxiolytics**) enhance the inhibitory effects of receptors for the transmitter GABA. Drugs affecting serotonergic synapses may also reduce anxiety. Review **Figure 16.26**

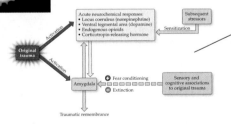

8 **Posttraumatic stress disorder** (**PTSD**) is characterized by an inability to forget horrible experiences. Temporal lobe atrophy in this disorder may be caused by exposure to stress hormones, such as cortisol, and prolonged sensitivity to those hormones. Review **Figure 16.27**

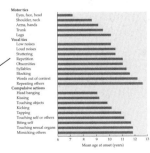

9 **Obsessive-compulsive disorder** (**OCD**) is characterized by changes in basal ganglia and frontal cortex and linked to serotonin. In **Tourette's syndrome**, overstimulation of dopamine receptors induces motor and verbal tics and compulsions. A restricted type of **psychosurgery** is sometimes used to treat the most severe cases of anxiety disorders. Review **Figure 16.24, Table 16.4, Box 16.3, Activity 16.1**

10 Difficulty in visually tracking moving objects may serve as an **endophenotype** for people at risk for schizophrenia. Review **Figure 16.29**

Cognitive Neuroscience

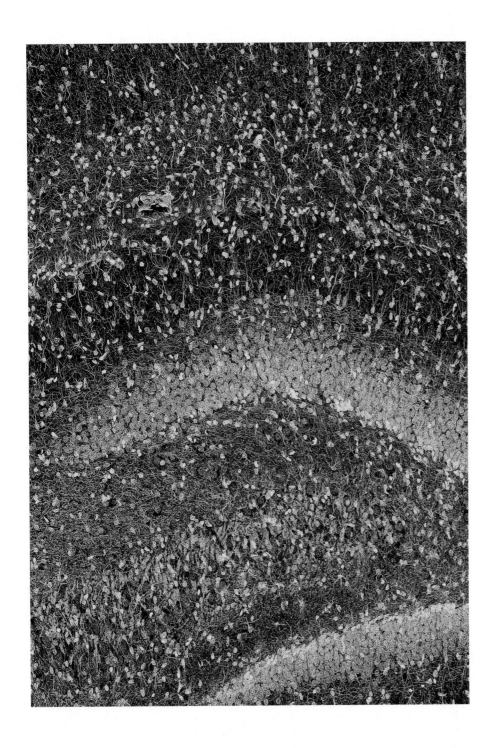

Rat hippocampus 2-photon fluorescence image of a rat's hippocampus showing the organization of glial cells (blue), neurofilaments in axons (green) and DNA in cell nuclei (yellow) within it. © Thomas Deerinck and Mark Ellisman, NCMIR, UCSD.

Learning and Memory

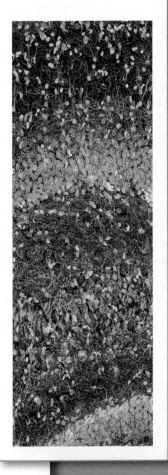

17

Henry Molaison, known to the world as *patient H.M.* in a classic series of research articles, was probably the most famous research subject in the history of brain science. Henry started to suffer seizures during adolescence, and by his late 20s, Henry's epilepsy was out of control. Because tests showed that his seizures began in both temporal lobes, a neurosurgeon removed most of the anterior temporal lobes, on both sides, in 1953.

Henry's surgery relieved his epilepsy, but that relief came at a terrible, unforeseen price: Henry had lost the ability to form new memories (Scoville and Milner, 1957). For more than 50 years after the surgery, until his death in 2008, Henry could retain any new fact only briefly; as soon as he was distracted, the newly acquired information vanished. Long after the surgery, he didn't know his age or the current date, that his parents had died years previously, or indeed any of the events that had transpired in the time since his surgery. His IQ remained a little above average (Corkin et al., 1997)—IQ tests don't require remembering new facts for more than a few minutes—but he knew that something was wrong with him.

> *Every day is alone in itself, whatever enjoyment I've had, and whatever sorrow I've had…. Right now, I'm wondering, have I done or said anything amiss? You see, at this moment everything looks clear to me, but what happened just before? That's what worries me. It's like waking from a dream. I just don't remember. (B. Milner, 1970, p. 37)*

Henry's inability to form new memories meant that he couldn't construct a lasting relationship with anybody new. No matter what experiences he might share with someone he met, Henry would have to start the acquaintance anew the following day, because he would have no recollection of ever meeting the person before.

What happened to Henry, and what does his experience teach us about learning and memory?

All the distinctively human aspects of our behavior are learned: the languages we speak, how we dress, the foods we eat and how we eat them, our skills and the ways we reach our goals. So much of our own individuality depends on **learning**, the process of acquiring new information, and on **memory**, the ability to store and retrieve that information. We begin this chapter with a discussion of the major types of memory because research in the twentieth century, including the case of H.M., revealed that there are fundamentally different types of memory, relying on varying networks of brain regions. In the second part of the chapter, we delve into what we know about how learning alters the structure of brain tissue at a more fine-grained cellular level.

Go to Brain Explorer
bn8e.com/17.1

Functional Perspectives on Learning and Memory

We can discover a great deal about learning and memory by examining how they fail. Clinical case studies show that memory can fail in very different ways, indicating that there are different *forms* of learning and memory, and that multiple brain regions are involved. The clinical research has guided further studies, using animal models and brain imaging; together, these diverse approaches are generating a comprehensive picture of brain mechanisms of learning and memory.

There Are Several Kinds of Learning and Memory

The terms *learning* and *memory* are so often paired that it sometimes seems as if one necessarily implies the other. We cannot be sure that learning has occurred unless a memory can be elicited later. Many kinds of brain damage, caused by disease or accidents, can produce highly specific types of memory impairment. We'll start our survey by looking at a few classic case studies of memory impairments and the brain damage that caused them.

For patient H.M., the present vanished into oblivion

Amnesia (Greek for "forgetfulness") is a severe impairment of memory, usually as a result of accident or disease. Loss of memories that formed prior to an event (such as surgery or trauma)—called **retrograde amnesia** (from the Latin *retro-*, "backward," and *gradi*, "to go")—is not uncommon. After an accident that damages the brain, people often have retrograde amnesia with regard to events that happened a few hours or days before the accident, or even a year. But despite dramatic depictions you may see on TV, it is unlikely that longer-term (or "complete") retrograde memory loss has ever occurred.

Patient H.M.—Henry Molaison, whom we met at the start of the chapter (**FIGURE 17.1**)—suffered from a far more unusual symptom: his apparent inability to retain *new* material for more than a brief period. The inability to form new memories *after* an event is called **anterograde amnesia** (the Latin *antero-* means "forward"). In Henry's case, most old memories remained intact, but he had difficulty recollecting any events after his surgery.

Over the very short term, Henry's memory was normal. If given a series of six or seven digits, he could immediately repeat the list back without error. But if he was given a list of words to study and then tested on them after other tasks had intervened, he could not repeat the list or even recall that there *was* a list. So Henry's case provided clear evidence that *short-term memory* differs from *long-term memory*—a distinction long recognized by biological psychologists on behavioral grounds (W. James, 1890) and which we will discuss in more depth later.

Henry's surgery removed the amygdala, most of the hippocampus, and some surrounding cortex from both temporal lobes (**FIGURE 17.2**). The memory deficit seemed to be caused by loss of the *medial temporal lobe*, including the hippocampus, because other surgical patients who had received the same type of damage to the amygdala, but less damage to the hippocampus, did not exhibit comparable memory impairment. But to the puzzlement of researchers, it seemed that bilateral hippocampal lesions in laboratory animals did not produce comparable memory deficits (Isaacson, 1972; Mumby, 2001). What might account for this apparent discrepancy between humans and lab animals?

An interesting finding about Henry's memory deficit offered a clue. When Henry was given a mirror-tracing task (**FIGURE 17.3A**), he improved considerably over ten trials (B. Milner, 1965). The next day the test was presented again. When asked if he recognized the task, Henry said no, yet his performance was better than at the start of the first day (**FIGURE 17.3B**). Over 3 successive days, Henry never recognized the task as something he had seen before, but his improved tracings showed evidence of memory, in the form of motor skill. Of course, we can't ask lab animals if they recognize a maze, so if an animal with comparable hippocampal damage shows

---

learning The process of acquiring new and relatively enduring information, behavior patterns, or abilities, characterized by modifications of behavior as a result of practice, study, or experience.

memory 1. The ability to retain information, based on the mental process of learning or encoding, retention across some interval of time, and retrieval or reactivation of the memory. 2. The specific information that is stored in the brain.

amnesia Severe impairment of memory.

retrograde amnesia Difficulty in retrieving memories formed before the onset of amnesia.

patient H.M. A person who, because of damage to medial temporal lobe structures, was unable to encode new declarative memories. Upon his death we learned his name was Henry Molaison.

anterograde amnesia The inability to form new memories beginning with the onset of a disorder.

declarative memory A memory that can be stated or described.

17.1 PATIENT H.M. Henry Molaison as a young man. (Courtesy of Dr. Suzanne Corkin.)

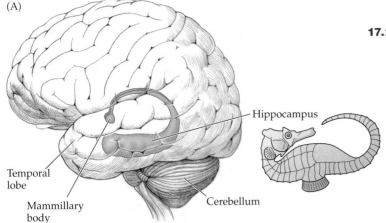

(A)

Hippocampus

Temporal lobe

Mammillary body

Cerebellum

17.2 BRAIN REGIONS CRUCIAL FOR MEMORY FORMATION
(A) The hippocampus, whose name means "sea horse" in Latin, was named for its resemblance to that animal. (B) MRI scans of a healthy person (left) and Henry (right) show that Henry's hippocampus (H) and entorhinal cortex (EC) were extensively damaged, bilaterally. Henry had a small amount of posterior hippocampus left, but the parahippocampal cortex (PH) was totally gone, and the cerebellum (Cer) was dramatically shrunken. (From Corkin et al., 1997.)

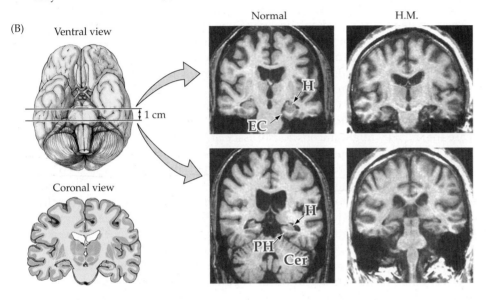

(B)

Ventral view

1 cm

Coronal view

Normal   H.M.

improvement on a task, we might prematurely conclude that the animal has normal memory.

So, was Henry's deficit simply an inability to learn verbal material? Probably not. First, people with brain damage like Henry's have difficulty reproducing or recognizing pictures and spatial designs that are not recalled in verbal terms. Second, although such individuals have difficulty with the specific content of verbal material, they can learn some kinds of information *about* verbal material (N. J. Cohen and Squire, 1980). For example, people with several kinds of amnesia can learn the *skill* of reading mirror-reversed text but show impaired learning of specific words (**FIGURE 17.4**).

Subsequent research confirmed that the important distinction is not between motor and verbal performances, but between two general categories of memory:

1. **Declarative memory** is what we usually think of as memory: facts and information acquired through learning. It is memory we are aware of accessing, which we can *declare* to others. This is the type of memory so profoundly impaired by Henry's surgery. Tests of declarative memory take the form

17.3 HENRY'S PERFORMANCE ON A MIRROR-TRACING TASK
(A) Henry was given this mirror-tracing task to test motor skill.
(B) His performance on this task progressively improved over 3 successive days, demonstrating a type of long-term memory. (After B. Milner, 1965.)

(A) The mirror-tracing task

(B) Performance of H.M. on mirror-tracing task

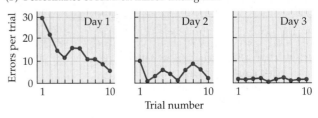

17.4 READING MIRROR-REVERSED TEXT People with amnesia like Henry's can learn to read mirror-reversed text well, even though they don't remember practicing this skill. This demonstrates that their problem is not verbal, but rather an inability to form declarative memories.

nondeclarative memory Also called procedural memory. A memory that is shown by performance rather than by conscious recollection.

delayed non-matching-to-sample task A test in which, on each trial, the participant must select the stimulus that they have not seen previously.

of requests for specific information that has been learned previously, such as a story or word list. It is the type of memory we use to answer "what" questions—and thus is difficult to test in animals.

2. **Nondeclarative memory**, or *procedural memory*—that is, memory about perceptual or motor procedures—is shown by *performance* rather than by conscious recollection. Examples of procedural memory include learning the mirror-tracing task at which Henry excelled, and the skill of mirror reading, along with more familiar skills such as riding a bicycle or juggling: things that you learn by *doing*. It is the type of memory we use for "how" problems, and is often (but not always) nonverbal. **FIGURE 17.5** illustrates this basic division of types of memory.

Medial temporal lobe structures are crucial for declarative memory

Publication of Henry Molaison's case prompted an intensive effort to develop methods for systematically studying declarative memory in monkeys and other lab animals. To get around the inability of lab animals to verbally report their memories, the **delayed non-matching-to-sample task** (**FIGURE 17.6**)—a test of *object recognition memory*—was developed. In this task, monkeys must identify which of two objects was *not* seen previously, with delays ranging from 8 seconds to 2 minutes (Spiegler and Mishkin, 1981). The important feature of this procedure is that the animal does *not* reach for the item that previously had a treat under it, because in that case the monkey might unconsciously associate reward with that object even if the animal had no conscious recollection of it. Instead, the monkey declares that it remembers the object by reaching for the *other* object, the one that was not associated with a reward previously. Monkeys with extensive damage to the medial temporal lobe, and thus similar to Henry, are severely impaired on this task, especially with the longer delays. But which specific temporal lobe structures are most important?

Selective removal of specific parts of the medial temporal lobes of monkeys revealed that the amygdala—one of the structures removed in Henry's surgery—was not crucial for performance on tests of declarative memory. However, removal of the adjacent hippocampus significantly impaired performance on these tests and, as shown in **FIGURE 17.7**, the deficit was even more pronounced when the hippocampal damage was paired with lesions of the nearby entorhinal and parahippocampal cortex, and much worse when lesions of perirhinal cortex were added (Zola-Morgan et al., 1994). Humans similarly show larger impairments when both the hippocampus and medial temporal cortex are damaged (Rempel-Clower et al., 1996; Zola-Morgan and Squire, 1986), confirming that Henry's symptoms resulted from the loss of the medial temporal lobe on both sides of the brain.

One modern formulation of declarative memory for facts and events takes the view that two interwoven processes are involved: *recollection* of the item in the specific context in which it was presented, and additionally the sense of *familiarity* with the features of the recalled item (Eichenbaum et al., 2007). Experimental evidence suggests that the two processes are served by differing components of the medial temporal lobe system. In this model, perirhinal cortex (see Figure 17.7A) is thought to be responsible for the sense of familiarity in memory, whereas recollection of

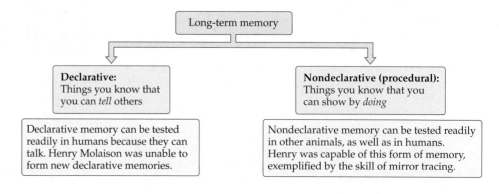

17.5 TWO MAIN KINDS OF MEMORY: DECLARATIVE AND NONDECLARATIVE

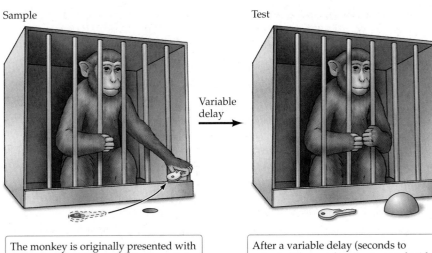

| The monkey is originally presented with a sample object. When he displaces it, he finds a pellet of food beneath. | After a variable delay (seconds to minutes) the monkey is presented with the original object and another object. | Over a series of trials with different pairs of objects, the monkey learns that food is present under the object that differs from the sample. |

17.6 THE DELAYED NON-MATCHING-TO-SAMPLE TASK

the item is the function of the hippocampus (Lech and Suchan, 2013; Suzuki and Naya, 2014). Processing of contextual aspects of memory (including spatial cognition, which we will discuss in more detail a little later) appears to depend especially on the parahippocampal cortex (Aminoff et al., 2013; Diana et al., 2013). In general, the performance of experimental animals suggests that the hippocampus acts as the final stage of convergence for adjacent regions of cortex (Squire et al., 2007; Zola et al., 2000), resulting in storage of declarative memories in the cortex. In keeping with this schema, people with specific hippocampal damage appear to have difficulties with recollection, while familiarity-based aspects of memory are spared (Addante et

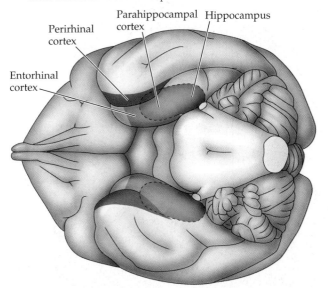

(A) Ventral view of monkey brain showing areas of different medial temporal lesions

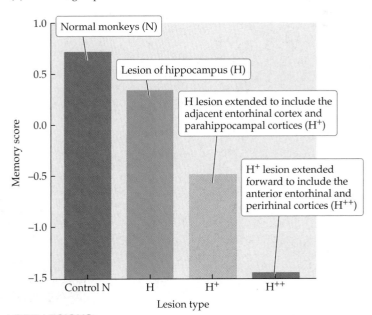

(B) Scores of groups with different lesions

Normal monkeys (N)

Lesion of hippocampus (H)

H lesion extended to include the adjacent entorhinal cortex and parahippocampal cortices (H⁺)

H⁺ lesion extended forward to include the anterior entorhinal and perirhinal cortices (H⁺⁺)

17.7 MEMORY PERFORMANCE AFTER MEDIAL TEMPORAL LOBE LESIONS
(A) In this ventral view of a monkey brain, the positions of the hippocampus, entorhinal cortex, perirhinal cortex, and parahippocampal cortex are shown in different colors. (B) Different bilateral lesions of the medial temporal lobe yielded different results in tests of memory. (After Squire and Zola-Morgan, 1991.)

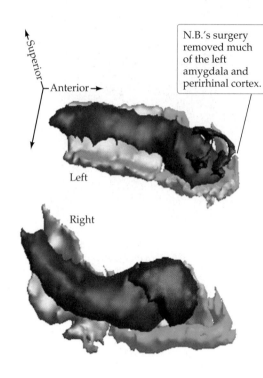

N.B.'s surgery removed much of the left amygdala and perirhinal cortex.

Left

Right

patient N.A. A person who is unable to encode new declarative memories, because of damage to the dorsal thalamus and the mammillary bodies.

mammillary body One of a pair of nuclei at the base of the brain, that connect to the hippocampus and play a role in memory.

17.8 IMPAIRED FAMILIARITY AFTER SURGERY Patient N.B. received surgical lesions in the left medial temporal lobe that selectively removed much of the amygdala (red in this reconstruction of the medial temporal lobes) and perirhinal cortex (green) while completely sparing the hippocampus (blue). Following surgery, N.B. experienced reduced feelings of familiarity in memory tests although recollection of details was unimpaired, supporting a two-process model of medial temporal lobe function. (From Bowles et al., 2007.)

al., 2012; Bowles et al., 2010). Conversely, people with surgical lesions that include the perirhinal cortex but not the hippocampus (**FIGURE 17.8**) experience impaired familiarity with stimuli despite preserved recollection (Bowles et al., 2007).

Damage to the medial diencephalon can also cause amnesia

In 1960, a young man now known to neuroscientists as **patient N.A.** suffered a bizarre accident in which a miniature sword injured his brain after entering through his nostril. He eventually recovered in most respects except that, like Henry Molaison, he was left with a profound anterograde amnesia, primarily for verbal material (Squire and Moore, 1979). He can give little information about events since his accident, although his memory for earlier events is near normal (Kaushall et al., 1981).

Studying N.A. with MRI (**FIGURE 17.9**) showed damage to several components of the diencephalon (thalamus and hypothalamus) that have connections to the hippocampus, especially the dorsomedial thalamus, and to both **mammillary bodies** (see Figure 17.2A), as well as probable damage to the mammillothalamic tract (Squire et al., 1989). Like Henry Molaison, N.A. shows normal short-term memory but is impaired in forming declarative (but not nondeclarative/procedural) long-term memories. The similarity in symptoms suggests that the medial temporal region damaged in Henry's brain and the midline diencephalic region damaged in N.A.

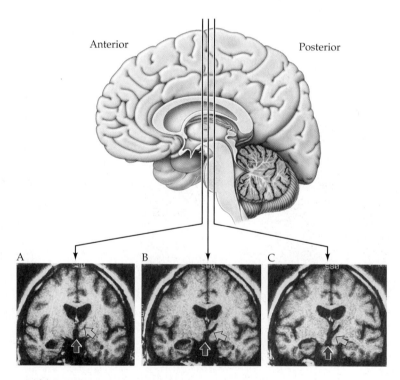

17.9 THE BRAIN DAMAGE IN PATIENT N.A. Successive MRI scans show a prominent diencephalic lesion on the left side of the brain (yellow arrows), as well as a lesion on the floor of the third ventricle (red arrows). The mammillary bodies should be present in B and C, but they are totally absent. (From Squire et al., 1989; MRI scans courtesy of Dr. Larry Squire.)

are normally parts of a larger memory system. Studies of people with surgical lesions of the fornix, which interconnects the hippocampus and mammillary bodies, confirm and extend this idea, as such individuals experience selective difficulty forming new declarative memories (Tsivilis et al., 2008).

That idea is reinforced by studies of people with **Korsakoff's syndrome**—named for its nineteenth-century discoverer, Russian neurologist Sergei Korsakoff—who also have anterograde amnesia for declarative memories. People with Korsakoff's syndrome frequently deny that anything is wrong with them, and they often **confabulate**—that is, fill a gap in memory with a falsification that they seem to accept as true. Temporal lobe structures, including the hippocampus, are typically normal in people with Korsakoff's syndrome (Mair et al., 1979). But their brains show shrunken, diseased mammillary bodies, as well as some damage in the dorsomedial thalamus (**FIGURE 17.10**). This damage is similar to that seen in N.A. The mammillary bodies may serve as a processing system connecting the medial temporal lobes (which were removed from Henry Molaison) to the thalamus via the mammillothalamic tract and, from there, to other cortical sites (Vann and Nelson, 2015). Damage to the basal frontal cortex, also found in people suffering from Korsakoff's syndrome, probably causes the denial and confabulation that differentiates them from other people who have amnesia, such as Henry.

The main cause of Korsakoff's syndrome is lack of the vitamin thiamine (or B_1). Alcoholics who obtain most of their calories from alcohol and neglect their diet often exhibit this deficiency. Treating them with thiamine can prevent further deterioration of memory functions but will not reverse the damage already done. If alcoholic beverages were supplemented with thiamine, then many new cases of Korsakoff's syndrome could be prevented (Price et al., 1987).

These studies make it clear that a brain circuit that includes the hippocampus, the mammillary bodies, and the dorsomedial thalamus is needed to *form* new declarative memories. But these case studies also clearly show that established declarative memories, formed before brain damage, are not *stored* in these structures. If the memories had been stored there, they would have been lost when the structures were damaged. So where are memories stored? Mathematical models based on the known connectivity patterns of cortical neurons indicate that the cortex is optimized for information storage (Brunel, 2016), and as we'll see next, clinical observations confirm that the cortex serves as a repository for memories.

The cortex is essential for long-term storage of memories

One striking case study indicates that the cortex is crucial for *storing* memories once they are formed, and also illustrates an important distinction between two subtypes of declarative memory. Profiled in numerous scientific reports as **patient K.C.**, Kent Cochran sustained serious brain damage in a motorcycle accident at age 30. For more than 30 years, from his accident until the day he died in 2014 at age 62, Kent was unable to retrieve any personal memory of his past, although his general knowledge remained good. He conversed easily and played a good game of chess (**FIGURE 17.11**), but he could not remember where he learned to play chess or who taught him the game. Detailed autobiographical declarative memory of this sort is known as **episodic memory**: you show episodic memory when you recall a specific episode in your life or relate an

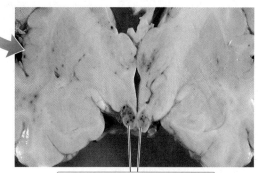

17.10 BRAIN DAMAGE IN PATIENTS WITH KORSAKOFF'S SYNDROME (Image courtesy of Dr. D. P. Agamanolis.)

These oval-shaped mammillary bodies are darkened as a result of bleeding and cell death.

Korsakoff's syndrome A memory disorder, related to a thiamine deficiency, that is generally associated with chronic alcoholism.

confabulate To fill in a gap in memory with a falsification. It often occurs in Korsakoff's syndrome.

patient K.C. A person who sustained damage to the cortex that rendered him unable to form and retrieve new episodic memories, especially autobiographical memories. Upon his death we learned that his name was Kent Cochran.

episodic memory Memory of a particular incident or a particular time and place.

17.11 PATIENT K.C. Kent Cochran lost the ability to form or retrieve episodic memories because of brain damage sustained in a motorcycle accident. (From Tulving, 2002.)

semantic memory Generalized memory—for instance, knowing the meaning of a word without knowing where or when you learned that word.

skill learning Learning to perform a task that requires motor coordination.

priming Also called repetition priming. The phenomenon by which exposure to a stimulus facilitates subsequent responses to the same or a similar stimulus.

associative learning A type of learning in which an association is formed between two stimuli or between a stimulus and a response; includes both classical and operant conditioning.

operant conditioning Also called instrumental conditioning. A form of associative learning in which the likelihood that an act (instrumental response) will be performed depends on the consequences (reinforcing stimuli) that follow it.

classical conditioning Also called Pavlovian conditioning. A type of associative learning in which an originally neutral (conditioned) stimulus acquires the power to elicit the response normally elicited by another (unconditioned) stimulus after the two stimuli are paired. A response elicited by the unconditioned stimulus (US) is called an unconditioned response (UR); a response elicited by the conditioned stimulus (CS) alone is called a conditioned response (CR).

event to a particular time and place. In contrast, **semantic memory** is generalized declarative memory, such as knowing the meaning of a word without knowing where or when you learned that word (Tulving, 1972). If care was taken to space out the trials to prevent interference among items, K.C. could acquire new *semantic* knowledge (Tulving et al., 1991), and like the lead character in the film *Memento*, he understood that time passes, and that he had a past, and that he also had a future to plan for (Craver et al., 2014). But even with careful training, K.C. could not acquire new *episodic* knowledge.

Brain scans of K.C. revealed extensive damage to the cerebral cortex and severe shrinkage of the hippocampus and nearby parahippocampal cortex (Rosenbaum et al., 2005). As with Henry, the bilateral hippocampal damage probably accounts for K.C.'s anterograde declarative amnesia. But that damage cannot account for the selective loss of nearly his entire autobiographical memory (i.e., retrograde episodic amnesia), because other people with damage restricted to the medial temporal lobes lack this symptom. K.C.'s inability to recall any autobiographical details of his life, even memories from years before his accident, may instead be a consequence of the extensive damage to his frontal and parietal cortex (Tulving, 1989).

There are a few rare individuals who have incredibly extensive episodic memories, who can tell you exactly what they had for breakfast on June 20, 2002, or any other date (Price, 2008). A group of 11 such people with extreme autobiographical memory were found to have larger temporal lobes, including a larger parahippocampal gyrus, than controls (LePort et al., 2012). We don't know whether these people were born with larger temporal lobes, and so had great autobiographical memory, or developed great autobiographical memory, which caused their temporal lobes to enlarge.

Different Forms of Nondeclarative Memory Involve Different Brain Regions

We have seen that there are two different kinds of declarative memory: semantic and episodic. Likewise, there are several forms of nondeclarative memory, and as we'll see, these depend on different neural systems.

Specific functions depend on different forms of nondeclarative memory

Unlike declarative memory, which we use to store the factual knowledge of ourselves and the world that we use in conversation and in our innermost thoughts, nondeclarative memories shape our abilities and responses to the world around us in ways that are difficult to express, but no less crucial for survival. Indeed, virtually every species of the animal kingdom seems capable of some sort of nondeclarative memory, even if very simple, indicating that it's an ancient evolutionary adaptation.

SKILL MEMORY   In **skill learning**, participants learn how to perform a challenging task by practicing it over and over again. Experimental tests like the mirror-tracing task performed by Henry Molaison (see Figure 17.3) or learning to read mirror-reversed text (see Figure 17.4) are examples of skill learning. So too are the everyday skills we acquire, like learning to ride a bike or to juggle (well, okay, maybe juggling isn't an "everyday" skill, but you get the idea).

Imaging studies have investigated learning and memory for different skill categories, especially *sensorimotor skills* (e.g., mirror tracing), *perceptual skills* (e.g., learning to read mirror-reversed text), and *cognitive skills* (e.g., puzzles like the Towers of Hanoi—which you can play on the website—that involve planning and problem solving). All three kinds of skill learning are impaired in people with damage to the basal ganglia; damage to other brain regions, especially the motor cortex and cerebellum, also affects aspects of some skills.

Neuroimaging studies in healthy people confirm that the basal ganglia, cerebellum, and motor cortex are important for sensorimotor skill learning (Grafton et al., 1992). For example, learning specific sequences of finger movements is associated with selective activation of motor cortex and the basal ganglia (Doyon et al., 1996; Hazeltine et al., 1997), with the cerebellum possibly providing error correction during learning (Flament et al., 1996). Often the activations shift among brain regions as performance changes during the course of learning, so learning appears to involve a complex set of interacting neural networks.

PRIMING A change in the processing of a stimulus, usually a word or a picture, as a result of prior exposure to the same stimulus or related stimuli is referred to as **priming** (or *repetition priming*). For example, if a person is shown the word *stamp* in a list and later is asked to complete the word stem *STA-*, he or she is more likely to reply "stamp" than is a person who was not exposed to that word. Priming does not require declarative memory of the stimulus—Henry Molaison and other people with amnesia have shown priming for words they don't remember seeing previously. In contrast to skill learning, researchers have found that priming is not impaired by damage to the basal ganglia.

In functional-imaging studies, perceptual priming (priming based on the visual *form* of words) has been related to *reduced* activity in bilateral occipitotemporal cortex (Schacter et al., 1996), presumably because the priming makes the task easier. Conceptual priming (priming based on word *meaning*) was associated with reduced activation of the left frontal cortex (Blaxton et al., 1996; Gabrieli et al., 1996; A. D. Wagner et al., 1997). And although it is primarily associated with declarative memory, evidence is mounting that the components of the medial temporal lobe memory system—notably the perirhinal cortex (Wang et al., 2010, 2014) and hippocampus (Addante, 2015)—are also involved in some forms of nondeclarative memory, including priming.

ASSOCIATIVE LEARNING Learning that involves relations between events—for example, between two or more stimuli, between a stimulus and a response, or between an action and its consequence—is called **associative learning**. In one form of associative learning, called **operant conditioning** (also called *instrumental conditioning*), an association is formed between the individual's behavior and the consequence(s) of that behavior. For example, lab animals can easily learn to press a lever to gain the reward of a tasty food pellet, using an apparatus like the one in **FIGURE 17.12**, often called a *Skinner box* after its famous originator, B. F. Skinner.

Many people are also familiar with another form of associative learning, termed **classical conditioning** (or *Pavlovian conditioning*), in which an initially neutral stimulus comes to *predict* an event. At the end of the nineteenth century, Ivan Pavlov (1849–1936) found that a dog would salivate when presented with an auditory or visual stimulus if the stimulus came to predict the presentation of food. So, as illustrated in **FIGURE 17.13**, repeatedly ringing a bell before putting meat powder in a dog's mouth will eventually cause the dog to start salivating when it hears the bell

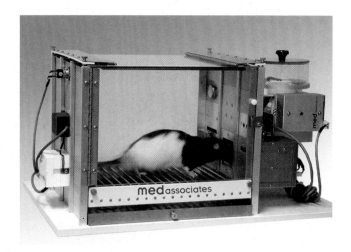

17.12 OPERANT CONDITIONING Animals in a Skinner box can learn to press a lever to gain food pellets or to avoid footshock, a form of associative learning called *operant* (or *instrumental*) *conditioning*.

17.13 CLASSICAL CONDITIONING In this famous experiment, by pairing food with the sound of a bell, Ivan Pavlov conditioned animals to eventually salivate to the sound of the bell alone.

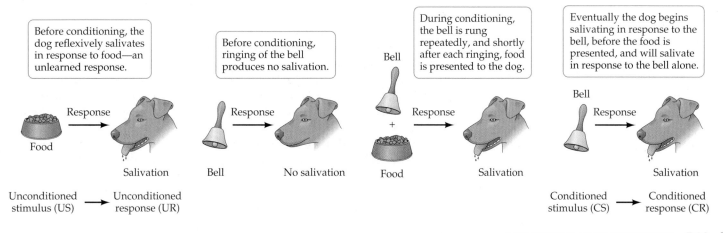

Before conditioning, the dog reflexively salivates in response to food—an unlearned response.

Food → Response → Salivation

Unconditioned stimulus (US) → Unconditioned response (UR)

Before conditioning, ringing of the bell produces no salivation.

Bell → Response → No salivation

During conditioning, the bell is rung repeatedly, and shortly after each ringing, food is presented to the dog.

Bell + Food → Response → Salivation

Eventually the dog begins salivating in response to the bell, before the food is presented, and will salivate in response to the bell alone.

Bell → Response → Salivation

Conditioned stimulus (CS) → Conditioned response (CR)

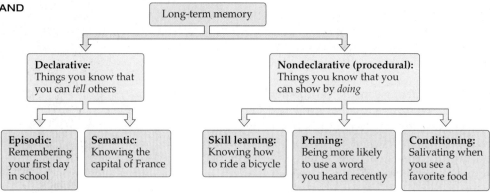

alone. In this case the meat powder in the mouth is the *unconditioned stimulus* (*US*), which already evokes an *unconditioned response* (*UR*; salivation in the example). The sound of the bell is the *conditioned stimulus* (*CS*), and the learned response to the CS alone (salivation in response to the bell) is called the *conditioned response* (*CR*).

Experimental evidence in lab animals shows that cerebellar circuits are crucial for simple eye-blink conditioning, in which a tone or other stimulus is associated with eye blinking in response to a puff of air. A PET study of human eye-blink conditioning (Logan and Grafton, 1995) found that in the course of conditioning, there was a progressive increase in activity in several regions of the brain, including not only the cerebellum, but also the hippocampus, the ventral striatum, and regions of the cerebral cortex. But activity in these other areas may not be *essential* for eye-blink conditioning in the way that the cerebellum is. For example, people with hippocampal lesions can acquire the conditioned eye-blink response, but people with unilateral cerebellar damage can acquire a conditioned eye-blink response only on the side where the cerebellum is intact (Papka et al., 1994). We'll look more closely at neural mechanisms of eye-blink conditioning later in the chapter, as well as the cellular and molecular underpinnings of a very simple type of memory—*nonassociative learning*—that is formed in basic neural circuits of even the simplest animals.

The taxonomy of memory we presented in Figure 17.5 is updated in **FIGURE 17.14**, where we have added the subtypes of declarative and nondeclarative memory described in this section, along with some examples.

Medial temporal mechanisms keep track of positions in spatial, temporal, and social networks

The caricature of the white-coated scientist watching rats run in mazes, a staple of cartoonists to this day, has its origins in the intensive memory research of the early twentieth century. The early work indicated that rats and other animals don't just learn a series of turns but instead form a **cognitive map** (an understanding of the *relative* spatial organization of objects and information) in order to solve a maze (Tolman, 1949). Animals apparently learn at least some of these details of their spatial environment simply by moving through it, a phenomenon that was termed *latent learning* (Tolman and Honzik, 1930).

We now know that, in parallel with its role in other types of declarative memory, the hippocampus is a crucial neural participant in spatial learning. Within the rat hippocampus are found many neurons that selectively encode spatial location (Leutgeb et al., 2005; O'Keefe and Dostrovsky, 1971). These **place cells** become active when the animal is in—or moving toward—a particular location (Pastalkova et al., 2008) (**FIGURE 17.15**). If the animal is placed in a new environment, its place cell activity indicates that the hippocampus remaps to the new locations (Moita et al., 2004). Lesions of this part of the hippocampus severely impair spatial learning in rats (McNaughton et al., 1996) and humans (Bartsch et al., 2010). The Nobel Prize in Physiology or Medicine for 2014 was awarded to John O'Keefe and the wife-and-husband team of May-Britt and Edvard Moser for their work on understanding hip-

cognitive map   A mental representation of a spatial relationship.

place cell   A neuron within the hippocampus that selectively fires when the animal is in a particular location.

pocampal place cells. Two types of cells discovered in nearby entorhinal cortex help the animal to learn the local spatial environment. **Grid cells** fire selectively when the animal crosses the intersection points of an abstract grid map of the local environment, acting like an innate system of latitude and longitude (Hafting et al., 2005). Cells that fire in the same pattern have also been discovered in humans (J. Jacobs et al., 2013). Arrival at the *perimeter* of the local spatial map is signaled by the activation of entorhinal **border cells** (Solstad et al., 2008).

Evidence is mounting that beyond its roles in forming declarative memories and keeping track of important locations in space, the hippocampus helps us to organize networks of data across multiple domains. For example, hippocampal function has been linked to mapping our *social* space—the web of social connections to other people that we navigate daily in our work and personal lives (Alexander et al., 2016; Tavares et al., 2015). Likewise, researchers have recently discovered hippocampal cells that appear to map locations in *time*, another important aspect of developing coherent memories (Eichenbaum, 2014; Schiller et al., 2015). In other words, the hippocampus helps organize the *what*, *where*, *when*, and *with whom* of memory.

SPATIAL MEMORY AND THE EVOLUTION OF HIPPOCAMPAL SIZE Careful comparisons of natural behavior and brain anatomy have revealed that for many species, their manner of making a living has left an imprint on the hippocampus. For example, not only does the monkey hippocampus contain place cells (Rolls and O'Mara, 1995), it also features *spatial view cells* that respond to the part of the environment that the monkey is *looking at*, perhaps reflecting the importance of vision for primates.

As another example, species of birds that hide caches of food in spatially scattered locations have larger hippocampi than noncaching species, even when the comparison species are very close relatives that have otherwise similar lifestyles (Krebs et al., 1989; Sherry, 1992; Sherry et al., 1989) (see Figure 6.6). Lesions of the hippocampus impair the ability of these birds to store and retrieve caches of food (Sherry and Vaccarino, 1989). Homing pigeons also have enlarged hippocampi relative to other varieties of pigeons, presumably serving the spatial demands of their prodigious navigational abilities (Rehkamper et al., 1988). A relationship between spatial cognition and hippocampal size is evident in mammals too. Just as with the food-caching birds, Merriam's kangaroo rat, which stashes food in scattered locations, has a significantly larger hippocampus than its noncaching cousin, the bannertail kangaroo rat (L. F. Jacobs and Spencer, 1994). (For additional fascinating examples of the relation between hippocampal volume and spatial behavior, see **A Step Further: Spatial Behavior and Hippocampal Structure in Humans and Other Species** on the website.)

Successive Processes Capture, Store, and Retrieve Information in the Brain

The span of time that a piece of information will be retained in the brain varies. Evidence suggests that there are as many as four different duration categories for memory. The briefest memories are held in **sensory buffers** (for visual stimuli, they are sometimes called *iconic memories*); an example is the fleeting impression of a glimpsed scene that vanishes from memory seconds later. These brief memories are thought to be residual sensory neural activity (**FIGURE 17.16**).

Somewhat more durable than the sensory buffers are **short-term memories** (**STMs**). If you look up a phone number and keep it in mind (perhaps through rehearsal) just long enough to make the phone call, you are using STM. In the absence

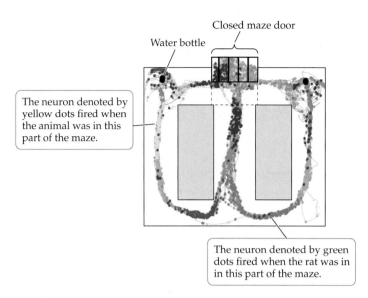

Water bottle
Closed maze door

The neuron denoted by yellow dots fired when the animal was in this part of the maze.

The neuron denoted by green dots fired when the rat was in in this part of the maze.

17.15 HIPPOCAMPAL PLACE CELLS In this simple maze, viewed from above, each colored dot represents the location of the rat when one specific place cell fired. Thus, all of the yellow dots represent one neuron, all of the green dots another neuron, and so on. As the figure plainly shows, place cells accurately encode a specific location in space. (Courtesy of Dr. Eva Pastalkova.)

grid cell A neuron that selectively fires when an animal crosses the intersection points of an abstract grid map of the local environment.

border cell A neuron that selectively fires when an animal arrives at the perimeter of a local spatial cognitive map.

sensory buffer An element of the type of memory that stores the sensory impression of a scene.

short-term memory (STM) A form of memory that usually lasts only for seconds, or as long as rehearsal continues, especially while being used during performance of a task.

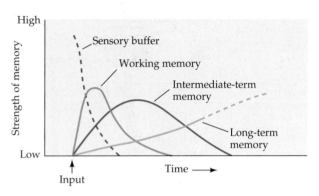

17.16 TEMPORAL STAGES OF MEMORY FORMATION

of rehearsal, STMs last only about 30 seconds (J. Brown, 1958; L. R. Peterson and Peterson, 1959). With rehearsal, you may be able to retain an STM until you turn to a new task a few minutes later, but when the STM is gone, it's gone for good. Many researchers now refer to this form of memory as **working memory**, in recognition of the way we use it; this is how we hold information in mind while we are working with it to solve a problem or are otherwise actively manipulating the information. One influential model (Baddeley, 2003) subdivides working memory into three complementary components:

1. A *phonological loop* that contains auditory information (such as speech); this is what you use to rehearse that phone number.

2. A so-called *visuospatial sketch pad* that holds visual impressions of stimuli; you use this to imagine the route back to your car in a parking building.

3. An *episodic buffer* that contains more-integrated information, spanning across sensory modalities, sort of like movie clips.

According to this model, the flow of information into and out of working memory is supervised by a fourth module, an *executive control*, which we'll discuss in Chapter 18.

Some memories last only a little longer than short-term memories. Chances are good that you can remember what you had for lunch today or yesterday, but not most of your lunches last week. You may recall today's weather forecast, but not that of a few days ago. These are examples of what some memory researchers identify as **intermediate-term memory**—that is, a memory that outlasts what we typically consider to be STM but is far from being permanent (M. R. Rosenzweig et al., 1993).

A variety of brain regions are involved in different attributes of working memory

Because they span verbal and nonverbal material, in multiple sensory modalities, for multiple purposes, working memories tend to have unique features or attributes. So, for example, an individual memory may include a mix of information about space, time, sensory perception, response, and/or emotional factors. Researchers have attempted to devise memory tasks that selectively tap some of these attributes of memory, in order to assess the relative contributions of different regions of the brain.

FIGURE 17.17 presents some examples of some well-known tests that researchers use to probe working memory (Kesner, 1998; Kesner et al., 1993). For testing *spatial* location memory, the eight-arm radial maze is commonly used (**FIGURE 17.17A**). To solve this task correctly and receive a food reward, rats must recognize and enter an arm of the maze that they went down shortly beforehand. Rats were tested following surgical lesions of the hippocampus, the caudate nucleus, or the extrastriate cortex (visual cortex outside the primary visual area). Only the animals with hippocampal lesions were impaired on this predominantly spatial task—a result that is consistent with the role of the hippocampus in spatial cognition that we discussed earlier. The test shown in **FIGURE 17.17B** was used to assess the memory of the same rats for their own *motor* behavior. Here the animal must use working memory to remember whether it made a left or right turn a few moments previously, and it receives a food reward only if it makes a turn in the same direction on a follow-up trial. Only the animals with lesions of the caudate nucleus were significantly impaired on this task. Finally, in the test depicted in **FIGURE 17.17C**, the rats were required to hold in working memory the *sensory* attributes of presented stimuli, identifying the novel stimulus in each pair of stimuli presented. Here, only the rats with extrastriate lesions were significantly impaired. This impressive lack of overlap between the symptoms of the different lesions nicely illustrates how memories involving different attributes are parceled out to diverse brain regions for storage.

working memory A type of short-term memory that holds information available for ready access during performance of a task.

intermediate-term memory (ITM) A form of memory that lasts longer than short-term memory, but not as long as long-term memory.

(A) Spatial-location recognition memory

In the study phase of each trial, the rat can choose any of the eight arms. In the test phase, doors block all but two arms: the arm entered in the study phase and one other. The rat obtains food only if it chooses the arm it entered in the study phase.

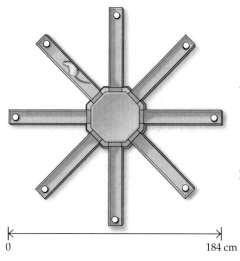

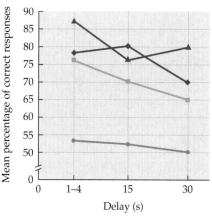

Brain region lesioned
- ● Hippocampus
- ■ Control
- ▲ Caudate nucleus
- ◆ Extrastriate visual cortex

Only rats with hippocampal lesions are impaired, relative to controls.

(B) Response recognition memory

In the first part of each trial, the rat is placed in the middle compartment on one side (2), and it finds food if it enters the compartment to either its right (1) or its left (3). In the second part of the trial, it is placed in the middle compartment on the other side (5), and it finds food only if it turns to the same side of its body as in the first part.

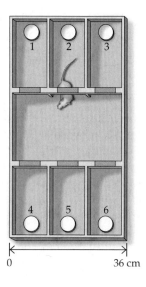

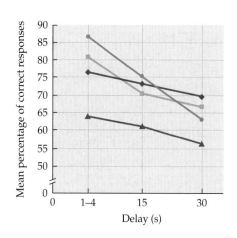

Brain region lesioned
- ● Hippocampus
- ■ Control
- ▲ Caudate nucleus
- ◆ Extrastriate visual cortex

Only rats with caudate nucleus lesions are impaired, relative to controls.

(C) Object recognition memory (non-matching-to-sample)

In the study phase of each trial, the rat obtains food by displacing a sample object over a small food well (top). In the test phase (bottom), the rat chooses between two objects and obtains food only if it chooses the object that does *not* match the sample.

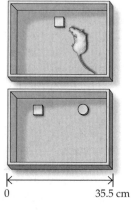

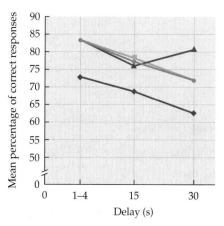

Brain region lesioned
- ● Hippocampus
- ■ Control
- ▲ Caudate nucleus
- ◆ Extrastriate visual cortex

Only rats with lesions of the extrastriate visual cortex are impaired, relative to controls.

17.17 TESTS OF SPECIFIC ATTRIBUTES OF MEMORY Brain lesion experiments testing spatial-location recognition (A), response recognition (B), and object recognition (C)—using the setups shown on the left—yielded the results shown on the right. (After Kesner et al., 1993.)

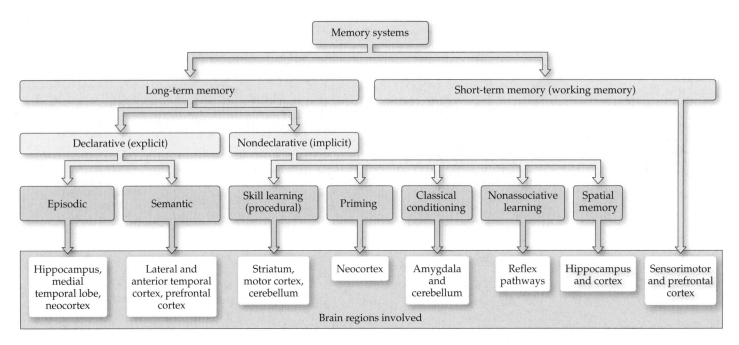

17.18 BRAIN REGIONS INVOLVED IN DIFFERENT KINDS OF LEARNING AND MEMORY (After Bartsch and Butler, 2013.)

It's perhaps not surprising that the brain regions that do the initial processing of the stimuli often also act as the memory buffers for holding the stimuli in working memory—visual information in visual cortex, motor information in motor areas, and so on. One additional common attribute of working memory is the passage of time—a delay between stimulus and response during which information must be held ready for further processing. Delayed-response tasks, which tap this aspect of working memory by varying the delay between the presentation and removal of a stimulus and the response, are especially associated with activity of the prefrontal cortex—particularly the dorsolateral parts—in humans and experimental animals (Funahashi, 2006; H. C. Leung et al., 2002, 2005).

Brain regions involved in learning and memory: A summary

FIGURE 17.18 provides a final update to the map of memory that we've been discussing. Several major conclusions should be apparent by now, especially (1) that many regions of the brain are involved in learning and memory; (2) that different forms of memory rely on at least partly different networks of brain mechanisms spanning several different regions of the brain; (3) that any one memory-related brain structure can be a part of the circuitry for several different forms of learning; and (4) that working memory relies on frontal and parietal cortical regions involved in sensory and motor processing. Next we'll discuss the stages by which memories, of any sort, can be preserved for a lifetime.

STM and LTM involve several different processes

As we have seen, really long-lasting declarative and nondeclarative memories—the address of your childhood home, how to ride a bike, your first kiss—are called **long-term memories** (**LTMs**), lasting from days to years. A substantial body of evidence indicates that STM and LTM, in particular, rely on different processes to store information. A classic demonstration involves learning lists of words or numbers. If you hear a series of ten words and then try to repeat them after a 30-second delay, you will probably do especially well with the earliest few words, which is termed a **primacy effect**; you will also do well with the last few words, termed a **recency effect**; and you will do less well with words in the middle of the list. **FIGURE 17.19**

long-term memory (LTM)
An enduring form of memory that lasts days, weeks, months, or years and has a very large capacity.

primacy effect The superior performance seen in a memory task for items at the start of a list; usually attributed to long-term memory.

recency effect The superior performance seen in a memory task for items at the end of a list; attributed to short-term memory.

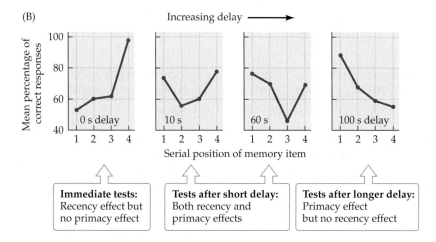

(A)

(B)

Increasing delay ⟶

Immediate tests: Recency effect but no primacy effect

Tests after short delay: Both recency and primacy effects

Tests after longer delay: Primacy effect but no recency effect

17.19 SERIAL POSITION CURVES FROM IMMEDIATE-RECALL EXPERIMENTS (A) These curves show the percentage of correct responses for immediate recall of a list of ten words. The people with amnesia (blue curve) performed as well on the most recent items (8–10) as the control group (red curve) did, but they performed significantly worse on earlier items. (B) Testing immediately after presenting the list prevents the primacy effect, while long delays between presentation and testing block the recency effect, as those last few items are no longer in short-term memory. (After Baddeley and Warrington, 1970.)

shows typical results from such an experiment: a U-shaped *serial position curve*. If the delay prior to recall is a few minutes instead of a few seconds, there is no recency effect; the recency effect is short-lived and thus attributed to working memory (or STM). The primacy effect, however, lasts longer and is usually attributed to LTM. Like humans, various experimental animals show U-shaped serial position functions (A. A. Wright et al., 1985)—a finding that confirms the basic distinction between working memory and LTM. People with amnesia caused by impairment of the hippocampus show a reduced primacy effect but retain the recency effect—their STM is intact. Pharmacological manipulations also reveal the different stages of memory, as reviewed in **A Step Further: Memories of Different Durations Form by Different Neurochemical Mechanisms** on the website.

So how much information do we hold in LTM? It is likely that LTM evolved not to give us a perfect record of our history, but rather to record important events that we can use to shape our future behavior in adaptive ways. It would be a waste of space to record every little detail of our lives, and indeed an important aspect of our memory system is the continual pruning of unimportant memories to preserve cognitive resources (Kuhl et al., 2007). Real-life cases of rare people with perfect recall show that an inability to forget details is confusing and exhausting (Luria, 1987; Parker et al., 2006). Nevertheless, we have the capability to retain enormous amounts of information. We take this capacity for granted and barely notice, for example, that knowledge of a language involves remembering at least 100,000 pieces of information. Most of us also store a huge assortment of information about faces,

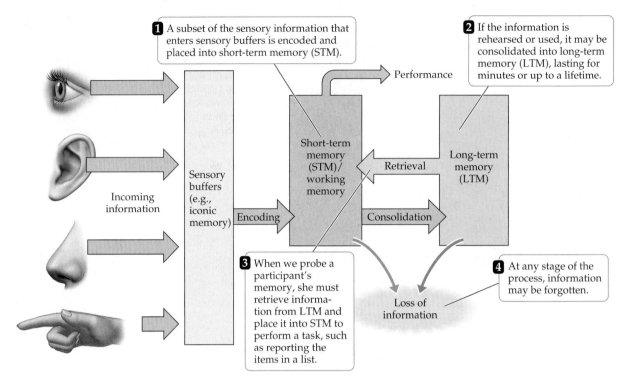

1 A subset of the sensory information that enters sensory buffers is encoded and placed into short-term memory (STM).

2 If the information is rehearsed or used, it may be consolidated into long-term memory (LTM), lasting for minutes or up to a lifetime.

3 When we probe a participant's memory, she must retrieve information from LTM and place it into STM to perform a task, such as reporting the items in a list.

4 At any stage of the process, information may be forgotten.

Incoming information

Sensory buffers (e.g., iconic memory)

Encoding

Short-term memory (STM)/ working memory

Performance

Retrieval

Consolidation

Long-term memory (LTM)

Loss of information

17.20 HYPOTHESIZED MEMORY PROCESSES: ENCODING, CONSOLIDATION, AND RETRIEVAL A problem at any stage can result in memory failure.

encoding A stage of memory formation in which the information entering sensory channels is passed into short-term memory.

tunes, odors, skills, stories, and so on. In one classic experiment, participants viewed long sequences of color photos of various scenes; several days later, the participants were shown pairs of images—in each case a new image plus one from the previous session—and were asked to identify the images seen previously. Astonishingly, the participants were highly accurate for series of up to 10,000 different stimuli (Standing, 1973), and researchers have since confirmed that LTM is so vast as to seem boundless (Brady et al., 2008), at least for some types of stimuli (Cunningham et al., 2015). Similar impressive feats of memory in our distant relatives, such as pigeons (Vaughan and Greene, 1984), illustrate that a great capacity for information storage is a general property of nervous systems across the animal kingdom.

The system for creating and retaining memories consists of three general stages (**FIGURE 17.20**):

1. *Encoding of raw information from sensory channels into short-term memory* Functional brain imaging indicates that while many brain areas participate in the initial processing of stimuli, fewer are associated with successful **encoding**, and these tend to reflect the specific characteristics of the stimuli. So, for example, encoding of the pictorial elements in photos involves greater activation of the right prefrontal cortex and the parahippocampal cortex in both hemispheres (Brewer et al., 1998). In the case of words (A. D. Wagner et al., 1998), the critical areas are the *left* prefrontal cortex and the *left* parahippocampal cortex. These results indicate that parahippocampal and prefrontal cortex are crucial for consolidation, and these mechanisms reflect the hemispheric specializations (left hemisphere for language and right hemisphere for spatial ability) that we'll discuss in Chapter 19. Although not depicted in the figure, this model suggests that the flow of information into and out of working memory is supervised by another part of the brain, a *central executive*, which we will discuss in more detail in Chapter 18.

2. *Consolidation of the volatile short-term memories into more-durable long-term memory* We know from cases like that of Henry Molaison (who could repeat STM items like word lists) that while the medial temporal lobe apparently is not

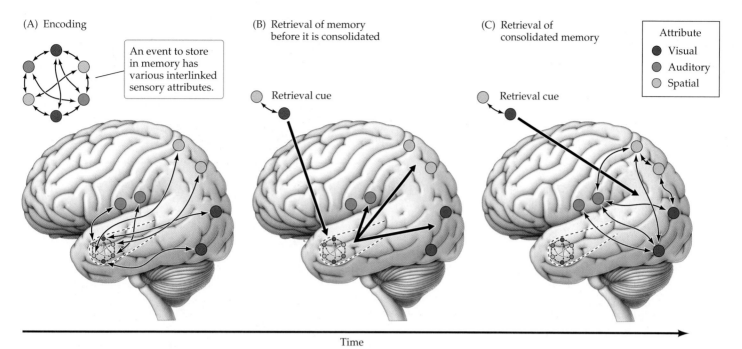

(A) Encoding

An event to store in memory has various interlinked sensory attributes.

(B) Retrieval of memory before it is consolidated

Retrieval cue

(C) Retrieval of consolidated memory

Retrieval cue

Attribute
● Visual
● Auditory
○ Spatial

Time

17.21 ENCODING, CONSOLIDATION, AND RETRIEVAL OF DECLARATIVE MEMORIES
(A) According to this model, medial temporal lobe processes distribute the various sensory attributes of an event, and linkages between them, in corresponding regions of cortex. (B) Before consolidation is complete, retrieval involves the hippocampus and other medial temporal structures. (C) After consolidation, retrieval may occur independent of the medial temporal system.

needed to encode sensory information into STM, it is crucial for **consolidation**, the conversion of memories from volatile STM into LTM, a different format that may endure for a lifetime (M. Lepage et al., 1998). And *where* are the new long-term memories—or more precisely their **engrams**, the physical changes that underlie LTM—actually being stored? Henry could recall events from before his surgery, and detailed studies in lab animals (Zola-Morgan and Squire, 1990) confirmed that LTM must be stored somewhere *other* than the hippocampus—namely, in the cortex. An important principle that has emerged from this area of research is that *permanent storage of information tends to be in the regions of the cortex where the information was first processed and held in short-term memory*. For example, visual cortex is crucial for visual object recognition memory (López-Aranda et al., 2009). After further processing that involves the medial temporal region, the permanent memory storage becomes independent and memories can be retrieved directly for use by other cognitive processes. This schema is illustrated in **FIGURE 17.21**.

3. *Retrieval of the stored information for use in future behavior* Information **retrieval** from long-term storage is under the direction of various cognitive processes, including attention, as we discuss in Chapter 18. Some evidence suggests that retrieval from LTM makes the memories temporarily plastic again and amenable to updating and strengthening, before they undergo *reconsolidation* and return to stable status (Eisenberg et al., 2003; Nader and Hardt, 2009). In fact, one of the best ways to improve learning is simply repeated retrieval (and thus, repeated reconsolidation) of the stored information (Karpicke and Blunt, 2011), as long as steps are taken to ensure the information being recalled is correct. But reconsolidation also has the potential to *distort* memories. For example, each time a memory trace is activated during recall, it is subject to changes and fluctuations, so with successive activations it may deviate more and more from its original form (Estes, 1997; Nader and Hardt, 2009). This may be why people sometimes "remember" events that never happened. We can create false memories by asking leading questions—"Did you see the broken headlight?" rather than "Was

consolidation A stage of memory formation in which information in short-term or intermediate-term memory is transferred to long-term memory.

engram The physical basis of a memory in the brain. Sometimes referred to as a memory trace on the assumption that it involves changes in a neural circuit rather than a single neuron.

retrieval A process in memory during which a stored memory is used by an organism.

Emotions and Memory

Almost everyone knows from personal experience that strong emotions can potently enhance memory formation and retrieval. Examples of memories enhanced in this way might include a strong association between special music and a first kiss, or uncomfortably vivid recollection of the morning of September 11, 2001. Interestingly, our memories about learning of such events, which seem so vivid and detailed, are not nearly as accurate as they seem (Hirst et al., 2009). Nevertheless, people who actually *experience* life-threatening events often develop **posttraumatic stress disorder** (**PTSD**), characterized as "reliving experiences such as intrusive thoughts, nightmares, dissociative flashbacks to elements of the original traumatic event, and ... preoccupation with that event" (Keane, 1998, p. 398) (see Chapter 16). For these people,

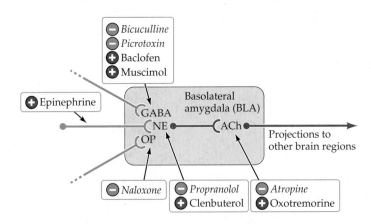

THE AMYGDALA AND MEMORY   The diagram shows sites of activity of drugs that affect different neuromodulator and neurotransmitter systems in the amygdala. *Antagonist/blocker*, blue; agonist/activator, red; ACh, acetylcholine; GABA, gamma-aminobutyric acid; NE, norepinephrine; OP, opioids. (After McGaugh, 2003.)

whether the details of their memories are accurate is irrelevant because their suffering is certainly real.

In animal models, stress and emotional arousal do enhance memory, and a suite of transmitters are involved, including the opioids, GABA (gamma-aminobutyric acid), and especially the adrenergic transmitters epinephrine and norepinephrine. Epi-

the headlight broken?"—or by providing misinformation via trusted channels (Loftus, 2003). For example, by burying false details in a biography provided to some participants, researchers found it relatively easy to plant a childhood memory of meeting a Bugs Bunny character at a Disney resort (Braun et al., 2002)—something that could never happen in real life (because Bugs is a Warner Bros. character). This distortion process has contributed to wrongful criminal convictions based on false "recovered memories" of victims or witnesses (McNally, 2003); alternatively, people can develop detailed but false memories of committing a crime in which they actually had no role (Shaw and Porter, 2015), potentially leading to false confessions.

Not all memories are created equal. We all know from firsthand experience that emotion can powerfully enhance our memory for past events. Some initial evidence in mice suggests that emotional enhancement of memory can even be transmitted epigenetically to subsequent generations (Dias and Ressler, 2014).

An emotionally arousing story is remembered significantly better than a closely matched but emotionally neutral story (Reisberg and Heuer, 1995). But if people are treated with propranolol (a beta-adrenergic antagonist, or beta-blocker, that blocks the effects of epinephrine), this emotional enhancement of memory vanishes. It's not that treated participants perceive the story as being any less emotional; in fact, treated participants rate the emotional content of the stories just the same as untreated participants do. Instead, the evidence indicates that propranolol directly interferes with the ability of adrenal stress hormones to act on the brain (Cahill et al., 1994), as discussed in **BOX 17.1**.

Neural Mechanisms of Memory Storage

What are the basic molecular, synaptic, and cellular events that store information in the nervous system? The remainder of this chapter concerns the cellular and physiological underpinnings of memory, what is called the *engram* or *memory trace*. We

nephrine (adrenaline), released by the adrenal glands during times of stress and strong emotion, appears to affect memory formation by influencing the amygdala, especially the basolateral amygdala (BLA). Injecting propranolol, a blocker of beta-adrenergic receptors, into the BLA blocks the memory-enhancing effects of stress (Cahill et al., 1994). A functional model of the BLA and the endogenous and exogenous compounds that affect this memory system is presented in the figure. In this model (McGaugh, 2003), activity in four main hormone/transmitter systems—adrenergic, opioid, GABA-ergic, and cholinergic inputs—converges on and is integrated in the BLA. Outputs of the BLA, in turn, project widely to brain regions, including the hippocampus, caudate, and cortex, influencing memory formation in these locations (McIntyre et al., 2005). Drugs that alter the biochemical messages to the BLA may potently alter the effect of emotion on memory. For example, if people who have just had a traumatic experience are given the beta-adrenergic antagonist propranolol, which blocks the effects of epinephrine, their memory for the event is significantly reduced when tested months later (Pitman et al., 2002).

In PTSD, each recurrence of the strong emotions and memories of the traumatic event may reactivate memories that, when reconsolidated in the presence of stress signals like epinephrine, become even stronger. Therefore, one strategy to treat PTSD could be to block the effects of epinephrine while the person is retrieving the traumatic memory, to blunt the emotional experience of the event and thereby weaken that aspect of the memory during reconsolidation. In a study of people suffering from PTSD, having them read aloud a written description of their ordeal while under the influence of propranolol reduced their symptoms (A. Brunet et al., 2014) such that most no longer met the diagnostic criteria for PTSD. They still remembered the details of the event, but they no longer found the memory so upsetting. If we cannot erase the traumatic memory altogether, perhaps we can reduce its sting.

posttraumatic stress disorder (PTSD) A disorder in which memories of an unpleasant episode repeatedly plague the victim.

will look at some of the ways in which new learning involves changes in the strength of existing synapses, and the biochemical signals that may produce those changes. We'll consider how the formation of memories may require the formation of new synapses, or even the birth of new neurons. The observation that **neuroplasticity** (or *neural plasticity*)—the ability of neurons and neural circuits to be remodeled by events—is found in virtually all animals indicates that it is an ancient and vital product of evolution.

neuroplasticity Also called neural plasticity. The ability of the nervous system to change in response to experience or the environment.

Memory Storage Requires Physical Changes in the Brain

In introducing the term *synapse*, Charles Sherrington (1897) speculated that synaptic alterations might be the basis of learning, anticipating an area of research that to this day is one of the most intensive efforts in all of neuroscience. Most current theories of the cellular basis of learning focus on plasticity of the structure and physiological functioning of synapses.

Plastic changes at synapses can be physiological or structural

Synaptic changes that may store information can be measured physiologically. The changes can be presynaptic, postsynaptic, or both (**FIGURE 17.22A**). Such changes include greater release of neurotransmitter molecules and/or greater effects because the receptor molecules become more numerous or more sensitive. These changes can alter in the size of the postsynaptic potential. Changes in the rate of inactivation of the transmitter (through reuptake or enzymatic degradation) can produce a similar effect.

Synaptic activity can also be modulated by inputs from other neurons (members of the same or other cell assemblies) causing extra depolarization or hyperpolarization of the axon terminals and changes in the amount of neurotransmitter released (**FIGURE 17.22B**).

Long-term memories may require changes in the nervous system so substantial that they can be directly observed (with the aid of a microscope, of course). Struc-

Before training

(A) Changes involving synaptic transmitters

After training

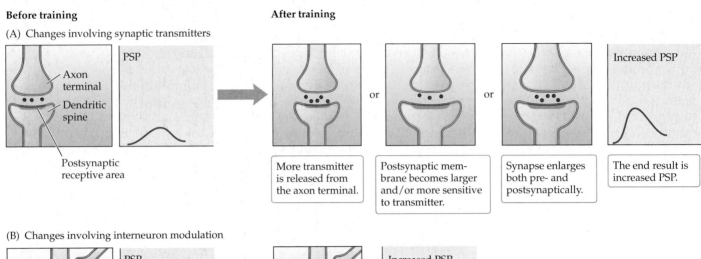

Axon terminal

Dendritic spine

Postsynaptic receptive area

PSP

More transmitter is released from the axon terminal.

or

Postsynaptic membrane becomes larger and/or more sensitive to transmitter.

or

Synapse enlarges both pre- and postsynaptically.

Increased PSP

The end result is increased PSP.

(B) Changes involving interneuron modulation

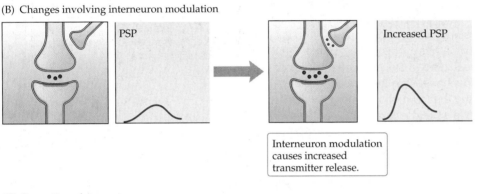

PSP

Increased PSP

Interneuron modulation causes increased transmitter release.

(C) Formation of new synapses

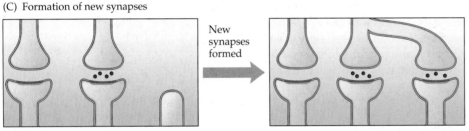

New synapses formed

(D) Rearrangement of synaptic input

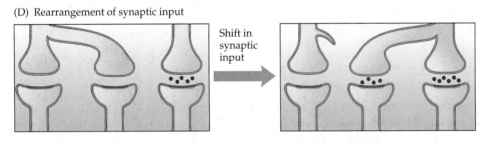

Shift in synaptic input

17.22 SYNAPTIC CHANGES THAT MAY STORE MEMORIES After training, each action potential in the relevant neural circuit causes increased release of transmitter molecules (red dots). The postsynaptic potential (PSP) therefore increases in size, as indicated by the graphs in (A) and (B). (A) Several different changes in the synapse each result in an increase in size of the PSP. (B) An interneuron modulates polarization of the axon terminal and causes the release of more transmitter molecules per nerve impulse. (C) A neural circuit that is used more often increases the number of synaptic contacts. For example, strong activity can induce a synapse to enlarge and eventually split, creating a "perforated synapse." (D) A more frequently used neural pathway takes over synaptic sites formerly occupied by a less active competitor.

tural changes resulting from use are apparent in other parts of the body. For example, exercise changes the mass and/or shape of muscles and bones. In a similar way, new synapses may form or synapses may be eliminated as a function of training (**FIGURE 17.22C**). Training may also lead to reorganization of synaptic connections. For example, training may cause a more used pathway to take over sites formerly occupied by a less active competitor (**FIGURE 17.22D**).

There is growing evidence that glia also play a role in learning and synaptic activity. For example, in some systems, nearby astrocytes mark which synapses will change in strength; blocking astrocyte activity prevents the synapse from changing (Min and Nevian, 2012). Also, people learning a new skill show changes in white matter that indicate changes in myelination from oligodendrocytes (Zatorre et al., 2012).

Varied experiences and learning cause the brain to change and grow

The remarkable plasticity of the brain is not all that difficult to demonstrate. Simply living in a complex environment, with its many opportunities for new learning, produces pronounced biochemical and anatomical changes in the brains of rats (E. L. Bennett et al., 1964, 1969; Renner and Rosenzweig, 1987; M. R. Rosenzweig, 1984; M. R. Rosenzweig et al., 1961). This area of research is covered in more detail in **A Step Further: Cerebral Changes Result from Training** on the website.

In standard studies of environmental enrichment, rats are randomly assigned to three housing conditions:

1. **Standard condition (SC)** Animals are housed in small groups in standard lab cages (**FIGURE 17.23A**). This is the typical environment for laboratory animals.

2. **Impoverished condition (IC)** Animals are housed individually in standard lab cages (**FIGURE 17.23B**).

3. **Enriched condition (EC)** Animals are housed in large social groups in special cages containing various toys and other interesting features (**FIGURE 17.23C**). This condition provides enhanced opportunities for learning perceptual and motor skills, social learning, and so on.

In dozens of studies over several decades, a variety of plastic changes in the brain have been linked to such environmental enrichment. For example, compared with IC animals (or SC animals in many cases), EC animals have heavier, thicker cortex (M. C. Diamond, 1967; M. R. Rosenzweig et al., 1962), with enhanced cholinergic activity (M. R. Rosenzweig et al., 1961). Cortical neurons in EC animals also have more dendritic branches, especially on dendrites closer to the cell body (called *basal dendrites*), than those from IC animals (Globus et al., 1973; Greenough, 1976) (**FIGURE 17.24**). Similarly, using structural MRI scans of the brain, researchers have found that human adolescents from advantageous socioeconomic environments have thicker cortex than adolescents from lower socioeconomic environments, independent of any other group differences, such as race or ethnicity differences (Mackey et al., 2015).

Similar effects on brain processes and behavior are seen in fishes, birds, mice, cats, and monkeys (Mohammed, 2001; Renner and Rosenzweig, 1987; van Praag et al., 2000). And the evidence indicates that the human brain is no exception: for example, we saw in Chapter 11 that the hand area of the motor cortex becomes larger in musicians, presumably because of their extensive practice. In another example, 100 children assigned to a 2-year enriched nursery school program showed improvements in tests of orienting and arousal when reassessed at age 11 (Raine et al., 2001).

Standard condition

Impoverished condition

Enriched condition

17.23 EXPERIMENTAL ENVIRONMENTS TO TEST THE EFFECTS OF ENRICHMENT ON LEARNING AND BRAIN MEASURES Interaction with an enriched environment has measurable effects on the brain, on stress reactions, and on learning.

standard condition (SC) The usual environment for laboratory rodents, with a few animals in a cage and adequate food and water but no complex stimulation.

impoverished condition (IC) Also called isolated condition. A condition in which laboratory rodents are housed singly in a small cage without complex stimuli.

enriched condition (EC) Also called complex environment. A condition in which laboratory rodents are group-housed with a wide variety of stimulus objects.

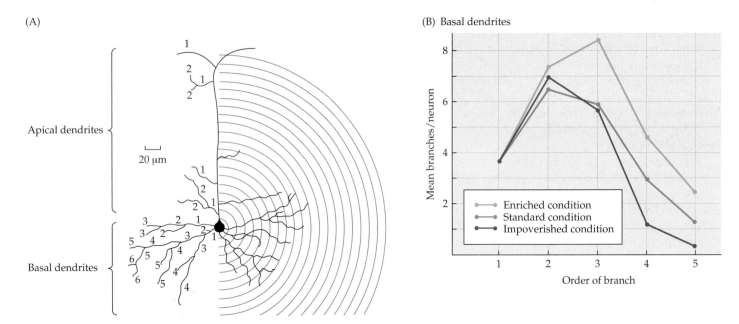

17.24 MEASUREMENT OF DENDRITIC BRANCHING (A) An enlarged image of a neuron is used to quantify branching, either by counts of the numbers of branches of different orders (left) or by counts of the numbers of intersections with concentric rings (right). (B) There are significant differences in branching, especially in the basal dendrites, among rats kept for 30 days in enriched, standard, or impoverished environments. (After Greenough, 1976.)

nonassociative learning A type of learning in which presentation of a particular stimulus alters the strength or probability of a response according to the strength and temporal spacing of that stimulus; includes habituation and sensitization.

habituation A form of nonassociative learning in which an organism becomes less responsive following repeated presentations of a stimulus.

dishabituation The restoration of response amplitude following habituation.

In fact, the ability to change in response to the environment is a pervasive quality of the brain, across the lifespan and across the animal kingdom, as we discuss in **A Step Further: Plasticity Is a Defining Feature of the Brain** on the website.

It is difficult to find the exact synaptic changes that underlie any particular instance of learning, because there are so many synapses (Merchán-Pérez et al., 2009). So instead, researchers made progress by studying simple learning in simple animals, as we discuss next.

Invertebrate Nervous Systems Show Plasticity

One fruitful research strategy has been to focus on memory mechanisms in the very simple nervous systems of certain invertebrates. Invertebrate nervous systems have relatively few neurons (on the order of hundreds to tens of thousands). Because these neurons are arranged identically in different individuals, it is possible to construct detailed neural circuit diagrams for particular behaviors and study the same few neurons in multiple individuals.

A Nobel Prize–winning program of research focused on *Aplysia* (Kandel, 2009; Kandel et al., 2014), sea slugs with a simple nervous system that is nonetheless capable of the simplest type of learning: **nonassociative learning**. In each of the three forms of nonassociative learning—habituation, dishabituation, and sensitization—a single stimulus is presented once or repeatedly. **Habituation** is a decrease in response to a stimulus as the stimulus is repeated (when the decrement cannot be attributed to sensory adaptation or motor fatigue). Sitting in a café, you may stop noticing the door chime when someone enters; in this case you have habituated to the chime. Once habituation has occurred, a strong stimulus (of the same sort, or even in another sensory modality) will often cause the response to the habituated stimulus to increase sharply; it may become even larger than the original response. The increase in response amplitude is called **dishabituation**. So, if a loud firecracker is set off behind you, the next ring of the door chime may startle you; in this case you have become temporarily dishabituated to the chime. Even a response that has

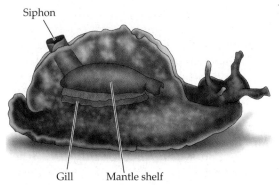

Siphon

Gill   Mantle shelf

17.25 THE SEA SLUG *APLYSIA* In the usual posture, the siphon is extended and the gill is spread out on the back. Ordinarily only the tip of the siphon would be visible in a lateral view; here, the rest of the siphon and the gill are shown as if the animal were transparent.

not been habituated may increase in amplitude after a strong stimulus. This effect is known as **sensitization**: the response is greater than the baseline level because of prior stimulation. After the firecracker, for example, you may overreact to someone standing up nearby. That horrible firecracker has sensitized you to many stimuli.

If you squirt water at a sea slug's siphon—a tube through which it draws water—the animal protectively retracts its delicate gill (**FIGURE 17.25**). But with repeated stimulation the animal retracts the gill less and less, as it learns that the stimulation represents no danger to the gill. Kandel and associates (1987, 2009) demonstrated that this habituation is caused by changes in the synapse between the sensory cell that detects the squirt of water and the motor neuron that retracts the gill. As this synapse releases less and less transmitter, the gill slowly stops retracting in response to the stimulation (**FIGURE 17.26A**) (M. Klein et al., 1980). So in this case the synaptic plasticity underlying learning is within the reflex circuit itself.

sensitization A form of nonassociative learning in which an organism becomes more responsive to most stimuli after being exposed to unusually strong or painful stimulation.

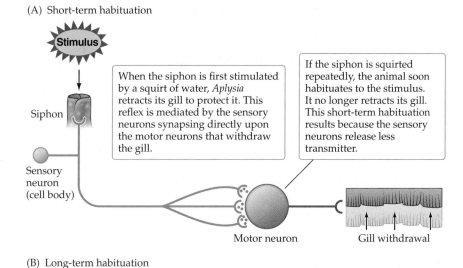

(A) Short-term habituation

Stimulus

Siphon

Sensory neuron (cell body)

When the siphon is first stimulated by a squirt of water, *Aplysia* retracts its gill to protect it. This reflex is mediated by the sensory neurons synapsing directly upon the motor neurons that withdraw the gill.

If the siphon is squirted repeatedly, the animal soon habituates to the stimulus. It no longer retracts its gill. This short-term habituation results because the sensory neurons release less transmitter.

Motor neuron   Gill withdrawal

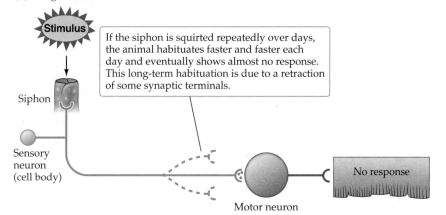

(B) Long-term habituation

Stimulus

Siphon

Sensory neuron (cell body)

If the siphon is squirted repeatedly over days, the animal habituates faster and faster each day and eventually shows almost no response. This long-term habituation is due to a retraction of some synaptic terminals.

No response

Motor neuron

17.26 SYNAPTIC PLASTICITY UNDERLYING HABITUATION IN *APLYSIA*

Similarly, both the number and the size of synaptic junctions vary with training in *Aplysia*. For example, if an *Aplysia* is tested in the habituation paradigm over a series of days, each successive day the animal habituates faster than it did the day before. This phenomenon represents long-term habituation (as opposed to the short-term habituation that we've already discussed), and in this case there is a reduction in the number of synapses between the sensory cell and the motor neuron (**FIGURE 17.26B**) (C. H. Bailey and Chen, 1983).

Elements of the *Aplysia* gill withdrawal system are similarly capable of sensitization in which strong stimulation anywhere on the skin causes subsequent stimulations of the siphon to produce *larger* gill withdrawals (N. Dale et al., 1988). The strong stimulation of the skin activates a facilitating neuron that releases the transmitter serotonin onto the presynaptic nerve terminals in the gill withdrawal reflex circuit shown in Figure 17.26A. Serotonin boosts the activity in the circuit by prolonging the activity of the sensory neuron's synapses onto the motor neuron, leading to a longer-lasting response (Y. Zhang et al., 2012).

The comparability of results obtained with diverse species of invertebrates indicates that, over a wide range of species, information can be stored in the nervous system by changes in both strength and number of synaptic contacts, confirming the hypotheses diagrammed in Figure 17.22. (For another example of memory research in invertebrates, see **A Step Further: In Drosophila, Each Stage in Memory Formation Depends on a Different Gene** on the website.) Next we'll consider a simple neural circuit in the mammalian brain in which neural activity alters the strength of synaptic connections.

Some Simple Learning in Mammals Relies on Circuits in the Cerebellum

Describing the complete circuit for even a simple learned behavior is very difficult in mammals because, in contrast to *Aplysia*, mammals have brains containing billions of neurons that are not organized in fixed circuits. So researchers focused on a very simple mammalian behavior: classical conditioning.

As we noted earlier, the cerebellum is crucial for some types of classical conditioning. When a puff of air is applied to the cornea of a rabbit, the animal reflexively blinks. If the air puff (US) immediately follows a tone (CS), a conditioned response develops rapidly: the rabbit comes to blink (CR) whenever the tone is sounded. The basic circuit of the eye-blink reflex is simple, involving cranial nerves and some interneurons that connect their nuclei (**FIGURE 17.27A**). Sensory fibers from the cornea run along cranial nerve V (the trigeminal nerve) to its nucleus in the brainstem. From there, some interneurons send axons to synapse on other cranial nerve motor nuclei (VI and VII), which in turn activate the muscles of the eyelids, causing them to close. While destruction of the hippocampus has little effect on the acquisition or retention of the conditioned eye-blink response in rabbits (Lockhart and Moore, 1975), researchers found learning-related increases in the activity of individual neurons of the cerebellum and associated structures. A large research effort eventually described a cerebellar circuit that is both necessary and sufficient for conditioning to aversive stimuli, including eye-blink conditioning (Poulos and Thompson, 2015).

The trigeminal (V) pathway that carries information about the corneal stimulation (the US) to the cranial motor nuclei also sends axons to the brainstem (specifically a structure called the *inferior olive*). These brainstem neurons, in turn, send axons called *climbing fibers* to synapse on cerebellar neurons in a region called the *interpositus nucleus*. The same cells also receive information about the auditory CS by a pathway through the auditory nuclei and other brainstem nuclei (**FIGURE 17.27B**). So the US and CS converge in the interpositus nucleus of the cerebellum. After conditioning, the occurrence of the CS—the tone—has an enhanced effect on the cerebellar neurons, so they now trigger eye blink even in the absence of an air puff (**FIGURE 17.27C**).

Local cooling or drugs that block the neurotransmitter GABA (gamma-aminobutyric acid, the transmitter used at synapses in the cerebellar circuit) have the effect of

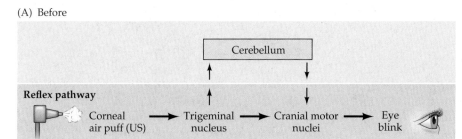

(A) Before

Cerebellum

Reflex pathway

Corneal air puff (US) → Trigeminal nucleus → Cranial motor nuclei → Eye blink

1 Before training, a puff of air on the surface of the eye triggers a reflexive eye blink.

2 Information about the puff of air is also sent (via a polysynaptic pathway) to the interpositus nucleus of the cerebellum. Although the cerebellum can send information to the cranial motor nuclei that trigger the eye blink, at this stage those synapses are inactive.

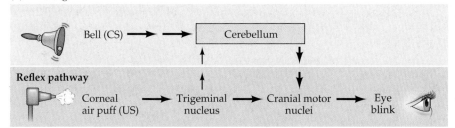

(B) Training

Bell (CS) → → Cerebellum

Reflex pathway

Corneal air puff (US) → Trigeminal nucleus → Cranial motor nuclei → Eye blink

3 During conditioning, information about the sound of the bell also reaches the cerebellum. There, impulses from this auditory signal and the air puff converge on particular neurons. With repeated pairings of bell (CS) and air puff (US), particular synapses within the cerebellum are strengthened.

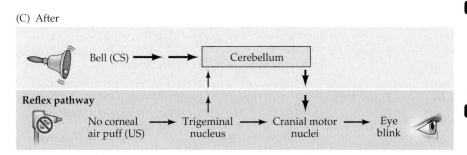

(C) After

Bell (CS) → → Cerebellum

Reflex pathway

No corneal air puff (US) → Trigeminal nucleus → Cranial motor nuclei → Eye blink

4 After training is complete, the sound of the bell now triggers activity in the cerebellum that drives the cranial motor nuclei to trigger an eye blink even if the air puff never happens. This is a conditioned response.

5 Repeated presentation of the bell without the air puff begins to weaken the cerebellar connections so that eventually the bell stops eliciting an eye blink.

17.27 FUNCTIONING OF THE NEURAL CIRCUIT FOR CONDITIONING OF THE EYE-BLINK REFLEX US, unconditioned stimulus; CS, conditioned stimulus. (After R. F. Thompson and Krupa, 1994.)

reversibly shutting down the interpositus nucleus. If this manipulation is performed at the beginning of training, then no conditioning occurs until after the effect wears off. Conversely, if animals are fully trained before treatment, subsequent injection of a GABA antagonist causes the conditioned behavior to disappear, along with its electrophysiological signature, until after the drug effect wears off. On the basis of these and other experiments, the complete eye-blink conditioning circuit is now understood, and the cerebellum's interpositus nucleus appears to be the key location for storing this type of memory (R. F. Thompson and Steinmetz, 2009).

As we discussed earlier, studies on human participants are consistent with the animal research on eye-blink conditioning. Unsurprisingly, other cases of conditioning also depend on cerebellar mechanisms. For example, conditioned leg flexion (in which the animal learns to withdraw a leg on hearing a tone) is cerebellum-dependent (Donegan et al., 1983; Voneida, 1990). Studies of humans with cerebellar damage indicate that the cerebellum is important for conditioning across several domains, including conditioning of emotions like fear and aspects of cognitive learning (Timmann et al., 2010).

Synaptic Plasticity Can Be Measured in Simple Hippocampal Circuits

Modern ideas about the role of neuroplasticity in memory have their origins in the theories of Donald Hebb (1949), who proposed that when a presynaptic neuron repeatedly activates a postsynaptic neuron, the synaptic connection between them will become stronger and more stable (the oft-repeated maxim "cells that fire together wire together" captures the basic idea). Ensembles of neurons, or **cell assemblies**, linked via synchronized activity of these **Hebbian synapses** (see also Figure 7.22) could then act together to store memories (Kelso and Brown, 1986).

cell assembly A large group of cells that tend to be active at the same time because they have been activated simultaneously or in close succession in the past.

Hebbian synapse A synapse that is strengthened when it successfully drives the postsynaptic cell.

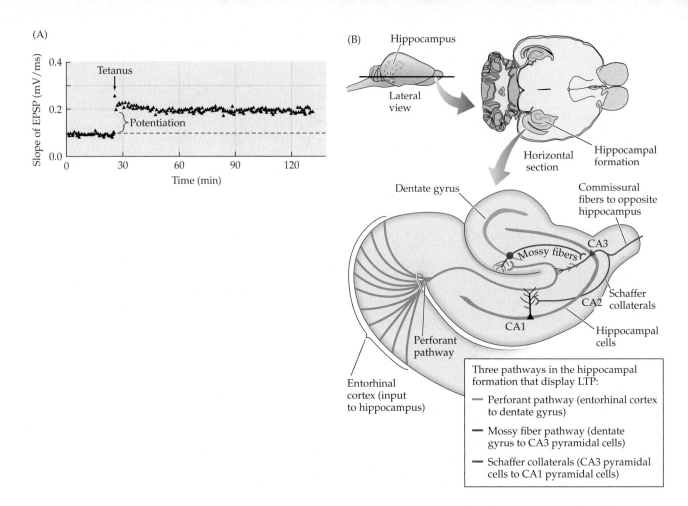

17.28 LONG-TERM POTENTIATION OCCURS IN THE HIPPOCAMPUS (A) If axons in the circuit are stimulated only once every second, the size of the response in the postsynaptic neurons is quite stable. However, after a brief tetanus (a burst of electrical stimulation triggering hundreds or thousands of action potentials over 1–2 seconds), the size of the excitatory postsynaptic potential (EPSP) responses increases markedly and remains high throughout the recording period. This greater responsiveness is called *long-term potentiation* (LTP). (B) The top diagram shows the location of the hippocampal formation in a whole rat brain and in a horizontal section. The bottom diagram of the right hippocampal formation shows various neural pathways found in the hippocampal formation, many of which display LTP. (See the text for an explanation of CA1, CA2, and CA3.)

tetanus An intense volley of action potentials.

long-term potentiation (LTP) A stable and enduring increase in the effectiveness of synapses following repeated strong stimulation.

In classic experiments in the 1970s, researchers probing the properties of hippocampal circuitry discovered an impressive form of neuroplasticity that appeared to confirm Hebb's theories about synaptic remodeling (Bliss and Lømo, 1973; Schwartzkroin and Wester, 1975). In these experiments, electrodes were placed within the rat hippocampus, positioned so that the researchers could stimulate a group of *presynaptic* axons and immediately record the electrical response of a group of *postsynaptic* neurons. Normal, low-level activation of the presynaptic cells produced stable and predictable excitatory postsynaptic potentials (EPSPs; see Chapter 3), as expected. But when the researchers applied a brief high-frequency burst of electrical stimuli (called a **tetanus**) to the presynaptic hippocampal neurons, thus inducing high rates of action potentials, the response of the postsynaptic neurons changed. Now the postsynaptic cells responded to normal levels of presynaptic activity by producing much larger EPSPs; in other words, the synapses appeared to have become stronger or more effective. This stable and long-lasting enhancement of synaptic transmission, termed **long-term potentiation** (LTP), is illustrated in **FIGURE 17.28A**.

Interestingly, a *weakening* of synaptic efficacy via a different mechanism—termed *long-term depression*—can also encode information. This phenomenon is discussed in **A Step Further: Long-Term Depression Is the Converse of Long-Term Potentiation** on the website.

We now know that LTP can be generated in conscious and freely behaving animals, in anesthetized animals, in many regions of the brain, and even in tissue slices. The fact that LTP is evident in a variety of invertebrate and vertebrate species suggests that it is an ancient evolutionary development, and probably a feature of all neural systems. Further, once formed, LTP lasts for weeks or more (Bliss and Gardner-Medwin, 1973). So, at least superficially, LTP appears to have all the hallmarks of a cellular mechanism of memory. This hint at a possible cellular basis of memory has prompted an intensive research effort, centered mainly on the rat hippocampus but also on the cortex, cerebellum, and elsewhere, aimed at understanding the molecular and physiological mechanisms that induce LTP.

LTP occurs at several sites in the hippocampal formation

The *hippocampal formation* (**FIGURE 17.28B**) consists of two interlocking C-shaped structures—the **hippocampus** itself and the **dentate gyrus**—along with the adjacent cortex (also called the *hippocampal gyrus*). On structural grounds, neuroscientists distinguish three major divisions within the hippocampus, labeled *CA1*, *CA2*, and *CA3*. It was in the main input pathway to the hippocampal formation (the *perforant* pathway, originating in nearby entorhinal cortex and terminating at synapses in dentate gyrus) that LTP was originally demonstrated. But LTP is also studied in other hippocampal pathways, which are illustrated in Figure 17.28B, and it may be a property of all excitatory synapses (Malenka and Bear, 2004).

In CA1, LTP occurs at synapses that use the excitatory neurotransmitter glutamate, and it is critically dependent on a glutamate receptor subtype called the **NMDA receptor** (after its selective ligand, *N*-*m*ethyl-**D**-*a*spartate). Treatment with drugs that selectively block NMDA receptors completely prevents new LTP in the CA1 region, but it does not affect LTP that has already been established. As you might expect, these postsynaptic NMDA receptors—working in conjunction with a related subtype of glutamate receptors called **AMPA receptors**—have some unique characteristics, which we discuss next.

NMDA receptors and AMPA receptors collaborate in LTP

During normal, low-level activity, the release of glutamate at a CA1 synapse activates only the AMPA receptors. The NMDA receptors cannot respond to the glutamate, because magnesium ions (Mg^{2+}) block the NMDA receptors' integral calcium ion (Ca^{2+}) channels (**FIGURE 17.29A**); thus, few Ca^{2+} ions can enter the neuron. The situation changes, however, if larger quantities of glutamate are released (in response to a barrage of action potentials), thus stimulating the AMPA receptors more strongly. Because AMPA receptors admit sodium ions (Na^+) when activated, the increased activation of AMPA receptors depolarizes the postsynaptic membrane, and if a threshold value of about −35 millivolts or so is reached, the Mg^{2+} plugs are driven from the central channels of the NMDA receptors (**FIGURE 17.29B**). The NMDA receptors are now able to respond to glutamate, admitting large amounts of Ca^{2+} into the postsynaptic neuron. Thus, NMDA receptors are fully active only when gated by a combination of voltage (depolarization via AMPA receptors) and the ligand (glutamate).

The large influx of Ca^{2+} at NMDA receptors activates intracellular enzymes, called **protein kinases**, that alter or activate a variety of other proteins. One of these protein kinases is CaMKII (calcium/calmodulin-dependent protein kinase II), which affects AMPA receptors in several important ways (**FIGURE 17.29B AND C**) (Kessels and Malinow, 2009; Lisman et al., 2012). Activated CaMKII causes more AMPA receptors to be produced and inserted into the postsynaptic membrane, and existing nearby AMPA receptors are induced to move to the active synapse (T. Takahashi

hippocampus A medial temporal lobe structure that is important for learning and memory.

dentate gyrus A strip of gray matter in the hippocampal formation.

NMDA receptor A glutamate receptor that also binds the glutamate agonist NMDA (N-methyl-D-aspartate) and that is both ligand-gated and voltage-sensitive.

AMPA receptor A glutamate receptor that also binds the glutamate agonist AMPA.

protein kinase An enzyme that adds phosphate groups (PO_4) to protein molecules, causing a functional change in the proteins.

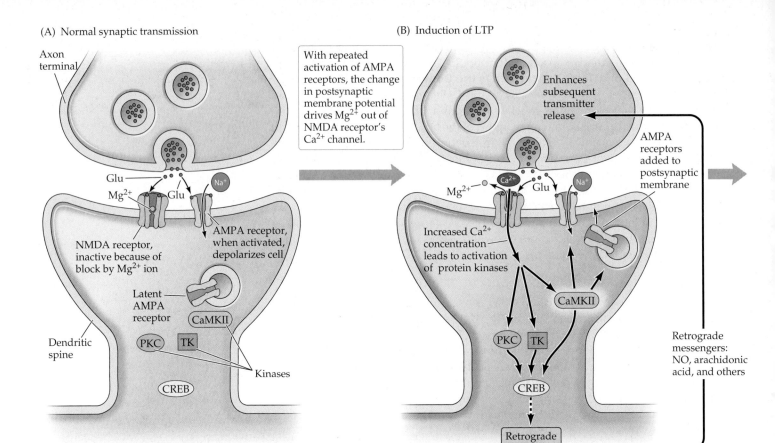

(A) Normal synaptic transmission

Axon terminal

Glu

Mg^{2+} — Glu

Na^+

NMDA receptor, inactive because of block by Mg^{2+} ion

AMPA receptor, when activated, depolarizes cell

Latent AMPA receptor

Dendritic spine

CaMKII

PKC TK

Kinases

CREB

(B) Induction of LTP

With repeated activation of AMPA receptors, the change in postsynaptic membrane potential drives Mg^{2+} out of NMDA receptor's Ca^{2+} channel.

Enhances subsequent transmitter release

Mg^{2+} Ca^{2+} Glu Na^+

Increased Ca^{2+} concentration leads to activation of protein kinases

AMPA receptors added to postsynaptic membrane

CaMKII

PKC TK

CREB

Retrograde signal generator

Retrograde messengers: NO, arachidonic acid, and others

CREB cAMP responsive element–binding protein. A protein that binds the promoter region of several genes involved in neural plasticity when activated by cyclic AMP (cAMP).

retrograde messenger Transmitter that is released by the postsynaptic region, travels back across the synapse, and alters the functioning of the presynaptic neuron.

et al., 2003). The membrane-bound AMPA receptors are also modified to increase their conductance of Na^+ and K^+ ions (Sanderson et al., 2008). The net effect of these changes, therefore, is to enhance the sensitivity of the synapse to released glutamate.

A second major effect of the activated protein kinases involves a substance called **CREB** (*c*AMP *r*esponsive *e*lement–*b*inding protein). CREB is a *transcription factor* (a protein that binds to the promoter region of genes and causes those genes to change their rate of expression) that is activated by protein kinases, including CaMKII and chemical cousins like MAPK (mitogen-activated protein kinase), PKC (protein kinase C), and TK (tyrosine kinase). So, as shown in **FIGURE 17.30**, a direct result of the activation of NMDA receptors is the activation of CREB and changes in the expression of genes encoding a wide range of proteins. Because the affected genes may encode anything from new receptors and kinases to the structural building blocks used for changing the shape of the cell, this action can have profound and long-lasting consequences for the neuron.

The long-term changes in neurons after LTP range from the formation of additional synapses, and enhancement of existing ones, to the construction of whole new dendritic branches and dendritic spines, through modifications of molecular components of the cell skeleton (Huang et al., 2013). In mice, genetic deletion of CREB impairs LTM but not STM (Bourtchuladze et al., 1994; Kogan et al., 1997). The earlier stages of LTP, lasting an hour or so, appear not to require protein synthesis, but thereafter, inhibition of protein synthesis prevents longer-lasting LTP (U. Frey et al., 1993; Krug et al., 1984). Furthermore, neurons can make proteins that selectively block CREB's actions (Genoux et al., 2002; Mioduszewska et al., 2003), possibly providing a means to erase or inhibit the formation of unwanted memories. Much remains to be discovered about the many controls on long-lasting components of LTP.

Not all of the changes in LTP are postsynaptic. When the postsynaptic cell is strongly stimulated and its NMDA receptors become active and admit Ca^{2+}, an intracellular process causes the postsynaptic cell to release a **retrograde messenger**—often a diffusible gas—that travels back across the synapse and alters the function-

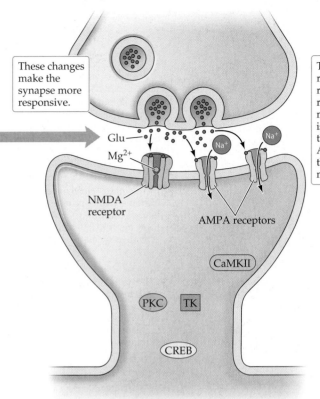

(C) Enhanced synapse, after induction of LTP

These changes make the synapse more responsive.

The synapse is now ready to give more-rapid and stronger response, because more transmitter is released and there are more AMPA receptors in the postsynaptic membrane.

Glu

Mg²⁺

Na⁺   Na⁺

NMDA receptor

AMPA receptors

CaMKII

PKC   TK

CREB

17.29 ROLES OF THE NMDA AND AMPA RECEPTORS IN THE INDUCTION OF LTP IN THE CA1 REGION (A) Normally, the NMDA channel is blocked by a Mg²⁺ ion and only the AMPA channel functions in excitation of the neuron. (B) With repeated activation of AMPA receptors, depolarization of the neuron drives Mg²⁺ out of the NMDA channel, and Ca²⁺ ions enter. The rapid increase of Ca²⁺ ions triggers processes that lead to LTP. Activation of the protein CaM kinase II (CaMKII) increases the conductance of AMPA receptors already present in the membrane and promotes the movement of AMPA receptors from the interior of the cell into the membrane. (C) The synapse is enhanced after induction of LTP. CREB, cAMP responsive element–binding protein; Glu, glutamate; PKC, protein kinase C; TK, tyrosine kinase.

Go to Animation 17.2
AMPA and NMDA Receptors
bn8e.com/17.2

ing of the *presynaptic* neuron (see Figure 17.29B). By affecting the presynaptic cell, the retrograde messenger ensures that more glutamate will be released into the synapse than previously, thereby strengthening the synapse. So, LTP involves active participation on both sides of the synapse. Nitric oxide (NO), carbon monoxide (CO), arachidonic acid, and nerve growth factor are among more than a dozen possible retrograde signals in LTP (J. R. Sanes and Lichtman, 1999).

In other locations in the hippocampus, such as the mossy fiber pathway (see Figure 17.28B), LTP can occur without NMDA receptor activity (E. W. Harris and Cotman, 1986), and some forms of LTP are blocked by drugs with completely different modes of action, such as opiate antagonists (Aroniadou et al., 1993; Derrick and Martinez, 1994). The diversity of mechanisms involved in LTP has complicated one of the central questions in LTP research, which we address next.

Is LTP a mechanism of memory formation?

Even the simplest learning involves circuits of multiple neurons and many synapses, and more-complex declarative and procedural memory traces must involve vast networks of neurons, so researchers don't view LTP as the only mechanism of learning. Instead, it is likely that LTP is an important part of a multifaceted system for storing information. Evidence from several research perspectives—as we defined way back in Figure 1.2—implicates LTP in memory:

- *Correlational observations*   The time course of LTP bears strong similarity to the time course of memory formation (Lynch et al., 1991; Staubli, 1995). Like memory, LTP can be induced within seconds, may last for days or weeks, and shows a labile consolidation period that lasts for several minutes after induction.

- *Somatic intervention experiments*   In general, pharmacological treatments that interfere with LTP tend to impair learning. So, for example, NMDA receptor blockade interferes with performance in the Morris water maze (a test of spatial memory) and other types of memory tests (R. G. Morris et al., 1989). Drugs that inhibit CaMKII

Go to Video 17.3
Morris Water Maze
bn8e.com/17.3

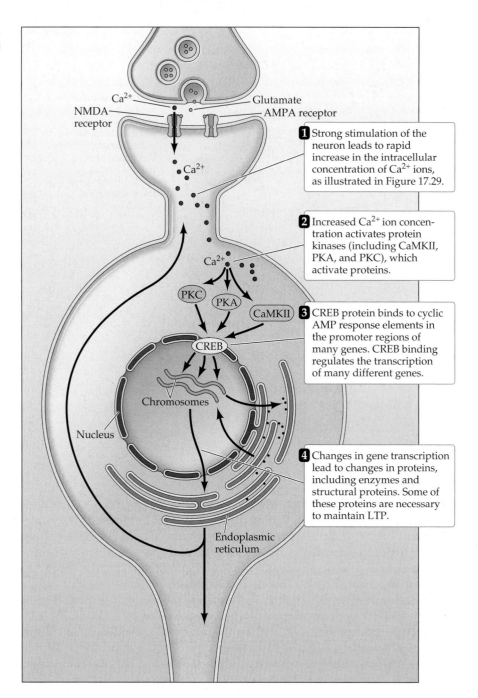

17.30 STEPS IN THE NEUROCHEMICAL CASCADE DURING THE INDUCTION OF LTP This illustration is based on LTP induction in the CA1 region of the hippocampus. PKA, protein kinase A.

NMDA receptor

Ca²⁺

Glutamate

AMPA receptor

Ca²⁺

Ca²⁺

PKC

PKA

CaMKII

CREB

Chromosomes

Nucleus

Endoplasmic reticulum

1 Strong stimulation of the neuron leads to rapid increase in the intracellular concentration of Ca²⁺ ions, as illustrated in Figure 17.29.

2 Increased Ca²⁺ ion concentration activates protein kinases (including CaMKII, PKA, and PKC), which activate proteins.

3 CREB protein binds to cyclic AMP response elements in the promoter regions of many genes. CREB binding regulates the transcription of many different genes.

4 Changes in gene transcription lead to changes in proteins, including enzymes and structural proteins. Some of these proteins are necessary to maintain LTP.

and other protein kinases also generally interfere with aspects of memory formation (M. R. Rosenzweig et al., 1992, 1993; Serrano et al., 1994). Because these same basic physiological processes are at work in many regions of the brain, in earlier research it was difficult to know exactly where and how the drugs were acting to affect memory. But more recently, regional genetic manipulations have enabled researchers to zero in on specific brain regions. Mice with one copy of the CaMKII gene knocked out can still form STMs, but they cannot form LTMs (Frankland et al., 2001). And knockout mice that lack functional NMDA receptors only in CA1 appear normal in many respects, but their hippocampi are incapable of LTP and their memory is impaired (Rampon et al., 2000). In a clever reversal, researchers have also shown that mice (called *Doogies*, see **A Step Further: How to Build a Doogie** on the website) engineered to overexpress NMDA receptors in the hippocampus have enhanced LTP, and better-than-normal long-term memory (Y. P. Tang et al., 1999, 2001). In fact, researchers have developed more than 30 different strains of genetically modified "smart mice," most of which exhibit enhanced LTP (Lehrer, 2009).

- *Behavioral intervention experiments*   In principle, the most convincing evidence for a link between LTP and learning would be "behavioral LTP": a demonstration that training an animal in a memory task can induce LTP in the brain. Such research is difficult because of uncertainty about exactly where to put the recording electrodes in order to detect any induced LTP. Nevertheless, several examples of successful behavioral LTP have been reported. Fear conditioning—for example, the repeated pairing of an aversive stimulus and a tone, eventually resulting in exaggerated reactions to the tone alone (see Figure 15.15)—produces clear LTP specifically in fear circuits in the amygdala and not elsewhere (McKernan and Shinnick-Gallagher, 1997; Rogan et al., 1997). And in the CA1 region of the hippocampus, a different form of aversive learning in rats produces exactly the same electrophysiological changes, as well as changes in AMPA receptor accumulation, that are seen with conventionally induced LTP (Whitlock et al., 2006). Furthermore, using optogenetic techniques (as described in *The Cutting Edge* in Chapter 3) to manipulate activity in the auditory inputs to the amygdala, researchers have succeeded in successively inactivating fear conditioning by inducing long-term *depression* (LTD) and then reactivating the memory by restoring the previous LTP in the same circuit (Nabavi et al., 2014).

Taken together, the research findings support the idea that LTP is a kind of synaptic plasticity that underlies (or is very similar to) certain forms of learning and memory.

In the Adult Brain, Newly Born Neurons May Aid Learning

There is now no doubt that new neurons are produced in the brains of adult mammals, including humans, as we discussed in Chapter 7 (C. G. Gross, 2000). This *adult neurogenesis* occurs primarily in the dentate gyrus of the hippocampal formation (**FIGURE 17.31**), although it is also observed in the olfactory bulbs and some cortical locations. New dentate neurons that survive and grow ultimately receive inputs from entorhinal cortex via the perforant pathway (see blue pathway in Figure 17.28B), extending their own axons and forming glutamatergic synapses (Toni et al., 2008). Anatomically, therefore, the new neurons appear to integrate into the functional circuitry of the hippocampus and adjacent cortex (Bruel-Jungerman et al., 2007), which we've seen play a role in forming new memories.

In experimental animals, neurogenesis and the survival of young neurons can be enhanced by a variety of factors, such as exercise, experience in an enriched environment, or training in a memory task (Opendak and Gould, 2015; Waddell and Shors, 2008). Reproductive hormones and experiences also potently influence neurogenesis (Galea, 2008; Hamson et al., 2013). What's more, newly generated neurons in the dentate gyrus are more plastic, showing enhanced LTP, compared with older neurons (Marín-Burgin et al., 2012). Although these observations are tantalizing, clear demonstrations that the new cells have significant functions in behavior—especially learning and memory—have been somewhat elusive.

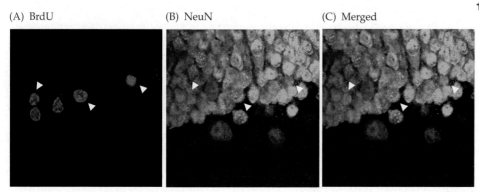

(A) BrdU   (B) NeuN   (C) Merged

20 µm

17.31 NEUROGENESIS IN THE DENTATE GYRUS   (A) BrdU (bromodeoxyuridine) is a label that is selectively incorporated into the DNA of cells that are about to divide. (B) NeuN (a neuron-specific nuclear protein) is used to selectively label neurons in order to distinguish them from other nearby cells, such as glial cells. (C) Merging the two images makes it clear that some of the newly born cells are in fact neurons (arrows). (From Bruel-Jungerman et al., 2007, courtesy of Drs. Elodie Bruel-Jungerman and Serge Laroche.)

conditional knockout A gene that can be selectively deactivated in specific tissues and/or at a specific stage of development.

Rats given a drug that is lethal to newly born neurons are reportedly impaired on tests of conditioning, but only when there is an interval between the CS and the US (Shors et al., 2001). As we discussed earlier, this form of conditioning is believed to rely on hippocampal function, so the finding that it is impaired when neurogenesis is prevented suggests that the role of neurogenesis in memory may be limited to hippocampus-dependent forms of memory. Neurogenesis has also been implicated in other forms of hippocampus-dependent learning, such as spatial memory (Lieberwirth et al., 2016) and fear conditioning (Barha and Galea, 2010; Saxe et al., 2006). In a study using mice with a **conditional knockout**—a gene that can be selectively deactivated in adulthood in specific tissues—researchers found that turning off neurogenesis in the brains of adults resulted in a marked impairment in spatial learning with little effect on other behaviors (C. L. Zhang et al., 2008).

The impaired learning that accompanies reduced adult neurogenesis, however it is caused, is consistent with a role for new neurons in learning. But it is always possible that the manipulations have a general effect—making the animals feel ill, for example—that might affect their performance. However, one lab used genetic manipulations to increase the survival of newly generated neurons in the dentate, resulting in *improved* performance (Sahay et al., 2011). These animals showed enhanced hippocampal LTP, which was expected since younger neurons display greater synaptic plasticity (Marín-Burgin et al., 2012). These mice were also better at one particular task: discriminating between two similar environments (Sahay et al., 2011). In parallel, activation of newly generated neurons in the olfactory bulbs enhances *olfactory* learning and memory (Alonso et al., 2012). Thus it seems clear that neurons born in adulthood play a role in learning and memory, and they do so in keeping with the primary functions of their anatomical location.

Learning and Memory Change as We Age

Understanding the impact of aging on cognition is a pressing issue; by 2030, there will be more than twice as many senior citizens alive as there were in 2000. In people and other mammals, normal aging brings a gradual decline in some but not all aspects of learning and memory (Lister and Barnes, 2009). For some tasks, differences in motivation, earlier education, and other confounding factors may masquerade as age-related memory problems. So experiments on memory in the elderly must be carefully constructed to control for alternate explanations.

What kinds of tasks reliably show decrements in performance with aging? Healthy elderly people tend to show some memory impairment in tasks of conscious recollection that require effort (Hasher and Zacks, 1979) and that rely primarily on internal generation of the memory rather than on external cues (Craik, 1985). Giving elderly participants easily organized task structures, or cues, can often raise their performance to the level of the young. Although working memory and the ability to form new episodic and declarative memories typically decline with age, existing memories such as autobiographical memory and semantic knowledge tend to remain stable (Hedden and Gabrieli, 2004). If vocabulary is tested in isolation, older adults outperform younger adults (D. C. Park et al., 2002), but on tests of executive function, even individuals in their 40s are likely to show age-related decline (Rhodes, 2004).

As we age, we also experience some decreases in spatial memory and navigational skills (Barnes and Penner, 2007). Similarly, aged rats show decrements in the eight-arm radial maze (see Figure 17.17A) compared with younger animals (Mizumori et al., 1996; M. A. Rossi et al., 2005). Along with other memory impairments, spatial memory problems may become much more severe in dementias like Alzheimer's disease (discussed in detail in Chapter 7), which is one of a family of dementing processes that result from inappropriate accumulations of protein in neurons (in the case of Alzheimer's, one of the prime culprits is called β-amyloid). People with these severe cases of dementia become disoriented and easily lose themselves even in familiar surroundings. Shown a familiar object in a new location, such people continue to search for it in the old location, even passing over the object in plain sight, as though they remember

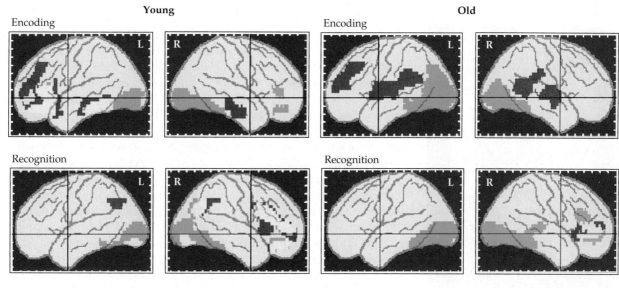

Encoding   Encoding

Recognition   Recognition

| ▨ Low activation | ■ Medium activation | □ High activation |

17.32 ACTIVE BRAIN REGIONS DURING ENCODING AND RETRIEVAL TASKS IN YOUNG AND OLD PEOPLE Lateral views of the cerebral hemispheres show regions of enhanced cerebral blood flow caused by encoding information (top) and retrieving it (bottom). (Courtesy of Dr. Cheryl Grady.)

the search procedure and not the object being sought (M. Moscovitch, 1985). New techniques that image β-amyloid plaques in the brain may help clinicians to identify people at risk for developing Alzheimer's (Ossenkoppele et al., 2016), perhaps allowing for earlier interventions that may help slow the progression of the disease.

Age-related impairments of memory have several causes

Why do some measures of learning and memory decline with age, while others remain intact? There are several ways in which neural changes may affect learning and memory during aging (Craik and Salthouse, 2007), including these major contributors:

- *Impairments of encoding and retrieval* Older people show less cortical activation than younger people when encoding or retrieval is self-initiated. In **FIGURE 17.32**, less frontal and temporal activity is seen in the older people while learning new faces (Grady et al., 1995), but when recognizing faces (a retrieval task that is not self-initiated, because retrieval is prompted by viewing stimuli), the elders' brain activity is comparable to that of the younger participants.

- *Loss of neurons and/or neural connections* The brain gradually loses weight after the age of 30, and some parts of the brain, such as frontal cortex (Raz, 2000), lose a larger proportion of volume or weight than other parts. Although not all investigators agree, age-related memory impairment may involve steady loss of synapses and neurons in the hippocampus and cortex (Geinisman et al., 1995; J. H. Morrison and Hof, 2007; Simic et al., 1997).

- *Problems with cholinergic neurotransmission* Two subcortical regions—known as the *septal complex* and the *nucleus basalis of Meynert* (NBM)—provide profuse cholinergic inputs to the hippocampus and cortex. Memory impairment in Alzheimer's disease seems to be caused by the loss of these cholinergic afferents to the cortex (McGeer et al., 1984; Rossor et al., 1982). Drug treatments that enhance acetylcholine transmission improve aspects of memory performance in human participants (Furey et al., 2000; Ricciardi et al., 2009).

Can the effects of aging on memory be prevented or alleviated?

The search for antiaging interventions and **nootropics**—drugs that enhance cognitive function—is an area of intense activity. Pharmacological approaches include the use of drugs, such as donepezil (Aricept), that inhibit acetylcholinesterase, the enzyme that breaks down acetylcholine. The resultant increase in cholinergic transmission in the forebrain has a positive effect on memory and cognition in mild to moderate cases of Alzheimer's (Ringman and Cummings, 2006). Compounds in a

nootropics A class of drugs that enhance cognitive function.

17.33 HENRY MOLAISON (PATIENT H.M.) Henry lived for over 50 years after the surgery that robbed him of any new declarative memories.

different class, called *ampakines*, act via glutamate receptors to improve hippocampal LTP (Rex et al., 2006); ampakines are under study as potential memory-enhancing therapeutics. Other possible drug targets are the family of protein kinases, such as PKMζ (the squiggle is the Greek letter *zeta*), that may contribute to long-term maintenance of memory traces (Shema et al., 2009) although, as with so much of the complicated molecular machinery of memory, many questions remain about their functioning (Lee et al., 2013). Given the complexity of the process, the list of possible targets for developing memory-boosting drugs grows longer every day.

Rats raised in enriched conditions show improved handling of stress, and the associated reduction in chronic glucocorticoid secretion reduces one source of life-style-related hippocampus damage (Sapolsky, 1993). And in humans there is good evidence that physical activity (Ngandu et al., 2015), mental activity (Suo et al., 2016), and adequate sleep (Gelber et al., 2015) can postpone cognitive decline in old age. Effortful learning—mastering a challenging new topic or skill over a period of time—enhances the survival of adult-born neurons, which may promote better memory performance (Shors, 2014). Similarly, longitudinal studies (e.g., Schaie, 1994) tracking thousands of people suggest several lifestyle factors that can more generally reduce cognitive decline as we age:

- *Living in favorable environmental circumstances* Getting an above-average education, pursuing occupations that involve high complexity and low routine, earning above-average income, and maintaining intact families

- *Involvement in complex and intellectually stimulating activities* Extensive reading, travel, attendance at cultural events, continuing-education activities, and participation in clubs and professional associations

- *Having a spouse/partner with high cognitive status*

Because so much of the brain is involved in the creation, storage, and retrieval of memories, a full understanding of learning and memory will require an enormous research effort at many levels of analysis, from experiments with molecular processes to cognitive studies of people like Henry Molaison. At age 82, more than 50 years after his life-shattering surgery, Henry died. In a final act of generosity to a field of science that he helped launch, Henry donated his brain for further study. Through webcasting technology, the slicing of Henry's brain into sections was viewed live by thousands of people, and a series of more than 2000 sections will eventually be made available. To the end, although he could remember so little of his entire adult life, Henry was courteous and concerned about other people (**FIGURE 17.33**). He remembered the surgeon he had met several times before his operation: "He did medical research on people.... What he learned about me helped others too, and I'm glad about that" (Corkin, 2002, p. 158). Henry never knew how famous he was, or how much his dreadful condition taught us about learning and memory; yet despite being deprived of one of the most important characteristics of a human being, he held fast to his humanity.

■ The Cutting Edge

Artificial Activation of an Engram

We've seen that experience can alter the strength of synapses, and for simple behaviors like habituation in a simple organism like *Aplysia*, we know exactly which synapse weakens as habituation proceeds. But in more-complicated animals like mammals, the physical basis of a memory formed by learning a particular task—the engram—probably involves changes in many neurons and in many synapses. In other words, the memory is more likely encoded by changes in the activity of a *circuit* of neurons, not just one neuron (much less one synapse). If so, then reactivating the neurons encoding the memory might be experienced as remembering. Several groups have tested this idea in mice, where genetic tools permit remarkable control over neuronal activity.

In one such demonstration, researchers were able to mark precisely the neurons that were activated when mice were subjected to fear conditioning (X. Liu et al., 2012). Mice

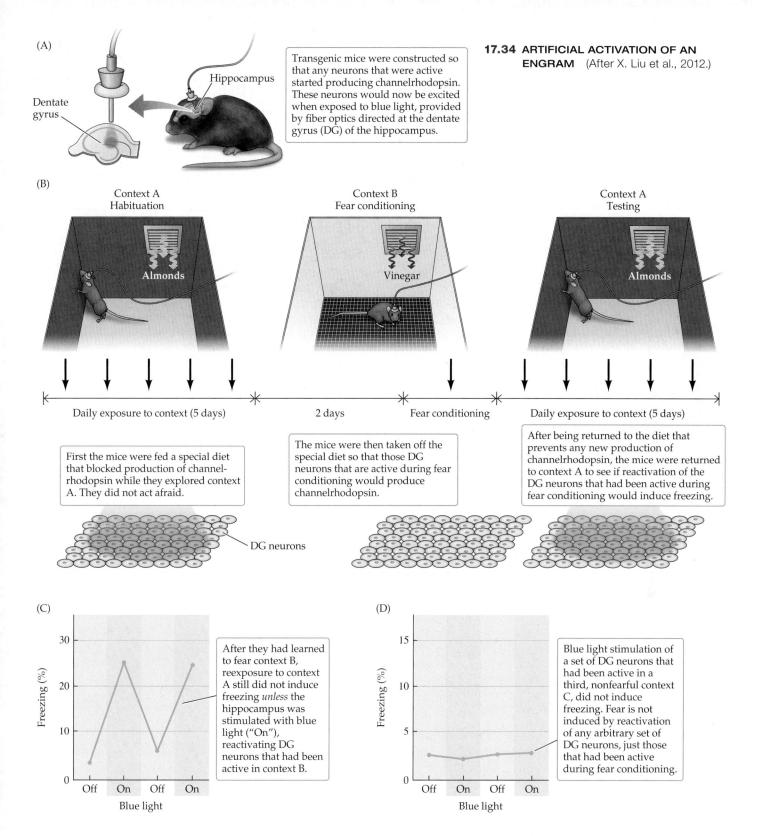

(A)

Dentate gyrus

Hippocampus

Transgenic mice were constructed so that any neurons that were active started producing channelrhodopsin. These neurons would now be excited when exposed to blue light, provided by fiber optics directed at the dentate gyrus (DG) of the hippocampus.

17.34 ARTIFICIAL ACTIVATION OF AN ENGRAM (After X. Liu et al., 2012.)

(B)

Context A
Habituation

Almonds

Context B
Fear conditioning

Vinegar

Context A
Testing

Almonds

Daily exposure to context (5 days) | 2 days | Fear conditioning | Daily exposure to context (5 days)

First the mice were fed a special diet that blocked production of channel-rhodopsin while they explored context A. They did not act afraid.

The mice were then taken off the special diet so that those DG neurons that are active during fear conditioning would produce channelrhodopsin.

After being returned to the diet that prevents any new production of channelrhodopsin, the mice were returned to context A to see if reactivation of the DG neurons that had been active during fear conditioning would induce freezing.

DG neurons

(C)

After they had learned to fear context B, reexposure to context A still did not induce freezing *unless* the hippocampus was stimulated with blue light ("On"), reactivating DG neurons that had been active in context B.

(D)

Blue light stimulation of a set of DG neurons that had been active in a third, nonfearful context C, did not induce freezing. Fear is not induced by reactivation of any arbitrary set of DG neurons, just those that had been active during fear conditioning.

were exposed to a particular context, A, placed in a box with a white plastic floor in a dimly lit room with black walls and a faint smell of almonds. The mice explored the chamber and showed no signs of being afraid (**FIGURE 17.34A AND B**). Next the mice were taught to be afraid of a very different context, B (a box with a wire grid floor in a brightly lit room with white walls and the smell of vinegar), by being exposed to an auditory tone followed by a mildly painful electrical shock to the feet. As expected, the mice quickly learned to freeze in response to the auditory tone (see Figure 15.15). Most important, these mice had received a genetic modification, controlled by a special diet, so that whenever neurons in the dentate gyrus (DG) of the hippocampus were active, they would start producing channelrhodopsin, a protein that would excite those cells, and only those cells, when exposed to blue light (see Figure 3.23)—an experimental technique called *optogenetic manipulation*. If the activity of this subset of DG neurons was responsible for the mice finding context B frightening, then reactivating those neurons should cause the mice to freeze in fear, even when they were in a completely different context.

To test this idea, the mice were put in context A, where they had never been shocked. As before, they showed no signs of being afraid. But, when fiber optics illuminated their DG with blue light, the mice froze, as if afraid. It was as though the mice were experiencing the other context, B, when the DG neurons that had been active in B were reactivated by the blue light. Turning the light off again caused the animals to resume activity, indicating that they remained unafraid of context A (**FIGURE 17.34C**). It wasn't just that light-induced activation of any random set of DG neurons induced fear, because when blue light reactivated DG neurons that had been active in a third (nonfearful) context, C, the animals did not freeze (**FIGURE 17.34D**). Rather, it appeared that the activity of that subset of DG neurons caused the mice to experience context B, which they had learned to fear—experimenters had activated an artificial memory. Evidence that electrical stimulation of discrete targets in the medial temporal lobe enhances memory formation in humans (Suthana et al., 2012) suggests that artificial memory is probably possible in our brains too.

Go to
bn8e.com
for study questions, quizzes, activities, and other resources

Recommended Reading

Baddeley, A. D. (2013). *Essentials of Human Memory.* London: Psychology Press.

Corkin, S. (2013). *Permanent Present Tense: The Unforgettable Life of the Amnesic Patient, H.M.* New York: Basic Books.

Gluck, M. A., Mercado, E., and Myers, C. E. (2013). *Learning and Memory: From Brain to Behavior* (2nd ed.). New York: Worth.

Kahana, M. J. (2012). *Foundations of Human Memory.* Oxford, England: Oxford University Press.

Lieberman, D. A. (2012). *Human Learning and Memory.* Cambridge, England: Cambridge University Press.

Martinez, J. L., and Kesner, R. P. (Eds.). (2014). *Learning and Memory: A Biological View* (2nd ed.). Cambridge, MA: Academic Press.

Rudy, J. W. (2013). *The Neurobiology of Learning and Memory* (2nd ed.). Sunderland, MA: Sinauer.

Squire, L. R., and Kandel, E. R. (2008). *Memory: From Mind to Molecules.* Greenwood Village, CO: Roberts and Company.

VISUAL SUMMARY

You should be able to relate each summary to the adjacent illustration, including structures and processes.
Go to **bn8e.com/vs17** for links to figures, animations, and activities that will help you consolidate the material.

1 The **hippocampus**, **mammillary bodies**, and dorsal thalamus are part of a network that must be intact to form new **declarative memories**—memories that we can declare to others. Damage to these regions can cause **amnesia**, the impairment of **memory**. Review **Figure 17.2**

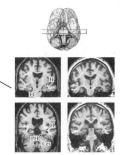

2 Removal of the hippocampus and nearby cortex left **patient H.M.** unable to form declarative memories that lasted more than a few minutes. He could, however, learn new **skills** such as mirror tracing, showing his **nondeclarative** (or *procedural*) **memory** for perceptual and motor behaviors was intact. Review **Figures 17.1–17.4**

3 Declarative memory consists of **semantic memory** of facts and **episodic memory** (or autobiographical memory) of particular incidents in the past. Brain damage can remove one type of declarative memory without affecting the other, indicating the two kinds of memories are stored separately. Review **Figures 17.5, 17.14, and 17.18, Activity 17.1**

4 Nondeclarative memory, which includes **skill learning**, **priming**, **operant conditioning** and **classical conditioning**, is demonstrated through performance. Most tests of memory in nonhuman animals are for nondeclarative memory, an exception being the **delayed non-matching-to-sample task** in monkeys. Review **Figures 17.6, 17.7, and 17.14**

5 Different kinds of **learning** depend on different brain regions. Spatial learning requires an intact hippocampus, while motor skills rely on the basal ganglia, and object recognition relies on the visual cortex. Review **Figures 17.17 and 17.18, Activity 17.2**

6 Memories are classified by how long they last. The **sensory buffers** retain only very brief impressions of sensations. **Short-term memory (STM)**, sometimes called **working memory**, lasts only a few minutes. Then the memory is either lost or transferred to **long-term memory (LTM)**, which may last a lifetime. The successive processes transferring information from one place to the other are **encoding**, **consolidation**, and **retrieval**. Memories are subject to distortion during recall and reconsolidation. Review **Figures 17.19–17.21**

7 **Nonassociative learning** includes **habituation**, while **associative learning** includes **classical conditioning** (*Pavlovian conditioning*) and **operant conditioning** (*instrumental conditioning*). Associative and nonassociative learning are forms of nondeclarative memory. In the sea slug *Aplysia*, habituation is due to a weakening of the synapse between the sensory neuron and the motor neuron. Review **Figures 17.25 and 17.26**

8 Conditioning of the eye-blink response in the rabbit is crucially dependent on the cerebellum. This simple mammalian system provides a model for understanding the formation of associations in the mammalian brain. Review **Figure 17.27**

9 **Long-term potentiation** (**LTP**) is a lasting increase in amplitude of the response of neurons, caused by brief high-frequency stimulation of their afferents (**tetanus**). In the hippocampus, LTP depends on the activation of **NMDA receptors**, which induces an increase in the number of postsynaptic **AMPA receptors** and greater neurotransmitter release. These are examples of **Hebbian synapses**, which become stronger if they successfully drive the postsynaptic cell, and weaker if they are unsuccessful. Review **Figures 17.28–17.30, Activity 17.3, Animation 17.2, Video 17.3**

10 Strong emotion can affect the strength of memories, as in **posttraumatic stress disorder** (**PTSD**). Review **Box 17.1**

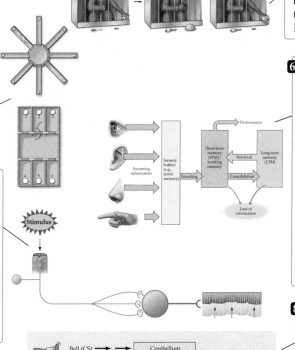

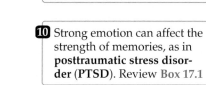

Attention and Higher Cognition

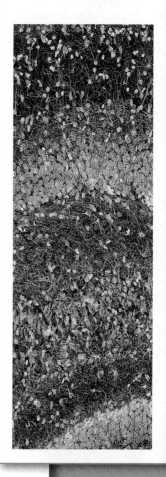

◼ One Thing at a Time

Everyone agreed that Parminder and her family were bighearted—generous and friendly to a fault—but they were also "bad"-hearted, in one sad sense. Many of Parminder's relatives had suffered early heart attacks and strokes, and now, in her 68th year, Parminder shared that unhappy fate. In February, and then again in September, a blood clot that originated in Parminder's heart found its way to the complex of arteries in her brain, eventually lodging like a cork and cutting off blood flow to the surrounding brain tissue: a *stroke*. But what made Parminder's case exceptional was that the two strokes were exact mirror images—they damaged identical regions of the left and right parietal lobes.

Parminder's unlikely lesions produced equally unlikely symptoms. A few weeks after her second stroke, Parminder had regained many of her intellectual powers—she could converse normally and remember things. Her visual fields were apparently normal too, but her visual perception was anything but normal. Parminder had lost the ability to see and pay attention to more than one thing at a time. For example, she could see her husband's face just fine, but she couldn't tell whether he had glasses on. She could see the glasses, or she could see the face, but couldn't see both at the same time. Shown a drawing of several overlapping items, Parminder could perceive and name only one at a time. Furthermore, she couldn't understand where the objects she saw were located. It was as if Parminder was lost in space, able to pay attention to only one object at a time, each alone in a world of its own. What could explain Parminder's symptoms?

William James, the great American psychologist, wrote in 1890:

> *Everyone knows what attention is. It is the taking possession by the mind, in clear and vivid form, of one out of what seem several simultaneously possible objects or trains of thought. Focalization, concentration, of consciousness are of its essence. It implies withdrawal from some things in order to deal effectively with others, and is a condition which has a real opposite in the confused, dazed, scatterbrained state.*

James understood that attention can be effortful, improves perception, and acts as a filter on the outside world. When we are alert and functioning normally, we are always paying attention to something. This continual shifting of our focus from one interesting stimulus to the next lies at the heart of our innermost conscious experiences and our awareness of the world around us and our place in it. So, we open this chapter by exploring the behavioral and neural dimensions of attention before broadening our focus to the second major topic of the chapter: consciousness.

◼ Go to **Brain Explorer**
bn8e.com/18.1

Attention

Attention Selects Stimuli for Processing

attention Also called *selective attention*. A state or condition of selective awareness or perceptual receptivity, by which specific stimuli are selected for enhanced processing.

arousal The global, nonselective level of alertness of an individual.

cocktail party effect The selective enhancement of attention in order to filter out distracters, such as while listening to one person talking in the midst of a noisy party.

Although she may delight in pretending otherwise, any average 5-year-old understands what it means when an exasperated parent shouts, "Pay attention!" We all share an intuitive understanding of the term *attention*, but to this day scientists have been unable to agree on a definition that goes much beyond the one provided by James—a testament to the great complexity and scope of the topic. In general, **attention** (or *selective attention*) is the process by which we select or focus on one or more specific stimuli—either sensory phenomena or internal thoughts—for enhanced processing and analysis. It is the *selective* quality of attention that distinguishes it from the related concept of **arousal**, the global level of alertness of the individual. Most of the time we orient our attention *overtly*, directing our senses and our attention toward the same target. For example, as you read this sentence, it is both the center of your visual gaze and (we hope) the main item that your brain has selected for attention. But if we choose to, we can shift the focus of our visual attention *covertly*; in classic research, Hermann von Helmholtz (1962; original work published in 1894) showed that we can keep our eyes fixed on one location while "secretly" scrutinizing some other location in peripheral vision (**FIGURE 18.1**).

Selective attention isn't restricted to visual stimuli. Imagine yourself chatting with an old friend at a noisy party. Despite the high levels of background noise, you would probably find it relatively easy to focus on what she was saying, even if she was speaking quietly, because paying close attention to your friend would enhance your processing of her speech and helps filter out distracters. This selective enhancement is known as the **cocktail party effect**, and it nicely illustrates how attention acts to *focus* cognitive processing resources on a particular target. Though it may feel effortless, in this scenario you are solving a very difficult information-processing problem: with loud fragments of speech coming from every direction, how do you know which sounds go together? Solving that problem requires that you maintain

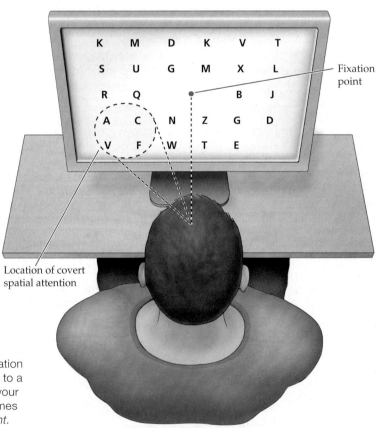

18.1 COVERT DIRECTION OF ATTENTION Holding your gaze steady on a central fixation point, you can direct your visual attention to a different spatial location without moving your eyes. This selective attention has sometimes been referred to as an *attentional spotlight*.

the focus of your attention on a single speech source, and if your attention drifts to a different auditory stimulus—for example, if you start eavesdropping on a more interesting conversation—it becomes virtually impossible to simultaneously follow your friend's conversation. Unsurprisingly, actually having cocktails exacerbates the problem because alcohol lowers sensitivity for speech-related frequencies, reducing your ability to distinguish your friend's speech from background noise (Upile et al., 2007). Maybe this is one reason that parties seem to get louder as the night wears on.

There are limits on attention

In a cocktail party setting you have a variety of extra clues, in different sensory modalities—the spatial origin of the speech sounds, the movements of your friend's face as she speaks, the unique tone of her voice, and so on—to help you focus on your friend's speech. But what if our attention is restricted to just a single type of stimulus? In now-classic experiments on the cocktail party effect (Cherry, 1953), extra cues were systematically excluded by having participants listen through headphones. Participants listened to two different streams of dialog delivered simultaneously to the left and right ears, a technique known as **dichotic presentation** (see Figure 19.16). People were asked to focus their attention on one ear or the other and to repeat aloud the material being presented to that ear. On this demanding task, called **shadowing**, participants could accurately report what they were hearing in the attended ear, but they could report very little that had been presented to the nonattended ear, aside from simple characteristics like the gender of the speaker. If a shadowing task is sufficiently difficult, then even advance warning that they will be quizzed later doesn't help people remember and report information from the nonattended auditory stream (Moray, 1959). In fact, even when the person's own name is presented in the nonattended ear, it is detected only about a third of the time (N. Wood and Cowan, 1995).

The cocktail party effect is not limited to speech (or parties!), of course. For example, musicians are better than nonmusicians at focusing attention on target notes and segregating them from multiple simultaneous musical sounds (Zendel and Alain, 2009). A shadowing procedure can be used to study visual attention too. In this case, participants are asked to attend to just one of two fully overlapping videos being presented simultaneously—imagine two movies being projected onto a single screen. As in the auditory shadowing experiments, participants are able to focus on one video only at the expense of the other; little of the nonattended video can be reported (Neisser and Becklen, 1975). Furthermore, if the attended visual stream is sufficiently complicated, people show **inattentional blindness**: a surprising failure to perceive nonattended stimuli that you'd think would be impossible to miss, like a gorilla strolling across the screen (Simons and Chabris, 1999; Simons and Jensen, 2009). It's a problem that can even bedevil experts: in one study, a clear image of a gorilla inserted into a CT scan of the lungs was missed by fully 83% of radiologists screening for lung cancer (Drew et al., 2013). (What's the deal with all the gorillas? We don't know, but you can try out some examples for yourself on the website.)

In general, **divided-attention tasks**—in which the person is asked to process two or more simultaneous stimuli—confirm that attention is a *limited* resource and that it's very difficult to attend to more than one thing at a time, particularly if the stimuli to be attended to are spatially separated (Bonnel and Prinzmetal, 1998). So, our limited selective attention generally acts like an **attentional spotlight**, which shifts around the environment, highlighting stimuli for enhanced processing. It's an adaptation that we share with many other species because, like us, they are confronted with the problem of extracting important signals from a noisy background (Bee and Micheyl, 2008). Birds, for example, must isolate the vocalizations of specific individuals from a cacophony of calls and other noises in the environment—an avian version of the cocktail party problem (Benney and Braaten, 2000). Having a single attentional spotlight helps us focus cognitive resources and behavioral responses toward the most important things in the environment at any given moment (the smell of smoke, the voice of a potential mate, a glimpse of a big spotty cat), while ignoring extraneous information.

dichotic presentation The simultaneous delivery of different stimuli to the right and the left ears.

shadowing A task in which the participant is asked to focus attention on one ear or the other while stimuli are being presented separately to both ears.

inattentional blindness The failure to perceive nonattended stimuli that seem so obvious as to be impossible to miss.

divided-attention task A task in which the participant is asked to simultaneously focus attention on two or more stimuli.

attentional spotlight The shifting of our limited selective attention around the environment to highlight stimuli for enhanced processing.

Go to Video 18.2
Change Blindness and Inattentional Blindness
bn8e.com/18.2

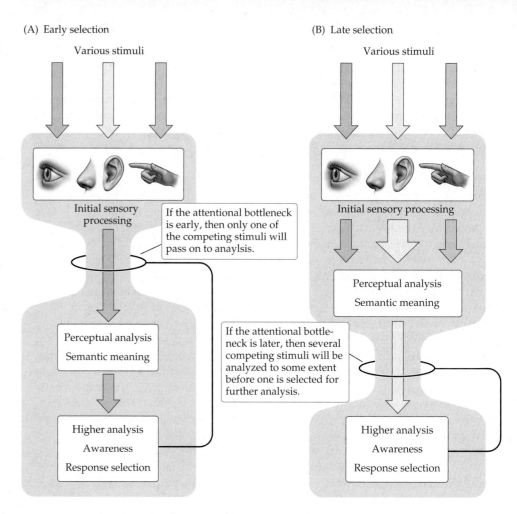

(A) Early selection

Various stimuli

Initial sensory processing

If the attentional bottleneck is early, then only one of the competing stimuli will pass on to anaylsis.

Perceptual analysis

Semantic meaning

Higher analysis

Awareness

Response selection

(B) Late selection

Various stimuli

Initial sensory processing

Perceptual analysis

Semantic meaning

If the attentional bottleneck is later, then several competing stimuli will be analyzed to some extent before one is selected for further analysis.

Higher analysis

Awareness

Response selection

attentional bottleneck   A filter that results from the limits intrinsic to our attentional processes, with the result that only the most important stimuli are selected for special processing.

early-selection model   A model of attention in which the attentional bottleneck filters out stimuli before even preliminary perceptual analysis has occurred.

late-selection model   A model of attention in which the attentional bottleneck filters out stimuli only after substantial analysis has occurred.

perceptual load   The immediate processing challenge presented by a stimulus.

One of the important functions of attention is to act as a filter, blocking unimportant stimuli and directing cognitive resources to only the most important events, and thereby protecting the brain from being overwhelmed by the world. But at what level of sensory processing is this **attentional bottleneck** evident? Initial research gave evidence of an **early-selection model** of attention (**FIGURE 18.2A**), in which unattended information is filtered out right away, at the level of the initial sensory input, as in the shadowing experiments (Broadbent, 1958). But other researchers noted that some important but unattended stimuli (such as your name) may undergo substantial unconscious processing right up to the level of semantic meaning and awareness, before suddenly capturing attention (N. Wood and Cowan, 1995). This is an example of a **late-selection model** of attention, in which the filtration imposed by the processing bottleneck occurs at a later point, filtering out stimuli only after substantial analysis has already occurred (**FIGURE 18.2B**). Many models of attention contain both early- and late-selection mechanisms (e.g., Wolfe, 1994), and vigorous debate continues over their relative importance.

A possible resolution to the debate over early versus late selection involves **perceptual load**—the immediate processing challenge presented by a stimulus. According to this view (N. Lavie et al., 2004), when we focus on a complex stimulus that requires a lot of perceptual processing, no perceptual resources remain for use on competing unattended items. So in this case, attention exerts early selection and excludes other stimuli from the outset. But when we focus on simpler stimuli, there is enough perceptual capacity to allow for processing of other stimuli, right up to the level of semantic meaning, recognition, and awareness (and thus, late selection) (N. Lavie et al., 2009). In other words, if we view attention as a limited resource, then we only have enough of it to do one complex task at a time, or several simple ones. These studies thus indicate that attention strikes a balance between early and late selection, according to the difficulty of the task at hand.

Attention Is Deployed in Several Different Ways

We've now seen that through an act of willpower we can direct our attention to specific stimulus sources without moving our eyes or otherwise reorienting. Early experiments on this phenomenon, like Helmholtz's, employed **sustained-attention tasks**, in which a single stimulus source or location must be held in the attentional spotlight for a protracted period (see Figure 18.1). Although these tasks are useful for studying basic phenomena, and for assessing attention problems due to neurological disorders, we need something more powerful to address key questions about attention. For example, how do we shift attention around? How does attention enhance the processing of stimuli, and which brain regions are involved? To answer these questions, researchers devised various clever tasks that employ **stimulus cuing** to control attention, revealing two general categories of attention, as we'll describe next.

We can decide where to direct our attention

The types of tasks that we have discussed thus far all involve **voluntary attention** (also called *consciously* or *endogenously controlled attention*). As the name implies, voluntary shifts of attention come from within; they are the conscious, *top-down* directing of attention toward specific aspects of the environment, according to our interests and goals.

By far the most common experimental procedure for studying voluntary attention is the **symbolic cuing task**, originated by Posner (1980). On this type of task, participants stare at a fixation point in the center of a computer screen and must press a key as soon as they see a specific target stimulus (the response being measured is therefore reaction time; **BOX 18.1**). Each trial is preceded by a cue that gives the

sustained-attention task A task in which a single stimulus source or location must be held in the attentional spotlight for a protracted period.

stimulus cuing A testing technique in which a cue to the stimulus location is provided before the stimulus itself.

voluntary attention Also called *consciously* or *endogenously controlled attention* or *top-down attention*. The voluntary direction of attention toward specific aspects of the environment, in accordance with our interests and goals.

symbolic cuing task An attention task in which a symbol indicates to the participant where to voluntarily direct attention in order to detect a stimulus.

Go to Animation 18.3
From Input to Output
bn8e.com/18.3

BOX 18.1
Reaction Time Responses, from Input to Output

Reaction time measures are a mainstay of cognitive neuroscience research. In tests of *simple reaction time*, participants make a single response—for example, pressing a button—in response to experimental stimuli (the appearance of a target, the solution to a problem, a tone, or whatever the experiment is testing). Tests of *choice reaction time* involve a slightly more complicated situation, in which a person is presented with alternatives and has to choose among them (e.g., right versus wrong, same versus different) by pressing one of two or more buttons.

Reaction times in an uncomplicated choice reaction time test, in which the participant indicates whether two stimuli are the same or different, average about 300–350 milliseconds (ms). The delay between stimulus and response varies depending on the amount of neural processing required between input and output. The stations involved in our sample task, and the timing of events, are illustrated in the figure. Brain activity proceeds

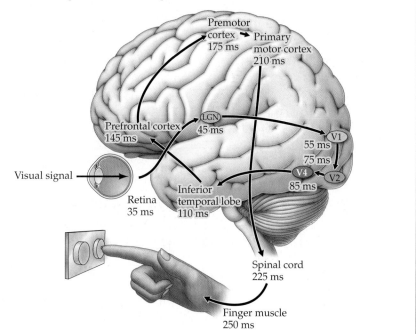

The sequence and timing of brain events that determine reaction time. LGN, lateral geniculate nucleus; V1, primary visual cortex; V2 and V4, extrastriate visual areas. (Timings based on Thorpe and Fabre-Thorpe, 2001.)

from the primary visual cortex through a ventral visual object identification pathway (see Chapter 10) to prefrontal cortex, and then through premotor

and primary motor cortex, down to the spinal motor neurons and out to the finger muscles. In the sequence

(continued)

BOX 18.1
Reaction Time Responses, from Input to Output (continued)

shown in the figure—proceeding from the presentation of visual stimuli to a discrimination response—notice that it takes about 110 ms for the sensory system (somewhere in the inferior temporal lobe) to recognize the stimulus, and about 35 ms more for that information to reach the prefrontal cortex. At this point, a decision about which

response to choose must be made; for very simple tasks this may take as little as 30 ms (Stanford et al., 2010), although for more-complex stimuli it may take longer. Then it takes about 75 ms for the movement to be executed (i.e., the time elapsed between the point at which the signal from the prefrontal cortex arrives in the premo-

tor cortex and the point at which the finger pushes the button). It is fascinating to think that something like this sequence of neural events happens over and over in more-complicated behaviors, such as recognizing a long-lost friend or composing an opera.

participant a hint as to where the stimulus will appear. So in our simple example (**FIGURE 18.3A**), participants fixate on the central point, and an arrow pointing left, right, or in both directions briefly flashes in a central location. Then, after a delay, the target stimulus flashes on the screen and the participant presses a key when he detects it. In most trials where there is a single arrow, it points in the correct direction and thus provides a *valid cue* about which side of the screen the target will appear on, but sometimes there's an *invalid cue*, where the arrow points in the opposite direction of where the target subsequently appears. The effects of these cues on reaction time are averaged over many trials and compared with trials with *neutral cues*, in which the cue provides no hint about subsequent target location.

As you can see in **FIGURE 18.3B**, people swiftly learn to use the cues to predict stimulus location, shifting their attention in the cued direction—*without shifting their gaze*—in anticipation of the appearance of the target stimulus. Reaction time is thus

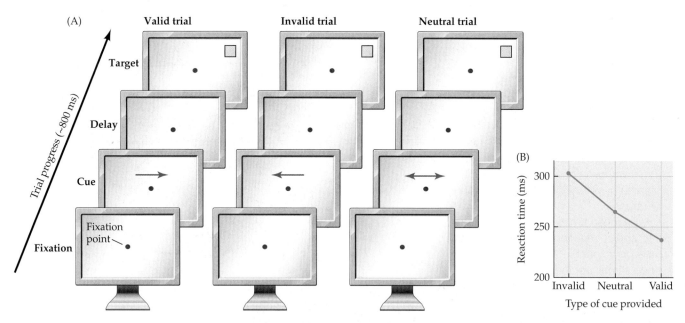

18.3 MEASURING THE EFFECTS OF VOLUNTARY SHIFTS OF ATTENTION (A) In symbolic cuing tasks, participants are provided with cues (the arrows) that accurately predict target locations (valid trials), provide inaccurate predictions (invalid trials), or provide no predictions (neutral trials). Participants are instructed to maintain visual fixation on a central point throughout the trial. (B) Whether the target appears to the left or the right of the fixation point, valid cues significantly enhance reaction time to detect the target, and invalid cues significantly impair reaction time. (After Posner, 1980.)

significantly faster for validly cued trials, compared with the uncued neutral condition, even when participants do not move their eyes to the cued location. And participants clearly pay a price on trials in which the cue is invalid, misdirecting attention to the wrong side of the display; they take more time to detect the target. So, directed attention helps us to perform better, faster, and with increased sensitivity to cues. Many variants of the symbolic cuing paradigm—changing the timing of the stimuli, altering their complexity, choosing between different responses (as in Box 18.1), and so on—have been employed to study the neurophysiological mechanisms of attention (R. D. Wright and Ward, 2008), as we'll discuss a little later in the chapter.

Some stimuli grab our attention

Everyone knows that attention to events in the surrounding environment involves more than just consciously steering your attentional spotlight around. Loud noise or sudden silence, flashes, moving objects—any striking or important change—can potently capture attention and draw it away from the task at hand, unless you are very focused (every conversation stops and every head swivels when someone drops a plate in a restaurant). This sort of involuntary reorientation toward a sudden or important event is an example of **reflexive attention** (or *exogenously controlled attention*). It is considered to be a *bottom-up* process because attention is being captured and controlled by sensory inputs from lower levels of the nervous system, rather than being the result of voluntary, conscious cognitive control by the forebrain.

The effects of reflexive shifts of attention on stimulus processing can be measured using a **peripheral spatial cuing task** (**FIGURE 18.4A**). Again, the participant fixates on a point and is asked to respond as quickly as possible when the target stimulus appears. But instead of a meaningful symbol to direct attention toward a target location, a simple *task-irrelevant* sensory stimulus (often a flash of light, but it could be a sound or other stimulus) is presented *in the location to which attention is to be drawn*. After a momentary delay, the target stimulus is presented, either in the same location

reflexive attention Also called *exogenously controlled attention* or *bottom-up attention*. The involuntary reorienting of attention toward the location of an unexpected object or event.

peripheral spatial cuing task An attention task where a visual stimulus is preceded by a simple sensory stimulus (like a flash) that reflexively captures attention.

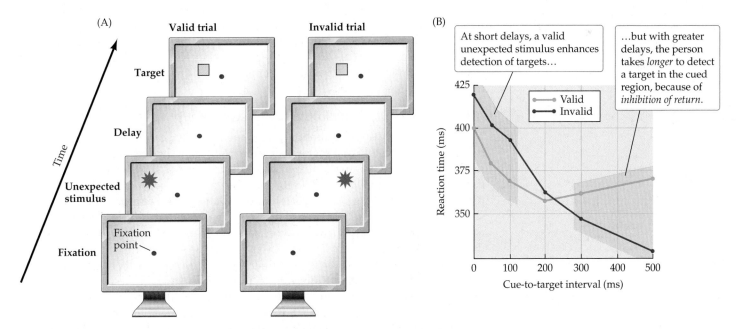

18.4 REFLEXIVE CAPTURE OF ATTENTION AND INHIBITION OF RETURN (A) In valid trials, a momentary flash appears in the location where a stimulus will appear soon. In invalid trials, the flash appears somewhere other than where the stimulus will appear. (B) Reaction times indicate that attention is focused on the cued location for less than about 200 ms. If the stimulus appears later, the person is *less* likely to detect it than if his attention had never been drawn to that region. This demonstrates the so-called inhibition of return (of attention). (After R. M. Klein, 2000.)

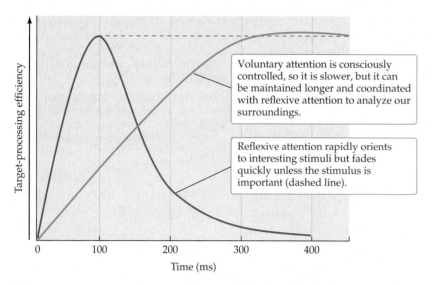

Voluntary attention is consciously controlled, so it is slower, but it can be maintained longer and coordinated with reflexive attention to analyze our surroundings.

Reflexive attention rapidly orients to interesting stimuli but fades quickly unless the stimulus is important (dashed line).

18.5 VOLUNTARY AND REFLEXIVE ATTENTION ARE COMPLEMENTARY Quick-reacting reflexive attention and slower, longer-lasting voluntarily controlled attention work together to direct our analysis of the environment.

inhibition of return The phenomenon in which detection of stimuli at the former location of a cue is impaired for latencies of 200 ms or more.

feature search A search for an item in which the target pops out right away because it possesses a unique attribute.

conjunction search A search for an item that is based on two or more features (e.g., size and color) that together distinguish the target from distracters that may share some of the same attributes.

as the cue (a valid trial) or somewhere else (an invalid trial). Reaction time measures for many such trials are averaged for each participant.

Two important effects are seen in such an experiment (**FIGURE 18.4B**). First, a valid cue captures attention and enhances processing of subsequent stimuli in the target location, but only when the interval between cue and target is brief—the cue draws attention toward the target location, but after 150 milliseconds (ms) or so, attention apparently wanders away again and the enhancement of processing is lost. And when the interval between cue and target becomes longer—about 200 ms onward—a curious phenomenon is observed: detection of stimuli at the location where the cue occurred is increasingly *impaired* (R. M. Klein, 2000; Posner and Cohen, 1984). It's as though attention has moved on from the flash and is reluctant to return to that location. This **inhibition of return** probably evolved to prevent reflexively controlled attention from settling on unimportant stimuli for more than an instant.

Normally, voluntary and reflexive attention work together in cognition (**FIGURE 18.5**), probably relying on somewhat overlapping neural mechanisms. Anyone who has watched a squirrel at work has seen that twitchy interplay. When it comes to single-mindedly searching for tasty morsels (an example of voluntarily controlled attention), a squirrel has few rivals. But even slight noises and movements (cues that reflexively capture attention) will cause it to stop and scan its surroundings—a sensible precaution if, like a squirrel, you are yourself a tasty morsel. Effective cues for reflexive attention can cross the boundaries between different sensory modalities in order to aid the processing of stimuli; a sudden sound coming from a particular location, for example, can improve the *visual* processing of a stimulus that appears there (Hillyard et al., 2016; McDonald et al., 2000), especially if the cue is associated with reward (Pooresmaeili et al., 2014). Cats are much better at localizing prey when they have a combination of cues to guide their attention (Schnupp et al., 2005), one of the many reasons that squirrels are twitchy.

Attention helps us to search a cluttered world for specific patterns

Another way that we use attention is to systematically scan the world, in order to find some specific item in a sea of distracters. If the sought item is different from all the distracters in some fundamental way—your friend in a red coat, in a crowd of dark-suited businesspeople—the search is easy and the target of the search immediately "pops out." This type of visual search is known as a **feature search**, and it seems effortless. But more often we must rely on a **conjunction search**: searching for an item on the basis of two or more features (e.g., size and color) that together distinguish the target from distracters that may share some of the same attributes.

The visual search tasks employed in attention labs typically consist of arrays of target stimuli that systematically vary in the number of attributes they share with nearby distracters, and also in the number of distracters that are present. In a simple feature search (**FIGURE 18.6A**), targets pop out right away, no matter how many distracters are present, with only a few exceptions (Joseph et al., 1997). Finding the target takes little effort and there is no need to scan the other items one by one. In contrast, performance on conjunction searches (**FIGURE 18.6B AND C**) is directly related to the number of distracters present. The results obtained from many such experiments (**FIGURE 18.6D**) suggest that in conjunction searches we are coordinating multiple cognitive *feature maps*—overlapping maps of the searched array, with each map focused on one particular stimulus attribute (color, shape, and so on).

(A) Feature search

Find a green object

Find a square

(B) Conjunction search:
    target present

Find a red circle

(C) Conjunction search:
    target absent

Find a green square

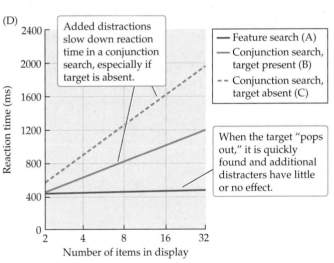

(D)

Added distractions slow down reaction time in a conjunction search, especially if target is absent.

— Feature search (A)
— Conjunction search, target present (B)
-- Conjunction search, target absent (C)

When the target "pops out," it is quickly found and additional distracters have little or no effect.

Reaction time (ms) — y-axis: 0, 400, 800, 1200, 1600, 2000, 2400

Number of items in display — x-axis: 2, 4, 8, 16, 32

This influential idea, called **feature integration theory** (A. M. Treisman and Gelade, 1980), helps us address an issue that has come to be known as the **binding problem** (A. M. Treisman, 1996). Namely, how does the brain know that a particular set of features combine to define a single object, considering that these different features are processed in different regions in the brain? According to feature integration theory, simple preattentive stimulus attributes (e.g., color, shape) guide our scanning of the environment, with higher-order processes coordinating the binding of features and, ultimately, conscious perception and selection. This may be why conjunction searches run much faster when you can direct your attention to a single basic attribute of the stimuli to be scanned (a **bottom-up process**: e.g., scan first for black things, then for cars, then Subarus, and so on, until you spot your car in the parking lot) rather than using systematic voluntary steering of the attentional spotlight using all attributes simultaneously (a **top-down process**: e.g., search for your black 2012 Subaru Forester) (Wolfe et al., 2000). Sustained attention to multiple

feature integration theory
The idea that conjunction searches involve multiple cognitive feature maps—overlapping representations of the search array based on individual stimulus attributes.

binding problem The question of how the brain understands which individual attributes blend together into a single object, when these different features are processed by different regions in the brain.

bottom-up process A process in which lower-order mechanisms, like sensory inputs, trigger additional processing by higher-order systems. There may be no conscious awareness until late in the process.

top-down process A process in which higher-order cognitive processes control lower-order systems, often reflecting conscious control.

temporal resolution The ability of an imaging technique to track changes in the brain over time.

spatial resolution The ability to observe the detailed structure of the brain.

features requires a large cognitive effort, and if the target objects appear only infrequently—as do weapons in luggage or tumors in X-rays—they may go undetected with alarmingly high frequency, even by highly trained screeners (Wolfe et al., 2005).

To uncover finer details of the brain's attentional mechanisms, neuroscientists take two complementary perspectives on attention. First, we can look at *consequences of attention* in the brain, asking how selective attention modifies brain activity to enhance processing of stimuli. Second, we can probe the *mechanisms of attention*, the brain regions that produce and control attention, shifting it between different stimuli in different sensory modalities. In selecting experimental techniques to address these objectives, researchers must juggle the need for good **temporal resolution**—the ability to track changes in the brain that occur very quickly—with the need for excellent **spatial resolution**, the ability to observe the detailed structure of the brain. Electrophysiological approaches offer the speed (temporal resolution) necessary to distinguish the consequences of attention from the mechanisms that direct it, and brain-imaging techniques like fMRI offer the anatomical detail (spatial resolution) to figure out exactly where these neural actions are taking place. This speed-accuracy trade-off permeates the research that we discuss in the following sections.

Attention Affects the Functioning of the Brain

When many cortical neurons work together to solve a complicated problem, their activity becomes synchronized to some degree. In Chapter 3 we described *electroencephalography* (EEG), in which sensitive recording electrodes are attached to the scalp at standardized locations (**FIGURE 18.7A**) to record moment-to-moment changes in brain electrical activity. So, you might think that the electrical activity of a network of millions of neurons working together on a specific problem would be easy to see in an EEG, but it isn't. That's because the contributions of multiple simultaneously active networks, regional differences in the timing of activity, and individual variation in the firing of neurons all contribute to the real-time EEG, making it look surprisingly random during the performance of any particular task. To solve this problem, researchers ask participants to do the same task over and over again (**FIGURE**

18.7 EVENT-RELATED POTENTIALS (A) Scalp electrodes record EEG activity during task performance. (B) The task is repeated many times; individual EEG segments for multiple trials show considerable random variation. (C) Averaging many such trials cancels out the random variation, leaving only task-related components, labeled as shown. Note that by convention, negative voltages are charted above the zero line. (Yes, it's kind of weird.)

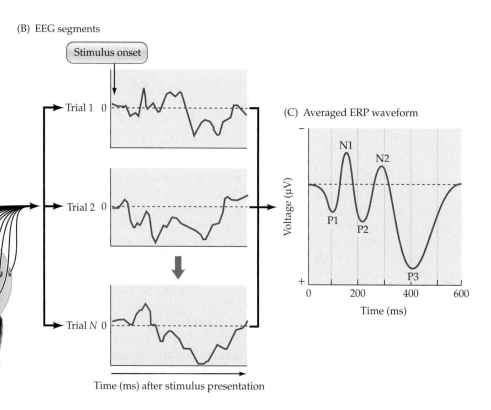

18.7B), and they average all the EEGs recorded during those repeated trials. Averaged over enough repetitions of the task, the variation due to the random firing of other neurons averages out, and what's left is the overall electrical activity specifically associated with the task being performed (**FIGURE 18.7C**). This averaged activity is called the **event-related potential** (**ERP**) (Luck, 2005), and it reveals regional changes in brain activity much faster than brain-imaging techniques like fMRI. For this reason, ERP has become the favorite tool of neuroscientists studying moment-to-moment consequences of attention in the brain, as we'll see.

Distinctive patterns of brain electrical activity mark shifts of attention

In one classic study of auditory attention (Hillyard et al., 1973), dichotic tones were presented to participants who were asked to attend to the stimuli arriving at one ear and to ignore the other ear. In half the trials, participants attended to the left; in the other half, to the right. EEGs were recorded and averaged into ERPs as already described. Thus, for each ear the researchers were able to compare ERPs for attended stimuli with ERPs for unattended stimuli. Overall, the ERPs for attended stimuli were larger in amplitude than when the same stimuli at the same ear were not being attended to. This effect was particularly evident in the ERP component called *N1*, a large negativity occurring 100–200 ms after stimulus onset. Because the only thing that changed between conditions was participants' attention to the stimuli, this auditory **N1 effect** must have been caused by selective attention somehow acting on neural mechanisms to enhance processing of information from that ear. Auditory attention also enhances much later ERP components, especially a wave called *P3* (or *auditory P300*; see Figure 18.7). P3 is believed to reflect higher-order cognitive processing of the stimulus (Herrmann and Knight, 2001)—semantic meaning of words, identification of the speaker, and so on—so the **P3 effect** is an example of a late-selection effect of auditory attention. In fact, some researchers view the P3 component as an electrophysiological marker of consciousness (Dehaene and Changeux, 2011), perhaps indicating that conscious awareness starts to emerge when P3 first appears in infants, at about 5 months of age (Kouider et al., 2013). Abnormal P3 responses are a reliable finding in people with schizophrenia, consistent with their difficulty filtering out distracting information (Ford, 1999).

Attention to *visual* stimuli is likewise reflected in ERPs, but because the neural systems involved in visual perception are different from those involved in audition, endogenous visual attention causes its own different, distinctive changes in the ERP. We can study these visual effects by collecting ERP data over occipital cortex—the primary visual area of the brain—while a participant performs a symbolic cuing task. **FIGURE 18.8** depicts this sort of experiment. On valid trials (remember, this is when the target appears as expected, in the location indicated by the cue, as in **FIGURE 18.8A**), electrodes over occipital cortex show a substantial enhancement of the ERP component called *P1*, the positive wave that occurs over auditory cortex about 70–100 ms after stimulus onset, often carrying over into an enhancement of the N1 component immediately afterward (**FIGURE 18.8B**). The visual **P1 effect** involves a large increase in the amplitude of P1 for attended stimuli, compared with ERPs for exactly the same stimulus presentation when attention is being directed elsewhere. The P1 effect is thought to reflect a crucial early-selection mechanism: an attentional bottleneck whereby attention selectively boosts the activity of occipital sensory processing (Mangun, 1995). Notice also that the visual P1 effect occurs over the *contralateral* occipital cortex; this is because information from the left visual field is processed in right occipital cortex, and vice versa, as we discussed in Chapter 10 (see Figure 10.10). A similar effect on P1 is evident when attention is instead oriented *reflexively* to a flash or sound (Hopfinger and Mangun, 1998; McDonald et al., 2005) but only when the interval between the cue and the appearance of the target is brief. At longer intervals, the P1 effect may actually be *reduced* as an electrophysiological manifestation of inhibition of return (McDonald et al., 1999). And for invalid trials in symbolic cuing experiments (see Figure 18.8A), where attention is being directed elsewhere, the **visual P1 effect** isn't evident at all, even though the visual stimulus is identical and in the same loca-

event-related potential (ERP) Averaged EEG recordings measuring brain responses to repeated presentations of a stimulus.

N1 effect A negative deflection of the event-related potential, occurring about 100 ms after stimulus presentation, that is enhanced for selectively attended input, compared with ignored input.

P3 effect A positive deflection of the event-related potential, occurring about 300–500 ms after stimulus presentation, that is associated with higher-order auditory stimulus processing and late attentional selection.

P1 effect A positive deflection of the event-related potential, occurring 70–100 ms after stimulus presentation, that is enhanced for selectively attended visual input, compared with ignored input.

visual P1 effect An increase in amplitude of the P1 component of event-related potentials that occurs for stimuli that are the focus of attention.

(A) Cued visual attention test

Attend left (valid cue)

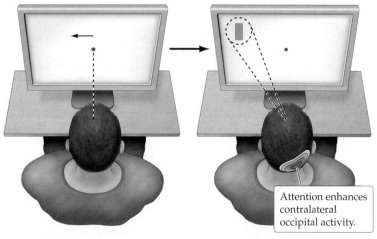

Attend right (invalid cue)

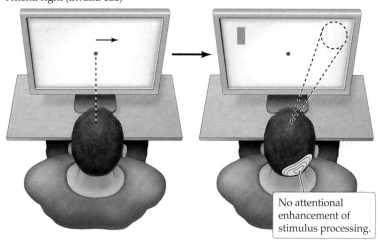

Attention enhances contralateral occipital activity.

No attentional enhancement of stimulus processing.

(B) Right occipital ERP

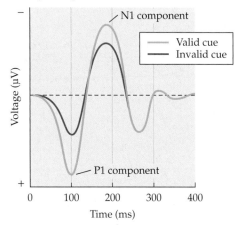

N1 component

Valid cue
Invalid cue

Voltage (μV)

P1 component

0   100   200   300   400

Time (ms)

18.8 ERP CHANGES IN CUED SHIFTS OF VISUAL ATTENTION (A) In this example, the participant maintains central fixation and covertly orients (dashed circle) in the direction indicated by a prior symbolic cue, pressing a key as soon as a stimulus appears. In most trials the cue is valid (left), but sometimes it misdirects attention to a different location (right). (B) This ERP, collected over the right occipital cortex while a stimulus was presented in the left visual field, shows that directing attention to the correct location significantly enhances neural processing and detection when the stimulus appears, reflected as large enhancements in the P1 and N1 components, starting 70–100 ms after stimulus presentation.

tion as in the valid trials. Attentional selection based on higher-order, complex properties of visual stimuli and combining multiple features—that is, late-selection tasks—is less associated with a P1 effect and instead is more likely to involve change in longer-latency ERP components (occurring as much as 400 ms after stimulus presentation; review Figure 18.7).

What happens to ERPs during visual search tasks, where we are directing attention so as to find a particular target in an array and ignore distracters (see Figure 18.6)? Under these conditions, a characteristic enhancement of a subcomponent of N2 (see Figure 18.7) is triggered at occipitotemporal sites contralateral to the visual search stimulus to which attention is being directed. In such studies, participants maintain fixation on a central point and the stimulus array is presented only briefly, so the visual search requires rapid, covert shifts of attention to the selected target. The wave form associated with this deployment of visual attention is called *N2pc* (short for **N2-p**osterior-**c**ontralateral) (Luck and Hillyard, 1994), but the question arose whether it reflected the selective processing of targets or the suppression of a response toward distracters. An experiment that addressed this question (Hickey et al., 2009) is depicted in **FIGURE 18.9**. Here, participants maintained central fixation and were briefly presented with a very simple array, consisting of only a red line at one of several possible locations on the left or right side of the display, and a green square that was always on the midline (**FIGURE 18.9A**). On some trials, participants were instructed to attend to the red line and report on its length. The line was isoluminant to the background (i.e., had the same brightness), so attention was not reflexively captured by this stimulus. In other trials, participants were instructed to attend to the green square and *ignore* the red line. The important thing is the displays were the same in both conditions; only the instruction to the participant varied. Comparing the visual N2 component of the ERPs for the ipsilateral and contralateral hemispheres (**FIGURE 18.9B**), it is evident that N2pc was associated with covert orientation toward the red line when it was the target, but furthermore, when the participant was instead instructed to ignore the red line, a different ERP component emerged: a large positivity over the occipital region, now known as P_D (for distracter positivity), that is associated with ignoring distracters, even if they are quite attention grabbing (Gaspar and McDonald, 2014; Hickey et al., 2009).

The neural mechanisms of visual attention are somewhat plastic: extensive experience with action video games, which rely heavily on visual attention, is associated with neural changes (Tanaka et al., 2013; West et al., 2015) and lasting enhancements of longer-latency ERP components (Latham et al., 2013; Mishra et al., 2011). Possible trade-offs for all this gaming, however, may include impairments in social

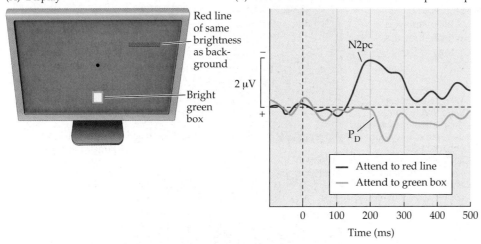

(A) Display

Red line of same brightness as background

2 µV

Bright green box

(B) Lateralized ERP waveforms over occipital scalp

N2pc

P_D

— Attend to red line
— Attend to green box

0   100   200   300   400   500

Time (ms)

18.9 DISTINCTIVE CHANGES IN BRAIN ACTIVITY IN VISUAL SEARCH In visual search tasks participants do not receive a cue to attend to a specific location; instead, they are told to find and attend to a specific target. (A) In this extremely simplified version of a visual search task, displays were flashed briefly on the screen while the participant fixated on the central dot, and the participant was told to either find the red line and ignore the green square, or find the green square and ignore the red line. (B) The ERP for the occipital region ipsilateral to the red line is subtracted from the ERP for the occipital region contralateral to the red stimulus. Because it is on the midline, the green square doesn't affect these difference scores (it would affect both hemispheres' visual areas). The results show that seeking and attending to a visual stimulus augments activity of contralateral visual areas, reflected in the ERP component known as *N2pc*. When attention is being used to seek a different stimulus (the green box in this example), the exact same visual display not only fails to trigger an N2pc in response to the red line, but in fact causes a distinctive ERP component (P_D) associated with *ignoring* the red line. (Based on Hickey et al., 2009; Courtesy of Dr. John McDonald.)

and emotional processing (no kidding: Bailey and West, 2013). And of course, some people could be drawn to video gaming simply because they are already good at visuospatial processing (Boot et al., 2008). Impressively, training with video games even enhances cognitive control—the ability to multitask—in older adults (60–85 year old), indicating that plasticity in attentional control systems is probably retained throughout life (Anguera et al., 2013).

Neuroimaging confirms that the anatomical foci of attention show augmented processing

Trading temporal resolution for spatial resolution, PET and fMRI studies have confirmed that a general consequence of attention is an enhancement of activity of the brain regions that process key aspects of the target stimuli. (PET, fMRI, and other brain imaging technologies are discussed in detail in Chapters 2 and 3.) In one such study, participants completed a simple spatial cuing task while both fMRI and ERP data were collected (McMains and Somers, 2004). By using ERP to decide *when* to collect fMRI images, the researchers found anatomically distinct regions of enhanced activity in visual cortex that corresponded to the spatial locations to which participants directed their covert attention (**FIGURE 18.10**). As participants shifted attention to other locations, the locus of enhanced activity within the retinotopic map of primary visual cortex also shifted (see Chapter 10). And dividing attention between two spatial locations resulted in two corresponding patches of neural enhancement.

An effect of attention on neural activation may even be observed in *subcortical* visual structures (K. A. Schneider and Kastner, 2009). Using a sustained-attention task, the researchers found fMRI enhancements in the superior colliculi and lateral geniculate nuclei (see Figure 10.10). This finding indicates that some degree of attentional selection may be occurring very early indeed, before visual information has even reached the cortex, in both subcortical visual pathways.

At later stages of the visual system, physiological effects of attention become even more pronounced. In one clever study, researchers devised stimuli composed of faces

These maps of visual cortex in two participants are displayed to correspond to visual space (in other words, they are retinotopic; see Chapter 10). (Image courtesy of Dr. David Somers.)

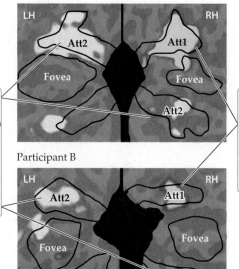

Participant A

Participant B

When participants were told to divide their attention between two spatial locations, enhancement of activity was evident for *two* corresponding regions of visual cortex (shown in red and yellow).

Covert attention to one location (Att1) produced increased activity on fMRI as targets appeared in that attended location, relative to control conditions.

overlaid on pictures of houses (O'Craven et al., 1999). When participants were asked to ignore the houses and direct attention to the faces, attention-related enhancement was seen in a cortical region specifically responsible for face processing, called the *fusiform face area* (see Figure 19.19). When participants were instead instructed to attend to the houses and ignore the faces—using the same stimuli—fMRI enhancement was seen in a different cortical area, one that is responsible for processing locations (the parahippocampal place area). This neuroimaging evidence of late attentional selection illustrates once again that the attentional bottleneck can vary, depending on task demands (N. Lavie et al., 2004).

Attention alters the functioning of individual neurons

As you'll recall from Chapter 10, visual neurons have distinctive receptive fields; visual stimuli falling within these fields can excite or inhibit the neurons, causing them to produce more or fewer action potentials. Similarly, the effects of visual attention can be studied, by recording the activity of individual visual cortex neurons while attention within the visual field is manipulated. In principle, there are three ways in which attention might affect single-cell recordings. One possibility is that selective attention to a cell's receptive field might globally *enhance or suppress* responses, increasing or decreasing the firing rate of that cell (**FIGURE 18.11A**). Al-

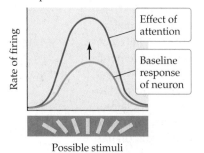

(A) Enhanced or suppressed response

Rate of firing

Effect of attention

Baseline response of neuron

Possible stimuli

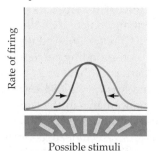

(B) Sharpened tuning to specific stimuli

Rate of firing

Possible stimuli

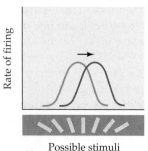

(C) Cell's tuning shifted to favor a different stimulus

Rate of firing

Possible stimuli

18.11 SOME WAYS THAT ATTENTION MIGHT CHANGE THE ACTIVITY OF INDIVIDUAL NEURONS

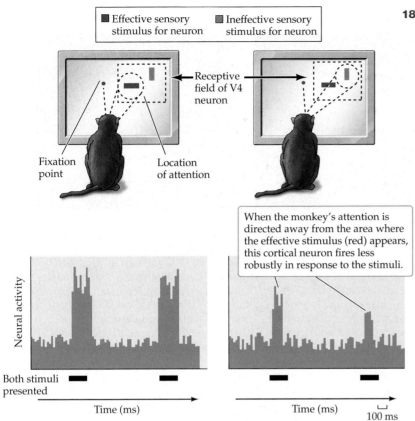

- ■ Effective sensory stimulus for neuron
- ■ Ineffective sensory stimulus for neuron

Receptive field of V4 neuron

Fixation point

Location of attention

When the monkey's attention is directed away from the area where the effective stimulus (red) appears, this cortical neuron fires less robustly in response to the stimuli.

Neural activity

Both stimuli presented

Time (ms)

Time (ms)

100 ms

A macaque monkey was trained to maintain central fixation while directing covert attention. Within the receptive field for the particular cortical neuron being recorded, the area being attended to is shown as a dashed circle. In the first condition (left) the area of attention within the cell's receptive field includes the effective stimulus (a red horizontal bar) and excludes the distracter (the green vertical bar that, by itself, has no effect on the cell's firing). The only difference in the second condition is that the monkey has moved its attentional spotlight away from the region where the effective stimulus will appear. Because (1) both stimuli are present in both conditions, (2) the fixation point hasn't changed, and (3) the same cell is being recorded from in both conditions, attentional mechanisms must have directly altered the cell's preferences and sensitivity. (After Moran and Desimone, 1985.)

ternatively, attention might *sharpen the tuning* of cortical neurons, causing them to focus more keenly on specific stimuli (**FIGURE 18.11B**). Or attention might induce a *shift in tuning* of the cell, indicating a change in the cell's preferred stimulus (**FIGURE 18.11C**). Furthermore, directed attention reduces variability and improves the signal-to-noise ratio in visual cortex, in part by adjusting the weighting of individual synapses (Briggs et al., 2013; Sprague et al., 2015).

In an important study (**FIGURE 18.12**), Moran and Desimone (1985) studied the effects of shifts in attention within the receptive fields of single neurons. Using a system of rewards, the researchers trained macaque monkeys to covertly attend to one spatial location or another (on the basis of symbolic cues) while recordings were made from single extrastriate visual neurons. In one condition, a display was presented that included the cell's most preferred stimulus, as well as an ineffective stimulus (one that, by itself, did not affect the cell's firing) a short distance away but still within the cell's visual field. Action potentials were counted while attention was covertly directed at the preferred stimulus, and as expected, a robust response was recorded. In the second condition, the same display was presented during recording from the same neuron, but this time the monkey's covert attention was shifted elsewhere within the neuron's receptive field. Because (1) the favored stimulus was present, (2) the same cell was being recorded, and (3) the animal's gaze had not shifted, you might expect that the rate of firing remained robust, but that was not the result. Instead, rates of firing were significantly diminished in the second condition. Only the shift in attention could account for this change (consistent with the process depicted in Figure 18.11A).

Conscious, voluntary direction of visual attention seems to continually tune the receptive fields of visual cortical neurons, enhancing their resolution (Anton-Erxleben and Carrasco, 2013; Womelsdorf et al., 2006). By repeatedly presenting a preferred visual stimulus, researchers can map a cortical visual neuron's sensitivity throughout its receptive field, as shown in **FIGURE 18.13A**. The researchers found that when the monkey covertly shifted attention from one cued location (S1 in the figure) to a different cued location (S2) still within the receptive field, without shift-

(A) 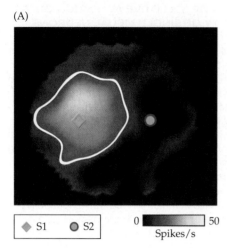 (B) 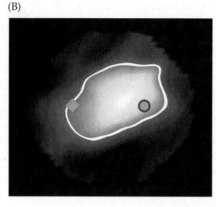 (C)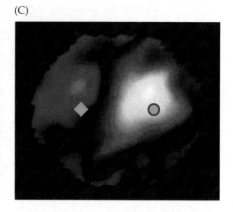

◆ S1   ● S2

0 ▮▮▮▮▮▮ 50
Spikes/s

18.13 ATTENTIONAL REMODELING OF A NEURON'S RECEPTIVE FIELD
Each image is a map from the same single neuron in extrastriate visual cortex, showing sensitivity to its preferred stimulus (S) throughout its receptive field. In (A), a region of heightened sensitivity is evident while the animal attends to a location cued by S1 (green diamond). In (B), stimuli are identical, except the animal is attending to the position cued by S2 (blue circle). Part (C) is a difference map, showing the net change in receptive-field characteristics as attention shifted from position S1 to position S2. The cell's receptive field has evidently been retuned by attentional processes. (Images courtesy of Drs. Thilo Womelsdorf and Stefan Treue.)

ing its gaze, the peak sensitivity within the receptive field for this neuron shifted right along with attention (**FIGURE 18.13B**). Furthermore, attention can apparently cause the overall size of receptive fields to shrink, as if sharpening a spotlight to exclude neighboring distracters (Womelsdorf et al., 2008), as depicted in Figure 18.11B. Studies such as these show that attention potently modifies the sensitivity of neurons throughout many of the vision-related areas of cortex.

A Network of Brain Sites Creates and Directs Attention

Whether attention comes reflexively, from the bottom up, or is controlled voluntarily, from the top down, it strongly affects neural processing in the brain, thereby augmenting electrophysiological activity. That doesn't mean that the *sources* of the various types of attention are identical, or even overlapping—just that their *consequences* are measurable and comparable. Probing the anatomical sources of attention requires different experimental approaches. Studies of lab animals, human brain imaging, and rare neurological disorders that impair attention all contribute to our understanding of the neural mechanisms of attention.

The superior colliculus guides attentional eye movements

Subcortical structures can be difficult to study because, situated in the center of the brain, they are difficult to probe using electrophysiological or neuroimaging techniques. Our knowledge of their roles in attention thus comes mostly from work with animals.

Single-cell recordings have implicated the **superior colliculus**, a midbrain structure (**FIGURE 18.14**), in the movement of the eyes toward objects of attention, especially overt attention (Wurtz and Goldberg, 1972; Wurtz et al., 1982). Comparable eye movements made *without* the attentional component are not associated with increased cell activity. Collicular neurons are particularly sensitive to relative motion in any direction (R. M. Davidson and Bender, 1991), perhaps because of the visual aspects of moving gaze around. A person with damage to one superior colliculus showed diminished inhibition of return for stimuli on the affected side; the superior colliculus may therefore help us avoid repeatedly returning to previously attended locations (Sapir et al., 1999).

superior colliculus A gray matter structure of the dorsal midbrain that receives visual information and is involved in direction of visual gaze and visual attention to intended stimuli.

Although implicated primarily in overt attention, the superior colliculus may help control covert attention too—a top-down task generally assigned to cortical mechanisms (as we'll discuss shortly). For example, reversible inactivation of the superior colliculus on one side abolishes monkeys' ability to utilize selective attention cues on the corresponding side of visual space (Lovejoy and Krauzlis, 2010).

The pulvinar drives shifts of attention

Making up approximately the posterior quarter of the thalamus in humans (see Figure 18.14), the **pulvinar** is heavily involved in visual processing, is organized retinotopically, and shares extensive connections with the superior colliculus, parietal cortex, and cingulate. The pulvinar is important for the orienting and shifting of attention. In one study, direct injections of GABA agonists and antagonists were used to reversibly inhibit or activate the pulvinar (recall that GABA is an inhibitory transmitter, so its antagonists tend to increase neural activity). Following injection of a GABA *agonist* into the pulvinar, monkeys reportedly had great difficulty orienting covert attention toward targets in the contralateral visual field (D. L. Robinson and Petersen, 1992). Injections of a GABA *antagonist*, however, enhanced covert shifting of attention. The pulvinar is also needed to filter out and ignore distracting stimuli while monkeys are engaged in covert attention tasks, and in general it serves as an information manager, directing and synchronizing relevant information and activity in large-scale cortical networks, in response to attentional demands (Saalmann et al., 2012). In humans, attention tasks with larger numbers of distracters induce greater activation of the pulvinar on fMRI (Buchsbaum et al., 2006), showing that the pulvinar is important for attention in humans too.

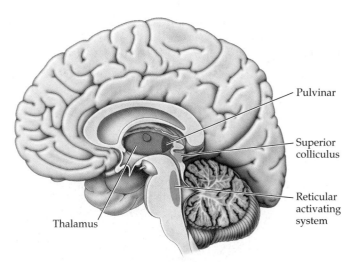

18.14 SUBCORTICAL SITES IMPLICATED IN VISUAL ATTENTION

pulvinar In humans, the posterior portion of the thalamus, heavily involved in visual processing and direction of attention.

lateral intraparietal area (LIP) A region in the monkey parietal lobe, homologous with the human intraparietal sulcus, that is especially involved in voluntary, top-down control of attention.

intraparietal sulcus (IPS) A region in the human parietal lobe, homologous with the monkey lateral intraparietal area, that is especially involved in voluntary, top-down control of attention.

Several cortical areas are crucial for generating and directing attention

We've already seen several ways in which the *effects* of attention are evident in the cortex. But what about the *generation and direction* of attention? The extensive connections between subcortical attention systems and regions of the parietal lobes, along with clinical observations, suggest that parietal cortex plays a special role in controlling attention. Initial work with single-cell recordings in monkeys confirmed that certain parietal cells selectively increase their firing rate when the animal identifies a target stimulus to which it will covertly attend, but not when the stimulus is in the same location in the absence of planning for covert attention (Wurtz et al., 1982). In other words, some cells in parietal cortex behave as though they are preparing to direct a shift of attention.

A region in the monkey parietal lobe called the **lateral intraparietal area (LIP)** is especially involved in the voluntary, top-down control of attention. The human homolog of this region is the **intraparietal sulcus (IPS)** (**FIGURE 18.15**). Activity of LIP neurons is correlated with the direction of attention to particular locations, and it is enhanced regardless of whether the attention is directed toward visual or auditory targets (Bisley and Goldberg, 2003; J. Gottlieb, 2007). By comparing the response of LIP cells to targets and distracters across space, researchers found that the LIP encodes a *salience map* (or *priority map*) that controls the direction of attention between important stimuli from one moment to the next (Bisley and Goldberg, 2006; Ipata et al., 2006). Neurons of the ventral LIP are primarily responsible for directing attention, while neurons in the dorsal LIP govern a complementary function: eye movement planning (Y. Liu et al., 2010).

Neurons of the human IPS appear to behave much like those in the monkey LIP. In covert attention tasks that are long enough to allow for fMRI analysis, IPS activity is greater while attention is being steered (Corbetta and Shulman, 1998). Conversely, interfering with the normal function of IPS through transcranial magnetic stimula-

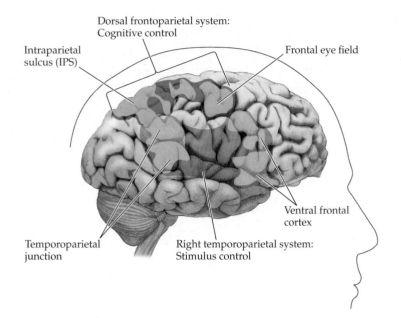

18.15 CORTICAL REGIONS IMPLICATED IN THE TOP-LEVEL CONTROL OF ATTENTION

Dorsal frontoparietal system: Cognitive control

Intraparietal sulcus (IPS)

Frontal eye field

Ventral frontal cortex

Temporoparietal junction

Right temporoparietal system: Stimulus control

frontal eye field (FEF) An area in the frontal lobe of the brain containing neurons important for establishing gaze in accordance with cognitive goals (top-down processes) rather than with any characteristics of stimuli (bottom-up processes).

temporoparietal junction (TPJ) The point in the brain where the temporal and parietal lobes meet that plays a role in shifting attention to a new location after target onset.

tion (see Chapter 2) makes it difficult for people to voluntarily shift their attention (Koch et al., 2005).

In conjunction with the LIP/IPS, an area in the frontal lobes of the brain called the **frontal eye field (FEF)** has been implicated in attention, because people with damage to the FEF have a very difficult time suppressing unwanted reorientation of the eyes toward peripheral distracters (Paus et al., 1991). Located in the premotor area of the frontal lobes (see Figure 18.15), neurons of the FEF are important for establishing gaze in accordance with cognitive goals (top-down processes) rather than with any characteristics of stimuli (bottom-up processes). This may be why the FEF has rich interconnections with the superior colliculus, which, as we discussed earlier, is important for planned eye movements. Furthermore, researchers using transcranial magnetic stimulation to temporarily disrupt activity of the FEF found that regions of visual cortex involved in processing target visual stimuli were likewise temporarily impeded (Zanto et al., 2011). This result confirmed, in humans, that top-down attentional systems (namely, in the FEF) act to bias neural activity in visual cortex.

Unlike the dorsal frontoparietal system (containing the IPS and FEF) just described for top-down voluntary control of attention, a more posterior and ventral system seems to be crucial for bottom-up, reflexive shifts in attention driven by characteristics of stimuli As its name implies, the **temporoparietal junction (TPJ)** lies at the junction of the parietal and temporal lobes (see Figure 18.15), including parts of the temporal lobe (specifically, the superior temporal gyrus) and parts of the inferior parietal lobe (namely, the supramarginal gyrus). Unlike the IPS/LIP, the TPJ plays a role in shifting attention to a new location *after* target onset, especially if the stimulus is unexpected. In one experiment, participants selectively attending to a specific location showed a significant increase in TPJ activity if a relevant stimulus suddenly appeared in a novel, unexpected location (Corbetta and Shulman, 2002). People with TPJ damage respond poorly to unanticipated targets (Friedrich et al., 1998). The role of the TPJ has been likened to an alerting signal or circuit breaker, overriding the current attentional priority in order to redirect to something new. Interestingly, this system is strongly lateralized to the right hemisphere, unlike the more dorsal system involving the IPS and FEF. This right-hemisphere dependence has implications for clinical conditions, which we'll discuss a little later.

Multiple brain regions collaborate in networks that govern attention

To produce our seamless experience of the world, continually selecting and shifting between objects of interest, the cortical and subcortical mechanisms of attention must all operate as a coordinated network. The individual attention-related mechanisms of the brain work together within two overall networks—dorsal frontoparietal and right temporoparietal.

A DORSAL FRONTOPARIETAL NETWORK FOR VOLUNTARY CONTROL OF ATTENTION A modified form of fMRI that allows partial tracking of activity during rapid events (called, unsurprisingly, *event-related fMRI*, or *ER-fMRI*) enables us to visualize network activities during top-down attentional processing (Corbetta et al., 2000; Hopfinger et al., 2000). **FIGURE 18.16** illustrates results from a typical experiment. **FIGURE 18.16A** shows patterns of activation during the cue presentation phase of the task. Enhanced activity was evident in the vicinity of the frontal eye fields (dorsolateral frontal cortex) and, simultaneously, in the IPS. By comparison, the target-processing phase of the trial (**FIGURE 18.16B**) was associated with activity of regions around the pre- and postcentral gyrus, reflecting response initia-

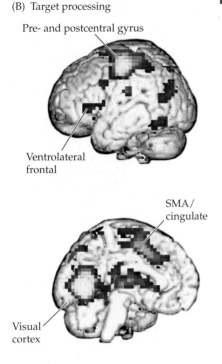

(A) Attentional control network

Dorsolateral frontal

Superior temporal

Posterior cingulate

Medial frontal

(B) Target processing

Pre- and postcentral gyrus

Ventrolateral frontal

SMA/ cingulate

Visual cortex

18.16 A FRONTOPARIETAL ATTENTIONAL CONTROL NETWORK While participants performed a spatial cued-attention task, ER-fMRI images were collected, tied to either (A) the cue-processing phase of the trial (thus, the covert direction of attention) or (B) the target-processing phase of the task (corresponding to target processing and selection of motor responses). In part A, the conscious direction of attention is associated with selective activations of the dorsolateral frontal cortex, corresponding to the frontal eye field, the intraparietal sulcus, and the temporoparietal junction (see text for details). (Images courtesy of Drs. Joe Hopfinger and George Mangun.)

tion, and activity in visual cortex reflected stimulus processing. Electrophysiological studies of the timing of activity in the network indicate that the attentional control–related activity is first seen in the frontal and parietal components, followed by anticipatory activation of visual cortex (if the expected stimulus is visual) or auditory cortex (if the stimulus is a sound) (Green et al., 2011; McDonald and Green, 2008). Taken together, studies to date thus support the view that a dorsal frontoparietal network provides top-down (voluntary) control of attention. Interestingly, application of top-down attention in this system during visual search appears to warp the tuning of target cortical regions so as to overrepresent the semantic category of the sought stimulus (e.g., boats) and related categories (cars, vehicles) at the expense of unrelated categories (e.g., humans, animals) (Çukur et al., 2013). This result suggests that the voluntary, top-down system is continually tuning visual sensitivity to align with attentional control.

A RIGHT TEMPOROPARIETAL NETWORK FOR REFLEXIVE ATTENTION Event-related fMRI studies confirm that a system in the temporoparietal junction is involved in steering attention to novel or unexpected stimuli (**FIGURE 18.17**). To investigate this system, researchers synchronized scans to the occasional appearance of novel stimuli in a stream of distracters. This system shows a strong right-hemisphere lateralization; activity is localized on the right TPJ regardless of whether the stimulus falls in left or right hemispace (Corbetta et al., 2000), as we will see a little later in Figure 18.19. The ventral temporoparietal system receives inputs from visual cortex (conveying stimulus properties) and also from ventral frontal cortex (VFC); VFC is implicated in working memory (see Chapter 17) and thus may provide crucial information about novelty by comparing the present state of stimuli with that of the recent past.

In order to smoothly integrate overall control of attention, the networks underlying voluntarily controlled attention and reflexive attention need to interact extensively and operate as a single coordinated system (Corbetta and Shulman, 2002). According to this model, voluntary control of attention depends on a dorsal stream of processing projecting from frontal cortex to the IPS region in posterior parietal

Left   Right

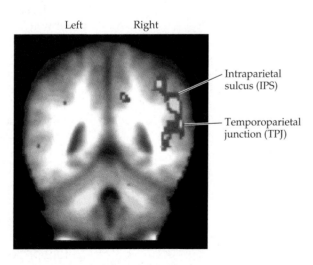

Intraparietal sulcus (IPS)

Temporoparietal junction (TPJ)

18.17 A RIGHT TEMPOROPARIETAL NETWORK FOR REFLEXIVE ATTENTION As described in the text, this pathway becomes more active when relevant stimuli appear unexpectedly. (Image courtesy of Dr. Maurizio Corbetta.)

18.18 THE CORTICAL ATTENTIONAL CONTROL NETWORK (A) Regions shaded blue are involved in voluntary control of attention. Regions in green are part of a right-hemisphere system for reorienting and reflexive direction of attention. Arrows indicate the presumed direction of control. Extensive interaction between the systems provides integrated control over attention. (B) Schematic of the attentional control network. Connections between the TPJ and IPS provide a means for novel stimuli to interrupt and reorganize attentional priorities. (After Corbetta and Shulman, 2002.)

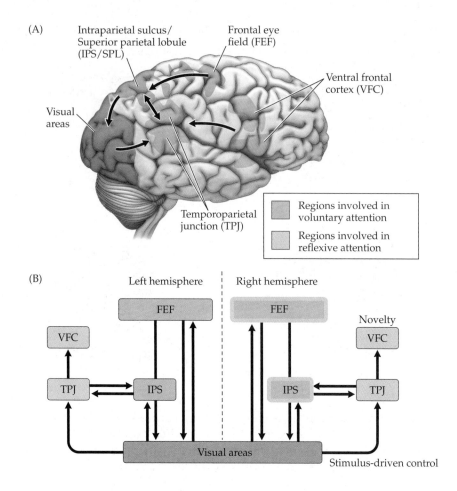

cortex (**FIGURE 18.18**). Operation of the dorsal stream seems to have two general effects: attentional modulation of neuronal function in visual areas, as we discussed earlier in the chapter (e.g., McMains and Somers, 2004), and coordination with the subcortical system (mediated by the pulvinar and superior colliculus) that steers attention. At the same time, projections from visual cortex to the TPJ help the right-sided ventral system to scan the environment for novel salient stimuli (which then draw reflexive attention), with the help of working memory inputs from the VFC.

The strong connections between IPS and TPJ allow for rapid reassignment of attention and give us the effortless awareness of environmental stimuli that we take for granted as we shift rapidly between intended objects of attention and the other interesting things that pop up around us. Although most research has focused on visuospatial stimuli, the frontoparietal cortical attention network appears to be active in other visual modalities (e.g., color, shape), temporal judgments (Kanwisher and Wojciulik, 2000), and auditory stimuli (Brunetti et al., 2008; Walther et al., 2010). As we've seen earlier, integration across sensory modalities is an important aid to attention—for example, attention drawn reflexively by an *auditory* stimulus enhances *visual* perception and associated ERPs in visual cortex (McDonald et al., 2000, 2003)—and the "supramodal" characteristics of the attention network are now the subject of intensive research efforts.

Studies of people with attention disorders implicate these same brain regions, as we'll see next.

Disorders Provide Clues about the Organization of Attention

A time-honored method for learning about the organization of the human brain is careful analysis of the impairments—sometimes subtle, sometimes profound—that accompany injuries and disorders of the brain. For example, by noting the behavioral consequences of damage to discrete neuroanatomical regions, we can make inferences about the affected regions' functions in the intact brain. It's an approach that has drawn back the curtain on the sources of attention and awareness, and their relationship to human consciousness.

Neglect of one side of the body and space can result from parietal lobe injury

One peculiar syndrome resulting from damage to the right inferior parietal cortex reinforces the notion that a special attentional mechanism resides in the right hemisphere, as we just discussed. The key feature of this disorder is a pervasive neglect of the left side of both the body and space (Rafal, 1994). People and objects to the left of the person's midline may be completely ignored, as if unseen, despite the absence of any visual-field defects. For example, the person may fail to dress the left side of her body, will not notice visitors if they approach from the left, and may fail to eat the food on the left side of her dinner plate. This phenomenon, called **hemispatial neglect**, can be revealed in simple test situations. A common test requires the person to copy drawings of familiar objects. In the typical result, a person with neglect who is asked to draw the face of a clock draws numbers on only the right side of the clock face (**FIGURE 18.19**) (Schenkerberg et al., 1980). Spontaneous drawings, where the patient is relying on memory rather than on a model, are similarly deranged. Curiously, people with hemispatial neglect even have difficulty with the "left side" of time: that is, they fail to attend to concepts that would appear on the left side of a provided timeline with arbitrary start, middle, and end points (Saj et al., 2014) and instead emphasize present and future events in the timeline.

Associated with hemispatial neglect is a feature called *extinction of simultaneous double stimulation*, or just **extinction**. Most healthy people have no trouble noticing when two stimuli are presented simultaneously on both sides of the body. People with right inferior parietal lesions, however, are unable to note the double nature of the stimulation and usually report only the stimulus presented to the right side. It is as if the normally balanced competition for attention between the two sides has become skewed and the input from the right side of the world now overrules or extinguishes the input from the left. This syndrome extends to visual imagery as well; for example, people with hemispatial neglect describe events from only one side of dream scenes, consistent with the observation that they make no leftward eye movements during REM sleep (Doricchi et al., 1991). Yet another striking feature of this syndrome is frequent **anosognosia** (denial of illness). People with hemispatial neglect may adamantly maintain that they are perfectly healthy and capable of engaging in their customary activities and do not recognize the impressive signs of unilateral neglect. They may even disclaim "ownership" of their own left arm or leg, rather than accepting that anything unusual is occurring.

Many people with right parietal damage do show recovery from hemispatial neglect, and researchers are working on rehabilitation therapies in which special prism glasses shift vision to the right during intense physical therapy, to recalibrate the visual attention system (Barrett et al., 2012; Goedert et al., 2015). However, even with recovery from neglect, the feature of extinction can be quite persistent. Although neglect and extinction are most dramatically evident in the visual domain, similar problems are reported with stimuli in other sensory modalities (e.g., Funk et al., 2010; Schindler et al., 2006), indicating that a supramodal attention control system has been compromised by the damage, with disconnections between high-level cognitive mechanisms (Bartolomeo, 2007; Mesulam, 1985). Lesion maps, averaged over numerous people with hemispatial neglect, fit with impressive precision over the model of the frontoparietal attention network we discussed earlier (**FIGURE 18.20**).

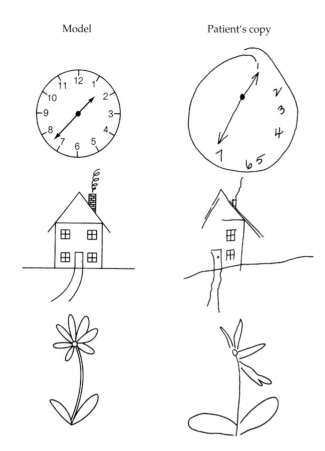

Model   Patient's copy

18.19 DIAGNOSTIC TEST FOR HEMISPATIAL NEGLECT When asked to duplicate drawings of common symmetrical objects, people suffering from hemispatial neglect ignore the left side of the model that they're copying. (From Kolb and Whishaw, 1990.)

hemispatial neglect A syndrome in which the person fails to pay any attention to objects presented to one side of the body and may even deny connection with that side.

extinction Short for *extinction of simultaneous double stimulation*. An inability to recognize the double nature of stimuli presented simultaneously to both sides of the body. People experiencing extinction report the stimulus from only one side.

anosognosia Denial of illness.

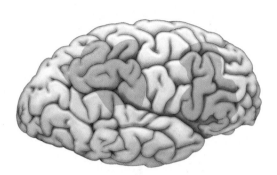

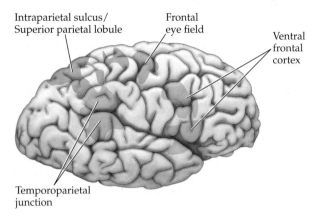

Intraparietal sulcus/ Superior parietal lobule

Frontal eye field

Ventral frontal cortex

Temporoparietal junction

18.20 BRAIN DAMAGE IN HEMISPATIAL NEGLECT   Note that the brain regions that are damaged in people with hemispatial neglect (A) roughly correspond to regions implicated in attentional control (B) earlier in the chapter.

Bálint's syndrome   Three co-occurring symptoms—simultagnosia, oculomotor apraxia, and optic ataxia—that may occur after bilateral lesions of cortical attentional systems.

oculomotor apraxia   A severe difficulty in voluntarily steering visual gaze toward specific targets.

optic ataxia   A spatial disorientation in which the affected person is unable to accurately reach for objects using visual guidance.

simultagnosia   A profound restriction of attention, often limited to a single item or feature.

attention deficit hyperactivity disorder (ADHD)   Syndrome of distractibility, impulsiveness, and hyperactivity that, in children, interferes with school performance.

In Bálint's syndrome, narrowed attention combines with spatial disorientation

Parminder, the stroke victim we met at the beginning of the chapter, had *bilateral* lesions of her posterior parietal and lateral occipital cortex, the attention-related regions we have been discussing. While rare, this sort of bilateral damage can produce an unusual and debilitating condition called **Bálint's syndrome** (after its discoverer, Hungarian neurologist Rezsö Bálint). There are three principal symptoms:

1. **Oculomotor apraxia**, a pronounced difficulty in voluntarily steering visual gaze toward specific targets

2. **Optic ataxia**, a spatial disorientation in which the patient is unable to accurately reach for objects using visual guidance

3. **Simultagnosia**, a profound restriction of attention, often limited to a single item or feature

The cardinal and most debilitating symptom in Bálint's syndrome, simultagnosia is like a dramatic narrowing of the metaphorical attentional spotlight described earlier, to the point that it can't encompass more than one object at a time. It's as though the patient is simply unable to see more than one thing at once, despite having little or no loss of vision. Bálint's syndrome thus illustrates the coordination of attention and awareness with mechanisms that orient us within our environment. Parminder's attention had become so narrow that most of the world around her was being excluded from processing; despite her normal vision, only one visual object at a time could make it into her conscious awareness.

Difficulty with sustained attention can sometimes be relieved with stimulants

At least 5% of all children in the United States are diagnosed with **attention deficit hyperactivity disorder (ADHD)**, characterized as difficulty with directing sustained attention to a task or activity, along with a higher degree of impulsivity than other children of the same age. Roughly 75% of affected children are male. Diagnosis of ADHD is complicated and very controversial; for example, research on ADHD prevalence has revealed that there are significant differences across the United States in both the rate of diagnosis of ADHD and the use of medication to treat it—with large differences observed even between neighboring states (Visser et al., 2014) (**FIGURE 18.21**)—raising serious questions about the reliability of current diagnostic practices (Fulton et al., 2009). Nevertheless, researchers have identified several neurological changes that are associated with this disorder. Affected children tend to have slightly reduced overall brain volumes (about 3–4% smaller than in unaffected children), with reductions most evident in the cerebellum and in the frontal lobes (Arnsten, 2006; Castellanos et al., 2002). As we'll discuss shortly, frontal lobe function is important for myriad complex cognitive processes, including the inhibition of impulsive behavior. (But remember, correlational studies like these are mute with regard to causation; we don't know whether the brain differences cause, or are caused by, the behavior.)

In addition to structural changes, ADHD has been associated with abnormalities in connectivity between brain regions (Cao et al., 2014). In fact, individual differences in the ability to sustain attention can be predicted with high accuracy from the strength of sets of brain connections (Rosenberg et al., 2016), even in the resting state, when the individual is not working on any particular task. This measure may provide both a physical marker for ADHD diagnosis and a new opportunity to understand the neural origins of ADHD. In addition to changes in connectivity, children with ADHD may have abnormal activity levels in some specific brain systems, such as the system that signals the rewarding aspects of activities (Volkow et al., 2009). Based on a model of ADHD that implicates impaired dopaminergic and noradrenergic neurotransmission, some researchers advocate treating children with ADHD with stimulant drugs like methylphenidate (Ritalin), which acts as a dopamine/norepinephrine reuptake inhibitor, or with selective norepinephrine reuptake inhibitors like atomexetine (Strattera) (Schwartz and Correll, 2014). Stimulant treatment often improves the focus and performance of children with ADHD in traditional school settings, but this treatment remains controversial because of significant risk of side effects. Furthermore, stimulant treatment improves attention in all individuals, not just people with ADHD, leading some researchers to question the orthodox view that impaired transmitter function is causative in ADHD (del Campo et al., 2013). In fact, some advocate the view that ADHD is simply one extreme on a continuum of normal behavior, consistent with the observation that simply allowing kids diagnosed with ADHD to engage in intense physical activity effectively reduces their symptoms and improves task performance (Hartanto et al., 2016).

There can be no denying the close relationship of attention and consciousness; indeed, attention is the foundation on which consciousness is built. So let's turn now to the topic of consciousness.

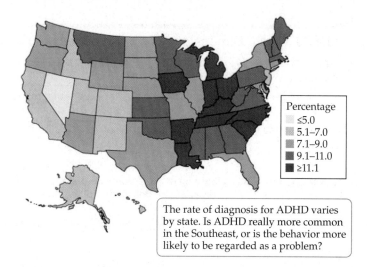

The rate of diagnosis for ADHD varies by state. Is ADHD really more common in the Southeast, or is the behavior more likely to be regarded as a problem?

Percentage
≤5.0
5.1–7.0
7.1–9.0
9.1–11.0
≥11.1

18.21 REGIONAL VARIATION IN ADHD PREVALENCE IN THE USA This map of ADHD diagnosis patterns reveals substantial differences across the United States: in some locations the reported prevalence is about 100% higher on one side of the state line than on the other side. This pattern suggests that the diagnosis of ADHD suffers from imprecision and unclear definition, possibly coupled with regional variation in sociocultural processes (such as expectations for children's behavior) and public policy. The fact that medication patterns closely follow the regional diagnosis map is cause for concern, as it implies that children may be overmedicated in some regions (or undermedicated in others). (After Visser et al., 2014.)

Consciousness, Thought, and Executive Function

Consciousness Is a Mysterious Product of the Brain

Whenever we are conscious, we are attending to *something*: other people, our innermost thoughts, the road ahead, music, and all the other important stimuli that make up our conscious experience of life. William James (1890) tried to capture the relationship of attention and consciousness when he wrote, "My experience is what I agree to attend to. Only those items which I notice, shape my mind—without selective interest, experience is an utter chaos." But while both attention and awareness are behavioral and experiential manifestations of consciousness, no one would accept them as synonymous. We've seen that attention to complex stimuli enhances activity in primary visual cortex (V1), but conscious awareness of the stimuli doesn't add any extra V1 activation (Watanabe et al., 2011). It seems that consciousness must inhabit a higher, heavily networked neural neighborhood. A more complete description of consciousness is freighted with the notion that we enjoy volitional control over experience—the belief that we can employ *free will* to direct our attention and

TABLE 18.1 Dimensions of Consciousness

ASPECT OF CONSCIOUSNESS	DEFINITION	SPECIES OTHER THAN HUMANS
Theory of mind	Insight into the mental lives of others; appreciation that beliefs, knowledge, and desires of others differ	Only chimpanzees, so far
Mirror recognition	Ability to recognize self as depicted in a mirror	All great apes; dolphins; elephants
Imitation	Ability to copy the actions of others; thought to be a stepping-stone to awareness and empathy	Many species, including cephalopods like the octopus
Empathy and emotion	Possession of complex emotions and the ability to imagine the feelings of other individuals	Most mammals, ranging from primates and dolphins, to hippos and rodents; most vertebrates able to experience pleasure (and other basic emotions)
Tool use	Ability to employ found objects to achieve ultimate goals	Chimps and other primates; other mammals such as elephants, otters, and dolphins; birds such as crows and gulls
Language	Use of a system of arbitrary symbols, associated with specific meanings and assembled according to a strict grammar, to convey information that may be concrete or abstract, on familiar or unfamiliar topics, to any other individual that has learned the same language	Generally considered to be an exclusively human ability, with controversy over the extent to which the great apes possess language skills (see Chapter 19)
Metacognition	"Thinking about thinking": the ability to consider the contents of one's own thoughts and cognitions	Nonhuman primates; dolphins

consciousness The state of awareness of one's own existence and experience.

default mode network The regions of the brain that are active when the brain is awake and at rest and attention is not being directed to external events.

ultimately make decisions about how to act. Add to this the observation that consciousness involves awareness of the passage of time, integration with memory of past events, and anticipation of future events, and we have a concept of immense scope. So as a rough approximation, we can define **consciousness** as the state of being *aware* that we are conscious and that we can perceive what is going on in our minds and all around us. This awareness is colored by events that affected our inner selves in the past and by our sense of what the future might hold. Some of the basic elements of consciousness—and some of the animals that may have conscious experiences resembling our own—are summarized in **TABLE 18.1**.

Which brain regions are active when we are conscious?

Despite the complexities of developing formal scientific definitions of conscious states, consciousness is an active area of research with many competing theoretical models but not, as yet, much hard neuroscientific data. One approach is to look for patterns of synchronized activity in dispersed neural networks as people engage in conscious, inwardly focused thought. Using fMRI, researchers have mapped a circuit of brain regions—collectively called the **default mode network**, consisting of parts of the frontal, temporal, and parietal lobes—that seems to be selectively activated when we are at our most introspective and reflective, and relatively deactivated during behavior directed toward external goals (Andrews-Hanna et al., 2014; Raichle, 2015). In some ways, you could think of it as a daydream network (and by thinking about it, you are also engaging in metacognition!) (see Table 18.1). Researchers suspect that dysfunction of the default mode network may contribute to diverse high-level cognitive problems, including ADHD, dementia, schizophrenia, and autism, affecting both children and adults (Sato et al., 2015; Whitfield-Gabrieli and Ford, 2012). Monkeys and lab rats have circuits that seem to function the same way the human default mode network does, suggesting that nonhuman species may likewise engage in self-reflection or other introspective mental activity (Mantini et al., 2011; Sierakowiak et al., 2015).

A practical alternative approach has been to define consciousness by reference to states in which it is absent. By studying the brains of people who appear to be unconscious, we might gain some insight into brain mechanisms of consciousness. Such investigation requires great care in identifying disorders or states with effects

(A)

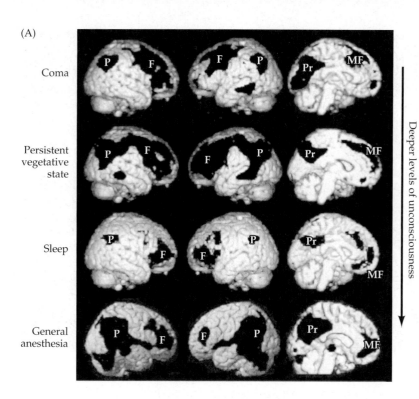

Coma

Persistent
vegetative
state

Sleep

General
anesthesia

Deeper levels of unconsciousness

(B)

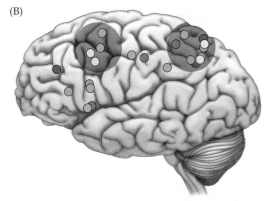

18.22 THE UNCONSCIOUS BRAIN (A) Functional-imaging studies of people in various states of diminished consciousness show impairment or reduced activity of a frontoparietal network including dorsolateral prefrontal cortex (F), medial frontal cortex (MF), posterior parietal cortex (P), and posterior cingulate (Pr). This general pattern of frontoparietal deactivation agrees well with a model (B) summarizing areas of activation in previous studies (indicated by different-colored dots) of visual awareness and consciousness. (Part A courtesy of Dr. Ralph Adolphs; B after Rees et al., 2002.)

limited to changes in consciousness; for example, damage to the brainstem can cause the entire cerebrum to shut down, but this is a global loss of brain function, not a selective impairment of consciousness. Using fMRI to track brain activity in conditions of diminished consciousness—ranging from sleep to persistent vegetative states due to head injuries—researchers have devised maps of cortical areas that appear to be deactivated in unconsciousness (Tsuchiya and Adolphs, 2007). The overlap in these maps suggests shared reliance on a frontoparietal network (**FIGURE 18.22**) that includes much of the attention network we have been discussing, as well as portions of medial frontal cortex and the cingulate. Some researchers have also suggested that the **claustrum** (**FIGURE 18.23**)—a slender sheet of neurons buried within the white matter of the forebrain lateral to the basal ganglia—plays a critical role in generating the experience of being conscious (Crick and Koch, 2005; Goll et al., 2015), by virtue of its remarkable reciprocal connections with virtually every area of cortex. In one case, a woman with a stimulating electrode in the claustrum experienced a "switching-off" of conscious awareness whenever a strong stimulation pulse was delivered through the electrode (Koubeissi et al., 2014).

Is clinical unconsciousness really the inverse of consciousness? Perhaps it's not that simple. In several cases, people in apparently deep and unresponsive comas were successfully instructed to use two different forms of mental imagery to create distinct "yes" and "no" patterns of activity on fMRI and then to use this mental activity to answer questions (**FIGURE 18.24**) (Fernández-Espejo and Owen, 2013; Monti et al., 2010). While it is not yet clear what proportion of people in comas have the ability to respond to commands in this fashion (Gibson et al., 2014)—studies like these suggest that it isn't accurate to view a coma as an exact inverse of what we experience as consciousness. Integrity of top-down feedback connections, from frontoparietal cortex to cortical sensory regions, seems to be crucial for even minimal levels of consciousness (Boly et al., 2011, 2012). But in any case, there seems to be more to consciousness than just being awake, aware, and attending. How can we identify and study the additional dimensions of consciousness?

claustrum A thin sheet of neurons, situated within the white matter lateral to the basal ganglia, that has been implicated in conscious awareness.

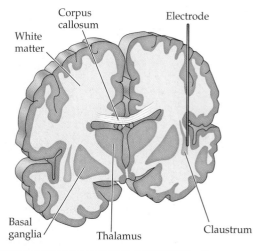

18.23 THE SEAT OF CONSCIOUSNESS? Some researchers have implicated the enigmatic gray matter band called the *claustrum* in the experience of conscious awareness. In one case study, a woman's conscious awareness was instantaneously switched off when a current was passed through an electrode planted in the region of the claustrum, and instantly restored when the electrode was turned off. (After Koubeissi et al., 2014.)

18.24 COMMUNICATION IN "UNCONSCIOUS" PEOPLE Functional MRI scans reveal distinctive patterns of brain activity obtained when a control participant (top) was asked to use two different mental images (playing tennis versus navigating) to signal yes or no answers to questions. The striking similarity of activation in the brain of a patient in a persistent vegetative state (bottom) who received the same instructions raises questions about the definition of unconsciousness. The patient was able to correctly answer a variety of questions using this technique, despite apparently deep unconsciousness due to profound brain damage (black regions on MRI scan) and lack of behavioral responses. (Images courtesy of Dr. Adrian Owen.)

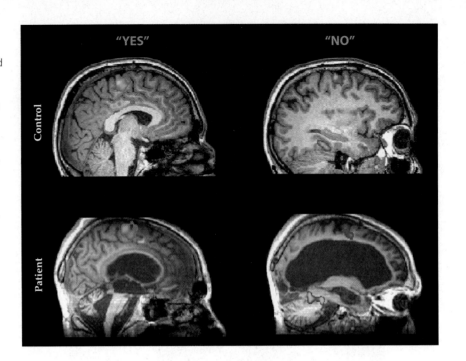

cognitively impenetrable Referring to data-processing operations of the central nervous system that are unconscious.

easy problem of consciousness The problem of how to read current conscious experiences directly from people's brains as they're happening.

hard problem of consciousness The problem of how to read people's subjective experience of consciousness and determine the qualia that accompany perception.

Some aspects of consciousness are easier to study than others

Most of the activity of the central nervous system is unconscious. In scientific language, these functions are said to be **cognitively impenetrable**: they involve basic neural processing operations that we cannot experience through introspection. We don't have conscious access to the subordinate components of perceptions—we see whole objects and can't even imagine what the primitive visual precursors of those perceptions could look like. Sweet food tastes sweet, and we can't mentally break it down any further than that. But those simpler mechanisms, operating below the surface of awareness, are the foundation that conscious experiences are built on. So in principle, we might someday develop technology that would let us directly reconstruct people's conscious experience—read their minds—by amalgamating lower-order brain activity into identifiable patterns.

Philosophers refer to this as the **easy problem of consciousness**: understanding how particular patterns of neural activity create *specific* conscious experiences. Of course, as a practical matter this undertaking is far from "easy," but at least we can reasonably say that some future brain-imaging technology may have enough speed and resolution to eavesdrop on large networks of neurons, in real time (**FIGURE 18.25A**). In fact, present-day technology offers a glimpse of that possible future. For example, if participants are repeatedly scanned while viewing several distinctive scenes, a computer can eventually learn to identify which of the scenes the participant is viewing on each trial, solely on the basis of the pattern of brain activation (Kay et al., 2008). Of course, this outcome relies on having the participants repeatedly view the same static images—hardly a normal state of consciousness. A more difficult problem is so-called constraint-free reconstruction of conscious experiences—that is, the ability to "read" what a person is perceiving rather than just identifying items on the basis of previous training. This sort of reconstruction has been accomplished for very simple stimuli, like letters and shapes (**FIGURE 18.25B**) (Miyawaki et al., 2008). We'll return to this topic in The Cutting Edge at the end of this chapter, but suffice it to say, we are still a very long way from directly reconstructing anything like a rich conscious experience. Still, at least it's conceivable.

Unsurprisingly, there is also the **hard problem of consciousness**: understanding the brain processes that result in a person's *subjective* experience of the contents of consciousness. To use a simple example, every person with normal color vision will identify a ripe tomato as being red because as children we all learned that a particular signal entering our consciousness from the color regions of the visual system is described as "red." We learn to relate labels to patterns of neural activity.

(A) Pattern identification

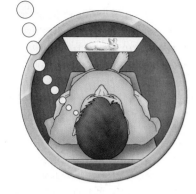

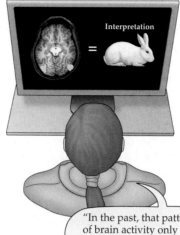

Interpretation

"In the past, that pattern of brain activity only appeared when he was looking at the rabbit."

(B) Visual reconstruction

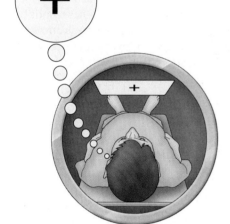

Reconstruction

"It looks like a 'plus' sign."

(C) Subjective experience

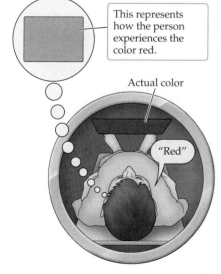

This represents how the person experiences the color red.

Actual color

"Red"

Both people instantly identify the color as red, but what differs is the way red *feels* in their minds.

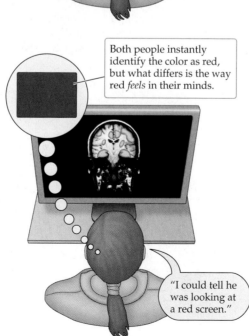

"I could tell he was looking at a red screen."

18.25 EASY AND HARD PROBLEMS OF CONSCIOUSNESS (A) When a participant is looking at one of 20 photographs, slightly different patterns of brain activity are elicited by different pictures. A computer can learn the patterns and eventually identify the scene being viewed. (B) In fact, vision scientists know enough about how different parts of the brain are activated by light striking the retina that they can even predict what sort of simple shape a person is viewing. (C) The "hard" problem goes beyond predicting what a person is seeing or thinking to knowing what that person's *subjective experience* is like. So, although the participant and the researcher would both use the label "red" to describe the color being viewed, how can we know their personal subjective experiences of that stimulus? It is difficult to see how we can ever be sure that we share any subjective experiences of consciousness. (Part A after Kay et al., 2008; B after Miyawaki et al., 2008.)

quale A purely subjective experience of perception.

But that doesn't mean that your friend's internal *personal* experience of "red" is the same as yours. These purely subjective experiences of perceptions are referred to as **qualia** (singular *quale*). Because they are subjective and impossible to communicate to others—how can your friend know if redness feels the same in your mind as it does in hers?—qualia may prove impossible to study (**FIGURE 18.25C**). At this point anyway, we are unable to even conceive of a technology that would make it possible.

Our subjective experience of consciousness is closely tied up with the notion of free will, or what are sometimes called *feelings of agency*: the perception (real or imagined) that our conscious self is the author of our actions and decisions. Aside from the issue of whether we actually have free will—a matter that won't be resolved anytime soon— there must be a neural substrate for the universal *feeling* of having free will. Conscious manipulations of intentions to act—an exercise in willful control of actions—result in selective fMRI activations of the pre–supplementary motor area (pre-SMA) in the frontal lobes of healthy participants, along with activations of the IPS (which we implicated earlier in top-down attention) and dorsal prefrontal cortex (Lau et al., 2004). However, research suggests that *conscious experiences* of intention may come relatively late in the process of deciding what to do. Early research (Libet, 1985), using EEG and a precise timer, found that an EEG component believed to signal movement preparation was evident 200 ms before participants consciously decided to move. Although controversy surrounded the assumptions and interpretation of the earlier study, more recent work using fMRI has strongly supported the idea that a decision can be made long before we have the conscious experience of making it, as described in **FIGURE 18.26** (Soon et al., 2008). Astonishingly, the results indicated that brain activity associated with making a decision was evident in the fMRI scans as much as 5–10 seconds before participants were consciously aware of making a choice. The earliest indications of this decision-making process are found in frontal cortex. Such involvement of prefrontal systems in most aspects of attention and consciousness, regardless of sensory modal-

18.26 ACT FIRST, THINK LATER Our brains may decide what we'll do before our conscious selves are aware of that decision. In this experiment, participants decided for themselves when to press a button with either the right hand or the left. Using brain MRI, the scientists found that they could predict beforehand when participants would "decide" to press the left or right button, and even *whether* they would press the left or the right button, up to 10 seconds before participants were aware of their own decisions. (After Soon et al., 2008.)

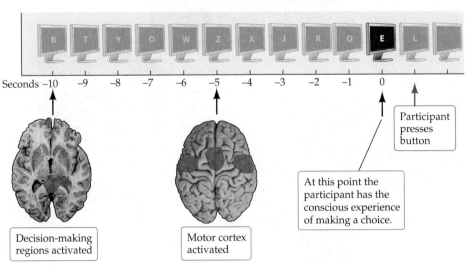

ity or emotional tone, suggests that the frontal cortex is the main source of goal-driven behaviors (E. K. Miller and Cohen, 2001), as we'll discuss next.

prefrontal cortex The anteriormost region of the frontal lobe.

The frontal lobes are a crucial part of the executive system that guides our thoughts, feelings, and choices

How do we decide what to do, and when to do it? Coordinated activity of a complex network of sites within the frontal lobes supports *hierarchical cognitive control*: the ability to direct shorter-term actions while simultaneously keeping longer-term goals in mind (Voytek et al., 2015). As noted in Chapter 6, humans are distinctive for the comparatively large size of our frontal lobes, about one-third of the entire cortical surface. We have already discussed key functions of the frontal lobes in several earlier chapters, in the context of such diverse behaviors as movement planning, memory performance, language, and psychopathology, but here we want to focus on some of the more enigmatic intellectual attributes of frontal systems. In part because of its size, the frontal region is regarded as the seat of intelligence and abstract thinking. Adding to the mystery of frontal lobe function is the unusual assortment of behavior changes that follows surgical or accidental lesions of this region.

On functional and anatomical grounds, researchers distinguish between several major divisions of the human frontal lobes. The posterior portion of frontal cortex includes the primary motor and premotor regions that we discussed in detail in Chapter 11. The more anterior portion, usually referred to as **prefrontal cortex**, is immensely interconnected with the rest of the brain and is especially associated with high-level cognition (Fuster, 1990; Mega and Cummings, 1994). It was prefrontal cortex that was surgically disrupted in frontal lobotomy: the notorious, now-discredited treatment for psychiatric disorders that we discussed in Chapter 16. Prefrontal cortex is further subdivided into a *dorsolateral* region and an *orbitofrontal* region (**FIGURE 18.27A**). The prefrontal cortex is especially prominent in humans and apes (Semendeferi et al., 2002), but it is a smaller portion of the cerebral cortex in other mammals (**FIGURE 18.27B**).

18.27 THE PREFRONTAL CORTEX
(A) The human prefrontal cortex can be subdivided into a dorsolateral region (blue) and an orbitofrontal region (green). Lesions in these different areas of prefrontal cortex have different effects on behavior. (B) The relative percentage of prefrontal cortex is greatest in humans and the great apes, such as the chimpanzees, but it decreases successively in monkeys, carnivores (such as cats), and rodents (not shown). The brains here are drawn to different scales. (Photographs courtesy of Drs. S. Mark Williams and Dale Purves.)

(A) The prefrontal cortex in humans

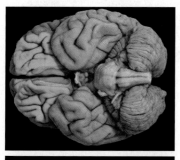

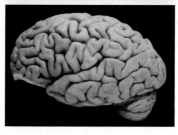

(B) Relative prefrontal cortex size in several mammals

Squirrel monkey
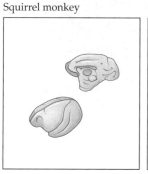
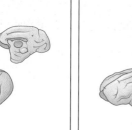

Cat

Rhesus monkey
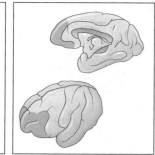

Chimpanzee
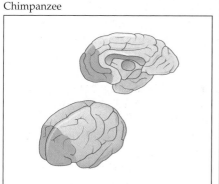

Human
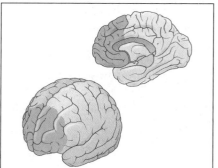

The study of prefrontal cortical function in animals began with Carlyle Jacobsen's work in the 1930s. In his experiments with chimpanzees, Jacobsen employed delayed-response learning. The animals were shown where food was hidden, but they had to wait before being allowed to reach for it. Chimpanzees with prefrontal lesions showed striking impairment on this simple task, compared with animals that sustained lesions in other brain regions. Jacobsen attributed the impairment to memory problems. But more recent observations, as we'll discuss next, suggest that the chimps were probably having trouble directing attention to the task and formulating a plan of action.

Frontal lobe injury in humans leads to emotional, motor, and cognitive changes

The complexity of change following prefrontal damage is epitomized by the case of Phineas Gage (**BOX 18.2**), one of neurology's most famous case studies. People with discrete prefrontal lesions express an unusual collection of emotional, motor, and cognitive changes. The emotional reactivity of these people shows a persistent strange apathy, broken by bouts of euphoria (an exalted sense of well-being). Ordinary social

BOX 18.2 — Phineas Gage

Phineas P. Gage was a sober, efficient, capable young man, respected by the workmen he supervised as they blasted rock to clear a path for a new railroad in northwestern Vermont. But one day in 1848, something went wrong. Gage was using a steel tamping rod to tightly pack explosives into a hole that had been drilled into the solid rock. The tamping rod—custom-made for Gage by a local blacksmith—was a cylinder about an inch and a quarter in diameter and three and a half feet long, flat at the bottom to tamp the charge, tapering to a point at the top. It resembled a javelin.

The iron rod must have struck a spark from the surrounding rock, because the charge went off unexpectedly, shooting the rod straight at Gage's head. The rod pierced his left cheek and passed behind his left eye and out the top of his skull, landing some 60 feet away. Gage was thrown onto his back, his limbs convulsing. Yet in a minute or two he spoke. With help from his men, he walked to a wagon, where he sat for the ride to town. There, Gage walked upstairs, unaided, to a doctor's office to have his wounds cleaned and dressed. No one expected him to live; an undertaker made a coffin for him (Macmillan, 2000).

In fact, Gage survived the injury—that's him in Figure A, in a recently

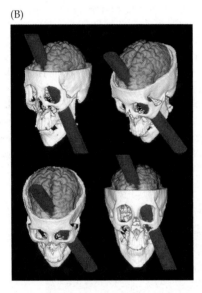

(A) Phineas Gage, holding the tamping rod. (B) The flight path of the tamping rod as it passed through Gage's head, reconstructed from studies of Gage's skull. (Courtesy of Dr. Hanna Damasio.)

discovered daguerreotype, holding the meter-long tamping rod. In fact, he was able to return to work—although not his old job—testifying to the remarkable plasticity and recuperative powers of the brain. Nevertheless, he was definitely a changed man. Reconstructions of the trajectory of the rod as it passed through Gage's head (shown in red in Figure B) reveal that it damaged both frontal lobes, especially the orbitofrontal regions. Although accounts of his symptoms clearly exaggerated his symptoms, it is still clear that after the accident his powers of attention and concentration were badly impaired, and compared with his old self he had become rude and aimless (Macmillan, 2000), prompting friends and relations to conclude that he was "no longer Gage." The historical account of Gage's case, now a neuroscience classic, closely agrees with the symptoms of modern people with frontal damage (H. Damasio et al., 1994; Wallis, 2007).

conventions are readily cast aside by impulsive behavior. Concern for the past or the future may be absent (Duffy and Campbell, 1994; Petrides and Milner, 1982). Forgetfulness is shown in many tasks requiring sustained attention. In fact, some of these people even forget their own warnings to "remember." However, standard IQ test performance often shows only slight changes after prefrontal injury or stroke.

Clinical examination of people with frontal lesions also reveals an array of strange impairments in their behavior, especially in the realm of **executive function**, the high-level control of other cognitive functions in order to attend to important stimuli and make suitable "plans" for action. For example, a patient with frontal lesions given a simple set of errands may be unable to complete them (if able to do any at all) without numerous false starts, backtracking, and confusion (Shallice and Burgess, 1991). Regions of dorsolateral prefrontal cortex, along with anterior portions of the cingulate, are closely associated with executive control. Dorsolateral prefrontal cortex is also crucial for working memory, the ability to hold information in mind while processing it or using the information to solve problems.

People with frontal lesions often struggle with *task shifting* and tend to **perseverate** (continue beyond a reasonable degree) in any activity (Alvarez and Emory, 2006; B. Milner, 1963). However, the overall level of motor activity—especially ordinary, spontaneous movements—is often quite diminished in people with frontal lesions. Along with movement of the head and eyes, facial expression of emotions may be greatly reduced.

One explanation for these disparate effects of prefrontal lesions is that this region of cortex may be important for organizing the diverse aspects of goal-directed behavior, including the capacity for prolonged attention and sensitivity to potential rewards and punishments. People with prefrontal lesions, like Phineas Gage, often have an inability to plan acts and use foresight. Their social skills may decline, especially the ability to inhibit inappropriate behaviors, and they may be unable to stay focused on any but short-term projects. They may agonize over even simple decisions. **TABLE 18.2** lists the main clinical features of people with lesions of the major subdivisions of the frontal lobes.

Studies of healthy people indicate that prefrontal cortex—especially the orbitofrontal region—is important for goal-directed behaviors. In monkeys, prefrontal cortical neurons become especially active when the animal has to make a decision that may provide a reward (Matsumoto et al., 2003), suggesting that prefrontal cortex controls goal-directed behaviors. In general, orbitofrontal cortex seems important for forming associations between hedonic experiences (such as the subjective pleasantness of eating gourmet food) and reward signals from elsewhere in the brain (Kringelbach, 2005); some researchers suggest that orbitofrontal cortex is actually more important for signaling expected outcomes (which is likewise related to reward) than for learning (Schoenbaum et al., 2009). In humans performing a task in which some stimuli have more reward value than others, the level of activation in prefrontal cortex (as measured by fMRI) correlates with how rewarding the stimulus is (Gottfried et al., 2003). In another testing situation that involved gambling,

executive function A neural and cognitive system that helps develop plans of action and organizes the activities of other high-level processing systems.

perseverate To continue to show a behavior repeatedly.

TABLE 18.2 Core Characteristics of the Regional Prefrontal Syndromes

SYNDROME TYPE	PREFRONTAL REGION AFFECTED	CHARACTERISTICS
Dysexecutive	Dorsolateral	Diminished judgment, planning, insight, and temporal organization; cognitive impersistence; motor programming deficits (possibly including aphasia and apraxia); diminished self-care
Disinhibited	Orbitofrontal	Stimulus-driven behavior; diminished social insight; distractibility; emotional lability
Apathetic	Mediofrontal	Diminished spontaneity; diminished verbal output (including mutism); diminished motor behavior (including akinesis); urinary incontinence; lower-extremity weakness and sensory loss; diminished spontaneous prosody; increased response latency

neuroeconomics The study of brain mechanisms at work during decision making.

ERPs indicated that prefrontal cortex was especially active when people were making choices that could cost them money (Gehring and Willoughby, 2002). In fact, understanding how we make decisions under conditions of risk is an active area of study, as we'll discuss next.

Frontal mechanisms sift alternatives, evaluate risk and reward, and guide decisions accordingly

To some extent, our inner lives are reflected in the choices we make. Should I have a Cobb salad for lunch? Or a smoked meat on rye sandwich? What happens in the brain when we make everyday decisions?

When asking people to make decisions in the lab, it is convenient to use monetary transactions because then you can vary how much money is at stake, how great a reward is offered, and so on, allowing for precise manipulation of the decision-making process. These studies show that most of us are very averse to loss and risk: we are more sensitive to losing a certain amount of money than we are to gaining that amount. In other words, losing $20 makes us feel a lot worse than gaining $20 makes us feel good. From a strictly logical point of view, the value of money, whether lost or gained, should be exactly the same. Our tendency to overemphasize loss is just one of several ways in which people fail to act rationally in the marketplace.

Neuroeconomics is the study of brain mechanisms at work during economic decision making, and our attention to environmental factors and evaluation of rewards has a tremendous impact on these decisions. For example, in monkeys playing these sorts of economic games (yes, monkeys—monkeys will gamble for apple juice, which they really, *really* like), neurons in the posterior cingulate cortex become more active when risky choices are being made (McCoy and Platt, 2005). In one study of humans, anterior cingulate cortex became more active when rewards were diminished, signaling that the participants should change how they played a game (Z. M. Williams et al., 2004). And when this brain region was lesioned (cingulotomy is occasionally performed in humans as a last-ditch attempt to control obsessive-compulsive disorder; see Figure 16.28), the participants made more errors, failing to switch strategies as if they did not fully experience the disappointment of a reduced reward.

Although neuroeconomics is a young field, enough data have been amassed to suggest theoretical models of the neural bases of decision making. Two main systems seem to underlie decision processes (Kable and Glimcher, 2009). The first, consisting of the ventromedial prefrontal cortex (including the anterior cingulate) plus the dopamine-based reward system of the basal forebrain (see Chapter 4), serves as a *valuation system*, a network that ranks choices on the basis of their perceived worth and potential reward. Impressively, using an optogenetic technique (see Chapter 3) to selectively activate neurons that express dopamine receptor D_2 in the nucleus accumbens—a central forebrain component of the brain's reward system—can instantaneously turn a risk-preferring rat into a risk-averse rat (Zalocusky et al., 2016)! Presumably, the activated cells cause the valuation system to devalue the choice relative to risk. Furthermore, *social* valuations in the context of decisions about affiliation and mate choice, or social components of material choices (such as co-owning a house, or choosing a business partner), seem to rely on much of the same neural machinery, especially the ventromedial prefrontal cortex system (Ruff and Fehr, 2014).

The second system, involving mostly dorsolateral prefrontal cortex, dorsal anterior cingulate cortex, and parietal regions (like LIP/IPS) that we have already discussed in the context of attention and awareness, is thought to be a *choice system*, sifting through the valuated alternatives and producing the conscious decision. Neuroeconomics research is confirming that the prefrontal cortex inhibits impulsive decisions, enforcing our loss aversion (Muhlert and Lawrence, 2015; Tom et al., 2007). As people are faced with more and more uncertainty, the prefrontal cortex becomes more and more active (Hsu et al., 2005; Huettel et al., 2006), and the dorsal anterior cingulate cortex is thought to help sharpen accuracy by delaying responses in situations that require time to complete complex processing of alternatives (Sheth et al., 2012). Likewise, when people have made wrong, costly decisions that they regret, activity increases in the amygdala and prefrontal cortex (Coricelli et al., 2005), probably reflecting the person's perception of diminished reward and increasing aversion to loss (**FIGURE 18.28**). Reflection on the accuracy of one's own decision-making processes is an aspect of metacognition (see Table 18.1), one of the central features of human consciousness. This sort of introspection is particularly associated with activity of the anterior prefrontal cortex (S. M. Fleming et al., 2012; Tsujimoto et al., 2011).

As we've seen in this chapter, our higher cognitive processes involve a constellation of mechanisms for attention, awareness, consciousness, and decision making that span most of the brain. Although we are just at the beginning of a long quest to understand the neural bases of attention, awareness, and consciousness, current research on these topics holds the promise of profound insights into brain processes that lie at the heart of human experience.

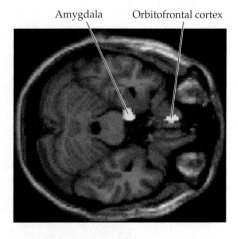

18.28 A POOR CHOICE A costly decision is associated with activation of the amygdala and orbitofrontal cortex, signaling diminished reward and aversion to loss. (From Coricelli et al., 2005, courtesy of Dr. Angela Sirigu.)

■ The Cutting Edge

Building a Better Mind Reader

Some sort of machine that can read and replay a person's thoughts and feelings is a staple of science fiction, but is it plausible? As we've discussed in this chapter, reading or reconstructing a person's visual experiences on the basis of patterns of brain activity, a so-called easy problem of consciousness, is at present very difficult. Using fMRI to track changes in the retinotopic map in primary visual cortex, researchers have had some success in determining whether people are viewing crosses, circles, or other large and simple stimuli (Miyawaki et al., 2008) (as in Figure 18.25B) or static pictures of faces or scenes (Naselaris et al., 2009). However, traditional fMRI is normally too slow to "read" anything more than relatively simple, static visual experiences. But of course visual perception is almost never static; it's a continuously rolling movie, directed by attention and powerfully shaping our consciousness.

So how can we sneak a look at peoples' internal movies? One clever approach involves building a huge library of predicted brain responses to visual scenes and using those to reconstruct visual experiences from recordings of brain activity. Researchers in Jack Gallant's lab at U.C. Berkeley (Nishimoto et al., 2011) began by themselves spending many, many hours watching two sets of training videos—Hollywood movie trailers—while fMRI data were recorded from the occipitotemporal visual cortex. These data were used to develop a mathematical model that predicts how shape and motion are encoded for every voxel in the visual cortex. (*Voxel* is short for *volumetric pixel*, and just as pixels define the two dimensions of a computer screen, voxels make up the three-dimensional volume of an imaged brain.)

Next, the researchers cut up a random assortment of YouTube videos into 18 million clips, each 1 second long, none of which were the same as the original training videos. Using a cutting-edge probability-based reconstruction algorithm, this library of short clips was fed into the computer program containing the model of brain activity, for each participant. The program created a prediction for the pattern of brain activity that each of the 18 million clips would produce.

Finally, a computer was used to compare the actual fMRI activity from the second set of test videos (again, movie trailers) with the *predicted* activity associated with the YouTube clips. For each 1-second "frame" of the test videos, a computer program selected the 100 clips whose predicted activity most closely matched the actual activity recorded when the participant viewed the original frame. These clips were then merged and processed and strung together frame by frame into a movie reconstruction. The results of this process are shown in **FIGURE 18.29** and on the website. For each of three test video clips (A, B, and C), three individual frames are shown across the top row. The next five rows show the five best-fitting YouTube frames, as selected by the modeled brain activity of the participant. Mostly, they don't much resemble the original frames, but when averaged together, as shown in the bottom row, a blurry but pretty strong resemblance begins to emerge. The accuracy of the reconstruction is much more evident when viewing the original and reconstructed videos playing side by side, which you can see on the website. It is almost unnerving. Researchers are now developing related techniques to reconstruct participants' mental imagery of various categories of complex stimuli, such as novel faces (Nestor et al., 2016) and natural visual scenes (Lescroart et al., 2015).

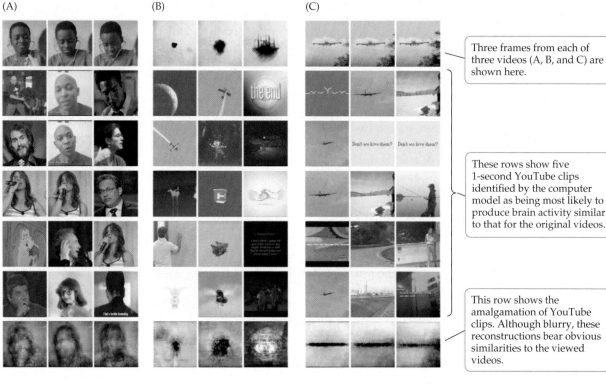

(A)　　　(B)　　　(C)

Three frames from each of three videos (A, B, and C) are shown here.

These rows show five 1-second YouTube clips identified by the computer model as being most likely to produce brain activity similar to that for the original videos.

This row shows the amalgamation of YouTube clips. Although blurry, these reconstructions bear obvious similarities to the viewed videos.

18.29 RECONSTRUCTION OF A MENTAL MOVIE (Courtesy of Drs. Shinji Nishimoto and Jack Gallant, University of California, Berkeley.)

So, we are making progress on the easy problem of consciousness: understanding how specific patterns of brain activity accompany specific conscious experiences and imagery. We are considerably further from ever being able to *implant* experiences and memories into consciousness, after the fashion of *The Matrix*, *Total Recall*, or *Inception*. But the technology to do so is at least conceivable; after all, we've seen that it's possible to noninvasively stimulate the brain with transcranial magnetic stimulation (TMS) (see Chapter 2). The same cannot be said for the hard problem of consciousness, however: any progress in reading the personal and subjective feelings that accompany conscious experiences lies in a distant, and largely unimagined, future.

Go to
bn8e.com
for study questions, quizzes, activities, and other resources

Recommended Reading

Bernat, J. L. (2009). Chronic consciousness disorders. *Annual Review of Medicine, 60,* 381–392.

Chun, M. M., Golomb, J. D., and Turk-Browne, N. B. (2011). A taxonomy of external and internal attention. *Annual Review of Psychology, 62,* 73–101.

Gazzaniga, M. S. (2012). *Who's in Charge? Free Will and the Science of the Brain.* New York: Ecco.

Glimcher, P. W., Camerer, C., Poldrack, R. A., and Fehr, E. (2008). *Neuroeconomics: Decision Making and the Brain.* San Diego, CA: Academic Press.

Goldberg, E. (2009). *The New Executive Brain: Frontal Lobes in a Complex World.* Oxford, England: Oxford University Press.

Koch, C. (2012). *Consciousness: Confessions of a Romantic Reductionist.* Cambridge, MA: MIT Press.

Mangun, G. R. (Ed.). (2012). *Neuroscience of Attention: Attentional Control and Selection.* Oxford, England: Oxford University Press.

Posner, M. I. (2011). *Cognitive Neuroscience of Attention* (2nd ed.). New York: Guilford.

Stuss, D. T., and Knight, R. T. (2012). *Principles of Frontal Lobe Function* (2nd ed.). Oxford, England: Oxford University Press.

Wright, R. D., and Ward, L. M. (2008). *Orienting of Attention.* Oxford, England: Oxford University Press.

VISUAL SUMMARY

You should be able to relate each summary to the adjacent illustration, including structures and processes.
Go to **bn8e.com/vs18** for links to figures, animations, and activities that will help you consolidate the material.

1 We can pay covert attention to stimuli or locations of our choosing. **Attention** helps us distinguish stimuli from distracters. Because we have limited processing capabilities, an **attentional bottleneck** limits incoming information. Review **Figures 18.1 and 18.2**, **Video 18.2**

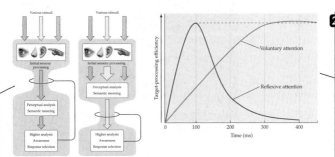

2 In **voluntary attention** we consciously select objects to attend to. **Reflexive attention** is the involuntary capture of attention by stimuli. In visual search, targets may pop out if they are distinctive on a particular feature (**feature search**). More often, we use **conjunction searches**, identifying target stimuli on the basis of two or more features. Review **Figures 18.3–18.6**, **Animation 18.3**

3 **Event-related potentials (ERPs)** are created by the averaging of many EEG recordings from repeated experimental trials. Endogenous visual attention enhances the **P1** component of the ERP, related to early attentional selection, and the **P3 effect**, which is related to later attentional selection. N2pc and P_D are contralateral occipital ERP components associated with searching visual scenes and ignoring distracters, respectively. Reflexive visual attention also enhances P1, but only for short delays between cue and stimulus. Review **Figures 18.7–18.9**

4 Selective attention causes enhanced activations of discrete regions of sensory cortex, such as primary visual cortex and extrastriate visual areas. Single-cell recordings in lab animals confirm that attention affects the responses of individual neurons. Review **Figures 18.10–18.13**

5 Subcortical mechanisms involving the **superior colliculi** and the **pulvinar** are crucial for shifting visual attention and gaze between important objects of attention. Review **Figure 18.14**, **Activity 18.1**

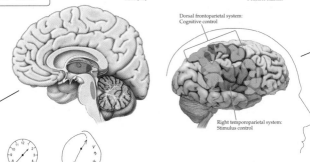

6 A dorsal frontoparietal attention network in the cortex is responsible for directing voluntary attention. A right-sided temporoparietal attentional system is responsible for detecting and shifting attention to novel stimuli. The two networks interact extensively. Review **Figures 18.15–18.18**, **Activities 18.2 and 18.3**

7 Damage to the right hemisphere involving the right parietal cortex can cause **hemispatial neglect**. Patients with this condition ignore the left side of the world. Review **Figures 18.19 and 18.20**

8 **Bálint's syndrome** is a rare consequence of bilateral parietal damage. In Bálint's syndrome, patients are spatially disoriented and experience a dramatic narrowing of attention, to the point that only one object at a time can be seen (**simultagnosia**). People in various unconscious states show reduced activity of frontoparietal regions. Review **Figures 18.22–18.24**

9 The **easy problem of consciousness** is the problem of how to read specific current conscious experiences directly from people's brains as they are happening. The **hard problem of consciousness** is the problem of how to read people's subjective experience of consciousness and determine the **qualia** that accompany perception. Review **Figure 18.25**

10 Feelings of free will may rely on the activity of specific frontal lobe mechanisms. But even if that's true, it's possible that unconscious mechanisms make many of our decisions well before we consciously realize it. Review **Figure 18.26**

(continued)

11 **Prefrontal cortex** consists of dorsolateral and orbitofrontal divisions; damage in these regions produces a distinctive set of symptoms. Medial aspects of the frontal lobes, including anterior cingulate regions, are associated with **executive function**. Prefrontal cortex appears to be essential for coordinating the resources needed for goal-directed behavior. **Neuroeconomics,** is concerned with the neural mechanisms responsible for decision making. A current model emphasizes a ventromedial frontal evaluation system and a dorsolateral choice network. Review **Figures 18.27 and 18.28, Box 18.2, Table 18.1**

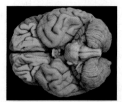
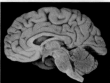
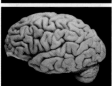

12 Thanks to powerful techniques for modeling brain activity while viewing visual scenes, we are getting closer to being able to use technology to reconstruct people's visual experiences. Review **Figure 18.29**

Language and Lateralization

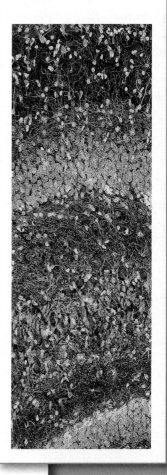

19

■ Silencing the Inner Voice ──────────────

We all have an inner voice: that sometimes-annoying mental narrator whose dialog runs the gamut from calm abstraction ("What is love?") to insistent directives ("Pizza now!") to harsh self-criticism ("Way to go, dork!"). Some researchers, observing that the development of a child's sense of self is inextricably linked to the acquisition of language, have proposed that the inner voice is essential for the self-awareness that defines our consciousness. Nevertheless, sometimes we wish our inner voice would just shut up for a while.

What would life be like if our inner voice actually *were* silenced? This is just what happened to Tinna Geula Phillips. Suddenly one day, Tinna lost the ability to communicate in any of the six languages (yes, *six*) that she had mastered; a devastating neurological event. But even more profound was the immediate silencing of Tinna's inner voice. For several months, Tinna was unable to process thoughts in the way we take for granted. Tinna's internal silence had robbed her of a critical tool for organizing her activities, weighing her emotions, processing abstract concepts, and considering her memories. She would later describe the experience as a near-total loss of identity. What could have happened to cause Tinna to lose the ability to talk to anyone, even herself?

───

Faces, coloration, smells, sounds—many species use physical and behavioral signals to engage in **communication**, the transmission of information between individuals. But we humans may be alone in our use of **language**, the highly specialized form of communication in which arbitrary symbols or behaviors are assembled and reassembled in almost infinite variety and associated with a vast range of things, actions, and concepts. Because the speakers of a language all understand the same strict set of rules, or **grammar**, language allows us to assemble and share information on any topic, linking thinkers of the past with those of the future. Our linguistic and aesthetic perception of the world gives us a mental life that appears to be unique among animal species.

In almost everyone, verbal abilities are especially associated with the left hemisphere of the brain, whereas the right hemisphere plays a special role in complex **spatial cognition**, our ability to process geometric relationships, to navigate, and to understand the spatial relationships between objects. In this chapter we survey the neuroscience of this **cerebral lateralization**, with a special emphasis on the acquisition of, use of, and brain mechanisms underlying speech and language. Much of what we know about human brain organization is derived from studies of people who have suffered strokes and other forms of brain injury, so we also look at the ways in which the damaged brain can be encouraged to recover and adapt.

Go to Brain Explorer
bn8e.com/19.1

Brain Asymmetry and Lateralization of Function

communication Information transfer between two individuals.

language The most sophisticated form of communication, in which a set of arbitrary sounds, tokens, or symbols can be arranged according to a grammar in order to convey an almost limitless variety of concepts.

grammar All of the rules for usage of a particular language.

spatial cognition Those mental processes that deal with the spatial relationship among objects.

cerebral lateralization Specialization of one cerebral hemisphere for a particular intellectual function.

lateralization The tendency for the right and left halves of a system to differ from one another.

split-brain individual An individual whose corpus callosum has been severed, halting communication between the right and left hemispheres.

The special role of the left hemisphere for language functions was well established by the mid-twentieth century, and it was often referred to as the *dominant hemisphere*, in recognition of the preeminence of language in our cognitive lives (Finger, 1994). However, the right hemisphere does not just idly sit within the skull, awaiting an occasional call to duty. In fact, most researchers have abandoned the notion of cerebral *dominance* in favor of models of hemispheric *specialization*, or **lateralization**. This emphasis implies that some functional systems are connected more to one side of the brain than the other—that is, that functions become lateralized—and that each hemisphere is specialized for particular ways of working. Keep in mind, however, that almost all types of behavior, from manual skills to intellectual activity, are performed better by the two hemispheres working together than by either hemisphere working alone. The idea that the two hemispheres are so different that they need separate instruction or that people can have personalities that are "left-brained" (supposedly more random, intuitive, and creative) or "right-brained" (ostensibly logical, sequential, and analytical) are notions that lack any scientific foundation.

The Left Brain Is Different from the Right Brain

The discovery that some brain functions are lateralized should not be especially surprising; after all, other body organs also show considerable asymmetry between the right and left sides. For example, in all vertebrates the heart is slightly to the left of the midline and the liver is on the right. Sometimes a person with a defect in one of the genes involved will develop with their organs reversed, a condition called *situs inversus* (Casey and Hackett, 2000).

When we study the *behavior* of healthy people, cerebral lateralization of function is masked by the rich neural connections between the hemispheres: they communicate with each other so quickly and so thoroughly that they seem to act as one. But by studying people whose interhemispheric pathways have been disconnected, researchers have been able to study the functioning of each hemisphere in isolation from the other.

Disconnection of the cerebral hemispheres reveals their individual specializations

Starting in the 1940s, a small group of people underwent a surgical procedure designed to provide relief from frequent, disabling epileptic seizures. In these people, epileptic activity that was initiated in one hemisphere spread to the other hemisphere via the corpus callosum, a large white matter tract containing hundreds of millions of axons that connect the two hemispheres. Surgically cutting the corpus callosum reduced the frequency and severity of such seizures. It is a very rare procedure; some people had only partial splits, and nowadays there are better medical alternatives, so only about ten **split-brain individuals** have been fully studied (A. M. Gazzaniga, 2008).

Studies at the time seemed to show that this remedy for seizures caused no apparent changes in brain function, as assessed by general measures like IQ tests. But this made little sense to researchers—how could hundreds of millions of axons be severed without affecting behavior?—and subsequent animal research soon confirmed that hemispheric disconnection actually has significant consequences.

In earlier studies on cats, both the corpus callosum and the optic chiasm were sectioned so that each eye was connected only to the ipsilateral hemisphere. Using the left eye (and hence the left hemisphere, because only the uncrossed axons of the optic nerve remained intact; see Chapter 10), the cats learned that a particular symbol was associated with a reward but that the inverted symbol was not. Using the right eye (and right hemisphere), the same cats simultaneously were able to learn the opposite—that the inverted symbol was rewarded rather than the upright symbol. Thus, each hemisphere remained ignorant of what the other had learned (Sperry et al., 1956).

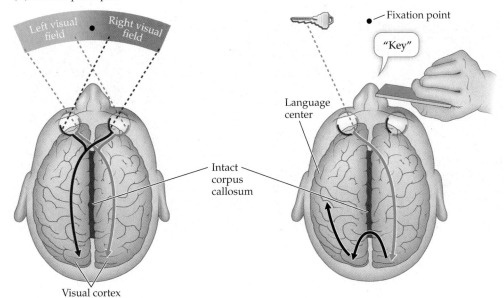

(A) Control participant

Left visual field · Right visual field

Intact corpus callosum

Visual cortex

Fixation point

"Key"

Language center

19.1 TESTING A SPLIT-BRAIN INDIVIDUAL Words or pictures projected to the left visual field activate the right visual cortex. (A) In intact individuals, activation of the right visual cortex excites corpus callosum fibers, which transmit verbal information to the left hemisphere, where the information is analyzed and language is produced. (B) In split-brain individuals, stimuli from the left visual field reach the right-hemisphere visual cortex via the subcortical visual pathways (they are independent of the corpus callosum). However, the split corpus callosum prevents right-hemisphere visual areas from communicating with the language areas of the left hemisphere, so verbal responses to the stimuli are impossible (left). In contrast, split-brain individuals are able to respond verbally to stimuli appearing in the right visual fields, because interhemispheric transfer is not required (right).

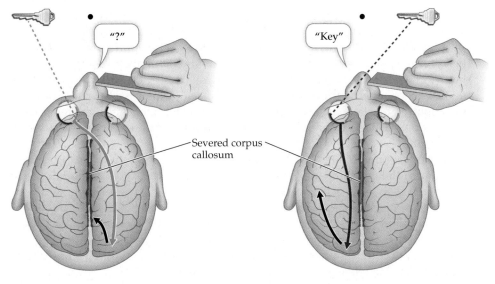

(B) Split-brain individual

"?"

"Key"

Severed corpus callosum

In Nobel Prize–winning research begun in the 1960s, Roger Sperry applied techniques that he had perfected in the split-brain cats to study split-brain humans. In the humans, as in the cats, stimuli are directed to either hemisphere. For example, objects that the person feels with the left hand stimulate activity in sensory neurons of the right hemisphere. Because the corpus callosum is cut in these people, most of the information sent to one hemisphere of the brain cannot travel to the other hemisphere. By controlling stimuli in this fashion—selectively presenting them to one hemisphere or the other—the experimenter can test the capabilities of each hemisphere.

In some of Sperry's studies, words were projected to either the left or the right hemisphere; that is, printed stimuli were presented in either the right or the left side of the visual field. The results were dramatic. Split-brain individuals could easily read and verbally communicate words projected to the left hemisphere (via the right visual field), but no such linguistic capabilities were evident when the words were directed to the right hemisphere (**FIGURE 19.1**). Although the right hemisphere in split-brain individuals does have minor linguistic capabilities—for example, recognition of very simple words, and processing of emotional content in verbal material (Zaidel, 1976)—in most people, vocabulary and grammar are the exclusive domain of the left hemisphere (left-handers occasionally show a reversed asymmetry).

19.2 CALLOSAL AGENESIS In contrast to the typical brain in (A), the brain in (B) failed to develop any vestige of a corpus callosum. Despite the absence of the hundreds of millions of axons that pass between the hemispheres through the corpus callosum, the activity of the two hemispheres of this individual remained coordinated. (From Tyszka et al., 2011; images courtesy of Drs. Lynn Paul and Mike Tyszka.)

(A)

Corpus callosum

(B)

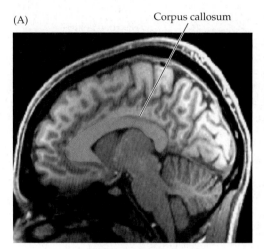 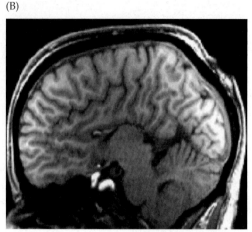

The capabilities of the "mute" right hemisphere thus required testing by nonverbal means. For example, a picture of a key might be projected to the left visual field and so reach only the right visual cortex. The person would then be asked to touch several different objects that she could not see and hold up the correct one. Such a task could be performed correctly by the left hand (controlled by the right hemisphere) but not by the right hand (controlled by the left hemisphere). So in this case, the left hemisphere literally does not know what the left hand is doing! In general, these and other studies with split-brain individuals provided early evidence that, in most people, the right hemisphere is specialized for processing spatial information. Right-hemisphere mechanisms are also crucial for face perception, for processing emotional aspects of language, and for controlling attention (as we discussed in Chapter 18).

As many as one in 4000 people are born either partially or totally lacking a corpus callosum. Although some individuals will show some behavioral consequences of this *callosal agenesis* (**FIGURE 19.2**), in general they lack the constellation of striking neuropsychological changes evident in surgical split-brain individuals (Sotiriadis and Makrydimas, 2012). Somehow, the developing nervous system compensates for the loss of the main connection between the hemispheres, perhaps by strengthening alternative subcortical routes of transmission (Tyszka et al., 2011). This observation highlights the incredible plasticity of the developing brain.

The two hemispheres process information differently in most humans

Most research on brain asymmetry in healthy people focuses on two sensory modalities: hearing and vision. That's because researchers have devised clever procedures for directing auditory or visual stimuli mostly to one hemisphere or the other, and then inferring hemispheric specializations from the behavioral responses made by the participants.

THE RIGHT-EAR ADVANTAGE   Through earphones, we can present different sounds to the two ears at the same time; this process is called **dichotic presentation**. So, for example, the participant may hear a particular speech sound in one ear and, at the same time, a different vowel, consonant, or word in the other ear. The task for the participant is to try to identify or recall both sounds. Although this procedure may seem designed to produce confusion, most data from dichotic presentation experiments indicate that right-handed persons identify verbal stimuli delivered to the right ear more accurately than verbal stimuli simultaneously presented to the left ear. This result is described as a *right-ear advantage* for verbal information. In contrast, about 50% of left-handed people reveal a reverse pattern, showing a left-ear advantage—more-accurate performance for verbal stimuli delivered to the left ear.

dichotic presentation   The simultaneous delivery of different stimuli to the right and the left ears.

tachistoscope test   A test in which stimuli are very briefly exposed in either the left or right visual half field.

planum temporale   A region of superior temporal cortex adjacent to the primary auditory area.

19.3 THE RIGHT-EAR ADVANTAGE IN DICHOTIC PRESENTATION
(A) A word delivered to the left ear results in stronger stimulation of the right auditory cortex. (B) A word delivered to the right ear results in stronger input to the left hemisphere. (C) When words are delivered to both ears simultaneously, the word to the right ear is the one usually perceived because the right ear has more-direct connections to the left hemisphere. (After Kimura, 1973.)

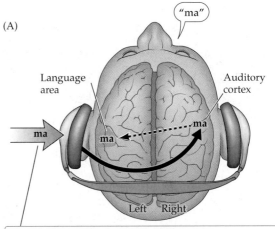

(A)

Language area

Auditory cortex

Left Right

Information to the left ear goes to right auditory cortex and then to the left hemisphere language area. Participant repeats word.

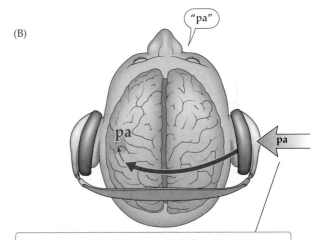

(B)

Information to the right ear goes to left auditory cortex and then to the left hemisphere language area. Participant repeats word.

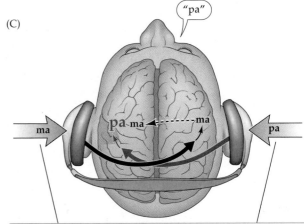

(C)

When conflicting information goes to both ears, the information to the right ear reaches the left hemisphere language area first. Participant repeats only the right-ear information.

As a consequence of the preferential connections between the right ear and left hemisphere, the right-ear advantage for verbal stimuli is probably a reflection of the left hemisphere's specialization for language (**FIGURE 19.3**). Although we can normally use either ear for processing speech sounds, speech presented to the right ear in dichotic presentation tests exerts stronger control over language mechanisms in the left hemisphere than does the speech simultaneously presented to the left ear (Kimura, 1973). The competition between the left- and right-ear inputs is the key; presentation of speech stimuli to one ear at a time (*monaural* presentation) does not produce a right-ear advantage. And the right-ear advantage in right-handers is restricted to particular kinds of speech sounds: those made for consonants like *b*, *d*, *t*, and *k* produce a right-ear effect, but vowel sounds do not (Tallal and Schwartz, 1980).

VISUAL PERCEPTION OF LINGUISTIC STIMULI A visual analog to the dichotic listening task is the **tachistoscope test**, in which a specialized apparatus (named, surprisingly, a *tachistoscope*) is used to present stimuli very briefly to either the left or right visual field (see Figures 10.11 and 19.1). If the stimulus exposure lasts less than 150 milliseconds (ms) or so, the input is received by only the contralateral hemisphere because there is not enough time for the eyes to shift their position to fix the stimulus in central vision. In healthy humans, of course, information may subsequently be passed to the other hemisphere via the corpus callosum, but the important thing is that, as with dichotic presentation, the stimuli have preferential access to one hemisphere.

Most tachistoscopic studies confirm the general division of labor between the hemispheres. Verbal stimuli (words and letters) are better recognized when they are presented to the right visual field and therefore left hemisphere than when they are presented to the left visual field/right hemisphere. Conversely, nonverbal visual stimuli (such as faces or geometric forms) presented to the left visual field/right hemisphere are better recognized than the same stimuli presented to the right visual field/left hemisphere. Simpler visual processing, such as detection of light, hue, or simple patterns, is performed equivalently by both hemispheres.

The left and right hemispheres differ in their auditory specializations

Anatomical studies of primary auditory cortex in the left and right hemispheres are consistent with the view that the two play different roles in auditory perception. In one early postmortem study of auditory cortex, the **planum temporale**—an auditory region on the superior surface of the temporal lobe—was

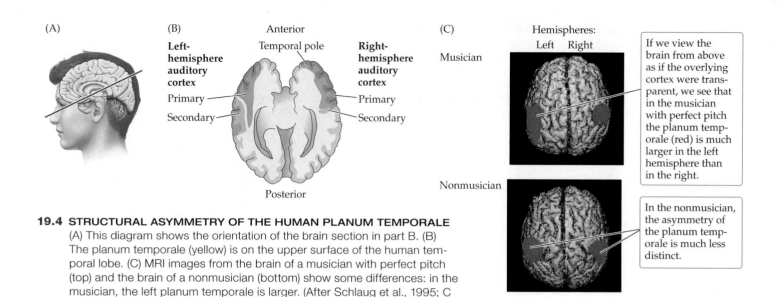

19.4 STRUCTURAL ASYMMETRY OF THE HUMAN PLANUM TEMPORALE
(A) This diagram shows the orientation of the brain section in part B. (B) The planum temporale (yellow) is on the upper surface of the human temporal lobe. (C) MRI images from the brain of a musician with perfect pitch (top) and the brain of a nonmusician (bottom) show some differences: in the musician, the left planum temporale is larger. (After Schlaug et al., 1995; C courtesy of Dr. Gottfried Schlaug.)

found to be larger in the left hemisphere than in the right in 65% of brains studied (**FIGURE 19.4A AND B**) (Geschwind and Levitsky, 1968). In only 11% of adults was the right side larger. The planum temporale includes part of Wernicke's area, which as we'll see shortly is crucial for speech, so it seems likely that the larger left planum temporale is related to the left hemisphere's language specialization. Direct evidence of this relationship, however, remains somewhat elusive: in one MRI study, for example, asymmetry of the planum temporale did not correlate with direct measures of language lateralization (Dorsaint-Pierre et al., 2006).

As in adults, the left planum temporale is larger than the right in the brains of infants (Wada et al., 1975), in agreement with the observation that speech activates the left cerebral hemisphere more than the right in infants as young as 3 months. This provides more evidence that there is probably an inborn aspect of cerebral specialization for language, because the asymmetry is evident before any substantial experience with speech has occurred. In fact, even in human fetuses of just 12–14 weeks of gestation, a variety of genes show asymmetrical expression in the brain (T. Sun et al., 2005). The planum temporale tends to be larger on the left than on the right in chimpanzees too (Gannon et al., 1998), and Broca's area—another cortical speech zone, as we'll see a little later—is larger on the left than on the right in chimps, bonobos, and gorillas, as well as in humans (Cantalupo and Hopkins, 2001). Furthermore, just as our left hemisphere is more activated than the right when we hear speech rather than other sounds, the left hemisphere of monkeys is more activated than the right when they hear monkey vocalizations rather than human speech (Poremba et al., 2004). These results suggest that other primates also possess a left-hemisphere specialization for some forms of communication (but not necessarily *language*, as we will discuss a little later).

In contrast, the auditory areas of the *right* hemisphere play a major role in the perception of music. Musical perception is impaired particularly by damage to the right hemisphere (Samson and Zatorre, 1994), and music activates the right hemisphere more than the left (Zatorre et al., 1994). But perfect pitch (the ability to identify any musical note without comparing it to a reference note) seems to involve the left rather than the right hemisphere. Schlaug et al. (1995) made MRI measurements of the planum temporale in three kinds of participants, all right-handed (because the larger size of the left planum temporale is seen especially in right-handed individuals): (1) musicians with perfect pitch, (2) musicians without perfect pitch, and (3) nonmusicians. The size of the left planum temporale was twice as large in musicians with perfect pitch than in nonmusicians (**FIGURE 19.4C**). The size of the left planum temporale in musicians without perfect pitch was intermediate, but closer to that of nonmusicians. Because perfect pitch requires both verbal ability (to name the pitch) and musical ability, perhaps it is not surprising to find that, like language, perfect pitch is associated with the left hemisphere.

Despite these data, we cannot assign the perception of speech entirely to the left hemisphere and the perception of music entirely to the right hemisphere. We have seen that the right hemisphere can play a role in speech perception even in people in whom the left hemisphere is dominant for speech. In addition, the perception of emotional tone-of-voice aspects of language, termed **prosody**, is a *right*-hemisphere specialization. Furthermore, although damage to the right hemisphere can impair the perception of music, it does not abolish it. Damage to *both* sides of the brain can completely wipe out musical perception (Samson and Zatorre, 1991). Thus, even though each hemisphere plays a greater role than the other in different kinds of auditory perception, the two hemispheres appear to collaborate in these functions, as well as in many others.

Handedness is associated with cerebral lateralization

Biological anthropologists speculate that the predominance of right-handedness in humans is an ancient trait. People portrayed in ancient cave paintings were generally portrayed clutching objects in their right hands, and Stone Age tools seem to be shaped for the right hand. Skull fractures of animals preyed on by ancient humans are usually on the animal's left side, so anthropologists conclude that most attackers held a club in the right hand. Handedness is a trait we share with our primate relatives: population-level hand preference is observed in gorillas, chimps, and bonobos (they're mostly right-handers) and orangutans (mostly lefties) (Hopkins et al., 2015; P. F. MacNeilage et al., 2009).

In previous ages, a variety of negative characteristics were attributed to left-handed people—from an evil personality to clumsiness to an association with black magic. Indeed, the Latin word for "left-handed"—*sinistra*—provides the root of not only the English term *sinistral*, meaning "left-handed," but also the negative word *sinister*. Various surveys of hand usage, such as the incidence of left-handed writing in American college populations (Spiegler and Yeni-Komshian, 1983), suggest that 10–15% of the population is left-handed. This percentage is viewed as a significant increase over prior generations, perhaps reflecting a relaxation of social pressures toward right-handedness and increased acceptance of left-handedness.

Handedness may have a genetic component, but if so it is not a simple, single-gene effect. Indirect evidence comes from the observation that hair on the back of the scalp forms a clockwise whorl in 93% of right-handers but hair direction is randomly clockwise and anticlockwise among non-right-handers, which has been hypothesized to reflect the operation of an unspecified gene that has a general influence on asymmetries in the body (Klar, 2003). One gene that may contribute to handedness is *LRRTM1* (Francks et al., 2007; Leach et al., 2014), a gene associated with glutamate neurotransmission that is also implicated in schizophrenia. Perhaps the co-occurrence of schizophrenic symptoms in a small minority of left-handers helped give rise to the historical negative view of left-handedness. Additionally, several studies have found that one form of the gene *PCSK6* is associated with right-handedness; *PCSK6* has a role in the development of the left-right axis in mammals, including the asymmetrical placement of internal organs (Brandler and Parrachini, 2013; Corballis, 2014).

The idea that left-handed people are "damaged" humans has been common in the past and has even found occasional support in research, such as observations that the incidence of left-handedness may be greater in clinical populations than in the general population (Silva and Satz, 1979), perhaps as a result of reorganization after injury or developmental problems in the fetal brain. However, studies of achievement, ability, and cognitive function in thousands of school-age children showed that left-handed children do not differ from right-handed children on any measure of cognitive performance (Hardyck et al., 1976). So while a few people may be left-handed because of early damage to the left hemisphere of the brain, this does not explain the handedness of the great majority of left-handers.

prosody   The perception of emotional tone-of-voice aspects of language.

The Wada Test

Given the incidence of aphasia after unilateral brain damage, scientists estimate that 90–95% of humans have a left-hemisphere specialization for language. But how can we be certain which hemisphere is specialized for language (or other functions, such as spatial memory or music perception) in people who haven't had a stroke? For example, it can be crucial to understand an individual's specific lateralization prior to brain surgery.

By injecting a short-acting anesthetic (sodium amytal) into the carotid artery on one side (as shown in Figure A), it is possible to simulate a massive stroke, shutting down the entire hemisphere on that side for a few minutes (Wada and Rasmussen, 1960). This is just long enough to use behavioral measures to document the specializations of that hemisphere. The same can be done for the other hemisphere several minutes later.

This **Wada test** confirms that most people have left-hemisphere specialization for language, regardless of handedness. The reverse pattern (right-hemisphere dominance for language) is very rare, but when it occurs, it is more common in left-handed people (Figure B). Comparable results can be obtained in healthy people by using TMS (Knecht et al., 2002) or fMRI. (Figure B after Epstein et al., 2000.)

Wada test   A test in which a short-lasting anesthetic is delivered into one carotid artery to determine which cerebral hemisphere principally mediates language.

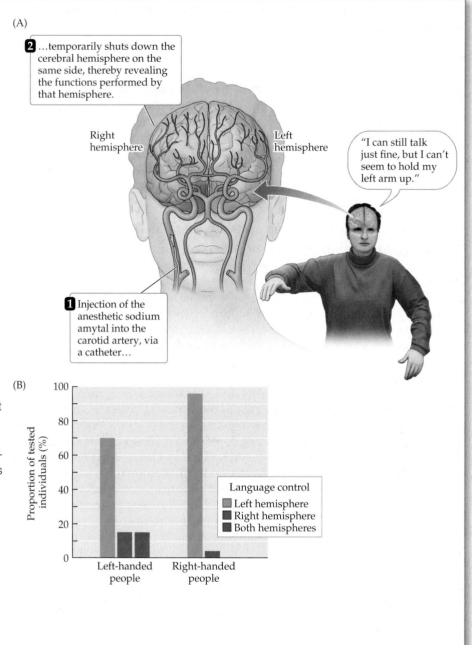

(A)

2 …temporarily shuts down the cerebral hemisphere on the same side, thereby revealing the functions performed by that hemisphere.

Right hemisphere

Left hemisphere

"I can still talk just fine, but I can't seem to hold my left arm up."

1 Injection of the anesthetic sodium amytal into the carotid artery, via a catheter…

(B)

Proportion of tested individuals (%)

Language control
- Left hemisphere
- Right hemisphere
- Both hemispheres

Left-handed people   Right-handed people

Techniques that allow the study of each hemisphere in isolation, such as the Wada test, reveal that as in right-handers, language is vested in the left hemisphere in the great majority of left-handers (**BOX 19.1**). However, in the rare case of right-hemisphere dominance for language, the person is more likely to be left-handed than right-handed. MRI studies show that the asymmetry of the planum temporale is also reduced in left-handed people (Steinmetz et al., 1991), reinforcing the idea that the planum temporale is involved in speech.

There are some rare circumstances in which a change in handedness may occur in adults. Two right-handed people who received double hand transplants after losing their own hands in accidents reportedly both became left-handers after the surgery (Vargas et al., 2009). One possible explanation is that the right hemisphere required less reorganization in order to take control of the contralateral hand, and that reconnection of the left hemisphere to the new right hand was initially hampered by the strong preexisting cortical representation of the former right hand. After getting an early start, perhaps the right hemisphere/left hand simply outcompeted the left hemisphere/right hand. Of course, no one yet knows if this process bears any relationship to the normal establishment of hand preference, but it suggests a surprising degree of flexibility in handedness.

How did hemispheric asymmetry and specialization evolve?

Some scientists believe that hemispheric specialization originated in the differential use of the limbs for many routine tasks. Picture early humans hunting. One hand holds the weapon and provides power; the other is used in more-delicate guidance or body balance. Perhaps powerful throwing, a strongly right-handed behavior in most right-handed people, was a particularly important evolutionary development, providing obvious advantages in hunting and defense. In time, the left-hemisphere neural specializations needed for programming throwing movements may have been co-opted to control language as well (Watson, 2001). However, other vertebrates—including toads (Vallortigara et al., 1999), crows (Hunt et al., 2001), walruses (Levermann et al., 2003), and chimpanzees (Corp and Byrne, 2004)—have been found to show preferences for using one limb or the other for particular behaviors, suggesting that handedness has additional adaptive advantages. (For other examples of the evolution of asymmetry, see **A Step Further: Evolution Favors Asymmetry under Some Conditions** on the website.) Some researchers go significantly further, arguing that hemispheric asymmetry reflects a left-right division of labor that, as a matter of processing efficiency, arose in the first vertebrates, hundreds of millions of years ago (P. F. MacNeilage et al., 2009). Reports that left-hemisphere neurons in mice differ from their right-hemisphere counterparts in both their expression of neurotransmitter receptors and their physiological functioning (Kohl et al., 2011; Shipton, et al., 2014) bolster this view; perhaps cerebral asymmetry is an ancient and ubiquitous adaptation.

Right-Hemisphere Damage Impairs Spatial Cognition

When studied with behavioral or imaging techniques that highlight hemispheric processing differences, people reliably demonstrate a right-hemisphere advantage for the processing of spatial stimuli. Geometric shapes and their relations, direction sense and navigation, face processing, imagined three-dimensional rotation of objects held in the mind's eye—these are a few examples of the kinds of stimuli that the right hemisphere preferentially processes. So it's no surprise that right-hemisphere lesions—especially more-posterior lesions that involve the temporal and parietal lobes—tend to produce a variety of striking impairments of spatial cognition, such as inability to recognize faces, spatial disorientation, failure to identify objects by touch, or the complete neglect of one side of the body that we discussed in Chapter 18 (see Figure 18.19).

The diversity of behavior changes following injury to the parietal lobe is related partly to its large expanse and its critical position, abutting all three of the other major lobes of the brain. The anterior end of the parietal region includes the postcentral gyrus, which is the primary cortical receiving area for somatic sensation. In addition to alterations in touch sensitivity on the opposite side of the body, brain injuries in this area can produce deficits involving much more complex sensory processing. For example, objects placed in the hand opposite the injured somatosensory cortex can be *felt* but cannot be identified by touch and active manipulation. This deficit is called **astereognosis** (from the Greek *a-*, "not"; *stereos*, "solid"; and *gnosis*, "knowledge").

More-extensive injuries in the parietal cortex, beyond the primary somatosensory cortex of the postcentral gyrus, affect interactions between sensory modalities, such as visual or tactile matching tasks, which require the participant to visually identify an object that is touched or to reach for an object that is first perceived visually.

In prosopagnosia, faces are unrecognizable

Suppose one day you look in the mirror and someone unfamiliar is looking back at you. As incredible as this scenario might seem, some individuals suffer this fate after brain damage. It's a rare syndrome called **prosopagnosia** (from the Greek *prosop-*,

astereognosis The inability to recognize objects by touching and feeling them.

prosopagnosia Also called *face blindness*. A condition characterized by the inability to recognize faces. *Acquired prosopagnosia* is caused by damage to the brain, particularly the fusiform gyrus. *Developmental* (or *congenital*) *prosopagnosia* is present from birth.

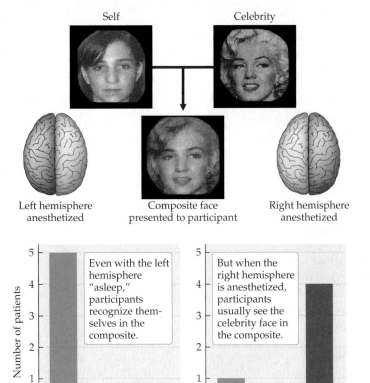

Self Celebrity

Left hemisphere
anesthetized

Composite face
presented to participant

Right hemisphere
anesthetized

Even with the left hemisphere "asleep," participants recognize themselves in the composite.

But when the right hemisphere is anesthetized, participants usually see the celebrity face in the composite.

19.5 USE OF THE RIGHT HEMISPHERE FOR FACIAL RECOGNITION Anesthetizing the left hemisphere in a Wada test (see Box 19.1) does not interfere with a participant's ability to recognize her own face in a picture that is a composite of her face and the face of a celebrity. But when the right hemisphere is anesthetized, the participant interprets the composite face as that of the celebrity. (From Keenan et al., 2001, courtesy of Dr. Julian Keenan.)

"face"; *a-*, "not"; and *gnosis*, "knowledge"), or sometimes *face blindness*. People with prosopagnosia fail to recognize not only their own faces but also the faces of relatives and friends. No amount of remedial training restores their ability to recognize anyone's face. In contrast, the ability to recognize *objects* may be retained, and the person may have no difficulty identifying familiar people by their voices.

Faces simply lack meaning in the person's life. No disorientation or confusion accompanies this condition, nor is there evidence of diminished intellectual abilities. Visual acuity is maintained, although the majority of people have a small visual-field defect—that is, an area of the visual field where they are blind. Most research indicates that the right hemisphere is more important than the left for recognizing faces. For example, shutting down the right hemisphere with anesthetic during the Wada test (see Box 19.1) can cause difficulty in recognizing faces, whereas anesthetizing the left hemisphere has less effect on facial recognition (**FIGURE 19.5**).

Similarly, split-brain individuals do a better job of recognizing faces if those faces are presented exclusively to the right hemisphere (M. S. Gazzaniga and Smylie, 1983). Still, data from split-brain individuals and functional imaging tests make it clear that both hemispheres have *some* capacity for recognizing faces. Thus, although damage restricted to the right hemisphere can impair face processing, the most complete cases of prosopagnosia are caused by *bilateral* damage. The **fusiform gyrus**, a region of cortex on the inferior surface of the brain where the occipital and temporal cortices meet (**FIGURE 19.6**), is crucial, and cases of prosopagnosia following brain damage almost always involve damage here.

Until recently, it was believed that prosopagnosia occurred solely as a result of brain damage (*acquired prosopagnosia*), but we now know that *congenital* (or *developmental*)

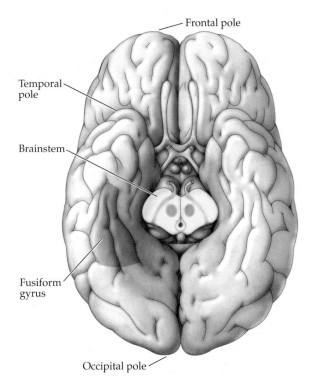

Frontal pole

Temporal pole

Brainstem

Fusiform gyrus

Occipital pole

19.6 THE FUSIFORM GYRUS In this view from below the brain, the cerebellum has been removed to reveal the region of cortex that normally lies opposite to it. The fusiform gyrus, at the juncture of the temporal and occipital lobes, is active during discrimination of objects in a large category, such as faces or birds or cars. Bilateral destruction of this region leads to prosopagnosia, the inability to recognize individual faces.

prosopagnosia—lifelong face blindness without brain damage—is surprisingly widespread. In fact, surveys indicate that about 2.5% of the general population is sufficiently impaired in processing faces to meet the criteria for congenital prosopagnosia (Duchaine et al., 2007; Kennerknecht et al., 2006), confirming the widespread belief that some people are just "bad with faces." This congenital form of prosopagnosia appears to run in families, suggesting a genetic aspect to the disorder (Grüter et al., 2008). Congenital prosopagnosia is associated with diminished activation of the fusiform gyrus and reduced white matter connectivity in the ventral occipitotemporal cortex, in keeping with the anatomical findings in acquired prosopagnosia that we already discussed. (You can learn more, and test yourself for prosopagnosia, at faceblind.org/facetests). At the other end of the spectrum, some people are exceptionally *good* with faces. These "super-recognizers," who are about as good with faces as people with prosopagnosia are bad, are actively recruited by some police forces (Robertson et al., 2016; Russell et al., 2009).

Prosopagnosia may be accompanied by additional forms of **agnosia** (an inability to identify items, in the absence of specific sensory impairments) (Gauthier et al., 1999). For example, people with prosopagnosia may also be unable to distinguish between different makes of cars, or to recognize their own. Bird watchers may lose the ability to distinguish between avian species. Indeed, fMRI studies of healthy participants show that the fusiform region is activated not only when people are identifying faces, but also when identifying birds, or cars (Gauthier et al., 2000). So it seems that the fusiform system may be crucial for identifying individual members of large categories (e.g., faces or birds or cars), especially when the members of the category have many things in common. It remains to be seen exactly how many distinct categories are individually represented in the brain, and the extent to which other brain regions may participate (Haxby, 2006); for example, fMRI evidence suggests that within the large category of animals, there is finer-pitched neural organization according to the type of animal (such as birds versus mammals) (Connolly et al., 2012).

Language Disorders Result from Region-Specific Brain Damage

We have known for millennia that localized brain damage can result in a specific impairment of language abilities, known as **aphasia**. Medical texts of ancient Egypt describe speech problems in people who had received blows to the side of the head (Finger, 1994), and many individual cases of speech loss after strokes, war wounds, and other brain injuries were recorded over the years. Some 25–50% of all people who suffer a stroke will experience aphasia as a primary symptom; that's why speech difficulty is considered to be one of the core warning signs of a stroke (see Figure 2.21), along with weakness or numbness on one side and dizziness, altered vision, or confusion. And in agreement with the evidence of left-hemisphere specialization for language, 90–95% of aphasia cases are the result of damage to the left cerebral hemisphere. Although some individuals will lose almost all capacity for speech, in cases where the left-hemisphere damage is less severe, the individual may instead show pronounced **paraphasia**—insertion of incorrect sounds or words—along with labored, effortful speech production. At times entirely novel nonsense words—called **neologisms**—may be generated via the insertion or substitution of one or more phonemes. Conversation reveals another important aspect of speech: its fluency or ease of production. **Nonfluent speech** is talking with considerable effort, in short sentences, and without the usual melodic character of conversational speech.

Most people with aphasia also have trouble with writing (**agraphia**) and reading (**alexia**). Brain damage that results in aphasia also produces a distinctive motor impairment called **apraxia** (see Chapter 11), characterized by great difficulty in executing precise *sequences* of movements that is not related to weakness, paralysis, a lack of coordination, or any kind of sensory problems. In fact, we'll see shortly that some researchers view aphasia as being primarily the result of problems with motor mechanisms. Curiously, people with aphasia seem to outperform in one domain: they are

fusiform gyrus A region on the inferior surface of the cortex, at the junction of temporal and occipital lobes, that has been associated with recognition of faces.

agnosia The inability to recognize objects, despite being able to describe them in terms of form and color; may occur after localized brain damage.

aphasia An impairment in language understanding and/or production that is caused by brain injury.

paraphasia A symptom of aphasia that is distinguished by the substitution of a word by a sound, an incorrect word, an unintended word, or a neologism (a meaningless word).

neologism An entirely novel word, sometimes produced by a person with aphasia.

nonfluent speech Talking with considerable effort, short sentences, and the absence of the usual melodic character of conversational speech.

agraphia The inability to write.

alexia The inability to read.

apraxia An impairment in the ability to begin and execute skilled voluntary movements, even though there is no muscle paralysis.

19.7 CORTICAL SPEECH AND LANGUAGE AREAS IN HUMANS Lesions in the anterior frontal region called *Broca's area* interfere with speech production; injury to an area of temporoparietal cortex called *Wernicke's area* interferes with language comprehension; injury to the supramarginal gyrus interferes with repetition of heard speech. For most individuals, these language-related systems are found only in the left hemisphere.

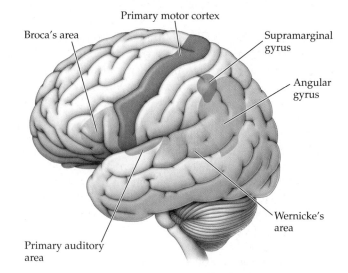

better than unaffected people at detecting when someone is lying (Etcoff et al., 2000). Perhaps this sensitivity to lying results from a focus on facial features of speakers: as we saw earlier, the undamaged right hemisphere is important for face processing.

Linking specific language disorders to damage in specific brain regions provides clues about the organization of the left-hemisphere language network. **FIGURE 19.7** shows some of the most important language-related regions of the left hemisphere of the brain. Damage in these regions tends to produce clusters of symptoms that define several distinct types of aphasia (**TABLE 19.1**). In the following sections, we look in more detail at the three primary aphasias.

Lesions of a left anterior speech zone cause nonfluent (or Broca's) aphasia

In the 1860s French neurologist Paul Broca (1824–1880) examined a man who had lost the ability to utter much more than the single syllable *tan*. Following postmortem analysis, Broca reported that this man, and other people with similar severe impairments of speech production, had suffered damage to a left inferior frontal region that now bears his name—**Broca's area** (**FIGURE 19.8**). Left anterior lesions that include Broca's area produce a type of aphasia known as **nonfluent aphasia**

Broca's area A region of the frontal lobe of the brain that is involved in the production of speech.

nonfluent aphasia Also called *Broca's aphasia*. A language impairment characterized by difficulty with speech production but not with language comprehension; related to damage in Broca's area.

TABLE 19.1 Language Symptomatology in Aphasia

TYPE OF APHASIA	BRAIN AREA AFFECTED	SPONTANEOUS SPEECH	COMPREHENSION	PARAPHASIA	REPETITION	NAMING
Nonfluent (Broca's) aphasia		Nonfluent	Good	Uncommon	Poor	Poor
Fluent (Wernicke's) aphasia		Fluent	Poor	Common	Poor	Poor
Global aphasia		Nonfluent	Poor	Variable	Poor	Poor
Conduction aphasia		Fluent	Good	Common	Poor	Poor
Subcortical aphasia	L R	Variable	Variable	Common	Good	Variable

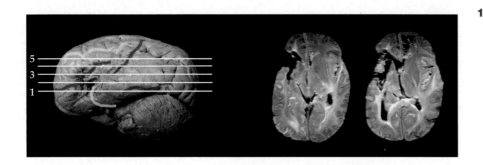

19.8 THE BRAIN OF "TAN" Photo and MRI image of the preserved brain of M. Leborgne, who could only utter the syllable *tan* after his brain injury. Study of this brain and similar cases led Paul Broca to identify a region in the anterior left hemisphere that is specialized for speech. The damage in what is now known as *Broca's area* is clearly evident in the photo (left) and in the horizontal MRI images (right) corresponding to levels 2 and 3 in the photo. (From Dronkers et al., 2007.)

(or *Broca's aphasia*). People with nonfluent aphasia have considerable difficulty producing speech, talking only in a labored and hesitant manner. Reading and writing are also impaired. The ability to utter automatic speech, however, is often preserved. Such speech includes greetings ("Hello"); short, common expressions ("Oh, my God!"); and swear words.

In contrast to their difficulty with speech production, *comprehension* of language is relatively preserved in nonfluent aphasics. Because of the proximity of primary and supplementary motor cortex to Broca's area (see Chapter 11), many people who suffer from nonfluent aphasia also have **hemiplegia**—paralysis of one side of the body (usually the right side, which is controlled by the left hemisphere). Sometimes there is unilateral weakness, termed **hemiparesis**, rather than full paralysis.

The CT scans in **FIGURE 19.9A AND B** map the lesion sites of several people with nonfluent aphasia. Seven years after a stroke, one such individual still spoke slowly, used mainly nouns and very few verbs or function words (a selective loss of action words, called *averbia*, sometimes occurs in nonfluent aphasia), and spoke only with great effort. When asked to repeat the phrase "Go ahead and do it if possible," she could say only, "Go to do it," with a pause after each word. People who suffer brain lesions as extensive as hers show little recovery of speech functions with the passage of time, but people with milder cases can show significant recovery.

Lesions of a left posterior speech zone cause fluent (or Wernicke's) aphasia

Not long after Broca's groundbreaking discovery of the left anterior speech zone, German neurologist Carl Wernicke (pronounced "VER-nih-keh") (1848–1905) described a different form of aphasia resulting from damage to a more posterior aspect of the left hemisphere, centered on a region of the superior temporal cortex that is now known as **Wernicke's area** (see Figure 19.7). Unlike the nonfluent aphasics, people who have this **fluent aphasia** (or *Wernicke's aphasia*) produce plenty of verbal output, but their utterances, although speechlike, tend to contain many paraphasias that make their speech unintelligible. Paraphasias may involve sound substitutions (e.g., "girl" becomes "curl") and/or word substitutions (e.g., *bread* becomes *cake*); neologisms are also common. Some fluent aphasias are marked by particular difficulty in naming persons or objects—an impairment referred to as **anomia**. Paraphasias and speech errors occur in a context that preserves syntactic structure, although sentences seem empty of content. The ability to repeat words and sentences is impaired. For this reason, people with fluent aphasia are believed to have difficulty *understanding* what they read or hear.

In fluent aphasia the most prominent brain lesions are in posterior regions of the left superior temporal gyrus and extend partially into adjacent parietal cortex, including the nearby supramarginal and angular gyri (**FIGURE 19.9C** and see Figure 19.7). When *word deafness* (the inability to understand spoken words) is more evident than reading impairment, damage is more likely in the superior temporal lobe and in tracts from the auditory cortex. In contrast, when *word blindness* (the inability to understand written words) predominates, greater destruction of the **angular gyrus** may be evident. Because the typical lesion spares the motor cortex of the precentral gyrus, people with fluent aphasia (unlike those with nonfluent aphasia) usually do not display hemiplegia.

hemiplegia Partial paralysis involving one side of the body.

hemiparesis Weakness of one side of the body.

Wernicke's area A region of temporoparietal cortex in the brain that is involved in the perception and production of speech.

fluent aphasia Also called *Wernicke's aphasia*. A language impairment characterized by fluent, meaningless speech and little language comprehension; related to damage in Wernicke's area.

anomia The inability to name persons or objects readily.

angular gyrus A brain region in which strokes can lead to word blindness.

19.9 BRAIN LESIONS THAT PRODUCE APHASIA The level of each CT scan slice is labeled according to the brain language region(s) shown by that slice: B, Broca's area; SM, supramarginal gyrus; W, Wernicke's area. (A) CT scans for one person with nonfluent aphasia, age 51, 7 years after a stroke. (B) Overlapping lesion maps for four individuals with nonfluent aphasia, at six levels of the brain. Large lesions (blue) are located in Broca's area on slices B and BW, and the peak amount of tissue damage occurred in the frontoparietal areas on slices SM and SM + 1. (C) Lesion sites for four cases of fluent aphasia. Lesions are located in Wernicke's area on slice W and in the supramarginal gyrus area on slice SM. (D) Lesion sites for five cases of global aphasia. Large lesions are present in every language area. (After Naeser and Hayward, 1978; CT scans courtesy of Dr. Margaret Naeser.)

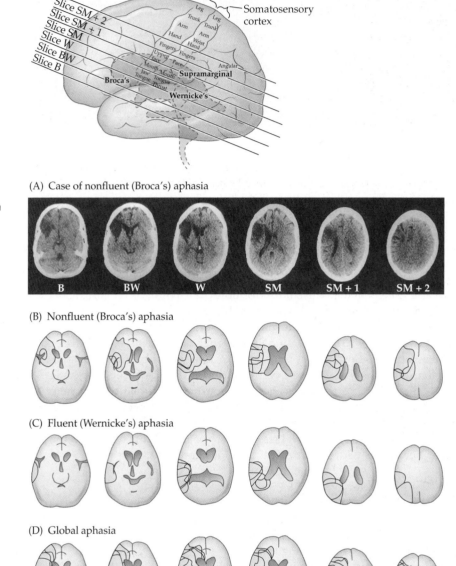

(A) Case of nonfluent (Broca's) aphasia

B   BW   W   SM   SM + 1   SM + 2

(B) Nonfluent (Broca's) aphasia

(C) Fluent (Wernicke's) aphasia

(D) Global aphasia

Slice B   Slice BW   Slice W   Slice SM   Slice SM + 1   Slice SM + 2

SPEECHLESS Tinna Guella Phillips suffered a stroke that robbed her of all language abilities, including her inner monologue.

Widespread left-hemisphere damage can obliterate language capabilities

In some people, brain injury or disease results in near-total loss of the ability to understand or produce language. This syndrome, called **global aphasia**, was the diagnosis in the case of Tinna, the woman whom we met at the beginning of the chapter. People suffering from global aphasia may retain some ability for automatic speechlike sounds, especially emotional exclamations. But they can utter very few words, and no semblance of syntax remains. Global aphasia generally results from very large left-hemisphere lesions that encompass both anterior and posterior language zones. Frontal, temporal, and parietal cortex—including Broca's area, Wernicke's area, and the supramarginal gyrus—are usually affected (**FIGURE 19.9D**). For nearly 2 years after suffering a massive left-hemisphere stroke in her 40s, it was unclear whether Tinna would ever regain the ability to communicate in any of her six languages, and even her inner monologue was banished for several months, taking with it her personal identity. Although Tinna has regained some degree of both outward and inward language, her verbal abilities remain quite impoverished. This is in keeping with the generally poor prognosis for language recovery in global aphasia. And because of the extent of their lesions, people with global aphasia often experience additional debilitating neurological impairments. Tinna and several other people with aphasia are profiled in a documentary entitled *Speechless*, by filmmaker Guillermo F. Florez; a theatrical trailer and information about the film are available at speechlessdoc.com.

global aphasia The total loss of ability to understand language, or to speak, read, or write.

connectionist model of aphasia The theory proposing that Wernicke's area and Broca's area, connected by the arcuate fasciculus, specialize in the receptive and expressive aspects of language respectively.

Competing Models Describe the Left-Hemisphere Language System

Considering how language is intertwined with so many other functions, it is not surprising that a complete description of the brain's language circuitry remains elusive, although steady progress has been made. The traditional **connectionist model of aphasia**—also known as the *Wernicke-Geschwind model* after its chief proponents Carl Wernicke and, later, Norman Geschwind (1926–1984)—views language deficits as resulting from *disconnection* between the brain regions in a language network. Each of these regions is viewed as a module that serves a particular feature of language analysis or production (**FIGURE 19.10A**). According to this view, when a word

19.10 THE TRADITIONAL CONNECTIONIST MODEL OF APHASIA (After Geschwind, 1976.)

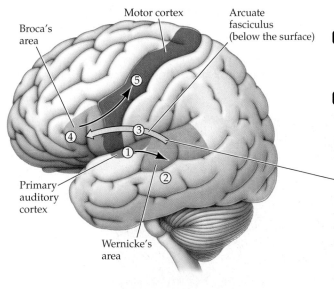

(A) Speaking a *heard* word

1 Information about the sound is analyzed by primary auditory cortex and transmitted to Wernicke's area.

2 Wernicke's area analyzes the sound information to determine the word that was said.

3 Under the connectionist model this information is transmitted via the arcuate fasciculus. (Note, however, that anatomical research casts doubt on this projection.)

Motor cortex

Broca's area

Arcuate fasciculus (below the surface)

Primary auditory cortex

Wernicke's area

4 Broca's area forms a motor plan to repeat the word and sends that information to motor cortex.

5 Motor cortex implements the plan, manipulating the larynx and related structures to say the word.

Lesions of the arcuate fasciculus disrupt the transfer from Wernicke's area to Broca's area, so the person has difficulty repeating spoken words (so-called conduction aphasia), but may retain comprehension of spoken language (because of intact Wernicke's area) and may still be able to speak spontaneously (because of intact Broca's area).

(B) Speaking a *written* word

1 Visual cortex analyzes the image and transmits the information about the image to the angular gyrus.

2 The angular gyrus decodes the image information to recognize the word and associate this visual form with the spoken form in Wernicke's area.

3 Information about the word is transmitted via the arcuate fasciculus to Broca's area.

Angular gyrus

Primary visual cortex

4 Broca's area formulates a motor plan to say the appropriate word and transmits that plan to motor cortex for implementation.

5 Motor cortex implements the plan, manipulating the larynx and related structures to say the word.

A lesion of the angular gyrus disrupts the flow of information from visual cortex, so the person has difficulty saying words he has seen but not words he has heard.

arcuate fasciculus A tract believed by some to connect Wernicke's area to Broca's area.

conduction aphasia An impairment in the repetition of words and sentences.

diffusion tensor imaging (DTI) A modified form of MRI imaging in which the diffusion of water in a confined space is exploited to produce images of axonal fiber tracts.

motor theory of language The theory proposing that the left-hemisphere language zones are motor control systems that are concerned with both the precise production and the perception of the extremely complex movements that go into speech.

or sentence is heard, the auditory cortex transmits information about the sounds to a speech reception mechanism in Wernicke's area, where the sounds are analyzed to decode what they mean. For the word to be spoken, Wernicke's area must transmit this information to the expressive mechanism in Broca's area, where a speech plan is activated. Broca's area then transmits this plan to adjacent motor cortex, which controls muscles of the chest, throat, and mouth that are used for speech production (Geschwind, 1972).

An important component in the connectionist model is a bundle of axons, called the **arcuate fasciculus** (from the Latin *arcuatus*, "bow-shaped," and *fasciculus*, "small bundle"), that is believed to convey information from Wernicke's area to Broca's area. According to the model, people with lesions of the arcuate fasciculus have relatively fluent speech and good comprehension of spoken words because Broca's and Wernicke's areas are intact. But they may display **conduction aphasia**, an impairment in the *repetition* of words and sentences. When these people attempt to repeat words they have heard, they are likely to produce incorrect phonemes substituting for correct sounds.

According to the connectionist model, saying the name of a *seen* object or word involves the transfer of visual information to the angular gyrus, which then arouses the auditory pattern in Wernicke's area. From Wernicke's area the auditory form is transmitted via the arcuate fasciculus to Broca's area. There the template for the spoken form is activated and transmitted to the face area of the motor cortex, and the word is then spoken (**FIGURE 19.10B**). In this model, lesions affecting the angular gyrus would thus disconnect the systems involved in visual and auditory language; individuals with lesions in this region would be expected to have difficulty reading aloud but would retain the ability to speak and understand speech.

Critics of the Wernicke-Geschwind connectionist model argue that it oversimplifies the neural mechanisms of language and prematurely attached functional labels to anatomical findings. For one thing, although anterior- and posterior-lesioned people with aphasia differ greatly with regard to fluency (D. F. Benson, 1967; Goodglass et al., 1964), the expressive versus receptive dichotomy of the Wernicke-Geschwind model doesn't hold up very well. Thus, anterior aphasics seem to have difficulty in comprehension of some aspects of speech in addition to their expression problems, and posterior aphasics make speech production errors despite their fluency (Kimura, 1993). Likewise, more modern fMRI data has confirmed that left hemisphere language zones are not as rigidly modular as was previously believed (Blumstein and Amso, 2013). Furthermore, tract-tracing studies using **diffusion tensor imaging** (**DTI**) (see Chapter 2) have shown that the arcuate fasciculus—long believed to connect Wernicke's area to Broca's area—actually terminates in the precentral gyrus (motor cortex), just short of Broca's area, in most people (**FIGURE 19.11**) (Bernal and Altman, 2010; Brown et al., 2014).

An alternative perspective—the **motor theory of language**—proposes that the left-hemisphere language zones are motor control systems that are concerned with both the precise production and the *perception* of the extremely complex movements that go into speech (Kimura, 1993; Lieberman, 1985). According to this view, the anterior left hemisphere programs the simple phonemic units of speech, and the posterior systems are re-

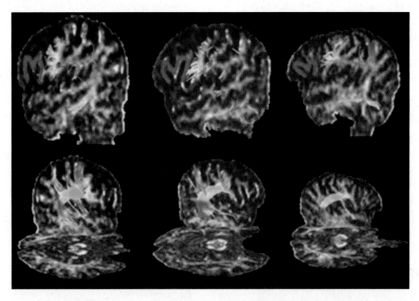

19.11 DTI AND THE CONNECTIONIST MODEL OF LEFT-HEMISPHERE LANGUAGE In these DTI tractography images of three different people, the region containing Broca's area (anatomically known as the *inferior frontal gyrus*) has been outlined in red. The two ends of the left arcuate fasciculus are colored in each upper image, and the entire course of the arcuate fasciculus is shown in each lower figure (in a mix of colors reflecting different fiber orientations). Note that in each case, the tractographic imaging reveals that the arcuate fasciculus terminates in the vicinity of the precentral gyrus, but well short of Broca's area. (From Bernal and Altman, 2010.)

sponsible for stringing speech sounds together into long sequences of movements (Kimura and Watson, 1989). Proponents of the motor theory further suggest that when we *listen* to speech, we are using elements of this same system to perceive the very rapid sequences of facial, throat, tongue, and respiratory movements that the speaker is making. So, in a way, speech sounds are simply an auditory representation of a series of rapid oral-facial movements that we perceive using our own oral-facial movement-making machinery. From an evolutionary perspective, this arrangement is economical because we can use the same evolved neural substrate—probably based on preexisting cortical and basal ganglia systems used for controlling other movements—to both produce and perceive speech sounds (Lieberman, 2002). It is possible that mirror neurons—specialized neurons that are active in both the production and perception of movements (see Chapters 10 and 11)—are an important part of this process, as one of the regions in which mirror neurons are found in the monkey brain corresponds to part of Broca's area in humans (Pulvermüller and Fadiga, 2010). Interestingly, deaf people who use American Sign Language (ASL)—a language based entirely on hand and arm movements—employ the same language-related regions of the left hemisphere while signing as hearing people use for spoken language (Neville et al., 1998; Petitto et al., 2000). Following focal left hemisphere damage, deaf signers also show highly similar language impairments: in most respects, aphasia in signers is the same as aphasia in speakers (Bellugi et al., 1983; Kimura, 1981).

In any event, detailed structural-imaging studies have revealed that the left hemisphere and the rest of the brain contain several speech areas well outside of the classical Broca's and Wernicke's areas (E. Bates et al., 2003; Dronkers et al., 2004), implying greater complexity than was proposed under the Wernicke-Geschwind model; damage that involves some of these areas likely explains the symptoms of conduction aphasia and other aspects of the traditional aphasia model (B. R. Buchsbaum et al., 2011). Further, recent evidence that low-level aspects of speech perception occur bilaterally (Cogan et al., 2014) and that semantic maps of natural speech are distributed across both hemispheres in a highly consistent manner (Huth et al., 2016) show that much remains to be determined about exactly what is, and what is not, the exclusive domain of the left-hemisphere language network. Whatever the details may be, it seems that the answer will involve a complex network of mechanisms that link perception to action.

Brain Mapping Provides Information about the Organization of Language in the Brain

In people with intact language capabilities, researchers can probe the organization of the brain's language circuitry through two general experimental approaches. In some studies, researchers stimulate discrete regions of the cortex and measure associated changes in language function. Conversely, researchers may ask participants to engage in specific verbal behaviors and measure associated changes in brain activity, using functional imaging. Together, these techniques have extended our understanding of the neural bases of language.

Cortical stimulation mapping provides precise identification of language areas

For some people with epilepsy, surgery to remove the source of abnormal electrical activity within the brain can provide lasting relief from seizures. In order to avoid disabling side effects, the neurosurgeon may use electrical stimulation during the surgery to locate—and thus avoid damaging—cortical regions devoted to critical functions like speech, movement, and memory. Once the brain is exposed, small stimulating electrodes are touched to the cortical surface, disrupting the normal functioning of neurons in the immediate vicinity. By observing changes in behavior during stimulation—the person is conscious, under local anesthesia—the surgeon can identify and map the brain regions serving various functions.

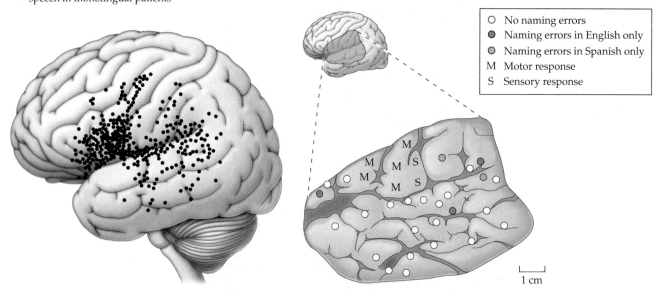

(A) Sites where stimulation interferes with speech in monolingual patients

(B) Sites where stimulation affects speech in a bilingual patient

○ No naming errors
● Naming errors in English only
● Naming errors in Spanish only
M Motor response
S Sensory response

1 cm

19.12 ELECTRICAL STIMULATION OF SOME BRAIN SITES CAN INTERFERE WITH LANGUAGE (A) This summary of data obtained from many monolingual individuals shows the brain sites where stimulation interferes with speech production. (B) This map highlights stimulation sites that affected the speech of a person who was bilingual—fluent in Spanish and English. Within this single region affecting speech, different subregions interfere with either one language or the other, but not both. (Part A after Penfield and Roberts, 1959; B after Ojemann and Whitaker, 1978.)

Pioneering work by Penfield and Roberts (1959) (see Chapter 2) provided an early map of language-related zones of the left hemisphere (**FIGURE 19.12A**). Pooled data from many individuals showed that stimulation anywhere within a large anterior zone often stops speech outright. Other forms of language interference, such as misnaming or impaired repetition of words, were evident from stimulation throughout the anterior and posterior cortical speech zones. Later researchers used more fine-grained electrical stimulation mapping to clarify the regions involved in discrete linguistic processes such as naming, reading, speech production, and verbal memory (Calvin and Ojemann, 1994). An interesting example of data collected with this technique is illustrated in **FIGURE 19.12B**, which shows the various locations in which cortical stimulation evoked naming errors in English versus Spanish, in a bilingual participant. Note that this very fine-grained approach revealed that different subregions appear to serve English versus Spanish language functions. People who are bilingual from an early age show a complete overlap of the English and Spanish language zones at the more gross anatomical level revealed in fMRI measures (Perani and Abutalebi, 2005) and an extended sensitive period for phoneme learning in early development (Petitto et al., 2012). In fact, evidence is mounting that bilingualism from an early age has an impact on brain organization for cognitive networks beyond purely linguistic ones (Costa and Sebastián-Gallés, 2014; Kroll et al., 2014).

Although electrical stimulation mapping provides excellent spatial resolution, it requires that the cortical surface be exposed during major brain surgery. However, it is also possible to stimulate cortical neurons noninvasively in healthy volunteers. As we described in Chapter 2, transcranial magnetic stimulation (TMS) provides a noninvasive method for altering the activity of cortical neurons located directly below a special electromagnet placed over the scalp (see Figure 2.22). By targeting this stimulation with reference to a baseline MRI, it is possible to use TMS as a sort of temporary brain lesion, disrupting the activity of targeted brain regions and noting the resultant changes in behavior. Depending on how it is applied, TMS can disrupt neural function for up to an hour. Alternatively, TMS can be used along with PET or fMRI to precisely localize regions of increased activity.

Studies with TMS mapping generally confirm and extend our understanding of the cortical organization of language functions (Devlin and Watkins, 2007). For example, TMS studies reveal that speech production is associated with activation of not only face areas in motor cortex but also hand areas, confirming the linkage and possible evolutionary relationship of hand gestures and speech (Meister et al., 2003). Speech *perception* apparently activates specific regions that TMS shows to be involved with speech *production* (S. K. Scott and Wise, 2004), supporting the motor theory of language, which we discussed earlier. And, impressively, the TMS temporary-lesion approach has revealed functional *sub*regions within Broca's area (**FIGURE 19.13**). Specifically, a more anterior and ventral division of Broca's area appears to be important for the semantic *meaning* of words, while a more posterior part of Broca's area is important for phonological processing: the patterning of speech *sounds* (Devlin and Watkins, 2007; Gough et al., 2005). A similar experimental approach indicated that the supramarginal gyrus, within the posterior speech zone, is involved in both semantic and phonological aspects of language (Stoeckel et al., 2009); previously, this structure was thought to be involved in phonological processes only. So the TMS procedure is providing new insights into the fine details of cortical organization of function, especially in conjunction with established neuroimaging techniques.

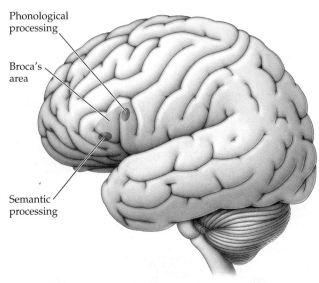

Phonological processing

Broca's area

Semantic processing

19.13 SUBREGIONS OF BROCA'S AREA REVEALED BY TMS TMS stimulation affects semantic processing (meaning) when applied to anterior regions of Broca's area, but similar stimulation of posterior regions of Broca's area affects phonological processing (sound patterns). (After Devlin and Watkins, 2007; Gough et al., 2005.)

Functional neuroimaging tracks activity in the brain's language zones

Different aspects of verbal processing produce noticeably different patterns of brain activation in PET scans (**FIGURE 19.14**). Passive viewing of words activates a posterior area within the left hemisphere (**FIGURE 19.14A**), but passive *hearing* of words shifts the focus of maximum brain activation to the temporal lobes (**FIGURE 19.14B**). Repeating the words orally activates the motor cortex of both sides, the supplementary motor cortex, and a portion of the cerebellum and insular cortex (**FIGURE 19.14C**). During word repetition or reading aloud, activity was relatively absent in Broca's area. But when participants were asked to generate an appropriate verb to go with a supplied noun, language-related regions in the left hemisphere, including Broca's area, were markedly activated (**FIGURE 19.14D**).

Interestingly, the brain regions activated during reading are slightly different in native Italian speakers than in native English speakers (Paulesu et al., 2000). One possible explanation for this is that Italian is perfectly phonetic—the sound associated with each letter and syllable is unvarying—whereas in English a given letter or letter combination may have very different sounds depending on the words it appears in. (For example, it has been noted that *ghoti* can be pronounced "fish" if you use the "gh" sound from *enough*, the "o" sound from *women*, and the "ti" sound from *nation*. Sheesh.) But overall, even languages that sound maximally different still tend to activate much the same brain regions in native speakers.

Silbo Gomero is a very unusual whistled language of the Canary Islands, used by shepherds (known as *silbadores*) to communicate over long distances. In Silbo, whistled notes serve as the phonemes and morphemes of a stripped-down form of Spanish (for an audio example of Silbo, with translation, see **A Step Further: Whistling Up Some Brain Activity** on the website). Functional MRI reveals that silbadores process Silbo using the same left-hemisphere mechanisms that they (and nonsilbadore control participants) use to process spoken language (Carreiras et al., 2005). Nonsilbadore controls, in contrast, process the whistle sounds of Silbo using completely different regions of the brain; for these people, of course, the whistle sounds have no linguistic content. The findings with silbadores illustrate that the brain's language systems are flexible enough to adapt to many types of signals.

(A) Passively viewing words

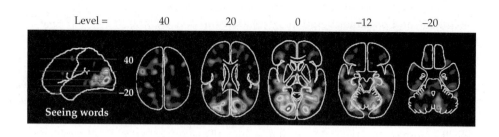

(B) Listening to words

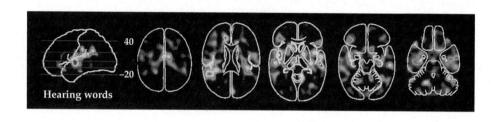

(C) Speaking words

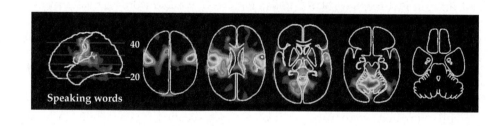

(D) Generating a verb associated with each noun shown

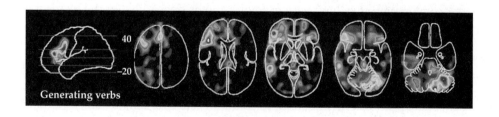

19.14 PET SCANS OF BRAIN ACTIVATION IN PROGRESSIVELY MORE COMPLEX LANGUAGE TASKS (Left) For clarity concerning the tasks, the participant is depicted here at a desk, but when the PET scans were made, the participants reclined with their heads in a PET scanner and viewed a specially mounted display. (Right) These PET scans correspond to the tasks at left; see the text for details of these results. (After Posner and Raichle, 1994; PET scans courtesy of Dr. Marcus Raichle.)

Event-related potentials (ERPs; see Chapters 3 and 18) can distinguish how different aspects of language are processed by the brain, from one millisecond to the next. Participants are asked to read a sentence in which they encounter a word that is grammatically correct but, because of its meaning, doesn't fit—for example, "The man started the car engine and stepped on the *pancake*." About 400 ms after the participant reads the word *pancake*, a negative wave is detected on the scalp (Kutas and Hillyard, 1980). Such "N400" responses (*N* denotes "negative," and the number represents the response time in milliseconds) to word meanings seem to be centered over the temporal lobe (Neville et al., 1992) and therefore may originate from temporoparietal cortex (including Wernicke's area). But *grammatically* inappropriate words elicit a positive potential about 600 ms after they are encountered (a "P600" response), suggesting that detection of this level of error requires an extra 200 ms of brain processing (Osterhout, 1997).

This propensity for humans to use their left cerebral hemisphere for language processing can be seen quite early. Even 3-month-old infants show more metabolic activity in the left hemisphere than in the right when exposed to speech (Dehaene-Lambertz et al., 2002). It seems that we are born with a predisposition to use the left brain for language.

Verbal Behavior: Speech and Reading

No one knows for sure how many languages are in use in the world; most estimates put the figure in the range of 6000–7000 languages, of which about 1000 have been formally studied (Wuethrich, 2000). By applying the tools of evolutionary biology to linguistics, it is possible to track the cultural evolution of language—this suggests a closer relation between languages than previously expected. For example, the seven major language families of Europe and Asia may trace back to a common ancestral language of only about 15,000 years ago (**FIGURE 19.15**) (Pagel et al., 2013). The remarkable profusion of languages since then may have served social roles, such as the identification of in-groups and the confounding of rivals, but now we seem to

19.15 THE EVOLUTION OF LANGUAGES This map shows the approximate distribution of the seven major language families of Europe and Asia; analysis of highly conserved features of these languages suggests that they shared a common ancestral language about 15,000 years ago—the time of the last Ice Age. (From Pagel et al., 2013, image courtesy of Dr. Mark Pagel.)

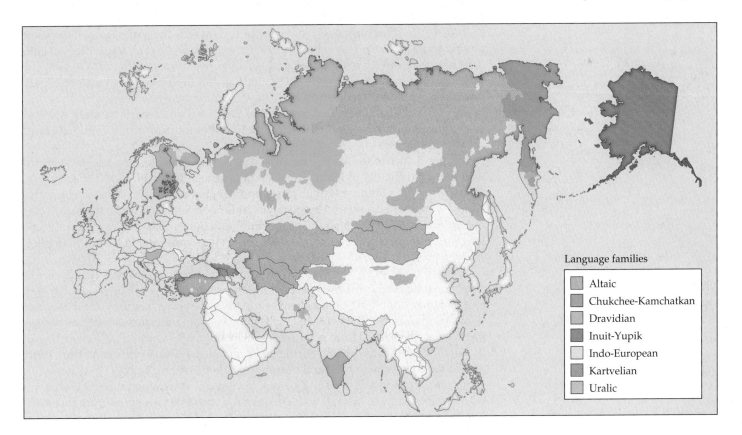

Language families

- Altaic
- Chukchee-Kamchatkan
- Dravidian
- Inuit-Yupik
- Indo-European
- Kartvelian
- Uralic

phoneme A sound that is produced for language.

morpheme The smallest grammatical unit of a language; a word or meaningful part of a word.

semantics The meanings or interpretation of words and sentences in a language.

syntax The grammatical rules for constructing phrases and sentences in a language.

pragmatics In linguistics, the context in which a speech sound is uttered.

sensitive period The period during development in which an organism can be permanently altered by a particular experience or treatment.

be inexorably sliding in the other direction as languages are lost or absorbed and we move toward a few common languages.

All human languages have similar basic elements, and each is composed of a set of sounds and symbols that have distinct meanings. Each language has basic speech sounds, or **phonemes**, that are assembled into simple units of meaning called **morphemes**. Morphemes are assembled into words (the word *unfathomable*, for example, consists of the morphemes *un-*, *fathom*, and *-able*), which have meaning (termed **semantics**), and in turn the words are assembled into meaningful strings (which may be complete sentences or just phrases) according to the language's **syntax** (rules for constructing phrases; one element of grammar). The transmission of information through language is colored and clarified both by the context of the utterance (known as **pragmatics** in linguistics) and by the emotional tone and emphasis (prosody) added by the speaker. But how does each of us end up with the right set of sounds and rules—the ones we need for our native language?

Language Has Both Learned and Unlearned Components

A child's brain is an incredible linguistic machine, rapidly acquiring the phonemes, vocabulary, and grammar of the local language without need of formal instruction. A newborn baby is able to discern all of the sounds of every language, from Icelandic to Inuktitut, and from Japanese to Javanese, and begins life babbling nearly all the known phonemes of all human languages. However, the baby soon starts to pay special attention to the particular speech sounds that she hears in use all around her and begins to use only that subset of phonemes in her preverbal babbling. The baby's developing language abilities are further shaped by "parentese," the singsong speech that parents universally use with their babies (Falk, 2004). The lilting qualities of parentese convey emotion and reward, helping to attach meaning to previously arbitrary speech sounds.

By 7 months of age, infants pay more attention to sentences with unfamiliar structure than to sentences with familiar structure (Marcus et al., 1999), indicating that they have already acquired a basic sense of the rules of the language being spoken around them and are actively looking out for exceptions. In rare, tragic cases of children rescued from long-term profound isolation (we discussed the case of Genie in Box 5.2), little or no language ever develops, pointing to the importance of experience during a **sensitive period** early in life. Similarly, when hearing was restored to an adult who had been deaf most of her life, she did not learn to speak (Curtiss, 1989), presumably because the sensitive period for language acquisition had closed many years earlier.

Further evidence for a sensitive period in language acquisition comes from the well-known difficulty of learning a second language in adulthood. Children seem to learn multiple languages with ease, and functional-imaging studies show that people who learned a second language in childhood tend to activate the same brain regions when using either language in adulthood. But people who learn their second language after about age 11 seem to use a different brain region for each language (K. H. Kim et al., 1997).

Because there is no fossil record to inform us about prehistoric language, the evolutionary antecedents of language are uncertain. One possibility is that speech and language were built on a system originally controlling gestures of the face and hands (Corballis, 2002; Hewes, 1973). Even today, hand movements facilitate speech: if people are prevented from gesturing, they make more slips and have more pauses in their speech (Krauss, 1998). Furthermore, people who have been blind from birth, and so have never seen the hand gestures of others, still make hand gestures while they speak (Iverson and Goldin-Meadow, 1998). And as we noted earlier, deaf people who communicate exclusively with gestures use the same part of the brain that hearing people use while speaking and listening. Deaf children raised without access to an established sign language will often invent one of their own, complete with struc-

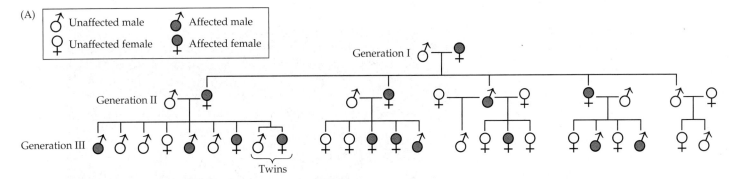

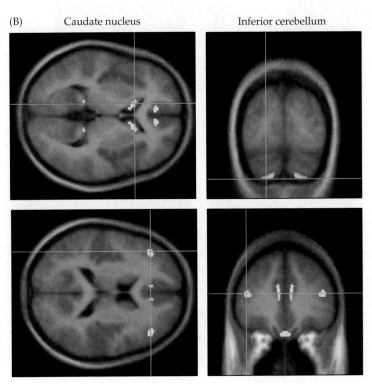

(B) Caudate nucleus   Inferior cerebellum

Inferior frontal gyrus from two perspectives

19.16 A HERITABLE LANGUAGE DISORDER (A) Three generations of the KE family, illustrating the transmission of a language disorder caused by mutation of the gene *FOXP2*. (B) Regions of thinned gray matter in the brains of affected members of the KE family. The blue crosshairs identify affected regions in the frontal cortex, basal ganglia, and cerebellum. (Part B courtesy of Dr. Faraneh Vargha-Khadem.)

tural features that characterize other spoken and sign languages (Goldin-Meadow, 2006). Studies like these provide additional hints of an ancient association between gestures and speech.

Analysis of a British family with a rare heritable language disorder—the KE family—identified a gene that appears to be important for the normal acquisition of language (**FIGURE 19.16**). Children with a specific mutation of the gene *FOXP2*[*] take a long time to learn to speak, and they display long-lasting difficulties with particular language tasks (such as learning verb tenses) (C. S. L. Lai et al., 2001). The pattern of brain activation in these individuals while performing a language task is different from that seen in typical speakers (Liégeois et al., 2003). More minor variations in the *FOXP2* gene are also associated with different patterns of activation in language-related areas of the brain (Pinel et al., 2012). Large-scale genetic screening revealed that *FOXP2* is a regulatory gene, meaning that its protein product is a transcription factor controlling the expression of a number of other genes, perhaps especially affecting the growth and interconnection of neurons during development (Vernes et al., 2011). That its structure and function differ from *FoxP2* in other primates, such as chimpanzees (G. Konopka et al., 2009; Maricic et al., 2013), suggests that this gene

---

* The several different versions of this gene name are no accident. By agreement, scientists use *FOXP2* for humans, *FoxP2* for nonhuman primates, and *Foxp2* for other species. This recognizes the minor variations that exist between the different forms of the gene, and of its product.

BOX 19.2

Williams Syndrome Offers Clues about Language

Williams syndrome, which occurs in approximately one out of 20,000 births (Bower, 2000), offers a fascinating dissociation between what we normally regard as intelligence and language. Individuals with Williams syndrome speak freely and fluently with a large vocabulary, yet they may be unable to draw simple images, arrange colored blocks to match an example, or tie shoelaces. The individuals are very sociable, ready to strike up conversation and smile. They may also display strong musical talent, either singing or playing an instrument.

The syndrome results from the deletion of about 28 genes from one of the two chromosomes numbered 7 (de Luis et al., 2000). No one understands why the remaining copies of these genes, on the other chromosome 7, do not compensate for the lost copies. The absence of one copy of the gene called *elastin* (which encodes a protein important for connective tissue in skin and ligaments) leads to pixie-like facial features. Several of the other missing genes are thought to lead to changes in brain development and to the behavioral features of the syndrome.

The psychological development of such individuals is complicated: As infants, they may display a greater understanding of numerosity than

VERBAL TALENT Ben Monkaba steals the show during the final performance at Williams Syndrome Camp. People with Williams Syndrome exhibit characteristic facial features, due to a problem with the *elastin* gene, along with high verbal fluency and mild mental disability due to deletion of other nearby genes.

other infants, but as adults they may show a poor grasp of numbers. Conversely, their language performance is poor in infancy but greatly improved by adulthood (Paterson et al., 1999). These findings suggest that the developmental process is distinctively altered in Williams syndrome. Impressively, possession of extra copies of the identified genes on chromosome 7—rather than deletions of these genes—produces a syndrome

that is, in many ways, the converse of Williams syndrome: very poor expressive language accompanied by unimpaired spatial abilities (Somerville et al., 2005).

Williams syndrome A disorder characterized by fluent linguistic function but poor performance on standard IQ tests and great difficulty with spatial processing.

has been evolving rapidly in humans, presumably because language is so adaptive in our species. When scientists remodeled the *Foxp2* gene of developing mice to add the human-specific changes present in *FOXP2*, the mice showed changes in connections between the cortex and basal ganglia as well as pronounced improvements in specific forms of learning that would be essential for language acquisition (Schreiweis et al., 2014). It is possible that some of the effects of *FOXP2* are accomplished indirectly via its regulation of other genes; for example, *Foxp2* modulates the expression of a gene called *SRPX2* that is involved in synapse formation in systems implicated in vocal behavior (Sia et al., 2013).

There's a genetic connection in language *production* too. Children born with the genetic disorder Williams syndrome have unusually good verbal abilities, as we discuss in **BOX 19.2**. But genetic abnormalities can also impair speech production, even in otherwise healthy individuals. Most of us have little trouble with *verbal articulation*, the mechanical process of moving the vocal tract to produce speech sounds, but some otherwise ordinary people tend to produce speech sounds only in fits and starts, tripping over certain syllables or unable to start vocalizing certain words. We call this difficulty *stuttering* or *stammering*. Scientists have long suspected that stuttering is at least partly heritable, and by again analyzing transmission within families, researchers have zeroed in on mutations in a set of three specific genes (C.

Kang et al., 2010). These genes—*GNPTAB, GNPTG,* and *NAGPA*—play a part in the normal functioning of lysosomes, organelles involved in the breakdown of cellular waste materials. It remains to be seen why a dysfunction in this basic and ubiquitous system should so specifically affect speech. But recall that, in Chapter 6, we asked how humans and chimpanzees could differ so little in their total genome yet behave so differently. Perhaps differences in a handful of genes—for example, the network of genes governed by *FOXP2* and the lysosomal stuttering genes—are enough to explain why we write books and give speeches, and chimpanzees do not.

Nonhuman primates engage in elaborate vocal behavior

Chirps, barks, meows, songs, and other sounds are among the many vocalizations produced by nonhuman animals, some of which are described in **BOX 19.3**. People have long tried to communicate with animals, sometimes quite successfully: anyone who has watched a sheepdog at work, responding to commands from its handler, has to acknowledge that the human is transmitting lots of information to a highly intelligent companion. Instilling *language* in a nonhuman is a different matter, however. Every day, you utter sentences that you have never said before, yet the meaning is clear to both you and your listener because you both understand the speech sounds and syntax involved. Animals generally are incapable of similar feats, instead requiring extensive training with each specific utterance (e.g., each voice command to the sheepdog) in order for communication to occur at all. In short, most animals appear to lack grammar. For this reason, scientists have focused the search for nonhuman language capabilities mostly on our nearest relatives, the other primate species.

Detailed analyses of the vocalizations of apes and monkeys (Ploog, 1992; Seyfarth and Cheney, 1997) show that a wide range of vocal behavior is employed for communication between individuals, particularly to relay emotional information like alarm or territoriality. The shrieking, purring, peeping, growling, and cackling sounds of squirrel monkeys, for example, can generally be related to specific social situations. Chimpanzees encountering model vipers issue alarm calls specifically to warn members of their group that are unaware of the threat (Crockford et al., 2012), and gibbons deploy a sizable repertoire of hooting calls that they recombine to communicate information about predators, social conditions, and mating opportunities (Clarke et al., 2015). But despite their apparent adaptive importance, most nonhuman primate vocalizations seem to have a somewhat "preprogrammed" quality, being repeatedly produced in much the same fashion and order. This suggests that in most primates, species-specific vocalizations are genetically determined, although close social contact between related individuals can fine-tune minor aspects of calls (Lemasson et al., 2011).

Direct electrical stimulation of subcortical regions in monkeys can elicit some calls (**FIGURE 19.17**), but stimulation of the cerebral cortex generally fails to elicit vocal behavior. Brain regions where stimulation generates vocalizations tend to be structures that are also involved in defense, attack, feeding, and sexual behaviors. These regions include sites in the limbic system and related structures. Just before vocalizing, monkeys display changes in electrical potential in cortical areas homologous to human speech areas (Gemba et al., 1995). Furthermore, monkeys, like people, are more likely to point the right ear (which has preferential connections with the left hemisphere) toward vocalizations from conspecifics (Ghazanfar and Hauser, 1999). Apes tend to favor gesturing with

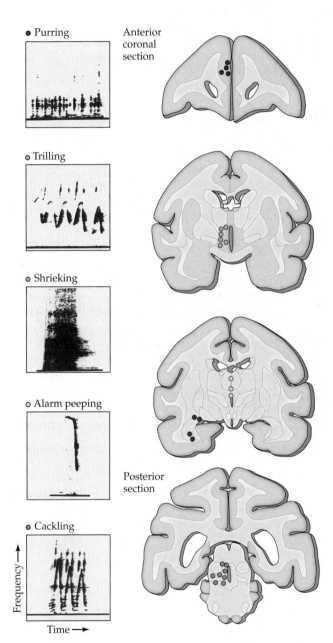

Purring

Trilling

Shrieking

Alarm peeping

Cackling

Frequency →

Time →

Anterior coronal section

Posterior section

19.17 ELICITATION OF VOCALIZATIONS BY ELECTRICAL STIMULATION OF THE MONKEY BRAIN Stimulation at different sites in the monkey brain results in different, species-typical vocalizations. The left column contains spectrograms of different vocalizations; the coronal sections in the right column show brain sites at which the different vocalizations are elicited. (After Ploog, 1992; spectrograms courtesy of Dr. Uwe Jürgens.)

Vocal Behavior in Birds and Other Species

Many nonprimate species engage in vocal behavior, sometimes elaborately, using sound to distinguish between local groups or species, to signal readiness to mate, or to alert kin to danger. Whales sing and may imitate songs that they hear from distant oceans (Noad et al., 2000), and some seal mothers recognize their pups' vocalizations even after 4 years of separation (Insley, 2000). In fact, many species—from elephants to bats to birds to dolphins—are capable of vocal learning and use their vocalizations to help form social bonds and identify individuals (Poole et al., 2005; Tyack, 2003). In the lab, measurement with special instruments reveals that rats and mice produce complex ultrasonic vocalizations that they use to communicate emotional information (Panksepp, 2005). These ultrasonic vocalizations are impaired in mice with mutations in the *Foxp2* gene (Shu et al., 2005), providing an intriguing parallel to the situation in humans. In particular, scientists have studied birdsong, not just because we humans find birdsong so pleasing, but also because these songs offer intriguing analogies to human language (Marler, 1970). Striking similarities exist between birdsong learning and human language development, at the behavioral, neurophysi-

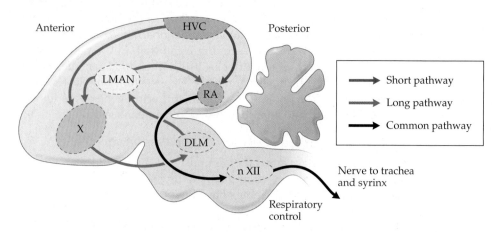

SONG CONTROL NUCLEI OF THE SONGBIRD BRAIN Two neural pathways control birdsong. A direct route from the high vocal center (HVC) to the nucleus robustus of the archistriatum (RA) to the nucleus of the twelfth cranial nerve (n XII) is crucial for song; lesions of any of these areas will disrupt song. (The nucleus labeled "X" is area X of the paraolfactory lobe, and the "DLM" is the medial dorsolateral nucleus of the thalamus.) The indirect path that includes the lateral magnocellular nucleus of the anterior neostriatum (LMAN) may play a role in song learning, although the memory of the tutor's song is probably stored elsewhere. (After A. P. Arnold, 1980.)

ological, and genetic levels—despite an evolutionary separation of more than 300 million years—suggestive of convergent evolution in these systems (Bolhuis et al., 2010; Pfenning et al., 2014).

Many birds produce only simple calls with limited communicative functions, but songbirds like canaries, zebra finches, and song sparrows produce complex vocalizations that are crucial for social behaviors and reproductive success. In most songbirds, only males of the species sing, and the song is *learned*—in much the same way that humans learn language (DeVoogd, 1994). Also like human language, birdsong relies principally on the left hemisphere of the brain (Moorman et al., 2012; Nottebohm, 1980). Birdsong learning has several distinct stages:

the right hand, and because the right hand has preferential connections with the left side of the brain, this observation provides additional behavioral evidence that the left hemisphere plays a special role in communicative behavior, just as in people (Meguerditchian and Vauclair, 2006; Taglialatela et al., 2006).

LANGUAGE TRAINING IN NONHUMAN PRIMATES   Nonhuman primates will never produce human speech, because they lack our vocal tracts and vocal repertoires. But can these animals be taught other forms of language, including the ability to represent objects with symbols and to manipulate those symbols according to rules of order? Can animals other than humans generate a novel string of symbols, such as a new sentence, in a grammatical form? Some researchers argue that language is a uniquely human adaptation that evolved, independently of other cognitive capabilities, in order to solve specific problems in our evolutionary past (Pinker and Jackendoff, 2005).

Chimpanzees, gorillas, and orangutans—the great apes—are our nearest primate relatives. Wild chimpanzees and other apes reportedly use a variety of hand gestures for communication (Hobaiter and Byrne, 2011), and apes are capable of learning hundreds of the hand gestures of American Sign Language (ASL), the standard-

1. Initial exposure to the song of a male tutor, usually the father, whose song becomes a stored model for the young bird's own singing

2. A trial-and-error period, during which the young bird makes successive approximations of the stored model

3. Fixing, or **crystallization**, of the song into a permanent form

Male songbirds raised in isolation fail to develop normal song, but even hearing a recording of species-typical song during the sensitive period allows for normal song development. Males deafened during the second stage of song learning never produce normal song (Konishi, 1985)—the male must first hear himself sing and compare his chirps with the memory of his father's song—but once the song has crystallized, deafening has little effect on singing. Furthermore, developing males prefer to learn the song of their own species and to employ species-typical phrasing (Baptista, 1996; T. J. Gardner et al., 2005), indicating a predisposition to learn the appropriate song.

A series of brain nuclei and their connections (shown in the Figure) control the production of song by the vocal organ, the **syrinx** (A. P. Arnold and Schlinger, 1993). First, a direct pathway from the high vocal center (HVC) to the nucleus robustus of the archistriatum (RA), and then on to the brainstem nucleus of the twelfth cranial nerve, controls the vocal organ. Lesions along this direct pathway at any stage of development will disrupt song. A second, less direct pathway from HVC to the brainstem includes several forebrain nuclei that may be involved in aspects of song acquisition. Early lesions of one of its components, called the *lateral magnocellular nucleus of the anterior neostriatum* (LMAN), will stop song development, but LMAN lesions in adulthood do not affect song performance (Bottjer et al., 1984). Vocal learning is accompanied by the generation in adulthood of new neurons (neurogenesis; see Chapter 7) in a variety of brain regions in songbirds (Walton et al., 2012).

Most female songbirds do not sing but store the songs of their fathers within the nuclei of the song control circuit, for use as models when selecting mates (Terpstra et al., 2006). But the females of some songbird species, such as the plain-tailed wren, take the lead in singing duets with males, in which the pair exchange notes so rapidly that it sounds like a single bird is singing. In these birds, the song control circuit encodes the *combined* song rather than a model of individual song (Fortune et al., 2011).

What about the *Foxp2* gene, which we've already discussed in the context of mouse vocalization and human language acquisition? The level of expression of *Foxp2* in the brains of birds is greater during song learning than before or after (Haesler et al., 2004). When researchers selectively silenced *Foxp2* expression in part of the song-learning pathway, called *area X* (see Figure), adolescent males failed to properly learn and recite the tutor's song, producing errors that resemble those in humans with abnormal *FOXP2* that we described earlier (Haesler et al., 2007). (For more on the complexity of birdsong and its social roles, see **A Step Further: Birdsong Broadcasts Information about the Singer** on the website.)

crystallization The final stage of birdsong formation, in which fully formed adult song is achieved.

syrinx The vocal organ in birds.

ized sign language used by deaf people in most of North America. Given enough training, apes may learn to use ASL signs spontaneously, sometimes in novel sequences (R. A. Gardner and Gardner, 1969, 1984; F. Patterson and Linden, 1981). Other researchers report that chimpanzees can learn to use arbitrary colored tokens or computerized symbols (**FIGURE 19.18**) in ways that seem to reflect an acquired ability to form short "sentences"—novel, meaningful chains made up of basic units of meaning—complete with concepts such as logical classifications, categorization, and negatives (e.g., Premack, 1971; Rumbaugh, 1977).

Critics of language research in apes argue that these sequences may simply be subtle forms of imitation (Terrace, 1979), perhaps unconsciously cued by the experimenter who is providing the training. Native ASL users viewing the signs made by apes have disputed their linguistic content, and Pinker (1994) insists, "Even putting aside vocabulary, phonology, morphology, and syntax, what impresses one the most about chimpanzee signing is that fundamentally, deep down, chimps just don't get it" (p. 349). Oth-

19.18 CHIMPANZEE USING SYMBOLS Although chimpanzees can learn to use arbitrary signs and/or symbols to communicate, it is questionable whether this usage is equivalent to human language. (Photograph courtesy of Dr. Sue Savage-Rumbaugh.)

ers, such as linguist Noam Chomsky, argue that teaching primates to emulate a quintessentially human behavior in which they do not naturally engage can tell us little about the behavior, other than the obvious conclusion that ape evolution did not favor the use of language.

Nevertheless, considering that apes can comprehend spoken words, produce novel combinations of words, and respond appropriately to sentences arranged according to a syntactic rule, it seems likely that the linguistic capacity of apes was underestimated historically (Savage-Rumbaugh, 1993). For example, a bonobo (or pygmy chimpanzee) named Kanzi, the focus of a long-term research program (Savage-Rumbaugh and Lewin, 1994), reportedly learned numerous symbols and ways to assemble them in novel combinations, entirely through observational learning rather than the usual intensive training. And in natural settings, monkeys combine certain vocalizations into higher-order, more complex calls, suggesting the presence of both syntax and semantic meaning, at least on a rudimentary level (K. Arnold and Zuberbühler, 2006; Ouattara et al., 2009). So although the debate is far from settled, the linguistic accomplishments of primates have at least forced investigators to sharpen their criteria of what constitutes language.

Reading Skills Are Difficult to Acquire and Frequently Impaired

Learning to read and write requires far more effort than learning to speak. This difference reflects the evolutionary heritage of our brains, which are more or less the same as those of prehistoric humans. Speaking is an ancient human adaptation, old enough that evolution has equipped our brain with inborn speech mechanisms. But reading and writing are relatively recent developments, just a few thousand years old, and too little time has passed for us to evolve the same sort of intrinsic mechanisms for these behaviors. This is probably why some primitive modern societies lack writing but none lack complex spoken language. Difficulty with reading is called **dyslexia** (from the Greek *dys*, "bad," and *lexis*, "word"), which can result from either developmental or neurological causes, as we'll see.

Brain damage may cause specific impairments in reading

Sometimes people who learned to read just fine as children suddenly become dyslexic in adulthood as a result of disease or injury, usually to the left hemisphere. This *acquired dyslexia* (sometimes called *alexia*) reveals hints about how the brain processes written language. One type of acquired dyslexia, known as **deep dyslexia**, is characterized by errors in which people read a word as another word that is related in meaning; for example, the printed word *cow* is read as *horse*. These individuals are also unable to read aloud words that are abstract, as opposed to concrete, and they make frequent errors in which they seem to fail to see small differences in words. It's as though they grasp words whole, without noting the details of the letters, so they have a hard time reading nonsense words.

In another form of acquired dyslexia, **surface dyslexia**, the person makes different types of errors when reading. These individuals can read nonsense words just fine, indicating that they know the rules of which letters make which sounds. But they find it difficult to recognize words in which the letter-to-sound rules are irregular. *The Tough Coughs as He Ploughs the Dough* by Dr. Seuss (1987), for example, would utterly confound them. In contrast to people with deep dyslexia, those with surface dyslexia have difficulties that are restricted to the details and sounds of letters. Interestingly, surface dyslexia doesn't occur in native speakers of languages that are perfectly phonetic (such as Italian). This finding indicates that what's lost in speakers of nonphonetic languages, like English, is purely a learned aspect of language. In contrast, deep dyslexia probably involves mechanisms that are important for all languages.

Other kinds of brain damage can impair reading. For example, individuals with hemispatial neglect following right parietal lobe damage (discussed in Chapter 18)

dyslexia A reading disorder attributed to brain impairment. *Acquired dyslexia* occurs as a result of injury or disease. *Developmental dyslexia* is associated with brain abnormalities present from birth.

deep dyslexia Acquired dyslexia in which the person reads a word as another word that is semantically related.

surface dyslexia Acquired dyslexia in which the person seems to attend only to the fine details of reading.

disregard the left half of the world, despite having otherwise normal vision. Such people also fail to notice the left halves of the words that they see, necessarily resulting in poor reading. One striking feature in some severe cases of acquired dyslexia is *letter-by-letter reading*, in which the person laboriously spells out each word to herself (aloud or silently). In these cases, it seems that conscious attention to the spelling of each word is the only way by which words can be identified, so reading speed is dramatically slower.

Some people struggle to read throughout their lives

Some children seem to take forever to learn to read. Their efforts are laden with frustration, and prolonged practice produces only small improvements. This *developmental dyslexia* is seen in nearly 5% of children in the general population; it is even more common in boys and in left-handed people. Children with dyslexia can have high IQs (B. Morris, 2002), and several have grown up to amass billion-dollar fortunes. Thus it appears that dyslexia is a specific problem with written language, specifically connecting reading with the more-ancient brain systems for speech, and not a general cognitive deficit.

A postmortem study of the brains of people with significant dyslexia revealed striking anomalies in the arrangement of cortical neurons, especially in frontal and temporal regions (Galaburda, 1994). These anomalies included unusual groupings of cells in outer layers of the cerebral cortex and distortions of the layers and columns in which cortex is normally organized (**FIGURE 19.19**). Many neurons were disoriented, and excessive cortical folding (**micropolygyria**) was observed. Nests of extra cells—**ectopias**—were seen. People showing MRI evidence of these abnormalities tend to have reading disorders (Chang et al., 2005). It is likely that these neural

micropolygyria A condition of the brain in which small regions are characterized by more gyri than usual.

ectopia Something out of place—for example, clusters of neurons seen in unusual positions in the cortex of someone suffering from dyslexia.

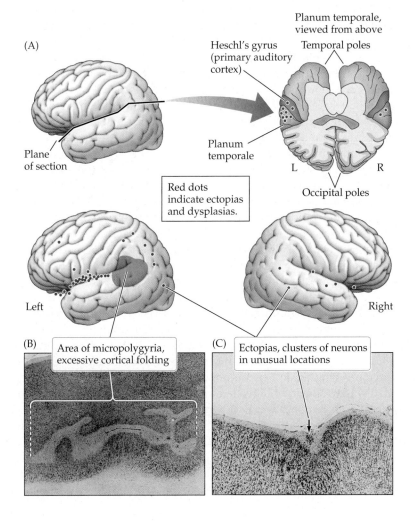

19.19 NEURAL DISORGANIZATION IN DYSLEXIA (A) (Top) Drawings of the left and right planum temporale (see Figure 19.4) from the brain of a person with dyslexia show these regions as nearly symmetrical; in most people the left planum temporale is considerably larger. The dots and the shaded area represent regions where microscopic anomalies called *ectopias*, *dysplasias*, and *micropolygyria* have been found in the brains of individuals with dyslexia. (Bottom) Anomalies in individuals with dyslexia are much more common in the left hemisphere, which is primarily responsible for language function. (B, C) These micrographs show (B) micropolygyria (literally "many tiny gyri") and (C) ectopias, clusters of neurons in unusual locations, such as this cluster in cortical layer I (arrow), which is normally devoid of neuronal cell bodies. (After Galaburda, 1994; micrographs courtesy of Dr. Albert Galaburda.)

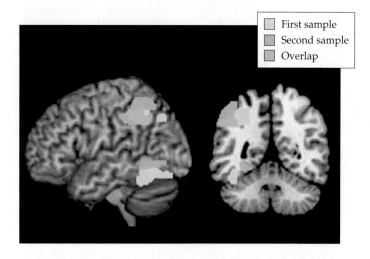

19.20 TROUBLE WITH PHONEMES In this experiment, researchers asked two different samples of children (about 10 years old) to complete a phonological reading task in which the rhyming of words is judged, thereby requiring accurate processing of phonemes. Compared with typical readers, children with dyslexia showed decreased activity in two left-hemisphere sites, as revealed in these composite fMRI images—the left inferior parietotemporal region and the left inferior fusiform region. This pattern appears to be independent of the IQs of the children. (After H. Tanaka et al., 2011, courtesy of Dr. Fumiko Hoeft.)

First sample
Second sample
Overlap

problems arise in fetal development, during a period in which cells are actively migrating into the cerebral cortex; defective neuronal migration has been implicated in unusual patterns of connectivity in language-related regions of the temporal cortex (Galaburda et al., 2006).

Functional-imaging studies further indicate differences in brain activity in dyslexia. Compared with control participants, people with dyslexia show diminished activation of left posterior speech zones that include the superior temporal lobe and angular gyrus (K. R. Pugh et al., 2000; Shaywitz et al., 1998, 2003), as well as the occipital lobe (Demb et al., 1998), along with relative overactivation of anterior regions of the brain. For tasks that especially focus on the phonological (phoneme-processing) aspects of dyslexia, abnormal patterns of activation are also seen in the nearby temporoparietal region and in the inferior fusiform area of the left temporal lobe (**FIGURE 19.20**) (Hoeft et al., 2006; H. Tanaka et al., 2011). In addition to differences in temporal *cortex*, brain imaging has revealed subtle changes in the fine structure of the temporoparietal white matter pathways in adult dyslexics (Klingberg et al., 2000). These results indicate possible problems with the axonal connections between language-related cortical areas. Researchers also find a consistent relationship between developmental dyslexia and cerebellar dysfunction (Stoodley and Stein, 2011). It is not yet clear exactly what role the cerebellum plays in reading, because cerebellar lesions later in life do not result in acquired dyslexia.

Taken together, imaging and behavioral studies indicate that our brains rely on two different language systems during reading: one focused on the sounds (*phonology*) of letters, the other on the meanings (*semantics*) of whole words (McCarthy and Warrington, 1990). Using fMRI, researchers have found that people with dyslexia often have a disconnection between these systems, impairing the coordination of sounds with their meanings (Boets et al., 2013). Presumably, these systems are shaped by training: as with learning any highly skilled behavior, our brains appear to mold themselves to accommodate our acquired expertise with written language. The observation that remedial training in people with dyslexia induces changes in the left-hemisphere systems that are used for reading (Temple et al., 2003) is consistent with this view. And intriguingly, there appears to be a cultural component to dyslexia: the specific brain regions involved may vary depending on the graphical form of the written language being learned. Most research implicates the left *temporoparietal* cortex as being centrally important in dyslexia, but in readers of Chinese—a language based on logographic symbols rather than an alphabet—dyslexia is especially associated with dysfunction of the left medial *frontal* cortex (Siok et al., 2004).

Developmental dyslexia appears to have a genetic component. By studying inheritance patterns in families, followed up with investigations in animals, researchers have identified several genes—*ROBO1*, *DYXC1*, *DCDC2*, and *KIAA0319*, for example—that are linked to reading disorders (Gabel et al., 2010; Hannula-Jouppi et al., 2005). *ROBO1* is known to be involved in guiding growing axons to their destinations. The precise function of *DYXC1* is not yet known, but it is estimated to be abnormal in 9% of individuals suffering from dyslexia in the general population (T. C. Bates et al., 2010; Taipale et al., 2003). Variation in the gene *DCDC2*, which is believed to participate in the migration of neurons into their positions in the cortex, predicted reading performance in a large analysis of families, indicating that the gene may be involved in normal reading ability and that mutations in the gene are a genetic risk factor for dyslexia (Lind et al., 2010). Finally, the gene *KIAA0319*, linked to processes of brain development, is also reported to be associated with developmental dyslexia (Cope et al., 2005; Harold et al., 2006). In rats, inhibition of *KIAA0319* causes cortical ectopias like those seen in humans with dyslexia, strongly supporting the idea that an early problem with neuronal migration can cause dyslexia (Peschansky et al., 2010).

Although more work will be needed before we really understand the genetic bases of the disorder, these discoveries raise the prospect of early identification of dyslexia via genetic screening. Such detection would allow for earlier, and more effective, intervention strategies, which could be critically important if some aspect of the visual or phonological problems experienced by people with dyslexia are actually a consequence of a lifetime of reduced experience with reading (Goswami, 2015). Furthermore, research is revealing additional, unexpected dimensions in dyslexia. For example, people with dyslexia are much worse than nondyslexic people when it comes to identifying the voices of speakers of their own language, but no worse than nondyslexic controls at identifying the voices of people speaking *other* languages (Perrachione et al., 2011). This result indicates that the phonological difficulties that dyslexics have in reading also affect their auditory speech perception. But there are also positive findings: evidence is accumulating that people with dyslexia actually outperform unaffected individuals in certain learning domains, such as aspects of spatial learning (Schneps et al., 2012). Findings like these may have important implications for developing new educational strategies in dyslexia.

Recovery of Function

Compared with the other organs of the body, it is all too easy to seriously damage the brain. This vulnerability is a consequence of the brain's extreme complexity coupled with its high metabolic demands, delicate structure, exposed location, and limited ability to regrow. In the United States alone, according to the 2012 National Health Interview Survey (Blackwell et al., 2014), almost 7 million adults are survivors of stroke, and many more are living with the consequences of other disease processes, such as tumors and brain trauma. In addition to diseases, motor vehicle accidents, horseback riding, diving, and contact sports such as football and boxing are major causes of injuries to the brain and spinal cord. So it's no surprise that discovering the mechanisms mediating **recovery of function** after brain damage, and developing new treatments to exploit those mechanisms, are topics of intense research activity.

Stabilization and Reorganization Are Crucial for Recovery of Function

In the months following a brain injury, people often show conspicuous improvements in behavior, as the injury site stabilizes, unaffected tissue reorganizes, and compensation occurs. For example, many people who become aphasic following brain injury will eventually regain some of the lost language abilities; language recovery following stroke in adults can be impressive and may continue for longer than 2 years after the initial brain injury, although the majority of recovery occurs during the first 3 months (**FIGURE 19.21**) (Kertesz et al., 1979). The relative extent of recovery from aphasia can be predicted from several factors. For example, recovery is better when brain damage is the result of trauma, such as a blow to the head, rather than a stroke. Individuals with more-severe language loss recover less. Left-handed people show better recovery than those who are right-handed. For some people, language recovery may depend on specific forms of speech therapy. Therapeutic ap-

recovery of function The recovery of behavioral capacity following brain damage from stroke or injury.

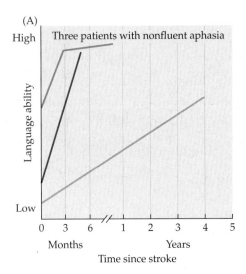

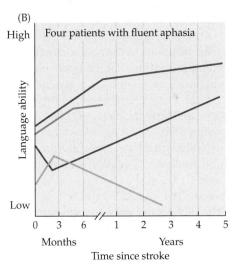

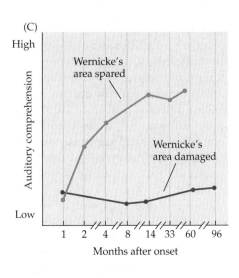

19.21 COURSES OF RECOVERY OF PEOPLE WITH APHASIA (A, B) The course of recovery from nonfluent (Broca's) aphasia (A) differs from the course of recovery from fluent (Wernicke's) aphasia (B). These graphs depict the aphasia quotient, a score derived from a clinical test battery. Higher scores indicate better language performance. (C) Here the course of recovery of the auditory comprehension of speech after a stroke in which Wernicke's area was damaged is compared with the course of recovery after a stroke in which Wernicke's area was spared. (Parts A and B after Kertesz et al., 1979; C after Naeser et al., 1990.)

proaches using alternate communication channels, such as singing, can be helpful in some cases (Racette et al., 2006).

Recovery can be downright amazing in children, thanks to their greater neural plasticity: A child may show extensive language recovery even after complete loss of the left hemisphere (**BOX 19.4**). These observations show that undamaged brain regions *can* take over functions of damaged regions, if impairment occurs early enough in life. But as we grow older, the brain slowly loses some of its ability to compensate for injury. Reversing this age-related decline in neuroplasticity is an important focus of research.

The brain regrows and reorganizes anatomically after being injured

We now know that the nervous system has much more potential for plasticity and recovery than was previously believed. For example, damaged neurons can regrow their connections under some circumstances, through a process called *collateral sprouting* (for more information on collateral sprouting, see **A Step Further: Some Nerve Fibers Can Be Regrown** on the website). And as we've discussed in several places in this book, it has become evident that the adult brain is capable of producing new neurons; perhaps we will learn how to bend these new neurons to our will and use them to replace damaged brain tissue.

One of the most exciting prospects for brain repair following stroke, injury, or many other neurological conditions is the use of **embryonic stem cells** (Casarosa et al., 2014). Derived from embryos, these cells have not yet differentiated into specific roles and therefore seem to be able to develop, under the control of local chemical cues, into the type of cell needed (see Chapter 7). We already know from the research on adult neurogenesis that new neurons can become integrated into functional brain circuits. Stem cells placed in the brain can be helped to survive and mature, and may migrate to the site of injury to take on their new roles (Emborg et al., 2013; Lindvall and Kokaia, 2006).

Although not all studies report encouraging results (Freed et al., 2001), in several studies implants of embryonic stem cells have been shown to reduce symptoms of Parkinson's disease (see Chapter 11) and stroke (Kondziolka et al., 2000). However, controversy surrounds the ethics of utilizing human embryos as cell donors, provid-

embryonic stem cell A cell, derived from an embryo, that has the capacity to form any type of tissue that a donor might produce.

BOX
19.4

The Amazing Resilience of a Child's Brain

Complications in pregnancy and fetal development occasionally result in children who are born with a terrible kind of epilepsy that can't be controlled by medication. These children may suffer paralysis on one side of the body, along with almost continual seizures. Sometimes, in these extreme cases, the only way to save the life of the child is to remove an entire brain hemisphere, as shown in this scan of a girl whose left hemisphere was completely removed when she was 7 years old.

Hemispherectomy surgery (see figure) removes the malfunctioning brain tissue and saves the life of the child, but it also produces severe symptoms of its own, such as complete paralysis of one side, speech loss, or visual impairments. However, provided the surgery occurs early enough, the child may show almost complete recovery of function over a long period

of time. The girl whose brain scan is shown in the figure experienced paralysis and complete speech loss after her surgery, but at follow-up a few years later, she had recovered language function and her paralysis had resolved almost completely.

Other people who have had childhood hemispherectomy have gone on to develop above-average IQs in adulthood, along with superior language and cognitive abilities (A. Smith and Sugar, 1975). So, although extensive hemispheric damage in an adult usually results in drastic and largely permanent functional and intellectual impairments, cases of childhood hemispherectomy vividly illustrate the amazing plasticity of the young brain.

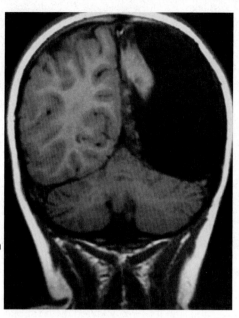

HEMISPHERECTOMY The brain can compensate even for the loss of a whole hemisphere, provided that this radical surgery is performed early enough in the individual's development. (From Borgstein and Grootendorst, 2002.)

ing impetus to find ways of creating stem cells from other sources. There are also difficulties associated with inducing implanted stem cells to form large functional populations of neurons at injury sites without triggering an immune reaction leading to tissue rejection (J. Y. Li, Christopherson, et al., 2008). Nevertheless, these issues are potentially surmountable, and stem cell grafts offer a very promising direction for future treatments. But despite some encouraging developments in the lab, prevention of brain injury is clearly better than treatment. (Additional discussion of mechanisms of brain damage, and the mitigation of brain injuries, is available on the website in **A Step Further: Different Strategies Aim to Reduce Brain Damage following Injury or Stroke**.)

Rehabilitation and retraining can help recovery from brain and spinal cord injury

Cognitive and/or perceptual handicaps that develop from brain impairments can be modified by training; similarly, intensive training may restore some measure of walking ability after certain spinal cord injuries (Barbeau et al., 1998). But it is important to distinguish restoration of function from compensation. It is well known that practice can significantly reduce the impact of brain injury by fostering compensatory behavior. For example, vigorous eye movements can make up for the *scotomas* (blind spots in the visual field) that result from strokes or other injuries that affect the visual cortex. Behavior strategies can be changed after a brain injury to enable successful performance on a variety of tasks.

As with recovery of language functions, a growing body of evidence shows that people can regain considerable use of limbs that have been paralyzed following brain injury, especially if they are *forced* to use the limb repeatedly. **Constraint-induced movement therapy** (**CIMT**) persuades people who have had a stroke to use the affected arm by simply tying the "good" arm to a splint for up to 90% of waking hours (Taub et al., 2002), in conjunction with daily rehabilitation therapy that includes practice moving the affected limb repeatedly (**FIGURE 19.22**). Many

constraint-induced movement therapy (CIMT) A therapy for recovery of limb movement after stroke or injury, in which the unaffected limb is constrained while the person is required to perform tasks with the affected contralateral limb.

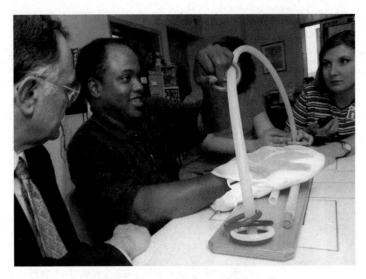

19.22 CONSTRAINT-INDUCED MOVEMENT THERAPY In this therapy, an unaffected limb is gently restrained (in this case in a white mitten) so that the person must use the limb that was affected by the stroke in a series of repetitive tasks. (Photograph courtesy of Dr. Edward Taub.)

individuals who received this treatment reportedly regained up to 75% of normal use of the paralyzed arm after only 2 weeks of therapy. Although the underlying mechanisms are not well understood—perhaps involving a remapping of the motor cortex—it's clear that CIMT offers substantial benefits that persist over the long term (Kwakkel et al., 2015; Liepert et al., 2000). Furthermore, combining physical retraining with a drug treatment that induces neural sprouting provides almost complete restoration of function in lab animals with experimental strokes (Wahl et al., 2014).

Another surprising use of experience for rehabilitation involves a simple mirror. Altschuler et al. (1999) treated people whose strokes had reduced their use of one arm by placing them before a mirror with only their "good" arm visible. To these people, it looked as though they were seeing the entire body, but now both arms were the good arm. The person was told to make symmetrical fluid motions with both arms. In the mirror, the motions looked perfectly symmetrical (of course), but surprisingly, most of the treated people soon learned to use the "weak" arm more extensively. It was as though the visible feedback, indicating that the weak arm was moving perfectly, overcame the brain's reluctance to use that arm. It is likely that the mirror neurons of the brain, discussed earlier and in Chapters 10 and 11, mediate some of the beneficial effects of this sort of rehearsal (Buccino et al., 2006).

Brain damage will remain a serious problem for the foreseeable future, one that will touch most of us as our friends and relations go through their lives. Perhaps the most important message to convey to victims of stroke and other nervous system damage is the encouragement that, with effort and perseverance, there is a very real prospect of recovering much of the lost behavioral capacity.

■ The Cutting Edge

Contact Sports Can Be Costly

Jarring blows to the head are common in a number of sports—football, hockey, and wrestling, for example—sometimes resulting in a **concussion** or *mild traumatic brain injury* (mTBI), with a range of possible symptoms including headache, altered mood, confusion, memory loss, or brief loss of consciousness. Even one concussion, and certainly repeated concussions, places the athlete at risk of permanent brain injury. Although uncomplicated concussions generally clear up with time, up to 25% of concussion cases may experience persistent cognitive symptoms (Ponsford, 2005), some of which may not become evident until later in an athlete's life (Montenigro et al., 2016; A. E. Thornton et al., 2008). In the United States alone, traumatic brain injuries result in more than 2.2 million hospital visits per year (CDC, 2015); many more go unreported.

Nowhere is the risk of brain injury more evident than in boxing, where the whole goal of the contest is to rain blows upon the head of the opponent. For too many boxers, the result of so many blows to the head is a debilitated state that was historically called *dementia pugilistica* (the Latin *pugil* means "boxer") or being *punch-drunk* (Erlanger et al., 1999) but nowadays is known as **chronic traumatic encephalopathy (CTE)**. Former athletes suffering from CTE have markedly impaired cognitive abilities, and striking abnormalities in the brain are common.

In one of the earliest studies, Casson et al. (1982) studied ten active professional boxers who had been knocked out. The group included boxers of championship caliber, as well as mediocre and poor boxers. At least five of the group had definitely abnormal CT scans, showing such conditions as generalized cortical atrophy, which in some cases included ventricular dilation. Only one boxer had a clearly normal brain picture. Sadly, the most successful boxers may have the most profound cortical atrophy: successful boxers have had the greatest number of high-caliber fights, and thus may have sustained the most punishment,

concussion Also called *minor traumatic brain injury (mTBI)*. An injury resulting from a blow to the head and associated with temporary neurological symptoms such as memory loss or other cognitive impairments, pain, and visual disturbances.

chronic traumatic encephalopathy (CTE) Also called *dementia pugilistica* or *punch-drunk*. The dementia that develops in boxers or other athletes who are subjected to repeat blows to the head.

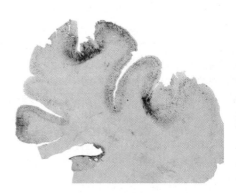
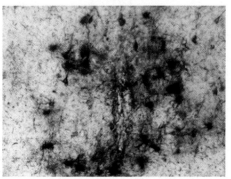

19.23 TAU PROTEIN IN THE BRAIN OF A BOXER SUFFERING FROM CTE (Left) Unmagnified section of cortex. (Right) Cortical gray matter magnified 350×. (Courtesy of Dr. Ann McKee.)

because they have participated in more matches. A large-scale CT study of 338 active boxers showed that scans were abnormal in 7% (showing brain atrophy) and borderline in 12% (B. D. Jordan et al., 1992).

Researchers have not yet agreed on a definitive diagnostic marker for CTE in living people—typically, it can be diagnosed only in postmortem analysis (McKee et al., 2016)—but one possible approach uses a special type of PET scan to detect abnormal expression of the cytostructural protein **Tau** in the brain (Barrio et al., 2015) (see Figure 7.28). Neuropathological evidence indicates that, like Alzheimer's disease, CTE in athletes is a type of *tauopathy*, in which excess Tau protein within neurons interferes with their functioning (McKee et al., 2009). **FIGURE 19.23** shows the brain of a former boxer who, by his mid-30s, was experiencing CTE-related symptoms including memory loss, confusion, and a tendency to fall. As in other cases of CTE, an excessive amount of Tau (brown in the photos) is evident in the brain, and it is found forming tangles within many neurons. At present, no effective treatments exist for CTE, although promising research is exploring novel ways of delivering anti-inflammatory medications and reducing abnormal tau expression (Kondo et al., 2015; Roth et al., 2014). So, while CTE may occur in other sports, including American football, only in boxing is significant head trauma an explicit goal—no small reason why many believe that boxing is a sport whose time has passed.

Tau A protein associated with neurofibrillary tangles in Alzheimer's disease.

Recommended Reading

Bradbury, J. W., and Vehrencamp, S. L. (2011). *Principles of Animal Communication* (2nd ed.). Sunderland, MA: Sinauer.

Ellard, C. (2009). *You Are Here: Why We Can Find Our Way to the Moon, but Get Lost in the Mall.* New York: Doubleday.

Fitch, W. T. (2010). *The Evolution of Language.* Cambridge, England: Cambridge University Press.

Gazzaniga, M. S. (2016). *Tales from Both Sides of the Brain: A Life in Neuroscience.* New York: Ecco.

Harrison, D. W. (2015). *Brain Asymmetry and Neural System: Foundations in Clinical Neuroscience and Neuropsychology.* New York: Springer.

Kolb, B., and Whishaw, I. Q. (2015). *Fundamentals of Human Neuropsychology* (7th ed.). New York: Worth.

Maynard-Smith, J., and Harper, D. (2004). *Animal Signals.* Oxford, England: Oxford University Press.

McManus, I. C. (2003). *Right Hand, Left Hand: The Origins of Asymmetry in Brains, Bodies, Atoms, and Cultures.* Cambridge, MA: Harvard University Press.

Meyer, J. (2015). *Whistled Languages: A Worldwide Enquiry on Human Whistled Speech.* New York: Springer.

Patel, A. (2007). *Music, Language, and the Brain.* Oxford, England: Oxford University Press.

Purves, D., Cabeza, R., Huettel, S. A., LaBar, K. S., et al. (2012). *Principles of Cognitive Neuroscience* (2nd ed.). Sunderland, MA: Sinauer.

Tomasello, M. (2010). *Origins of Human Communication.* Cambridge, MA: Bradford Press / MIT Press.

Zeigler, H. P., and Marler, P. (2008). *Neuroscience of Birdsong.* Cambridge, England: Cambridge University Press.

Go to **bn8e.com** for study questions, quizzes, activities, and other resources

19
VISUAL SUMMARY
You should be able to relate each summary to the adjacent illustration, including structures and processes.
Go to **bn8e.com/vs19** for links to figures, animations, and activities that will help you consolidate the material.

1 **Split-brain individuals** show striking examples of hemispheric specialization (**lateralization**). Most words projected only to the right hemisphere, for example, cannot be read, but the same stimuli directed to the left hemisphere can be read. Spatial tasks, however, are performed better by the right hemisphere than by the left. Because of asymmetrical organization of the brain, humans typically show an advantage for verbal stimuli presented to the right ear or right visual field. Review **Figures 19.1–19.3**

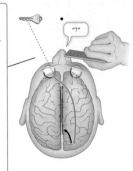

2 Anatomical asymmetry of the hemispheres is seen in some structures in the human brain. Especially striking is the large size difference in the **planum temporale** (which is larger in the left hemisphere than in the right hemisphere of most right-handed individuals). Nevertheless, in most cases mental activity depends on interactions between the cerebral hemispheres. Review **Figure 19.4**

3 In most patients, parietal cortical injuries produce perceptual changes, including alterations in sensory and spatial processing. Damage to the **fusiform gyrus** can produce acquired **prosopagnosia**, a dramatic inability to recognize the faces of familiar people. A congenital form of prosopagnosia affects about 2.5% of the population. Review **Figures 19.5 and 19.6**

4 Left inferior frontal lesions produce an impairment in speech production called **nonfluent** (or **Broca's**) **aphasia**. More-posterior lesions, involving the temporoparietal cortex, cause **fluent** (or **Wernicke's**) **aphasia**. Extensive destruction of the left hemisphere causes a more complete loss of language called **global aphasia**. Review **Figures 19.7–19.9**, **Table 19.1**, **Activity 19.1**

Broca's area — Primary motor cortex — Supramarginal gyrus — Angular gyrus — Wernicke's area — Primary auditory area

5 The Wernicke-Geschwind model of aphasia emphasizes a loop from a posterior speech reception zone to an anterior expressive zone, but tract-tracing studies are causing a reevaluation of this model. In contrast, the **motor theory of language** suggests that the entire circuit serves motor control and is used for both production and perception. Nonhuman primates lack this specialization. Review **Figure 19.10 and 19.11**, **Activity 19.2**

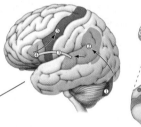

6 Mapping studies have confirmed the left-hemisphere organization for language functions. Stimulation within anterior regions causes speech arrest, while stimulation in other locations causes misnaming and other speech errors. Review **Figures 19.12 and 19.13**

7 Studies using ERP, PET, and fMRI reveal that distinct regions of the left hemisphere are active during viewing, hearing, repeating, or assembling verbal material. Review **Figure 19.14**

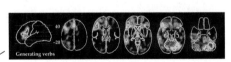
Generating verbs

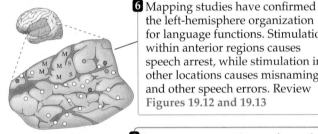

8 Languages are made up of speech sounds, called **phonemes** and **morphemes**, that are assembled into words and sentences according to **syntax**, and colored through context (pragmatics) and **prosody**. Humans are born with an innate mechanism for acquiring language during an early **sensitive period**. Aspects of language acquisition appear to be controlled by genes like *FOXP2*. Other genes appear to be crucial for language articulation. Review **Figures 19.15 and 19.16**

9 Nonhumans lack the peripheral apparatus to produce speech, but nonhuman primates like the chimpanzee can learn to use the signs of American Sign Language. However, controversy surrounds claims that these animals can arrange signs in novel orders to create new sentences. Review **Figure 19.17**, **Activity 19.3**

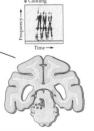
Cackling
Frequency
Time

Temporal poles
Occipital poles
L   R

10 Acquired **dyslexia** is a difficulty with reading resulting from brain damage, usually in the left hemisphere. In **deep dyslexia** there is a disturbance in reading whole words; **surface dyslexia** involves a difficulty with the sounds of words. Several brain systems have been identified in developmental dyslexia. Review **Figures 19.19 and 19.20**

11 Much of the area damaged by brain injury can show at least partial **recovery of function**, especially during the first year or so, as the damaged brain stabilizes. Retraining is a significant part of functional recovery and may involve both compensation, by establishing new solutions to adaptive demands, and reorganization of surviving networks. Review **Figures 19.21 and 19.22**

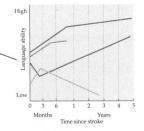
High
Language ability
Low
0   3   6   1   2   3   4   5
Months   Years
Time since stroke

Appendix
Molecular Biology: Basic Concepts and Important Techniques

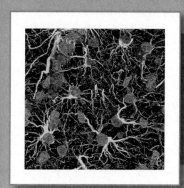

Genes Carry Information That Encodes the Synthesis of Proteins

The most important characteristic of **genes** is that they are pieces of information, inherited from parents, that affect the development and function of our cells. Information carried by the genes is a very specific sort: each gene codes for the construction of a specific string of amino acids to form a **protein** molecule. This is *all* that genes do; they do not *directly* encode intelligence, or memories, or any other sort of complex behavior. The various proteins, each encoded by its own gene, make up the physical structure and most of the constituents of cells, such as enzymes. These proteins make complex behavior possible, and in that context they are also the targets upon which the forces of evolution act.

Enzymes are protein molecules that allow particular chemical reactions to occur in our cells. For example, only cells that have liver-typical proteins will look like a liver cell and be able to perform liver functions. Neurons are cells that make neuron-typical proteins so that they can look and act like neurons. The genetic information for making these various proteins is crucial for an animal to live and for a nervous system to work properly.

One thing we hope this book will help you understand is that everyday experience can affect whether and when particular genetic recipes for making various proteins are used. But first let's review how genetic information is stored and how proteins are made. Our discussion will be brief, but many online tutorials can provide you with more detailed information (see **A Step Further: Molecular Biology Online** on the website).

Genetic information is stored in molecules of DNA

The information for making all of our proteins could, in theory, be stored in any sort of format—on sheets of paper, a DVD, an iPod—but organisms on this planet store their genetic information in a chemical called **deoxyribonucleic acid**, or **DNA**. Each molecule of DNA consists of a long strand of chemicals called **nucleotides** strung one after the other. DNA has only four nucleotides: guanine, cytosine, thymine, and adenine (abbreviated G, C, T, and A). The particular sequence of nucleotides (e.g., GCTTACC or TGGTCC or TGA) holds the information that will eventually make a protein. Because many millions of these nucleotides can be joined one after the other, a tremendous amount of information can be stored in very little space—on a single molecule of DNA.

A set of nucleotides that has been strung together can snuggle tightly against another string of nucleotides if it has the proper sequence: T nucleotides preferentially link with A nucleotides, and G nucleotides link with C nucleotides. Thus, T nucleotides are said to be complementary to A nucleotides, and C nucleotides are complementary to G nucleotides. In fact, most of the time our DNA consists not of a single strand of nucleotides, but of two complementary strands of nucleotides wrapped around one another.

gene A length of DNA that encodes the information for constructing a particular protein.

protein A long string of amino acids; the basic building material of organisms.

enzyme A complicated protein whose action increases the probability of a specific chemical reaction.

deoxyribonucleic acid (DNA) A nucleic acid that is present in the chromosomes of cells and encodes hereditary information.

nucleotide A portion of a DNA or RNA molecule that is composed of a single base and the adjoining sugar-phosphate unit of the strand.

A.1 DUPLICATION OF DNA Before cell division, the genome must be duplicated as illustrated here so that each daughter cell has the full complement of genetic information.

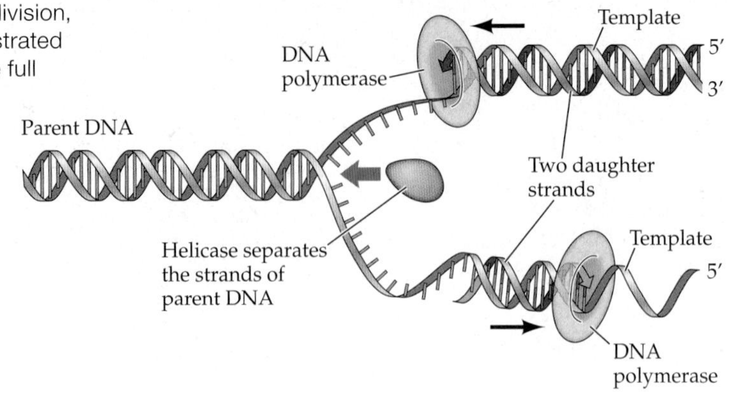

hybridization The process by which a string of nucleotides becomes linked to a complementary series of nucleotides.

chromosome A complex of condensed strands of DNA and associated protein molecules; found in the nucleus of cells.

eukaryote Any organism whose cells have the genetic material contained within a nuclear envelope.

nucleus Here, the spherical central structure of a cell that contains the chromosomes.

ribonucleic acid (RNA) A nucleic acid that implements information found in DNA.

transcription The process during which mRNA forms bases complementary to a strand of DNA. The resulting message (called a *transcript*) is then used to translate the DNA code into protein molecules.

messenger RNA (mRNA) A strand of RNA that carries the code of a section of a DNA strand to the cytoplasm.

transcript The mRNA strand that is produced when a stretch of DNA is "read."

stop codon A trio of nucleotides in DNA to mark the end of transcription.

ribosomes Structures in the cell body where genetic information is translated to produce proteins.

translation The process by which amino acids are linked together (directed by an mRNA molecule) to form protein molecules.

codon A set of three nucleotides that uniquely encodes one particular amino acid.

peptide A short string of amino acids. Longer strings of amino acids are called *proteins*.

The two strands of nucleotides are said to **hybridize** with one another, coiling slightly to form the famous double helix (**FIGURE A.1**). The double-stranded DNA twists and coils further, becoming visible in microscopes as **chromosomes**, which resemble twisted lengths of yarn. Humans and many other organisms are known as **eukaryotes** because we store our chromosomes in a membranous sphere called a **nucleus** (plural *nuclei*) inside each cell. You may remember that the ability of DNA to exist as two complementary strands of nucleotides is crucial for the duplication of the chromosomes, but that story will not concern us here. Just remember that, with very few exceptions, every cell in your body has a faithful copy of all the DNA you received from your parents.

DNA is transcribed to produce messenger RNA

The information from DNA is used to assemble another molecule—**ribonucleic acid**, or **RNA**—that serves as a template for later steps in protein synthesis. Like DNA, RNA is made up of a long string of four different nucleotides. For RNA, those nucleotides are G and C (which, you recall, are complementary to each other) and A and U (uracil), which are also complementary to each other. Note that the T nucleotide is found only in DNA, and the U nucleotide is found only in RNA.

When a particular gene becomes active, the double strand of DNA unwinds enough so that one strand becomes free of the other and becomes available to special cellular machinery (including an enzyme called *transcriptase*) that begins **transcription**—the construction of a specific string of RNA nucleotides that are complementary to the exposed strand of DNA (**FIGURE A.2**). This length of RNA goes by several names: **messenger RNA (mRNA)**, **transcript**, or sometimes, *message*. Each DNA nucleotide encodes a specific RNA nucleotide (an RNA G for every DNA C, an RNA C for every DNA G, an RNA U for every DNA A, and an RNA A for every DNA T). Transcription stops when the assembly reaches a trio of DNA nucleotides, called a **stop codon**, that signals the end. This transcript is made in the nucleus where the DNA resides; then the mRNA molecule moves to the cytoplasm, where protein molecules are assembled.

RNA molecules direct the formation of protein molecules

In the cytoplasm are special organelles, called **ribosomes**, that attach themselves to a molecule of mRNA, "read" the sequence of RNA nucleotides, and, using that information, begin linking together amino acids to form a protein molecule. The structure and function of a protein molecule depend on which particular amino acids are put together and in what order. The decoding of an RNA transcript to manufacture a particular protein is called **translation** (see Figure A.2), as distinct from *transcription*, the construction of the mRNA molecule.

Each trio of RNA nucleotides, or **codon**, encodes one of 20 or so different amino acids. Special molecules associated with the ribosome recognize the codon and bring a molecule of the appropriate amino acid so that the ribosome can fuse that amino acid to the previous one. If the resulting string of amino acids is short (say, 50 amino acids or so), it is called a **peptide**; if it is long, it is called a *protein*. Thus the ribosome assembles a very particular sequence of amino acids at the behest of a very particular sequence of RNA nucleotides, which were themselves encoded in the DNA inherited from our parents. In short, the secret of life is that DNA makes RNA, and RNA makes protein.

There are fascinating amendments to this short story. Often the information from separate stretches of DNA is spliced together to make a single transcript; so-called alternative splicing can create different transcripts from the same gene. Sometimes a protein is modified extensively after translation ends; special chemical processes can cleave long proteins to create one or several active peptides.

Within a population, different individuals will inherit slightly different versions of any given gene, including versions that result in different amino acids at any particular position in the protein. These different versions of a given gene are known as **alleles**. Different alleles may produce proteins that vary in structure and function, including protein products that are completely dysfunctional, or even harmful to the cell and therefore the individual.

Keep in mind that each cell has the complete library of genetic information (collectively known as the **genome**) but makes only a fraction of all the proteins encoded in that DNA. In modern biology we say that each cell **expresses** only some genes; that is, the cell transcribes certain genes and makes the corresponding gene products (protein molecules). Thus, each cell must come to express all the genes needed to perform its function. Modern biologists refer to the expression of a particular subset of the genome as **cell differentiation**: the process by which different types of cells acquire their unique appearance and function. During development, individual cells appear to become more and more specialized, expressing progressively fewer genes. Many molecular biologists are striving to understand which cellular and molecular mechanisms "turn on" or "turn off" gene expression, in order to understand development and pathologies such as cancer, or to provide crucial proteins to afflicted organs in a variety of diseases.

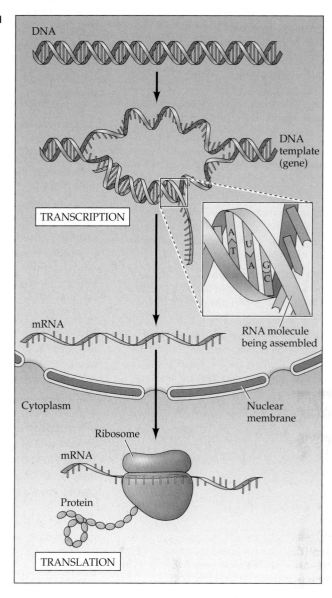

Molecular Biologists Have Craftily Enslaved Microorganisms and Enzymes

Many basic methods of molecular biology are not explicitly discussed in the text, so we will not describe them in detail here. However, you should understand what some of the terms *mean*, even if you don't know exactly how the methods are performed.

Molecular biologists have found ways to incorporate DNA from other species into the DNA of microorganisms such as bacteria and viruses. After the foreign DNA is incorporated, the microorganisms are allowed to reproduce rapidly, producing more and more copies of the (foreign) gene of interest. At this point the gene is said to be **cloned** because the researcher can make as many copies as she likes. To ensure that the right gene is being cloned, the researcher generally clones many, many different genes—each into different bacteria—and then "screens" the bacteria rapidly to find the rare one that has incorporated the gene of interest.

When enough copies of the DNA have been made, the microorganisms are ground up and the DNA extracted. If sufficient DNA has been generated, chemical steps can then determine the exact sequence of nucleotides found in that stretch of

allele A particular version of a given gene. Different alleles may differ in the functionality of the protein produced.

genome Also called *genotype*. All the genetic information that one specific individual has inherited.

expression The process by which a cell makes an mRNA transcript of a particular gene.

cell differentiation The developmental stage in which cells acquire distinctive characteristics, such as those of neurons, as the result of expressing particular genes.

clones Here, the reproduction of a gene so that it can be sequenced and/or manipulated.

DNA sequencing The process by which the order of nucleotides in a gene, or amino acids in a protein, is determined.

polymerase chain reaction (PCR) Also called *gene amplification*. A method for reproducing a particular RNA or DNA sequence manyfold, allowing amplification for sequencing or manipulating the sequence.

transgenic Referring to an animal in which a new or altered gene has been deliberately introduced into the genome.

probe A manufactured sequence of DNA or RNA that is made to include a label (a colorful or radioactive molecule) that lets us track its location.

gel electrophoresis A method of separating molecules of differing size or electrical charge by forcing them to flow through a gel.

blotting Transferring DNA, RNA, or protein fragments to nitrocellulose following separation via gel electrophoresis. The blotted substance can then be labeled.

DNA—a process known as **DNA sequencing**. Once the sequence of nucleotides has been determined, the sequence of complementary nucleotides in the messenger RNA for that gene can be inferred. The sequence of mRNA nucleotides tells the investigator the sequence of amino acids that will be made from that transcript because biologists know which amino acid is encoded by each trio of DNA nucleotides. For example, scientists discovered the amino acid sequence of neurotransmitter receptors by this process.

The business of obtaining many copies of DNA has been boosted by a technique called the **polymerase chain reaction**, or **PCR**. This technique exploits a special type of polymerase enzyme that, like other such enzymes, induces the formation of a DNA molecule that is complementary to an existing single strand of DNA (see Figure A.1). Because this particular polymerase enzyme (called *Taq polymerase*) evolved in bacteria that inhabit geothermal hot springs, it can function in a broad range of temperatures. By heating double-stranded DNA, we can cause the two strands to separate, making each strand available to polymerase enzymes that, when the temperature is cooled enough, construct a new "mate" for each strand so that they are double-stranded again. The first PCR yields only double the original number of DNA molecules; repeating the process results in four times as many molecules as at first. Repeatedly heating and cooling the DNA of interest in the presence of this heat-resistant polymerase enzyme soon yields millions of copies of the original DNA molecule, which is why this process is also referred to as *gene amplification*. In practice, PCR usually requires the investigator to provide primers: short nucleotide sequences synthesized to hybridize on either side of the gene of interest to amplify that particular gene more than others.

With PCR, sufficient quantities of DNA are produced for chemical analysis or other manipulations, such as introducing DNA into cells. For example, we might inject some of the DNA encoding a protein of interest into a fertilized mouse egg (a zygote) and then return the zygote to a pregnant mouse to grow. Occasionally the injected DNA becomes incorporated into the zygote's genome, resulting in a **transgenic** mouse that carries and expresses the foreign gene (see Box 7.3).

Southern blots identify particular genes

Suppose we want to know whether a particular individual or a particular species carries a certain gene. Because all cells contain a complete copy of the genome, we can gather DNA from just about any kind of cell population: blood, skin, or muscle, for example. After the cells are ground up, a chemical extraction procedure isolates the DNA (discarding the RNA and protein). Finding a particular gene in that DNA just boils down to finding a particular sequence of DNA nucleotides. To do that, we can exploit the tendency of nucleic acids to hybridize with one another.

If we were looking for the DNA sequence GCT, for example, we could manufacture the sequence CGA (there are machines to do that), which would then stick to (hybridize with) any DNA sequence of GCT. The manufactured sequence CGA is called a **probe** because it is made to include a label (a colorful or radioactive molecule) that lets us track its location. Of course, such a short length of nucleotides will be found in many genes. In order for a probe to recognize one particular gene, it has to be about 15 nucleotides long.

When we extract DNA from an individual, it's convenient to let enzymes cut up the very long stretches of DNA into more manageable pieces of 1000 to 20,000 nucleotides each. A process called **gel electrophoresis** uses electrical current to separate these millions of pieces more or less by size (**FIGURE A.3**). Large pieces move slowly through a tube of gelatin-like material, and small pieces move rapidly. The tube of gel is then sliced and placed on top of a sheet of paperlike material called *nitrocellulose*. When fluid is allowed to flow through the gel and nitrocellulose, DNA molecules are pulled out of the gel and deposited on the waiting nitrocellulose. This process of making a "sandwich" of gel and nitrocellulose and using fluid to move molecules from the former to the latter is called **blotting** (see Figure A.3).

If the gene that we're looking for is among those millions of DNA fragments sitting on the nitrocellulose, our labeled probe should recognize and hybridize to the

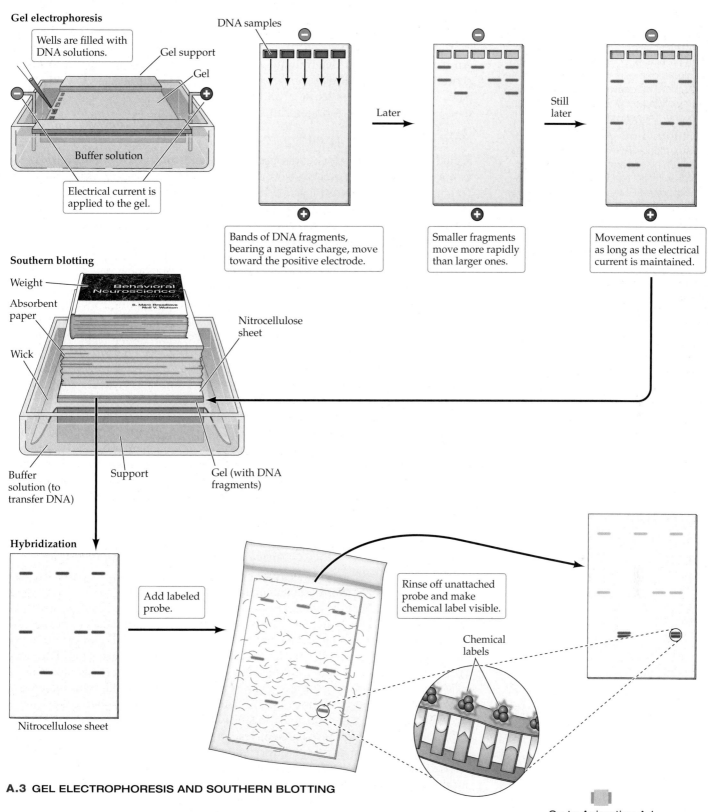

Gel electrophoresis

Wells are filled with DNA solutions.

Gel support

Gel

DNA samples

Buffer solution

Electrical current is applied to the gel.

Later

Still later

Bands of DNA fragments, bearing a negative charge, move toward the positive electrode.

Smaller fragments move more rapidly than larger ones.

Movement continues as long as the electrical current is maintained.

Southern blotting

Weight

Absorbent paper

Wick

Buffer solution (to transfer DNA)

Support

Nitrocellulose sheet

Gel (with DNA fragments)

Behavioral Neuroscience
Eighth Edition
S. Marc Breedlove
Neil V. Watson

Hybridization

Nitrocellulose sheet

Add labeled probe.

Rinse off unattached probe and make chemical label visible.

Chemical labels

A.3 GEL ELECTROPHORESIS AND SOUTHERN BLOTTING

Go to Animation A.1
Gel Electrophoresis
bn8e.com/a.1

sequence. The nitrocellulose sheet is soaked in a solution containing our labeled probe; we wait for the probe to find and hybridize with the gene of interest (if it is present), and we rinse the sheet to remove probe molecules that did not find the gene. Then we *visualize* the probe, either by causing the label to show its color or, if radioactive, by letting the probe expose photographic film to identify the locations where the probe has accumulated. In either case, if the probe has found the gene, a labeled band will be evident, corresponding to the size of DNA fragment that contained the gene (see Figure A.3).

Southern blot A method of detecting a particular DNA sequence in the genome of an organism, by separating DNA with gel electrophoresis, blotting the separated DNAs onto nitrocellulose, and then using a nucleotide probe to hybridize with, and highlight, the gene of interest.

Northern blot A method of detecting a particular RNA transcript in a tissue or organ, by separating RNA from that source with gel electrophoresis, blotting the separated RNAs onto nitrocellulose, and then using a nucleotide probe to hybridize with, and highlight, the transcript of interest.

in situ hybridization A method for detecting particular RNA transcripts in tissue sections by providing a nucleotide probe that is complementary to, and will therefore hybridize with, the transcript of interest.

antibody Also called *immunoglobulin*. A large protein that recognizes and permanently binds to particular shapes, normally as part of the immune system attack on foreign particles.

This process of looking for a particular sequence of DNA is called a **Southern blot**, named after the man who developed the technique, Edward Southern. Southern blots are useful for determining whether related individuals share a particular gene or for assessing the evolutionary relatedness of different species. The developed blots, with their lanes of labeled bands (see Figure A.3), are often seen in popular-media accounts of "DNA fingerprinting" of individuals.

Northern blots identify particular mRNA transcripts

A method more relevant for our discussions is the **Northern blot** (whimsically named as the opposite of the Southern blot). A Northern blot can identify which tissues are making a particular RNA transcript. If liver cells are making a particular protein, for example, then some transcripts for the gene that encodes that protein should be present. So we can take the liver, grind it up, and use chemical processes to isolate most of the RNA (discarding the DNA and protein). The resulting mixture consists of RNA molecules of many different sizes: long, medium, and short transcripts. Gel electrophoresis will separate the transcripts by size, and we can blot the size-sorted mRNAs onto nitrocellulose sheets; the process is very similar to the Southern blot procedure.

To see whether the particular transcript that we're looking for is among the mRNAs, we construct a labeled probe (of either DNA nucleotides or RNA nucleotides) that is complementary to the mRNA transcript of interest and long enough that it will hybridize only to that particular transcript. We incubate the nitrocellulose in the probe, allow time for the probe to hybridize with the targeted transcript (if present), rinse off any unused probe molecules, and then visualize the probe as before. If the transcript of interest is present, we should see a band on the film (see Figure A.3). The presence of several bands indicates that the probe has hybridized to more than one transcript and we may need to make a more specific probe or alter chemical conditions to make the probe less likely to bind similar transcripts.

Because different gene transcripts are of different lengths, the transcript of interest should have reached a particular point in the electrophoresis gel: small transcripts should have moved far; large transcripts should have moved only a little. If our probe has found the right transcript, the single band of labeling should be at the point that is appropriate for a transcript of that length.

In situ hybridization localizes mRNA transcripts within specific cells

Northern blots can tell us whether a particular *organ* has transcripts for a particular gene product. For example, Northern blot analyses have indicated that thousands of genes are transcribed only in the brain. Presumably the proteins encoded by these genes are used exclusively in the brain. But such results alone are not very informative, because the brain consists of so many different kinds of glial and neuronal cells. We can refine Northern blot analyses somewhat, by dissecting out a particular part of the brain—say, the hippocampus—to isolate mRNAs. Sometimes, though, it is important to know *exactly which cells* are making the transcript. In that case we use **in situ hybridization**.

With in situ hybridization we use the same sort of labeled probe, constructed of nucleotides that are complementary to (and will therefore hybridize with) the targeted transcript, as in Northern blots. Instead of using the probe to find and hybridize with the transcript on a sheet of nitrocellulose, however, we use the probe to find the transcripts "in place" (*in situ* in Latin)—that is, on a section of tissue. After rinsing off the probe molecules that didn't find a match, we visualize the probe right in the tissue section. Any cells in the section that were transcribing the gene of interest will have transcripts in the cytoplasm that should have hybridized with our labeled probe (**FIGURE A.4**) (see Box 2.1). In situ hybridization therefore can tell us exactly which cells are expressing a particular gene.

Western blots identify particular proteins

Sometimes we wish to study a particular protein rather than its transcript. In such cases we can use antibodies. **Antibodies** are large, complicated molecules (proteins, in fact) that our immune system adds to the bloodstream to identify and fight invading microbes, thereby arresting and preventing disease (see Figure 15.27). But if

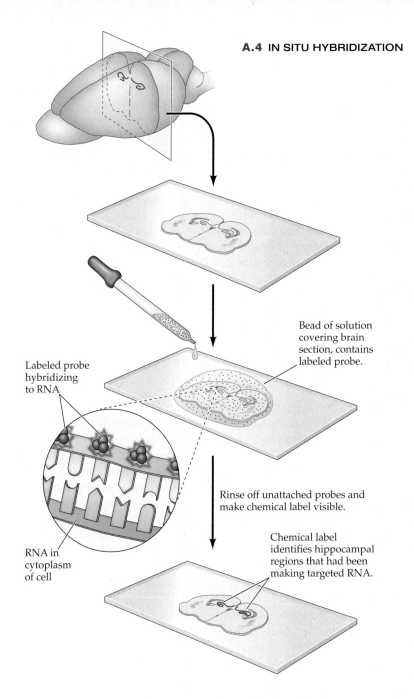

Bead of solution covering brain section, contains labeled probe.

Labeled probe hybridizing to RNA

Rinse off unattached probes and make chemical label visible.

Chemical label identifies hippocampal regions that had been making targeted RNA.

RNA in cytoplasm of cell

we inject a rabbit or mouse with a sample of a protein of interest, we can induce the animal to create antibodies that recognize and attach to that particular protein, just as if it were an invader.

Once these antibodies have been purified and chemically labeled, we can use them to search for the target protein. We grind up an organ, isolate the proteins (discarding the DNA and RNA), and separate them by means of gel electrophoresis. Then we blot these proteins out of the gel and onto nitrocellulose. Next we use the antibodies to tell us whether the targeted protein is among those made by that organ. If the antibodies identify only the protein we care about, there should be a single band of labeling (if there are two or more, then the antibodies recognize more than one protein). Because proteins come in different sizes, the single band of label should be at the position corresponding to the size of the protein that we're studying. Such blots are called **Western blots**.

To review, Southern blots identify particular DNA pieces (genes), Northern blots identify particular RNA pieces (transcripts), and Western blots identify particular proteins (sometimes called *products*).

Western blot A method of detecting a particular protein molecule in a tissue or organ, by separating proteins from that source with gel electrophoresis, blotting the separated proteins onto nitrocellulose, and then using an antibody that binds, and highlights, the protein of interest.

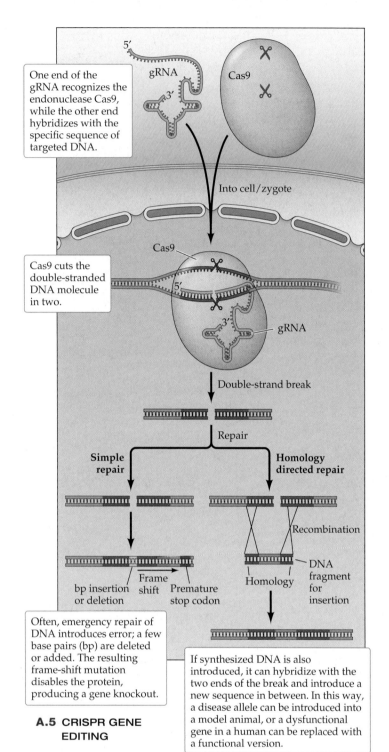

One end of the gRNA recognizes the endonuclease Cas9, while the other end hybridizes with the specific sequence of targeted DNA.

Cas9 cuts the double-stranded DNA molecule in two.

Into cell/zygote

Double-strand break

Repair

Simple repair

Homology directed repair

Recombination

bp insertion or deletion

Frame shift

Premature stop codon

Homology

DNA fragment for insertion

Often, emergency repair of DNA introduces error; a few base pairs (bp) are deleted or added. The resulting frame-shift mutation disables the protein, producing a gene knockout.

If synthesized DNA is also introduced, it can hybridize with the two ends of the break and introduce a new sequence in between. In this way, a disease allele can be introduced into a model animal, or a dysfunctional gene in a human can be replaced with a functional version.

A.5 CRISPR GENE EDITING

Antibodies can also tell us which cells possess a particular protein

If we need to know which particular cells within an organ such as the brain are making a particular protein, we can use the same sorts of antibodies that we use in Western blots, but in this case directed at that protein in tissue sections. We slice up the brain, expose the sections to the antibodies, allow time for them to find and attach to the protein, rinse off unattached antibodies, and use chemical treatments to visualize the antibodies. Cells that were making the protein will be labeled from the chemical treatments (see Box 2.1).

Because antibodies from the *immune* system are used to identify *cells* with the aid of *chemical* treatment, this method is called **immunocytochemistry**, or **ICC**. This technique can even tell us where, within the cell, the protein is found. Such information can provide important clues about the function of the protein. For example, if the protein is found in axon terminals, it may be a neurotransmitter.

Gene Editing Enables the Creation of Model Organisms

In Chapter 7 we discuss the use of "knockout" organisms, where a particular gene has been disabled, and "transgenic" organisms, where a new gene has been introduced (see Box 7.3). These animal models are powerful means of investigating the influence of genes on the nervous system and behavior. A recent breakthrough in molecular biology has made it much easier to produce such models in organisms as diverse as worms and monkeys.

Like many other biotech innovations, such as optogenetics (see Figure 3.24), this one exploits a mechanism that evolved in simple organisms. Unicellular organisms like bacteria become infected with viruses that insert their invasive genes into the host organism's DNA. In response, bacteria have evolved mechanisms to identify and remove, or at least disable, the invasive genes. One mechanism is a stretch of DNA known as **CRISPR**, for *c*lustered *r*egularly *i*nterspaced *s*hort *p*alindromic *r*epeats. The RNA transcribed from a CRISPR site will serve as a guide to target the invasive DNA and so is referred to as a **guide RNA** (**gRNA**). The palindromic sequences in the front of the gRNA cause it to fold up in a distinctive shape that binds to an enzyme, an endonuclease called **Cas9** (CRISPR-*as*sociated enzyme *9*), while the "tail" of the gRNA is complementary to the invasive sequence and so will hybridize with it. Then the associated Cas9 enzyme breaks the host's double-stranded DNA at that point. This type of break in double-stranded DNA is relatively rare, but all organisms have machinery in place to repair it. The thing is, this emergency repair often introduces an error, either adding or subtracting a few nucleotides. That in turn will introduce a frameshift mutation, with the result that the wrong sequence of amino acids will be assembled and eventually a premature stop codon (the trio of nucleotides that normally signal the end of transcription) will end the transcription entirely (**FIGURE A.5**). The combination of improper amino acids and curtailed transcription means the invasive viral protein won't work, and the infection will be undone.

Eukaryotes like worms and mice lack the CRISPR mechanism and so normally do not produce Cas9. But we can introduce the gene for Cas9 into a zygote (of a worm, a fly, a mouse, or a monkey), and we can also introduce DNA custom made to produce a gRNA directed at whatever gene we choose. In that case, the gRNA will direct Cas9 to break the DNA within the targeted gene. Then the imperfect repair of that DNA will effectively knock out the gene in the individual that results from this zygote. Or the same system can be used to knock out the gene in particular cells in a mature individual. An enormous advantage of the CRISPR system is that one can introduce several different gRNAs simultaneously to knock out several different genes at once (H. Wang et al., 2013).

Scientists have also exploited the CRISPR system for gene editing. In this variant, the scientist again introduces DNA to cause the cell or zygote to express Cas9 and a specific gRNA, but also provides synthesized DNA fragments that are homologous to the cut ends of the host's DNA. Then when the break is repaired, the synthesized DNA fragment recombines into the host's genome, a case of *homology-directed repair*. Now, instead of knocking out the targeted gene, the scientist has replaced that section of the gene, effectively producing a new allele. In this way, a mutated allele can be introduced into the fly, mouse, zebrafish, or monkey, producing a transgenic animal (more specifically, a "knockin" animal, where a new allele has been put in place of the endogenous allele). There is also great hope that this method may someday be used for gene therapy in humans, to replace dysfunctional genes that cause disease, such as the *dystrophin* gene in Duchenne muscular dystrophy (see Chapter 11).

Another bacterial mechanism to get rid of viral infection is to insert a specific series of nucleotides, called **loxP** sites, to mark the invasive DNA. A bacterial enzyme, called **Cre-recombinase**, then binds to two such loxP sites (as long as they are not too far apart), cuts out the DNA between them, and joins the cut ends of DNA back together, a process called *recombination*. This severe editing renders the viral gene product worthless, thwarting the infection. Multicellular organisms normally do not have this Cre-lox system, but scientists can insert them into the genome of flies/zebrafish/mice to manipulate genes. For example, we can insert lox sites into the DNA of a targeted gene (we might use the CRISPR homology-directed repair to do this) in such a way that the gene still functions normally despite the lox sites. Now we can inject viruses into a particular brain site to infect cells there to express Cre-recombinase. That means the loxP-flanked, or "floxed" gene will be knocked out only in that brain region. Or for another approach, we might cross animals carrying the floxed allele with animals carrying a transgene for Cre-recombinase. This transgene might include a promoter that causes the enzyme to be expressed only in neurons, or only in astrocytes, or only in motor neurons. That means the floxed gene will be disrupted only in those particular classes of cells, not the whole organism (**FIGURE A.6**). Using these methods, scientists are able to test more and more specific hypotheses about how gene expression alters the brain and therefore behavior.

immunocytochemistry (ICC) A method for detecting a particular protein in tissues in which an antibody recognizes and binds to the protein and then chemical methods are used to leave a visible reaction product around each antibody.

CRISPR *c*lustered *r*egularly *i*nterspaced *s*hort *p*alindromic *r*epeats. A system of gene manipulation that evolved in single-celled organisms and is exploited by scientists for gene editing.

guide RNA (gRNA) A strand of RNA designed to hybridize with a targeted nucleotide sequence in DNA in order to guide the Cas9 enzyme to break the DNA at that site.

Cas9 *C*RISPR *as*sociated enzyme *9*. A bacterial enzyme that induces a break in double-stranded DNA as part of the CRISPR system.

loxP A specific sequence of nucleotides recognized by the enzyme Cre-recombinase. If the enzyme encounters a pair of loxP sites in a gene, it will remove the DNA between the two sites and recombine the gene, usually rendering the gene product dysfunctional.

Cre-recombinase A bacterial enzyme that recognizes loxP, which is a specific sequence of nucleotides, and recombines the DNA at loxP sites.

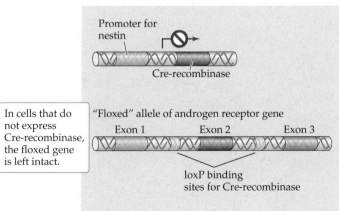

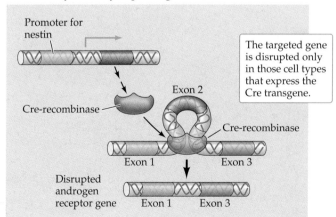

A.6 CRE-LOX SYSTEMS FOR KNOCKING OUT GENES IN SPECIFIC CELLS

Glossary

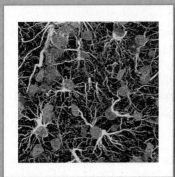

Numbers in brackets refer to the chapter(s) where the term is introduced.

17β-estradiol or estradiol The primary type of estrogen that is secreted by the ovary. **[5]**

5α-reductase An enzyme that converts testosterone into dihydrotestosterone (DHT). **[12]**

5-HT See *serotonin*.

A

A1 See primary auditory cortex.

absence attack See *simple partial seizure*.

absolute refractory phase A brief period of complete insensitivity to stimuli. **[3]**

accommodation The process of focusing by the ciliary muscles and the lens to form a sharp image on the retina. **[10]**

acetylcholine (ACh) A neurotransmitter produced and released by parasympathetic postganglionic neurons, by motor neurons, and by neurons throughout the brain. **[2, 3, 4, 11]**

acetylcholinesterase (AChE) An enzyme that inactivates the transmitter acetylcholine both at synaptic sites and elsewhere in the nervous system. **[4]**

ACh See *acetylcholine*.

AChE See *acetylcholinesterase*.

acid See *LSD*.

ACTH See *adrenocorticotropic hormone*.

actin A protein that, along with myosin, mediates the contraction of muscle fibers. **[11]**

action potential The propagated electrical message of a neuron that travels along the axon to the presynaptic axon terminals. **[3]**

activational effect A temporary change in behavior resulting from the administration of a hormone to an adult animal. **[12]**

acupuncture The insertion of needles at designated points on the skin in an attempt to alleviate pain or physiological malfunction, or alter behavior. **[8]**

adaptation 1. A trait that increases the probability that an individual will leave offspring in subsequent generations. **[6]** 2. The progressive loss of receptor sensitivity as stimulation is maintained. **[8, 10]**

addiction See *dependence*.

adenohypophysis See *anterior pituitary*.

adenosine An endogenous neuromodulator that generally reduces neural activity. Caffeine interferes with adenosine binding. In the context of neural transmission, adenosine alters synaptic activity. **[4,14]**

adequate stimulus The type of stimulus for which a given sensory organ is particularly adapted. **[8]**

Aδ fiber A moderately large, myelinated, and therefore fast-conducting axon, usually transmitting pain information. **[8]**

ADH See *arginine vasopressin*.

ADHD See *attention deficit hyperactivity disorder*.

adipose tissue Tissue made up of fat cells. **[13]**

adrenal cortex The outer rind of the adrenal gland, which secretes steroid hormones, including cortisol. **[5, 15]**

adrenal gland An endocrine gland atop the kidney. **[5]**

adrenal medulla The inner core of the adrenal gland, which secretes epinephrine and norepinephrine. **[5, 15]**

adrenal steroids See *adrenocorticoids*.

adrenaline See *epinephrine*.

adrenocorticoids Also called *adrenal steroids*. A class of steroid hormones that are secreted by the adrenal cortex, including glucocorticoids such as cortisol and mineralocorticoids such as aldosterone. **[5, 15]**

adrenocorticotropic hormone (ACTH) A tropic hormone secreted by the anterior pituitary gland that controls the production and release of hormones of the adrenal cortex. **[5]**

adult neurogenesis The creation of new neurons in the brain of an adult. **[7]**

afferent In reference to axons, carrying action potentials from a sensory organ to the central nervous system or from one region to another region of interest. Compare *efferent*. **[2]**

affinity See *binding affinity*.

afterpotential The positive or negative change in membrane potential that may follow an action potential. **[3]**

agnosia The inability to recognize objects, despite being able to describe them in terms of form and color. It may occur after localized brain damage. **[19]**

agonist A molecule, usually a drug, that binds a receptor molecule and initiates a response like that of another molecule, usually a neurotransmitter. **[3, 4]**

agraphia The inability to write. **[19]**

AIS See *androgen insensitivity syndrome*.

alarm reaction The initial response to stress. [15]

aldosterone A mineralocorticoid hormone, a steroid secreted by the adrenal cortex, that induces the kidneys to conserve sodium ions. [5, 13]

alexia The inability to read. [19]

allele One of two or more versions of a given gene or genetic locus. Different alleles may differ in the functionality of the protein produced. [6, App]

allocortex Cortical tissue with three layers or unlayered organization, in contrast with six-layered neocortex. [2]

allomone A chemical signal that is released outside the body by one species and affects the behavior of other species. [5]

allopregnanolone A naturally occurring steroid that modulates GABA receptor activity in much the same way that benzodiazepine anxiolytics do. [4]

all-or-none property The fact that the amplitude of the action potential is independent of the magnitude of the stimulus. [3]

allostasis A coordinated set of behavioral and physiological changes to maintain homeostasis. [13]

α-fetoprotein A protein found in the plasma of fetuses. In rodents, α-fetoprotein binds estrogens and prevents them from entering the brain. [12]

α-melanocyte-stimulating hormone (α-MSH) A peptide that binds the melanocortin receptor. [13]

alpha motor neuron A motor neuron that controls the main contractile fibers (extrafusal fibers) of a muscle. [11]

α-MSH See *α-melanocyte-stimulating hormone*.

alpha rhythm A brain potential of 8–12 Hz that occurs during relaxed wakefulness. [14]

α-synuclein A protein that has been implicated in Parkinson's disease. [11]

ALS See *amyotrophic lateral sclerosis*.

altricial Referring to animals that are born in an undeveloped state and depend on maternal care, as human infants do. [12]

Alzheimer's disease A form of dementia that may appear in middle age but is more frequent among the aged. [7]

amacrine cells Specialized retinal neurons that contact both the bipolar cells and the ganglion cells and are especially significant in inhibitory interactions within the retina. [10]

amblyopia Reduced visual acuity of one eye, that is not caused by optical or retinal impairments. [7, 10]

AMH See *anti-müllerian hormone*.

amine hormones Also called *monoamine hormones*. A class of hormones, each composed of a single amino acid that has been modified into a related molecule, such as melatonin or epinephrine. [5]

amine neurotransmitter A neurotransmitter based on modifications of a single amino acid. Examples include acetylcholine, serotonin, and dopamine. [4]

amino acid neurotransmitter A neurotransmitter that is itself an amino acid. Examples include GABA, glycine, and glutamate. [4]

amnesia Severe impairment of memory. [17]

AMPA receptor A glutamate receptor that also binds the glutamate agonist AMPA. [17]

amphetamine A molecule that resembles the structure of the catecholamine transmitters and enhances their activity. [4]

amphetamine psychosis A delusional and psychotic state, closely resembling acute schizophrenia, that is brought on by repeated use of high doses of amphetamine. [16]

amplitude Magnitude or strength. In acoustics, the force sound exerts per unit area, usually measured as dynes per square centimeter. [9]

ampulla An enlarged region of each semicircular canal that contains the receptor cells (hair cells) of the vestibular system. [9]

amusia A disorder characterized by the inability to discern tunes accurately. [9]

amygdala A group of nuclei in the medial anterior part of the temporal lobe. [2, 15]

amyloid plaques See *senile plaques*.

amyloid precursor protein (APP) A protein that, when cleaved by several enzymes, produces β-amyloid. [7]

amyotrophic lateral sclerosis (ALS) Also called *Lou Gehrig's disease*. A disease in which motor neurons and their target muscles waste away. [11]

analgesia Absence of or reduction in pain. [8]

analgesic Referring to painkilling properties. [4]

analogy Similarity of function, although the structures of interest may look different. The human hand and an elephant's trunk are analogous features. [6]

anandamide An endogenous substance that binds the cannabinoid receptor molecule. [4]

androgen insensitivity syndrome (AIS) A syndrome caused by a mutation of the androgen receptor gene that renders tissues insensitive to androgenic hormones like testosterone. Affected XY individuals are phenotypic females, but they have internal testes and regressed internal genital structures. [12]

androgens A class of hormones that includes testosterone and other male hormones. [5]

androstenedione The chief sex hormone secreted by the human adrenal cortex. [5]

angel dust See *phencyclidine*.

angiography A brain-imaging technique in which a specialized X-ray image of the head is taken shortly after the cerebral blood vessels have been filled with a radiopaque dye by means of a catheter. [2]

angiotensin II A substance that is produced in the blood by the action of renin and that may play a role in the control of thirst. [13]

angular gyrus A brain region in which strokes can lead to word blindness. [19]

anion A negatively charged ion, such as a protein or chloride ion. [3]

annulospiral ending See *primary sensory ending*.

anomia The inability to name persons or objects readily. [19]

anorexia nervosa A syndrome in which individuals severely deprive themselves of food. [13]

anorexigenic neurons Neurons of the hypothalamic appetite system that inhibit feeding behavior. [13]

anosmia The inability to smell. [9]

anosognosia Denial of illness. [18]

ANP See *atrial natriuretic peptide.*

antagonist 1. A molecule, usually a drug, that interferes with or prevents the action of a transmitter. **[3, 4]** 2. A muscle that counteracts the effect of another muscle. **[11]**

anterior Also called *rostral.* In anatomy, toward the head end of an organism. Compare *posterior.* **[2]**

anterior cerebral arteries Two large arteries, arising from the internal carotid arteries, that provide blood to the anterior poles and medial surfaces of the cerebral hemispheres. **[2]**

anterior pituitary Also called *adenohypophysis.* The front division of the pituitary gland. It secretes tropic hormones. **[5]**

anterograde amnesia The inability to form new memories beginning with the onset of a disorder. **[17]**

anterograde degeneration Also called *Wallerian degeneration.* The loss of the distal portion of an axon resulting from injury to the axon. **[7]**

anterolateral system or spinothalamic system A somatosensory system that carries most of the pain and temperature information from the body to the brain. **[8]**

antibody Also called *immunoglobulin.* A large protein that recognizes and permanently binds to particular shapes, normally as part of the immune system attack on foreign particles. **[15, App]**

antidepressants A class of drugs that relieve the symptoms of depression. **[4]**

antidiuretic hormone (ADH) See *arginine vasopressin.*

anti-müllerian hormone (AMH) A protein hormone secreted by the fetal testis that inhibits müllerian duct development. **[12]**

antipsychotics Also called *neuroleptics.* A class of drugs that alleviate the symptoms of schizophrenia, typically by blocking dopamine receptors. **[4, 16]**

anxiety disorder Any of a class of psychological disorders that include recurrent panic states and generalized anxiety disorders. **[16]**

anxiolytics A class of substances that are used to combat anxiety. Examples include alcohol, opiates, barbiturates, and the benzodiazepines. **[4, 16]**

aphagia Refusal to eat. **[13]**

aphasia An impairment in language understanding and/or production that is caused by brain injury. **[19]**

apical dendrite The type of dendrite that extends from a pyramidal cell to the outermost surface of the cortex. **[2]**

apolipoprotein E (ApoE) A protein that may help break down amyloid. **[7]**

apoptosis See *cell death.*

APP See *amyloid precursor protein.*

appetitive behavior The second stage of mating behavior. It helps establish or maintain sexual interaction. **[12]**

apraxia An impairment in the ability to begin and execute skilled voluntary movements, even though there is no muscle paralysis. **[11, 19]**

aquaporins Channels spanning the cell membrane that are specialized for conducting water molecules into or out of the cell. **[13]**

arachnoid The thin covering (one of the three meninges) of the brain that lies between the dura mater and pia mater. **[2]**

arborization The elaborate branching of the dendrites of some neurons. **[2]**

arcuate fasciculus A tract believed by some to connect Wernicke's area to Broca's area. **[19]**

arcuate nucleus An arc-shaped hypothalamic nucleus implicated in appetite control. **[13]**

area 17 See *primary visual cortex.*

arginine vasopressin (AVP) Also called *vasopressin* or *antidiuretic hormone (ADH).* A peptide hormone from the posterior pituitary that promotes water conservation. **[5, 13]**

aromatase An enzyme that converts some androgens into estrogens. **[5, 12]**

aromatization The chemical reaction that converts testosterone to estradiol, and other androgens to other estrogens. **[12]**

aromatization hypothesis The hypothesis that testicular androgens enter the brain and are converted there into estrogens to masculinize the developing nervous system in some rodents. **[12]**

arousal The global, nonselective level of alertness of an individual. **[18]**

ASD See *autism spectrum disorder.*

aspartate An amino acid transmitter that is excitatory at many synapses. **[4]**

associative learning A type of learning in which an association is formed between two stimuli or between a stimulus and a response. It includes both classical and operant conditioning. **[17]**

astereognosis The inability to recognize objects by touching and feeling them. **[19]**

astrocyte A star-shaped glial cell with numerous processes (extensions) that run in all directions. **[2]**

ataxia An impairment in the direction, extent, and rate of muscular movement. It is often caused by cerebellar pathology. **[11]**

atrial natriuretic peptide (ANP) A hormone, secreted by the heart, that normally reduces blood pressure, inhibits drinking, and promotes the excretion of water and salt at the kidneys. **[13]**

attention Also called *selective attention.* A state or condition of selective awareness or perceptual receptivity, by which specific stimuli are selected for enhanced processing. **[8, 18]**

attention deficit hyperactivity disorder (ADHD) Syndrome of distractibility, impulsiveness, and hyperactivity that, in children, interferes with school performance. **[18]**

attentional bottleneck A filter that results from the limits intrinsic to our attentional processes, with the result that only the most important stimuli are selected for special processing. **[18]**

attentional spotlight The shifting of our limited selective attention around the environment to highlight stimuli for enhanced processing. **[18]**

atypical antipsychotics Also called *atypical neuroleptics.* A class of antischizophrenic drugs that have actions other than or in addition to the dopamine D_2 receptor antagonism that characterizes the typical antipsychotics. **[4, 16]**

aura In epilepsy, the unusual sensations or premonition that may precede the beginning of a seizure. **[3]**

australopithecine Referring to *Australopithecus*, a primate genus, known only from the fossil record, thought to be an ancestor to humans. [6]

autism spectrum disorder (ASD) A disorder, which can run from mild to severe, characterized by deficits in social communication and interaction, accompanied by restricted, repetitive behaviors and interests. [5]

autocrine Referring to a signal that is secreted by a cell into its environment and that feeds back to the same cell. [5]

autoimmune disorder A disorder caused when the immune system mistakenly attacks a person's own body, thereby interfering with normal functioning. [11]

autonomic ganglia Collections of nerve cell bodies, belonging to the autonomic division of the peripheral nervous system, that are found in various locations and innervate the major organs. [2]

autonomic nervous system The part of the peripheral nervous system that supplies neural connections to glands and to smooth muscles of internal organs. [2]

autoradiography A histological technique that shows the distribution of radioactive chemicals in tissues. [2, 5]

autoreceptor A receptor for a synaptic transmitter that is located in the presynaptic membrane, telling the axon terminal how much transmitter has been released. [3, 4]

AVP See *arginine vasopressin*.

axo-axonic Referring to a synapse in which a presynaptic axon terminal synapses onto another axon's terminal. [3]

axo-dendritic Referring to a synapse in which a presynaptic axon terminal synapses onto a dendrite of the postsynaptic neuron, either via a dendritic spine or directly onto the dendrite itself. [3]

axon A single extension from the nerve cell that carries action potentials from the cell body to other neurons. [2]

axon collateral A branch of an axon from a single neuron. [2]

axon hillock A cone-shaped area from which the axon originates out of the cell body; functionally, the integration zone of the neuron. [2, 3]

axon terminal Also called *synaptic bouton*. The end of an axon or axon collateral, which forms a synapse on a neuron or other target cell. [2]

axonal transport The transportation of materials from the neuronal cell body to distant regions in the dendrites and axons, and from the axon terminals back to the cell body. [2]

axo-somatic Referring to a synapse in which a presynaptic axon terminal synapses onto the cell body (soma) of the postsynaptic neuron. [3]

B

B cell or B lymphocyte An immune system cell, formed in the bone marrow (hence the *B*), that mediates humoral immunity. [15]

Bálint's syndrome Three co-occurring symptoms—simultagnosia, oculomotor apraxia, and optic ataxia—that may occur after bilateral lesions of cortical attentional systems. [18]

ballistic movement A rapid muscular movement that is generally preprogrammed. [11]

bar detector See *simple cortical cell*.

barbiturate A powerful sedative anxiolytic derived from barbituric acid, with dangerous addiction and overdose potential. [4]

bariatric Having to do with treatment of obesity. [13]

baroreceptor A pressure receptor in the heart or a major artery that detects a fall in blood pressure. [13]

basal dendrite One of several dendrites on a pyramidal cell that extend horizontally from the cell body. [2]

basal forebrain A ventral region in the forebrain that has been implicated in consciousness and sleep. [14]

basal ganglia A group of forebrain nuclei, including caudate nucleus, globus pallidus, and putamen, found deep within the cerebral hemispheres. [2, 11]

basal metabolism The consumption of energy by the basic life-sustaining functions of the body. [13]

basilar artery An artery, formed by the fusion of the vertebral arteries, that supplies blood to the brainstem and to the posterior cerebral arteries. [2]

basilar membrane A membrane in the cochlea that contains the principal structures involved in auditory transduction. [9]

bass An aspect of pitch corresponding to the subjective experience of low-frequency sounds (especially musical sounds like those from a bass guitar). [9]

batrachotoxin A toxin, secreted by poison arrow frogs, that selectively interferes with Na^+ channels. [3]

Bcl-2 A family of proteins that regulate apoptosis. [7]

BDNF See *brain-derived neurotrophic factor*.

behavioral intervention An approach to finding relations between body variables and behavioral variables that involves intervening in the behavior of an organism and looking for resultant changes in body structure or function. [1]

behavioral medicine See *health psychology*.

behavioral neuroscience Also called *biological psychology*. The study of the neural bases of behavior and mental processes. [1]

behavioral teratology The study of impairments in behavior that are produced by embryonic or fetal exposure to toxic substances. [7]

Bell's palsy A disorder, usually caused by viral infection, in which the facial nerve on one side stops conducting action potentials, resulting in paralysis on one side of the face. [15]

benzodiazepine agonists A class of antianxiety drugs that bind to sites on $GABA_A$ receptors. [4]

benzodiazepines A class of antianxiety drugs that bind with high affinity to receptor molecules in the central nervous system. One example is diazepam (Valium). [16]

beta activity See *desynchronized EEG*.

β-amyloid A protein that accumulates in senile plaques in Alzheimer's disease. [7]

β-secretase An enzyme that cleaves amyloid precursor protein, forming β-amyloid, which can lead to Alzheimer's disease. [7]

binaural Referring to two ears. [9]

binding affinity Also called simply *affinity*. The propensity of molecules of a drug (or other ligand) to bind to receptors. [4]

binding problem The question of how the brain understands which individual attributes blend together into a single object, when these different features are processed by different regions in the brain. [18]

binge eating The paroxysmal intake of large quantities of food, often of poor nutritional value and high in calories. [13]

binocular deprivation Depriving both eyes of form vision, as by sealing the eyelids. **[7]**

bioavailable Referring to a substance, usually a drug, that is present in the body in a form that is able to interact with physiological mechanisms. **[4]**

biological psychology See *behavioral neuroscience*.

biotransformation The process in which enzymes convert a drug into a metabolite that is itself active, possibly in ways that are substantially different from the actions of the original substance. **[4]**

bipolar cells A class of interneurons of the retina that receive information from rods and cones and pass the information to retinal ganglion cells. **[10]**

bipolar disorder Formerly called *manic-depressive illness*. A psychiatric disorder characterized by periods of depression that alternate with excessive, expansive moods. **[16]**

bipolar neuron A nerve cell that has a single dendrite at one end and a single axon at the other end. **[2]**

blind spot The portion of the visual field from which light falls on the optic disc. Because there are no receptors in this region, light striking it cannot be seen. **[10]**

blood-brain barrier The mechanisms that make the movement of substances from blood vessels into brain cells more difficult than exchanges in other body organs, thus affording the brain greater protection from exposure to some substances found in the blood. **[2, 4]**

blotting Transferring DNA, RNA, or protein fragments to nitrocellulose following separation via gel electrophoresis. The blotted substance can then be labeled. **[App]**

border cell A neuron that selectively fires when an animal arrives at the perimeter of a local spatial cognitive map. **[17]**

bottom-up attention See *reflexive attention*.

bottom-up process A process in which lower-order mechanisms, like sensory inputs, trigger additional processing by higher-order systems. There may be no conscious awareness until late in the process. **[18]**

botulinum toxin A toxin that cleaves SNAREs (Soluble *NSF Attachment Protein REceptors*), such as t-SNAREs and v-SNAREs, disabling neurotransmitter release. **[3]**

bovine spongiform encephalopathy (BSE) Also called *mad cow disease*. A disorder caused by improperly formed prion proteins, leading to dementia and death. **[11]**

brain self-stimulation The process in which animals will work to provide electrical stimulation to particular brain sites, presumably because the experience is very rewarding. **[15]**

brain-derived neurotrophic factor (BDNF) A protein purified from the brains of animals that can keep some classes of neurons alive. **[7]**

brainstem The region of the brain that consists of the midbrain, the pons, and the medulla. **[2]**

Broca's aphasia See *nonfluent aphasia*.

Broca's area A region of the frontal lobe of the brain that is involved in the production of speech. **[19]**

BSE See *bovine spongiform encephalopathy*.

bulimia Also called *bulimia nervosa*. A syndrome in which individuals periodically gorge themselves, usually with "junk food," and then either vomit or take laxatives to avoid weight gain. **[13]**

bungarotoxin A neurotoxin from the venom of the banded krait that selectively blocks acetylcholine receptors. **[3]**

C

C fiber A small, unmyelinated axon that conducts pain information slowly and adapts slowly. **[8]**

Ca²⁺ See *calcium ion*.

caffeine A stimulant compound found in coffee, cacao, and other plants. **[4]**

CAH See *congenital adrenal hyperplasia*.

calcium ion (Ca²⁺) A calcium atom that carries a double positive charge because it has lost two electrons. **[3]**

CAM See *cell adhesion molecule*.

cAMP See *cyclic adenosine monophosphate*.

Cannon-Bard theory The theory that our experience of emotion is independent of the simultaneous physiological changes that accompany it. **[15]**

capsaicin A compound synthesized by various plants to deter predators by mimicking the experience of burning. **[8]**

carotid arteries The major arteries that ascend the left and right sides of the neck to the brain, supplying blood to the anterior and middle cerebral arteries. **[2]**

Cas9 *C*RISPR *as*sociated enzyme *9*. A bacterial enzyme that induces a break in double-stranded DNA as part of the CRISPR system. **[App]**

caspases A family of proteins that regulate cell death (apoptosis). **[7]**

castration Removal of the gonads, usually the testes. **[5, 12]**

CAT or CT See *computerized axial tomography*.

cataplexy Sudden loss of muscle tone, leading to collapse of the body without loss of consciousness. **[14]**

catecholamines A class of monoamines that serve as neurotransmitters, including dopamine and norepinephrine. **[4]**

cation A positively charged ion, such as a potassium or sodium ion. **[3]**

caudal See *posterior*.

caudate nucleus One of the basal ganglia. It has a long extension or tail. **[2]**

CBT See *cognitive behavioral therapy*.

CCK See *cholecystokinin*.

cell adhesion molecule (CAM) A protein found on the surface of a cell that guides cell migration and/or axonal pathfinding. **[7]**

cell assembly A large group of cells that tend to be active at the same time because they have been activated simultaneously or in close succession in the past. **[17]**

cell body Also called *soma*. The region of a neuron that is defined by the presence of the cell nucleus. **[2]**

cell death Also called *apoptosis*. The developmental process during which "surplus" cells die. **[7]**

cell differentiation The developmental stage in which cells acquire distinctive characteristics, such as those of neurons, as the result of expressing particular genes. **[7, App]**

cell membrane The lipid bilayer that ensheathes a cell. **[3]**

cell migration The movement of cells from site of origin to final location. **[7]**

cell nucleus The spherical central structure of a cell that contains the chromosomes. [2]

cell-autonomous Referring to cell processes that are directed by the cell itself rather than being under the influence of other cells. [7]

cell-cell interactions The general process during development in which one cell affects the differentiation of other, usually neighboring, cells. [7]

central deafness A hearing impairment that is related to lesions in auditory pathways or centers, including sites in the brainstem, thalamus, or cortex. [9]

central nervous system (CNS) The portion of the nervous system that includes the brain and the spinal cord. [2]

central pattern generator Neural circuitry that is responsible for generating the rhythmic pattern of a behavior such as walking. [11]

central sulcus A fissure that divides the frontal lobe from the parietal lobe. [2]

cerebellum A structure located at the back of the brain, dorsal to the pons, that is involved in the central regulation of movement. [2]

cerebral cortex Also called simply *cortex*. The outer covering of the cerebral hemispheres that consists largely of neuronal cell bodies and their branches. [2, 6]

cerebral hemispheres The right and left halves of the forebrain. [2]

cerebral lateralization Specialization of one cerebral hemisphere for a particular intellectual function. [19]

cerebrocerebellum The lowermost part of the cerebellum, consisting especially of the lateral part of each cerebellar hemisphere. [11]

cerebrospinal fluid (CSF) The fluid that fills the cerebral ventricles. [2]

cervical Referring to the topmost eight segments of the spinal cord, in the neck region. [2]

cGMP See *cyclic guanosine monophosphate*.

channelopathy A genetic abnormality of ion channels, causing a variety of symptoms. [3]

channelrhodopsin A protein that, in response to light of the proper wavelength, opens a channel to admit sodium ions, which results in excitation of the neuron. [3]

ChAT See *choline acetyltransferase*.

chemical transmitter See *neurotransmitter*.

chemically gated ion channel See *ligand-gated ion channel*.

chemoaffinity hypothesis The notion that each cell has a chemical identity that directs it to synapse on the proper target cell during development. [7]

chemoattractants Compounds that attract particular classes of axonal growth cones. [7]

chemorepellents Compounds that repel particular classes of axonal growth cones. [7]

choline acetyltransferase (Chat) An important enzyme involved in the synthesis of the neurotransmitter acetylcholine. [4]

cholinergic Referring to cells that use acetylcholine as their synaptic transmitter. [3, 4]

choroid plexus A highly vascular portion of the lining of the ventricles that secretes cerebrospinal fluid. [2]

chromosome A complex of condensed strands of DNA and associated protein molecules, found in the nucleus of cells. [6, App]

chronic traumatic encephalopathy (CTE) Also called *dementia pugilistica* or *punch-drunk*. The dementia that develops in boxers or other athletes who are subjected to repeated blows to the head. [19]

ciliary muscle One of the muscles that controls the shape of the lens inside the eye, focusing an image on the retina. [10]

cilium A hairlike cellular extension. [9]

cingulate cortex Also called *cingulum*. A region of medial cerebral cortex that lies dorsal to the corpus callosum. [8]

cingulate gyrus A cortical portion of the limbic system, found in the frontal and parietal midline. [2]

cingulum See *cingulate cortex*.

circadian rhythm A pattern of behavioral, biochemical, or physiological fluctuation that has a 24-hour period. [14]

circannual Occurring on a roughly annual basis. [14]

circle of Willis A vascular structure at the base of the brain that is formed by the joining of the carotid and basilar arteries. [2]

circumvallate papillae One of three types of small structures on the tongue that contain taste receptors, located in the back of the tongue. [9]

circumventricular organ An organ that lies in the wall of a cerebral ventricle and monitors the composition of body fluids. [13]

CJD See *Creutzfeldt-Jakob disease*.

Cl⁻ See *chloride ion*.

classical conditioning Also called *Pavlovian conditioning*. A type of associative learning in which an originally neutral (conditioned) stimulus acquires the power to elicit the response normally elicited by another (unconditioned) stimulus after the two stimuli are paired. A response elicited by the *unconditioned stimulus* (US) is called an *unconditioned response* (UR); a response elicited by the *conditioned stimulus* (CS) alone is called a *conditioned response* (CR). [17]

claustrum A thin sheet of neurons, situated within the white matter lateral to the basal ganglia, that has been implicated in conscious awareness. [18]

cloacal exstrophy A rare medical condition in which XY individuals are born completely lacking a penis. [12]

clone 1. An asexually produced organism that is genetically identical to the organism it was grown from. [7] 2. To reproduce a gene so that it can be sequenced and/or manipulated. [App]

closed-loop control mechanism A control mechanism that provides a flow of information from whatever is being controlled to the device that controls it. [11]

clozapine An atypical antipsychotic. [16]

CMR1 See *cool-menthol receptor 1*.

CNS See *central nervous system*.

cocaine A drug of abuse, derived from the coca plant, that acts by potentiating catecholamine stimulation. [4]

coccygeal Referring to the lowest spinal vertebra (also called the *tailbone*). [2]

cochlea A snail-shaped structure in the inner ear that contains the primary receptor cells for hearing. [9]

cochlear implant An electromechanical device that detects sounds and selectively stimulates nerves in different regions of the cochlea via surgically implanted electrodes. [9]

cochlear nuclei Brainstem nuclei that receive input from auditory hair cells and send output to the superior olivary complex. [9]

cocktail party effect The selective enhancement of attention in order to filter out distracters, such as while listening to one person talking in the midst of a noisy party. [18]

coding The rules by which action potentials in a sensory system reflect a physical stimulus. [8]

codon A set of three nucleotides that uniquely encodes one particular amino acid. [App]

cognitive attribution model The theory that our emotional experience results from cognitive analysis of the context around us, such that physiological changes may accentuate emotions but not specify which emotion we experience. [15]

cognitive behavioral therapy (CBT) Psychotherapy aimed at correcting negative thinking and improving interpersonal relationships. [16]

cognitive map A mental representation of a spatial relationship. [17]

cognitively impenetrable Referring to data-processing operations of the central nervous system that are unconscious. [18]

coincidence detector A device that senses the co-occurrence of two events. [9]

coitus See *copulation.*

co-localization Also called *co-release.* In neurons, the appearance of more than one neurotransmitter in a given presynaptic terminal. [4]

communication Information transfer between two individuals. [19]

comorbid Referring to the tendency of certain diseases or disorders to occur together in individuals. [16]

competitive ligand A substance that directly competes with the endogenous ligand for the same binding site on a receptor molecule. [4]

complex cortical cell A cell in the visual cortex that responds best to a bar of a particular size and orientation anywhere within a particular area of the visual field. [10]

complex environment See *enriched condition.*

complex partial seizure In epilepsy, a type of seizure that doesn't involve the entire brain and therefore can cause a wide variety of symptoms. [3]

computerized axial tomography (CAT or CT) A noninvasive technique for examining brain structure in humans through computer analysis of X-ray absorption at several positions around the head. [2]

concentration gradient Variation of the concentration of a substance within a region. [3]

concordant Referring to any trait that is seen in both individuals of a pair of twins. [16]

concussion Also called *minor traumatic brain injury* (*mTBI*). An injury resulting from a blow to the head and associated with temporary neurological symptoms such as memory loss or other cognitive impairments, pain, and visual disturbances. [19]

conditional knockout A gene that can be selectively deactivated in specific tissues and/or at a specific stage of development. [17]

conduction aphasia An impairment in the repetition of words and sentences. [19]

conduction deafness A hearing impairment that is associated with pathology of the external-ear or middle-ear cavities. [9]

conduction velocity The speed at which an action potential is propagated along the length of an axon (or section of peripheral nerve). [3]

conduction zone The part of the neuron over which the nerve's electrical signal may be actively propagated. It usually corresponds to the cell's axon. [2]

cones A class of photoreceptor cells in the retina that are responsible for color vision. [10]

confabulate To fill in a gap in memory with a falsification. It often occurs in Korsakoff's syndrome. [17]

congenital adrenal hyperplasia (CAH) Any of several genetic mutations that can result in exposure of a female fetus to adrenal androgens, which results in a clitoris that is larger than normal at birth. [12]

congenital hypothyroidism See *cretinism.*

congenital insensitivity to pain The condition of being born without the ability to perceive pain. [8]

conjunction search A search for an item that is based on two or more features (e.g., size and color) that together distinguish the target from distracters that may share some of the same attributes. [18]

connectionist model of aphasia The theory proposing that Wernicke's area and Broca's area, connected by the arcuate fasciculus, specialize in the receptive and expressive aspects of language, respectively. [19]

connexon A protein assembly that provides an open ion channel between two neurons, forming an electrical synapse between them. [3]

consciousness The state of awareness of one's own existence and experience. [1, 18]

consciously controlled attention See *voluntary attention.*

conserved In the context of evolution, referring to a trait that is passed on from a common ancestor to two or more descendant species. [1]

consolidation A stage of memory formation in which information in short-term or intermediate-term memory is transferred to long-term memory. [17]

constraint-induced movement therapy A therapy for recovery of limb movement after stroke or injury, in which the unaffected limb is constrained while the person is required to perform tasks with the affected contralateral limb. [19]

contralateral In anatomy, pertaining to a location on the opposite side of the body. Compare *ipsilateral.* [2]

convergence The phenomenon of neural connections in which many cells send signals to a single cell. [3]

convergent evolution The evolutionary process by which responses to similar ecological features bring about similarities in behavior or structure among animals that are only distantly related (i.e., that differ in genetic heritage). [6]

Coolidge effect The propensity of an animal that has appeared sexually satiated with a present partner to resume sexual activity when provided with a novel partner. [12]

cool-menthol receptor 1 (CMR1) Also called *TRPM8*. A sensory receptor, found in some free nerve endings, that opens an ion channel in response to a mild temperature drop or exposure to menthol. [8]

copulation Also called *coitus*. The sexual act. [12]

copulatory lock Reproductive behavior in which the male's penis swells after ejaculation so that the male and female are forced to remain joined for 5–15 minutes. It occurs in dogs and some rodents, but not in humans. [12]

co-release See *co-localization*.

cornea The transparent outer layer of the eye, whose curvature is fixed. It bends light rays and is primarily responsible for forming the image on the retina. [10]

coronal plane Also called *frontal plane* or *transverse plane*. The plane that divides the body or brain into front and back parts. Compare *horizontal plane* and *sagittal plane*. [2]

corpora lutea The structures formed from collapsed ovarian follicles subsequent to ovulation. The corpora lutea are a major source of progesterone. [5]

corpus callosum The main band of axons that connects the two cerebral hemispheres. [2]

correlation The covariation of two measures. [1]

cortex See *cerebral cortex*.

cortical column One of the vertical columns that constitute the basic organization of the neocortex. [2]

cortical deafness A hearing impairment that is caused by a fault or defect in the cortex. [9]

corticospinal system See *pyramidal system*.

cortisol A glucocorticoid stress hormone of the adrenal cortex. [5, 15]

cranial nerve A nerve that is connected directly to the brain. [2]

CREB *c*AMP *r*esponsive *e*lement-*b*inding protein. A protein that binds the promoter region of several genes involved in neural plasticity when activated by cyclic AMP (cAMP). [17]

Cre-recombinase A bacterial enzyme normally made by bacteria that recognizes loxP, which is a specific sequence of nucleotides, removes a segment of DNA flanked by two loxP sites, and then recombines the DNA at those loxP sites. [11, App]

cretinism Also called *congenital hypothyroidism*. Reduced stature and intellectual disability caused by thyroid deficiency during early development. [5]

Creutzfeldt-Jakob disease (CJD) A brain disorder in humans, leading to dementia and death, that is caused by improperly folded prion proteins; the human equivalent of mad cow disease. [11]

crib death See *sudden infant death syndrome*.

CRISPR *c*lustered *r*egularly *i*nterspaced *s*hort *p*alindromic *r*epeats. A system of gene manipulation that evolved in single-celled organisms and is exploited by scientists for gene editing. [App]

cross-tolerance A condition in which the development of tolerance for one drug causes an individual to develop tolerance for another drug. [4]

crystallization The final stage of birdsong formation, in which fully formed adult song is achieved. [19]

CSF See *cerebrospinal fluid*.

CT or CAT See *computerized axial tomography*.

CTE See *chronic traumatic encephalopathy*.

cue-induced drug use An increased likelihood to use a drug (especially an addictive drug) because of the presence of environmental stimuli that were present during previous use of the same drug. [4]

cupula A small gelatinous structure, containing hair cells that detect fluid movement within the semicircular canals of the the vestibular system. [9]

curare An alkaloid neurotoxin that causes paralysis by blocking acetylcholine receptors in muscle. [3]

Cushing's syndrome A condition in which levels of adrenal glucocorticoids are abnormally high. [16]

cyclic adenosine monophosphate (cyclic AMP, or cAMP) A second messenger activated in many target cells in response to synaptic or hormonal stimulation. [5]

cyclic guanosine monophosphate (cyclic GMP, or cGMP) A second messenger activated in some target cells in response to synaptic or hormonal stimulation. [5]

cytokine A protein that induces the proliferation of other cells, as in the immune system. [15]

cytoplasm See *intracellular fluid*.

D

DA See *dopamine*.

dB See *decibel*.

DBS See *deep brain stimulation*.

deafness Hearing loss so profound that speech perception is lost. [9]

death gene A gene that is expressed only when a cell becomes committed to natural cell death (apoptosis). [7]

decibel (dB) A measure of sound intensity. [9]

declarative memory A memory that can be stated or described. [17]

decomposition of movement Difficulty of movement in which gestures are broken up into individual segments instead of being executed smoothly. It is a symptom of cerebellar lesions. [11]

decorticate rage Also called *sham rage*. Sudden intense rage characterized by actions (such as snarling and biting in dogs) that lack clear direction. [15]

deep brain stimulation (DBS) Mild electrical stimulation through an electrode that is surgically implanted deep in the brain. [11, 16]

deep dyslexia Acquired dyslexia in which the person reads a word as another word that is semantically related. [19]

default mode network The regions of the brain that are active when the brain is awake and at rest and attention is not being directed to external events. [18]

degradation The chemical breakdown of a neurotransmitter into inactive metabolites. [3, 4]

delayed non-matching-to-sample task A test in which, on each trial, the participant must select the stimulus not seen previously. [17]

Δ9-tetrahydrocannabinol (THC) The major active ingredient in marijuana. [4]

delta wave The slowest type of EEG wave, about 1 Hz, characteristic of stage 3 sleep. [14]

delusion A false belief strongly held in spite of contrary evidence. [16]

dementia Drastic failure of cognitive ability, including memory failure and loss of orientation. [7]

dementia pugilistica See *chronic traumatic encephalopathy.*

dendrite One of the extensions of the cell body that are the receptive surfaces of the neuron. [2]

dendritic knob A portion of an olfactory receptor cell present in the olfactory epithelium. [9]

dendro-dendritic Referring to a synapse in which a synaptic connection forms between the dendrites of two neurons. [3]

dentate gyrus A strip of gray matter in the hippocampal formation. [17]

deoxyribonucleic acid (DNA) A nucleic acid that is present in the chromosomes of cells and encodes hereditary information. [App]

dependence Also called *addiction.* In the context of drugs, the strong desire to self-administer a drug of abuse. [4]

dependent variable The factor that an experimenter measures to monitor a change in response to manipulation of an independent variable. [1]

depolarization A reduction in membrane potential (the interior of the neuron becomes less negative). [3]

depressants A class of drugs that act to reduce neural activity. [4]

depression A psychiatric condition characterized by such symptoms as an unhappy mood; loss of interests, energy, and appetite; and difficulty concentrating. [16]

dermatome A strip of skin innervated by a particular spinal nerve. [8]

dermis The middle layer of skin, between the epidermis and the hypodermis. [8]

designer receptors exclusively activated by designer drugs (DREADDs) Engineered G protein receptors made to respond only to synthetic ligands so that scientists can selectively activate neurons made to express those receptors. [5]

desynchronized EEG Also called *beta activity.* EEG activity seen in wakefulness, comprising a mix of many different high frequencies with low amplitude. [14]

dexamethasone suppression test A test of pituitary-adrenal function in which the participant is given dexamethasone, a synthetic glucocorticoid hormone, which should cause a decline in the production of adrenal corticosteroids. [16]

dfMRI See *dyadic functional MRI.*

DHT See *dihydrotestosterone.*

diabetes mellitus Excessive glucose in the urine, caused by the failure of insulin to induce glucose absorption by the body. [13]

Diablo A protein released by mitochondria, in response to high calcium levels, that activates apoptosis. [7]

dichotic presentation The simultaneous delivery of different stimuli to the right and the left ears. [18, 19]

diencephalon The posterior part of the forebrain, including the thalamus and hypothalamus. [2]

diffusion The spontaneous spread of molecules of one substance among molecules of another substance until a uniform concentration is achieved. [3, 13]

diffusion tensor imaging (DTI) A modified form of MRI in which the diffusion of water in a confined space is exploited to produce images of axonal fiber tracts. [2, 9, 19]

digestion The process by which food is broken down to provide energy and nutrients. [13]

dihydrotestosterone (DHT) The 5α-reduced metabolite of testosterone; a potent androgen that is principally responsible for the masculinization of the external genitalia in mammalian sexual differentiation. [12]

dimer A complex of two proteins that have bound together. [14]

discordant Referring to any trait that is seen in only one individual of a pair of twins. [16]

dishabituation The restoration of response amplitude following habituation. [17]

dissociative drug A type of drug that produces a dreamlike state in which consciousness is partly separated from sensory inputs. [4]

dissociative thinking A condition, seen in schizophrenia, that is characterized by disturbances of thought and difficulty relating events properly. [16]

distal In anatomy, toward the periphery of an organism or the end of a limb. Compare *proximal.* [2]

diurnal Active during the light periods of the daily cycle. [14]

divergence The phenomenon of neural connections in which one cell sends signals to many other cells. [3]

divided-attention task A task in which the participant is asked to simultaneously focus attention on two or more stimuli. [18]

dizygotic Referring to twins derived from separate eggs (*fraternal* twins). Such twins are no more closely related genetically than are other full siblings. [16]

DNA See *deoxyribonucleic acid.*

DNA sequencing The process by which the order of nucleotides in a gene, or amino acids in a protein, is determined. [App]

dopamine (DA) A monoamine transmitter found in the midbrain—especially the substantia nigra—and basal forebrain. [4]

dopamine hypothesis The hypothesis that schizophrenia results from either excessive levels of synaptic dopamine or excessive postsynaptic sensitivity to dopamine. [16]

dorsal In anatomy, toward the back of the body or the top of the brain. Compare *ventral.* [2]

dorsal column nuclei Collection of neurons in the medulla that receive somatosensory information via the dorsal columns of the spinal cord. These neurons send their axons across the midline and to the thalamus. [8]

dorsal column system A somatosensory system that delivers most touch stimuli via the dorsal columns of spinal white matter to the brain. [8]

dorsal root The branch of a spinal nerve, entering the dorsal horn of the spinal cord, that carries sensory information from the peripheral nervous system to the spinal cord. [2]

dose-response curve (DRC) A formal plot of a drug's effects (on the y-axis) versus the dose given (on the x-axis). [4]

Down syndrome A syndrome caused by inheriting an extra copy of chromosome 21, usually accompanied by intellectual disability. [7]

down-regulation A compensatory reduction in receptor availability at the synapses of a neuron. [3, 4]

DRC See *dose-response curve.*

DREADDs See *designer receptors exclusively activated by designer drugs.*

DTI See *diffusion tensor imaging.*

DTI tractography Also called *fiber tracking.* Visualization of the orientation and terminations of white matter tracts in the living brain via diffusion tensor imaging. [2]

dual dependence Dependence for emergent drug effects that occur only when two drugs are taken simultaneously. [4]

dualism Within the concept of separation of soul and body, the notion promoted by René Descartes that the mind is subject only to spiritual interactions while the body is subject only to material interactions. [1]

duplex theory A theory that we localize sound by combining information about intensity differences and latency differences between the two ears. [9]

dura mater The outermost of the three meninges that surround the brain and spinal cord. [2]

dyadic functional MRI (dfMRI) An fMRI technique in which the brains of two interacting individuals are simultaneously imaged. [2]

dynorphins One of three kinds of endogenous opioids, substances that reduce pain perception. [4, 8]

dyskinesia Difficulty or distortion in voluntary movement. [16]

dyslexia A reading disorder attributed to brain impairment. *Acquired dyslexia* occurs as a result of injury or disease. *Developmental dyslexia* is associated with brain abnormalities present from birth. [19]

dysphoria Unpleasant feelings; the opposite of euphoria. [4]

dystrophin A protein that is needed for normal muscle function. [11]

E

ear canal A tube leading from the pinna to the middle ear. [9]

eardrum See *tympanic membrane.*

early-selection model A model of attention in which the attentional bottleneck filters out stimuli before even preliminary perceptual analysis has occurred. [18]

easy problem of consciousness The problem of how to read current conscious experiences directly from people's brains as they're happening. [18]

EC See *enriched condition.*

ecological niche The unique assortment of environmental opportunities and challenges to which each organism is adapted. [6, 14]

Ecstasy See *MDMA.*

ectoderm The outer cellular layer of the developing embryo, giving rise to the skin and the nervous system. [7]

ectopia Something out of place—for example, clusters of neurons seen in unusual positions in the cortex of someone suffering from dyslexia. [19]

ectopic transmission Cell-cell communication based on release of neurotransmitter in regions outside traditional synapses. [3]

ectotherm An animal whose body temperature is regulated by, and whose heat comes mainly from, the environment. Examples include snakes and bees. [13]

edema The swelling of tissue, such as in the brain, in response to injury. [2]

edge detector See *simple cortical cell.*

EEG See *electroencephalogram* and *electroencephalography.*

efferent In reference to axons, carrying information from the central nervous system to the periphery. Compare *afferent.* [2]

efficacy Also called *intrinsic activity.* The extent to which a drug activates a response when it binds to a receptor. [4]

ejaculation The forceful expulsion of semen from the penis. [12]

electrical synapse Also called *gap junction.* The region between neurons where the membranes are so close that changes in potential can flow from one to the other without being translated into a chemical message. [3]

electroencephalogram (EEG) A recording of gross electrical activity of the brain recorded from electrodes placed on the scalp. [3]

electroencephalography (EEG) The recording and study of gross electrical activity of the brain recorded from electrodes placed on the scalp. [14]

electromyography (EMG) The electrical recording of muscle activity. [11, 14]

electro-oculography (EOG) The electrical recording of eye movements. [14]

electrostatic pressure The propensity of charged molecules or ions to move toward areas with the opposite charge. [3]

embryo The earliest stage in a developing animal. [7]

embryonic stem cell A cell, derived from an embryo, that has the capacity to form any type of tissue that a donor might produce. [19]

EMG See *electromyography.*

emotion A subjective mental state that is usually accompanied by distinctive behaviors, feelings, and involuntary physiological changes. [15]

emotional dyscontrol syndrome A condition consisting of temporal lobe disorders that may underlie some forms of human violence. [15]

encephalization factor A measure of brain size relative to body size. [6]

encoding In memory formation, the stage in which the information entering sensory channels is passed into short-term memory. [17]

endocannabinoid An endogenous ligand of cannabinoid receptors, thus an analog of marijuana that is produced by the brain. [4, 13]

endocast A cast of the cranial cavity of a skull, especially useful for studying fossils of extinct species. [6]

endocrine Referring to glands that release chemicals to the interior of the body. These glands secrete the principal hormones. [5]

endocrine gland A gland that secretes hormones into the bloodstream to act on distant targets. [5]

endogenous Produced inside the body. [4]

endogenous ligand Any substance that is produced within the body and selectively binds to the type of receptor that is under study. [3]

endogenous opioids A family of peptide transmitters that have been called the body's own narcotics. The three kinds are enkephalins, endorphins, and dynorphins. [4, 8]

endogenously controlled attention See *voluntary attention.*

endophenotype Behavioral or physical characteristics accompanying susceptibility to a particular disorder, which may be used to identify those at risk. [16]

endorphins One of three kinds of endogenous opioids, substances that reduce pain perception. [4, 8]

endotherm An animal whose body temperature is regulated chiefly by internal metabolic processes. Examples include mammals and birds. [13]

engram The physical basis of a memory in the brain. Sometimes referred to as a *memory trace* on the assumption that it involves changes in a neural circuit rather than a single neuron. [17]

enkephalins One of three kinds of endogenous opioids, substances that reduce pain perception. [4, 8]

enriched condition (EC) Also called *complex environment.* A condition in which laboratory rodents are group-housed with a wide variety of stimulus objects. [17]

enteric nervous system An extensive mesh-like system of neurons that governs the functioning of the gut. [2]

enterotype Each individual's personal composition of gut microbiota. [13]

entrainment The process of synchronizing a biological rhythm to an environmental stimulus. [14]

enzyme A complicated protein whose action increases the probability of a specific chemical reaction. [App]

EOG See *electro-oculography.*

ependymal layer See *ventricular zone.*

epidemiology The statistical study of patterns of disease in a population. [16]

epidermis The outermost layer of skin, over the dermis. [8]

epigenetic regulation Process affecting the expression of a particular gene or genes without affecting the sequence of nucleotides making up the gene itself. [15]

epigenetic transmission The passage of epigenetic modifications of a gene from one generation to another. [13]

epigenetics The study of factors that affect gene expression without making any changes in the nucleotide sequence of the genes themselves. [6, 7]

epilepsy A brain disorder marked by major sudden changes in the electrophysiological state of the brain that are referred to as seizures. [3]

epinephrine Also called *adrenaline.* A compound that acts both as a hormone (secreted by the adrenal medulla under the control of the sympathetic nervous system, which prepares the body for action) and as a synaptic transmitter. [5, 15]

episodic memory Memory of a particular incident or a particular time and place. [17]

EPSP See *excitatory postsynaptic potential.*

equilibrium In a neuron, the state in which the number of ions crossing the cell membrane in one direction is matched by the number crossing in the opposite direction. [3]

equilibrium potential The voltage across a permeable membrane that exactly counteracts the movement of ions from the side with a high concentration to the side with a low concentration. [3]

ERP See *event-related potential.*

estradiol See *17β-estradiol.*

estrogens A class of steroid hormones produced by female gonads. [5]

estrus The period during which female animals are sexually receptive. [12]

eukaryote Any organism whose cells have the genetic material contained within a nuclear envelope. [App]

event-related potential (ERP) Also called *evoked potential.* Averaged EEG recordings measuring brain responses to repeated presentations of a stimulus. [3, 18]

evoked potential See *event-related potential.*

evolution In biology, the process by which a population of interbreeding individuals changes over long periods of time. [6]

evolution by natural selection The Darwinian theory that evolution proceeds by differential success in reproduction. [6]

evolutionary psychology A field devoted to asking how natural selection has shaped behavior in humans and other animals. [6, 15]

excitatory postsynaptic potential (EPSP) A depolarizing potential in the postsynaptic neuron that is caused by excitatory connections. EPSPs increase the probability that the postsynaptic neuron will fire an action potential. [3]

excitotoxicity The property by which neurons die when overstimulated, as with large amounts of glutamate. [4]

executive function A neural and cognitive system that helps develop plans of action and organizes the activities of other high-level processing systems. [18]

exocrine gland A gland whose secretions exit the body via ducts. [5]

exocytosis In neurons, the process by which a synaptic vesicle fuses with the presynaptic terminal membrane to release neurotransmitter into the synaptic cleft. [3]

exogenous Arising from outside the body. [4]

exogenous ligand Any substance that originates outside the body and selectively binds to the type of receptor that is under study. [3]

exogenously controlled attention See *reflexive attention.*

expression The process by which a cell makes an mRNA transcript of a particular gene. [7, App]

external ear The part of the ear that we readily see (the pinna) and the canal that leads to the eardrum. [9]

external fertilization The process by which eggs are fertilized outside of the female's body, as in many fishes and amphibians. [12]

extinction Also called *extinction of simultaneous double stimulation.* In the context of neurology, an inability to recognize the double nature of stimuli presented simultaneously to both sides of the body. People experiencing extinction report the stimulus from only one side. [18]

extracellular compartment The fluid space of the body that exists outside the cells. [13]

extracellular fluid The fluid in the spaces between cells (interstitial fluid) and in the vascular system. [3]

extrafusal fiber One of the ordinary muscle fibers that lie outside the spindles and provide most of the force for muscle contraction. [11]

extraocular muscle One of the muscles attached to the eyeball that control its position and movements. [10]

extrapyramidal system A motor system that includes the basal ganglia and some closely related brainstem structures. [11]

extrastriate cortex Visual cortex outside of the primary visual (striate) cortex. [10]

F

FA See *fractional anisotropy*.

face blindness See *prosopagnosia*.

facial feedback hypothesis The hypothesis that our emotional experience is affected by the sensory feedback we receive during particular facial expressions, such as smiling. [15]

FAS See *fetal alcohol syndrome*.

fast-twitch muscle fiber A type of striated muscle that contracts rapidly but fatigues readily. [11]

fatal familial insomnia An inherited disorder in which humans sleep normally at the beginning of their life but stop sleeping in midlife and die 7–24 months later. [14]

fear conditioning A type of classical conditioning where a previously neutral stimulus is repeatedly paired with shock or some other unpleasant experience, causing the individual to act fearful in response to the stimulus. [15, 16]

feature integration theory The idea that conjunction searches involve multiple cognitive feature maps—overlapping representations of the search array based on individual stimulus attributes. [18]

feature search A search for an item in which the target pops out right away because it possesses a unique attribute. [18]

fecal transplantation A medical procedure in which gut microbiota, via fecal matter, are transferred from a donor to a host. [13]

FEF See *frontal eye field*.

fetal alcohol syndrome (FAS) A disorder, including intellectual disability and characteristic facial anomalies, that affects children exposed to too much alcohol (through maternal ingestion) during fetal development. [4, 7]

fetus A developing individual after the embryo stage. [7]

fiber tracking See *DTI tractography*.

filopodia Very fine, tubular outgrowths from the growth cone of an axon or dendrite. [7]

final common pathway The information-processing pathway consisting of all the motor neurons in the body. Motor neurons are known by this collective term because they receive and integrate all motor signals from the brain and then direct movement accordingly. [11]

flaccid paralysis A loss of reflexes below the level of transection of the spinal cord. [11]

flower spray ending See *secondary sensory ending*.

fluent aphasia Also called *Wernicke's aphasia*. A language impairment characterized by fluent, meaningless speech and little language comprehension. It is related to damage in Wernicke's area. [19]

fMRI See *functional MRI*.

foliate papillae One of three types of small structures on the tongue that contain taste receptors, located along the sides of the tongue. [9]

follicles Ovarian structures containing immature ova. [5]

follicle-stimulating hormone (FSH) A gonadotropin, named for its actions on ovarian follicles. [5]

forebrain Also called *prosencephalon*. The anterior division of the brain, containing the cerebral hemispheres, the thalamus, and the hypothalamus. [2, 7]

fornix A fiber tract that extends from the hippocampus to the mammillary body. [2]

Fourier analysis The mathematical decomposition of a complex pattern into a sum of sine waves. [9]

fourth ventricle The passageway within the pons that receives cerebrospinal fluid from the third ventricle and releases it to surround the brain and spinal cord. [2]

fovea The central portion of the retina, packed with the most photoreceptors and therefore the center of our gaze. [10]

fractional anisotropy (FA) The tendency of water to diffuse more readily along the long axis of an enclosed space, such as an axon. It is the basis of diffusion tensor imaging. [2]

fragile X syndrome A condition that is a frequent cause of inherited intellectual disability. It is produced by a fragile site on the X chromosome that seems prone to breaking because the DNA there is unstable. [7]

free nerve ending An axon that terminates in the skin without any specialized cell associated with it and that detects pain and/or changes in temperature. [8]

free-running Referring to a rhythm of behavior shown by an animal deprived of external cues about time of day. [14]

frequency The number of cycles per second in a sound wave, measured in hertz (Hz). [9]

frontal eye field (FEF) An area in the frontal lobe of the brain containing neurons important for establishing gaze in accordance with cognitive goals (top-down processes) rather than with any characteristics of stimuli (bottom-up processes). [18]

frontal lobe The most anterior portion of the cerebral cortex. [2]

frontal plane See *coronal plane*.

FSH See *follicle-stimulating hormone*.

functional MRI (fMRI) Magnetic resonance imaging that detects changes in blood flow and therefore identifies regions of the brain that are particularly active during a given task. [2]

functional tolerance Decreased responding to a drug after repeated exposures, generally as a consequence of up- or down-regulation of receptors. [4]

fundamental The predominant frequency of an auditory tone or a visual scene. [9]

fungiform papillae One of three types of small structures on the tongue that contain taste receptors, located in the front of the tongue. [9]

fusiform gyrus A region on the inferior surface of the cortex, at the junction of temporal and occipital lobes, that has been associated with recognition of faces. [19]

G

G protein-coupled receptors (GPCRs) Cell surface receptors that, when activated extracellularly, initiate G protein signaling mechanisms inside the cell. **[4]**

G proteins A class of proteins that reside next to the intracellular portion of a receptor and that are activated when the receptor binds an appropriate ligand on the extracellular surface. **[3]**

GABA See *gamma-aminobutyric acid.*

gamete A sex cell (sperm or ovum) that contains only unpaired chromosomes and therefore has only half the usual number of chromosomes in other cells. **[12]**

gamma efferent See *gamma motor neuron.*

gamma motor neuron Also called *gamma efferent.* A motor neuron that innervates the contractile tissue (the intrafusal fiber) in a muscle spindle. **[11]**

gamma-aminobutyric acid (GABA) A widely distributed amino acid transmitter; the main inhibitory transmitter in the mammalian nervous system. **[4]**

ganglion cells A class of cells in the retina whose axons form the optic nerve. **[10]**

gap junction See *electrical synapse.*

gas neurotransmitter A soluble gas, such as nitric oxide or carbon monoxide, that is produced and released by a neuron to alter the functioning of another neuron. **[4]**

gel electrophoresis A method of separating molecules of differing size or electrical charge by forcing them to flow through a gel. **[App]**

gene A length of DNA that encodes the information for constructing a particular protein. **[6, App]**

gene amplification See *polymerase chain reaction.*

general anesthetic A drug that renders an individual unconscious. **[14]**

generator potential See *receptor potential.*

genetics The study of inheritance, including the genes encoded in DNA. **[6]**

genome Also called *genotype.* All the genetic information that one specific individual has inherited. **[7, App]**

genotype See *genome.*

genus A group of species that resemble each other because of shared inheritance. **[6]**

GH See *growth hormone.*

ghrelin A peptide hormone emanating from the gut. **[13]**

glial cells Also called *glia* or *neuroglia.* Nonneuronal brain cells that provide structural, nutritional, and other types of support to the brain. **[2]**

global aphasia The total loss of ability to understand language or to speak, read, or write. **[19]**

globus pallidus One of the basal ganglia. **[2]**

glomerulus A complex arbor of dendrites from a group of olfactory cells. **[9]**

glucagon A hormone, released by alpha cells in the islets of Langerhans, that increases blood glucose. **[13]**

glucocorticoids A class of steroid hormones, released by the adrenal cortex, that affect carbohydrate metabolism and inflammation. **[5]**

glucodetector A cell that detects and informs the nervous system about levels of circulating glucose. **[13]**

gluconeogenesis The metabolism of body fats and proteins to create glucose. **[13]**

glucose A sugar molecule used by the body and brain for energy. **[13]**

glucose transporter A molecule that conducts glucose molecules through the external membrane of a cell for use inside. **[13]**

glutamate An amino acid transmitter, the most common excitatory transmitter. **[4, 8]**

glutamate hypothesis The hypothesis that schizophrenia may be caused, in part, by understimulation of glutamate receptors. **[16]**

glutamatergic Referring to cells that use glutamate as their synaptic transmitter. **[4]**

glycine An amino acid transmitter, often inhibitory. **[4]**

glycogen A complex carbohydrate derived from glucose. **[13]**

glycogenesis The physiological process by which glycogen is produced. **[13]**

glycogenolysis The conversion of glycogen back into glucose, triggered when blood concentrations of glucose drop too low. **[13]**

GnIH See *gonadotropin-inhibiting hormone.*

GnRH See *gonadotropin-releasing hormone.*

goiter A swelling of the thyroid gland resulting from iodine deficiency. **[5]**

Goldman equation An equation predicting the potential difference across a membrane based on the concentrations of ions on opposite sides of the membrane, as well as its relative permeability to each ion. **[3]**

Golgi stain A cell stain that fills a small proportion of neurons with a dense dark product. **[2]**

Golgi tendon organ One of the receptors located in tendons that send action potentials to the central nervous system reporting muscle tension. **[11]**

gonadotropin An anterior pituitary hormone that selectively stimulates the cells of the gonads to produce sex steroids and gametes. **[5]**

gonadotropin-inhibiting hormone (GnIH) A hypothalamic peptide hormone that reduces gonadotropin secretion from the pituitary. **[5]**

gonadotropin-releasing hormone (GnRH) A hypothalamic hormone that controls the release of luteinizing hormone and follicle-stimulating hormone from the pituitary. **[5]**

gonads The sexual organs (ovaries in females, testes in males), which produce gametes for reproduction. **[5]**

grammar All of the rules for usage of a particular language. **[19]**

grand mal seizure See *tonic-clonic seizure.*

granule cell A type of small nerve cell. **[2]**

gray matter Areas of the brain that are dominated by cell bodies and are devoid of myelin. **[2]**

grid cell A neuron that selectively fires when an animal crosses the intersection points of an abstract grid map of the local environment. **[17]**

gRNA See *guide RNA.*

gross neuroanatomy Anatomical features of the nervous system that are apparent to the naked eye. [2]

growth cone The growing tip of an axon or a dendrite. [7]

growth hormone (GH) Also called *somatotropin* or *somatotropic hormone*. A tropic hormone, secreted by the anterior pituitary, that influences the growth of cells and tissues. [5]

guevedoces Literally, "eggs at 12" (in Spanish). A nickname for individuals who are raised as girls but at puberty change appearance and begin behaving as boys do. [12]

guide RNA (gRNA) A strand of RNA designed to hybridize with a targeted nucleotide sequence in DNA in order to guide the Cas9 enzyme to break the DNA at that site. [App]

gustatory system The taste system. [9]

gut microbiota Also called *normal flora*. The microorganisms that normally inhabit the digestive tract. [13]

gyrus A ridged or raised portion of a convoluted brain surface. [2]

H

habituation A form of nonassociative learning in which an organism becomes less responsive following repeated presentations of a stimulus. [17]

hair cell A cochlear auditory receptor cell. [9]

hallucinogens A class of drugs that alter sensory perception and produce peculiar experiences. [4]

halorhodopsin A protein that, in response to light of the proper wavelength, opens a channel to admit chloride ions, which results in inhibition of neurons. [3]

hard problem of consciousness The problem of how to read people's subjective experience of consciousness and determine the qualia that accompany perception. [18]

harmonics Multiples of a particular frequency called the *fundamental*. [9]

health psychology Also called *behavioral medicine*. A field that studies psychological influences on health-related processes, such as why people become ill or how they remain healthy. [15]

hearing loss Decreased sensitivity to sound, in varying degrees. [9]

Hebbian synapse A synapse that is strengthened when it successfully drives the postsynaptic cell. [7, 17]

hemiparesis Weakness of one side of the body. [19]

hemiplegia Partial paralysis involving one side of the body. [19]

hemispatial neglect A syndrome in which the person fails to pay any attention to objects presented to one side of the body and may even deny connection with that side. [18]

hermaphrodite An individual possessing the reproductive organs of both sexes, either simultaneously or at different points in time. [12]

heroin Diacetylmorphine; an artificially modified, very potent form of morphine. [4]

hertz (Hz) Cycles per second, as of an auditory stimulus. [9]

hindbrain Also called *rhombencephalon*. The rear division of the brain, which in the mature vertebrate contains the cerebellum, pons, and medulla. [2, 7]

hippocampus A medial temporal lobe structure that is important for learning and memory. [2, 17]

histology The scientific study of the composition of tissues. [2]

homeostatic Referring to the active process of maintaining a particular physiological parameter relatively constant. [13]

hominin The subgroup of Hominidae that contains modern humans and their ancestral species. [6]

homology A physical resemblance that is based on common ancestry, such as the similarity in forelimb structures of different mammals. [6]

homoplasy A physical resemblance between physical or behavioral characteristics due to convergent evolution, such as the similar body forms of tuna and dolphins. [6]

horizontal cells Specialized retinal neurons that contact both the receptor cells and the bipolar cells. [10]

horizontal plane The plane that divides the body or brain into upper and lower parts. Compare *coronal plane* and *sagittal plane*. [2]

hormone A chemical secreted by cells that is conveyed by the bloodstream and regulates target organs or tissues. [5]

hostility In psychology, the angry, antagonistic personality characteristic associated with a greater risk for heart disease. [15]

hue A dimension of light perception, varying around the color circle through blue, green, yellow, orange, and red. [10]

hunger The internal state of an animal seeking food. [13]

huntingtin A protein produced by a gene (called *HTT*) that, when containing too many trinucleotide repeats, results in Huntington's disease in a carrier. [11]

Huntington's disease Also called *Huntington's chorea*. A progressive genetic disorder characterized by abrupt, involuntary movements and profound changes in mental functioning. [11]

hybridization The process by which a string of nucleotides becomes linked to a complementary series of nucleotides. [App]

hyperphagia Excessive eating. [13]

hyperpolarization An increase in membrane potential (the interior of the neuron becomes even more negative). [3]

hypertonic Referring to a solution with a higher concentration of salt than that found in interstitial fluid and blood plasma (more than about 0.9% salt). [13]

hypocretins See *orexins*.

hypodermis Also called *subcutaneous tissue*. The innermost layer of skin, under the dermis. [8]

hypofrontality hypothesis The hypothesis that schizophrenia may result from underactivation of the frontal lobes. [16]

hypophyseal portal system A system of capillaries spanning between the neurosecretory cells of the hypothalamus and the secretory tissue of the anterior pituitary. [5]

hypophysis See *pituitary gland*.

hypothalamus Part of the diencephalon, lying ventral to the thalamus. [2]

hypotonic Referring to a solution with a lower concentration of salt than that found in interstitial fluid and blood plasma (less than about 0.9% salt). [13]

hypovolemic thirst A desire to ingest fluids that is stimulated by a reduced volume of extracellular fluid. [13]

hypoxia A lack of oxygen. [7]

Hz See *hertz*.

I

IAPs See *inhibitors of apoptosis proteins.*

IC See *impoverished condition.*

ideational apraxia An impairment in the ability to carry out a sequence of actions, even though each element or step can be done correctly. [11]

ideomotor apraxia The inability to carry out a simple motor activity in response to a verbal command, even though this same activity is readily performed spontaneously. [11]

IHC See *immunohistochemistry* and *inner hair cell.*

immunocytochemistry (ICC) A method for detecting a particular protein in tissues in which an antibody recognizes and binds to the protein and then chemical methods are used to leave a visible reaction product around each antibody. [5, App]

immunoglobulin See *antibody.*

immunohistochemistry (IHC) A technique in which labeled antibodies are used to visualize the histological distribution of specific proteins. [2]

impoverished condition (IC) Also called *isolated condition.* A condition in which a laboratory rodent is housed singly in a small cage without complex stimuli. [17]

in situ hybridization A method to detect cells that express specific messenger RNA transcripts by using a labeled nucleotide probe that is complementary to, and will therefore hybridize with, the transcript of interest. [2, 5, App]

in vitro Literally, "in glass" (in Latin). Outside the body, usually in a laboratory dish. [7]

inattentional blindness The failure to perceive nonattended stimuli that seem so obvious as to be impossible to miss. [18]

incus Latin for "anvil." A middle-ear bone situated between the malleus and the stapes. [9]

independent variable The factor that is manipulated by an experimenter. [1]

indifferent gonads The undifferentiated gonads of the early vertebrate fetus, which will eventually develop into either testes or ovaries. [12]

individual response stereotypy The tendency of individuals to show the same response pattern to particular situations throughout their life span. [15]

indoleamine neurotransmitters A class of monoamines, including serotonin and melatonin, that serve as neurotransmitters. [4]

induction The process by which one set of cells influences the fate of neighboring cells, usually by secreting a chemical factor that changes gene expression in the target cells. [7]

inferior In anatomy, pertaining to the lower of two locations. Compare *superior.* [2]

inferior colliculi Paired gray matter structures of the dorsal midbrain that receive auditory information. [2, 9]

infradian Referring to a rhythmic biological event whose period is longer than that of a circadian rhythm—that is, longer than a day. [14]

infrasound Very low-frequency sound, generally below the threshold for human hearing (about 20 Hz). [9]

infundibulum See *pituitary stalk.*

inhibition of return The phenomenon in which detection of stimuli at the former location of a cue is impaired for latencies of 200 ms or more. [18]

inhibitors of apoptosis proteins (IAPs) A family of proteins that inhibit caspases and thereby stave off apoptosis. [7]

inhibitory postsynaptic potential (IPSP) A hyperpolarizing potential in the postsynaptic neuron that is caused by inhibitory connections. IPSPs decrease the probability that the postsynaptic neuron will fire an action potential. [3]

inner ear The cochlea and vestibular apparatus. [9]

inner hair cell (IHC) One of the two types of cochlear receptor cells for hearing. [9]

innervate To provide neural input. [2]

innervation ratio The ratio expressing the number of muscle fibers innervated by a single motor axon. [11]

inositol triphosphate (IP3) A member of a class of second-messenger compounds (*phosphoinositides*) common in postsynaptic cells. [5]

input zone The part of a neuron that receives information from other neurons or from specialized sensory structures, usually corresponding to the cell's dendrites. [2]

instrumental conditioning See *operant conditioning.*

insula A region of cortex lying below the surface, within the lateral sulcus, of the frontal, temporal, and parietal lobes. [4]

insulin A hormone, released by beta cells in the islets of Langerhans, that lowers blood glucose. [13]

integration zone The part of the neuron that initiates nerve electrical activity, usually corresponding to the neuron's axon hillock. It is described in detail in Chapter 3. [2]

intellectual disability A disability characterized by significant limitations in intellectual functioning and adaptive behavior. [7]

intensity differences Perceived differences in loudness between the two ears, which can be used to localize a sound source. [9]

intermale aggression Aggression between males of the same species. [15]

intermediate long-term memory A form of memory that lasts longer than short-term memory, but not as long as long-term memory. [17]

internal fertilization The process by which sperm fertilize eggs inside the female's body, as in all mammals, birds, and reptiles. [12]

interneuron A neuron that is neither a sensory neuron nor a motor neuron but receives input from and sends output to other neurons. [2]

intersex Referring to an individual with atypical genital development and sexual differentiation that generally resembles a form intermediate between typical male and typical female genitals. [12]

intracellular compartment The fluid space of the body that is contained within cells. [13]

intracellular fluid Also called *cytoplasm.* The watery solution found within cells. [3]

intrafusal fiber One of the small muscle fibers that lie within each muscle spindle. [11]

intraparietal sulcus (IPS) A region in the human parietal lobe, homologous with the monkey lateral intraparietal area, that is especially involved in voluntary, top-down control of attention. [18]

intrinsic activity See *efficacy.*

intromission Insertion of the erect penis into the vagina during copulation. [12]

inverse agonist A substance that binds to a receptor and causes it to do the opposite of what the naturally occurring transmitter does. [4]

ion An atom or molecule that has acquired an electrical charge by gaining or losing one or more electrons. [3]

ion channel A pore in the cell membrane that permits the passage of certain ions through the membrane when the channel is open. [3]

ionotropic receptor A receptor protein that includes an ion channel that is opened when the receptor is bound by an agonist. [3, 4]

IP3 See *inositol triphosphate.*

IPS See *intraparietal sulcus.*

ipsilateral In anatomy, pertaining to a location on the same side of the body. Compare *contralateral.* [2]

IPSP See *inhibitory postsynaptic potential.*

iris The circular structure of the eye that provides an opening to form the pupil. [10]

isolated brain Sometimes referred to by the French term *encéphale isolé.* An experimental preparation in which an animal's brainstem has been separated from the spinal cord by a cut below the medulla. [14]

isolated condition See *impoverished condition.*

isolated forebrain Sometimes referred to by the French term *cerveau isolé.* An experimental preparation in which an animal's nervous system has been cut in the upper midbrain, dividing the forebrain from the brainstem. [14]

isotonic Referring to a solution with a concentration of salt that is the same as that found in interstitial fluid and blood plasma (about 0.9% salt). [13]

J

James-Lange theory The theory that our experience of emotion is a response to the physiological changes that accompany it. [15]

K

K complex A sharp negative EEG potential that is seen in stage 2 sleep. [14]

K⁺ See *potassium ion.*

ketamine A dissociative anesthetic drug, similar to PCP, that acts as an NMDA receptor antagonist. [4, 16]

ketones A metabolic fuel source liberated by the breakdown of body fats and proteins. [13]

khat Also spelled *qat.* An African shrub that, when chewed, acts as a stimulant. [4]

kindling A method of experimentally inducing an epileptic seizure by repeatedly stimulating a brain region. [3]

kisspeptin A hypothalamic peptide hormone that increases gonadotropin secretion by facilitating the release of gonadotropin-releasing hormone. [5]

Klüver-Bucy syndrome A condition, brought about by bilateral amygdala damage, that is characterized by dramatic emotional changes including reduction in fear and anxiety. [15]

knee-jerk reflex A variant of the stretch reflex in which stretching of the tendon below the knee leads to an upward kick of the leg. [3]

knockout organism An individual in which a particular gene has been disabled by an experimenter. [5, 7]

Korsakoff's syndrome A memory disorder, related to a thiamine deficiency, that is generally associated with chronic alcoholism. [17]

L

labeled lines The concept that each nerve input to the brain reports only a particular type of information. [8, 9]

lamellated corpuscle See *Pacinian corpuscle.*

language The most sophisticated form of communication, in which a set of arbitrary sounds, tokens, or symbols can be arranged according to a grammar in order to convey an almost limitless variety of concepts. [19]

latency differences Differences between the two ears in the time of arrival of a sound, which can be employed by the nervous system to localize sound sources. [9]

latent learning Learning that has taken place but has not (yet) been demonstrated by performance. [17]

lateral In anatomy, toward the side of the body. Compare *medial.* [2]

lateral geniculate nucleus (LGN) The part of the thalamus that receives information from the optic tract and sends it to visual areas in the occipital cortex. [10]

lateral hypothalamus (LH) A hypothalamic region involved in the control of appetite and other functions. [13]

lateral inhibition The phenomenon by which interconnected neurons inhibit their neighbors, producing contrast at the edges of regions. [10]

lateral intraparietal area (LIP) A region in the monkey parietal lobe, homologous with the human intraparietal sulcus, that is especially involved in voluntary, top-down control of attention. [18]

lateral sulcus See *Sylvian fissure.*

lateral ventricle A complexly shaped lateral portion of the ventricular system within each hemisphere of the brain. [2]

lateralization The tendency for the right and left halves of a system to differ from one another. [19]

lateral-line system A sensory system, found in many kinds of fishes and some amphibians, that informs the animal of water motion in relation to the body surface. [9]

late-selection model A model of attention in which the attentional bottleneck filters out stimuli only after substantial analysis has occurred. [18]

L-dopa The immediate precursor of the transmitter dopamine. [11]

learned helplessness In the context of experimentation, a learning paradigm in which individuals are subjected to inescapable, unpleasant conditions. [16]

learning The process of acquiring new and relatively enduring information, behavior patterns, or abilities, characterized by modifications of behavior as a result of practice, study, or experience. [17]

lens A structure in the eye that helps focus an image on the retina. [10]

leptin A peptide hormone released by fat cells. [13]

lesions Regions of damage. [2]

levels of analysis The scope of experimental approaches. A scientist may try to understand behavior by monitoring molecules, nerve cells, brain regions, or social environments, or some combination of these levels of analysis. [1]

LGN See *lateral geniculate nucleus*.

LH See *lateral hypothalamus* and *luteinizing hormone*.

lie detector See *polygraph*.

ligand A substance that binds to receptor molecules, such as those at the surface of the cell. [3, 4]

ligand-gated ion channel Also called *chemically gated ion channel*. An ion channel that opens or closes in response to the presence of a particular chemical. [3]

limbic system A loosely defined, widespread group of brain nuclei that innervate each other to form a network. These nuclei are implicated in emotions. [2, 15]

LIP See *lateral intraparietal area*.

lipid bilayer The structure of the neuronal cell membrane, which consists of two layers of lipid molecules. Various specialized proteins, such as ion channels and receptors, are embedded within the membrane. [3]

lipids Large molecules (commonly called *fats*) consisting of fatty acids and glycerol that are insoluble in water. [13]

lithium An element that, when administered as a drug, often relieves the symptoms of bipolar disorder. [16]

lobotomy The surgical detachment of a portion of the frontal lobe from the rest of the brain. It was once used as a treatment for schizophrenia and many other ailments. [16]

local anesthetic A drug, such as procaine or lidocaine, that blocks sodium channels to stop neural transmission in pain fibers. [4]

local potential An electrical potential that is initiated by stimulation at a specific site and that is a graded response that spreads passively across the cell membrane, decreasing in strength with time and distance. [3]

locus coeruleus Literally, "blue spot." A small nucleus in the brainstem whose neurons produce norepinephrine. [4]

long-term memory (LTM) An enduring form of memory that lasts days, weeks, months, or years and has a very large capacity. [17]

long-term potentiation (LTP) A stable and enduring increase in the effectiveness of synapses following repeated strong stimulation. [17]

lordosis A female receptive posture in quadrupeds in which the hindquarters are raised and the tail is turned to one side, facilitating intromission by the male. [12]

Lou Gehrig's disease See *amyotrophic lateral sclerosis*.

loudness The subjective experience of the pressure level of a sound. [9]

loxP A specific sequence of nucleotides recognized by the enzyme Cre-recombinase. If the enzyme encounters a pair of loxP sites in a gene, it will remove the DNA between the two sites and recombine the gene, usually rendering the gene product dysfunctional. [11, App]

LSD Also called *acid*. Lysergic acid diethylamide, a hallucinogenic drug. [4]

LTM See *long-term memory*.

LTP See *long-term potentiation*.

lumbar Referring to the five spinal segments that make up the upper part of the lower back. [2]

luteinizing hormone (LH) A gonadotropin, named for its stimulatory effects on the ovarian corpora lutea. [5]

M

M1 See *primary motor cortex*.

macular degeneration A progressive loss of central vision due to death or obstruction of photoreceptors in the retina. [10]

mad cow disease See *bovine spongiform encephalopathy*.

magnetic resonance imaging (MRI) A noninvasive technique that uses magnetic energy to generate images that reveal some structural details in the living brain. [2]

magnetoencephalography (MEG) A passive and noninvasive functional brain-imaging technique that measures the tiny magnetic fields produced by active neurons, in order to identify regions of the brain that are particularly active during a given task. [2]

magnocellular Referring to relatively large cells. [10]

malleus Latin for "hammer." A middle-ear bone that is connected to the tympanic membrane. [9]

mammillary body One of a pair of nuclei at the base of the brain that connect to the hippocampus and play a role in memory. [2, 17]

MAO See *monoamine oxidase*.

marijuana Dried leaves and flowers of the plant *Cannabis sativa*, typically smoked to obtain THC for a psychoactive effect. [4, 8]

MBSR See *mindfulness-based stress reduction*.

MC4Rs See *melanocortin type-4 receptors*.

MD See *muscular dystrophy*.

MDMA Also called *Ecstasy*. A drug of abuse, 3,4-methylenedioxymethamphetamine. [4]

medial In anatomy, toward the middle of an organism. Compare *lateral*. [2]

medial amygdala A portion of the amygdala that receives olfactory and pheromonal information. [12]

medial forebrain bundle A collection of axons traveling in the midline region of the forebrain. [15]

medial geniculate nuclei Nuclei in the thalamus that receive input from the inferior colliculi and send output to the auditory cortex. [9]

medial preoptic area (mPOA) A region of the anterior hypothalamus implicated in the control of many behaviors, including thermoregulation, sexual behavior, and gonadotropin secretion. [12]

median eminence Midline feature on the base of the brain marking the point at which the pituitary stalk exits the hypothalamus to connect to the pituitary. It contains elements of the hypophyseal portal system. [5]

medulla Also called *myelencephalon*. The posterior part of the hindbrain, continuous with the spinal cord. [2]

medullary reticular formation The hindmost portion of the brainstem reticular formation, implicated in motor control and copulatory behavior. [12]

MEG See *magnetoencephalography*.

Meissner's corpuscle A skin receptor cell type that detects light touch. [8]

melanocortin type-4 receptors (MC4Rs) A specific subtype of melanocortin receptor. [13]

melanocortins One category of endogenous opioid peptides. [13]

melanopsin A photopigment found within particular retinal ganglion cells that project to the suprachiasmatic nucleus. [14]

melatonin An amine hormone that is released by the pineal gland. [5]

memory 1. The ability to retain information, based on the mental process of learning or encoding, retention across some interval of time, and retrieval or reactivation of the memory. 2. The specific information that is stored in the brain. [17]

meninges The three protective sheets of tissue—dura mater, pia mater, and arachnoid—that surround the brain and spinal cord. [2]

meningiomas Several classes of noncancerous tumors arising from the meninges. [2]

meningitis An acute inflammation of the meninges, usually caused by a viral or bacterial infection. [2]

Merkel's disc A skin receptor cell type that detects fine touch. [8]

mesencephalon See *midbrain*.

mesolimbocortical pathway A set of dopaminergic axons arising in the midbrain and innervating the limbic system and cortex. [4]

mesostriatal pathway A set of dopaminergic axons arising from the midbrain and innervating the basal ganglia, including those from the substantia nigra to the striatum. [4]

messenger RNA (mRNA) A strand of RNA that carries the code of a section of a DNA strand to the cytoplasm. [App]

metabolic tolerance The form of drug tolerance that arises when repeated exposure to the drug causes the metabolic machinery of the body to become more efficient at clearing the drug. [4]

metabotropic receptor A receptor protein that does not contain an ion channel but may, when activated, use a G protein system to alter the functioning of the postsynaptic cell. [3, 4]

metencephalon A subdivision of the hindbrain that includes the cerebellum and the pons. [2]

methylation A chemical modification of DNA that does not affect the nucleotide sequence of a gene but makes that gene less likely to be expressed. [7]

microbiome The collective term for the population of microbes found in the gut. [13]

microelectrode An especially small electrode used to record electrical potentials from living cells. [3]

microglial cells Also called *microglia*. Extremely small glial cells that remove cellular debris from injured or dead cells. [2]

micropolygyria A condition of the brain in which small regions are characterized by more gyri than usual. [19]

midbrain Also called *mesencephalon*. The middle division of the brain. [2, 7]

middle canal See *scala media*.

middle cerebral arteries Two large arteries, arising from the internal carotid arteries, that provide blood to most of the lateral surfaces of the cerebral hemispheres. [2]

middle ear The cavity between the tympanic membrane and the cochlea. [9]

migraines Intense headaches, typically perceived from one half of the head, that recur regularly and can be difficult to treat. [8]

milk letdown reflex The reflexive release of milk in response to suckling or to stimuli associated with suckling. [5]

millivolt (mV) A thousandth of a volt. [3]

mindfulness-based stress reduction (MBSR) A therapy to reduce stress that pairs relaxation with efforts to focus attention on the present moment, rather than past or future problems. [15]

mineralocorticoids A class of steroid hormones, released by the adrenal cortex, that affect ion concentrations in body tissues. [5]

minimal discriminable frequency difference The smallest change in frequency that can be detected reliably between two tones. [9]

minor traumatic brain injury (mTBI) See *concussion*.

mirror neuron A neuron that is active both when an individual makes a particular movement and when that individual sees another individual make that same movement. [10, 11]

mitochondrion A cellular organelle that provides metabolic energy for the cell's processes. [2]

mitosis The process of division of somatic cells that involves duplication of DNA. [7]

mitral cell A type of cell in the olfactory bulb that conducts smell information from the glomeruli to the rest of the brain. [9]

modulatory site A portion of a receptor that, when bound by a compound, alters the receptor's response to its transmitter. [4]

monoamine hormones See *amine hormones*.

monoamine hypothesis The hypothesis that depression is caused by reduced activity of one or more monoamine transmitters, such as serotonin. [16]

monoamine oxidase (MAO) An enzyme that breaks down and thereby inactivates monoamine transmitters. [4, 16]

monocular deprivation Depriving one eye of light. [7]

monopolar neuron See *unipolar neuron*.

monozygotic Referring to twins derived from a single fertilized egg (*identical* twins). Such individuals have the same genotype. [16]

morpheme The smallest grammatical unit of a language; a word or meaningful part of a word. [19]

morphine An opiate compound derived from the poppy flower. [4]

motion sickness The experience of nausea brought on by unnatural passive movement, as in a car or boat. [9]

motivation With respect to homeostasis, a psychological drive state that prompts behaviors that restore balance. [13]

motoneuron See *motor neuron*.

motor nerve A nerve that conveys neural activity to muscle tissue and causes it to contract. [2]

motor neuron Also called *motoneuron*. A neuron in the brain or spinal cord that transmits motor messages, stimulating a muscle or gland. [2, 11]

motor plan Also called *motor program*. A plan for action in the nervous system. [11]

motor program See *motor plan*.

motor protein A specialized kinetic protein molecule that conveys a load, such as a vesicle, from one location to another within a cell. [2]

motor theory of language The theory proposing that the left-hemisphere language zones are motor control systems that are concerned with both the precise production and the perception of the extremely complex movements that go into speech. [19]

motor unit A single motor axon and all the muscle fibers that it innervates. [11]

mPOA See *medial preoptic area*.

MRI See *magnetic resonance imaging*.

mRNA See *messenger RNA*.

mTBI See *concussion*.

müllerian ducts A duct system in the embryo that will develop into female reproductive structures (oviduct, uterus, and inner vagina) if testes are not present. [12]

multiple sclerosis Literally, "many scars." A disorder characterized by widespread degeneration of myelin. [2, 7]

multipolar neuron A nerve cell that has many dendrites and a single axon. [2]

muscarinic Referring to cholinergic receptors that respond to the chemical muscarine as well as to acetylcholine. [4]

muscle fiber A collection of large cylindrical cells, making up most of a muscle, that can contract in response to neurotransmitter released from a motor neuron. [11]

muscle spindle A muscle receptor that lies parallel to a muscle and sends action potentials to the central nervous system when the muscle is stretched. [11]

muscular dystrophy (MD) A disease that leads to degeneration of and functional changes in muscles. [11]

musth An annual period of heightened aggressiveness and sexual activity in male elephants. [12]

mutation A change in the nucleotide sequence of a gene as a result of unfaithful replication. [6, 7]

mV See *millivolt*.

myasthenia gravis A disorder characterized by a profound weakness of skeletal muscles, caused by a loss of acetylcholine receptors. [11]

myelencephalon See *medulla*.

myelin The fatty insulation around an axon, formed by glial cells, that improves the speed of conduction of action potentials. [2]

myelination The process of myelin formation. [2, 7]

myopia Nearsightedness; the inability to focus the retinal image of objects that are far away. [10]

myosin A protein that, along with actin, mediates the contraction of muscle fibers. [11]

N

N1 effect A negative deflection of the event-related potential, occurring about 100 ms after stimulus presentation, that is enhanced for selectively attended input, compared with ignored input. [18]

Na⁺ See *sodium ion*.

naloxone A potent antagonist of opiates that is often administered to people who have taken drug overdoses. It blocks receptors for endogenous opioids. [8]

narcolepsy A disorder that involves frequent, intense episodes of sleep, which last from 5 to 30 minutes and can occur anytime during the usual waking hours. [14]

natriuretic polypeptide B (Nppb) A peptide neurotransmitter used by neurons reporting itch to the spinal cord. [8]

naturalist A student of the forms and classification of organisms. [6]

Na$_V$1.7 Also called *SCN9A*. A voltage-gated sodium channel used almost exclusively by nociceptors to initiate action potentials. [8]

NE See *norepinephrine*.

negative feedback The property by which some of the output of a system feeds back to reduce the effect of input signals. [5, 13]

negative polarity A negative electrical-potential difference relative to a reference electrode. [3]

negative symptom In psychiatry, a symptom that reflects insufficient functioning. Examples include emotional and social withdrawal, blunted affect, and slowness and impoverishment of thought and speech. [16]

neocortex Cerebral cortex that is made up of six distinct layers. [6]

neologism An entirely novel word, sometimes produced by a person with aphasia. [19]

neonatal Referring to newborns. [12]

Nernst equation An equation predicting the equilibrium potential for a given ion based on the concentrations of the ion on opposite sides of a permeable membrane. [3]

nerve A collection of axons bundled together outside the central nervous system. [2]

nerve cell See *neuron*.

nerve growth factor (NGF) A substance that markedly affects the growth of neurons in spinal ganglia and in the ganglia of the sympathetic nervous system. [7]

neural chain A simple kind of neural circuit in which neurons are attached linearly, end to end. [3]

neural groove In the developing embryo, the groove between the neural folds. [7]

neural plasticity See *neuroplasticity*.

neural tube An embryonic structure with subdivisions that correspond to the future forebrain, midbrain, and hindbrain. [2, 7]

neurochemistry The branch of neuroscience concerned with the fundamental chemical composition and processes of the nervous system. [4]

neurocrine Referring to secretory functions of neurons, especially pertaining to synapse transmission. [5]

neuroeconomics The study of brain mechanisms at work during decision making. [18]

neuroendocrine cell Also called *neurosecretory cell*. A neuron that releases hormones into local or systemic circulation. [5]

neurofibrillary tangle An abnormal whorl of neurofilaments within nerve cells. [7]

neurogenesis The mitotic division of nonneuronal cells to produce neurons. [7]

neuroglia See *glial cells.*

neurohypophysis See *posterior pituitary.*

neuroleptics See *antipsychotics.*

neuromodulator A substance that influences the activity of synaptic transmitters. [5]

neuromuscular junction (NMJ) The region where the motor neuron terminal and the adjoining muscle fiber meet; the point where the nerve transmits its message to the muscle fiber. [11]

neuron Also called *nerve cell.* The basic unit of the nervous system, each composed of a cell body, receptive extension(s) (dendrites), and a transmitting extension (axon). [1, 2]

neuron doctrine The hypothesis that the brain is composed of separate cells that are distinct structurally, metabolically, and functionally. [2]

neuropathic pain Pain caused by damage to peripheral nerves. It is often difficult to treat. [8]

neuropeptide Also called *peptide neurotransmitter.* A peptide that is used by neurons for signaling. [5]

neuropeptide Y (NPY) A peptide neurotransmitter that may carry some of the signals for feeding. [13]

neuropharmacology Also called *psychopharmacology.* The scientific field concerned with the discovery and study of compounds that selectively affect the functioning of the nervous system. [4]

neurophysiology The study of electrical and chemical processes in neurons. [3]

neuroplasticity Also called *neural plasticity.* The ability of the nervous system to change in response to experience or the environment. [1, 2, 17]

neuroscience The study of the nervous system. [1]

neurosecretory cell See *neuroendocrine cell.*

neurosteroids Steroid molecules produced within the brain that affect neurons. [4, 5]

neurotransmitter Also called *synaptic transmitter, chemical transmitter,* or simply *transmitter.* The chemical released from the presynaptic axon terminal that serves as the basis of communication between neurons. [2, 3]

neurotrophic factor Also called *trophic factor.* A target-derived chemical that acts as if it "feeds" certain neurons to help them survive. [7, 13]

neurotrophins A family of proteins, including NGF and BDNF, that prevent different classes of neurons from dying. [7]

NGF See *nerve growth factor.*

nicotine A compound found in plants, including tobacco, that acts as an agonist on a large class of cholinergic receptors. [4]

nicotinic Referring to cholinergic receptors that respond to nicotine as well as to acetylcholine. [4]

night terror A sudden arousal from stage 3 slow-wave sleep that is marked by intense fear and autonomic activation. [14]

nightmare A long, frightening dream that awakens the sleeper from REM sleep. [14]

Nissl stain A cell stain that reveals all cell bodies by staining RNA. [2]

nitric oxide (NO) A soluble gas that serves as a retrograde gas neurotransmitter in the nervous system. [4]

NMDA receptor A glutamate receptor that also binds the glutamate agonist NMDA (*N*-methyl-D-aspartate) and that is both ligand-gated and voltage-sensitive. [17]

NMJ See *neuromuscular junction.*

NO See *nitric oxide.*

nociceptor A receptor that responds to stimuli that produce tissue damage or pose the threat of damage. [8]

nocturnal Active during the dark periods of the daily cycle. [14]

node of Ranvier A gap between successive segments of the myelin sheath where the axon membrane is exposed. [2, 3]

nonassociative learning A type of learning in which presentation of a particular stimulus alters the strength or probability of a response according to the strength and temporal spacing of that stimulus. It includes habituation and sensitization. [17]

noncompetitive ligand Also called *neuromodulator.* A substance that alters the response to an endogenous ligand without interacting with the endogenous ligand's recognition site. [4]

nondeclarative memory Also called *procedural memory.* A memory that is shown by performance rather than by conscious recollection. [17]

nondirected synapse A type of synapse in which the presynaptic and postsynaptic cells are not in close apposition; instead, neurotransmitter is released by axonal varicosities and diffuses away to affect wide regions of tissue. [3]

nonfluent aphasia Also called *Broca's aphasia.* A language impairment characterized by difficulty with speech production but not with language comprehension. It is related to damage in Broca's area. [19]

nonfluent speech Talking with considerable effort, short sentences, and the absence of the usual melodic character of conversational speech. [19]

nongenomic effect An effect of a steroid hormone that is not mediated by direct changes in gene expression. [5]

nonprimary motor cortex Frontal lobe regions adjacent to the primary motor cortex that contribute to motor control and modulate the activity of the primary motor cortex. [11]

nonprimary sensory cortex See *secondary sensory cortex.*

non-REM (NREM) sleep Stage of sleep without rapid eye movements. In humans this is divided into stages 1, 2, and 3 sleep. [14]

nootropics A class of drugs that enhance cognitive function. [17]

noradrenaline See *norepinephrine.*

noradrenergic Referring to systems using norepinephrine (noradrenaline) as a transmitter. [4]

norepinephrine (NE) Also called *noradrenaline.* A chemical that acts as a transmitter in the brain and sympathetic nervous system, and also as a circulating adrenal hormone that prepares the body for action. [2, 4, 5, 15]

normal flora See *gut microbiota.*

Northern blot A method of detecting a particular RNA transcript in a tissue or organ by separating RNA from that source with gel electrophoresis, blotting the separated RNAs onto nitrocellulose, and then using a nucleotide probe to hybridize with, and highlight, the transcript of interest. [App]

notochord A midline structure arising early in the embryonic development of vertebrates. [7]

Nppb See *natriuretic polypeptide B.*

NPY See *neuropeptide Y.*

NPY neurons Neurons involved in the hypothalamic appetite control system, so named because they produce neuropeptide Y (NPY) along with agouti-related peptide (AgRP). [13]

NREM 1 See *stage 1 sleep.*

NREM 2 See *stage 2 sleep.*

NREM 3 See *slow-wave sleep.*

NREM sleep See *non-REM (NREM) sleep.*

NST See *nucleus of the solitary tract.*

nucleotide A portion of a DNA or RNA molecule that is composed of a single base and the adjoining sugar-phosphate unit of the strand. [App]

nucleus 1. A collection of neurons within the central nervous system (e.g., the caudate nucleus). [2] 2. The spherical central structure of a cell that contains the chromosomes. [App]

nucleus accumbens A region of the forebrain that receives dopaminergic innervation from the ventral tegmental area. [4]

nucleus of the solitary tract (NST) A brainstem nucleus that receives visceral and taste information via several cranial nerves. [13]

nutrient A chemical that is needed for growth, maintenance, and repair of the body but is not used as a source of energy. [13]

O

obligatory losses Unavoidable loss of regulated variables, such as energy, water, or temperature, as a consequence of life processes. [13]

obsessive-compulsive disorder (OCD) A syndrome in which the affected individual engages in recurring, repetitive acts that are carried out without rhyme, reason, or the ability to stop. [16]

occipital lobe Large region of cortex covering much of the posterior part of each cerebral hemisphere, specialized for visual processing. [2, 10]

OCD See *obsessive-compulsive disorder.*

ocular dominance column A region of cortex in which one eye or the other provides a greater degree of synaptic input. [10]

ocular dominance histogram A graph that portrays the strength of response of a brain neuron to stimuli presented to either the left eye or the right eye. [7]

ocular dominance slab A slab of visual cortex, about 0.5 mm wide, in which the neurons of all layers respond preferentially to stimulation of one eye. [10]

oculomotor apraxia A severe difficulty in voluntarily steering visual gaze toward specific targets. [18]

off-center bipolar cell A retinal bipolar cell that is inhibited by light in the center of its receptive field. [10]

off-center ganglion cell A retinal ganglion cell that is activated when light is presented to the periphery, rather than the center, of the cell's receptive field. [10]

off-center/on-surround Referring to a concentric receptive field in which the center inhibits the cell of interest while the surround excites it. [10]

OHC See *outer hair cell.*

olfactory bulb An anterior projection of the brain that terminates in the upper nasal passages and, through small openings in the skull, receives axons from olfactory receptor neurons. [2, 9]

olfactory epithelium A sheet of cells, including olfactory receptors, that lines the dorsal portion of the nasal cavities and adjacent regions, including the septum that separates the left and right nasal cavities. [9]

olfactory receptor neuron A type of neuron, found in the olfactory epithelium, that senses airborne odorants via specialized receptor proteins. [9]

oligodendrocyte A type of glial cell that forms myelin in the central nervous system. [2]

on-center bipolar cell A retinal bipolar cell that is excited by light in the center of its receptive field. [10]

on-center ganglion cell A retinal ganglion cell that is activated when light is presented to the center, rather than the periphery, of the cell's receptive field. [10]

on-center/off-surround Referring to a concentric receptive field in which the center excites the cell of interest while the surround inhibits it. [10]

ontogeny The process by which an individual changes in the course of its lifetime—that is, grows up and grows old. [1]

Onuf's nucleus The human homolog of the spinal nucleus of the bulbocavernosus (SNB) in rats. [12]

open-loop control mechanism A control mechanism in which feedback from the output of the system is not provided to the input control. [11]

operant conditioning Also called *instrumental conditioning.* A form of associative learning in which the likelihood that an act (instrumental response) will be performed depends on the consequences (reinforcing stimuli) that follow it. [17]

opiates A class of compounds that exert an effect like that of opium, including reduced pain sensitivity. [8]

opioid peptide A type of endogenous peptide that mimics the effects of morphine in binding to opioid receptors and producing marked analgesia and reward. [4]

opioid receptor A receptor that responds to endogenous and/or exogenous opiates. [4, 8]

opioids A class of peptides produced in various regions of the brain that bind to opioid receptors and act like opiates. [8]

opium A heterogeneous extract of the seedpod juice of the opium poppy, *Papaver somniferum.* [4]

opponent-process hypothesis The theory that color vision depends on systems that produce opposite responses to light of different wavelengths. [10]

opsin One of the two components of photopigments in the retina. [10]

optic ataxia A spatial disorientation in which the affected person is unable to accurately reach for objects using visual guidance. [10, 18]

optic chiasm The point at which the two optic nerves meet. [10]

optic disc The region of the retina devoid of receptor cells because ganglion cell axons and blood vessels exit the eyeball there. [10]

optic nerve Cranial nerve II, the collection of ganglion cell axons that extend from the retina to the optic chiasm. [10]

optic radiation Axons from the lateral geniculate nucleus that terminate in the primary visual areas of the occipital cortex. [10]

optic tract The axons of retinal ganglion cells after they have passed the optic chiasm. Most terminate in the lateral geniculate nucleus. [10]

optical imaging A method for visualizing brain activity in which near-infrared light is passed through the scalp and skull. [2]

optogenetics The use of genetic tools to induce neurons to become sensitive to light, such that experimenters can excite or inhibit a cell by exposing it to light. [3]

oral contraceptive A birth control pill, typically consisting of steroid hormones to prevent ovulation. [5]

orexigenic neurons Neurons of the hypothalamic appetite system that promote feeding behavior. [13]

orexins Also called *hypocretins*. Neuropeptides produced in the hypothalamus that are involved in switching between sleep states, in narcolepsy, and in the control of appetite. [13, 14]

organ of Corti A structure in the inner ear that lies on the basilar membrane of the cochlea and contains the hair cells and terminations of the auditory nerve. [9]

organizational effect A permanent alteration of the nervous system, and thus permanent change in behavior, resulting from the action of a steroid hormone on an animal early in its development. [12]

organum vasculosum of the lamina terminalis (OVLT) One of the circumventricular organs. [13]

orgasm The climax of sexual experience, marked by extremely pleasurable sensations. [12]

orientation column A column of visual cortex that responds to rod-shaped stimuli of a particular orientation. [10]

orphan receptor Any receptor for which no endogenous ligand has yet been discovered. [4]

osmolality The number of solute particles per unit volume of solvent. [13]

osmosensory neuron A specialized neuron that measures the movement of water into and out of cells. [13]

osmosis The passive movement of water molecules from one place to another until a uniform concentration is achieved. [13]

osmotic pressure The tendency of a solvent to move through a membrane in order to equalize the concentration of solute. [13]

osmotic thirst A desire to ingest fluids that is stimulated by a high concentration of solute (like salt) in the extracellular compartment, reducing intracellular fluid. [13]

ossicles Three small bones (incus, malleus, and stapes) that transmit sound across the middle ear, from the tympanic membrane to the oval window. [9]

otoacoustic emission A sound produced by the cochlea itself, either spontaneously or in response to an environmental noise. [9]

otolith A small crystal on the gelatinous membrane in the vestibular system. [9]

ototoxic Toxic to the ears, especially the middle or inner ear. [9]

outer hair cell (OHC) One of the two types of cochlear receptor cells for hearing. [9]

output zone The part of a neuron, usually corresponding to the axon terminals, at which the cell sends information to another cell. [2]

oval window The location on the surface of the cochlea at which vibrations are received from the ossicles. [9]

ovaries The female gonads, which produce eggs for reproduction. [5]

OVLT See *organum vasculosum of the lamina terminalis*.

ovulation The production and release of an egg (ovum). [12]

ovulatory cycle The periodic occurrence of ovulation. [12]

ovum An egg, the female gamete. [12]

oxytocin A hormone, released from the posterior pituitary, that triggers milk letdown in the nursing female. [5]

P

P1 effect A positive deflection of the event-related potential, occurring 70–100 ms after stimulus presentation, that is enhanced for selectively attended visual input, compared with ignored input. [18]

P3 effect A positive deflection of the event-related potential, occurring about 300–500 ms after stimulus presentation, that is associated with higher-order auditory stimulus processing and late attentional selection. [18]

Pacinian corpuscle Also called *lamellated corpuscle*. A skin receptor cell type that detects vibration. [8]

pain The discomfort normally associated with tissue damage. [8]

pair bond A durable and exclusive relationship between a male and a female. [12]

papilla A small bump that projects from the surface of the tongue. Papillae contain most of the taste receptor cells. [9]

parabiotic Referring to a surgical preparation that joins two animals to share a single blood supply. [12]

paracrine Referring to cellular communication in which a chemical signal diffuses to nearby target cells through the extracellular space. [5]

paradoxical sleep See *rapid-eye-movement (REM) sleep*.

paragigantocellular nucleus (PGN) A region of the brainstem reticular formation implicated in sleep and modulation of spinal reflexes. [12]

parallel fiber One of the axons of the granule cells that form the outermost layer of the cerebellar cortex. [2]

paraphasia A symptom of aphasia that is distinguished by the substitution of a word by a sound, an incorrect word, an unintended word, or a neologism (a meaningless word). [19]

parasympathetic nervous system A component of the autonomic nervous system that arises from both the cranial nerves and the sacral spinal cord. [2, 15]

paraventricular nucleus (PVN) A nucleus of the hypothalamus implicated in the release of oxytocin and vasopressin, and in the control of feeding and other behaviors. [5, 13]

parental behavior Behavior of adult animals with the goal of enhancing the well-being of their own offspring, often at some cost to the parents. [12]

paresis Partial paralysis. [11]

parietal lobe Large region of cortex lying between the frontal and occipital lobes of each cerebral hemisphere. [2]

parkin A protein that has been implicated in Parkinson's disease. [11]

Parkinson's disease A degenerative neurological disorder, characterized by tremors at rest, muscular rigidity, and reduction in voluntary movement, that involves dopaminergic neurons of the substantia nigra. [11]

parthenogenesis "Virgin birth," a process of reproduction by which a female produces live offspring without need of a male. [12]

partial agonist A drug that, when bound to a receptor, has less effect than the endogenous ligand would. [4]

parvocellular Referring to relatively small cells. [10]

patch clamp To use voltage clamping to monitor the flow of current across a tiny patch of membrane taken from a neuron. [3]

patient H.M. A person who, because of damage to medial temporal lobe structures, was unable to encode new declarative memories. Upon his death we learned his name was Henry Molaison. [17]

patient K.C. A person who sustained damage to the cortex that rendered him unable to form and retrieve new episodic memories, especially autobiographical memories. Upon his death we learned that his name was Kent Cochrane.[17]

patient N.A. A person who is unable to encode new declarative memories, because of damage to the dorsal thalamus and the mammillary bodies. [17]

pattern coding Coding of information in sensory systems based on the temporal pattern of action potentials. [9]

Pavlovian conditioning See *classical conditioning*.

PCP See *phencyclidine*.

PCR See *polymerase chain reaction*.

peptide A short string of amino acids. Longer strings of amino acids are called *proteins*. [App]

peptide hormones A class of hormones, molecules of which consist of a string of amino acids. If the string of amino acids is long enough, it may be called a *protein hormone*. [5]

peptide neurotransmitter Also called *neuropeptide*. A neurotransmitter consisting of a short chain of amino acids. Examples include neuropeptide Y, galanin, and VIP (vasoactive intestinal polypeptide). [4]

perceptual load The immediate processing challenge presented by a stimulus. [18]

periaqueductal gray The neuronal body–rich region of the midbrain surrounding the cerebral aqueduct that connects the third and fourth ventricles. It is involved in pain perception. [4, 8, 12]

period The interval of time between two similar points of successive cycles, such as sunset to sunset. [14]

peripheral nervous system The portion of the nervous system that includes all the nerves and neurons outside the brain and spinal cord. [2]

peripheral spatial cuing task An attention task where a visual stimulus is preceded by a simple sensory stimulus (like a flash) that reflexively captures attention. [18]

perseverate To continue to show a behavior repeatedly. [5, 18]

PET See *positron emission tomography*.

PGN See *paragigantocellular nucleus*.

phagocyte An immune system cell that engulfs invading molecules or microbes. [15]

phallus The clitoris or penis. [12]

pharmacodynamics Collective name for the factors that affect the relationship between a drug and its target receptors, such as affinity and efficacy. [4]

pharmacokinetics Collective name for all the factors that affect the movement of a drug into, through, and out of the body. [4]

phase shift A shift in the activity of a biological rhythm, typically provided by a synchronizing environmental stimulus. [14]

phasic receptor A receptor in which the frequency of action potentials drops rapidly as stimulation is maintained. [8]

phencyclidine (PCP) Also called *angel dust*. An anesthetic agent that is also a psychedelic drug. PCP makes many people feel dissociated from themselves and their environment. [16]

phenotype The sum of an individual's physical characteristics at one particular time. [7]

phenylketonuria (PKU) An inherited disorder of protein metabolism in which the absence of an enzyme leads to a toxic buildup of certain compounds, causing intellectual disability. [7]

pheromone A chemical signal that is released outside the body of an animal and affects other members of the same species. [5, 9, 12]

phobic disorder An intense, irrational fear that becomes centered on a specific object, activity, or situation that a person feels compelled to avoid. [16]

phoneme A sound that is produced for language. [19]

photon A quantum of electromagnetic energy in the range of wavelengths we call light. [10]

photopic system A system in the retina that operates at high levels of light, shows sensitivity to color, and involves the cones. [10]

photoreceptor adaptation The tendency of rods and cones to adjust their light sensitivity to match ambient levels of illumination. [10]

photoreceptors Neural cells in the retina that respond to light. [10]

phrenology The outmoded belief that bumps on the skull reflect enlargements of brain regions responsible for certain behavioral faculties. [1]

phylogeny The evolutionary history of a particular group of organisms. [6]

pia mater The innermost of the three meninges that surround the brain and spinal cord. [2]

Piezo2 A receptor protein in touch receptors that responds to mechanical stretch by opening channels to let cations in to depolarize the cell. [8]

pineal gland The secretory gland in the brain, at midline, that is the source of melatonin release. [5, 14]

pinna The external part of the ear. [9]

pitch A dimension of auditory experience in which sounds vary from low to high. [9]

pituitary gland Also called *hypophysis*. A small, complex endocrine gland located in a socket at the base of the skull. [5]

pituitary stalk Also called *infundibulum*. A thin piece of tissue that connects the pituitary gland to the hypothalamus. [5]

PKU See *phenylketonuria*.

place cell A neuron within the hippocampus that selectively fires when the animal is in a particular location. [17]

place coding The encoding of sound frequency as a function of the location on the basilar membrane that is most stimulated by that sound. [9]

placebo A substance that is known to be ineffective or inert, but when administered like a drug can sometimes brings relief. [8]

planum temporale A region of superior temporal cortex adjacent to the primary auditory area. [19]

plegia Paralysis, the loss of the ability to move. [11]

polioviruses A class of viruses that destroy motor neurons of the spinal cord and brainstem. [11]

polygraph Also called a *lie detector*. A device that measures several bodily responses, such as heart rate and blood pressure. [15]

polymerase chain reaction (PCR) Also called *gene amplification*. A method for reproducing a particular RNA or DNA sequence manyfold, allowing amplification for sequencing or manipulating the sequence. [App]

polymodal Involving several sensory modalities. [8]

POMC neurons Neurons involved in the hypothalamic appetite control system, so named because they produce pro-opiomelanocortin (POMC) along with cocaine- and amphetamine-related transcript (CART). [13]

pons A portion of the metencephalon; part of the brainstem connecting midbrain to medulla. [2]

positive symptom In psychiatry, a behavior that is gained in a disorder. Examples include hallucinations, delusions, and excited motor behavior in schizophrenia. [16]

positron emission tomography (PET) A technique for examining brain function by combining tomography with injections of radioactive substances used by the brain. [2]

postcentral gyrus The strip of parietal cortex, just behind the central sulcus, that receives somatosensory information from the entire body. [2]

postcopulatory behavior The final stage in mating behavior. Species-specific postcopulatory behaviors include rolling (in the cat) and grooming (in the rat). [12]

posterior Also called *caudal*. In anatomy, toward the tail end of an organism. Compare *anterior*. [2]

posterior cerebral arteries Two large arteries, arising from the basilar artery, that provide blood to posterior aspects of the cerebral hemispheres, cerebellum, and brainstem. [2]

posterior pituitary Also called *neurohypophysis*. The rear division of the pituitary gland. [5]

postganglionic Literally, "after the ganglion." Referring to neurons in the autonomic nervous system that run from the autonomic ganglia to various targets in the body. [2]

postpartum depression A bout of depression that afflicts a woman around the time that she gives birth. [16]

postsynaptic Referring to the region of a synapse that receives and responds to neurotransmitter. [2]

postsynaptic membrane The specialized membrane on the surface of the cell that receives information by responding to neurotransmitter from a presynaptic neuron. [2]

postsynaptic potential A local potential that is initiated by stimulation at a synapse, can vary in amplitude, and spreads passively across the cell membrane, decreasing in strength with time and distance. [3]

posttraumatic stress disorder (PTSD) Formerly called *combat fatigue, war neurosis,* or *shell shock*. A disorder in which memories of an unpleasant episode repeatedly plague the victim. [16, 17]

potassium ion (K⁺) A potassium atom that carries a positive charge because it has lost one electron. [3]

pragmatics In linguistics, the context in which a speech sound is uttered. [19]

precentral gyrus The strip of frontal cortex, just in front of the central sulcus, that is crucial for motor control. [2]

precocial Referring to animals that are born in a relatively developed state and that are able to survive with relatively little maternal care. [12]

prefrontal cortex The anteriormost region of the frontal lobe. [18]

preganglionic Literally, "before the ganglion." Referring to neurons in the autonomic nervous system that run from the central nervous system to the autonomic ganglia. [2]

premotor cortex A region of nonprimary motor cortex just anterior to the primary motor cortex. [11]

presenilin An enzyme that cleaves amyloid precursor protein, forming β-amyloid, which can lead to Alzheimer's disease. [7]

prestin A motor protein that allows outer hair cells to change length. [9]

presynaptic Referring to the region of a synapse that releases neurotransmitter. [2]

presynaptic membrane The specialized membrane of the axon terminal of the neuron that transmits information by releasing neurotransmitter. [2]

primacy effect The superior performance seen in a memory task for items at the start of a list. It is usually attributed to long-term memory. [17]

primary auditory cortex (A1) The region of superior temporal cortex in which auditory processing occurs. [9]

primary motor cortex (M1) The apparent executive region for the initiation of movement, primarily the precentral gyrus. [11]

primary sensory cortex For a given sensory modality, the region of cortex that receives most of the information about that modality from the thalamus or, in the case of olfaction, directly from the secondary sensory neurons. [8]

primary sensory ending Also called *annulospiral ending*. The axon that transmits information from the central portion of a muscle spindle. [11]

primary somatosensory cortex (S1) Also called *somatosensory 1*. The gyrus just posterior to the central sulcus, in the parietal lobe, where sensory receptors on the body surface are mapped; primary cortex for receiving touch and pain information. [8]

primary visual cortex (V1) Also called *striate cortex* or *area 17*. The region of the occipital lobe where most visual information first arrives in the cortex. [10]

priming Also called *repetition priming*. The phenomenon by which exposure to a stimulus facilitates subsequent responses to the same or a similar stimulus. [17]

prion A protein that can become improperly folded and thereby can induce other proteins to follow suit, leading to long protein chains that impair neural function. **[11]**

probe A manufactured sequence of DNA or RNA that is made to include a label (a colorful or radioactive molecule) that lets us track its location. **[App]**

procedural memory See *nondeclarative memory*.

proceptive Referring to a state in which an animal advertises its readiness to mate through species-typical behaviors, such as ear wiggling in the female rat. **[12]**

progesterone The primary type of progestin secreted by the ovary. **[5]**

progestins A major class of steroid hormones that are produced by the ovary, including progesterone. **[5]**

prolactin A peptide hormone, produced by the anterior pituitary, that promotes mammary development for lactation in female mammals. **[5]**

proprioception Body sense; information about the position and movement of the body that is sent to the brain. **[11]**

prosencephalon See *forebrain*.

prosody The perception of emotional tone-of-voice aspects of language. **[19]**

prosopagnosia Also called *face blindness*. A condition characterized by the inability to recognize faces. *Acquired prosopagnosia* is caused by damage to the brain, particularly the fusiform gyrus. *Developmental* (or *congenital*) *prosopagnosia* is present from birth. **[19]**

protein A long string of amino acids; the basic building material of organisms. **[App]**

protein kinase An enzyme that adds phosphate groups (PO_4) to protein molecules, causing a functional change in the proteins. **[17]**

proximal In anatomy, near the trunk or center of an organism. Compare *distal*. **[2]**

psychoneuroimmunology The study of the immune system and its interaction with the nervous system and behavior. **[15]**

psychopath An individual incapable of experiencing remorse. **[15]**

psychopharmacology See *neuropharmacology*.

psychosocial dwarfism Reduced stature caused by stress early in life that inhibits growth. **[5]**

psychosomatic medicine A field of study that emphasizes the role of psychological factors in disease. **[15]**

psychosurgery Surgery in which brain lesions are produced to alleviate severe psychiatric disorders. **[16]**

psychotomimetic A drug that induces a state resembling schizophrenia. **[16]**

PTSD See *posttraumatic stress disorder*.

pulvinar In humans, the posterior portion of the thalamus, heavily involved in visual processing and direction of attention. **[18]**

punch-drunk See *chronic traumatic encephalopathy*.

pupil The aperture, formed by the iris, that allows light to enter the eye. **[10]**

pure tone A tone with a single frequency of vibration. **[9]**

Purkinje cell A type of large nerve cell in the cerebellar cortex. **[2]**

putamen One of the basal ganglia. **[2]**

PVN See *paraventricular nucleus*.

pyramidal cell A type of large nerve cell, found in the cerebral cortex, that has a roughly pyramid-shaped cell body. **[2]**

pyramidal system Also called *corticospinal system*. The motor system that includes neurons within the cerebral cortex that send axons to form the pyramidal tract. **[11]**

PYY$_{3-36}$ A peptide hormone, secreted by the intestines, that probably acts on hypothalamic appetite control mechanisms to suppress appetite. **[13]**

Q

quale A purely subjective experience of perception. **[18]**

quantum (pl. quanta) A discrete unit of electromagnetic energy. **[10]**

R

radial glial cells Glial cells that form early in development, spanning the width of the emerging cerebral hemispheres, and guide migrating neurons. **[7]**

radioimmunoassay (RIA) A technique that uses antibodies to measure the concentration of a substance, such as a hormone, in blood. **[5]**

range fractionation A hypothesis of stimulus intensity perception stating that a wide range of intensity values can be encoded by a group of cells, each of which is a specialist for a particular range of stimulus intensities. **[8, 10]**

raphe nuclei A string of nuclei in the midline of the midbrain and brainstem that contain most of the serotonergic neurons of the brain. **[4]**

rapid-eye-movement (REM) sleep Also called *paradoxical sleep*. A stage of sleep characterized by small-amplitude, fast-EEG waves, no postural tension, and rapid eye movements. *REM* rhymes with "gem." **[14]**

RBD See *REM behavior disorder*.

recency effect The superior performance seen in a memory task for items at the end of a list. It is attributed to short-term memory. **[17]**

receptive field The stimulus region and features that affect the activity of a cell in a sensory system. **[8, 10]**

receptor See *receptor molecule*.

receptor cell A specialized cell that responds to a particular energy or substance in the internal or external environment and converts this energy into a change in the electrical potential across its membrane. **[8]**

receptor isoform A subtype of a receptor protein whose slight differences in structure give it different functional properties. **[5]**

receptor molecule Also called *receptor*. A protein that binds and reacts to molecules of a neurotransmitter or hormone. **[2, 3, 4]**

receptor potential Also called *generator potential*. A local change in the resting potential of a receptor cell that mediates between the impact of stimuli and the initiation of action potentials. **[8]**

receptor subtype Any type of receptor having functional characteristics that distinguish it from other types of receptors for the same neurotransmitter. **[4]**

reconsolidation The return of a memory trace to stable long-term storage after it has been temporarily made volatile during the process of recall. [17]

recovery of function The recovery of behavioral capacity following brain damage from stroke or injury. [19]

red nucleus A brainstem structure related to motor control. [2, 11]

reductionism The scientific strategy of breaking a system down into increasingly smaller parts in order to understand it. [1]

reflex A simple, highly stereotyped, and unlearned response to a particular stimulus (e.g., an eye blink in response to a puff of air). [11]

reflexive attention Also called *exogenously controlled attention* or *bottom-up attention*. The involuntary reorienting of attention toward the location of an unexpected object or event. [18]

refraction The bending of light rays by a change in the density of a medium, such as the cornea and the lens of the eye. [10]

refractory Referring to transiently inactivated or exhausted axonal membranes. [3]

refractory period A period following copulation during which an individual cannot recommence copulation. [12]

regulation An adaptive response to early injury, as when developing individual cells compensate for missing or injured cells. [7]

relative refractory phase A period of reduced sensitivity during which only strong stimulation produces an action potential. [3]

releasing hormones A class of hormones, produced in the hypothalamus, that traverse the hypothalamic-pituitary portal system to control the pituitary's release of tropic hormones. [5]

REM behavior disorder (RBD) A sleep disorder in which a person physically acts out a dream. [14]

REM sleep See *rapid-eye-movement (REM) sleep*.

repetition priming See *priming*.

reserpine A drug that causes the depletion of monoamines and can lead to depression. [16]

resting membrane potential A difference in electrical potential across the membrane of a nerve cell during an inactive period. [3]

reticular formation An extensive region of the brainstem (extending from the medulla through the thalamus) that is involved in arousal (waking) and motor control. [2, 11, 14]

reticulospinal tract A tract of axons arising from the brainstem reticular formation and descending to the spinal cord to modulate movement. [11, 12]

retina The receptive surface inside the eye that contains photoreceptors and other neurons. [10]

RETINAL Abbreviation for *retinaldehyde*, one of the two components of photopigments in the retina. Also called *vitamin A aldehyde*. [10]

retinaldehyde See RETINAL.

retinohypothalamic pathway The projection of retinal ganglion cells to the suprachiasmatic nuclei. [14]

retrieval A process in memory during which a stored memory is used by an organism. [17]

retrograde amnesia Difficulty in retrieving memories formed before the onset of amnesia. [17]

retrograde degeneration Destruction of the nerve cell body following injury to its axon. [7]

retrograde messenger Transmitter that is released by the postsynaptic region, travels back across the synapse, and alters the functioning of the presynaptic neuron. [17]

retrograde synapse A synapse in which a signal (usually a gas neurotransmitter) flows from the postsynaptic neuron to the presynaptic neuron, thus counter to the usual direction of synaptic communication. [3]

retrograde transmitter A neurotransmitter that diffuses from the postsynaptic neuron back to the presynaptic neuron. [4]

Rett syndrome A rare genetic disorder, occurring almost exclusively in girls, of slowing development resulting in intellectual disability, stereotyped movements, and loss of language. [7]

reuptake The process by which released synaptic transmitter molecules are taken up and reused by the presynaptic neuron, thus stopping synaptic activity. [3]

rhodopsin The photopigment in rods that responds to light. [10]

rhombencephalon See *hindbrain*.

RIA See *radioimmunoassay*.

ribonucleic acid (RNA) A nucleic acid that implements information found in DNA. [App]

ribosomes Structures in the cell body where genetic information is translated to produce proteins. [2, App]

rods A class of light-sensitive receptor cells (photoreceptors) in the retina that are most active at low levels of light. [10]

rostral See *anterior*.

round window A membrane separating the cochlear duct from the middle-ear cavity. [9]

rubrospinal tract A tract of axons arising from the red nucleus in the midbrain and innervating neurons of the spinal cord. [11]

Ruffini's ending A skin receptor cell type that detects stretching of the skin. [8]

S

S1 See *primary somatosensory cortex*.

S2 See *secondary somatosensory cortex*.

saccades Fast movements of the eyes that present various parts of the visual scene to the fovea. When we fix our gaze, small saccades that we are unaware of avert photoreceptor adaptation. [10]

saccule A small, fluid-filled sac under the utricle in the vestibular system that responds to static positions of the head. [9]

sacral Referring to the five spinal segments that make up the lower part of the lower back. [2]

SAD See *seasonal affective disorder*.

sagittal plane The plane that bisects the body or brain into right and left portions. Compare *coronal plane* and *horizontal plane*. [2]

saltatory conduction The form of conduction that is characteristic of myelinated axons, in which the action potential jumps from one node of Ranvier to the next. [3]

saxitoxin (STX) An animal toxin that blocks sodium channels when applied to the outer surface of the cell membrane. [3]

SC See *standard condition.*

scala media Also called *middle canal.* The central of the three canals running the length of the cochlea, situated between the scala vestibuli and the scala tympani. [9]

scala tympani Also called *tympanic canal.* One of the three canals running the length of the cochlea. [9]

scala vestibuli Also called *vestibular canal.* One of the three canals running the length of the cochlea. [9]

schizophrenia A severe psychopathology characterized by negative symptoms such as emotional withdrawal and impoverished thought, and by positive symptoms such as hallucinations and delusions. [16]

Schwann cell The glial cell that forms myelin in the peripheral nervous system. [2]

SCN See *suprachiasmatic nucleus.*

SCN9A See *Na_v1.7.*

scotoma A region of blindness caused by injury to the visual pathway or brain. [10]

scotopic system A system in the retina that operates at low levels of light and involves the rods. [10]

SDN-POA See *sexually dimorphic nucleus of the preoptic area.*

seasonal affective disorder (SAD) A depression putatively brought about by the short days of winter. [16]

second messenger A slow-acting substance in a target cell or postsynaptic cell that amplifies the effects of synaptic or hormonal activity and regulates chemical activity within that cell. [3, 5]

secondary sensory cortex Also called *nonprimary sensory cortex.* For a given sensory modality, the cortical regions receiving direct projections from primary sensory cortex for that modality. [8]

secondary sensory ending Also called *flower spray ending.* The axon that transmits information from the ends of a muscle spindle. [11]

secondary somatosensory cortex (S2) Also called *somatosensory 2.* The region of cortex that receives direct projections from primary somatosensory cortex. [8]

seizure An epileptic episode. [3]

selective attention See *attention.*

selective permeability The property of a membrane that allows some substances to pass through, but not others. [3]

selective serotonin reuptake inhibitors (SSRIs) A class of drugs that block the reuptake of transmitter at serotonergic synapses. They are commonly used to treat depression. [4, 16]

semantic memory Generalized memory—for instance, knowing the meaning of a word without knowing where or when you learned that word. [17]

semantics The meanings or interpretation of words and sentences in a language. [19]

semen A mixture of fluids and sperm that is released during ejaculation. [12]

semicircular canal One of the three fluid-filled tubes in the inner ear that are part of the vestibular system. Each of the tubes, which are at right angles to each other, detects angular acceleration. [9]

senile dementia A neurological disorder of the aged that is characterized by progressive behavioral deterioration, including personality change and profound intellectual decline. It includes, but is not limited to, Alzheimer's disease. [7]

senile plaques Also called *amyloid plaques.* Small areas of the brain that have abnormal cellular and chemical patterns. Senile plaques correlate with senile dementia. [7]

sensitive period The period during development in which an organism can be permanently altered by a particular experience or treatment. [7, 12, 19]

sensitization 1. A process in which the body shows an enhanced response to a given drug after repeated doses. [4] 2. A form of nonassociative learning in which an organism becomes more responsive to most stimuli after being exposed to unusually strong or painful stimulation. [17]

sensorineural deafness A hearing impairment that originates from cochlear or auditory nerve lesions. [9]

sensory buffer An element of the type of memory that stores the very brief sensory impression of a scene. [17]

sensory conflict theory A theory of motion sickness suggesting that discrepancies between vestibular information and visual information simulate food poisoning and therefore trigger nausea. [9]

sensory nerve A nerve that conveys sensory information from the periphery into the central nervous system. [2]

sensory neuron A neuron that is directly affected by changes in the environment, such as light, odor, or touch. [2]

sensory pathway The chain of neural connections from sensory receptor cells to the cortex. [8]

sensory receptor organ An organ (such as the eye or ear) specialized to receive particular stimuli. [8]

sensory transduction The process in which a receptor cell converts the energy in a stimulus into a change in the electrical potential across its membrane. [8]

septal nuclei A collection of gray matter structures lying medially below the corpus callosum, implicated in the perception of reward. [2]

serotonergic Referring to neurons that use serotonin as their synaptic transmitter. [4]

serotonin (5-HT) A synaptic transmitter that is produced in the raphe nuclei and is active in structures throughout the cerebral hemispheres. [4]

serotonin syndrome Syndrome of confusion, muscle spasms, and fever that may occur when brain levels of serotonin are too high. It is a risk of taking SSRIs. [16]

serotonin-norepinephrine reuptake inhibitor (SNRI) A drug that blocks the reuptake of transmitter at both serotonergic and noradrenergic synapses. [4]

set point The point of reference in a feedback system. An example is the setting of a thermostat. [13]

set zone The range of a variable that a feedback system tries to maintain. [13]

sex determination The process that initiates either male or female development in an embryo or fetus. [12]

sex steroids Steroid hormones secreted by the gonads: androgens, estrogens, and progestins. [5]

sexual attraction The first step in the mating behavior of many animals, in which animals emit stimuli that attract members of the opposite sex. [12]

sexual differentiation The process by which individuals develop either male-like or female-like bodies and behavior. [12]

sexual dimorphism The condition in which males and females show pronounced sex differences in appearance. [12]

sexual selection A form of evolution through natural selection in which members of one sex favor specific heritable traits in the other sex when choosing a reproductive partner. [6]

sexually dimorphic nucleus of the preoptic area (SDN-POA) A region of the preoptic area that is 5 to 6 times larger in volume in male rats than in females. [12]

sexually receptive Referring to the state in which an individual (in mammals, typically the female) is willing to copulate. [12]

SFO See *subfornical organ.*

shadowing A task in which the participant is asked to focus attention on one ear or the other while stimuli are being presented separately to both ears. [18]

sham rage See *decorticate rage.*

short-term memory (STM) A form of memory that usually lasts only for seconds, or as long as rehearsal continues, especially while being used during performance of a task. [17]

SIDS See *sudden infant death syndrome.*

simple cortical cell Also called *bar detector* or *edge detector*. A cell in the visual cortex that responds best to an edge or a bar that has a particular width, as well as a particular orientation and location in the visual field. [10]

simple partial seizure Also called *absence attack*. A seizure that is characterized by a spike-and-wave EEG and often involves a loss of awareness and inability to recall events surrounding the seizure. [3]

simultagnosia A profound restriction of attention, often limited to a single item or feature. [18]

single-nucleotide polymorphisms A minor variation within a gene, or neighboring noncoding DNA, where one nucleotide has been substituted for another. [6]

site-directed mutagenesis A technique in molecular biology that changes the sequence of nucleotides in an existing gene. [7]

skill learning Learning to perform a task that requires motor coordination. [17]

sleep apnea A sleep disorder in which respiration slows or stops periodically, waking the person. Excessive daytime sleepiness results from the frequent nocturnal awakening. [14]

sleep cycle A period of slow-wave sleep followed by a period of REM sleep. In humans, a sleep cycle lasts 90–110 minutes. [14]

sleep deprivation The partial or total prevention of sleep. [14]

sleep enuresis Bed-wetting. [14]

sleep hygiene Habits, such as avoiding caffeine shortly before bedtime, that promote healthy sleep. [14]

sleep paralysis A state during the transition to or from sleep, in which the ability to move or talk is temporarily lost. [14]

sleep recovery The process of sleeping more than is normal, after a period of sleep deprivation, as though in compensation. [14]

sleep spindle A characteristic 14- to 18-Hz wave in the EEG of a person in stage 2 sleep. [14]

sleep state misperception Commonly, a person's perception that he has not been asleep when in fact he has. It typically occurs at the start of a sleep episode. [14]

sleep-maintenance insomnia Difficulty in staying asleep. [14]

sleep-onset insomnia Difficulty in falling asleep. [14]

slow-twitch muscle fiber A type of striated muscle fiber that contracts slowly but does not fatigue readily. [11]

slow-wave sleep (SWS) Also called *NREM 3*. A stage of NREM sleep characterized by large-amplitude delta waves (in humans, this is also called *stage 3 sleep*). [14]

SMA See *supplementary motor area.*

smooth muscle A type of muscle fiber, as in the heart, that is controlled by the autonomic nervous system rather than by voluntary control. [11]

SNB See *spinal nucleus of the bulbocavernosus.*

SNRI See *serotonin-norepinephrine reuptake inhibitor.*

social neuroscience The use of neuroscience techniques to understand the neural bases of social processes. [2]

sodium ion (Na⁺) A sodium atom that carries a positive charge because it has lost one electron. [3]

sodium-potassium pump The energetically expensive mechanism that pushes sodium ions out of a cell, and potassium ions in. [3]

soma See *cell body.*

somatic intervention An approach to finding relations between body variables and behavioral variables that involves manipulating body structure or function and looking for resultant changes in behavior. [1]

somatic nerve See *spinal nerve.*

somatic nervous system The part of the peripheral nervous system that provides neural connections to the skeletal musculature. [2]

somatomedins A group of proteins, released from the liver in response to growth hormone, that aid body growth and maintenance. [5]

somatosensory Referring to body sensation, particularly touch and pain sensation. [8]

somatosensory 1 See *primary somatosensory cortex.*

somatosensory 2 See *secondary somatosensory cortex.*

somatotropic hormone See *growth hormone.*

somatotropin See *growth hormone.*

somnambulism Sleepwalking. [14]

Southern blot A method of detecting a particular DNA sequence in the genome of an organism, by separating DNA with gel electrophoresis, blotting the separated DNAs onto nitrocellulose, and then using a nucleotide probe to hybridize with, and highlight, the gene of interest. [App]

spasticity Markedly increased rigidity in response to forced movement of the limbs. [11]

spatial cognition Those mental processes that deal with the spatial relationships among objects. [19]

spatial resolution The ability to observe the detailed structure of the brain. [18]

spatial summation The summation at the axon hillock of postsynaptic potentials from across the cell body. If this summation reaches threshold, an action potential is triggered. [3]

spatial-frequency filter model A model of pattern analysis that emphasizes Fourier analysis of visual stimuli. [10]

species A group of individuals that can readily interbreed to produce fertile offspring. **[6]**

specific nerve energies The doctrine that the receptors and neural channels for the different senses are independent and operate in their own special ways and can produce only one particular sensation each. **[8]**

spectral filtering Alteration of the amplitude of some, but not all, frequencies in a sound. **[9]**

spectrally opponent cell A visual receptor cell that has opposite firing responses to different regions of the spectrum. **[10]**

sperm The gamete produced by males for fertilization of eggs (ova). **[12]**

spinal animal An animal whose spinal cord has been surgically disconnected from the brain to enable the study of behaviors that do not require brain control. **[11]**

spinal nerve Also called *somatic nerve*. A nerve that emerges from the spinal cord. **[2]**

spinal nucleus of the bulbocavernosus (SNB) A group of motor neurons in the spinal cord of rats that innervate striated muscles controlling the penis. **[12]**

spinocerebellum The uppermost part of the cerebellum, consisting mostly of the vermis and anterior lobe. **[11]**

spinothalamic system See *anterolateral system*.

split-brain individual An individual whose corpus callosum has been severed, halting communication between the right and left hemispheres. **[19]**

***SRY* gene** A gene on the Y chromosome that directs the developing gonads to become testes. The name *SRY* stands for *s*ex-determining *r*egion on the *Y* chromosome. **[12]**

SSRI See *selective serotonin reuptake inhibitor*.

stage 1 sleep Also called *NREM 1*. The initial stage of NREM sleep, which is characterized by small-amplitude EEG waves of irregular frequency, slow heart rate, and reduced muscle tension. **[14]**

stage 2 sleep Also called *NREM 2*. A stage of NREM sleep that is defined by bursts of regular 14- to 18-Hz EEG waves called *sleep spindles*. **[14]**

stage 3 sleep Also called *NREM 3*. A stage of NREM sleep that is defined by the presence of large-amplitude, very slow waves (delta waves). **[14]**

standard condition (SC) The usual environment for laboratory rodents, with a few animals in a cage and adequate food and water but no complex stimulation. **[17]**

stapedius A middle-ear muscle that is attached to the stapes. **[9]**

stapes Latin for "stirrup." A middle-ear bone that is connected to the oval window. **[9]**

stem cell A cell that is undifferentiated and therefore can take on the fate of any cell that a donor organism can produce. **[7]**

stereocilium A relatively stiff hair that protrudes from a hair cell in the auditory or vestibular system. **[9]**

steroid hormones A class of hormones, each of which is composed of four interconnected rings of carbon atoms. **[5]**

steroid receptor cofactors Proteins that affect the cell's response when a steroid hormone binds its receptor. **[5]**

stimulus A physical event that triggers a sensory response. **[8]**

stimulus cuing A testing technique in which a cue to the stimulus location is provided before the stimulus itself. **[18]**

STM See *short-term memory*.

stop codon A trio of nucleotides in DNA to mark the end of transcription. **[App]**

stress Any circumstance that upsets homeostatic balance. **[15]**

stress immunization The concept that mild stress early in life makes an individual better able to handle stress later in life. **[15]**

stretch reflex The contraction of a muscle in response to stretch of that muscle. **[11]**

stria terminalis A limbic pathway connecting the amygdala and hypothalamus. **[2]**

striate cortex See *primary visual cortex*.

striated muscle A type of muscle with a striped appearance, generally under voluntary control. **[11]**

striatum The caudate nucleus and putamen together. **[4, 11]**

stroke Damage to a region of brain tissue that results from blockage or rupture of vessels that supply blood to that region. **[2]**

STX See *saxitoxin*.

subcoeruleus A brain region just ventral to the locus coeruleus, associated with REM sleep. **[14]**

subcutaneous tissue See *hypodermis*.

subfornical organ (SFO) One of the circumventricular organs. **[13]**

substance abuse A maladaptive pattern of substance use that has lasted more than a month but does not fully meet the criteria for dependence. **[4]**

substance P A peptide transmitter implicated in pain transmission. **[8]**

substantia nigra Literally, "black substance." A group of pigmented neurons in the midbrain that provides dopaminergic projections to areas of the forebrain, especially the basal ganglia. **[2, 4, 11]**

subthalamic nucleus A nucleus just ventral to the thalamus that interacts with the basal ganglia. It is a favored site for deep brain stimulation to treat Parkinson's disease. **[11]**

sudden infant death syndrome (SIDS) Also called *crib death*. The sudden, unexpected death of an apparently healthy human infant who simply stops breathing, usually during sleep. **[14]**

sulcus A furrow of a convoluted brain surface. **[2]**

superior In anatomy, pertaining to the higher of two locations. Compare *inferior*. **[2]**

superior colliculus (pl. colliculi) A gray matter structure of the dorsal midbrain that receives visual information and is involved in direction of visual gaze and visual attention to intended stimuli. **[2, 18]**

superior olivary nuclei Brainstem nuclei that receive input from both right and left cochlear nuclei and provide the first binaural analysis of auditory information. **[9]**

supersensitivity psychosis An exaggerated psychosis that may emerge when doses of antipsychotic medication are reduced, probably as a consequence of the up-regulation of receptors that occurred during drug treatment. **[16]**

supplementary motor area (SMA) A region of nonprimary motor cortex that receives input from the basal ganglia and modulates the activity of the primary motor cortex. **[11]**

suprachiasmatic nucleus (SCN) A small region of the hypothalamus above the optic chiasm that is the location of a circadian oscillator. [14]

supraoptic nucleus A hypothalamic nucleus containing neuroendocrine cells that send axons to the posterior pituitary to release oxytocin or vasopressin. [5]

surface dyslexia Acquired dyslexia in which the person seems to attend only to the fine details of reading. [19]

sustained-attention task A task in which a single stimulus source or location must be held in the attentional spotlight for a protracted period. [18]

SWS See *slow-wave sleep.*

Sylvian fissure Also called *lateral sulcus.* A deep fissure that demarcates the temporal lobe. [2]

symbolic cuing task An attention task in which a symbol indicates to the participant where to voluntarily direct attention in order to detect a stimulus. [18]

sympathetic chain A chain of ganglia that runs along each side of the spinal column and is part of the sympathetic nervous system. [2]

sympathetic nervous system A component of the autonomic nervous system that arises from the thoracic and lumbar spinal cord. [2, 15]

synapse rearrangement Also called *synaptic remodeling.* The loss of some synapses and the development of others; a refinement of synaptic connections that is often seen in development. [7]

synapse The tiny gap between neurons where information is passed from one to the other. [2]

synaptic bouton See *axon terminal.*

synaptic cleft The space between the presynaptic and postsynaptic elements. [2]

synaptic delay The brief delay between the arrival of an action potential at the axon terminal and the creation of a postsynaptic potential. [3]

synaptic remodeling See *synapse rearrangement.*

synaptic transmitter See *neurotransmitter.*

synaptic vesicle A small, spherical structure that contains molecules of neurotransmitter. [2]

synaptogenesis The establishment of synaptic connections as axons and dendrites grow. [7]

synaptotagmin A specialized protein that responds to calcium ions to trigger vesicular exocytosis. [3]

synergist A muscle that acts together with another muscle. [11]

synesthesia A condition in which stimuli in one modality evoke the involuntary experience of an additional sensation in another modality. [8]

syntax The grammatical rules for constructing phrases and sentences in a language. [19]

syrinx The vocal organ in birds. [12, 19]

T

T cell See *T lymphocyte.*

T lymphocyte Also called *T cell.* An immune system cell, formed in the thymus (hence the *T*), which includes killer T cells that attack foreign microbes, and helper T cells that secrete cytokines. [15]

T1R A family of taste receptor proteins that, when particular members heterodimerize, form taste receptors for sweet flavors and umami flavors. [9]

T2R A family of bitter taste receptors. [9]

TAARs See *trace amine–associated receptors.*

tachistoscope test A test in which stimuli are very briefly exposed in either the left or right visual half field. [19]

tactile Of or relating to touch. [8]

tardive dyskinesia A disorder characterized by involuntary movements, especially involving the face, mouth, lips, and tongue. It can be caused by prolonged use of antipsychotic drugs, such as chlorpromazine. [16]

tastant A substance that can be tasted. [9]

taste bud A cluster of 50–150 cells that detects tastes. Taste buds are found in papillae. [9]

taste pore The small aperture through which tastant molecules are able to access the sensory receptors of the taste bud. [9]

Tau A protein associated with neurofibrillary tangles in Alzheimer's disease. [7, 19]

taxonomy The classification of organisms. [6]

tectorial membrane A membrane that sits atop the organ of Corti in the cochlear duct. [9]

tectum The dorsal portion of the midbrain, including the inferior and superior colliculi. [2]

telencephalon The frontal subdivision of the forebrain that includes the cerebral hemispheres when fully developed. [2]

temporal coding The encoding of sound frequency in terms of the number of action potentials per second produced by an auditory nerve. [9]

temporal lobe Large lateral cortical region of each cerebral hemisphere, continuous with the parietal lobe posteriorly and separated from the frontal lobe by the Sylvian fissure. [2]

temporal resolution The ability of an imaging technique to track changes in the brain over time. [18]

temporal summation The summation of postsynaptic potentials that reach the axon hillock at different times. The closer in time the potentials occur, the more complete the summation. [3]

temporoparietal junction (TPJ) The point in the brain where the temporal and parietal lobes meet that plays a role in shifting attention to a new location after target onset. [18]

tendon Strong tissue that connects muscle to bone. [11]

tensor tympani The muscle attached to the malleus that modulates mechanical linkage to protect the delicate receptor cells of the inner ear from damaging sounds. [9]

testes The male gonads, which produce sperm and androgenic steroid hormones. [5]

testosterone A hormone, produced by male gonads, that controls a variety of bodily changes that become visible at puberty. [5]

tetanus An intense volley of action potentials. [17]

tetanus toxin A toxin that cleaves SNAREs, disabling neurotransmitter release. [3]

tetrodotoxin (TTX) A toxin from puffer fish ovaries that blocks the voltage-gated sodium channel, preventing action potential conduction. [3]

thalamus The brain regions surrounding the third ventricle at the top of the brainstem that trade information with the cortex. [2, 8]

THC See Δ9-tetrahydrocannabinol.

thermogenin Also called *UCP1*. A specialized protein that allows mitochondria to turn energy directly into heat. [13]

thermoregulation The active process of closely regulating body temperature around a set value. [13]

third ventricle The midline ventricle that conducts cerebrospinal fluid from the lateral ventricle to the fourth ventricle. [2]

thoracic Referring to the 12 spinal segments below the cervical (neck) portion of the spinal cord, corresponding to the chest. [2]

threshold The stimulus intensity that is just adequate to trigger an action potential. [3, 8]

thyroid gland An endocrine gland, located in the throat, that regulates cellular metabolism throughout the body. [5]

thyroid hormones Two hormones, triiodothyronine and thyroxine (also called *tetraiodothyronine*), released from the thyroid gland that have widespread effects, including growth and maintenance of the brain. [5]

thyroid-stimulating hormone (TSH) A tropic hormone, released by the anterior pituitary gland, that signals the thyroid gland to secrete its hormones. [5]

thyrotropin-releasing hormone (TRH) A hypothalamic hormone that regulates the release of thyroid-stimulating hormone from the anterior pituitary. [5]

timbre The characteristic sound quality of a musical instrument, as determined by the relative intensities of its various harmonics. [9]

tinnitus A sensation of noises or ringing in the ears. [9]

tip link A fine, threadlike fiber that runs along and connects the tips of stereocilia. [9]

TMS See *transcranial magnetic stimulation.*

tolerance A condition in which, with repeated exposure to a drug, an individual becomes less responsive to a constant dose. [4]

tonic receptor A receptor in which the frequency of action potentials declines slowly or not at all as stimulation is maintained. [8]

tonic-clonic seizure Also called *grand mal seizure*. A type of generalized epileptic seizure in which nerve cells fire in high-frequency bursts. [3]

tonotopic organization A major organizational feature in auditory systems in which neurons are arranged as an orderly map of stimulus frequency, with cells responsive to high frequencies located at a distance from those responsive to low frequencies. [9]

top-down attention See *voluntary attention.*

top-down process A process in which higher-order cognitive processes control lower-order systems, often reflecting conscious control. [8, 18]

Tourette's syndrome A heightened sensitivity to tactile, auditory, and visual stimuli that may be accompanied by the buildup of an urge to emit verbal or phonic tics. [16]

TPJ See *temporoparietal junction.*

trace amine–associated receptors (TAARs) A family of probable pheromone receptors produced by neurons in the main olfactory epithelium. [9]

tract A bundle of axons found within the central nervous system. [2]

tract tracer A compound used to identify the routes and interconnections of neuronal projections. [2]

transcranial magnetic stimulation (TMS) Localized, noninvasive stimulation of cortical neurons through the application of strong magnetic fields. [2]

transcript The mRNA strand that is produced when a stretch of DNA is "read." [App]

transcription factor A substance that binds to recognition sites on DNA and alters the rate of expression of particular genes. [5]

transcription The process during which mRNA forms bases complementary to a strand of DNA. The resulting message (called a *transcript*) is then used to translate the DNA code into protein molecules. [App]

transduction The conversion of one form of energy to another. [9]

transgenic Referring to an animal in which a new or altered gene has been deliberately introduced into the genome. [7, App]

transient receptor potential type M3 (TRPM3) A receptor, found in some free nerve endings, that opens its channel in response to rising temperatures. [8]

transient receptor potential vanilloid type 1 (TRPV1) Also called *vanilloid receptor 1*. A receptor that binds capsaicin to transmit the burning sensation from chili peppers and normally detects sudden increases in temperature. [8]

translation The process by which amino acids are linked together (directed by an mRNA molecule) to form protein molecules. [App]

transmitter See *neurotransmitter.*

transmitter reuptake The reabsorption of synaptic transmitter by the axon terminal from which it was released. [4]

transporter Specialized receptor in the presynaptic membrane that recognizes transmitter molecules and returns them to the presynaptic neuron for reuse. [3, 4]

transverse plane See *coronal plane.*

treble An aspect of pitch corresponding to the subjective experience of high-frequency sounds (especially musical sounds, such as cymbals). [9]

TRH See *thyrotropin-releasing hormone.*

trichromatic hypothesis A hypothesis of color perception stating that there are three different types of cones, each excited by a different region of the spectrum and each having a separate pathway to the brain. [10]

tricyclics or tricyclic antidepressants A class of drugs that act by increasing the synaptic accumulation of serotonin and norepinephrine. [4, 16]

trigeminal nerve Cranial nerve V, which receives information from the face and controlling jaw musculature. [15]

trinucleotide repeat Repetition of the same three nucleotides within a gene, which can lead to dysfunction, as in the cases of Huntington's disease and fragile X syndrome. [7, 11]

trophic factor See *neurotrophic factor.*

tropic hormones A class of anterior pituitary hormones that affect the secretion of other endocrine glands. [5]

TRPM3 See *transient receptor potential type M3.*

TRPM8 See *cool-menthol receptor 1.*

TRPV1 See *transient receptor potential vanilloid type 1.*

TSH See *thyroid-stimulating hormone.*

t-SNARE Specialized protein anchored to the presynaptic "target" membrane to bind v-SNAREs to dock vesicles, making them ready for release. [3]

TTX See *tetrodotoxin.*

tuberomammillary nucleus A region of the basal hypothalamus, near the pituitary stalk, that plays a role in generating SWS. [14]

tuning curve A graph of the responses of a single auditory nerve fiber or neuron to sounds that vary in frequency and intensity. [9]

Turner's syndrome A condition seen in individuals carrying a single X chromosome but no other sex chromosome. [12]

two-photon excitation microscopy Method of providing many low-energy photons that can penetrate deep into tissues, such that the simultaneous arrival of two photons at a fluorescent molecule is sufficient to elicit a visible photon in response. [15]

tympanic canal See *scala tympani.*

tympanic membrane Also called *eardrum.* The partition between the external ear and the middle ear. [9]

typical antipsychotics Also called *typical neuroleptics.* A major class of antischizophrenic drugs that share an antagonist activity at dopamine D_2 receptors. [4, 16]

U

UCP1 See *thermogenin.*

ultradian Referring to a rhythmic biological event whose period is shorter than that of a circadian rhythm, usually from several minutes to several hours long. [14]

ultrasound High-frequency sound, generally above the threshold for human hearing, at about 20,000 Hz. [9]

umami One of the five basic tastes (along with salty, sour, sweet, and bitter), probably mediated by amino acids in foods. [9]

unipolar neuron Also called *monopolar neuron.* A nerve cell with a single branch that leaves the cell body and then extends in two directions: one end is the receptive pole, the other end the output zone. [2]

up-regulation A compensatory increase in receptor availability at the synapses of a neuron. [3, 4]

utricle A small, fluid-filled sac in the vestibular system above the saccule that responds to static positions of the head. [9]

V

V1 See *primary visual cortex.*

vaccination Injection of a foreign substance, such as deactivated viruses or conjugated molecules of drugs of abuse like cocaine, in order to provoke the production of antibodies against the foreign substance. [4]

vagus nerve Cranial nerve X, which regulates the viscera (organs) and transmits signals from the viscera to the brain. [13]

vanilloid receptor 1 See *transient receptor potential vanilloid type 1.*

varicosity The axonal swelling from which neurotransmitter diffuses in a nondirected synapse. [3]

vasopressin See *arginine vasopressin.*

ventral In anatomy, toward the belly or front of the body, or the bottom of the brain. Compare *dorsal.* [2]

ventral root The branch of a spinal nerve, arising from the ventral horn of the spinal cord, that carries motor messages from the spinal cord to the peripheral nervous system. [2]

ventral tegmental area (VTA) A portion of the midbrain that projects dopaminergic fibers to the nucleus accumbens. [4]

ventricular system A system of fluid-filled cavities inside the brain. [2]

ventricular zone Also called *ependymal layer.* A region lining the cerebral ventricles that displays mitosis, providing neurons early in development and glial cells throughout life. [7]

ventromedial hypothalamus (VMH) A hypothalamic region involved in eating, sexual, and aggressive behaviors. [12, 13, 15]

vertebral arteries Arteries that ascend the vertebrae, enter the base of the skull, and join together to form the basilar artery. [2]

vertex spike A sharp-wave EEG pattern that is seen during stage 1 slow-wave sleep. [14]

vestibular canal See *scala vestibuli.*

vestibular nuclei Brainstem nuclei that receive information from the vestibular organs through cranial nerve VIII (the vestibulocochlear nerve). [9]

vestibular system The inner ear system that encodes the orientation and acceleration of the head in three axes, crucial for the sense of balance. [9]

vestibulocerebellum The middle portion of the cerebellum, sandwiched between the spinocerebellum and the cerebrocerebellum and consisting of the nodule and the flocculus. [11]

vestibulocochlear nerve Cranial nerve VIII, which runs from the cochlea to the brainstem auditory nuclei. [9]

vestibulo-ocular reflex (VOR) The brainstem mechanism that maintains gaze on a visual object despite movements of the head. [9]

visual acuity Sharpness of vision. [10]

visual field The whole area that you can see without moving your head or eyes. [10]

visual P1 effect An increase in amplitude of the P1 component of event-related potentials that occurs for stimuli that are the focus of attention. [18]

vitamin A aldehyde See RETINAL.

VMH See *ventromedial hypothalamus.*

VNO See *vomeronasal organ.*

voltage clamping The use of electrodes to inject current into an axon or neuron to keep the membrane potential at a set value. The apparatus measures how much current must be injected to counteract any ion channel openings. [3]

voltage-gated Na^+ channel A Na^+-selective channel that opens or closes in response to changes in the voltage of the local membrane potential and mediates the action potential. [3]

voluntary attention Also called *consciously* or *endogenously controlled attention* or *top-down attention.* The voluntary direction of attention toward specific aspects of the environment, in accordance with our interests and goals. **[18]**

vomeronasal organ (VNO) A collection of specialized receptor cells, near to but separate from the olfactory epithelium, that detect pheromones and send electrical signals to the accessory olfactory bulb in the brain. **[9, 12]**

vomeronasal system A specialized chemical detection system that detects pheromones and transmits information to the brain. **[9]**

VOR See *vestibulo-ocular reflex.*

v-SNARE Specialized protein anchored to vesicles to aid their fusing to the presynaptic membrane to release neurotransmitter. **[3]**

VTA See *ventral tegmental area.*

W

Wada test A test in which a short-lasting anesthetic is delivered into one carotid artery to determine which cerebral hemisphere principally mediates language. **[19]**

Wallerian degeneration See *anterograde degeneration.*

wavelength The length between two peaks in a repeated stimulus such as a wave, light, or sound. **[10]**

Wernicke's aphasia See *fluent aphasia.*

Wernicke's area A region of temporoparietal cortex in the brain that is involved in the perception and production of speech. **[19]**

Western blot A method of detecting a particular protein molecule in a tissue or organ, by separating proteins from that source with gel electrophoresis, blotting the separated proteins onto nitrocellulose, and then using an antibody that binds, and highlights, the protein of interest. **[App]**

white matter A pale-colored layer underneath the cortex that consists largely of axons with white myelin sheaths. **[2]**

Williams syndrome A disorder characterized by fluent linguistic function but poor performance on standard IQ tests and great difficulty with spatial processing. **[19]**

withdrawal symptom An uncomfortable symptom that arises when a person stops taking a drug that he or she has used frequently, especially at high doses. **[4]**

wolffian ducts A duct system in the embryo that will develop into male structures (the epididymis, vas deferens, and seminal vesicles) if testes are present. **[12]**

word deafness The specific inability to hear words, although other sounds can be detected. **[9]**

working memory A type of short-term memory that holds information available for ready access during performance of a task. **[17]**

Z

zeitgeber Literally, "time giver" (in German). The stimulus (usually the light-dark cycle) that entrains circadian rhythms. **[14]**

zygote The fertilized egg. **[7, 12]**

Illustration Credits

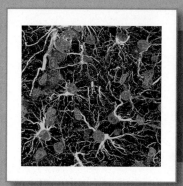

CHAPTER 1 1.1: © Dwayne Godwin 2011. 1.10: © Santa Cruz Sentinel/ZUMAPRESS.com. 1.12: Reproduced with gracious permission of Her Majesty Queen Elizabeth II, copyright reserved. 1.14A: © The Print Collector/Alamy Stock Photo. 1.15: © iStock.com/Roman Sigaev.

CHAPTER 2 2.5C: © Dennis Kunkel Microscopy, Inc. 2.8B: From Gray's Anatomy, 35th ed., Figure 2.9, page 807. Reprinted with permission of the publisher, Churchill Livingstone. Dissection by M. C. E. Hutchinson, photograph by Kevin Fitzpatrick, Guy's Hospital Medical School, London. 2.21A: © Scott Camazine/Alamy Stock Photo. 2.21B: © iStock.com/Mark Herreid. 2.21D: Courtesy of Dr. Jamie Eberling. 2.24: Courtesy of Dr. Mario Liotti and Dr. Anthony Herdman, Simon Fraser University, and the Down Syndrome Research Foundation. 2.27: Courtesy of Dr. R. F. Lee, Princeton University.

CHAPTER 3 3.20: Courtesy of Neuroscan Labs, a division of Neurosoft, Inc. 3.21: Courtesy of Dr. Hal Blumenfeld, Dr, Rik Stokking, Dr. Susan Spencer, and Dr. George Zubal, Yale School of Medicine. 3.25A: © Carnett/Getty Images. Box 3.2 *frog*: © iStock.com/John Arnold. Box 3.2 *scorpion*: © iStock.com/Julie de Leseleuc. Box 3.2 *puffer*: © iStock.com/Kerry Werry.

CHAPTER 4 4.14: © South West Images Scotland/Alamy Stock Photo. 4.16: © Blaine Harrington III/Getty Images. 4.22: Art by Wes Black, courtesy of www.blotterart.com.

CHAPTER 5 5.4: © Tom Vezo/Naturepl.com. 5.20: © Thomas & Pat Leeson/Science Source. p. 155 *Jepsen*: © John B. Carnett/Bonnier Corporation/Getty Images.

CHAPTER 6 6.5: Cartoon by Dan Piraro, www.bizarro.com, courtesy of King Features Syndicate. 6.21: © Cyril Ruoso/Minden Pictures/Getty Images. 6.21: © Konrad Wothe/Minden Pictures/Getty Images. 6.25: © iStock.com/Paul Tessier. Box 6.1 *owl*: © Kevin Schafer/Getty Images. Box 6.1 *howler*: © Tim Laman/Getty Images. Box 6.3: © Ashley Cooper/Alamy Stock Photo.

CHAPTER 7 7.18A: © Moodboard Stock Photography Ltd./Getty Images. 7.18B: Courtesy of the National Fragile X Foundation. p. 218, *May*: © Florence Low.

CHAPTER 8 8.1A: © The Natural History Museum/Alamy Stock Photo. 8.1B: Courtesy of Matthew Haskins and Brianna Matthews. 8.1C: © iStock.com/Vitaly Titov. 8.1D: © Stockbyte/PictureQuest. 8.25: © Monkey Business Images/Getty Images. 8.29A: © Jose Luis Pelaez Inc/Getty Images. 8.29B: © iStock.com/al wekelo. Box 8.1: Courtesy of R. Berry/MyToysRyourToys/Etsy. p. 251, *Blocker*: © Jeff Riedel/Contour/Getty Images.

CHAPTER 9 9.1 *sea lion*: © marima-design/Getty Images. 9.1 *chimp*: © DLILLC/Corbis/VCG/Getty Images. 9.1 *rabbit*: © Nature/UIG/Getty Images. 9.1 *elephant*: © Thomas Dressler/Getty Images. 9.12: © Dave Watts/Alamy Stock Photo. 9.17: Micrographs by H. Engstrom and B. Engstrom, courtesy of Widex. 9.21: David McIntyre. 9.22: © Astrid & Hanns-Frieder Michler/Science Source.

CHAPTER 10 10.5: © Paul Parker/SPL/Science Source. 10.17: © Gerry Ellis/DigitalVision. 10.23C: Dress photo © Cecilia Bleasdale. 10.30: Courtesy of Patch Pals, www.PatchPals.com. Box 10.3A: Photo by David McIntyre; simulation created using software from Vischeck (www.vischeck.com). Box 10.3B: © Brand X Pictures/Alamy Stock Photo.

CHAPTER 11 11.24: © Danita Delimont/Alamy Stock Photo. Box 11.1C: © Dan Kitwood/Getty Images. Box 11.2: Courtesy of the USDA Animal and Plant Health Inspection Service.

CHAPTER 12 12.2: © Jane Burton/Naturepl.com. 12.7: © FLPA/Andrew Forsyth/AGE Fotostock. 12.15: © The Wellcome Photo Library. 12.16: Courtesy of Kimberly Saviano/AISSG-USA. Box 12.1: © Laurence Frank, courtesy of Stephen Glickman.

CHAPTER 13 13.2A: David McIntyre. 13.2B: © Jeff Rotman/Alamy Stock Photo. 13.2C: © Sam Chadwick/Alamy Stock Photo. 13.10: © Rod Planck/Science Source. 13.22: © John Sholtis/Rockefeller University. 13.26A: © Gregg DeGuire/WireImage/Getty Images. 13.26B: Kunsthistorisches Museum, Vienna.

CHAPTER 14 14.11A: © iStock.com/Tomo Jesenicnik. 14.11B: © iStock.com/Ira Bachinskaya. 14.20: © iStock.com/ariwasabi. 14.23: © Hoberman Collection/Alamy Stock Photo. 14.25: Courtesy of Ray Meddis.

CHAPTER 15 15.4A: © blickwinkel/Alamy Stock Photo. 15.4B: © Nic van Oudtshoorn/Alamy Stock Photo. 15.5: © iStock.com/NuStock. 15.7: © Sinauer Associates. 15.11A: © Richard Green/Commercial/Alamy Stock Photo. 15.11B: Courtesy of Jennifer Basil-Whitaker. 15.12: © Dr. P. Marazzi/SPL/Science Source. 15.21: © Bill Frakes/Time & Life Pictures/Getty Images. 15.27: © Biology Pics/Science Source.

CHAPTER 16 16.2: © EFE/Zuma Press. 16.11: Courtesy of Howard Dully. Box 16.1: Courtesy of Steven J Frucht. p. 514: Courtesy of Eleanor Longden.

CHAPTER 17 17.10: Courtesy of D.P. Agamanolis, neuropathology-web.org. 17.12: Courtesy of Med Associates. 17.33: Courtesy of Dr. Suzanne Corkin.

CHAPTER 18 Box 18.2A: From the collection of Jack and Beverly Wilgus.

CHAPTER 19 Box 19.2: © Tampa Bay Times/Zuma Press. p. 622, *Phillips*: © Guillermo F. Florez.

References

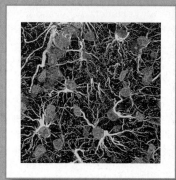

A

Aaronson, S. T., Rashed, S., Biber, M. P., and Hobson, J. A. (1982). Brain state and body position. A time-lapse video study of sleep. *Archives of General Psychiatry, 39,* 330–335.

Abbott, A. (2011). A problem for our age. *Nature, 475,* S2–S4.

Abe, N., Suzuki, M., Mori, E., Itoh, M., et al. (2007). Deceiving others: Distinct neural responses of the prefrontal cortex and amygdala in simple fabrication and deception with social interactions. *Journal of Cognitive Neuroscience, 19,* 287–295.

Abel, E. L. (1984). Prenatal effects of alcohol. *Drug and Alcohol Dependence, 14,* 1–10.

Abelson, J. F., Kwan, K. Y., O'Roak, B. J., Baek, D. Y., et al. (2005). Sequence variants in *SLITRK1* are associated with Tourette's syndrome. *Science, 310,* 317–320.

Adams, C. S., Korytko, A. I., and Blank, J. L. (2003). A novel mechanism of body mass regulation. *Journal of Experimental Biology, 206,* 2535–2536.

Addante, R. J. (2015). A critical role of the human hippocampus in an electrophysiological measure of implicit memory. *Neuroimage, 109,* 515–528.

Addante, R. J., Ranganath, C., Olichney, J., and Yonelinas, A. P. (2012). Neurophysiological evidence for a recollection impairment in amnesia patients that leaves familiarity intact. *Neuropsychologia, 50*(13), 3004–3014.

Ader, R. (2001). Psychoneuroimmunology. *Current Directions in Psychological Science, 10,* 94–98.

Adhikari, A., Lerner, T. N., Finkelstein, J., Pak, S., et al. (2015). Basomedial amygdala mediates top-down control of anxiety and fear. *Nature, 527,* 179–185.

Adler, E., Hoon, M. A., Mueller, K. L., Chandrashekar, J., et al. (2000). A novel family of mammalian taste receptors. *Cell, 100,* 693–702.

Adler, N., and Matthews, K. (1994). Health psychology: Why do some people get sick and some stay well? *Annual Review of Psychology, 45,* 229–259.

Adolphs, R., Gosselin, F., Buchanan, T. W., Tranel, D., et al. (2005). A mechanism for impaired fear recognition after amygdala damage. *Nature, 433,* 68–72.

Aflalo, T., Kellis, S., Klaes, C., Lee, B., et al. (2015). Neurophysiology: Decoding motor imagery from the posterior parietal cortex of a tetraplegic human. *Science, 348*(6237), 906–910.

Agmon-Snir, H., Carr, C. E., and Rinzel, J. (1998). The role of dendrites in auditory coincidence detection. *Nature, 393,* 268–272.

Agnew, H. W., Jr., Webb, W. B., and Williams, R. L. (1966). The first night effect: An EEG study of sleep. *Psychophysiology, 2*(3), 263–266.

Agre, P., King, L. S., Yasui, M., Guggino, W. B., et al. (2002). Aquaporin water channels: From atomic structure to clinical medicine. *Journal of Physiology, 542,* 3–16.

Agulhon, C., Fiacco, T. A., and McCarthy, K. D. (2010). Hippocampal short- and long-term plasticity are not modulated by astrocyte Ca^{2+} signaling. *Science, 327,* 1250–1254.

Ahmari, S. E., Spellman, T., Douglass, N. L., Kheirbek, M. A., et al. (2013). Repeated cortico-striatal stimulation generates persistent OCD-like behavior. *Science, 340,* 1234–1239.

Ahmed, E. I., Zehr, J. L., Schulz, K. M., Lorenz, B. H., et al. (2008). Pubertal hormones modulate the addition of new cells to sexually dimorphic brain regions. *Nature Neuroscience, 11,* 995–997.

Ajslev, T. A., Andersen, C. S., Gamborg, M., Sørensen, T. I., et al. (2011). Childhood overweight after establishment of the gut microbiota: The role of delivery mode, pre-pregnancy weight and early administration of antibiotics. *International Journal of Obesity (London), 35*(4), 522–529.

Akil, O., Seal, R. P., Burke, K., Wang, C., et al. (2012). Restoration of hearing in the *VGLUT3* knockout mouse using virally mediated gene therapy. *Neuron, 75*(2), 283–293.

Albanese, A., Hamill, G., Jones, J., Skuse, D., et al. (1994). Reversibility of physiological growth hormone secretion in children with psychosocial dwarfism. *Clinical Endocrinology (Oxford), 40,* 687–692.

al-Barazanji, K. A., Buckingham, R. E., Arch, J. R., Haynes, A., et al. (1997). Effects of intracerebroventricular infusion of leptin in obese Zucker rats. *Obesity Research, 5,* 387–394.

Alberts, J. R. (1978). Huddling by rat pups: Multisensory control of contact behavior. *Journal of Comparative and Physiological Psychology, 92,* 220–230.

Al-Chalabi, A., and Hardiman, O. (2013). The epidemiology of ALS: A conspiracy of genes, environment and time. *Nature Reviews Neurology, 9*(11), 617–628.

Aldrich, M. A. (1993). The neurobiology of narcolepsy-cataplexy. *Progress in Neurobiology, 41,* 533–541.

Alexander, G. M., Farris, S., Pirone, J. R., Zheng, C., et al. (2016). Social and novel contexts modify hippocampal CA2 representations of space. *Nature Communications, 7,* 10300.

Alivisatos, A. P., Andrews, A. M., Boyden, E. S, Chun, M., et al. (2013). Nanotools for neuroscience and brain activity mapping. *ACS Nano, 7*(3), 1850–1866.

Alkire, M. T., Hudetz, A. G., and Tononi, G. (2008). Consciousness and anesthesia. *Science, 322*, 876–880.

Allard, J. S., Heilbronn, L. K., Smith, C., Hunt, N. D., et al. (2008). In vitro cellular adaptations of indicators of longevity in response to treatment with serum collected from humans on calorie restricted diets. *PLOS ONE, 15*, e3211.

Alle, H., Rother, A., and Geiger, J. (2009). Energy-efficient action potentials in hippocampal mossy fibers. *Science, 325*, 1405–1408.

Almada, S. J., Zonderman, A. B., Shekelle, R. B., Dyer, A. R., et al. (1991). Neuroticism and cynicism and risk of death in middle-aged men: The Western Electric Study. *Psychosomatic Medicine, 53*, 165–175.

Alonso, M., Lepousez, G., Wagner, S., Bardy, C., et al. (2012). Activation of adult-born neurons facilitates learning and memory. *Nature Neuroscience, 15*, 897–904.

Alpert, M., and Friedhoff, A. J. (1980). An un-dopamine hypothesis of schizophrenia. *Schizophrenia Bulletin, 6*, 387–390.

Altman, J. (1969). Autoradiographic and histological studies of postnatal neurogenesis. IV. Cell proliferation and migration in the anterior forebrain, with special reference to persisting neurogenesis in the olfactory bulb. *Journal of Comparative Neurology, 137*, 433–457.

Altschuler, E. L., Wisdom, S. B., Stone, L., Foster, C., et al. (1999). Rehabilitation of hemiparesis after stroke with a mirror. *Lancet, 353*, 2035–2036.

Alvarez, J. A., and Emory, E. (2006). Executive function and the frontal lobes: A meta-analytic review. *Neuropsychology Review, 16*, 17–42.

American Psychiatric Association. (2013). *Diagnostic and Statistical Manual of Mental Disorders* (5th ed.). Arlington, VA: American Psychiatric Publishing.

Aminoff, E. M., Kveraga, K., and Bar, M. (2013). The role of the parahippocampal cortex in cognition. *Trends in Cognitive Science, 17*(8), 379–390.

Amoroso, T. (2015). The psychopharmacology of ±3,4 methylenedioxymethamphetamine and its role in the treatment of posttraumatic stress disorder. *Journal of Psychoactive Drugs, 47*, 337–344.

Amunts, K., Schlaug, G., Jaencke, L., Steinmetz, H., et al. (1997). Motor cortex and hand motor skills: Structural compliance in the human brain. *Human Brain Mapping, 5*, 206–215.

Anand, B. K., and Brobeck, J. R. (1951). Localization of a "feeding center" in the hypothalamus of the rat. *Proceedings of the Society for Experimental Biology and Medicine, 77*, 323–324.

Andersen, B. B., Korbo, L., and Pakkenberg, B. (1992). A quantitative study of the human cerebellum with unbiased stereological techniques. *Journal of Comparative Neurology, 326*, 549–560.

Andersen, P. M., Nilsson, P., Ala-Hurula, V., Keranen, M. L., et al. (1995). Amyotrophic lateral sclerosis associated with homozygosity for an Asp90Ala mutation in CuZn-superoxide dismutase. *Nature Genetics, 10*, 61–66.

Anderson, M. A., Burda, J. E., Ren, Y., Ao, Y., et al. (2015). Astrocyte scar formation aids central nervous system axon regeneration. *Nature, 532*(7598), 195–200.

Andreasen, N. C. (1991). Assessment issues and the cost of schizophrenia. *Schizophrenia Bulletin, 17*, 475–481.

Andreasen, N. C. (1994). Changing concepts of schizophrenia and the ahistorical fallacy. *American Journal of Psychiatry, 151*, 1405–1407.

Andreasen, N. C., Flaum, M., Swayze, V. O. D. S., Alliger, R., et al. (1993). Intelligence and brain structure in normal individuals. *American Journal of Psychiatry, 150*, 130–134.

Andreasen, N., Nassrallah, H. A., Dunn, V., Olson, S. C., et al. (1986). Structural abnormalities in the frontal system in schizophrenia. *Archives of General Psychiatry, 43*, 136–144.

Andrews-Hanna, J. R., Smallwood, J., and Spreng, R. N. (2014). The default network and self-generated thought: Component processes, dynamic control, and clinical relevance. *Annals of the New York Academy of Sciences, 1316*, 29–52.

Anggono, V., and Huganir, R. L. (2012). Regulation of AMPA receptor trafficking and synaptic plasticity. *Current Opinions in Neurobiology, 22*, 461–469.

Anguera, J. A., Boccanfuso, J., Rintoul, J. L., Al-Hashimi, O., et al. (2013). Video game training enhances cognitive control in older adults. *Nature, 501*(7465), 97–101.

Anson, R. M., Guo, Z., de Cabo, R., Iyun, T., et al. (2003). Intermittent fasting dissociates beneficial effects of dietary restriction on glucose metabolism and neuronal resistance to injury from calorie intake. *Proceedings of the National Academy of Sciences, USA, 100*, 6216–6220.

Anstey, M. L., Rogers, S. M., Ott, S. R., Burrows, M., et al. (2009). Serotonin mediates behavioral gregarization underlying swarm formation in desert locusts. *Science, 323*, 627–630.

Antle, M. C., and Silver, R. (2005). Orchestrating time: Arrangements of the brain circadian clock. *Trends in Neurosciences, 28*(3), 145–151.

Anton-Erxleben, K., and Carrasco, M. (2013). Attentional enhancement of spatial resolution: Linking behavioural and neurophysiological evidence. *Nature Reviews Neuroscience, 14*(3), 188–200.

Apkarian, A. V., Sosa, Y., Sonty, S., Levy, R. M., et al. (2004). Chronic back pain is associated with decreased prefrontal and thalamic gray matter density. *Journal of Neuroscience, 24*, 10410–10415.

Archer, G. S., Friend, T. H., Piedrahita, J., Nevill, C. H., et al. (2003). Behavioral variation among cloned pigs. *Applied Animal Behaviour Science, 82*, 151–161.

Archer, J. (2006). Testosterone and human aggression: An evaluation of the challenge hypothesis. *Neuroscience and Biobehavioral Reviews, 30*, 319–345.

Ardiel, E. L., and Rankin, C. H. (2010). An elegant mind: Learning and memory in *Caenorhabditis elegans*. *Learning and Memory, 17*, 191–201.

Argyll-Robertson, D. M. C. L. (1869). On an interesting series of eye symptoms in a case of spinal disease, with remarks on the action of belladonna on the iris. *Edinburgh Medical Journal, 14*, 696–708.

Arnold, A. P. (1980). Sexual differences in the brain. *American Scientist, 68*, 165–173.

Arnold, A. P., and Schlinger, B. A. (1993). Sexual differentiation of brain and behavior: The zebra finch is not just a flying rat. *Brain, Behavior and Evolution, 42*, 231–241.

Arnold, K., and Zuberbühler, K. (2006). Language evolution: Semantic combinations in primate calls. *Nature, 441*, 303.

Arnone, D., Cavanagh, J., Gerber, D., Lawrie, S. M., et al. (2009). Magnetic resonance imaging studies in bipolar disorder and schizophrenia: Meta-analysis. *British Journal of Psychiatry, 195*, 194–201.

Arnsten, A. F. (2006). Fundamentals of attention-deficit/hyperactivity disorder: Circuits and pathways. *Journal of Clinical Psychiatry, 67*, 7–12.

Aroniadou, V. A., Maillis, A., and Stefanis, C. C. (1993). Dihydropyridine-sensitive calcium channels are involved in the induction of N-methyl-D-aspartate receptor-independent long-term potentiation in visual cortex of adult rats. *Neuroscience Letters, 151*, 77–80.

Aschner, M., and Ceccatelli, S. (2010). Are neuropathological conditions relevant to ethylmercury exposure? *Neurotoxicity Research, 1,* 59–68.

Aschwanden, C. (2013). The curious lives of people who feel no fear. *New Scientist, 217,* 36–39.

Aserinsky, E., and Kleitman, N. (1953). Regularly occurring periods of eye motility, and concomitant phenomena, during sleep. *Science, 118,* 273–274.

Ashmore, J. F. (1994). The cellular machinery of the cochlea. *Experimental Physiology, 79,* 113–134.

Aspelund, A., Antila, S., Proulx, S. T., Karlsen, T. V., et al. (2015). A dural lymphatic vascular system that drains brain interstitial fluid and macromolecules. *Journal of Experimental Medicine, 212*(7), 991–999.

Audero, E., Coppi, E., Mlinar, B., Rossetti, T., et al. (2008). Sporadic autonomic dysregulation and death associated with excessive serotonin autoinhibition. *Science, 321,* 130–133.

Aungst, J. L., Heyward, P. M., Puche, A. C., Karnup, S. V., et al. (2003). Centre-surround inhibition among olfactory bulb glomeruli. *Nature, 426,* 623–629.

Avan, P., Loth, D., Menguy, C., and Teyssou, M. (1992). Hypothetical roles of middle ear muscles in the guinea-pig. *Hearing Research, 59,* 59–69.

Avanzini, G., Depaulis, A., Tassinari, A., and de Curtis M. (2013). Do seizures and epileptic activity worsen epilepsy and deteriorate cognitive function? *Epilepsia, 54*(Suppl. 8), 14–21.

Aviezer, H., Trope, Y., and Todorov, A. (2012). Body cues, not facial expressions, discriminate between intense positive and negative emotions. *Science, 338,* 1225–1229.

Azevedo, F. A., Carvalho, L. R., Grinberg, L. T., Farfel, J. M., et al. (2009). Equal numbers of neuronal and nonneuronal cells make the human brain an isometrically scaled-up primate brain. *Journal of Comparative Neurology, 513,* 532–541.

B

Baddeley, A. (2003). Working memory: Looking back and looking forward. *Nature Review. Neuroscience, 4,* 829–839.

Baddeley, A. D., and Warrington, E. K. (1970). Amnesia and the distinction between long- and short-term memory. *Journal of Verbal Learning and Verbal Behavior, 9,* 176–189.

Bagemihl, B. (1999). *Biological exuberance: Animal homosexuality and natural diversity.* New York: St. Martin's.

Bagni, C., and Greenough, W. T. (2005). From mRNP trafficking to spine dysmorphogenesis: The roots of fragile X syndrome. *Nature Reviews Neuroscience, 6,* 376–387.

Bailey, C. H., and Chen, M. (1983). Morphological basis of long-term habituation and sensitization in *Aplysia. Science, 220,* 91–93.

Bailey, H. R., Zacks, J. M., Hambrick, D. Z., Zacks, R. T., et al. (2013). Medial temporal lobe volume predicts elders' everyday memory. *Psychological Science, 24*(7), 1113–1122. doi:10.1177/0956797612466676

Bailey, J. M., Pillard, R. C., Neale, M. C., and Agyei, Y. (1993). Heritable factors influence sexual orientation in women. *Archives of General Psychiatry, 50,* 217–223.

Bailey, K., and West, R. (2013). The effects of an action video game on visual and affective information processing. *Brain Research, 1504,* 35–46.

Bakker, J., De Mees, C., Douhard, Q., Balthazart, J., et al. (2006). Alpha-fetoprotein protects the developing female mouse brain from masculinization and defeminization by estrogens. *Nature Neuroscience, 9,* 220–226.

Baldermann, J. C., Schüller, T., Huys, D., Becker, I., et al. (2016). Deep brain stimulation for Tourette-syndrome: A systematic review and meta-analysis. *Brain Stimulation, 9,* 296–304.

Baldwin, M. W., Toda, Y., Nakagita, T., O'Connell, M. J., et al. (2014). Sensory biology: Evolution of sweet taste perception in hummingbirds by transformation of the ancestral umami receptor. *Science, 345*(6199), 929–933.

Balter, M. (2004). Evolution of behavior: Seeking the key to music. *Science, 306,* 1120–1122.

Balter, M. (2005). Are human brains still evolving? Brain genes show signs of selection. *Science, 309*(5741), 1662–1663.

Bancaud, J., Brunet-Bourgin, F., Chauvel, P., and Halgren, E. (1994). Anatomical origin of deja vu and vivid "memories" in human temporal lobe. *Brain, 117,* 71–90.

Baptista, L. F. (1996). Nature and its nurturing in avian vocal development. In D. E. Kroodsma and E. H. Miller (Eds.), *Ecology and evolution of acoustic communication in birds* (pp. 39–60). Ithaca, NY: Cornell University Press.

Barasa, A. (1960). Forma, grandezza e densita dei neuroni della corteccia cerebrale in mammiferi di grandezza corporea differente. *Zeitschrift für Zellforschung, 53,* 69–89.

Barbeau, H., Norman, K., Fung, J., Visintin, M., et al. (1998). Does neurorehabilitation play a role in the recovery of walking in neurological populations? *Annals of the New York Academy of Sciences, 860,* 377–392.

Barha, C. K., and Galea, L. A. (2010). Influence of different estrogens on neuroplasticity and cognition in the hippocampus. *Biochimica et Biophysica Acta, 1800*(10), 1056–1067.

Barker, R. A., Drouin-Ouellet, J., and Parmar, M. (2015). Cell-based therapies for Parkinson disease: Past insights and future potential. *Nature Reviews Neurology, 11*(9), 492–503.

Barlow, H. B., and Levick, W. R. (1965). The mechanism of directionally selective units in rabbit's retina. *Journal of Physiology, 178,* 477–504.

Barnea, G., O'Donnell, S., Mancia, F., Sun, X., et al. (2004). Odorant receptors on axon termini in the brain. *Science, 304,* 1468.

Barnes, C. A., and Penner, M. R. (2007). Memory changes with age: Neurobiological correlates. In R. P. Kesner and J. L. Martinez (Eds.), *Neurobiology of learning and memory* (2nd ed., pp. 483–517). San Diego, CA: Elsevier.

Barrett, A. M., Goedert, K. M., and Basso, J. C. (2012). Prism adaptation for spatial neglect after stroke: Translational practice gaps. *Nature Reviews Neurology, 8*(10), 567–577.

Barrett, L. F., Mesquita, B., and Gendron, M. (2011). Context in emotion perception. *Current Directions in Psychological Science, 20*(5), 286–290.

Barrio, J. R., Small, G. W., Wong, K. P., Huang, S. C., et al. (2015). In vivo characterization of chronic traumatic encephalopathy using [F-18]FDDNP PET brain imaging. *Proceedings of the National Academy of Sciences, USA, 112*(16), E2039–2047.

Bar-Shira, O., Maor, R., and Chechik, G. (2015). Gene expression switching of receptor subunits in human brain development. *PLOS Computational Biology, 11,* e1004559.

Bartels, A., and Zeki, S. (2000). The neural basis of romantic love. *Neuroreport, 11,* 3829–3834.

Bartolomeo, P. (2007). Visual neglect. *Current Opinion in Neurology, 20,* 381–386.

Bartoshuk, L. M. (1993). Genetic and pathological taste variation: What can we learn from animal models and human disease? In D. Chadwick, J. Marsh, and J. Goode (Eds.), *The molecular basis of smell and taste transduction* (pp. 251–267). New York: Wiley.

Bartoshuk, L. M., and Beauchamp, G. K. (1994). Chemical senses. *Annual Review of Psychology, 45*, 419–449.

Bartsch, T., and Butler, C. (2013). Transient amnesic syndromes. *Nature Reviews Neurology, 9*, 86–97. doi:10.1038/nrneurol.2012.264

Bartsch, T., Schönfeld, R., Müller, F. J., Alfke, K., et al. (2010). Focal lesions of human hippocampal CA1 neurons in transient global amnesia impair place memory. *Science, 328*, 1412–1415.

Basbaum, A., and Fields, H. L. (1984). Endogenous pain control systems: Brainstem spinal pathways and endorphin circuitry. *Annual Review of Neuroscience, 7*, 309–339.

Basson, R. (2001). Human sex-response cycles. *Journal of Sex & Marital Therapy, 27*, 33–43.

Basson, R. (2008). Women's sexual function and dysfunction: Current uncertainties, future directions. *International Journal of Impotence Research, 20*, 466–478.

Bates, E., Wilson, S. M., Saygin, A. P., Dick, F., et al. (2003). Voxel-based lesion-symptom mapping. *Nature Neuroscience, 6*, 448–450.

Bates, G. P., Dorsey, R., Gusella, J. F., Hayden, M. R., et al. (2015). Huntington disease. *Nature Reviews Disease Primers, 1*, 15005.

Bates, T. C., Lind, P. A., Luciano, M., Montgomery, G. W., et al. (2010). Dyslexia and DYX1C1: Deficits in reading and spelling associated with a missense mutation. *Molecular Psychiatry, 12*, 1190–1196.

Batterham, R. L., and Bloom, S. R. (2003). The gut hormone peptide YY regulates appetite. *Annals of the New York Academy of Sciences, 994*, 162–168.

Batterham, R. L., Cohen, M. A., Ellis, S. M., Le Roux, C. W., et al. (2003). Inhibition of food intake in obese subjects by peptide YY_{3-36}. *New England Journal of Medicine, 349*, 941–948.

Baumeister, D., Barnes, G., Giaroli, G., and Tracy, D. (2014). Classical hallucinogens as antidepressants? A review of pharmacodynamics and putative clinical roles. *Therapeutic Advances in Psychopharmacology, 4*, 156–169.

Bautista, D. M., Siemens, J., Glazer, J. M., Tsuruda, P. R., et al. (2007). The menthol receptor TRPM8 is the principal detector of environmental cold. *Nature, 448*, 204–208.

Baynes, K. C., Dhillo, W. S., and Bloom, S. R. (2006). Regulation of food intake by gastrointestinal hormones. *Current Opinion in Gastroenterology, 22*, 626–631.

Beach, F. A. (1977). *Human sexuality in four perspectives.* Baltimore: Johns Hopkins University Press.

Beall, A. T., and Tracy, J. L. (2013). Women are more likely to wear red or pink at peak fertility. *Psychological Science, 24*(9), 1837–1841.

Beauchamp, G. K., Cowart, B. J., Mennella, J. A., and Marsh, R. R. (1994). Infant salt taste: Developmental, methodological, and contextual factors. *Developmental Psychobiology, 27*, 353–365.

Bee, M. A., and Micheyl, C. (2008). The cocktail party problem: What is it? How can it be solved? And why should animal behaviorists study it? *Journal of Comparative Psychology, 122*, 235–251.

Beecher, H. K. (1956). Relationship of significance of wound to pain experienced. *Journal of the American Medical Association, 161*(17), 1609–1613.

Beeli, G., Esslen, M., and Jäncke, L. (2005). When coloured sounds taste sweet. *Nature, 434*, 38.

Beggs, S., Trang, T., and Salter, M. W. (2012). P2X4R+ microglia drive neuropathic pain. *Nature Neuroscience, 15*, 1068–1073.

Beggs, W. D., and Foreman, D. L. (1980). Sound localization and early binaural experience in the deaf. *British Journal of Audiology, 14*, 41–48.

Behr, C., Goltzene, M. A., Kosmalski, G., Hirsch, E., et al. (2016). Epidemiology of epilepsy. *Revue Neurologique (Paris), 172*, 27–36.

Belelli, D., and Lambert, J. J. (2005). Neurosteroids: Endogenous regulators of the GABA(A) receptor. *Nature Reviews Neuroscience, 6*, 565–575.

Belleville, S., Clément, F., Mella, S., Gilbert, B., et al. (2011). Training-related brain plasticity in subjects at risk of developing Alzheimer's disease. *Brain, 134*(Pt. 6), 1623–1634.

Bellinger, D. L., Ackerman, K. D., Felten, S.Y., and Felten, D. L. (1992). A longitudinal study of age-related loss of noradrenergic nerves and lymphoid cells in the rat spleen. *Experimental Neurology, 116*, 295–311.

Bellugi, U., Poizner, H., and Klima, E. S. (1983). Brain organization for language: Clues from sign aphasia. *Human Neurobiology, 2*, 155–171.

Belluscio, L., Gold, G. H., Nemes, A., and Axel, R. (1998). Mice deficient in G(olf) are anosmic. *Neuron, 20*, 69–81.

Belvederi, M. M., Pariante, C., Mondelli, V., Masotti, M., et al. (2014). HPA axis and aging in depression: systematic review and meta-analysis. *Psychoneuroendocrinology, 41*, 46–62. doi: 10.1016/j.psyneuen.2013.12.004

Bennett, E. L., Diamond, M. L., Krech, D., and Rosenzweig, M. R. (1964). Chemical and anatomical plasticity of brain. *Science, 146*, 610–619.

Bennett, E. L., Rosenzweig, M. R., and Diamond, M. C. (1969). Rat brain: Effects of environmental enrichment on wet and dry weights. *Science, 163*, 825–826.

Bennett, W. (1983). The nicotine fix. *Rhode Island Medical Journal, 66*, 455–458.

Benney, K. S., and Braaten, R. F. (2000). Auditory scene analysis in estrildid finches (*Taeniopygia guttata* and *Lonchura striata domestica*): A species advantage for detection of conspecific song. *Journal of Comparative Psychology, 114*, 174–182.

Bensafi, M., Porter, J., Pouliot, S., Mainland, J., et al. (2003). Olfactomotor activity during imagery mimics that during perception. *Nature Neuroscience, 6*, 1142–1144.

Bensmaia, S. J., and Miller, L. E. (2014). Restoring sensorimotor function through intracortical interfaces: Progress and looming challenges. *Nature Reviews Neuroscience, 15*(5), 313–325.

Benson, D. F. (1967). Fluency in aphasia: Correlation with radioactive scan localization. *Cortex, 3*, 373–394.

Benson, P. J., Beedie, S. A., Shephard, E., Giegling, I., et al. (2012). Simple viewing tests can detect eye movement abnormalities that distinguish schizophrenia cases from controls with exceptional accuracy. *Biological Psychiatry, 72*, 716–724.

Berenbaum, S. A. (2001). Cognitive function in congenital adrenal hyperplasia. *Endocrinology and Metabolism Clinics of North America, 30*, 173–192.

Berger, L. R., de Ruiter, D. J., Churchill, S. E, Schmid, P., et al. (2010). *Australopithecus sediba*: A new species of Homo-like australopith from South Africa. *Science, 328*(5975), 195–204.

Bergfeld, I. O., Mantione, M., Hoogendoorn, M. L. C., Ruhé, H. G., et al. (2016). Deep brain stimulation of the ventral anterior limb of the internal capsule for treatment resistant depression: A randomized clinical trial. *JAMA Psychiatry.* doi:10.1001/jamapsychiatry.2016.0152

Berglund, E. D, Liu, T., Kong, X., Sohn, J. W., et al. (2014). Melanocortin 4 receptors in autonomic neurons regulate thermogenesis and glycemia. *Nature Neuroscience, 17*, 911–913.

Bernal, B., and Altman, N. (2010). The connectivity of the superior longitudinal fasciculus: A tractography DTI study. *Magnetic Resonance Imaging, 28*(2), 217–225.

Berneche, S., and Roux, B. (2001). Energetics of ion conduction through the K+ channel. *Nature, 414*, 73–77.

Bernhardt, P. C. (1997). Influences of serotonin and testosterone in aggression and dominance: Convergence with social psychology. *Current Directions in Psychological Science, 2*(6), 44–48.

Bernhardt, P. C., Dabbs, J. M., Jr., Fielden, J. A., and Lutter, C. D. (1998). Testosterone changes during vicarious experiences of winning and losing among fans at sporting events. *Physiology & Behavior, 65*, 59–62.

Bernstein, H. G., Steiner, J., Guest, P. C., Dobrowolny, H., et al. (2015). Glial cells as key players in schizophrenia pathology: Recent insights and concepts of therapy. *Schizophrenia Research, 161*(1), 4–18.

Bernstein, I. S., and Gordon, T. P. (1974). The function of aggression in primate societies. *American Scientist, 62*, 304–311.

Bernstein, L. E., Auer, E. T., Jr., Moore, J. K., Ponton, C. W., et al. (2002). Visual speech perception without primary auditory cortex activation. *Neuroreport, 13*, 311–315.

Bernstein-Goral, H., and Bregman, B. S. (1993). Spinal cord transplants support the regeneration of axotomized neurons after spinal cord lesions at birth: A quantitative double-labeling study. *Experimental Neurology, 123*, 118–132.

Berton, O., and Nestler, E. J. (2006). New approaches to antidepressant drug discovery: Beyond monoamines. *Neuroscience, 7*, 137–151.

Bertram, L., and Tanzi, R. E. (2008). Thirty years of Alzheimer's disease genetics: The implications of systematic meta-analyses. *Nature Reviews Neuroscience, 9*, 768–778.

Beurg, M., Fettiplace, R., Nam, J.-H., and Ricci, A. J. (2009). Localization of inner hair cell mechanotransducer channels using high-speed calcium imaging. *Nature Neuroscience, 12*, 553–558.

Bezanilla, F., and Correa, A. M. (1995). Single-channel properties and gating of Na+ and K+ channels in the squid giant axon. In N. J. Abbott, R. Williamson, and L. Maddock (Eds.), *Cephalopod neurobiology* (pp. 131–151). New York: Oxford University Press.

Binder, J. R., Rao, S. M., Hammeke, T. A., Yetkin, F. Z., et al. (1994). Functional magnetic resonance imaging of human auditory cortex. *Annals of Neurology, 35*, 662–672.

Birch, L. L., Fisher, J. O., and Davison, K. K. (2003). Learning to overeat: Maternal use of restrictive feeding practices promotes girls' eating in the absence of hunger. *American Journal of Clinical Nutrition, 78*, 215–220.

Bird, C. D., and Emery, N. J. (2009). Insightful problem solving and creative tool modification by captive nontool-using rooks. *Proceedings of the National Academy of Sciences, USA, 106*, 10370–10375.

Bishop, N. A., and Guarente, L. (2007). Genetic links between diet and lifespan: Shared mechanisms from yeast to humans. *Nature Reviews Genetics, 8*, 835–844.

Bisley, J. W., and Goldberg, M. E. (2003). Neuronal activity in the lateral intraparietal area and spatial attention. *Science, 299*, 81–86.

Bisley, J. W., and Goldberg, M. E. (2006). Neural correlates of attention and distractibility in the lateral intraparietal area. *Journal of Neurophysiology, 95*, 1696–1717.

Bjorness, T. E., and Greene, R. W. (2009). Adenosine and sleep. *Current Neuropharmacology, 7*(3), 238–245.

Blackwell, D. L., Lucas, J. W., and Clarke, T. C. (2014). Summary health statistics for U.S. adults: National Health Interview Survey. *Vital and Health Statistics, 10*(260), 1–161.

Blake, D. J., Weir, A., Newey, S. E., and Davies, K. E. (2002). Function and genetics of dystrophin and dystrophin-related proteins in muscle. *Physiology Review, 82*, 291–329.

Blanchard, R., Cantor, J. M., Bogaert, A. F., Breedlove, S. M., et al. (2006). Interaction of fraternal birth order and handedness in the development of male homosexuality. *Hormones and Behavior, 49*, 405–414.

Blaxton, T. A., Bookheimer, S. Y., Zeffiro, T. A., Figlozzi, C. M., et al. (1996). Functional mapping of human memory using PET: Comparisons of conceptual perceptual tasks. *Canadian Journal of Experimental Psychology, 50*, 42–56.

Blehar, M. C., and Rosenthal, N. E. (1989). Seasonal affective disorders and phototherapy. Report of a National Institute of Mental Health-sponsored workshop. *Archives of General Psychiatry, 46*, 469–474.

Bleuler, E. (1950). *Dementia praecox; or, The group of schizophrenias* (J. Zinkin, Trans.). New York: International Universities Press.

Bliss, T. V. P., and Gardner-Medwin, A. R. (1973). Long-lasting potentiation of synaptic transmission in the dentate area of the unanaesthetized rabbit following stimulation of the perforant path. *Journal of Physiology (London), 232*, 357–374.

Bliss, T. V. P., and Lømo, T. (1973). Long-lasting potentiation of synaptic transmission in the dentate area of the anaesthetized rabbit following stimulation of the perforant path. *Journal of Physiology (London), 232*, 331–356.

Bliwise, D. L. (1989). Neuropsychological function and sleep. *Clinics in Geriatric Medicine, 5*, 381–394.

Blue, M. E., and Parnavelas, J. G. (1983). The formation and maturation of synapses in the visual cortex of the rat. II. Quantitative analysis. *Journal of Neurocytology, 12*, 697–712.

Blumberg, M. S. (2015). Developing sensorimotor systems in our sleep. *Current Directions in Psychological Science, 24*(1), 32–37.

Blumberg, M. S., Sokoloff, G., and Kirby, R. F. (1997). Brown fat thermogenesis and cardiac rate regulation during cold challenge in infant rats. *American Journal of Physiology, 272*, R1308–R1313.

Blumstein, S. E., and Amso, D. (2013). Dynamic functional organization of language: Insights from functional neuroimaging. *Perspectives on Psychological Science, 8*(1), 44–48.

Boets, B., Op de Beeck, H. P., Vandermosten, M., Scott, S. K., et al. (2013). Intact but less accessible phonetic representations in adults with dyslexia. *Science, 342*(6163), 1251–1254.

Bogaert, A. F. (2006). Biological versus nonbiological older brothers and men's sexual orientation. *Proceedings of the National Academy of Sciences, USA, 103*, 10771–10774.

Bogaert, A. F. (2007). Extreme right-handedness, older brothers, and sexual orientation in men. *Neuropsychology, 21*, 141–148.

Bogenschutz, M. P., and Johnson, M. W. (2016). Classic hallucinogens in the treatment of addictions. *Progress in Neuro-Psychopharmacology Biological Psychiatry, 64*, 250–258.

Bogin, B. (1997). Evolutionary hypotheses for human childhood. *Yearbook of Physical Anthropology, 40*, 63–89.

Bohrn, I., Carbon, C.-C., and Hutzler, F. (2010). Mona Lisa's smile: perception or deception? *Psychological Science, 21*, 378–380.

Bolhuis, J. J., Okanoya, K., and Scharff, C. (2010). Twitter evolution: Converging mechanisms in birdsong and human speech. *Nature Reviews Neuroscience, 11*(11), 747–759.

Boly, M., Garrido, M. I., Gosseries, O., Bruno, M. A., et al. (2011). Preserved feedforward but impaired top-down processes in the vegetative state. *Science, 332,* 858–862.

Boly, M., Moran, R., Murphy, M., Boveroux, P., et al. (2012). Connectivity changes underlying spectral EEG changes during propofol-induced loss of consciousness. *Journal of Neuroscience, 32*(20),7082–7090.

Bonhoeffer, T., and Grinvald, A. (1991). Iso-orientation domains in cat visual cortex are arranged in pinwheel-like patterns. *Nature, 353,* 429–431.

Bonini, F., Burle, B., Liégeois-Chauvel, C., Régis, J., et al. (2014). Action monitoring and medial frontal cortex: Leading role of supplementary motor area. *Science, 343*(6173), 888–891.

Bonnel, A. M., and Prinzmetal, W. (1998). Dividing attention between the color and the shape of objects. *Perception & Psychophysics, 60,* 113–124.

Boolell, M., Gepi-Attee, S., Gingell, J. C., and Allen, M. J. (1996). Sildenafil, a novel effective oral therapy for male erectile dysfunction. *British Journal of Urology, 78,* 257–261.

Boot, W. R., Kramer, A. F., Simons, D. J., Fabiani, M., et al. (2008). The effects of video game playing on attention, memory, and executive control. *Acta Psychologica, 129,* 387–398.

Booth, W., Smith, C. F., Eskridge, P. H., Hoss, S. K., et al. (2012). Facultative parthenogenesis discovered in wild vertebrates. *Biology Letters, 8,* 983–985.

Borgstein, J., and Grootendorst, C. (2002). Clinical picture: Half a brain. *Lancet, 359,* 473.

Borota, D., Murray, E., Keceli, G., Chang, A., et al. (2014). Post-study caffeine administration enhances memory consolidation in humans. *Nature Neuroscience, 17,* 201–203.

Boström, P., Wu, J., Jedrychowski, M. P., Korde, A., et al. (2012). A PGC1-α-dependent myokine that drives brown-fat-like development of white fat and thermogenesis. *Nature, 481*(7382), 463–468.

Bottjer, S. W., Miesner, E. A., and Arnold, A. P. (1984). Forebrain lesions disrupt development but not maintenance of song in passerine birds. *Science, 224,* 901–903.

Bourane, S., Duan, B., Koch, S. C., Dalet, A., et al. (2015). Gate control of mechanical itch by a subpopulation of spinal cord interneurons. *Science, 350*(6260), 550–554.

Bouret, S. G., Draper, S. J., and Simerly, R. B. (2004). Trophic action of leptin on hypothalamic neurons that regulate feeding. *Science, 304,* 108–110.

Bourque, C. W. (2008). Central mechanisms of osmosensation and systemic osmoregulation. *Nature Reviews Neuroscience, 9,* 519–531.

Bourtchuladze, R., Frenguelli, B., Blendy, J., Cioffi, D., et al. (1994). Deficient long-term memory in mice with a targeted mutation of the cAMP-responsive element-binding protein. *Cell, 79,* 59–68.

Bouton, C. E., Shaikhouni, A., Annetta, N.V., Bockbrader, M. A., et al. (2016). Restoring cortical control of functional movement in a human with quadriplegia. *Nature, 533*(7602), 247–250.

Bower, B. (2000). Genes to grow on. *Science News, 157*(9), 142.

Bower, B. (2003).Vision seekers. *Science News, 164,* 331–333.

Bower, B. (2006). Prescription for controversy: Medications for depressed kids spark scientific dispute. *Science News, 169,* 168–172.

Bowles, B., Crupi, C., Mirsattari, S. M., Pigott, S. E., et al. (2007). Impaired familiarity with preserved recollection after anterior temporal-lobe resection that spares the hippocampus. *Proceedings of the National Academy of Sciences, USA, 104*(41), 16382–16387.

Bowles, B., Crupi, C., Pigott, S., Parrent, A., et al. (2010). Double dissociation of selective recollection and familiarity impairments following two different surgical treatments for temporal-lobe epilepsy. *Neuropsychologia, 48*(9), 2640–2647.

Boyd, C. A. (2010). Cerebellar agenesis revisited. *Brain, 133*(Pt. 3), 941–944.

Brady, T. F., Konkle, T., Alvarez, G. A., and Oliva, A. (2008).Visual long-term memory has a massive storage capacity for object details. *Proceedings of the National Academy of Sciences, USA, 105*(38), 14325–14329.

Brain, P. F. (1994). Neurotransmission, the individual and the alcohol/aggression link. Commentary on Miczek et al. "Neuropharmacological characteristics of individual differences in alcohol effects on aggression in rodents and primates." *Behavioural Pharmacology, 5,* 422–424.

Brainard, D. H., Roorda, A.,Yamauchi,Y., Calderone, J. B., et al. (2000). Functional consequences of the relative numbers of L and M cones. *Journal of the Optical Society of America. Part A, Optics, Image Science and Vision, 17,* 607–614.

Brancaleoni, G., Nikitenkova, E., Grassi, L., and Hansen,V. (2009). Seasonal affective disorder and latitude of living. *Epidemiologia e Psichiatria Sociale, 18,* 336–343.

Brandler, W. M., and Paracchini, S. (2014). The genetic relationship between handedness and neurodevelopmental disorders. *Trends in Molecular Medicine, 20*(2), 83–90.

Brandon, N. J., and Sawa, A. (2011). Linking neurodevelopment and synaptic theories of mental illness through DISC1. *Nature Reviews Neuroscience, 12,* 707–722.

Branson, R., Potoczna, N., Kral, J. G., Lentes, K. U., et al. (2003). Binge eating as a major phenotype of melanocortin 4 receptor gene mutations. *New England Journal of Medicine, 348,* 1096–1103.

Braun, K. A., Ellis, R., and Loftus, E. F. (2002). Make my memory: How advertising can change our memories of the past. *Psychology and Marketing, 19,* 1–23.

Bray, G. A. (1969). Effect of caloric restriction on energy expenditure in obese patients. *Lancet, 2,* 397–398.

Breedlove, S. M. (2010). Minireview: Organizational hypothesis: Instances of the fingerpost. *Endocrinology, 151*(9), 4116–4122.

Breier, A., Malhotra, A. K., Pinals, D. A., Weisenfeld, N. I., et al. (1997). Association of ketamine-induced psychosis with focal activation of the prefrontal cortex in healthy volunteers. *American Journal of Psychiatry, 154,* 805–811.

Bremer, F. (1938). L'activité électrique de l'écorce cérébrale. *Actualités Scientifiques et Industrielles, 658,* 3–46.

Bremner, J. D., Randall, P., Scott, T. M., Bronen, R. A., et al. (1995). MRI-based measurement of hippocampal volume in patients with combat-related posttraumatic stress disorder. *American Journal of Psychiatry, 152,* 973–981.

Bremner, J. D., Scott, T. M., Delaney, R. C., Southwick, S. M., et al. (1993). Deficits in short-term memory in posttraumatic stress disorder. *American Journal of Psychiatry, 150,* 1015–1019.

Brennan, S. C., Davies, T. S., Schepelmann, M., and Riccardi, D. (2014). Emerging roles of the extracellular calcium-sensing receptor in nutrient sensing: Control of taste modulation and intestinal hormone secretion. *British Journal of Nutrition, 111*(Suppl. 1), S16–S22.

Brewer, J. B., Zhao, Z., Desmond, J. E., Glover, G. H., et al. (1998). Making memories: Brain activity that predicts how well visual experience will be remembered. *Science, 281,* 1185–1187.

Bridgham, J. T., Carroll, S. M., and Thornton, J. W. (2006). Evolution of hormone-receptor complexity by molecular exploitation. *Science, 312,* 97–101.

Brien, J. A. (1993). Ototoxicity associated with salicylates. A brief review. *Drug Safety, 9*, 143–148.

Brigande, J. V., and Heller, S. (2009). *Quo vadis*, hair cell regeneration? *Nature Neuroscience, 12*, 679–685.

Briggs, F., and Usrey, W. M. (2008). Emerging views of corticothalamic function. *Current Opinion in Neurobiology, 18*, 403–407.

Briggs, F., Mangun, G. R., and Usrey, W. M. (2013). Attention enhances synaptic efficacy and the signal-to-noise ratio in neural circuits. *Nature, 499*(7459), 476–480.

Bril, B., Smaers, J., Steele, J., Rein, R., et al. (2012). Functional mastery of percussive technology in nut-cracking and stone-flaking actions: Experimental comparison and implications for the evolution of the human brain. *Philosophical Transactions of the Royal Society of London. Series B: Biological Sciences, 367*(1585), 59–74.

Broadbent, D. A. (1958). *Perception and communication.* New York: Pergamon.

Broberg, D. J., and Bernstein, I. L. (1989). Cephalic insulin release in anorexic women. *Physiology & Behavior, 45*, 871–874.

Brodin, T., Fick, J., Jonsson, M., and Klaminder, J. (2013). Dilute concentrations of a psychiatric drug alter behavior of fish from natural populations. *Science, 339*, 814–815.

Brody, A. L., Mandelkern, M. A., London, E. D., Olmstead, R. E., et al. (2006). Cigarette smoking saturates brain alpha 4 beta 2 nicotinic acetylcholine receptors. *Archives of General Psychiatry, 63*, 907–915.

Brody, G. H., Beach, S. R., Philibert, R. A., Chen, Y. F., et al. (2009). Parenting moderates a genetic vulnerability factor in longitudinal increases in youths' substance abuse. *Journal of Consulting and Clinical Psychology, 77*, 1–11.

Brohawn, S. G., Campbell, E. B., and MacKinnon, R. (2014). Physical mechanism for gating and mechanosensitivity of the human TRAAK K$^+$ channel. *Nature, 516*(7529), 126–130.

Brooks, J. X., Carriot, J., and Cullen, K. E. (2015). Learning to expect the unexpected: Rapid updating in primate cerebellum during voluntary self-motion. *Nature Neuroscience, 18*(9), 1310–1317.

Broughton, R. (1985). Slow-wave sleep awakenings in normal and in pathology: A brief review. In W. P. Koella, E. Ruther, and H. Schulz (Eds.), *Sleep '84* (pp. 164–167). Stuttgart, Germany: Gustav Fischer.

Broughton, R., Billings, R., Cartwright, R., Doucette, D., et al. (1994). Homicidal somnambulism: A case report. *Sleep, 17*, 253–264.

Brown, A. S. (2011). Exposure to prenatal infection and risk of schizophrenia. *Frontiers in Psychiatry, 2*, 63.

Brown, A. S., and Susser, E. S. (2008). Prenatal nutritional deficiency and risk of adult schizophrenia. *Schizophrenia Bulletin, 34*, 1054–1063.

Brown, C. (2003, February 2). The man who mistook his wife for a deer. *The New York Times*, Section 6, p. 32.

Brown, E. C., Jeong, J. W., Muzik, O., Rothermel, R., et al. (2014). Evaluating the arcuate fasciculus with combined diffusion-weighted MRI tractography and electrocorticography. *Human Brain Mapping, 35*(5), 2333–2347.

Brown, J. (1958). Some tests of the decay theory of immediate memory. *Quarterly Journal of Experimental Psychology, 10*, 12–21.

Brownlee, S., and Schrof, J. M. (1997). The quality of mercy. Effective pain treatments already exist. Why aren't doctors using them? *U.S. News & World Report, 122*, 54–67.

Bruel-Jungerman, E., Rampon, C., and Laroche S. (2007). Adult hippocampal neurogenesis, synaptic plasticity and memory: Facts and hypotheses. *Review in the Neurosciences, 18*, 93–114.

Brunel, N. (2016). Is cortical connectivity optimized for storing information? *Nature Neuroscience, 19*(5), 749–755.

Brunet, A., Thomas, É., Saumier, D., Ashbaugh, A. R., et al. (2014). Trauma reactivation plus propranolol is associated with durably low physiological responding during subsequent script-driven traumatic imagery. *Canadian Journal of Psychiatry, 59*(4), 228–232.

Brunet, L. J., Gold, G. H., and Ngai, J. (1996). General anosmia caused by a targeted disruption of the mouse olfactory cyclic nucleotide-gated cation channel. *Neuron, 17*, 681–693.

Brunetti, M., Della Penna, S., Ferretti, A., Del Gratta, C., et al. (2008). A frontoparietal network for spatial attention reorienting in the auditory domain: A human fMRI/MEG study of functional and temporal dynamics. *Cerebral Cortex, 18*, 1139–1147.

Brunoni, A. R., Moffa, A. H., Fregni, F., Palm, U., et al. (2016). Transcranial direct current stimulation for acute major depressive episodes: Meta-analysis of individual patient data. *British Journal of Psychiatry*. doi:10.1192/bjp.bp.115.164715

Bu, G. (2009). Apolipoprotein E and its receptors in Alzheimer's disease: Pathways, pathogenesis and therapy. *Nature Reviews Neuroscience, 10*, 333–344.

Buccino, G., Lui, F., Canessa, N., Patteri, I., et al. (2004). Neural circuits involved in the recognition of actions performed by nonconspecifics: An fMRI study. *Journal of Cognitive Neuroscience, 16*, 114–126.

Buccino, G., Solodkin, A., and Small, S. L. (2006). Functions of the mirror neuron system: Implications for neurorehabilitation. *Cognitive and Behavioral Neurology, 19*, 55–63.

Buchsbaum, B. R., Baldo, J., Okada, K., Berman, K. F., et al. (2011). Conduction aphasia, sensory-motor integration, and phonological short-term memory: An aggregate analysis of lesion and fMRI data. *Brain and Language, 119*(3), 119–128.

Buchsbaum, M. S., Buchsbaum, B. R., Chokron, S., Tang, C., et al. (2006). Thalamocortical circuits: fMRI assessment of the pulvinar and medial dorsal nucleus in normal volunteers. *Neuroscience Letters, 404*, 282–287.

Buchsbaum, M. S., Mirsky, A. F., DeLisi, L. E., Morihisa, J., et al. (1984). The Genain quadruplets: Electrophysiological, positron emission and X-ray tomographic studies. *Psychiatry Research, 13*, 95–108.

Buck, L., and Axel, R. (1991). A novel multigene family may encode odorant receptors: A molecular basis for odor recognition. *Cell, 65*, 175–187.

Buhr, E. D., Yoo, S. H., and Takahashi, J. S. (2010). Temperature as a universal resetting cue for mammalian circadian oscillators. *Science, 330*(6002), 379–385.

Bullock, T. H. (1986). Some principles in the brain analysis of important signals: Mapping and stimulus recognition. *Brain, Behavior and Evolution, 28*, 145–156.

Bullock, T. H., Bennett, M. V. L., Johnston, D., Josephson, R., et al. (2005). Neuroscience: The neuron doctrine, redux. *Science, 310*, 791–793.

Burgdorf, J., Kroes, R. A., Moskal, J. R., Pfaus, J. G., et al. (2008). Ultrasonic vocalizations of rats (*Rattus norvegicus*) during mating, play, and aggression: Behavioral concomitants, relationship to reward, and self-administration of playback. *Journal of Comparative Psychology, 122*, 357–367.

Burguière, E., Monteiro, P., Feng, G., and Graybiel, A. M. (2013). Optogenetic stimulation of lateral orbitofronto-striatal pathway suppresses compulsive behaviors. *Science, 340*, 1243–1246.

Burke, L. K., and Heisler, L. K. (2015). 5-Hydroxytryptamine medications for the treatment of obesity. *Journal of Neuroendocrinology, 27,* 389–398.

Burke, T. M., Markwald, R. R., McHill, A. W., Chinoy, E. D., et al. (2015). Effects of caffeine on the human circadian clock in vivo and in vitro. *Science Translational Medicine, 7*(305), 305ra146.

Burnett, A. L. (2006). Nitric oxide in the penis: Science and therapeutic implications from erectile dysfunction to priapism. *Journal of Sexual Medicine, 3,* 578–582.

Burton, S. (2006). Symptom domains of schizophrenia: The role of atypical antipsychotic agents. *Journal of Psychopharmacology, 20*(6 Suppl.), 6–19.

Bushdid, C., Magnasco, M. O., Vosshall, L. B., and Keller, A. (2014). Humans can discriminate more than 1 trillion olfactory stimuli. *Science, 343*(6177), 1370–1372.

Bushman, J. D., Ye, W., and Liman, E. R. (2015). A proton current associated with sour taste: Distribution and functional properties. *FASEB Journal, 7,* 3014–3026.

Buss, D. M. (2000). *The dangerous passion: Why jealousy is as necessary as love and sex.* New York: Free Press.

Butler, A. C., Chapman, J. E., Forman, E. M., and Beck, A. T. (2006). The empirical status of cognitive-behavioral therapy: A review of meta-analyses. *Clinical Psychology Review, 26,* 17–31.

Buzsáki, G., Anastassiou, C. A., and Koch, C. (2012). The origin of extracellular fields and currents: EEG, ECoG, LFP and spikes. *Nature Reviews Neuroscience, 13*(6), 407–420.

C

Cacioppo, J. T., Berntson, G. G., Larsen, J. T., Poehlmann, K. M., et al. (2000). The psychophysiology of emotion. In M. Lewis and J. M. Haviland-Jones (Eds.), *Handbook of emotions* (2nd ed., pp. 173–191). New York: Guilford.

Cadoret, R. J., O'Gorman, T., Troughton, E., and Heywood, E. (1986). An adoption study of genetic and environmental factors in drug abuse. *Archives of General Psychiatry, 43,* 1131–1136.

Cahill, L., Prins, B., Weber, M., and McGaugh, J. L. (1994). Beta-adrenergic activation and memory for emotional events. *Nature, 371,* 702–704.

Caldwell, J. A. (2012). Crew schedules, sleep deprivation, and aviation performance. *Current Directions in Psychological Science, 21*(2), 85–89.

Calvert, G. A., Bullmore, E. T., Brammer, M. J., Campbell, R., et al. (1997). Activation of auditory cortex during silent lipreading. *Science, 276,* 593–596.

Calvin, W. H., and Ojemann, G. A. (1994). *Conversations with Neil's brain: The neural nature of thought and language.* Reading, MA: Addison-Wesley.

Campbell, F. W., and Robson, J. G. (1968). Application of Fourier analysis to the visibility of gratings. *Journal of Physiology (London), 197,* 551–566.

Campbell, S. S., and Tobler, I. (1984). Animal sleep: A review of sleep duration across phylogeny. *Neuroscience and Biobehavioral Reviews, 8,* 269–301.

Canli, T., Zhao, Z., Kang, E., Gross, J., et al. (2001). An fMRI study of personality influences on brain reactivity to emotional stimuli. *Behavioral Neuroscience, 115,* 33–42.

Cannon, W. B. (1929). *Bodily changes in pain, hunger, fear and rage.* New York: Appleton.

Cantalupo, C., and Hopkins, W. D. (2001). Asymmetric Broca's area in great apes. *Nature, 414,* 505.

Cantor, J. M., Blanchard, R., Paterson, A. D., and Bogaert, A. F. (2002). How many gay men owe their sexual orientation to fraternal birth order? *Archives of Sexual Behavior, 31,* 63–71.

Cao, M., Shu, N., Cao, Q., Wang, Y., et al. (2014). Imaging functional and structural brain connectomics in attention-deficit/hyperactivity disorder. *Molecular Neurobiology, 50*(3), 1111–1123.

Cao, Y. Q., Mantyh, P. W., Carlson, E. J., Gillespie, A. M., et al. (1998). Primary afferent tachykinins are required to experience moderate to intense pain. *Nature, 392,* 390–394.

Capitão, L. P., Murphy, S. E., Browning, M., Cowen, P. J., et al. (2015). Acute fluoxetine modulates emotional processing in young adult volunteers. *Psychological Medicine, 45*(11), 2295–2308.

Caramazza, A., Anzellotti, S., Strnad, L., and Lingnau, A. (2014). Embodied cognition and mirror neurons: A critical assessment. *Annual Review of Neuroscience, 37,* 1–15.

Cardno, A. G., and Gottesman, I. I. (2000). Twin studies of schizophrenia: From bow-and-arrow concordances to star wars Mx and functional genomics. *American Journal of Medical Genetics, 97,* 12–17.

Carhart-Harris, R. L., Erritzoe, D., Williams, T., Stone, J. M., et al. (2012). Neural correlates of the psychedelic state as determined by fMRI studies with psilocybin. *Proceedings of the National Academy of Sciences, USA, 109,* 2138–2143.

Carhart-Harris, R. L., Leech, R., Williams, T. M., Erritzoe, D., et al. (2012). Implications for psychedelic-assisted psychotherapy: Functional magnetic resonance imaging study with psilocybin. *British Journal of Psychiatry, 200,* 238–244.

Carmichael, M. S., Warburton, V. L., Dixen, J., and Davidson, J. M. (1994). Relationships among cardiovascular, muscular, and oxytocin responses during human sexual activity. *Archives of Sexual Behavior, 23,* 59–79.

Carpen, J. D., Archer, S. N., Skene, D. J., Smits, M., et al. (2005). A single-nucleotide polymorphism in the 5'-untranslated region of the *hPER2* gene is associated with diurnal preference. *Journal of Sleep Research, 14,* 293–297.

Carreiras, M., Lopez, J., Rivero, F., and Corina, D. (2005). Linguistic perception: Neural processing of a whistled language. *Nature, 433,* 31–32.

Carroll, J., McMahon, C., Neitz, M., and Neitz, J. (2000). Flicker-photometric electroretinogram estimates of L:M cone photoreceptor ratio in men with photopigment spectra derived from genetics. *Journal of the Optical Society of America. Part A, Optics, Image Science, and Vision, 17,* 499–509.

Carter, C. S. (1992). Oxytocin and sexual behavior. *Neuroscience and Biobehavioral Reviews, 16,* 131–144.

Cartwright, R. D. (1979). The nature and function of repetitive dreams: A survey and speculation. *Psychiatry, 42,* 131–137.

Casarosa, S., Bozzi, Y., and Conti, L. (2014). Neural stem cells: Ready for therapeutic applications? *Molecular and Cellular Therapies, 2,* 31.

Casey, B., and Hackett, B. P. (2000). Left-right axis malformations in man and mouse. *Current Opinion in Genetics and Development, 10,* 257–261.

Caspi, A., Moffitt, T. E., Cannon, M., McClay, J., et al. (2005). Moderation of the effect of adolescent-onset cannabis use on adult psychosis by a functional polymorphism in the catechol-O-methyltransferase gene: Longitudinal evidence of a gene X environment interaction. *Biological Psychiatry, 57,* 1117–1127.

Caspi, A., Sugden, K., Moffitt, T. E., Taylor, A., et al. (2003). Influence of life stress on depression: Moderation by a polymorphism in the 5-HTT gene. *Science, 301,* 386–389.

Cassens, G., Wolfe, L., and Zola, M. (1990). The neuropsychology of depressions. *Journal of Neuropsychiatry and Clinical Neurosciences, 2,* 202–213.

Casson, I. R., Sham, R., Campbell, E. A., Tarlau, M., et al. (1982). Neurological and CT evaluation of knocked-out boxers. *Journal of Neurology, Neurosurgery and Psychiatry, 45,* 170–174.

Castellanos, F. X., Lee, P. P., Sharp, W., Jeffries, N. O., et al. (2002). Developmental trajectories of brain volume abnormalities in children and adolescents with attention-deficit/hyperactivity disorder. *Journal of the American Medical Association, 288,* 1740–1748.

Catania, K. C. (2001). Early development of a somatosensory fovea: A head start in the cortical space race? *Nature Neuroscience, 4,* 353–354.

Caterina, M. J., Leffler, A., Malmberg, A. B., Martin, W. J., et al. (2000). Impaired nociception and pain sensation in mice lacking the capsaicin receptor. *Science, 288,* 306–313.

Caterina, M. J., Schumacher, M. A., Tominaga, M., Rosen, T. A., et al. (1997). The capsaicin receptor: A heat-activated ion channel in the pain pathway. *Nature, 389,* 816–824.

Catterall, W. A., and Yu, F. H. (2006). Painful channels. *Neuron, 52,* 743–744.

Centers for Disease Control and Prevention (CDC). (2010). Current depression among adults: United States, 2006 and 2008. *Morbidity and Mortality Weekly Report, 59*(38), 1229–1235.

Centers for Disease Control and Prevention (CDC). (2015). *Report to Congress on traumatic brain injury in the United States: Epidemiology and rehabilitation.* Atlanta, GA: National Center for Injury Prevention and Control; Division of Unintentional Injury Prevention.

Chamberlain, S. R., Menzies, L., Hampshire, A., Suckling, J., et al. (2008). Orbitofrontal dysfunction in patients with obsessive-compulsive disorder and their unaffected relatives. *Science, 321,* 421–422.

Champagne, F., Diorio, J., Sharma, S., and Meaney, M. J. (2001). Naturally occurring variations in maternal behavior in the rat are associated with differences in estrogen-inducible central oxytocin receptors. *Proceedings of the National Academy of Sciences, USA, 98,* 12736–12741.

Chandrashekar, J., Hoon, M. A., Ryba, N. J., and Zuker, C. S. (2006). The receptors and cells for mammalian taste. *Nature, 444,* 288–294.

Chandrashekar, J., Mueller, K. L., Hoon, M. A., Adler, E., et al. (2000). T2Rs function as bitter taste receptors. *Cell, 100,* 703–711.

Chandrashekar, J., Yarmolinsky, D., von Buchholtz, L., Oka, Y., et al. (2009). The taste of carbonation. *Science, 326,* 443–445.

Chang, B. S., Ly, J., Appignani, B., Bodell, A., et al. (2005). Reading impairment in the neuronal migration disorder of periventricular nodular heterotopia. *Neurology, 64,* 799–803.

Chapman, C. D., Dono, L. M., French, M. C., Weinberg, Z. Y., et al. (2012). Paraventricular nucleus anandamide signaling alters eating and substrate oxidation. *Neuroreport, 23*(7), 425–429.

Charney, D. S., Deutch, A. Y., Krystal, J. H., Southwick, S. M., et al. (1993). Psychobiologic mechanisms of posttraumatic stress disorder. *Archives of General Psychiatry, 50,* 295–305.

Chase, J. E., and Gidal, B. E. (1997). Melatonin: Therapeutic use in sleep disorders. *Annals of Pharmacotherapy, 31,* 1218–1226.

Chasman, D. I., Schürks, M., Anttila, V., deVries, B., et al. (2011). Genome-wide association study reveals three susceptibility loci for common migraine in the general population. *Nature Genetics, 43,* 695–698.

Chatzigeorgiou, M., Bang, S., Hwang, S. W., and Schafer, W. R. (2013). *Tmc-1* encodes a sodium-sensitive channel required for salt chemosensation in *C. elegans. Nature, 494*(7435), 95–99.

Chaudhari, N., Landin, A. M., and Roper, S. D. (2000). A metabotropic glutamate receptor variant functions as a taste receptor. *Nature Neuroscience, 3,* 113–119.

Chelikani, P. K., Haver, A. C., and Reidelberger, R. D. (2005). Intravenous infusion of peptide YY(3-36) potently inhibits food intake in rats. *Endocrinology, 146,* 879–888.

Chemelli, R. M., Willie, J. T., Sinton, C. M., Elmquist, J. K., et al. (1999). Narcolepsy in orexin knockout mice: Molecular genetics of sleep regulation. *Cell, 98,* 437–451.

Chen, S.-K., Badea, T. C., Hattar, S. (2011). Photoentrainment and pupillary light reflex are mediated by distinct populations of ipRGCs. *Nature, 476,* 92–95.

Chen, X., Gabitto, M., Peng, Y., Ryba, N. J., et al. (2011). A gustotopic map of taste qualities in the mammalian brain. *Science, 333*(6047), 1262–1266.

Chenn, A., and Walsh, C. A. (2002). Regulation of cerebral cortical size by control of cell cycle exit in neural precursors. *Science, 297,* 365–369.

Cherry, E. C. (1953). Some experiments on the recognition of speech, with one and with two ears. *Journal of the Acoustical Society of America, 25,* 975–979.

Cheyne, J. A. (2002). Situational factors affecting sleep paralysis and associated hallucinations: Position and timing effects. *Journal of Sleep Research, 11,* 169–177.

Chittka, L., and Peng, F. (2013). Caffeine boosts bees' memories. *Science, 339,* 1157–1159.

Cho, I., Yamanishi, S., Cox, L., Methé, B. A., et al. (2012). Antibiotics in early life alter the murine colonic microbiome and adiposity. *Nature, 488*(7413), 621–626.

Cho, K. (2001). Chronic "jet lag" produces temporal lobe atrophy and spatial cognitive deficits. *Nature Neuroscience, 4,* 567–568.

Choquet, D., and Triller, A. (2013). The dynamic synapse. *Neuron, 80,* 691–703.

Chung, W. S., Clarke, L. E., Wang, G. X., Stafford, B. K., et al. (2013). Astrocytes mediate synapse elimination through MEGF10 and MERTK pathways. *Nature, 504*(7480), 394–400.

Chung, Y., Jacobson, A., He, G., van Erp, T. G., et al. (2015). Prodromal symptom severity predicts accelerated gray matter reduction and third ventricle expansion among clinically high risk youth developing psychotic disorders. *Molecular Neuropsychiatry, 1,* 13–22.

Ciccocioppo, R., Martin-Fardon, R., and Weiss, F. (2004). Stimuli associated with a single cocaine experience elicit long-lasting cocaine-seeking. *Nature Neuroscience, 7,* 495–496.

Cirulli, E. T., Lasseigne, B. N., Petrovski, S., Sapp, P. C., et al. (2015). Exome sequencing in amyotrophic lateral sclerosis identifies risk genes and pathways. *Science, 347*(6229), 1436–1441.

Clapham, J. C., Arch, J. R. S., Chapman, H., Haynes, A., et al. (2000). Mice overexpressing human uncoupling protein-3 in skeletal muscle are hyperphagic and lean. *Nature, 406,* 415–418.

Clapper, J. R., Moreno-Sanz, G., Russo, R., Guijarro, A., et al. (2010). Anandamide suppresses pain initiation through a peripheral endocannabinoid mechanism. *Nature Neuroscience, 13,* 1265–1270.

Clarke, E., Reichard, U. H., and Zuberbühler, K. (2015). Context-specific close-range "hoo" calls in wild gibbons (*Hylobates lar*). *BMC Evolutionary Biology, 15,* 56.

Clarke, M. C., Tanskanen, A., Huttunen, M., Leon, D. A., et al. (2011). Increased risk of schizophrenia from additive interaction between infant motor developmental delay and obstetric complications: Evidence from a population-based longitudinal study. *American Journal of Psychiatry, 168,*1295–1302.

Classen, J., Liepert, J., Wise, S. P., Hallett, M., et al. (1998). Rapid plasticity of human cortical movement representation induced by practice. *Journal of Neurophysiology, 79,* 1117–1123.

Clemens, L. G., Gladue, B. A., and Coniglio, L. P. (1978). Prenatal endogenous androgenic influences on masculine sexual behavior and genital morphology in male and female rats. *Hormones and Behavior, 10,* 40–53.

Clemente, C. D., and Sterman, M. B. (1967). Limbic and other forebrain mechanisms in sleep induction and behavioral inhibition. *Progress in Brain Research, 27,* 34–37.

Clutton-Brock, T. H., and Harvey, P. H. (1980). Primates, brains and ecology. *Journal of Zoology, 190,* 309–323.

Cnotka, J., Güntürkün, O., Rehkämper, G., Gray, R. D., et al. (2008). Extraordinary large brains in tool-using New Caledonian crows (*Corvus moneduloides*). *Neuroscience Letters, 433,* 241–245.

Coelho, M., and Ferreira, J. J. (2012). Late-stage Parkinson disease. *Nature Reviews Neurology, 8,* 435–442.

Cogan, G. B., Thesen, T., Carlson, C., Doyle, W., et al. (2014). Sensory-motor transformations for speech occur bilaterally. *Nature, 507*(7490), 94–98.

Coggan, J. S., Bartol, T. M., Esquenazi, E., Stiles, J. R., et al. (2005). Evidence for ectopic neurotransmission at a neuronal synapse. *Science, 309,* 446–451.

Coghill, R. C., McHaffie, J. G., and Yen, Y.-F. (2003). Neural correlates of interindividual differences in the subjective experience of pain. *Proceedings of the National Academy of Sciences, USA, 100,* 8538–8542.

Cohen, A. H., Baker, M. T., and Dobrov, T. A. (1989). Evidence for functional regeneration in the adult lamprey spinal cord following transection. *Brain Research, 496,* 368–372.

Cohen, A. J., and Leckman, J. F. (1992). Sensory phenomena associated with Gilles de la Tourette's syndrome. *Journal of Clinical Psychiatry, 53,* 319–323.

Cohen, N. J., and Squire, L. R. (1980). Preserved learning and retention of pattern-analyzing skill in amnesia: Dissociation of knowing how and knowing what. *Science, 210,* 207–210.

Cohen, S., Alper, C. M., Doyle, W. H., Treanor, J. J., et al. (2006). Positive emotional style predicts resistance to illness after experimental exposure to Rhinovirus or Influenza A virus. *Psychosomatic Medicine, 68,* 809–815.

Cohen, S., Doyle, W. J., Alper, C. M., Janicki-Deverts, D., et al. (2009). Sleep habits and susceptibility to the common cold. *Archive of Internal Medicine, 169,* 62–67.

Cohen, S., Janicki-Deverts, D., Turner, R. B., and Doyle, W. J. (2015). Does hugging provide stress-buffering social support? A study of susceptibility to upper respiratory infection and illness. *Psychological Science, 26,* 135–147.

Cole, J. (1995). *Pride and a daily marathon.* Cambridge, MA: MIT Press.

Collings, V. B. (1974). Human taste response as a function of locus of stimulation on the tongue and soft palate. *Perception and Psychophysics, 16,* 169–174.

Colman, R. J., Anderson, R. M., Johnson, S. C., Kastman, E. K., et al. (2009). Caloric restriction delays disease onset and mortality in rhesus monkeys. *Science, 325*(5937), 201–204.

Colman, R. J., Beasley, T. M., Kemnitz, J. W., Johnson, S. C., et al. (2014). Caloric restriction reduces age-related and all-cause mortality in rhesus monkeys. *Nature Communications, 5,* 3557.

Colom, R., Burgaleta, M., Román, F. J., Karama, S., et al. (2013). Neuroanatomic overlap between intelligence and cognitive factors: Morphometry methods provide support for the key role of the frontal lobes. *Neuroimage, 72,* 143–152.

Coltman, D. W., O'Donoghue, P., Jorgenson, J. T., Hogg, J. Y., et al. (2003). Undesirable evolutionary consequences of trophy hunting. *Nature, 426,* 655–658.

Colwell, C. S. (2010). Preventing dehydration during sleep. *Nature Neuroscience, 13*(4), 403–404.

Conel, J. L. (1939). *The postnatal development of the human cerebral cortex: Vol. 1. The cortex of the newborn.* Cambridge, MA: Harvard University Press.

Conel, J. L. (1947). *The postnatal development of the human cerebral cortex: Vol. 3. The cortex of the three-month infant.* Cambridge, MA: Harvard University Press.

Conel, J. L. (1959). *The postnatal development of the human cerebral cortex: Vol. 6. The cortex of the twenty-four-month infant.* Cambridge, MA: Harvard University Press.

Confer, J. C., Easton, J. A., Fleischman, D. S., Goetz, C. D., et al. (2010). Evolutionary psychology. Controversies, questions, prospects, and limitations. *American Psychologist, 65,* 110–126.

Conn, M. P., and Parker, J. V. (2008). *The animal research war.* New York: Palgrave Macmillan.

Connolly, A. C., Guntupalli, J. S., Gors, J., Hanke, M., et al. (2012). The representation of biological classes in the human brain. *Journal of Neuroscience, 32*(8), 2608–2618.

Conrad, A. J., Abebe, T., Austin, R., Forsythe, S., et al. (1991). Hippocampal pyramidal cell disarray in schizophrenia as a bilateral phenomenon. *Archives of General Psychiatry, 48,* 413–417.

Conrad, K. L., Tseng, K. Y., Uejima, J. L., Reimers, J. M., et al. (2008). Formation of accumbens GlurR2-lacking AMPA receptors mediates incubation of cocaine craving. *Nature, 454,* 118–121.

Constantine-Paton, M., Cline, H. T., and Debski, E. (1990). Patterned activity, synaptic convergence, and the NMDA receptor in developing visual pathways. *Annual Review of Neuroscience, 13,* 129–154.

Cooke, B. M., Breedlove, S. M., and Jordan, C. L. (2003). Both estrogen receptors and androgen receptors contribute to testosterone-induced changes in the morphology of the medial amygdala and sexual arousal in male rats. *Hormones and Behavior, 43,* 336–346.

Cooke, B. M., Chowanadisai, W., and Breedlove, S. M. (2000). Post-weaning social isolation of male rats reduces the volume of the medial amygdala and leads to deficits in adult sexual behavior. *Behavioural Brain Research, 117,* 107–113.

Cooke, B. M., Tabibnia, G., and Breedlove S. M. (1999). A brain sexual dimorphism controlled by adult circulating androgens. *Proceedings of the National Academy of Sciences, USA, 96,* 7538–7540.

Cope, N., Harold, D., Hill, G., Moskvina, V., et al. (2005). Strong evidence that KIAA0319 on chromosome 6p is a susceptibility gene for developmental dyslexia. *American Journal of Human Genetics, 76,* 581–591.

Corballis, M. C. (2002). *From hand to mouth: The origins of language.* Princeton, NJ: Princeton University Press.

Corballis, M. C. (2014). Left brain, right brain: Facts and fantasies. *PLOS Biology, 12*(1), e1001767.

Corbetta, M., Kincade, J. M., Ollinger, J. M., McAvoy, M. P., et al. (2000). Voluntary orienting is dissociated from target detection in human posterior parietal cortex. *Nature Neuroscience, 3,* 292–297.

Corbetta, M., and Shulman, G. L. (1998). Human cortical mechanisms of visual attention during orienting and search. *Philosophical Transactions of the Royal Society of London. Series B: Biological Sciences, 353,* 1353–1362.

Corbetta, M., and Shulman, G. L. (2002). Control of goal-directed and stimulus-driven attention in the brain. *Nature Reviews Neuroscience, 3,* 201–215.

Corcoran, A. J., Barber, J. R., and Conner, W. E. (2009). Tiger moth jams bat sonar. *Science, 325,* 325–327.

Coricelli, G., Critchley, H. D., Joffily, M., O'Doherty, J. P., et al. (2005). Regret and its avoidance: A neuroimaging study of choice behavior. *Nature Neuroscience, 8,* 1255–1262.

Corkin, S. (2002). What's new with the amnesic patient H.M.? *Neuroscience, 3,* 153–159.

Corkin, S., Amaral, D. G., Gonzalez, R. G., Johnson, K. A., et al. (1997). H.M.'s medial temporal lobe lesion: Findings from magnetic resonance imaging. *Journal of Neuroscience, 17,* 3964–3979.

Correa, A. M., and Bezanilla, F. (1994). Gating of the squid sodium channel at positive potentials. II. Single channels reveal two open states. *Biophysical Journal, 66,* 1864–1878.

Coryell, W., Noyes, R., Jr., and House, J. D. (1986). Mortality among outpatients with anxiety disorders. *American Journal of Psychiatry, 143,* 508–510.

Cosmides, L., and Tooby, J. (2000). Evolutionary psychology and the emotions. In M. Lewis and J. M. Haviland-Jones (Eds.), *Handbook of emotions* (2nd ed., pp. 91–115). New York: Guilford.

Costa, A., and Sebastián-Gallés, N. (2014). How does the bilingual experience sculpt the brain? *Nature Reviews Neuroscience, 15*(5), 336–345.

Costanzo, R. M. (1991). Regeneration of olfactory receptor cells. *CIBA Foundation Symposium, 160,* 233–242.

Counotte, D. S., Goriounova, N. A., Li, K. W., Loos, M., et al. (2011). Lasting synaptic changes underlie attention deficits caused by nicotine exposure during adolescence. *Nature Neuroscience, 14*(4), 417–419.

Courtiol, A., Pettay, J. E., Jokela, M., Rotkirch, A., et al. (2012). Natural and sexual selection in a monogamous historical human population. *Proceedings of the National Academy of Sciences, USA, 109*(21), 8044–8049.

Courtney, S., Ungerleider, L., Keil, K., and Haxby, J. (1996). Object and spatial visual working memory activate separate neural systems in human cortex. *Cerebral Cortex, 6,* 39–49.

Cowan, W. M. (1979). The development of the brain. *Scientific American, 241*(3), 112–133.

Cox, J. J., Reimann, F., Nicholas, A. K., Thornton, G., et al. (2006). An SCN9A channelopathy causes congenital inability to experience pain. *Nature, 444,* 894–898.

Cragg, B. G. (1975). The development of synapses in the visual system of the cat. *Journal of Comparative Neurology, 160,* 147–166.

Craig, A. D., Reiman, E. M., Evans, A., and Bushnell, M. C. (1996). Functional imaging of an illusion of pain. *Nature, 384,* 258–260.

Craik, F. I. M. (1985). Paradigms in human memory research. In L.-G. Nilsson and T. Archer (Eds.), *Perspectives on learning and memory* (pp. 197–221). Hillsdale, NJ: Erlbaum.

Craik, F. I. M., and Salthouse, T. A. (2007). *The handbook of aging and cognition* (3rd ed.). London: Psychology Press.

Craver, C. F., Kwan, D., Steindam, C., and Rosenbaum, R. S. (2014). Individuals with episodic amnesia are not stuck in time. *Neuropsychologia, 57,* 191–195.

Crick, F. C., and Koch, C. (2005). What is the function of the claustrum? *Philosophical Transactions of the Royal Society of London. Series B: Biological Sciences, 360*(1458), 1271–1279.

Crockford, C., Wittig, R. M., Mundry, R., and Zuberbühler, K. (2012). Wild chimpanzees inform ignorant group members of danger. *Current Biology, 22*(2), 142–146.

Crowell, A., Riva-Posse, P., Garlow, S., and Mayberg, H. (2014). Toward an understanding of the neural circuitry of major depressive disorder through the clinical response to deep brain stimulation of different anatomical targets. *Current Behavioral Neuroscience Reports, 1,* 55–63.

Cruce, J. A. F., Greenwood, M. R. C., Johnson, P. R., and Quartermain, D. (1974). Genetic versus hypothalamic obesity: Studies of intake and dietary manipulation in rats. *Journal of Comparative and Physiological Psychology, 87,* 295–301.

Cryan, J. F., and Dinan, T. G. (2012). Mind-altering microorganisms: The impact of the gut microbiota on brain and behaviour. *Nature Reviews Neuroscience, 13,* 701–712.

Cryns, K., and Van Camp, G. (2004). Deafness genes and their diagnostic applications. *Audiology & Neurotology, 9,* 2–22.

Cui, G., Jun, S. B., Jin, X., Pham, M. D., et al. (2013). Concurrent activation of striatal direct and indirect pathways during action initiation. *Nature, 494*(7436), 238–242.

Cui, M., Jiang, P., Maillet, E., Max, M., et al. (2006). The heterodimeric sweet taste receptor has multiple potential ligand binding sites. *Current Pharmaceutical Design, 12,* 4591–4600.

Çukur, T., Nishimoto, S., Huth, A. G., and Gallant, J. L. (2013). Attention during natural vision warps semantic representation across the human brain. Nature Neuroscience, 16(6), 763–770.

Cummings, D. E. (2006). Ghrelin and the short- and long-term regulation of appetite and body weight. *Physiology & Behavior, 89,* 71–84.

Cummings, J. L. (1995). Dementia: The failing brain. *Lancet, 345,* 1481–1484.

Cunningham, C. A., Yassa, M. A., and Egeth, H. E. (2015). Massive memory revisited: Limitations on storage capacity for object details in visual long-term memory. *Learning and Memory, 22*(11), 563–566.

Curcio, C. A., Sloan, K. R., Packer, O., Hendrickson, A. E., et al. (1987). Distribution of cones in human and monkey retina: Individual variability and radial asymmetry. *Science, 236,* 579–582.

Currie, P. J., John, C. S., Nicholson, M. L., Chapman, C. D., et al. (2010). Hypothalamic paraventricular 5-hydroxytryptamine inhibits the effects of ghrelin on eating and energy substrate utilization. *Pharmacology, Biochemistry, and Behavior, 97*(1), 152–155.

Curtiss, S. (1989). The independence and task-specificity of language. In M. H. Bornstein and J. S. Bruner (Eds.), *Interaction in human development* (pp. 105–137). Hillsdale, NJ: Erlbaum.

Cypess, A. M, Lehman, S., Williams, G., Tal, I., et al. (2009). Identification and importance of brown adipose tissue in adult humans. *New England Journal of Medicine, 360,* 1509–1517.

Czech-Damal, N. U., Liebschner, A., Miersch, L., Klauer, G., et al. (2012). Electroreception in the Guiana dolphin (*Sotalia guianensis*). *Proceedings: Biological Sciences, 279,* 663–668.

Czeisler, C. A., Duffy, J. F., Shanahan, T. L., Brown, E. N., et al. (1999). Stability, precision, and near-24-hour period of the human circadian pacemaker. *Science, 284,* 2177–2181.

D

D'Ardenne, K., McClure, S. M., Nystrom, L. E., and Cohen, J. D. (2008). BOLD responses reflecting dopaminergic signals in the human ventral tegmental area. *Science, 319,* 1264–1267.

Dabbs, J. M., and Morris, R. (1990). Testosterone, social class, and antisocial behavior in a sample of 4,462 men. *Psychological Science, 1,* 209–211.

Dabbs, J. M., Ruback, R. B., Frady, R. L., Hopper, C. H., et al. (1988). Saliva testosterone and criminal violence among women. *Personality and Individual Differences, 9,* 269–275.

Dale, N., Schacher, S., and Kandel, E. R. (1988). Long-term facilitation in *Aplysia* involves increase in transmitter release. *Science, 239,* 282–285.

Dale, R. C., Heyman, I., Giovannoni, G., and Church, A. W. (2005). Incidence of anti-brain antibodies in children with obsessive-compulsive disorder. *British Journal of Psychiatry, 187,* 314–319.

Dalley, J. W., Fryer, T. D., Brichard, L., Robinson, E. S. J., et al. (2007). Nucleus accumbens D2/3 receptors predict trait impulsivity and cocaine reinforcement. *Science, 315,* 1267–1270.

Damak, S., Rong, M., Yasumatsu, K., Kokrashvili, Z., et al. (2003). Detection of sweet and umami taste in the absence of taste receptor T1r3. *Science, 301,* 850–853.

Damasio, A. R., Grabowski, T. J., Bechara, A., Damasio, H., et al. (2000). Subcortical and cortical brain activity during the feeling of self-generated emotions. *Nature Neuroscience, 3,* 1049–1056.

Damasio, H., Grabowski, T., Frank, R., Galaburda, A. M., et al. (1994). The return of Phineas Gage: Clues about the brain from the skull of a famous patient. *Science, 264,* 1102–1105.

Daneman, R., Zhou, L., Kebede, A. A., and Barres, B. A. (2010). Pericytes are required for blood-brain barrier integrity during embryogenesis. *Nature, 468,* 562–566.

Daniels, D., and Marshall, A. (2012). Evaluating the potential for rostral diffusion in the cerebral ventricles using angiotensin II–induced drinking in rats. *Brain Research, 1486,* 62–67.

Dantz, B., Edgar, D. M., and Dement, W. C. (1994). Circadian rhythms in narcolepsy: Studies on a 90 minute day. *Electroencephalography and Clinical Neurophysiology, 90,* 24–35.

Dantzer, R., O'Connor, J. C., Freund, G. G., Johnson, R. W., et al. (2008). From inflammation to sickness and depression: When the immune system subjugates the brain. *Nature Reviews Neuroscience, 9,* 46–56.

Dapretto, M., Davies, M. S., Pfeifer, J. H., Scott, A. A., et al. (2006). Understanding emotions in others: Mirror neuron dysfunction in children with autism spectrum disorders. *Nature Neuroscience, 9,* 28–30.

Dark, J., Forger, N. G., and Zucker, I. (1984). Rapid recovery of body mass after surgical removal of adipose tissue in ground squirrels. *Proceedings of the National Academy of Sciences, USA, 81,* 2270–2272.

Darwin, C. (1859). *On the origin of species by means of natural selection, or, The preservation of favoured races in the struggle for life.* London: J. Murray.

Darwin, C. (1871). *The descent of man, and selection in relation to sex.* London: J. Murray.

Darwin, C. (1872). *The expression of the emotions in man and animals.* London: J. Murray.

Dauvilliers, Y., Siegel, J. M., Lopez, R., Torontali, Z. A., et al. (2014). Cataplexy: Clinical aspects, pathophysiology and management strategy. *Nature Reviews Neurology, 10*(7), 386–395.

Davalos, D., Grutzendler, J., Yang, G., Kim, J. V., et al. (2005). ATP mediates rapid microglial response to local brain injury in vivo. *Nature Neuroscience, 8,* 752–758.

Davey-Smith, G., Frankel, S., and Yarnell, J. (1997). Sex and death: Are they related? Findings from the Caerphilly Cohort Study. *British Medical Journal (Clinical Research Edition), 315,* 1641–1644.

David, L. A., Maurice, C. F., Carmody, R. N., Gootenberg, D. B., et al. (2014). Diet rapidly and reproducibly alters the human gut microbiome. *Nature, 505,* 559–563.

Davidson, J. M., Camargo, C. A., and Smith, E. R. (1979). Effects of androgen on sexual behavior in hypogonadal men. *Journal of Clinical Endocrinology & Metabolism, 48,* 955–958.

Davidson, R. M., and Bender, D. B. (1991). Selectivity for relative motion in the monkey superior colliculus. *Journal of Neurophysiology, 65,* 1115–1133.

Davies, M. J., Baer, D. J., Judd, J. T., Brown, E. D., et al. (2002). Effects of moderate alcohol intake on fasting insulin and glucose concentrations and insulin sensitivity in postmenopausal women: A randomized controlled trial. *Journal of the American Medical Association, 287,* 2559–2562.

Davis, J. I., Senghas, A., Brandt, F., and Ochsner, K. N. (2010). The effects of BOTOX injections on emotional experience. *Emotion, 10,* 433–440.

Davis, J. I., Senghas, A., and Ochsner, K. N. (2009). How does facial feedback modulate emotional experience? *Journal of Research in Personality, 43,* 822–829.

Dawson, D., and Encel, N. (1993). Melatonin and sleep in humans. *Journal of Pineal Research, 15,* 1–12.

Day, N. L., Leech, S. L., Richardson, G. A., Cornelius, M. D., et al. (2002). Prenatal alcohol exposure predicts continued deficits in offspring size at 14 years of age. *Alcoholism: Clinical and Experimental Research, 26,* 1584–1591.

De Felipe, C., Herrero, J. F., O'Brien, J. A., Palmer, J. A., et al. (1998). Altered nociception, analgesia and aggression in mice lacking the receptor for substance P. *Nature, 392,* 394–397.

de Gelder, B., Hortensius, R., and Tamietto, M. (2012). Attention and awareness each influence amygdala activity for dynamic bodily expressions: A short review. *Frontiers in Integrative Neuroscience, 6,* 54. doi:10.3389/fnint.2012.00054

de Groot, C. M., Janus, M. D., and Bornstein, R. A. (1995). Clinical predictors of psychopathology in children and adolescents with Tourette syndrome. *Journal of Psychiatric Research, 29,* 59–70.

de Hemptinne, C., Swann, N. C., Ostrem, J. L., Ryapolova-Webb, E. S., et al. (2015). Therapeutic deep brain stimulation reduces cortical phase-amplitude coupling in Parkinson's disease. *Nature Neuroscience, 18*(5), 779–786.

de Luis, O., Valero, M. C., and Jurado, L. A. (2000). WBSCR14, a putative transcription factor gene deleted in Williams-Beuren syndrome: Complete characterisation of the human gene and the mouse ortholog. *European Journal of Human Genetics, 8,* 215–222.

de Paiva, A., Poulain, B., Lawrence, G. W., Shone, C. C., et al. (1993). A role for the interchain disulfide or its participating thiols in the internalization of botulinum neurotoxin A revealed by a toxin derivative that binds to ecto-acceptors and inhibits transmitter release intracellularly. *Journal of Biological Chemistry, 268,* 20838–20844.

De Valois, R. L., and De Valois, K. K. (1980). Spatial vision. *Annual Review of Psychology, 31,* 309–341.

De Valois, R. L., and De Valois, K. K. (1988). *Spatial vision.* New York: Oxford University Press.

De Valois, R. L., and De Valois, K. K. (1993). A multi-stage color model. *Vision Research, 33,* 1053–1065.

Dearborn, G. V. N. (1932). A case of congenital general pure analgesia. *Journal of Nervous and Mental Disease, 75,* 612–615.

Debanne, D., Campanac, E., Bialowas, A., Carlier, E., et al. (2011). Axon physiology. *Physiological Reviews, 91*(2), 555–602.

Dehaene, S., and Changeux, J. P. (2011). Experimental and theoretical approaches to conscious processing. *Neuron, 70*(2), 200–227.

Dehaene-Lambertz, G., Dehaene, S., and Hertz-Pannier, L. (2002). Functional neuroimaging of speech perception in infants. *Science, 298,* 2013–2015.

Dehkordi, O., Rose, J. E., Fatemi, M., Allard, J. S., et al. (2012). Neuronal expression of bitter taste receptors and downstream signaling molecules in the rat brainstem. *Brain Research, 1475,* 1–10.

Deisseroth, K. (2015). Optogenetics: 10 years of microbial opsins in neuroscience. *Nature Neuroscience, 18*(9), 1213–1225.

del Campo, N., Fryer, T. D., Hong, Y. T., Smith, R., et al. (2013). A positron emission tomography study of nigro-striatal dopaminergic mechanisms underlying attention: Implications for ADHD and its treatment. *Brain, 136*(Pt. 11), 3252–3270.

Delbarco-Trillo, J., Burkert, B. A., Goodwin, T. E., and Drea, C. M. (2011). Night and day: The comparative study of strepsirrhine primates reveals socioecological and phylogenetic patterns in olfactory signals. *Journal of Evolutionary Biology, 24*(1), 82–98.

DelBello, M. P., Zimmerman, M. E., Mills, N. P., Getz, G. E., et al. (2004). Magnetic resonance imaging analysis of amygdala and other subcortical brain regions in adolescents with bipolar disorder. *Bipolar Disorder, 6,* 43–52.

DeLong, M. R., Georgopoulos, A. P., Crutcher, M. D., Mitchell, S. J., et al. (1984). Functional organization of the basal ganglia: Contributions of single-cell recording studies. *CIBA Foundation Symposium, 107,* 64–82.

Demb, J. B., Boynton, G. M., and Heeger, D. J. (1998). Functional magnetic resonance imaging of early visual pathways in dyslexia. *Journal of Neuroscience, 18,* 6939–6951.

Dement, W. C. (1974). *Some must watch while some must sleep.* San Francisco: Freeman.

Demyttenaere, K., Bruffaerts, R., Posada-Villa, J., Gasquet, I., et al. (2004). Prevalence, severity, and unmet need for treatment of mental disorders in the World Heatlh Organization World Mental Health Surveys. *Journal of American Medical Association, 291,* 2581–2590.

Dennis, S. G., and Melzack, R. (1983). Perspectives on phylogenetic evolution of pain expression. In R. L. Kitchell, H. H. Erickson, E. Carstens, and L. E. Davis (Eds.), *Animal pain* (pp. 151–161). Bethesda, MD: American Physiological Society.

Denton, D., Shade, R., Zamarippa, F., Egan, G., et al. (1999). Neuroimaging of genesis and satiation of thirst and an interoceptor-driven theory of origins of primary consciousness. *Proceedings of the National Academy of Sciences, USA, 96,* 5304–5309.

Depaepe, V., Suarez-Gonzalez, N., Dufour, A., Passante, L., et al. (2005). Ephrin signalling controls brain size by regulating apoptosis of neural progenitors. *Nature, 435,* 1244–1250.

Derecki, N., Cronk, J. C., Lu, Z., Xu, E., et al. (2012). Wild-type microglia arrest pathology in a mouse model of Rett syndrome. *Nature, 484,* 105–109.

Derrick, B. E., and Martinez, J. L. (1994). Frequency-dependent associative long-term potentiation at the hippocampal mossy fiber-CA3 synapse. *Proceedings of the National Academy of Sciences, USA, 91,* 10290–10294.

DeRubeis, R. J., Siegle, G. J., and Hollon, S. D. (2008). Cognitive therapy versus medication for depression: Treatment outcomes and neural mechanisms. *Nature, 9,* 788–796.

Descartes, R. (1662). *De homine.* Paris: Petrvm Leffen & Franciscvm Moyardvm.

Deshpande, D. A., Wang, W. C., McIlmoyle, E. L., Robinett, K. S., et al. (2010). Bitter taste receptors on airway smooth muscle bronchodilate by localized calcium signaling and reverse obstruction. *Nature Medicine, 16,* 1299–1304.

DeSisto, M. J., Harding, C. M., McCormick, R. V., Ashikaga, T., et al. (1995). The Maine and Vermont three-decade studies of serious mental illness. I. Matched comparison of cross-sectional outcome. *British Journal of Psychiatry, 167,* 331–338.

Devane, W. A., Dysarz, F. A., Johnson, M. R., Melvin, L. S., et al. (1988). Determination and characterization of a cannabinoid receptor in rat brain. *Molecular Pharmacology, 34,* 605–613.

Devane, W. A., Hanus, L., Breuer, A., Pertwee, R. G., et al. (1992). Isolation and structure of a brain constituent that binds the cannabinoid receptor. *Science, 258,* 1946–1949.

Devinsky, O., and Bear, D. (1984). Varieties of aggressive behavior in temporal lobe epilepsy. *American Journal of Psychiatry, 141,* 651–656.

Devlin, J. T., and Watkins, K. E. (2007). Stimulating language: Insights from TMS. *Brain, 130*(Pt. 3), 610–622.

DeVoogd, T. J. (1994). Interactions between endocrinology and learning in the avian song system. *Annals of the New York Academy of Sciences, 743,* 19–41.

DeWall, C. N., MacDonald, G., Webster, G. D., Masten, C. L., et al. (2010). Acetaminophen reduces social pain: Behavioral and neural evidence. *Psychological Science, 21*(7), 931–937.

Dewan, A., Pacifico, R., Zhan, R., Rinberg, D., et al. (2013). Non-redundant coding of aversive odours in the main olfactory pathway. *Nature, 497*(7450), 486–489.

Dewsbury, D. A. (1972). Patterns of copulatory behavior in male mammals. *Quarterly Review of Biology, 47,* 1–33.

Di Marzo, V., Goparaju, S. K., Wang, L., Liu, J., et al. (2001). Leptin-regulated endocannabinoids are involved in maintaining food intake. *Nature, 410,* 822–825.

Di Marzo, V., and Matias, I. (2005). Endocannabinoid control of food intake and energy balance. *Nature Neuroscience, 8,* 585–589.

Di Pelligrino, G., Fadiga, L., Fogassi, L., Galese, V., et al. (1992). Understanding motor events: A neurophysiological study. *Experimental Brain Research, 91,* 176–180.

Diamond, M. C. (1967). Extensive cortical depth measurements and neuron size increases in the cortex of environmentally enriched rats. *Journal of Comparative Neurology, 131,* 357–364.

Diana, R. A., Yonelinas, A. P., and Ranganath, C. (2013). Parahippocampal cortex activation during context reinstatement predicts item recollection. *Journal of Experimental Psychology, 142*(4), 1287–1297.

Dias, B. G., and Ressler, K. J. (2014). Parental olfactory experience influences behavior and neural structure in subsequent generations. *Nature Neuroscience, 17*(1), 89–96.

Dichgans, J. (1984). Clinical symptoms of cerebellar dysfunction and their topodiagnostical significance. *Human Neurobiology, 2,* 269–279.

Dickson, B. J., and Gilestro, G. F. (2006). Regulation of commissural axon pathfinding by slit and its Robo receptors. *Annual Review of Cell and Developmental Biology, 22,* 651–675. doi:10.1146/annurev.cellbio.21.090704.151234

Diekelmann, S., and Born, J. (2010). The memory function of sleep. *Nature Reviews Neuroscience, 11,* 114–126.

Diekelmann, S., Büchel, C., Born, J., and Rasch, B. (2011). Labile or stable: Opposing consequences for memory when reactivated during waking and sleeping. *Nature Neuroscience, 14,* 381–386.

Dietz, P. M., Williams, S. B., Callaghan, W. M., Bachman, D. J., et al. (2007). Clinically identified maternal depression before, during, and after pregnancies ending in live births. *American Journal of Psychiatry, 164,* 1457–1459.

DiFranza, J. R., Savageau, J. A., Fletcher, K., O'Loughlin, J., et al. (2007). Symptoms of tobacco dependence after brief intermittent use: The Development and Assessment of Nicotine Dependence in Youth-2 study. *Archives of Pediatrics & Adolescent Medicine, 161,* 704–710.

Dloniak, S. M., French, J. A., and Holekamp, K. E. (2006). Rank-related maternal effect of androgens on behaviour in wild spotted hyenas. *Nature, 440,* 1190–1193.

Dlugos, C., and Pentney, R. (1997). Morphometric evidence that the total number of synapses on Purkinje neurons of old f344 rats is reduced after long-term ethanol treatment and restored to control levels after recovery. *Alcohol and Alcoholism, 32,* 161–172.

Do, M. T. H., Kang, S. H., Zue, T., Zhong, H., et al. (2009). Photon capture and signalling by melanopsin retinal ganglion cells. *Nature, 457,* 281–287.

Dodd, M. L., Klos, K. J., Bower, J. H., Geda, Y. E., et al. (2005). Pathological gambling caused by drugs used to treat Parkinson disease. *Archives of Neurology, 62,* 1377–1381.

Dohanich, G. (2003). Ovarian steroids and cognitive function. *Current Directions in Psychological Science, 12,* 57–61.

Dohrenwend, B. P., Turner, J. B., Turse, N. A., Adams, B. G., et al. (2006). The psychological risks of Vietnam for U.S. veterans: A revisit with new data and methods. *Science, 313,* 979–982.

Dolan, R. J. (2002). Emotion, cognition, and behavior. *Science, 298,* 1191–1194.

Dolder, C. R., and Nelson, M. H. (2008). Hypnosedative-induced complex behaviours: Incidence, mechanisms and management. *CNS Drugs, 22,* 1021–1036.

Domínguez-Rodrigo, M., Pickering, T. R., Semaw, S., and Rogers, M. J. (2005). Cutmarked bones from Pliocene archaeological sites at Gona, Afar, Ethiopia: Implications for the function of the world's oldest stone tools. *Journal of Human Evolution, 48,* 109–121.

Dominici, N., Ivanenko, Y. P., Cappellini, G., d'Avella, A., et al. (2011). Locomotor primitives in newborn babies and their development. *Science, 334,* 997–999.

Domjan, M., and Purdy, J. E. (1995). Animal research in psychology: More than meets the eye of the general psychology student. *American Psychologist, 50,* 496–503.

Do-Monte, F. H., Manzano-Nieves, G., Quiñones-Laracuente, K., Ramos-Medina, L., et al. (2015). Revisiting the role of infralimbic cortex in fear extinction with optogenetics. *Journal of Neuroscience, 35,* 3607–3615.

Donaldson, Z. R., and Young, L. J. (2008). Oxytocin, vasopressin, and the neurogenetics of sociality. *Science, 322,* 900–903.

DonCarlos, L. L., Sarkey, S., Lorenz, B., Azcoitia, I., et al. (2006). Novel cellular phenotypes and subcellular sites for androgen action in the forebrain. *Neuroscience, 138,* 801–807.

Donegan, N. H., Lowery, R. W., and Thompson, R. F. (1983). Effects of lesioning cerebellar nuclei on conditioned leg-flexion responses. *Society for Neuroscience Abstracts, 9,* 331.

Donelson, N. C., and Sanyal, S. (2015). Use of *Drosophila* in the investigation of sleep disorders. *Experimental Neurology, 274*(Pt. A), 72–79.

Doricchi, F., Guariglia, C., Paolucci, S., and Pizzamiglio, L. (1991). Disappearance of leftward rapid eye movements during sleep in left visual hemi-inattention. *Neuroreport, 2,* 285–288.

Doroudchi, M. M., Greenberg, K. P., Liu, J., Silka, K. A., et al. (2011). Virally delivered channelrhodopsin-2 safely and effectively restores visual function in multiple mouse models of blindness. *Molecular Therapy, 19,* 1220–1229.

Dorsaint-Pierre, R., Penhune, V. B., Watkins, K. E., Neelin, P., et al. (2006). Asymmetries of the planum temporale and Heschl's gyrus: Relationship to language lateralization. *Brain, 129,* 1164–1176.

Dosenbach, N. U. F., Petersen, S. E., and Schlaggar, B. L. (2013). The teenage brain: Functional connectivity. *Current Directions in Psychological Science, 22*(3): 101–107.

Doty, R. L. (2010). *The great pheromone myth.* Baltimore: Johns Hopkins University Press.

Dougherty, D. D., Rezai, A. R., Carpenter, L. L., Howland, R. H., et al. (2015). A randomized sham-controlled trial of deep brain stimulation of the ventral capsule/ventral striatum for chronic treatment-resistant depression. *Biological Psychiatry, 78,* 240–248.

Doyle, S., and Menaker, M. (2007). Circadian photoreception in vertebrates. *Cold Spring Harbor Symposia on Quantitative Biology, 72,* 499–508.

Doyon, J., Owen, A. M., Petrides, M., Sziklas, V., et al. (1996). Functional anatomy of visuomotor skill learning in human subjects examined with positron emission tomography. *European Journal of Neuroscience, 8,* 637–648.

Drea, C. M., Weldele, M. L., Forger, N. G., Coscia, E. M., et al. (1998). Androgens and masculinization of genitalia in the spotted hyaena (*Crocuta crocuta*). 2. Effects of prenatal anti-androgens. *Journal of Reproduction and Fertility, 113,* 117–127.

Drevets, W. C. (1998). Functional neuroimaging studies of depression: The anatomy of melancholia. *Annual Review of Medicine, 49,* 341–361.

Drew, T., Võ, M. L., and Wolfe, J. M. (2013). The invisible gorilla strikes again: Sustained inattentional blindness in expert observers. *Psychological Science, 24*(9), 1848–1853.

Drickamer, L. C. (1992). Behavioral selection of odor cues by young female mice affects age of puberty. *Developmental Psychobiology, 25,* 461–470.

Dronkers, N. F., Plaisant, O., Iba-Zizen, M. T., and Cabanis, E. A. (2007). Paul Broca's historic cases: High resolution MR imaging of the brains of Leborgne and Lelong. *Brain, 130*(Pt. 5), 1432–1441.

Dronkers, N. F., Wilkins, D. P., Van Valin, R. D., Jr., Redfern, B. B., et al. (2004). Lesion analysis of the brain areas involved in language comprehension. *Cognition, 92,* 145–177.

Druckman, D., and Bjork, R. A. (1994). *Learning, remembering, believing: Enhancing human performance.* Washington, DC: National Academy Press.

Du, J. L., and Poo, M. M. (2004). Rapid BDNF-induced retrograde synaptic modification in a developing retinotectal system. *Nature, 429,* 878–882.

Duchaine, B., Germine, L., and Nakayama, K. (2007). Family resemblance: Ten family members with prosopagnosia and within-class object agnosia. *Cognitive Neuropsychology, 24,* 419–430.

Duchamp-Viret, P., Chaput, M. A., and Duchamp, A. (1999). Odor response properties of rat olfactory receptor neurons. *Science, 284,* 2171–2174.

Dudai, Y. (1988). Neurogenic dissection of learning and short term memory in *Drosophila. Annual Review of Neuroscience, 11,* 537–563.

Duffy, J. D., and Campbell, J. J. (1994). The regional prefrontal syndromes: A theoretical and clinical overview. *Journal of Neuropsychiatry and Clinical Neurosciences, 6,* 379–387.

Dulac, C., O'Connell, L. A., and Wu, Z. (2014). Neural control of maternal and paternal behaviors. *Science, 345*(6198), 765–770.

Dulac, C., and Torello, A. T. (2003). Molecular detection of pheromone signals in mammals, from genes to behaviour. *Nature Reviews Neuroscience, 4,* 551–562.

Dully, H., and Fleming, C. (2007). *My lobotomy.* New York: Crown.

Duman, J. G. (2015). Animal ice-binding (antifreeze) proteins and glycolipids: An overview with emphasis on physiological function. *Journal of Experimental Biology, 218,* 1846–1855.

Dunbar, R. I. M. (1998). The social brain hypothesis. *Evolutionary Anthropology, 6*(5), 178–190.

Dunbar, R. I. M. (2009). The social brain hypothesis and its implications for social evolution. *Annals of Human Biology, 36,* 562–572.

Dunlop, J., and Brandon, N. J. (2015). Schizophrenia drug discovery and development in an evolving era: Are new drug targets fulfilling expectations? *Journal of Psychopharmacology, 29,* 230–238.

Durkheim, E. (1897). *Le suicide.* Paris: Alcan.

Dvir, Y., and Smallwood, P. (2008). Serotonin syndrome: A complex but easily avoidable condition. *General Hospital Psychiatry, 30,* 284–287.

E

Eagleman, D. M., Kagan, A. D., Nelson, S. S., Sagaram, D., et al. (2007). A standardized test battery for the study of synesthesia. *Journal of Neuroscience Methods, 159,* 139–145.

Earnshaw, W. C., Martins, L. M., and Kaufmann, S. H. (1999). Mammalian caspases: Structure, activation, substrates, and functions during apoptosis. *Annual Review of Biochemistry, 68,* 383–424.

Eberhard, W. G. (1977). Aggressive chemical mimicry by a bolas spider. *Science, 198,* 1173–1175.

Edinger, J. D., and Krystal, A. D. (2003). Subtyping primary insomnia: Is sleep state misperception a distinct clinical entity. *Sleep Medicine Reviews, 7*(3), 203–214.

Edwards, R. R., Grace, E., Peterson, S., Klick, B., et al. (2009, January 23). Sleep continuity and architecture: Associations with pain-inhibitory processes in patients with temporomandibular joint disorder. *European Journal of Pain, 13,* 1043–1047.

Egeland, M., Zunszain, P. A., and Pariante, C. M. (2015). Molecular mechanisms in the regulation of adult neurogenesis during stress. *Nature Reviews Neuroscience, 16,* 189–200.

Ehrenberg, R. (2010). Stomach's sweet tooth. *Science News, 177,* 22–25.

Eichenbaum, H. (2014). Time cells in the hippocampus: A new dimension for mapping memories. *Nature Reviews Neuroscience, 15*(11), 732–744.

Eichenbaum, H., Yonelinas, A. P., and Ranganath, C. (2007). The medial temporal lobe and recognition memory. *Annual Review of Neuroscience, 30,* 123–152.

Eippert, F., Finsterbusch, J., Bingel, U., and Büchel, C. (2009). Direct evidence for spinal cord involvement in placebo analgesia. *Science, 326,* 404.

Eisenberg, M., Kobilo, T., Berman, D. E., and Dudai, Y. (2003). Stability of retrieved memory: Inverse correlation with trace dominance. *Science, 301,* 1102–1104.

Eisenberger, N. I. (2012). Broken hearts and broken bones: A neural perspective on the similarities between social and physical pain. *Psychological Science, 21*(1), 42–47.

Eisenberger, N. I., and Lieberman, M. D. (2004). Why rejection hurts: A common neural alarm system for physical and social pain. *Trends in Cognitive Sciences, 8,* 294–300.

Eklund, A., Nichols, T. E., and Knutsson, H. (2016). Cluster failure: Why fMRI inferences for spatial extent have inflated false-positive rates. *Proceedings of the National Academy of Sciences, USA, 113*(28), 7900–7905.

El Mestikawy, S., Wallén-Mackenzie, A., Fortin, G. M., Descarries, L., et al. (2011). From glutamate co-release to vesicular synergy: Vesicular glutamate transporters. *Nature Reviews Neuroscience, 12,* 204–216.

Elbert, T., Pantev, C., Wienbruch, C., Rockstroh, B., et al. (1995). Increased cortical representation of the fingers of the left hand in string players. *Science, 270,* 305–307.

Ellenbogen, J. M., Hu, P. T., Payne, J. D., Titone, D., et al. (2007). Human relational memory requires time and sleep. *Proceedings of the National Academy of Sciences, USA, 104,* 7317–7318.

Elster, A. D., and Burdette, J. H. (2001). *Magnetic resonance imaging.* Philadelphia: Mosby.

Emborg, M. E., Liu, Y., Xi, J., Zhang, X., et al. (2013). Induced pluripotent stem cell–derived neural cells survive and mature in the nonhuman primate brain. *Cell Reports, 3*(3), 646–650.

Emery, N. J., Capitanio, J. P., Mason, W. A., Machado, C. J., et al. (2001). The effects of bilateral lesions of the amygdala on dyadic social interactions in rhesus monkeys (*Macaca mulatta*). *Behavioral Neuroscience, 115,* 515–544.

Enard, W., Khaitovich, P., Klose, J., Zollner, S., et al. (2002). Intra- and interspecific variation in primate gene expression. *Science, 296,* 340–343.

Engel, J., Jr. (1992). Recent advances in surgical treatment of temporal lobe epilepsy. *Acta Neurologica Scandinavica. Supplementum, 140,* 71–80.

English, P. J., Ghatei, M. A., Malik, I. A., Bloom, S. R., et al. (2002). Food fails to suppress ghrelin levels in obese humans. *Journal of Clinical Endocrinology & Metabolism, 87,* 2984–2987.

Eom, T. Y., Li, J., and Anton, E. S. (2010). Going tubular in the rostral migratory stream: Neurons remodel astrocyte tubes to promote directional migration in the adult brain. *Neuron, 67*(2), 173–175. doi:10.1016/j.neuron.2010.07.013

Epstein, C. M., Woodard, J. L., Stringer, A. Y., Bakay, R. A., et al. (2000). Repetitive transcranial magnetic stimulation does not replicate the Wada test. *Neurology, 55*(7), 1025–1027.

Erickson, J. T., Conover, J. C., Borday, V., Champagnat, J., et al. (1996). Mice lacking brain-derived neurotrophic factor exhibit visceral sensory neuron losses distinct from mice lacking NT4 and display a severe developmental deficit in control of breathing. *Journal of Neuroscience, 16,* 5361–5371.

Erickson, K. I., Voss, M. W., Prakash, R. S., Basak, C., et al. (2011). Exercise training increases size of hippocampus and improves memory. *Proceedings of the National Academy of Sciences, USA, 108,* 3017–3022.

Eriksson, A., and Lacerda, F. (2007). Charlatanry in forensic speech science: A problem to be taken seriously. *International Journal of Speech Language and the Law, 14,* 169–193.

Eriksson, P. S., Perfilieva, E., Björk-Eriksson, T., Alborn, A. M., et al. (1998). Neurogenesis in the adult human hippocampus. *Nature Medicine, 4,* 1313–1317.

Erlanger, D. M., Kutner, K. C., Barth, J. T., and Barnes, R. (1999). Neuropsychology of sports-related head injury: Dementia pugilistica to post concussion syndrome. *Clinical Neuropsychologist, 13,* 193–209.

Ernst, T., Chang, L., Leonido-Yee, M., and Speck, O. (2000). Evidence for long-term neurotoxicity associated with methamphetamine abuse: A 1H MRS study. *Neurology, 54,* 1344–1349.

Erren, T. C., Morfeld, P., Stork, J., Knauth, P., et al. (2009). Shift work, chronodisruption and cancer? The IARC 2007 challenge for research and prevention and 10 theses from the Cologne Colloquium 2008. *Scandinavian Journal of Work, Environment & Health, 35,* 74–79.

Estes, W. K. (1997). Processes of memory loss, recovery, and distortion. *Psychological Review, 104,* 148–169.

Etcoff, N. L., Ekman, P., Magee, J. J., and Frank, M. G. (2000). Lie detection and language comprehension. *Nature, 405,* 139.

Euston, D. R., Tatsuno, M., and McNaughton, B. L. (2007). Fast-forward playback of recent memory sequences in prefrontal cortex during sleep. *Science, 318,* 1147–1150.

Evans, P. D., Anderson, J. R., Vallender, E. J., Gilbert, S. L., et al. (2004). Adaptive evolution of *ASPM,* a major determinant of cerebral cortical size in humans. *Human Molecular Genetics, 13,* 489–494.

Everitt, B. J. (1990). Sexual motivation: A neural and behavioural analysis of the mechanisms underlying appetitive and copulatory responses of male rats. *Neuroscience and Biobehavioral Reviews, 14*(2), 217–232.

Everitt, B. J., and Stacey, P. (1987). Studies of instrumental behavior with sexual reinforcement in male rats (*Rattus norvegicus*): II. Effects of preoptic area lesions, castration, and testosterone. *Journal of Comparative Psychology, 101,* 407–419.

Everson, C. A. (1993). Sustained sleep deprivation impairs host defense. *American Journal of Physiology, 265,* R1148–R1154.

Everson, C. A., Bergmann, B. M., and Rechtschaffen A. (1989). Sleep deprivation in the rat: III. Total sleep deprivation. *Sleep, 12,* 13–21.

Everson, C. A., Thalacker, C. D., and Hogg, N. (2008). Phagocyte migration and cellular stress induced in liver, lung, and intestine during sleep loss and sleep recovery. *American Journal of Physiology. Regulatory, Integrative and Comparative Physiology, 295*(6), R2067–R2074.

F

Faix, A., Lapray, J. F., Courtieu, C., Maubon, A., et al. (2001). Magnetic resonance imaging of sexual intercourse: Initial experience. *Journal of Sex and Marital Therapy, 27*(5), 475–482.

Falk, D. (1993). Sex differences in visuospatial skills: Implications for hominid evolution. In K. R. Gibson and T. Ingold (Eds.), *Tools, language and cognition in human evolution* (pp. 216–229). Cambridge, England: Cambridge University Press.

Falk, D. (2004). Prelinguistic evolution in early hominins: Whence motherese? *Behavioral and Brain Sciences, 27,* 491–503.

Falkner, A. L., Grosenick, L., Davidson, T. J., Deisseroth, K., et al. (2016). Hypothalamic control of male aggression-seeking behavior. *Nature Neuroscience, 19,* 596–604.

Faraone, S.V., Glatt, S. J., Su, J., and Tsuang, M. T. (2004). Three potential susceptibility loci shown by a genome-wide scan for regions influencing the age at onset of mania. *American Journal of Psychiatry, 161,* 625–630.

Farbman, A. I. (1994). The cellular basis of olfaction. *Endeavour, 18,* 2–8.

Fay, R. R. (1988). *Hearing in vertebrates: A psychophysics databook.* Winnetka, IL: Hill-Fay Associates.

Feder, H. H., and Whalen, R. E. (1965). Feminine behavior in neonatally castrated and estrogen-treated male rats. *Science, 147,* 306–307.

Feinstein, J. S., Adolphs, R., Damasio, A., and Tranel, D. (2011). The human amygdala and the induction and experience of fear. *Current Biology, 21,* 34–38.

Feinstein, J. S., Buzza, C., Hurlemann, R., Follmer, R. L., et al. (2013). Fear and panic in humans with bilateral amygdala damage. *Nature Neuroscience, 16*(3), 270–272.

Fenstemaker, S. B., Zup, S. L., Frank, L. G., Glickman, S. E., et al. (1999). A sex difference in the hypothalamus of the spotted hyena. *Nature Neuroscience, 2,* 943–945.

Ferguson, J. N., Young, L. J., Hearn, E. F., Matzuk, M. M., et al. (2000). Social amnesia in mice lacking the oxytocin gene. *Nature Genetics, 25,* 284–288.

Fernald, R. D. (2000). Evolution of eyes. *Current Opinion in Neurobiology, 10,* 444–450.

Fernández-Espejo, D., and Owen, A. M. (2013). Detecting awareness after severe brain injury. *Nature Reviews Neuroscience, 14*(11), 801–809.

Fernández-López, D., Faustino, J., Daneman, R., Zhou, L., et al. (2012). Blood-brain barrier permeability is increased after acute adult stroke but not neonatal stroke in the rat. *Journal of Neuroscience, 32,* 9588–9600.

Fields, R. D., and Stevens-Graham, B. (2002). New insights into neuron-glia communication. *Science, 298,* 556–562.

Fields, S. (1990). Pheromone response in yeast. *Trends in Biochemical Sciences, 15,* 270–273.

Figee, M., Luigjes, J., Smolders, R., Valencia-Alfonso, C. E., et al. (2013). Deep brain stimulation restores frontostriatal network activity in obsessive-compulsive disorder. *Nature Neuroscience, 16,* 386–387.

Finch, C. E., and Kirkwood, T. B. L. (2000). *Chance, development, and aging.* New York: Oxford University Press.

Finger, S. (1994). *Origins of neuroscience: A history of explorations into brain function.* New York: Oxford University Press.

Fink, A. J., Croce, K. R., Huang, Z. J., Abbott, L. F., et al. (2014). Presynaptic inhibition of spinal sensory feedback ensures smooth movement. *Nature, 509*(7498), 43–48.

Fink, H., Rex, A., Voits, M., and Voigt, J. P. (1998). Major biological actions of CCK: A critical evaluation of research findings. *Experimental Brain Research, 123,* 77–83.

Fink, M., and Taylor, M. A. (2007). Electroconvulsive therapy: Evidence and challenges. *JAMA, 298,* 330–332.

Finlay, B. L., and Darlington, R. B. (1995). Linked regularities in the development and evolution of mammalian brains. *Science, 268,* 1578–1584.

Finlay, B. L., Franco, E. C. S., Yamada, E. S., Crowley, J. C., et al. (2008). Number and topography of cones, rods and optic nerve axons in New and Old World primates. *Visual Neuroscience, 25,* 289–299.

Fischer, H., Andersson, J. L., Furmark, T., and Fredrikson, M. (1998). Brain correlates of an unexpected panic attack: A human positron emission tomographic study. *Neuroscience Letters, 251,* 137–140.

Fishman, R. B., Chism, L., Firestone, G. L., and Breedlove, S. M. (1990). Evidence for androgen receptors in sexually dimorphic perineal muscles of neonatal male rats. Absence of androgen accumulation by the perineal motoneurons. *Journal of Neurobiology, 21,* 694–704.

Fitzsimmons, J. T. (1998). Angiotensin, thirst, and sodium appetite. *Physiological Reviews, 78,* 583–686.

Flament, D., Ellermann, J. M., Kim, S. G., Ugurbil, K., et al. (1996). Functional magnetic resonance imaging of cerebellar activation during the learning of a visuomotor dissociation task. *Human Brain Map, 4,* 210–226.

Fleming, A. S., Kraemer, G. W., Gonzalez, A., Lovic, V., et al. (2002). Mothering begets mothering: The transmission of behavior and its neurobiology across generations. *Pharmacology, Biochemistry, and Behavior, 73,* 61–75.

Fleming, S. M., Huijgen, J., and Dolan, R. J. (2012). Prefrontal contributions to metacognition in perceptual decision making. *Journal of Neuroscience, 32,* 6117–6125.

Flor, H., Nikolajsen, L., and Jensen, T. S. (2006). Phantom limb pain: A case of maladaptive CNS plasticity? *Nature Neuroscience, 7,* 873–881.

Foa, E. B., Gillihan, S. J., and Bryant, R. A. (2013). Challenges and successes in dissemination of evidence-based treatments for posttraumatic stress disorder: Lessons learned from prolonged exposure therapy for PTSD. *Psychological Science in the Public Interest, 14,* 65–111.

Fogassi, L., Francesco Ferrari, P., Gesierich, B., Rozzi, S., et al. (2005). Parietal lobe: From action organization to intention understanding. *Science, 308,* 662–666.

Fonseca, L. M., Yokomizo, J. E., Bottino, C. M., and Fuentes, D. (2016). Frontal lobe degeneration in adults with Down syndrome and Alzheimer's disease: A review. *Dementia and Geriatric Cognitive Disorders, 41*(3–4), 123–136. doi:10.1159/000442941

Ford, J. M. (1999). Schizophrenia: The broken P300 and beyond. *Psychophysiology, 36,* 667–682.

Forger, N. G., and Breedlove, S. M. (1986). Sexual dimorphism in human and canine spinal cord: Role of early androgen. *Proceedings of the National Academy of Sciences, USA, 83,* 7527–7531.

Forger, N. G., and Breedlove, S. M. (1987). Seasonal variation in mammalian striated muscle mass and motoneuron morphology. *Journal of Neurobiology, 18,* 155–165.

Forger, N. G., Frank, L. G., Breedlove, S. M., and Glickman, S. E. (1996). Sexual dimorphism of perineal muscles and motoneurons in spotted hyenas. *Journal of Comparative Neurology, 375,* 333–343.

Forger, N. G., Howell, M., Bengston, L., Mackenzie, L., et al. (1997). Sexual dimorphism in the spinal cord is absent in mice lacking the ciliary neurotrophic factor receptor. *Journal of Neuroscience, 17,* 9605–9612.

Fortune, E. S., Rodríguez, C., Li, D., Ball, G. F., et al. (2011). Neural mechanisms for the coordination of duet singing in wrens. *Science, 334,* 666–670.

Foster, G. D., Wyatt, H. R., Hill, J. O., McGuckin, B. G., et al. (2003). A randomized trial of a low-carbohydrate diet for obesity. *New England Journal of Medicine, 348,* 2082–2090.

Foster, N. L., Cahse, T. N., Mansi, L., Brooks, R., et al. (1984). Cortical abnormalities in Alzheimer's disease. *Annals of Neurology, 16,* 649–654.

Fothergill, E., Guo, J., Howard, L., Kerns, J. C., et al. (2016). Persistent metabolic adaptation 6 years after "The Biggest Loser" competition. *Obesity.* doi:10.1002/oby.21538. PubMed PMID: 27136388.

Fournier, J. C., DeRubeis, R. J., Hollon, S. D., Dimidjian, S., et al. (2010). Antidepressant drug effects and depression severity: A patient-level meta-analysis. *JAMA, 303,* 47–53.

Fraint, A., and Pal, G. (2015). Deep brain stimulation in Tourette's syndrome. *Frontiers in Neurology, 6,* 170. doi:10.3389/fneur.2015.00170

Francis, D. D., Szegda, K., Campbell, G., Martin, W. D., et al. (2003). Epigenetic sources of behavioral differences in mice. *Nature Neuroscience, 6,* 445–446.

Francks, C., Maegawa, S., Laurén, J., Abrahams, B. S., et al. (2007). LRRTM1 on chromosome 2p12 is a maternally suppressed gene that is associated paternally with handedness and schizophrenia. *Molecular Psychiatry, 12*(12), 1129–1139.

Frank, L. G., Glickman, S. E., and Licht, P. (1991). Fatal sibling aggression, precocial development, and androgens in neonatal spotted hyenas. *Science, 252,* 702–704.

Frank, M. J., Samanta, J., Moustafa, A. A., and Sherman, S. J. (2007). Hold your horses: Impulsivity, deep brain stimulation, and medication in parkinsonism. *Science, 318,* 1309–1312.

Franken, T. P., Roberts, M. T., Wei, L., Golding, N. L., et al. (2015). In vivo coincidence detection in mammalian sound localization generates phase delays. *Nature Neuroscience, 18*(3), 444–452.

Frankenhaeuser, M. (1978). Psychoneuroendocrine approaches to the study of emotion as related to stress and coping. *Nebraska Symposium on Motivation, 26,* 123–162.

Frankland, P. W., O'Brien, C., Masuo, O., Kirkwood, A., et al. (2001). α-CaMKII-dependent plasticity in the cortex is required for permanent memory. *Nature, 411,* 309–312.

Franklin, T. R., Acton, P. D., Maldjian, J. A., Gray, J. D., et al. (2002). Decreased gray matter concentration in the insular, orbitofrontal, cingulate, and temporal cortices of cocaine patients. *Biological Psychiatry, 51,* 134–142.

Franks, N. P. (2008). General anaesthesia: From molecular targets to neuronal pathways of sleep and arousal. *Nature, 9,* 370–386.

Franz, S. I. (1902). On the functions of the cerebrum: I. The frontal lobes in relation to the production and retention of simple sensory-motor habits. *American Journal of Physiology, 8,* 1–22.

Freed, C. R., Greene, P. E., Breeze, R. E., Tsai, W.-Y., et al. (2001). Transplantation of embryonic dopamine neurons for severe Parkinson's disease. *New England Journal of Medicine, 344,* 710–719.

Freedman, M. S., Lucas, R. J., Soni, B., von Schantz, M., et al. (1999). Regulation of mammalian circadian behavior by non-rod, non-cone, ocular photoreceptors. *Science, 284,* 502–504.

Freeman, J., Ziemba, C. M., Heeger, D. J., Simoncelli, E. P., et al. (2013). A functional and perceptual signature of the second visual area in primates. *Nature Neuroscience, 16,* 974–981.

Freitag, J., Ludwig, G., Andreini, P., Roessler, P., et al. (1998). Olfactory receptors in aquatic and terrestrial vertebrates. *Journal of Comparative Physiology, 183,* 635–650.

Freiwald, W. A., Tsao, D.Y., and Livingstone, M. S. (2009). A face feature space in the macaque temporal lobe. *Nature Neuroscience, 12,* 1187–1196.

Frenda, S. J., Patihis, L., Loftus, E. F., Lewis, H. C., et al. (2014). Sleep deprivation and false memories. *Psychological Science, 25*(9), 1674–1681.

Frey, S. H., Bogdanov, S., Smith, J. C., Watrous, S., et al. (2008). Chronically deafferented sensory cortex recovers a grossly typical organization after allogenic hand transplantation. *Current Biology, 18,* 1530–1534.

Frey, U., Huang, Y.-Y., and Kandel, E. R. (1993). Effects of cAMP simulate a late stage of LTP in hippocampal CA1 neurons. *Science, 260,* 1661–1664.

Fridlund, A. J. (1994). *Human facial expression: An evolutionary view.* San Diego, CA: Academic Press.

Fried, I., Wilson, C. L., MacDonald, K. A., and Behnke, E. J. (1998). Electric current stimulates laughter. *Nature, 391,* 650.

Friedman, L., and Jones, B. E. (1984). Study of sleep-wakefulness states by computer graphics and cluster analysis before and after lesions of the pontine tegmentum in the cat. *Electroencephalography and Clinical Neurophysiology, 57,* 43–56.

Friedman, M., and Rosenman, R. H. (1974). *Type A behavior and your heart.* New York: Knopf.

Friedrich, F. J., Egly, R., Rafal, R. D., and Beck, D. (1998). Spatial attention deficits in humans: A comparison of superior parietal and temporal-parietal junction lesions. *Neuropsychology, 12,* 193–207.

Fritz, J., Shamma, S., Elhilali, M., and Klein, D. (2003). Rapid task-related plasticity of spectrotemporal receptive fields in primary auditory cortex. *Nature Neuroscience, 6,* 1216–1223.

Fromer, M., Pocklington, A. J., Kavanagh, D. H., Williams, H. J., et al. (2014). De novo mutations in schizophrenia implicate synaptic networks. *Nature, 506,* 179–184.

Frumin, I., Sobel, N., and Gilad, Y. (2014). Does a unique olfactory genome imply a unique olfactory world? *Nature Neuroscience, 17*(1), 6–8.

Fukuda, K., Ogilvie, R. D., Chilcott, L., Vendittelli, A.-M., et al. (1998). The prevalence of sleep paralysis among Canadian and Japanese college students. *Dreaming: Journal of the Association for the Study of Dreams, 8*(2), 59–66.

Fuller, P. M., Lu, J., and Saper C. B. (2008). Differential rescue of light- and food-entrainable circadian rhythms. *Science, 320,* 1074–1077.

Fulton, B. D., Scheffler, R. M., Hinshaw, S. P., Levine, P., et al. (2009). National variation of ADHD diagnostic prevalence and medication use: Health care providers and education policies. *Psychiatric Services, 60*(8), 1075–1083.

Fulton, S., Woodside, B., and Shizgal, P. (2000). Modulation of brain reward circuitry by leptin. *Science, 287,* 125–128.

Funahashi, S. (2006). Prefrontal cortex and working memory processes. Neuroscience, 139, 251–261.

Funahashi, S. (2006). Prefrontal cortex and working memory processes. *Neuroscience, 139,* 251–261.

Funk, J., Finke, K., Müller, H. J., Preger, R., et al. (2010). Systematic biases in the tactile perception of the subjective vertical in patients with unilateral neglect and the influence of upright vs. supine posture. *Neuropsychologia, 48,* 298–308.

Furey, M. L., Pietrini, P., and Haxby, J. V. (2000). Cholinergic enhancement and increased selectivity of perceptual processing during working memory. *Science, 290,* 2315–2319.

Fuster, J. M. (1990). Prefrontal cortex and the bridging of temporal gaps in the perception-action cycle. *Annals of the New York Academy of Sciences, 608,* 318–336.

G

Gabel, L. A., Gibson, C. J., Gruen, J. R., and LoTurco, J. J. (2010). Progress towards a cellular neurobiology of reading disability. *Neurobiology of Disease, 38*(2), 173–180.

Gabrieli, J. D. E., Sullivan, E. V., Desmond, J. E., Stebbins, G. T., et al. (1996). Behavioral and functional neuroimaging evidence for preserved conceptual implicit memory in global amnesia. *Society for Neuroscience, 22,* 1449.

Gage, S. H., Hickman, M., and Zammit, S. (2015). Association between cannabis and psychosis: Epidemiologic evidence. *Biological Psychiatry,* pii: S0006-3223(15)00647-2. doi:10.1016/j.biopsych.2015.08.001

Gainetdinov, R. R., Wetsel, W. C., Jones, S. R., Levin E. D., et al. (1999). Role of serotonin in the paradoxical calming effect of psychostimulants on hyperactivity. *Science, 283,* 397–401.

Galaburda, A. M. (1994). Developmental dyslexia and animal studies: At the interface between cognition and neurology. *Cognition, 56,* 833–839.

Galaburda, A. M., LoTurco, J., Ramus, F., Fitch, R. H., et al. (2006). From genes to behavior in developmental dyslexia. *Nature Neuroscience, 9,* 1213–1217.

Galea, L. A. (2008). Gonadal hormone modulation of neurogenesis in the dentate gyrus of adult male and female rodents. *Brain Research Reviews, 57,* 332–341.

Gallant, J. L., Braun, J., and Van Essen, D. C. (1993). Selectivity for polar, hyperbolic, and Cartesian gratings in macaque visual cortex. *Science, 259,* 100–103.

Gangwisch, J. E., Heymsfield, S. B., Boden-Albala, B., Buijs, R. M., et al. (2007). Sleep duration as a risk factor for diabetes incidence in a large U.S. sample. *Sleep, 30,* 1667–1673.

Gannon, P. J., Holloway, R. L., Broadfield, D. C., and Braun, A. R. (1998). Asymmetry of chimpanzee planum temporale: Humanlike pattern of brain language area homolog. *Science, 279,* 220–222.

Gaoni, Y., and Mechoulam, R. (1964). Isolation, structure, and partial synthesis of an active constituent of hashish. *Journal of the American Chemical Society, 86,* 1646–1647.

Gardner, L. I. (1972). Deprivation dwarfism. *Scientific American, 227*(1), 76–82.

Gardner, R. A., and Gardner, B. T. (1969). Teaching sign language to a chimpanzee. *Science, 165,* 664–672.

Gardner, R. A., and Gardner, B. T. (1984). A vocabulary test for chimpanzees (*Pan troglodytes*). *Journal of Comparative Psychology, 98,* 381–404.

Gardner, T. J., Naef, F., and Nottebohm, F. (2005). Freedom and rules: The acquisition and reprogramming of a bird's learned song. *Science, 308,* 1046–1049.

Garfield, A. S., Li, C., Madara, J. C., Shah, B. P., et al. (2015). A neural basis for melanocortin-4 receptor-regulated appetite. *Nature Neuroscience, 18,* 863–871.

Garver, D. L., Holcomb, J. A., and Christensen, J. D. (2000). Heterogeneity of response to antipsychotics from multiple disorders in the schizophrenia spectrum. *Journal of Clinical Psychiatry, 61,* 964–972.

Gaspar, J. M., and McDonald, J. J. (2014). Suppression of salient objects prevents distraction in visual search. *Journal of Neuroscience, 34*(16), 5658–5666.

Gasser, P., Holstein, D., Michel, Y., Doblin, R., et al. (2014). Safety and efficacy of lysergic acid diethylamide-assisted psychotherapy for anxiety associated with life-threatening diseases. *Journal of Nervous and Mental Disease, 202,* 513–520.

Gaulin, S. J. C, and Fitzgerald, R. W. (1989). Sexual selection for spatial-learning ability. *Animal Behaviour, 37*, 322–331.

Gauthier, I., Behrmann, M., and Tarr, M. J. (1999). Can face recognition really be dissociated from object recognition? *Journal of Cognitive Neuroscience, 11*, 349–370.

Gauthier, I., Skudlarski, P., Gore, J. C., and Anderson, A. W. (2000). Expertise for cars and birds recruits brain areas involved in face recognition. *Nature Neuroscience, 3*, 191–197.

Gawande, A. (2008, June 30). The itch. *The New Yorker*.

Gazzaniga, A. M. (2008). *Human: The science behind what makes us unique.* New York: HarperCollins.

Gazzaniga, M. S., and Smylie, C. S. (1983). Facial recognition and brain asymmetries: Clues to underlying mechanisms. *Annals of Neurology, 13*, 536–540.

Geers, A. E., and Sedey, A. L. (2011). Language and verbal reasoning skills in adolescents with 10 or more years of cochlear implant experience. *Ear and Hearing, 32*(Suppl. 1), 39S–48S.

Gehring, W. J., and Willoughby, A. R. (2002). The medial frontal cortex and the rapid processing of monetary gains and losses. *Science, 295*, 2279–2280.

Geinisman, Y., Detoledo-Morrell, L., Morrell, F., and Heller, R. E. (1995). Hippocampal markers of age-related memory dysfunction: Behavioral, electrophysiological and morphological perspectives. *Progress in Neurobiology, 45*, 223–252.

Gelber, R. P., Redline, S., Ross, G. W., Petrovitch, H., (2015). Associations of brain lesions at autopsy with polysomnography features before death. *Neurology, 84*(3), 296–303.

Gelstein, S., Yeshurun, Y., Rozenkrantz, L., Shushan, S., et al. (2011). Human tears contain a chemosignal. *Science, 331*(6014), 226–230.

Gemba, H., Miki, N., and Sasaki, K. (1995). Cortical field potentials preceding vocalization and influences of cerebellar hemispherectomy upon them in monkeys. *Brain Research, 697*, 143–151.

Genoux, D., Haditsch, U., Knobloch, M., Michalon, A., et al. (2002). Protein phosphatase 1 is a molecular constraint on learning and memory. *Nature, 418*, 970–975.

George, A. L., Jr. (2005). Inherited disorders of voltage-gated sodium channels. *Journal of Clinical Investigation, 115*, 1990–1999.

Georgiadis, J. R., and Holstege, G. (2005). Human brain activation during sexual stimulation of the penis. *Journal of Comparative Neurology, 493*(1), 33–38.

Georgiadis, J. R., Farrell, M. J., Boessen, R., Denton, D. A., et al. (2010). Dynamic subcortical blood flow during male sexual activity with ecological validity: A perfusion fMRI study. *Neuroimage, 50*(1), 208–216.

Georgiadis, J. R., Reinders, A. A., Paans, A. M., Renken, R., et al. (2009). Men versus women on sexual brain function: Prominent differences during tactile genital stimulation, but not during orgasm. *Human Brain Mapping, 10*, 3089–3101.

Georgopoulos, A. P., Kalaska, J. F., Caminiti, R., and Massey, J. T. (1982). On the relations between the direction of two-dimensional arm movements and cell discharge in primate motor cortex. *Journal of Neuroscience, 2*, 1527–1537.

Georgopoulos, A. P., Taira, M., and Lukashin, A. (1993). Cognitive neurophysiology of the motor cortex. *Science, 260*, 47–52.

Gerard, C. M., Mollereau, C., Vassart, G., and Parmentier, M. (1991). Molecular cloning of a human cannabinoid receptor which is also expressed in testis. *Biochemical Journal, 279*, 129–134.

Gerashchenko, D., Kohls, M. D., Greco, M. A., Waleh, N. S., et al. (2001). Hypocretin-2-saporin lesions of the lateral hypothalamus produce narcoleptic-like sleep behavior in the rat. *Neuroscience, 21*, 7273–7283.

Geschwind, N. (1972). Language and the brain. *Scientific American, 226*(4), 76–83.

Geschwind, N. (1976). Language and cerebral dominance. In T. N. Chase (Ed.), *Nervous system: Vol. 2. The clinical neurosciences* (pp. 433–439). New York: Raven.

Geschwind, N., and Levitsky, W. (1968). Human brain: Left-right asymmetries in temporal speech region. *Science, 161*, 186–187.

Ghazanfar, A. A., and Hauser, M. D. (1999). The neuroethology of primate vocal communication: Substrates for the evolution of speech. *Trends in Cognitive Sciences, 3*, 377–384.

Gibson, R. M., Fernández-Espejo, D., Gonzalez-Lara, L. E., Kwan, B. Y., et al. (2014). Multiple tasks and neuroimaging modalities increase the likelihood of detecting covert awareness in patients with disorders of consciousness. *Frontiers in Human Neuroscience, 8*, 950.

Gilad, Y., Bustamante, C. D., Lancet, D., and Pääbo, S. (2003). Natural selection on the olfactory receptor gene family in humans and chimpanzees. *America Journal of Human Genetics, 73*(3), 489–501.

Gilbert, A. N., and Wysocki, C. J. (1987). The smell survey results. *National Geographic, 172*, 514–525.

Gilbert, A. N., Yamazaki, K., Beauchamp, G. K., and Thomas, L. (1986). Olfactory discrimination of mouse strains (*Mus musculus*) and major histocompatibility types by humans (*Homo sapiens*). *Journal of Comparative Psychology, 100*, 262–265.

Gilbertson, M. W., Shenton, M. E., Ciszewski, A., Kasai, K., et al. (2002). Smaller hippocampal volume predicts pathologic vulnerability to psychological trauma. *Nature Neuroscience, 5*, 1242–1247.

Gilissen, C., Hehir-Kwa, J. Y., Thung, D. T., van de Vorst, M., et al. (2014). Genome sequencing identifies major causes of severe intellectual disability. *Nature, 511*(7509), 344–347. doi:10.1038/nature13394

Gill, R. E., Tibbitts, T. L., Douglas, D. C., Hanel, C. M., et al. (2009). Extreme endurance flights by landbirds crossing the Pacific Ocean: Ecological corridor rather than barrier? *Proceedings: Biological Sciences, 276*, 447–457.

Gitelman, D. R., Alpert, N. M., Kosslyn, S., Daffner, K., et al. (1996). Functional imaging of human right hemispheric activation for exploratory movements. *Annals of Neurology, 39*, 174–179.

Glantz, L. A., and Lewis, D. A. (2000). Decreased dendritic spine density on prefrontal cortical pyramidal neurons in schizophrenia. *Archives of General Psychiatry, 57*, 65–73.

Glantz, M., and Pickens, R. (1992). *Vulnerability to drug abuse.* Washington, DC: American Psychological Association.

Glaser, R., Rice, J., Speicher, C. E., Stout, J. C., et al. (1986). Stress depresses interferon production by leukocytes concomitant with a decrease in natural killer cell activity. *Behavioral Neuroscience, 100*, 675–678.

Glendinning, J. I., Yiin, Y. M., Ackroff, K., and Sclafani, A. (2008). Intragastric infusion of denatonium conditions flavor aversions and delays gastric emptying in rodents. *Physiology & Behavior, 93*(4–5), 757–765.

Glenn, A. L., and Raine, A. (2014). Neurocriminology: Implications for the punishment, prediction and prevention of criminal behaviour. *Nature Reviews Neuroscience, 15*, 54–63.

Glickman, S. E. (1977). Comparative psychology. In P. Mussen and M. R. Rosenzweig (Eds.), *Psychology: An introduction* (2nd ed., pp. 625–703). Lexington, MA: Heath.

Glickman, S. E., Frank, L. G., Davidson, J. M., Smith, E. R., et al. (1987). Androstenedione may organize or activate sex-reversed traits in female spotted hyenas. *Proceedings of the National Academy of Sciences, USA, 84,* 344–347.

Glimcher, P. W. (2011). Understanding dopamine and reinforcement learning: The dopamine reward prediction error hypothesis. *Proceedings of the National Academy of Sciences, USA, 108*(Suppl. 3), 15647–15654.

Globus, A., Rosenzweig, M. R., Bennett, E. L., and Diamond, M. C. (1973). Effects of differential experience on dendritic spine counts in rat cerebral cortex. *Journal of Comparative and Physiological Psychology, 82,* 175–181.

Gnad, T., Scheibler, S., von Kügelgen, I., Scheele, C., et al. (2014). Adenosine activates brown adipose tissue and recruits beige adipocytes via A2A receptors. *Nature, 516,* 395–399.

Goebel, T. (2007). The missing years for modern humans. *Science, 315,* 194–196.

Goedert, K. M., Zhang, J.Y., and Barrett, A. M. (2015). Prism adaptation and spatial neglect: The need for dose-finding studies. *Frontiers in Human Neuroscience, 9,* 243.

Gogtay, N., Giedd, J. N., Lusk, L., Hayashi, K. M., et al. (2004). Dynamic mapping of human cortical development during childhood through early adulthood. *Proceedings of the National Academy of Sciences, USA, 101,* 8174–8179.

Golden, R. N., Gaynes, B. N., Ekstrom, R. D., Hamer, R. M., et al. (2005). The efficacy of light therapy in the treatment of mood disorders: A review and meta-analysis of the evidence. *American Journal of Psychiatry, 162,* 656–662.

Goldin, P. R., and Gross, J. J. (2010). Effects of mindfulness-based stress reduction (MBSR) on emotion regulation in social anxiety disorder. *Emotion, 10,* 83–91.

Goldin-Meadow, S. (2006). Talking and thinking with our hands. *Current Directions in Psychological Science, 15,* 34–39.

Goldstein, J. M., Seidman, L. J., Horton, N. J., Makris, N., et al. (2001). Normal sexual dimorphism of the adult human brain assessed by in vivo magnetic resonance imaging. *Cerebral Cortex, 11,* 490–497.

Goldstein, R. Z., and Volkow N. D. (2011). Dysfunction of the prefrontal cortex in addiction: Neuroimaging findings and clinical implications. *Nature Reviews Neuroscience, 12,* 652–669.

Goll, Y., Atlan, G., and Citri, A. (2015). Attention: The claustrum. *Trends in Neurosciences, 38*(8), 486–495.

Golomb, J., de Leon, M. J., George, A. E., Kluger, A., et al. (1994). Hippocampal atrophy correlates with severe cognitive impairment in elderly patients with suspected normal pressure hydrocephalus. *Journal of Neurology, Neurosurgery and Psychiatry, 57,* 590–593.

González-Maeso, J., Ang, R. L., Yuen, T., Chan, P., et al. (2008). Identification of a serotonin/glutamate receptor complex implicated in psychosis. *Nature, 452,* 93–97.

Goodale, M. A., and Haffenden, A. (1998). Frames of reference for perception and action in the human visual system. *Neuroscience and Biobehavioral Reviews, 22,* 161–172.

Goodale, M. A., and Milner, A. D. (1992). Separate visual pathways for perception and action. *Trends in Neurosciences, 15*(1), 20–25.

Goodale, M. A., Milner, A. D., Jakobson, L. S., and Carey, D. P. (1991). A neurological dissociation between perceiving objects and grasping them. *Nature, 349,* 154–156.

Goodglass, H., Quadfasel, F. A., and Timberlake, W. H. (1964). Phrase length and the type and severity of aphasia. *Cortex, 1,* 133–153.

Goodman, C. (1979). Isogenic grasshoppers: Genetic variability and development of identified neurons. In X. O. Breakefeld (Ed.), *Neurogenetics* (pp. 101–151). New York: Elsevier.

Gooley, J. J., Rajaratnam, S. M., Brainard, G. C., Kronauer, R. E., et al. (2010). Spectral responses of the human circadian system depend on the irradiance and duration of exposure to light. *Science Translational Medicine, 2*(31), 31ra33.

Gordon, N. S., Burke, S., Akil, H., Watson, S. J., et al. (2003). Socially-induced brain "fertilization": Play promotes brain derived neurotrophic factor transcription in the amygdala and dorsolateral frontal cortex in juvenile rats. *Neuroscience Letters, 341,* 17–20.

Gorski, R. A., Gordon, J. H., Shryne, J. E., and Southam, A. M. (1978). Evidence for a morphological sex difference within the medial preoptic area of the rat brain. *Brain Research, 148,* 333–346.

Gorzalka, B. B., Mendelson, S. D., and Watson, N.V. (1990). Serotonin receptor subtypes and sexual behavior. *Annals of the New York Academy of Sciences, 600,* 435–444.

Gosselin, R. D., Suter, M. R., Ji, R. R., and Decosterd, I. (2010). Glial cells and chronic pain. *Neuroscientist, 16,* 519–531.

Goswami, U. (2015). Sensory theories of developmental dyslexia: Three challenges for research. *Nature Reviews Neuroscience, 16*(1), 43–54.

Gotlib, I. H., Joormann, J., and Foland-Ross, L. C. (2014). Understanding familial risk for depression: A 25 year perspective. *Perspectives on Psychological Science, 9,* 94–108.

Gottesman, I. I. (1991). *Schizophrenia genesis: The origins of madness.* New York: Freeman.

Gottfried, J. A., O'Doherty, J., and Dolan, R. J. (2003). Encoding predictive reward value in human amygdala and orbitofrontal cortex. *Science, 301,* 1104–1107.

Gotti, S., Caricati, E., and Panzica, G. (2011). Alterations of brain circuits in Down syndrome murine models. *Journal of Chemical Neuroanatomy, 42*(4), 317–326. doi:10.1016/j.jchemneu.2011.09.002

Gottlieb, J. (2007). From thought to action: The parietal cortex as a bridge between perception, action, and cognition. *Neuron, 53,* 9–16.

Gough, P. M., Nobre, A. C., and Devlin, J. T. (2005). Dissociating linguistic processes in the left inferior frontal cortex with transcranial magnetic stimulation. *Journal of Neuroscience, 25,* 8010–8016.

Gougoux, F., Zatorre, R. J., Lassonde, M., Voss, P., et al. (2005). A functional neuroimaging study of sound localization: Visual cortex activity predicts performance in early-blind individuals. *PLOS Biology, 3,* 324–332.

Gould, E., Reeves, A. J., Graziano, M. S., and Gross, C. G. (1999). Neurogenesis in the neocortex of adult primates. *Science, 286,* 548–552.

Gould, S. J. (1981). *The mismeasure of man.* New York: Norton.

Gourévitch, B., Edeline, J. M., Occelli, F., and Eggermont, J. J. (2014). Is the din really harmless? Long-term effects of non-traumatic noise on the adult auditory system. *Nature Reviews Neuroscience, 15*(7), 483–491.

Goutman, J. D., Elgoyhen, A. B., and Gómez-Casati, M. E. (2015). Cochlear hair cells: The sound-sensing machines. *FEBS Letters, 589*(22), 3354–3361.

Grados, M. A., Walkup, J., and Walford, S. (2003). Genetics of obsessive-compulsive disorders: New findings and challenges. *Brain & Development, 25*(Suppl. 1), S55–S61.

Grady, C. L., McIntosh, A. R., Horowitz, B., Maisog, J. M., et al. (1995). Age-related reductions in human recognition memory due to impaired encoding. *Science, 269,* 218–221.

Graeber, M. B. (2010). Changing face of microglia. *Science, 330,* 783–788.

Grafton, S. T., Mazziotta, J. C., Presty, S., Friston, K. J., et al. (1992). Functional anatomy of human procedural learning determined with regional cerebral blood flow and PET. *Journal of Neuroscience, 12,* 2542–2548.

Graham, D. L., Edwards, S., Bachtell, R. K., DiLeone, R., et al. (2007). Dynamic BDNF activity in nucleus accumbens with cocaine use increases self-administration and relapse. *Nature Neuroscience, 10,* 1029–1037.

Grant, P. R., and Grant, B. R. (2006). Evolution of character displacement in Darwin's finches. *Science, 313,* 224–226.

Gratton, G., and Fabiani, M. (2001). Shedding light on brain function: The event-related optical signal. *Trends in Cognitive Sciences, 5,* 357–363.

Gray, N. S., MacCulloch, M. J., Smith, J., Morris, M., et al. (2003). Violence viewed by psychopathic murderers. *Nature, 423,* 497.

Graybiel, A. M., Aosaki, T., Flaherty, A. W., and Kimura, M. (1994). The basal ganglia and adaptive motor control. *Science, 265,* 1826–1831.

Graziano, M. S. [A.], and Aflalo, T. N. (2007). Mapping behavioral repertoire onto the cortex. *Neuron, 56,* 239–251.

Graziano, M. S. [A.], Hu, X. T., and Gross, C. G. (1997). Coding the locations of objects in the dark. *Science, 277,* 239–241.

Green, E., and Craddock, N. (2003). Brain-derived neurotrophic factor as a potential risk locus for bipolar disorder: Evidence, limitations, and implications. *Current Psychiatry Reports, 5,* 469–476.

Green, J. J., Doesburg, S. M., Ward, L. M., and McDonald, J. J. (2011). Electrical neuroimaging of voluntary audiospatial attention: Evidence for a supramodal attention control network. *Journal of Neuroscience, 31*(10), 3560–3564.

Green, M. F., Horan, W. P., and Lee, J. (2015). Social cognition in schizophrenia. *Nature Reviews Neuroscience, 16,* 620–631.

Green, W. H., Campbell, M., and David, R. (1984). Psychosocial dwarfism: A critical review of the evidence. *Journal of the American Academy of Child Psychiatry, 23,* 39–48.

Greenough, W. T. (1976). Enduring brain effects of differential experience and training. In M. R. Rosenzweig and E. L. Bennett (Eds.), *Neural mechanisms of learning and memory* (pp. 255–278). Cambridge, MA: MIT Press.

Gregory, R. L., and Wallace, J. G. (1963). Recovery from early blindness: A case study. *Experimental Psychology Society Monograph, 2,* 1–44.

Grenham, S., Clarke, G., Cryan, J. F., and Dinan, T. G. (2011). Brain-gut-microbe communication in health and disease. *Frontiers in Physiology, 2,* 94.

Griebel, G., and Holmes, A. (2013). 50 years of hurdles and hope in anxiolytic drug discovery. *Nature Reviews Drug Discovery, 12,* 667–687.

Griffin, D. M., Hoffman, D. S., and Strick, P. L. (2015). Corticomotoneuronal cells are "functionally tuned." *Science, 350*(6261), 667–670.

Griffin, G. D., and Flanagan-Cato, L. M. (2011). Ovarian hormone action in the hypothalamic ventromedial nucleus: Remodelling to regulate reproduction. *Journal of Neuroendocrinology, 23*(6), 465–471.

Griffin, L. D., and Mellon, S. H. (1999). Selective serotonin reuptake inhibitors directly alter activity of neurosteroidogenic enzymes. *Proceedings of the National Academy of Sciences, USA, 96,* 13512–13517.

Grimbos, T., Dawood, K., Burriss, R. P., Zucker, K. J., et al. (2010). Sexual orientation and the second to fourth finger length ratio: A meta-analysis in men and women. *Behavioral Neuroscience, 124*(2), 278–287.

Grimm, D. (2014, March 12). Animal rights extremists increasingly targeting individuals. *Science.* (www.sciencemag.org/news/2014/03/animal-rights-extremists-increasingly-targeting-individuals)

Grimm, S., and Bajbouj, M. (2010). Efficacy of vagus nerve stimulation in the treatment of depression. *Expert Review of Neurotherapeutics, 19,* 87–92.

Grob, C. S., Danforth, A. L., Chopra, G. S., Hagerty, M., et al. (2011). Pilot study of psilocybin treatment for anxiety in patients with advanced-stage cancer. *Archives of General Psychiatry, 68,* 71–78.

Gropp, E., Shanabrough, M., Borok, E., Xu, A. W., et al. (2005). Agouti-related peptide-expressing neurons are mandatory for feeding. *Nature Neuroscience, 8,* 1289–1291.

Grosjean, Y., Grillet, M., Augustin, H., Ferveur, J. F., et al. (2008). A glial amino-acid transporter controls synapse strength and courtship in Drosophila. *Nature Neuroscience, 11,* 54–61.

Gross, C. G. (2000). Neurogenesis in the adult brain: Death of a dogma. *Nature Reviews Neuroscience, 1,* 67–73.

Gross, C. T., and Canteras, N. S. (2012). The many paths to fear. *Nature Reviews Neuroscience, 13,* 651–658.

Grothe, B. (2003). New roles for synaptic inhibition in sound localization. *Nature Reviews Neuroscience, 4,* 540–550.

Grover, G. J., Mellstrom, K., Ye, L., Malm, J., et al. (2003). Selective thyroid hormone receptor-β activation: A strategy for reduction of weight, cholesterol, and lipoprotein (a) with reduced cardiovascular liability. *Proceedings of the National Academy of Sciences, USA, 100,* 10067–10072.

Grumbach, M. M., and Auchus, R. J. (1999). Estrogen: Consequences and implications of human mutations in synthesis and action. *Journal of Clinical Endocrinology & Metabolism, 84*(12), 4677–4694.

Grunt, J. A., and Young, W. C. (1953). Consistency of sexual behavior patterns in individual male guinea pigs following castration and androgen therapy. *Journal of Comparative and Physiological Psychology, 46,* 138–144.

Grüter T., Grüter, M., and Carbon, C. C. (2008). Neural and genetic foundations of face recognition and prosopagnosia. *Journal of Neuropsychology, 2,* 79–97.

Grutzendler, J., Kasthuri, N., and Gan, W.-B. (2002). Long-term dendritic spine stability in the adult cortex. *Nature, 420,* 812–816.

Guan, Z., Kuhn, J. A., Wang, X., Colquitt, B., et al. (2016). Injured sensory neuron-derived CSF1 induces microglial proliferation and DAP12-dependent pain. *Nature Neuroscience, 19*(1), 94–101.

Guarner, F., and Malagelada, J. R. (2003). Gut flora in health and disease. *Lancet, 361*(9356), 512–519.

Gulevich, G., Dement, W., and Johnson, L. (1966). Psychiatric and EEG observations on a case of prolonged (264 hours) wakefulness. *Archives of General Psychiatry, 15,* 29–35.

Gunn, B. G., Cunningham, L., Mitchell, S. G., Swinny, J. D., et al. (2015). GABA$_A$ receptor-acting neurosteroids: A role in the development and regulation of the stress response. *Frontiers in Neuroendocrinology, 36,* 28–48.

Guo, J. U., Ma, D. K., Mo, H., Ball, M. P., et al. (2011). Neuronal activity modifies the DNA methylation landscape in the adult brain. *Nature Neuroscience, 14*, 1345–1351.

Gurney, M. E., and Konishi, M. (1979). Hormone induced sexual differentiation of brain and behavior in zebra finches. *Science, 208*, 1380–1382.

Gurney, M. E., Pu, H., Chiu, A. Y., Dal Canto, M. C., et al. (1994). Motor neuron degeneration in mice that express a human Cu,Zn superoxide dismutase mutation. *Science, 264*, 1772–1775.

Gusella, J. F., and MacDonald, M. E. (1993). Hunting for Huntington's disease. *Molecular Genetic Medicine, 3*, 139–158.

H

Haász, J., Westlye, E. T., and Fjær, S. (2013). General fluid-type intelligence is related to indices of white matter structure in middle-aged and old adults. *Neuroimage, 83*, 372–383.

Hackman, D. A., Farah, M. J., and Meaney, M. J. (2010). Socio-economic status and the brain: Mechanistic insights from human and animal research. *Nature Reviews Neuroscience, 11*, 651–659.

Haesler, S., Rochefort, C., Georgi, B., Licznerski, P., et al. (2007). Incomplete and inaccurate vocal imitation after knockdown of FoxP2 in songbird basal ganglia nucleus Area X. *PLOS Biology, 5*, e321.

Haesler, S., Wada, K., Nshdejan, A., Morrisey, E. E., et al. (2004). FoxP2 expression in avian vocal learners and non-learners. *Journal of Neuroscience, 24*, 3164–3175.

Hafting, T., Fyhn, M., Molden, S., Moser, M. B., and Moser, E. I. (2005). Microstructure of a spatial map in the entorhinal cortex. *Nature, 436*, 801–806.

Haga, S., Hattori, T., Sato, T., Sato, K., et al. (2010). The male mouse pheromone ESP1 enhances female sexual receptive behaviour through a specific vomeronasal receptor. *Nature, 466*(7302), 118–122.

Hagstrum, J. T. (2000). Infrasound and the avian navigational map. *Journal of Experimental Biology, 203*, 1103–1111.

Hahn-Holbrook, J., and Haselton, M. (2014). Is postpartum depression a disease of modern civilization? *Psychological Science, 23*, 395–400.

Håkansson, M. L., Brown, H., Ghilardi, N., and Skoda, R. C., et al. (1998). Leptin receptor immunoreactivity in chemically defined target neurons of the hypothalamus. *Journal of Neuroscience, 18*, 559–572.

Halsband, U., Matsuzaka, Y., and Tanji, J. (1994). Neuronal activity in the primate supplementary, pre-supplementary and premotor cortex during externally and internally instructed sequential movements. *Neuroscience Research, 20*, 149–155.

Hamburger, V. (1958). Regression versus peripheral control of differentiation in motor hypoplasia. *American Journal of Anatomy, 102*, 365–410.

Hamburger, V. (1975). Cell death in the development of the lateral motor column of the chick embryo. *Journal of Comparative Neurology, 160*, 535–546.

Hamer, D. H., Hu, S., Magnuson, V. L., Hu, N., et al. (1993). A linkage between DNA markers on the X chromosome and male sexual orientation. *Science, 261*, 321–327.

Hamson, D. K., Csupity, A. S., Ali, F. M., and Watson, N. V. (2009). Partner preference and mount latency are masculinized in androgen insensitive rats. *Physiology & Behavior, 98*, 25–30.

Hamson, D. K., Wainwright, S. R., Taylor, J. R., Jones, B. A. et al. (2013). Androgens increase survival of adult-born neurons in the dentate gyrus by an androgen receptor-dependent mechanism in male rats. *Endocrinology, 154*(9), 3294–3304.

Hamson, D. K., and Watson, N. V. (2004). Regional brainstem expression of Fos associated with sexual behavior in male rats. *Brain Research, 1006*, 233–240.

Han, S. K., Gottsch, M. L., Lee, K. J, Popa, S. M., et al. (2005). Activation of gonadotropin-releasing hormone neurons by kisspeptin as a neuroendocrine switch for the onset of puberty. *Journal of Neuroscience, 25*, 11349–11356.

Hanakawa, T., Immisch, I., Toma, K., Dimyan, M. A., et al. (2003). Functional properties of brain areas associated with motor execution and imagery. *Journal of Neurophysiology, 89*, 989–1002.

Hanaway, J., Woolsey, T. A., Gado, M. H., and Roberts, M. P. (1998). *The brain atlas.* Bethesda, MD: Fitzgerald Science.

Hanchar, H. J., Dodson, P. D., Olsen, R. W., Otis, T. S., et al. (2005). Alcohol-induced motor impairment caused by increased extrasynaptic GABA(A) receptor activity. *Nature Neuroscience, 8*, 339–345.

Haney, M., Gunderson, E. W., Jiang, H., Collins, E. D., et al. (2010, January 1). Cocaine-specific antibodies blunt the subjective effects of smoked cocaine in humans. *Biological Psychiatry, 67*(1), 59–65.

Hannula-Jouppi, K., Kaminen-Ahola, N., Taipale, M., Eklund, R., et al. (2005). The axon guidance receptor gene ROBO1 is a candidate gene for developmental dyslexia. *PLOS Genetics, 1*, e50.

Harder, B. (2003). Unproven elixir: Hormone therapy tempts aging men, but its risks haven't yet been reckoned. *Science News, 163*, 296–301.

Hardingham, G. E., and Do, K. Q. (2016). Linking early-life NMDAR hypofunction and oxidative stress in schizophrenia pathogenesis. *Nature Reviews Neuroscience, 17*, 125–134.

Hardyck, C., Petrinovich, L., and Goldman, R. (1976). Left-handedness and cognitive deficit. *Cortex, 12*, 226–279.

Hare, R. D., Harpur, T. J., Hakstian, A. R., Forth, A. E., et al. (1990). The revised psychopathy checklist: Descriptive statistics, reliability, and factor structure. *Psychological Assessment, 2*, 338–341.

Harold, D., Paracchini, S., Scerri, T., Dennis, M., et al. (2006). Further evidence that the KIAA0319 gene confers susceptibility to developmental dyslexia. *Molecular Psychiatry, 11*, 1085–1091, 1061.

Harris, D. S., Everhart, E. T., Mendelson, J., and Jones, R. T. (2003). The pharmacology of cocaethylene in humans following cocaine and ethanol administration. *Drug and Alcohol Dependence, 72*, 169–182.

Harris, E. W., and Cotman, C. W. (1986). Long-term potentiation of guinea pig mossy fiber responses is not blocked by N-methyl D-aspartate antagonists. *Neuroscience Letters, 70*, 132–137.

Harrow, M., Jobe, T. H., and Faull, R. N. (2012, February 17). Do all schizophrenia patients need antipsychotic treatment continuously throughout their lifetime? A 20-year longitudinal study. *Psychological Medicine, 42*, 2145–2155.

Hart, B. L. (1988). Biological basis of the behavior of sick animals. *Neuroscience and Biobehavioral Reviews, 12*, 123–137.

Hartanto, T. A., Krafft, C. E., Iosif, A. M., and Schweitzer, J. B. (2016). A trial-by-trial analysis reveals more intense physical activity is associated with better cognitive control performance in attention-deficit/hyperactivity disorder. *Child Neuropsychology, 22*(5), 618–626.

Hartmann, E. (1978). *The sleeping pill.* New Haven, CT: Yale University Press.

Hartmann, E. (1984). *The nightmare: The psychology and biology of terrifying dreams.* New York: Basic Books.

Harvey, P. H., and Krebs, J. R. (1990). Comparing brains. *Science, 249,* 140–146.

Hasher, L., and Zacks, R. T. (1979). Automatic and effortful processes in memory. *Journal of Experimental Psychology: General, 108,* 356–358.

Haxby, J. V. (2006). Fine structure in representations of faces and objects. *Nature Neuroscience, 9,* 1084–1086.

Hayashi, Y., Kashiwagi, M., Yasuda, K., Ando, R., et al. (2015). Cells of a common developmental origin regulate REM/non-REM sleep and wakefulness in mice. *Science, 350*(6263), 957–961.

Haynes, K. F., Gemeno, C., Yeargan, K. V., Millar, J. G., et al. (2002). Aggressive chemical mimicry of moth pheromones by a bolas spider: How does this specialist predator attract more than one species of prey? *Chemoecology, 12,* 99–105.

Hazeltine, E., Grafton, S. T., and Ivry, R. (1997). Attention and stimulus characteristics determine the locus of motor-sequence encoding. A PET study. *Brain, 120,* 123–140.

He, D. Z., Lovas, S., Ai, Y., Li, Y., et al. (2014). Prestin at year 14: Progress and prospect. *Hearing Research, 311,* 25–35.

Health Quality Ontario. (2016). Repetitive transcranial magnetic stimulation for treatment-resistant depression: A systematic review and meta-analysis of randomized controlled trials. *Ontario Health Technology Assessment Series, 16,* 1–66.

Heath, R. G. (1972). Pleasure and brain activity in man. *Journal of Nervous and Mental Diseases, 154,* 3–18.

Hebb, D. O. (1949). *The organization of behavior.* New York: Wiley.

Hebron, M. L., Lonskaya, I., and Moussa, C. E. (2015). Tyrosine kinase inhibition facilitates autophagic SNCA/α-synuclein clearance. *Autophagy, 9*(8), 1249–1250.

Heckert, J. (2012, November 15). The hazards of growing up painlessly. *The New York Times, Sunday Magazine,* MM26.

Hedden, T., and Gabrieli, J. D. (2004). Insights into the ageing mind: A view from cognitive neuroscience. *Current Opinion in Neurology, 18,* 740–747.

Heffner, H. E., and Heffner, R. S. (1989). Unilateral auditory cortex ablation in macaques results in a contralateral hearing loss. *Journal of Neurophysiology, 62,* 789–801.

Heidenreich, M., Lechner, S. G., Vardanyan, V., Wetzel, C., et al. (2012). KCNQ4 K$^+$ channels tune mechanoreceptors for normal touch sensation in mouse and man. *Nature Neuroscience, 15,* 138–145.

Heinrichs, R. W. (2003). Historical origins of schizophrenia: Two early madmen and their illness. *Journal for the History of Behavioral Sciences, 39,* 349–363.

Held, R. (1993). Binocular vision: Behavioral and neuronal development. In M. H. Johnson (Ed.), *Brain development and cognition: A reader* (pp. 152–166). Oxford, England: Blackwell.

Helmchen, F., and Denk, W. (2005). Deep tissue two-photon microscopy. *Nature Methods, 2,* 932–940.

Helmholtz, H. von. (1962). *Treatise on physiological optics* (J. P. C. Southall, Trans.). New York: Dover. (Original work published 1894)

Hemmingsen, A. M. (1960). Energy metabolism as related to body size and respiratory surfaces, and its evolution. *Reports of Steno Memorial Hospital, Copenhagen, 9,* 1–110.

Herbert, J. (2013). Cortisol and depression: Three questions for psychiatry. *Psychological Medicine, 3,* 449–469.

Herbst, C. T., Stoeger, A. S., Frey, R., Lohscheller, J., et al. (2012). How low can you go? Physical production mechanism of elephant infrasonic vocalizations. *Science, 337*(6094), 595–599.

Herculano-Houzel, S. (2012). The remarkable, yet not extraordinary, human brain as a scaled-up primate brain and its associated cost. *Proceedings of the National Academy of Sciences, USA, 109*(Suppl. 1), 10661–10668.

Herculano-Houzel, S. (2014). The glia/neuron ratio: How it varies uniformly across brain structures and species and what that means for brain physiology and evolution. *Glia, 62*(9), 1377–1391.

Herek, G. M., and McLemore, K. A. (2013). Sexual prejudice. *Annual Review of Psychology, 64,* 309–333.

Herrada, G., and Dulac, C. (1997). A novel family of putative pheromone receptors in mammals with a topographically organized and sexually dimorphic distribution. *Cell, 90,* 763–773.

Herrmann, C., and Knight, R. (2001). Mechanisms of human attention: Event-related potentials and oscillations. *Neuroscience and Biobehavioral Reviews, 25,* 465–476.

Herrup, K. (2015). The case for rejecting the amyloid cascade hypothesis. *Nature Neuroscience, 18*(6), 794–799. doi:10.1038/nn.4017

Hertel, P., Fagerquist, M. V., and Svensson, T. H. (1999). Enhanced cortical dopamine output and antipsychotic-like effects of raclopride by alpha-2 adrenoceptor blockade. *Science, 286,* 105–107.

Herzfeld, D. J., Kojima, Y., Soetedjo, R., and Shadmehr, R. (2015). Encoding of action by the Purkinje cells of the cerebellum. *Nature, 526*(7573), 439–442.

Hetherington, A. W., and Ranson, S. W. (1940). Hypothalamic lesions and adiposity in the rat. *Anatomical Record, 78,* 149–172.

Hewes, G. (1973). Primate communication and the gestural origin of language. *Current Anthropology, 14,* 5–24.

Heyes, C. (2012). New thinking: The evolution of human cognition. *Philosophical Transactions of the Royal Society of London. Series B: Biological Sciences, 367*(1599), 2091–2096.

Hickey, C., Di Lollo, V., and McDonald, J. J. (2009). Electrophysiological indices of target and distractor processing in visual search. *Journal of Cognitive Neuroscience, 21*(4), 760–775.

Hickey, M., Elliott, J., and Davison, S. L. (2012). Hormone replacement therapy. *British Medical Journal, 344,* e763.

Hicks, M. J., De, B. P., Rosenberg, J. B., Davidson, J. T., et al. (2011). Cocaine analog coupled to disrupted adenovirus: A vaccine strategy to evoke high-titer immunity against addictive drugs. *Molecular Therapy, 19,* 612–619.

Higley, J. D., Mehlman, P. T., Taub, D. M., Higley, S. B., et al. (1992). Cerebrospinal fluid monoamine and adrenal correlates of aggression in free-ranging rhesus monkeys. *Archives of General Psychiatry, 49,* 436–441.

Hill, R. S., and Walsh, C. A. (2005). Molecular insights into human brain evolution. *Nature, 437,* 64–67.

Hillis, D. M., Moritz, C., and Mable, B. K. (Eds.). (1996). *Molecular systematics* (2nd ed.). Sunderland, MA: Sinauer.

Hillyard, S. A., Hink, R. F., Schwent, V. L., and Picton, T. W. (1973). Electrical signs of selective attention in the human brain. *Science, 182,* 177–180.

Hillyard, S. A., Störmer, V. S., Feng, W., Martinez, A., et al. (2016). Cross-modal orienting of visual attention. *Neuropsychologia, 83,* 170–178.

Himle, M. B., Woods, D. W., Piacentini, J. C., and Walkup, J. T. (2006). Brief review of habit reversal training for Tourette syndrome. *Journal of Child Neurology, 21,* 719–725.

Hines, M. (2010). Sex-related variation in human behavior and the brain. *Trends in Cognitive Sciences, 14*(10), 448–456.

Hingson, R., Heeren, T., Winter, M., and Weschler, H. (2005). Magnitude of alcohol-related mortality and morbidity among U.S. college students ages 18–24: Changes from 1998 to 2001. *Annual Review of Public Health, 26,* 259–279.

Hirsch, E., Moye, D., and Dimon, J. H. (1995). Congenital indifference to pain: Long-term follow-up of two cases. *Southern Medical Journal, 88,* 851–857.

Hirst, W., Phelps, E. A., Buckner, R. L., Budson, A. E., et al. (2009). Long-term memory for the terrorist attack of September 11: Flashbulb memories, event memories, and the factors that influence their retention. *Journal of Experimental Psychology General, 138*(2), 161–176.

Hirtz, D., Thurman, D. J., Gwinn-Hardy, K., Mohamed, M. et al. (2007). How common are the "common" neurologic disorders? *Neurology, 68,* 326–337.

Hitt, E. (2007). Careers in neuroscience: From protons to poetry. *Science, 318,* 661–665.

Ho, S.Y., and Duchêne, S. (2014). Molecular-clock methods for estimating evolutionary rates and timescales. *Molecular Ecology, 23,* 5947–5965.

Hobaiter, C., and Byrne, R. W. (2011). The gestural repertoire of the wild chimpanzee. *Animal Cognition, 14*(5), 745–767.

Hochberg, L. R., Bacher, D., Jarosiewicz, B., Masse, N.Y., et al. (2012). Reach and grasp by people with tetraplegia using a neurally controlled robotic arm. *Nature, 485*(7398), 372–375.

Hodes, G. E., Kana, V., Menard, C., Merad, M., et al. (2015). Neuroimmune mechanisms of depression. *Nature Neuroscience, 18,* 1386–1393.

Hoeft, F., Hernandez, A., McMillon, G., Taylor-Hill, H., et al. (2006). Neural basis of dyslexia: A comparison between dyslexic and nondyslexic children equated for reading ability. *Journal of Neuroscience, 26,* 10700–10708.

Hofmann, A. (1981). *LSD: My problem child.* New York: McGraw-Hill.

Hofmann, S. G., Sawyer, A. T., Witt, A. A., and Oh, D. (2010). The effect of mindfulness-based therapy on anxiety and depression: A meta-analytic review. *Journal of Consulting and Clinical Psychology, 78,* 169–183.

Hohmann, A. G., Suplita, R. L., Bolton, N. M., Neely, M. H., et al. (2005). An endocannobinoid mechanism for stress-induced analgesia. *Nature, 435,* 1108–1112.

Hohmann, G. W. (1966). Some effects of spinal cord lesions on experienced emotional feelings. *Psychophysiology, 3,* 143–156.

Hollander, E. (1999). Managing aggressive behavior in patients with obsessive-compulsive disorder and borderline personality disorder. *Journal of Clinical Psychiatry, 60*(Suppl.), 38–44.

Hollon, S. D., Thase, M. E., and Markowitz, J. C. (2002). Treatment and prevention of depression. *Psychological Science in the Public Interest, 3,* 39–77.

Holmes, B. (2005). Evolution: Blink and you'll miss it. *NewScientist, 2507,* 28–31.

Holmes, C., Boche, D., Wilkinson, D., Yadegarfar, G., et al. (2008). Long-term effects of Abeta42 immunisation in Alzheimer's disease: Follow-up of a randomized, placebo-controlled phase I trial. *Lancet, 372,* 216–223.

Holstege, G., Georgiadis, J. R., Paans, A. M., Meiners, L. C., et al. (2003). Brain activation during human male ejaculation. *Journal of Neuroscience, 23*(27), 9185–9193.

Holt-Lunstad, J., Smith, T. B., and Layton, J. B. (2010). Social relationships and mortality risk: A meta-analytic review. *PLOS Medicine, 7,* e1000316.

Holy, T. E., and Guo, Z. (2005). Ultrasonic songs of male mice. *PLOS Biology, 3*(12), e386. doi:10.1371/journal.pbio.0030386

Holzenberger, M., Dupont, J., Ducos, B., Leneuve, P., et al. (2003). IGF-1 receptor regulates lifespan and resistance to oxidative stress in mice. *Nature, 421,* 182–187.

Honey, G. D., Bullmore, E. T., Soni, W., Varatheesan, M., et al. (1999). Differences in frontal cortical activation by a working memory task after substitution of risperidone for typical antipsychotic drugs in patients with schizophrenia. *Proceedings of the National Academy of Sciences, USA, 96,* 13432–13437.

Hopfinger, J. B., Buonocore, M. H., and Mangun, G. R. (2000). The neural mechanisms of top-down attentional control. *Nature Neuroscience, 3,* 284–291.

Hopfinger, J., and Mangun, G. (1998). Reflexive attention modulates processing of visual stimuli in human extrastriate cortex. *Psychological Science, 6,* 441–447.

Hopkins, W. D., Misiura, M., Pope, S. M., and Latash, E. M. (2015). Behavioral and brain asymmetries in primates: A preliminary evaluation of two evolutionary hypotheses. *Annals of the New York Academy of Sciences, 1359,* 65–83.

Hopper, K., and Wanderling, J. (2000). Revisiting the developed versus developing country distinction in course and outcome in schizophrenia: Results from ISoS, the WHO collaborative followup project. International Study of Schizophrenia. *Schizophrenia Bulletin, 26,* 835–846.

Horikawa, T., Tamaki, M., Miyawaki, Y., and Kamitani, Y. (2013). Neural decoding of visual imagery during sleep. *Science, 340*(6132), 639–642.

Horton, J. C., and Adams, D. L. (2005). The cortical column: A structure without a function. *Philosophical Transactions of the Royal Society of London. Series B: Biological Sciences, 360,* 837–862.

Howard-Jones, P. A. (2014). Neuroscience and education: Myths and messages. *Nature Reviews Neuroscience, 15*(12), 817–824.

Hsu, M., Bhatt, M., Adolphs, R., Tranel, D., et al. (2005). Neural systems responding to degrees of uncertainty in human decision-making. *Science, 310,* 1680–1683.

Huang, A. L., Chen, X., Hoon, M. A., Chandrashekar, J., et al. (2006). The cells and logic for mammalian sour taste detection. *Nature, 442,* 934–938.

Huang, C. C., and Tesmer, J. J. (2011). Recognition in the face of diversity: Interactions of heterotrimeric G proteins and G protein–coupled receptor (GPCR) kinases with activated GPCRs. *Journal of Biological Chemistry, 286* (10), 7715–7721.

Huang, W., Zhu, P. J., Zhang, S., Zhou, H., et al. (2013). mTORC2 controls actin polymerization required for consolidation of long-term memory. *Nature Neuroscience, 16*(4), 441–448.

Huang, Z. J., and Luo, L. (2015). It takes the world to understand the brain. *Science, 350*(6256), 42–44.

Hubel, D. H., and Wiesel, T. N. (1959). Receptive fields of single neurones in the cat's striate cortex. *Journal of Physiology (London), 148,* 573–591.

Hubel, D. H., and Wiesel, T. N. (1965). Binocular interaction in striate cortex kittens reared with artificial squint. *Journal of Neurophysiology, 28,* 1041–1059.

Hubel, D. H., Wiesel, T. N., and LeVay, S. (1977). Plasticity of ocular dominance in monkey striate cortex. *Philosophical Transactions of the Royal Society of London. Series B: Biological Sciences, 278,* 377–409.

Huber, E., Webster, J. M., Brewer, A. A., MacLeod, D. I., et al. (2015). A lack of experience-dependent plasticity after more than a decade of recovered sight. *Psychological Science, 26*(4), 393–401. doi:10.1177/0956797614563957

Hudspeth, A. J. (1992). Hair-bundle mechanics and a model for mechanoelectrical transduction by hair cells. *Society of General Physiologists Series, 47*, 357–370.

Hudspeth, A. J. (2014). Integrating the active process of hair cells with cochlear function. *Nature Reviews Neuroscience, 15*(9), 600–614.

Huettel, S. A., Stowe, C. J., Gordon, E. M., Warner, B. T., et al. (2006). Neural signatures of economic preferences for risk and ambiguity. *Neuron, 49*, 765–775.

Huffman, K. J., Nelson, J., Clarey, J., and Krubitzer, L. (1999). Organization of somatosensory cortex in three species of marsupials, *Dasyurus hallucatus, Dactylopsila trivirgata*, and *Monodelphis domestica*: Neural correlates of morphological specializations. *Journal of Comparative Neurology, 403*, 5–32.

Hughes, J., Smith, T. W., Kosterlitz, H. W., Fothergill, L. A., et al. (1975). Identification of two related pentapeptides from the brain with potent opiate agonist activity. *Nature, 258*, 577–580.

Huizink, A. C., and Mulder, E. J. (2006). Maternal smoking, drinking or cannabis use during pregnancy and neurobehavioral and cognitive functioning in human offspring. *Neuroscience and Biobehavioral Reviews, 30*, 24–41.

Hunt, G. R., Corballis, M. C., and Gray, R. D. (2001). Laterality in tool manufacture by crows. *Nature, 414*, 707.

Huntington, G. (1872). On chorea. *Medical and Surgical Reporter, 26*, 317–321.

Hurtado, M. D., Sergeyev, V. G., Acosta, A., Spegele, M., et al. (2013). Salivary peptide tyrosine-tyrosine 3-36 modulates ingestive behavior without inducing taste aversion. *Journal of Neuroscience, 33*, 18368–18380.

Huth, A. G., de Heer, W. A., Griffiths, T. L., Theunissen, F. E., et al. (2016). Natural speech reveals the semantic maps that tile human cerebral cortex. *Nature, 532*(7600), 453–458.

Huttenlocher, P. R., deCourten, C., Garey, L. J., and Van der Loos, H. (1982). Synaptogenesis in human visual cortex: Evidence for synapse elimination during normal development. *Neuroscience Letters, 33*, 247–252.

Hyde, J. S. (2005). The gender similarities hypothesis. *American Psychologist, 60*(6), 581–592.

Hyde, K. L., and Peretz I. (2004). Brains that are out of tune but in time. *Psychological Science, 15*, 356–360.

Hyde, K. L., Zatorre, R. J., Griffiths, T. D., Lerch, J. P., et al. (2006). Morphometry of the amusic brain: A two-site study. *Brain, 129*, 2562–2570.

Hyde, T. M., Aaronson, B. A., Randolph, C., Rickler, K. C., et al. (1992). Relationship of birth weight to the phenotypic expression of Gilles de la Tourette's syndrome in monozygotic twins. *Neurology, 42*, 652–658.

Hyde, T. M., and Weinberger, D. R. (1990). The brain in schizophrenia. *Seminars in Neurology, 10*, 276–286.

I

Imai, T., Yamazaki, T., Kobayakawa, R., Kobayakawa, K., et al. (2009). Pre-target axon sorting establishes the neural map topography. *Science, 325*, 585–590.

Imeri, L, and Opp, M. R. (2009). How (and why) the immune system makes us sleep. *Nature Reviews Neuroscience, 10*, 199–210.

Imperato-McGinley, J., Guerrero, L., Gautier, T., and Peterson, R. E. (1974). Steroid 5α-reductase deficiency in man: An inherited form of male pseudohermaphroditism. *Science, 86*, 1213–1215.

Infurna, F. J., and Luthar, S. S. (2016). Resilience to major life stressors is not as common as thought. *Perspectives on Psychological Science, 11*, 175–194.

Insley, S. J. (2000). Long-term vocal recognition in the northern fur seal. *Nature, 406*, 404–405.

Institute of Medicine. (1990). *Broadening the base of treatment for alcohol problems.* Washington, DC: National Academy Press.

Ipata, A. E., Gee, A. L., Goldberg, M. E., and Bisley, J. W. (2006). Activity in the lateral intraparietal area predicts the goal and latency of saccades in a free-viewing visual search task. *Journal of Neuroscience, 26*, 3656–3661.

Irish, L. A., Kline, C. E., Gunn, H. E., Buysse, D. J., et al. (2015). The role of sleep hygiene in promoting public health: A review of empirical evidence. *Sleep Medicine Reviews, 22*, 23–36.

Isaacson, R. L. (1972). Hippocampal destruction in man and other animals. *Neuropsychologia, 10*, 47–64.

Isles, A. R., Baum, M. J., Ma, D., Keverne, E. B., et al. (2001). Urinary odour preferences in mice. *Nature, 409*, 783–784.

Iverson, J. M., and Goldin-Meadow, S. (1998). Why people gesture when they speak. *Nature, 396*, 228.

J

Jablensky, A., Sartorius, N., Ernberg, G., Anker, M., et al. (1992). Schizophrenia: Manifestations, incidence and course in different cultures. A World Health Organization ten-country study. *Psychological Medicine. Monograph Supplement, 20*, 1–97.

Jackson, H., and Parks, T. N. (1982). Functional synapse elimination in the developing avian cochlear nucleus with simultaneous reduction in cochlear nerve axon branching. *Journal of Neuroscience, 2*, 1736–1743.

Jacobs, G. H. (1993). The distribution and nature of colour vision among the mammals. *Biological Reviews of the Cambridge Philosophical Society, 68*, 413–471.

Jacobs, G. H., Williams, G. A., Cahill, H., and Nathans, J. (2007). Emergence of novel color vision in mice engineered to express a human cone photopigment. *Science, 315*, 1723–1725.

Jacobs, J., Weidemann, C. T., Miller, J. F., Solway, A., et al. (2013). Direct recordings of grid-like neuronal activity in human spatial navigation. *Nature Neuroscience, 16*(9), 1188–1190.

Jacobs, L. F., Gaulin, S. J., Sherry, D. F., and Hoffman, G. E. (1990). Evolution of spatial cognition: Sex-specific patterns of spatial behavior predict hippocampal size. *Proceedings of the National Academy of Sciences, USA, 87*, 6349–6352.

Jacobs, L. F., and Spencer, W. D. (1994). Natural space-use patterns and hippocampal size in kangaroo rats. *Brain, Behavior and Evolution, 44*, 125–132.

Jaffe, A. E., Gao, Y., Deep-Soboslay, A., Tao, R., et al. (2016). Mapping DNA methylation across development, genotype and schizophrenia in the human frontal cortex. *Nature Neuroscience, 19*, 40–47.

James, T. W., Culham, J., Humphery, G. K., Milner, A. D., et al. (2003). Ventral occipital lesions impair object recognition but not object-directed grasping: An fMRI study. *Brain, 126*, 2464–2475.

James, W. (1890). *Principles of psychology.* New York: Holt.

Jamieson, D., and Roberts, A. (2000). Responses of young *Xenopus laevis* tadpoles to light dimming: Possible roles for the pineal eye. *Journal of Experimental Biology, 203*, 1857–1867.

Jang, H. J., Kokrashvili, Z., Theodorakis, M. J., Carlson, O. D., et al. (2007). Gut-expressed gustducin and taste receptors regulate secretion of glucagon-like peptide-1. *Proceedings of the National Academy of Sciences, USA, 104*(38), 15069–15074.

Janssen, S., Laermans, J., Verhulst, P. J., Thijs, T., et al. (2011). Bitter taste receptors and α-gustducin regulate the secretion of ghrelin with functional effects on food intake and gastric emptying. *Proceedings of the National Academy of Sciences, USA, 108*(5), 2094–2099.

Jaremka, L. M., Fagundes, C. P., Peng, J., Bennett, J. M., et al. (2013). Loneliness promotes inflammation during acute stress. *Psychological Science, 24,* 1089–1097.

Jaskiw, G. E., and Popli, A. P. (2004). A meta-analysis of the response to chronic L-dopa in patients with schizophrenia: Therapeutic and heuristic implications. *Psychopharmacology (Berlin), 171,* 365–374.

Jaspers, L., Feys, F., Bramer, W. M., Franco, O. H., et al. (2016). Efficacy and safety of flibanserin for the treatment of hypoactive sexual desire disorder in women: A systematic review and meta-analysis. *JAMA Internal Medicine, 176*(4), 453–462. doi:10.1001/jamainternmed.2015.8565

Jaunmuktane, Z., Mead, S., Ellis, M., Wadsworth, J. D., et al. (2015). Evidence for human transmission of amyloid-beta pathology and cerebral amyloid angiopathy. *Nature, 525*(7568), 247–250. doi:10.1038/nature15369

Javitt, D. C., and Sweet, R. A. (2015). Auditory dysfunction in schizophrenia: Integrating clinical and basic features. *Nature Reviews Neuroscience, 16,* 535–550.

Jeffress, L. A. (1948). A place theory of sound localization. *Journal of Comparative and Physiological Psychology, 41,* 35–39.

Jenike, M. A., Baer, L., Ballantine, T., Martuza, R. L., et al. (1991). Cingulotomy for refractory obsessive-compulsive disorder. A long-term follow-up of 33 patients. *Archives of General Psychiatry, 48,* 548–555.

Jenkins, J., and Dallenbach, K. (1924). Oblivescence during sleep and waking. *American Journal of Psychology, 35,* 605–612.

Jensen, M. P., Day, M. A., and Miró, J. (2014). Neuromodulatory treatments for chronic pain: Efficacy and mechanisms. *Nature Reviews Neurology, 10*(3), 167–178.

Jentsch, J. D., Redmond, D. E., Jr., Elsworth, J. D., Taylor, J. R., et al. (1997). Enduring cognitive deficits and cortical dopamine dysfunction in monkeys after long-term administration of phencyclidine. *Science, 277,* 953–955.

Jentsch, T. J., Maritzen, T., and Zdebik, A. A. (2005). Chloride channel diseases resulting from impaired transepithelial transport or vesicular function. *Journal of Clinical Investigation, 115,* 2039–2046.

Jepsen, M. L. (2013, November 24). Bringing back my real self with hormones. *The New York Times,* p. SR6. www.nytimes.com/2013/11/24/opinion/sunday/bringing-back-my-real-self-with-hormones.html

Jerison, H. J. (1991). *Brain size and the evolution of mind.* New York: American Museum of Natural History.

Ji, D., and Wilson, M. A. (2007). Coordinated memory replay in the visual cortex and hippocampus during sleep. *Nature Neuroscience, 10*(1), 100–107.

Johansson, R. S., and Flanagan, J. R. (2009). Coding and use of tactile signals from the fingertips in object manipulation tasks. *Nature Reviews Neuroscience, 10,* 345–358.

Johnson, K. O., and Hsiao, S. S. (1992). Neural mechanisms of tactual form and texture perception. *Annual Review of Neuroscience, 15,* 227–250.

Johnson, L. C. (1969). Psychological and physiological changes following total sleep deprivation. In A. Kales (Ed.), *Sleep: Physiology and pathology.* Philadelphia: Lippincott.

Jones, B. A., Shimell, J. J., and Watson, N. V. (2011). Pre- and postnatal bisphenol A treatment results in persistent deficits in the sexual behavior of male rats, but not female rats, in adulthood. *Hormones and Behavior, 59*(2), 246–251.

Jones, B. A., and Watson, N. V. (2012). Perinatal BPA exposure demasculinizes males in measures of affect but has no effect on water maze learning in adulthood. *Hormones and Behavior, 61*(4), 605–610.

Jones, J. R., Tackenberg, M. C., and McMahon, D. G. (2015). Manipulating circadian clock neuron firing rate resets molecular circadian rhythms and behavior. *Nature Neuroscience, 18*(3), 373–375.

Jones, P. B., Barnes, T. R. E., Davies, L., Dunn, G., et al. (2006). Randomized controlled trial of the effect on Quality of Life of second- vs first-generation antipsychotic drugs in schizophrenia. *Archives of General Psychiatry, 39,* 1079–1087.

Jordan, B. D., Jahre, C., Hauser, W. A., Zimmerman, R. D., et al. (1992). CT of 338 active professional boxers. *Radiology, 185,* 509–512.

Jordan, C. L., Breedlove, S. M., and Arnold, A. P. (1991). Ontogeny of steroid accumulation in spinal lumbar motoneurons of the rat: Implications for androgen's site of action during synapse elimination. *Journal of Comparative Neurology, 313,* 441–448.

Jordan, G., Deeb, S. S., Bosten, J. M., and Mollon, J. D. (2010). The dimensionality of color vision in carriers of anomalous trichromacy. *Journal of Vision, 10,* 12.

Jordt, S.-E., Bautista, D. M., Chuang, H., McKemy, D. D., et al. (2004). Mustard oils and cannabinoids excite sensory nerve fibres through the TRP channel ANKTM1. *Nature, 427,* 260–265.

Joris, P. X., Smith, P. H., and Yin, T. C. (1998). Coincidence detection in the auditory system: 50 years after Jeffress. *Neuron, 21*(6), 1235–1238.

Joseph, J. S., Chun, M. M., and Nakayama, K. (1997). Attentional requirements in a "preattentive" feature search task. *Nature, 387,* 805–807.

Ju, Y. E., Lucey, B. P., and Holtzman, D. M. (2014). Sleep and Alzheimer disease pathology: A bidirectional relationship. Nature Reviews Neurology, 10(2), 115–119. doi:10.1038/nrneurol.2013.269

Julian, T., and McKenry, P. C. (1979). Relationship of testosterone to men's family functioning at mid-life: A research note. *Aggressive Behavior, 15,* 281–289.

K

Kaar, G. F., and Fraher, J. P. (1985). The development of alpha and gamma motoneuron fibres in the rat. I. A comparative ultrastructural study of their central and peripheral axon growth. *Journal of Anatomy, 141,* 77–88.

Kaas, J. H., and Hackett, T. A. (1999). "What" and "where" processing in auditory cortex. *Nature Neuroscience, 2,* 1045–1047.

Kable, J. W., and Glimcher, P. W. (2009). The neurobiology of decision: Consensus and controversy. *Neuron, 63,* 733–745.

Kagan, J. (1997). Temperament and the reactions to unfamiliarity. *Child Development, 68,* 139–143.

Kaji, I., Karaki, S., Fukami, Y., Terasaki, M., et al. (2009). Secretory effects of a luminal bitter tastant and expressions of bitter taste receptors, T2Rs, in the human and rat large intestine. *American*

Journal of Physiology: Gastrointestinal and Liver Physiology, 296(5), G971–981. doi:10.1152/ajpgi.90514.2008

Kakei, S., Hoffman, D. S., and Strick, P. L. (1999). Muscle and movement representations in the primary motor cortex. *Science, 285*, 2136–2139.

Kales, A., and Kales, J. (1970). Evaluation, diagnosis and treatment of clinical conditions related to sleep. *JAMA, 213*, 2229–2235.

Kales, A., and Kales, J. D. (1974). Sleep disorders. Recent findings in the diagnosis and treatment of disturbed sleep. *New England Journal of Medicine, 290*, 487–499.

Kamm, G. B., Pisciottano, F., Kliger, R., and Franchini, L. F. (2013). The developmental brain gene *NPAS3* contains the largest number of accelerated regulatory sequences in the human genome. *Molecular Biology and Evolution, 30*, 1088–1102.

Kandel, E. R. (2009). The biology of memory: A forty-year perspective. *Journal of Neuroscience, 29*, 12748–12756.

Kandel, E. R., Castellucci, V. F., Goelet, P., and Schacher, S. (1987). 1987 cell-biological interrelationships between short-term and long-term memory. *Research Publications—Association for Research in Nervous and Mental Disease, 65*, 111–132.

Kandel, E. R., Dudai, Y., and Mayford, M. R. (2014). The molecular and systems biology of memory. *Cell, 157*(1), 163–186.

Kandler, K., Clause, A., and Noh, J. (2009). Tonotopic reorganization of developing auditory brainstem circuits. *Nature Neuroscience, 12*, 711–716.

Kang, C., Riazuddin, S., Mundorff, J., Krasnewich, D., et al. (2010). Mutation in the lysosomal enzyme–targeting pathway and persistent stuttering. *New England Journal of Medicine, 362*, 677–685.

Kang, H. J., Imperato-McGinley, J., Zhu, Y. S., Cai, L. Q., et al. (2011). The first successful paternity through in vitro fertilization-intracytoplasmic sperm injection with a man homozygous for the 5α-reductase-2 gene mutation. *Fertility and Sterility, 95*(6), 2125. e5–2125.e8.

Kanwisher, N., and Wojciulik, E. (2000). Visual attention: Insights from brain imaging. *Nature Reviews Neuroscience, 1*, 91–100.

Karlin, A. (2002). Emerging structure of the nicotinic acetylcholine receptors. *Nature Reviews Neuroscience, 3*, 102–114.

Karlsgodt, K. H., Sun, D., and Cannon, T. D. (2010). Structural and functional brain abnormalities in schizophrenia. *Current Directions in Psychological Science, 19*, 226–231.

Karmiloff-Smith, A., Al-Janabi, T., D'Souza, H., Groet, J., et al. (2016). The importance of understanding individual differences in Down syndrome. *F1000Research, 5*. doi:10.12688/f1000research.7506.1

Karp, L. E. (1976). *Genetic engineering, threat or promise?* Chicago: Nelson-Hall.

Karpicke, J. D, and Blunt, J. R. (2011). Retrieval practice produces more learning than elaborative studying with concept mapping. *Science, 331*(6018), 772–775.

Karra, E., Chandarana, K., and Batterham, R. L. (2009). The role of peptide YY in appetite regulation and obesity. *Journal of Physiology, 587*, 19–25.

Kass, R. S. (2005). The channelopathies: Novel insights into molecular and genetic mechanisms of human disease. *Journal of Clinical Investigation, 115*, 1986–1989.

Kato, H. E., Zhang, F., Yizhar, O., Ramakrishnan, C., et al. (2012). Crystal structure of the channelrhodopsin light-gated cation channel. *Nature, 482*, 369–374.

Katsiki, N., Tziomalos, K., and Mikhailidis, D. P. (2014). Alcohol and the cardiovascular system: A double-edged sword. *Current Pharmaceutical Design, 20*, 6276–6288.

Katz, D. B., and Steinmetz, J. E. (2002). Psychological functions of the cerebellum. *Behavioral Cognitive Neuroscience Review, 1*, 229–241.

Katzenberg, D., Young, T., Finn, L., Lin, L., et al. (1998). A CLOCK polymorphism associated with human diurnal preference. *Sleep, 21*, 569–576.

Kaufman, M. T., Churchland, M. M., Ryu, S. I., and Shenoy, K. V. (2014). Cortical activity in the null space: Permitting preparation without movement. *Nature Neuroscience, 17*(3), 440–448.

Kaushall, P. I., Zetin, M., and Squire, L. R. (1981). A psychosocial study of chronic, circumscribed amnesia. *Journal of Nervous and Mental Disease, 169*, 383–389.

Kay, K. N., Naselaris, T., Prenger, R. J., and Gallant, J. L. (2008). Identifying natural images from human brain activity. *Nature, 452*, 352–355.

Kaye, W. H., Fudge, J. L., and Paulus, M. (2009). New insights into symptoms and neurocircuit function of anorexia nervosa. *Nature Reviews Neuroscience, 10*, 573–584.

Keane, T. M. (1998). Psychological and behavioral treatments of post-traumatic stress disorder. In P. E. Nathan, and J. M. Gorman (Eds.), *A guide to treatments that work* (pp. 398–407). New York: Oxford University Press.

Keenan, J. P., Nelson, A., O'Connor, M., and Pascual-Leone, A. (2001). Self-recognition and the right hemisphere. *Nature, 409*, 305.

Keesey, R. E. (1980). A set-point analysis of the regulation of body weight. In A. J. Stunkard (Ed.), *Obesity* (pp. 144–165). Philadelphia: Saunders.

Keesey, R. E., and Boyle, P. C. (1973). Effects of quinine adulteration upon body weight of LH-lesioned and intact male rats. *Journal of Comparative and Physiological Psychology, 84*, 38–46.

Kell, C. A., von Kriegstein, K., Rösler, A., Kleinschmidt, A., et al. (2005). The sensory cortical representation of the human penis: Revisiting somatotopy in the male homunculus. *Journal of Neuroscience, 25*(25), 5984–5987.

Keller, M. C., and Visscher, P. M. (2015). Genetic variation links creativity to psychiatric disorders. *Nature Neuroscience, 18*(7), 928–929.

Kelly, J. P. (2011). Cathinone derivatives: A review of their chemistry, pharmacology and toxicology. *Drug Testing and Analysis, 3*, 439–453.

Kelly, J. R., Clarke, G., Cryan, J. F., and Dinan, T. G., et al. (2016). Brain-gut-microbiota axis: Challenges for translation in psychiatry. *Annals of Epidemiology, 26*(5), 366–372.

Kelso, S. R., and Brown, T. H. (1986). Differential conditioning of associative synaptic enhancement in hippocampal brain slices. *Science, 232*, 85–87.

Keltner, D., and Ekman, P. (2000). Facial expression of emotion. In M. Lewis and J. M. Haviland-Jones (Eds.), *Handbook of emotions* (2nd ed., pp. 236–250). New York: Guilford.

Kemp, M. (2001). The harmonious hand. Marin Mersenne and the science of memorized music. *Nature, 409*, 666.

Kendler, K. S., Gardner, C. O., and Prescott, C. A. (1999). Clinical characteristics of major depression that predict risk of depression in relatives. *Archives of General Psychiatry, 56*, 322–327.

Kendler, K. S., Karkowski, L. M., Neale, M. C., and Prescott, C. A. (2000). Illicit psychoactive substance use, heavy use, abuse, and dependence in a US population-based sample of male twins. *Archives of General Psychiatry, 57,* 261–269.

Kennedy, D. P., and Adolphs, R. (2011). Impaired fixation to eyes following amygdala damage arises from abnormal bottom-up attention. *Neuropsychologia, 49,* 589–595.

Kennedy, D. P., Gläscher, J., Tyszka, J. M., and Adolphs, R. (2009). Personal space regulation by the human amygdala. *Nature Neuroscience, 12,* 1226–1227.

Kennerknecht, I., Grueter, T., Welling, B., Wentzek, S., et al. (2006). First report of prevalence of non-syndromic hereditary prosopagnosia (HPA). *American Journal of Medical Genetics. Part A, 140,* 1617–1622.

Kertesz, A., Harlock, W., and Coates, R. (1979). Computer tomographic localization, lesion size, and prognosis in aphasia and nonverbal impairment. *Brain and Language, 8,* 34–50.

Kesner, R. P. (1998). Neurobiological views of memory. In J. L. Martinez, Jr., and R. P. Kesner (Eds.), *Neurobiology of learning and memory* (3rd ed., pp. 361–416). San Diego, CA: Harcourt Brace.

Kesner, R. P., Bolland, B. L., and Dakis, M. (1993). Memory for spatial locations, motor responses, and objects: Triple dissociation among the hippocampus, caudate nucleus, and extrastriate visual cortex. *Experimental Brain Research, 93,* 462–470.

Kessels, H. W., and Malinow, R. (2009). Synaptic AMPA receptor plasticity and behavior. *Neuron, 61,* 340–350.

Kessler, R. C., Berglund, P., Demler, O., Jin, R., et al. (2005). Lifetime prevalence and age-of-onset distributions of *DSM-IV* disorders in the National Comorbidity Survey Replication. *Archives of General Psychiatry, 62,* 593–602.

Kessler, R. C., Chiu, W. T., Demler, O., Merikangas, K. R., et al. (2005). Prevalence, severity, and comorbidity of 12-month DSM-IV disorders in the National Comorbidity Survey Replication. *Archives of General Psychiatry, 62,* 617–627.

Kessler, R. C., Chiu, W. T., Demler, O., and Walters, E. E. (2005). Prevalence, severity, and comorbidity of 12-month *DSM-IV* disorders in the National Comorbidity Survey Replication. *Archives of General Psychiatry, 62,* 617–627.

Kety, S. S., Wender, P. H., Jacobsen, B., Ingraham, L. J., et al. (1994). Mental illness in the biological and adoptive relatives of schizophrenic adoptees. Replication of the Copenhagen Study in the rest of Denmark. *Archives of General Psychiatry, 51,* 442–455.

Khalsa, S. S., Feinstein, J. S., Li ,W., Feusner, J. D., et al. (2016). Panic anxiety in humans with bilateral amygdala lesions: Pharmacological induction via cardiorespiratory interoceptive pathways. *Journal of Neuroscience, 36,* 3559–3566.

Khankan, R. R., Griffis, K. G., Haggerty-Skeans, J. R., Zhong, H., et al. (2016). Olfactory ensheathing cell transplantation after a complete spinal cord transection mediates neuroprotective and immunomodulatory mechanisms to facilitate regeneration. *Journal of Neuroscience, 36*(23), 6269–6286.

Kiang, N. Y. S. (1965). *Discharge patterns of single fibers in the cat's auditory nerve.* Cambridge, MA: MIT Press.

Kiehn, O. (2016). Decoding the organization of spinal circuits that control locomotion. *Nature Reviews Neuroscience, 17*(4), 224–238.

Kim, D. R., Pesiridou, A., and O'Reardon, J. P. (2009). Transcranial magnetic stimulation in the treatment of psychiatric disorders. *Current Psychiatry Reports, 11,* 447–452.

Kim, H. J., Jeon, B. S., Yoon, M. Y., Park, S. S., et al. (2012). Increased expression of α-synuclein by SNCA duplication is associated with resistance to toxic stimuli. *Journal of Molecular Neuroscience, 47*(2), 249–255.

Kim, K. H., Relkin, N. R., Lee, K. M., and Hirsch, J. (1997). Distinct cortical areas associated with native and second languages. *Nature, 388,* 171–174.

Kimura, D. (1973). The asymmetry of the human brain. *Scientific American, 228*(3), 70–78.

Kimura, D. (1981). Neural mechanisms in manual signing. *Sign Language Studies, 33,* 291–312.

Kimura, D. (1993). *Neuromotor mechanisms in human communication.* Oxford, England: Oxford University Press.

Kimura, D., and Watson, N. V. (1989). The relation between oral movement control and speech. *Brain and Language, 37,* 565–590.

King, A. (2013, August 24). The nose knows: How to train a canine conservationist. *New Scientist* (www.newscientist.com).

King, S., St-Hilaire, A., and Heidkamp, D. (2010). Prenatal factors in schizophrenia. *Current Directions in Psychological Science, 19,* 209–213.

Kingsbury, S. J., and Garver, D. L. (1998). Lithium and psychosis revisited. *Progress in Neuro-Psychopharmacology & Biological Psychiatry, 22,* 249–263.

Kinney, H. C. (2009). Brainstem mechanisms underlying the sudden infant death syndrome: Evidence from human pathologic studies. *Developmental Psychobiology, 51,* 223–233.

Kinsey, A. C., Pomeroy, W. B., and Martin, C. E. (1948). *Sexual behavior in the human male.* Philadelphia: Saunders.

Kinsey, A. C., Pomeroy, W. B., Martin, C. E., and Gebhard, P. H. (1953). *Sexual behavior in the human female.* Philadelphia: Saunders.

Kivell, T. L., Kibii, J. M., Churchill, S. E., Schmid, P., et al. (2011). *Australopithecus sediba* hand demonstrates mosaic evolution of locomotor and manipulative abilities. *Science, 333*(6048), 1411–1417.

Klar, A. J. (2003). Human handedness and scalp hair-whorl direction develop from a common genetic mechanism. *Genetics, 165,* 269–276.

Kleiber, M. (1947). Body size and metabolic rate. *Physiological Reviews, 15,* 511–541.

Klein, M., Shapiro, K. M., and Kandel, E. R. (1980). Synaptic plasticity and the modulation of the Ca^{2+} current. *Journal of Experimental Biology, 89,* 117–157.

Klein, R. M. (2000). Inhibition of return. *Trends in Cognitive Science, 4,* 138–147.

Kleitman, N. (1969). Basic rest-activity cycle in relation to sleep and wakefulness. In A. Kales (Ed.), *Sleep: Physiology and pathology.* Philadelphia: Lippincott.

Kleitman, N., and Engelmann, T. (1953). Sleep characteristics of infants. *Journal of Applied Physiology, 6,* 269–282.

Klingberg, T., Hedehus, M., Temple, E., Salz, T., et al. (2000). Microstructure of temporo-parietal white matter as a basis for reading ability: Evidence from diffusion tensor magnetic resonance imaging. *Neuron, 25,* 493–500.

Kluger, M. J. (1978). The evolution and adaptive value of fever. *American Scientist, 66,* 38–43.

Klump, K. L., Miller, K. B., Keel, P. K., McGue, M., et al. (2001). Genetic and environmental influences on anorexia nervosa syndromes in a population-based twin sample. *Psychological Medicine, 31,* 737–740.

Klüver, H., and Bucy, P. C. (1938). An analysis of certain effects of bilateral temporal lobectomy in the rhesus monkey, with special reference to "psychic blindness." *Journal of Psychology, 5,* 33–54.

Knecht, S., Flöel, A., Dräger, B., Breitenstein, C., et al. (2002). Degree of language lateralization determines susceptibility to unilateral brain lesions. *Nature Neuroscience, 5,* 695–699.

Knepper, M. A., Kwon, T. H., and Nielsen, S. (2015). Molecular physiology of water balance. *New England Journal of Medicine, 372,* 1349–1358.

Knibestol, M., and Valbo, A. B. (1970). Single unit analysis of mechanoreceptor activity from the human glabrous skin. *Acta Physiologica Scandinavica, 80,* 178–195.

Knuth, N. D., Johannsen, D. L., Tamboli, R. A., Marks-Shulman, P. A., et al. (2014). Metabolic adaptation following massive weight loss is related to the degree of energy imbalance and changes in circulating leptin. *Obesity, 22,* 2563–2569.

Koch, G., Oliveri, M., Torriero, S., and Caltagirone, C. (2005). Modulation of excitatory and inhibitory circuits for visual awareness in the human right parietal cortex. *Experimental Brain Research, 160,* 510–516.

Koch, M., Varela, L., Kim, J. G., Kim, J. D., et al. (2015). Hypothalamic POMC neurons promote cannabinoid-induced feeding. *Nature, 519,* 45–50.

Kodama, T., Lai, Y. Y., and Siegel, J. M. (2003). Changes in inhibitory amino acid release linked to pontine-induced atonia: An *in vivo* microdialysis study. *Journal of Neuroscience, 23,* 1548–1554.

Kogan, J. H., Frankland, P. W., Blendy, J. A., Coblentz, J., et al. (1997). Spaced training induces normal long-term memory in CREB mutant mice. *Current Biology, 7,* 1–11.

Koh, K., Joiner, W. J., Wu, M. N., Yue, Z., et al. (2008). Identification of SLEEPLESS, a sleep-promoting factor. *Science, 321,* 372–376.

Kohl, M. M., Shipton, O. A., Deacon, R. M., Rawlins, J. N., et al. (2011). Hemisphere-specific optogenetic stimulation reveals left-right asymmetry of hippocampal plasticity. *Nature Neuroscience, 14*(11), 1413–1415.

Kojima, M., Hosoda, H., Date, Y., Nakazato, M., et al. (1999). Ghrelin is a growth-hormone-releasing acylated peptide from stomach. *Nature, 402,* 656–660.

Kokrashvili, Z., Mosinger, B., and Margolskee, R. F. (2009). T1r3 and α-gustducin in gut regulate secretion of glucagon-like peptide-1. *Annals of the New York Academy of Sciences, 1170,* 91–94.

Kolata, G. (2016, May 2). After "The Biggest Loser," their bodies fought to regain weight. *The New York Times,* Health Section (www.nytimes.com/2016/05/02/health/biggest-loser-weight-loss.html?ref=topics&_r=1).

Kolb, B., and Whishaw, I. Q. (1990). *Fundamentals of human neuropsychology.* San Francisco: Freeman.

Komisaruk, B. R, and Whipple, B. (2005). Functional MRI of the brain during orgasm in women. *Annual Review of Sex Research, 16,* 62–86.

Kondo, A., Shahpasand, K., Mannix, R., Qiu, J., et al. (2015). Antibody against early driver of neurodegeneration cis P-tau blocks brain injury and tauopathy. *Nature, 523*(7561), 431–436.

Kondo, Y., Sachs, B. D., and Sakuma, Y. (1997). Importance of the medial amygdala in rat penile erection evoked by remote stimuli from estrous females. *Behavioural Brain Research, 88,* 153–160.

Kondratova, A. A., and Kondratov, R. V. (2012). The circadian clock and pathology of the ageing brain. *Nature Reviews Neuroscience, 13,* 325–335.

Kondziolka, D., Wechsler, L., Goldstein, S., Meltzer, C., et al. (2000). Transplantation of cultured human neuronal cells for patients with stroke. *Neurology, 55,* 565–569.

Kong, A., Frigge, M. L., Masson, G., Besenbacher, S., et al. (2012). Rate of de novo mutations and the importance of father's age to disease risk. *Nature, 488,* 471–475.

Konishi, M. (1985). Birdsong: From behavior to neuron. *Annual Review of Neuroscience, 8,* 125–170.

Konopka, G., Bomar, J. M., Winden, K., Coppola, G., et al. (2009). Human-specific transcriptional regulation of CNS development genes by FOXP2. *Nature, 462,* 213–217.

Konopka, R. J., and Benzer, S. (1971). Clock mutants of *Drosophila melanogaster. Proceedings of the National Academy of Sciences, USA, 68,* 2112–2116.

Kopell, B. H., Machado, A. G., and Rezai, A. R. (2005). Not your father's lobotomy: Psychiatric surgery revisited. *Clinical Neurosurgery, 52,* 315–330.

Kopin, I. J., and Markey, S. P. (1988). MPTP toxicity: Implications for research in Parkinson's disease. *Annual Review of Neuroscience, 11,* 81–96.

Kordower, J. H., Chu, Y., Hauser, R. A., Freeman, T. B., et al. (2008). Lewy body-like pathology in long-term embryonic nigral transplants in Parkinson's disease. *Nature Medicine, 14,* 504–506.

Kosslyn, S. M., Alpert, N. M., Thompson, W. L., Maljkovic, V., et al. (1993). Visual mental imagery activates topographically organized visual cortex. *Journal of Cognitive Neuroscience, 5,* 263–287.

Kosslyn, S. M., Pascual-Leone, A., Felician, O., Camposano, S., et al. (1999). The role of Area 17 in visual imagery: Convergent evidence from PET and RTMS. *Science, 208,* 167–170.

Koubeissi, M. Z., Bartolomei, F., Beltagy, A., and Picard, F. (2014). Electrical stimulation of a small brain area reversibly disrupts consciousness. *Epilepsy and Behavior, 37,* 32–35.

Kouider, S., Stahlhut, C., Gelskov, S. V., Barbosa, L. S., et al. (2013). A neural marker of perceptual consciousness in infants. *Science, 340*(6130), 376–380.

Kovelman, J. A., and Scheibel, A. B. (1984). A neurohistological correlate of schizophrenia. *Biological Psychiatry, 19,* 1601.

Koya, E., Golden, S. A., Harvey, B. K., Guez-Barber, D. H., et al. (2009). Targeted disruption of cocaine-activated nucleus accumbens neurons prevents context-specific sensitization. *Nature Neuroscience, 12,* 1069–1073.

Koyama, S., Chase, S. M., Whitford, A. S., Velliste, M., et al. (2010). Comparison of brain-computer interface decoding algorithms in open-loop and closed-loop control. *Journal of Comparative Neurology, 29*(1–2), 73–87.

Kraepelin, E. (1919). *Dementia praecox and paraphrenia.* Edinburgh, Scotland: Livingstone.

Kraft, S., Hsu, C., Brough, D. E., and Staecker, H. (2013). Atoh1 induces auditory hair cell recovery in mice after ototoxic injury. *Laryngoscope, 123*(4), 992–999.

Krashes, M. J., Lowell, B. B., and Garfield, A. S. (2016). Melanocortin-4 receptor-regulated energy homeostasis. *Nature Neuroscience, 19,* 206–219.

Krauss, R. M. (1998). Why do we gesture when we speak? *Current Directions in Psychological Science, 7*(2), 54–60.

Kraut, R. E., and Johnston, R. E. (1979). Social and emotional messages of smiling: An ethological approach. *Journal of Personality and Social Psychology, 37,* 1539–1553.

Kravitz, D. J., Saleem, K. S., Baker, C. I., and Mishkin, M. (2011). A new neural framework for visuospatial processing. *Nature Reviews Neuroscience, 12,* 217–230.

Krebs, J. R., Sherry, D. F., Healy, S. D., Perry, V. H., et al. (1989). Hippocampal specialisation of food-storing birds. *Proceedings of the National Academy of Sciences, USA, 86,* 1388–1392.

Kriegsfeld, L. J. (2006). Driving reproduction: RFamide peptides behind the wheel. *Hormones and Behavior, 50,* 655–666.

Kril, J., Halliday, G., Svoboda, M., and Cartwright, H. (1997). The cerebral cortex is damaged in chronic alcoholics. *Neuroscience, 79,* 983–998.

Kring, A. M. (1999). Emotion in schizophrenia: Old mystery, new understanding. *Current Directions in Psychological Science, 8*(5), 160–163.

Kring, A. M., and Caponigro, J. M. (2010). Emotion in schizophrenia: Where feeling meets thinking. *Current Directions in Psychological Science, 19,* 255–259.

Kringelbach, M. L. (2005). The human orbitofrontal cortex: Linking reward to hedonic experience. *Nature Reviews Neuroscience, 6,* 691–702.

Kringelbach, M. L., Jenkinson, N., Owen, S. L. F., and Aziz, T. Z. (2007). Translational principles of deep brain stimulation. *Nature Reviews Neuroscience, 8,* 623–634.

Kripke, D. F., Garfinkel, L., Wingard, D. L., Klauber, M. R., et al. (2002). Mortality associated with sleep duration and insomnia. *Archives of General Psychiatry, 59,* 131–136.

Kroll, J. F., Bobb, S. C., and Hoshino, N. (2014). Two languages in mind: Bilingualism as a tool to investigate language, cognition, and the brain. *Current Directions in Psychological Science, 23*(3), 159–163.

Krubitzer, L. A., Manger, P., Pettigrew, J. D., and Calford, M. B. (1995). The organization of neocortex in monotremes: In search of the prototypical plan. *Journal of Comparative Neurology, 348,* 1–45.

Krubitzer, L. A., and Seelke, A. M. (2012). Cortical evolution in mammals: The bane and beauty of phenotypic variability. *Proceedings of the National Academy of Sciences, USA, 109*(Suppl. 1), 10647–10654.

Krug, M., Lössner, B., and Ott, T. (1984). Anisomycin blocks the late phase of long-term potentiation in the dentate gyrus of freely moving rat. *Brain Research Bulletin, 13,* 39–42.

Krystal, A., Krishnan, K. R., Raitiere, M., Poland, R., et al. (1990). Differential diagnosis and pathophysiology of Cushing's syndrome and primary affective disorder. *Journal of Neuropsychiatry and Clinical Neurosciences, 2,* 34–43.

Kuhl, B. A., Dudukovic, N. M., Kahn, I., and Wagner, A. D. (2007). Decreased demands on cognitive control reveal the neural processing benefits of forgetting. *Nature Neuroscience, 10,* 908–914.

Kuiper, G. G., Enmark, E., Pelto-Huikko. M., Nilsson, S., et al. (1996). Cloning of a novel receptor expressed in rat prostate and ovary. *Proceedings of the National Academy of Sciences, USA, 93,* 5925–5930.

Kulkarni, A., and Colburn, H. S. (1998). Role of spectral detail in sound-source localization. *Nature, 396,* 747–749.

Kumar, D. K.V., Choi, S. H., Washicosky, K. J., Eimer, W. A., et al. (2016). Amyloid-β peptide protects against microbial infection in mouse and worm models of Alzheimer's disease. *Science Translational Medicine, 8(340),* 340ra72. doi:10.1126/scitranslmed.aaf1059

Kutas, M., and Hillyard, S. A. (1980). Reading senseless sentences: Brain potentials reflect semantic incongruity. *Science, 207,* 203–205.

Kuyken, W., Warren, F. C., Taylor, R. S., Whalley, W., et al. (2016). Efficacy of mindfulness-based cognitive therapy in prevention of depressive relapse: An individual patient data meta-analysis from randomized trials. *JAMA Psychiatry.* doi:10.1001/jamapsychiatry.2016.0076

Kwakkel, G., Veerbeek, J. M., van Wegen, E. E., and Wolf, S. L. (2015). Constraint-induced movement therapy after stroke. *Lancet Neurology, 14*(2), 224–234.

L

LaBar, K. S., Gatenby, J. C., Gore, J. C., LeDoux, J. E., et al. (1998). Human amygdala activation during conditioned fear acquisition and extinction: A mixed-trial fMRI study. *Neuron, 20,* 937–945.

Lacey, J. I., and Lacey, B. C. (1970). Some autonomic-central nervous system interrelationships. In P. Black (Ed.), *Physiological correlates of emotion* (pp. 205–227). New York: Academic Press.

Lafer-Sousa, R., Hermann, K. L., and Conway, B. R. (2015). Striking individual differences in color perception uncovered by 'The Dress' photograph. *Current Biology, 25,* R545–546.

Lai, C. S. L., Fisher, S. E., Hurst, J. A., Vargha-Khadem, F., et al. (2001). A forkhead-domain gene is mutated in a severe speech and language disorder. *Nature, 413,* 519–523.

Lai, C. S.-W., Franke, T. F., and Gan, W.-B. (2012). Opposite effects of fear conditioning and extinction on dendritic spine remodelling. *Nature, 483,* 87–90.

LaMotte, R. H., Dong, X., and Ringkamp, M. (2014). Sensory neurons and circuits mediating itch. *Nature Reviews Neuroscience, 15*(1), 19–31.

Lampert, K. P., and Schartl, M. (2010). A little bit is better than nothing: The incomplete parthenogenesis of salamanders, frogs and fish. *BMC Biology, 8,* 78. doi:10.1186/1741-7007-8-78

Landau, B., and Levy, R. M. (1993). Neuromodulation techniques for medically refractory chronic pain. *Annual Review of Medicine, 44,* 279–287.

Lang, B. T., Cregg, J. M., DePaul, M. A., Tran, A. P., et al. (2015). Modulation of the proteoglycan receptor PTPσ promotes recovery after spinal cord injury. *Nature, 518*(7539), 404–408.

Langergraber, K. E., Prüfer, K., Rowney, C., Boesch, C., et al. (2012). Generation times in wild chimpanzees and gorillas suggest earlier divergence times in great ape and human evolution. *Proceedings of the National Academy of Sciences, USA, 109,* 15716–15721.

Langleben, D. D., Schroeder, L., Maldjian, J. A., Gur, R. C., et al. (2002). Brain activity during simulated deception: An event-related functional magnetic resonance study. *Neuroimage, 15,* 727–732.

Larroche, J.-C. (1977). *Developmental pathology of the neonate.* Amsterdam: Excerpta Medica.

Larrondo, L. F., Olivares-Yañez, C., Baker, C. L., Loros, J. J., et al. (2015). Circadian rhythms: Decoupling circadian clock protein turnover from circadian period determination. *Science, 347*(6221), 1257277.

Larsson, J., Gulyas, B., and Roland, P. E. (1996). Cortical representation of self-paced finger movement. *Neuroreport, 7,* 463–468.

Larsson, M., and Willander, J. (2009). Autobiographical odor memory. *Annals of the New York Academy of Sciences, 1170,* 318–323.

Latham, A. J., Patston, L. L., Westermann, C., Kirk, I. J., et al. (2013). Earlier visual N1 latencies in expert video-game players: A temporal basis of enhanced visuospatial performance? *PLOS ONE, 8*(9), e75231.

Lau, H. C., Rogers, R. D., Haggard, P., and Passingham, R. E. (2004). Attention to intention. *Science, 303,* 1208–1210.

Laverty, P. H., Leskovar, A., Breur, G. J., Coates, J. R., et al. (2004). A preliminary study of intravenous surfactants in paraplegic dogs:

Polymer therapy in canine clinical SCI. *Journal of Neurotrama, 21,* 1767–1777.

Lavie, N., Hirst, A., de Fockert, J. W., and Viding, E. (2004). Load theory of selective attention and cognitive control. *Journal of Experimental Psychology. General, 133,* 339–354.

Lavie, N., Lin, Z., Zokaei, N., and Thoma, V. (2009). The role of perceptual load in object recognition. *Journal of Experimental Psychology. Human Perception and Performance, 35,* 1346–1358.

Lavie, P., and Kripke, D. F. (1981). Ultradian circa 1 1/2 hour rhythms: A multioscillatory system. *Life Sciences, 29,* 2445–2450.

Lazeyras F., Boex, C., Sigrist, A., Seghier, M. L., et al. (2002). Functional MRI of auditory cortex activated by multisite electrical stimulation of the cochlea. *Neuroimage, 17,* 1010–1017.

Le Grand, R., Mondloch, C. J., Maurer, D., and Brent, H. P. (2001). Early visual experience and face processing. *Nature, 410,* 890.

Le Grange, D. (2005). The Maudsley family-based treatment for adolescent anorexia nervosa. *World Psychiatry, 4,* 142–146.

Leach, E. L., Prefontaine, G., Hurd, P. L., and Crespi, B. J. (2014). The imprinted gene *LRRTM1* mediates schizotypy and handedness in a nonclinical population. *Journal of Human Genetics, 59*(6), 332–336.

Leber, S. M., Breedlove, S. M., and Sanes, J. R. (1990). Lineage, arrangement, and death of clonally related motoneurons in chick spinal cord. *Journal of Neuroscience, 10,* 2451–2462.

Lebrun, C. J., Blume, A., Herdegen, T., Seifert, K., et al. (1995). Angiotensin II induces a complex activation of transcription factors in the rat brain: Expression of Fos, Jun and Krox proteins. *Neuroscience, 65,* 93–99.

Lech, R. K., and Suchan, B. (2013). The medial temporal lobe: Memory and beyond. *Behavioural Brain Research, 254,* 45–49.

Ledent, C., Valverde, O., Cossu, G., Petitet, F., et al. (1999). Unresponsiveness to cannabinoids and reduced addictive effects of opiates in CB$_1$ receptor knockout mice. *Science, 283,* 401–404.

Lederbogen, F., Kirsch, P., Haddad, L., Streit, F., et al. (2011). City living and urban upbringing affect neural social stress processing in humans. *Nature, 474,* 498–501.

LeDoux, J. E. (1994). Emotion, memory and the brain. *Scientific American, 270*(6), 50–57.

LeDoux, J. E. (1995). Emotion: Clues from the brain. *Annual Review of Psychology, 46,* 209–235.

LeDoux, J. E. (1996). *The emotional brain: The mysterious underpinnings of emotional life.* London: Simon & Schuster.

Lee, A. M., Kanter, B. R., Wang, D., Lim, J. P., et al. (2013). *Prkcz* null mice show normal learning and memory. *Nature, 493*(7432), 416–419.

Lee, C.-K., Weindruch, R., and Prolla, T. A. (2000). Gene-expression profile of the ageing brain in mice. *Nature Genetics, 25,* 294–297.

Lee, E. B., Lee, V. M.-Y., and Trojanowski, J. Q. (2012). Gains or losses: Molecular mechanisms of TDP43-mediated neurodegeneration. *Nature Reviews Neuroscience, 13,* 38–50.

Lee, H. M., Giguere, P. M., and Roth, B. L. (2014). DREADDs: Novel tools for drug discovery and development. *Drug Discovery Today, 19*(4), 469–473.

Lee, H., Kim, D. W., Remedios, R., Anthony, T. E., et al. (2014). Scalable control of mounting and attack by Esr1+ neurons in the ventromedial hypothalamus. *Nature, 509,* 627–632.

Lee, J.Y., and Petratos, S. (2013). Multiple sclerosis: Does Nogo play a role? *Neuroscientist, 19*(4), 394–408. doi:10.1177/1073858413477207

Lee, R. F., Dai, W., and Jones, J. (2012). Decoupled circular-polarized dual-head volume coil pair for studying two interacting human brains with dyadic fMRI. *Magnetic Resonance in Medicine, 68,* 1087–1096.

Lee, R. J., and Cohen, N. A. (2015). Taste receptors in innate immunity. *Cellular and Molecular Life Sciences, 72*(2), 217–236.

Lee, S.-Y., and MacKinnon, R. (2004). A membrane-access mechanism of ion channel inhibition by voltage sensor toxins from spider venom. *Nature, 430,* 232–235.

Lefebvre, L., Whittle, P., Lascaris, E., and Finkelstein, A. (1997). Feeding innovations and forebrain size in birds. *Animal Behavior, 53,* 549–560.

Leggett, J. D., Aspley, S., Beckett, S. R., D'Antona, A. M., et al. (2004). Oleamide is a selective endogenous agonist of rat and human CB1 cannabinoid receptors. *British Journal of Pharmacology, 141,* 253–262.

Lehrer, J. (2009). Small, furry … and smart. *Nature, 461*(7266), 862–864.

Leinders-Zufall, T., Lane, A. P., Puche, A. C., Ma, W., et al. (2000). Ultrasensitive pheromone detection by mammalian vomeronasal neurons. *Nature, 405,* 792–796.

Lemasson, A., Ouattara, K., Petit, E. J., and Zuberbühler, K. (2011). Social learning of vocal structure in a nonhuman primate? *BMC Evolutionary Biology, 11,* 362.

Lepage, J. F., and Theoret, H. (2006). EEG evidence for the presence of an action observation-execution matching system in children. *European Journal of Neuroscience, 23,* 2505–2510.

Lepage, M., Habib, R., and Tulving, E. (1998). Hippocampal PET activations of memory encoding and retrieval: The HIPER model. *Hippocampus, 8,* 313–322.

LePort, A. K., Mattfield, A. T., Dickinson-Anson, H., Fallon, H., et al. (2012). Behavioral and neuroanatomical investigation of Highly Superior Autobiographical Memory (HSAM). *Neurobiology of Learning and Memory, 98,* 78–92.

Leroi, I., Sheppard, J. M., and Lyketsos, C. G. (2002). Cognitive function after 11.5 years of alcohol use: Relation to alcohol use. *American Journal of Epidemiology, 156,* 747–752.

LeRoith, D., Shemer, J., and Roberts, C. T., Jr. (1992). Evolutionary origins of intercellular communication systems: Implications for mammalian biology. *Hormone Research, 38,* 1–6.

Lescroart, M. D., Stansbury, D. E., and Gallant, J. L. (2015). Fourier power, subjective distance, and object categories all provide plausible models of BOLD responses in scene-selective visual areas. *Frontiers in Computational Neuroscience, 9,* 135.

Lesku, J. A., Rattenborg, N. C., Valcu, M., Vyssotski, A. L., et al. (2012). Adaptive sleep loss in polygynous pectoral sandpipers. *Science, 337*(6102),1654–1658.

Leuner, B., Glasper, E. R., and Gould E. (2010). Sexual experience promotes adult neurogenesis in the hippocampus despite an initial elevation in stress hormones. *PLOS ONE, 5*(7): e11597. doi:10.1371/journal.pone.0011597

Leung, C. T., Coulombe, P. A., and Reed, R. R. (2007). Contribution of olfactory neural stem cells to tissue maintenance and regeneration. *Nature Neuroscience, 10,* 720–726.

Leung, H. C., Gore, J. C., and Goldman-Rakic, P. S. (2002). Sustained mnemonic response in the human middle frontal gyrus during on-line storage of spatial memoranda. *Journal of Cognitive Neuroscience, 14,* 659–671.

Leung, H. C., Gore, J. C., and Goldman-Rakic, P. S. (2005). Differential anterior prefrontal activation during the recognition stage of a spatial working memory task. *Cerebral Cortex, 15,* 1742–1749.

Leutgeb, S., Leutgeb, J. K., Barnes, C. A., Moser, E. I., et al. (2005). Independent codes for spatial and episodic memory in hippocampal neuronal ensembles. *Science, 309,* 619–623.

LeVay, S. (1991). A difference in hypothalamic structure between heterosexual and homosexual men. *Science, 253,* 1034–1037.

LeVay, S. (1996). *Queer science: The use and abuse of research into homosexuality.* Cambridge, MA: MIT Press.

Levenson, R. W., Ekman, P., and Friesen, W. V. (1990). Voluntary facial action generates emotion-specific autonomic nervous system activity. *Psychophysiology, 27,* 363–384.

Levermann, N., Galatius, A., Ehlme, G., Rysgaard, S., et al. (2003). Feeding behaviour of free-ranging walruses with notes on apparent dextrality of flipper use. *BMC Ecology, 3,* 9.

Levi-Montalcini, R. (1963). Growth and differentiation in the nervous system. In J. Allen (Ed.), *The nature of biological diversity* (pp. 261–296). New York: McGraw-Hill.

Levi-Montalcini, R. (1982). Developmental neurobiology and the natural history of nerve growth factor. *Annual Review of Neuroscience, 5,* 341–362.

Levine, J. D., Gordon, N. C., and Fields, H. L. (1978). The mechanism of placebo analgesia. *Lancet, 2,* 654–657.

Levine, S., Haltmeyer, G. C., and Karas, G. G. (1967). Physiological and behavioral effects of infantile stimulation. *Physiology & Behavior, 2,* 55–59.

Lewis, D. O. (1990). Neuropsychiatric and experiential correlates of violent juvenile delinquency. *Neuropsychology Review, 1,* 125–136.

Lewis, R. (1998). Flies invade human genetics. *Scientist, 12,* 1, 4–5.

Lewy, A. J., Bauer, V. K., Cutler, N. L., Sack, R. L., et al. (1998). Morning vs evening light treatment of patients with winter depression. *Archives of General Psychiatry, 55,* 890–896.

Li, B., Piriz, J., Mirrione, M., Chung, C., et al. (2011). Synaptic potentiation onto habenula neurons in the learned helplessness model of depression. *Nature, 470,* 535–539.

Li, F., and Zhou, M. (2012). Depletion of bitter taste transduction leads to massive spermatid loss in transgenic mice. *Molecular Human Reproduction, 18*(6), 289–297.

Li, J.Y., Christophersen, N. S., Hall, V., Soulet, D., et al. (2008). Critical issues of clinical human embryonic stem cell therapy for brain repair. *Trends in Neuroscience, 31,* 146–153.

Li, N., Lee, B., Rong-Jian, L., Banasr, M., et al. (2010). mTOR-dependent synapse formation underlies the rapid antidepressant effects of NMDA antagonists. *Science, 329,* 959–964.

Li, R., Polat, U., Makous, W., and Bavelier, D. (2009). Enhancing the contrast sensitivity function through action video game training. *Nature Neuroscience, 12,* 549–551.

Li, S., and Tator, C. H. (2000). Action of locally administered NMDA and AMPA/kainate receptor antagonists in spinal cord injury. *Neurological Research, 22,* 171–180.

Li, X., Glaser, D., Li, W., Johnson, W. E., et al. (2009). Analyses of sweet receptor gene (Tas1r2) and preference for sweet stimuli in species of Carnivora. *Journal of Heredity, 100*(Suppl. 1), S90–S100.

Liberles, S. D., and Buck, L. B. (2006). A second class of chemosensory receptors in the olfactory epithelium. *Nature, 442,* 645–650.

Libet, B. (1985). Unconscious cerebral initiative and the role of conscious will in voluntary action. *Behavioral and Brain Sciences, 8,* 529–566.

Licht, P., Frank, L. G., Pavgi, S., Yalcinkaya, T. M., et al. (1992). Hormonal correlates of "masculinization" in female spotted hyenas (*Crocuta crocuta*). 2. Maternal and fetal steroids. *Journal of Reproduction and Fertility, 95,* 463–474.

Lichtenstein, P., Yip, B. H., Björk, C., Pawitan, Y., et al. (2009). Common genetic determinants of schizophrenia and bipolar disorder in Swedish families: A population-based study. *Lancet, 373*(9659), 234–239.

Lichtman, J. W., Pfister, H., and Shavit, N. (2014). The big data challenges of connectomics. *Nature Neuroscience, 17*(11), 1448–1454.

Lichtman, J. W., and Purves, D. (1980). The elimination of redundant preganglionic innervation to hamster sympathetic ganglion cells in early post-natal life. *Journal of Physiology (London), 301,* 213–228.

Lieberman, P. (1985). On the evolution of human syntactic ability: Its pre-adaptive bases: Motor control and speech. *Journal of Human Evolution, 14,* 657–668.

Lieberman, P. (2002). On the nature and evolution of the neural bases of human language. *American Journal of Physical Anthropology, Suppl. 35,* 36–62.

Lieberwirth, C., Pan, Y., Liu, Y., Zhang, Z., et al. (2016). Hippocampal adult neurogenesis: Its regulation and potential role in spatial learning and memory. *Brain Research, 1644,* 127–140.

Liégeois, F., Baldeweg, T., Connelly, A., Gadian, D. G., et al. (2003). Language fMRI abnormalities associated with FOXP2 gene mutation. *Nature Neuroscience, 6,* 1230–1237.

Liepert, J., Bauder, H., Wolfgang, H. R., Miltner, W. H., et al. (2000). Treatment-induced cortical reorganization after stroke in humans. *Stroke, 31,* 1210–1216.

Lieving, L. M., Cherek, D. R., Lane, S. D., Tcheremissine, O.V., et al. (2008). Effects of acute tiagabine administration on aggressive responses of adult male parolees. *Journal of Psychopharmacology, 22,* 144–152.

Lim, M. M., and Young, L. J. (2006). Neuropeptidergic regulation of affiliative behavior and social bonding in animals. *Hormones and Behavior, 50,* 506–557.

Lim, M. M., Wang, Z., Olazabal, D. E., Ren, X., et al. (2004). Enhanced partner preference in a promiscuous species by manipulating the expression of a single gene. *Nature, 429,* 754–757.

Lin, F. H., Witzel, T., Hamalainen, M. S., Dale, A. M., et al. (2004). Spectral spatiotemporal imaging of cortical oscillations and interactions in the human brain. *Neuroimage, 23,* 582–595.

Lin, L., Faraco, J., Li, R., Kadotani, H., et al. (1999). The sleep disorder canine narcolepsy is caused by a mutation in the hypocretin (orexin) receptor 2 gene. *Cell, 98,* 365–376.

Lind, P. A., Luciano, M., Wright, M. J., Montgomery, G. W., et al. (2010). Dyslexia and DCDC2: Normal variation in reading and spelling is associated with DCDC2 polymorphisms in an Australian population sample. *European Journal of Human Genetics, 6,* 668–673.

Linde, K., Allais, G., Brinkhaus, B., Manheimer, E., et al. (2009). Acupuncture for tension-type headache. *Cochrane Database of Systematic Reviews, 1,* CD007587.

Lindemann, B. (1995). Sweet and salty: Transduction in taste. *News in Physiological Sciences, 10,* 166–170.

Lindskog, M., Svenningsson, P., Pozzi, L., Kim, Y., et al. (2002). Involvement of DARPP-32 phosphorylation in the stimulant action of caffeine. *Nature, 418,* 774–778.

Lindvall, O., and Kokaia, Z. (2006). Stem cells for the treatment of neurological disorders. *Nature, 441,* 1094–1096.

Lisabeth, L., and Bushnell, C. (2012). Stroke risk in women: The role of menopause and hormone therapy. *Lancet Neurology, 11,* 82–91.

Lisk, R. D. (1962). Diencephalic placement of estradiol and sexual receptivity in the female rat. *American Journal of Physiology, 203,* 493–496.

Lisman, J., Yasuda, R., and Raghavachari, S. (2012). Mechanisms of CaMKII action in long-term potentiation. *Nature Reviews Neuroscience, 13,* 169–182.

Lister, J. P., and Barnes, C. A. (2009). Neurobiological changes in the hippocampus during normative aging. *Archives of Neurology, 66,* 829–833.

Lister, R., Mukamel, E. A., Nery, J. R., Urich, M., et al. (2013). Global epigenomic reconfiguration during mammalian brain development. *Science, 341*(6146), 1237905. doi:10.1126/science.1237905

Liu, D., Diorio, J., Tannenbaum, B., Caldji, C., et al. (1997). Maternal care, hippocampal glucocorticoid receptors, and hypothalamic-pituitary-adrenal responses to stress. *Science, 277,* 1659–1662.

Liu, X., Ramirez, S., Pang, P. T., Puryear, C. B., et al. (2012). Optogenetic stimulation of a hippocampal engram activates fear memory recall. *Nature, 484,* 381–385.

Liu, Y., Gao, J. H., Liotti, M., Pu, Y., et al. (1999). Temporal dissociation of parallel processing in the human subcortical outputs. *Nature, 400,* 364–367.

Liu, Y., Gao, J.-H., Liu, H.-L., and Fox, P. T. (2000). The temporal response of the brain after eating revealed by functional MRI. *Nature, 405,* 1058–1062.

Liu, Y., Yttri, E. A., and Snyder, L. H. (2010). Intention and attention: Different functional roles for LIPd and LIPv. *Nature Neuroscience, 13*(4), 495–500.

Livingstone, M. S. (2000). Is it warm? Is it real? Or just low spatial frequency? *Science, 290,* 1299.

Lloyd, J. A. (1971). Weights of testes, thymi, and accessory reproductive glands in relation to rank in paired and grouped house mice (*Mus musculus*). *Proceedings of the Society for Experimental Biology and Medicine, 137,* 19–22.

Lockhart, M., and Moore, J. W. (1975). Classical differential and operant conditioning in rabbits (*Orycytolagus cuniculus*) with septal lesions. *Journal of Comparative and Physiological Psychology, 88,* 147–154.

Loconto, J., Papes, F., Chang, E., Stowers, L., et al. (2003). Functional expression of murine V2R pheromone receptors involves selective association with the M10 and M1 families of MHC class Ib molecules. *Cell, 112,* 607–618.

Loewenstein, W. R. (1971). Mechano-electric transduction in the Pacinian corpuscle. Initiation of sensory impulses in mechanoreception. In *Handbook of sensory physiology: Vol. 1. Principles of receptor physiology* (pp. 269–290). Berlin: Springer.

Loftus, E. F. (2003). Make-believe memories. *American Psychologist, 58,* 867–873.

Logan, C. G., and Grafton, S. T. (1995). Functional anatomy of human eyeblink conditioning determined with regional cerebral glucose metabolism and positron emission tomography. *Proceedings of the National Academy of Sciences, USA, 92,* 7500–7504.

Logothetis, N. K. (2008). What we can do and what we cannot do with fMRI. *Nature, 453,* 869–878.

Long, M. A., Jutras, M. J., Connors, B. W., and Burwell, R. D. (2005). Electrical synapses coordinate activity in the suprachiasmatic nucleus. *Nature Neuroscience, 8,* 61–66.

Longden, E. (2013). Listening to voices. *Scientific American Mind, 24,* 34–39.

Longden, E., and Read, J. (2016a). Social adversity in the etiology of psychosis: A review of the evidence. *American Journal of Psychotherapy, 70*(1), 5–33.

Longden, E., and Read, J. (2016b). Assessing and reporting the adverse effects of antipsychotic medication: A systematic review of clinical studies, and prospective, retrospective, and cross-sectional research. *Clinical Neuropharmacology, 39*(1), 29–39.

Lonstein, J. S., and Stern, J. M. (1997). Role of the midbrain periaqueductal gray in maternal nurturance and aggression: *c-fos* and electrolytic lesion studies in lactating rats. *Journal of Neuroscience, 17,* 3364–3378.

López-Aranda, M. F., López-Téllez, J. F., Navarro-Lobato, I., Masmudi-Martín, M., et al. (2009). Role of layer 6 of V2 visual cortex in object-recognition memory. *Science, 325,* 87–89.

Loui, P., Alsop, D., and Schlaug, G. (2009). Tone deafness: A new disconnection syndrome? *Journal of Neuroscience, 29,* 10215–10220.

Louveau, A., Smirnov, I., Keyes, T. J., and Eccles, J. D. (2015). Structural and functional features of central nervous system lymphatic vessels. *Nature, 523*(7560), 337–341.

Lovejoy, L. P., and Krauzlis, R. J. (2010). Inactivation of primate superior colliculus impairs covert selection of signals for perceptual judgments. *Nature Neuroscience, 13,* 261–266.

Lozano, R., Rosero, C. A., and Hagerman, R. J. (2014). Fragile X spectrum disorders. *Intractable and Rare Disease Research, 3*(4), 134–146. doi:10.5582/irdr.2014.01022

Lu, L., Hope, B. T., Dempsey, J., Liu, S. Y., et al. (2005). Central amygdala ERK signaling pathway is critical to incubation of cocaine craving. *Nature Neuroscience, 8,* 212–219.

Lu, L., Koya, E., Zhai, H., Hope, B. T., et al. (2006). Role of ERK in cocaine addiction. *Trends in Neurosciences, 29,* 695–703.

Lübke, K. T., and Pause, B. M. (2015). Always follow your nose: The functional significance of social chemosignals in human reproduction and survival. *Hormones and Behavior, 68,* 134–144.

Lucas, R. J., Hattar, S., Takao, M., Berson, D. M., et al. (2003). Diminished pupillary light reflex at high irradiances in melanopsin-knockout mice. *Science, 299,* 245–247.

Luck, S. J. (2005). *An introduction to the event-related potential technique.* Cambridge, MA: MIT Press.

Luck, S. J., and Hillyard, S. A. (1994). Electrophysiological correlates of feature analysis during visual search. *Psychophysiology, 31*(3), 291–308.

Lucking, C. B., Durr, A., Bonifati, V., Vaughan, J., et al. (2000). Association between early-onset Parkinson's disease and mutations in the parkin gene. *New England Journal of Medicine, 342,* 1560–1567.

Lumpkin, E. A., and Caterina, M. J. (2007). Mechanisms of sensory transduction in the skin. *Nature, 445,* 858–865.

Luna, E., and Luk, K. C. (2015). Bent out of shape: ⍺-Synuclein misfolding and the convergence of pathogenic pathways in Parkinson's disease. *FEBS Letters, 589*(24 Pt. A), 3749–3759.

Luria, A. R. (1987). *The mind of a mnemonist.* Cambridge, MA: Harvard University Press.

Lush, I. E. (1989). The genetics of tasting in mice. VI. Saccharin, acesulfame, dulcin and sucrose. *Genetical Research, 53,* 95–99.

Lyall, V., Heck, G. L., Vinnikova, A. K., Ghosh, S., et al. (2004). The mammalian amiloride-insensitive non-specific salt taste receptor is a vanilloid receptor-1 variant. *Journal of Physiology (London), 558,* 147–159.

Lyamin, O., Pryaslova, J., Lance, V., and Siegel, J. (2005). Continuous activity in cetaceans after birth: The exceptional wakefulness of newborn whales and dolphins has no ill-effect on their development. *Nature, 435,* 1177.

Lynch, G., Larson, J., Staubli, U., and Granger, R. (1991). Variants of synaptic potentiation and different types of memory operations in hippocampus and related structures. In L. R. Squire, N. M. Weinberger, G. Lynch, and J. L. McGaugh (Eds.), *Memory: Organization and locus of change* (pp. 330–363). New York: Oxford University Press.

Lyons, J. I., Kerr, G. R., and Mueller, P. W. (2015). Fragile X syndrome: Scientific background and screening technologies. *Journal of Molecular Diagnostics.* doi:10.1016/j.jmoldx.2015.04.006

M

Ma, L., Wu, Y., Qiu, Q., Scheerer, H., et al. (2014). A developmental switch of axon targeting in the continuously regenerating mouse olfactory system. *Science, 344*(6180), 194–197.

Mace, G. M., Gittleman, J. L., and Purvis, A. (2003). Preserving the tree of life. *Science, 300,* 1707–1709.

Mace, G. M., Harvey, P. H., and Clutton-Brock, T. H. (1981). Brain size and ecology in small mammals. *Journal of Zoology, 193,* 333–354.

Mackey, A. P., Finn, A. S., Leonard, J. A., Jacoby-Senghor, D. S., et al. (2015). Neuroanatomical correlates of the income-achievement gap. *Psychological Science, 26*(6), 925–933.

MacLean, P. D. (1949). Psychosomatic disease and the "visceral brain": Recent developments bearing on the Papez theory of emotion. *Psychosomatic Medicine, 11,* 338–353.

Macmillan, M. (2000). *An odd kind of fame: Stories of Phineas Gage.* Cambridge, MA: MIT Press.

MacNeilage, P. F., Rogers, L. J., and Vallortigara, G. (2009). Origins of the left & right brain. *Scientific American, 301*(1), 60–67.

MacNeilage, P. R., Banks, M. S., Berger, D. R., and Bülthoff, H. H. (2007). A Bayesian model of the disambiguation of gravitoinertial force by visual cues. *Experimental Brain Research, 179,* 263–290.

Madden, J. (2001). Sex, bowers and brains. *Proceedings of the Royal Society of London. Series B: Biological Sciences, 268,* 833–838.

Maggioncalda, A. N., and Sapolsky, R. M. (2002). Disturbing behaviors of the orangutan. *Scientific American, 286*(6), 60–65.

Mair, W. G. P., Warrington, E. K., and Wieskrantz, L. (1979). Memory disorder in Korsakoff's psychosis. *Brain, 102,* 749–783.

Mak, G. K., Enwere, E. K., Gregg, C., Pakarainen, T., et al. (2007). Male pheromone-stimulated neurogenesis in the adult female brain: Possible role in mating behavior. *Nature Neuroscience, 10,* 1003–1011.

Maki, P. M., and Resnick, S. M. (2000). Longitudinal effects of estrogen replacement therapy on pet cerebral blood flow and cognition. *Neurobiology of Aging, 21,* 373–383.

Maldonado, R., and Rodríguez de Fonseca, F. (2002). Cannabinoid addiction: Behavioral models and neural correlates. *Journal of Neuroscience, 22,* 3326–3331.

Malenka, R. C., and Bear, M. F. (2004). LTP and LTD: An embarrassment of riches. *Neuron, 44,* 5–21.

Malone, D. T., Hill, M. N., and Rubino, T. (2010). Adolescent cannabis use and psychosis: Epidemiology and neurodevelopmental models. *British Journal of Pharmacology, 160,* 511–522.

Malpas, C. B., Genc, S., Saling, M. M., Velakoulis, D., et al. (2016). MRI correlates of general intelligence in neurotypical adults. *Journal of Clinical Neuroscience, 24,* 128–134.

Mancuso, K., Hauswirth, W. W., Li, Q., Connor, T. B., et al. (2009). Gene therapy for red-green colour blindness in adult primates. *Nature, 461,* 784–788.

Manetto, V., Medori, R., Cortelli, P., Montagna, P., et al. (1992). Fatal familial insomnia: Clinical and pathologic study of five new cases. *Neurology, 42,* 312–319.

Manfredi, M., Bini, G., Cruccu, G., Accornero, N., et al. (1981). Congenital absence of pain. *Archives of Neurology, 38,* 507–511.

Manger, P. R., Collins, R., and Pettigrew, J. D. (1998). The development of the electroreceptors of the platypus (*Ornithorhynchus anatinus*). *Philosophical Transactions of the Royal Society of London. Series B: Biological Sciences, 353,* 1171–1186.

Mangun, G. R. (1995). Neural mechanisms of visual selective attention. *Psychophysiology, 32,* 4–18.

Mani, S. K., Mermelstein, P. G., Tetel, M. J., and Anesetti, G. (2012). Convergence of multiple mechanisms of steroid hormone action. *Hormone and Metabolic Research, 44,* 569–576.

Mantini, D., Gerits, A., Nelissen, K., Durand, J. B., et al. (2011). Default mode of brain function in monkeys. *Journal of Neuroscience, 31*(36), 12954–12962.

Mantyh, P. W., Rogers, S. D., Honore, P., Allen, B. J., et al. (1997). Inhibition of hyperalgesia by ablation of lamina I spinal neurons expressing the substance P receptor. *Science, 278,* 275–279.

March, J., Silva, S., Petrychi, S., Curry, J., et al. (2004). Fluoxetine, cognitive-behavioral therapy, and their combination for adolescents with depression: Treatment for adolescents with depression study (TADS) randomized controlled trial. *JAMA, 292,* 807–820.

Marcus, G. F., Vijayan, S., Bandi Rao, S., and Vishton, P. M. (1999). Rule learning by seven-month-old infants. *Science, 283,* 77–80.

Maren, S., and Quirk, G. J. (2004). Neuronal signalling of fear memory. *Nature, 5,* 844–852.

Mariani, J., and Changeaux, J.-P. (1981). Ontogenesis of olivocerebellar relationships. I. Studies by intracellular recordings of the multiple innervation of Purkinje cells by climbing fibers in the developing rat cerebellum. *Journal of Neuroscience, 1,* 696–702.

Maricic, T., Günther, V., Georgiev, O., Gehre, S., et al. (2013). A recent evolutionary change affects a regulatory element in the human *FOXP2* gene. *Molecular Biology and Evolution, 30*(4), 844–852.

Maricich, S. M., Wellnitz, S. A., Nelson, A. M., and Lesniak, D. R. (2009). Merkel cells are essential for light-touch responses. *Science, 324,* 1580–1582.

Marín-Burgin, A., Mongiat, L. A., Pardi, M. B., and Schinder, A. F. (2012). Unique processing during a period of high excitation/inhibition balance in adult-born neurons. *Science, 335,* 1238–1242.

Mark, V. H., and Ervin, F. R. (1970). *Violence and the brain.* New York: Harper & Row.

Marler, P. (1970). Birdsong and speech development: Could there be parallels? *American Scientist, 58,* 669–673.

Marler, P., and Sherman, V. (1983). Song structure without auditory feedback: Emendations of the auditory template hypothesis. *Journal of Neuroscience, 3,* 517–531.

Marler, P., and Sherman, V. (1985). Innate differences in singing behaviour of sparrows reared in isolation from adult conspecific song. *Animal Behavior, 33,* 57–71.

Marshall, C. B., Fletcher, G. L., and Davies, P. L. (2004). Hyperactive antifreeze protein in a fish. *Nature, 429,* 153.

Marshall, L., Helgadóttir, H., Mölle, M., and Born, J. (2006). Boosting slow oscillations during sleep potentiates memory. *Nature, 444,* 610–613.

Marsicano, G., Goodenough, S., Monory, K., Hermann, H., et al. (2003). CB1 cannabinoid receptors and on-demand defense against excitotoxicity. *Science, 302,* 84–88.

Marsicano, G., Wotjak, C. T., Azad, S. C., Bisogno, T., et al. (2002). The endogenous cannabinoid system controls extinction of aversive memories. *Nature, 418,* 530–532.

Martin, C. K., Heilbronn, L., de Jonge, L., Delany, J. P., et al. (2007). Effect of calorie restriction on resting metabolic rate and spontaneous physical activity. *Obesity (Silver Spring), 15,* 2964–2973.

Martin, J. T., and Nguyen, D. H. (2004). Anthropometric analysis of homosexuals and heterosexuals: Implications for early hormone exposure. *Hormones and Behavior, 45,* 31–39.

Martinez-Conde, S., Otero-Millan, J., and Macknik, S. L. (2013). The impact of microsaccades on vision: Towards a unified theory of saccadic function. *Nature Reviews Neuroscience, 14,* 83–96.

Martinez-Vicente, M., Talloczy, Z., Wong, E., Tang, G., et al. (2010). Cargo recognition failure is responsible for inefficient autophagy in Huntington's disease. *Nature Neuroscience, 13,* 567–576.

Martuza, R. L., Chiocca, E. A., Jenike, M. A., Giriunas, I. E., et al. (1990). Stereotactic radiofrequency thermal cingulotomy for obsessive compulsive disorder. *Journal of Neuropsychiatry and Clinical Neurosciences, 2,* 331–336.

Marucha, P. T., Kiecolt-Glaser, J. K., and Favagehi, M. (1998). Mucosal wound healing is impaired by examination stress. *Psychosomatic Medicine, 60,* 362–365.

Maruyama, M., Shimada, H., Suhara, T., Shinotoh, H., et al. (2013). Imaging of tau pathology in a tauopathy mouse model and in Alzheimer patients compared to normal controls. *Neuron, 79*(6), 1094–1108. doi:10.1016/j.neuron.2013.07.037

Maruyama, Y., Pereira, E., Margolskee, R. F., Chaudhari, N., et al. (2006). Umami responses in mouse taste cells indicate more than one receptor. *Journal of Neuroscience, 26,* 2227–2234.

Marzani, D., and Wallman, J. (1997). Growth of the two layers of the chick sclera is modulated reciprocally by visual conditions. *Investigative Ophthalmology & Visual Science, 38,* 1726–1739.

Maskos, U., Molles, B. E., Pons, S., Besson, M., et al. (2005). Nicotine reinforcement and cognition restored by targeted expression of nicotinic receptors. *Nature, 436,* 103–107.

Masters, W. H., and Johnson, V. E. (1966). *Human sexual response.* Boston: Little, Brown.

Masters, W. H., and Johnson, V. E. (1970). *Human sexual inadequacy.* Boston: Little, Brown.

Masters, W. H., Johnson, V. E., and Kolodny, R. C. (1994). *Heterosexuality.* New York: HarperCollins.

Masterton, R. B. (1993). Central auditory system. *Journal of Oto-Rhino-Laryngology and Its Related Specialties, 55,* 159–163.

Mastrianni, J. A., Nixon, R., Layzer, R., Telling, G. C., et al. (1999). Prion protein conformation in a patient with sporadic fatal insomnia. *New England Journal of Medicine, 340,* 1630–1638.

Mateo, J. M., and Johnston, R. E. (2000). Kin recognition and the "armpit effect": Evidence of self-referent phenotype matching. *Proceedings of the Royal Society of London. Series B: Biological Sciences, 267,* 695–700.

Matsumoto, K., Suzuki, W., and Tanaka, K. (2003). Neuronal correlates of goal-based motor selection in the prefrontal cortex. *Science, 301,* 229–232.

Matsunami, H., Montmayeur, J. P., and Buck, L. B. (2000). A family of candidate taste receptors in human and mouse. *Nature, 404*(6778), 601–604.

Matthews, K. A. (2005). Psychological perspectives on the development of coronary heart disease. *American Psychology, 60,* 783–796.

Mattson, S. N., Riley, E. P., Gramling, L., Delis, D. C., et al. (1998). Neuropsychological comparison of alcohol-exposed children with or without physical features of fetal alcohol syndrome. *Neuropsychology, 12,* 146–153.

Maurer, P., and Bachmann, M. F. (2007). Vaccination against nicotine: An emerging therapy for tobacco dependence. *Expert Opinion on Investigational Drugs, 16,* 1775–1783.

Mayberg, H. S., Lozano, A. M., Voon, V., McNeely, H. E., et al. (2005). Deep brain stimulation for treatment-resistant depression. *Neuron, 45,* 651–660.

Mayfield, R. D., Lewohl, J. M., Dodd, P. R., Herlihy, A., et al. (2002). Patterns of gene expression are altered in the frontal and motor cortices of human alcoholics. *Journal of Neurochemistry, 81,* 802–813.

Mazur, A., and Booth, A. (1998). Testosterone and dominance in men. *Behavioral and Brain Sciences, 21,* 353–363.

McAllister, A. K., Katz, L. C., and Lo, D. C. (1997). Opposing roles for endogenous BDNF and NT-3 in regulating cortical dendritic growth. *Neuron, 18,* 767–778.

McAlpine, D., Jiang, D., and Palmer, A. R. (2001). A neural code for low-frequency sound localization in mammals. *Nature Neuroscience, 4,* 396–401.

McBurney, D. H., Smith, D.V., and Shick, T. R. (1972). Gustatory cross adaptation: Sourness and bitterness. *Perception & Psychophysics, 11,* 2228–2232.

McCall, W. V., and Edinger, J. D. (1992). Subjective total insomnia: An example of sleep state misperception. *Sleep, 15,* 71–73.

McCarthy, M. M., and Nugent, B. M. (2015). At the frontier of epigenetics of brain sex differences. *Frontiers in Behavioral Neuroscience, 9,* 221. doi:10.3389/fnbeh.2015.00221

McCarthy, R. A., and Warrington, E. K. (1990). *Cognitive neuropsychology: A clinical introduction.* San Diego, CA: Academic Press.

McComb, K., Moss, C., Sayialel, S., and Baker, L. (2000). Unusually extensive networks of vocal recognition in African elephants. *Animal Behavior, 59,* 1103–1109.

McCoy, A. N., and Platt, M. L. (2005). Risk-sensitive neurons in macaque posterior cingulate cortex. *Nature Neuroscience, 8,* 1220–1227.

McCrae, C. S., Rowe, M. A., Tierney, C. G., Dautovich, N. D., et al. (2005). Sleep complaints, subjective and objective sleep patterns, health, psychological adjustment, and daytime functioning in community-dwelling older adults. *Journals of Gerontology. Series B, Psychological Sciences and Social Sciences, 60*(4), P182–P189.

McDonald, J. J., and Green, J. J. (2008). Isolating event-related potential components associated with voluntary control of visuo-spatial attention. *Brain Research, 1227,* 96–109.

McDonald, J. J., Teder-Sälejärvi, W. A., Di Russo, F., and Hillyard, S. A. (2003). Neural substrates of perceptual enhancement by crossmodal spatial attention. *Journal of Cognitive Neuroscience, 15,* 10–19.

McDonald, J. J., Teder-Sälejärvi, W. A., Di Russo, F., and Hillyard, S. A. (2005). Neural basis of auditory-induced shifts in visual time-order perception. *Nature Neuroscience, 8*(9), 1197–1202.

McDonald, J. J., Teder-Sälejärvi, W. A., and Hillyard, S. A. (2000). Involuntary orienting to sound improves visual perception. *Nature, 407,* 906–908.

McDonald, J. J., Ward, L. M., and Kiehl, K. A. (1999). An event-related brain potential study of inhibition of return. *Perception and Psychophysics, 61*(7), 1411–1423.

McEwen, B. S. (2012). Brain on stress: How the social environment gets under the skin. *Proceedings of the National Academy of Sciences, USA, 109*(Suppl. 2), 17180–17185.

McEwen, B. S., and Akil, H. (2011). Introduction to social neuroscience: Gene, environment, brain, body. *Annals of the New York Academy of Science, 1231*, vii–ix.

McEwen, B. S., Bowles, N. P., Gray, J. D., Hill, M. N., et al. (2015). Mechanisms of stress in the brain. *Nature Neuroscience, 1*, 1353–1363.

McEwen, B. S., and Wingfield, J. C. (2010). What is in a name? Integrating homeostasis, allostasis and stress. *Hormones and Behavior, 57*, 105–111.

McFadden, D., and Champlin, C. A. (1990). Reductions in overshoot during aspirin use. *Journal of the Acoustical Society of America, 87*, 2634–2642.

McFadden, D., and Pasanen, E. (1998). Comparison of the auditory systems of heterosexuals and homosexuals: Click-evoked otoacoustic emissions. *Proceedings of the National Academy of Sciences, USA, 95*, 2709–2713.

McGaugh, J. L. (2003). *Memory and emotions: The making of lasting memories.* New York: Columbia University Press.

McGeer, P., McGeer, E., Suzuki, J., Dolman, C., et al. (1984). Aging, Alzheimer's disease, and the cholinergic system of the basal forebrain. *Neurology, 34*, 741–745.

McGinty, D. J., and Sterman, M. B. (1968). Sleep suppression after basal forebrain lesions in the cat. *Science, 160*, 1253–1255.

McGowan, P. O., Sasaki, A., D'Alessio, A. C., Dymov, S., et al. (2009). Epigenetic regulation of the glucocorticoid receptor in human brain associates with childhood abuse. *Nature Neuroscience, 12*, 342–348.

McGue, M. (1999). The behavioral genetics of alcoholism. *Current Trends in Psychological Science, 8*, 109–115.

McGuigan, F. J., and Lehrer, P. M. (2007). Progressive relaxation: Origins, principles and clinical application. In P. M. Lehrer, R. L. Woolfolk, and W. E. Sime (Eds.), *Principles and practices of stress management* (pp. 57–87). New York: Guilford Press.

McIntyre, C. K., Miyashita, T., Setlow, B., Marjon, K. D., et al. (2005). Memory-influencing intra-basolateral amygdala drug infusions modulate expression of Arc protein in the hippocampus. *Proceedings of the National Academy of Sciences, USA, 102*, 10718–10723.

McKee, A. C., Cairns, N. J., Dickson, D. W., Folkerth, R. D., et al. (2016). The first NINDS/NIBIB consensus meeting to define neuropathological criteria for the diagnosis of chronic traumatic encephalopathy. *Acta Neuropathologica, 131*(1), 75–86.

McKee, A. C., Cantu, R. C., Nowinski, C. J., Hedley-Whyte, E. T., et al. (2009). Chronic traumatic encephalopathy in athletes: Progressive tauopathy after repetitive head injury. *Journal of Neuropathology and Experimental Neurology, 68*, 709–735.

McKenna, K. (1999). The brain is the master organ in sexual function: Central nervous system control of male and female sexual function. *International Journal of Impotence Research, 11*(Suppl. 1), S48–S55.

McKeown, S. J., Wallace, A. S., and Anderson, R. B. (2013). Expression and function of cell adhesion molecules during neural crest migration. *Developmental Biology, 373*(2), 244–257. doi:10.1016/j.ydbio.2012.10.028

McKernan, M. G., and Shinnick-Gallagher, P. (1997). Fear conditioning induces a lasting potentiation of synaptic currents in vitro. *Nature, 390*, 607–611.

McKim, W. A. (1991). *Drugs and behavior: An introduction to behavioral pharmacology* (2nd ed.). Englewood Cliffs, NJ: Prentice Hall.

McKinley, M. J., and Johnson, A. K. (2004). The physiological regulation of thirst and fluid intake. *News in Physiological Sciences, 19*, 1–6.

McKinney, T. D., and Desjardins, C. (1973). Postnatal development of the testis, fighting behavior, and fertility in house mice. *Biology of Reproduction, 9*, 279–294.

McLaughlin, S. K., McKinnon, P. J., Spickofsky, N., Danho, W., et al. (1994). Molecular cloning of G proteins and phosphodiesterases from rat taste cells. *Physiology & Behavior, 56*, 1157–1164.

McMahon, H. T., Foran, P., Dolly, J. O., Verhage, M., et al. (1992). Tetanus toxin and botulinum toxins type A and B inhibit glutamate, gamma-aminobutyric acid, aspartate, and met-enkephalin release from synaptosomes. Clues to the locus of action. *Journal of Biological Chemistry, 267*, 21338–21343.

McMains, S., and Somers, D. (2004). Multiple spotlights of attentional selection in human visual cortex. *Neuron, 42*, 677–686.

McNally, R. J. (2003). Recovering memories of trauma: A view from the laboratory. *Current Directions in Psychological Science, 12*, 32–35.

McNamara, J. O. (1984). Role of neurotransmitters in seizure mechanisms in the kindling model of epilepsy. *Federation Proceedings, 43*, 2516–2520.

McNaughton, B. L., Barnes, C. A., Gerrard, J. L., Gothard, K., et al. (1996). Deciphering the hippocampal polyglot: The hippocampus as a path integration system. *Journal of Experimental Biology, 199*(Pt. 1), 173–185.

Meddis, R. (1975). On the function of sleep. *Animal Behavior, 23*, 676–691.

Meddis, R. (1977). *The sleep instinct.* London: Routledge & Kegan Paul.

Mednick, S. A., Huttunen, M. O., and Machon, R. A. (1994). Prenatal influenza infections and adult schizophrenia. *Schizophrenia Bulletin, 20*, 263–267.

Medori, R., Montagna, P., Tritschler, H. J., LeBlanc, A., et al. (1992). Fatal familial insomnia: A second kindred with mutation of prion protein gene at codon 178. *Neurology, 42*, 669–670.

Mega, M. S., and Cummings, J. L. (1994). Frontal-subcortical circuits and neuropsychiatric disorders. *Journal of Neuropsychiatry and Clinical Neurosciences, 6*, 358–370.

Meguerditchian, A., and Vauclair, J. (2006). Baboons communicate with their right hand. *Behavioural Brain Research, 171*, 170–174.

Mei, L., and Xiong, W.-C. (2008). Neuregulin 1 in neural development, synaptic plasticity and schizophrenia. *Nature Reviews Neuroscience, 9*, 437–452.

Meier, M. H., Caspi, A., Ambler, A., Harrington, H., et al. (2012). Persistent cannabis users show neuropsychological decline from childhood to midlife. *Proceedings of the National Academy of Sciences, USA, 109*, E2657–E2664.

Meisel, R. L., and Luttrell, V. R. (1990). Estradiol increases the dendritic length of ventromedial hypothalamic neurons in female Syrian hamsters. *Brain Research Bulletin, 25*, 165–168.

Meisel, R. L., and Sachs, B. D. (1994). The physiology of male sexual behavior. In E. Knobil and J. D. Neill (Eds.), *The physiology of reproduction* (2nd ed., Vol. 1, pp. 3–105). New York: Raven.

Meister, I. G., Boroojerdi, B., Foltys, H., Sparing, R., et al. (2003). Motor cortex hand area and speech: Implications for the development of language. *Neuropsychologia, 41*, 401–406.

Melcangi, R. C., and Panzica, G. C. (2014). Allopregnanolone: State of the art. *Progress in Neurobiology, 113*, 1–5.

Mellars, P. (2006). A new radiocarbon revolution and the dispersal of modern humans in Eurasia. *Nature, 439*, 931–935.

Melmed, S., Polonsky, K. S., Larsen, P. R., and Kronenberg, H. M. (2016). *Williams textbook of endocrinology* (13th ed.). Philadelphia: Elsevier.

Melzack, R. (1984). Neuropsychological basis of pain measurement. *Advances in Pain Research, 6*, 323–341.

Melzack, R., and Wall, P. D. (1965). Pain mechanisms: A new history. *Science, 150*, 971–979.

Mendel, G. (1967). *Experiments in plant hybridisation* (Royal Horticultural Society of London, Trans.). Cambridge, MA: Harvard University Press.

Menninger, W. C. (1948). Facts and statistics of significance for psychiatry. *Bulletin of the Menninger Clinic, 12*, 1–25.

Menzies, F. M., Fleming, A., and Rubinsztein, D. C. (2015). Compromised autophagy and neurodegenerative diseases. *Nature Reviews Neuroscience, 16*(6), 345–357.

Merchán-Pérez, A., Rodriguez, J. R., Alonso-Nanclares, L., Schertel, A., et al. (2009). Counting synapses using FIB/SEM microscopy: A true revolution for ultrastructural volume reconstruction. *Frontiers in Neuroanatomy, 3*, 18.

Mersch, P. P., Middendorp, H. M., Bouhuys, A. L., Beersma, D. G., et al. (1999). Seasonal affective disorder and latitude: A review of the literature. *Journal of Affective Disorders, 53*, 35–48.

Mertens, J., Wang, Q. W., Kim, Y., Yu, D. X., et al. (2015). Differential responses to lithium in hyperexcitable neurons from patients with bipolar disorder. *Nature, 527*, 95–99.

Merzenich, M. M., and Jenkins, W. M. (1993). Reorganization of cortical representations of the hand following alterations of skin inputs induced by nerve injury, skin island transfers, and experience. *Journal of Hand Therapy, 6*, 89–104.

Meshberger, F. L. (1990). An interpretation of Michelangelo's *Creation of Adam* based on neuroanatomy. *JAMA, 264*(14), 1837–1841.

Messias, E., Kirkpatrick, B., Bromet, E., Ross, D., et al. (2004). Summer birth and deficit schizophrenia: A pooled analysis from 6 countries. *Archives of General Psychiatry, 61*, 985–989.

Mesulam, M.-M. (1985). Attention, confusional states and neglect. In M.-M. Mesulam (Ed.), *Principles of behavioral neurology.* Philadelphia: Davis.

Michael, J., Sandberg, K., Skewes, J., Wolf, T., et al. (2014). Continuous theta-burst stimulation demonstrates a causal role of premotor homunculus in action understanding. *Psychological Science, 25*(4), 963–972.

Michael, N., and Erfurth, A. (2004). Treatment of bipolar mania with right prefrontal rapid transcranial magnetic stimulation. *Journal of Affective Disorders, 78*, 253–257.

Miczek, K. A., Fish, E. W., De Bold, J. F., and De Almeida, R. M. (2002). Social and neural determinants of aggressive behavior: Pharmacotherapeutic targets at serotonin, dopamine and gamma-aminobutyric acid systems. *Psychopharmacology (Berlin), 163*, 434–458.

Mignot, E. (2013). The perfect hypnotic? *Science, 340*(6128), 36–38.

Miller, E. K., and Cohen, J. D. (2001). An integrative theory of prefrontal cortex function. *Annual Review of Neuroscience, 24*, 167–202.

Miller, G. (2010). fMRI lie detection fails a legal test. *Science, 328*, 1336–1337.

Miller, G. A. (2010). Mistreating psychology in the decades of the brain. *Perspectives on Psychological Science, 5*, 716–743.

Miller, G. F. (2000). *The mating mind: How sexual choice shaped the evolution of human nature.* New York: Doubleday.

Miller, N. E., Sampliner, R. I., and Woodrow, P. (1957). Thirst-reducing effects of water by stomach fistula versus water by mouth measured by both a consummatory and an instrumental response. *Journal of Comparative Physiology and Psychology, 50*, 1–5.

Mills, K. L., Lalonde, F., Clasen, L. S., Giedd, J. N., et al. (2014). Developmental changes in the structure of the social brain in late childhood and adolescence. *Social Cognitive and Affective Neuroscience, 9*(1), 123–131. doi:10.1093/scan/nss113

Milner, A. D., Perrett, D. I., Johnston, R. S., Benson, P. J., et al. (1991). Perception and action in "visual form agnosia." *Brain, 114*, 405–428.

Milner, B. (1963). Effect of different brain lesions on card sorting. *Archives of Neurology, 9*, 90–100.

Milner, B. (1965). Memory disturbance after bilateral hippocampal lesions. In P. M. Milner and S. E. Glickman (Eds.), *Cognitive processes and the brain; an enduring problem in psychology* (pp. 97–111). Princeton, NJ: Van Nostrand.

Milner, B. (1970). Memory and the medial temporal regions of the brain. In D. H. Pribram and D. E. Broadbent (Eds.), *Biology of memory* (pp. 29–50). New York: Academic Press.

Milner, P. M. (1993). The mind and Donald O. Hebb. *Scientific American, 268*(1), 124–129.

Milot, E., Mayer, F. M., Nussey, D. H., Boisvert, M., et al. (2011). Evidence for evolution in response to natural selection in a contemporary human population. *Proceedings of the National Academy of Sciences, USA, 108*(41), 17040–17045.

Min, R., and Nevian, T. (2012). Astrocyte signaling controls spike timing-dependent depression at neocortical synapses. *Nature Neuroscience, 15*, 746–753.

Minzenberg, M. J., Laird, A. R., Thelen, S., Carter, C. S., et al. (2009). Meta-analysis of 41 functional neuroimaging studies of executive function in schizophrenia. *Archives of General Psychiatry, 66*, 811–822.

Mioduszewska, B., Jaworski, J., and Kaczmarek, L. (2003). Inducible cAMP early repressor (ICER) in the nervous system: A transcriptional regulator of neuronal plasticity and programmed cell death. *Journal of Neurochemistry, 87*, 1313–1320.

Miras, M., Serrano, M., Durán, C., Valiño, C., et al. (2015). Early experience with customized, meal-triggered gastric electrical stimulation in obese patients. *Obesity Surgery, 25*, 174–179.

Mirescu, C., Peters, J. D., and Gould, E. (2004). Early life experience alters response of adult neurogenesis to stress. *Nature Neuroscience, 7*, 841–846.

Miri, A., Azim, E., and Jessell, T. M. (2013). Edging toward entelechy in motor control. *Neuron, 80*(3), 827–834. doi:10.1016/j.neuron.2013.10.049

Mirsky, A. F., and Duncan, C. C. (1986). Etiology and expression of schizophrenia: Neurobiological and psychosocial factors. *Annual Review of Psychology, 37*, 291–321.

Mishkin, M., and Ungerleider, L. (1982). Contribution of striate inputs to the visuospatial functions of parieto-preoccipital cortex in monkeys. *Behavioural Brain Research, 6*, 57–77.

Mishra, J., Zinni, M., Bavelier, D., and Hillyard, S. A. (2011). Neural basis of superior performance of action videogame players in an attention-demanding task. *Journal of Neuroscience, 31*(3), 992–998.

Mishra, S. K., and Hoon, M. A. (2013). The cells and circuitry for itch responses in mice. *Science, 340*(6135), 968–971.

Mistlberger, R. E. (2005). Circadian regulation of sleep in mammals: Role of the suprachiasmatic nucleus. *Brain Research Reviews, 49,* 429–454.

Mistlberger, R. E., and Skene, D. J. (2004). Social influences on mammalian circadian rhythms: Animal and human studies. *Biological Reviews of the Cambridge Philosophical Society, 79,* 533–556.

Mithoefer, M. C., Wagner, M. T., Mithoefer, A. T., Jerome, L., et al. (2013, January). Durability of improvement in post-traumatic stress disorder symptoms and absence of harmful effects or drug dependency after 3,4-methylenedioxymethamphetamine-assisted psychotherapy: A prospective long-term follow-up study. *Journal of Psychopharmacology, 27*(1), 28–39.

Miyata, S. (2015). New aspects in fenestrated capillary and tissue dynamics in the sensory circumventricular organs of adult brains. *Frontiers in Neuroscience, 9*, 390.

Miyawaki, Y., Uchida, H., Yamashita, O., Sato, M. A., et al. (2008). Visual image reconstruction from human brain activity using a combination of multiscale local image decoders. *Neuron, 60,* 915–929.

Mizumori, S. J., Lavoie, A. M., and Kalyani, A. (1996). Redistribution of spatial representation in the hippocampus of aged rats performing a spatial memory task. *Behavioral Neuroscience, 110,* 1006–1016.

Moghaddam, B., and Adams, B. W. (1998). Reversal of phencyclidine effects by a group II metabotropic glutamate receptor agonist in rats. *Science, 281,* 1349–1352.

Mogil, J. S., and Chanda, M. L. (2005). The case for the inclusion of female subjects in basic science studies of pain. *Pain, 117,* 1–5.

Mogil, J. S., Wilson, S. G., Chesler, E. J., Rankin, A. L., et al. (2003). The melanocortin-1 receptor gene mediates female-specific mechanisms of analgesia in mice and humans. *Proceedings National Academy of Sciences, USA, 100,* 4867–4872.

Mohammed, A. (2001). *Enrichment and the brain. Plasticity in the adult brain: From genes to neurotherapy.* 22nd International Summer School of Brain Research, Amsterdam, Netherlands.

Moita, M. A., Rosis, S., Zhou, Y., LeDoux, J. E., et al. (2004). Putting fear in its place: Remapping of hippocampal place cells during fear conditioning. *Journal of Neuroscience, 24,* 7015–7023.

Molenda-Figueira, H. A., Williams, C. A., Griffin, A. L., Rutledge, E. M., et al. (2006). Nuclear receptor coactivators function in estrogen receptor- and progestin receptor-dependent aspects of sexual behavior in female rats. *Hormones and Behavior, 50,* 383–392.

Money, J., and Ehrhardt, A. A. (1972). *Man and woman, boy and girl.* Baltimore: Johns Hopkins University Press.

Monfils, M. H., Plautz, E. J., and Kleim, J. A. (2005). In search of the motor engram: Motor map plasticity as a mechanism for encoding motor experience. *Neuroscientist, 11,* 471–483.

Monks, D. A., and Watson N. V. (2001). N-cadherin expression in motoneurons is directly regulated by androgens: A genetic mosaic analysis in rats. *Brain Research, 895,* 73–79.

Monks, T. J., Jones, D. C., Bai, F., and Lau, S. S. (2004). The role of metabolism in 3,4-(+)-methylenedioxyamphetamine and 3,4-(+)-methylenedioxymethamphetamine (ecstasy) toxicity. *Therapeutic Drug Monitoring, 26,* 132–136.

Montague, C. T., Farooqi, I. S., Whitehead, J. P., Soos, M. A., et al. (1997). Congenital leptin deficiency is associated with severe early-onset obesity in humans. *Nature, 387,* 903–908.

Montenigro, P. H., Alosco, M. L., Martin, B., Daneshvar, D. H., et al. (2016). Cumulative head impact exposure predicts later-life depression, apathy, executive dysfunction, and cognitive impairment in former high school and college football players. *Journal of Neurotrauma.* PubMed PMID: 27029716. [Epub ahead of print]

Monti, M. M., Vanhaudenhuyse, A., Coleman, M. R., Boly, M., et al. (2010). Willful modulation of brain activity in disorders of consciousness. *New England Journal of Medicine, 362,* 579–589.

Moon, R. Y. (2011). SIDS and other sleep-related infant deaths: Expansion of recommendations for a safe infant sleeping environment. Task Force on Sudden Infant Death Syndrome. *Pediatrics, 125*(5), 1030–1039.

Moore, C. L., Dou, H., and Juraska, J. M. (1992). Maternal stimulation affects the number of motor neurons in a sexually dimorphic nucleus of the lumbar spinal cord. *Brain Research, 572,* 52–56.

Moore, G. J., Bebchuk, J. M., Wilds, I. B., Chen, G., et al. (2000). Lithium-induced increase in human brain grey matter. *Lancet, 356,* 241–242.

Moore, R. Y. (1983). Organization and function of a central nervous system circadian oscillator: The suprachiasmatic nucleus. *Federation Proceedings, 42,* 2783–2789.

Moore, R. Y., and Eichler, V. B. (1972). Loss of circadian adrenal corticosterone rhythm following suprachiasmatic lesions in the rat. *Brain Research, 42,* 201–206.

Moorhead, T. W., McKirdy, J., Sussmann, J. E., Hall, J., et al. (2007). Progressive gray matter loss in patients with bipolar disorder. *Biological Psychiatry, 62,* 894–900.

Moorman, S., Gobes, S. M., Kuijpers, M., Kerkhofs, A., et al. (2012). Human-like brain hemispheric dominance in birdsong learning. *Proceedings of the National Academy of Sciences, USA,* 109(31), 12782–12787.

Moran, J., and Desimone, R. (1985). Selective attention gates visual processing in the extrastriate cortex. *Science, 229,* 782–784.

Moray, N. (1959). Attention in dichotic listening: Affective cues and the influence of instructions. *Quarterly Journal of Experimental Psychology, 11,* 56–60.

Mori, K., Nagao, H., and Yoshihara, Y. (1999). The olfactory bulb: Coding and processing of odor molecule information. *Science, 286,* 711–715.

Morihisa, J., and McAnulty, G. B. (1985). Structure and function: Brain electrical activity mapping and computed tomography in schizophrenia. *Biological Psychiatry, 20,* 3–19.

Moriya, J., Takimoto, Y., Yoshiuchi, K., Shimosawa, T., et al. (2006). Plasma agouti-related protein levels in women with anorexia nervosa. *Psychoneuroendocrinology, 31,* 1057–1061.

Morran, L. T., Schmidt, O. G., Gelarden, I. A., Parrish, R. C., 2nd, et al. (2011). Running with the Red Queen: Host-parasite coevolution selects for biparental sex. *Science, 333*(6039), 216–218.

Morris, B. (2002). Overcoming dyslexia. *Fortune, 145*(10), 1–7.

Morris, R. G., Halliwell, R. F., and Bowery, N. (1989). Synaptic plasticity and learning. II: Do different kinds of plasticity underlie different kinds of learning? *Neuropsychologia, 27,* 41–59.

Morrison, A. P., Turkington, D., Pyle, M., Spencer, H., et al. (2014). Cognitive therapy for people with schizophrenia spectrum disorders not taking antipsychotic drugs: A single-blind randomised controlled trial. *Lancet, 383,* 1395–1403.

Morrison, A. R. (1983). A window on the sleeping brain. *Scientific American, 248*(4), 94–102.

Morrison, A. R., Sanford, L. D., Ball, W. A., Mann, G. L., et al. (1995). Stimulus-elicited behavior in rapid eye movement sleep without atonia. *Behavioral Neuroscience, 109*(5), 972–979.

Morrison, J. H., and Hof, P. R. (2007). Life and death of neurons in the aging cerebral cortex. *International Review of Neurobiology, 81,* 41–57.

Mortenson, P. B., Pedersen, C. B., Westergaard, T., Wohlfahrt, J., et al. (1999). Effects of family history and place and season of birth on the risk of schizophrenia. *New England Journal of Medicine, 340,* 603–608.

Moruzzi, G. (1972). The sleep-waking cycle. *Ergebnisse der Physiologie, biologischen Chemie und experimentellen Pharmakologie, 64,* 1–165.

Moruzzi, G., and Magoun, H. W. (1949). Brain stem reticular formation and activation of the EEG. *Clinical Neurophysiology, 1,* 455–473.

Moscovitch, A., Blashko, C. A., Eagles, J. M., Darcourt, G., et al. (2004). A placebo-controlled study of sertraline in the treatment of outpatients with seasonal affective disorder. *Psychopharmacology (Berlin), 171,* 390–397.

Moscovitch, M. (1985). Memory from infancy to old age: Implications for theories of normal and pathological memory. *Annals of the New York Academy of Sciences, 444,* 78–96.

Mott, F. W. (1895). Experimental inquiry upon the afferent tracts of the central nervous system of the monkey. *Brain, 18,* 1–20.

Mountcastle, V. B. (1979). An organizing principle for cerebral function: The unit module and the distributed system. In F. O. Schmitt and F. G. Worden (Eds.), *The neurosciences: Fourth study program* (pp. 21–24). Cambridge, MA: MIT Press.

Mountcastle, V. B., Andersen, R. A., and Motter, B. C. (1981). The influence of attentive fixation upon the excitability of the light-sensitive neurons of the posterior parietal cortex. *Journal of Neuroscience, 1,* 1218–1235.

Mowry, B. J., Holmans, P. A., Pulver, A. E., Gejman, P. V., et al. (2004). Multicenter linkage study of schizophrenia loci on chromosome 22q. *Molecular Psychiatry, 9,* 784–795.

Muhlert, N., and Lawrence, A. D. (2015). Brain structure correlates of emotion-based rash impulsivity. *NeuroImage, 115,* 138–146.

Mukerji, S., Windsor, A. M., and Lee, D. J. (2010). Auditory brainstem circuits that mediate the middle ear muscle reflex. *Trends in Amplification, 14*(3), 170–191.

Mukhametov, L. M. (1984). Sleep in marine mammals. In A. Borbely and J. L. Valatx (Eds.), *Experimental Brain Research. Supplementum: 8. Sleep mechanisms.* Berlin: Springer.

Mumby, D. G. (2001). Perspectives on object-recognition memory following hippocampal damage: Lessons from studies in rats. *Behavioral Brain Research, 127*(1–2), 159–181.

Münte, T. F. (2002). Brains out of tune. *Nature, 415,* 589–590.

Münte, T. F., Altenmüller, E., and Jäncke, L. (2002). The musician's brain as a model of neuroplasticity. *Nature Reviews Neuroscience, 3,* 473–478.

Münte, T. F., Kohlmetz, C., Nager, W., and Altenmüller, E. (2001). Superior auditory spatial tuning in conductors. *Nature, 409,* 580.

Murphy, D. N., Boggio, P., and Fregni, F. (2009). Transcranial direct current stimulation as a therapeutic tool for the treatment of major depression: Insights from past and recent clinical studies. *Current Opinion in Psychiatry, 22,* 306–311.

Murphy, M. L., Slavich, G. M., Chen, E., and Miller, G. E. (2015). Targeted rejection predicts decreased anti-inflammatory gene expression and increased symptom severity in youth with asthma. *Psychological Science, 26,* 111–121.

Murray, R. M., Morrison, P. D., Henquet, C., and Di Forti, M. (2007). Cannabis, the mind and society: The hash realities. *Nature Reviews Neuroscience, 8,* 885–895.

Muthukrishna, M., and Henrich, J. (2016). Innovation in the collective brain. *Philosophical Transactions of the Royal Society of London. Series B: Biological Sciences, 371,* pii: 20150192. doi:10.1098/rstb.2015.0192

Myers, N. L. (2010). Culture, stress and recovery from schizophrenia: Lessons from the field for global mental health. *Culture, Medicine and Psychiatry, 34,* 500–528.

N

Nabavi, S., Fox, R., Proulx, C. D., Lin, J. Y., et al. (2014). Engineering a memory with LTD and LTP. *Nature, 511*(7509), 348–352.

Nader, K., and Hardt, O. (2009). A single standard for memory: The case for reconsolidation. *Nature Reviews Neuroscience, 10,* 224–234.

Naeser, M., Gaddie, A., Palumbo, C., and Stiassny-Eder, D. (1990). Late recovery of auditory comprehension in global aphasia. Improved recovery observed with subcortical temporal isthmus lesion vs. Wernicke's cortical area lesion. *Archives of Neurology, 47,* 425–432.

Naeser, M., and Hayward, R. (1978). Lesion localization in aphasia with cranial computed tomography and the Boston Diagnostic Aphasia Exam. *Neurology, 28,* 545–551.

Nagai, M., Re, D. B., Nagata, T., Chalazonitis, A., et al. (2007). Astrocytes expressing ALS-linked mutated SOD1 release factors selectively toxic to motor neurons. *Nature Neuroscience, 10*(5), 615–622.

Nair, K. S., Rizza, R. A., O'Brien, P., Dhatariya, K., et al. (2006). DHEA in elderly women and DHEA or testosterone in elderly men. *New England Journal of Medicine, 355,* 1647–1659.

Najmabadi, H., Hu, H. Garshasbi, M., Zemojtel, T., et al. (2011). Deep sequencing reveals 50 novel genes for recessive cognitive disorders. *Nature, 478,* 57–63.

Nakazato, M., Murakami, N., Date, Y., Kojima, M., et al. (2001). A role for ghrelin in the central regulation of feeding. *Nature, 409,* 194–198.

Namburi, P., Beyeler, A., Yorozu, S., Calhoon, G. G., et al. (2015). A circuit mechanism for differentiating positive and negative associations. *Nature, 520,* 675–678.

Naqvi, N. H., Rudrauf, D., Damasio, H., and Bechara, A. (2007). Damage to the insula disrupts addiction to cigarette smoking. *Science, 315,* 531–534.

Naselaris, T., Prenger, R. J., Kay, K. N., Oliver, M., et al. (2009). Bayesian reconstruction of natural images from human brain activity. *Neuron, 63*(6), 902–915.

Nation, E. F. (1973). William Osler on penis captivus and other urologic topics. *Urology, 2,* 468–470.

National Academy of Sciences. (2003). *The polygraph and lie detection.* Washington, DC: National Academies Press (www.nap.edu/openbook.php?isbn=0309084369).

Nature Neuroscience. (2015). Inhumane treatment of nonhuman primate researchers [Editorial]. *Nature Neuroscience, 18*(6), 787.

Nauhaus, I., Nielsen, K. J., Disney, A. A., and Callaway, E. M. (2012). Orthogonal micro-organization of orientation and spatial frequency in primate primary visual cortex. *Nature Neuroscience, 15,* 1683–1690.

Nave, K. A. (2010). Myelination and the trophic support of long axons. *Nature Reviews Neuroscience, 11*, 275–283.

Neale, G. (2006, December 3). Peter Singer: Monkey business. *Independent* (http://news.independent.co.uk/people/profiles/article2035119.ece).

Neary, M. T., and Batterham, R. L. (2009). Gut hormones: Implications for the treatment of obesity. *Pharmacology & Therapeutics, 124*, 44–56.

Neff, W. D., and Casseday, J. H. (1977). Effects of unilateral ablation of auditory cortex on monaural cat's ability to localize sound. *Journal of Neurophysiology, 40*, 44–52.

Neisser, U., and Becklen, R. (1975). Selective looking: Attending to visually specified events. *Cognitive Psychology, 7*, 480–494.

Neitz, M., Kraft, T. W., and Neitz, J. (1998). Expression of L cone pigment gene subtypes in females. *Vision Research, 38*(21), 3221–3225.

Neitz, M., and Neitz, J. (2014). Curing color blindness: Mice and nonhuman primates. *Cold Spring Harbor Perspectives in Medicine, 4*, a017418.

Nelissen, K., Luppino, G., Vanduffel, W., Rizzolatti, G., et al. (2005). Observing others: Multiple action representation in the frontal lobe. *Science, 310*, 332–336.

Nelson, G., Chandrashekar, J., Hoon, M. A., Feng, L., et al. (2002). An amino-acid taste receptor. *Nature, 416*, 199–202.

Nelson, G., Hoon, M. A., Chandrashekar, J., Zhang, Y., et al. (2001). Mammalian sweet taste receptors. *Cell, 106*, 381–390.

Nelson, R. J., Demas, G. E., Huang, P. L., Fishman, M. C., et al. (1995). Behavioural abnormalities in male mice lacking neuronal nitric oxide synthase. *Nature, 378*, 383–386.

Nestler, E. J., and Hyman, S. E. (2010). Animal models of neuropsychiatric disorders. *Nature Neuroscience, 13*, 1161–1169.

Nestor, A., Plaut, D. C., and Behrmann, M. (2016). Feature-based face representations and image reconstruction from behavioral and neural data. *Proceedings of the National Academy of Sciences, USA, 113*(2), 416–421.

Neumeister, A., Bain, E., Nugent, A. C., Carson, R. E., et al. (2004). Reduced serotonin type 1A receptor binding in panic disorder. *Journal of Neuroscience, 24*, 589–591.

Neves-Pereira, M., Mundo, E., Muglia, P., King, N., et al. (2002). The brain-derived neurotrophic factor gene confers susceptibility to bipolar disorder: Evidence from a family-based association study. *American Journal of Human Genetics, 71*, 651–655.

Neville, H. J., Bavelier, D., Corina, D., Rauschecker, J., et al. (1998). Cerebral organization for language in deaf and hearing subjects: Biological constraints and effects of experience. *Proceedings of the National Academy of Sciences, USA, 95*, 922–929.

Neville, H. J., Mills, D. L., and Lawson, D. S. (1992). Fractionating language: Different neural subsystems with different sensitive periods. *Cerebral Cortex, 2*, 244–258.

Newsome, W. T., Wurtz, R. H., Dursteler, M. R., and Mikami, A. (1985). Deficits in visual motion processing following ibotenic acid lesions of the middle temporal visual area of the macaque monkey. *Journal of Neuroscience, 5*, 825–840.

Ng, S. F., Lin, R. C., Laybutt, D. R., Barres, R., et al. (2010). Chronic high-fat diet in fathers programs β-cell dysfunction in female rat offspring. *Nature, 467*(7318), 963–966.

Ngandu, T., Lehtisalo, J., Solomon, A., Levälahti, E., et al. (2015). A 2 year multidomain intervention of diet, exercise, cognitive training, and vascular risk monitoring versus control to prevent cognitive decline in at-risk elderly people (FINGER): A randomised controlled trial. *Lancet, 385*(9984), 2255–2263.

Nichols, M. J., and Newsome, W. T. (1999). The neurobiology of cognition. *Nature, 402*, C35–C38.

Niel, L., Shah, A. H., Lewis, G. A., Mo, K., et al. (2009). Sexual differentiation of the spinal nucleus of the bulbocavernosus is not mediated solely by androgen receptors in muscle fibers. *Endocrinology, 150*, 3207–3213.

Nielsen, H. H., Qiu, J., Friis, S., Wermuth, L., et al. (2012). Treatment for Helicobacter pylori infection and risk of Parkinson's disease in Denmark. *European Journal of Neurology, 19*(6), 864-869.

Nietzel, M. T. (2000). Police psychology. In A. E. Kazdin (Ed.), *Encyclopedia of psychology* (Vol. 6, pp. 224–226). Washington, DC: American Psychological Association.

Nishida, M., and Walker, M. P. (2007). Daytime naps, motor memory consolidation and regionally specific sleep spindles. *PLOS ONE, 2*, e341.

Nishimoto, S., Vu, A. T., Naselaris, T., Benjamini, Y., et al. (2011). Reconstructing visual experiences from brain activity evoked by natural movies. *Current Biology, 21*(19), 1641–1646.

Nitz, D. A., Van Swinderen, B., Tononi, G., and Greenspan, R. J. (2002). Electrophysiological correlates of rest and activity in *Drosophila melanogaster*. *Current Biology, 12*, 1934–1940.

Nixon, K., and Crews, F. T. (2002). Binge ethanol exposure decreases neurogenesis in adult rat hippocampus. *Journal of Neurochemistry, 83*, 1087–1093.

Noad, M. J., Cato, D. H., Bryden, M. M., Jenner, M.-N., et al. (2000). Cultural revolution in whale songs. *Nature, 408*, 537–538.

Nobre, A. C., Sebestyen, G. N., Gitelman, D. R., Mesulam, M. M., et al. (1997). Functional localization of the system for visuospatial attention using positron emission tomography. *Brain, 120*, 515–533.

Nordeen, E. J., Nordeen, K. W., Sengelaub, D. R., and Arnold, A. P. (1985). Androgens prevent normally occurring cell death in a sexually dimorphic spinal nucleus. *Science, 229*, 671–673.

Norenzayan, A., Shariff, A. F., Gervais, W. M., Willard, A. K., et al. (2016). Parochial prosocial religions: Historical and contemporary evidence for a cultural evolutionary process. *Behavioral and Brain Sciences, 39*, e29.

Norton, T. T., and Siegwart, J. T., Jr. (2013). Light levels, refractive development, and myopia: A speculative review. *Experimental Eye Research, 114*, 48–57.

Nottebohm, F. (1980). Brain pathways for vocal learning in birds: A review of the first 10 years. *Progress in Psychobiology and Physiological Psychology, 9*, 85–124.

Nottebohm, F., and Arnold, A. P. (1976). Sexual dimorphism in vocal control areas of the songbird brain. *Science, 194*, 211–213.

NRC Committee on Animals as Monitors of Environmental Hazards. (1991). *Animals as sentinels of environmental health hazards.* Washington, DC: National Academy Press.

Nudo, R. J., Milliken, G. W., Jenkins, W. M., and Merzenich, M. M. (1996). Use-dependent alterations of movement representations in primary motor cortex of adult squirrel monkeys. *Journal of Neuroscience, 16*, 785–807.

Numan, M., and Numan. M. J. (1991). Preoptic-brainstem connections and maternal behavior in rats. *Behavioral Neuroscience, 105*, 1010–1029.

Nutt, D. J., Lingford-Hughes, A., Erritzoe, D., and Stokes, P. R. (2015). The dopamine theory of addiction: 40 years of highs and lows. *Nature Reviews Neuroscience, 16*, 305–312.

O

O'Brien, C. P., Childress, A. R., Ehrman, R., and Robbins, S. J. (1998). Conditioning factors in drug abuse: Can they explain compulsion? *Journal of Psychopharmacology*, *12*, 15–22.

O'Connell-Rodwell, C. E. (2007). Keeping an "ear" to the ground: Seismic communication in elephants. *Physiology (Bethesda)*, *22*, 287–294.

O'Connor, D. B., Archer, J., and Wu, F. C. (2004). Effects of testosterone on mood, aggression, and sexual behavior in young men: A double-blind, placebo-controlled, cross-over study. *Journal of Clinical Endocrinology & Metabolism*, *89*, 2837–2845.

O'Craven, K. M., Downing, P. E., and Kanwisher, N. (1999). fMRI evidence for objects as the units of attentional selection. *Nature*, *401*, 584–587.

O'Keefe, J., and Dostrovsky, J. (1971). The hippocampus as a spatial map. Preliminary evidence from unit activity in the freely-moving rat. *Brain Research, 34*, 171–175.

Oades, R. D., and Halliday, G. M. (1987). Ventral tegmental (A10) system: Neurobiology. 1. Anatomy and connectivity. *Brain Research Reviews, 12*, 117–165.

Oberlander, T. F., Papsdorf, M., Brain, U. M., Misri, S., et al. (2010). Prenatal effects of selective serotonin reuptake inhibitor antidepressants, serotonin transporter promoter genotype (SLC6A4), and maternal mood on child behavior at 3 years of age. *Archives of Pediatric & Adolescent Medicine, 164*, 444–451.

Obernier, J. A., White, A. M., Swartzwelder, H. S., and Crews, F. T. (2002). Cognitive deficits and CNS damage after a 4-day binge ethanol exposure in rats. *Pharmacology, Biochemistry and Behavior, 72*, 521–532.

Ogden, J. (2012). *Health psychology.* New York: Open University Press.

Ohno, K., and Sakurai, T. (2008). Orexin neuronal circuitry: Role in the regulation of sleep and wakefulness. *Frontiers in Neuroendocrinology, 29*, 70–87.

Ojemann, G. A., and Whitaker, H. A. (1978). The bilingual brain. *Archives of Neurology, 35*, 409–412.

Oka, Y., Butnaru, M., von Buchholtz, L., Ryba, N. J., et al. (2013). High salt recruits aversive taste pathways. *Nature, 494*(7438), 472–475.

Oka, Y., Ye, M., and Zuker, C. S. (2015). Thirst driving and suppressing signals encoded by distinct neural populations in the brain. *Nature, 520*, 349–352.

Okano, H., Ogawa, Y., Nakamura, M., Kaneko, S., et al. (2003). Transplantation of neural stem cells into the spinal cord after injury. *Seminars in Cell and Developmental Biology, 14*, 191–198.

Olanow, C. W., Goetz, C. G., Kordower, J. H., Stoessl, A. J., et al. (2003). A double-blind controlled trial of bilateral fetal nigral transplantation in Parkinson's disease. *Annals of Neurology, 54*, 403–414.

Olatunji, B. O., Davis, M. L., Powers, M. B., and Smits, J. A. (2013). Cognitive-behavioral therapy for obsessive-compulsive disorder: A meta-analysis of treatment outcome and moderators. *Journal of Psychiatric Research, 47*(1), 33–41.

Olds, J., and Milner, P. (1954). Positive reinforcement produced by electrical stimulation of septal area and other regions of the rat brain. *Journal of Comparative and Physiological Psychology, 47*, 419–427.

Oler, J. A., Fox, A. S., Shelton, S. E., Rogers, J., et al. (2010). Amygdalar and hippocampal substrates of anxious temperament differ in their heritability. *Nature, 466*, 864–868.

Olfson, M., Marcus, S. C., and Shaffer, D. (2006). Antidepressant drug therapy and suicide in severely depressed children and adults: A case-control study. *Archives of General Psychiatry, 63*, 865–872.

Olsen, E. M., Heino, M., Lilly, G. R., Morgan, M. J., et al. (2004). Maturation trends indicative of rapid evolution preceded the collapse of northern cod. *Nature, 428*, 899–900.

Olsen, K. L. (1979). Androgen-insensitive rats are defeminised by their testes. *Nature, 279*, 238–239.

Olson, S. (2004). Making sense of Tourette's. *Science, 305*, 1390–1392.

Olsson, A., and Phelps, E. A. (2007). Social learning of fear. *Nature Neuroscience, 10*, 1095–1102.

Oman, C. M. (2012). Are evolutionary hypotheses for motion sickness "just-so" stories? *Journal of Vestibular Research, 22*(2), 117–127.

Opendak, M., and Gould, E. (2015). Adult neurogenesis: A substrate for experience-dependent change. Trends in Cognitive Sciences, *19*(3), 151–161. doi:10.1016/j.tics.2015.01.001

Ophir, A. G., Phelps, S. M., Sorin, A. B., and Wolff, J. O. (2008). Social but not genetic monogamy is associated with greater breeding success in prairie voles. *Animal Behavior, 75*, 1143–1154.

Orive, G., Anitua, E., Pedraz, J. L., and Emerich, D. F. (2009). Biomaterials for promoting brain protection, repair and regeneration. *Nature Reviews Neuroscience, 10*, 682–692.

Oroszi, G., Anton, R. F., O'Malley, S., Swift, R., et al. (2009). OPRM1 Asn40Asp predicts response to naltrexone treatment: A haplotype-based approach. *Alcoholism: Clinical and Experimental Research, 33*, 383–393.

Orson, F. M., Wang, R., Brimijoin, S., Kinsey, B. M., et al. (2014). The future potential for cocaine vaccines. *Expert Opinion on Biological Therapy, 14*, 1271–1283.

Ortigue, S., Grafton, S. T., and Bianchi-Demicheli, F. (2007). Correlation between insula activation and self-reported quality of orgasm in women. *Neuroimage, 37*(2), 551–560.

Ossenkoppele, R., Schonhaut, D. R., Schöll, M., Lockhart, S. N., et al. (2016). Tau PET patterns mirror clinical and neuroanatomical variability in Alzheimer's disease. *Brain, 139*(Pt. 5), 1551–1567.

Osterhout, L. (1997). On the brain response to syntactic anomalies: Manipulations of word position and word class reveal individual differences. *Brain and Language, 59*, 494–522.

Ostrovsky, Y., Meyers, E., Ganesh, S., Mathur, U., et al. (2009). Visual parsing after recovery from blindness. *Psychological Science, 20*, 1484–1491.

Ostrovsky, Y., Meyers, E., Ganesh, S., Mathur, U., et al. (2009). Visual parsing after recovery from blindness. *Psychological Science, 20*, 1484–1491.

Ouattara, K., Lemasson, A., and Zuberbühler, K. (2009). Campbell's monkeys concatenate vocalizations into context-specific call sequences. *Proceedings of the National Academy of Sciences, USA, 22*, 22026–22031.

Overstreet, D. H. (1993). The Flinders sensitive line rats: A genetic animal model of depression. *Neuroscience and Biobehavioral Reviews, 17*, 51–68.

Owen, A. M., Coleman, M. R., Boly, M., Davis, M. H., et al. (2006). Detecting awareness in the vegetative state. *Science, 313*, 1402.

P

Pack, A. I. (2003). Should a pharmaceutical be approved for the broad indication of excessive sleepiness? *American Journal of Respiratory and Critical Care Medicine, 167*, 109–111.

Paddock, R. C., and La Ganga, M. (2008, August 5). Officials decry attacks on UC staff. *Los Angeles Times* (http://articles.latimes.com/2008/aug/05/local/me-attacks5).

Pagel, J. F., and Helfter, P. (2003). Drug induced nightmares: An etiology based review. *Human Psychopharmacology, 18*, 59–67.

Pagel, M., Atkinson, Q. D., Calude, A. S., and Meade, A. (2013). Ultraconserved words point to deep language ancestry across Eurasia. *Proceedings of the National Academy of Sciences, USA, 110*(21), 8471–8476.

Paik, S.-B., and Ringach, D. L. (2011). Retinal origin of orientation maps in visual cortex. *Nature Neuroscience, 14*, 919–925.

Palmer, T. D., Schwartz, P. H., Taupin, P., Kaspar, B., et al. (2001). Progenitor cells from human brain after death. *Nature, 411*, 42–43.

Panksepp, J. (1998). *Affective neuroscience.* New York: Oxford University Press.

Panksepp, J. (2005). Beyond a joke: From animal laughter to human joy? *Science, 308*, 62–63.

Panksepp, J. (2007). Neuroevolutionary sources of laughter and social joy: Modeling primal human laughter in laboratory rats. *Behavioural Brain Research, 182*, 231–244.

Panowski, S. H., Wolff, S., Aguilaniu, H., Durieux, J., et al. (2007). PHA-4/Foxa mediates diet-restriction-induced longevity of C. elegans. *Nature, 447*, 550–555.

Pantev, C., Oostenveld, R., Engelien, A., Ross, B., et al. (1998). Increased auditory cortical representation in musicians. *Nature, 392*, 811–814.

Papez, J. W. (1937). A proposed mechanism of emotion. *Archives of Neurology and Psychiatry, 38*, 725–745.

Papka, M., Ivry, R., and Woodruff-Pak, D. S. (1994). Eyeblink classical conditioning and time production in patients with cerebellar damage. *Society of Neuroscience Abstracts, 20*, 360.

Pare, M., Behets, C., and Cornu, O. (2003). Paucity of presumptive ruffini corpuscles in the index finger pad of humans. *Journal of Comparative Neurology, 456*, 260–266.

Park, D. C., Lautenschlager, G., Hedden, T., Davidson, N. S., et al. (2002). Models of visuospatial and verbal memory across the adult life span. *Psychology of Aging, 17*, 299–320.

Park, H., and Poo, M. M. (2013). Neurotrophin regulation of neural circuit development and function. *Nature Reviews Neuroscience, 14*(1), 7–23. doi:10.1038/nrn3379

Park, S., Como, P. G., Cui, L., and Kurlan, R. (1993). The early course of the Tourette's syndrome clinical spectrum. *Neurology, 43*, 1712–1715.

Parker, G., Cahill, L., and McGaugh, J. L. (2006). A case of unusual autobiographical remembering. *Neurocase, 12*, 35–49.

Parkes, J. D. (1985). *Sleep and its disorders.* Philadelphia: Saunders.

Parnavelas, J. G., Anderson, S. A., Lavdas, A. A., Grigoriou, M., et al. (2000). The contribution of the ganglionic eminence to the neuronal cell types of the cerebral cortex. *Novartis Foundation Symposium, 228*, 129–139; discussion 139–147.

Parrott, A. C. (2013). Human psychobiology of MDMA or "Ecstasy": An overview of 25 years of empirical research. *Human Psychopharmacology, 28*, 289–307.

Parrott, A. C. (2014). The potential dangers of using MDMA for psychotherapy. *Journal of Psychoactive Drugs, 46*, 37–43.

Parsons, L. H., and Hurd, Y. L. (2015). Endocannabinoid signalling in reward and addiction. *Nature Reviews Neuroscience, 16*, 579–594.

Parton, L. E., Ye, C. P., Coppari, R., Enriori, P. J., et al. (2007). Glucose sensing by POMC neurons regulates glucose homeostasis and is impaired in obesity. *Nature, 449*, 228–232.

Pastalkova, E., Itskov, V., Amarasingham, A., and Buzsáki, G. (2008). Internally generated cell assembly sequences in the rat hippocampus. *Science, 321*(5894),1322–1327.

Paterson, S. J., Brown, J. H., Gsödl, M. K., Johnson, M. H., et al. (1999). Cognitive modularity and genetic disorders. *Science, 286*, 2355–2358.

Patterson, F., and Linden, E. (1981). *The education of Koko.* New York: Holt, Rinehart, and Winston.

Patterson, P. H. (2007). Maternal effects on schizophrenia risk. *Science, 318*, 576–578.

Paulesu, E., McCrory, E., Fazio, F., Menoncello, L., et al. (2000). A cultural effect on brain function. *Nature Neuroscience, 3*, 91–96.

Pauls, D. L. (2003). An update on the genetics of Gilles de la Tourette syndrome. *Journal of Psychosomatic Research, 55*, 7–12.

Pauls, D. L., Abramovitch, A., Rauch, S. L., and Geller, D. A. (2014). Obsessive-compulsive disorder: An integrative genetic and neurobiological perspective. *Nature Reviews Neuroscience, 15*, 410–424.

Paus, T., Kalina, M., Patocková, L., Angerová, Y., et al. (1991). Medial vs lateral frontal lobe lesions and differential impairment of central-gaze fixation maintenance in man. *Brain, 114*, 2051–2067.

Paus, T., Keshavan, M., and Giedd, J. N. (2008). Why do many psychiatric disorders emerge during adolescence? *Nature Reviews Neuroscience, 9*, 947–956.

Pearson, R. A., Barber, A. C., Rizzi, M., Hippert, C., et al. (2012). Restoration of vision after transplantation of photoreceptors. *Nature, 485*, 99–103.

Pecho-Vrieseling, E., Rieker, C., Fuchs, S., Bleckmann, D., et al. (2014). Transneuronal propagation of mutant huntingtin contributes to non-cell autonomous pathology in neurons. *Nature Neuroscience, 17*(8), 1064–1072.

Pedersen, C. B., and Mortensen, P. B. (2001). Evidence of a dose-response relationship between urbanicity during upbringing and schizophrenia risk. *Archives of General Psychiatry, 58*, 1039–1046.

Pediatric Eye Disease Investigator Group. (2005). Randomized trial of treatment of amblyopia in children aged 7 to 17 years. *Archives of Ophthalmology, 13*, 437–447.

Pedreira, C., Mormann, F., Kraskov, A., Cerf, M., et al. (2010). Responses of human medial temporal lobe neurons are modulated by stimulus repetition. *Journal of Neurophysiology, 103*, 97–107.

Pegna, A. J., Khateb, A., Lazeyras, F., and Seghier, M. L. (2005). Discriminating emotional faces without primary visual cortices involves the right amygdala. *Nature Neuroscience, 8*, 24–25.

Pelvig, D. P., Pakkenberg, H., Stark, A. K., and Pakkenberg, B. (2008). Neocortical glial cell numbers in human brains. *Neurobiology of Aging, 29*, 1754–1762.

Peñagarikano, O., Lázaro, M. T., Lu, X. H., Gordon, A., et al. (2015). Exogenous and evoked oxytocin restores social behavior in the *Cntnap2* mouse model of autism. *Science Translational Medicine, 7*(271), 271ra8.

Penfield, W., and Rasmussen, T. (1950). *The cerebral cortex in man.* New York: Macmillan.

Penfield, W., and Roberts, L. (1959). *Speech and brain-mechanisms.* Princeton, NJ: Princeton University Press.

Peng, Y., Gillis-Smith, S., Jin, H., Tränkner, D., et al. (2015). Sweet and bitter taste in the brain of awake behaving animals. *Nature, 527*(7579), 512–515.

Pennisi, E. (2003). Systems biology: Tracing life's circuitry. *Science, 302*, 1646–1649.

Pennisi, E. (2012). Genomics. ENCODE project writes eulogy for junk DNA. *Science, 337*(6099), 1159, 1161. doi:10.1126/science.337.6099.1159

Peplau, L. A. (2003). Human sexuality: How do men and women differ? *Current Directions in Psychological Science, 12*, 37–40.

Perani, D., and Abutalebi, J. (2005). The neural basis of first and second language processing. *Current Opinion in Neurobiology, 15*, 202–206.

Perea, G., Navarrete, M., and Araque, A. (2009). Tripartite synapses: Astrocytes process and control synaptic information. *Trends in Neuroscience, 32*, 421–431.

Pereda, A. E. (2014). Electrical synapses and their functional interactions with chemical synapses. *Nature Reviews Neuroscience, 15*(4), 250–263.

Perenin, M. T., and Vighetto, A. (1988). Optic ataxia: A specific disruption in visuomotor mechanisms. I. Different aspects of the deficit in reaching for objects. *Brain, 111*, 643–674.

Peretz, I., and Hyde, K. L. (2003). What is specific to music processing? Insights from congenital amusia. *Trends in Cognitive Sciences, 7*, 362–367.

Perilloux, C., Easton, J. A., and Buss, D. M. (2012). The misperception of sexual interest. *Psychological Science, 23*(2), 146–151.

Peris, J., Boyson, S. J., Cass, W. A., Curella, P., et al. (1990). Persistence of neurochemical changes in dopamine systems after repeated cocaine administration. *Journal of Pharmacology and Experimental Therapeutics, 253*, 38–44.

Pernía-Andrade, A. J., Kato, A., Witschi, R., Nyilas, R., et al. (2009). Spinal endocannabinoids and CB_1 receptors mediate C-fiber–induced heterosynaptic pain sensitization. *Science, 325*, 760–764.

Perrachione, T. K., Del Tufo, S. N., and Gabrieli, J. D. (2011). Human voice recognition depends on language ability. *Science, 333*, 595.

Perrin, J. S., Merz, S., Bennett, D. M., Currie, J., et al. (2012). Electroconvulsive therapy reduces frontal cortical connectivity in severe depressive disorder. *Proceedings of the National Academy of Sciences, USA, 109*, 5464–5468.

Perrin, S. (2014). Preclinical research: Make mouse studies work. *Nature, 507*(7493), 423–425.

Perry, V. H., and Holmes, C. (2014). Microglial priming in neurodegenerative disease. *Nature Reviews Neurology, 10*(4), 217–224.

Pertwee, R. G. (1997). Pharmacology of cannabinoid CB1 and CB2 receptors. *Pharmacology & Therapeutics, 74*, 129–180.

Peschansky, V. J., Burbridge, T. J., Volz, A. J., Fiondella, C., et al. (2010). The effect of variation in expression of the candidate dyslexia susceptibility gene homolog Kiaa0319 on neuronal migration and dendritic morphology in the rat. *Cerebral Cortex, 20*, 884–897.

Petanjek, Z., Judaš, M., Šimic, G., Rasin, M. R., et al. (2011). Extraordinary neoteny of synaptic spines in the human prefrontal cortex. *Proceedings of the National Academy of Sciences, USA, 108*(32), 13281–13286.

Peterhans, E., and von der Heydt, R. (1989). Mechanisms of contour perception in monkey visual cortex. II. Contours bridging gaps. *Journal of Neuroscience, 9*, 1749–1763.

Peters, A., Palay, S. L., and Webster, H. deF. (1991). *The fine structure of the nervous system: Neurons and their supporting cells* (3rd ed.). New York: Oxford University Press.

Petersen, J. L., and Hyde, J. S. (2011). Gender differences in sexual attitudes and behaviors: A review of meta-analytic results and large datasets. *Journal of Sex Research, 48*(2–3), 149–165.

Peterson, B. S., Warner, V., Bansal, R., Zhu, H., et al. (2009). Cortical thinning in persons at increased familial risk for major depression. *Proceedings of the National Academy of Sciences, USA, 106*, 6273–6278.

Peterson, L. R., and Peterson, M. J. (1959). Short-term retention of individual verbal items. *Journal of Experimental Psychology, 58*, 193–198.

Petit, C., and Richardson, G. P. (2009). Linking genes underlying deafness to hair-bundle development and function. *Nature Neuroscience, 12*, 703–710.

Petit, D., Pennestri, M. H., Paquet, J., Desautels, A., et al. (2015). Childhood sleepwalking and sleep terrors: A longitudinal study of prevalence and familial aggregation. *JAMA Pediatrics, 169*(7), 653–658.

Petitto, L. A., Berens, M. S., Kovelman, I., Dubins, M. H., et al. (2012). The "Perceptual Wedge Hypothesis" as the basis for bilingual babies' phonetic processing advantage: New insights from fNIRS brain imaging. *Brain and Language, 121*(2), 130–143.

Petitto, L. A., Zatorre, R. J., Gauna, K., Nikelski, E. J., et al. (2000). Speech-like cerebral activity in profoundly deaf people processing signed languages: Implications for the neural basis of human language. *Proceedings of the National Academy of Sciences, USA, 97*, 13961–13966.

Petrelli, F., Pucci, L., and Bezzi, P. (2016). Astrocytes and microglia and their potential link with autism spectrum disorders. *Frontiers in Cellular Neuroscience, 10*, 21. doi:10.3389/fncel.2016.00021

Petrides, M., and Milner, B. (1982). Deficits on subject-ordered tasks after frontal- and temporal-lobe lesions in man. *Neuropsychologia, 20*, 249–262.

Petrof, E. O., Gloor, G. B., Vanner, S. J., Weese, S. J., et al. (2013). Stool substitute transplant therapy for the eradication of *Clostridium difficile* infection: "RePOOPulating" the gut. *Microbiome, 1*, 3.

Petrovic, P., Kalso, E., Petersson, K. M., and Ingvar, M. (2002). Placebo and opioid analgesia imaging: A shared neuronal network. *Science, 295*, 1737–1740.

Pettit, H. O., and Justice, J. B., Jr. (1991). Effect of dose on cocaine self-administration behavior and dopamine levels in the nucleus accumbens. *Brain Research, 539*, 94–102.

Petty, F., Kramer, G., Wilson, L., and Jordan, S. (1994). In vivo serotonin release and learned helplessness. *Psychiatry Research, 52*, 285–293.

Pfaff, D. W. (1980). *Estrogens and brain function: Neural analysis of a hormone-controlled mammalian reproductive behavior.* New York: Springer.

Pfaff, D. W. (1997). Hormones, genes, and behavior. *Proceedings of the National Academy of Sciences, USA, 94*, 14213–14216.

Pfaus, J. G., Damsma, G., Nomikos, G. G., Wenkstern, D. G., et al. (1990). Sexual behavior enhances central dopamine transmission in the male rat. *Brain Research, 530*(2), 345–348.

Pfaus, J. G., Kippin, T. E., and Centeno, S. (2001). Conditioning and sexual behavior: A review. *Hormones and Behavior, 40*, 291–321.

Pfefferbaum, A., Sullivan, E. V., Mathalon, D. H., Shear, P. K., et al. (1995). Longitudinal changes in magnetic resonance imaging brain volumes in abstinent and relapsed alcoholics. *Alcoholism: Clinical and Experimental Research, 19*, 1177–1191.

Pfenning, A. R., Hara, E., Whitney, O., Rivas, M. V., et al. (2014). Convergent transcriptional specializations in the brains of humans and song-learning birds. *Science, 346*(6215). doi:10.1126/science.1256846

Pfrieger, F. W., and Barres, B. A. (1997). Synaptic efficacy enhanced by glial cells in vitro. *Science, 277*, 1684–1687.

Philips, T., and Rothstein, J. D. (2015). Rodent models of amyotrophic lateral sclerosis. *Current Protocols in Pharmacology, 69*, 5.67.1–5.67.21. *doi:10.1002/0471141755.ph0567s69*

Phillips, J. R., Johansson, R. S., and Johnson, K. O. (1990). Representation of braille characters in human nerve fibres. *Experimental Brain Research, 81*, 589–592.

Phoenix, C. H., Goy, R. W., Gerall, A. A., and Young, W. C. (1959). Organizing action of prenatally administered testosterone propionate on the tissues mediating mating behavior in the female guinea pig. *Endocrinology, 65*, 369–382.

Picard, N., Matsuzaka, Y., and Strick, P. L. (2013). Extended practice of a motor skill is associated with reduced metabolic activity in M1. *Nature Neuroscience, 16*(9), 1340–1347.

Pickens, R., and Thompson, T. (1968). Drug use by U.S. Army enlisted men in Vietnam: A followup on their return home. *Journal of Pharmacology and Experimental Therapeutics, 161*, 122–129.

Pietrobon, D., and Moskowitz, M. A. (2014). Chaos and commotion in the wake of cortical spreading depression and spreading depolarizations. *Nature Reviews Neuroscience, 15*(6), 379–393.

Pinel, P., Fauchereau, F., Moreno, A., Barbot, A., et al. (2012). Genetic variants of FOXP2 and KIAA0319/TTRAP/THEM2 locus are associated with altered brain activation in distinct language-related regions. *Journal of Neuroscience, 32*(3), 817–825.

Pines, J. (1992). Cell proliferation and control. *Current Opinion in Cell Biology, 4*(2), 144–148.

Pinker, S. (1994). *The language instinct.* New York: Morrow.

Pinker, S., and Jackendoff, R. (2005). The faculty of language: What's special about it? *Cognition, 95*, 201–236.

Pirastu, N., Kooyman, M., Traglia, M., Robino, A., et al. (2016, April 30). Genome-Wide Association Study in isolated populations reveals new genes associated to common food likings. *Reviews in Endocrine and Metabolic Disorders.* doi:10.1007/s11154-016-9354-3 [Epub ahead of print]

Pitman, R. K., Sanders, K. M., Zusman, R. M., Healy, A. R., et al. (2002). Pilot study of secondary prevention of posttraumatic stress disorder with propranolol. *Biological Psychiatry, 51*, 189–192.

Pleim, E. T., and Barfield, R. J. (1988). Progesterone versus estrogen facilitation of female sexual behavior by intracranial administration to female rats. *Hormones and Behavior, 22*, 150–159.

Pletnikov, M. V., Ayhan, Y., Nikolskaia, O., Xu, Y., et al. (2008). Inducible expression of mutant human DISC1 in mice is associated with brain and behavioral abnormalities reminiscent of schizophrenia. *Molecular Psychiatry, 13*, 13–186.

Ploog, D. W. (1992). Neuroethological perspectives on the human brain: From the expression of emotions to intentional signing and speech. In A. Harrington (Ed.), *So human a brain: Knowledge and values in the neurosciences* (pp. 3–13). Boston: Birkhauser.

Plutchik, R. (1994). *The psychology and biology of emotion.* New York: HarperCollins.

Polleux, F., Morrow, T., and Ghosh, A. (2000). Semaphorin 3A is a chemoattractant for cortical apical dendrites. *Nature, 404*, 567–573.

Polymeropoulos, M. H., Lavedan, C., Leroy, E., Ide, S. E., et al. (1997). Mutation in the alpha-synuclein gene identified in families with Parkinson's disease. *Science, 276*, 2045–2047.

Pompili, M., Serafini, G., Innamorati, M., Möller-Leimkühler, A. M., et al. (2010). The hypothalamic-pituitary-adrenal axis and serotonin abnormalities: A selective overview for the implications of suicide prevention. *European Archives of Psychiatry and Clinical Neuroscience, 260*, 583–600.

Ponsford, J. (2005). Rehabilitation interventions after mild head injury. *Current Opinion in Neurology, 18*, 692–697.

Poole, J. H., Tyack, P. L., Stoeger-Horwath, A. S., and Watwood, S. (2005). Animal behaviour: Elephants are capable of vocal learning. *Nature, 434*, 455–456.

Pooresmaeili, A., FitzGerald, T. H., Bach, D. R., Toelch, U., et al. (2014). Cross-modal effects of value on perceptual acuity and stimulus encoding. *Proceedings of the National Academy of Sciences, USA, 111*(42), 15244–15249.

Pope, H. G., Jr., Kouri, E. M., and Hudson, J. I. (2000). Effects of supraphysiologic doses of testosterone on mood and aggression in normal men: A randomized controlled trial. *Archives of General Psychiatry, 57*, 133–140.

Poremba, A., Malloy, M., Saunders, R. C., Carson, R. E., et al. (2004). Species-specific calls evoke asymmetric activity in the monkey's temporal poles. *Nature, 427*, 448–451.

Poritsky, R. (1969). Two and three dimensional ultrastructure of boutons and glial cells on the motoneuronal surface in the cat spinal cord. *Journal of Comparative Neurology, 135*, 423–452.

Porta, M., Brambilla, A., Cavanna, A. E., Servello, D., et al. (2009). Thalamic deep brain stimulation for treatment-refractory Tourette syndrome: Two-year outcome. *Neurology, 73*, 1375–1380.

Porter, J., Craven, B., Khan, R. H., Chang, S.-J., et al. (2007). Mechanisms of scent-tracking in humans. *Nature Neuroscience, 10*, 27–29.

Posner, M. I. (1980). Orienting of attention. *Quarterly Journal of Experimental Psychology, 32*, 3–25.

Posner, M. I., and Cohen, Y. (1984). Components of visual orienting. In H. Bouma and D. Bowhuis (Eds.), *Attention and performance: Vol 10. Control of language processes* (pp. 531–556). Hillsdale, NJ: Erlbaum.

Posner, M. I., and Raichle, M. E. (1994). *Images of mind.* New York: Scientific American Library.

Posthuma, D., De Geus, E. J. C., Baaré, W. F. C., Hulshoff Pol, H. E., et al. (2002). The association between brain volume and intelligence is of genetic origin. *Nature Neuroscience, 5*, 83–84.

Postuma, R. B., Gagnon, J. F., Vendette, M., Fantini, M. L., et al. (2009). Quantifying the risk of neurodegenerative disease in idiopathic REM sleep behavior disorder. *Neurology, 72*, 1296–1300.

Poulet, J. F. A., and Petersen, C. C. H. (2008). Internal brain state regulates membrane potential synchrony in barrel cortex of behaving mice. *Nature, 454*, 881–885.

Poulos, A. M., and Thompson, R. F. (2015). Localization and characterization of an essential associative memory trace in the mammalian brain. *Brain Research, 1621*, 252–259.

Powell, S. B. (2010). Models of neurodevelopmental abnormalities in schizophrenia. *Current Topics in Behavioral Neurosciences, 4*, 435–481.

Power, R. A., Steinberg, S., Bjornsdottir, G., Rietveld, C. A., et al. (2015). Polygenic risk scores for schizophrenia and bipolar disorder predict creativity. *Nature Neuroscience, 18*, 953–955.

Powers, R. J., Roy, S., Atilgan, E., Brownell, W. E., et al. (2012). Stereocilia membrane deformation: Implications for the gating spring and mechanotransduction channel. *Biophysical Journal, 102*(2), 201–210.

Powley, T. L. (2000). Vagal circuitry mediating cephalic-phase responses to food. *Appetite, 34*, 184–188.

Premack, D. (1971). Language in a chimpanzee? *Science, 172*, 808–822.

Price, J. (2008). *The woman who can't forget.* New York: Free Press.

Price, J., Kerr, R., Hicks, M., and Nixon, P. F. (1987). The Wernicke-Korsakoff syndrome: A reappraisal in Queensland with special reference to prevention. *Medical Journal of Australia, 147*(11–12), 561–565.

Price, M. A., and Vandenbergh, J. G. (1992). Analysis of puberty-accelerating pheromones. *Journal of Experimental Zoology, 264,* 42–45.

Pruszynski, J. A., and Johansson, R. S. (2014). Edge-orientation processing in first-order tactile neurons. *Nature Neuroscience, 17*(10), 1404–1409.

Ptáček, L. J. (2015). Episodic disorders: Channelopathies and beyond. *Annual Review of Physiology, 77,* 475–479.

Pugh, E. N., Jr., and Lamb, T. D. (1990). Cyclic GMP and calcium: The internal messengers of excitation and adaptation in vertebrate photoreceptors. *Vision Research, 30,* 1923–1948.

Pugh, E. N., Jr., and Lamb, T. D. (1993). Amplification and kinetics of the activation steps in phototransduction. *Biochimica et Biophysica Acta, 1141,* 111–149.

Pugh, K. R., Mencl, W. E., Shaywitz, B. A., Shaywitz, S. E., et al. (2000). The angular gyrus in developmental dyslexia: Task-specific differences in functional connectivity within posterior cortex. *Psychological Science, 11,* 51–56.

Puighermanal, E., Busquets-Garcia, A., Maldonado, R., and Ozaita, A. (2012). Cellular and intracellular mechanisms involved in the cognitive impairment of cannabinoids. *Philosophical Transactions of the Royal Society of London. Series B: Biological Sciences, 367,* 3254–3263.

Pulvermüller, F., and Fadiga, L. (2010). Active perception: Sensorimotor circuits as a cortical basis for language. *Nature Reviews Neuroscience, 11*(5), 351–360.

Purves, D., Augustine, G. J., Fitzpatrick, D., LaMantia, A.-S., et al. (Eds.). (2017). *Neuroscience* (6th. ed.). Sunderland, MA: Sinauer.

Purves, D., and Lotto, R. B. (2010). *Why we see what we do redux: A wholly empirical theory of vision.* Sunderland, MA: Sinauer.

Putman, C. T., Xu, X., Gillies, E., Maclean, I. M., et al. (2004). Effects of strength, endurance and combined training on myosin heavy chain content and fibre-type distribution in humans. *European Journal of Applied Physiology, 92,* 376–384.

Q

Quill, T. E., and Meier, D. E. (2006). The big chill: Inserting the DEA into end-of-life care. *New England Journal of Medicine, 354,* 1–3.

R

Racette, A., Bard, C., and Peretz, I. (2006). Making non-fluent aphasics speak: Sing along! *Brain, 129,* 2571–2584.

Racine, E., Bar-Ilan, O., and Illes, J. (2005). fMRI in the public eye. *Nature Reviews Neuroscience, 6,* 159–164.

Radley, J. J., and Sawchenko, P. E. (2011). A common substrate for prefrontal and hippocampal inhibition of the neuroendocrine stress response. *Journal of Neuroscience, 31,* 9683–9695.

Rafal, R. D. (1994). Neglect. *Current Opinion in Neurobiology, 4,* 231–236.

Rahman, Q. (2005). The neurodevelopment of human sexual orientation. *Neuroscience and Biobehavioral Reviews, 29,* 1057–1066.

Raichle, M. E. (2015). The brain's default mode network. *Annual Review of Neuroscience, 38,* 433–447.

Raine, A., Reynolds, C., Venables, P. H., and Mednick, S. A. (2002). Stimulation seeking and intelligence: A prospective longitudinal study. *Journal of Personality and Social Psychology, 82,* 663–674.

Raine, A., Venables, P. H., Dalais, C., Mellingen, K., et al. (2001). Early educational and health enrichment at age 3–5 years is associated with increased autonomic and central nervous system arousal and orienting at age 11 years: Evidence from the Mauritius Child Health Project. *Psychophysiology, 38,* 254–266.

Rainville, P., Duncan, G. H., Price, D. D., Carrier, B., et al. (1997). Pain affect encoded in human anterior cingulate but not somatosensory cortex. *Science, 277,* 968–971.

Raisman, G., and Field, P. M. (1971). Sexual dimorphism in the preoptic area of the rat. *Science, 173,* 731–733.

Raisman, G., and Li, Y. (2007). Repair of neural pathways by olfactory ensheathing cells. *Nature Reviews Neuroscience, 8,* 312–319.

Rakel, R. E. (2009). Clinical and societal consequences of obstructive sleep apnea and excessive daytime sleepiness. *Postgraduate Medicine, 121,* 86–95.

Rakic, P. (1971). Guidance of neurons migrating to the fetal monkey neocortex. *Brain Research, 33,* 471–476.

Rakic, P. (1985). Mechanisms of neuronal migration in developing cerebellar cortex. In G. M. Edelman, W. M. Cowan, and E. Gull (Eds.), *Molecular basis of neural development* (pp. 139–160). New York: Wiley.

Ralph, M. R., and Menaker, M. (1988). A mutation of the circadian system in golden hamsters. *Science, 241,* 1225–1227.

Ralph, M. R., Foster, R. G., Davis, F. C., and Menaker, M. (1990). Transplanted suprachiasmatic nucleus determines circadian period. *Science, 247,* 975–978.

Ramachandran, V. S., and Hubbard, E. M. (2001). Psychophysical investigations into the neural basis of synthaesthesia. *Proceedings of the Royal Society of London. Series B: Biological Sciences, 268,* 979–983.

Ramachandran, V. S., and Rogers-Ramachandran D. (2000). Phantom limbs and neural plasticity. *Archives of Neurology, 57,* 317–320.

Ramchandani, P. (2004). A question of balance: How safe are the medicines that are prescribed to children? *Nature, 430,* 401–402.

Ramon, F., Hernandex-Falcon, J., Nguyen, B., and Bullock, T. H. (2004). Slow wave sleep in crayfish. *Proceedings of the National Academy of Sciences, USA, 101,* 11857–11861.

Rampon, C., Tang, Y. P., Goodhouse, J., Shimizu, E., et al. (2000). Enrichment induces structural changes and recovery from nonspatial memory deficits in CA1 NMDAR1-knockout mice. *Nature Neuroscience, 3,* 238–244.

Ranade, S. S., Woo, S. H., Dubin, A. E., Moshourab, R. A., et al. (2014). Piezo2 is the major transducer of mechanical forces for touch sensation in mice. *Nature, 516*(7529), 121–125.

Ranaldi, R., and Beninger, R. J. (1994). The effects of systemic and intracerebral injections of D1 and D2 agonists on brain stimulation reward. *Brain Research, 651,* 283–292.

Rand, M. N., and Breedlove, S. M. (1987). Ontogeny of functional innervation of bulbocavernosus muscles in male and female rats. *Brain Research, 430,* 150–152.

Rasmussen, L. E., and Greenwood, D. R. (2003). Frontalin: A chemical message of musth in Asian elephants (*Elephas maximus*). *Chemical Senses, 28,* 433–446.

Rasmussen, L. E., Riddle, H. S., and Krishnamurthy, V. (2002). Chemical communication: Mellifluous matures to malodorous in musth. *Nature, 415,* 975–976.

Rathelot, J. A., and Strick, P. L. (2006). Muscle representation in the macaque motor cortex: An anatomical perspective. *Proceedings of the National Academy of Sciences, USA, 103,* 8257–8262.

Rattenborg, N. C. (2006). Do birds sleep in flight? *Naturwissenschaften, 93*, 413–425.

Rauch, S. L., Shin, L. M., and Wright, C. I. (2003). Neuroimaging studies of amygdala function in anxiety disorders. *Annals of the New York Academy of Sciences, 985*, 389–410.

Raz, N. (2000). Aging of the brain and its impact on cognitive performance: Integration of structural and functional findings. In F. I. M. Craik and T. A. Salthouse (Eds.), *The handbook of aging and cognition* (2nd ed., pp. 1–90). Mahwah, NJ: Erlbaum.

Reader, S. M., and Laland, K. N. (2002). Social intelligence, innovation, and enhanced brain size in primates. *Proceedings of the National Academy of Sciences, USA, 99*, 4436–4441.

Recanzone, G. H., and Cohen, Y. E. (2010). Serial and parallel processing in the primate auditory cortex revisited. *Behavioural Brain Research, 206*, 1–7.

Rechtschaffen, A., and Bergmann, B. M. (1995). Sleep deprivation in the rat by the disk-over-water method. *Behavioural Brain Research, 69*, 55–63.

Rechtschaffen, A., and Kales, A. (1968). *A manual of standardized terminology, techniques and scoring system for sleep stages of human subjects.* Bethesda, MD: U.S. National Institute of Neurological Diseases and Blindness, Neurological Information Network.

Redcay, E., Dodell-Feder, D., Pearrow, M. J., Mavros, P. L., et al. (2010). Live face-to-face interaction during fMRI: A new tool for social cognitive neuroscience. *Neuroimage, 50*(4), 1639–1647.

Redican, W. K. (1982). An evolutionary perspective on human facial displays. In P. Ekman (Ed.), *Emotion in the human face* (2nd ed., pp. 212–280). Elmsford, NY: Pergamon.

Reed, L. I., DeScioli, P., and Pinker S. A. (2014). The commitment function of angry facial expressions. *Psychological Science, 25*, 1511–1517.

Rees, G., Kreiman, G., and Koch, C. (2002). Neural correlates of consciousness in humans. *Nature Reviews Neuroscience, 3*, 261–270.

Rehkamper, G., Haase, E., and Frahm, H. D. (1988). Allometric comparison of brain weight and brain structure volumes in different breeds of the domestic pigeon, *Columba livia* f. d. (fantails, homing pigeons, strassers). *Brain, Behavior and Evolution, 31*, 141–149.

Reiner, W. G., and Gearhart, J. P. (2004). Discordant sexual identity in some genetic males with cloacal exstrophy assigned to female sex at birth. *New England Journal of Medicine, 350*, 333–341.

Reisberg, D., and Heuer, F. (1995). Emotion's multiple effects on memory. In J. L. McGaugh, N. M. Weinberger, and G. Lynch (Eds.), *Brain and memory: Modulation and mediation of neuroplasticity* (pp. 84–92). New York: Oxford University Press.

Rempel-Clower, N. L., Zola, S. M., Squire, L. R., and Amaral, D. G. (1996). Three cases of enduring memory impairment after bilateral damage limited to the hippocampal formation. *Journal of Neuroscience, 16*, 5233–5255.

Renner, M. J., and Rosenzweig, M. R. (1987). *Enriched and impoverished environments: Effects on brain and behavior.* New York: Springer.

Reppert, S. M., Perlow, M. J., Tamarkin, L., and Klein, D. C. (1979). A diurnal melatonin rhythm in primate cerebrospinal fluid. *Endocrinology, 104*, 295–301.

Reuter, J., Raedler, T., Rose, M., Hand, I., et al. (2005). Pathological gambling is linked to reduced activation of the mesolimbic reward system. *Nature Neuroscience, 8*, 147–148.

Revel, F. G., Masson-Pévet, M., Pévet, P., Mikkelsen, J. D., et al. (2009). Melatonin controls seasonal breeding by a network of hypothalamic targets. *Neuroendocrinology, 90*, 1–14.

Rex, C. S., Lauterborn, J. C., Lin, C.Y., Kramár, E. A., et al. (2006). Restoration of long-term potentiation in middle-aged hippocampus after induction of brain-derived neurotrophic factor. *Journal of Neurophysiology, 96*, 677–685.

Rhodes, M. G. (2004). Age-related differences in performance on the Wisconsin card sorting test: A meta-analytic review. *Psychology of Aging, 19*, 482–494.

Ribeiro, R. C., Kushner, P. J., and Baxter, J. D. (1995). The nuclear hormone receptor gene superfamily. *Annual Review of Medicine, 46*, 443–453.

Ricciardi, E., Pietrini, P., Schapiro, M. B., Rapoport, S. I., et al. (2009). Cholinergic modulation of visual working memory during aging: A parametric PET study. *Brain Research Bulletin, 79*, 322–332.

Richman, D. P., and Agius, M. A. (2003). Treatment of autoimmune myasthenia gravis. *Neurology, 61*, 1652–1661.

Richter, C. (1967). Sleep and activity: Their relation to the 24-hour clock. *Proceedings of the Association for Research in Nervous and Mental Diseases, 45*, 8–27.

Ridley, M. (2003). *Nature via nurture: Genes, experience, and what makes us human.* New York: HarperCollins.

Ringman, J. M., and Cummings, J. L. (2006). Current and emerging pharmacological treatment options for dementia. *Behavioral Neurology, 17*, 5–16.

Risch, N., Herrell, R., Lehner, T., Liang, K.Y., et al. (2009). Interaction between the serotonin transporter gene (5-HTTLPR), stressful life events, and risk of depression: A meta-analysis. *JAMA, 301*, 2462–2471.

Rizzolatti, G., and Craighero, L. (2004). The mirror-neuron system. *Annual Review of Neuroscience, 27*, 169–192.

Rizzolatti, G., Fogassi, L., and Gallese, V. (2006). Mirrors of the mind. *Scientific American, 295*(5), 54–61.

Robel, S., and Sontheimer, H. (2015). Glia as drivers of abnormal neuronal activity. *Nature Neuroscience, 19*(1), 28–33.

Roberts, C. G., and Ladenson, P. W. (2004). Hypothyroidism. *Lancet, 363*, 793–803.

Roberts, E. K., Lu, A., Bergman, T. J., and Beehner, J. C. (2012). A Bruce effect in wild geladas. *Science, 335*(6073), 1222–1225.

Robertson, D. J., Noyes, E., Dowsett, A. J., Jenkins, R., et al. (2016). Face recognition by metropolitan police super-recognisers. *PLOS ONE, 11*(2), e0150036.

Robino, A., Mezzavilla, M., Pirastu, N., Dognini, M., et al. (2014). A population-based approach to study the impact of PROP perception on food liking in populations along the Silk Road. *PLOS ONE, 9*(3), e91716.

Robins, L. N., and Regier, D. A. (1991). *Psychiatric disorders in America: The epidemiologic catchment area study.* New York: Free Press.

Robins, L. N., and Slobodyan, S. (2003). Post-Vietnam heroin use and injection by returning US veterans: Clues to preventing injection today. *Addiction, 98*, 1053–1060.

Robinson, D. L., and Petersen, S. E. (1992). The pulvinar and visual salience. *Trends in Neuroscience, 15*, 127–132.

Robinson, R. (2009). Intractable depression responds to deep brain stimulation. *Neurology Today, 9*, 7–10.

Rocca, W. A., Hofman, A., Brayne, C., Breteler, M. M., et al. (1991). The prevalence of vascular dementia in Europe: Facts and fragments from 1980–1990 studies. *Annals of Neurology, 30*, 817–824.

Roenneberg, T. (2013). Chronobiology: The human sleep project. *Nature, 498*(7455), 427–428.

Roenneberg, T., Kuehnle, T., Pramstaller, P. P., Ricken, J., et al. (2004). A marker for the end of adolescence. *Current Biology, 14*, R1038–R1039.

Roffwarg, H. P., Muzio, J. N., and Dement, W. C. (1966). Ontogenetic development of the human sleep-dream cycle. *Science, 152*, 604–619.

Rogan, M. T., Staubli, U. V., and LeDoux, J. E. (1997). Fear conditioning induces associative long-term potentiation in the amygdala. *Nature, 390*, 604–607.

Rogawski, M. A., and Löscher, W. (2004). The neurobiology of antiepileptic drugs. *Nature Reviews Neuroscience, 5*, 553–564.

Roland, P. E. (1984). Metabolic measurements of the working frontal cortex in man. *Trends in Neurosciences, 7*, 430–436.

Roland, P. E. (1993). *Brain activation.* New York: Wiley-Liss.

Rolls, E. T., and O'Mara, S. M. (1995). View-responsive neurons in the primate hippocampal complex. *Hippocampus, 5*, 409–424.

Romanski, L. M., Tian, B., Fritz, J., Mishkin, M., et al. (1999). Dual streams of auditory afferents target multiple domains in the primate prefrontal cortex. *Nature Neuroscience, 2*, 1131–1136.

Rorabaugh, W. J. (1976). Estimated U.S. alcoholic beverage consumption, 1790–1860. *Journal of Studies on Alcohol, 37*, 357–364.

Rosci, C., Chiesa, V., Laiacona, M., and Capitani, E. (2003). Apraxia is not associated to a disproportionate naming impairment for manipulable objects. *Brain and Cognition, 53*, 412–415.

Rose, K. A., Morgan, I. G., Smith, W., Burlutsky, G., et al. (2008). Myopia, lifestyle, and schooling in students of Chinese ethnicity in Singapore and Sydney. *Archives of Ophthalmology, 126*(4), 527–530.

Roselli, C. E., Larkin, K., Resko, J. A., Stellflug, J. N., et al. (2004). The volume of a sexually dimorphic nucleus in the ovine medial preoptic area/anterior hypothalamus varies with sexual partner preference. *Endocrinology, 145*, 475–477.

Roselli, C. E., and Stormshak, F. (2009). The neurobiology of sexual partner preferences in rams. *Hormones and Behavior, 55*, 611–620.

Rosenbaum, R. S., Köhler, S., Schacter, D. L., Moscovitch, M., et al. (2005). The case of K.C.: Contributions of a memory-impaired person to memory theory. *Neuropsychologia, 43*, 989–1021.

Rosenberg, M. D., Finn, E. S., Scheinost, D., Papademetris, X., et al. (2016). A neuromarker of sustained attention from whole-brain functional connectivity. *Nature Neuroscience, 19*(1), 165–171.

Rosenfield, P. J., Kleinhaus, K., Opler, M., Perrin, M., et al. (2010). Later paternal age and sex differences in schizophrenia symptoms. *Schizophrenia Research, 116*, 191–195.

Rosengren, A., Tibblin, G., and Wilhelmsen, L. (1991). Self-perceived psychological stress and incidence of coronary artery disease in middle-aged men. *American Journal of Cardiology, 68*, 1171–1175.

Rosenkranz, M. A., Jackson, D. C., Dalton, K. M., Dolski, I., et al. (2003). Affective style and in vivo immune response: Neurobehavioral mechanisms. *Proceedings of the National Academy of Sciences, USA, 100*, 11148–11152.

Rosenzweig, M. R. (1946). Discrimination of auditory intensities in the cat. *American Journal of Psychology, 59*, 127–136.

Rosenzweig, M. R. (1984). Experience, memory, and the brain. *American Psychologist, 39*, 365–376.

Rosenzweig, M. R., and Bennett, E. L. (1977). Effects of environmental enrichment or impoverishment on learning and on brain values in rodents. In A. Oliveno (Ed.), *Genetics, environment, and intelligence* (pp. 1–2). Amsterdam: Elsevier/North-Holland.

Rosenzweig, M. R., and Bennett, E. L. (1978). Experimental influences on brain anatomy and brain chemistry in rodents. In G. Gottlieb (Ed.), *Studies on the development of behavior and the nervous system: Vol. 4. Early influences* (pp. 289–327). New York: Academic Press.

Rosenzweig, M. R., Bennett, E. L., Colombo, P. J., Lee, D. W., et al. (1993). Short-term, intermediate-term, and long-term memory. *Behavioural Brain Research, 57*, 193–198.

Rosenzweig, M. R., Bennett, E. L., Martinez, J. L., Colombo, P. J., et al. (1992). Studying stages of memory formation with chicks. In L. R. Squire and N. Butters (Eds.), *Neuropsychology of memory* (2nd ed., pp. 533–546). New York: Guilford.

Rosenzweig, M. R., Krech, D., and Bennett, E. L. (1961). Heredity, environment, brain biochemistry, and learning. In *Current trends in psychological theory* (pp. 87–110). Pittsburgh, PA: University of Pittsburgh Press.

Rosenzweig, M. R., Krech, D., Bennett, E. L., and Diamond, M. C. (1962). Effects of environmental complexity and training on brain chemistry and anatomy: A replication and extension. *Journal of Comparative and Physiological Psychology, 55*, 429–437.

Roses, A. D. (1995). On the metabolism of apolipoprotein E and the Alzheimer diseases. *Experimental Neurology, 132*, 149–156.

Rossi, M. A., Mash, D. C., and deToledo-Morrell, I. (2005). Spatial memory in aged rats is related to PKCγ-dependent G-protein coupling of the M1 receptor. *Neurobiology of Aging, 26*, 53–68.

Rossor, M., Garrett, N., Johnson, A., Mountjoy, C., et al. (1982). A post-mortem study of the cholinergic and GABA systems in senile dementia. *Brain, 105*, 313–330.

Rotarska-Jagiela, A., Schönmeyer, R., Oertel, V., Haenschel, C., et al. (2008). The corpus callosum in schizophrenia-volume and connectivity changes affect specific regions. *NeuroImage, 39*, 1522–1532.

Roth, T. L., Nayak, D., Atanasijevic, T., Koretsky, A. P., et al. (2014). Transcranial amelioration of inflammation and cell death after brain injury. *Nature, 505*(7482), 223–228.

Rouw, R., and Scholte, H. S. (2007). Increased structural connectivity in grapheme-color synesthesia. *Nature Neuroscience, 10*, 792–797.

Row, B. W., Kheirandish, L., Cheng, Y., Rowell, P. P., et al. (2007). Impaired spatial working memory and altered choline acetyltransferase (CHAT) immunoreactivity and nicotinic receptor binding in rats exposed to intermittent hypoxia during sleep. *Behavioural Brain Research, 177*, 308–314.

Rowe, A. H., Xiao, Y., Rowe, M. P., Cummins, T. R., et al. (2013). Voltage-gated sodium channel in grasshopper mice defends against bark scorpion toxin. *Science, 342*(6157), 441–446.

Rowe, M. K., and Chuang, D. M. (2004). Lithium neuroprotection: Molecular mechanisms and clinical implications. *Expert Reviews in Molecular Medicine, 18*, 1–18.

Rozanski, A. (2014). Behavioral cardiology: Current advances and future directions. *Journal of the American College of Cardiology, 64*, 100–110.

Rück, C., Karlsson, A., Steele, J. D., Edman, G., et al. (2008). Capsulotomy for obsessive-compulsive disorder: Long-term follow-up of 25 patients. *Archives of General Psychiatry, 65*, 914–921.

Rueda-Orozco, P. E., and Robbe, D. (2015). The striatum multiplexes contextual and kinematic information to constrain motor habits execution. *Nature Neuroscience, 18*(3), 453–460.

Ruff, C. C., and Fehr, E. (2014). The neurobiology of rewards and values in social decision making. *Nature Reviews Neuroscience, 15*(8), 549–562.

Rumbaugh, D. M. (1977). *Language learning by a chimpanzee: The LANA project.* New York: Academic Press.

Rupnick, M. A., Panigrahy, D., Zhang, C. Y., Dallabrida, S. M., et al. (2002). Adipose tissue mass can be regulated through the vasculature. *Proceedings of the National Academy of Sciences, USA, 99,* 10730–10735.

Rupprecht, R., Rammes, G., Eser, D., Baghai, T. C., et al. (2009). Translocator protein (18 kD) as target for anxiolytics without benzodiazepine-like side effects. *Science, 325,* 490–493.

Rusak, B., and Zucker, I. (1979). Neural regulation of circadian rhythms. *Physiological Reviews, 59,* 449–526.

Ruschel, J., Hellal, F., Flynn, K. C., Dupraz, S., et al. (2015). Axonal regeneration: Systemic administration of epothilone B promotes axon regeneration after spinal cord injury. *Science, 348*(6232), 347–352.

Russell, J. A. (1994). Is there universal recognition of emotion from facial expressions? A review of the cross-cultural studies. *Psychological Bulletin, 115,* 102–141.

Russell, R., Duchaine, B., and Nakayama, K. (2009). Super-recognizers: People with extraordinary face recognition ability. *Psychological Bulletin Review, 16*(2): 252–257.

Russo, E. B., Jiang, H. E., Li, X., Sutton, A., et al. (2008). Phytochemical and genetic analyses of ancient cannabis from Central Asia. *Journal of Experimental Botany, 59,* 4171–4182.

Russo, S. J., Murrough, J. W., Han, M.-H., Charney, D. S., et al. (2012). Neurobiology of resilience. *Nature Neuroscience, 15,* 1475–1484.

Ruthazer, E. S., Akerman, C. J., and Cline, H. T. (2003). Control of axon branch dynamics by correlated activity in vivo. *Science, 301,* 66–70.

Rymer, R. (1993). *Genie: An abused child's flight from silence.* New York: HarperCollins.

Rypma, B., Berger, J. S., Genova, H. M., Rebbechi, D., et al. (2005). Dissociating age-related changes in cognitive strategy and neural efficiency using event-related fMRI. *Cortex, 41,* 582–594.

S

Saab, A. S., Neumeyer, A., Jahn, H. M., Cupido, A., et al. (2012). Bergman glial AMPA receptors are required for fine motor coordination. *Science, 337,* 749–753.

Saalmann, Y. B., Pinsk, M. A., Wang, L., Li, X., et al. (2012). The pulvinar regulates information transmission between cortical areas based on attention demands. *Science, 337*(6095), 753–756.

Sabeti, P. C., Schaffner, S. F., Fry, B., Lohmueller, J., et al. (2006). Positive natural selection in the human lineage. *Science, 312*(5780), 1614–1620.

Sack, R. L., Blood, M. L., and Lewy, A. J. (1992). Melatonin rhythms in night shift workers. *Sleep, 15,* 434–441.

Sáenz de Miera, C., Monecke, S., Bartzen-Sprauer, J., Laran-Chich, M. P., et al. (2014). A circannual clock drives expression of genes central for seasonal reproduction. *Current Biology, 24*(13), 1500–1506.

Sage, C., Huang, M., Vollrath, M. A., Brown, M. C., et al. (2006). Essential role of retinoblastoma protein in mammalian hair cell development and hearing. *Proceedings of the National Academy of Sciences, USA, 103,* 7345–7350.

Sahay, A., and Hen, R. (2007). Adult hippocampal neurogenesis in depression. *Nature Neuroscience, 10,* 1110–1114.

Sahay, A., Scobie, K. N., Hill, A. S., O'Carroll, C. M., et al. (2011). Increasing adult hippocampal neurogenesis is sufficient to improve pattern separation. *Nature, 472,* 466–470.

Saj, A., Fuhrman, O., Vuilleumier, P., and Boroditsky, L. (2014). Patients with left spatial neglect also neglect the "left side" of time. *Psychological Science, 25*(1), 207–214.

Sakurai, T., Amemiya, A., Ishii, M., Matsuzaki, I., et al. (1998). Orexins and orexin receptors: A family of hypothalamic neuropeptides and G protein–coupled receptors that regulate feeding behavior. *Cell, 92,* 573–585.

Salazar, H., Llorente, I., Jara-Oseguera, A., García-Villegas, R., et al. (2008). A single N-terminal cysteine in TRPV1 determines activation by pungent compounds from onion and garlic. *Nature Neuroscience, 11,* 255–260.

Salimpoor, V. N., van den Bosch, I., Kovacevic, N., McIntosh, A. R., et al. (2013). Interactions between the nucleus accumbens and auditory cortices predict music reward value. *Science, 340*(6129), 216–219.

Salvini-Plawen, L. V., and Mayr, E. (1977). On the evolution of photoreceptors and eyes. *Evolutionary Biology, 10,* 207–263.

Samad, T. A., Moore, K. A., Sapirstein, A., Billet, S., et al. (2001). Interleukin-1β-mediated induction of Cox-2 in the CNS contributes to inflammatory pain hypersensitivity. *Nature, 410,* 471–475.

Samaha, F. F., Iqbal, N., Seshadri, P., Chicano, K. L., et al. (2003). A low-carbohydrate as compared with a low-fat diet in severe obesity. *New England Journal of Medicine, 348,* 2074–2081.

Samson, S., and Zatorre, R. J. (1991). Recognition memory for text and melody of songs after unilateral temporal lobe lesion: Evidence for dual encoding. *Journal of Experimental Psychology. Learning, Memory, and Cognition, 17,* 793–804.

Samson, S., and Zatorre, R. J. (1994). Contribution of the right temporal lobe to musical timbre discrimination. *Neuropsychologia, 32,* 231–240.

Samuels, B. A., Anacker, C., Hu, A., Levinstein, M. R., et al. (2015). 5-HT1A receptors on mature dentate gyrus granule cells are critical for the antidepressant response. *Nature Neuroscience, 18,* 1606–1616.

Sanders, A. R., Martin, E. R., Beecham, G. W., Guo, S., et al. (2015). Genome-wide scan demonstrates significant linkage for male sexual orientation. *Psychological Medicine, 45*(7), 1379–1388.

Sanderson, D. J., Good, M. A., Seeburg, P. H., Sprengel, R., et al. (2008). The role of the GluR-A (GluR1) AMPA receptor subunit in learning and memory. *Progress in Brain Research, 169,* 159–178.

Sanes, J. N., and Donoghue, J. P. (2000). Plasticity and primary motor cortex. *Annual Review of Neuroscience, 23,* 393–415.

Sanes, J. R., and Lichtman, J. W. (1999). Can molecules explain long-term potentiation? *Nature Neuroscience, 2,* 597–604.

Santhanam, F., Ryu, S. I., Yu, B. M., Afshar, A., et al. (2006) A high-performance brain–computer interface. *Nature, 442,* 195–198.

Sapir, A., Soroker, N., Berger, A., and Henik, A. (1999). Inhibition of return in spatial attention: Direct evidence for collicular generation. *Nature Neuroscience, 2,* 1053–1054.

Sapolsky, R. M. (1992). Neuroendocrinology of the stress response. In J. B. Becker, S. M. Breedlove, and D. Crews (Eds.), *Behavioral endocrinology* (pp. 287–324). Cambridge, MA: MIT Press.

Sapolsky, R. M. (1993). Potential behavioral modification of glucocorticoid damage to the hippocampus [Special issue: Alzheimer's disease: Animal models and clinical perspectives]. *Behavioural Brain Research, 57,* 175–182.

Sapolsky, R. M. (2004). *Why zebras don't get ulcers* (3rd ed.). New York: Holt.

Sartorius, N., Shapiro, R., Kimura, M., and Barrett, K. (1972). WHO international pilot study of schizophrenia. *Psychological Medicine, 2,* 422–425.

Satinoff, E. (1978). Neural organization and evolution of thermal regulation in mammals. *Science, 201,* 16–22.

Satinoff, E., and Rutstein, J. (1970). Behavioral thermoregulation in rats with anterior hypothalamic lesions. *Journal of Comparative and Physiological Psychology, 71,* 77–82.

Satinoff, E., and Shan, S.Y. (1971). Loss of behavioral thermoregulation after lateral hypothalamic lesions in rats. *Journal of Comparative and Physiological Psychology, 77,* 302–312.

Sato, J. R., Salum, G. A., Gadelha, A., Crossley, N., et al. (2015). Default mode network maturation and psychopathology in children and adolescents. *Journal of Child Psychology and Psychiatry, 57*(1), 55–64.

Saul, S. (2006, March 8). Some sleeping pill users range far beyond bed. *The New York Times.*

Savage-Rumbaugh, E. S. (1993). *Language comprehension in ape and child.* Chicago: University of Chicago Press.

Savage-Rumbaugh, [E.] S., and Lewin, R. (1994). *Kanzi: The ape at the brink of the human mind.* New York: Wiley.

Sawamoto, K., Wichterle, H., Gonzalez-Perez, O., Cholfin, J. A., et al. (2006). New neurons follow the flow of cerebrospinal fluid in the adult brain. *Science, 311,* 629–632.

Sawin, C. T. (1996). Arnold Adolph Berthold (1803–1861). *Endocrinologist, 6,* 164–168.

Saxe, M. D., Battaglia, F., Wang, J. W., Malleret, G., et al. (2006). Ablation of hippocampal neurogenesis impairs contextual fear conditioning and synaptic plasticity in the dentate gyrus. *Proceedings of the National Academy of Sciences, USA, 103,* 17501–17506.

Saxena, S., Brody, A. L., Ho, M. L., Alborzian, S., et al. (2001). Cerebral metabolism in major depression and obsessive-compulsive disorder occurring separately and concurrently. *Biological Psychiatry, 50,* 159–170.

Scammell, T. E. (2015). Narcolepsy. *New England Journal of Medicine, 373,* 2654–2662.

SCENIHR (Scientific Committee on Emerging and Newly Identified Health Risks). (2008, September 23). Scientific opinion on the potential health risks of exposure to noise from personal music players and mobile phones including a music playing function.

Schachter, S. (1975). Cognition and peripheralist-centralist controversies in motivation and emotion. In M. S. Gazzaniga and C. Blakemore (Eds.), *Handbook of psychobiology* (pp. 529–564). New York: Academic Press.

Schachter, S., and Singer, J. (1962). Cognitive, social, and physiological determinants of emotional state. *Psychological Review, 69,* 379–399.

Schacter, D. L., Alpert, N. M., Savage, C. R., Rauch, S. L., et al. (1996). Conscious recollection and the human hippocampal formation: Evidence from positron emission tomography. *Proceedings of the National Academy of Sciences, USA, 93,* 321–325.

Schaie, K. W. (1994). The course of adult intellectual development. *American Psychologist, 49,* 304–313.

Schaller, M., Miller, G. E., Gervais, W. M., Yager, S., et al. (2010). Mere visual perception of other people's disease symptoms facilitates a more aggressive immune response. *Psychological Science, 21,* 649–652.

Schatzberg, A. F., Rothschild, A. J., Stahl, J. B., Bond, T. C., et al. (1983). The dexamethasone suppression test: Identification of subtypes of depression. *American Journal of Psychiatry, 140*(1): 88–91.

Scheibel, M. E., Tomiyasu, U., and Scheibel, A. B. (1977). The aging human Betz cells. *Experimental Neurology, 56,* 598–609.

Scheibert, J., Leurent, S., Prevost, A., and Debrégeas, G. (2009). The role of fingerprints in the coding of tactile information probed with a biomimetic sensor. *Science, 323,* 1503–1506.

Schein, S. J., and Desimone, R. (1990). Spectral properties of V4 neurons in the macaque. *Journal of Neuroscience, 10,* 3369–3389.

Schenck, C. H., and Mahowald, M. W. (2002). REM sleep behavior disorder: Clinical, developmental, and neuroscience perspectives 16 years after its formal identification in *Sleep. Sleep, 25,* 120–138.

Schenkerberg, T., Bradford, D. C., and Ajax, E. T. (1980). Line bisection and unilateral visual neglect in patients with neurologic impairment. *Neurology, 30,* 509–518.

Schiffman, S. S., Simon, S. A., Gill, J. M., and Beeker, T. G. (1986). Bretylium tosylate enhances salt taste. *Physiology & Behavior, 36,* 1129–1137.

Schildkraut, J. J., and Kety, S. S. (1967). Biogenic amines and emotion. *Science, 156,* 21–30.

Schiller, D., Eichenbaum, H., Buffalo, E. A., Davachi, L., et al. (2015). Memory and space: Towards an understanding of the cognitive map. *Journal of Neuroscience, 35*(41), 13904–13911.

Schindler, E. A., Gottschalk, C. H., Weil, M. J., Shapiro, R. E., et al. (2015). Indoleamine hallucinogens in cluster headache: Results of the clusterbusters medication use survey. *Journal of Psychoactive Drugs, 47,* 372–381.

Schindler, I., Clavagnier, S., Karnath, H. O., Derex, L., et al. (2006). A common basis for visual and tactile exploration deficits in spatial neglect? *Neuropsychologia, 44,* 1444–1451.

Schizophrenia Working Group of the Psychiatric Genomics Consortium. (2014). Biological insights from 108 schizophrenia-associated genetic loci. *Nature, 511,* 421–427.

Schlaug, G., Jancke, L., Huang, Y., and Steinmetz, H. (1995). In vivo evidence of structural brain asymmetry in musicians. *Science, 267,* 699–701.

Schlosburg, J. E., Vendruscolo, L. F., Bremer, P. T., Lockner, J. W., et al. (2013). Dynamic vaccine blocks relapse to compulsive intake of heroin. *Proceedings of the National Academy of Sciences, USA, 110,* 9036–9041.

Schmidt-Nielsen, K. (1960). *Animal physiology.* Englewood Cliffs, NJ: Prentice-Hall.

Schnapf, J. L., and Baylor, D. A. (1987). How photoreceptor cells respond to light. *Scientific American, 256*(4), 40–47.

Schneider, D. M., Nelson, A., and Mooney, R. (2014). A synaptic and circuit basis for corollary discharge in the auditory cortex. *Nature, 513*(7517), 189–194.

Schneider, K. A., and Kastner, S. (2009). Effects of sustained spatial attention in the human lateral geniculate nucleus and superior colliculus. *Journal of Neuroscience, 29,* 1784–1795.

Schneider, P., Scherg, M., Dosch, H. G., Specht, H. J., et al. (2002). Morphology of Heschl's gyrus reflects enhanced activation in the auditory cortex of musicians. *Nature Neuroscience, 5,* 688–694.

Schneps, M. H., Brockmole, J. R., Sonnert, G., and Pomplun, M. (2012). History of reading struggles linked to enhanced learning in low spatial frequency scenes. *PLOS ONE, 7*(4), e35724.

Schnupp, J. W., Dawe, K. L., and Pollack, G. L. (2005). The detection of multisensory stimuli in an orthogonal sensory space. *Experimental Brain Research, 162,* 181–190.

Schoenbaum, G., Roesch, M. R., Stalnaker, T. A., and Takahashi, Y. K. (2009). A new perspective on the role of the orbitofrontal cortex in adaptive behaviour. *Nature Reviews Neuroscience, 10*(12), 885–892.

Schreiweis, C., Bornschein, U., Burguière, E., Kerimoglu, C., et al. (2014). Humanized Foxp2 accelerates learning by enhancing transitions from declarative to procedural performance. *Proceedings of the National Academy of Sciences, USA, 111*(39), 14253–14258.

Schuckit, M. A., and Smith, T. L. (1997). Assessing the risk for alcoholism among sons of alcoholics. *Journal of Studies on Alcohol, 58*, 141–145.

Schulman, C. I., Namias, N., Doherty, J., Manning, R. J., et al. (2005). The effect of antipyretic therapy upon outcomes in critically ill patients: A randomized, prospective study. *Surgical Infections, 6*(4), 369–375.

Schultz, W. W., van Andel, P., Sabelis, I., and Mooyaart, E. (1999). Magnetic resonance imaging of male and female genitals during coitus and female sexual arousal. *British Medical Journal, 319*(7225), 1596–1600.

Schummers, J., Yu, H., and Sur, M. (2008). Tuned responses of astrocytes and their influence on hemodynamic signals in the visual cortex. *Science, 320*, 1638–1643.

Schuster, C. R. (1970). Psychological approaches to opiate dependence and self-administration by laboratory animals. *Federation Proceedings, 29*, 1–5.

Schwartz, C. E., Wright, C. I., Shin, L. M., Kagan, J., et al. (2003). Inhibited and uninhibited infants "grown up": Adult amygdalar response to novelty. *Science, 300*, 1952–1953.

Schwartz, S., and Correll, C. U. (2014). Efficacy and safety of atomoxetine in children and adolescents with attention-deficit/hyperactivity disorder: Results from a comprehensive meta-analysis and metaregression. *Journal of the American Academy of Child and Adolescent Psychiatry, 53*(2), 174–187.

Schwartz, S. D., Hubschman, J. P., Heilwell, G., Franco-Cardenas, V., et al. (2012). Embryonic stem cell trials for macular degeneration: A preliminary report. *Lancet, 379*, 713–720.

Schwartzkroin, P. A., and Wester, K. (1975). Long-lasting facilitation of a synaptic potential following tetanization in the in vitro hippocampal slice. *Brain Research, 89*, 107–119.

Sclafani, A., Springer, D., and Kluge, L. (1976). Effects of quinine adulteration on the food intake and body weight of obese and nonobese hypothalamic hyperphagic rats. *Physiology & Behavior, 16*, 631–640.

Scott, D. J., Stohler, C. S., Egnatuk, C. M., Wang, H., et al. (2008). Placebo and nocebo effects are defined by opposite opioid and dopaminergic responses. *Archives of General Psychiatry, 65*, 220–231.

Scott, N., Prigge, M., Yizhar, O., and Kimchi, T. (2015). A sexually dimorphic hypothalamic circuit controls maternal care and oxytocin secretion. *Nature, 525*(7570), 519–522.

Scott, S. K., and Wise, R. J. (2004). The functional neuroanatomy of prelexical processing in speech perception. *Cognition, 92*, 13–45.

Scoville, W. B., and Milner, B. (1957). Loss of recent memory after bilateral hippocampal lesions. *Journal of Neurology, Neurosurgery and Psychiatry, 20*, 11–21.

Scudellari, M. (2015). The science myths that will not die. *Nature, 528*, 322–325.

Scullin, M. K., and Bliwise, D. L. (2015). Sleep, cognition, and normal aging: Integrating a half century of multidisciplinary research. *Perspectives on Psychological Science, 10*(1), 97–137.

Seeman, P. (1990). Atypical neuroleptics: Role of multiple receptors, endogenous dopamine, and receptor linkage. *Acta Psychiatrica Scandinavica. Supplementum, 358*, 14–20.

Seiden, R. H. (1978). Where are they now? A follow-up study of suicide attempters from the Golden Gate Bridge. *Suicide and Life Threatening Behavior, 8*, 203–216.

Seif, T., Chang, S. J., Simms, J. A., Gibb, S. L., et al. (2013). Cortical activation of accumbens hyperpolarization-active NMDARs mediates aversion-resistant alcohol intake. *Nature Neuroscience, 16*, 1094–1100.

Seil, F. J., Kelly, J. M., and Leiman, A. L. (1974). Anatomical organization of cerebral neocortex in tissue culture. *Experimental Neurology, 45*, 435–450.

Sekar, A., Bialas, A. R., de Rivera, H., Davis, A., et al. (2016). Schizophrenia risk from complex variation of complement component 4. *Nature, 530*, 177–183.

Seligman, M. E., and Beagley, G. (1975). Learned helplessness in the rat. *Journal of Comparative and Physiological Psychology, 88*, 534–541.

Selye, H. (1956). *The stress of life.* New York: McGraw-Hill.

Semaw, S. (2000). The world's oldest stone artefacts from Gona, Ethiopia: Their implications for understanding stone technology and patterns of human evolution between 2.6–1.5 million years ago. *Journal of Archaeolical Science, 27*, 1197–1214.

Semendeferi, K., Lu, A., Schenker, N., and Damasio, H. (2002). Humans and great apes share a large frontal cortex. *Nature Neuroscience, 5*, 272–276.

Sendtner, M., Holtmann, B., and Hughes, R. A. (1996). The response of motoneurons to neurotrophins. *Neurochemical Research, 21*, 831–841.

Senju, A., Southgate, V., White, S., and Frith, W. (2009). Mindblind eyes: An absence of spontaneous theory of mind in Asperger syndrome. *Science, 325*, 883–885.

Seok, J., Warren, H. S., Cuenca, A. G., Mindrinosa, M. N., et al. (2013). Genomic responses in mouse models poorly mimic human inflammatory diseases. *Proceedings of the National Academy of Sciences, USA, 110*(9), 3501–3512.

Seretis, K., Goulis, D. G., Koliakos, G., and Demiri, E. (2015). Short- and long-term effects of abdominal lipectomy on weight and fat mass in females: A systematic review. *Obesity Surgery, 25*, 1950–1958.

Serrano, P. A., Beniston, D. S., Oxonian, M. G., Rodriguez, W. A., et al. (1994). Differential effects of protein kinase inhibitors and activators on memory formation in the 2-day-old chick. *Behavioral and Neural Biology, 61*, 60–72.

Serviere, J., Webster, W. R., and Calford, M. B. (1984). Isofrequency labelling revealed by a combined [14C]-2-deoxyglucose, electrophysiological, and horseradish peroxidase study of the inferior colliculus of the cat. *Journal of Comparative Neurology, 228*, 463–477.

Seuss, Dr. (1987). *The tough coughs as he ploughs the dough: Early writings and cartoons by Dr. Seuss.* New York: Morrow.

Sexton, C. E., Mackay, C. E., and Ebmeier, K. P. (2013). A systematic review and meta-analysis of magnetic resonance imaging studies in late-life depression. *American Journal of Geriatric Psychiatry, 2*, 184–195.

Seyfarth, R. M., and Cheney, D. L. (1997). Behavioral mechanisms underlying vocal communication in nonhuman primates. *Animal Learning & Behavior, 25*, 249–267.

Shah, A., Carreno, F. R., and Frazer, A. (2014). Therapeutic modalities for treatment resistant depression: Focus on vagal nerve stimulation and ketamine. *Clinical Psychopharmacology and Neuroscience, 12*, 83–93.

Shallice, T., and Burgess, P. W. (1991). Deficits in strategy application following frontal lobe damage in man. *Brain, 114*, 727–741.

Shank, S. S., and Margoliash, D. (2009). Sleep and sensorimotor integration during early vocal learning in a songbird. *Nature, 458,* 73–77.

Shapiro, R. M. (1993). Regional neuropathology in schizophrenia: Where are we? Where are we going? *Schizophrenia Research, 10,* 187–239.

Shaw, J., and Porter, S. (2015). Constructing rich false memories of committing crime. *Psychological Science, 26*(3), 291–301.

Shaw, P., Greenstein, D., Lerch, J., Clasen, L., et al. (2006). Intellectual ability and cortical development in children and adolescents. *Nature, 440,* 676–679.

Shaw, P. J., Tononi, G., Greenspan, R. J., and Robinson, D. F. (2002). Stress response genes protect against lethal effects of sleep deprivation in *Drosophila. Nature, 417,* 287–291.

Shaywitz, S. E., Shaywitz, B. A., Fulbright, R. K., Skudlarski, P., et al. (2003). Neural systems for compensation and persistence: Young adult outcome of childhood reading disability. *Biological Psychiatry, 54,* 25–33.

Shaywitz, S. E., Shaywitz, B. A., Pugh, K. R., Fulbright, R. K., et al. (1998). Functional disruption in the organization of the brain for reading in dyslexia. *Proceedings of the National Academy of Sciences, USA, 95,* 2636–2641.

Shema, R., Hazvi, S., Sacktor, T. C., and Dudai, Y. (2009). Boundary conditions for the maintenance of memory by PKMzeta in neocortex. *Learning & Memory, 16,* 122–128.

Shenoy, K. V., Sahani, M., and Churchland, M. M. (2013). Cortical control of arm movements: A dynamical systems perspective. *Annual Review of Neuroscience, 36,* 337–359.

Sherrington, C. S. (1897). *A textbook of physiology. Part III. The Central Nervous System* (7th ed.), M. Foster (Ed.). London: Macmillan.

Sherrington, C. S. (1898). Experiments in examination of the peripheral distribution of the fibres of the posterior roots of some spinal nerves. *Philosophical Transactions, 190,* 45–186.

Sherry, D. F. (1992). Memory, the hippocampus, and natural selection: Studies of food-storing birds. In L. R. Squire and N. Butters (Eds.), *Neuropsychology of memory* (2nd ed., pp. 521–532). New York: Guilford.

Sherry, D. F., and Vaccarino, A. L. (1989). Hippocampus and memory for food caches in black-capped chickadees. *Behavioral Neuroscience, 103,* 308–318.

Sherry, D. F., Vaccarino, A. L., Buckenham, K., and Herz, R. S. (1989). The hippocampal complex of food-storing birds. *Brain Behavior and Evolution, 34,* 308–317.

Sherwin, B. B. (1998). Use of combined estrogen-androgen preparations in the postmenopause: Evidence from clinical studies. *International Journal of Fertility and Women's Medicine, 43*(2), 98–103.

Sherwin, B. B. (2002). Randomized clinical trials of combined estrogen-androgen preparations: Effects on sexual functioning. *Fertility and Sterility, 77*(Suppl. 4), 49–54.

Sheth, S. A., Mian, M. K., Patel, S. R., Asaad, W. F., et al. (2012). Human dorsal anterior cingulate cortex neurons mediate ongoing behavioural adaptation. *Nature, 488*(7410), 218–221.

Shih, R. A., Belmonte, P. L., and Zandi, P. P. (2004). A review of the evidence from family, twin and adoption studies for a genetic contribution to adult psychiatric disorders. *International Review of Psychiatry, 16,* 260–283.

Shimura, H., Schlossmacher, M. G., Hattori, N., Frosch, M. P., et al. (2001). Ubiquitination of a new form of α-synuclein by parkin from human brain: Implications for Parkinson's disease. *Science, 293,* 263–269.

Shingo, T., Gregg, C., Enwere, E., Fujikawa, H., et al. (2003). Pregnancy-stimulated neurogenesis in the adult female forebrain mediated by prolactin. *Science, 299,* 117–120.

Shipton, O. A., El-Gaby, M., Apergis-Schoute, J., Deisseroth, K., et al. (2014). Left-right dissociation of hippocampal memory processes in mice. *Proceedings of the National Academy of Sciences, USA, 111*(42), 15238–15243.

Shors, T. J. (2014). The adult brain makes new neurons, and effortful learning keeps them alive. *Current Directions in Psychological Science, 23*(5), 311–318.

Shors, T. J., Miesegaes, G., Beylin, A., Zhao, M., et al. (2001). Neurogenesis in the adult is involved in the formation of trace memories. *Nature, 410,* 372–376.

Shu, W., Cho, J. Y., Jiang, Y., Zhang, M., et al. (2005). Altered ultrasonic vocalization in mice with a disruption in the Foxp2 gene. *Proceedings of the National Academy of Sciences, USA, 102,* 9643–9648.

Sia, G. M., Clem, R. L., and Huganir, R. L. (2013). The human language-associated gene *SRPX2* regulates synapse formation and vocalization in mice. *Science, 342*(6161), 987–991.

Siegel, J. M. (1994). Brainstem mechanisms generating REM sleep. In M. H. Kryger, T. Roth, and W. C. Dement (Eds.), *Principles and practice of sleep medicine* (2nd ed., pp. 125–144). Philadelphia: Saunders.

Siegel, J. M. (2005). Clues to the function of mammalian sleep. *Nature, 437,* 1264–1271.

Siegel, J. M. (2009). Sleep viewed as a state of adaptive inactivity. *Nature Reviews Neuroscience, 10,* 747–753.

Siegel, J. M. (2012). Evolution: Suppression of sleep for mating. *Science, 337*(6102), 1610–1611.

Siegel, J. M., Manger, P. R., Nienhuis, R., Fahringer, H. M., et al. (1999). Sleep in the platypus. *Neuroscience, 91,* 391–400.

Siegel, J. M., Nienhuis, R., Gulyani, S., Ouyang, S., et al. (1999). Neuronal degeneration in canine narcolepsy. *Journal of Neuroscience, 19,* 248–257.

Siemens, J., Zhou, S., Piskorowski, R., Nikai, T., et al. (2006). Spider toxins activate the capsaicin receptor to produce inflammatory pain. *Nature, 444,* 208–212.

Sierakowiak, A., Monnot, C., Aski, S. N., Uppman, M., et al. (2015). Default mode network, motor network, dorsal and ventral basal ganglia networks in the rat brain: Comparison to human networks using resting state-fMRI. *PLOS ONE, 10*(3), e0120345.

Siever, L. J. (2008). Neurobiology of aggression and violence. *American Journal of Psychiatry, 165,* 429–442.

Sikich, L, Frazier, J. A., McClellan, J., Findling, R. L., et al. (2008). Double-blind comparison of first- and second-generation antipsychotics in early-onset schizophrenia and schizo-affective disorder: Findings from the treatment of early-onset schizophrenia spectrum disorders (TEOSS) study. *American Journal of Psychiatry, 165,* 1420–1431.

Sikl, R., Simecek, M., Porubanova-Norquist, M., Bezdicek, O., et al. (2013). Vision after 53 years of blindness. *i-Perception, 4*(8), 498–507. doi:10.1068/i0611

Sileno, A. P., Brandt, G. C., Spann, B. M., and Quay, S. C. (2006). Lower mean weight after 14 days intravenous administration peptide YY_{3-36} (PYY_{3-36}) in rabbits. *International Journal of Obesity, 30,* 68–72.

Silva, D. A., and Satz, P. (1979). Pathological left-handedness. Evaluation of a model. *Brain and Language, 7,* 8–16.

Silver, R., LeSauter, J., Tresco, P. A., and Lehman, M. N. (1996). A diffusible coupling signal from the transplanted suprachiasmatic nucleus controlling circadian locomotor rhythms. *Nature,* *382*(6594), 810–813.

Simic, G., Kostovic, I., Winblad, B., and Bogdanovic, N. (1997). Volume and number of neurons of the human hippocampal formation in normal aging and Alzheimer's disease. *Journal of Comparative Neurology, 379,* 482–494.

Simmons, R. (2003). *Odd girl out: The hidden culture of aggression in girls.* New York: Harcourt.

Simner, J., Mulvenna, C., Sagiv, N., Tsakanikos, E., et al. (2006). Synaesthesia: The prevalence of atypical cross-modal experiences. *Perception, 35,* 1024–1033.

Simons, D. J., and Chabris, C. F. (1999). Gorillas in our midst: Sustained inattentional blindness for dynamic events. *Perception, 28,* 1059–1074.

Simons, D. J., and Jensen, M. S. (2009). The effects of individual differences and task difficulty on inattentional blindness. *Psychonomic Bulletin & Review, 16,* 398–403.

Singer, P. (1975). *Animal liberation: A new ethics for our treatment of animals.* New York: New York Review.

Singer, T., Seymour, B., O'Doherty, J., Kaube, H., et al. (2004). Empathy for pain involves the affective but not sensory components of pain. *Science, 303,* 1157–1162.

Singh, D. (2002). Female mate value at a glance: Relationship of waist-to-hip ratio to health, fecundity and attractiveness. *Neuroendocrinology Letters, 23*(Suppl. 4), 81–91.

Siok, W. T., Perfetti, C. A., Jin, Z., and Tan, L. H. (2004). Biological abnormality of impaired reading is constrained by culture. *Nature, 431,* 71–76.

Sirotnak, A. P., Grigsby, T., and Krugman, R. D. (2004). Physical abuse of children. *Pediatrics in Review, 25,* 264–277.

Sjöbeck, M., Dahlén, S., and Englund, E. (1999). Neuronal loss in the brainstem and cerebellum--part of the normal aging process? A morphometric study of the vermis cerebelli and inferior olivary nucleus. The Journals of Gerontology Series *A Biological Science, 54,* (9), B363–368.

Skinner, M., Holden, L., and Holden, T. (1997). Parameter selection to optimize speech recognition with the nucleus implant. *Otolaryngology and Head and Neck Surgery, 117,* 188–195.

Skolnick, P. (2015). Biologic approaches to treat substance-use disorders. *Trends in Pharmacological Sciences, 36,* 628–635.

Slee, S. J., and Young, E. D. (2011). Information conveyed by inferior colliculus neurons about stimuli with aligned and misaligned sound localization cues. *Journal of Neurophysiology, 106*(2), 974–985.

Smale, L. (1988). Influence of male gonadal hormones and familiarity on pregnancy interruption in prairie voles. *Biology of Reproduction, 39,* 28–31.

Smale, L., Holekamp, K. E., and White, P. A. (1999). Siblicide revisited in the spotted hyaena: Does it conform to obligate or facultative models? *Animal Behaviour, 58,* 545–551.

Smith, A., and Sugar, O. (1975). Development of above normal language and intelligence 21 years after hemispherectomy. *Neurology, 25,* 813–818.

Smith, C. (1995). Sleep states and memory processes. *Behavioural Brain Research, 69,* 137–145.

Smith, C. M., and Luskin, M. B. (1998). Cell cycle length of olfactory bulb neuronal progenitors in the rostral migratory stream. *Developmental Dynamics, 213,* 220–227.

Smith, D. E., Roberts, J., Gage, F. H., and Tuszynski, M. H. (1999). Age-associated neuronal atrophy occurs in the primate brain and is reversible by growth factor gene therapy. *Proceedings of the National Academy of Sciences, USA, 96,* 10893–10898.

Smith, J. T., Clifton, D. K., amd Steiner, R. A. (2006). Regulation of the neuroendocrine reproductive axis by kisspeptin-GPR54 signaling. *Reproduction, 131,* 623–630.

Smith, M. A., Brandt, J., and Shadmehr, R. (2000). Motor disorder in Huntington's disease begins as a dysfunction in error feedback control. *Nature, 403,* 544–549.

Smith, P. B., Compton, D. R., Welch, S. P., Razdan, R. K., et al. (1994). The pharmacological activity of anandamide, a putative endogenous cannabinoid, in mice. *Journal of Pharmacology and Experimental Therapeutics, 270,* 219–227.

Smith, S. (1997, September 2). Dreaming awake. Part 1: Living with narcolepsy. *Minnesota Public Radio News* (http://news.minnesota.publicradio.org/features/199709/02_smiths_narcolepsy/narco_1.shtml).

Smoller, J. W., and Finn, C. T. (2003). Family, twin, and adoption studies of bipolar disorder. *American Journal of Medical Genetics. Part C, Seminars in Medical Genetics, 123,* 48–58.

Smyth, K. A., Pritsch, T., Cook, T. B., McClendon, M. J., et al. (2004). Worker functions and traits associated with occupations and the development of AD. *Neurology, 63,* 498–503.

Snyder, J. S., Soumier, A., Brewer, M., Pickel, J., et al. (2011). Adult hippocampal neurogenesis buffers stress responses and depressive behaviour. *Nature, 476,* 458–461.

Sobel, N., Khan, R. M., Saltman, A., Sullivan, E.V., et al. (1999). The world smells different to each nostril. *Nature, 402,* 35.

Sobel, N., Prabhakaran, V., Zhao, Z., Desmond, J. E., et al. (2000). Time course of odorant-induced activation in the human primary olfactory cortex. *Journal of Neurophysiology, 83,* 537–551.

Sol, D., Duncan, R. P., Blackburn, T. M., Casey, P., et al. (2005). Big brains, enhanced cognition, and response of birds to novel environments. *Proceedings of the National Academy of Sciences, USA, 102,* 5460–5465.

Soldner, F., Stelzer, Y., Shivalila, C. S., Abraham, B. J., et al. (2016). Parkinson-associated risk variant in distal enhancer of α-synuclein modulates target gene expression. *Nature, 533*(7601), 95–99.

Solomon, A. (2001). *The noonday demon: An atlas of depression.* New York: Scribner.

Solstad, T., Boccara, C. N., Kropff, E., Moser, M. B., et al. (2008). Representation of geometric borders in the entorhinal cortex. *Science, 322,* 1865–1868.

Soltis, J., King, L. E, Douglas-Hamilton, I., Vollrath, F., et al. (2014). African elephant alarm calls distinguish between threats from humans and bees. *PLOS ONE, 9*(2), e89403.

Somel, M., Liu, X., and Khaitovich, P. (2013). Human brain evolution: Transcripts, metabolites and their regulators. *Nature Reviews Neuroscience, 14,* 112–127.

Somerville, M. J., Mervis, C. B., Young, E. J., Seo, E. J., et al. (2005). Severe expressive-language delay related to duplication of the Williams-Beuren locus. *New England Journal of Medicine, 353,* 1694–1701.

Sone, T., Nakaya, N., Ohmori, K., Shimazu, T., et al. (2008). Sense of life worth living (*ikigai*) and mortality in Japan: Ohsaki Study. *Psychosomatic Medicine, 70,* 709–715.

Soon, C. S., Brass, M., Heinze, H. J., and Haynes, J. D. (2008). Unconscious determinants of free decisions in the human brain. *Nature Neuroscience, 11,* 543–545.

Sorensen, P. W., and Goetz, F. W. (1993). Pheromonal and reproductive function of F prostaglandins and their metabolites in teleost fish. *Journal of Lipid Mediators, 6,* 385–393.

Sotiriadis, A., and Makrydimas, G. (2012). Neurodevelopment after prenatal diagnosis of isolated agenesis of the corpus callosum: An integrative review. *American Journal of Obstetrics and Gynecology, 206*(4), 337, e1–5.

Sowell, E. R., Kan, E., Yoshii, J., Thompson, P. M., et al. (2008). Thinning of sensorimotor cortices in children with Tourette syndrome. *Nature Neuroscience, 11,* 637–639.

Spalding, K. L., Bergmann, O., Alkass, K., Bernard, S., et al. (2013). Dynamics of hippocampal neurogenesis in adult humans. *Cell, 153*(6):1219–1227.

Sperry, R. W., Stamm, J., and Miner, N. (1956). Relearning tests for interocular transfer following division of optic chiasma and corpus callosum in cats. *Journal of Comparative and Physiological Psychology, 49,* 529–533.

Spiegler, B. J., and Mishkin, M. (1981). Evidence for the sequential participation of inferior temporal cortex and amygdala in the acquisition of stimulus-reward associations. *Behavioural Brain Research, 3,* 303–317.

Spiegler, B. J., and Yeni-Komshian, G. H. (1983). Incidence of left-handed writing in a college population with reference to family patterns of hand preference. *Neuropsychologia, 21,* 651–659.

Sporns, O. (2011). The human connectome: A complex network. *Annals of the New York Academy of Science, 1224,* 109–125.

Sprague, T. C., Saproo, S., and Serences, J. T. (2015). Visual attention mitigates information loss in small- and large-scale neural codes. *Trends in Cognitive Sciences, 19*(4), 215–226.

Squire, L. R., Amaral, D. G., Zola-Morgan, S., and Kritchevsky, M. P. G. (1989). Description of brain injury in the amnesic patient N.A. based on magnetic resonance imaging. *Experimental Neurology, 105,* 23–35.

Squire, L. R., and Moore, R. Y. (1979). Dorsal thalamic lesion in a noted case of chronic memory dysfunction. *Annals of Neurology, 6,* 503–506.

Squire, L. R., Wixted, J. T., and Clark, R. E. (2007). Recognition memory and the medial temporal lobe: A new perspective. *Nature Reviews Neuroscience, 8,* 872–883.

Squire, L. R., and Zola-Morgan, S. (1991). The medial temporal lobe memory system. *Science, 253,* 1380–1386.

Squitieri, F. (2013). Neurodegenerative disease: "Fifty shades of grey" in the Huntington disease gene. *Nature Reviews Neurology, 9*(8), 421–422.

St. John, S. J., and Spector, A. C. (1998). Behavioral discrimination between quinine and KCl is dependent on input from the seventh cranial nerve: Implications for the functional roles of the gustatory nerves in rats. *Journal of Neurophysiology, 18*(11), 4353–4362.

Standing, L. G. (1973). Learning 10,000 pictures. *Quarterly Journal of Experimental Psychology, 25,* 207–222.

Stanford, T. R., Shankar, S., Massoglia, D. P., Costello, M. G., et al. (2010). Perceptual decision making in less than 30 milliseconds. *Nature Neuroscience, 13*(3), 379–385.

Stanovich, K. E. (2009). *What intelligence tests miss: The psychology of rational thought.* New Haven, CT: Yale University Press.

Stanton, S. J., Beehner, J. C., Saini, E. K., Kuhn, C. M., et al. (2009). Dominance, politics, and physiology: Voters' testosterone changes on the night of the 2008 United States presidential election. *PLOS ONE, 4,* e7543.

Staubli, U. V. (1995). Parallel properties of long-term potentiation and memory. In J. L. McGaugh, N. M. Weinberger, and G. Lynch (Eds.), *Brain and memory: Modulation and mediation of neuroplasticity* (pp. 303–318). New York: Oxford University Press.

Stearns, S. C., Byars, S. G., Govindaraju, D. R., and Ewbank, D. (2010). Measuring selection in contemporary human populations. *Nature Reviews Genetics, 11*(9), 1611–1622.

Stefansson, H., Ophoff, R. A., Steinberg, S. Andreassen, O. A., et al. (2009). Common variants conferring risk of schizophrenia. *Nature, 460,* 744–747.

Stein, B., and Meredith, M. A. (1993). *The merging of the senses.* Cambridge, MA: MIT Press.

Stein, B. E., and Stanford, T. R. (2008). Multisensory integration: Current issues from the perspective of the single neuron. *Nature Reviews Neuroscience, 9,* 255–266.

Stein, M., and Miller, A. H. (1993). Stress, the hypothalamic-pituitary-adrenal axis, and immune function. *Advances in Experimental Medicine and Biology, 335,* 1–5.

Stein, M., Miller, A. H., and Trestman, R. L. (1991). Depression, the immune system, and health and illness. Findings in search of meaning. *Archives of General Psychiatry, 48,* 171–177.

Steiner, J. E. (1974). Discussion paper: Innate, discriminative human facial expressions to taste and smell stimulation. *Annals of the New York Academy of Sciences, 27,* 237–233.

Steinmetz, H., Volkmann, J., Jancke, L., and Freund, H. J. (1991). Anatomical left-right asymmetry of language-related temporal cortex is different in left- and right-handers. *Annals of Neurology, 29,* 315–319.

Stella, N., Schweitzer, P., and Piomelli, D. (1997). A second endogenous cannabinoid that modulates long-term potentiation. *Nature, 388,* 773–778.

Stephan, F. K., and Zucker, I. (1972). Circadian rhythms in drinking behavior and locomotor activity of rats are eliminated by hypothalamic lesions. *Proceedings of the National Academy of Sciences, USA, 69,* 1583–1586.

Stephan, H., Frahm, H., and Baron, G. (1981). New and revised data on volumes of brain structures in insectivores and primates. *Folia Primatologica, 35,* 1–29.

Stern, K., and McClintock, M. (1998). Regulation of ovulation by human pheromones. *Nature, 392,* 177–179.

Stoeckel, C., Gough, P. M., Watkins, K. E., and Devlin, J. T. (2009). Supramarginal gyrus involvement in visual word recognition. *Cortex, 45,* 1091–1096.

Stoerig, P., and Cowey, A. (1997). Blindsight in man and monkey. *Brain, 120,* 535–559.

Stoodley, C. J., and Stein, J. F. (2011). The cerebellum and dyslexia. *Cortex, 1, 101–116.*

Stowers, L., Holy, T. E., Meister, M., Dulac, C., et al. (2002). Loss of sex discrimination and male-male aggression in mice deficient for TRP2. *Science, 295,* 1493–1500.

Stranahan, A. M., Khalil, D., and Gould, E. (2006). Social isolation delays the positive effects of running on adult neurogenesis. *Nature Neuroscience, 9,* 526–533.

Stuber, G. D., and Wise, R. A. (2016). Lateral hypothalamic circuits for feeding and reward. *Nature Neuroscience, 19,* 198–205.

Stuve, T. A., Friedman, L., Jesberger, J. A., Gilmore, G. C., et al. (1997). The relationship between smooth pursuit performance, motion perception and sustained visual attention in patients with schizophrenia and normal controls. *Psychological Medicine, 27,* 143–152.

Substance Abuse and Mental Health Services Administration. (2011). *Results from the 2010 National Survey on Drug Use and Health: Summary of National Findings, NSDUH Series H-41, HHS Publication No. (SMA) 11-4658.* Rockville, MD: Substance Abuse and Mental Health Services Administration.

Substance Abuse and Mental Health Services Administration. (2014). *Results from the 2013 National Survey on Drug Use and Health: Summary of National Findings, NSDUH Series H-48, HHS Publication No. (SMA) 14-4863.* Rockville, MD: Substance Abuse and Mental Health Services Administration.

Sugawara, N., Yasui-Furukori, N., Ishii, N., Iwata, N., et al. (2013). Lithium in tap water and suicide mortality in Japan. *International Journal of Environmental Research and Public Health, 10,* 6044–6048.

Suk, I., and Tamargo, R. J. (2010). Concealed neuroanatomy in Michelangelo's *Separation of Light from Darkness* in the Sistine Chapel. *Neurosurgery, 66*(5), 851–861.

Sumbre, G., Fiorito, G., Flash, T., and Hochner, B. (2005). Motor control of flexible octopus arms. *Nature, 443,* 595–596.

Sumnall, H. R., and Cole, J. C. (2005). Self-reported depressive symptomatology in community samples of polysubstance misusers who report Ecstasy use: A meta-analysis. *Journal of Psychopharmacology, 19,* 84–92.

Sun, T., Patoine, C., Abu-Khalil, A., Visvader, J., et al. (2005). Early asymmetry of gene transcription in embryonic human left and right cerebral cortex. *Science, 308,* 1794–1798.

Sunn, N., Egli, M., Burazin, T. C. D., Burns, P., et al. (2002). Circulating relaxin acts on subfornical organ neurons to stimulate water drinking in the rat. *Proceedings of the National Academy of Sciences, USA, 99,* 1701–1706.

Sunstein, C. R., and Nussbaum, M. C. (Eds.) (2004). *Animal rights: Current debates and new directions.* Oxford, England: Oxford University Press.

Suo, C., Singh, M. F., Gates, N., Wen, W., et al. (2016). Therapeutically relevant structural and functional mechanisms triggered by physical and cognitive exercise. *Molecular Psychiatry.* PubMed PMID: 27001615. doi:10.1038/mp.2016.19 [Epub ahead of print]

Sutcliffe, J. G., and de Lecea, L. (2002). The hypocretins: Setting the arousal threshold. *Nature Reviews Neuroscience, 3,* 339–349.

Suthana, N., Haneef, Z., Stern, J., Mukamel, R., et al. (2012). Memory enhancement and deep-brain stimulation of the entorhinal area. *New England Journal of Medicine, 366*(6), 502–510.

Suzuki, S., Brown, C. M., and Wise, P. M. (2009). Neuroprotective effects of estrogens following ischemic stroke. *Frontiers in Neuroendocrinology, 30,* 201–211.

Suzuki, W. A., and Naya, Y. (2014). The perirhinal cortex. *Annual Review of Neuroscience, 37,* 39–53.

Swedo, S. E., Rapoport, J. L., Leonard, H., Lenane, M., et al. (1989). Obsessive-compulsive disorder in children and adolescents: Clinical phenomenology of 70 consecutive cases. *Archives of General Psychiatry, 46*(4), 335–341.

Swick, T. J. (2015). Treatment paradigms for cataplexy in narcolepsy: Past, present, and future. *Nature and Science of Sleep, 7,* 159–169.

Symonds, M. E., Pope, M., and Budge, H. (2015). The ontogeny of brown adipose tissue. *Annual Review of Nutrition, 35,* 295–320.

Szalavitz, M. (2004, March 25). The accidental addict: Clearing away the myths surrounding the OxyContin "epidemic." *Slate* (http://slate.msn.com/id/2097786).

Szarfman, A., Doraiswamy, P. M., Tonning, J. M., and Levine, J. G. (2006). Association between pathologic gambling and parkinsonian therapy as detected in the Food and Drug Administration Adverse Event database. *Archives Neurology, 62,* 299–300.

Székely, T., Catchpole, C. K., DeVoogd, A., Marchl, Z., et al. (1996). Evolutionary changes in a song control area of the brain (HVC) are associated with evolutionary changes in song repertoire among European warblers (Sylviidae). *Proceedings of the Royal Society of London. Series B: Biological Sciences, 263,* 607–610.

Szente, M., Gajda, Z., Said Ali, K., and Hermesz, E. (2002). Involvement of electrical coupling in the in vivo ictal epileptiform activity induced by 4-aminopyridine in the neocortex. *Neuroscience, 115,* 1067–1078.

T

Taglialatela, J. P., Cantalupo, C., and Hopkins, W. D. (2006). Gesture handedness predicts asymmetry in the chimpanzee inferior frontal gyrus. *Neuroreport, 17,* 923–927.

Taipale, M., Kaminen, N., Nopola-Hemmi, J., Haltia, T., et al. (2003). A candidate gene for developmental dyslexia encodes a nuclear tetratricopeptide repeat domain protein dynamically regulated in brain. *Proceedings of the National Academy of Sciences, USA, 100,* 11553–11558.

Tait, S. W., and Green, D. R. (2010). Mitochondria and cell death: Outer membrane permeabilization and beyond. *Nature Reviews Molecular Cell Biology, 11*(9), 621–632. doi:10.1038/nrm2952

Takahashi, H., Kato, M., Matsuura, M., Mobbs, D., et al. (2009). When your gain is my pain and your pain is my gain: Neural correlates of envy and schadenfreude. *Science, 323,* 937–939.

Takahashi, J. S. (1995). Molecular neurobiology and genetics of circadian rhythms in mammals. *Annual Review of Neuroscience, 18,* 531–554.

Takahashi, T., Svoboda, K., and Malinow, R. (2003). Experience strengthening transmission by driving AMPA receptors into synapses. *Science, 299,* 1585–1588.

Tallal, P., and Schwartz, J. (1980). Temporal processing, speech perception and hemispheric asymmetry. *Trends in Neurosciences, 3,* 309–311.

Tam, J., Duda, D. G., Perentes, J. Y., Quadri, R. S., et al. (2009). Blockade of VEGFR2 and not VEGFR1 can limit diet-induced fat tissue expansion: Role of local versus bone marrow-derived endothelial cells. *PLOS ONE, 4,* e4974.

Tamaki, M., Bang, J. W., Watanabe, T., and Sasaki, Y. (2016). Night watch in one brain hemisphere during sleep associated with the first-night effect in humans. *Current Biology, 26.* doi:10.1016/j.cub.2016.02.063

Tamás, G., Lörincz, A., Simon, A., and Szabadics, J. (2003). Identified sources and targets of slow inhibition in the neocortex. *Science, 299,* 1902–1905.

Tamgüney, G., Miller, M. W., Wolfe, L. L., Sirochman, T. M., et al. (2009). Asymptomatic deer excrete infectious prions in faeces. *Nature, 461,* 529–532.

Tamminga, C. A., and Schulz, S. C. (1991). *Schizophrenia research.* New York: Raven.

Tanaka, H., Black, J. M., Hulme, C., Stanley, L. M., et al. (2011). The brain basis of the phonological deficit in dyslexia is independent of IQ. *Psychological Science, 22*(11), 1442–1451.

Tanaka, K. (1993). Neuronal mechanisms of object recognition. *Science, 262,* 685–688.

Tanaka, S., Ikeda, H., Kasahara, K., Kato, R., et al. (2013). Larger right posterior parietal volume in action video game experts: A behavioral and voxel-based morphometry (VBM) study. *PLOS ONE, 8,* e66998.

Tanaka, Y., Kamo, T., Yoshida, M., and Yamadori, A. (1991). "So-called" cortical deafness. Clinical, neurophysiological and radiological observations. *Brain, 114,* 2385–2401.

Tanda, G., Munzar, P., and Goldberg, S. R. (2000). Self-administration behavior is maintained by the psychoactive ingredient of marijuana in squirrel monkeys. *Nature Neuroscience, 3,* 1073–1074.

Tang, Y. P., Shimizu, E., Dube, G. R., Rampon, C., et al. (1999). Genetic enhancement of learning and memory in mice. *Nature, 401,* 63–69.

Tang, Y. P., Wang, H., Feng, R., Kyin, M., et al. (2001). Differential effects of enrichment on learning and memory function in NR2B transgenic mice. *Neuropharmacology, 41,* 779–790.

Tanigawa, H., Lu, H. D., and Roe, A. W. (2010). Functional organization for color and orientation in macaque V4. *Nature Neuroscience, 13,* 1542–1548.

Tanji, J. (2001). Sequential organization of multiple movements: Involvement of cortical motor areas. *Annual Review of Neuroscience, 24,* 631–651.

Tannenbaum, P. L., Tye, S. J., Stevens, J., Gotter, A. L., et al. (2016). Inhibition of orexin signaling promotes sleep yet preserves salient arousability in monkeys. *Sleep, 39*(3), 603–612.

Taub, E. (1976). Movement in nonhuman primates deprived of somatosensory feedback. *Exercise and Sport Sciences Reviews, 4,* 335–374.

Taub, E., Uswatte, G., and Elbert, T. (2002). New treatments in neurorehabilitation founded on basic research. *Nature Reviews Neuroscience, 3,* 228–235.

Tavares, R. M., Mendelsohn, A., Grossman, Y., Williams, C. H., et al. (2015). A map for social navigation in the human brain. *Neuron, 87*(1), 231–243.

Tavernise, S. (2016, February 29). Female Viagra only modestly increases sexual satisfaction, study finds. *The New York Times,* p. A20.

Temple, E., Deutsch, G. K., Poldrack, R. A., Miller, S. L., et al. (2003). Neural deficits in children with dyslexia ameliorated by behavioral remediation: Evidence from functional MRI. *Proceedings of the National Academy of Sciences, USA, 100,* 2860–2865.

Terburg, D., Aarts, H., and van Honk, J. (2012). Testosterone affects gaze aversion from angry faces outside of conscious awareness. *Psychological Science, 23,* 459–463.

Terkel, J., and Rosenblatt, J. S. (1972). Humoral factors underlying maternal behavior at parturition: Cross transfusion between freely moving rats. *Journal of Comparative and Physiological Psychology, 80,* 365–371.

Terman, G. W., Shavit, Y., Lewis, J. W., Cannon, J. T., et al. (1984). Intrinsic mechanisms of pain inhibition: Activation by stress. *Science, 226,* 1270–1277.

Terpstra, N. J., Bolhuis, J. J., Riebel, K., van der Burg, J. M., et al. (2006). Localized brain activation specific to auditory memory in a female songbird. *Journal of Comparative Neurology, 494,* 784–791.

Terrace, H. S. (1979). *Nim.* New York: Knopf.

Tessier-Lavigne, M., Placzek, M., Lumsden, A. G., Dodd, J., et al. (1988). Chemotropic guidance of developing axons in the mammalian central nervous system. *Nature, 336,* 775–778.

Tetel, M. J. (2000). Nuclear receptor coactivators in neuroendocrine function. *Journal of Neuroendocrinology, 12,* 927–932.

Tewksbury, J. J., and Nabhan, G. P. (2001). Seed dispersal: Directed deterrence by capsaicin in chillies. *Nature, 412,* 403–404.

Thannickal, T. C., Moore, R. Y., Nienhuis, R., Ramanathan, L., et al. (2000). Reduced number of hypocretin neurons in human narcolepsy. *Neuron, 27,* 469–474.

Theillet, F. X., Binolfi, A., Bekei, B., Martorana, A., et al. (2016). Structural disorder of monomeric α-synuclein persists in mammalian cells. *Nature, 530*(7588), 45–50.

Theunissen, F. E., and Elie, J. E. (2014). Neural processing of natural sounds. *Nature Reviews Neuroscience, 15*(6), 355–366.

Thimgan, M. S., Seugnet, L., Turk, J., and Shaw, P. J. (2015). Identification of genes associated with resilience/vulnerability to sleep deprivation and starvation in *Drosophila. Sleep, 38*(5), 801–814.

Thoen, H. H., How, M. J., Chiou, T. H., and Marshall, J. (2014). A different form of color vision in mantis shrimp. *Science, 343,* 411–413.

Thompson, P. M., Vidal, C., Giedd, J. N., Gochman, P., et al. (2001). Mapping adolescent brain change reveals dynamic wave of accelerated gray matter loss in very early-onset schizophrenia. *Proceedings of the National Academy of Sciences, USA, 98,* 11650–11655.

Thompson, R. F., and Krupa, D. J. (1994). Organization of memory traces in the mammalian brain. *Annual Review of Neuroscience, 17,* 519–549.

Thompson, R. F., and Steinmetz, J. E. (2009). The role of the cerebellum in classical conditioning of discrete behavioral responses. *Neuroscience, 162,* 732–755.

Thompson, T., and Schuster, C. R. (1964). Morphine self-administration, food reinforced and avoidance behaviour in rhesus monkeys. *Psychopharmacologia, 5,* 87–94.

Thornton, A. E., Cox, D. N., Whitfield, K., and Fouladi, R. T. (2008). Cumulative concussion exposure in rugby players: Neurocognitive and symptomatic outcomes. *Journal of Clinical and Experimental Neuropsychology, 30,* 398–409.

Thornton-Jones, Z. D., Kennett, G. A., Benwell, K. R., Revell, D. F., et al. (2006). The cannabinoid CB1 receptor inverse agonist, rimonabant, modifies body weight and adiponectin function in diet-induced obese rats as a consequence of reduced food intake. *Pharmacology, Biochemistry, and Behavior, 84,* 353–359.

Thorpe, S. J., and Fabre-Thorpe, M. (2001). Seeking categories in the brain. *Science, 291,* 260–263.

Timmann, D., Drepper, J., Frings, M., Maschke, M., et al. (2010). The human cerebellum contributes to motor, emotional and cognitive associative learning. A review. *Cortex, 7,* 845–857.

Tissir, F., and Goffinet, A. M. (2003). Reelin and brain development. *Nature Reviews Neuro-science, 4,* 496–505.

Tizzano, M., and Finger, T. E. (2013). Chemosensors in the nose: Guardians of the airways. *Physiology, 28*(1), 51–60.

Tobias, P. V. (1980). L'evolution du cerveau humain. *La Recherche, 11,* 282–292.

Todorov, A., Said, C. P., Engell, A. D., and Oosterhof, N. N. (2008). Understanding evaluation of faces on social dimensions. *Trends in Cognitive Science, 12,* 455–460.

Tolman, E. C. (1949). There is more than one kind of learning. *Psychological Review, 56,* 144–155.

Tolman, E. C., and Honzik, C. H. (1930). Introduction and removal of reward, and maze performance in rats. *University of California Publications in Psychology, 4,* 257–275.

Tom, S. M., Fox, C. R., Trepel, C., and Poldrack, R. A. (2007). The neural basis of loss aversion in decision-making under risk. *Science, 315,* 515–518.

Tomizawa, K., Iga, N., Lu, Y. F., Moriwaki, A., et al. (2003). Oxytocin improves long-lasting spatial memory during motherhood through MAP kinase cascade. *Nature Neuroscience, 6,* 384–390.

Tomonari, H., Miura, H., Nakayama, A., Matsumura, E., et al. (2012). Gα-gustducin is extensively coexpressed with sweet and bitter taste receptors in both the soft palate and fungiform papillae but has a different functional significance. *Chemical Senses, 37*(3), 241–251.

Toni, N., Laplagne, D. A., Zhao, C., Lombardi, G., et al. (2008). Neurons born in the adult dentate gyrus form functional synapses with target cells. *Nature Neuroscience, 11,* 901–907.

Tootell, R. B., Silverman, M. S., Hamilton, S. L., De Valois, R. L., et al. (1988). Functional anatomy of macaque striate cortex. III. Color. *Journal of Neuroscience, 8,* 1569–1593.

Tootell, R. B., Silverman, M. S., Switkes, E., and De Valois, R. L. (1982). Deoxyglucose analysis of retinotopic organization in primate striate cortex. *Science, 218,* 902–904.

Tootell, R. B., Tsao, D., and Vanduffel, W. (2003). Neuroimaging weighs in: Humans meet macaques in "primate" visual cortex. *Journal of Neuroscience, 23,* 3981–3989.

Tootell, R. B. H., Hadjikhani, N. K., Vanduffel, W., Liu, A. K., et al. (1998). Functional analysis of primary visual cortex (V1) in humans. *Proceedings of the National Academy of Sciences, USA, 95,* 811–817.

Tordoff, M., Rawson, N., and Friedman, M. (1991). 2,5-Anhydro-d-mannitol acts in liver to initiate feeding. *American Journal of Physiology, 261,* R283–R288.

Torrey, E. F., Bowler, A. E., Taylor, E. H., and Gottesman, I. I. (1994). *Schizophrenia and manic depressive disorder.* New York: Basic Books.

Trachtenberg, J. T., Chen, B. E., Knott, G. W., Feng, G., et al. (2002). Long-term in vivo imaging of experience-dependent synaptic plasticity in adult cortex. *Nature, 420,* 788–794.

Traffanstedt, M. K., Mehta, S., and LoBello, S. G. (2016). Major depression with seasonal variation: Is it a valid construct? *Clinical Psychological Science.* doi:10.1177/2167702615615867

Trasande, L., Blustein, J., Liu, M., Corwin, E., et al. (2013). Infant antibiotic exposures and early-life body mass. *International Journal of Obesity (London), 37*(1), 16–23.

Travers, S. P., and Geran, L. C. (2009). Bitter-responsive brainstem neurons: Characteristics and functions. *Physiology & Behavior, 97*(5), 592–603.

Treesukosol, Y., Lyall, V., Heck, G. L., Desimone, J. A., et al. (2007). A psychophysical and electrophysiological analysis of salt taste in *Trpv1* null mice. *American Journal of Physiology. Regulatory, Integrative, and Comparative Physiology, 292,* R1799–R1809.

Treesukosol, Y., and Spector, A. C. (2012). Orosensory detection of sucrose, maltose, and glucose is severely impaired in mice lacking T1R2 or T1R3, but Polycose sensitivity remains relatively normal. *American Journal of Physiology: Regulatory, Integrative, and Comparative Physiology, 303*(2), R218–R235.

Treisman, A. [M]. (1996). The binding problem. *Current Opinion in Neurobiology, 6,* 171–178.

Treisman, A. M., and Gelade, G. (1980). A feature-integration theory of attention. *Cognitive Psychology, 12,* 97–136.

Treisman, M. (1977). Motion sickness: Evolutionary hypotheses. *Science, 197,* 493–495.

Trimble, M. R. (1991). Interictal psychoses of epilepsy. *Advances in Neurology, 55,* 143–152.

Trinh, J., and Farrer, M. (2013). Advances in the genetics of Parkinson disease. *Nature Reviews Neurology, 9*(8), 445–454.

Trojanowski, N. F., and Raizen, D. M. (2016). Call it worm sleep. *Trends in Neurosciences, 39*(2), 54–62.

Tronick, R., and Reck, C. (2009). Infants of depressed mothers. *Harvard Review of Psychiatry, 17,* 147–156.

Truitt, W. A., and Coolen, L. M. (2002). Identification of a potential ejaculation generator in the spinal cord. *Science, 297,* 1566–1569.

Ts'o, D. Y., Frostig, R. D., Lieke, E. E., and Grinvald, A. (1990). Functional organization of primate visual cortex revealed by high resolution optical imaging. *Science, 249,* 417–420.

Tsai, L., and Barnea, G. (2014). A critical period defined by axon-targeting mechanisms in the murine olfactory bulb. *Science, 344*(6180), 197–200.

Tsivilis, D., Vann, S. D., Denby, C., Roberts, N., et al. (2008). A disproportionate role for the fornix and mammillary bodies in recall versus recognition memory. *Nature Neuroscience, 11*(7), 834–842.

Tsuboi, D., Kuroda, K., Tanaka, M., Namba, T., et al. (2015). Disrupted-in-schizophrenia 1 regulates transport of *ITPR1* mRNA for synaptic plasticity. *Nature Neuroscience, 18,* 698–707.

Tsuchiya, N., and Adolphs, R. (2007). Emotion and consciousness. *Trends in Cognitive Sciences, 11,* 158–167.

Tsujimoto, S., Genovesio, A., and Wise, S. P. (2011). Frontal pole cortex: Encoding ends at the end of the endbrain. *Trends in Cognitive Sciences, 15*(4), 169–176.

Tsutsui, K., Bentley, G. E., Ubuka, T., Saigoh, E., et al. (2006). The general and comparative biology of gonadotropin-inhibitory hormone (GnIH). *General and Comparative Endocrinology, 153,* 365–370.

Tuller, D. (2002, January 8). A quiet revolution for those prone to nodding off. *The New York Times* (http://query.nytimes.com/gst/fullpage.html?sec=health&res=980DE5DD1439F93BA35752C0A9649C8B63).

Tulving, E. (1972). Episodic and semantic memory. In E. Tulving and W. Donaldson (Eds.), *Organization of memory* (pp. 381–403). New York: Academic Press.

Tulving, E. (1989). Memory: Performance, knowledge, and experience. *European Journal of Cognitive Psychology, 1,* 3–26.

Tulving, E., Hayman, C. A., and Macdonald, C. A. (1991). Long-lasting perceptual priming and semantic learning in amnesia: A case experiment. *Journal of Experimental Psychology: Learning, Memory, and Cognition, 17,* 595–617.

Turner, E. H., Matthews, A. M., Linardatos, E., Tell, R. A., et al. (2008). Selective publication of antidepressant trials and its influence on apparent efficacy. *New England Journal of Medicine, 358,* 252–260.

Twenge, J. M. (2015). Time period and birth cohort differences in depressive symptoms in the U.S., 1982–2013. *Social Indicators Research, 121*(2), 437–454.

Twenge, J. M., Gentile, B., DeWall, C. N., Ma, D., et al. (2010). Birth cohort increases in psychopathology among young Americans, 1938–2007: A cross-temporal meta-analysis of the MMPI. *Clinical Psychology Review, 30*(2), 145–154.

Tyack, P. L. (2003). Dolphins communicate about individual-specific social relationships. In F. de Waal and P. L. Tyack (Eds.), *Animal social complexity: Intelligence, culture, and individualized societies* (pp. 342–361). Cambridge, MA: Harvard University Press.

Tye, K. M., and Deisseroth, K. (2012). Optogenetic investigation of neural circuits underlying brain disease in animal models. *Nature Reviews Neuroscience, 13,* 251–266.

Tyszka, J. M., Kennedy, D. P., Adolphs, R., and Paul, L. K. (2011). Intact bilateral resting-state networks in the absence of the corpus callosum. *Journal of Neuroscience, 31*(42), 15154–15162.

Tyzio, R., Cossart, R., Khalilov, I., Minlebaeve, M., et al. (2006). Maternal oxytocin triggers a transient inhibitory switch in GABA signaling in the fetal brain during delivery. *Science, 314,* 1788–1792.

U

Umilta, M. A., Kohler, E., Galiese, V., Fogassi, L., et al. (2001). I know what you are doing: A neurophysiological study. *Neuron, 31,* 155–165.

Underwood, E. (2016). A shot at migraine. *Science, 351*(6269), 116–119.

Ungerleider, L. G., Courtney, S. M., and Haxby, J.V. (1998). A neural system for human visual working memory. *Proceedings of the National Academy of Sciences, USA, 95,* 883–890.

Upile, T., Sipaul, F., Jerjes, W., Singh, S., et al. (2007). The acute effects of alcohol on auditory thresholds. *BMC Ear, Nose, and Throat Disorders, 7,* 4.

Urban, D. J., and Roth, B. L. (2015). DREADDs (designer receptors exclusively activated by designer drugs): Chemogenetic tools with therapeutic utility. *Annual Review of Pharmacology and Toxicology, 55,* 399–417.

Ursin, H., Baade, E., and Levine, S. (1978). *Psychobiology of stress: A study of coping men.* New York: Academic Press.

V

Vallortigara, G., Rogers, L. J., and Bisazza, A. (1999). Possible evolutionary origins of cognitive brain lateralization. *Brain Research. Brain Research Reviews, 30,* 164–175.

van Anders, S. M., and Watson, N.V. (2006). Social neuroendocrinology: Effects of social contexts and behaviors on sex steroids in humans. *Human Nature, 17,* 212–237.

Van Dongen, H. P., Maislin, G., Mullington, J. M., and Dinges, D. F. (2003). The cumulative cost of additional wakefulness: Dose-response effects on neurobehavioral functions and sleep physiology from chronic sleep restriction and total sleep deprivation. *Sleep, 26,* 117–126.

Van Essen, D. C. (2013). Cartography and connectomes. *Neuron, 80*(3), 775–790.

Van Essen, D. C., and Drury, H. A. (1997). Structural and functional analyses of human cerebral cortex using a surface-based atlas. *Journal of Neuroscience, 17,* 7079–7102.

Van Gaal, L. F., Rissanen, A. M., Scheen, A. J., Ziegler, O., et al. (2005). Effects of the cannabinoid-1 receptor blocker rimonabant on weight reduction and cardiovascular risk factors in overweight patients: 1-year experience from the RIO-Europe study. *Lancet, 365,* 1389–1397.

van Nas, A., Guhathakurta, D., Wang, S. S., Yehya, N., et al. (2009). Elucidating the role of gonadal hormones in sexually dimorphic gene coexpression networks. *Endocrinology, 150,* 1235–1249.

van Os, J., and Kapur, S. (2009). Schizophrenia. *Lancet, 374*(9690), 635–645.

van Os, J., Kenis, G., and Rutten, B. P. F. (2010). The environment and schizophrenia. *Nature, 468,* 203–212.

van Praag, H., Kempermann, G., and Gage, F. H. (2000). Neural consequences of environmental enrichment. *Nature Reviews Neuroscience, 1,* 191–198.

van Tol, M. J., van der Wee, N. J., van den Heuvel, O. A., Nielen, M. M., et al. (2010). Regional brain volume in depression and anxiety disorders. *Archives of General Psychiatry, 67,* 1002–1011.

Van Valen, L. (1974). Brain size and intelligence in man. *American Journal of Physical Anthropology, 40,* 417–423.

van Westen, M., Rietveld, E., Figee, M., and Denys, D. (2015). Clinical outcome and mechanisms of deep brain stimulation for obsessive-compulsive disorder. *Current Behavioral Neuroscience Reports, 2,* 41–48.

Van Winkel, R., and Genetic Risk and Outcome of Psychosis (GROUP) Investigators. (2011). Family-based analysis of genetic variation underlying psychosis-inducing effects of cannabis: Sibling analysis and proband follow-up. *Archives of General Psychiatry, 68,* 148–157.

Van Zoeren, J. G., and Stricker, E. M. (1977). Effects of preoptic, lateral hypothalamic, or dopamine-depleting lesions on behavioral thermoregulation in rats exposed to the cold. *Journal of Comparative and Physiological Psychology, 91,* 989–999.

Vandermosten, M., Boets, B., Wouters, J., and Ghesquière, P. (2012). A qualitative and quantitative review of diffusion tensor imaging studies in reading and dyslexia. *Neuroscience and Biobehavioral Reviews, 36*(6), 1532–1552.

VanDoren, M. J., Matthews, D. B., Janis, G. C., Grobin, A. C., et al. (2000). Neuroactive steroid 3 alpha-hydroxy-5alpha-pregnan-20-one modulates electrophysiological and behavioral actions of ethanol. *Journal of Neuroscience, 20,* 1982–1989.

Vann, S. D., and Nelson, A. J. (2015). The mammillary bodies and memory: More than a hippocampal relay. *Progress in Brain Research, 219,* 163–185.

Vargas, C. D., Aballéa, A., Rodrigues, E. C., Reilly, K. T., et al. (2009). Re-emergence of hand-muscle representations in human motor cortex after hand allograft. *Proceedings of the National Academy of Sciences, USA, 106,* 7197–7202.

Vasey, P. L. (1995). Homosexual behaviour in primates: A review of evidence and theory. *International Journal of Primatology, 16,* 173–204.

Vassar, R., Ngai, J., and Axel, R. (1993). Spatial segregation of odorant receptor expression in the mammalian olfactory epithelium. *Cell, 74,* 309–318.

Vaughan, W., and Greene, S. L. (1984). Pigeon visual memory capacity. *Journal of Experimental Psychology: Animal Behavior Processes, 10,* 256–271.

Velliste, M., Perel, S., Spalding, M. C., Whitford, A. S., et al. (2008). Cortical control of a prosthetic arm for self-feeding. *Nature, 453,* 1098–1101.

Vernes, S. C., Oliver, P. L., Spiteri, E., Lockstone, H. E., et al. (2011). Foxp2 regulates gene networks implicated in neurite outgrowth in the developing brain. *PLOS Genetics, 7*(7), e1002145. doi:10.1371/journal.pgen.1002145

Vialou, V., Feng, J., Robison, A. J., Ku, S. M., et al. (2012). Serum response factor and cAMP response element binding protein are both required for cocaine induction of ΔFosB. *Journal of Neuroscience, 32,* 7577–7584.

Vierbuchen, T., Ostermeier, A., Pang, Z. P., Kokubu, Y., et al. (2010). Direct conversion of fibroblasts to functional neurons by defined factors. *Nature, 463,* 1035–1041.

Villalobos, M. E., Mizuno, A., Dahl, B. C., Kemmotsu, N., et al. (2005). Reduced functional connectivity between V1 and inferior frontal cortex associated with visuomotor performance in autism. *Neuroimage, 25,* 916–925.

Villringer, A., and Chance, B. (1997). Non-invasive optical spectroscopy and imaging of human brain function. *Trends in Neurosciences, 20,* 435–442.

Vincus, A. A., Ringwalt, C., Harris, M. S., and Shamblen, S. R. (2010). A short-term, quasi-experimental evaluation of D.A.R.E.'s revised elementary school curriculum. *Journal of Drug Education, 40,* 37–49.

Visser, S. N., Danielson, M. L., Bitsko, R. H., Holbrook, J. R., et al. (2014). Trends in the parent-report of health care provider-diagnosed and medicated attention-deficit/hyperactivity disorder: United States, 2003–2011. *Journal of the American Academy of Child and Adolescent Psychiatry, 53*(1), 34–46.e2.

Vita, A., De Peri, L., and Sacchetti, E. (2015). Lithium in drinking water and suicide prevention: A review of the evidence. *International Clinical Psychopharmacology, 30,* 1–5.

Vitali, P., Di Perri, C., Vaudano, A. E., Meletti, S., et al. (2015). Integration of multimodal neuroimaging methods: A rationale for clinical applications of simultaneous EEG-fMRI. *Functional Neurology, 30*(1), 9–20.

Vogt, B. A. (2005). Pain and emotion interactions in subregions of the cingulate gyrus. *Nature Reviews Neuroscience, 6,* 533–544.

Volkow, N. D., Wang, G. J., Kollins, S. H., Wigal, T. L., et al. (2009). Evaluating dopamine reward pathway in ADHD: Clinical implications. *JAMA, 302,* 1084–1091.

Volkow, N. D., Wang, G-J., Telang, F., Fowler, J. S., et al. (2006). Cocaine cues and dopamine in dorsal striatum: Mechanism of craving in cocaine addiction. *Journal of Neuroscience, 26,* 6583–6588.

Volkow, N. D., and Wise, R. A. (2005). How can drug addiction help us understand obesity? *Nature Neuroscience, 8,* 555–560.

Vollenweider, F. X., and Kometer, M. (2010). The neurobiology of psychedelic drugs: Implications for the treatment of mood disorders. *Nature Reviews Neuroscience, 11,* 642–651.

von Helmholtz, H. (1852). On the theory of compound colours. *Philosophical Magazine, 4,*(4), 519–535.

Vonck, K., Raedt, R., Naulaerts, J., De Vogelaere, F., et al. (2014). Vagus nerve stimulation … 25 years later! What do we know about the effects on cognition? *Neuroscience and Biobehavioral Reviews, 45,* 63–71.

Voneida, T. J. (1990). The effect of rubrospinal tractotomy on a conditioned limb response in the cat. *Society for Neuroscience Abstracts, 16,* 279.

Voytek, B., Kayser, A. S., Badre, D., Fegen, D., et al. (2015). Oscillatory dynamics coordinating human frontal networks in support of goal maintenance. *Nature Neuroscience, 18*(9), 1318–1324.

Vriens, J., Nilius, B., and Voets, T. (2014). Peripheral thermosensation in mammals. *Nature Reviews Neuroscience, 15,* 573–589.

Vrieze, A., Van Nood, E., Holleman, F., Salojärvi, J., et al. (2012). Transfer of intestinal microbiota from lean donors increases insulin sensitivity in individuals with metabolic syndrome. *Gastroenterology, 143*(4), 913–916.e7.

Vrontou, E., Nilsen, S. P., Demir, E., Kravitz, E. A., et al. (2006). *fruitless* regulates aggression and dominance in *Drosophila. Nature Neuroscience, 9,* 1469–1471.

Vyazovskiy, V. V., and Harris, K. D. (2013). Sleep and the single neuron: The role of global slow oscillations in individual cell rest. *Nature Reviews Neuroscience, 14*(6), 443–451.

Vyazovskiy, V. V., Olcese, U., Hanlon, E. C., Nir, Y. et al. (2011). Local sleep in awake rats. *Nature, 472*(7344), 443–447.

Vyazovskiy, V. V., Olcese, U., Hanlon, E. C., Nir, Y., et al. (2011). Local sleep in awake rats. *Nature, 472,* 443–447.

W

Wada, J. A., Clarke, R., and Hamm, A. (1975). Cerebral hemispheric asymmetry in humans. Cortical speech zones in 100 adults and 100 infant brains. *Archives of Neurology, 32,* 239–246.

Wada, J. A., and Rasmussen, T. (1960). Intracarotid injection of sodium amytal for the lateralization of cerebral speech dominance: Experimental and clinical observations. *Journal of Neurosurgery, 17,* 266–282.

Waddell, J., and Shors, T. J. (2008). Neurogenesis, learning and associative strength. *European Journal of Neuroscience, 27,* 3020–3028.

Wager, T. D., and Atlas, L. Y. (2015). The neuroscience of placebo effects: Connecting context, learning and health. *Nature Reviews Neuroscience, 16*(7), 403–418.

Wager, T. D., Rilling, J. K., Smith, E. E., Sokolik, A., et al. (2004). Placebo-induced changes in fMRI in the anticipation and experience of pain. *Science, 303,* 1162–1167.

Wager, T. D., Scott, D. J., and Zubieta, J. K. (2007). Placebo effects on human mu-opioid activity during pain. *Proceedings of the National Academy of Sciences, USA, 104,* 11056–11061.

Wagner, A. D., Desmond, J. E., Demb, J. B., Glover, G. H., et al. (1997). Semantic repetition priming for verbal and pictorial knowledge: A functional MRI study of left inferior prefrontal cortex. *Journal of Cognitive Neuroscience, 9,* 714–726.

Wagner, A. D., Schacter, D. L., Rotte, M., Koutstaal, W., et al. (1998). Building memories: Remembering and forgetting of verbal experiences as predicted by brain activity. *Science, 281,* 1188–1191.

Wagner, G. C., Beuving, L. J., and Hutchinson, R. R. (1980). The effects of gonadal hormone manipulations on aggressive target-biting in mice. *Aggressive Behavior, 6,* 1–7.

Wagner, U., Gais, S., Haider, H., Verleger, R., et al. (2004). Sleep inspires insight. *Nature, 427,* 352–355.

Wahl, A. S., Omlor, W., Rubio, J. C., Chen, J. L., et al. (2014). Neuronal repair: Asynchronous therapy restores motor control by rewiring of the rat corticospinal tract after stroke. *Science, 344*(6189), 1250–1255.

Wahlstrom, J. (2002). Changing times: Findings from the first longitudinal study of later high school start times. *National Association of Secondary School Principals Bulletin, 86,* 3–21.

Waldrop, M. M. (2012). Brain in a box. *Nature, 482*(7386), 456–458.

Walker, E. F. (1991). *Schizophrenia: A life-course developmental perspective.* San Diego, CA: Academic Press.

Wallis, J. D. (2007). Orbitofrontal cortex and its contribution to decision-making. *Annual Review of Neuroscience, 30,* 31–56.

Walsh, D. M., and Selkoe, D. J. (2016). A critical appraisal of the pathogenic protein spread hypothesis of neurodegeneration. *Nature Reviews Neuroscience, 17*(4), 251–260.

Walsh, E. J., Wang, L. M., Armstrong, D. L., Curro, T., et al. (2003). Acoustic communication in *Panthera tigris*: A study of tiger vocalization and auditory receptivity. In Special Session on: Nature's orchestra: Acoustics of singing and calling animals: Production and reception of sound for communication by underwater and terrestrial animals. *Journal of the Acoustical Society of America, 113,* 2275.

Walters, R. J., Hadley, S. H., Morris, K. D. W., and Amin, J. (2000). Benzodiazepines act on $GABA_A$ receptors via two distinct and separable mechanisms. *Nature Neuroscience, 3,* 1273–1280.

Walther, S., Goya-Maldonado, R., Stippich, C., Weisbrod, M., et al. (2010). A supramodal network for response inhibition. *Neuroreport, 21,* 191–195.

Walton, C., Pariser, E., and Nottebohm, F. (2012). The zebra finch paradox: Song is little changed, but number of neurons doubles. *Journal of Neuroscience, 32*(3), 761–774.

Wang, F., Nemes, A., Mendelsohn, M., and Axel, R. (1998). Odorant receptors govern the formation of a precise topographic map. *Cell, 93,* 47–60.

Wang, H., Yang, H., Shivalila, C. S., Dawlaty, M. M., et al. (2013). One-step generation of mice carrying mutations in multiple genes by CRISPR/Cas-mediated genome engineering. *Cell, 153*(4), 910–918.

Wang, H., Yu, M., Ochani, M., Amella, C. A., et al. (2003). Nicotinic acetylcholine receptor α7 subunit is an essential regulator of inflammation. *Nature, 421*, 384–388.

Wang, S., Liu, B., Zhang, H., Dong, R., et al. (2013). Mandarin lexical tone recognition in sensorineural hearing-impaired listeners and cochlear implant users. *Acta Oto-Laryngologica, 133*(1), 47–54.

Wang, W. C., Lazzara, M. M., Ranganath, C., Knight, R. T., et al. (2010). The medial temporal lobe supports conceptual implicit memory. *Neuron, 68*(5), 835–842.

Wang, W. C., Ranganath, C., and Yonelinas, A. P. (2014). Activity reductions in perirhinal cortex predict conceptual priming and familiarity-based recognition. *Neuropsychologia, 52*, 19–26.

Wang, Y., and Mandelkow, E. (2016). Tau in physiology and pathology. *Nature Reviews Neuroscience, 17*(1), 5–21. doi:10.1038/nrn.2015.1

Watanabe, M., Cheng, K., Murayama, Y., Ueno, K., et al. (2011). Attention but not awareness modulates the BOLD signal in the human V1 during binocular suppression. *Science, 334*, 829–831.

Watanabe, S., Trimbuch, T., Camacho-Pérez, M., Rost, B. R., et al. (2014). Clathrin regenerates synaptic vesicles from endosomes. *Nature, 515*(7526), 228–233.

Watson, N. V. (2001). Sex differences in throwing: Monkeys having a fling. *Trends in Cognitive Sciences, 5*, 98–99.

Watson, N. V., Freeman, L. M., and Breedlove, S. M. (2001). Neuronal size in the spinal nucleus of the bulbocavernosus: Direct modulation by androgen in rats with mosaic androgen insensitivity. *Journal of Neuroscience, 21*, 1062–1066.

Waxman, S. G., and Zamponi, G. W. (2014). Regulating excitability of peripheral afferents: Emerging ion channel targets. *Nature Neuroscience, 17*(2), 153–163.

Weber, F., Chung, S., Beier, K. T., Xu, M., et al. (2015). Control of REM sleep by ventral medulla GABAergic neurons. *Nature, 526*(7573), 435–438.

Wehr, T. A., Sack, D. A., Duncan, W. C., Mendelson, W. B., et al. (1985). Sleep and circadian rhythms in affective patients isolated from external time cues. *Psychiatry Research, 15*, 327–339.

Wei, W., Nguyen, L. N., Kessels, H. W., Hagiwara, H., et al. (2010). Amyloid beta from axons and dendrites reduces local spine number and plasticity. *Nature Neuroscience, 13*, 190–196.

Weinberger, D. R., Aloia, M. S., Goldberg, T. E., and Berman, K. F. (1994). The frontal lobes and schizophrenia. *Journal of Neuropsychiatry and Clinical Neurosciences, 6*, 419–427.

Weinberger, N. M. (1998). Physiological memory in primary auditory cortex: Characteristics and mechanisms. *Neurobiology of Learning and Memory, 70*, 226–251.

Weindruch, R., and Walford, R. L. (1988). *The retardation of aging and disease by dietary restriction.* Springfield, IL: Thomas.

Weiner, R. D. (1994). Treatment optimization with ECT. *Psychopharmacology Bulletin, 30*, 313–320.

Weiss, J., Pyrski, M., Jacobi, E., Bufe, B., et al. (2011). Loss-of-function mutations in sodium channel Nav1.7 cause anosmia. *Nature, 472*, 186–190.

Weiss, L. A., Arking, D. E., and The Gene Discovery Project of Johns Hopkins & the Autism Consortium. (2009). A genome-wide linkage and association scan reveals novel loci for autism. *Nature, 461*, 802–808.

Weitzman, E. D. (1981). Sleep and its disorders. *Annual Review of Neurosciences, 4*, 381–417.

Weitzman, E. D., Czeisler, C. A., Zimmerman, J. C., and Moore-Ede, M. C. (1981). Biological rhythms in man: Relationship of sleep-wake, cortisol, growth hormone, and temperature during temporal isolation. In J. B. Martin, S. Reichlin, and K. L. Bick (Eds.), *Neurosecretion and brain peptides* (pp. 475–499). New York: Raven.

Wersinger, E., and Fuchs, P. A. (2011). Modulation of hair cell efferents. *Hearing Research, 279*(1–2), 1–12.

Wesensten, N. J., Belenky, G., Kautz, M. A., Thorne, D. R., et al. (2002). Maintaining alertness and performance during sleep deprivation: Modafinil versus caffeine. *Psychopharmacology (Berlin), 159*, 238–247.

Wessberg, J., Stambaugh, C. R., Kralik, J. D., Beck, P. D., et al. (2000). Real-time predictions of hand trajectory by ensembles of cortical neurons in primates. *Nature, 408*, 361–365.

West, G. L., Drisdelle, B. L., Konishi, K., Jackson, J., et al. (2015). Habitual action video game playing is associated with caudate nucleus-dependent navigational strategies. *Proceedings: Biological Sciences, 282*(1808), 20142952.

West, S. L., and O'Neal, K. K. (2004). Project D.A.R.E. outcome effectiveness revisited. *American Journal of Public Health., 94*, 1027–1029.

Wever, R. A. (1979). Influence of physical workload on freerunning circadian rhythms of man. *Pflügers Archiv European Journal of Physiology, 381*, 119–126.

Wexler, N. S., Rose, E. A., and Housman, D. E. (1991). Molecular approaches to hereditary diseases of the nervous system: Huntington's disease as a paradigm. *Annual Review of Neuroscience, 14*, 503–529.

Whitaker, D., and McGraw, P. V. (2000). Long-term visual experience recalibrates human orientation perception. *Nature Neuroscience, 3*, 13.

White, N. M., and Milner, P. M. (1992). The psychobiology of reinforcers. *Annual Review of Psychology, 43*, 443–471.

White, N. R., Gonzales, R. N., and Barfield, R. J. (1993). Do vocalizations of the male rat elicit calling from the female? *Behavioral and Neural Biology, 59*(1), 76–78.

White, P. M., Doetzlhofer, A., Lee, Y. S., Groves, A. K., et al. (2006). Mammalian cochlear supporting cells can divide and trans-differentiate into hair cells. *Nature, 441*, 984–987.

Whitfield-Gabrieli, S., and Ford, J. M. (2012). Default mode network activity and connectivity in psychopathology. *Annual Review of Clinical Psychology, 8*, 49–76.

Whitlock, J. R., Heynen, A. J., Shuler, M. G., and Bear, M. F. (2006). Learning induces long-term potentiation in the hippocampus. *Science, 313*, 1093–1097.

Wiesel, T. N., and Hubel, D. H. (1965). Extent of recovery from the effects of visual deprivation in kittens. *Journal of Neurophysiology, 28*, 1060–1072.

Wildman, D. E., Uddin, M., Liu, G., Grossman, L. I., et al. (2003). Implications of natural selection in shaping 99.4% nonsynonymous DNA identity between humans and chimpanzees: Enlarging genus *Homo. Proceedings of the National Academy of Sciences, USA, 100*, 7181–7188.

Williams, J. H., Waiter, G. D., Gilchrist, A., Perrett, D. I., et al. (2006). Neural mechanisms of imitation and "mirror neuron" functioning in autistic spectrum disorder. *Neuropsychologia, 44*, 610–621.

Williams, N. R., and Schatzberg, A. F. (2016). NMDA antagonist treatment of depression. *Current Opinion in Neurobiology, 36*, 112–117. doi:10.1016/j.conb.2015.11.001

Williams, S. R., and Stuart, G. J. (2003). Role of dendritic synapse location in the control of action potential output. *Trends in Neurosciences, 26*, 147–154.

Williams, T. J., Pepitone, M. E., Christensen, S. E., Cooke, B. M., et al. (2000). Finger-length ratios and sexual orientation. *Nature, 404*, 455–456.

Williams, Z. M., Bush, G., Rauch, S. I., Cosgrove, G. R., et al. (2004). Human anterior cingulate neurons and the integration of monetary reward with motor responses. *Nature Neuroscience, 7*, 1370–1374.

Wilson, M. L., Boesch, C., Fruth, B., Furuichi, T., et al. (2014). Lethal aggression in *Pan* is better explained by adaptive strategies than human impacts. *Nature, 513*, 414–417.

Wilson, S. R., Gerhold, K. A., Bifolck-Fisher, A., Liu, Q., et al. (2011). TRPA1 is required for histamine-independent, Mas-related G protein–coupled receptor–mediated itch. *Nature Neuroscience, 14*, 595–602.

Wingfield, J. C., Ball, G. F., Dufty, A. M., Hegner, R. E., et al. (1987). Testosterone and aggression in birds. *American Scientist, 75*, 602–608.

Winslow, J. T., and Insel, T. R. (2002). The social deficits of the oxytocin knockout mouse. *Neuropeptides, 36*, 221–229.

Wise, R. A., Bauco, P., Carlezon, W. A., Jr., and Trojniar, W. (1992). Self-stimulation and drug reward mechanisms. *Annals of the New York Academy of Sciences, 654*, 192–198.

Wiseman, F. K., Al-Janabi, T., Hardy, J., Karmiloff-Smith, A., et al. (2015). A genetic cause of Alzheimer disease: Mechanistic insights from Down syndrome. *Nature Reviews Neuroscience, 16*(9), 564–574. doi:10.1038/nrn3983

Wittchen, H. U., Jacobi, F., Rehm, J., Gustavsson, A., et al. (2011). The size and burden of mental disorders and other disorders of the brain in Europe 2010. *European Neuropsychopharmacology, 21*(9), 655–679.

Witthoft, N., and Winawer, J. (2013). Learning, memory, and synesthesia. *Psychological Science, 24*(3), 258–265.

Wolf, S. S., Jones, D. W., Knable, M. B., Gorey, J. G., et al. (1996). Tourette syndrome: Prediction of phenotypic variation in monozygotic twins by caudate nucleus D2 receptor binding. *Science, 273*, 1225–1227.

Wolfe, J. M. (1994). Guided search 2.0: A revised model of visual search. *Psychonomic Bulletin & Review, 1*, 202–238.

Wolfe, J. M., Alvarez, G. A., and Horowitz, T. S. (2000). Attention is fast but volition is slow. *Nature, 406*, 691.

Wolfe, J. M., Horowitz, T. S., and Kenner, N. M. (2005). Cognitive psychology: Rare items often missed in visual searches. *Nature, 435*, 439–440.

Wolk, D. A., Price, J. C., Saxton, J. A., Snitz, B. E., et al. (2009). Amyloid imaging in mild cognitive impairment subtypes. *Annals of Neurology, 65*, 557–568.

Womelsdorf, T., Anton-Erxleben, K., Pieper, F., and Treue, S. (2006). Dynamic shifts of visual receptive fields in cortical area MT by spatial attention. *Nature Neuroscience, 9*, 1156–1160.

Womelsdorf, T., Anton-Erxleben, K., and Treue, S. 2008. Receptive field shift and shrinkage in macaque middle temporal area through attentional gain modulation. *Journal of Neuroscience, 28*, 8934–8944.

Wong, M., and Martin, L. J. (2010). Skeletal muscle-restricted expression of human SOD1 causes motor neuron degeneration in transgenic mice. *Human Molecular Genetics, 19*, 2284–2302.

Woo, S. H., Lukacs, V., de Nooij, J. C., Zaytseva, D., et al. (2015). Piezo2 is the principal mechanotransduction channel for proprioception. *Nature Neuroscience, 18*(12), 1756–1762.

Wood, J. M., Bootzin, R. R., Kihlstrom, J. F., and Schacter, D. L. (1992). Implicit and explicit memory for verbal information presented during sleep. *Psychological Science, 3*, 236–239.

Wood, N., and Cowan, N. (1995). The cocktail party phenomenon revisited: How frequent are attention shifts to one's name in an irrelevant auditory channel? *Journal of Experimental Psychology. Learning, Memory, and Cognition, 21*, 255–260.

Woolf, C. J., and Salter, M. W. (2000). Neuronal plasticity: Increasing the gain in pain. *Science, 288*, 1765–1769.

World Health Organization. (2001). *The world health report.* Geneva, Switzerland: World Health Organization.

World Health Organization. (2004). *Burden of disease in DALYs by cause, sex, and mortality stratum in WHO regions, estimates for 2002.* Geneva, Switzerland: World Health Organization.

Wren, A. M., Seal, L. J., Cohen, M. A., Brynes, A. E., et al. (2001). Ghrelin enhances appetite and increases food intake in humans. *Journal of Clinical Endocrinology & Metabolism, 86*, 5992–5995.

Wren, A. M., Small, C. J., Ward, H. L., Murphy, K. G., et al. (2000). The novel hypothalamic peptide ghrelin stimulates food intake and growth hormone secretion. *Endocrinology, 141*, 4325–4328.

Wright, A. A., Santiago, H. C., Sands, S. F., Kendrick, D. F., et al. (1985). Memory processing of serial lists by pigeons, monkeys, and people. *Science, 229*, 287–289.

Wright, R. D., and Ward, L. M. (2008). *Orienting of attention.* New York: Oxford University Press.

Wu, G. D., Chen, J., Hoffmann, C., Bittinger, K., et al. (2011). Linking long-term dietary patterns with gut microbial enterotypes. *Science, 334*(6052), 105–108.

Wu, L.-Q., and Dickman, J. D. (2012). Neural correlates of a magnetic sense. *Science, 336*, 1054–1057.

Wu, P. C., Tsai, C. L., Wu, H. L., Yang, Y. H., et al. (2013). Outdoor activity during class recess reduces myopia onset and progression in school children. *Ophthalmology, 120*, 1080–1085.

Wu, S. V., Rozengurt, N., Yang, M., Young, S. H., et al. (2002). Expression of bitter taste receptors of the T2R family in the gastrointestinal tract and enteroendocrine STC-1 cells. *Proceedings of the National Academy of Sciences, USA, 99*(4), 2392–2397.

Wuethrich, B. (2000). Learning the world's languages—before they vanish. *Science, 288*, 1156–1159.

Wunderink, L., Nieboer, R. M., Wiersma, D., Sytema, S., et al. (2013). Recovery in remitted first-episode psychosis at 7 years of follow-up of an early dose reduction/discontinuation or maintenance treatment strategy: Long-term follow-up of a 2-year randomized clinical trial. *JAMA Psychiatry, 70*(9), 913–920.

Wurtz, R. H., and Goldberg, M. E. (1972). Activity of superior colliculus in behaving monkey. 3. Cells discharging before eye movements. *Journal of Neurophysiology, 35*, 575–586.

Wurtz, R. H., Goldberg, M. E., and Robinson, D. L. (1982). Brain mechanisms of visual attention. *Scientific American, 246*(6), 124–135.

X

Xerri, C., Coq, J., Merzenich, M., and Jenkins, W. (1996). Experience-induced plasticity of cutaneous maps in the primary somatosensory cortex of adult monkeys and rats. *Journal de Physiologie, 90*, 277–287.

Xerri, C., Stern J. M., and Merzenich, M. M. (1994). Alterations of the cortical representation of the rat ventrum induced by nursing behavior. *Journal of Neuroscience, 14*, 1710–1721.

Xie, L., Kang, H., Xu, Q., Chen, M. J., et al. (2013). Sleep drives metabolite clearance from the adult brain. *Science, 342*(6156), 373–377.

Xu, H., Delling, M., Jun, J. C., and Clapham, D. E. (2006). Oregano, thyme and clove-derived flavors and skin sensitizers activate specific TRP channels. *Nature Neuroscience, 9*, 628–635.

Xu, J., Cao, J., Iguchi, N., Riethmacher, D., et al. (2013). Functional characterization of bitter-taste receptors expressed in mammalian testis. *Molecular Human Reproduction, 19*(1), 17–28.

Xu, L., Furukawa, S., and Middlebrooks, J. C. (1999). Auditory cortical responses in the cat to sounds that produce spatial illusions. *Nature, 399*, 688–691.

Xu, M., Chung, S., Zhang, S., Zhong, P., et al. (2015). Basal forebrain circuit for sleep-wake control. *Nature Neuroscience, 18*(11), 1641–1647.

Xue, T., Do, M. T. H., Riccio, A., Jiang, Z., et al. (2011). Melanopsin signalling in mammalian iris and retina. *Nature, 479*, 67–73.

Xue, Y., Xu, X., Zhang, X. Q., Farokhzad, O. C., et al. (2016). Preventing diet-induced obesity in mice by adipose tissue transformation and angiogenesis using targeted nanoparticles. *Proceedings of the National Academy of Sciences, USA, 113*, 5552–5557.

Y

Yaffe, K., Lui, L. Y., Zmuda, J., and Cauley, J. (2002). Sex hormones and cognitive function in older men. *Journal of the American Geriatrics Society, 50*, 707–712.

Yanagisawa, K., Bartoshuk, L. M., Catalanotto, F. A., Karrer, T. A., et al. (1992). Anesthesia of the chorda tympani nerve: Insights into a source of dysgeusia. *Chemical Senses, 17*, 724.

Yang, G., Lai, C. S., Cichon, J., Ma, L., et al. (2014). Sleep promotes branch-specific formation of dendritic spines after learning. *Science, 344*(6188), 1173–1178.

Yang, T. T., Gallen, C. C., Ramachandran, V. S., Cobb, S., et al. (1994). Noninvasive detection of cerebral plasticity in adult human somatosensory cortex. *Neuroreport, 5*, 701–704.

Yang, Y., and Raine, A. (2009). Prefrontal structural and functional brain imaging findings in antisocial, violent, and psychopathic individuals: A meta-analysis. *Psychiatry Research, 174*, 81–88.

Yang, Z., Slavin, M. J., and Sachdev, P. S. (2013). Dementia in the oldest old. *Nature Reviews Neurology, 9*(7), 382–393. doi:10.1038/nrneurol.2013.105

Yehuda, R. (2002). Post-traumatic stress disorder. *New England Journal of Medicine, 346*, 108–114.

Yetish, G., Kaplan, H., Gurven, M., Wood, B., et al. (2015). Natural sleep and its seasonal variations in three pre-industrial societies. *Current Biology, 25*(21), 2862–2868.

Young, K. D., Erickson, K., Nugent, A. C., Fromm, S. J., et al. (2011). Functional anatomy of autobiographical memory recall deficits in depression. *Psychological Medicine, 29*, 1–13.

Young, L. J. (2009). Being human: love: Neuroscience reveals all. *Nature, 457*, 148.

Yttri, E. A., and Dudman, J. T. (2016). Opponent and bidirectional control of movement velocity in the basal ganglia. *Nature, 533*(7603), 402–406.

Yu, F., Jiang, Q. J., Sun, X. Y., and Zhang, R. W. (2015). A new case of complete primary cerebellar agenesis: Clinical and imaging findings in a living patient. *Brain, 138*(Pt. 6), e353.

Yuan, J., Gong, H., Li, A., Li, X., et al. (2015). Visible rodent brain-wide networks at single-neuron resolution. *Frontiers in Neuroanatomy, 9*, 70.

Yue, Y., Pan, X., Hakim, C. H., Kodippili, K., et al. (2015). Safe and bodywide muscle transduction in young adult Duchenne muscular dystrophy dogs with adeno-associated virus. *Human Molecular Genetics, 24*(20), 5880–5890.

Yuste, R. and Church, G. M. (2014). The new century of the brain. *Scientific American, 310*(3), 38–45.

Z

Zadikoff, C., and Lang, A. E. (2005). Apraxia in movement disorders. *Brain, 128*, 1480–1497.

Zaidel, E. (1976). Auditory vocabulary of the right hemisphere following brain bisection or hemidecortication. *Cortex, 12*, 191–211.

Zalocusky, K. A., Ramakrishnan, C., Lerner, T. N., Davidson, T. J., et al. (2016). Nucleus accumbens D2R cells signal prior outcomes and control risky decision-making. *Nature, 531*(7596), 642–646.

Zanto, T. P., Rubens, M. T., Thangavel, A., and Gazzaley, A. (2011). Causal role of the prefrontal cortex in top-down modulation of visual processing and working memory. *Nature Neuroscience, 14*(5), 656–661.

Zatorre, R. J., Evans, A. C., and Meyer, E. (1994). Neural mechanisms underlying melodic perception and memory for pitch. *Journal of Neuroscience, 14*, 1908–1919.

Zatorre, R. J., Fields, R. D., and Johansen-Berg, H. (2012). Plasticity in gray and white: Neuroimaging changes in brain structure during learning. *Nature Neuroscience, 15*, 528–536.

Zawilska, J. B. (2014). Mephedrone and other cathinones. *Current Opinion in Psychiatry, 27*, 256–262.

Zeki, S., Watson, J. D., Lueck, C. J., Friston, K. J., et al. (1991). A direct demonstration of functional specialization in human visual cortex. *Journal of Neuroscience, 11*, 641–649.

Zeman, A. (2002). *Consciousness: A user's guide.* New Haven, CT: Yale University Press.

Zendel, B. R., and Alain, C. (2009). Concurrent sound segregation is enhanced in musicians. *Journal of Cognitive Neuroscience, 21*, 1488–1498.

Zendel, B. R., Lagrois, M. É., Robitaille, N., and Peretz, I. (2015). Attending to pitch information inhibits processing of pitch information: The curious case of amusia. *Journal of Neuroscience, 35*(9), 3815–3824.

Zhang, C. L., Zou, Y., He, W., Gage, F. H., et al. (2008). A role for adult TLX-positive neural stem cells in learning and behaviour. *Nature, 451*, 1004–1007.

Zhang, F., Aravanis, A. M., Adamantidis, A., deLecea, L., et al. (2007). Circuit-breakers: Optical technologies for probing neural signals and systems. *Nature Reviews Neuroscience, 8*, 577–581.

Zhang, Q., Li, Y., and Tsien, R. W. (2009). The dynamic control of kiss-and-run and vesicular reuse probed with single nanoparticles. *Science, 323*, 1448–1453.

Zhang, T. Y., and Meaney, M. J. (2010). Epigenetics and the environmental regulation of the genome and its function. *Annual Review of Psychology, 61*, C1–C3.

Zhang, Y., Liu, R.-Y., Heberton, G. A., Smolen, P., et al. (2012). Computational design of enhanced learning protocols. *Nature Neuroscience, 15*, 294–297.

Zhang, Y., Proenca, R., Maffei, M., Barone, M., et al. (1994). Positional cloning of the mouse obese gene and its human homologue. *Nature, 372*, 425–432.

Zhang, Z., and Bourque, C. W. (2003). Osmometry in osmosensory neurons. *Nature Neuroscience, 6*, 1021–1022.

Zhao, G. Q., Zhang, Y., Hoon, M. A., Chandrashekar, J., et al. (2003). The receptors for mammalian sweet and umami taste. *Cell, 115,* 255–266.

Zhao, H., Yang, J. R., Xu, H., and Zhang, J. (2010). Pseudogenization of the umami taste receptor gene *Tas1r1* in the giant panda coincided with its dietary switch to bamboo. *Molecular Biology and Evolution, 27*(12), 2669–2673.

Zhao, Z. Q. (2008). Neural mechanism underlying acupunture analgesia. *Progress in Neurobiology, 85,* 355–375.

Zheng, J., Shen, W., He, D. Z., Long, K. B., et al. (2000). Prestin is the motor protein of cochlear outer hair cells. *Nature, 405,* 149–155.

Zhou, Q., Lai, Y., Bacaj, T., Zhao, M., et al. (2015). Architecture of the synaptotagmin-SNARE machinery for neuronal exocytosis. *Nature, 525*(7567), 62–67.

Ziauddeen, H., Farooqi, I. S., and Fletcher, P. C. (2012). Obesity and the brain: How convincing is the addiction model? *Nature Reviews Neuroscience, 13*(4), 279–286.

Zihl, J., von Cramon, D., and Mai, N. (1983). Selective disturbance of movement vision after bilateral brain damage. *Brain, 106,* 313–340.

Zilioli, S., Ponzi, D., Henry, A., Kubicki, K., et al. (2015). Interest in babies negatively predicts testosterone responses to sexual visual stimuli among heterosexual young men. *Psychological Science, 27*(1), 114–118.

Zimmer, C. (2004). *The soul made flesh: The discovery of the brain—and how it changed the world.* New York: Basic Books.

Zimmerman, A. W., and Connors, S. L. (2014). Could autism be treated prenatally? *Science, 343*(6171), 620–621.

Zola, S. M., Squire, L. R., Teng, E., Stefanacci, L., et al. (2000). Impaired recognition memory in monkeys after damage limited to the hippocampal region. *Journal of Neuroscience, 20,* 451–463.

Zola-Morgan, S. [M.], and Squire, L. R. (1986). Memory impairment in monkeys following lesions of the hippocampus. *Behavioral Neuroscience, 100,* 155–160.

Zola-Morgan, S. M., and Squire, L. R. (1990). The primate hippocampal formation: Evidence for a time-limited role in memory storage. *Science, 250,* 288–290.

Zola-Morgan, S. [M.], Squire, L. R., and Ramus, S. J. (1994). Severity of memory impairment in monkeys as a function of locus and extent of damage within the medial temporal lobe memory system. *Hippocampus, 4,* 483–495.

Zucker, I. (1976). Light, behavior, and biologic rhythms. *Hospital Practice, 11,* 83–91.

Zucker, I. (1988). Seasonal affective disorders: Animal models non fingo. *Journal of Biological Rhythms, 3,* 209–223.

Zucker, I., Boshes, M., and Dark, J. (1983). Suprachiasmatic nuclei influence circannual and circadian rhythms of ground squirrels. *American Journal of Physiology, 244,* R472–R480.

Author Index

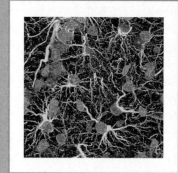

Earnshaw, W. C., 203
Ebbinghaus, H., 18
Eberhard, W. G., 135
Edinger, J. D., 459
Edwards, R. R., 451
Egeland, M., 495
Ehrenberg, R., 297
Ehrhardt, A. A., 388
Eichenbaum, H., 538, 545
Eichler, V. B., 435
Eippert, F., 258
Eisenberg, M., 551
Eisenberger, N. I., 254, 255
Eklund, A., 56
Ekman, P., 474
El Mestikawy, S., 100
Elbert, T., 246
Elie, J. E., 277
Ellenbogen, J. M., 452
Elster, A. D., 53
Emborg, M. E., 640
Emery, N. J., 183, 479
Emory, E., 603
Enard, W., 185
Encel, N., 460
Engel, J. Jr., 481, 487
Engelmann, T., 445
Eom, T.Y., 198
Epstein, C. M., 616
Erfurth, A., 515
Erickson, J. T., 213
Erickson, K. I., 223
Eriksson, A., 471
Eriksson, P. S., 198
Erlanger, D. M., 642
Ernst, T., 118
Erren, T. C., 451
Ervin, F. R., 487
Estes, W. K., 551
Etcoff, N. L., 620
Euston, D. R., 452
Evans, P. D., 185
Everitt, B. J., 377
Everson, C. A., 448, 449

F

Fabiani, M., 54
Fabre-Thorpe, M., 577
Fadiga, L., 625
Faix, A., 399
Falk, D., 180, 630
Falkner, A. L., 487
Faraone, S.V., 515

Farbman, A. I., 293
Farrer, M., 362
Fay, R. R., 231
Feder, H. H., 390
Fehr, E., 604
Feinstein, J. S., 467, 483
Fennema, C., 364
Fenstemaker, S. B., 391
Ferguson, J. N., 155
Fernald, R. D., 312, 313
Fernández-Espejo, D., 597
Ferreira, J. J., 362
Field, P. M., 392
Fields, R. D., 34
Fields, S., 378
Figee, M., 527
Finch, C. E., 215
Finger, S., 297, 610, 619
Fink, A. J., 348
Fink, H., 425
Fink, M., 517
Finlay, B. L., 179
Finn, C. T., 515
Fischer, H., 8
Fishman, R. B., 393
Fitzsimmons, J.T., 412
Flament, D., 543
Flanagan, J. R., 243
Flanagan-Cato, L. M., 376
Fleming, C., 508
Fleming, S. M., 605
Foa, E. B., 525
Fogassi, L., 357
Fonseca, L. M., 212
Ford, J. M., 583
Foreman, D. L., 277
Forger, N. G., 203, 391, 393, 394
Fortune, E. S., 635
Foster, G. D., 418
Foster, N. L., 222
Fothergill, E., 403, 416
Fournier, J. C., 518
Fraher, J. P., 344
Fraint, A., 529
Francis, D. D., 215
Francks, C., 615
Frank, L. G., 391
Frank, M. J., 364
Franken, T. B., 276
Frankenhaeuser, M., 489, 490
Frankland, P. W., 564
Franklin, T. R., 117

Franks, N. P., 453
Franz, S. I., 18
Freed, C. R., 640
Freedman, M. S., 437
Freeman, J., 320
Freitag, J., 291
Freiwald, W. A., 317
Frenda, S. J., 452
Frey, S. H., 246
Frey, U., 562
Fridlund, A. J., 475
Fried, I., 6
Friedhoff, A. J., 509
Friedman, L., 455
Friedman, M., 491
Friedrich, F. J., 590
Fritz, J., 277
Fromer, M., 504
Fuchs, P. A., 82
Fukuda, K., 458
Fuller Torrey, E., 13
Fuller, P. M., 435
Fulton, B. D., 594
Fulton, S., 427
Funahashi, S., 548
Funk, J., 593
Furey, M. L., 567
Fuster, J. M., 601

G

Gabel, L. A., 638
Gabrieli, J. D., 566
Gabrieli, J.D.E., 543
Gage, S. H., 115
Galaburda, A. M., 637, 638
Galea, L. A., 565, 566
Gallant, J., 605
Gallant, J. L., 321
Gangwisch, J. E., 451
Gannon, P. W., 614
Gaoni,Y., 115
Gardner, B. T., 635
Gardner, L. I., 149
Gardner, R. A., 635
Gardner, T. J., 635
Garfield, A. S., 424
Garver, D. L., 504, 515
Gaspar, J. M., 584
Gauthier, I., 619
Gawande, A., 251
Gazzaniga, A. M., 610
Gazzaniga, M. S., 618
Gearhart, J. P., 371, 397

Geers, A. E., 282
Geinisman,Y., 567
Gelade, G., 581
Gelber, R. P., 568
Gemba, H., 633
Genoux, D., 562
George, A. L. Jr., 74
Georgiadis, J. R., 381, 400
Georgopolous, A. P., 352
Georgopoulos, A. P., 353
Geran, L. C., 289
Gerard, C. M., 115
Gerashchenko, D., 457
Gerometta, J., 90
Geschwind, N., 614, 623, 624
Ghazanfar, S. A., 633
Gibson, 2014, 597
Gidal, B. E., 460
Gilad,Y., 293
Gilbert, A. N., 291
Gilbertson, M. W., 524
Gilestro, G. F., 202
Gilissen, C., 212
Gill, R. E., 445
Gitelman, D. R., 240
Glantz, L. A., 508
Glantz. M., 122
Glaser, R., 494
Glendinning, J. I., 297
Glenn, A. L., 488
Glickman, S. E., 391, 485
Glimcher, P. W., 102, 604
Globus, 1973, 555
Gnad, T., 427
Godwin, D., 2
Goedert, K. M., 593
Goetz, F. W., 378
Goffinet, A. M., 212
Gogtay, N., 206, 207
Goldberg, M. E., 588, 589
Golden, R. N., 522
Goldin, P. R., 495
Goldin-Meadow, S., 630, 631
Goldstein, J. M., 396
Goldstein, R. Z., 124
Goll,Y., 597
Golomb, J., 221
González-Maeso, J., 512
Goodale, M. A., 277, 301, 347
Goodglass, H., 624
Goodman, C., 215
Goodman, C. S., 202
Gooley, J. J., 437, 461

Reck, C., 521
Redcay, E., 57
Redican, W. K., 472
Reed, L. I., 476
Rees, G., 597
Reeves, A. J., 198
Regier, D. A., 520
Rehkamper, G., 545
Reiner, W. G., 371, 397
Reisberg, D., 552
Rempel-Clower, N. L., 538
Renner, M. J., 555
Reppert, S. M., 154
Resnick, S. M., 153
Ressler, K. J., 552
Reuter, J., 124
Revel, F. G., 154
Rex, C. S., 568
Rhodes, M. G., 566
Ribeiro, R. C., 139
Ricciardi, E., 567
Richardson, G. P., 280
Richman, D. P., 345
Richter, C., 435
Ringach, D. L., 323
Ringman, J. M., 567
Risch, N., 516
Rizzolatti, G., 330, 357
Robbe, D., 359
Roberts, A., 436
Roberts, C. G., 151
Roberts, E. K., 379
Roberts, L., 626
Robertson, D. J., 619
Robino, A., 286
Robins, L. N., 126, 520
Robinson, D. L., 589
Robinson, R., 519
Robson, J. G., 318
Rocca, W. A., 221
Rodríguez de Fonseca, F., 115
Roenneberg, T., 461
Roffwarg, H. P., 446
Rogan, M. T., 565
Rogawski, M. A., 90
Rogers-Ramachandran, D., 253
Roland, P. E., 53, 356
Rolls, E. T., 545
Romanski, L. M., 277
Rorabaugh, W. J., 122
Rosci, C., 361

Rose, K. A., 331
Roselli, C. E., 397, 398
Rosenbaum, R. S., 542
Rosenberg, M. D., 595
Rosengren, A., 491
Rosenkranz, M. A., 492
Rosenman, R. H., 491
Rosenthal, N. E., 522
Rosenzweig, M. R., 217, 277, 407, 546, 555, 564
Roses, A. D., 222
Rossi, M. A., 566
Rossor, M., 567
Rota-Donahue, C., 90
Rotarska-Jagiela, A., 506
Roth, B. L., 157
Roth, T. L., 643
Rothstein, J. D., 350
Rouw, R., 241
Roux, B., 74
Row, B. W., 460
Rowe, A., 260
Rowe, M., 260
Rowe, M. K., 260, 515
Rozanski, A., 491
Rück, C., 527
Rueda-Orozco, P. E., 359
Ruff, C. C., 604
Rumbaugh, D. M., 635
Rupnick, M. A., 427
Rupprecht, R., 524
Rusak, B., 435, 436
Ruschel, J., 349
Russell, J. A., 475
Russell, R., 619
Russo, E. B., 115
Russo, S. J., 491
Ruthazer, E. S., 218
Rutstein, J., 406
Rymer, R., 149
Rypma, B., 53

S

Saab, A. S., 366, 367
Saalmann, Y. B., 589
Sabeti, P. C., 188
Sachs, B. D., 377
Sack, R. L., 155
Sáenz de Miera, C., 440
Sage, C., 282
Sahay, A., 517, 566
Saj, A., 593
Sakurai, T., 424

Salazar, H., 250
Salimpoor, V., 278
Salter, M. W., 253
Salthouse, T. A., 567
Salvini-Plawen, L. V., 312
Samad, T. A., 492
Samaha, F. F., 418
Samson, S., 614, 615
Samuels, B. A., 517
Sanders, A. R., 399
Sanderson, D. J., 562
Sanes, J. N., 355
Sanes, J. R., 563
Santhanam, F., 355
Sanyal, S., 444
Sapir, A., 588
Sapolsky, R. M., 373, 495, 568
Sartorius, N., 514
Satinoff, E., 406
Sato, J. R., 596
Satz. P., 615
Saul, S., 460
Savage-Rumbaugh, E. S., 636
Sawa, A., 504
Sawamoto, K., 198
Sawchenko, P. E., 495
Sawin, C. T., 133
Saxe, M. D., 566
Scammell, T. E., 457
Schacter, D. L., 543
Schacter, S., 469
Schale, K. W., 568
Schaller, M., 492
Schartl, M., 374
Schatzberg, A. F., 120, 520
Scheibel, A. B., 506
Scheibel, M. E., 221
Scheibert, J., 242
Schein, S. J., 328
Schenck, C. H., 459
Schenkerberg, T., 593
Schiffman, S. S., 288
Schildkraut, J. J., 517
Schiller, D., 545
Schindler, I., 593
Schlaug, G., 614
Schlinger, B. A., 635
Schlosburg, J. E., 128
Schmidt-Nelsen, K., 412
Schnapf, J. L., 306
Schneider, D. M., 277
Schneider, K. A., 585
Schneider, P., 278

Schneps, M. H., 639
Schnupp, J. W., 580
Schoenbaum, G., 603
Scholte, H. S., 241
Schreiweis, C., 632
Schrof, J. M., 126, 257
Schuckit, M. A., 119
Schulman, C. I., 406
Schultz, W. W., 399
Schulz, S. C., 502
Schummers, J., 34
Schuster, C. R., 124
Schwartz, C. E., 474
Schwartz, J., 613
Schwartz, S., 595
Schwartz, S. D., 332
Schwartzkroin, P. A., 560
Sclafani, A., 420
Scott, S. K., 627
Scoville, W. B., 535
Scudellari, M., 178
Scullin, M. K., 447
Sebastián-Gallés, N., 626
Sedey, A. L., 282
Seelke, A. M., 173
Seeman, P., 511
Seiden, R. H., 516
Seif, T., 119
Seil, F. J., 200
Sekar, A., 504
Seligman, M. E., 522
Selkoe, D. J., 363
Selye, H., 488
Semaw, S., 180
Semendeferi, K., 601
Sendtner, M., 213
Senju, A., 157
Seok, J., 5
Seretis, K., 426
Serrano, P. A., 564
Serviere, J., 272
Sexton, C. E., 517
Seyfarth, R. M., 633
Shah, A., 519
Shakespeare, W., 448
Shallice, T., 603
Shan, S.Y., 406
Shank, S. S., 452
Shapiro, R. M., 506
Shaw, J., 552
Shaw, P., 18, 207
Shaw, P. J., 448
Shaywitz, S. E., 638

Subject Index

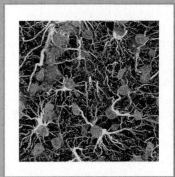

Page numbers followed by *f* refer to figures; those followed by *t* refer to tables.

amino acids, synaptic transmission and, 99t

"Ammon's horn,"506f

amnesiac mutation, 212

amnesias, 116, 536, 571f

AMPA receptors
    accumulation of, 565
    Bergmann glia and, 366–367, 367f
    description, 561
    glutamergic transmission and, 99
    LTP and, 561
    number of, 571f
    roles of, 563f

ampakines, 568

amphetamine psychosis, 509

amphetamines (meth, speed), 116, 117–118, 129f, 458, 508

amphibians, 179f, 282, 374

amplitude, of waves, 264, 265

ampulla, 284

amusia, 278

amygdala, 498f
    cholinergic projections, 100
    decision making and, 605
    emotions and, 47
    fear circuitry, 479–483
    function of, 46f
    location of, 46f

amyloid precursor protein (AAP), 222, 223f

β-amyloid protein, 222, 226f, 566

amyotrophic lateral sclerosis (ALS), 350, 368f

analgesia, 255
    shock-induced, 259

analgesics, 114

analogy, definition, 165

anandamide, 116, 129f

androgen insensitivity syndrome (AIS), 386, 387f, 396

androgen receptors, dysfunctional, 386–387

androgens. *See also specific* androgens
    aggression and, 485–487
    birdsong and, 392
    copulatory behavior and, 375f
    description of, 159f
    effects of, 144t
    function of, 152f
    male reproductive behavior and, 376–377
    masculine behavior and, 389–390
    prenatal, 395, 398, 398f
    production of, 151
    regulation of, 152

androstenedione, 150

androstenedione, effects of, 144t

anger, brain activation in, 484f

angiogenesis, 427

angiography, 51

angiotensin cascade, 412f

angiotensin II, 412

angular gyrus, 621

anhedonia, 127

Animal Liberation (Singer), 13

animal magnetism, 55f

animal models. *See also specific* animals

animal research, 13

Animalia, 167f

anions, definition, 62

annulospiral endings, 345

anomia, 621

anorexia nervosa, 428

anorexigenic neurons, 424

anosmia, 291

anosognosia, 593

ansomia, 395

antagonists
    description of, 81, 97
    drug action and, 98f
    function of, 129f, 341, 368f

antegrade labeling, 31

anterior, definition of, 42

anterior cerebral arteries, 50

anterior cingulate cortex, 483

anterior lobe, 365

anterior pituitary
    description of, 144, 159f
    functions of, 132f, 143, 146–147
    hormone release by, 147f
    hormones and effects, 144t
    secretions of, 148f

anterograde amnesia, 536

anterograde degeneration, 199

anterolateral system, 252, 262

anteroventral periventricular nucleus (AVPV), 383

anti-inflammatory drugs, 257t

anti-müllerian hormone (AMI), 385

antibodies, 128, 492, A.6

anticipation, 412, 435

antidepressants, 112, 113, 129f, 518f. *See also specific* drugs

antidiuretic hormone (ADH). *See* vasopressin (AVP)

antiepileptic drugs, 90

"antifreeze" molecules, 405

antigens, vaccination and, 128

antihistamines, 251

antipsychotic drugs, 112, 508–510, 510, 511f, 531f

antisocial behaviors, 486

anxiety, 113–114, 523

anxiety disorders, 500t, 523–528

anxiolytics, 113, 523

apathetic syndromes, 603t

apes. *See also* primates, nonhuman
    family tree of, 168f
    language capacity of, 635–636
    vocalizations, 633–634

aphagia, 419

aphasias, 619, 620t, 623f, 640f

apical dendrites, 46

Aplysia (sea slug), 172f, 556, 557f, 568

apolipoprotein E (ApoE), 222–223, 226f

apoptosis, 202, 203

appetite control, 420–424, 426–427

appetitive behavior, 373, 401f

apraxia, 361, 594, 619

aquaporins, 409

2-arachidonylglycerol (2-AG), 116

arachionic acid, 84

arachnoid, 49

arctic ground squirrels, 405f

arcuate fasciculus, 624

arcuate nucleus, 420, 422–424

arginine vasopressin (AVP), 145

Argyll-Robertson pupils, 499

Aristotle, 133

aromatase, 390

aromatase gene, 391

aromatases, 142

aromatization, 390

aromatization hypothesis, 390, 390f

arousal, 47, 574

artificial selection, 186

aspartate, 99

ASPM gene, 184–185, 189t

associative learning, 543–544, 571f

astereognosis, 617

astrocytes, 34f

ataxia, 365, 594

Ativan, 523

Atlantic cod, 187

Atoh1 gene, 282

atomexetine (Stratera), 595

atrial natriuretic peptide (ANP), 144t, 412

atropine, 100, 460

attention
    bottlenecks in, 576f
    brain regions in, 240f, 582–588
    consequences of, 582
    control of, 590f
    cortical areas in, 589–590
    covert direction of, 574f
    deployment of, 577–582
    description of, 239–240, 261f, 574, 607f
    directed, 47, 577–579, 587–592
    EEG responses, 582, 582f, 583
    limits on, 575–576
    macaque monkey, 587f
    mechanisms of, 582
    neuron functioning and, 586–588, 586f
    organization of, 592–595
    patterns and, 580–582
    reflexive, 579, 591f
    spatial cuing of, 585–586
    stimuli for, 574–577
    voluntary shifts in, 578f

attention-deficit hyperactivity disorder (ADHD), 116, 528–529, 594–595, 595f

attentional bottlenecks, 576, 576f, 607f

attentional control network, 591f

attentional spotlights, 574f, 575, 586f

attraction, 372

atypical antipsychotics, 112, 510

atypical neuroleptics, 531f

auditory cortex, 173f, 277–279, 277f, 278

auditory-evoked brainstem potentials, 90–91

auditory information, 43
auditory nerve fibers, 269f
auditory neurons, tuning curves, 271f
auditory P300, 583
auditory perception, 277–279, 277f
auras, seizures and, 89
australopithecines, 180
Australopithecus species, 181
autism, management of, 157–158
autism spectrum disorder (ASD), 157–158
autobiographical memory, 542
autocrine communication, 134, 134f, 159f
autoimmune disorders, 345
autonomic ganglia, 38
autonomic nervous system, 36, 38–40, 58f, 489f
autoradiograms, 141f
autoradiography, 31, 140f, 141
autoreceptors, 84, 110
aversion to loss, 605f
axo-axonic synapses, 85
axo-dendritic synapses, 84
axo-synaptic, 84
axon collaterals, 27
axon hillocks, 32, 69
axonal fibers, 53
axonal tracts, 48
axonal transport, 32, 33f
axons, 61
    action potential conduction, 72
    blockade of transport, 109f
    dendrites and, 33t
    depolarization of, 96
    description of, 2, 27, 34f, 58f
    electrical signals, 35
    giant, 72
    growth cones, 201f, 202f
    hillocks, 93
    membranes, 69
azimuth, definition of, 274, 276

B

B lymphocytes, 492, 493f
babies. sleep, 445f
Babinski reflex, 360
Bálint, Rezsö, 594
Bálint's syndrome, 594, 607f
ballistic movements, 338, 339
banded krait (*Bundarus multicinctus*), 81
bar detectors, 315
barbiturates, 113, 460
Bard, Phillip, 469
bariatric, definition of, 428
bark scorpions, 259
baroreceptors, 411f, 412
basal dendrites, 46
basal forebrain, 455, 464f
basal ganglia
    activation of, 542
    components of, 368f
    description of, 46, 358
    electrical stimulation of, 363

in Huntington's disease, 364–365
    motor control and, 340, 359–360, 360f
    movement and, 46f, 59f, 358–359
basal metabolism, 416
basilar artery, 50f, 51
basilar membrane, 268, 268f, 298f
bass, 273
"bath salts," 116
batrachotoxin, 74
bats, 170, 231, 264, 274, 276f
Bcl-2, 202
Bcl-2 proteins, 203, 203f
BDNF (brain-derived neurotrophic factor), 515
A Beautiful Mind (film), 501f
beauty, ideals of, 429f
bed wetting, 458
bees, 231, 407f
behavior
    biological mechanisms, 6
    brain and, 6–8
    descriptions of, 4
    development of, 193–226
    evolution of, 4
    hormones and, 155
    lifespan and, 4, 6
    midbrain and, 47
    synchronization of, 435
    types of, 4t
behavioral disorders. *See also specific*
    disorders
behavioral endocrinology, 133f, 140–141
behavioral interventions, 6, 7f, 21f, 565
behavioral neuroscience
    advances in, 20, 20f
    animal research, 13
    approaches to the study of, 7f
    definition, 2–3, 3f
    description of, 3f, 21f
    human disorders and, 12–13
    levels of analysis, 10, 10f
behavioral teratology, 210
behaviors, evolution of, 166, 175–179
belladonna, 302
Bell's palsy, 477, 477f
benzodiazepine agonists, 113
benzodiazepine receptors, 524f
benzodiazepines, 126, 460, 523, 531f
Bergmann glia, 366–367
Bernal, B., 52
Berthold, Arnold Adolph, 133
beta activity, 440–441
Betz cells, 221
Biggest Loser program, 422
bighorn rams, horn size, 186, 186f
bilateral, definition of, 45
bilateral symmetry, 174
bilious personalities, 132
binaural, description, 272, 274
binaural hearing, 275f
binding affinities, 105, 105f, 129f
binding problems, 581
binge eating, 429

bingeing, alcohol, 119
binocular deprivation, 217
bioavailability, definition, 108
biological factors, addictive behavior and, 126
biological psychology, 2–6
biological rhythms, 433–440. *See also*
    circadian rhythms
biotransformation, 108
bipolar cells, 303, 313f, 334f
bipolar disorders, 514–516, 515f, 516f, 531f
bipolar neurons, 27
bird song, 264
birds
    brain of, 176f
    color vision, 323
    food storing by, 170f
    hippocampal size and, 170f
    sleep patterns, 445
    TRPV1, 250
    visual perception, 176, 231
    vocal behavior in, 575–576, 634
birdsong, 170, 170f, 634
birth order, fraternal, 399f
bisphenol A, 395
bitter taste, 287–288, 289
black-capped chickadees, 170
blackfly (*Simulium samnosum*), 230f
Bleuler, Eugen, 501
blind spots, 308
blindness, 193, 264
blindsight, 311–312
blink responses, 544
Blocker, Ashlyn, 229, 251f
blood-brain barrier (BBB), 51, 59f, 108
blood-oxygen-level-dependent (BOLD)
    signals, 53
blood pressure, 40
blotting, A.4
blues, color vision, 323
body, human, orientations for viewing, 42
body fluids, 408–414
body mass index (BMI), 426t
body restoration, sleep and, 449, 451
"body sense," 337
body size, metabolism and, 416
body weight
    brain weight and, 177f, 178f, 181
    hypothalamic lesions and, 420f
    regulation of, 421t
BOLD (blood-oxygen-level-dependent)
    signals, 53
bonobos, 473f
border cells, 545
Botox injections, 477
bottom-up processes, 581
botulinum toxin (Botox), 80, 81, 110
bovine spongiform encephalopathy (BSE,
    mad cow disease), 362–363, 362f
bowerbird nest, 184f
boxing, brain injury and, 643
Braille, 244f

brain
- aging of, 220–221
- alcohol and, 119*f*
- asymmetry of, 610–629
- behavior and, 6–8
- cannabinoid receptors in, 116*f*
- cells of, 30*f*
- cholinergic pathways, 100*f*
- cocaine-binding sites, 117*f*
- complicated lives and, 170–171
- development of, 44–45, 44*f*, 193–226
- developmental disorders of, 210–214
- dopaminergic pathways, 102*f*
- electrical stimulation of, 478
- evolution of, 163–191
- fetal development, 182*f*
- gene expression in, 214–217
- growth of, 555
- hormone receptors in, 141
- hormones and, 131–159
- imaging techniques, 51–56
- language disorders, 619–623
- left *versus* right, 610–617
- lesions, 55–56
- limbic areas, 114
- local sleep in, 462*f*
- localization of function, 16, 16*f*
- mapping, 625–629
- masculinization of, 401*f*
- newly born neurons in, 565–566
- noradrenergic pathways, 102*f*
- number of synapses, 26
- by the numbers, 2*f*
- object recognition centers, 329*f*
- opioid receptors, 114*f*
- placebo effects, 258*f*, 259*f*
- recovery from injuries, 641–642
- regrowth, 640–641
- reward system, 127
- serotonergic pathways, 103*f*
- sexual differentiation of, 402*f*
- size of, 17–18, 29*f*, 173, 176–177, 183
- sleep and restoration of, 451
- specialization within, 45–49
- support systems for, 49–51
- transection of, 454*f*
- transplants of, 436*f*
- unconscious, 597*f*
- weights, 177*f*, 178*f*
brain, cat, prefrontal cortex, 601*f*
brain, chimpanzee, 163, 178, 601*f*
brain, fish, 176*f*
brain, frog, 176*f*
brain, human
- aphasia inducing lesions, 622*f*
- auditory pathways, 271*f*
- basal view, 50*f*
- benzodiazepine receptors, 524*f*
- blood supply to, 50–51, 50*f*
- chimpanzee brains and, 163
- divisions of, 44*f*
- internal anatomy, 43*f*
- language areas, 620*f*, 627–629
- lateral view of, 41*f*, 50*f*
- midsagittal view, 41*f*, 50*f*
- orientations for viewing, 42
- prefrontal cortex, 601*f*
- rat brain *versus*, 173, 174*f*
- sexual dimorphism, 396*f*
- speech areas, 620*f*
- synapse rearrangement in, 207*f*
- ventral view, 41*f*
- visual pathways, 311*f*, 319–321, 320*f*
brain, macaque, 320*f*
brain, monkey, 185, 601*f*
- cocaine-binding sites, 117*f*
- lateral geniculate nucleus (LGN), 327
- ocular dominance columns, 322*f*
- visual pathways, 319–321, 320*f*
- vocalizations, 633*f*
brain, mouse, 186*f*
brain, prairie vole, 155*f*
brain, rat, 114*f*, 116*f*, 173, 174*f*
brain, Rhesus monkey, 601*f*
brain, squirrel monkey, 601*f*
brain, vertebrate, 172–175, 176*f*
Brain Activity Map (BAM), 49
brain-computer interfaces, 355
brain-derived neurotrophic factor (BDNF), 204, 213–214
brain scans, 54
brain self-stimulation, 478, 478*f*
brainstem, 252*f*
- arousal system, 455
- central apnea, 459
- description of, 45
- embryology of, 44
- executive brain and, 182
- motor control and, 340
- motor nuclei, 351*f*
- sensory processing and, 237*f*
- in sleep, 453
- vestibulocochlear nerve, 284–285
Bremer, Frédéric, 454
brightness, perception of, 309*f*
Broca, Paul, 16, 620
Broca's aphasia, 620*t*, 622*f*, 644*f*
Broca's area, 620, 625*f*
Bruce effect, 379
bulbocavernosus (BC) muscles, 393–394
bulimia nervosa, 429
bullying, 255
Bundy, Theodore, 487*f*
bungarotoxin, 81
buspirone (Buspar), 524

C

C fibers, 250
c-fos gene, 30
Caenorhabditis elegans, 172, 196–197, 197*f*, 201
caffeine, 110, 116, 129*f*, 289, 459
calcitonin, 144*t*, 150
calcium/calmodulin-dependent protein kinase II (CaMKII), 561–562
calcium channel blockers, 110
calcium ion (Ca^{2+}) channels, 96

calcium ions (Ca^{2+}), 66, 307
callosal agenesis, 612*f*
caloric restriction, 417*f*
Canidae, 167*f*
cannabinoid receptors, 115, 116*f*
cannabinoids, 115–116, 257*t*
Cannabis sativa, 257, 425
Cannon, Walter B., 469
Cannon-Bard theory, 469, 498*f*
capacitance, 66
capsaicin, 249, 250
carbon monoxide, 85
cardiac function, emotions and, 491
cardiovascular disease, anxiety and, 523
Caribbean tarantula, 250
carnivores, 167*f*, 179*f*
carotid arteries, description of, 50
Cas9, A.8, A.9
caspases, 202, 203
castration, 133, 375, 486
cataplexy, 456, 458, 464*f*
catecholamine transmitters, 117
catecholamines, 101, 144*t*
β-catenin, 186*f*
cathinones, 116
cations, definition of, 62
cats
- attention by, 580
- auditory cortex, 277
- color vision, 325
- prefrontal cortex, 601*f*
- REM sleep, 456
- sleep postures, 442*f*
- visual cortex development, 217*f*
- visual system, 316*f*
cauda equina, 36*f*
caudal, definition of, 42
caudate nuclei, 102
- description of, 46
- location of, 46*f*
- movement modulation and, 46*f*
- in OCD, 526
- in Parkinson's disease, 361
CCR5 gene, 189*t*
cell adhesion molecules (CAM), 198, 199, 201, 202
cell assemblies, 559
cell-autonomous, 200
cell body, neuronal, 27, 58*f*
cell-cell interactions, 197, 200–201, 203, 226*f*
cell death, 202. *See also* apoptosis
cell differentiation, 200, 226*f*, A.3
cell growth, hormones and, 137–138
cell membranes, 62, 74
cell migration, 195, 196*f*, 198, 226*f*
cell nuclei, 26
central apnea, 459
central deafness, 280*f*, 281, 298*f*
central gray stimulation, 257*t*
central injection, 108*t*
central nervous system (CNS)
- components, 58*f*
- description of, 36, 40–43

fibers linking receptors to, 244*f*
localization of function, 175
structure of, 36*f*
central pattern generator, 348
central sulcus, 41, 239
cerebellar cortex, 115
cerebellum, 59*f*
cellular arrangement in, 48*f*
damage to, 542
description of, 45
embryology of, 44
function of, 47–48
motor control and, 340, 359–360, 360*f*
mouse mutants, 213*f*
organization of, 365*f*
cerebral aqueduct, 49*f*
cerebral cortex, 40, 59*f*
atrophy of, 221
cannabinoid receptors, 115
development of, 200*f*
layers of, 45–46, 45*f*
motor impairments and, 360–361
receptive fields, 238–239
cerebral hemispheres, 40, 59*f*
asymmetry of, 617
auditory specialization, 613–615
bilateral symmetry, 174
disconnection of, 610–612
dyslexia and, 638
hierarchical control, 174
information processing, 612–613
language capabilities, 622–623
specialization of, 617
cerebral lateralization, 609, 610
cerebral palsy, toll of, 12*f*
cerebral ventricles, 49*f*
cerebrocerebellum, 365, 365*f*, 368*f*
cerebrospinal fluid (CSF), 49, 59*f*
cervical spinal cord, 38, 38*f*, 246*f*
channelopathies, 74
channelrhodopsin, 91, 92, 332, 570
chemical communications, 134–135
chemical sensory system, 231*t*
chemical synapses, 79*f*, 83*f*
chemoaffinity hypothesis, 208, 209
chemoattractants, 202
chemorepellants, 202
chemosensation, 296
child abuse, 490–491
chimpanzees, 634–635
brain of, 178
humans and, 163, 185
prefrontal cortex, 601*f*
prefrontal lesions, 602
symbol use by, 635*f*
tool making by, 180
chloride channel disorders, 74
chloride ions (Cl⁻), 76
chlorpromazine (Thorazine), 508, 509, 511*f*
choice systems, 604, 605*f*
cholecystokinin (CCK), 103, 144*t*, 421*t*, 424
choleric personalities, 132
cholesterol, 137

choline acetyltransferase (ChAT), 101
cholinergic, definition, 82, 100
cholinergic pathways, brain, 100*f*
cholinesterase inhibitors, 111
Chomsky, Noam, 636
Chordata, 167*f*
choroid plexus, 49, 49*f*
chromosomes, 166, A.2
chronic back pain, 253
chronic traumatic encephalopathy (CTE),
642, 643*f*
cigarettes, nicotine from, 116–117
cilia, 291
ciliary muscles, 302, 302*f*
ciliary neurotrophic factor (CNTF), 204
cingulate cortex, 240, 252*f*, 253, 254, 484*f*,
526
cingulate gyrus, 46*f*
cingulotomy, 527
circadian clock, 435
circadian rhythms, 306, 433–435, 437–439,
437*f*, 448, 464*f*
circannual rhythms, 439
circle of Willis, 50*f*, 51
circulating messages, 147
circumvallate papillae, 286
circumventricular organs, 412*f*
citalopram (Celexa), 113
city living, schizophrenia risk and, 513*f*
Clark's nutcracker, 170
classical conditioning, 542, 543, 558, 571*f*
claustrum, 597, 597*f*
climbing fibers, 558
clitoris, 380, 384
cloacal exstrophy, 371, 397
Clock protein, 438, 464*f*
clomipramine (Anafranil), 526
clones, 214, A.3
closed-loop control mechanisms, 338, 339,
340*f*, 368*f*
Clostridium difficile, 430
clove, 250
clozapine, 112, 510, 511*f*
Cntnap2 gene, 157, 158
co-localization, 99
coca-cola, 117
coca shrubs, 117
cocaethylene, 117
cocaine, 116, 117
cocaine and amphetamine-regulated
transcript (CART), 422
coccygeal vertebra, 38, 38*f*, 246*f*
cochlea, 267, 270, 280*f*, 298*f*
cochlear implants, 282*f*, 298*f*
cochlear nuclei, 271, 298*f*
Cochran, Kent, 541*f*
cocktail party effect, 574
coding, 234, 235, 261*f*
codons, A.2
cognitive attribution model, 469, 498*f*
cognitive behavioral therapy (CBT), 515,
519, 525, 531*f*

cognitive disorders, 500
cognitive function
aging and, 568
cerebellum and, 365–366
cortex and, 41
emotions and, 470*f*
estrogens and, 153
frontal lobe and, 602–604
hierarchical control of, 601
in Huntington's disease, 364
localization of, 21*f*
Parkinson's disease and, 364
sex differences, 395–396, 396*t*
cognitive maps, 544
cognitive skills, 542
cognitive therapies, for pain relief, 257*t*
cognitively impenetrable functions, 598
coincidence detectors, 275
coitus. *See* copulation
collateral sprouting, 640–641
color, perception of, 19*f*, 310
color blindness, 323, 326, 326*f*
color perception, 324*f*, 327–328
color vision, 323–328
coma, fMRI in, 597*f*
coma consciousness, 55
combat fatigue. *See* posttraumatic stress
disorder (PTSD)
communications, 4*t*, 609, 610
comorbid, definition of, 527
competition, testosterone in, 9, 486
competitive ligands, 98
complex cortical cells, 315
complex partial seizures, 89
compulsions, 525
compulsive obsessive disorder, 531*f*
computerized axial tomography (CAT
scans), 51, 52, 52*f*, 59*f*
computerized tomography (CT), 52*f*
concentration gradients, 63, 93
concordant, definition of, 502–503
concussion, 642
conditional knockout, 566
conditioned responses (CR), 542, 544
conditioned stimulus (CS), 542, 544
conditioning, 147
condoms, 381
conduction aphasia, 620*t*, 624
conduction deafness, 279, 280*f*, 298*f*
conduction velocities, 72
conduction zones, 27
cone photoreceptors, 302–303, 308,
324–325, 334*f*
confabulation, 541
conflict, social support and, 492
congenital adrenal hyperplasia (CAH), 386,
396
congenital insensitivity to pain, 248
conjunction search, 580, 581*f*, 607*f*
connectionist model of aphasia, 623, 624*f*
consciousness, 18–19
altered by drugs, 115–121
the brain and, 595–605

in coma, 55f
dimensions of, 596t
seat of, 597f
study of, 598–601
conserved, definition of, 4
consolidation, 551, 551f, 571f
conspecifics, 166
constraint-induced movement therapy, 641, 642f
continuous positive airway pressure (CPAP), 459
contours, perception of, 321, 321f
contralateral, definition of, 42, 45
convergence, description of, 86
convergent evolution, 165, 190f, 312
cool-menthol receptor 1 (CMR1), 250
Coolidge effect, 373f
"coolness" receptors, 250
cooperative homeostasis, 407
coordination, 359, 365f, 366–367, 367f
copper/zinc superoxide dismutase, 350
copulation, 373, 401f
copulatory behaviors, 485
copulatory locks, 374
cornea, description, 302, 302f
coronal plane, 42, 42f, 43f
corpora lutea, 148
corpus callosum, 43, 210, 506
correlation, definition, 7, 21f
correlation coefficient, 17
cortex, 177, 190f, 261f
cortical attentional control network, 592f
cortical columns, 46
cortical deafness, 281
cortical maps, plasticity in, 246, 247f
cortical thinning, 207, 207f
cortical tracts, 48f
corticospinal system, 350–351, 368f
cortisol, 144t, 150, 488, 519–520
cortisone, 144t
courtship behaviors, 156
"crack," 117
cranial nerves (CN)
CN I (olfactory), 37f
CN II (optic), 37f, 208, 303, 309, 334
CN III (oculomotor), 37f
CN IV (trochlear), 37f
CN IX (glossopharyngeal), 37f, 290
CN V (trigeminal), 37f, 477, 498f, 558
CN VI (abducens), 37f
CN VII (facial), 37f, 290, 476, 498f
CN VIII (vestibulocochlear), 37f, 48, 271, 284–285
CN X (vagus), 37f, 290, 428
CN XI (spinal accessory), 37f, 48
CN XII (hypoglossal), 37f, 48
functions of, 37f
motor pathways, 36–37
nuclei of, 48
peripheral nervous system and, 58f
sensory pathways, 36
Cre-Lox systems, A.9f
Cre-recombinase, 366, A.9

CREB (cAMP responsive element-binding protein), 562
cretinism, 151
Creutzfeldt-Jakob disease (CJD), 363
crib death, 460
CRISPR, 213–214, A.8–A.9, A.8f
cross-tolerance, 107
crows, 170
cryptochrome (cry) gene, 438
crystallization, 635
cue-induced drug use, 126
cues, 578
culture, transmission of, 183f
cupulae, 284
curare, 81, 111, 111f
Cushing's syndrome, 519
Cycle gene, 448
Cycle protein, 438, 464f
cyclic adenosine monophosphate (cAMP), 84, 138, 293
cyclic guanosine monophosphate (cGMP), 139, 305–306
cyclothymia, 515
CYP3A gene, 189t
cytokines, 492

D

D$_1$ receptors, 510, 511f
D$_2$ receptors, 509, 510, 511f
da Vinci, Leonardo, 14, 15f
Damasio, Antonio, 483
Darwin, Charles, 164, 165, 472
Darwin's finches, 186
DCDC2 gene, 638–639
De Homine (Descartes), 14
deafness, 74, 264, 279–282, 280f, 630
death genes, 202, 203
decibels (dBs), 265, 281f
decision making, 604–605, 607f
declarative memory, 536, 537, 538f, 544f, 551f, 571f
decomposition of movement, 365
decorticate rage, 478
decussation, 351
deep brain stimulation (DBS), 362, 363f, 519, 527, 529
deep dyslexia, 636, 644f
default mode network, 596
degradation, 84, 111
dehydration, response to, 412–413
delayed non-matching-to-sample task, 538, 571f
delta (δ) receptor, 115
delta waves, 441, 464f
delusion, 500
Dement, William, 453
dementia praecox. See schizophrenia
dementia pugilistica, 642
dementias, 221, 459, 566
denaturing, protein, 404
dendrites
axons and, 33t

branching, 190f, 556f
description, 27
function of, 78
growth cones, 201f, 202f
dendritic interaction zones, 78
dendritic knob, 291
dendritic spines, 496f
dendro-dentritic contacts, 84, 85
dentate gyrus, 561, 565f
deoxycorticosterone, 144t
2-deoxyglucose (2-DG), 272
deoxyribonucleic acid (DNA), A.1–A.2, A.2f
dependence, definition of, 123
dependent variables, 6
depolarization, 66–67, 93
depolarizing stimuli, 67f
depots, drug, 108
depressants, 113
depression, 516–523, 531f
animal models of, 522–523
in bipolar disorder, 515
brain changes in, 517, 517f
drug-resistant, 517
drugs in treatment of, 518t
gender and, 520–521
hypothalamic-pituitary-adrenal axis and, 519–520, 520f
immune system and, 493–494
inheritance of, 516
seasonality of, 522
sleep and, 521f
treadmill of, 519
treatments for, 517–519
dermatomes, 245, 246f
dermis, 242
Descartes, René, 14, 15, 154
designer receptors exclusively activated by designer drugs (DREADDs), 157, 157f
desynchronized EEG, 440–441
developmental disorders, 210–214
dexamethasone suppression test, 520
diabetes mellitus, 418–419
Diablo protein, 202, 203
diacylglycerol, 84
Diagnostic and Statistical Manual of Mental Disorders 5th ed (DSM V), 429
diazepam (Valium), 113, 523
dichotic presentation, 575, 612
diencephalon, 44, 59f, 195, 540–541
diffusion, 63, 409
diffusion tensor imaging (DTI), 52f, 53, 59f, 278, 624, 624f
digestion, 40, 416
dihydrotestosterone (DHT), 144t, 385
dimers, description, 438
dinosaur joke, 178f
DISC1 gene, 505
discordant, definition, 503
disease, definition of, 122
disease model of substance abuse, 122–123
dishabituation, 556
disinhibited syndromes, 603t
dissociative drugs, 121

stress management and, 568
enzymes, A.1
epidemiology, 500
epidermis, description, 242
epidural administration, 256
epigenetic regulation, 216–217, 226f, 490
epigenetic transmission, 426
epigenetics, 166, 214, 215–216, 215f
epilepsy, 35, 61, 88, 113, 169, 610, 625–626
epinephrine, 143, 144t, 149–150, 150f, 488, 498f
episodic buffer, 546
episodic memory, 541, 571f
equilibrium, description of, 64
equilibrium potentials, 64, 93
ergot, 95
essential amino acids, 415
estradiol, 153
    description of, 159f
    effects of, 144t
    enzymatic conversion to, 142, 142f
    structure of, 137f
    synthesis of, 390
estrogen receptors, 139, 391
estrogen replacement therapy, 153
estrogens
    description of, 153, 159f
    effects of, 144t
    egg release and, 372–373
    function of, 152f
    ventromedial hypothalamus and, 376
estrone, effects of, 144t
estrus, 373
eukaryotes, A.2
eunuchs, 133
euphoria, 602
European Warblers, 170
event-related potentials (ERPs), 90f, 94, 582f, 583, 607f
    auditory attention and, 90
    definition, 90
    visual search and, 584f, 585f
evolution
    brain, 163–191
    continuing, 186–187
    description of, 164
evolution by natural selection, 164, 190f
evolutionary psychology, 184, 185
excitatory postsynaptic potentials (EPSPs), 75f, 96f, 560, 560f
    characteristics of, 78t
    definition, 75
    IPSPs and, 77f
    visual summary, 93
excitotoxicity, 100
executive brain, 182
executive control, 546
executive function, 603, 608f
exocrine glands, 132
exocytosis, 80, 80f
exogenous ligands, 81
exogenous substances, 95, 96

experience, epigenetic regulation and, 216–217
expression, 200, A.3
The Expression of the Emotions in Man and Animals (Darwin), 472
external ear, 265, 298f
external fertilization, 374
extinction, 593
extracellular compartments, 409
extracellular fluids, 62, 408f, 410
extrafusal fiber, 345
extraocular muscles, 302
extrapyramidal motor system, 358, 368f
extrapyramidal systems, 358–360
extrastriate cortex, 310, 334f
eye-blink reflex, conditioning, 559f, 571f
eye-blink responses, 398, 544
eyes
    abnormal movements, 528–530
    function of, 302
    human, 302f
    movement control, 365f
    suprachiasmatic nucleus and, 436
    variety of, 230f

F

face blindness. *See* prosopagnosia
facial expressions
    cultural differences in, 475f
    emotions and, 472, 472f
    mediators of, 476–477
    nonhuman primates, 473f
    universal, 475f
facial feedback hypothesis, 477, 498f
facial muscles, 476–477, 476f
facial nerve (CN VII), 37f, 290, 476, 498f
facial nucleus, 351f
facial recognition, 617–618, 618f
false-climb illusion, 285
false memories, 452
familiarity, feelings of, 540f
families, addictive behavior and, 126
family studies of schizophrenia, 502
famines, 415
fast-twitch muscle fibers, 342
fat, surgical removal of, 426
fat tissue, inhibition of, 427
fatal familial insomnia, 448f, 449
fear, 481f, 482f, 484f
fear conditioning, 479, 496f, 525, 565, 569f
fearlessness, 467
feature integration theory, 581
feature search, 580, 581f, 607f
fecal transplantation, 430, 430f
fentanyl, 114
fetal alcohol syndrome (FAS), 118, 210, 211f
fetal development, 182f
fetus, definition, 195
fevers, generation of, 406
fiber tracking, 53
fight-or-flight response, 149

filopodia, 201
final common pathway, 344
finches, 164
fine motor skills, sex differences in, 396t
finger lengths, 398f
fish, 176f, 282, 323, 374
fitness advantage, 181
5α-reductase, 385, 387
flaccid paralysis, 348
flavors, perception of, 286
Flinders-sensitive animals, 523
flocculus, 366
Florez, Guillermo F., 623
flower spray endings, 345
fluent aphasia, 620t, 621, 622f
fluid regulation, 408–414, 414f
fluoxetine (Prozac), 113, 524, 526
fluvoxamine (Luvox), 526
foliate papillae, 286
follicle-stimulating hormone (FSH), 144t, 147, 159f
follicles, description, 147
food regulation, 415–429
football, brain injury and, 643
forebrain, 44, 182–183, 195, 226f, 453
forebrain (prosencephalon), 195
forebrain (telencephalon), 59f
forelimbs, homology, 164f
form, perception of, 310
fornix, 46f, 47
fossils, evolutionary tree and, 168
Fourier analyses, 265, 317
fourth ventricle, 49f, 50
fovea, 307, 308f, 334f
Fox, Michael J., 361, 361f
FOXP2 gene, 189t, 631–632, 644f
Foxp2 gene, 631–627–24
fractional anisotropy (FA), 52f, 53
fragile X syndrome, 211f, 212, 226f
Franz, Shepard I., 18
free nerve endings, 233f, 249, 261f
free-run, in humans, 440f
free-running rhythms, 434
free will, 595, 607f
frequency, of waves, 264, 264, 265, 273
frogs, 176f, 208
frontal cortex
    addictive behavior and, 125
    dyslexia and, 638
    effects of alcohol on, 118
    holes in, 448f
    mirror neurons in, 357
frontal eye field (FEF), 590, 590f
frontal horn, 49f
frontal lobes, 40, 43, 239
    effects of alcohol on, 119
    information processed by, 43
    injury to, 602–604
    in schizophrenia, 506
frontal lobotomy, 257t
frontalin (pheromone), 379
fruit flies (*Drosophila melanogaster*), 166, 169, 202f, 399, 444

functional magnetic resonance imaging (fMRI), 52*f*, 53, 56*f*, 59*f*, 90, 627–629
functional neuroanatomy, 25–59
functional neuroimaging, 627–629
functional tolerance, 106
fundamentals, of sound, 264, 265
fungiform papillae, 286
Fuseli, Henry, 444*f*
fusiform face area, 586
fusiform gyrus, 618*f*, 619, 644*f*

G

G-protein-coupled receptors (GPCRs), 97, 100, 154
G proteins, 83, 293
GABA (gamma-aminobutyric acid), 83, 129*f*, 455, 487, 523
GABA (gamma-aminobutyric acid) antagonists, 589
GABA (gamma-aminobutyric acid) receptors, 104*t*, 113, 113*f*, 118
Gage, Phineas P., 602, 603
galanin, 383
Galápagos islands, 164
Galapagos marine iguana, 407*f*
Galen, 14
Galileo, 15
Gallant, Jack, 605
Galton, Sir Francis, 17
gambling addiction, 603–604
gametes, 151, 374
gamma-aminobutyric acid (GABA). *See* GABA
gamma efferents, 346
gamma motor neurons, 346
γ-hydroxybutyrate (GBH), 458
ganglion cells, 303, 306, 334*f*
gap junctions, 280
gas neurotransmitters, 99, 103
gases, synaptic transmission and, 99*t*
gastric bypass surgery, 422, 428*f*
gastrin, 144*t*
gated ion channels, 83–84
gay men, 397–399
gel electrophoresis, A.4
gelada, 379
gender
    definition of, 388
    depression and, 520–521
    drug addiction and, 126
gender identity, 385, 396*t*
gene expression, 210–217
general anesthetics, 453, 597*f*
generalized anxiety disorder, 113, 523
generator potentials, 233
genes, 166, 190*f*, A.1–A.3. *See also specific genes*
genetic sex, 385, 401*f*
genetics, 165–166
genital tract development, 384–385
genital tubercle, 384
genomes, A.3

genomic effects, 112
genotypes, 211
gentamicin, ototoxicity, 280
genus, definition, 166
geologists, 164
Geschwind, Norman, 623
ghrelin, 144*t*, 421*t*, 422, 423*f*
giant axons, 72
giant pandas, 289–290
giant tortoises, 164
GJB2 gene, 280
glial cells, 58*f*
    CNS regeneration and, 349
    description, 26, 34*f*, 196*f*
    development of, 195
    function of, 33–36, 78
    glial tumors and, 208
    motor coordination and, 366–367, 367*f*
    precursors of, 197*f*
glial tumors, 208
global aphasia, 620*t*, 622–623, 622*f*, 644*f*
globus pallidus, 46, 46*f*, 363*f*
glomeruli, olfactory, 294
glomerulus, 299*f*
glossopharyngeal nerve (CN IX), 37*f*, 290
glucagon, 144*t*, 417
glucocorticoids, 144*t*, 150, 216
glucodetectors, 418
gluconeogenesis, 418
glucose, 53, 143, 416
glucose transporters, 418
glutamate, 99, 104*t*, 252–253, 289, 314
glutamate hypothesis, 511
glutamate receptors, 454*f*
glutamatergic transmission, 99
glycine, 100
glycogen, 417
glycogenesis, 417
glycogeolysis, 417
GNPTAB gene, 633
GNPTG gene, 633
goal-directed behaviors, 603
goiter, causes of, 151
goldfish, pheromones in, 378
Goldman equation, 65
Golgi, Camillo, 26
Golgi stains, 30
Golgi tendon organs, 345, 346–347, 368*f*
gonadal hormones, 153–155, 401*f*. *See also specific* hormones
gonadal sex, 385
gonadotropin-inhibiting hormone (GnIH), 151
gonadotropin-releasing hormone (GnRH), 151, 159*f*
gonadotropins, 147
gonads, 132*f*, 144*t*, 151. *See also* ovaries; testes
gorillas, language training for, 634–635
Gorski, Roger, 392
Gotthelf, Jeremias, 151*f*
G6PD gene, 189*t*
graded responses, 66

grammar, 609, 610, 611
grand mal seizures, 89
granule cell layer, 48, 49
grasshopper mice, 259–260
gravity, perception of, 283
gray matter, 43, 253, 506, 507*f*
grid cells, 545
gross neuroanatomy, 36
gross potentials, 88*f*
growth cones, 201*f*, 202*f*
growth hormone (GH), 144*t*, 148
guanosine diphosphate (GDP), 84
guanosine triphosphate (GTP), 84
guevedoces, 387–388, 387*f*, 396–397
guide RNA (gRNA), A.8–A.9, A.8*f*
Guinea pigs, 373*f*
gustatory system, 290, 290*f*, 299*f*
gustducin, 296
gut microbiota, 429
gyri, 40

H

habituation, 556, 557*f*, 569*f*
hair cells, 268, 269
Halcion, 460, 523
hallucinations, auditory, 514
hallucinogens, 119, 121*t*, 129*f*
haloperidol (Haldol), 112, 509, 511*f*, 529
halorhodopsin, 91, 92
Hamburger, Viktor, 202
hamsters, free-run rhythms in, 440
handedness, 615–617
hands, loss of, 246, 247*f*
haplotypes, 188
happiness, 484*f*
hard problem of consciousness, 598, 599*f*, 607*f*
harmonics, 265
Hawking, Stephen, 350
HBC gene, 189*t*
head trauma, 12*f*, 639–640
health psychology, 490, 491
hearing, 264–283
    loss of, 279–282, 280*f*
    passive, 627
    pressure waves as, 264–271
    testing in infants, 90*f*
hearing aids, 281
heart, hormones and, 144*t*
heart disease, 491*f*
heart rates, 40
Hebb, Donald O., 18, 218, 559
Hebbian synapses, 18, 218, 559, 571*f*
height, adult, 396*t*
Helicobacter pylori, 430
Helmholtz, Hermann von, 323–324
helper T cells, 492
hemiparesis, 360, 621
hemiplegia, 360, 621
hemispatial neglect, 312, 593, 593*f*, 594*f*, 607*f*, 636–637
hemispherectomy, 641*f*

hemispheric asymmetry, 610
heredity, 165, 168
Hering, Ewald, 324
heroin (diacetylmorphine), 114, 126, 129f
Herophilus, 14
hertz (Hz), 264, 265
Heschl's gyrus, 278f
heterocyclic antidepressants, 518t
hibernation, 405f
hierarchical control, 174
higher vocal centers (HVCs), 170, 171, 392,
    634
hillocks, axon, 93
hindbrain (rhombencephalon), 44, 59f,
    195, 226f
hippocampal formation (HF), 220–221, 561
hippocampus, 46f
    bird, 170f
    cannabinoid receptors, 115
    cholinergic projections, 100
    description, 561, 571f
    evolution of size of, 545
    function of, 46f, 538–539
    learning and, 47
    long-term potentiation in, 560f
    NMDA expression, 564
    shrinkage of, 221f
histamines, 249
histology, description of, 30
HMS Beagle, 164
Hodgkin, Alan, 68
Hofmann, Albert, 95, 120f
home heating systems, 404f
homeostasis, 403–432
homeostatic, definition of, 404
homeostatic balance, 488
homing pigeons, 274
hominins, 180, 181–183
Homo erectus, 180f, 181
Homo habilis, 180f
Homo sapiens. See humans (Homo sapiens)
homology, definition, 165
homology-directed repair, A.9
homoplasy, 165
homosexual behaviors, 397–399
homosexuality, 399
homunculus, 239f, 352f
horizontal cells, 303, 334f
horizontal plane, 42, 42f, 43f
hormones. See also specific hormones
    actions of, 132–137, 135f
    behavior and, 157f
    brain and, 131–159
    cellular action of, 137–145
    classes of, 137t
    classification of, 136–137
    communication of, 134f
    description of, 132, 159f
    feeding and, 425t
    fetal exposure and adult behavior,
        395–399
    mechanism of action, 138f
    sexual development and, 384

stress-activated, 488f
hostility, 490, 498f
house sparrows, 170
howler monkey, 169f
Hubel, David, 315
hues, 323, 335f
Human Brain Project, 19f, 49
humans (Homo sapiens), 181. See also brain,
    human
    brain size, 179f
    cerebral volume, 180f
    colonization by, 187f
    continuing evolution of, 187–189
    cortex expansion, 179f
    ears, 267f
    family tree of, 168f
    prenatal brain development, 194f
    reproductive anatomy, 380f
    sexual behavior diversity, 379–382
    sexual differentiation in, 384f
    sexual response patterns, 380f
    sleep cycles, 445, 446f
    sleep requirements of, 453
    sleep stages in, 440–444
    thermoregulation in, 405f
hummingbirds, 290
hunger, 47, 419, 424
Hunter, John, 133
huntingtin, 364, 365
Huntington, George, 364
Huntington's disease, 12f, 339f, 358, 360,
    364–365, 368f
Huxley, Andrew, 68
hybridization, A.2
hydrocortisone, 144t
hyenas, aggression in, 485
hyperphagia, 419
hyperpolarization, 66, 67f, 76
hypersexuality, 479
hypertonic, definition, 410
hypnosis, pain relief, 257t
hypocretins, 424, 456, 457
hypodermia, 242
hypofrontality hypothesis, 507, 507f
hypoglossal nerve (CN XII), 37f, 48
hypoglossal nuclei, 351f
hypoglycemia, 419
hypomania, 515
hypophyseal portal system, 146, 159f
hypophysis. See pituitary gland
hypothalamic-pituitary-adrenal axis,
    519–520, 520f
hypothalamic system, 453
hypothalamus
    appetite control and, 423f
    circadian clock in, 435
    description of, 159f
    embryology of, 44
    function of, 47, 132f
    hormones and effects, 144t
    lesions, 420f
    sexual differences, 392f
    sleep center, 456–458

system coordination by, 419–425, 420f
hypovolemic thirst, 410, 411f, 412
hypoxia, 210

I

iconic memory, 545
ideational apraxia, 361
identical twins, 13f
ideomotor apraxia, 361
iguanas, temperature control, 406f
imipramine (Tofranil), 113
imitation, consciousness and, 596t
immediate early genes (IEGs), 31
immediate recall, 549f
immune system
    components of, 493f
    psychological stress and, 493–494
    stress and, 491–495
    system interactions, 492
    vaccination and, 127
immunocytochemistry (ICC), 141, 141f,
    A.8, A.9
immunoglobulins, 492
immunohistochemistry (IHC), 31
impoverished condition (IC), 555
impulsive behaviors, 364
in situ hybridization, 31, 141, A.6
in vitro, definition, 200
inattentional blindness, 575
incus, 266
independent variables, 6
indifferent gonads, 383
individual response stereotypy, 473
indolamines, 101
induction, 200
infants, 445–446, 474f
inferior, definition of, 42
inferior colliculi, 47, 272, 298f
inferior fusiform area, 638
inferior olive, 221, 558
inferior salivary nuclei, 351f
information processing, 61, 76, 550–551
infradian rhythms, 439
infrasound, 274
infundibulum. See pituitary stalk
ingestion, of drugs, 108t
inhalation, of drugs, 108t
inhibition of return, 580
inhibitors of apoptosis proteins (IAPs), 202,
    203
inhibitory postsynaptic potentials (IPSPs),
    75f, 76, 77f, 78t, 93, 96f
injection, of drugs, 108t
inner ear, 267, 281, 283
inner hair cells (IHCs), 268, 270, 298f
innervate, 32
innervation ratios, 343
inositol triphosphate (IP3), 139
input zones, 27
insectivores, 179f
insomnia, 446–447, 459–460, 464f
instrumental conditioning, 543

insula, 125, 483
insulin, 143, 144*t*, 417–419, 417*f*, 421*t*
integration, visual, 306
integration zone, 27
intellectual disability, 210, 224, 226*f*
intelligence, brain size and, 17–18
intensions, conscious experiences of, 600
intensity, sound, 264
intensity coding, 235*f*
intensity differences, 274, 298*f*
intermale aggression, 485, 498*f*
intermediate-term memory (ITM), 546
internal clocks, 434–435
internal fertilization, 374
interneurons, 28, 348
interpositus nucleus, 558
intersex phenotypes, 386*f*
interstitial nucleus of the anterior
    hypothalamus (INAH-3), 398, 398*f*
intracellular compartments, 409
intracellular fluid, 62
intrafusal fiber, 345
intraparietal sulcus (IPS), 589, 590*f*
intrathecal administration, 256
intrinsic activity, 105
intromissions, 373
inverse agonists, 97, 129*f*
invertebrates, 171–172, 190*f*, 444, 556–558
iodized salt, 151
ion channels, 63. *See also specific* ions
ionotropic receptors, 83, 83*f*, 97, 97*f*
ions, definition of, 62
ipsilateral, definition of, 42
iris, 302, 302*f*
isocarboxazid (Marplan), 113
isocortex, 45
isolated brain (*encéphale isolé*), 455
isolated forebrain (*cerveau isolé*), 455
isotonic, definition, 410
isotropy, 53
itch, sensation of, 244*f*, 251

J

James, William, 8, 17, 468, 573, 595
James-Lange theory, 468, 470, 477, 498*f*
Jeffress model of sound localization, 276
joints, movements and, 341*f*
Jolie, Angelina, 429*f*
joy, parasympathetic activation, 468
juvenile-onset diabetes, 418–419

K

K complexes, 441
kainate receptors, 99
kappa (κ) receptor, 115, 255
Keller, Helen, 264
ketamine (special K), 120, 121*t*, 511
ketones, 418
khat, 116
KIAA0319 gene, 638–639
kidney problems, 74
kindling of seizures, 90

"kiss and run" process, 80
kisspeptin, functions of, 151
Kleiber, Max, 416
Klüver-Bucy syndrome, 479
knee-jerk reflex, 86, 87*f*
knockout organisms, 140, 141, 213–214
Komodo dragons, 374
Korsakoff's syndrome, 118, 541
Kraepelin, Emil, 501

L

L-dopa, 362–363
labeled lines, 232, 232*f*, 261*f*, 291
lactase genes, 189*t*
lamellated corpuscles, 233
lamprey, brain, 176*f*
Lange, Carl G., 468
language
    basic speech, 630
    brain regions, 173, 626*f*
    comprehension of, 621
    consciousness and, 596*t*
    definition of, 609, 610
    disorders, 619–623
    evolution of, 629*f*
    heritable disorders of, 631*f*
    lateralization and, 609–644
    learned components, 630–636
    processing of, 627
    research perspectives, 4*t*
language areas, 625–627
large ground finch (*Geospiza magnirostris*),
    187
Lashley, Karl S., 18
late-selection model, 576
latency differences, 275, 298*f*
latent learning, 544
lateral, definition of, 43*f*
lateral geniculate nucleus (LGN), 310,
    314–315, 315*f*, 326, 327, 334*f*
lateral hypothalamus, (LH) 419
lateral inhibition, 308, 309*f*, 334*f*
lateral intraparietal area (LIP), 589
lateral-line system, 284
lateral magnocellular nucleus of the
    anterior neostratum (LMAN), 634
lateral planes, 42
lateral superior olive (LSO), 276
lateral ventricles, 49, 49*f*
lateralization, 609–644, 644*f*
learned helplessness, 522–523
learning
    aging and, 566–568
    brain regions involved in, 46*f*, 548*f*
    cerebellar circuits in, 359
    conditioned responses, 147
    control of, 365*f*
    definition, 535, 536
    enrichment and, 555*f*
    functional perspectives on, 536–552
    kinds of, 536–542, 571*f*
    memory and, 535–571
    primary motor cortex and, 354–356

research perspectives, 4*t*
lemur, 179*f*
lenses, eye, 302, 302*f*, 312–313
leptin, 421, 421*t*, 422
lesbians, 397–399
lesions, brain, 55
letter-by-letter reading, 637
LeVay, Simon, 398
levels of analysis, 10*f*, 21*f*
Lewy bodies, 362
lie detection, 471–472
lies, detection of, 620
life spans. *See also* age/aging
    behavior over, 193–226
    brain development over, 193–226
    sleep patterns over, 445–447, 447*f*
ligand-gated ion channels, 83, 97*f*
ligands, 81, 97, 129*f*
light, sensitivity to, 306*f*
limbic seizures, 487
limbic system, 59*f*, 479, 498*f*
    components of, 46*f*
    description of, 46
    projections to, 102
    in schiziphrenia, 505–506
linear regressions, 177
Linnaeus, Carolus, 166
lipid bilayers, 62
lipids, storage of, 418
lithium, 515, 531*f*
lithium chloride, 112
lizards, thermoregulation in, 406*f*
lobotomy, 508, 527
local anesthetics, 109
local potentials, 66, 93
location, perception of, 310
locus coeruleus, 102, 114
Loewi, Otto, 82, 100
Longden, Eleanor, 514*f*
long-term depression (LTD), 565
long-term memory (LTM), 536, 538, 548,
    549, 571*f*
long-term potentiation (LTP), 560*f*, 561,
    564*f*, 571*f*
lorazepam (Ativan), 113
lordosis, 375, 375*f*, 376–378, 401*f*
Lou Gehrig's disease, 350
loudness, 264, 265, 274, 281*f*
loxP, 366, A.9
LRRTM1 gene, 615
LSD (lysergic acid diethylamide, acid), 111*f*,
    112, 119, 120*f*, 121*t*, 509
LSD: My Problem Child (Hofmann), 120
lumbar spinal cord, 38, 38*f*, 246*f*
Lunesta, 460
luteinizing hormone (LH), 148, 159*f*

M

macaque, 320*f*, 587, 587*f*
MacLean, Paul, 478
macular degeneration, 332–333

magnetic resonance imaging (MRI), 52, 52f, 59f

magnetoencephalography (MEG), 55, 55f, 59f

magnocellular layer, 315

magpies, 170

male courtship behaviors, 485

malleus, 266

malnutrition, 210

Mammalia, 167f

mammals. *See also specific* mammals
  auditory system, 231
  brain of, 176f
  color vision, 325–326
  ears of, 266f
  fossils of, 175–176
  hair cells, 282
  learning circuits in, 558–559
  nervous system, 172f
  sleep states in, 444f
  spinal cord in, 393–394
  temperature control, 407, 407t
  vocalizations, 274

mammillary bodies, 46f, 47, 540, 540f, 571f

mammillothalamic tract, 541

manic-depressive illness, 515. *See also* bipolar disorders

MAOA gene, 189t

MAPK (mitogen-activated protein kinase), 562

marijuana, 115, 116, 129f, 257

marine mammals, sleep patterns, 445f

masculine behaviors, 389–390

masculinization, 388–389, 395, 401f

mast cells, 251

maternal behaviors, 383, 490

math abilities, 395

math concepts, sex differences in, 396t

Maudsley therapy, 429

May, Michael, 193, 218–220

McGill Pain Questionnaire, 248

MDMA (3,4-methylenedioxymetham-phetamine, ecstasy), 120–121, 121t

meaning, priming and, 543

mechanical sensory system, 231t

mechanical stimuli, 233–234

mechanosensory pain, 249

MeCP2 gene, 224

Meddis, Ray, 453

medial amygdala, 378

medial forebrain bundle, 102, 125f, 478

medial geniculate nuclei, 272, 298f

medial planes, 42

medial preoptic area (mPOA), 376, 377, 397–398, 401f

medial superior olive (MSO), 276

medial temporal (MT) area, 321, 328

medial temporal lobe, 536, 538–540

median eminence, 146, 159f

medium ground finch (*Geospiza fortis*), 186–187

medulla (myelencephalon), 45, 48–49, 179, 195

medullary reticular formation, 376, 401f

Meissner's corpuscles, 233f, 242, 243f, 261f

melanocortin receptors, 427

melanocortin type-4 receptors (MC4Rs), 424

melanocortins, 424

α-melanocyte-stimulating hormone (α-MSH), 424

melanopsin, 436, 461

melatonin, 144t, 154–155, 460

membrane potentials, 67, 74–78

membranes, permeability, 409

Memento (film), 542

memories
  consolidation of, 550–551
  false, 452
  formation of, 546f, 563–565
  physical basis of, 568
  storage of, 554f

memory
  aging and, 566–568
  attributes of, 547f
  brain regions involved in, 46f, 537f, 548f
  consolidation, 449, 451–452
  control of, 365f
  decline of, 221f
  definition, 535, 536
  emotions and, 552–553
  functional perspectives on, 536–552
  impairment, 571f
  kinds of, 536–542
  learning and, 535–571
  neurogenesis and, 566
  processes, 550f
  research perspectives, 4t
  storage of, 552–568
  traces, 552

men, 325–326, 382

Mendel, Gregor Johann, 165

meninges, 49, 59f

meningiomas, 49

meningitis, 49

menopause, 153

mental illnesses, U.S. adults, 501f

mental retardation. *See* intellectual disability

meprobamate (Miltown), 523

Merkel's discs, 233f, 242, 243f, 261f

mescaline (peyote), 120

mesencephalon, 195. *See also* forebrain

mesolimbocortical pathway, 101

mesostriatal pathway, 101

messenger RNA (mRNA), A.2

metabolic adaptation, 416, 416f

metabolic rates, 445, 450

metabolic tolerance, 106

metabolism, 221–223, 416

metabotropic receptors, 83, 83f, 94, 97, 100, 115

metacognition, 596t

metencephalon, 44, 195

methadone, 127

methamphetamines, 118f

methylation, 216

methylphenidate (Ritalin), 116

mice, 213f, 438f, 634

Michelangelo, 14

microbiome, 429

microelectrodes, 62

microglial cells, 34f, 35, 224

micropolygyria, 637f

midbrain (mesencephalon), 44, 47, 59f, 195, 226f, 484f

middle canal, ear, 267

middle cerebral arteries, 50

middle ear, 266, 298f

migraines, 254

mild traumatic brain injury, 642

milk letdown reflex, 145, 146f, 382

Miller, Geoffrey F., 183, 185

millivolts (mV), 63

mindfulness-based stress reduction (MBSR), 495

mineralocorticoids, 144t, 150

minimal discriminable frequency difference, 273

mirror neurons, 330, 357–358, 357f, 358f, 368f

mirror recognition, 596t

mirror-reversed texts, 538f

mirror-tracing tasks, 537f

Mishkin, Mortimer, 329

mitochondria, 26

mitosis, 195

mitral cells, 294

modafinil (Provigil), 458

modulatory sites, 98

Molaison, Henry, 535, 536, 568f. *See also* patient H. M.

molecular clocks, 438, 438f

Mona Lisa (da Vinci), 318, 319f

monaural, definition, 613

monkeys, 185. *See also* primates, nonhuman
  aggressive behavior in, 487
  caloric restriction in, 417f
  color vision, 323
  default mode network in, 596
  gambling by, 604
  lateral geniculate nucleus (LGN), 327
  verbalizations, 264
  visual pathways, 311, 319, 320f
  vocalizations, 633

monoamine hypothesis, 517

monoamine oxidases (MAOs), 101, 112, 113, 517, 518t

monoamine transmitters, 101–103

monoamine transporters, 117

monoamines, 99t

monocular deprivation, 218

monogamy, 372

monozygotic, definition, 502, 503

mood disorders, 113, 117, 169, 500t, 516–523

mood-stabilizers, 111f

Moore, Celia, 395

moral model of substance abuse, 122

morphemes, 630, 644f

morphine, 114, 114f, 129f, 255, 256, 289
Moser, Edward, 544–545
Moser, May-Britt, 544–545
mossy fiber pathways, 563
motion, perception of, 321, 328
motion sickness, 285
motivation, 404
motoneurons, 341
motor control, 358–360, 602–604
motor cortex, 340f, 353f, 356f, 542
motor homunculus, 352f
motor learning, 356f
motor neurons, 28, 36, 341
    neuromuscular junctions and, 344f
    pathology of, 350
    skeletal muscle, 368f
    SNB, 393
    spinal, 206
motor nucleus of vagus, 351f
motor plans, 338, 339f, 365f
motor proteins, 32
motor skills, sex differences in, 396t
motor theory of language, 624, 644f
motor units, 343
mounting behaviors, 390. See also lordosis
mouse models, 213–214
movement, 46–47, 310, 340f
mu (β) receptor, 115, 255
Müller, Johannes, 232
Müllerian ducts, 384
multiple sclerosis, 35, 208
multipolar neurons, 27
mummification, 14f
muscarine, 81
muscarinic, definition, 100
muscle contractions, 342f
muscle fibers, 342, 368f
muscle receptors, 345f
muscle spindles, 345, 345f, 368f
muscle tone, 365f
muscular dystrophy (MD), 343, 368f
music, 263, 278, 278f, 355, 615
musicians, perfect pitch and, 614
mustard oils, 250
musth, definition, 379f
mutations, 165, 190f, 212, 226f. See also
    specific genes
myasthenia gravis, 344
myelencephalon (medulla), 59f, 195
myelin, 35, 93, 209f
myelin sheaths, 72
myelination, 35, 73f, 208, 226f
myopia, 330, 335f
myosin, 342

N

N1 effects, 583, 584f
NAGPA gene, 633
naloxone (Narcan), 115, 127, 258
naltrexone (ReVia), 115
narcolepsy, 169, 456, 457f, 464f
nasal cavity, odor receptors, 292–294

nasal hemiretina, 309
Nash, John, 501f
National Survey on Drug Use and Health,
    2013, 122
natriuretic polypeptide B (Nppb), 251
natural selection, 164, 165–166, 165f, 188f,
    190f
naturalists, 164
$Na_v1.7$, 259–260
$Na_v1.8$, 260
$Na_v1.7$ gene, 251
navigational skills, aging and, 566
negative feedback, 143, 159f, 404–405, 404f
negative polarity, 63
negative selection pressures, 181–183
negative symptoms, 500
neglect, 593–594
neocortex, 45, 177
neologisms, 619
neonatal period, 389
Nernst equation, 64
nerve cells. See neurons
nerve growth factor (NGF), 204, 204f
nervous systems
    comparative view, 172f
    development of, 73
    divisions in humans, 44f
    divisions of, 36–45
    effects of stimulants in, 116–118
    embryonic development of, 194f
    endocrine system and, 156–157, 156f
    fetal development of, 194f
    gross potentials, 88f
    make up of, 26–35
    sexual dimorphism, 392
    stages of development, 195
    system interactions, 492
nervous tissue degeneration, 199
nervous tissue regeneration, 199
NeuN protein, 565f
neural chains, 86
neural circuitry representations, 88f
neural conduction, drugs and, 109–112
neural development, 196f, 220t
neural groove, 195
neural plasticity, 31, 58f, 640
neural tube, 44, 174, 195, 196f, 226f
neuralgia, 253
neuroactive drugs, 112–115
neuroanatomy, functional, 25–59
neurochemistry, 95, 96
neurocrine communication, 134
neuroeconomics, 604, 608f
neuroendocrine cells, 135–136, 136f, 159f
neurofibrillary tangles, 222, 223f, 226f
neurogenesis, 195, 226f, 565, 565f, 566
neurohypophysis. See posterior pituitary
neuroleptics. See antipsychotic drugs
neurological disorders, 21f
neuromodulators, 98, 129f, 136
neuromuscular junctions (NMJ), 343–345,
    344f, 368f
neuron doctrine, 26, 33

neuronal cell death, 195
neurons
    apoptosis, 202
    classification of, 27–28
    collateral sprouting, 640–641
    components of, 27f
    description of, 2, 26, 36, 58f
    development of, 195
    differentiation of, 200–201
    diversity of, 28f
    drawings of, 26f
    electrical signaling, 63f, 65f
    electrical signals, 78t
    growth of, 204
    information processing, 61, 76
    loss during aging, 567
    mature human brain, 193
    migration of, 198–199
    motor, 28
    off-line, 461–463
    oxytocinergic, 158
    precursors of, 197f
    prenatal growth of, 193
    receptive fields, 261f, 588f
    sensory, 28
    single-cell recordings, 607f
    species differences, 175f
    structural divisions, 26–27
    synapses and, 86–88
    unipolar, 28
neuropathic pain, 253
neuropeptide Y (NPY), 103, 251, 422
neuropeptides, 99t, 136, 249
neuropharmacology, 95, 96
neurophysiology, 61, 62
neuroplasticity, 8–9, 97, 553
neuroscience, 2, 21f
neurosteroids, 114, 142
neurotensin, 103
neurotransmitter receptors, 94, 104t
neurotransmitters, 30
    action of, 96f
    brain arrays, 99–103
    categories, 129f
    clearance of, 110–111
    definition, 75
    description of, 61
    feeding and, 425t
    gas, 85
    general anesthetics and, 454f
    inhibition of synthesis, 109f
    re-uptake of, 109f, 111
    receptor subtypes, 80–83
    release of, 80, 84–86, 109f, 110
    reuptake of, 79f
    storage of, 109f
    synthesis of, 79f, 101
    versatility of, 97f
neurotrophic factors, 204, 205f, 218, 226f,
    349
neurotrophins, 204
niche adaptation, sleep and, 449–451
nicotine, 111f, 116–117, 127, 129f, 289

nicotinic, definition, 100
nicotinic ACh receptors, 117
night terror, 443, 444f
The Nightmare (Fuseli), 444f
nightmares, 443
Nissl stain, 30
nitric oxide (NO), 85, 103
nitrocellulose, A.4
NMDA receptors, 99, 119, 511, 512f, 571f
    description, 561
        LTP and, 561
        roles of, 563f
nociceptors, 249, 251, 261f
nocturnal animals, 434
nocturnal owl monkey, 169f
nodes of Ranvier, 34f, 35, 72, 93
nodule, 366
Noguchi, Hideyo, 499
noise pollution, 280
non-matching-to-sample task, 539f
non-REM (NREM) sleep, 440–441, 442t,
    452, 464f
nonassociative learning, 544, 556, 571f
noncompetitive ligands, 98
nondeclarative memory, 538, 538f, 542–
    545, 544f, 571f
nondirected synapses, 85
nonfluent aphasia, 620, 620t, 622f, 644f
nonfluent speech, 619
nongenomic effects, 142
nonprimary motor cortex, 356–357, 368f
nonprimary sensory cortex, 239
nonsleepers, 453f
nootropics, 567
noradrenaline. *See* norepinephrine (NE)
noradrenergic, definition of, 102
noradrenergic pathways, brain, 102f
norepinephrine (NE), 40, 102, 129f, 150f,
    488, 498f
    effects of, 144t
        hormones produced by, 149–150
        receptor subtypes, 104t
norepinephrine (NE) receptors, 102–103
Northern blots, A.6
notochord, 200
NPAS3 gene, 189t
N2pc (N2-posterior-contralateral), 584,
    585f, 607f
NPY neurons, 422
nuclei (brain), 45
nucleotides, A.1–A.2
nucleus, 58f, A.2
nucleus accumbens, 124, 125f, 527, 604
nucleus ambiguus, 351f
nucleus basalis, 100
nucleus basalis of Meynert (NBM), 567
nucleus laminaris, 275
nucleus of the solitary tract (NST), 418
nucleus robustus of the archistriatum, 634
nutrient regulation, 415–418
nutrients, 415, 416

O

obesity, 421f, 426–428, 428f, 459
object recognition centers, 329f
object recognition memory, 538, 547f
obligatory losses, 404
obsessions, symptoms, 525
obsessive-compulsive disorder (OCD),
    500t, 525–526, 526t, 531f
obstructive apnea, 459
occipital cortex, 334f, 583
occipital horn, 49f
occipital lobes, 41, 43, 310
occipitotemporal cortex, 619
ocular dominance columns, 218, 321, 322f
ocular dominance histograms, 219f
ocular dominance slab, 321
oculomotor apraxia, 594
oculomotor nerve (CNIII), 37f
oculomotor nuclei, 351f
odor sensations, 291–296, 372–373, 452,
    452f
odorants, 292–294
off-axis sounds, 274
off-center bipolar cells, 312, 313, 334f
off-center ganglion cells, 314
off-center/on-surround, 314, 334f
offspring survival, 382–383
O'Keefe, John, 544
olfactory bulb, 294, 299f
    function of, 46f
    innervation of, 291–292
    learning and, 566
    location of, 46f
    neurogenesis in, 565
    smell and, 47
olfactory ensheathing cells, 349
olfactory epithelium, 291, 294f, 299f
olfactory nerve (CN I), 37f
olfactory receptor neurons, 291, 299f
olfactory system, 292f, 293f
oligodendrocytes, 35
on-center bipolar cells, 312, 313, 334f
on-center ganglion cells, 314
on-center/off-surround, 314
On the Origin of Species (Darwin), 164
ongoing phase disparity, 275
onset disparity, 275
ontogeny, 4
Onuf's nucleus, 394
open-loop control mechanisms, 338, 339,
    368f
operant conditioning, 542, 543f, 571f
opiate drugs, 255–257
opiates, 113, 255, 257t
opioid peptides, 99t, 103
opioid receptors, 114, 114f, 255
opioids, 255, 262f, 487
opium, 114f, 255, 460
opossum, 175
opponent-process hypothesis, 324
opsin, 305
optic ataxia, 329, 594

optic chiasm, 309, 334f
optic disc, 308
optic nerve (CN II), 37f, 208, 303, 309, 334f
optic radiation, 310
optic tract, 310
optical illusions, 220f
optical imaging, 53, 54, 59f
optogenetic manipulation, 570
optogenetic proteins, 91f
optogenetic tools, 91f
optogenetics, 91, 92
oral contraceptives, 153
orangutans, language training, 634–635
orbit, eye, 302
orbitofrontal cortex, 526, 603
oregano, 250
orexigenic neurons, 424
orexins, 424
organ of Corti, 268, 269f, 298f
The Organization of Behavior (Hebb), 18
organizational effects, 388–391, 389f, 395,
    401f
organum vasculosum of the lamina
    terminalis (OVLT), 412
orgasm, 380–381, 400f, 401f
orientation columns, 322, 322f
orlistat (Xenical), 427
orphan receptors, 114
osmolality, 410
osmosensory neurons, 410, 411f
osmosis, 409, 409f
osmotic pressure, 410
osmotic thirst, 410, 411f
ossicles, 266, 298f
otoacoustic emissions, 270, 398
otoliths, 283f, 284
ototoxic, definition of, 280
outer hair cells (OHCs), 268, 270, 298f
output zone, 27
oval window, 266
ovaries, 132f, 144t, 153
ovulation, 374
ovulatory cycles, 376, 376f
ovum, 374
owls, directional perception, 264
oxycodone (OxyContin), 114
oxytocin, 103, 121, 145, 376, 382, 487
    autism management and, 157–158
    description of, 145, 159f
    effects of, 144t
    social behavior and, 155

P

P1 effect, 35, 583, 584f, 607f
P3 effect, 583, 607f
Pacinian corpuscles, 233, 234f, 243f, 261f
pain
    ascending pathways, 256f
    brain response to, 9f
    character of, 248f
    definition of, 248
    descending pathways, 256f

emotional component of, 254–255
  insensitivity to, 248f
  interventions, 257t
  long-lasting, 248
  peripheral mediation of, 249, 249f
  short-lasting, 248
  as a social signal, 248
pain management, 114–115, 255–259
pain receptors, 232f, 244f, 250f, 251
pair bonds, 372
pancreas, 132f, 144t
panic attacks, 113, 523
panic disorders, 523
panther chameleon, 230f
Papez, James W., 478
Papez circuit, 478
papilla, 286
papillae, 299f
parabiotic, definition, 382
parabiotic exchange, 383f
paracrine communication, 134, 134f
paradoxical sleep, 442
paragigantocellular nucleus (PGN), 377
parahippocampal cortex, 539, 550
parallel fibers, 48, 49
paralytic dementia, 499
paraphasia, 619
parasympathetic nervous system, 39f, 40,
  58f, 468
paraventricular nucleus (PVN), 146, 424
parental behaviors, 382, 401f
paresis, 360
parietal cortex, 43, 221, 357, 589
parietal lobes, 41, 43, 239
  damage to, 636–637
  information processed by, 43
  injury to, 593–594
parkin, 362
Parkinson, James, 361
Parkinson's disease, 47, 102, 368f, 430, 477
  basal ganglia degeneration in, 358,
    361–364
  basal ganglia in, 360
  deep brain stimulation for, 363f
  REM behavior disorder and, 459
  toll of, 12f
paroxetine (Paxil), 524
parthenogenesis, 374
partial agonists, 105
parvocellular layers, 315
patch clamping, 70–71, 71f
patient H. M., 536, 571f. See also Molaison,
  Henry
patient K. C., 541–542
patient N. A., 540, 540f
pattern coding, 290
pattern identification, 599f
patterns, attention to, 580–582
Pavlov, Ivan P., 18, 543
Pavlovian conditioning, 543
PCSK6 gene, 615
peahens, 184f
peer groups, drug addiction and, 126

Penfield, Wilder, 25
penile erections, 377
penis, development of, 384, 385
peptide hormones, 136, 137f, 159f
peptide neurotransmitters, 99, 103, 104t,
  129f
peptides, A.2
Per/Cry proteins, 438
perception, 263–299
perceptual load, 576
perceptual skills, 542
perforant pathway, 565
periaqueductal gray, 114, 115, 252f, 256,
  376, 383, 401f
period (per) gene, 437
Period protein, 464f
periods, definition of, 434
peripheral injection, 108t
peripheral nerve cord severing, 257t
peripheral nervous system, 36, 36f, 58f,
  208–209
peripheral spatial cueing tasks, 579
perirhinal cortex, 538, 543
perseverate, 157, 603
persistent vegetative state, 597f
personal traits
  addictive behavior and, 126
  sex differences in, 396t
peyote plant, 120
phagocytes, 492, 492f
phallus, 380
phantom limb pain, 253, 253f
pharmacodynamics, 106
pharmacokinetics, 108
pharmacological intervention, 257t
phase shifts, 435
phasic receptors, 236, 261f
phencyclidine (PCP, angel dust), 511, 512f
phenotypes, 211
phenotypic sex, 385
phenylketonuria (PKU), 212–214, 226f
phenylthiocarbamide (PTC), 289
pheromones, 134f, 135, 159f, 299f, 378–379
Philippine tarsier, 230f
Phillips, Tinna Guela, 609, 622f
phlegmatic personalities, 132
phobias, 113
phobic disorders, 523
phonemes, 630, 638f, 644f
phonological loop, 546
phosphodiesterase (PDE), 305
photons, 304, 304
photopic system, 303, 304t, 334f
photopigments, 324, 325f
photoreception, 244f
photoreceptors, 302, 303
  adaptation, 307
  evolution of, 306
  function of, 304–306
  hyperpolarization of, 305f, 313
  transplanted, 332, 333f
  types of, 334f
phototherapy, 522

phrenology, 16, 16f, 21f
phylogeny, 166
physical model of drug abuse, 123–124
pia mater, 49
Piezo2, 243
pig, color vision, 325
pineal gland, 132f, 144t, 154, 154f, 436
pinnae, 265
pit vipers, fertilization in, 374
pitch, 264, 265
pitch, of sounds, 273–274
pitocin. See oxytocin
Pittsburgh Blue, 222
pituitary gland, 131, 132f, 144–146
pituitary portal system, 146
pituitary stalk, 145, 159f
place cells, 544
place coding, 273, 298f
placebo effects, 258t, 259f, 262f, 518, 518f
placebos, 257–258, 257t
planum temporale, 612–614, 614f, 616, 644f,
  1014
plasticity
  in auditory perception, 277f
  cortical maps, 246, 247f
  motor cortex, 355
  neural, 8–9, 31, 58f, 97, 553, 640
platypus (Ornithorhynchus anatinus), 171
play, importance of, 9f
pleasure and reward, 400f
plegia, description, 360
polioviruses, 350
polyethylene glycol, 349
polygraphs, 471, 471–472, 498f
polymerase chain reactions (PCR), A.4
polymodal, definition, 241
POMC/CART neurons, 422, 424
pons, 44, 45, 48, 455–456, 484f
pontine system in sleep, 453
poppy, opium-producing, 114
positive reward model, 124–125
positive selection pressures, 181–183
positive symptoms, 500
positron emission tomography (PET), 52f,
  53, 54, 59f, 506, 628f
postcentral gyrus, 43
postcopulatory behavior, 373, 401f
posterior, definition of, 42
posterior cerebral arteries, 50
posterior pituitary, 132f, 144t, 145, 145f, 159f
postganglionic neurons, 38, 39f
postpartum depression, 521
postsynaptic, definition, 28
postsynaptic membrane, 29, 30, 58f
postsynaptic potentials (PSPs), 75, 93, 554f
posttraumatic stress disorder (PTSD), 524–
  525, 531f, 553, 571f
potassium ion (K+), 69, 93
potassium ions (K+), 63
pragmatics, 630
prairie voles (Microtus ochrogaster), 155f

pre-supplementary motor area (pre-SMA), 600
precentral gyrus, 43, 351, 624
precocial, definition, 382
prefrontal cortex, 601, 601f, 608f
  decision making and, 604–605
  emotion and, 483
  encoding by, 550
  goal-directed behaviors, 603
  shrinkage in age, 253
  working memory and, 603
prefrontal syndromes, 603t
preganglionic neurons, 38, 39f
pregnancy, hormones and, 153
premotor cortex, 356, 356f, 357–358, 368f
prenatal stress, 512–514
preoptic area (POA), 392–393, 406
presenilin, 222, 226f
pressure waves, 264
prestin, 270, 298f
presynaptic, definition, 28
presynaptic membrane, 28
presynoptic neurons, 563
primacy effect, 548
primary auditory cortex (A.1), 272, 298f
primary motor cortex (M1), 340, 351–356, 352f, 356f, 368f
primary sensory cortex, 239, 239f
primary sensory ending, 345
primary somatosensory cortex (S1), 261f
primary visual cortex (VI), 310–311, 312f, 319–322, 334f
primates, nonhuman
  aromatase gene function, 391
  color vision, 325
  cortex expansion, 179f
  diurnal, 451f
  facial expressions, 473f
  gene expression in, 184–186
  human gene expression and, 185f
  language training, 634–635
  lateral geniculate nucleus (LGN), 314, 315f
  retina, 328f
priming, 542, 543, 571f
Principles of Psychology (James), 17
prion diseases, 362–363
prion proteins, 449
priority maps, 589
pro-opiomelanocortin (POMC), 422
probes, A.4
procedural memory, 538
proceptive, definition, 373
proceptive behavior, 376
process outgrowth, 201
progesterone, 144t, 152f, 153, 159f
progestin receptors, 153
progestins, 144t, 153, 159f
Project D.A.R.E., 122
prolactin, 144t, 148
propranolol, 552
proprioception, 345
6-*n*-propylthiouracil (PROP), 289

prosencephalon (forebrain), 195
prosody, 615, 630, 644f
prosopagnosia, 617, 619, 644f
prostaglandins, 249
proteases, 203
protein hormones, 138f
protein kinase Mξ (PKMξ), 568
protein kinases, 561
protein synthesis, A.1–A.3
proteins
  denaturing of, 404
  synthesis of, A.3f
proteolytic enzymes, 249
proximal, definition of, 42
Prozac, 103, 517
psilocybin (magic mushrooms), 119–121, 121t
psychiatric disorders. *See also specific* disorders
  impacts of, 21f
  prevalence, 500t
  toll of, 500
psychoactive drugs, 103–104, 123
psychogenic interventions, 257t
psychoneuroimmunology, 490, 491–492
psychopathology, 499–531
psychopaths, 487, 487f
psychosocial dwarfism, 149
psychosomatic medicine, 490, 491
psychosurgery, 508, 531f
psychotomimetics, 511
puberty, androgens in, 485–486
PubMed, 20
puffer fish toxins, 74
pulvinar, 589, 589f, 607f
punch drunk, 642
pupils, 302, 302f, 306
pure tones, 264, 265
Purkinje cells, 359
  cerebellar, 48, 48f
  dendrites, 366–367
  description of, 47
  effects of alcohol on, 118
purpose, sense of, 491f
putamen, 46, 46f, 102, 361
pyramidal cells, 46, 118
pyramidal system, 350–351, 352f, 368f
PYY$_{3-36}$, 421t, 422–424, 423f, 427

Q

quale, 600
qualia, 607f
quanta, definition of, 304
quaternary amines, 99t

R

raclopride, 511f
radial glial cells, 198
radioimmunoassay (RIA), 140
Ramachandran, Vilayanur, 253
Ramón y Cajal, Santiago, 26
range fractionation, 234, 235, 306

raphe nuclei, 102–103
rapid-eye-movement (REM) sleep, 440–441, 464f
  depression and, 521–522
  evolution of, 444–445
  neuronal activity in, 452
  properties of, 442t
rat pups, temperature control, 407
rats (*Rattus norvegicus*), 171
  androgen insensitivity in, 393
  copulation in, 375f
  enriched environment, 568
  ovulatory cycles, 376f
  preoptic area, 392–393
  sleep patterns in, 445
  vocal behavior in, 634
Rb1 gene, 282
reaching movements, 339f
reaction times, 577–578
reading, verbal behaviors, 629–639
reading skill impairment, 636–639
recency effect, 548, 549
receptive fields, 238–239, 238f, 312, 313, 334f, 586, 588f
receptor cells, 230, 232–242
receptor fields, 261f
receptor isoforms, 139
receptor molecules, 81
receptor potentials, 233, 261f
receptor subtypes, 97
receptors, 31
  definition of, 96
  description of, 159f
  for hormones, 138–139
  regulation by drugs, 107f
  suppression of, 236–237
recollections, 538
reconsolidation, 551
recovery of function, 639–642, 644f
red deer antlers, 153f
red nucleus, 47, 358
"red tide," 74
redheaded women, 255
reds, color vision, 323
reductionism, 10
redundancy, 405–406
reeler mutation, 212
reflexes, 15f, 86, 87f, 338, 368f. *See specific* reflexes
reflexive attention, 579, 580f, 591f, 607f
refraction, description, 69, 302, 334f
refractory periods, 373
regulation, definition, 200, 201
relative refractory phase, 69, 93
releasing hormones, 143, 144t, 146, 159f
REM behavior disorder (RBD), 459
REM sleep. *See* rapid-eye-movement (REM) sleep
remoxipride, 511f
renin-angiotensin system, 412f
repetition priming, 543
reproductive anatomy, 380f, 384f

cat, 316f
color vision, 323–328
deficiencies, 330–332
extent of, 301–309
processing pathways, 329f
receptive fields, 313–321
visuomotor skills, 335f
visuospatial sketch pads, 546
vocabulary, 396t, 611
vocalizations, elephant, 264
voltage clamping, 70–71, 70f, 71
voltage-gated channels, 74, 96, 251
voltage-gated Na$^+$ channel, 68, 69
voluntary attention, 577, 578f, 580f, 607f
vomeronasal organ (VNO), 296, 299f, 378, 401f
von Bayer, Adolph, 460
von Helmholtz, Herman, 574
voxels, 605
Vries, Hugo de, 165
Vulpes spp., 167f

W

Wada test, 616
wakefulness, brain and, 454
waking, sleeping and, 440–461
Walker, Elaine, 503
Wallace, Alfred Russel, 164

war neurosis. *See* posttraumatic stress disorder (PTSD)
warblers songs, 170
wasabi, 250
water
  balance, 410t
  homeostatic regulation, 411–412
  loss of, 412
  movement through membranes, 409
wavelength, definition, 304
weaver mutation, 212
weight loss, 416f
Wernicke, Carl, 621
Wernicke-Geschwind model of aphasia, 623
Wernicke's aphasia, 620t, 621, 622f, 644f
Wernicke's area, 621
Western blots, A.6–A.7, A.7f
white matter, 43
whole cell recording, 70
Wiesel, Torsten, 315
Williams syndrome, 632
withdrawal
  avoidance model, 123–124
  lessening discomfort of, 126
  symptoms, 107
wolffian ducts, 384, 386

women, 325–326, 381–382, 381f
word blindness, 621
word deafness, 281, 621
working memory, 546–548, 591–592, 603

X

Xanax, 523

Y

young adults, psychiatric disorders in, 500
YouTube videos, 605

Z

zebra finches, song control, 392
Zeiman, Adam, 19
zeitgeber, 435
Zucker, Irving, 439
zygotes, 195, 374

About the Book

Editor: Sydney Carroll

Production Editor: Kathaleen Emerson

Copy Editor: Lou Doucette

Production Manager: Christopher Small

Book Production: Joanne Delphia

Art: Dragonfly Media Group

Photo Researcher: David McIntyre

Book and Cover Design: Joanne Delphia

Book and Cover Manufacturer: R. R. Donnelley